Handbook of Economic Expectations

Handbook of Economic Expectations

Edited by

Rüdiger Bachmann
University of Notre Dame
Notre Dame, IN, United States

Giorgio Topa
Federal Reserve Bank of New York
New York, NY, United States

Wilbert van der Klaauw
Federal Reserve Bank of New York
New York, NY, United States

ACADEMIC PRESS
An imprint of Elsevier

Academic Press is an imprint of Elsevier
125 London Wall, London EC2Y 5AS, United Kingdom
525 B Street, Suite 1650, San Diego, CA 92101, United States
50 Hampshire Street, 5th Floor, Cambridge, MA 02139, United States
The Boulevard, Langford Lane, Kidlington, Oxford OX5 1GB, United Kingdom

Notices

Knowledge and best practice in this field are constantly changing. As new research and experience broaden our understanding, changes in research methods, professional practices, or medical treatment may become necessary.

Practitioners and researchers must always rely on their own experience and knowledge in evaluating and using any information, methods, compounds, or experiments described herein. In using such information or methods they should be mindful of their own safety and the safety of others, including parties for whom they have a professional responsibility.

To the fullest extent of the law, neither the Publisher nor the authors, contributors, or editors, assume any liability for any injury and/or damage to persons or property as a matter of products liability, negligence or otherwise, or from any use or operation of any methods, products, instructions, or ideas contained in the material herein.

ISBN: 978-0-12-822927-9

For information on all Academic Press publications
visit our website at https://www.elsevier.com/books-and-journals

Publisher: Joseph P. Hayton
Acquisitions Editor: Kathryn Eryilmaz
Editorial Project Manager: Rupinder K. Heron
Production Project Manager: Selvaraj Raviraj / Punithavathy Govindaradjane
Cover Designer: Christian J. Bilbow

Typeset by VTeX

Contents

PART 1 EXPECTATION ELICITATION

---

† Deceased.

PART 3 EXPECTATIONS AND ECONOMIC THEORY

PART 4 THEORIES OF EXPECTATIONS

PART 5   OPEN ISSUES

Contributors

Klaus Adam
University of Mannheim, Mannheim, Germany
CEPR, London, United Kingdom
CESIfo, Munich, Germany

George-Marios Angeletos
MIT, Cambridge, MA, United States
NBER, Cambridge, MA, United States

Rüdiger Bachmann
University of Notre Dame, Notre Dame, IN, United States
CEPR, London, United Kingdom
CESifo, Munich, Germany
ifo, Munich, Germany

Isaac Baley
University of Pompeu Fabra, Barcelona, Spain
Center for Research in International Economics, Barcelona, Spain
Barcelona School of Economics, Barcelona, Spain
CEPR, London, United Kingdom

Federico Bassetti
Polytechnic University of Milan, Milan, Italy

Christiane Baumeister
University of Notre Dame, Notre Dame, IN, United States
University of Pretoria, Pretoria, South Africa
NBER, Cambridge, MA, United States
CEPR, London, United Kingdom

Benjamin Born
Frankfurt School of Finance and Management, Frankfurt am Main, Germany
CEPR, London, United Kingdom
CESifo, Munich, Germany
ifo, Munich, Germany

Wändi Bruine de Bruin
University of Southern California, Los Angeles, CA, United States

Bernardo Candia
University of California at Berkeley, Berkeley, CA, United States

Christopher Carroll
Johns Hopkins University, Baltimore, MD, United States

Kai Carstensen
University of Kiel, Kiel, Germany
CESifo, Munich, Germany
ifo, Munich, Germany

Roberto Casarin
Ca' Foscari University of Venice, Venice, Italy

Alycia Chin
U.S. Securities and Exchange Commission, Washington, DC, United States

Michael P. Clements
University of Reading, Reading, United Kingdom

Olivier Coibion
University of Texas at Austin, Austin, TX, United States
NBER, Cambridge, MA, United States

Richard K. Crump
Federal Reserve Bank of New York, New York, NY, United States

Francesco D'Acunto
Georgetown University, Washington, DC, United States

Adeline Delavande
University of Technology Sydney, Broadway, NSW, Australia
Nova School of Business and Economics, Carcavelos, Portugal

Marco Del Negro
Federal Reserve Bank of New York, New York, NY, United States

Anthony M. Diercks
Federal Reserve Board, Washington, DC, United States

Jeff Dominitz
ECONorthwest, Portland, OR, United States

Zeno Enders
Heidelberg University, Heidelberg, Germany
CESifo, Munich, Germany

Stefano Eusepi

University of Texas at Austin, Austin, TX, United States

Andreas Fuster

EPFL, Swiss Finance Institute, Lausanne, Switzerland

CEPR, London, United Kingdom

Pamela Giustinelli

Bocconi University, Milan, Italy

Yuriy Gorodnichenko

University of California at Berkeley, Berkeley, CA, United States

NBER, Cambridge, MA, United States

Péter Hudomiet

RAND, Santa Monica, CA, United States

Michael D. Hurd

RAND, Santa Monica, CA, United States

NBER, Cambridge, MA, United States

NETSPAR, Tilburg, the Netherlands

Cosmin Ilut

Duke University, Durham, NC, United States

NBER, Cambridge, MA, United States

Haitham Jendoubi

Federal Reserve Bank of New York, New York, NY, United States

Gábor Kézdi[†]

University of Michigan, Ann Arbor, MI, United States

Gizem Koşar

Federal Reserve Bank of New York, New York, NY, United States

CESifo, Munich, Germany

Theresa Kuchler

New York University, New York, NY, United States

NBER, Cambridge, MA, United States

CEPR, London, United Kingdom

Chen Lian

University of California at Berkeley, Berkeley, CA, United States

NBER, Cambridge, MA, United States

[†] Deceased.

Ulrike Malmendier

University of California at Berkeley, Berkeley, CA, United States

CEPR, London, United Kingdom

NBER, Cambridge, MA, United States

Charles F. Manski

Northwestern University, Evanston, IL, United States

Fabio Milani

University of California at Irvine, Irvine, CA, United States

Emanuel Moench

Frankfurt School of Finance and Management, Frankfurt am Main, Germany

CEPR, London, United Kingdom

Andreas I. Mueller

University of Texas at Austin, Austin, TX, United States

NBER, Cambridge, MA, United States

CEPR, London, United Kingdom

IZA, Bonn, Germany

Gernot J. Müller

University of Tübingen, Tübingen, Germany

CEPR, London, United Kingdom

CESifo, Munich, Germany

Stefan Nagel

University of Chicago, Chicago, IL, United States

NBER, Cambridge, MA, United States

CEPR, London, United Kingdom

CESIfo, Munich, Germany

Knut Niemann

University of Tübingen, Tübingen, Germany

Cormac O'Dea

Yale University, New Haven, CT, United States

IFS, London, United Kingdom

NBER, Cambridge, MA, United States

Evi Pappa

Universidad Carlos III de Madrid, Madrid, Spain

CEPR, London, United Kingdom

Monika Piazzesi
Stanford University, Stanford, CA, United States
NBER, Cambridge, MA, United States
CEPR, London, United Kingdom

Bruce Preston
University of Melbourne, Parkville, VIC, Australia

Morten O. Ravn
University College London, London, United Kingdom
CEPR, London, United Kingdom

Robert W. Rich
Federal Reserve Bank of Cleveland, Cleveland, OH, United States

Susann Rohwedder
RAND, Santa Monica, CA, United States
NETSPAR, Tilburg, the Netherlands

Martin Schneider
Stanford University, Stanford, CA, United States
NBER, Cambridge, MA, United States

Matthew D. Shapiro
University of Michigan, Ann Arbor, MI, United States

Johannes Spinnewijn
London School of Economics, London, United Kingdom
CEPR, London, United Kingdom

Vincent Sterk
University College London, London, United Kingdom
CEPR, London, United Kingdom

Johannes Stroebel
New York University, New York, NY, United States
NBER, Cambridge, MA, United States
CEPR, London, United Kingdom

Joseph S. Tracy
Federal Reserve Bank of Dallas, Dallas, TX, United States

Wilbert van der Klaauw
Federal Reserve Bank of New York, New York, NY, United States

Laura Veldkamp
Columbia University, New York, NY, United States
NBER, Cambridge, MA, United States
CEPR, London, United Kingdom

Tao Wang
Johns Hopkins University, Baltimore, MD, United States

Michael Weber
University of Chicago, Chicago, IL, United States
CEPR, London, United Kingdom
NBER, Cambridge, MA, United States

Basit Zafar
University of Michigan, Ann Arbor, MI, United States
NBER, Cambridge, MA, United States

Preface

When we were first approached about editing a Handbook focusing on economic expectations, one of the first thoughts we had was: isn't all of Economics about expectations? Indeed, one could argue that expectations – individuals having beliefs and perhaps an opinion about the future, which then guide their actions today – are the defining characteristic of the subject matter of Economics, perhaps of all of the Social Sciences. Atoms, molecules, even biological species do not appear to be having a notion of the future and thus have no expectations. Formally, in the field of Economics, it is natural to use models with difference or differential equations that feature expectation operators. None other than the German philosopher Martin Heidegger expressed this in his characteristic language in Being and Time: "An Existenziale of Dasein is temporality. Dasein is care, being-ahead-of-itself."

Yet, the field of Economics and expectations did not always have a smooth relationship, even though the start was promising. After WW2, as Chapters 1 (on household expectation surveys) and 2 (on firm expectation surveys) show, rich research programs were developed around the world concerning the measurement of expectations of economic agents. However, doubts emerged in the profession during the 1960s regarding the value of expectations data for predicting household- and firm-level choices. With the advent of the rational expectations revolution in the 1970s, the importance of having reliable measures of agents' expectations took a back seat: the rational expectations approach provided an elegant and powerful way of "closing the model" through model-internal and model-consistent expectations. This was exacerbated by a strong behaviorist undercurrent in Economics according to which only what people do, not what they think and say, counts as reliable data. Whatever one's favorite expectation theory was, it was a convenient way to eschew thinking hard about measurement issues. To remain fair to our predecessors: theory was ahead of measurement at the time, and economists could not always wait for everything to be measured carefully. Nevertheless, we should remind ourselves that measurement issues are not limited to expectations data alone, they affect data on realizations as well: think of how the measurement of even the most basic economic concepts like GDP is fraught with issues and subject to revisions!

Fast-forward to today: expectations have become respectable economic data again! Starting in the late 1980s, we now have a renewed interest and more than three decades of robust data collection efforts to directly elicit subjective expectations of economic agents. We believe that we also have to thank our sister social sciences, sociology, psychology, and the political sciences, for this development. Data on subjective expectations allow us to make progress on fundamental questions around the formation and updating of expectations by economic agents and about the content of their information sets; to study the heterogeneity and potential biases in expectations, analyzing their impact on behavior; and to deepen our understanding of the role expectations play in decision making under uncertainty.

The first part of this Handbook highlights the advances that have been made in the elicitation of subjective expectations data from households, firms, and professional forecasters. New methodologies have been developed to elicit forecast distributions and to construct measures of individual forecast uncertainty. Innovative ways of conducting field experiments in surveys have enabled researchers to shed a brighter light on how agents form and update their expectations in response to new information, including their willingness to pay for such information. The use of hypothetical scenarios has also allowed us to causally infer how agents' expectations respond to various possible counterfactual scenarios in the economic environment.

The second part of the Handbook reviews what we have learned about expectations data in a broad range of economic areas of interest. These chapters discuss the measurement and role of expectations about inflation; expectations about housing market variables; expectations in the areas of education, development and health economics; expectations of older households about retirement and late life outcomes; firm-level expectations, both about the macroeconomy and about their own plans and decisions; and expectations of financial market participants.

In the third part of the Handbook, our contributors have written about how this new body of data on subjective expectations has changed the way in which expectations operate in a broad range of models, spanning asset pricing and the term structure of various assets; dynamic stochastic general equilibrium (DSGE) models; models with incomplete markets, incomplete information, and bounded rationality; and structural micromodels of behavior, in particular labor market models. In all cases, the availability of expectations data has enhanced researchers' ability to add more nuances to the role of expectations in these models, enriching the full-information rational expectations (FIRE) framework and germinating models with departures from that framework.

In the fourth part of the Handbook, canonical theories of expectations formation and dissemination are presented: learning, ambiguity, and epidemiological approaches. We were struck by how rich the theoretical landscape is that economists can already rely on and are sure that this landscape will thrive even more with the new expectations data that are being collected.

In the final chapter of this Handbook, Chuck Manski, one of the pioneers in this area and a strong advocate for the revival of the collection and use of expectations data in Economics, offers some concluding thoughts on open questions. Much remains to be done, including on the measurement of imprecise probabilities about future events, on expectation formation, and on how to elicit expectations when agents confound beliefs and preferences. Measurement issues still abound and more and more refined theory still needs to be developed, taking into account what we have learned about expectations. What is, in our view, no longer justifiable, however, is the status of FIRE environments as some sort of "natural benchmark." FIRE models should now be evaluated against the expectations data, just like any deviation from FIRE should.

In closing, we wish to express our heartfelt thanks to the many contributors that have brought this Handbook to life: this was made especially difficult by the timing of the Handbook, which took shape under difficult circumstances during a worldwide pandemic. COVID-19 also prevented us from having an in-person conference about the Handbook submissions, but we, nevertheless, were able to hold a virtual conference that yielded great discussion and useful insights for all contributors.

When we discussed what we wanted from our Handbook contributors, the one recurring theme was always: How can we help a graduate student get into expectational research and its subfields? What are the open questions that they might want to address? We hope that this Handbook provides this help and guidance and that, in any future volume of this Handbook of Economic Expectations, we will have some of this exciting work presented.

Rüdiger Bachmann, Giorgio Topa, and Wilbert van der Klaauw

PART

1

Expectation elicitation

Household surveys and probabilistic questions

1

Wändi Bruine de Bruin[a]**, Alycia Chin**[b,e]**, Jeff Dominitz**[c]**, and Wilbert van der Klaauw**[d,f]

[a]*University of Southern California, Los Angeles, CA, United States*
[b]*U.S. Securities and Exchange Commission, Washington, DC, United States*
[c]*ECONorthwest, Portland, OR, United States*
[d]*Federal Reserve Bank of New York, New York, NY, United States*

1.1 History and motivation for measuring household economic expectations

1.1.1 Why economists started to elicit qualitative subjective expectations

The history of household surveys eliciting subjective economic expectations started at the University of Michigan's Survey Research Center. In the 1940s, psychologist George Katona and his Michigan colleagues launched national household surveys, including the University of Michigan's Surveys of Consumers (henceforth "Michigan Survey of Consumers") and the Survey of Consumer Finances (SCF) funded by the Federal Reserve Board. Expectations questions asked consumers whether or not they intended to purchase a car, expected their household income to increase or decrease or stay about the same, and expected that they would be better off or worse off financially. The Michigan Survey of Consumers also asked for point forecasts of next-year and long-term inflation, or the outcome regarded as most likely (Section 1.3.1).

In one of the earliest publications about this research, Katona and Rensis Likert assessed the value of using subjective data, along with objective data, to predict choice behavior. In this paper, they critique the idea that behavioral predictions should be based solely on observed historical relationships among economic variables:

> At times, people in general tend to act as they did before, and knowing how people acted in the past may yield the best clue at such times concerning how they will act in the future. But there are times when people change their behavior—sometimes rapidly—and then information on intervening variables, motives, attitudes, etc., must be relied upon to supplement behavioral data for purposes of prediction (Katona and Likert, 1946, p. 199).

---

[e] The Securities and Exchange Commission disclaims responsibility for any private publication or statement of any SEC employee or Commissioner. This research expresses the author's views and does not necessarily reflect those of the Commission, the Commissioners, or other members of the staff.

[f] The views expressed in this paper are those of the authors and do not necessarily reflect the position of the Federal Reserve Bank of New York or the Federal Reserve System.

This work led to the creation of Michigan's well-known Index of Consumer Sentiment, and its subindex, the Index of Consumer Expectations. Both have been reported monthly since 1966, and are utilized by The Conference Board in its Index of Leading Economic Indicators. Thus, subjective economic expectations were incorporated in aggregate measures that seemed relevant for economic research and policy makers.

By the 1950s, Katona had teamed up with Lawrence Klein, a future recipient of the Nobel Prize in economics (Katona and Klein, 1952). They pointed to the value of household expectations data for the purposes of (i) predicting choice behavior, (ii) understanding how these choices are made, and (iii) understanding how expectations are formed. Charles F. Manski mentioned these same three points a half-century later, in his Fisher–Schulz lecture at the European meeting of the Econometrics Society. In the intervening time period, "the profession for many years enforced something of a prohibition on the collection of subjective data" (Manski, 2004, p. 1337). Doubts had been raised about the value of qualitative expectations data for predicting individual choice decisions, including by the so-called Smithies committee report on the SCF (Federal Reserve Consultant Committee on Consumer Survey Statistics, 1955). The rational expectations revolution had circumvented the need for such data. Dominitz and Manski (1997a, 1999) describe this history.

1.1.2 Why economists started to elicit subjective probabilities

The early 1990s saw a resurgence of household surveys on subjective expectations. Our focus in this chapter will be on probabilistic questions, but questions also asked for point forecasts or most likely outcomes. We will touch on some important limitations of point forecasts below, but acknowledge that they have been found valuable, especially in aggregated form, in capturing changes in household expectations (e.g., Stanislawska et al., 2019).

Modern economic theory models economic agents as forming expectations as subjective probability distributions. Subjective probabilities may therefore be directly utilized in econometric models to replace strong assumptions on expectations that are typically not testable in the absence of these data. Furthermore, these subjective probabilities may be utilized by policy makers and others to monitor subjective well-being (Dominitz and Manski, 1997b).

Manski (2004) makes a clear case for eliciting quantitative expectations in the form of subjective probabilities:

> If persons can express their expectations in probabilistic form, elicitation of subjective probability distributions should have compelling advantages relative to verbal questioning. Perhaps the most basic attraction is that probability provides a well-defined absolute numerical scale for responses; hence, there is reason to think that responses may be interpersonally comparable. Another attraction is that empirical assessment of the internal consistency of respondents' expectations is possible. A researcher can use the algebra of probability (Bayes Theorem, the Law of Total Probability, etc.) to examine the internal consistency of respondent's expectations about different events (p. 1339).

Initial evidence that people can express their expectations in probabilistic form and that these probabilities have predictive value comes from Juster (1966). His empirical analyses show that directly eliciting the subjective probability of buying a good is more informative than eliciting a yes/no intention. In the 1990s, Juster became Principal Investigator of the University of Michigan's Health and Retirement Study (HRS). This longitudinal study of households in the United States (US) includes numerous subjective probability questions. A 10-point scale was used initially but it was replaced with a 0–100 "percent chance" scale in subsequent waves.

Analyses of these early surveys demonstrated the value of expectations data. For instance, HRS participants' expectations of living until specific ages were found to predict how long they ended up living (Hurd and McGarry, 2002). Similarly, adolescents who completed the 1997 National Longitudinal Study of Youth reported probabilities of significant life events that were associated with actual life events reported concurrently and several years later (Bruine de Bruin et al., 2007; Fischhoff et al., 2000). At about the same time, other US household surveys also elicited subjective probabilities (Survey of Economic Expectations, Dominitz and Manski, 1997b) and in Europe (Bank of Italy's Survey of Household Income and Wealth, Guiso et al., 1992).

Interest in expectations data grew for two additional reasons. First, subjective measures, such as those collected in the Michigan Survey of Consumers and The Conference Board's Consumer Confidence surveys, were found to have predictive power in forecasting changes in consumption and inflation (Carroll et al., 1994; Ludvigson, 2004; Ang et al., 2007). Second, researchers started questioning the popular assumption that expectations are rational. Psychologists Daniel Kahneman and Amos Tversky (Kahneman et al., 1982) found that individuals typically lack complete information and do not consistently follow the rules of rational decision making. Their work promoted economic research that incorporated enhancements and deviations from rational expectations, including models with bounded rationality, rational inattention, imperfect knowledge, and adaptive learning. This led to increased recognition of the value of expectations data for testing rationality of expectations and for estimating models with and without rational expectations. Examples of empirical studies using consumers' subjective expectations to test for rationality include Bernheim (1990); Das and van Soest (1997, 1999); Das et al. (1999); Souleles (2004); Benitez-Silva and Dwyer (2005, 2006); Benitez-Silva et al. (2008); Case et al. (2012); D'Haultfoeuille et al. (2021).

1.1.3 **Widespread adoption of subjective probability elicitation**

Research on subjective expectations has continued to expand. In the early 2000s, expectations questions were included in the English Longitudinal Study of Ageing (ELSA) and the European Survey of Health, Ageing and Retirement (SHARE). In 2006, expectations questions about personal life events were incorporated into the 1979 cohort of the National Longitudinal Survey of Youth, a representative sample of US youth born between 1957 and 1964 (Table 1.1).

Since 2005, expectations questions have been regularly incorporated in online surveys administered through RAND's American Life Panel (ALP), covering topics like inflation, asset prices, employment, retirement, health, life expectancy, H1N1 infection risk, voting and elections. Since 2014 the USC Understanding America Study (UAS) has also included online surveys with expectations questions on retirement, longevity, medical expenditures, health, inheritance, job loss, home values, insurance product choices, income, and saving. The ALP and the UAS were both launched under the leadership of Arie Kapteyn, whose efforts (which included the earlier Dutch VSB Panel, which later became the CentER Savings Survey) have been invaluable for research on subjective expectations.

In the 2010s, at least three central banks started running large, representative surveys on consumer expectations. The Spanish Survey of Household Finances (EFF) incorporated house price expectations in 2011, and probabilistic expectations for household income in 2014. In 2013, the Federal Reserve Bank of New York launched the Survey of Consumer Expectations (SCE), a monthly survey that asks

Table 1.1 Selection of Surveys that Contain Probabilistic Expectations Questions.

Survey	Home Values	Income	Work	Inflation	Stocks/ Mutual Funds	Other Expectations Questions
Centralized, nationally representative surveys:						
1 University of Michigan Surveys of Consumers (https://data.sca.isr.umich.edu/reports.php) **Background:** Founded in 1946, this survey currently runs monthly, with responses from at least 500 adult men and women living in households in the coterminous U.S. **Format:** Repeated cross-section with a rotating panel: the total sample typically includes 60% new respondents (an independent cross section), and 40% who are being interviewed for the second time. **Method:** Telephone.		X	X		X	Social security/pension income
2 Health and Retirement Study (https://hrs.isr.umich.edu/about) **Background:** Founded in 1992, this survey has expanded to become a representative sample of approximately 20,000 people (aged 50+) in the U.S. It currently asks for respondent and household level data every 2 years. **Format:** Longitudinal panel. **Method:** Starting in 2006, interviews are conducted in-person and over the phone. The in-person sample reports physical/biological and psychosocial measures.	XT		XT		XT	Mental clarity, survival [T], inheritance [T], nursing home, Social Security/Medicare benefits, medical expenses [T]
3 Survey of Consumer Expectations (FRB-New York) (https://www.newyorkfed.org/microeconomics/sce#/) **Background:** The SCE launched in 2013. It is fielded monthly to a representative sample of approximately 1300 household heads (defined as the person in the household who owns, is buying, or rents the home). In addition, there are triannual surveys on Credit Access, Household Spending, Labor Market and Public Policy, and annual Housing Market surveys. **Format:** Rotating panel. Respondents participate for up to 12 months, with a roughly equal number rotating in and out of the panel each month. **Method:** Internet-based.	XD	XD	X	XD	X	Spending, moving, interest rates, US unemployment, government debt, your business will hire more workers, credit applications, taxes and generosity of assistance programs.
4 Bank of Italy's Survey on Household Income and Wealth (https://www.bancaditalia.it/statistiche/tematiche/indagini-famiglie-imprese/bilanci-famiglie/index.html) **Background:** This survey started in the 1960s, and currently runs every 2 years. Respondents include approx. 8000 households (20,000 individuals) over 300 Italian municipalities, covering the official resident population of Italy. **Format:** A panel started in 1989 and covers about 50% of the sample. **Method:** Starting in 1998, data are collected through a computer-assisted electronic questionnaire. The remaining surveys collected on paper.	XD		X	XD		
5 Bank of Canada's Survey of Consumer Expectations (https://www.bankofcanada.ca/publications/canadian-survey-of-consumer-expectations/canadian-survey-of-consumer-expectations-overview/) **Background:** The survey was launched in 2014 and runs quarterly. It is nationally representative of adult residents of Canada aged 18+. The survey is offered in both English and French. **Format:** Rotating panel. Respondents participate for up to a year, with a roughly equal number joining and leaving each quarter. **Method:** Online.			X	XD		

continued on next page

Table 1.1 (*continued*)

Survey	Home Values	Income	Work	Inflation	Stocks/ Mutual Funds	Other Expectations Questions
6 National Longitudinal Survey of Youth (1979) (https://www.nlsinfo.org/content/cohorts/nlsy79) **Background:** The survey started in 1979, and expectations questions added in 2006. The sample contains U.S. youth born between 1957 and 1964. It originally included 12,686 respondents; now, 9964 respondents remain eligible. They are interviewed every 2 years. **Format:** Panel. **Method:** Mixed phone and in-person. However, the vast majority (95% as of 2018) are phone.			X			Health limiting ability to work, inheritance, survival, nursing home moves, working age [T]
7 National Longitudinal Survey of Youth (1997) (https://www.nlsinfo.org/content/cohorts/nlsy97) **Background:** Sample of youth born between 1980 and 1984 who are interviewed every 2 years. The sample originally included 8984 respondents. **Format:** Panel **Method:** Mix of in-person and phone.			X			Life events (e.g., arrested, die, get pregnant, have children, get married, move)
8 English Longitudinal Study of Ageing (ELSA) (https://www.elsa-project.ac.uk/) **Background:** The survey launched in 2002 and runs every two years. It is a representative survey of adults aged 50+ in England. **Format:** Panel **Method:** Interviews are conducted face-to-face, with some additional questionnaires completed by respondents on paper.	X		XT			Moving, survival [T], running out of money, inheritance/bequests, nursing home, long term care
9 Survey of Health, Ageing and Retirement in Europe (SHARE) (http://www.share-project.org/home0.html) **Background:** The survey launched in 2004. It targets all persons aged 50+ who have their regular domicile in one of the 29 countries covered by SHARE. **Format:** Panel of primary respondents, plus interviews for household members. **Method:** Interviews are primarily face-to-face, with some paper questionnaires and telephone interviews.			X			Survival, government benefits
10 Banco de España's Survey of Household Finances (https://www.bde.es/bde/en/areas/estadis/estadisticas-por/encuestas-hogar/relacionados/Encuesta_Financi/) **Background:** The survey launched in 2002 and is conducted every three years. It is representative of the Spanish population with an oversample of high wealth households. **Format:** Respondents include both new participants and repeat participants. Each household is limited from repeating more than a certain number of times. **Method:** Phone	XD	X				
11 Deutsche Bundesbank's Survey on Consumer Expectations (https://www.bundesbank.de/en/bundesbank/research/survey-on-consumer-expectations/survey-on-consumer-expectations-794568) **Background:** The survey started in 2019. For each wave, around 2000 members of the general public are asked to respond, yielding estimates that are representative of the online population. **Format:** Some repeat and some new respondents. **Method:** Online.	D	D		DE		Default on a debt

continued on next page

Table 1.1 (*continued*)

Survey	Home Values	Income	Work	Inflation	Stocks/ Mutual Funds	Other Expectations Questions
12 European Central Bank's Consumer Expectations Survey (https://www.ecb.europa.eu/stats/ecb_surveys/consumer_exp_survey/ html/index.en.html) **Background:** The survey began in January 2020 and includes over 10,000 respondents from Belgium, France, Germany, Italy, the Netherlands, and Spain. **Format:** Some repeat and some new respondents. **Method:** Online.	D	D		D		
Historical surveys and decentralized surveys:						
13 Survey of Economic Expectations (SEE) (https://www.disc.wisc.edu/archive/econexpect/index.html#:~: text=The%20Survey%20of%20Economic%20Expectations%20(SEE) %20is%20a%20nationwide%20survey,University%20of% 20Wisconsin%20Survey%20Center) **Background:** From 1994 to 2002, the survey was a module in WISCON, a telephone survey conducted by the University of Wisconsin Survey Center. It was representative of currently working residential telephone numbers in the continental U.S. Each wave had between 230 and 1000 respondents. **Format:** Repeated cross-section. **Method:** Phone.		T	T		T	Crime, health insurance coverage, Social Security benefits [T]
14 RAND's American Life Panel (https://alpdata.rand.org/) **Background:** The ALP contains over 6000 adults aged 18+. Content is customized to individual researchers' studies. **Format:** Panel. **Method:** Online.						Varies across studies
15 USC's Understanding America Study (https://uasdata.usc.edu/index.php) **Background:** The UAS includes approximately 9500 adults aged 18+. Content is customized to individual researchers' studies. **Format:** Panel. **Method:** Online.						Varies across studies

Note. *X designates the presence of an expectations question in the standard, 0–100% format. D designates the presence of a probability density question, which asks respondents to assign 100 points across multiple outcome bins. T designates the presence of cumulative distribution questions, which ask respondents to report expectations at thresholds (e.g., survival to 75, 85, and 95). Finally, E designates an experimental treatment.*

about household and macroeconomic indicators, including income, spending, work status, inflation, home price growth, stock market movements, and US unemployment rates. In the following year, the Bank of Canada launched a quarterly survey which adapted questions from the SCE, including on work status and inflation.

Currently, subjective probability questions are included in least six ongoing nationally representative surveys in the US. Additional surveys with expectations questions are running in Europe and Canada. Table 1.1 presents a list of key surveys. Due to this growing subject of inquiry, it is impossible to provide a complete list. The majority of listed surveys sample adult household decision-makers. However, surveys eliciting subjective probabilities have expanded to include businesses (see Chapters 2, 12, and 11 in this Handbook) and adolescents (such as the National Longitudinal Studies of

Youth). Since 2019, the Deutsche Bundesbank has been conducting its online survey to elicit expectations from Germany's members of the public. In 2020, the European Central Bank launched their Consumer Expectations Survey (CES) in Belgium, France, Germany, Italy, the Netherlands, and Spain. Both surveys incorporate features taken from the New York Fed's SCE.

Table 1.1 contains additional details about the surveys mentioned in this section. The top panel describes established, nationally representative surveys from different countries. The bottom panel describes historical surveys and those that are "decentralized," meaning that the content varies depending on individual research teams. The columns describe the content of each survey. Specifically, we highlight whether surveys contain expectations questions pertaining to five common topics: income changes, inflation, home values, work-related outcomes (including job loss), and changes in stock market or mutual fund values. The rightmost column notes additional topics, including public benefits (e.g., Social Security), personal events (e.g., crime victimization, having a child, moving to a different residence or nursing home), and macroeconomic events (e.g., interest rate changes).

Table 1.1 suggests that work-related expectations are a key topic of household expectations surveys. Another common topic is inflation, which is a focus of central banks in the US, Canada, and Europe. In these latter surveys, inflation expectations are elicited in a manner that provides policymakers with information on the distribution of respondent beliefs (i.e., subjective uncertainty), as discussed further below. Given the predominant role of households in aggregate as drivers of economic activity, monitoring and managing consumers' inflation expectations are primary goals of policymakers and central components of modern monetary policy (Armantier et al., 2017; Chapter 5 in this Handbook). These surveys also facilitate deeper analysis of how expectations are formed.

Table 1.1 shows variation in how frequently nationally representative surveys are fielded (ranging from monthly to every three years) and their interview mode (telephone, in-person, online, or a combination). All of the nationally representative surveys listed in Table 1.1 are structured as longitudinal or rotating panels, except for the Michigan Survey of Consumers, which is more accurately characterized as a repeated cross-sectional survey that includes a limited panel component. Across surveys, there is some variation in the proportion of the sample that is repeatedly interviewed versus newly sampled, as well as how many times respondents are asked to participate before rotating off of the panel.

The bottom section of Table 1.1 describes surveys that have varied over time in terms of content, format, and methodology. This variation may be due to the decentralized nature of these surveys.

1.1.4 Main takeaway

National household surveys of economic expectations have been administered for about three-quarters of a century, beginning with the Survey of Consumer Finances at the University of Michigan in the late 1940s. Following a general rejection of expectations data in economics beginning in the early 1960s, elicitation of subjective probabilities began again in the 1990s, with widespread adoption of subjective probability elicitation beginning in the early 2000s.

Economists have recognized the value of expectations data for the purposes of (i) predicting choice behavior, (ii) understanding how choices are made, and (iii) understanding how expectations are formed. The widespread adoption seen today can be attributed to efforts that clarified the inherent limitations of qualitative as opposed to quantitative expectations data, demonstrations of the feasibility of eliciting quantitative expectations in the form of subjective probabilities, and growing recognition of the untenability of strong assumptions of rational expectations that are made in the absence of expectations data. The remainder of this chapter provides methodological details to inform the design, administration, and analysis of household surveys on economic expectations, and illustrates how these methods have been utilized in a wide range of recent applications.

1.2 Methodological considerations when developing surveys of expectations

Surveys are a form of communication between question designers and respondents who answer questions (Bruine de Bruin, 2011; Schwarz, 1996). Effective communication occurs when respondents interpret questions as intended by the researchers and are able to provide responses that reflect their relevant beliefs (also referred to as "mental models"; Bruine de Bruin and Bostrom, 2013; Andre et al., 2021; Ferrario and Stantcheva, 2022). When researchers and respondents agree on what questions ask about, questions are said to have *face validity*. When respondents give answers that are correlated with other relevant beliefs, questions are said to have *construct validity*. When respondents give answers that are correlated with behaviors, questions are said to have *predictive validity*. Designing survey questions carefully tends to improve these types of validity.

We begin this section by discussing methods for pretesting survey questions in order to enhance data quality. These best-practice recommendations should be useful for designing surveys of expectations on a variety of topics, including panel surveys, cross-sectional surveys, survey-based experiments, and ad-hoc surveys. We also consider the relative benefits of including expectations questions in panel surveys as opposed to cross-sectional (or repeated cross-sectional) surveys.

1.2.1 Survey pretesting

Poorly designed questions that are difficult to understand will generate less valid responses, if participants answer at all (Chin and Bruine de Bruin, 2018; Knäuper et al., 1997; Velez and Ashworth, 2007). When respondents attempt to answer confusing questions, they may end up guessing at how to answer. If respondents misunderstand the researchers' intentions, then their guesses may not reflect their actual economic expectations, or correlate with other relevant beliefs and behaviors. In some instances, respondents may even report a "fifty–fifty" or 50% chance of an event happening, when they actually mean to say that they do not know what to answer (Bruine de Bruin and Carman, 2012).

Fortunately, there is a social science of survey design that provides evidence about how to best design survey questions (Dillman, 2011). Here, we discuss two methodological approaches that have informed the design of expectations questions: (1) randomized survey-based experiments and (2) cognitive interviews with follow-up surveys. We subsequently discuss how these methods were utilized in the design of a national household survey of economic expectations.

1.2.1.1 *Randomized survey-based experiments*

Insights from the survey design literature have been based on randomized survey-based experiments, in which participants are randomly assigned to different versions of the same question. For example, studies have examined how participants respond to simplified (versus original) versions of the same expectations question (Chin and Bruine de Bruin, 2018), or how responses vary with open-ended questions as compared to questions accompanied by 0–100% response scales (Bruine de Bruin and Carman, 2018). To find out which version leads to more informative responses, the different versions are systematically compared in terms of their effect on, for example, missing responses, the relationship of reported expectations with relevant behaviors, and respondents' reported confidence in their answers.

One insight from randomized experiments is that survey questions will be less likely to be skipped if they are easy to understand (Chin and Bruine de Bruin, 2018). As a rule of thumb, words of 1–2 syllables (vs. more) are less likely to reflect jargon, and are more commonly used in everyday language. Additionally, average adult literacy in the US are at the 7th–9th grade level (Neuhauser and Paul, 2011). This means that surveys that are written at a higher reading level may be too hard for many respondents to understand. Microsoft Word's grammar check and several online tools provide ways to assess the readability of a survey.

However, writing questions in simple wording will not avoid confusion if survey designers and respondents interpret simple words differently. For example, respondents who are cohabiting in a heterosexual relationship may not recognize that survey designers want them to check that they are "married or living with a partner" if they think that "partner" refers to same-sex relationships (Hunter, 2005). Such a misunderstanding is difficult to catch when conducting a survey. Therefore, survey designers recommend conducting cognitive interviews with individuals who are selected from among the intended survey population.

1.2.1.2 *Cognitive interviews with follow-up surveys*

To find out whether respondents interpret survey questions in the way that researchers intended, the survey design literature suggests conducting *cognitive interviews* (Bruine de Bruin, 2011; Bruine de Bruin and Bostrom, 2013; Dillman, 2011). In cognitive interviews, participants are asked to read each survey question out loud, and think out loud while generating their answer. Participants' explanations will reveal when they get confused. In general, even a few interviews reveal the most common causes of confusion. If cognitive interviews show serious difficulties with understanding, survey designers can revise the question and try another round of cognitive interviews. In cases where improvements are not straightforward, a follow-up survey can be conducted to examine how different question interpretations are associated with responses. A randomized survey-based experiment could be used to examine whether changes in the question design are successfully addressing any undesirable effects on responses.

1.2.1.3 *Example*

The Federal Reserve Bank of New York's Survey of Consumer Expectations was informed by cognitive interviews and randomized survey-based experiments conducted during a 6-year development and testing period. This Household Inflation Expectations Project started by asking 30 people to think out loud while answering the Michigan Survey of Consumers' qualitative expectations question about inflation (henceforth "the Michigan question"). The Michigan question had been the standard for assessing inflation expectations in the US for more than 50 years (Curtin, 2006). As recommended by the survey design literature, it uses relatively straightforward wording:

> During the next 12 months, do you think prices in general will go up, go down, or stay where they are now?

Participants who report that prices will go up or down are then asked by what percent they think prices will change. We found that some interviewees interpreted the question as asking about *infla-*

tion, whereas others interpreted it as asking about *prices they pay* (Armantier et al., 2013). Although the term "inflation" refers to a relatively complex economic concept, people tend to have a basic understanding of what it means (Leiser and Drori, 2005; Svenson and Nilsson, 1986; van der Klaauw et al., 2008).

Interviewees who thought of their personal price experiences (as opposed to general inflation) seemed more likely to think of prices that have increased rather than prices that have decreased or stayed the same – perhaps because price increases are more memorable than decreases. A similar issue arose during the introduction of the euro. Although economists were unable to measure an effect of the euro introduction on general inflation in Germany, Germans believed that prices had increased (Jungermann et al., 2007). Indeed, psychological theories suggest that price increases are more memorable than price decreases, especially if they are large and frequently experienced (Brachinger, 2008; Christandl et al., 2011; Jungermann et al., 2007; Greitemeyer et al., 2005; Ranyard et al., 2008).

To examine whether respondents' interpretations of the Michigan question were associated with reported expectations, a follow-up survey was administered in December 2007 with a larger sample recruited through RAND's American Life Panel. All respondents received the Michigan question about prices in general. They were then asked to indicate how much they were thinking of different question interpretations taken directly from cognitive interviews, including "the prices of things you spend money on" and "inflation." Thinking relatively more about personal price experiences when answering questions about expectations for prices in general is associated with reporting expectations of larger price increases (Bruine de Bruin et al., 2012), due to extreme experiences with prices for food and gas being most likely to come to mind (Bruine de Bruin et al., 2011b).

In a subsequent survey-based experiment, participants were randomly assigned to the original Michigan question about "prices in general" or a version that instead asked about "inflation" (Bruine de Bruin et al., 2012). The question wording had little to no effect on the nonresponse rate. However, participants who were asked to report their expectations for "inflation" gave responses that were more in line with historical inflation rates and agreed more with each other (seen in lower dispersion of responses), as compared to participants who were asked to report their expectations for "prices in general." The greater disagreement in expectations for "prices in general" reflects differences in interpretation with some respondents thinking the question asks about inflation and others thinking it asks about specific prices they pay. Given these findings, we recommend the "inflation" wording instead of the "prices in general" wording.

1.2.2 Panel vs. cross-sectional surveys

One key design decision that researchers must make in advance of administering an expectations survey is whether or not to elicit expectations from the same individuals over time. In *panel* (or longitudinal) surveys, responses are repeatedly elicited from the same respondents over time, whereas in *cross-sectional* surveys, responses are elicited from different respondents each time. For nonpersonal outcomes, including macroeconomic variables, panel surveys offer the benefit of being able to determine how a given set of individuals revise expectations over time.

Panel data are needed to evaluate whether respondents' reported expectations predict later future experiences, because subsequent survey waves can ask follow-up questions about those experiences. Panel data on individual-level expectations have also proved valuable for analyzing changes in expectations over time. For instance, Zafar (2011) shows that there is considerable heterogeneity in how students use new information about academic ability and "match quality" to revise their beliefs about college-major specific outcomes. Similarly, Armand et al. (2019) show that parents in the Republic of Macedonia exhibit considerable heterogeneity in the way they update expectations about the returns to secondary school education in response to changes in the local labor market conditions. Heiss et al. (2019) find persistent heterogeneity in stock market return expectations and in the way respondents use information on past stock market returns to form expectations.

A few studies identified a potential downside of panel surveys, and propose using repeated cross-sectional surveys instead. Specifically, repeated survey waves have been found to influence respondents' answers – and potentially their behaviors – over time (Fitzsimons and Morwitz, 1996; Halpern-Manners et al., 2014). For example, Kim and Binder (in press) find that average inflation point forecasts and inflation uncertainty in the Survey of Consumer Expectations decline with survey experience. This finding is consistent with evidence reported in Armantier et al. (2017). Kim and Binder argue that this effect is due to respondents seeking information about inflation to inform their answers to subsequent surveys. As a result, panel-survey participants' inflation expectations may no longer reflect inflation expectations held by the general population.

Panel conditioning may also indicate a reduction in measurement error as respondents gain survey experience. For example, when considering inflation expectations, measurement errors may stem from respondents' cognitive efforts to formalize, retrieve and report their true underlying beliefs. Respondents may become better at formalizing and retrieving their true beliefs through introspection over time, reducing noise in their responses. Given the well-documented finding that measurement errors tend to be positively correlated with responses, and that some respondents appear to see inflation expectations as bounded at zero, this would result in a decline in average expectations with panel tenure. Reported beliefs could then become more accurate with respondents' survey experience. Whether changes in expectations tend to reflect information acquisition or reduced measurement error is an empirical question that requires further investigation.

Concerns about panel conditioning effects are often addressed by combining cross-sectional and panel data within the same survey (Table 1.1). For instance, the Federal Reserve Bank of New York SCE has a rotating panel, where participants are invited to answer surveys for 12 months. Each month, roughly the same proportion of participants rotate on and off of the panel. The number of months of participation in the survey is held stable over time, mitigating the impact of conditioning on the time series of average or median expectations. New respondents can be treated as a new cross-section, whereas responses by repeat-participants can be used to analyze the updating and revision of expectations, and panel effects.

1.2.3 **Main takeaway**

Researchers face a number of survey design decisions before launching household surveys of economic expectations. Before investing in a survey, we strongly recommended conducting cognitive interviews and randomized survey-based experiments. Without such investments, longitudinal surveys may run for decades with poor questions that elicit low-quality expectations data. In Section 1.3 below, we will discuss additional applications of these approaches for designing probabilistic-expectation questions.

Of course, not all projects will have the resources to conduct randomized survey-based experiments to test their survey questions. PhD students who are designing their own surveys may therefore look to the survey design literature for practical guidance about survey design (Bergman et al., 2020; Dillman,

2011). Additionally, conducting a few cognitive interviews before implementing a survey should reveal the most common misunderstandings participants may have.

1.3 Insights and methodological advances

In this section, we describe new insights and methodological advances for eliciting and analyzing subjective expectations. Generally, these developments are grounded in the survey pretesting methodology described in Section 1.2. Our goal here is to describe approaches for conducting research involving subjective expectations, and to highlight issues requiring further study.

1.3.1 Point forecasts versus probabilistic expectations

While intuitive and direct, asking for a point forecast (e.g., "what do you think will be" or "by how much do you expect") has important drawbacks. First, it is not clear whether the estimates respondents provide reflect the mean, mode, median, or another central-tendency measure of the subjective distribution. As discussed in Section 1.3.8, some point forecasts reflect none of these, but rather capture varying degrees of loss aversion. Second, point forecasts contain no information about respondents' uncertainty about their beliefs. Third, as discussed in Section 1.3.2, reported point forecasts are sensitive to the wording and context of the survey question.

Asking whether or not an event is expected to occur has limited informativeness. For example, when respondents report an expectation that a binary outcome will happen (or not), we only know that the underlying subjective probability of that outcome exceeds the threshold of 0.5. This argument was made by Juster (1966) and formalized by Manski (1990).

Another approach is to ask respondents to judge the likelihood of an uncertain event on a Likert scale, with response options for "very likely", "fairly likely", "not too likely", and "not at all likely". Considerable effort has been devoted to convert these responses into quantitative measures (Pesaran and Weale, 2006). A concern is that the interpretation of verbal probabilities varies across respondents, and, for a given respondent, across events of interest (Beyth-Marom, 1982).

Alternatively, the probabilistic question format asks respondents to assess the quantitative "percent chance" of an event happening. The simplest version of a probabilistic question asks about a binary event, such as whether household income will increase in the next year or not. A more complex version asks for respondents' full subjective probability distribution of next-year's household income, including the percent chance that household income will be greater than, say, $10,000, that it will be between $10,000 and $20,000, and so on. If respondents are willing and able to report probabilities, then these responses should capture beliefs and subjective uncertainty in a way that is comparable across respondents.

Before discussing the formulation and application of the probabilistic question format in greater detail, we first discuss findings related to the importance of question wording in the elicitation of point forecasts.

1.3.2 Question wording and framing of point forecasts

As discussed in Section 1.2, in designing probabilistic expectations questions, attention should be devoted to their wording and framing. We expand on that discussion here using two examples from the

Household Inflation Expectations Project that informed the Survey of Consumer Expectations at the Federal Reserve Bank of New York.

The first example is about capturing negative and positive changes in expectations. To do so, the inflation-expectations question in the Michigan Survey consist of two parts. The first part asks whether respondents expect prices in general to go up, go down, or stay the same. The second part asks those respondents who expected prices to go up or down about the expected magnitude of that change. A relatively large share of respondents tends to answer "stay the same" to the first part. Upon probing of respondents who report "stay the same", Armantier et al. (2017) find that a substantial fraction then changes their answers to numbers that are substantially different from 0. Thus, incorrectly interpreting "stay the same" as point forecasts of zero inflation would be problematic.

Experimenting with alternative question formats in the SCE, Armantier et al. (2017) use a question format that does not include the "stay the same" option. For example, their spending expectations question first asks whether respondents expect their household spending to increase by 0% or more or decrease by 0% or more. Respondents are then asked for the expected magnitude of the change, and are told that 0% responses are allowed. This question generates a substantially lower fraction of 0% responses, as compared to a question that offers a "stay the same" option. Initial evidence collected through probing suggests that Armantier et al. (2017)'s question format is better at capturing respondents' beliefs. Related findings are reported by Palmqvist and Strömberg (2004) at the Sveriges Riksbank.

The second example pertains to follow-up questions that ask respondents to reconsider their answers. The Michigan Survey of Consumers' expectations question about year-ahead inflation provides respondents who report a point forecast in excess of 5% up or down with this follow-up "probe":

> Let me make sure I have that correct. You said that you expect prices to go [up/down] during the next 12 months by [x] percent. Is that correct?

Bruine de Bruin et al. (2017) find that this probe causes some respondents to revise their expectations downward. If it is thought that the probe is needed to encourage respondents to think harder about their answer, then it should also be given to all respondents. Bruine de Bruin et al. find that if the follow-up question is instead applied uniformly, then it results in a broader downward shift in the response distribution.

Of course, these are just two examples illustrating that the answer to a question can be influenced by the way response options are framed. Other question design features, such as presenting a "Don't know" option (or not) may also be consequential (Schuman and Presser, 1996).

1.3.3 Introductory framing for probabilistic expectations questions

To help respondents understand how to respond to probabilistic questions, it is common to present a brief introduction about how to use numerical probabilities. For example, adapting wording proposed by Juster (1966) and Dominitz and Manski (1997a), the SCE includes the following introduction:

> In some of the following questions, we will ask you to think about the *percent chance* of something happening in the future. Your answers can range from 0 to 100, where 0 means there is absolutely no chance, and 100 means that it is absolutely certain. For example, numbers like 2 and 5 percent may indicate "almost no chance"; 18 percent or so may mean "not much chance"; 47 or 52 percent chance may be a "pretty even chance"; 83 percent or so may mean a "very good chance"; 95 or 98 percent chance may be "almost certain."

The HRS uses a similar introduction:

> Next we would like to ask your opinion about how likely you think various events might be. When I ask a question I'd like for you to give me a number from 0 to 100, where "0" means that you think there is absolutely no chance, and "100" means that you think the event is absolutely sure to happen.

1.3.4 Rounding, bunching and ambiguity

When reporting probabilistic expectations, it is common for respondents to round their responses to answers ending in 0 or 5. The extent of rounding varies across respondents, with some respondents using coarser rounding than others. Several approaches have been proposed to account for differential rounding when analyzing probabilistic expectations (Manski and Molinari, 2010; Kleinjans and van Soest, 2014). Using different econometric approaches, De Bresser and van Soest (2013) and Giustinelli et al. (in press) exploit patterns in rounding across questions and survey waves to identify and account for heterogeneity in rounding.

In addition to using responses ending in 0 or 5, a common feature of responses to probabilistic questions is heaping at zero, 50 and 100 percent (Lillard and Willis, 2001; Hudomiet and Willis, 2013). Initial studies focused on heaped responses at 50%, and argued that some respondents use 50% to indicate that they do not know what to answer (Fischhoff and Bruine de Bruin, 1999; Bruine de Bruin et al., 2000). Bruine de Bruin and Carman (2012) ask participants to explain their probability responses and find that participants who report 50% are more likely to say that they do not know what to answer as compared to participants who report other values. In another application, over 60 percent of respondents who stated a 50% chance of survival beyond age 75 on the 2006 HRS also said that they were unsure about their survival chances. When such unsure explanations predominate, it may be appropriate to treat 50% responses as "don't know" responses.

Yet, 50%-responses can also be meaningful. For example, Niu and van Soest (2014) find that about 70 percent of homeowners in the ALP who report a 50%-chance that their home's value will increase over the next year choose "equally likely" instead of "unsure" to explain their 50%-response. Hurd et al. (2011) argue that the fraction of 50%-responses declines with survey experience, and Bruine de Bruin and Carman (2012) find that 50%-responses are less likely among respondents with higher numeracy. Currently, the HRS asks participants who report a 50%-chance to explain their answer for questions related to work expectations, survival, and changes in mutual fund values, allowing for continued exploration of this issue.

It is possible that economic agents may make decisions based on uncertain or imprecise probabilistic expectations. If so, then perhaps surveys of expectations should attempt to elicit such beliefs. Giustinelli et al. (2021) find that nearly half of the respondents in the HRS reported imprecise expectations for late-onset dementia. Their approach builds on earlier work by Manski and Molinari (2010) and Giustinelli and Pavoni (2017) and enables respondents to convey a specific probability or a *probability interval* (such as "between 30 and 60 percent"). Those who initially provide a specific probability are asked whether it represented an exact number or was rounded or an approximation. When not an exact number, a second probe then permits the respondent to give a specific probability or a probability interval. Elicitation of probability intervals would also enable respondents to directly express ambiguity instead of reporting 50% as a "fifty–fifty" or "don't know" answer. Empirical studies of the extent of belief ambiguity and its role in choice decisions under uncertainty is an important area of research, discussed in more detail in Chapters 24 and 26 in this Handbook.

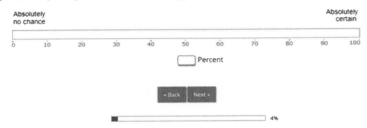

For example, what do you think is the percent chance that over the next 12 months you will move to a different primary residence (that is, the place where you usually live)?
Please enter your answer by clicking on the scale below or entering your response in the box below the scale.

FIGURE 1.1 Example of a visual response scale used to elicit probabilistic expectations.

Source: New York Fed Survey of Consumer Expectations.

1.3.5 Use of visual response scales

Probabilistic questions in mail surveys and internet surveys are often accompanied by a 0–100% visual linear response scale. Presenting a visual linear scale instead of an open-ended answer box can reduce the use of focal responses such as 0%, 50%, and 100%, as well as improve response validity (Bruine de Bruin and Carman, 2018). In the SCE, respondents see a scale and an answer box, where the 0–100 scale has labels of "absolutely no chance" and "absolutely certain" at the 0 and 100 tick marks, respectively (Fig. 1.1). Respondents are then given the instruction that they could either enter a number (on 0–100 scale) directly into the box or click anywhere on the sliding scale. To prevent respondents from anchoring their response at the original location of the cursor, no marker appears on the scale until the respondent clicks somewhere on it. Delavande and Rohwedder (2008) and Delavande et al. (2011b) test additional ways of presenting visual response scales.

1.3.6 Elicitation of probability distributions

Probabilistic questions permit elicitation of quantitative measures of belief and uncertainty typically required in estimating economic models. They assess probabilistic expectations about events that have many possible outcomes, thus capturing respondents' subjective probability distributions. Below, we discuss two main approaches for collecting subjective probability distributions, referred to as the probability density format and the cumulative distribution format (Manski, 2018). In practice, either method could be mathematically translated to the other, as long as reported beliefs are internally consistent with respect to the laws of probability. Morgan and Henrion (1990) discuss the practical advantages and disadvantages of different procedures for eliciting subjective distributions.

1.3.6.1 Elicitation of probability density functions

Questions that elicit probability density functions ask respondents to assess the probabilities of nonoverlapping outcome categories (or "bins") representing the full range of possible values. Probability density functions have long been elicited to gather data on macroeconomic variables in surveys of professional forecasters such as the Livingston Survey and the Survey of Professional Forecasters. To

And in your view, what would you say is the percent chance that, over the next 12 months, the average home price nationwide will...

*(Please note: The numbers need to add up to **100**.)*

increase by 12% or more	⬜ percent chance
increase by 8% to 12%	⬜ percent chance
increase by 4% to 8%	⬜ percent chance
increase by 2% to 4%	⬜ percent chance
increase by 0% to 2%	⬜ percent chance
decrease by 0% to 2%	⬜ percent chance
decrease by 2% to 4%	⬜ percent chance
decrease by 4% to 8%	⬜ percent chance
decrease by 8% to 12%	⬜ percent chance
decrease by 12% or more	⬜ percent chance
	TOTAL:0

FIGURE 1.2 Example of a Probability Density Function Format, used for eliciting home price expectations.

Source: New York Fed Survey of Consumer Expectations.

the best of our knowledge, the Bank of Italy's Survey of Household Income and Wealth (SHIW) was the first household survey to use it. The 1989 and 1991 waves elicited beliefs about future inflation, nominal earnings, and pension growth (Guiso et al., 1992). For example, the question about future earnings asked:

> We are interested in knowing your opinion about labor earnings or pensions 12 months from now. Suppose now that you have 100 points to be distributed between these intervals. Are there intervals which you definitely exclude? Assign zero points to these intervals. How many points do you assign to each of the remaining intervals?

The intervals shown with this question (as well as the inflation question) were: >25%, 20%–25%, 15%–20%, 13%–15%, 10%–13%, 8–10%, 7%–8%, 6%–7%, 5%–6%, 3%–5%, 0%–3%, <0%. Guiso et al. (1992) use the responses to measure subjective earnings uncertainty.

Similarly, the SCE elicits density forecasts for inflation at 1- and 3-year horizons, home price growth, and earnings growth. Respondents are asked for the percent chance of outcomes falling in various intervals, while ensuring that responses add up to 100%. As discussed in more detail later these bin probabilities are then used to construct individual measures of central tendency (e.g., the density mean or median), uncertainty, and perceived tail risks (e.g., probability of extreme positive or negative outcomes). Fig. 1.2 shows the density forecast for year-ahead national home price changes.

As respondents enter their answers, they can see the running "TOTAL" of responses. Respondents who give answers that do not add up to 100% receive the notice "Please change the numbers in the table so they add up to 100."

Other examples of national surveys that elicit an entire probability density include the Canadian and German Surveys of Consumer Expectations (Table 1.1). Chapter 2 in this Handbook provides additional examples.

When designing probability density questions, researchers must choose the location, number, and width of bins, as well as how the bins are visually presented. Too few bins spread over a large domain will generally reduce potential information quality, while many bins may become burdensome for respondents. The range of the bins and how they are centered may also lead to anchoring. Preliminary questions may be asked to establish a subjective lower and upper bound on possible outcomes, and to inform the location and width of the bins. Dominitz and Manski (1997a) adopted such an approach to customize the assessed distribution. While they argue that their approach is helpful, they warn against interpreting reports of the "lowest possible" and "highest possible" values literally as the minimum and maximum possible values. Delavande et al. (2011a) indicate that respondents tend to report the 90th or 95th percentile of the subjective distribution of beliefs when asked about a maximum. Notwithstanding this caveat, Morgan and Henrion (1990) argue that preliminary questions may help to reduce anchoring problems.

An advantage of using self-anchored support is that respondents are only asked about the range of values which they consider relevant. Fewer bins may be required when they are personalized rather than predetermined. Allowing for heterogeneity in the assessment of subjective distributions permits researchers to zoom in and collect more detailed information on the distribution. However, this variation in questioning across respondents may reduce the interpersonal comparability of responses.

Limited information is available about the sensitivity of density forecasts to the choice of bins. As part of the Household Inflation Expectations Project, New York Fed economists conducted randomized experiments comparing a symmetric 10-bin version of an inflation expectations question with an 8-bin version in which the three lowest bins were combined into one lower bin representing deflation of 4% or more. They find relatively little difference between the fitted densities derived from the two versions. They also ran an experiment on their earnings growth expectation question, to assess the effect of splitting the 0%–2% bin into two separate 0%–1% and 1%–2% bins. Again, they find relatively small differences in fitted densities derived from the reported bin probabilities.

In a study with boat owners in India, Delavande et al. (2011b) report similar robustness to variations in the elicitation design. Individuals were asked to distribute a number of bins across possible future fish catches. They were randomly assigned to using 10 or 20 bins, and to self-anchored or personalized assessment of distributions. Results were remarkably robust to both variations. Nevertheless, the best results were obtained when using 20 bins and a predetermined support.

Delavande and Rohwedder (2011) elicit density forecasts of future Social Security benefits, conditional upon receiving them. They asked HRS internet survey respondents to allocate 20 balls across 7 bins. Respondents who allocated all balls into one or two adjacent bins were presented with a follow-up screen. That screen split the chosen range into a set of narrower bins of equal width. Respondents were then asked to distribute the 20 balls across these bins. Findings indicate that this is an effective way of obtaining more precise answers about respondents' distributions of beliefs.

More research is needed to assess the effects of bin design on responses. Delavande and Rohwedder (2008) conduct a randomized experiment to examine anchoring biases, comparing the subjective probability density functions obtained from two differently centered bins-and-balls formats. They find strikingly similar subjective distributions, suggesting that there is no anchoring bias toward the middle in the bins-and-balls format used in their survey. Chapter 9 in this Handbook discusses the density question format in further detail.

Another new area of research is the elicitation of joint distributions of expected future outcomes for two or more variables, such as inflation and unemployment. While there are multiple ways of eliciting joint distributions. researchers at the New York Fed have successfully experimented with questions asking for density forecasts of one variable, conditional on ranges of outcomes for another. These conditional probability distributions, together with the outcome probabilities for the conditioning variables, can be used to recover the subjective joint distribution for each respondent. This approach was adopted in the New York Fed's Survey of Primary Dealers to elicit the joint distribution for the future size of the Federal Reserve's balance sheet and the future rate of unemployment (Potter et al., 2017). The SCE team has also used this approach to elicit the subjective joint distribution of future price and wage inflation.

1.3.6.2 *Elicitation of cumulative distribution functions*

An alternative to eliciting a subjective probability density function is to elicit the subjective cumulative distribution function. This approach typically involves a sequence of questions about the percent chance that an outcome will be less (or greater) than some threshold, which increases over the sequence. The elicited percentiles are then used to fit the entire CDF. Dominitz and Manski (1997a) used this approach to elicit year-ahead household income expectations, in the Survey of Economic Expectations. Dominitz (1998) elicited subjective future earnings distributions. Specifically, respondents were asked the following sequence questions with increasing threshold values $W_1, W_2, ..., W_k, ..., W_K$:

> Still thinking about your own earnings if you are currently working for pay one year from now...
> What do you think is the percent chance (or what are the chances out of 100) that your earnings, before deductions, will be less than $\$W_k$ per week?

The thresholds $\{W_k\}$ were determined partly by respondents' answers to two preliminary questions asking about the "lowest possible" and "highest possible" weekly earnings one year from now, conditional on working for pay at that time. To ensure logical consistency, respondents were informed of violations of monotonicity, or when they reported a probability at a higher threshold that was smaller than that at a lower threshold.

Other assessments of respondents' subjective cumulative distribution function are reported by Juster and Suzman (1995), McKenzie et al. (2007), Attanasio and Kaufmann (2008, 2009, 2014), Attanasio and Augsburg (2016), Manski (2018), Leemann et al. (2020) and Crossley et al. (2021) for income expectations; Dominitz and Manski (2006) and Delavande and Rohwedder (2008) on future Social Security benefits in the SEE and HRS, respectively; and Bover (2015) for homeowners' expected change in the price of their homes over the next 12 months. The HRS regularly asks for probabilities over multiple thresholds, for example for home price growth expectations.

Morgan and Henrion (1990) provide evidence that people find it easier to work with densities than with cumulative distributions, because it is easier to visualize certain properties of the distribution like location and symmetry. However, the sequential CDF elicitation approach of asking a set of probabilistic questions of binary events may be especially convenient in the case of telephone surveys, such as the SEE, in which visual aids are not feasible.

In the HRS internet-survey, Delavande and Rohwedder (2008, 2011) conducted a similar exercise to elicit subjective distributions of future Social Security benefits, conditional upon receiving them. They compared a balls-and-bins allocation for subjective probability-density elicitation to one based on a standard CDF-elicitation approach with a sequence of probabilistic questions asking about the "percent chance" of outcomes below different thresholds. They find that the two elicitation methods yield similar response rates, survey time and precision of responses. Furthermore, uncertainty about future Social

Security benefits was found to correlate with other sources of uncertainty in the expected direction for both designs. While the density-elicitation generated usable answers for almost all respondents, CDF-elicitation produced a significant fraction of inconsistent answers – that is, violations of monotonicity.

1.3.7 Fitting distributions and measuring uncertainty

After data on a set of bin probabilities or a sequence of distribution percentiles have been collected, researchers typically adopt a distributional assumption to calculate moments of the respondent's belief distribution. Dominitz and Manski (1997a) fit a log-normal CDF to expectations of household income, by minimizing the residual sum of squares between observed and fitted probabilities at four thresholds. Crossley et al. (2021) instead fit a stepwise uniform distribution. Bover (2015) apply a similar approach to a set of bin probabilities, connecting observed cumulative probabilities using straight lines so that the CDF is piecewise linear with a flat density within segments. Bellemare et al. (2012) interpolate using cubic splines. The fitted CDF can then be used to calculate all quantiles by linear extrapolation.

An alternative approach for fitting a distribution to elicited bin probabilities was popularized by Engelberg et al. (2009). They fit a four-parameter generalized beta distribution for cases with positive probabilities allocated to three or more bins, and fit an isosceles triangular distribution in case of only one or two bins with positive probability. While flexible, the approach assumes a unimodal density. As in the log-normal case, each respondent's distribution can be obtained by minimizing the sum of squared differences between observed and fitted cumulative probabilities at the bin end points. This approach is used in fitting all probability density distributions in regularly published reports based on SCE data (Armantier et al., 2017, New York Fed Press Releases).

Engelberg et al. (2009) also use nonparametric methods to derive bounds on the median, mean and mode of the subjective distribution based on reported probability density bin probabilities. Bissonnette and de Bresser (2018) derive nonparametric bounds on the CDF. Relatively little is known about the impact of alternative parametric assumptions when fitting distributions for inference based on reported probability distributions. This topic deserves further investigation. Chapters 3 and 4 in this Handbook provide additional discussion of the inference problem in using survey-based subjective probability distributions. Chapter 15 in this Handbook discusses a Bayesian nonparametric approach.

Distribution-based measures of uncertainty, such as the variance and interquartile range of a fitted distribution, have been found to be strongly correlated with other individual-level measures and sources of uncertainty (Bruine de Bruin et al., 2011a; Delavande and Rohwedder, 2008, 2011). An advantage of distribution-based measures of uncertainty is the comparability across individuals and over time. Bruine de Bruin et al. (2011a) report strong persistence in individual-level uncertainty over time and find that those who are more uncertain about the future tend to make larger revisions to their point forecasts over time. Their findings are roughly consistent with Bayesian updating, where a more diffuse prior at a point in time is associated with larger subsequent revisions in point forecasts. Zafar (2011) similarly finds updating behavior consistent with Bayesian learning.

In the absence of direct information on subjective uncertainty, economists have, perhaps mistakenly, used cross-sectional dispersion (or "disagreement") in point forecasts to measure aggregate uncertainty. Bruine de Bruin et al. (2011a) compare estimates of aggregate uncertainty based on individual subjective distributions to estimates based on a disagreement measure and find the latter to be an unreliable proxy for forecast uncertainty. Their findings are consistent with similar evidence from professional forecasters, reported by Rich and Tracy (2010, 2021). Although the two measures are positively correlated, these results indicate that disagreement and uncertainty are entirely distinct concepts.

An interesting alternative approach was proposed by Binder (2017). Arguing that rounding of point forecasts can be seen as an expression of uncertainty, she constructs an inflation uncertainty index based on the extent of rounding to multiples of five in the Michigan Survey of Consumers. The measure is shown to be countercyclical and positively correlated with inflation disagreement, volatility, and uncertainty as measured in the SCE.

1.3.8 Density-based forecasts versus point forecasts

Several studies have compared point forecasts to measures of central tendency derived from subjective probability distributions for the same respondents (Engelberg et al., 2009, for professional forecasters; Delavande and Rohwedder, 2011, and Bruine de Bruin et al., 2011a, for consumers). Generally, the two measures are close for most respondents. However, for a substantial share of respondents, point forecasts fall in the tail of the subjective probability distribution or even outside it – suggesting inconsistency. This heterogeneity across respondents causes average point forecasts to differ from the average central tendency of their distributions.

An important potential advantage of using the mean (or the median) of the density is that it captures the same measure of central tendency for each respondent. In contrast, as noted above, point forecasts may represent for some respondents the density mean, while for others it may represent the density median, mode, or some other moment in their subjective distribution. Similarly, another potential advantage of probability elicitation is that it permits common measurement of subjective uncertainty. Yet, we do not have a full understanding for why some point forecasts differ from the central tendency of the respondent's probability distribution. In an investment experiment conducted by Armantier et al. (2015), the relationship between reported inflation expectations and investment choices was similar when using point forecasts or density means. More research is needed to assess more generally which measure better captures the beliefs that respondents act upon in decision making. Chapters 9, 3, and 15 in this Handbook provide additional discussion of this issue.

1.3.9 Individual differences in expectations and uncertainty

Subjective expectations tend to show systematic variation in beliefs and uncertainty across respondents by gender, age, education, income and geography. Researchers have examined the extent to which such differences stem from differences in information, circumstances, experiences and preferences. For example, Jacobson et al. (2014) examine gender differences in optimism and asset allocation, Wiswall and Zafar (2018) and Reuben et al. (2017) investigate gender differences in wage expectations; however, Bruine de Bruin et al. (2010) found no significant gender differences in inflation expectations. D'Acunto et al. (2020) and Kuchler and Zafar (2019) establish the importance of personal experiences in explaining gender differences in expectations about a range of macrofinance variables, including inflation (see also Chapter 5 in this Handbook). Furthermore, these differences in expectations have been found to be persistent (see Chapter 3 in this Handbook) and meaningful in that they are associated with differences in choice decisions and updating behavior. For example, in the investment choice experiment conducted by Armantier et al. (2015), the majority of respondents were found to act on their inflation expectations in a manner consistent with economic theory. Across respondents, differences in behavior could be explained to a large extent by expectations, self-reported risk tolerances and subjective uncertainty about future inflation.

One source of differences in reported expectations that deserves special attention is the respondent's numeracy and financial literacy. Numeracy refers to the ability to use numbers (Peters et al., 2006) and financial literacy refers to the ability to understand financial numbers and information (Lusardi and Mitchell, 2005, 2007). Both of these skills are highly correlated, and lower among individuals who are less educated, poorer and older (Bruine de Bruin et al., 2010). People who find it difficult to understand numbers are less motivated to think hard about complex numerical problems (Bruine de Bruin et al., 2015). People who have lower numeracy are more likely to answer "50–50" when asked for subjective probabilities, and to explain their responses to subjective probability questions by stating that they do not know the chances (Bruine de Bruin and Carman, 2012). Individuals with lower numeracy and financial literacy also tend to show more uncertainty in their responses (seen in using wider intervals for their subjective probabilities), as well as more disagreement with each other (seen in dispersion of responses across participants) (Bruine de Bruin et al., 2011a). Finally, there may be a weaker link between low-numerate respondents' expectations and behavior. Armantier et al. (2015) found that respondents whose expectations and behavior in their investment experiment were most difficult to reconcile with standard economic theory tended to exhibit specific characteristics: they were less educated, they had lower numeracy and financial literacy, and they took longer to complete the survey. Recent work by D'Acunto et al. (2019) reports similar results when differentiating respondents by cognitive ability (IQ), finding those with higher IQ to display lower forecast errors, less rounding, fewer outliers and more persistence in inflation forecasts, and a closer link between inflation expectations and economic and financial decisions. There is much to be learned about reasons for the heterogeneity in beliefs across individuals and across outcomes, about the roles of differences in information and the way it is processed.

1.3.10 Use of expectations data in economic analysis

A comprehensive review of recent economic analysis of survey data on probabilistic expectations is beyond the scope for this chapter. Much of this work is covered in greater detail in other chapters in this Handbook. Here, we would like to provide a brief overview of various ways in which expectations data have been collected and used to study economic behavior. Specifically, we would like to highlight a few approaches we consider particularly impactful.

Much research on subjective expectations has focused on properties (such as rationality), heterogeneity and determinants or predictors of expectations and how expectations respond to new information. Examples include Bernheim (1988, 1990). Dominitz (1998), Smith et al. (2001), Attanasio et al. (2005), Benitez-Silva and Dwyer (2005), Bruine de Bruin et al. (2007), McKenzie et al. (2007), Delavande (2008b), Fischhoff et al. (2000), Giné et al. (2008, 2015), Hurd and McGarry (2002), Lochner (2007), and Dominitz and Manski (2011). These and other studies discussed throughout this Handbook generally find that expectations are responsive to new information in systematic ways, while also finding substantial heterogeneity across respondents in how the information is used.

Another line of research uses individual-level expectations data to improve our understanding of economic choice behavior, including the relationship between expectations of future returns and choice behavior (or intentions). Examples include Delavande (2008a), Arcidiacono et al. (2012), Stinebrickner and Stinebrickner (2014), Schweri and Hartog (2017), Wiswall and Zafar (2015b), Delavande and Zafar (2019), Cecere et al. (2018), and Armona et al. (2019).

An important challenge in both lines of work is to establish causality. Two approaches that appear particularly promising are experiments that examine how information affects expectations, and stated choice experiments using probabilistic expectations. In the former, survey participants are typically asked about their subjective expectations regarding some future outcome. Frequently they are asked about their intentions or likelihood of making future decisions, as well as the expected outcomes or returns associated with those decisions. Participants in these experiments are subsequently randomly assigned to receive information, and asked how this information affects their expectations and future choice probabilities. For example, Armantier et al. (2016) analyze how information about recent price changes and professional forecasts affect inflation expectations. Wiswall and Zafar (2015a,b), Ruder and Van Noy (2017), and Baker et al. (2018) conducted experiments to study the impact of labor market information on students' beliefs about the returns to education and on their college major choices. Bleemer and Zafar (2018) similarly analyzed the impact of information about "college returns" and "college costs" on intended college attendance, while Dizon-Ross (2019) studied how information on children's academic performance affects parent's beliefs and their investment in their children's education. Haaland et al. (2021) discuss best practices for designing information-provision experiments.

Several papers have used the stated choice methodology initially used in Blass et al. (2010)'s study of preferences for the reliability of electricity services. Here, respondents are asked to assign a probability of choosing among a fixed set of alternatives. This approach is an important innovation over the common practice of asking participants to select their most preferred choice or, to rank a set of alternatives. It addresses the incompleteness of typical choice scenario descriptions in stated-choice experiments (with respondents given only a subset of the information they would have in actual choice settings). Furthermore, choice probabilities allow respondents to express uncertainty about future behavior and to rank their choices. Choice probabilities have been elicited to study voting behavior and preferences for political candidates (Delavande and Manski, 2015; Galesic et al., 2018), preferences for long-term care insurance products (Boyer et al., 2017), preferences for workplace attributes (Wiswall and Zafar, 2018) and preferences for residential location attributes and moving costs (Kosar et al., in press).

There are important design issues regarding the provision of information and the description of conditioning events when eliciting conditional expectations in hypothetical scenarios (so-called vignettes) (Dominitz, 1997; Manski, 1999; Blass et al., 2010), an important area for future research. More details on the use of information experiments in studying expectations formation and the elicitation of counterfactual choice probabilities in hypothetical choice experiments can be found in Chapters 4 and 21 in this Handbook.

1.3.11 **Main takeaway**

Much effort and substantial resources have been expended to collect and analyze subjective data on a wide range of economic behaviors and outcomes over the past three decades. As documented here, much has been learned about best practices in this endeavor, and favorable evidence has been found that these surveys generate valuable information that would be unavailable in their absence.

In any new survey of economic expectations, attention must be paid to the potential impact of question wording and framing. Further, decisions must be made regarding how to elicit features of subjective probability distributions, such as by elicitation of densities or CDFs, and then how to use these data to fit a distribution and measure uncertainty, if so desired. As discussed in Section 1.2, pretesting should be utilized whenever possible. When resources or time limit the extent to which sufficient pretesting may be conducted, researchers should look to the research discussed here to inform the survey design.

1.4 Concluding remarks

We have described here the long history of and recent expansion in efforts to measure economic expectations via household surveys. In Section 1.1, we discussed the history and motivation for measuring household economic expectations. We include an overview of major ongoing expectations surveys and their focal topics. In Section 1.2, we described methodological considerations about how to design surveys of economic expectations, and how to test what works. We presented best practice guidelines that included pretesting surveys in randomized survey-based experiments and cognitive interviews with follow-up surveys so as to ensure that survey questions are easy for respondents to understand and yield valid responses. These recommendations should be useful for designing surveys of expectations on a variety of topics, including panel surveys, cross-sectional surveys, and survey-based experiments of expectations, as well as ad-hoc surveys. Section 1.3 discusses recent advances in measuring probabilistic expectations, and suggested topics for future research.

It is important to note that what is the best practice at one point in time may not hold up later as, for instance, survey technologies and survey modes change, and as the composition and attributes of responding populations change. Further, innovations in economic theory and empirical practice will likely lead to new avenues for research on household expectations, such as we have seen from the impact of behavioral economics and, more recently, from work on imprecise probabilities and ambiguity.

References

Andre, P., Haaland, I., Roth, C., Wohlfart, J., 2021. Inflation Narratives. CEBI Working Paper 18/21.

Ang, A., Bekaert, G., Wei, M., 2007. Do macro variables, asset markets, or surveys forecast inflation better? Journal of Monetary Economics 54 (4), 1163–1212.

Arcidiacono, P., Hotz, V.J., Kang, S., 2012. Modeling college major choice using elicited measures of expectations and counterfactuals. Journal of Econometrics 166 (1), 3–16.

Armand, A., Carneiro, P., Toppeta, A., 2019. Local Labour Market and Parental Perceived Returns to Schooling: Evidence from panel data. Manuscript.

Armantier, O., Bruine de Bruin, W., Potter, S., Topa, G., van der Klaauw, W., Zafar, B., 2013. Measuring inflation expectations. Annual Review of Economics 5 (1), 273–301.

Armantier, O., Bruine de Bruin, W., Topa, G., van der Klaauw, W., Zafar, B., 2015. Inflation expectations and behavior: do survey respondents act on their beliefs? International Economic Review 56, 505–536. https://doi.org/10.1111/iere.12113.

Armantier, O., Topa, G., van der Klaauw, W., Zafar, B., 2016. The price is right: updating inflation expectations in a randomized price information experiment. Review of Economics and Statistics 98, 503–523.

Armantier, O., Topa, G., van der Klaauw, W., Zafar, B., 2017. An overview of the survey of consumer expectations. FRBNY Economic Policy Review, 51–72.

Armona, L., Fuster, A., Zafar, B., 2019. Home price expectations and behavior: evidence from a randomized information experiment. The Review of Economic Studies 86 (4), 1371–1410.

Attanasio, O.P., Augsburg, B., 2016. Subjective expectations and income processes in rural India. Economica 83 (331), 416–442.

Attanasio, O.P., Kaufmann, K.M., 2008. Subjective Returns to Schooling and Risk Perceptions of Future Earnings – Elicitation and Validation of Subjective Distributions of Future Earnings. Mimeo.

Attanasio, O.P., Kaufmann, K.M., 2009. Educational choices, subjective expectations, and credit constraints. NBER Working Paper No. 15087.

Attanasio, O.P., Kaufmann, K.M., 2014. Education choices and returns to schooling: Mothers' and youths' subjective expectations and their role by gender. Journal of Development Economics 109 (C), 203–216.

Attanasio, O.P., Meghir, C., Vera-Hernandez, M., 2005. Elicitation, Validation, and Use of Probability Distributions of Future Income in Developing Countries. Paper presented at the 2005 Econometric Society Meeting.

Baker, R., Bettinger, E., Jacob, B., Marinescu, I., 2018. The effect of labor market information on community college students' major choice. Economics of Education Review 65, 18–30.

Bellemare, C., Bissonnette, L., Kröger, S., 2012. Flexible approximation of subjective expectations using probability questions: an application to the investment game. Journal of Business and Economic Statistics 30 (1), 125–131.

Benitez-Silva, H., Dwyer, D.S., 2005. The rationality of retirement expectations and the role of new information. Review of Economics and Statistics 87 (3), 587–592.

Benitez-Silva, H., Dwyer, D.S., 2006. Expectation formation of older married coupled and the rational expectations hypothesis. Labour Economics 13 (2), 191–218.

Benitez-Silva, H., Dwyer, D.S., Gayle, W., Muench, R., 2008. Expectations in micro data: rationality revisited. Empirical Economics 34 (2), 381–416.

Bergman, A., Chinco, A., Hartzman, S.M., Sussman, A., 2020. Survey Curious? Start-up Guide and Best Practices for Online Survey Experiments. Working paper. University of Chicago – Booth School of Business.

Bernheim, B.D., 1988. Social security benefits: an empirical study of expectations and realizations. In: Lazear, E., Ricardo-Campbell, R. (Eds.), Issues in Contemporary Retirement. Hoover Institution, Stanford, pp. 312–348.

Bernheim, B.D., 1990. How do the elderly form expectations? An analysis of responses to new information. In: Wise, D. (Ed.), Issues in the Economics of Aging. University of Chicago Press, Chicago, pp. 259–285.

Beyth-Marom, R., 1982. How probable is probable? A numerical translation of verbal probability expressions. Journal of Forecasting 1, 257–269.

Binder, C.C., 2017. Measuring uncertainty based on rounding. Journal of Monetary Economics 90, 1–12.

Bissonnette, L., de Bresser, J., 2018. Eliciting subjective survival curves: lessons from partial identification. Journal of Business & Economic Statistics 36 (3), 505–515.

Blass, A.A., Lach, S., Manski, C.F., 2010. Using elicited choice probabilities to estimate random utility models: preferences for electricity reliability. International Economic Review 51 (2), 421–440.

Bleemer, Z., Zafar, B., 2018. Intended college attendance: evidence from an experiment on college returns and costs. Journal of Public Economics 157, 184–211.

Bover, O., 2015. Measuring expectations from household surveys: new results on subjective probabilities of future house prices. SERIEs 6 (4), 361–405.

Boyer, M., De Donder, P., Fluet, C., Leroux, M.-L., Michaud, P.-C., 2017. Long-Term Care Insurance: Knowledge Barriers, Risk Perception and Adverse Selection. Working Paper 23918. National Bureau of Economic Research.

Brachinger, H.W., 2008. A new index of perceived inflation: assumptions, method, and application to Germany. Journal of Economic Psychology 29, 433–457.

Bruine de Bruin, W., 2011. Framing effects in survey design: how respondents make sense of the questions we ask. In: Keren, G. (Ed.), Perspectives on Framing. Taylor & Francis, London, UK, pp. 303–324.

Bruine de Bruin, W., Bostrom, A., 2013. Addressing what to address in science communication. Proceedings of the National Academy of Sciences of the United States of America 110 (Supplement 3), 14062–14068.

Bruine de Bruin, W., Carman, K.G., 2012. Measuring risk perceptions: what does the excessive use of 50% mean? Medical Decision Making 32 (2), 232–236.

Bruine de Bruin, W., Carman, K.G., 2018. Measuring subjective probabilities: the effect of response mode on the use of focal responses, validity, and respondents' evaluations. Risk Analysis 38 (10), 2128–2143.

Bruine de Bruin, W., Fischhoff, B., Millstein, S.G., Halpern-Felsher, B.L., 2000. Verbal and numerical expressions of probability: "it's a fifty–fifty chance". Organizational Behavior and Human Decision Processes 81, 115–131.

Bruine de Bruin, W., Manski, C.F., Topa, G., van der Klaauw, W., 2011a. Measuring consumer uncertainty about future inflation. Journal of Applied Econometrics 26 (3), 454–478.

Bruine de Bruin, W., McNair, S., Taylor, A.L., Summers, B., Strough, J., 2015. Thinking about numbers is not my idea of fun: need for cognition mediates age differences in numeracy performance. Medical Decision Making 35 (1), 22–26.

Bruine de Bruin, W., Parker, A.M., Fischhoff, B., 2007. Can adolescents predict significant life events? Journal of Adolescent Health 41, 208–210.

Bruine de Bruin, W., van der Klaauw, W., Downs, J.S., Fischhoff, B., Topa, G., Armantier, O., 2010. Expectations of inflation: the role of financial literacy and demographic variables. The Journal of Consumer Affairs 44, 381–402.

Bruine de Bruin, W., van der Klaauw, W., Topa, G., 2011b. Expectations of inflation: the biasing effect of thoughts about specific prices. Journal of Economic Psychology 32 (5), 834–845.

Bruine de Bruin, W., van der Klaauw, W., Topa, G., Downs, J.S., Fischhoff, B., Armantier, O., 2012. The effect of question wording on consumers' reported inflation expectations. Journal of Economic Psychology 33 (4), 749–757.

Bruine de Bruin, W., van der Klaauw, W., van Rooij, M., Teppa, F., de Vos, K., 2017. Measuring expectations of inflation: effects of survey mode, wording, and opportunities to revise. Journal of Economic Psychology 59, 45–58.

Carroll, D.C., Fuhrer, J.C., Wilcox, D.W., 1994. Does consumer sentiment forecast household spending? If so, why? The American Economic Review 84 (5), 1397–1408.

Case, K.E., Shiller, R.J., Thompson, A.K., 2012. What Have They Been Thinking? – Homebuyer Behavior in Hot and Cold Markets. Brookings Papers on Economic Activity, 265–298.

Cecere, G., Corrocher, N., Guerzoni, M., 2018. Price or performance? A probabilistic choice analysis of the intention to buy electric vehicles in European countries. Energy Policy 118, 19–32.

Chin, A., Bruine de Bruin, W., 2018. Eliciting stock market expectations: the effects of question wording on survey experience and response validity. The Journal of Behavioral Finance 19 (1), 101–110.

Christandl, F., Fetchenhauer, D., Hoelzl, E., 2011. Price perception and conformation bias in the context of a VAT increase. Journal of Economic Psychology 32 (1), 131–141.

Crossley, T.F., Gong, Y., Stinebrickner, T., Stinebrickner, R., 2021. Examining Income Expectations in the College and Early Post-College Periods: New Distributional Tests of Rational Expectations. CESifo Working Paper No. 8834.

Curtin, R., 2006. Inflation Expectations: Theoretical Models and Empirical Tests. Paper presented at the National Bank of Poland Workshop on the Role of Inflation Expectations in Modeling and Monetary Policy Making, Warsaw, February 9–10.

D'Acunto, F., Hoang, D., Paloviita, M., Weber, M., 2019. IQ, Expectations, and Choice. NBER Working Paper 25496.

D'Acunto, F., Malmendier, U., Weber, M., 2020. Gender Roles and the Gender Expectations Gap. CESifo Working Paper Series 8158.

Das, M., Dominitz, J., van Soest, A., 1999. Comparing predictions and outcomes: theory and application to income changes. Journal of the American Statistical Association 94 (445), 75–85.

Das, M., van Soest, A., 1997. Expected and realized income changes: evidence from the Dutch socio-economic panel. Journal of Economic Behavior & Organization 32, 137–154.

Das, M., van Soest, A., 1999. A panel data model for subjective information on household income growth. Journal of Economic Behavior & Organization 40, 409–426.

De Bresser, J., van Soest, A., 2013. Survey response in probabilistic questions and its impact on inference. Journal of Economic Behavior & Organization 96, 65–84.

Delavande, A., 2008a. Pill, patch, or shot? Subjective expectations and birth control choice. International Economic Review 49 (3), 999–1042.

Delavande, A., 2008b. Measuring revisions to subjective expectations. Journal of Risk and Uncertainty 36 (1), 43–82.

Delavande, A., Gine, X., McKenzie, D., 2011a. Measuring subjective expectations in developing countries: a critical review and new evidence. Journal of Development Economics 94, 151–163.

Delavande, A., Gine, X., McKenzie, D., 2011b. Eliciting probabilistic expectations with visual aids in developing countries: how sensitive are answers to variations in elicitation design? Journal of Applied Econometrics 26 (3), 479–497.

Delavande, A., Manski, C.F., 2015. Using elicited choice probabilities in hypothetical elections to study decisions to vote. Electoral Studies 38, 28–37.

Delavande, A., Rohwedder, S., 2008. Eliciting subjective probabilities in Internet surveys. Public Opinion Quarterly 72 (5), 866–891.

Delavande, A., Rohwedder, S., 2011. Individuals' uncertainty about future social security benefits and portfolio choice. Journal of Applied Econometrics 26 (3), 498–519.

Delavande, A., Zafar, B., 2019. University choice: the role of expected earnings, non-pecuniary outcomes and financial constraints. Journal of Political Economy 127 (5), 2343–2393.

D'Haultfoeuille, X., Gaillac, C., Maurel, A., 2021. Rationalizing rational expectations: characterizations and tests. Quantitative Economics 12 (3), 817–842.

Dillman, D.A., 2011. Mail and Internet Surveys: The Tailored Design Method—2007 Update with New Internet, Visual, and Mixed-Mode Guide. John Wiley & Sons.

Dizon-Ross, R., 2019. Parents' beliefs about their children's academic ability: implications for educational investments. The American Economic Review 109 (8), 2728–2765.

Dominitz, J., 1997. The Role of Conditioning Information in Reports of Subjective Phenomena. Paper prepared for presentation at EML/NSF Symposium on Preference Elicitation.

Dominitz, J., 1998. Earnings expectations, revisions, and realizations. Review of Economics and Statistics 80, 374–388.

Dominitz, J., Manski, C.F., 1997a. Using expectations data to study subjective income expectations. Journal of the American Statistical Association 92, 855–867.

Dominitz, J., Manski, C.F., 1997b. Perceptions of economic insecurity. Public Opinion Quarterly 61 (2), 261–287.

Dominitz, J., Manski, C.F., 1999. The several cultures of research on subjective expectations. In: Smith, James P., Willis, Robert J. (Eds.), Wealth, Work, and Health. University of Michigan Press, Ann Arbor, MI.

Dominitz, J., Manski, C.F., 2006. Measuring pension-benefit expectations probabilistically. Labour 20 (2), 201–236.

Dominitz, J., Manski, C.F., 2011. Measuring and interpreting expectations of equity returns. Journal of Applied Econometrics 26 (3), 352–370.

Engelberg, J., Manski, C.F., Williams, J., 2009. Comparing the point predictions and subjective probability distributions of professional forecasters. Journal of Business & Economic Statistics 27 (1), 30–41.

Federal Reserve Consultant Committee on Consumer Survey Statistics, 1955. Smithies Committee Report in Reports of the Federal Reserve Committees on Economic Statistics. Hearings of the Subcommittee on Economic Statistics of the Joint Committee on the Economic Report, 84th US Congress.

Ferrario, B., Stantcheva, S., 2022. Eliciting People's First-Order Concerns: Text Analysis of Open-Ended Survey Questions. NBER working paper 29686.

Fischhoff, B., Bruine de Bruin, W., 1999. Fifty−fifty=50%? Journal of Behavioral Decision Making 12 (2), 149–163.

Fischhoff, B., Parker, A.M., Bruine de Bruin, W., Downs, J.S., Palmgren, C., Dawes, R., Manski, C., 2000. Teen expectations for significant life events. Public Opinion Quarterly 64, 189–205.

Fitzsimons, G.J., Morwitz, V.G., 1996. The effect of measuring intent on brand-level purchase behavior. Journal of Consumer Research 23 (1), 1–11.

Galesic, M., Bruine de Bruin, W., Dumas, M., Kapteyn, A., Darling, J.E., Meijer, E., 2018. Asking about social circles improves election predictions. Nature Human Behaviour 2, 187–193.

Giné, X., Townsend, R., Vickery, J., 2008. Rational Expectations? Evidence from Planting Decisions in Semi-arid India. BREAD Working Paper No. 166.

Giné, X., Townsend, R., Vickery, J., 2015. Forecasting when it matters: evidence from semi-arid India. Unpublished manuscript.

Giustinelli, P., Manski, C.F., Molinari, F., in press. Tail and center rounding of probabilistic expectations in the Health and Retirement Study, Journal of Econometrics.

Giustinelli, P., Manski, C.F., Molinari, F., 2021. Precise or imprecise probabilities? Evidence from survey response related to late-onset dementia. Journal of the European Economic Association 20 (1), 187–221. https://doi.org/10.1093/jeea/jvab023.

Giustinelli, P., Pavoni, N., 2017. The evolution of awareness and belief ambiguity in the process of high school track choice. Review of Economic Dynamics, Elsevier for the Society for Economic Dynamics 25, 93–120.

Greitemeyer, T., Schulz-Hardt, S., Traut-Mattausch, E., Frey, D., 2005. The influence of price trend expectations on price trend estimates: why the euro seems to make life more expensive. Journal of Economic Psychology 26, 541–548.

Guiso, L., Jappelli, T., Terlizzese, D., 1992. Earnings uncertainty and precautionary saving. Journal of Monetary Economics 30, 307–337.

Haaland, I., Roth, C., Wohlfart, J., 2021. Designing information provision experiments. Journal of Economic Literature.

Halpern-Manners, A., Warren, J.R., Torche, F., 2014. Panel conditioning in a longitudinal study of illicit behaviors. Public Opinion Quarterly 78 (3), 565–590. https://doi.org/10.1093/poq/nfu029.

Heiss, F., Hurd, M., Rossmann, T., van Rooij, M., Winter, J.K., 2019. Dynamics and Heterogeneity of Subjective Stock Market Expectations. Manuscript.

Hudomiet, P., Willis, R.J., 2013. Estimating second order probability beliefs from subjective survival data. Decision Analysis 10 (2), 152–170.

Hunter, J., 2005. Report on Cognitive Testing of Cohabitation Questions. Study Series Report (Survey Methodology #2550-06). Unpublished report. U.S. Census Bureau, Statistical Research Division.

Hurd, M.D., McGarry, K., 2002. The predictive validity of subjective probabilities of survival. The Economic Journal 112 (482), 966–985.

Hurd, M.D., van Rooij, M., Winter, J., 2011. Stock market expectations of Dutch households. Journal of Applied Econometrics 26 (3), 416–436.

Jacobson, B., Lee, J.B., Marquering, W., Zhang, C.Y., 2014. Gender differences in optimism and asset allocation. Journal of Economic Behavior & Organization 107 (PB), 630–651.

Jungermann, H., Brachinger, H.W., Belting, J., Grinberg, K., Zacharias, E., 2007. The euro changeover and the factors influencing perceived inflation. Journal of Consumer Policy 30, 405–419.

Juster, F.T., 1966. Consumer buying intentions and purchase probability: an experiment in survey design. Journal of the American Statistical Association 61, 658–696.

Juster, F.T., Suzman, R., 1995. An overview of the health and retirement study. The Journal of Human Resources 30, S7–S56.

Kahneman, D., Slovic, P., Tversky, A., 1982. Judgment Under Uncertainty: Heuristics and Biases. Cambridge University Press.

Katona, G., Klein, L.R., 1952. Psychological data in business cycle research. American Journal of Economics and Sociology 12 (1), 11–22.

Katona, G., Likert, R., 1946. Relationship between consumer expenditures and savings: the contribution of survey research. Review of Economics and Statistics 28 (4), 197–199.

Kim, G.M., Binder, C., in press. Learning-through-survey in inflation expectations, American Economic Journal: Macroeconomics.

Kleinjans, K.J., van Soest, A., 2014. Rounding, focal point answers and nonresponse to subjective probability questions. Journal of Applied Econometrics 29 (4), 567–585.

Knäuper, B., Belli, R.F., Hill, D.H., Herzog, A.R., 1997. Question difficulty and respondents' cognitive ability: the effect on data quality. Journal of Official Statistics 13, 181–199.

Kosar, G., Ransom, T., van der Klaauw, W., in press. Understanding migration aversion using elicited counterfactual choice probabilities, Journal of Econometrics.

Kuchler, T., Zafar, B., 2019. Personal experiences and expectations about aggregate outcomes. The Journal of Finance 74 (5), 2491–2542.

Leemann, L., Stoetzer, L.F., Traunmueller, R., 2020. Eliciting beliefs as distributions in online surveys. Political Analysis 5, 1–17.

Leiser, D., Drori, S., 2005. Naïve understanding of inflation. The Journal of Socio-Economics 34 (2), 179–198.

Lillard, L.A., Willis, R.J., 2001. Cognition and Wealth: the Importance of Probabilistic Thinking. Presented at the Third Annual Joint Conference for the Retirement Research Consortium "Making Hard Choices About Retirement," May 17-18, 2001, Washington, DC.

Lochner, L., 2007. Individual perceptions of the criminal justice system. The American Economic Review 97 (1), 444–460.

Ludvigson, S.C., 2004. Consumer confidence and consumer spending. The Journal of Economic Perspectives 18 (2), 29–50.

Lusardi, A., Mitchell, O.S., 2005. Financial Literacy and Planning: Implications for Retirement Wellbeing. Working Paper WP 2005-18. University of Michigan Retirement Research Center, Ann Arbor.

Lusardi, A., Mitchell, O.S., 2007. Financial literacy and retirement preparedness: evidence and implications for financial education. Business Economics 42 (1), 35–44.

Manski, C.F., 1990. The use of intentions data to predict behavior: a best case analysis. Journal of the American Statistical Association 84, 934–940.

Manski, C.F., 1999. Analysis of choice expectations in incomplete scenarios. Journal of Risk and Uncertainty 19, 49–65.

Manski, C.F., 2004. Measuring expectations. Econometrica 72 (5), 1329–1376.

Manski, C.F., 2018. Survey measurement of probabilistic macroeconomic expectations: 47 progress and promise. NBER Macroeconomics Annual 32 (1), 411–471.

Manski, C.F., Molinari, F., 2010. Rounding probabilistic expectations in surveys. Journal of Business & Economic Statistics 28 (2), 219–231.

McKenzie, D., Gibson, J., Stillman, S., 2007. A land of milk and honey with streets paved with gold: do emigrants have over-optimistic expectations about incomes abroad? World Bank Policy Research Working Paper No. 4141.

Morgan, G.M., Henrion, M., 1990. Uncertainty a Guide to Dealing with Uncertainty in Quantitative Risk and Policy Analysis. Cambridge University Press, Cambridge.

Neuhauser, L., Paul, K., 2011. Readability, comprehension, and usability. In: Communicating Risks and Benefits: An Evidence-Based User's Guide, pp. 129–148.

Niu, G., van Soest, A.H., 2014. House price expectations. IZA Discussion Paper No. 8536. Available at SSRN: https://ssrn.com/abstract=2514729.

Palmqvist, S., Strömberg, L., 2004. Households' inflation opinions – a tale of two surveys. Sveriges Riksbank Economic Review 4, 23–42.

Pesaran, H.M., Weale, M., 2006. Survey expectations. In: Elliott, G., Granger, C.W.J., Timmermann, A. (Eds.), Handbook of Economic Forecasting. North-Holland, Amsterdam.

Peters, E., Västfjäll, D., Slovic, P., Mertz, C.K., Mazzocco, K., Dickert, S., 2006. Numeracy and decision making. Psychological Science 17 (5), 407–413.

Potter, S., Del Negro, M., Topa, G., van der Klaauw, W., 2017. The advantages of probabilistic survey questions. Review of Economic Analysis 9, 1–32.

Ranyard, R., Del Missier, F., Bonini, N., Duxbury, D., Summers, B., 2008. Perceptions and expectations of price changes and inflation: a review and conceptual framework. Journal of Economic Psychology 29, 378–400.

Reuben, E., Wiswall, M., Zafar, B., 2017. Preferences and biases in education choices and labor market expectations: shrinking the black box of gender. The Economic Journal 127 (604), 2153–2186.

Rich, R.W., Tracy, J., 2010. The relationship among expected inflation, disagreement, and uncertainty: evidence from matched point and density forecasts. Review of Economics and Statistics 92, 200–207.

Rich, R.W., Tracy, J., 2021. A closer look at the behavior of uncertainty and disagreement: micro evidence from the euro area. Journal of Money, Credit, and Banking 53 (1), 233–253.

Ruder, A.I., Van Noy, M., 2017. Knowledge of earnings risk and major choice: evidence from an information experiment. Economics of Education Review 57 (1), 80–90.

Schuman, H., Presser, S., 1996. Questions and Answers on Attitude Surveys: Experiments on Question Form, Wording, and Context. Sage.

Schwarz, N., 1996. Cognition and Communication: Judgmental Biases, Research Methods, and the Logic of Conversation. Erlbaum, Hillsdale, NJ.

Schweri, J., Hartog, J., 2017. Do wage expectations predict college enrollment? Evidence from healthcare. Journal of Economic Behavior & Organization 141 (3), 135–150.

Smith, K.V., Taylor, D.H., Sloan, F.A., 2001. Longevity expectations and death: can people predict their own demise? The American Economic Review 91 (4), 1126–1134.

Souleles, N., 2004. Expectations, heterogeneous forecast errors, and consumption: micro evidence from the Michigan consumer sentiment surveys. Journal of Money, Credit, and Banking 36 (1), 39–72.

Stanislawska, E., Paloviita, M., Lyziak, T., 2019. Assessing reliability of aggregated inflation views in the European Commission consumer survey. Bank of Finland Research Discussion Paper 10/2019.

Stinebrickner, R., Stinebrickner, T., 2014. Academic performance and college dropout: using longitudinal expectations data to estimate a learning model. Journal of Labor Economics 32 (3), 601–644.

Svenson, O., Nilsson, G., 1986. Mental economics: subjective representations of factors related to expected inflation. Journal of Economic Psychology 7 (3), 327–349.

van der Klaauw, W., Bruine de Bruin, W., Topa, G., Potter, S., Bryan, M.F., 2008. Rethinking the Measurement of Household Inflation Expectations: Preliminary Findings. FRB of New York Staff Report 359.

Velez, P., Ashworth, S., 2007. The impact of item readability on the endorsement of the midpoint response in surveys. Survey Research Methods 1 (2), 69–74.

Wiswall, M., Zafar, B., 2015a. How do college students respond to public information about earnings? Journal of Human Capital 9 (2), 117–169.

Wiswall, M., Zafar, B., 2015b. Determinants of college major choice: identification using an information experiment. The Review of Economic Studies 82 (2), 791–824.

Wiswall, M., Zafar, B., 2018. Preference for the workplace, investment in human capital, and gender. The Quarterly Journal of Economics 133 (1), 457–507.

Zafar, B., 2011. How do college students form expectations? Journal of Labor Economics 29 (2), 301–348.

Firm surveys ☆

Kai Carstensen[a,b,c] **and Rüdiger Bachmann**[d,e,b,c]
[a] University of Kiel, Kiel, Germany
[b] CESifo, Munich, Germany
[c] ifo, Munich, Germany
[d] University of Notre Dame, Notre Dame, IN, United States
[e] CEPR, London, United Kingdom

2.1 Introduction

This chapter surveys firm surveys, specifically surveys of expectations of putative decision makers in firms. Expectational surveys directed at households were introduced in the previous Chapter 1, and surveys directed at experts will be introduced in the following Chapter 3. The chapter focuses on the historical development of firm surveys in the U.S., where business surveys date back to the 19th century, Europe, and Japan, and gives a brief and necessarily incomplete overview of their current state and the recent literature that has made use of them to answer economic research questions. Chapters 11 and 12 in this Handbook complement this chapter by surveying the current state of knowledge about firms' expectations. These chapters also contain overview tables of the many different firm surveys in the world, including many not from the U.S. and from non-European countries.

A long-standing debate specifically in the literature on firm surveys is whether they should elicit the answers on a qualitative, often trichotomous scale—some variation of "up," "stay the same," and "down"—or be quantitative in nature; see, e.g., the discussion in Piatier (1953), Marquardt and Strigel (1959), and Trebing (1998) who stress the simplicity of qualitative surveys as a virtue. Perhaps surprisingly, as we will show, this debate was not settled in favor of qualitative surveys early on. In fact, there existed quantitative firm surveys in the early days of firm surveys. Yet, with the loss of academic research interest in expectational data that accompanied the rational expectations revolution, the needs of business cycle forecasters came to determine the design of firm surveys, and qualitative so-called business tendency surveys started to dominate the landscape. Firm surveys needed to be answerable quickly and without much intrusion into both the time and the confidential knowledge of decision makers at the firms; lack of quantitative detail was not considered a problem because, for business cycle forecasting, only the aggregate results of these surveys were needed (this is not to say that the qualitative microdata was entirely uninteresting to academic researchers, as we will show below). This has recently changed with the reestablishment of quantitative firm surveys or firm survey modules. Correspondingly, the in-

---

☆ We are grateful to Christian Gayer and Enrico Giovannini for helpful information, and to Buket Bozduman, Lukas Baumann, and Francesco Nienhaus for excellent research assistance.

Handbook of Economic Expectations. https://doi.org/10.1016/B978-0-12-822927-9.00008-2
33

terest of academic researchers in the microdata of such surveys has dramatically increased in recent years.

2.2 Quantification of qualitative survey answers

Since in the days before the rational expectations revolution academic research with expectation data was considered reputable and important, the literature gave some thought into quantifying the existing qualitative firm-level survey data. The problem of quantifying qualitative survey information is probably as old as the survey business itself (see Anderson, 1952, for an early attempt). How can trichotomous information—positive, neutral, and negative—be turned into meaningful quantitative statements?

This quantification problem has been studied for a long time. The oldest, and until today most common, approach is to compute the share of all three categories and then subtract the share of negatives from the share of positives. This is a balance statistic,[1] which typically tracks quantitative business cycle indicators well (Anderson, 1952; Moore, 1955; Theil, 1955).[2] Consider a survey that asks firms for their recent price change and provides the following answer options: "up," "same," and "down." Now suppose that each firm draws its price change from some distribution and reports "same" if the change falls in a symmetric indifference interval around zero and "up" ("down") if it falls above (below) this interval. Assume, further, that both the thresholds and the distribution are the same for all firms at a given point in time. If this distribution is rectangular, the balance statistic is proportional to its mean, i.e., to the underlying quantitative aggregate price change (Theil, 1952). Carlson and Parkin (1975), more realistically, assume that the unknown distribution is normal and show that, in this case, the balance statistic needs to be replaced by a nonlinear function of the "up" and "down" shares. This has become known as the probability approach.[3] Alternatively, Pesaran (1984) suggests regressing the quantitative aggregate target index on these shares and then to use this regression model to track the target index. Detailed surveys of these approaches (and others) can be found in Pesaran and Weale (2006) and Mitchell et al. (2004).

Another strand of the literature attempts to quantify qualitative survey information at the firm level. While Lui et al. (2010) document for the U.K. that quantitative firm information reported to the statistical office and trichotomous answers to a business survey provided by the same firm are significantly related, it is often important to construct plan revisions or expectation errors. This amounts to computing a difference between, or at least to compare, two categorical variables and thus requires some kind of quantification. Lui et al. (2011) construct nonparametric tests to examine the nexus between qualitative expectations and realizations. Many authors study the cross-tabulation of such qualitative,

---

[1] Moore (1955) and Hastay (1960) call it diffusion index. However, this term is used more broadly in the business cycle literature as a variable that measures the share of rising disaggregate indicators as a percentage of all indicators in a given set; see Moore (1961). Stock and Watson (2002) call a diffusion index a factor that summarizes the overall movement of a set of business cycle indicators.

[2] Bachmann et al. (2013) argue that a related measure of forecast dispersion, which uses the variance of trichotomous answers originally discussed by Theil (1955), is a useful proxy for uncertainty.

[3] Mankiw et al. (2003) use this probability approach. Many refinements have been discussed in the literature. Seitz (1988), Smith and McAleer (1995), and Henzel and Wollmershäuser (2005); and Breitung and Schmeling (2013) relax the symmetry assumption of the probability approach concerning the indifference interval and show that the bounds are asymmetric.

trichotomous variables (Anderson et al., 1954, 1958; Nerlove, 1983; Kawasaki and Zimmermann, 1986). Others combine qualitative and quantitative information. For example, Bachmann and Elstner (2015) and Bachmann et al. (2019) use qualitative answers for expectations and quantitative answers for capacity utilization from the same survey to compute quantitative production expectation errors. Botsis et al. (2020) merge quantitative balance sheet data to qualitative survey expectations to study the Rational Expectations Hypothesis.

2.3 Historic business expectation surveys in the U.S.

Expectation surveys of firms are not new. Probably the earliest examples are in the agricultural sector. The Consultant Committee on General Business Expectations (1955a) refers to surveys of farmers' intentions to plant and farmers' crop yield estimates of the U.S. Department of Agriculture that started in the 19th century. This was not exclusive to the United States. For example, Strigel (1989) reports that 19th century farmer surveys in Germany used qualitative expectational questions similar to those used today in business tendency surveys. The manufacturing and services sectors followed later, with a few exceptions, after 1945.[4] Informational needs must have been enormous at that time: The Consultant Committee on General Business Expectations (1955a) conducted a survey among nationwide U.S. trade associations and found that a large majority of the 437 respondents provided business outlooks for which 43 used opinion surveys among their member firms. Official statistics followed closely behind. In particular, the Federal Reserve Board, at the behest of the United States Congress, initiated five consultant committees on economic statistics in 1954, three of which were concerned with expectational surveys (Hart et al., 1960).[5]

In this section, we focus on a few well-known early firm surveys in the manufacturing and services sectors that are often cited in the literature and on which the first analyses of firms' expectations are based. We first describe what might be called business outlook surveys as they are primarily concerned with eliciting short-term expectational or planning information about core variables of the firm such as sales, orders, inventories, and prices. Subsequently, we turn to business investment surveys which focus on plant and equipment expenditures and which are arguably particularly dependent on medium-term business expectations. We sketch only the most important characteristics of these surveys and refer the interested reader to the Consultant Committee on General Business Expectations (1955a) and the Consultant Committee on Plant and Equipment Expenditure Expectations (1955b) for a comprehensive description.

---

[4] One of the earliest business expectation surveys was initiated in Sweden in 1930 eliciting capital outlay plans (Modigliani and Weingartner, 1958).

[5] Probably the most well-known of these committees is the Consultant Committee of Consumer Survey Statistics chaired by Arthur Smithies. More relevant for this chapter are the Consultant Committee on Business Plant and Equipment Expenditure Expectations and the Consultant Committee on General Business Expectations. The two remaining committees were the Consultant Committee on Savings Statistics and the Consultant Committee on Inventory Statistics. The reports and hearings of all five committees to the Joint Committee on the Economic Report of U.S. Congress can be found at https://www.jec.senate.gov/public/index.cfm/1956/12/report-8438cbd4-c85f-4568-9bdd-e832fe5e5aa4.

2.3.1 Surveys of the general business outlook

Probably the earliest regular U.S. business expectation survey was conducted by the Car Service Division of the American Railroad Association. It started in the third quarter of 1927 and produced commodity-specific forecasts of railroad freight car needs. This information was collected and aggregated from local shippers by regional Shippers' Advisory Boards, see Hultgren (1942, 1955). While the questionnaires were sent to individual shippers, and thus firms, the forecasts were aggregated to the national level and then published by the Car Service Division in an outlet called the *National Forecast of the Regional Shippers' Advisory Boards* (Modigliani and Sauerlender, 1955). Since not all shippers were members of the Advisory Boards and not all members responded to the survey, the forecasts were not based on a random sample. Nevertheless, the response rates in terms of commodity-specific regional freight volumes typically was above 50% (Consultant Committee on General Business Expectations, 1955a).[6]

Informational needs both by the government and the business community led to the establishment of several expectations surveys in the postwar period. The Dun and Bradstreet Corporation started a quarterly *Survey of Businessmen's Expectations* in spring 1947 at the request of the Joint Committee on the Economic Report of the United States Congress, see Lehman and Knowles (1960). The survey focused on small and medium-sized firms and included more than 1,000 firms per survey round (Modigliani and Sauerlender, 1955). Firms were asked to report both expectations and realizations concerning changes in sales, employment, inventories, prices, profits, and orders. Respondents typically came from the top management. While the survey initially elicited percent changes (an early example of a quantitative business survey), it later switched to a trichotomous tendency scale ("increase," "no change," "decrease"), see Bonhoeffer and Strigel (1966). Unfortunately, only the unweighted aggregate tendency results of the expectational questions were published in *Dun's Review and Modern Industry* while the realizations were exclusively used for internal purposes (Consultant Committee on General Business Expectations, 1955a). Moreover, the trustworthiness of the answers might have suffered from the fact that Dun and Bradstreet, at the same time, produced credit ratings of the surveyed firms (Hastay, 1960).

The Fortune magazine conducted several expectational surveys of business executives. The *Forum of Executive Opinion* included, from November 1946 to May 1950, a series of semiannual expectational questions relating both to aggregate developments (GDP, production, inflation) and the firm-specific outlooks (e.g., sales), see Modigliani and Sauerlender (1955). The survey was directed to a very large number of top executives of medium-sized and large firms, yielding 4,000 to 5,000 respondents per wave. Several smaller surveys by Fortune, like the semiannual *Business Expectations and Mood Survey*, *Retail Survey*, and *Capital Goods Survey* and the quarterly *Inventory Survey* started at the beginning of the 1950s, see the Consultant Committee on General Business Expectations (1955a). They all were typically based on 150–200 responses of, in the view of the local interviewers, "representative" firms in select cities and/or branches. The *Business Expectations and Mood Survey* elicited, on a trichotomous tendency scale, the firms' business situation and expectations, its inventory situation, and a general economic outlook. The *Retail Survey* asked car, home goods, and apparel dealers for both realized and

---

[6]   This highlights a more general issue with firm surveys, the so-called nonresponse bias, that is, nonrandom nonresponse, which, for example, can arise when firms in distress do not find the time to answer a survey. This problem has been discussed by Graham and Harvey (2015) for the Fuqua–Duke CEO survey and Seiler (2010) for the ifo survey.

expected sales changes in percent, and for expected prices, inventories, and order policies on a trichotomous tendency scale. The *Capital Goods Survey* was targeted at the largest producers of machinery and equipment. It elicited, on a quantitative scale, the recent change in sales, new orders, and unfilled orders, as well as a four-quarter outlook on production. Finally, the *Inventory Survey* focused on realized and expected changes in inventories in percent, recent and expected levels of inventories in US dollars, and expected sales changes in percent.

The National Association of Purchasing Agents (NAPA)—renamed into Institute for Supply Management (ISM) in 2002—started a monthly survey among members in 1931. It is known best today for its Purchasing Manager's Index (PMI) created jointly with the U.S. Department of Commerce in 1988 (Arnseth, 2015; Marquardt and Strigel, 1959). Even though the Consultant Committee on General Business Expectations (1955a) reports that, in the 1950s, its questionnaire occasionally included questions regarding the business outlook of the firm, it has always been rather focused on current developments in the form of an ordered trichotomous scale, with respect to, e.g., production, orders, inventories, employment, prices, and buying policy. Therefore, the survey underlying the PMI is, strictly speaking, not expectational.

2.3.2 Business investment surveys

The *Plant and Equipment Survey* was conducted by the U.S. Department of Commerce in collaboration with the Securities and Exchange Commission from 1945 to 1988, which is why it is often called Commerce-SEC survey in the early literature, and by the Census Bureau from 1988 to 1994 when it was discontinued.[7] The survey elicited, on a quarterly frequency, the participating firms' realized and planned spending on structures and equipment, both per quarter and per year, from which quarterly and annual forecasts were derived. Starting in 1947, it also asked for expected and realized sales (Foss and Natrella, 1957b).[8] All answer scales were quantitative. Coverage and representativeness were high: while not being a random sample—for large firms registered with the Securities and Exchange Commission participation was mandatory, for smaller firms it was voluntary—almost two-thirds of total corporate assets in the U.S. industry were accounted for by the sample already in 1948 even though only 2,100 firms participated (Friend and Bronfenbrenner, 1950; Bridge, 1951). In later years, participation increased step by step by including more small firms to broadly cover manufacturing and nonmanufacturing sectors.[9] Representativeness is suggested by the high correlation of 0.89 between nominal annual investment growth derived from the survey and nonresidential fixed investment growth from the national accounts in 1948–1993 (Lamont, 2000). Aggregate and branch-specific results were regularly published in the *Survey of Current Business* (see https://apps.bea.gov/scb/issues.htm).

The *McGraw-Hill Survey of Business' Plans for New Plants and Equipment* was started in 1947 as an annual survey and later extended to the semiannual frequency (Keezer et al., 1960). To the best

---

[7] After termination of the Plant and Equipment Survey, expectations and plans continued to be surveyed for two more years by the Census Bureau's Investment Plan Survey, see https://www.census.gov/econ/overview/mu2300.html for more information.

[8] A supplementary annual survey collected additional information such as price expectations but was discontinued in 1984 (Landefeld and Seskin, 1984).

[9] The Consultant Committee on Plant and Equipment Expenditure Expectations (1955b) reports 3,000 participating firms, which increased to 8,000-9,000 firms according to Bonhoeffer and Strigel (1966). On its website the Census Bureau mentions 15,000 firms (see https://www.census.gov/econ/overview/mu1000.html).

of our knowledge, it was discontinued in 1988 (Morin and Stevens, 2004). The survey questionnaire included, over different sample periods, a multitude of questions concerning both plans or expectations, and realizations. With respect to investment in plants and equipment, it asked for plans for the current and the following three years as well as the realization in the previous year. Similar questions concerned expected and realized sales and physical capacity. The survey also elicited the capacity utilization rate which was used, e.g., by the Federal Reserve Board (Morin and Stevens, 2004). While the *McGraw-Hill Survey* included fewer firms than the Commerce-SEC *Plant and Equipment Survey*—according to Bonhoeffer and Strigel (1966) around 500 firms—it nevertheless covered, in terms of employment, a notable fraction of the U.S. nonfarm business.[10]

Finally, the *Lionel D. Edie Survey of Business Plant and Equipment Spending Plans* seems to have been well-known in the 1960s and 1970s among forecasters (see, e.g., Bischoff, 1971). It is referred to in a Greenbook (Board of Governors of the Federal Reserve System, 1975), in a letter by the U.S. President (Johnson, 1966), and in articles of the New York Times and the Time magazine. However, this survey appears to have been defunct now for some time and we could not find any academic literature referring to it.

2.3.3 Findings of the early literature

When regular expectational firm surveys became more and more available at the beginning of the 1950s, hopes seemed to have been that their results would significantly improve the accuracy of aggregate economic forecasts. Indeed, as the reports from Consultant Committee on Plant and Equipment Expenditure Expectations (1955b) and the Consultant Committee on General Business Expectations (1955a) show, forecasting of aggregates was the main intended use of these firm surveys, and not the better understanding of firm decision making at the micro level. It was probably not by accident that the 1951 NBER Conference on Research in Income and Wealth in Ann Arbor, which was devoted to short-term economic forecasting, mainly included papers that used firm or consumer expectation surveys. Klein (1955), in his Introduction to the conference volume, describes the optimistic spirit of that conference as follows: "There were an air of enthusiasm and a sense of achievement, a feeling that the papers revealed distinct progress in transforming the fine art of forecasting into a science."

However, the predictive content of expectational surveys turned out to be more meager than anticipated. The NBER conference on the Quality and Economic Significance of Anticipations Data held in Princeton 1957 took stock in a much more nuanced and partly even pessimistic way. In their Introduction to the conference volume, Hart et al. (1960) concede that anticipations data should not be used as direct forecasts, and Bossons and Modigliani (1960) even state: "Analyses of several surveys of businessmen's short-run expectations have consistently revealed a surprising degree of inaccuracy in the forecasts. Accordingly economists have tended to write them off as containing little useful information. As a result, the resources allocated to several such surveys have been sharply reduced."

What happened between these two conferences? A series of papers showed that especially short-term business outlook surveys that elicited forecasts of railway traffic or expected sales yielded, once aggregated, very imprecise forecasts of industry or economy-wide developments and were easily outperformed by naive prediction models. In addition, economists appeared to be surprised by how large

---

[10] In 1956, the coverage rate was 30% on average but much higher in capital-intensive industries like iron and steel (70%), autos, trucks, and parts (95%), and petroleum (83%), see Keezer et al. (1960).

firms' expectation errors concerning their own sales were. We will review this literature first and then turn to survey evidence that in our view was more of a success.

At the beginning of the 1950s, the Shippers' quarterly forecasts of railway traffic was the only time series of aggregated survey expectations of reasonable length.[11] Given that aggregate forecasting was the major aim of the early literature and railway traffic was closely related to the business cycle (Hultgren, 1942), it is not surprising that several papers evaluate their predictive content in detail. Ferber (1953) and Hultgren (1955) document that the Shippers' forecasts are biased, always miss the turning points, lead to large aggregate forecast errors, and are outperformed by simple extrapolation models that take the large seasonal variation in the railway traffic into account.

Evidence concerning other business outlook surveys was at least partly more favorable. While Modigliani and Sauerlender (1955) classify the Dun and Bradstreet surveys as a failure similar to the Shippers' forecasts, Hastay (1954) concludes that they add information beyond that already embodied in aggregate indicators known at the time of the forecast. Hastay (1960) uses diffusion indices derived from the Dun and Bradstreet surveys and estimates models of inventory adjustments intended by firms. While his interpretation of aggregate statistical relationships as behavioral might be difficult to defend from today's perspective, he, nevertheless, obtains sensible parameter estimates and claims that firms plan in a rational way. In addition, Modigliani and Sauerlender (1955) attest the expectations collected in the Fortune surveys strong superiority over simple extrapolation rules, even though forecast errors are large. For the sales anticipations and realizations elicited by the Commerce-SEC survey, they document a fairly strong predictive content at the firm level using the earliest annual survey waves available. A few years later, with a time series of eight annual observations, Modigliani and Weingartner (1958) find that the sales anticipations outperform naive forecasting models and get the direction—but not the magnitude—of change right and thereby confirm a tentative result by Eisner (1958) who uses McGraw-Hill survey data.[12] Internationally, early evidence from the surveys of German firms by the ifo Institute suggests that the aggregate survey results help to forecast producer prices well, except that turning points are missed (Anderson, 1952).

To summarize: while not entirely negative, taken together the literature at the time found considerable and persistent biases, large forecast errors, and missed turning points. From today's perspective perhaps somewhat odd, the literature at the time was also concerned with the "regressivity" of aggregate forecasts. Recall that this was a time when rational expectation formation was not a leading paradigm in Economics. Accordingly, economists expected that, on average, firms would use a simple extrapolation of their most recent trend when forming expectations. In the (quarterly) aggregate data, however, they typically found trend reversals which they called "regressive forecasts."[13] Ferber (1953) first documents this feature for the Shippers' railway traffic forecasts. While Hart (1960) tries to explain it by the specific way these forecasts are collected and compiled and proposes to use a corrected aggregate

---

[11] As a cautionary note, we should add that all aggregate results reported in the early literature must be taken with great care as they were typically based on very few time series observations, typically much less than 20, often around or even below 10. In addition, regression models were mostly specified in levels of nonstationary variables.

[12] One explanation brought forward by Pashigian (1964) is that firms, when asked by the Commerce-SEC survey in January or February for their annual sales outlook, focus on the next few months. In fact, he shows that the association of annual expectations with monthly sales of that year tends to be smaller as the horizon increases.

[13] More technically, extrapolative and regressive forecasts were defined as follows. Suppose y_t is a target variable such as the level of sales and $f_{t|t-1}$ is a forecast based on information available in $t-1$. If $f_{t|t-1} - y_{t-1}$ had the same sign as $y_{t-1} - y_{t-2}$, it was called extrapolative. If it had the opposite sign, it was called regressive.

series, Bossons and Modigliani (1960) show that Dun and Bradstreet's sales expectations exhibit a similar regressivity even at the firm level and conclude that it is an inherent property of the expectational data. In fact, Bossons and Modigliani (1963) document that actual firm-specific sales are also regressive which is why regressive forecasts may not be irrational from the firm's perspective. At the time, this perceived puzzle remained unsolvable, and the initially hopeful enthusiasm about expectational survey data turned soon into pessimism and considerably less research activity (perhaps interestingly in this regard, Bossons and Modigliani (1963) remained, to the best of our knowledge, a working paper).

In terms of the further development of the literature, while the regressivity debate itself is probably not particularly interesting from today's perspective, it exemplifies how the evidence from firm surveys influenced the study of belief formation. In fact, Muth (1961) already cites an early version of Bossons and Modigliani (1963) and suggests that rational expectations might be one way to explain their results, and Pashigian (1964) demonstrates that the null of rational expectations cannot be rejected with aggregate anticipation data. By contrast, Bossons and Modigliani (1966) argue that the type of regressivity they observe at the firm level does not get along well with Muth's rational expectations hypothesis, and Carlson (1967) shows that aggregate anticipations may be interpreted as being adaptive.

Firm surveys yielded interesting results in other dimensions than sales forecasting. Investment plans—in contrast to sales expectations—appeared useful for aggregate forecasting (Okun, 1962) which might be one reason why investment surveys have been continued for a much longer time. For the Commerce-SEC survey, Friend and Bronfenbrenner (1950, 1955) and Foss and Natrella (1957b) document that one-year-ahead expectations of nominal annual plant and equipment expenditures constitute good aggregate forecasts both in terms of the level and the direction of change (Friend and Bronfenbrenner, 1950, 1955; Foss and Natrella, 1957b). For the McGraw-Hill survey, Keezer et al. (1960) show a similarly good performance. Even planned changes in plant capacity are fairly accurate at the aggregate level.[14] A good summary paper of the evidence collected at that time is Friend (1958).[15]

The availability of firm-level data also spurred the microeconometric research on the "behavioral side" of macroeconomics. It started with the question of why firms are such bad forecasters. To this end, Friend and Bronfenbrenner (1950) analyze, in quite some detail, the deviations between quantitative planned and realized capital expenditures at the firm level elicited in the Commerce-SEC survey. They appear to be among the first to study the cross-sectional dimension of firm surveys. One notable result is that, at the firm level—in contrast to the aggregate—, nominal capital expenditure expectations are typically quite inaccurate; only slightly more than one quarter of the firms report an absolute forecast error of less than 20%. Forecast errors are particularly large for small firms and relatively small investment projects (as a fraction of installed capital), see also Friend and Bronfenbrenner (1955) for a discussion. Foss and Natrella (1957b,a, 1960) largely confirm these results.

Given that firms appeared to be bad forecasters, interest turned to explain forecast errors to better understand how firms react to shocks.[16] Foss and Natrella (1957b, 1960) sent special questionnaires to

---

[14] The Canadian Bureau of Statistics' survey of investment intentions yields comparably favorable results (Firestone, 1955).

[15] We did not find out whether these data, which were available at the U.S. Department of Commerce and at the Census Bureau, are still there. These data were rich: different types of expectations and subsequent realizations (investment, sales, inventories), all at the firm level. They might prove to be a great resource for papers studying, say, the stagflation episode, the oil price shocks, the Volcker era, the subsequent disinflation period, etc.

[16] In the terminology of Modigliani and Cohen (1958) and Modigliani and Weingartner (1958), interest focused on the *realization function* which measures the firm's reaction to deviations from expected developments.

the firms in the sample of the Commerce-SEC survey to elicit the reasons for investing more or less in plants and equipment than planned. According to the survey answers, revisions in investment plans are strongly related to the changes in the sales and earnings outlook. This confirms results of Eisner (1958) who analyzes the 1948–1950 cross-sections of firms from the McGraw-Hill survey and finds that, first, investment anticipations significantly explain a considerable share of subsequent capital expenditures even after controlling for initial conditions (e.g., previous capital expenditures and profits) and, second, that both sales changes and sales expectation errors help explain the discrepancy between investment anticipations and realizations. In addition, Greenberg (1964) matches survey data of the McGraw-Hill plant and equipment survey with balance sheet information at the firm level and shows that a stock-adjustment model, which includes expected sales over current capacity, can explain investment plans.

Survey data also informed the then hot debate on the role of inventories in the business cycle. Modigliani and Sauerlender (1955) show that expected sales elicited by the Dun and Bradstreet survey for 1948 and 1949 help explain inventory investment (in a cross-section of 46 firms). Brown (1961), using aggregate and industry-specific time series of 11 observations from the Fortune survey, finds little predictive content of anticipation variables with respect to quarterly inventory investment, once he controls for realizations such as unfilled orders. By contrast, Pashigian (1965) uses 13 years of data from the Commerce-SEC survey and finds sales anticipations to be both relevant and significant in the framework of a stock-adjustment model of inventories. Based on a cross-section of 149 firms from the 1957–1958 McGraw-Hill survey, Orr (1966) confirms that unplanned inventory investment can be explained, in the framework of a simple accelerator model, by the difference between expected and realized sales.

2.4 Ongoing business expectation surveys in the U.S.

In the following, we present select U.S. business expectation surveys which are still ongoing and have proven useful in empirical research.[17]

2.4.1 Manufacturing Business Outlook Survey

The Federal Reserve Bank of Philadelphia established a monthly business tendency survey of the manufacturing industry in the Third Federal Reserve District in 1968.[18] Today, it is known as the Manufacturing Business Outlook Survey (MBOS). The Philadelphia Fed maintains a panel of 250 firms of which the same individual—typically, the CEO or other high-level management personnel—is requested each month to fill out the questionnaire. The panel is not chosen randomly but its composition reflects the industry structure in the Third District.[19] Initially, it included only large firms with at least

---

[17] We note that Canada also has a relatively long-running survey with quantitative expectational questions, the Capital Expenditure Survey. Dave (2011) explains the details and uses this data to test a number of expectation forming hypothesis, arriving at the conclusion that Canadian firms exhibit regressive expectations.

[18] The Third Federal Reserve District includes Delaware and parts of New Jersey and Pennsylvania.

[19] Trebing and Fenske (2018) report the following composition: final business equipment producers 18%, final consumer goods producers 26%, materials producers 20%, equipment parts and components producers 18%, intermediate goods producers 11%, and unclassified 7%.

500 employees but the threshold has been reduced considerably over time to account for structural change in the economy (Trebing and Fenske, 2018). To adjust to these changes and compensate for dropouts, the panel is replenished from time to time. Since participation is voluntary, the response rate varies around 50% (Trebing, 1998). As in most firm surveys, answers are treated confidentially.

Except for a few special questions that change from month to month, the questionnaire of the MBOS has remained largely unchanged since 1968. The regular questions concern important firm indicators such as orders, shipments, inventories, prices, employees, and capital expenditures. A single question asks the participants to assess general business activity but the answers are highly correlated with the answers to the shipment question, which is why Trebing (1998) argues that they primarily reflect firm-specific information. All regular questions elicit an evaluation with respect to the most recent month-over-month change and to the expected change six months ahead. Answers are given on a trichotomous scale ("decrease," "no change," "increase"). The Federal Reserve Bank of Philadelphia publishes the time series of the fractions of firms in each answer category.

The special questions partly require a quantitative answer and are often asked at a quarterly frequency. For example, in 2015 the quarterly Philadelphia Inflation Expectations Survey was added as a module to the MBOS (Trebing and Fenske, 2018), eliciting past and expected rates of price and wage changes. Another quarterly special module asks for the capacity utilization rate and the quarterly change in production on quantitative interval scales.

In 2011, the Federal Reserve Bank of Philadelphia launched the Nonmanufacturing Business Outlook Survey (NBOS) to reflect the decreasing relevance of manufacturing in production and employment (Sen, 2014). It is generally designed and constructed in the same way as the MBOS, featuring regular standard questions to be answered on a trichotomous scale and alternating special question which are partly answered on a quantitative or interval scale.

Given the small number of respondents, representativeness of the answers is a major issue. Supportive evidence is typically based on the comparison of MBOS diffusion indexes with aggregate indicators. Schiller and Trebing (2003), Deitz and Steindel (2005), and Kerr et al. (2014) show that the headline MBOS index relates closely to, and has predictive power for, the growth rate in U.S. manufacturing production. More recently, Trebing and Fenske (2018) find a relatively strong correlation between MBOS indexes and comparable subcomponents of the Purchasing Managers' Index (PMI). However, the MBOS indexes appear more erratic than the PMI, which is based on a larger sample.

Given the length and consistency of the survey in the time dimension, it is uniquely suitable for time series analysis. For example, Giannone et al. (2008) show that the MBOS has a large marginal impact on the nowcast of both inflation and real variables. Bachmann et al. (2013) argue that dispersion indices based on the MBOS can proxy for business uncertainty in manufacturing.

Today, similar surveys are conducted by other regional Federal Reserve Banks in their districts. Examples are the New York Fed's Empire State Manufacturing Survey for the manufacturing sector and the Business Leaders Survey for the services sector, the Richmond Fed's Fifth District Surveys of Manufacturing and Service Sector Activity, the Chicago Fed Survey of Business Conditions, the Minneapolis Fed's general business conditions survey, the Kansas City Fed's Survey of Tenth District Manufacturers, and the Dallas Fed's Texas Manufacturing and Service Sector Outlook Surveys.

2.4.2 CFO Survey

In 1996, Duke University's Fuqua School of Business initiated a quarterly survey of Chief Financial Officers (CFOs), the Duke Global Business Outlook, to elicit quantitative expectations both for their firm and the U.S. economy. Until 2004, Duke conducted the survey jointly with Financial Executives International, an organization of financial executives with 14,000 members—typically, CFOs, treasurers, and controllers—at 8,000 companies throughout the U.S. and Canada. Every quarter, these executives were polled with a one-page survey on important topical issues. From 2005, Duke partnered with CFO Magazine and polled both the members of Duke's own mailing lists and the CFO subscribers that met the criteria for policy-making positions. The typical response rate was 5%–8% (Graham and Harvey, 2001, 2015). Since 2020, Duke has continued the survey in collaboration with the Federal Reserve Banks of Richmond and Atlanta, now concentrating on U.S. firms and calling it CFO Survey.

Survey participants are not sampled randomly. The aim is, however, to have them representative in terms of geographic, sectoral, and size distributions which requires ongoing recruitment efforts (Graham et al., 2020). In terms of firm characteristics, the survey gathers location and sector information. In addition, the firms are asked to provide their level of employment, their current dollar revenues, and their export share. The answers are treated confidentially.

The questionnaire has always included a set of core quarterly questions which ask about the firm's optimism, its expectations with respect to own key indicators, and its expectations of macroeconomic variables. Since there were some changes in 2020 when the cooperation with the Federal Reserve Banks of Richmond and Atlanta started, we discuss the expectational parts of the most recent version of the questionnaire, see Graham et al. (2020) for details. The first question asks respondents to rate, on a scale between 0 and 100, their optimism with respect to their own firm and the U.S. macroeconomy. Another question elicits expected, but not realized, annual growth rates of revenues, prices, wage and nonwage compensations, and unit costs of the main product both in the current and next calendar year. It also asks for the level of employment in the current quarter, at the end of the current calendar year, and at the end of the next calendar year. Hence, only for employment is it possible to compare expectations with realizations. Concerning the macroeconomy, the survey elicits a one-year forecast distribution of GDP growth. It also asks for the firm's best case, most likely, and worst case estimate of the average annual S&P 500 returns both at the one- and ten-year horizons. Once per year, some questions concerning the firm's capital expenditures are included which elicit, inter alia, the current book value of the firm's property, plants, and equipment as well as the dollar value of the purchases of land, structures, and equipment planned for the next six months.

2.4.3 Survey of Business Uncertainty

The Federal Reserve Bank of Atlanta in cooperation with Nick Bloom (Stanford University) and Steven Davis (Chicago Booth School of Business) established the monthly Survey of Business Uncertainty (SBU) in July 2014. The Atlanta Fed maintains a panel of 1,300 firms which were obtained from a list of firms acquired from a supplier of business information. The list was constructed by stratified random sampling such that the mix of firms reflected the sectoral composition of U.S. GDP. In terms of the size distribution, large firms are somewhat underrepresented. The usual contact person within firms is a senior executive such as CEO, CFO, or controller. Approximately 50% of the firms contacted agree to join the panel. The average monthly response rate of the firms in the panel is again near 50% (Altig et al., 2020c).

The aim of the SBU is to elicits past, current, and future firm-specific outcomes with a particular focus on subjective probability distributions of future sales growth rates and employment levels that can, inter alia, be used to construct measures of subjective uncertainty (Altig et al., 2020b). The number and specification of questionnaires and the assignment of firms to them have changed over time, see Altig et al. (2020c). Since August 2020, a sales questionnaire and an employment questionnaire have been in use. The sales questionnaire elicits the current dollar value of sales, its growth rate over the past 12 months, and a five-point discrete probability distribution of the anticipated sales growth rate over the following four quarters. Importantly, the five points of the discrete support are chosen by the firm as representing the scenarios "lowest sales growth," "low sales growth," "middle sales growth," "high sales growth," and "highest sales growth." By thus avoiding any anchoring bias and accounting for the typical cross-sectional heterogeneity in both the central tendency and the range of the support, the SBU allows each firm to state a meaningful distribution. The employment questionnaire elicits the level of employment currently and 12 months ago, and a five-point discrete probability distribution of the anticipated level of employment 12 months ahead defined in the same way as in the sales questionnaire. Both questionnaires are typically augmented by one or more special questions.

To keep the burden on the respondents low, firms do not answer both questionnaires in the same month. Instead, they are randomly allocated to two groups. Members of the first group receive the sales questionnaire in even-numbered months and the employment questionnaire in odd-numbered month, and vice versa for members of the second group (Altig et al., 2020c).

2.4.4 Business Inflation Expectations Survey

The Federal Reserve Bank of Atlanta has been conducting the monthly Business Inflation Expectations (BIE) survey[20] among private nonfarm sector businesses headquartered in the Sixth Federal Reserve District since 2011.[21] According to Bryan et al. (2015) and Meyer et al. (2021) the panel comprises 400–500 firms sampled such that the industry composition largely resembles that of the U.S. economy while oversampling firms with 100 employees or more and from cyclical sensitive industries. Indeed, small firms with less than 100 employees account for only 50% of the panel but for more than three quarters of the establishments in the U.S. and in the Sixth District. By contrast, firms with 100–499 employees are heavily, and firms with 500 employees or more slightly overrepresented. This overrepresentation of medium-sized and large firms might be justified by the fact that they account for roughly two thirds of the employment in the U.S. and in the Sixth District. The usual contact person within the firms is a senior executive such as CEO, CFO, director, or controller. The average monthly response rate of the firms in the panel is usually around 40% (Meyer et al., 2021).

The BIE survey features, inter alia, four monthly standard questions and three quarterly questions. Two of the standard questions focus on unit costs as a measure of inflation that is meaningful to the firm. One elicits, on a five-point interval scale, the percent change in current unit costs compared to one year ago. The interval limits are given as "less than -1%," "-1% to 1%," "1.1% to 3%," "3.1% to 5%," and "more than 5%." Another considers the anticipated one-year-ahead percent change in unit costs

---

[20] There is a second important inflation expectation survey on U.S. businesses, which has been in the field since 2018. It has been conducted by Olivier Coibion and Yuriy Gorodnichenko; see http://firm-expectations.org/ for more detailed information. This survey asks firms about their 12-months-ahead inflation expectations, long-term inflation expectations, perceptions of recent inflation rates, inflation uncertainty, and belief about the Federal Reserve's inflation target. The survey covers firms in manufacturing and services. Since Chapter 11 in this Handbook discusses this survey and results from it in more detail, for the sake of brevity, we limit ourselves here to this footnote.

[21] The Sixth Federal Reserve District includes Alabama, Florida, Georgia, and parts of Louisiana, Mississippi, and Tennessee.

and asks to assign probabilities to the five events defined by the aforementioned intervals. In addition, one of the quarterly questions asks for the distribution of anticipated inflation per year over the next 5 to 10 years, using the same five events and another quarterly question elicits the relevance of factors affecting future price setting by the firm.

The remaining questions are designed to assess the firm's current business environment. Two standard questions ask participants to compare, on a qualitative five-point scale, current to normal sales levels and profit margins, while a quarterly question elicits the percent difference between current and normal unit sales levels.

There is a potential issue with the two central questions that elicit a forecast distribution defined on five pre-specified intervals. In particular, fixed interval limits can lead to anchoring bias and may be of little use when firms experience very heterogeneous evolutions of their unit costs. However, Meyer et al. (2021) conclude from a comparison with a similar (but retired) question of the SBU that these problems are not severe in their sample.

2.4.5 ManpowerGroup Employment Outlook Survey

The international Employment Outlook Survey (EOS) measures firms' hiring and firing intentions and has been conducted quarterly by the ManpowerGroup since 1962. According to ManpowerGroup (2021) the EOS is conducted in 43 countries and based on samples of firms not necessarily related to its customer base. Each country panel is designed such that it reflects the national labor market in terms of the distribution of industries and organization sizes. In the fourth quarter of 2021, more than 45,000 public and private employers participated.[22] The typical respondent within the firm is the head of HR, an HR manager, a general manager, or a senior executive such as the CEO.

The questionnaire features one main question which elicits the anticipated change in the employment level in the next three months as compared to the current quarter. Responses can be given on a trichotomous tendency scale with options "increase," "unchanged," and "decrease." Up to six special questions are added, but they change quarterly. In particular, there is no regular backward-looking question that elicits realized employment change which could be used to compute expectation errors and to validate the results against external data sources. However, ManpowerGroup (2021) reports that the country-specific diffusion indexes of employment intentions are closely related to the realized employment dynamics published by official statistics.

2.4.6 Management and Organizational Practices Survey

The Management and Organizational Practices Survey (MOPS) has been conducted on a large sample of U.S. firms by the U.S. Census Bureau at five-year intervals since 2010.[23] Both the MOPS 2010 and 2015 were sent to a sample of about 50,000 manufacturing establishments also used for the Annual Survey of Manufactures (ASM) conducted by Census Bureau (Buffington et al., 2017). An important feature of this sample is that it is updated annually with new establishments. In addition, it can be linked to the results of the ASM and other surveys of the Census Bureau which provides researchers with a

---

[22] Unsurprisingly, the number of respondents varies considerably over time. For example, Ernst and Viegelahn (2014) report that the EOS is based on 66,000 employers across 42 countries.

[23] Presumably because of issues related to the COVID-19 pandemic, the 2020 survey became a 2021 survey.

plethora of information at the plant level. Being a mandatory survey, the response rate was relatively high at 78% in 2010 and 71% in 2015 of all successfully delivered questionnaires (Buffington et al., 2017; Bloom et al., 2020). Given the large sample and the careful sampling strategy (see Buffington et al., 2016, 2018, for details), the sample should be representative in term of size, branch and geographical location unless nonresponse is highly selective. The typical respondent within the plant is a manager or controller. Senior executives like CEO or CFO are rather rare but this is most probably the consequence of targeting establishments as opposed to firms.

While the general objective of the MOPS is to better understand current and evolving management and organizational practices, a module in the 2015 MOPS included a set of expectational questions. These questions relate to shipments, capital expenditures, materials expenditures (all in dollars), and the number of employees. For each variable, the respondent is first asked to quantify the level of the previous and current year. Subsequently, similar to the SBU, a subjective five-point forecast distribution for the next year is elicited. To this end, respondents are given five scenarios denoted as "lowest," "low," "medium," "high," and "highest." Then they are requested to state what each scenario means to them in quantitative terms and which probabilities they attach to each scenario. The 2021 MOPS only contains expectational questions with respect to shipments and number of employees.

2.4.7 Small Business Economic Trends Survey

The National Federation of Independent Businesses (NFIB), a small business advocacy group, established the Small Business Economic Trends (SBET) survey in 1973 as an instrument to communicate with the White House (Dennis Jr. and Dunkelberg, 2001). Initially, it was conducted in every first month of a quarter, in 1986 the frequency was increased to monthly. The sampling frame is the universe of members which has varied in size but always included several hundred thousand firms. While NFIB members are not representative of the population of small firms in the U.S. in all dimensions—NFIB member firms are on average more rural and older—, they reasonably reflect other characteristics such as sector and size (Dennis Jr. and Dunkelberg, 2001).

Each month a sample is drawn randomly from the list of members, hence there is no panel structure that would allow researchers to follow individual firms over time. Samples in the first month of a quarter have a size of 1,400–1,800 firms and are deliberately larger than in the subsequent two months when the size is around 500–800. The response rate declined from more than 30% in the first 20 years to currently near 10% (Dunkelberg and Wade, 2021). Nevertheless, Dennis Jr. and Dunkelberg (2001) did not find any nonresponse bias in terms of sector, size, and geographic distribution of members who respond and members who do not.

Important characteristics of the sampled firms such as sector, size, geographic region, and organizational form in each month since 1986 are available at http://www.nfib-sbet.org/micro-data/. Most importantly, firms are typically very small. In 2020, nearly 45% of them have less than 9 employees and only 8% have at least 38 employees. The predominant sectors are retail (21.5%), construction (18.5%), and services (17%).

The questionnaire includes expectational (mostly three-months-ahead) and backward-looking questions and offers various answer scales. For example, changes in the general economy, earnings, real sales, inventories, loan rate, and employee compensation are elicited on a five-point tendency scale, while for the change in selling prices, capital expenditures, and the number of employees quantitative interval scales are used.[24]

2.5 Firm surveys in Europe

In the following, we first briefly describe the beginnings of regular firm surveys in post WWII Europe with a focus on Germany, France, and Italy, where long-running business tendency surveys were initiated around 1950. We also cover the UK which started a few years later. We then discuss the current harmonized firm surveys of the EU Commission which are regularly conducted in all EU member countries.

2.5.1 Germany: ifo surveys

The Munich-based ifo Institute conducts the oldest regular European business survey, originally called the "Konjunkturtest," and provides researchers with access to the underlying microdata in its research data center.[25] Therefore, we describe the ifo surveys in some detail.[26] We start with its historic development, then turn to the current state of the two main surveys, the monthly business cycle survey and the semiannual investment survey, and conclude with recent attempts to elicit quantitative information.

2.5.1.1 *The history of the ifo surveys*

The ifo Institute for Economic Research launched the first regular large firm survey in Europe. ifo was founded in 1949 through a merger of two smaller institutes. One of them, the Information and Research

---

[24] The U.S. Chamber of Commerce, in cooperation with MetLife, has been conducting a survey among small firms with less than 500 employees since 2017 with the explicit goal "to give small business owners a voice," see MetLife and U.S. Chamber of Commerce (2017). It is fielded as a telephone survey of 1,000 small business owners and operators based on a stratified random sample drawn from a business directory. Poststratification weighting is used to adequately reflect the population characteristics of small firms regarding region, industry, and size. The questionnaire features ten questions, three of which are expectational. Two ask whether the firm plans to change its number of employees and its investment in the subsequent year, one elicits a one-year-ahead expectation concerning revenues. All three questions are answered on a trichotomous tendency scale ("increase," "same," "decrease").

[25] We note that the microdata are available from 1980 only. The Economics & Business Data Center is jointly operated by the ifo Institute and the University of Munich. It grants access to the anonymized microdata of the ifo Surveys as well as to linked balance sheet data, see Seiler (2012). More information, especially full lists of variables can be found online at https://www.ifo.de/EBDC.

[26] To our knowledge, there are two other surveys fielding expectational questions to German firms: (i) the IAB Betriebspanel at https://www.iab.de/de/erhebungen/iab-betriebspanel.aspx, which is an annual panel survey of approximately 16,000 establishments, fielded since 1993, mostly focusing on labor market questions, but with two qualitative and quantitative expectational questions on sales volume and number of employees (the survey also asks retrospectively about sales volume and number of employees, so that yearly expectation errors can be computed); and (ii) the brand new Bundesbank Online Panel – Firmen (BOP-F) at https://www.bundesbank.de/de/bundesbank/forschung/fdsz/forschungsdaten/bop-f-831640, which started in 2020 at the quarterly frequency as a survey of approximately 10,000 firms, and is now a monthly survey with rolling panels of approximately 3,000 firms, and which asks expectational questions on intermediate input availability, short-run liquidity, access to financing, inventory development, and inflation, thus providing a welcome complement to the ifo surveys. In Switzerland, the Swiss National Bank runs a firm survey with expectational questions, which has been used, e.g., in Hunziker et al. (2022) to study inflation expectations. The Swiss-equivalent survey to the ifo Business Cycle Survey is administered at KOF, an institute at the ETH Zurich: https://kof.ethz.ch/umfragen/konjunkturumfragen.html.

Center for Economic Monitoring at the Bavarian Statistical Office had conducted an interview survey of manufacturing firms—explicitly referring to George Gallup and Elmo Roper who pioneered opinion polls and market research in the U.S.—in 1948 just after the currency reform in order to obtain business cycle information ahead of the (at that time scarce) official statistics (Marquardt and Strigel, 1959; Knoche, 2018). The ifo Institute turned this into a postal survey in 1949, termed it *Konjunkturtest*,[27] and has since conducted it on a monthly basis. The results of the Konjunkturtest were published in the outlets *ifo Schnelldienst* and *ifo Konjunkturperspektiven* and soon became an important and reliable source of business cycle information for Germany, relating closely to the official statistics (see Anderson, 1952, for a first check).[28]

The Konjunkturtest elicits information about the current business situation and the business outlook of the participating firms which helps to derive a timely picture of the business cycle situation both in the aggregate and at the industry level. From the start, the questionnaire has been short and simple, and offered answers on a trichotomous ordinal tendency scale of the type "good," "average/satisfactory," "bad," regarding level variables, and "increase," "unchanged," "decrease," regarding change variables. The guiding principle was to design a one-page questionnaire that the director of a firm would be willing and able to answer within a few minutes without the need to look up numbers or to consider seasonal effects and accounting issues (Langelütke and Marquardt, 1951; Marquardt and Strigel, 1959). Therefore, all questions relate to a certain product, typically the main product of the firm.[29]

The questionnaire comprised a body of standard questions and a few special questions (see Marquardt and Strigel, 1959, for a comprehensive overview). The standard questions for manufacturing firms included (a) the recent monthly change in production, inventories, orders, and sales prices, (b) the recent change in sales against the previous year, (c) an appraisal of the current business stance, inventory size, export situation, and order book, (d) expected production, new orders, and sales prices in the next month, and (e) a six-months-ahead business outlook. Trade and construction firms received similar questions. Special questions changed from month to month. Some of them related to topical developments like labor scarcity or energy prices. Others were included regularly but not monthly, especially a few quantitative questions which presumably put a larger workload on the respondent. In particular, the number of employees was elicited once per year, and capacity utilization rates once per quarter.

While ifo started surveying exclusively manufacturing firms in 1949, it soon included retail, wholesale, and construction firms step by step between 1950 and 1956, targeting each of them with specialized questionnaires. Representativeness was an ongoing concern, which is why the sample started with larger or more important firms and was enlarged step by step. ifo started with 88 manufacturing firms in 1949 but already in 1950 they received 1328 responses. In 1958, more than 6,000 firms participated altogether (manufacturing, 3578; construction, 488; wholesale, 1124; retail, 1137). The market shares of the included firms relative to total sales of their industries varied between 15% (bricks) and almost 100% (automobiles, window glass) in manufacturing while it was much lower in wholesale (6%) and retail (5%) because of the more atomistic firm structure in these sectors at that time, see Marquardt and Strigel (1959). In the 1960s, about 12,000 firms participated in the survey (manufacturing, 6000;

---

[27] The name *Konjunkturtest* means "business cycle test" in English and was chosen to characterize it as a business cycle screening or test procedure (Langelütke and Marquardt, 1951; Laumer, 1989).

[28] The *ifo Schnelldienst* is available online since 2001 and the *ifo Konjunkturperspektiven* since 2005 at https://www.ifo.de/.

[29] Therefore, large firms with several main products may submit more than one questionnaire.

construction, 1300; wholesale, 2500; retail, 2000), and the firms surveyed by the ifo Institute accounted for 44% of the total production volume in manufacturing (Gerstenberger et al., 1969).

In addition to the monthly Konjunkturtest which focused on providing timely data to assess the current state of the business cycle, the ifo Institute started an annual investment survey, the *Investitionstest*, for the manufacturing sector in 1955, in order to obtain better ex post information about business investment. However, it was planned from the beginning to also include anticipations questions which was implemented a few years later after a special question posed in 1958 revealed that the large majority of firms had a planning horizon of one year ahead or even more (Sauer and Wohlrabe, 2020). In the subsequent years, the investment survey was expanded to both trade and construction, and in 1977 leasing firms were included as they started to become an important player (Strigel, 1989).

In 1979 the ifo started an annual innovation survey in the manufacturing sector (Seiler, 2012) to better understand innovation activities of German firms and their determining factors. The questionnaire was very detailed and elicited quantitative and qualitative information about the types and goals of the innovation activities, innovation expenditures, education, and know-how of the employees, as well as factors stimulating or impeding innovation. The innovation survey was discontinued in 2015.

2.5.1.2 *The ifo Konjunkturtest today*

Today, ifo uses the more general term "ifo Business Cycle Survey" instead of Konjunkturtest. It covers the manufacturing, construction, trade, and, since 2001, services sectors. The total size of the firm panel is 11,400 firms (manufacturing, 3200; construction, 900; trade, 3000; services, 4300) and the average response rate is around 61% (manufacturing, 66%; construction, 72%; trade, 67%; services, 52%). Hence, on average 7,000 firms participate in the surveys. Since multiproduct firms may supply more than one questionnaire per product, the ifo collects around 9,000 answers per month; see Sauer and Wohlrabe (2020) for a very detailed description of the surveys (in German) and Link (2020) for a harmonization procedure that integrates the industry-specific surveys into one unified data set.

The panel[30] includes firms from all parts of Germany and of all sizes, including large ones. In particular, more than 10% of the firms in the manufacturing panel employed 1,000 persons or more in 2017, see Table 2.1. For the trade panel, ifo measures the size in terms of the sales volume per year. Large retail and wholesale firms with sales above 25 million euros account for 19% and 42% of the panel, respectively.

While a majority of firms participate in the survey via a web interface or email, a nonnegligible portion still prefers paper questionnaires which are typically returned by fax. In fact, 31% of the firms in the manufacturing panel (construction, 56%; trade, 41%; services, 17%) return a paper questionnaire.

The survey results are summarized in the ifo Business Climate Index, which is a major leading indicator of the German business cycle. It is widely publicized and regularly used in applied forecasting; see Carstensen et al. (2020) and Lehmann (2020) for the high forecasting quality of this index and its components.

The monthly core questions have not changed much compared to the beginnings, even though the details have been adjusted from time to time, and the answer scale is still predominantly trichotomous. In our view, this can partly be explained by the empirical success of the survey-based business cycle

---

[30] The ifo surveys are not balanced panels but, conditional on deciding to stay with the survey after the first attempt, the firms often stay with the surveys for years.

Table 2.1 Size distribution of the ifo surveys in 2017.

	Number of employees				
	1–99	**100–249**	**250–499**	**500–999**	**1000 or more**
Manufacturing	44.7%	23.7%	13.1%	8.2%	10.2%
	Sales (in million euros)				
	below 1	**1–below 5**	**5–below 25**	**25–below 1000**	**1000 or more**
Retail trade	11%	38%	32%	17%	2%
Wholesale trade	3%	18%	39%	39%	3%

Notes: The numbers are taken from Sauer and Wohlrabe (2020) and slightly aggregated.

indicators and partly by ifo's participation in the harmonized EU surveys which aim to produce long time series and favor qualitative questions. We present the harmonized core questions in Section 2.5.5 below.

Besides the monthly core questions, many supplementary questions, some of which quantitative, are included regularly but mostly at lower frequencies. For example, all surveys elicit current credit conditions and factors impeding business activity such as insufficient demand or shortage of workers four times per year.

In addition, the manufacturing survey elicits, inter alia, information about the competition on home and foreign markets, short-term work, and production capacities including the quantitative capacity utilization rate (in percent of the technical capacity) every quarter. Twice a year, manufacturing firms answer questions concerning their profit situation which includes two quantitative questions: firms state their return on sales of the previous year in May and their expected return on sales of the current year in September. Once per year, the questionnaire elicits the number of employees as another quantitative information. Other annual questions pertain to investment and innovation activities. The latter include the percentage of employees in F&E activities and F&E expenditures as a percentage of total sales.

The construction survey also includes additional regular questions not present in the harmonized core questionnaire. Most notably, the capacity utilization rate is elicited on a monthly frequency. On a yearly basis, the number of employees, staffing issues and construction-specific topics such as the share of rented machines, the relevance of subcontractors, and the types of construction activities are elicited.

The trade survey also includes additional questions especially with respect to investment. In May, firms are asked to provide qualitative information about the change in investment in the previous and in the current year. In November, firms update on the change in investment in the current year and provide their qualitative expectations for the next year. On a yearly basis, they quantitatively state the number of employees and total annual sales (on a interval scale, in euros).

The services survey elicits the following additional questions: At a quarterly frequency, firms are asked by how much in percent they could increase their activities with the current capacity, thus providing an analogue to the capacity utilization rate elicited in manufacturing and construction. Once per year, firms are asked to assess the change in investment in the previous year and forecast it for the current year, both on a qualitative basis. They also state the number of employees and total annual sales (on a interval scale, in euros) once per year.

Furthermore, the ifo Institute has included, and stored, a large number of one-time or very infrequent questions that inform about various characteristics, beliefs, and activities of the firms. Some of these special questions inform about the type of the firm, e.g., the self-characterization as a family business

Table 2.2 Topics of one-time special questions elicited by the ifo Institute.

Topic	Survey	Sector included			
		Manuf.	Constr.	Trade	Services
Effects of climate change	01/2013	yes	yes	yes	yes
Potential of hiring refugees	10/2015	yes	yes	yes	yes
Implications of the German minimum wage	03/2016	yes	yes	yes	yes
Demand for loans	06/2016	yes	yes	yes	yes
Implications of Brexit	06/2016	yes			
Activities in online trade	08/2016			yes	
Expectations with respect to US trade policy	02/2017	yes			
Effects of negative interest rates	06/2017	yes	yes	yes	yes
Implications of the US tax reform	03/2018	yes		yes	yes
Export of services	08/2018				yes
Impact of extreme weather events	05/2019	yes	yes	yes	yes
Relevance of online platforms	08/2019			yes	
Dimensions and consequences of uncertainty	09/2019ff.	yes		yes	yes
Opinions about the retirement age	02/2020	yes	yes	yes	yes
Effects of the COVID-19 pandemic	03/2020ff.	yes	yes	yes	yes

Notes: A more comprehensive overview until 2018 is provided by Sauer and Wohlrabe (2020). A detailed list of questions is provided by the Economics & Business Data Center, see EBDC-BEP (2020). The topic "Dimensions and consequences of uncertainty" was included in the questionnaires for manufacturing in 09/2019 and 01/2020, for trade in 12/2019, for services in 01/2020. The topic "Effects of the Corona pandemic" has been included in various months since 03/2020.

(included in 02/2014) and the founding year (08–09/2018), and the characteristics of the responding person (11–12/2018). Typically, however, the special questions relate to a topical issue of that time. A list of examples is given in Table 2.2. For instance, since March 2020 the ifo Institute has included a series of questions relating to the COVID-19 pandemic in order to obtain timely information about the economic situation and inform policy makers. Bachmann et al. (2020c) use this information to show how relevant the pandemic-induced uncertainty is for the crisis-struck firms; see also Balleer et al. (2020), Buchheim et al. (2022a), and Buchheim et al. (2022b).

The ifo Institute has documented the high quality of the answers in its Business Cycle Survey. In the overwhelming majority of participating manufacturing firms, the survey respondent is a member of top management. Sauer and Wohlrabe (2019) document that 73% of firms mention CEO, CFO, or COO, and an additional 13% of survey units refer to a "division head." For large firms with more than 500 employees, the shares are only slightly lower: 65% CEOs, CFOs, or COOs, and 15% division heads. The findings are consistent with an earlier metastudy conducted by ifo about the trade sector (Abberger et al., 2011). Second, the identity of the responder within the firm changes rarely. A special survey fielded by ifo in fall 2019 asks who filled out the questionnaire in the past; 83% of firms indicate the responder is "always the same person," 15% say "mostly the same person," and less than 2% mention a team of people or that the responder "changes frequently" (Bachmann et al., 2020a). Link et al. (2021) provide additional evidence for the case of aggregate economic conditions that, in general, survey answers by firms are of high quality.

In terms of economic research, the ifo Business Cycle Survey has seen an increased use in recent years: Carstensen et al. (2013) use expectation data from the ifo Business Cycle Survey to analyze to what extent oil market developments contributed to the German recession in 2009. Strasser (2013) investigates, using the export expectation and credit availability questions of the ifo survey, how exchange rate pass-through depends on firms' credit conditions. Bachmann et al. (2013) compute qualitative forecast errors from the ifo microdata about production changes and study the business cycle properties of their cross-sectional dispersion as a proxy for time-varying business uncertainty. Bachmann and Elstner (2015) combine the monthly qualitative production change data with the quantitative quarterly capacity utilization data from the survey in order to extract quantitative expectations errors at the firm level. They then study the aggregate misallocation consequences for capital and labor of such errors. Buchheim and Link (2017) study whether firms' expectations reflect rather aggregate, industrywide or disaggregate information. Huber (2018) uses the aforementioned questions about credit availability and what constrains business activity to study the transmission of a banking crisis through the production sector. Massenot and Pettinicchi (2018) study the overextrapolation behavior of firms in the ifo survey. Bachmann et al. (2019) build on the work computing quantitative firm-level production expectation errors from the ifo survey to study the influence of micro uncertainty and volatility on the price setting of firms. Enders et al. (2019a) study how monetary policy announcements shape firms' production and price expectations and document nonlinear effects. Enders et al. (2019b) investigate how firms' expectations about future production influence their current production and pricing decisions. Importantly, they show that firms' expectations matter even when they turn out to be incorrect ex post. Link (2019) uses the price and employment expectation questions to analyze how the introduction of the minimum wage in Germany impacted firms' pricing and employment decisions. Finally, Link et al. (2021) use the firm-level ifo data to compare the degree of information frictions at the firm level with that at the household level, finding that firms' expectations are much closer to those of experts than those of households.

2.5.1.3 *The ifo Investment Survey today*

Currently, the ifo Investment Survey is focused on the manufacturing sector alone. It is conducted twice per year in spring and fall. The sample has decreased over time from 3,000 in 1970 to 1,800 in the recent years, partly reflecting the increasing concentration in this sector. Nevertheless, the ifo Institute takes care to replace exiting firms in order to keep the sample representative. In fact, according to Sauer and Wohlrabe (2020), the sample accounts for 46% of the sales and 56% of the investment expenditures in manufacturing due to oversampling of large firms.

The spring survey elicits annual expenditures for investments in structures and equipment for the two previous years as well as, as a point forecast, planned investment in the current year (all in euros). It also asks the firms to state qualitatively to which end they primarily invest: expansion of capacities, rationalization, or replacement.

The fall survey elicits total investment in the previous year, estimated investment in the current year, and, again as a point forecast, planned investment for the next year, all in euros. For the current and next year, firms give a breakdown of the percent shares of total investment due to expansion of capacities, restructuring, rationalization, and replacement. They also state, on a five-point scale, which factors stimulate or dampen investment (demand, financing conditions, profits, technical factors, economic policy). In both spring and fall, firms report employment and sales of the previous year.

In terms of economic research, the ifo Investment Survey has been used by Bachmann et al. (2017) to characterize empirically the business cycle properties of the cross section of quantitative investment expectation errors. This is made possible by the long time series of quantitative expectational and realized investment data at the firm level. They find that the cross-sectional dispersion of investment surprises is countercyclical, as is their average within-firm time series volatility, and both are highly correlated. This justifies, in part, strategies in the literature to use cross-sectional moments for the calibration of heteroscedasticity. At the same time, the cross-sectional dispersion of investment is procyclical, suggesting a nonsmooth capital adjustment friction at the microlevel. There is substantial dispersion in within-firm volatility, a feature consistent with a recent literature on information frictions at the firm-level. Finally, the aforementioned second moments of investment innovations are Granger-caused by recessions, but not vice versa, rendering simple exogenous uncertainty shocks less plausible as drivers of business cycles. Bachmann and Zorn (2020) use the information about which factors stimulated or dampened investment for firms to extract business cycle shocks for the German economy. They find that the bulk of investment fluctuations are driven by aggregate demand shocks. Consistent with neoclassical views, however, technological factors are the most important investment determinant on average. Finally, Link et al. (2022) use investment plan revisions from the ifo Investment Survey and combine them with administrative tax data to study the deleterious investment effect of corporate tax hikes.

2.5.1.4 *Quantitative answer scales*

While the ifo Business Cycle Survey mainly features easy-to-answer trichotomous answer scales, the rise of the internet allowed ifo to experiment and, for some questions, introduce a much finer answer scale, the Visual Analog Scale (VAS), in 2005. Since then, the VAS has been used for two questions—the appraisal of the current business situation and the six-months-ahead business outlook—in the online part of the manufacturing survey.[31] The respondents are given the option to answer using, in addition to the usual trichotomous scale, a slider on a visual scale which has two endpoints and a middle anchor. For the current business situation the endpoints are labeled "bad" and "good," while the middle anchor is labeled "satisfactory." For the six-months-ahead outlook the endpoint labels are "worse" and "better," while the middle anchor is "more or less unchanged." The position of the slider chosen by the respondent is converted to numbers between 0 and 100. While the VAS was new in business tendency surveys in 2005, it had a long history in medical interviews to elicit, e.g., a degree of feelings or pain (Stangl, 2008).

While it turned out that the VAS does not make a big difference for aggregate indices of business sentiment compared to the trichotomous scale, it allows firms to answer on a much finer scale. This also holds for the calculation of expectation errors and revisions and is thus interesting for researchers using firm-level data. Additionally, the parallel use of a trichotomous scale and a VAS allows researchers to study how firms think about the three categories of the former. Three results are particularly noteworthy, see Stangl (2008) for details. First, the answers given in the VAS seem to follow a nonnormal distribution in the cross-section of firms with the degree of asymmetry changing over the business cycle. Second, firm-specific thresholds to switch from the middle category into the upper or lower category appear symmetric for the current business situation but asymmetric for the business outlook. Third,

---

[31] In 2017, the VAS was also introduced in the online parts of the construction, trade, and services surveys.

choosing the middle category of the trichotomous scale, say "more or less unchanged" for the business outlook, can have two reasons: either the respondent really expects a broadly unchanged business situation or she does not have a good idea. This effect is known from probability scales where respondents choose the value of 50 when they really feel "epistemic" uncertainty which may lead to an overrepresentation of this value in surveys (de Bruin et al., 2000). Indeed, the VAS answer distribution clearly shows a spike at exactly 50 which suggests that epistemically uncertain firms put their slider to the middle anchor when they use a VAS and similarly use the middle category when they use a trichotomous tendency scale.

   In 2013, the ifo Institute finally added a quarterly online module of quantitative questions to elicit subjective firm uncertainty and ambiguity in the manufacturing sector. In the first years, firms had to affirm that they also want to fill in the uncertainty questionnaire after finishing the regular Business Cycle Survey. Nevertheless, participation was stable between 300 and 400 firms per wave in the first years. In 2019, the module was fully integrated into the regular Business Cycle Survey and extended to all sectors which is why participation increased considerably. The new questions elicit, in the first month of a quarter, the sales growth rate of the previous quarter and, for the current quarter, the expected sales growth rate together with best case and worst case growth rates. The distance between the latter two can be interpreted as a robust measure of uncertainty (Bachmann et al., 2020a). In addition, firms are requested to state the probabilities that sales increase, stay the same, and decrease in the current quarter; they can state either a probability or a range of probabilities. Firms choosing the latter can be termed ambiguous or Knightian since they are unable to state a single probability for an event (Bachmann et al., 2020b).

2.5.2 **France: INSEE survey**

The Institut National de la Statistique et des Études Économiques (INSEE)—the French Statistical Authority—launched their first firm survey in 1951 inspired by the aforementioned U.S. Fortune surveys (INSEE, 1951; Malhomme, 1969). Its purpose was, similarly to the ifo Institute, to obtain faster and more comprehensive business cycle data than the official "hard" statistics, but also to collect ex ante information to better understand the business cycle (Piatier, 1953). Results were published in the journal *Etudes et conjoncture*.[32]

   The initial sample was not random but focused on large and important firms of all nonfarm sectors, partly because the company heads and their addresses were more easily available in a time that lacked an appropriate business register, partly because INSEE suspected that the questions could be too difficult to be answered by possibly less educated heads of smaller firms. However, to have a good geographical balance, also medium-sized and a few small firms were included. In total, the questionnaire was sent out to 3,308 firms, of which 1,670 responded. Thirty percent of firm respondents had less than 100 employees, 51% had 100 to 1,000 employees, and 16% had more than 1,000 employees (see INSEE, 1951, for more details).

   INSEE's initial questionnaire resembled ifo's in important dimensions (see INSEE, 1951, for the full questionnaire). In particular, it comprised both backward-looking and expectational questions, and it predominantly posed tendency questions. However, there were also important differences. Unlike the

---

[32] All issues can be browsed online at https://www.persee.fr/collection/estat. In 1969, INSEE discontinued the journal and started to publish the survey results in, inter alia, *Les collections de l'INSEE – Série E* (Ripert, 1969).

ifo, INSEE asked about product groups and elicited annual developments. In addition, firms also had to provide tendency forecasts for the macroeconomy (e.g., production, exports, employment, and prices). Finally, INSEE originally used a five-point interval scale. For example, the expected annual change in sales revenues could be answered with "strong increase (more than 15%)," "moderate increase (5% to 15%)," "no appreciable change (between −5% and 5%)," "moderate decrease (between 5% and 15%)," and "strong decrease (15% or more)."

By 1958, INSEE had changed several aspects of the survey (Marquardt and Strigel, 1959; Malhomme, 1969; INSEE, 1957; Jankeliowitch, 1957, 1958a,b,c). In particular, INSEE skipped the quantitative interval limits making it a purely qualitative ordered five-point scale. However, in 1957 INSEE added an annex to their main questionnaire which elicited percent changes for some categories so that, effectively, respondents answered on both a tendency and a quantitative scale. Other changes included focusing on company-specific questions, increasing the survey frequency to three times per year, and targeting solely the manufacturing and trade sectors for which specialized questionnaires were introduced. Finally, the sample size increased to 1,659 respondents in manufacturing of which 27% had less than 100 employees, 59% had 100 to 1,000 employees, and 14% had more than 1,000 employees; and to 673 respondents in wholesale and retail trade of which 14% had annual sales of less than 100 million francs, 61% had annual sales between 100 million and 1 billion francs, and 25% had annual sales of more than 1 billion francs.[33]

In 1962, as part of the European harmonization discussed in Section 2.5.5 below, INSEE added a monthly manufacturing survey with a reduced questionnaire, but continued the more detailed survey it conducted three times a year. The remaining surveys were conducted less frequently (trade, 5 p.a.; construction, 2–4 p.a.; consumers, 3 p.a.), see Malhomme (1969) for details.

Also, since the early 1990s, the Banque de France has conducted a monthly Business Outlook Survey, the *Enquete Mensuelle de Conjoncture*. It is a short survey with qualitative questions about firms' perceptions and expectations about their own activity, demand and prices during the current month and over the next three months. The interviews take place the last week of each month (most answers are collected over two or three days). More recently in 2020, an inflation expectations module was added to this survey, see Savignac et al. (2021) for details.

2.5.3 Italy: from ISCO to Istat

In 1949, the Italian Union of Chambers of Commerce, Industry, and Agriculture started a monthly survey among the local Chambers of Commerce of manufacturing, trade, and agriculture. These local entities, in turn, either asked their member firms formally with regular questionnaires or elicited firm sentiments through informal contacts (Pagani, 1959). Initially, the questionnaire focused on ex post questions, but since 1952 it also elicited plans and expectations, all on a trichotomous tendency scale. The results were published in the journal *Sintesi Economico* (Marquardt and Strigel, 1959).

Inspired by the Fortune surveys in the U.S., the Institute for Economic Studies (Istituto per gli Studi Economia, ISE) started a semiannual survey in 1952 (Pagani, 1959). It was targeted at businessmen, financiers, and experts who were chosen by name and replaced individually after dropout. Hence, it was rather an expert survey, and it was biased towards the more developed northern Italy. It initially

---

[33] To put these numbers into perspective, according to the Jordà–Schularick–Taylor Macrohistory Database (https://www.macrohistory.net/database/) the exchange rate in 1958 was 4.59 francs per US-dollar.

elicited information about the general economic situation and outlook, e.g., the expectations for the upcoming half-year with respect to the general business situation, demand, exports, and prices. From 1956 to 1959, it also included questions regarding the respective sectors the respondents had expertise in. Firm-specific questions were avoided on purpose. The answer scale was a five-point interval scale similar to that of INSEE. The sample size was 1,200–1,300 persons from all parts of the business sector (agriculture and manufacturing, 40%; trade, 25%; finance, 20%; experts, 15%). Results were published in the periodical *Mondo Economico*.

In 1959, the National Institute for the Study of the Business Cycle (Istituto Nazionale per lo Studio della Congiuntura, ISCO) in cooperation with *Mondo Economico* decided to introduce a proper firm survey (Pagani, 1959). Initially, it was quarterly and focused on the manufacturing sector (trade and construction followed later). The sample was not random but intended to include "leading firms," in particular large incorporated companies, which were assumed to reflect the evolution of the economy better than others, and included 2,600 firms (Martelli, 1998; Martelli et al., 2014). However, the basic idea was already in 1959 that size groups, branches, and geographical regions should be well represented in the survey (Pagani, 1959). Results were published in *Mondo Economico* which was discontinued in 1997.

The ISCO questionnaire followed the ifo principles. It was printed on one page, contained easy-to-answer questions and a trichotomous answer scale. It elicited, inter alia, information about the firms' employment, capacity utilization, inventories, orders, and sales prices, both for the most recent and for the upcoming quarter.

In 1962, as part of the European harmonization, the survey frequency was increased to monthly and the sample size was stabilized at around 4,000 firms (Malgarini et al., 2005). Since 1986, a carefully designed stratified sampling procedure has been applied to reflect the industry, size, and regional structure of the Italian economy (Malgarini et al., 2005). In 1999, ISCO was merged with another research institute to the Institute of Economic Studies and Analysis (Istituto di Studi e Analisi Economica, ISAE), and in 2011 ISAE was merged into the National Statistical Institute of Italy (Istat) which has since then conducted the firm surveys (Martelli et al., 2014).

As in Germany and France, there is also a parallel firm survey structure in Italy at the national central bank, with the Banca d'Italia administering at least two surveys with expectational information: there is the annual Survey on Investment in Manufacturing (SIM), started in 1996, whose question on expected sales growth Guiso and Parigi (1999) used in a seminal contribution to study empirically the effects of firm uncertainty on investment; this study was repeated and extended on by Bontempi et al. (2010). There is also the Survey on Inflation and Growth Expectations (SIGE), a quarterly business expectations survey started in 1999, which has been used by, e.g., Grasso and Ropele (2018), Bartiloro et al. (2019), Coibion et al. (2019), and Conflitti and Zizza (2021).

2.5.4 UK: CBI Industrial Trends Survey

The Federation of British Industries (FBI) started a business survey known as Industrial Trends Enquiry in 1958 (Shepherd, 1963). Initially, it was conducted only three times per year but otherwise resembled ifo's Konjunkturtest quite closely. In particular, it was targeted at the top management level of the manufacturing industry, included a relatively short questionnaire with both backward-looking and expectational questions, and used a trichotomous answer scale. It elicited, inter alia, information about the firms' output, orders, exports, stocks, employment, hours, prices, and profits both for the most recent and for the upcoming four-month period, and capital expenditure in the upcoming 12 months.[34] The sample started with 550 firms and increased over time to 1,100 firms in 1965 (Board of Trade, 1965). The sample was not random but its composition mimicked the industry structure. However, the FBI aggregated the answers without weighting which resulted in an underrepresentation of large firms in terms of employment and output (Shepherd, 1963). The FBI published the aggregate results of the backward-looking questions but unfortunately not of the expectational questions (Shepherd, 1963; NIESR, 1961).

In 1965, the FBI was merged with two other industry associations into the Confederation of British Industry (CBI). The survey remained largely unaffected and has since been known as Industrial Trends Survey. The panel further increased to 2,000 firms in 1967 and represented 30% of total manufacturing employment and 40% of exports (Glynn, 1969). Moreover, a weighting scheme was introduced that took the firms' size and industry into account. In 1972, the CBI changed the survey frequency to quarterly but otherwise left the questionnaire unchanged (Klein and Moore, 1981). In 1973, the UK joined the European Community and therefore started to participate in its harmonized survey program described in Section 2.5.5 below. As one consequence, the CBI introduced an additional monthly survey with a reduced questionnaire (Low, 1997). In later years, the CBI broadened the survey to wholesale and retail trade (1983), financial services (1989), and consumer and business services (1998). Boneva et al. (2019) use the Industrial Trends Survey to empirically characterize firms' expectations at the microlevel. They find, for example, that UK firms do not form rational expectations.

Again, as in the other European countries also the Bank of England now conducts its own expectational survey, the Decision Maker Panel, which was launched in 2016 in cooperation with the Universities of Nottingham and Stanford and which surveys approximately 8,000 firms on a monthly frequency.[35] On a rolling basis, the survey focuses on one of three topics: firms' expectations and uncertainty for the year ahead in their sales and prices, firms' employment, and firms' capital expenditures. Bloom et al. (2019) use this survey to study the impact of Brexit on UK firms, especially how uncertain they perceive their environment to be after Brexit, and Altig et al. (2020a) use this survey, in addition to many others, to characterize the impact of the COVID-19 pandemic on the uncertainty of British firms. Finally, there is a Management and Expectations Survey executed by the UK Office for National Statistics and designed after the MOPS survey in the U.S.; see Bloom et al. (2021) for details and an analysis of the question whether firms with better forecasts also perform better.

2.5.5 European harmonization of business surveys

European cooperation with respect to business surveys started as early as 1952 when the heads of INSEE (André Piatier), the ifo Institute (Karl Wagner), and the Italian Union of Chambers of Commerce, Industry, and Agriculture (Guglielmo Tagliacarne) met in Paris and founded the Comité International pour l'Etude des Méthodes Conjoncturelles (Marquardt and Strigel, 1959). Piatier (1953) emphasized the unifying features of the three surveys, namely, qualitative answer scales and expectational questions that asked decision makers to look into the future. For the time, his ideas were quite modern: "The starting point of any business cycle analysis must be that the decisions of economic agents are

---

[34] A sample questionnaire is shown in the Appendix of Board of Trade (1965).

[35] Information can be found at https://www.bankofengland.co.uk/statistics/research-datasets and https://decisionmaker-panel.co.uk/.

much more important in foreshadowing the economic future than the statistical recording of the results of the past period. ... The study of these decisions or, in a broader sense, of the behavior of economic units of all dimensions ... must have a relevance at least equal to that of the statistical study of the past." (own translation of Piatier, 1953).

Soon experts from other European countries joined the Comité. In 1953, the ifo Institute organized the first European conference on business tendency surveys which was attended by 18 participants from seven countries who discussed six papers (Ziegler, 1989). The conference was repeated biannually, initially in Germany (1955 in Kiel, 1957 and 1959 in Munich), with quickly increasing numbers of participants.

To deepen this cooperation, several European survey institutes founded the Centre for International Research on Economic Tendency Surveys (CIRET, initially known under the French name Contact International des Recherches Economiques Tendancielles) in 1960 (Ziegler, 1989). Henri Theil became the first director, and CIRET was equipped with a research center at Theil's Econometric Institute at the University of Rotterdam until 1966.[36] The next conference on business tendency surveys took place in Nordwijk aan Zee in the Netherlands in 1961 and thus the first time outside of Germany and has since been organized by CIRET.

Political cooperation in Europe led to the Treaty of Rome which constituted the European Economic Community (EEC) in 1957. The Commission of the EEC decided in 1961 to establish a joint business survey of industrial firms within the six member countries which started in 1962 on a monthly frequency.[37] The centerpiece of the joint survey was a harmonized questionnaire that allowed cross-country comparisons and EEC-wide aggregation of the national results (Commission of the European Communities, 2006). Monthly surveys for other sectors were added step by step: construction in 1966, retail trade in 1984, consumer and business services in 1996, and financial services in 2007. Moreover, in 1966 a semiannual investment survey of the manufacturing sector was started (European Commission, 2021). With the enlargement of the EEC and later the EU, the geographical coverage has increased significantly to 32 countries in 2021, including the EU candidate countries.

The Commission has never conducted an own survey; instead it commissioned national institutions, typically those with long-standing expertise, and supported them with grants that covered up to 50% of the costs (Commission of the European Communities, 2006) which is why these institutions must have a "self interest" in conducting these surveys. It is thus no surprise that the ifo Institute has conducted most of the harmonized firm surveys in Germany, INSEE in France, ISCO-ISAE-Istat in Italy and—for the time the UK was part of the EEC and later the EU—the CBI in the United Kingdom. As an unfortunate consequence of the commissioning, the Commission only obtains results aggregated to the industry level from the national institutions but has no access to the microdata. This means that there exists no European expectational firm microdata set to this day.

We describe the harmonized European firm surveys in the following, taking European Commission (2021) as our primary source. All results, time series, methodological guidelines, sample questionnaires and information about the survey institutions are available on the website of the European Commis-

---

[36] Afterwards, the research center moved to the University of Mannheim and later to the ifo Institute in Munich (Strigel and Ziegler, 1988). Since 1999 CIRET has been located at the ETH Zurich.

[37] The Netherlands did not participate in the first years, partly because the firms feared that company secrets could be compromised (Kommission der EWG, 1966).

sion.[38] Importantly, harmonization does not mean uniformity. For example, the sample questionnaires may be augmented by national institutes with their own questions and thus define a minimum set of questions posed all over Europe. Moreover, aspects like the sampling design, the sample size, and the survey mode are not fixed by the European Commission but may be carefully chosen by the national institutes as long as they ensure representative surveys without much noise in the aggregates. Nevertheless, the European Commission (2014) has published a "best practice list" which includes many recommendations concerning the sampling methodology. For example, the EU aims at a high response rate. Currently, it averages around 70%, which is a good value internationally.[39]

The manufacturing survey is conducted monthly as a classical business tendency survey, almost exclusively featuring tendency questions to be answered on a trichotomous scale. The questionnaire is sent out to 38,000 firms. It contains questions asking for (a) the recent 3-month change in production, (b) an assessment of current orders and inventories, and (c) the expected 3-months-ahead changes in production, employment, and selling prices. A relatively new question concerns the predictability of the future business situation which might be taken as a measure of uncertainty. The answer is given on a four-point scale with options "easy to predict," "moderately easy to predict," "moderately difficult to predict," and "difficult to predict." Some questions are added every first month of a quarter including the only two quantitative ones eliciting the capacity utilization rate (in percent) and the number of months for which production has been secured.

The monthly construction survey is conducted among 21,500 firms. The questionnaire elicits (a) the recent 3-month change in building activity, (b) an assessment of current orders, (c) the main factors currently limiting building activity, and (d) the expected 3-months-ahead changes in employment and selling prices, all on a trichotomous scale. In addition, it asks about the predictability of the future business situation as in the manufacturing survey. On a quarterly basis, firms are requested to state the number of months for which production is secured which is the only quantitative question in the construction survey.

The retail trade survey is entirely qualitative. Each month, 27,500 retailers receive a questionnaire which asks about (a) the development of business activity over the past three months, (b) an assessment of current inventories, and (c) the expected 3-months-ahead changes in business activity, employment, selling prices and orders placed with suppliers. Again it also includes the question concerning the predictability of the future business situation to be answered on a four-point scale.

The services survey is the largest monthly survey of the EU. The questionnaire is sent out to 47,000 firms each month. It contains questions concerning (a) the recent 3-month change in demand, employment, and the business situation, (b) the predictability of the future business situation, and (c) the expected 3-months-ahead changes in demand, employment, and selling prices. In the first month of a quarter, firms are additionally asked about the main factors currently limiting business and the maximum increase in business activity possible with the present resources.

In spring and fall, manufacturing and services firms are additionally requested to provide information concerning their investment activity. The spring survey elicits, on the usual trichotomous scale, the annual change in investment in the previous year and in the year just begun, both overall and with respect to the asset classes (a) machinery and equipment, (b) land, building, and infrastructure, and (c)

---

[38] https://ec.europa.eu/info/business-economy-euro/indicators-statistics/economic-databases/business-and-consumer-surveys.

[39] The survey website of the European Commission provides breakdowns by survey and country which show that response rates vary considerably, especially across countries.

intangibles like R&D, software, and intellectual property. The fall survey asks, again on a trichotomous scale, about the annual change in total investment in the current and next year. It also elicits the main factors stimulating investment with answer options being "demand," "financial conditions," "technical factors," and "other factors." Finally, it requests to state the main objectives of investment (replacement, extension of capacity, streamlining production, and other objectives).

2.6 Firm surveys in Japan: the TANKAN

The *Tanki Keizai Kansoku Chousa* (in English – Short-Term Economic Survey of Enterprises in Japan) is the leading business tendency survey of Japan, generally known as TANKAN.[40],[41] Using the ifo Konjunkturtest as a role model, it was launched by the Industrial Bank of Japan in 1951 as Short-Term Survey of the Industries.[42] The Bank of Japan took over the survey in 1957 and renamed it to Principal Enterprises TANKAN. At that time, it was conducted on a semiannual basis and included 524 firms. In the subsequent years and decades, the Bank of Japan increased the survey frequency to quarterly and extended its coverage step by step to about 10,000 firms in the recent years.

Unlike the ifo Konjunkturtest, the TANKAN has long elicited both qualitative and quantitative answers. Currently, it is largely structured into a judgemental part which includes tendency questions to be answered on a qualitative three-point scale; a projection part which asks for quantitative forecasts and realizations of sales, exports, exchange rates, profits, and investment with a specific block of questions regarding overseas business activities; and an inflation part which elicits expected rates of change in both the firm's sales prices and in general consumer prices over one to five years.[43] Morikawa (2016a) uses the TANKAN to study the relationship between firm-level uncertainty and investment.

More generally, Japan has a number of other expectational firm surveys at various institutions: (i) the Annual Survey of Corporate Behavior conducted by the Economic and Social Research Institute in the Cabinet Office of Japan. Individual firm identifiers are available only after 1989. In each year, the survey questionnaire was sent to all listed firms on the Tokyo and Nagoya Stock Exchanges. This amounts to about 2,200 firms on average. The response rate of the survey is 53% on average. The survey is conducted annually between mid-December and mid-January. Respondents are required to answer questions regarding their business outlook for GDP and industry demand, and their business plans for investment and employment. The forecasts are made for multiple horizons; see Tanaka et al. (2020) (and also Kaihatsu and Shiraki, 2016; Koga and Kato, 2017); (ii) the Survey of Production Forecast, a monthly survey of Japanese manufacturers conducted by the Ministry of Economy, Trade,

---

[40] "Tan" is Japanese for "short-term" and "Kan" means "survey" (Yoshino, 1995).

[41] Handbook chapters necessarily have to select and be limited in size and scope. This means that we have not done justice to the many firm surveys with expectational questions which are not from the U.S. or Europe. This very brief section on Japan is thus meant as a pars pro toto. Chapters 11 and 12 in this Handbook complement this attempt somewhat. Perhaps the one other non-U.S./non-European country, in addition to the long-standing survey tradition in Japan, worth pointing out separately here is New Zealand, which has been a recent laboratory for studying firms' inflation expectations: Kumar et al. (2015), Coibion et al. (2018), and Kumar et al. (2022).

[42] Yoshino (1995) reports that the head of the Department of Economics of the Industrial Bank of Japan traveled to Western Europe in 1951, learned about ifo's Konjunkturtest, and established the first firm survey in the same year. For additional details, see the https://www.boj.or.jp/en/statistics/outline/exp/tk/faqtk04.htm/#p0109 provided by the Bank of Japan.

[43] Sample questionnaires are available online at https://www.boj.or.jp/en/statistics/outline/exp/tk/extk01.htm.

and Industry, asking about quantitative information on ex ante production forecasts and ex post realized production at the firm-product-level; see Morikawa (2019); (iii) the Research Institute of Economy, Trade, and Industry conducts ad-hoc surveys on a somewhat regular basis: the Survey on the Outlook of the Japanese Economy and Economic Policy from February to March 2013, with a questionnaire sent to 2,309 listed manufacturing and nonmanufacturing firms in Japan with a response rate of 12.7% (see Morikawa, 2021); and the Survey of Corporate Management and Economic Policy from October to December 2015 with 15,000 firms being surveyed and a response rate of 22.9% (see Morikawa, 2016b).

2.7 International cooperation

Business tendency surveys expanded quickly after they proved to be useful for the construction of early cyclical indicators. Even before the fall of the iron curtain, Strigel and Ziegler (1988) list 160 surveys in 42 countries. To benchmark best practices but also to make results comparable across countries, there is ongoing international cooperation which we very briefly review in this section.

2.7.1 Centre for International Research on Economic Tendency Surveys

The Centre for International Research on Economic Tendency Surveys (CIRET), originally founded to foster cooperation between European survey institutes as described in Section 2.5.5, started to expand overseas in 1983 and to Eastern Europe in 1991. Currently, it has more than 150 members from 23 countries and international organizations covering Europe, Asia, Africa, North and South America.[44]

CIRET conferences were initially held in Europe but the perspective widened to other continents in the 1980s. The conference took place the first time in North America (Washington, USA) in 1983, in Asia (Osaka, Japan) in 1989, in Africa (Stellenbosch, South Africa) in 1993, in Oceania (Wellington, New Zealand) in 1999, and in South America (Santiago, Chile) in 2008. The most recent conference was held in Rio de Janeiro and discussed the special topic "The use of Big Data in Economic Cycle Statistics and Research."

2.7.2 OECD and UN

The OECD has long reported confidence indicators based on business tendency surveys as part of its Main Economic Indicators. To foster international comparison, the OECD also established a harmonized system of business tendency surveys that is recommended to non-OECD countries and published it in form of a Handbook (OECD, 2003). It largely reflects the EU survey program described in Section 2.5.5, perhaps unsurprisingly, as it is the product of a cooperation with the EU Commission. This cooperation is ongoing as a joint conference series shows.[45]

More recently, the UN published a Handbook on Economic Tendency Surveys (United Nations, 2015), which has a similar structure to the OECD Handbook but is more broadly targeted at all types of

---

[44] For more details, see https://www.ciret.org/.
[45] See https://www.oecd.org/sdd/leading-indicators/businesstendencyandconsumersurveysmeetingpapers.htm for a list of conferences and topics.

tendency surveys including those targeted at consumers. Interestingly, the UN Handbook was prepared, after extensive international consultations, by the United Nations Statistics Division as a reaction to the gaps in short-term economic statistics that became apparent during the Great Recession 2007–2009. This shows that business tendency surveys are widely appreciated as a useful tool to monitor the business cycle.

2.8 Conclusion

In many dimensions, for firms, both the available survey infrastructure as well as the expectational research conducted with its help are somewhat behind the state-of-the-art on the household survey side and the corresponding academic literature. This can be explained by firms having higher opportunity costs of filling out detailed surveys—especially if respondents need to be in the top management, which often will only trust larger institutions with an existing strong reputation—as well as by the interests of the institutions that conduct firm surveys, which often view their core mission as business cycle forecasting for which they only use aggregate survey results, rather than providing microdata for economic research. However, this appears to be changing: After a very promising start in the 1950s and 1960s, subsequent frustrations and neglect, having to do—from the academic side—with the rational expectations revolution, (expectational) firm surveys are back on stage with the promise of telling us in ever more detail how firms think, view their future, and act. To fulfill this promise, we need to press on, however, and continue to improve firm surveys. A few dimensions come to mind: (1) quantitative expectation and realization questions, in conjunction with the traditional tendency questions, need to become the norm; (2) access and the possibility of merging expectational firm surveys with other firm data sets need to become less onerous across the globe; (3) the feasibility of survey experiments needs to become standard rather than the exception (see Savignac et al., 2021; Kumar et al., 2022), as is the case now in the household expectation literature; (4) probabilistic and multidimensional distribution elicitation should be developed; (5) nonprobabilistic (scenario- and range-based) answer possibilities should be investigated further; (6) fast, monthly firm surveys with rotating panels and questions have been an innovation of late, we would like to see more, etc.

For those graduate students out there looking for a dissertation topic in the field, investigate, if you are historically interested, whether some of the historical expectational microdata we mentioned in this chapter still exist and can be used to study historical episodes, perhaps with the goal of achieving better identification; pick surveys that have just recently been fielded so that the research community on them is not yet so crowded (and there are many of such surveys); look to other countries: as we could only intimate in this chapter, Japan has a large and diverse firm survey infrastructure, which is likely to have been underused in academic research; maybe you are from a country with contacts into their official statistical or policy community and can set up your own firm survey; maybe you can add one our two questions to existing surveys by contacting institutes and researchers who run them and thus getting into this community: a few well-thought out questions on a new topic can sometimes go pretty far; in such projects, think about how the expectational data you want to collect also might help those institutions/other researchers with their own goals which may range from characterizing expectations data at the firm level to disciplining structural economic models to forecasting; finally, the household survey literature has seen increased use of self-designed online surveys at reasonable cost, perhaps this new technology can be adapted to small firms or business units in developing countries. The barriers to entry into research with firm surveys are still high, certainly higher than on the household side, but they have arguably never been lower.

References

Abberger, K., Sauer, S., Seiler, C., 2011. Der Test des Tests im ifo Konjunkturtest Handel. ifo Forschungs-berichte 52.

Altig, D., Baker, S., Barrero, J.M., Bloom, N., Bunn, P., Chen, S., Davis, S.J., Leather, J., Meyer, B., Mihaylov, E., Mizen, P., Parker, N., Renault, T., Smietanka, P., Thwaites, G., 2020a. Economic uncertainty before and during the COVID-19 pandemic. Journal of Public Economics 191, 104–274.

Altig, D., Barrero, J.M., Bloom, N., Davis, S., Meyer, B., Parker, N., 2020b. Surveying business uncertainty. Journal of Econometrics. Forthcoming.

Altig, D., Barrero, J.M., Bloom, N., Davis, S.J., Meyer, B.H., Mihaylov, E., Parker, N., 2020c. Survey of business uncertainty. https://www.atlantafed.org/-/media/documents/research/surveys/business-uncertainty/sbu-methodology.pdf.

Anderson, O., 1952. The business test of the ifo-Institute for economic research, Munich, and its theoretical model. Revue de l'Institut International de Statistique / Review of the International Statistical Institute 20, 1–17.

Anderson, O., Bauer, R.K., Fels, E., 1954. On the accuracy of short-term entrepreneurial expectations. In: Proceedings of the Business and Economic Statistics Section, pp. 124–147.

Anderson, O., Bauer, R.K., Führer, H., Petersen, J.P., 1958. On short-term entrepreneurial reaction patterns. Weltwirtschaftliches Archiv 81, 243–264.

Arnseth, L., 2015. 100 years of learning, 100 years of leading. Inside Supply Management Magazine 26, 18–27.

Bachmann, R., Born, B., Elstner, S., Grimme, C., 2019. Time-varying business volatility and the price setting of firms. Journal of Monetary Economics 101, 82–99.

Bachmann, R., Carstensen, K., Lautenbacher, S., Schneider, M., 2020a. Uncertainty and change: Survey evidence of firms' subjective beliefs. Mimeo. Stanford University.

Bachmann, R., Carstensen, K., Lautenbacher, S., Schneider, M., 2020b. Uncertainty is more than risk – survey evidence on Knightian and Bayesian firms. Mimeo. University of Notre Dame.

Bachmann, R., Carstensen, K., Lautenbacher, S., Schneider, M., 2020c. Unsicherheit und Beschäftigungsabbau in der Coronakrise. ifo Schnelldienst Digital 1.

Bachmann, R., Elstner, S., 2015. Firms' optimism and pessimism. European Economic Review 79, 297–325.

Bachmann, R., Elstner, S., Hristov, A., 2017. Surprise, surprise – measuring firm-level investment innovations. Journal of Economic Dynamics and Control 83, 107–148.

Bachmann, R., Elstner, S., Sims, E.R., 2013. Uncertainty and economic activity: evidence from business survey data. American Economic Journal: Macroeconomics 5, 217–249.

Bachmann, R., Zorn, P., 2020. What drives aggregate investment? Evidence from German survey data. Journal of Economic Dynamics and Control 115, 103–873.

Balleer, A., Link, S., Menkhoff, M., Zorn, P., 2020. Demand or supply? Price adjustment during the COVID-19 pandemic. CESifo Working Paper 8394.

Bartiloro, L., Bottone, M., Rosolia, A., 2019. The heterogeneity of the inflation expectations of Italian firms along the business cycle. International Journal of Central Banking 15, 175–205.

Bischoff, C.W., 1971. The outlook for investment in plant and equipment. Brookings Papers on Economic Activity 1971, 735–753.

Bloom, N., Bunn, P., Chen, S., Mizen, P., Smietanka, P., Thwaites, G., 2019. The impact of Brexit on UK firms. NBER Working Paper 26218. National Bureau of Economic Research.

Bloom, N., Davis, S.J., Foster, L., Lucking, B., Ohlmacher, S., Saporta-Eksten, I., 2020. Business-Level Expectations and Uncertainty. NBER Working Paper 28259. National Bureau of Economic Research.

Bloom, N., Kawakubo, T., Meng, C., Mizen, P., Riley, R., Senga, T., Van Reenen, J., 2021. Do Well Managed Firms Make Better Forecasts? NBER Working Paper 29591. National Bureau of Economic Research.

Board of Governors of the Federal Reserve System, 1975. Current economic and financial conditions – summary and outlook. https://www.federalreserve.gov/monetarypolicy/files/FOMC19751021gbpt119751015.pdf. Prepared for the Federal Open Market Committee by the staff of the Board of Governors of the Federal Reserve System, October 15, 1975.

Board of Trade, 1965. Some of the results of the industrial surveys of the Federation of British Industries compared with official statistics. Economic Trends 143, 68–84. https://escoe-website.s3.amazonaws.com/wp-content/uploads/2020/01/01235759/ET-143-Some-of-the-results-of-the-Industrial-Surveys-of-the-Federation-of-British-Industries-compared-with-official-statistics-Sep-1965.pdf.

Boneva, L., Cloyne, J., Weale, M., Wieladek, T., 2019. Firms' price, cost and activity expectations: evidence from micro data. The Economic Journal 130, 555–586.

Bonhoeffer, F.O., Strigel, W.H., 1966. Amerikanische Unternehmer- und Verbraucherbefragungen – Ergebnisse einer Studienreise. Duncker and Humblot.

Bontempi, M.E., Golinelli, R., Parigi, G., 2010. Why demand uncertainty curbs investment: evidence from a panel of Italian manufacturing firms. Journal of Macroeconomics 32, 218–238.

Bossons, J., Modigliani, F., 1960. The source of regressiveness in surveys of businessmen's short-run expectations. In: Universities-National Bureau (1960), pp. 239–262. http://www.nber.org/chapters/c6599.

Bossons, J., Modigliani, F., 1963. On the reasonableness of regressive expectations. Paper presented at the 2nd international meeting of CIRET in Vienna No. 10-63. https://dspace.mit.edu/bitstream/handle/1721.1/48690/onreasonableness00boss.pdf?sequence=1.

Bossons, J., Modigliani, F., 1966. Statistical vs. structural explanations of understatement and regressivity in "rational" expectations. Econometrica 34, 347–353.

Botsis, A., Görtz, C., Sakellaris, P., 2020. Quantifying Qualitative Survey Data: New Insights on the (Ir)Rationality of Firms' Forecasts. CESifo Working Paper 8148. CESifo, Munich.

Bowman, M.J. (Ed.), 1958. Expectations, Uncertainty, and Business Behavior. Social Science Research Council, New York.

Breitung, J., Schmeling, M., 2013. Quantifying survey expectations: what's wrong with the probability approach? International Journal of Forecasting 29, 142–154.

Bridge, L., 1951. Capital expenditures by manufacturing industries in the postwar period. Survey of Current Business 31, 15–22.

Brown, M., 1961. Ex ante and ex post data in inventory investment. Journal of the American Statistical Association 56, 518–534.

Bryan, M.F., Meyer, B.H., Parker, N.B., 2015. The inflation expectations of firms: What do they look like, are they accurate, and do they matter? Federal Reserve Bank of Atlanta Working paper 2014-27a, revised January 2015.

Buchheim, L., Dovern, J., Krolage, C., Link, S., 2022a. Sentiment and firm behavior during the Covid-19 pandemic. Journal of Economic Behavior & Organization 195, 186–198.

Buchheim, L., Krolage, C., Link, S., 2022b. Sudden stop: when did firms anticipate the potential consequences of COVID-19? German Economic Review 23, 79–119.

Buchheim, L., Link, S., 2017. The Effect of Disaggregate Information on the Expectation Formation of Firms. CESifo Working Paper 6768. CESifo.

Buffington, C., Foster, L., Jarmin, R., Ohlmacher, S., 2017. The management and organizational practices survey (MOPS): an overview. Journal of Economic and Social Measurement 42, 1–26.

Buffington, C., Hennessy, A., Ohlmacher, S., 2018. The Management and Organizational Practices Survey (MOPS): Collection and Processing. CES Working Paper 18-51. U.S. Census Bureau, Center for Economic Studies.

Buffington, C., Herrell, K., Ohlmacher, S., 2016. The Management and Organizational Practices Survey (MOPS): Cognitive Testing. CES Working Paper 16-53. U.S. Census Bureau, Center for Economic Studies.

Carlson, J.A., 1967. Forecasting errors and business cycles. The American Economic Review 57, 462–481.

Carlson, J.A., Parkin, M., 1975. Inflation expectations. Economica 42, 123–138.

Carstensen, K., Elstner, S., Paula, G., 2013. How much did oil market developments contribute to the 2009 recession in Germany? Scandinavian Journal of Economics 115, 695–721.

Carstensen, K., Heinrich, M., Reif, M., Wolters, M.H., 2020. Predicting ordinary and severe recessions with a three-state Markov-switching dynamic factor model: an application to the German business cycle. International Journal of Forecasting 36, 829–850.

Coibion, O., Gorodnichenko, Y., Kumar, S., 2018. How do firms form their expectations? New survey evidence. The American Economic Review 108, 2671–2713.

Coibion, O., Gorodnichenko, Y., Ropele, T., 2019. Inflation expectations and firm decisions: new causal evidence. The Quarterly Journal of Economics 135, 165–219.

Commission of the European Communities, 2006. Joint harmonized EU programme of business and consumer surveys. https://eur-lex.europa.eu/legal-content/EN/TXT/PDF/?uri=CELEX:52006DC0379&from=EL. Communication from the Commission, COM(2006) 379 final.

Conference on Research in Income and Wealth, 1955. Short-Term Economic Forecasting. Studies in Income and Wealth. Princeton University Press. http://www.nber.org/books/unkn55-1.

Conflitti, C., Zizza, R., 2021. What's behind firms' inflation forecasts? Empirical Economics 61, 2449–2475.

Consultant Committee on General Business Expectations, 1955a. An appraisal of data and research on businessmen's expectations about outlook and operating variables. In: Federal Reserve Consultant Committees on Economic Statistics (1955), pp. 493–722. https://www.jec.senate.gov/public/index.cfm/1956/12/report-8438cbd4-c85f-4568-9bdd-e832fe5e5aa4.

Consultant Committee on Plant and Equipment Expenditure Expectations, 1955b. Statistics on business plant and equipment expenditure expectations. In: Federal Reserve Consultant Committees on Economic Statistics (1955), pp. 3–42. https://www.jec.senate.gov/public/index.cfm/1956/12/report-8438cbd4-c85f-4568-9bdd-e832fe5e5aa4.

Dave, C., 2011. Are investment expectations rational, adaptive or regressive? Economic Inquiry 49, 212–225.

de Bruin, W.B., Fischhoff, B., Millstein, S.G., Halpern-Felsher, B.L., 2000. Verbal and numerical expressions of probability: "It's a fifty–fifty chance". Organizational Behavior and Human Decision Processes 81, 115–131.

Deitz, R., Steindel, C., 2005. The predictive abilities of the New York Fed's Empire State manufacturing survey. Federal Reserve Bank of New York, Current Issues in Economics and Finance 11, 1–7.

Dennis Jr., W.J., Dunkelberg, W.C., 2001. Small business economic trends: a quarter century longitudinal data base of small business economic activity. In: Databases for the Study of Entrepreneurship. In: Advances in Entrepreneurship, Firm Emergence and Growth, vol. 4. Emerald Group Publishing Limited, Bingley, pp. 31–50.

Dunkelberg, W.C., Wade, H., 2021. Small business economic trends. September 2021, National Federation of Independent Businesses.

EBDC-BEP, 2020. Business Expectations Panel 01/1980–06/2020. LMU-ifo Economics & Business Data Center, Munich. https://www.ifo.de/node/61412.

Eisner, R., 1958. Expectations, plans, and capital expenditures: a synthesis of ex post and ex ante data. In: Bowman (1958), pp. 165–188.

Enders, Z., Hünnekes, F., Müller, G.J., 2019a. Firm expectations and economic activity. CESifo Working Paper 7623.

Enders, Z., Hünnekes, F., Müller, G.J., 2019b. Monetary policy announcements and expectations: evidence from German firms. Journal of Monetary Economics 108, 45–63.

Ernst, E., Viegelahn, C., 2014. Hiring uncertainty: a new labour market indicator. SSRN Working Paper 2411299.

European Commission, 2014. The Joint Harmonised EU Programme of Business and Consumer Surveys – List of 'best practice' for the conduct of business and consumer surveys. https://ec.europa.eu/info/sites/default/files/file_import/bcs_best_practice_en_0.pdf. Directorate-General for Economic and Financial Affairs, 21 March 2014.

European Commission, 2021. The Joint Harmonised EU Programme of Business and Consumer Surveys – User guide (updated July 2021). https://ec.europa.eu/info/sites/default/files/bcs_user_guide.pdf. Directorate-General for Economic and Financial Affairs.

Federal Reserve Consultant Committees on Economic Statistics, 1955. Reports of the Federal Reserve Consultant Committees on Economic Statistics. Government Printing Office, Washington. https://www.jec.senate.gov/public/index.cfm/1956/12/report-8438cbd4-c85f-4568-9bdd-e832fe5e5aa4.

Ferber, R., 1953. Measuring the accuracy and structure of businessmen's expectations. Journal of the American Statistical Association 48, 385–413.

Firestone, O.J., 1955. Investment forecasting in Canada. In: Conference on Research in Income and Wealth (1955), pp. 113–260. http://www.nber.org/chapters/c2902.

Foss, M.F., Natrella, V., 1957a. Investment plans and realization. Survey of Current Business 37, 12–18.

Foss, M.F., Natrella, V., 1957b. Ten years' experience with business investment anticipations. Survey of Current Business 37, 16–24.

Foss, M.F., Natrella, V., 1960. The structure and realization of business investment anticipations. In: Universities-National Bureau (1960), pp. 387–406. http://www.nber.org/chapters/c6605.

Friend, I., 1958. Critical evaluation of surveys of expectations, plans, and investment behavior. In: Bowman (1958), pp. 189–198.

Friend, I., Bronfenbrenner, J., 1950. Business investment programs and their realization. Survey of Current Business 30, 11–22.

Friend, I., Bronfenbrenner, J., 1955. Plant and equipment programs and their realization. In: Conference on Research in Income and Wealth (1955), pp. 53–112. http://www.nber.org/chapters/c2901.

Gerstenberger, W., Nerb, G., Schittenhelm, S., 1969. Unternehmerische Urteile und Antizipationen über den Bedarf an Arbeitskräften. Mitteilungen aus der Arbeitsmarkt- und Berufsforschung 9, 671–697.

Giannone, D., Reichlin, L., Small, D., 2008. Nowcasting: the real-time informational content of macroeconomic data. Journal of Monetary Economics 55, 665–676.

Glynn, D.R., 1969. The CBI industrial trends survey. Applied Economics 1, 183–196.

Graham, J.R., Harvey, C.R., 2001. Expectations of equity risk premia, volatility and asymmetry from a corporate finance perspective. NBER Working Paper 8678.

Graham, J.R., Harvey, C.R., 2015. The equity risk premium in 2015. SSRN Working Paper 2611793.

Graham, J.R., Meyer, B., Parker, N., Waddell, S.R., 2020. The CFO survey. https://www.richmondfed.org/-/media/RichmondFedOrg/research/national_economy/cfo_survey/the_cfo_survey_methods.pdf. Methodology paper.

Grasso, A., Ropele, T., 2018. Firms' inflation expectations and investment plans. Bank of Italy Temi di Discussione (Working Paper) No 1203.

Greenberg, E., 1964. A stock-adjustment investment model. Econometrica 32, 339–357.

Guiso, L., Parigi, G., 1999. Investment and demand uncertainty. The Quarterly Journal of Economics 114, 185–227.

Hart, A.G., 1960. Quantitative evidence for the interwar period on the course of business expectations: a revaluation of the railroad shippers' forecast. In: Universities-National Bureau (1960), pp. 205–238. http://www.nber.org/chapters/c6598.

Hart, A.G., Modigliani, F., Orcutt, G., 1960. Introduction to the quality and economic significance of anticipations data. In: Universities-National Bureau (1960), pp. 3–8. http://www.nber.org/chapters/c6591.

Hastay, M., 1954. The Dun and Bradstreet survey of businessmen's expectations. In: Proceedings of the Business and Economic Statistics Section, 114th Annual Meeting of the American Statistical Association. Montreal, pp. 93–123.

Hastay, M., 1960. The formation of business expectations about operating variables. In: Universities-National Bureau (1960), pp. 91–148. http://www.nber.org/chapters/c6595.

Henzel, S., Wollmershäuser, T., 2005. Quantifying inflation expectations with the Carlson–Parkin method. Journal of Business Cycle Measurement and Analysis 2, 321–352.

Huber, K., 2018. Disentangling the effects of a banking crisis: evidence from German firms and counties. The American Economic Review 108, 868–898.

Hultgren, T., 1942. Railway Freight Traffic in Prosperity and Depression. Occasional Paper 5. National Bureau of Economic Research. http://www.nber.org/chapters/c9309.

Hultgren, T., 1955. Forecasts of railway traffic. In: Conference on Research in Income and Wealth (1955), pp. 363–380. http://www.nber.org/chapters/c2904.

Hunziker, H.U., Raggi, C., Rosenblatt-Wisch, R., Zanetti, A., 2022. The impact of guidance, short-term dynamics and individual characteristics on firms' long-term inflation expectations. Journal of Macroeconomics 71, 103–380.

INSEE, 1951. Les perspectives économiques en France à la fin de 1951, d'après les chefs d'entreprises. Etudes et Conjoncture – Union Française 6, 8–37. https://doi.org/10.3406/estat.1951.8551.

INSEE, 1957. La situation économique au printemps 1957. Etudes et Conjoncture – Union Française 12, 575–700. https://doi.org/10.3406/estat.1957.8450.

Jankeliowitch, R., 1957. Les perspectives économiques en France pour le deuxième semestre 1957 d'après les chefs d'entreprises. Etudes et Conjoncture – INSEE 12, 809–835. https://doi.org/10.3406/estat.1957.8455.

Jankeliowitch, R., 1958a. Les perspectives économiques en France pour le premier semestre 1958 d'après les chefs d'entreprises. Etudes et Conjoncture – INSEE 13, 103–135. https://doi.org/10.3406/estat.1958.9041.

Jankeliowitch, R., 1958b. Situation et perspectives dans l'industrie et le commerce en juin 1958 d'après les chefs d'entreprises. Etudes et Conjoncture – INSEE 13, 846–869. https://doi.org/10.3406/estat.1958.9102.

Jankeliowitch, R., 1958c. Situation et perspectives dans l'industrie et le commerce en mars 1958 d'après les chefs d'entreprises. Etudes et Conjoncture – INSEE 13, 575–596. https://doi.org/10.3406/estat.1958.9080.

Johnson, L.B., 1966. Letter to the Chairman, House Committee on Banking and Currency, on receiving a forecast of business investment plans, March 07, 1966. Online by Gerhard Peters and John T. Woolley, The American Presidency Project. https://www.presidency.ucsb.edu/node/238455.

Kaihatsu, S., Shiraki, N., 2016. Firms' inflation expectations and wage-setting behaviors. Bank of Japan Working Paper 16-E-10. Bank of Japan.

Kawasaki, S., Zimmermann, K.F., 1986. Testing the rationality of price expectations for manufacturing firms. Applied Economics 18, 1335–1347.

Keezer, D., Ulin, R., Greenwald, D., Matulis, M., 1960. Observations on the predictive quality of McGraw-Hill surveys of business' plans for new plants and equipment. In: Universities-National Bureau (1960), pp. 369–386. http://www.nber.org/chapters/c6604.

Kerr, E., Orrenius, P., Wang, J., Cañas, J., 2014. Fed manufacturing surveys provide insight into national economy. Federal Reserve Bank of Dallas Economic Letter 9, 1–4.

Klein, L.R., 1955. Introduction to short-term economic forecasting. In: Conference on Research in Income and Wealth (1955), pp. 1–6. http://www.nber.org/chapters/c2899.

Klein, P.A., Moore, G.H., 1981. Industrial surveys in the UK: Part I New orders. Applied Economics 13, 167–179.

Knoche, M., 2018. Ludwig Erhard, Adolf Weber und die schwierige Geburt des ifo Instituts. ifo Schnelldienst 71, 14–60.

Koga, M., Kato, H., 2017. Behavioral biases in firms' growth expectations. Bank of Japan Working Paper 17-E-9. Bank of Japan.

Kommission der EWG, 1966. Konjunkturerhebung in der Wirtschaft – Antwort auf die schriftliche Anfrage Nr. 110 von Herrn Vredeling an die Kommission der EWG. Amtsblatt der Europäischen Gemeinschaften 9, 612–613. https://eur-lex.europa.eu/legal-content/DE/TXT/PDF/?uri=OJ:P:1966:045:FULL&from=PL.

Kumar, S., Afrouzi, H., Coibion, O., Gorodnichenko, Y., 2015. Inflation targeting does not anchor inflation expectations: evidence from firms in New Zealand. Brookings Papers on Economic Activity 2015, 151–225.

Kumar, S., Gorodnichenko, Y., Coibion, O., 2022. The Effect of Macroeconomic Uncertainty on Firm Decisions. NBER Working Paper 30288. National Bureau of Economic Research.

Lamont, O.A., 2000. Investment plans and stock returns. The Journal of Finance 55, 2719–2745.

Landefeld, J.S., Seskin, E.P., 1984. Plant and equipment expenditures, first and second quarters and second half of 1984. Survey of Current Business 64, 26–31.

Langelütke, H., Marquardt, W., 1951. Das Konjunkturtest-Verfahren. Schriftenreihe des ifo Instituts für Wirtschaftsforschung, vol. 13. ifo Institut, pp. 2–24.

Laumer, H., 1989. Zielsetzung der ifo-Umfragen. In: Oppenländer and Poser (1989), pp. 3–6.

Lehman, J.W., Knowles, J.W., 1960. Comment on forecasting in its relation to government policy-making. In: Universities-National Bureau (1960), pp. 44–50. http://www.nber.org/chapters/c6593.

Lehmann, R., 2020. The Forecasting Power of the ifo Business Survey. CESifo Working Paper 8291. CESifo, Munich.

Link, S., 2019. The Price and Employment Response of Firms to the Introduction of Minimum Wages. CESifo Working Paper 7575. CESifo, Munich.

Link, S., 2020. Harmonization of the ifo business survey's micro data. Journal of Economics and Statistics 240, 543–555.

Link, S., Menkhoff, M., Peichl, A., Schüle, P., 2022. Downward Revision of Investment Decisions after Corporate Tax Hikes. CESifo Working Paper 9786. CESifo, Munich.

Link, S., Peichl, A., Roth, C., Wohlfart, J., 2021. Information Frictions among Firms and Households. CESifo Working Paper 8969. CESifo, Munich.

Low, W., 1997. Expectations and U.K. firms' employment and production plans: Microeconometric analysis of the CBI's Business Survey. London School of Economics and Political Science, Department of Economics. PhD (London) thesis. http://etheses.lse.ac.uk/2232/1/U615179.pdf.

Lui, S., Mitchell, J., Weale, M., 2010. Qualitative business surveys: signal or noise? Journal of the Royal Statistical Society. Series A. Statistics in Society 174, 327–348.

Lui, S., Mitchell, J., Weale, M., 2011. The utility of expectational data: firm-level evidence using matched qualitative-quantitative UK surveys. International Journal of Forecasting 27, 1128–1146.

Malgarini, M., Margani, P., Martelli, B.M., 2005. Re-engineering the ISAE manufacturing survey. ISAE Working Paper 47. Istituto di Studi e Analisi Economica.

Malhomme, C., 1969. L'enquête mensuelle de conjoncture auprès des industriels. Economie et Statistique, 37–52.

Mankiw, N.G., Reis, R., Wolfers, J., 2003. Disagreement about inflation expectations. NBER Macroeconomics Annual 18, 209–248.

ManpowerGroup, 2021. Strongest global hiring outlooks reported since beginning of the pandemic – talent shortages remain at 15-year high. https://go.manpowergroup.com/hubfs/MPG_MEOS_Q4_2021_Global_Report.pdf. ManpowerGroup Employment Outlook Survey. Q4, 2021.

Marquardt, W., Strigel, W., 1959. Der Konjunkturtest – Eine neue Methode der Wirtschaftsbeobachtung. Schriftenreihe des ifo Instituts für Wirtschaftsforschung, vol. 38. Duncker and Humblot.

Martelli, B.M., 1998. The ISCO short term surveys: methodological aspects. ISCO (Institute of short term analysis), MPRA Paper No. 16331.

Martelli, B.M., Bruno, G., Chiodini, P.M., Manzi, G., Verrecchia, F., 2014. Fifty years of business confidence surveys on manufacturing sector. In: Crescenzi, F., Mignani, S. (Eds.), Statistical Methods and Applications from a Historical Perspective. In: Studies in Theoretical and Applied Statistics. Springer, pp. 1–11.

Massenot, B., Pettinicchi, Y., 2018. Can firms see into the future? Survey evidence from Germany. Journal of Economic Behavior & Organization 145, 66–79.

MetLife, U.S. Chamber of Commerce, 2017. Small business index – the voices of small business owners. https://www.uschamber.com/sbindex/uploads/SBI_2017_Q2.pdf. Q2 2017.

Meyer, B.H., Parker, N.B., Sheng, X.S., 2021. Unit cost expectations and uncertainty: Firms' perspectives on inflation. Federal Reserve Bank of Atlanta Working Paper No. 2021.

Mitchell, J., Mouratidis, K., Weale, M., 2004. The impact of survey aggregation methods on the quality of business survey indicators. ECFIN/2003/A3-04 Final Report. National Institute of Economic and Social Research.

Modigliani, F., Cohen, K.J., 1958. The significance and uses of ex ante data. In: Bowman (1958), pp. 151–164.

Modigliani, F., Sauerlender, O.H., 1955. Economic expectations and plans of firms in relation to short-term forecasting. In: Conference on Research in Income and Wealth (1955), pp. 261–362. http://www.nber.org/chapters/c2903.

Modigliani, F., Weingartner, H.M., 1958. Forecasting uses of anticipatory data on investment and sales. The Quarterly Journal of Economics 72, 23–54.

Moore, G.H., 1955. Diffusion indexes: a comment. American Statistician 9, 13–30.

Moore, G.H., 1961. Leading and confirming indicators of general business changes. In: Business Cycle Indicators, vol. 1. Princeton University Press, pp. 45–109. Chapter 3. http://www.nber.org/chapters/c0723.

Morikawa, M., 2016a. Business uncertainty and investment: evidence from Japanese companies. Journal of Macroeconomics 49, 224–236.

Morikawa, M., 2016b. How uncertain are economic policies? New evidence from a firm survey. Economic Analysis and Policy 52, 114–122.

Morikawa, M., 2019. Uncertainty over production forecasts: an empirical analysis using monthly quantitative survey data. Journal of Macroeconomics 60, 163–179.

Morikawa, M., 2021. Firms' subjective uncertainty and forecast errors: survey evidence from Japan. Applied Economics Letters, 1–4.

Morin, N., Stevens, J., 2004. Estimating Capacity Utilization from Survey Data. Finance and Economics Discussion Series 2004-49. Federal Reserve Board.

Muth, J.F., 1961. Rational expectations and the theory of price movements. Econometrica 29, 315–335.

Nerlove, M., 1983. Expectations, plans, and realizations in theory and practice. Econometrica 51, 1251–1279.

NIESR, 1961. The economic situation. National Institute Economic Review, 4–17.

OECD, 2003. Business Tendency Surveys – A Handbook. OECD. https://www.oecd.org/sdd/leading-indicators/31837055.pdf.

Okun, A.M., 1962. The predictive value of surveys of business intentions. The American Economic Review 52, 218–225.

Oppenländer, K.H., Poser, G. (Eds.), 1989. Handbuch der Ifo-Umfragen: Vierzig Jahre Unternehmensbefragungen des Ifo-Instituts für Wirtschaftsforschung. Duncker and Humblot, München.

Orr, L.D., 1966. Expected sales, actual sales, and inventory-investment realization. Journal of Political Economy 74, 46–54.

Pagani, B., 1959. Les enquêtes de conjoncture en Italie. Manuscript. In: 4th International Conference on Problems of Business Tendency Surveys. Munich, 17–19 September 1959.

Pashigian, B.P., 1964. The accuracy of the Commerce-S.E.C. sales anticipations. Review of Economics and Statistics 46, 398–405.

Pashigian, B.P., 1965. The relevance of sales anticipatory data in explaining inventory investment. International Economic Review 6, 65–91.

Pesaran, M.H., 1984. Expectations formation and macroeconomic modelling. In: Malgrange, P., Muet, P. (Eds.), Contemporary Macroeconomic Modelling. Blackwell, pp. 27–53.

Pesaran, M.H., Weale, M., 2006. Survey expectations. Handbook of Economic Forecasting 1, 715–776.

Piatier, A., 1953. Nouvelles méthodes pour l'étude de la conjoncture. Kyklos 6, 35–51.

Ripert, J., 1969. La réforme des publications de l'Insee. Economie et Statistique, 3–5.

Sauer, S., Wohlrabe, K., 2019. Chef oder Praktikant — wer beantwortet eigentlich die Fragebögen in den ifo Konjunkturumfragen? ifo Schnelldienst 72.

Sauer, S., Wohlrabe, K., 2020. Ifo Handbuch der Konjunkturumfragen. ifo Beiträge zur Wirtschaftsforschung, vol. 88. Ifo Institut, Munich. https://www.ifo.de/node/52384.

Savignac, F., Gautier, E., Gorodnichenko, Y., Coibion, O., 2021. Firms' Inflation Expectations: New Evidence from France. Working Paper 29376. National Bureau of Economic Research.

Schiller, T., Trebing, M., 2003. Taking the measure of manufacturing. Federal Reserve Bank of Philadelphia Business Review Q4/2003, 24–37.

Seiler, C., 2010. Dynamic Modelling of Nonresponse in Business Surveys. ifo Working Paper 93. ifo Institute – Leibniz Institute for Economic Research at the University of Munich.

Seiler, C., 2012. The Data Sets of the LMU-ifo Economics & Business Data Center – A Guide for Researchers. Working Paper 138. Ifo Institute.

Seitz, H., 1988. The estimation of inflation forecasts from business survey data. Applied Economics 20, 427–438.

Sen, E., 2014. Introducing the Philadelphia Fed nonmanufacturing survey. Federal Reserve Bank of Philadelphia Business Review 97, 15–22.

Shepherd, J.R., 1963. The FBI industrial trends enquiry. National Institute Economic Review 26, 63–74.

Smith, J., McAleer, M., 1995. Alternative procedures for converting qualitative response data to quantitative expectations: an application to Australian manufacturing. Journal of Applied Econometrics 10, 165–185.

Stangl, A., 2008. Essays on the Measurement of Economic Expectations. PhD Thesis. Ludwig-Maximilians-Universität, München. https://edoc.ub.uni-muenchen.de/9823/1/Stangl_Anna.pdf.

Stock, J.H., Watson, M.W., 2002. Macroeconomic forecasting using diffusion indexes. Journal of Business & Economic Statistics 20, 147–162.

Strasser, G., 2013. Exchange rate pass-through and credit constraints. Journal of Monetary Economics 60, 25–38.

Strigel, W.H., 1989. Die Entwicklung der Ifo-Umfragen seit 1949. In: Oppenländer and Poser (1989), pp. 6–13.

Strigel, W.H., Ziegler, M., 1988. Cyclical business and consumer surveys—the current state of the art. In: Fildes, R., Crissanthaki, T. (Eds.), World Index of Economic Forecasts, third edition. Gower Publishing Company, pp. 18–52.

Tanaka, M., Bloom, N., David, J.M., Koga, M., 2020. Firm performance and macro forecast accuracy. Journal of Monetary Economics 114, 26–41.

Theil, H., 1952. On the time shape of economic microvariables and the Munich Business Test. Revue de l'Institut International de Statistique / Review of the International Statistical Institute 20, 105–120.

Theil, H., 1955. Recent experiences with the Munich Business Test: an expository article. Econometrica 23, 184–192.

Trebing, M.E., 1998. What's happening in manufacturing: "Survey says...". Federal Reserve Bank of Philadelphia Business Review September/October 1998, 15–29.

Trebing, M.E., Fenske, C.B., 2018. The "Philly Fed Index" turns 50 with steadfast success. Economic Insights 3, 8–21.

United Nations, 2015. Handbook on Economic Tendency Surveys. Statistical Papers, Series M, vol. 96. UN. https://www.un-ilibrary.org/content/books/9789210577199#.Yd2Kfisbeok.mailto.

Universities-National Bureau, 1960. The Quality and Economic Significance of Anticipations Data. Princeton University Press. http://www.nber.org/books/univ60-1.

Yoshino, T., 1995. Die Entwicklung von "Tankan" durch die japanische Nationalbank. In: Oppenländer, K.H. (Ed.), Konjunkturindikatoren. R. Oldenbourg Verlag, pp. 45–61.

Ziegler, M., 1989. CIRET – Ein internationaler Erfahrungsaustausch. In: Oppenländer and Poser (1989), pp. 21–26.

Surveys of professionals[☆],[☆☆]

3

Michael P. Clements[a], Robert W. Rich[b], and Joseph S. Tracy[c]

[a] University of Reading, Reading, United Kingdom
[b] Federal Reserve Bank of Cleveland, Cleveland, OH, United States
[c] Federal Reserve Bank of Dallas, Dallas, TX, United States

3.1 Surveys of professional forecasters

3.1.1 Interest and attractiveness of eliciting professional forecasters' expectations

Expectations play a critical role in agents' decision-making processes and are a key determinant of many economic and financial variables. This chapter considers professional forecasters, who are typically assumed to possess extensive and largely homogeneous information sets, as well as sophisticated and comparable processing capabilities. Surveys of households and firms are covered in Chapters 1 and 2 in this Handbook respectively. Chapter 15 in this Handbook focuses on conducting inference and complements this chapter.

Professional forecasters are an attractive source of expectations data for researchers and policymakers. For example, Keane and Runkle (1990) argue that testing for rationality might be more appropriately applied to professional forecasters rather than to other respondents. Professional forecasters should be better informed and better able to respond to technical questions, such as the formulation and reporting of "probabilistic beliefs" using histograms. In addition, professional forecasters mitigate the need to control for demographics and other individual-specific characteristics. Consequently, surveys of professional forecasters provide data that are useful in monitoring movements in expectations and evaluating their influence. Surveys of professionals can also be used to monitor central bank credibility (see, e.g., Beechey et al., 2011, and Dovern and Kenny, 2020), evaluate their influence on private-sector expectations (e.g., Carroll, 2003), and incorporate direct measures of expectations into economic models (see, e.g., Smets et al., 2014).

This chapter examines surveys of professional forecasters, with a focus on the U.S. Survey of Professional Forecasters and the European Central Bank Survey of Professional Forecasters. A distinguishing feature of these surveys is that they collect point and density forecasts and make the data publicly available. We discuss the history and design of the surveys, issues involved in using the data,

[☆] The views expressed in the paper are those of the authors and do not necessarily reflect those of the Federal Reserve Bank of Cleveland, the Federal Reserve Bank of Dallas, or the Federal Reserve System.

[☆☆] We are grateful to the Handbook editors, as well as Dean Croushore and Geoff Kenny for helpful comments. We would also like to thank Amber Sherman for her assistance with the Appendix table that accompanies this chapter.

and the construction of measures such as disagreement and uncertainty. An Appendix table is available that provides background information on a large set of primary surveys of professional forecasters. The chapter also summarizes the findings of studies that have used surveys of professional forecasters to explore a wide range of issues. These include heterogeneity and persistence in individual forecast behavior, comparisons of the properties of point and density forecasts, and the reliability of using disagreement as a proxy for uncertainty.

3.1.2 Surveys of professional forecasters

U.S. survey of professional forecasters

The U.S. Survey of Professional Forecasters (US-SPF) is a survey of U.S. macrovariables. The survey began in the fourth quarter of 1968 and was initially conducted by the American Statistical Association and the National Bureau of Economic Research, but from 1990 to the present day, it has been run by the Federal Reserve Bank of Philadelphia. See Zarnowitz (1969) on the original objectives of the survey, and Croushore (1993) and Croushore and Stark (2019) on the revival of the survey by the Federal Reserve Bank of Philadelphia. The survey is conducted each quarter after the release of the advance report of the national income and product accounts (NIPA) from the Bureau of Economic Analysis (BEA). Since 1990:Q2, the deadlines for responses have been around the middle of each quarter, before the BEA's second report. The average number of panelists has been around 40 since the Philadelphia Fed has overseen the survey. The respondents are anonymous but have identifiers allowing the forecasts of a given individual to be identified across surveys. There is a quarterly report summarizing the results of the survey and the data are available on the Federal Reserve Bank of Philadelphia's website.

European Central Bank survey of professional forecasters

The European Central Bank Survey of Professional Forecasters (ECB-SPF) provides a survey of forecasts for the euro area. The survey began in January 1999 and draws respondents from both financial and nonfinancial institutions, with most, but not all, located in the euro area. The principal aim of the survey is to elicit expectations about inflation, real GDP growth, and unemployment, although the questionnaire also contains a noncompulsory section asking participants for their expectations of additional variables and to provide qualitative comments that inform their quantitative forecasts.[1] The survey is typically fielded in February, May, August, and November, with a little under 60 respondents on average per survey.[2] While there is a listing of the respondents' names and institutions, individual responses are anonymous and tracked across surveys by an assigned identification number. Similar to the US-SPF, there is a quarterly report summarizing the results of the survey and the data are available on the ECB's website. For additional details about the ECB-SPF, see Garcia (2003) and Bowles et al. (2007).

Generally, we do not know how the respondents make their forecasts in any specific instance. An ad hoc US-SPF survey by Stark (2013) found the majority "use a mathematical/computer model plus subjective adjustments to that model in reporting their projections." No information is available in the US-SPF on forecaster characteristics, except whether the company is in the financial or non-financial

---

[1] The additional expectations pertain to variables such as wage growth, the price of oil, and the exchange rate. See Meyler (2020).

[2] The actual average of 58 panelists per survey is based on the history of the ECB-SPF, although there has been some decline in participation over time.

services sector (if known). Special surveys conducted by the ECB in 2008, 2013, and 2018 indicate that most participants report judgment-based forecasts, although the number of model-based forecasts appears to be increasing over time. The ECB-SPF does not provide any information on forecaster characteristics. The respondent anonymity of each survey may discourage respondents from strategic reporting of forecasts.

3.1.3 Nature of survey expectations and concepts

The US-SPF and ECB-SPF elicit point forecasts for specified variables and horizons. Point forecasts provide direct measures of expectations and avoid the challenges of model-based measures (for example, the specification of regression equations and information sets). In addition, even among professional forecasters there is disagreement as evidenced by the dispersion in predictions.

There are, however, limitations to point forecast data. One is their interpretation: a point forecast may represent a mean, median, or mode, or some other construct from the respondent's subjective probability distribution. Because surveys do not provide any guidance on loss functions, it is unclear for any given respondent what the point forecast represents and the degree to which the possible representations may vary across respondents.[3] We return to this issue in Section 3.4.

The US-SPF and ECB-SPF also ask forecasters to report density forecasts using histograms with a set of intervals provided in the survey instrument. Density forecasts provide a basis for constructing measures of uncertainty, and the shape of a density forecast can be informative about the respondent's balance of risks. The extent of skewness displayed by a density forecast reflects the respondent's assessment of upside or downside risks. Through the ability to convey uncertainty and balance of risks, density forecasts provide survey participants with a medium in which to describe their outlook in more detail and allow for a more thorough analysis of forecast properties than can be carried out using point forecasts alone. Nevertheless, it is worth noting that histogram-based density forecasts also present respondents and researchers with several challenges, which we discuss below.

3.2 Point and density forecasts: data features, measures, and properties
3.2.1 Background
Respondent participation patterns/survey design

The US-SPF and ECB-SPF involve panels of forecasters whose composition changes as some respondents leave and new respondents are added. The panels are unbalanced due both to entry and exit and to the fact that there are occasions when respondents do not provide responses to all or part of the survey questionnaire. Respondents' numerical identifiers allow their forecasts to be tracked over time.[4] This supports individual-level analyses of forecast behavior and allows comparisons between forecasters,

---

[3] If the respondent chooses to minimize a squared-error loss function, then the conditional mean will be reported as the forecast. The three special ECB surveys in 2008, 2013, and 2018 also asked participants if their reported point forecasts refer to the mean, median, or mode of their subjective probability distributions. While most participants initially indicated that the point forecasts refer to the mean, the median and the mode are now being reported more often. Comparable information for the US-SPF is not available.

[4] It is not always clear whether the identifiers are associated with the individuals or the companies that employ them, and what happens to the identifier when an employee changes firms. In its documentation, the US-SPF states that the identifier either moves

such as whether some respondents are relatively more accurate or tend to be more contrarian or more uncertain compared to others.

The coverage of many surveys has expanded over time, with questions added to elicit expectations about new variables, concepts (such as the natural rate of unemployment), as well as density forecasts of some variables and longer-horizon forecasts.[5] Nevertheless, forecasts may not be available at the specific times and horizons required by the survey user. An example is when the analyst requires a series of fixed-horizon forecasts, but the forecast data are instead fixed-event, such as with year-on-year calendar growth rates. As discussed below, various techniques have been suggested to deal with these limitations.

The vague phrasing of survey questionnaires may complicate the task of the survey respondents and users in various ways. First, respondents forecasting target variables subject to revision are not provided guidance about the specific vintage to consider. In the case of GDP, for example, it is not clear whether an individual should provide his or her "best" estimate of the first release (i.e., advance estimate), the first quarterly revised estimate, or the final estimate for the target variable. Only a few variables are not subject to revision, while many are heavily revised.[6] Second, as already noted, it is unclear how the respondents' point forecasts relate to their (assumed) subjective distributions of the target variables. We discuss this in Section 3.4.

Less obviously, the question of what the forecasts represent also applies to the density forecasts. For example, an analyst might evaluate a respondent's density forecasts using a popular scoring rule, such as the quadratic probability score (QPS: Brier (1950)) or the ranked probability score (RPS: Epstein (1969)), and find in favor of an alternative set of forecasts, such as benchmark forecasts. But the respondent might be driven by motives other than maximizing QPS or RPS, such as ensuring that the realized outcomes fall well within the likely range of outcomes implied by their probability assessments.

Target variables and forecast horizons

The surveys typically include a mixture of fixed- and rolling-event (or fixed-horizon) forecasts. For example, the US-SPF asks for density forecasts of the annual rate of GDP deflator inflation in the year of the survey relative to the previous year and of the next year relative to the current year, that is, of the percentage rate of change in the annual GDP deflator between years. This means that there are eight "fixed-event" histogram forecasts of annual inflation in 2016, compared to 2015. The first was made in response to the 2015:Q1 survey, with a horizon of nearly two years. The second was made in 2015:Q2, and so on, down to the last one made in 2016:Q4 (with a horizon of just under a quarter). An *annual* series of fixed-horizon histograms of approximately one year can be constructed using the first-quarter survey responses. However, some analyses require quarterly rather than annual series.

A simple way of constructing an approximate series of quarterly year-ahead forecasts has been proposed by D'Amico and Orphanides (2008). They suggest using the first-quarter current-year forecast, the second-quarter current-year forecast, the third-quarter next-year forecast, and the fourth-quarter

---

with the individual or stays with the company depending on whether "a forecast seems associated more with the firm than the individual."

[5] For example, the US-SPF began asking for forecasts of the natural rate of unemployment in 1996:Q3 (for the third-quarter surveys), density forecasts for the unemployment rate in 2009:Q2, and forecasts for 10-year annual-average real GDP growth and productivity growth in 1992:Q1 (for first-quarter surveys).

[6] Reviews of data revisions and real-time analysis are provided by Croushore (2006, 2011a,b) and Clements and Gálvao (2019).

Table 3.1 The Fixed-Event/Fixed-Horizon Nature of the US-SPF Point forecasts.

Survey/Target	y_{t-2}	y_{t-1}	y_t	y_{t+1}	y_{t+2}	y_{t+3}	y_{t+4}	y_{t+5}	
⋮									
$t-2$	$y_{t-2\mid t-2}$	$y_{t-1\mid t-2}$	$y_{t\mid t-2}$	$y_{t+1\mid t-2}$	$y_{t+2\mid t-2}$				
$t-1$		$y_{t-1\mid t-1}$	$y_{t\mid t-1}$	$y_{t+1\mid t-1}$	$y_{t+2\mid t-1}$	$y_{t+3\mid t-1}$			
t			$y_{t\mid t}$	$y_{t+1\mid t}$	$y_{t+2\mid t}$	$y_{t+3\mid t}$	$y_{t+4\mid t}$		
$t+1$				$y_{t+1\mid t+1}$	$y_{t+2\mid t+1}$	$y_{t+3\mid t+1}$	$y_{t+4\mid t+1}$	$y_{t+5\mid t+1}$	
$t+2$					$y_{t+2\mid t+2}$	$y_{t+3\mid t+2}$	$y_{t+4\mid t+2}$	$y_{t+5\mid t+2}$	⋱
$t+3$						$y_{t+3\mid t+3}$	$y_{t+4\mid t+3}$	$y_{t+5\mid t+3}$	⋱
$t+4$							$y_{t+4\mid t+4}$	$y_{t+5\mid t+4}$	⋱
$t+5$								$y_{t+5\mid t+5}$	⋱
⋮									⋱

next-year forecast. This gives a quarterly-frequency series of forecasts, although from the first to the fourth quarters the actual horizons are 4, 3, 6, and 5, and the target moves from the current to the next year's growth rate between the second and third quarters. An alternative solution is to take a weighted average of the current and next year's forecasts, where the weights vary with the quarter of the year of the survey, reflecting the distances of the forecasts from the desired forecast horizon, as suggested by D'Amico and Orphanides (2014). A recent contribution by Ganics et al. (2020) suggests weighting together the fixed-event density forecasts to obtain uniformity of the probability integral transform of the combined (fixed-horizon) density. The aim is to obtain a correctly calibrated fixed-horizon density forecast.

In terms of point forecasts, the US-SPF typically provides forecasts of the current quarter (i.e., of the quarter in which the survey is held) and of each of the next four quarters, as well as the current year and the following year (including density forecasts). If we denote the survey quarter by t, the forecast horizons are $h = 0, 1, 2, 3, 4$, where $h = 4$ indicates a forecast of the same quarter of the year (as the quarter of the survey) in the following year. Hence, we have quarterly series of rolling-event forecasts, or fixed-horizon forecasts, for $h = 0, 1, 2, 3, 4$. But when the data are linked to earlier surveys, forecasts with a fixed-event structure also arise.

The nature of the US-SPF point forecasts is as described in Table 3.1, where $y_{t+h\mid t}$ denotes a forecast of y_{t+h} made at time t.

The five diagonals give the fixed-horizon forecasts, with the bottom diagonal containing the $h = 0$ forecasts, the one above the $h = 1$ forecasts, and so on up to the top diagonal containing the longest-horizon forecasts. The fixed-event forecasts are given by the columns. For example, reading the column headed y_{t+3}, from bottom to top gives the $h = 0$ to $h = 4$ forecasts of y_{t+3}.

In the context of obtaining fixed-horizon point forecasts from fixed-event point forecasts, Knüppel and Vladu (2016) cite a large number of papers that have used ad hoc weights. They provide a general framework for obtaining optimal approximations—in the sense of minimizing the mean-squared error—to fixed-horizon forecasts when the requisite forecasts are not provided. They illustrate by calculating one-year-ahead inflation and growth forecasts from Consensus Economics quarterly forecasts of annual inflation and growth in the current year and the next year.

The ECB-SPF provides fixed- and rolling-event forecasts at short-, medium-, and longer-term horizons. In terms of fixed-event horizons, the survey asks for forecasts of the current calendar year and the next two calendar years. For inflation and growth, the forecasts for the current calendar year and the next calendar year parallel those in the US-SPF. For unemployment, the current calendar year and the next calendar year refer to the average of monthly unemployment rates in the current year and the subsequent year of the survey, respectively. The remaining calendar year horizon for inflation, growth, and unemployment follows analogously with the appropriate shifting forward of reference years.

Compared to the US-SPF, the ECB-SPF provides four additional fixed-event forecasts of the target variables due to the horizon extending out to a maximum of three years. There are two other important differences between the surveys. First, the ECB-SPF provides both point and density forecasts for the calendar year horizons allowing for matched series across all 12 fixed-event forecasts for a particular calendar year. Second, the ECB-SPF also provides matched point and density rolling-event forecasts for inflation, growth, and unemployment at the one-year-ahead and the one-year/one-year-forward horizons. This structure yields *quarterly* series of fixed horizon forecasts that offer a three-fold increase in the number of observations compared to the US-SPF.[7]

3.2.2 **Point forecasts**

Measures at the aggregate and individual levels

While surveys of professional forecasters record expectations data at the individual level, the fielding agencies typically report aggregate responses, such as the mean or median of the individual responses. These measures may suffice for empirical studies that only require observations on a "consensus" forecast. On other occasions, the individual responses are required, as when testing the implications of expectations models for features of forecast behavior such as disagreement. For example, disagreement cannot arise under rational expectations when the structure of the economy is known to all forecasters and all information is common. Disagreement, however, may arise for various reasons, including information rigidities (see, e.g., Coibion and Gorodnichenko (2012, 2015b)); differential interpretation of public information (see, e.g., Manzan (2011)); some forecasters receiving superior signals; differential rates of learning in non-stationary environments; and differential loss functions (see, e.g., Capistrán and Timmermann (2009)).

The interest in forecaster disagreement is not limited to its relevance for expectations models. As we discuss later in this section, it remains common practice in empirical studies to use disagreement as a proxy for uncertainty when direct measures for uncertainty are not available. In addition, differences in agents' expectations have been cited as an important channel through which monetary policy can affect real activity [Woodford (2003), Mankiw and Reis (2002), and Lorenzoni (2009)] and a key factor influencing the effect of public information signals (Morris and Shin (2002), and Amador and Weill (2010)). The role of heterogeneous beliefs has also been advanced in terms of explaining the evolutions that led to the global financial crisis [Sims (2009), Tomura (2013), Favara and Song (2014), Tian and Yan (2009), and Geanakoplos (2010)].

---

[7] The ECB-SPF also provides matched longer-term point and density forecasts that correspond to a 4- to 5-year-ahead forecast horizon.

Disagreement – measures of dispersion

Disagreement is measured by the distance between (point) forecasts, where different choices of the distance metric give rise to alternative disagreement measures. A common measure of disagreement is the cross-sectional standard deviation of the point forecasts (using the squared distance norm from the mean of the point forecasts):

$$s_{t+h|t} = \sqrt{\frac{1}{N_t - 1} \sum_{i=1}^{N_t} \left(y_{i,t+h|t} - \bar{y}_{t+h|t} \right)^2}, \tag{3.1}$$

where $y_{i,t+h|t}$ denotes the h-step-ahead point prediction of forecaster i at time t and $\bar{y}_{t+h|t} = N_t^{-1} \sum_{i=1}^{N_t} y_{i,t+h|t}$ denotes the mean (or "consensus") forecast.

Disagreement can also be measured using the average absolute value distance from the consensus forecast or by range-based statistics that are more robust to outliers. With regard to the latter, Abel et al. (2016), Glas and Hartmann (2016), and Lahiri and Sheng (2010) use the interquartile range (IQR) of the point forecasts,

$$y_{t+h|t}^{IQR} = y_{t+h|t}^{0.75} - y_{t+h|t}^{0.25}, \tag{3.2}$$

where $y_{t+h|t}^{0.75}$ and $y_{t+h|t}^{0.25}$ denote the 75th and 25th percentiles of the ordered array of point forecasts. Giordani and Söderlind (2003) and Boero et al. (2015) use the quasistandard deviation – half the distance between the 84th and 16th percentiles of the cross-sectional distribution – which equals one standard deviation if the point forecasts are normally distributed.

Almost all survey-based measures of disagreement are constructed at the aggregate level. Rich and Tracy (2021b), however, have proposed univariate disagreement measures for individual ECB-SPF respondents. Specifically, they define the average absolute point disagreement (AAPD) measure for the ith respondent as

$$AAPD_{i,t+h|t} = \frac{1}{N_t - 1} \sum_{j \neq i} \left| y_{j,t+h|t} - y_{i,t+h|t} \right|. \tag{3.3}$$

The AAPD measure uses an individual forecaster's point prediction as the reference point for the calculation.[8] In particular, the extent of conformity in (3.3) is based on pairwise comparisons between a respondent's point forecast and those of all the other respondents.

Clements (2022) constructs multivariate disagreement measures for individual US-SPF respondents. The measure accounts for beliefs about potential interdependencies in the set of variables being forecast. Following Banternghansa and McCracken (2009), the cross-sectional forecast covariance matrix is

$$\mathbf{S}_{t+h|t} = N_t^{-1} \sum_{i=1}^{N_t} \left(\mathbf{y}_{i,t+h|t} - \bar{\mathbf{y}}_{t+h|t} \right) \left(\mathbf{y}_{i,t+h|t} - \bar{\mathbf{y}}_{t+h|t} \right)', \tag{3.4}$$

---

[8] As discussed in Rich and Tracy (2021b), the squared distance norm can be used as an alternative in (3.3) to construct a measure of individual disagreement.

where $\mathbf{y}_{i,t+h|t}$ is the vector of forecasts made by respondent i at time t for the target variables $\mathbf{y}_{t+h}$, N_t is the number of participants at time t, and $\bar{\mathbf{y}}_{t+h|t} = N_t^{-1} \sum_{i=1}^{N_t} \mathbf{y}_{i,t+h|t}$ is the cross-sectional average. For respondent i, the multivariate disagreement measure is given by

$$D_{i,t+h|t} = \sqrt{\left(\mathbf{y}_{i,t+h|t} - \bar{\mathbf{y}}_{t+h|t}\right)' \mathbf{S}_{t+h|t}^{-1} \left(\mathbf{y}_{i,t+h|t} - \bar{\mathbf{y}}_{t+h|t}\right)}. \tag{3.5}$$

To understand the form of (3.5), start by supposing $\mathbf{S}_{t+h|t}$ is a diagonal matrix, with the diagonal consisting of the cross-sectional variances $\{S_{jj,t+h|t}\}$, for $j = 1, ..., n$, where n is the number of variables. Then the measure simplifies to

$$D_{i,t+h|t} = \sqrt{\sum_{j=1}^{n} \frac{\left(\mathbf{y}_{j,i,t+h|t} - \bar{\mathbf{y}}_{j,t+h|t}\right)^2}{S_{jj,t+h|t}}}. \tag{3.6}$$

That is, it is the sum of individual i's squared deviations of each variable from the consensus, divided by the cross-sectional variance. When $n = 1$, the measure further simplifies to the distance between the forecast and consensus, divided by the cross-sectional standard deviation. But when $n > 1$, and $\mathbf{S}_{t+h|t}$ is nondiagonal, the value of the multivariate measure will be reduced (increased) when the vector of differences of individual i's forecasts is consistent with (at odds with) the interdependencies as measured by the cross-sectional forecast covariance matrix.

The univariate and multivariate individual measures of disagreement in (3.3) and (3.6) permit analysis of the heterogeneity and persistence of individual disagreement that are masked at the aggregate level.

3.2.3 Density forecasts

Background and general discussion

Many surveys of professional forecasters do not provide information about the degree of confidence that respondents attach to their point forecasts. There are, however, a smaller number of surveys, including the US-SPF and ECB-SPF, that report both point and density forecasts. Density forecasts provide a basis for constructing measures of uncertainty and studying their properties. While density forecasts are not the only source for measures of uncertainty, they have potential advantages compared to model-based measures, such as those derived from time series conditional variance models (following the seminal contribution by Engle (1982)). As noted by Giordani and Söderlind (2003), model-based estimates of uncertainty may lag those derived from surveys when there are structural breaks.

The implementation of density forecasts, however, can also introduce complications. For example, the ECB-SPF 2009:Q1 one-year-ahead real GDP growth forecasts witnessed a "pile-up" of probabilities in the lower open interval because the survey design failed to provide sufficient histogram coverage to accommodate respondents' shift toward a very pessimistic outlook for growth. Consequently, it can be especially challenging to calculate uncertainty estimates for GDP growth from the density forecasts for this specific survey.

Another complication is that the number, location, and widths of the bins used to define the histogram for the density forecasts occasionally change over time. In the case of the GDP-deflator inflation density forecasts for the US-SPF, the survey initially offered 15 interior bins with a width of 1%

(1968:Q4 to 1981:Q2), with the locations of the bins changing in 1973:Q2 and 1974:Q4. From 1981:Q3 to 1991:Q4, the survey presented respondents with only 6 interior bins with a width of 2% (and a change in locations in 1985:Q2). From 1992:Q1 to 2013:Q4, the histogram consisted of 10 interior bins with a 1% width, and from 2014:Q1 the width was reduced to half a percentage point.[9] This type of change to the structure of the survey instrument makes it problematic for some measures derived from the density forecasts to have a consistent interpretation over time.

Uncertainty and density forecasts

Uncertainty reflects the confidence attached to a prediction and is determined from the distribution of probabilities that a forecaster attaches to the different possible outcomes (or the outcomes to different percentiles) of the target variable. In the case of the surveys, this is typically reported in the form of a histogram where increases (decreases) in the spread of the reported predictive probabilities are indicative of higher (lower) uncertainty.

Uncertainty at the individual level

Surveys that elicit density forecasts typically ask respondents to assign a sequence of probabilities, $p_i(k)$, to a set of $k = 1, ..., K$ prespecified outcome intervals where each closed interval is characterized by a lower bound, l_k, and an upper bound, u_k.[10] To facilitate discussion, we assume that the number of bins and the number of respondents do not change over time, and therefore, we omit a time subscript for these terms here as well as going forward.

One approach to calculating the mean and uncertainty associated with a density forecast is to use formulas for the mean and variance of a histogram. This approach, however, requires addressing two issues. The first is that density forecasts typically contain open intervals on each end of the histogram that, if the respondent assigned a probability to either, must be closed to calculate the mean and variance. A typical—although ad hoc—practice is to assign the same or twice the width of the interior closed intervals to the open intervals. The degree to which this will impact any estimate depends on the amount of assigned probability to each open interval.

The second issue concerns the location of the probability mass within a specified closed interval. For example, some studies [Boero et al. (2008b), Rich and Tracy (2010), Kenny et al. (2015), and Poncela and Senra (2017)] assume that the probability mass is located at the midpoint of each bin. Under this assumption, the mean and variance of forecaster i's histogram are given, respectively, by

$$\mu_{i,t+h|t} = \sum_{k=1}^{K} p_{i,t+h|t}(k) \times mid(k), \tag{3.7}$$

---

[9] Recently, the COVID-19 pandemic resulted in marked changes in some of the histograms for the US-SPF and ECB-SPF starting with the 2020:Q2 survey. For example, lower and upper open limits were pushed out, and the histogram widths were made much wider in the tails than around the (assumed) center of the distribution. Because survey operators may not be able to anticipate every occasion when respondents will significantly shift their density forecasts, an alternative survey design would be to ask respondents to provide selective percentiles of their subjective distributions, but this is a complex issue (see, e.g., O'Hagan et al. (2006)).

[10] The probabilities are assumed to sum to unity.

$$\sigma^2_{i,t+h|t} = \sum_{k=1}^{K} p_{i,t+h|t}(k) \times [mid(k) - \mu_{i,t+h|t}]^2, \tag{3.8}$$

where $p_{i,t+h|t}(k)$ is the probability that forecaster i assigns to the kth interval corresponding to an h-step-ahead prediction from a survey conducted in period t and $mid(k) = (u_k + l_k)/2$ is the midpoint of the kth bin.

Several studies [Zarnowitz and Lambros (1987), Abel et al. (2016), and Rich and Tracy (2021b)] instead assume that the probability is distributed uniformly within each interval. While the mean of the histogram derived under this assumption is identical to that in (3.7), the variance is now given by

$$\sigma^2_{i,t+h|t} = \left[\sum_{k=1}^{K} p_{i,t+h|t}(k) \times \left(\frac{u_k^3 - l_k^3}{3(u_k - l_k)} \right) \right] - \left[\sum_{k=1}^{K} p_{i,t+h|t}(k) \times \left(\frac{u_k^2 - l_k^2}{2(u_k - l_k)} \right) \right]^2. \tag{3.9}$$

Recent work by Glas (2020) suggests that the variance estimates are not particularly sensitive to using method (3.8) or (3.9).

An alternative approach is to first fit a continuous parametric distribution to the individual histogram. This practice involves selecting a respondent-specific parameter vector $\theta_{i,t,h}$ for a proposed distribution that solves the following minimization problem:

$$\min_{\theta_{i,t,h}} \sum_{k=1}^{K} \left[F(u_k, \theta_{i,t,h}) - P_{i,t+h|t}(k) \right]^2, \tag{3.10}$$

where F is the cumulative distribution function (CDF) of the proposed distribution and $P_{i,t+h|t}(k) = \sum_{s=1}^{k} p_{i,t+h|t}(s)$ is the CDF corresponding to the reported histogram. Depending on the proposed distribution, the mean and variance of the histogram are obtained either directly or indirectly via the estimated parameter vector $\hat{\theta}_{i,t,h}$.

Most studies adopt either the normal distribution [Giordani and Söderlind (2003), Lahiri and Liu (2006), D'Amico and Orphanides (2008), Söderlind (2011), and Boero et al. (2015)] or the generalized beta distribution with fixed support [Engelberg et al. (2009), Glas and Hartmann (2016), Liu and Sheng (2019), and Glas (2020)]. Other choices include a gamma distribution [D'Amico and Orphanides (2008)] and a two-piece normal distribution [Krüger (2017)]. Importantly, Engelberg et al. (2009) note that the approach in (3.10) requires forecasters to assign nonzero probabilities to at least three bins. If a respondent assigns probability only to one or two bins, they suggest fitting triangular distributions and outline a method of doing so for two-bin histograms.

The IQR provides an alternative measure of individual uncertainty.[11] Following Abel et al. (2016) and Glas (2020), we can define this measure as

$$p^{IQR}_{i,t+h|t} = p^{0.75}_{i,t+h|t} - p^{0.25}_{i,t+h|t}, \tag{3.11}$$

---

[11] The IQR is typically more robust than a standard deviation/variance estimate to situations when respondents place probability in open intervals. The IQR is unaffected unless the respondent places more than a 25% probability in an open interval.

where $p_{i,t+h|t}^{0.75}$ and $p_{i,t+h|t}^{0.25}$ denote the 75th and 25th percentiles, respectively, of respondent i's density forecast. The quartiles in (3.11) can be derived under the "mass-at-midpoint" and uniform distribution assumptions, as well as the parametric approach.[12]

Uncertainty at the aggregate level

A measure of aggregate uncertainty can be calculated as the mean of the standard deviations calculated from the individual density forecasts (see, e.g., Zarnowitz and Lambros (1987)),

$$\bar{\sigma}_{t+h|t} = N^{-1} \sum_{i=1}^{N} \sqrt{\sigma_{i,t+h|t}^2}.$$ (3.12)

Batchelor and Dua (1996) and Boero et al. (2008a, 2015) adopt the root mean subjective variance (RMSV) of the individual variances,

$$RMSV_{t+h|t} = \sqrt{N^{-1} \sum_{i=1}^{N} \sigma_{i,t+h|t}^2}.$$ (3.13)

An IQR-based measure of aggregate uncertainty has also been proposed based on an ordered array of the individual IQR values in (3.11). Abel et al. (2016) and Glas (2020) consider the cross-sectional median value for the uniform distribution and parametric approach. In the case of the "mass-at-midpoint" approach, Glas (2020) argues for the use of the cross-sectional average.

The individual density forecast data can be combined into an aggregate density forecast, from which various summary statistics such as the mean and standard deviation/variance can be calculated.[13] Wallis (2005) demonstrates that a measure of aggregate uncertainty can be obtained as the difference between the variance of the aggregate density forecast and dispersion in the individual point forecasts. Using the finite mixture distribution to characterize the statistical properties of the aggregate density forecast, Wallis (2005) derives the following decomposition:

$$VAR\left(\phi_{t+h|t}\right) = N^{-1} \sum_{i=1}^{N_t} \sigma_{i,t+h|t}^2 + N^{-1} \sum_{i=1}^{N_t} \left(y_{i,t+h|t} - \bar{y}_{t+h|t}\right)^2$$

$$= \bar{\sigma}_{t+h|t}^2 + \tilde{s}_{t+h|t}^2,$$ (3.14)

where $VAR\left(\phi_{t+h|t}\right)$ is the variance of the aggregate density forecast, $\bar{\sigma}_{t+h|t}^2$ is the average variance of the individual density forecasts, and $\tilde{s}_{t+h|t}^2$ is a measure of the cross-sectional variance of the individual point forecasts. As shown in (3.14), the variance of the aggregate density forecast reflects a combination of both average uncertainty and disagreement. Consequently, the spread of the aggregate density

---

[12] Under the "mass-at-midpoint" assumption, the quartiles in (3.11) are defined as the midpoint of the bin where the empirical CDF, $P_{i,t+h|t}(k)$, first exceeds the relevant threshold. In the case of the uniform distribution, linear interpolation is used to derive the quartiles.

[13] The aggregate density forecast typically is constructed as an equally weighted combination of the individual density forecasts.

forecast <u>should not</u> be interpreted as a measure of aggregate uncertainty due to the additional influence of forecast dispersion.[14]

Given estimates of $VAR\left(\phi_{t+h|t}\right)$ and values of $\tilde{s}^2_{t+h|t}$, measures of aggregate uncertainty $\bar{\sigma}^2_{t+h|t}$ can be backed out from (3.14). An advantage of the approach is that the fitting of parametric distributions is facilitated by the fact that nonzero probabilities are almost always assigned to more than three bins of the aggregate density forecast. Boero et al. (2008a) and Rich and Tracy (2010) adopt this approach for their analyses of the Bank of England Survey of External Forecasters (BOE-SEF) and the US-SPF, respectively.

Skew/risk

Density forecasts also convey the shape of the subjective probability distribution and thereby provide an assessment about the respondent's balance of risks. That is, a respondent can report a symmetric histogram suggesting balanced risks to a forecast or a skewed histogram indicating upside or downside risks. Taken together, these additional features of density forecasts are important to policymakers and market participants as they allow for a richer characterization of forecasts and offer a more informed outlook.

3.2.4 A closer look at disagreement and uncertainty

Heterogeneity and persistence at the individual level

Aggregate measures of expectations and/or uncertainty from surveys cannot speak to issues related to the forecast behavior of individual respondents in the cross-section or over time. Consequently, panel data on individual forecasts are attractive for the construction of key variables of interest and for assessing differences across respondents and the statistical properties of those differences.

Underlying the earlier discussion of measures of disagreement is the observation that there is marked dispersion across the cross-sectional distribution of point forecasts. Turning to the individual density forecasts, various studies [D'Amico and Orphanides (2008), Boero et al. (2008b,a, 2015), Clements (2014b), Glas (2020), Rich and Tracy (2021b)] also find considerable heterogeneity in the cross-sectional distributions of the first- and second moments of the density forecasts. That is, respondents display notable differences in the mean and confidence of their reported outlooks.

The notion of forecaster disagreement can be extended to their density forecasts. Specifically, Rich and Tracy (2021b) propose an individual density disagreement measure using the Wasserstein distance (WD) measure for histograms (see Arroyo and Mate (2009)). Specifically, the WD disagreement measure between respondent j and respondent i is given by

$$WD_{j,i,t+h|t} = \int_0^1 \left| F^{-1}_{j,t+h|t}(z) - F^{-1}_{i,t+h|t}(z) \right| dz, \tag{3.15}$$

---

[14] Another problematic aspect associated with using the spread of the aggregate density forecast as a measure of aggregate uncertainty is that Wallis (2005) shows that changes in the variance of aggregate density forecasts principally reflect shifts in disagreement and not individual uncertainty.

where $F_{i,t+h|t}^{-1}$ denotes the inverse CDF for respondent i in the survey at date t.[15] They then define the average absolute density disagreement (AADD) measure for respondent i as follows:

$$AADD_{i,t+h|t} = \frac{1}{N-1} \sum_{j \neq i} WD_{j,i,t+h|t}. \qquad (3.16)$$

The expression in (3.16) has several attractive features. First, the measure uses the same density forecasts as those used for the individual uncertainty measure. Second, the measure captures any differences across respondents' density forecasts by focusing on the entire cumulative distribution function.

As previously discussed, the evidence from cross-sectional distributions indicates heterogeneity in respondents' point and density forecasts. However, the heterogeneity does not reveal the degree to which respondents move within the distributions over time. In particular, the distributions do not indicate whether there are persistent patterns in individual respondents' forecast behavior and, if so, the sources for such persistence. The availability of measures of uncertainty and disagreement at the individual level allows for an exploration into the issue of persistence for these features of forecast behavior.

On the confidence of respondents' predictions, Boero et al. (2015) and Rich and Tracy (2021b) find strong evidence of persistence in individual uncertainty. Moreover, Rich and Tracy (2021b) find that individual uncertainty appears to be associated with a prominent respondent effect. That is, while there are marked differences across forecasters in the confidence attached to their predictions, forecasters' confidence changes slowly over time.

Turning to disagreement, Clements (2022) adopts the individual multivariate disagreement measure in (3.5) to determine whether some individuals in the US-SPF are persistently more contrarian than others. Using a split sample analysis, he ranks forecasters in each period based on the extent of their disagreement. His results document a positive correlation between the ranks in the two periods, indicating persistence in disagreement. Rich and Tracy (2021b) examine data from the ECB-SPF and adopt the personal disagreement measure in (3.3). For each survey period, they assign forecasters to quartiles based on the extent of their disagreement and then examine the transitions between quartiles over time. The results indicate that forecasters tend to remain in the same quartile, also indicating persistence in disagreement. In contrast to their analysis of uncertainty, Rich and Tracy (2021b) find that individual disagreement is associated with a prominent time effect.

Taken together, individual data reveal notable heterogeneity and persistence in uncertainty and disagreement. Moreover, this evidence is consistent with other work documenting heterogeneity and persistence in the relative level of point forecasts [Patton and Timmermann (2010), and Boero et al. (2015)]. These properties do not support full information rational expectations (FIRE) models, which cannot generate heterogeneity, nor models that incorporate informational rigidities, such as Coibion and Gorodnichenko (2012, 2015b). At least in their baseline versions, these latter models assume homogeneous signal qualities (noisy information) or propensities to update (sticky information) and therefore cannot generate systematic differences across forecasters. Rather, the observed properties of individual forecast behavior cited above would argue for the development of expectations models that feature persistent heterogeneity.

---

[15] The squared distance norm can be used as an alternative to the absolute value norm in (3.15).

Is disagreement a reliable proxy for uncertainty?

Empirical studies attempting to quantify the effects of uncertainty face the challenge of constructing measures of uncertainty.[16] While researchers may find appropriate density forecasts from surveys, absent this situation they will need to select a proxy to measure uncertainty. In practice, the dispersion of point forecasts has been used for this purpose. However, the validity of this practice requires a significant positive association between disagreement and uncertainty. Zarnowitz and Lambros (1987) show that it is possible for disagreement and uncertainty to display a negative relationship or no relationship. Essentially, for this reason, Manski (2011) and others are critical of the use of disagreement to proxy uncertainty.

Whether there is a meaningful correlation between disagreement and uncertainty is an empirical question and several studies have investigated this relationship. These studies, however, have largely been conducted at the aggregate level and have relied mainly on data from the US-SPF. The following regression model is typically used to assess the association between uncertainty and disagreement:

$$Uncertainty_{t+h|t} = \alpha + \beta(Disagreement_{t+h|t}) + \varepsilon_{t+h|t}, \tag{3.17}$$

where the measures of aggregate uncertainty and disagreement (expressed in comparable units) are selected from the various candidate series previously discussed. The issue of whether disagreement is a valid proxy for uncertainty rests on both statistical and economic significance. Specifically, the determination is based on a one-tailed test that $\beta > 0$ and the R^2 from the estimation of (3.17).

The evidence from the US-SPF has been mixed. Zarnowitz and Lambros (1987) report a modest positive association between disagreement and uncertainty. Giordani and Söderlind (2003) extend the sample period of Zarnowitz and Lambros and report a positive association between disagreement and uncertainty that is both economically and statistically significant, although some studies have argued that their conclusion is problematic.[17] Examining matched point and density forecasts from the US-SPF Rich and Tracy (2010) find a very weak relationship between disagreement and uncertainty. Recent analyses that have examined data from other surveys featuring point and density forecasts, such as Boero et al. (2008a) for the BOE-SEF and Abel et al. (2016) and Glas (2020) for the ECB-SPF, have found little support for the use of disagreement as a proxy for uncertainty.[18]

Lahiri and Sheng (2010) suggest the disagreement-uncertainty relationship may be episodic and that the strength of the disagreement–uncertainty relationship is inversely related to the volatility of

---

[16] There is an extensive literature investigating the effects of uncertainty on economic activity and financial variables. Early work focused on the dynamics of uncertainty and capital investment [Bernanke (1983), Dixit (1989), Abel and Eberly (1994), and Dixit and Pindyck (1994)], with more recent work by Leahy and Whited (1996) and Bloom et al. (2007) linking lower investment to stock market volatility. In addition, uncertainty can affect the hiring decisions of firms [Bloom (2009), Schaal (2017)] and serves as an important source for business cycle fluctuations [Bloom et al. (2018)]. Campbell (2000) discusses how uncertainty is a fundamental determinant of asset prices. Turning to the international sphere, uncertainty can affect export dynamics [Novy and Taylor (2020)] or the decisions of firms to enter and invest in new export markets [Handley and Limao (2015, 2017)].

[17] Rich and Tracy (2010) and Boero et al. (2015) discuss the problems with Giordani and Söderlind (2003) fitting normal distributions to two-bin histograms. Rich and Tracy (2010) also raise concerns about deriving a disagreement measure from the (estimated) means of the density forecasts rather than the point forecasts.

[18] Boero et al. (2015) find a strong positive correlation between disagreement and uncertainty when they extend their 2008 analysis of the BOE-SEF to include the global financial crisis period. However, they note that the results are largely driven by observations associated with the initial onset of the crisis.

the forecasting environment. Lahiri and Sheng find some support using the US-SPF data. Rich and Tracy (2021b) construct measures of disagreement and uncertainty at the individual level for the ECB-SPF and use a panel data model to test the relationship between the measures and any changes in the strength of the relationship across time. They find an economically insignificant relationship between the variables in both the pre- and post-financial crisis periods, with their results corroborating the preponderance of evidence at the aggregate level that disagreement is not a reliable proxy for uncertainty. Moreover, they argue that the weak linkage between uncertainty and disagreement could reflect the divergent properties of the variables discussed in the preceding section in which uncertainty is characterized by prominent respondent effects and disagreement is characterized by prominent time effects.

Ex ante vs. ex post uncertainty

A histogram-based measure of uncertainty is an *ex ante* measure in that it is available before the realization of the target variable becomes known. *Ex post* measures of forecast uncertainty, such as the root mean squared forecast error (RMSFE), only become available when the realizations are known. A number of studies have sought to compare the two uncertainty measures as a way to address questions relating to whether respondents' *perceptions* of uncertainty are accurate, that is, whether the *ex ante* and *ex post* measures broadly match.

Clements (2014b) looks at both individual and aggregate forecasts for the US-SPF, exploiting the point and histogram forecasts to calculate perceived (*ex ante*) and realized, or actual, (*ex post*) uncertainty. He finds that respondents tend to be under-confident in their probability assessments of both inflation and GDP growth at horizons up to one year ahead. For forecasts of the *next* year the probability assessments display over-confidence.

A similar dependence on the forecast horizon (or the "term structure") is found by Knüppel and Schultefrankenfeld (2019). In their study of central banks' inflation uncertainty forecasts (they consider the Bank of England, the Banco Central do Brasil, the Magyar Nemzeti Bank, and the Sveriges Riksbank), they find that the banks' forecasts also tend to display under-confidence at short horizons and over-confidence at longer horizons.

3.3 **Evaluation of forecaster performance**

3.3.1 **Data revisions**

Most of the target variables in surveys of professional forecasters are subject to revision over time. In these cases, which vintage of data should be taken as the "actual values" for calculating forecast errors, given that the analyst is ignorant about the respondent's choice of vintage? A forecast might be reasonably close to the advance estimate but end up deviating considerably from a revised estimate. This problem is obviously dependent on the size of the revisions. For example, Croushore (2011a, p. 249, Fig. 9.1) illustrates, with an admittedly extreme case, the revisions to the 1976:Q3 growth rate of U.S. real residential investment. A plot of the initial release and of all subsequent estimates (up to those made in 2009) show that the estimates of the annual rate rose from less than 3% to nearly 16%, before ending up at around −5%!

Using later estimates for actual values might be advised on the grounds that these are more accurate estimates of the "true" values, which are of primary interest, and *ought* to be the focus of respondents. On the other hand, Keane and Runkle (1990, p. 715) argue that the use of revised data in tests of forecaster rationality might lead to misleading results, since it rests on incorrect assumptions "about what the forecasters tried to predict and what they knew when they made their predictions."

In addition to the magnitude of revisions, a key consideration is whether revisions are predictable (see, e.g., Mankiw and Shapiro (1986)). Clements and Gālvao (2017a) show that revisions can sometimes be predicted using general information sets, and Clements (2019) shows that under certain conditions it is possible in principle to determine the vintage of the data being targeted.

3.3.2 Rationality/efficiency of point forecasts

Starting with Turnovsky and Wachter (1972), both aggregate and individual survey expectations have been used to determine whether economic agents form their expectations rationally.

Rational expectations is the hypothesis that:

"expectations, since they are informed predictions of future events, are essentially the same as the predictions of the relevant economic theory" (Muth (1961, p. 316)).

This statement assumes that all agents have access to all relevant information. Several authors have balked at this assumption (see, e.g., Pesaran (1987)), and it may be more reasonable to ask whether agents make efficient use of the information they possess. This more limited notion of forecast efficiency proposed by Mincer and Zarnowitz (1969) can be tested by regressing actual values on forecasts,

$$y_t = \alpha_i + \beta_i \, y_{i,t|t-h} + \mu_{i,t}, \tag{3.18}$$

where $y_{i,t|t-h}$ is the forecast made by individual i at $t-h$ of the target variable y_t, and the data range over t for a fixed horizon h. The null of forecast efficiency is that $\alpha_i = 0$ and $\beta_i = 1$. Consider the covariance between the forecast error and the forecast,

$$Cov\left(y_t - y_{i,t|t-h}, \, y_{i,t|t-h}\right) = Cov\left((\beta_i - 1) \, y_{i,t|t-h} + \mu_{i,t}, \, y_{i,t|t-h}\right). \tag{3.19}$$

Unless $\beta_i = 1$, the covariance will be nonzero and could be exploited to adjust the forecasts to improve their accuracy. Hence, the original forecasts do not make optimal use of the information available to the forecaster, where "information" in this context simply refers to the respondent's own forecast. (If $\alpha_i \neq 0$ when $\beta_i = 1$, the forecasts are clearly biased.) For multistep forecasts, $h > 1$, heteroscedasticity, and autocorrelation consistent (HAC) standard errors are used to account for the overlapping forecasts phenomenon, which induces serial correlation in $\mu_{i,t}$ in (3.18).

Should the test for forecast efficiency be applied to aggregate or individual forecasts? The aggregate may appear a better choice, since it avoids the vagaries of any given forecaster, but the comment on Figlewski and Wachtel (1981) by Dietrich and Joines (1983), and the rejoinder by Figlewski and Wachtel (1983), establish that for the aggregate, $\beta < 1$ (when $\beta_i = 1$ for all i, unless the forecasts are identical across individuals). That is, an aggregate of forecast-efficient individuals will appear to be inefficient.

A related finding is the under-reaction of the consensus forecasts to new information, as predicted by models of dispersed noisy information or rational inattention. This literature regresses the aggregate forecast error on the revision to the aggregate forecast and shows that the slope coefficient should be positive. Individual forecasters correctly down-weight their information because it is noisy, but this results in an underresponse of the average forecasts. Regressions of this type have recently generated much interest (see Coibion and Gorodnichenko (2015b), Broer and Kohlhas (2018), Bordalo et al. (2020) and Angeletos et al. (2020), inter alia).

More demanding tests of rationality would require the forecast error to be orthogonal to variables in the agent's information set at time $t - h$. A term such as $g'_{i,t-h}\theta_i$ could be included in (3.18), where $g_{i,t-h}$ denotes a vector of variables in the agent's information set at time $t - h$. The null specified above is then augmented by the requirement that $\theta_i = 0$.

As noted in Section 3.2, some surveys have a fixed-event dimension. Patton and Timmermann (2012) propose a test that exploits this dimension of the forecast data by essentially testing whether the long-horizon forecast error is systematically related to revisions to more recent forecasts of the target variable (their "optimal revision regression"). The concern that inference may be affected by an erroneous choice of the outcome vintage can be countered by replacing the realization of the target variable by a short-horizon forecast. Chapter 17 in this Handbook presents a model of the relationship between different horizon forecasts.[19]

Tests of efficiency or rationality might fail to detect alternating periods of underprediction and overprediction, such as the tendency of U.S. inflation forecasts to under-predict in the 1970s but to overpredict in the 1980s and 1990s. Rossi and Sekhposyan (2016) use the US-SPF inflation forecasts and the Federal Reserve's Greenbook forecasts to test for forecast optimality allowing for instabilities. The null hypothesis of rationality is not rejected in the standard setting, but rationality is rejected for both sets of forecasts after allowing for instabilities.

3.3.3 Scoring rules

Point forecasts

In practice, point forecasts are often evaluated using the absolute or squared forecast error averaged over the set of forecasts and realizations. In Section 3.4, we discuss loss functions for point forecasts that do not penalize equal under- and overpredictions the same. Allowing for asymmetric loss might be viewed as a small step in the direction of evaluating forecast errors in terms of economic costs (see, e.g., Granger and Machina (2006)).

Density forecasts

A large and growing body of work focuses on the properties of density forecasts: their accuracy, whether they are calibrated (in the sense of closely matching the true densities), and whether survey participants' reported density forecasts are overly optimistic or pessimistic.

Density forecast accuracy is typically evaluated using a scoring rule, which can also be used to rank competing forecasts. In line with the histogram format of the survey instruments considered here, we can describe this approach for respondent i at time t for a target variable at time $t + h$ as follows. We assume that there are K bins associated with the histogram at time t and let $p_{i,t+h|t}(k)$ denote the probability assigned by respondent i to the kth bin. While there are several candidates for a density-based accuracy measure, the ranked probability score (RPS) [Epstein (1969)] is a popular choice and

---

[19] These tests are closely related to the weak efficiency tests of Nordhaus (1987) and the property that forecast revisions should be unpredictable from earlier revisions.

can be defined as follows:

$$RPS_{i,t+h|t} = \frac{1}{K-1} \sum_{j=1}^{K} \left(\sum_{k=1}^{j} p_{i,t+h|t}(k) - \sum_{k=1}^{j} I_{t+h}(k) \right)^2, \tag{3.20}$$

where $I_{t+h}(k)$ denotes an indicator variable that takes a value of one if the actual outcome in period $t+h$ is in the kth interval of the histogram from the survey at date t. The forecast performance metric in (3.20) can then be averaged over all surveys in which respondent i participated to produce an overall score. Boero et al. (2011) provide an overview of scoring rules.

3.3.4 Using the probability integral transform to assess density forecast coverage

Density forecasts can also be evaluated using the probability integral transform (PIT), as surveyed in Diebold et al. (1998) (see also Dawid (1984) and Rosenblatt (1952)). Let $\{f_t(y_t)\}_{t=1}^{m}$ be the sequence of true conditional densities governing the target variable y_t, $\{y_t\}_{t=1}^{m}$ the sequence of realizations of y_t, and let $\{\Omega_t(y_t)\}_{t=1}^{m}$ be the corresponding sequence of one-step-ahead density forecasts. Then z_t is the series of probability integral transforms defined by

$$\{z_t\}_{t=1}^{m} = \left\{ \int_{-\infty}^{y_t} \Omega_t(u)\, du \right\}_{t=1}^{m}. \tag{3.21}$$

A sequence of density forecasts is consistent with the data-generating process for the target variable, i.e., $\{\Omega_t(y_t)\}_{t=1}^{m} = \{f_t(y_t)\}_{t=1}^{m}$, if $\{z_t\}_{t=1}^{m}$ is i.i.d. $U(0,1)$. Various testing procedures are available. Berkowitz (2001) suggests taking the inverse normal transformation of $\{z_t\}_{t=1}^{m}$, and testing whether this is an i.i.d. drawing from a standard normal, using likelihood ratio tests based on Gaussian likelihoods. See also Knüppel (2015) for an alternative approach.

Two sets of forecast densities can also be compared against each other. Bao et al. (2007) show that the difference between the Kullback–Leibler information criterion (KLIC) calculated for two rival forecast densities can be used as the basis for a test of equal predictive ability using the Diebold and Mariano (1995) approach. (A similar approach has been developed by Amisano and Giacomini (2007).)

The evidence concerning the coverage rates of respondents' density forecasts is mixed. For example, Diebold et al. (1999) and Giordani and Söderlind (2003, 2006) examine the US-SPF and find that forecasters are "over-confident" when reporting their probabilistic assessment of target variables. Kenny et al. (2014) and Krüger (2017) find similar results examining the ECB-SPF, while Clements (2004) examines the Bank of England Inflation Reports and finds the one-year-ahead forecasts unduly pessimistic in that too much probability mass is allocated to high rates of inflation, whereas the current and next quarter forecasts are better calibrated.

Clements (2018) compares the US-SPF GDP deflator inflation and real GDP growth histograms against a set of benchmark forecasts, both at an individual level and in the aggregate, using the approach of Bao et al. (2007). The benchmark forecasts are constructed from the SPF historical median forecast errors and are unconditional in nature. The SPF forecasts are generally not more informative than the benchmark forecasts.

3.3.5 Balanced vs. unbalanced panels

Missing observations from non-response complicate individual-level analyses of forecaster behavior, as well as the calculation of aggregate measures. Due to the unbalanced panel structure, analyses of individual-level forecast performance may need to control for distortions that arise from respondents participating at different times, especially if these times are characterized by different economic conditions.

Calculating an aggregate measure from a series of individual responses can be regarded as a forecast combination problem. That is, the optimal combination will depend on the loss function, and the weights attached to the individual forecasts will depend on the relative accuracy of the individual forecasts and the correlations between the individual forecast errors.[20]

In practice, the cross-sectional median or mean ("equal weights") is routinely used. Genre et al. (2013) consider whether it is possible to do better than "the simple average" for the ECB-SPF. As noted by Capistrán and Timmermann (2009), missing forecast values imply there may be relatively few observations on which to estimate optimal combination weights. Uncertainty in the optimal weights might favor the use of theoretically suboptimal equal weighting of the individual forecasts. Capistrán and Timmermann (2009) consider "filling in" missing data before combining. They use the EM algorithm and a simple model for individual forecasts to back-fill missing forecasts, although such approaches are not common in the survey expectations literature.

Engelberg et al. (2011) focus on how to interpret changes in the consensus forecast when the composition of the panel is changing over time. For example, compositional effects may mean that the aggregate changes in ways that are at odds with changes in the consensus of the ever-present forecasters. Engelberg et al. (2011, p. 1061) argue that changing panel composition can only be ignored "if it were credible to assume that panel members are randomly recruited from a stable population of potential forecasters and that participation in the survey after recruitment is statistically independent of forecasters' beliefs about inflation." They propose replacing missing forecasts with imputed upper and lower values, such that the implied changes between periods are no more extreme than the observed changes in the forecasts of those who responded in both periods. This generates a bound on the change in the aggregate. Consistent with the views expressed in Manski (2007), in this instance a more "credible" assumption concerning the missing data leads to a bound as opposed to a point estimate of the change in the aggregate.

Clements (2021a) considers whether joiners and leavers differ from incumbents for the US-SPF and finds some evidence that joiners' density forecasts are less accurate. However, it is difficult to gauge the reliability of this finding due to the relatively small number of joiners to each survey.

3.3.6 Are some forecasters better than others?

Compared to households or firms, professional forecasters are often viewed as a homogeneous group. Nevertheless, researchers have investigated whether some forecasters are better/worse than others. Early studies by Stekler (1987) and Batchelor (1990) report contradictory findings for the Blue Chip

---

[20] See Bates and Granger (1969), Granger and Ramanathan (1984), and Clements and Harvey (2009) for a review. Although in general the optimal weights will differ for asymmetric loss, Elliott and Timmermann (2004) show that under certain conditions the weights are identical to the squared-error loss weights, and the degree of asymmetry is accommodated by the constant term in the combination.

survey, with the different conclusions related to the debate about the appropriate test statistic for the analysis. Christensen et al. (2008) examine the US-SPF and develop a test for equal forecasting accuracy based on the forecast comparison test of Diebold and Mariano (1995). Their analysis yields mixed results, with tests suggesting equal predictive performance for some variables and not others. However, they are only able to study three individual respondents because their approach requires a balanced panel and a long time series of forecasts.

D'Agostino et al. (2012) point out that there are notable drawbacks to the approaches used in these previous studies. First, the requirement of a balanced panel can significantly reduce the sample size. Second, when respondents participate at different times, inter-respondent comparisons need to control for differences over time in the forecasting environment. To do this, they suggest using a normalized forecast error. If $e_{i,t+h|t}$ is the forecast error made by individual i forecasting y_{t+h} at survey date t, the normalized forecast error is

$$\tilde{e}_{i,t+h|t} = \frac{e_{i,t+h|t}}{\sqrt{\frac{1}{N_t} \sum_{j=1}^{N_t} e_{j,t+h|t}^2}} = \frac{e_{i,t+h|t}}{\sqrt{\left(\overline{e_{t+h|t}^2}\right)}}, \tag{3.22}$$

where N_t is the number of respondents at survey date t.

D'Agostino et al. (2012) compare the empirical distribution of forecaster performance (using the normalized errors) to a simulated distribution calculated under the null hypothesis of equal ability, constructed by randomly assigning forecasts to forecasters. Their approach also accounts for the unbalanced nature of the panel. They find little evidence to suggest that some US-SPF forecasters are notably better than others, once a set of poorly performing forecasters is removed. Meyler (2020) finds similar results for the ECB-SPF. However, Clements (2020) finds systematic differences in the accuracy of the US-SPF histogram forecasts.

Rich and Tracy (2021a) use a regression approach to examine forecasts from the ECB-SPF. Specifically, they adopt a panel data specification for each respondent i and survey in period t,

$$FP_{i,t+h|t} = \alpha_i + \lambda_i \left(\overline{FP_{t+h|t}}\right) + \varepsilon_{i,t+h|t}, \tag{3.23}$$

where $FP_{i,t+h|t}$ and $\overline{FP_{t+h|t}}$ denote a forecast performance (FP) metric at the individual and average (cross-sectional) level, respectively, and $\varepsilon_{i,t+h|t}$ is a mean-zero error term. An important feature of (3.23) is that it allows for two sources of heterogeneity in forecast performance across survey respondents through a fixed effect (α_i) and an individual loading factor (λ_i). They find strong evidence that respondents do not display equal forecast accuracy. Moreover, their results indicate that some respondents display higher relative accuracy in more tranquil environments, while others display higher relative accuracy in more volatile environments.

3.3.7 Professionals versus models (and other sources of forecasts)

The predictions of professional forecasters have been compared to alternative sources of forecasts, including surveys of consumers and firms, as well as forecasts from empirical models, financial markets, and prediction markets (see, e.g., Snowberg et al. (2013) and Grothe and Meyler (2018) on the last two). Some earlier studies showed survey forecasts outperforming model forecasts for nominal variables such as inflation (see, e.g., Ang et al. (2007), Faust and Wright (2009, 2013), Aiolfi et al. (2011), and Clements (2015)), with more equivocal findings for real variables such as output. However, even for inflation, the evidence is mixed, with a recent study by Berge (2018) finding that an ARIMA(1,1) produces more accurate inflation forecasts than professional forecasters over 1990 to 2015.

A possible reason why survey-based forecasts might outperform those from models is that they are likely to benefit from a superior reading of the state of the economy and ongoing trends at the time the forecasts are made. They may also be able to react more rapidly than model-based forecasts to structural change. Against this, as discussed earlier, recent theories of expectations formation suggest that survey forecasts may not efficiently incorporate new information which might be expected to adversely affect accuracy.

A growing literature suggests using survey expectations in conjunction with empirical models. For example, Chan et al. (2018) use long-run inflation survey forecasts in a model of inflation, and Coibion et al. (2018) argue for a greater use of survey data in macroeconomic analyses, with a focus on the New Keynesian Phillips curve. That said, Coibion and Gorodnichenko (2015a) argue for the primacy of firms' expectations over those of professional forecasters in Phillips curve models of inflation, and of using consumers' expectations to proxy firms' expectations when the latter are unavailable.

Some studies have compared surveys and other sources of forecasts in terms of density forecasts. Alternative sources of density forecasts are rarer, with the exception of model-based forecasts. In addition to Clements (2018) discussed earlier, there are comparisons of variances derived from the histograms to model forecasts. These include Giordani and Söderlind (2003) and Clements and Gálvao (2017b). Clements and Gálvao (2017b) found that model-based uncertainty assessments were more accurate than those of the US-SPF.

3.4 Consistency of point and density forecasts

When both point and density forecasts are available, a natural question is whether the two are consistent. We consider reasons why a respondent's forecasts may appear inconsistent and discuss formal evaluation for this property.

3.4.1 Calculating bounds on the central moments of histograms

Comparisons between point forecasts and density forecasts are complicated by the respondent only imperfectly revealing the underlying density forecast, and ignorance of what the point forecast represents (e.g., the mean of the subjective density, or the optimal forecast for an asymmetric loss function, and so on). Engelberg et al. (2009) suggest a way of dealing with the first consideration without introducing any auxiliary assumptions by calculating bounds on a given measure of the central tendency of the histogram (such as the mean, for example). If the point prediction lies within the bounds on a particular moment, such as the mean, then it is consistent with that moment of the underlying distribution.

The calculation of bounds on the mean, as well as the mode and median, can be explained by an example. Suppose a respondent assigns non-zero probabilities to three bins. The probability that inflation (say) is in the interval [2, 3] is 0.5, in the interval [3, 4] is 0.3, and is in the interval [4, 5] is 0.2. For the mean, the lower (upper) bound is obtained if all the probability is assumed to be at the lower (upper) limit of the histogram intervals. Then the lower bound is $0.5 \times 2 + 0.3 \times 3 + 0.2 \times 4 = 2.7$, and the upper bound is $0.5 \times 3 + 0.3 \times 4 + 0.2 \times 5 = 3.7$. Hence, a value of the point forecast in the interval [2.7, 3.7] could plausibly be interpreted as the respondent's (conditional) mean forecast. For the median, the bounds are given by the lower and upper values of the histogram intervals that contain 50% of the cumulative probability. But since the [2.0, 3.0] interval contains exactly 50% of the cumulative probability, the bound is increased to include the next bin; so for this histogram, the bound on the median is [2.0, 4.0]. The mode is given by the bin with the maximum probability; so here the bound on the mode is [2.0, 3.0].

Based on the percentages of point forecasts for the US-SPF (across respondents and surveys) that are within, below, and above the bounds calculated on the mean, median, and mode, Engelberg et al. (2009) conclude that point predictions may have a systematic, favorable bias in that when the point forecast does not lie within the bounds of any of the three central moments, the point forecasts are generally below the bounds for inflation and above the bounds for real GDP growth. However, an alternative interpretation is that the inaccuracy of the probabilistic forecasts is the source of this mismatch between the point predictions and the bounds (see Clements (2009, 2010, 2014a)).

3.4.2 Nature of loss functions – symmetric vs. asymmetric

Individuals may attach different costs to over- and under-predicting by the same amount. If their loss functions are asymmetric, then, as is well known, their forecasts will be biased (see, e.g., Granger (1969) and Zellner (1986)). The literature considers whether forecasts are rational once we allow forecasters to have asymmetric loss functions.

Under certain conditions on the data-generating process and the loss function, Patton and Timmermann (2007) show that the optimal forecast is given by

$$y_{i,t+h|t} = \mu_{i,t+h|t} + \phi_{ih} \cdot \sigma_{i,t+h|t}, \qquad (3.24)$$

where $\mu_{i,t+h|t}$ is respondent i's conditional mean, and $\sigma_{i,t+h|t}$ is the forecast standard deviation (or possibly the variance). The term ϕ_{ih} is a constant that depends on the form of the data-generating process and the loss function (e.g., the degree of asymmetry). As shown in (3.24), the conditional mean and optimal forecast will differ when point forecasts are optimal for an asymmetric loss function. This is a prima facie explanation of discrepancies between histogram means and point forecasts. The conditional mean and forecast standard deviation can of course be calculated from the histograms, provided we are prepared to make the sorts of assumptions that were avoided by the bounds approach.

Elliot et al. (2008) test for rationality allowing for a general loss function using the approach of Elliot et al. (2005). They find that rationality is rejected for fewer US-SPF respondents under asymmetric loss than when quadratic loss is imposed. However, Clements (2009, 2010) finds little evidence in favor of the asymmetric loss explanation for histogram/point forecast inconsistencies.

3.4.3 Rounding of point and density forecasts

Although there is evidence that consumers round their (point) forecasts to a striking degree (see, e.g., Binder (2017)), there is much less evidence that professional forecasters round their point forecasts to the same extent (Clements (2021b)). The literature has focused on the rounding of probability forecasts by professionals based on the observed reporting in histograms and, in the case of the US-SPF, the probability of GDP decline forecasts. Engelberg et al. (2009, Appendix, pp. 40–41) consider whether rounding of the histogram probabilities could explain apparent inconsistencies between the histograms and point forecasts. They propose a strategy to "undo" any presumed rounding of the histograms, but find that their results concerning the patterns of inconsistency are qualitatively unchanged.

Clements (2011) considers whether allowing for "plausible" patterns of rounding behavior affects the finding that one in three pairs of probability forecasts of a decline in real output and histograms for annual real output growth is not consistent. One aspect of his approach is to replace a point probability of a decline by an interval, when there is evidence that an individual reports rounded forecasts. This is based on the assumption that a respondent applies the same rounding rule each time he or she responds to an SPF survey question on the probability of decline (cf. Manski and Molinari (2010)). Allowing for rounding reduces the rate of inconsistent pairs of forecasts from one in three to one in four. While rounding has an effect, it is only a partial explanation of the observed inconsistencies. Glas and Hartmann (2022) find that rounders tend to understate uncertainty relative to non-rounders, especially at longer horizons. They undertake the same exercise as in Clements (2014b), comparing *ex ante* histogram uncertainty to *ex post* uncertainty, but separately for rounders and non-rounders, and find that the variance misalignment is less at longer horizons for non-rounders. That is, the degree of over-confidence at longer horizons is less for non-rounders.

3.5 Conclusion

Taken together, surveys of professional forecasters have provided critical insights into the expectations formation process. The surveys serve both to inform the development of expectations models and to test their implications, with the wide range of topics and extensive literature associated with the surveys indicating the extent of their contributions. The analysis of uncertainty afforded by the availability of density forecasts continues to draw considerable attention. Related issues such as the relationship between *ex ante* and *ex post* measures of uncertainty and the reliability of using forecast dispersion measures to proxy uncertainty remain areas of ongoing interest. The surveys also provide a basis for comparing the alignment of point forecasts and (estimated) means of the density forecasts as well as assessing the nature of forecasters' loss functions.

While surveys of professional forecasters have often been used for analyses at the aggregate level, interesting and important features emerge from examining the data at the individual level. For example, there is notable heterogeneity in forecast behavior that extends beyond first moments to include uncertainty, the degree of contrarianism, and accuracy. Moreover, and perhaps more importantly, there is growing evidence to suggest that this heterogeneity is persistent in nature. The possibility that these observed differences are systematic has important implications. At a minimum, this finding would call into question the view that professional forecasters can be treated as essentially identical and interchangeable, and future research should look to determine the source(s) of the persistent heterogeneity. This finding would also motivate studies to explore whether systematic differences in predictive behavior are unique to professional forecasters or if this characteristic extends to households and firms. If persistent heterogeneity is a general property, then this consideration would argue for the development of a new class of expectations models that are not only capable of generating differential forecast behavior but also providing mechanisms that can sustain such differences across time.

Appendix 3.A Appendix table: surveys of professional forecasters

This table provides a list of surveys of professional forecasters along with as much information on features of the surveys that we were able to locate. Some links direct the reader to a website, while in other cases the links direct the reader to a report or a research paper that discusses the survey in some capacity. Some categories may be incomplete.

Bank of England: *Survey of External Forecasters*

- *Background*   Started in Feb 1996, quarterly, with 23–38 participants
- *Forecast variables* GDP, Inflation, Unemployment Rate, Policy Rate, Exchange Rate
- *Horizons*   1-, 2-, and 3-year-ahead forecasts
- *Density forecasts*   Quarterly for GDP, inflation, unemployment rate, policy rate, and exchange rate at all horizons listed above, histogram
- *Data availability*   Micro panel data are available
- *Information from*   http://wrap.warwick.ac.uk/1421/, https://academic.oup.com/ej/article/118/530/1107/5088816, and https://onlinelibrary.wiley.com/doi/10.1002/jae.2400

Central Bank of Argentina: *Market Expectations Survey (REM)*

- *Background*   Started in Jan 2004, monthly, approximately 34 participants
- *Forecast variables* Inflation, Interest Rate, Nominal Exchange Rate, External Sector: Exports and Imports of Goods or Merchandise, Unemployment Rate, Activity: Growth Rate, Primary Result of the National Non-Financial Public Sector (NFPS)
- *Horizons*   2-month, current & 1-qtr-ahead, current & 1-yr-ahead
- *Density forecasts*   Not known
- *Data availability*   Aggregated data are available; micro panel data are not disclosed
- *Information from*   http://www.bcra.gob.ar/PublicacionesEstadisticas/Relevamiento_Expectativas_de_Mercado_i.asp and https://www.bis.org/ifc/publ/ifcb30i.pdf

Central Bank of Brazil: *Market Expectations – Focus Survey*

- *Background*   Started in May 1999; data can be submitted daily but respondent must submit at least once a month to be included in published reports; approximately 140 respondents
- *Forecast variables* GDP, Inflation, Short-Term Interest Rates, Exchange Rate, Balance of Payments, Trade Balance, FDI, Net Public Sector Debt
- *Horizons*   Inflation over next 12, 13–24 months
- *Density forecasts*   Not collected
- *Data availability*   Micro data are available for respondents providing consent with a one-year lag; weekly, monthly, and annual reports
- *Information from*   https://www.bcb.gov.br/en/monetarypolicy/marketexpectations and FAQ – Market Expectations System (bcb.gov.br)

Central Bank of Iceland: *Survey of Market Expectations*

- *Background*   Started in 2012, quarterly, approximately 31 respondents
- *Forecast variables* Inflation, Policy Rate, Exchange Rate

- *Horizons*   Current, 1-qtr & 2-qtr-ahead, inflation—2- & 10-year-ahead
- *Density forecasts*   Not known
- *Data availability*   Micro panel data are not available
- *Information from*   https://www.cb.is/statistics/various-measures-of-inflation-expectations/survey-of-market-expectations/

Central Bank of Indonesia: *Consensus Forecasts*

- *Background*   Started in 2001, quarterly, approximately 200 economists
- *Forecast variables*   GDP, Inflation, Exchange Rates
- *Horizons*   Average for current and 1-yr-ahead, 4-qtr average
- *Density forecasts*   Not known
- *Data availability*   Micro panel data availability is not known
- *Information from*   https://www.bis.org/ifc/events/7ifcconf_wuryandani_mardiani.pdf

Central Bank of Israel: *Macroeconomic Staff Forecast*

- *Background*   Started in 2001, daily (at least for some variables), approximately 14 respondents
- *Forecast variables*   Inflation, Bank of Israel Policy Rate, Exchange Rates; GDP Added in 2017
- *Horizons*   Current, 1-, 2- & 12-month-ahead; current & 1-year-ahead
- *Density forecasts*   Not collected
- *Data availability*   Micro panel data are available upon request
- *Information from*   https://www.sciencedirect.com/science/article/pii/S1059056021001350#

Central Bank of Turkey: *Survey of Market Participants*

- *Background*   Started in 2001, monthly since 2013, approximately 57 respondents
- *Forecast variables*   Inflation, Exchange Rates, Current Account Balance, GDP, Repo & Reverse Repo Rates
- *Horizons*   Inflation—Current, 1-, 2-month-ahead; end of current, 1- & 2-yr-ahead current account—current & 1-yr-ahead GDP—current & 1-yr-ahead average; Repo rates—end of current month
- *Density forecasts*   12-month-ahead annual consumer inflation expectations and 24-month-ahead annual consumer inflation expectations
- *Data availability*   Micro panel data are not available
- *Information from*   Email correspondence and https://www.tcmb.gov.tr/wps/wcm/connect/EN/TCMB+EN/Main+Menu/Statistics/Tendency+Surveys/Survey+of+Market+Participants/

Conference Board of Canada: *Survey of Forecasters*

- *Background*   Started in 1999 Q4, quarterly, 500 firms
- *Forecast variables*   GDP, Consumption Spending, and the Current Account Balance
- *Horizons*   2 year
- *Density forecasts*   Not collected
- *Data availability*   Aggregate data available with subscription; micro panel data are not available
- *Information from*   Email correspondence and https://www.bankofcanada.ca/wp-content/uploads/2010/06/cunningham.pdf

Consensus Economics: *Consensus Forecasts*

- *Background*   Started in 1989, monthly, approximately 700 economists
- *Forecast variables*   GDP, Inflation, Short-Term Interest Rates, Exchange Rate
- *Horizons*   Vary by forecast variable
- *Density forecasts*   No
- *Data availability*   Micro panel data are not available; consensus estimates are available on a subscription basis
- *Information from*   https://www.consensuseconomics.com/

Dutch National Bank: *Inflation Expectations Survey*

- *Background*   Started in July 2010, weekly with approximately 25 respondents
- *Forecast variables*   Euro area inflation
- *Horizons*   Current year, next year, and 10-yr-ahead
- *Density forecasts*   Quarterly for short- & long-term inflation expectations, histogram
- *Data availability*   Aggregate data available; micro panel data are not available
- *Information from*   https://www.bis.org/publ/work809.pdf

European Central Bank: *Survey of Professional Forecasters*

- *Background*   Started in January 1999, quarterly, approximately 60 respondents
- *Forecast variables*   GDP, Inflation, and Unemployment Rate, with Non-Compulsory Section on Wage Growth, Price of Oil, and Exchange Rate
- *Horizons*   Current calendar year, next calendar year, the calendar year after that, 1-year-ahead, 1-year/1-year forward, and a longer horizon
- *Density forecasts*   Quarterly for inflation, core inflation, GDP growth, and unemployment rate at all horizons listed above, histogram
- *Data availability*   Micro panel data are available
- *Information from*   https://www.ecb.europa.eu/stats/ecb_surveys/survey_of_professional_forecasters/html/index.en.html

Federal Reserve Bank of Philadelphia: *Survey of Professional Forecasters*

- *Background*   Started in Q4 1968, quarterly, approximately 40 respondents
- *Forecast variables*   GDP, Inflation, Unemployment Rate, Various Business Indicators, and Components of Real GDP
- *Horizons*   1-5-quarter-ahead levels and growth rates, Q4/Q4 growth, year-over-year growth, and a longer horizon
- *Density forecasts*   Quarterly for real GDP growth, inflation, and unemployment rate at varying short- and medium-run horizons
- *Data availability*   Micro panel data are available
- *Information from*   https://www.philadelphiafed.org/research-and-data/real-time-center/survey-of-professional-forecasters

Federal Reserve Bank of Philadelphia: *Livingston Survey*

- *Background*   Started in June 1946, semi-annual (June & Dec), 10–20 respondents

- *Forecast variables*   Quarterly: GDP, Non-Residential FI, After-Tax Corporate Profits; Monthly: IP, Housing Starts, PPI, CPI, Unemployment Rate, Avg Weekly Earnings in Mfg., Retail Sales, Auto Sales, Prime Interest Rate; 3-Month T-Bill Rate, 10-Year T-Note Rate, S&P 500
- *Forecast horizons*   Quarterly: current, 1-, 2-, & 4-qtrs-ahead, June—current & 1-yr-ahead, Dec—current yr, 1- & 2-yr-ahead; Monthly: current, 6- & 12-mth, June—current & 1-yr-ahead, Dec—current, 1- & 2-yr-ahead; June 1990—10-yr GDP & inflation
- *Density forecasts*   No
- *Data availability*   Micro panel data are available, and summaries are published semi-annually
- *Information from*   Livingston Survey (philadelphiafed.org)

Japan Center for Economic Research: *ESPF Survey*

- *Background*   Started in April 2004, monthly, approximately 40 respondents
- *Forecast variables*   GDP, Inflation Less Fresh Food, Unemployment Rate
- *Horizons*   GDP – quarter to quarter changes for current, 1-, 2- & 3-quarter-ahead; Inflation – year-on-year change
- *Density forecasts*   Not known
- *Data availability*   Aggregated data are available
- *Information from*   https://www.jcer.or.jp/en/esp-forecast-top and dp2017-04.pdf (kanagawa-u.ac.jp)

Ministry of Finance of the Czech Republic: *Survey of Macroeconomic Forecasts*

- *Background*   Started 1996, 2x/year, approximately 14 institutions
- *Forecast variables*   GDP, Inflation, Oil Price, Exchange Rates, Interest Rates, Employment, Unemployment Rate, Wages
- *Horizons*   3 years
- *Density forecasts*   Not known
- *Data availability*   Not known
- *Information from*   https://www.mfcr.cz/en/statistics/survey-of-macroeconomic-forecasts

Monetary Authority of Singapore: *Survey of Professional Forecasters*

- *Background*   Started in 1999 Q4, quarterly, approximately 20–30 respondents
- *Forecast variables*   GDP and Components, Headline and Core Inflation, Unemployment Rate, Short-Term Interest Rates, Exchange Rate
- *Horizons*   Annual average for current and next year, rolling horizon for quarters left in current year
- *Density forecasts*   GPP in 2001 Q3, inflation in 2017 Q1; histogram
- *Data availability*   Micro panel data are available
- *Information from*   Survey of Professional Forecasters Data Documentation (mas.gov.sg)

National Association for Business Economics: *NABE Outlook*

- *Background*   Started in 1965, quarterly with approximately 50 respondents
- *Forecast variables*   Macro variables

- *Horizons* — Not known
- *Density forecasts* — Not collected
- *Data availability* — Micro panel data are not available; consensus estimates are available on a sub-scription basis
- *Information from* — https://www.nabe.com/NABE/Surveys/Outlook_Surveys/december-2021-Outlook-Survey-Summary.aspx

National Bank of Poland: *Survey of Professional Forecasters*

- *Background* — Started in 2001, quarterly, approximately 20–30 respondents
- *Forecast variables* — GDP, Inflation, Unemployment Rate Exchange Rate, Oil Prices, Average Wage Growth, Euro Area GDP
- *Horizons* — Point forecasts – current year, 1-year, 2-year; Density forecasts – current year, 1-year, 2-year, annual average over next 5 years
- *Density forecasts* — Cumulative density – 5%, median, 95%
- *Data availability* — Micro panel data are available
- *Information from* — https://amakro.nbp.pl/amakro-forecaster/pages/about.nbp

National Bank of Ukraine: Survey of Experts

- *Background* — Started in July 2014, 6x/year, approximately 17 respondents
- *Forecast variables* — Inflation, Exchange Rate
- *Horizons* — 1- and 3-year
- *Density forecasts* — No
- *Data availability* — Aggregated and micro panel data are available
- *Information from* — https://voxukraine.org/en/inflation-expectations-in-ukraine-a-long-path-to-anchoring-en/ and https://bank.gov.ua/en/statistic/nbusurvey

Wolters Kluwer: *Blue Chip Economic Indicators*

- *Background* — Started in 1976, monthly, approximately 50 respondents
- *Forecast variables* — GDP, Inflation, Unemployment Rate, IP, Disposable Income, Non-Residential Fixed Investment, Pre-Tax Corporate Profits, 3-Month T-Bill Rate, Housing Starts, Auto and Light Truck Sales, Net Exports
- *Horizons* — Inflation 0 to 7 quarters ahead for the United States, 1 to 2 years ahead for other major economies
- *Density forecasts* — Not collected
- *Data availability* — Micro panel data available with subscription
- *Information from* — https://www.wolterskluwer.com/en/solutions/vitallaw-law-firms/blue-chip

Reserve Bank of Australia: *Survey of Market Economists*

- *Background* — Started in 1993, quarterly, approximately 10–20 respondents
- *Forecast variables* — Inflation
- *Horizons* — Year-end for current year and next year are asked in June and December, 5–10-year average added in mid-2015
- *Density forecasts* — No

- *Data availability*   Micro panel data are available
- *Information from*   https://www.rba.gov.au/publications/rdp/2016/pdf/rdp2016-02.pdf

Reserve Bank of India: *Survey of Professional Forecasters*

- *Background*   Started in Sept 2007, quarterly, approximately 40 respondents
- *Forecast variables*   GDP, Inflation, Consumption, Fixed Capital Formation, Imports, Exports, Current Account Deficit, Gross Value Added
- *Horizons*   Annual and quarterly averages
- *Density forecasts*   For GDP and inflation
- *Data availability*   Micro panel data are not available
- *Information from*   https://rbidocs.rbi.org.in/rdocs/Publications/PDFs/
                         SPF06022020E68670BBBFD5479B8B5785AD4F85FB43.PDF

Reserve Bank of New Zealand: *Survey of Expectations*

- *Background*   Started in 1987, quarterly, approximately 179 respondents
- *Forecast variables*   Inflation, Policy Rate, 10-Yr Gov't Bond Rate, GDP, Annual Wage Growth, Unemployment Rate, Exchange Rate, House Price Index
- *Horizons*   Inflation—1-, 2-, 5-yr-ahead; policy rate—current qtr, 1-yr-ahead; 10-yr gov't bond rate—end qtr, 1-yr-ahead; GDP, annual wage growth, unemployment rate, house price index—1- & 2-yr-ahead
- *Density forecasts*   Not known
- *Data availability*   Micro panel data are not available
- *Information from*   https://www.rbnz.govt.nz/statistics/m14

South African Reserve Bank: *Inflation Expectations Survey*

- *Background*   Started in Sept 2000, quarterly, approximately 40 financial sector respondents
- *Forecast variables*   Headline & Core Inflation, GDP, Prime Interest Rate, Exchange Rate, Gov't Bond Rate, M3 Supply Growth, Capacity Utilization in Mfg., Wage and Salary Growth
- *Horizons*   Current, 1- & 2-year-ahead; wage & salary – current & 1-yr-ahead
- *Density forecasts*   Expected inflation
- *Data availability*   Aggregated data are available; access to micro panel data is limited
- *Information from*   https://www.ber.ac.za/Reasearch/Method/Inflation-expectations/#IEShow

ZEW: *Financial Market Survey*

- *Background*   Started in 1991, monthly, approximately 270 (German) respondents
- *Forecast variables*   GDP, Inflation, Exchange Rates, Oil Prices for Eurozone, Germany, Japan, U.S., U.K., France, and Italy
- *Horizons*   Year-end for current year and next year are asked in June and December, 5–10-year average added in mid-2015
- *Density forecasts*   No
- *Data availability*   Micro panel data are not available

• *Information from* https://ftp.zew.de/pub/zew-docs/div/Kurzinfo_English.pdf and https://www.zew.de/en/publications/zew-expertises-research-reports/research-reports/business-cycle/zew-financial-market-survey

---

References

Abel, Andrew B., Eberly, Janice C., 1994. A unified model of investment under uncertainty. The American Economic Review 84, 1369–1384.

Abel, Joshua, Rich, Robert, Song, Joseph, Tracy, Joseph, 2016. The measurement and behavior of uncertainty: evidence from the ECB survey of professional forecasters. Journal of Applied Econometrics 31, 533–550.

Aiolfi, Marco, Capistrán, Carlos, Timmermann, Allan, 2011. Forecast combinations. In: Clements, Michael P., Hendry, David F. (Eds.), The Oxford Handbook of Economic Forecasting. Oxford University Press, Oxford, pp. 355–388.

Amador, Manuel, Weill, Pierre-Oliver, 2010. Learning from prices: public communication and welfare. Journal of Political Economy 118, 866–907.

Amisano, Gianni, Giacomini, Raffaella, 2007. Comparing density forecasts via weighted likelihood ratio tests. Journal of Business and Economic Statistics 25, 177–190.

Ang, Andrew, Bekaert, Geert, Wei, Min, 2007. Do macro variables, asset markets, or surveys forecast inflation better? Journal of Monetary Economics 54, 1163–1212.

Angeletos, George-Marios, Huo, Zhen, Sastry, Karthik A., 2020. Imperfect macroeconomic expectations: evidence and theory. In: Eichenbaum, Martin, Hurst, Erik (Eds.), Macroeconomic Annual, vol. 35. University of Chicago Press, Chicago, pp. 1–86.

Arroyo, Javier, Mate, Carlos, 2009. Forecasting histogram time-series with K-nearest neighbors methods. International Journal of Forecasting 25, 192–207.

Banternghansa, Chanont, McCracken, Michael W., 2009. Forecast Disagreement Among FOMC Members. Working Paper 2009-059. Federal Reserve Bank of Saint Louis.

Bao, Yong, Lee, Tae-Hwy, Saltoglu, Burak, 2007. Comparing density forecast models. Journal of Forecasting 26, 203–225.

Batchelor, Roy, Dua, Pami, 1996. Empirical measures of inflation uncertainty: a cautionary note. Applied Economics 28, 333–341.

Batchelor, Roy A., 1990. All forecasters are equal. Journal of Business and Economic Statistics 8, 143–144.

Bates, J.M., Granger, Clive W.J., 1969. The combination of forecasts. Operations Research Quarterly 20 (4), 451–468.

Beechey, Meredith J., Johannsen, Benjamin K., Levin, Andrew T., 2011. Are long-run inflation expectations anchored more firmly in the euro area than in the United States? American Economic Journal: Macroeconomics 3, 104–129.

Berge, Travis J., 2018. Understanding survey-based inflation expectations. International Journal of Forecasting 34, 788–801.

Berkowitz, Jeremy, 2001. Testing density forecasts with application to risk management. Journal of Business and Economic Statistics 19 (4), 465–474.

Bernanke, Ben S., 1983. Irreversibility, uncertainty, and cyclical investment. The Quarterly Journal of Economics 98, 85–106.

Binder, Carola C., 2017. Measuring uncertainty based on rounding: new method and application to inflation expectations. Journal of Monetary Economics 90, 1–12.

Bloom, Nicholas, 2009. The impact of uncertainty shocks. Econometrica 77, 623–685.

Bloom, Nicholas, Bond, Stephen, van Reenen, John, 2007. Uncertainty and investment dynamics. The Review of Economic Studies 74, 391–415.

Bloom, Nicholas, Floetotto, Max, Jaimovich, Nir, Saporata-Eksten, Itay, Terry, Stephen J., 2018. Really uncertain business cycles. Econometrica 86, 1031–1065.

Boero, Gianna, Smith, Jeremy, Wallis, Kenneth F., 2008a. Uncertainty and disagreement in economic prediction: the bank of England survey of external forecasters. The Economic Journal 118, 1107–1127.

Boero, Gianna, Smith, Jeremy, Wallis, Kenneth F., 2008b. Evaluating a three-dimensional panel of point forecasts: the bank of England survey of external forecasters. International Journal of Forecasting 24, 354–367.

Boero, Gianna, Smith, Jeremy, Wallis, Kenneth F., 2011. Scoring rules and survey density forecasts. International Journal of Forecasting 27, 379–393.

Boero, Gianna, Smith, Jeremy, Wallis, Kenneth F., 2015. The measurement and characteristics of professional forecasters' uncertainty. Journal of Applied Econometrics 30, 1029–1046.

Bordalo, Pedro, Gennaioli, Nicola, Ma, Yueran, Schleifer, Andrei, 2020. Overreaction in macroeconomic expectations. The American Economic Review 110, 2748–2782.

Bowles, Carlos, Friz, Roberta, Genre, Veronique, Kenny, Geoff, Meyler, Aidan, Rautanen, Tuomas, 2007. The ECB Survey of Professional Forecasters (SPF): a Review After Eight Years' Experience. ECB Occasional Paper No 59. European Central Bank.

Brier, Glenn W., 1950. Verification of forecasts expressed in terms of probability. Monthly Weather Review 78 (1), 1–3.

Broer, Tobias, Kohlhas, Alexandre N., 2018. Forecaster (Mis-)Behavior. Discussion Papers 12898. C.E.P.R.

Campbell, John Y., 2000. Asset pricing at the millennium. The Journal of Finance 55, 1515–1567.

Capistrán, Carlos, Timmermann, Allan, 2009. Forecast combination with entry and exit of experts. Journal of Business and Economic Statistics 27 (4), 428–440.

Carroll, Christopher D., 2003. Macroeconomic expectations of households and professional forecasters. The Quarterly Journal of Economics 118, 269–298.

Chan, Joshua C.C., Clark, Todd E., Koop, Gary, 2018. A new model of inflation, trend inflation, and long run inflation expectations. Journal of Money, Credit, and Banking 50, 5–53.

Christensen, Jens H., Diebold, Francis X., Strasser, George H., Rudebusch, Glenn D., 2008. Multivariate Comparisons of Predictive Accuracy. Federal Reserve Bank of San Francisco, Working Paper.

Clements, Michael P., 2004. Evaluating the bank of England density forecasts of inflation. The Economic Journal 114, 844–866.

Clements, Michael P., 2009. Internal consistency of survey respondents' forecasts: evidence based on the survey of professional forecasters. In: Castle, Jennifer L., Shephard, Neal (Eds.), The Methodology and Practice of Econometrics, a Festschrift in Honour of David F. Hendry. Oxford University Press, Oxford, pp. 206–226.

Clements, Michael P., 2010. Explanations of the inconsistencies in survey respondents' forecasts. European Economic Review 54, 536–549.

Clements, Michael P., 2011. An empirical investigation of the effects of rounding on the SPF probabilities of decline and output growth histograms. Journal of Money, Credit, and Banking 43, 207–220.

Clements, Michael P., 2014a. Probability distributions or point predictions? Survey forecasts of US output growth and inflation. International Journal of Forecasting 30, 99–117.

Clements, Michael P., 2014b. Forecast uncertainty – ex ante and ex post: US inflation and output growth. Journal of Business and Economic Statistics 32, 206–216.

Clements, Michael P., 2015. Are professional macroeconomic forecasters able to do better than forecasting trends? Journal of Money, Credit, and Banking 47, 349–381.

Clements, Michael P., 2018. Are macroeconomic density forecasts informative? International Journal of Forecasting 34, 181–198.

Clements, Michael P., 2019. Do forecasters target first or later releases of national accounts data? International Journal of Forecasting 35, 1240–1249.

Clements, Michael P., 2020. Are some forecasters' probability assessments of macro variables better than those of others? Econometrics MDPI 8, 16.

Clements, Michael P., 2021a. Do survey joiners and leavers differ from regular participants? International Journal of Forecasting 37, 634–646.

Clements, Michael P., 2021b. Rounding behaviour of professional macro-forecasters. International Journal of Forecasting 37, 1614–1631.

Clements, Michael P., 2022. Forecaster efficiency, accuracy and disagreement: evidence using individual-level survey data. Journal of Money, Credit, and Banking 54, 537–567.

Clements, Michael P., Gálvao, Ana Beatriz, 2017a. Predicting early data revisions to US GDP and the effects of releases on equity markets. Journal of Business and Economic Statistics 35, 389–406.

Clements, Michael P., Gálvao, Ana Beatriz, 2017b. Model and survey estimates of the term structure of US macroeconomic uncertainty. International Journal of Forecasting 33, 591–604.

Clements, Michael P., Gálvao, Ana Beatriz, 2019. Data revisions and real-time forecasting. In: The Oxford Research Encyclopedia of Economics and Finance. Oxford University Press, Oxford.

Clements, Michael P., Harvey, David I., 2009. Forecasting combination and encompassing. In: Mills, T.C., Patterson, K. (Eds.), Handbook of Econometrics. Palgrave MacMillan, London, pp. 169–198.

Coibion, Olivier, Gorodnichenko, Yuriy, 2012. What can survey forecasts tell us about information rigidities? Journal of Political Economy 120, 116–159.

Coibion, Olivier, Gorodnichenko, Yuriy, 2015a. Is the Phillips curve alive and well after all? Inflation expectations and the missing disinflation. American Economic Journal: Macroeconomics 7, 197–232.

Coibion, Olivier, Gorodnichenko, Yuriy, 2015b. Information rigidity and the expectations formation process: a simple framework and new facts. The American Economic Review 105, 2644–2678.

Coibion, Olivier, Gorodnichenko, Yuriy, Kamdar, Rupal, 2018. The formation of expectations, inflation, and the Phillips curve. Journal of Economic Literature 56, 1447–1491.

Croushore, Dean, 1993. Introducing: the Survey of Professional Forecasters. Federal Reserve Bank of Philadelphia Business Review. pp. 3–15.

Croushore, Dean, 2006. Forecasting with real-time macroeconomic data. In: Elliott, Graham, Granger, Clive, Timmermann, Allan (Eds.), Handbook of Economic Forecasting, vol. 1. Elsevier, North Holland, pp. 961–982.

Croushore, Dean, 2011a. Forecasting with real-time data vintages. In: Clements, Michael P., Hendry, David F. (Eds.), The Oxford Handbook of Economic Forecasting. Oxford University Press, Oxford, pp. 247–267.

Croushore, Dean, 2011b. Frontiers of real-time data analysis. Journal of Economic Literature 49, 72–100.

Croushore, Dean, Stark, Tom, 2019. Fifty years of professional forecasters. Economic Inquiry, 1–11.

D'Agostino, Antonello, McQuinn, Kieran, Whelan, Karl, 2012. Are some forecasters really better than others? Journal of Money, Credit, and Banking 44, 715–732.

D'Amico, Stefania, Orphanides, Athanasios, 2008. Uncertainty and Disagreement in Economic Forecasting. Finance and Economics Discussion Series 2008-56. Federal Reserve Board, Washington DC.

D'Amico, Stefania, Orphanides, Athanasios, 2014. Inflation Uncertainty and Disagreement in Bond Risk Premia. Working Paper Series WP-2014-24. Federal Reserve Bank of Chicago.

Dawid, A.P., 1984. Statistical theory: the prequential approach. Journal of the Royal Statistical Society 147, 278–292.

Diebold, Francis X., Gunther, Todd A., Tay, Anthony S., 1998. Evaluating density forecasts with applications to financial risk management. International Economic Review 39, 863–883.

Diebold, Francis X., Mariano, Roberto S., 1995. Comparing predictive accuracy. Journal of Business and Economic Statistics 13, 253–263.

Diebold, Francis X., Tay, Anthony S., Wallis, Kenneth F., 1999. Evaluating density forecasts of inflation: the survey of professional forecasters. In: Engle, Robert F., White, Halbert (Eds.), Cointegration, Causality, and Forecasting: A Festschrift in Honour of Clive W. J. Granger. Oxford University Press, Oxford and New York, pp. 76–90.

Dietrich, J. Kimball, Joines, Douglas H., 1983. Rational expectations, informational efficiency, and tests using survey data: a comment. Review of Economics and Statistics 65, 525–529.

Dixit, Avinash K., 1989. Entry and exit decisions under uncertainty. Journal of Political Economy 97, 620–638.

Dixit, Avinash K., Pindyck, Robert S., 1994. Investment Under Uncertainty. Princeton University Press, Princeton.

Dovern, Jonas, Kenny, Geoff, 2020. Anchoring inflation expectations in unconventional times: micro evidence for the euro area. International Journal of Central Banking 16, 309–347.

Elliot, Graham, Komunjer, Ivana, Timmermann, Allan, 2005. Estimation and testing of forecast rationality under flexible loss. The Review of Economic Studies 72, 1107–1125.

Elliot, Graham, Komunjer, Ivana, Timmermann, Allan, 2008. Biases in macroeconomic forecasts: irrationality or asymmetric loss? Journal of the European Economic Association 6 (1), 122–157.

Elliott, Graham, Timmermann, Allan, 2004. Optimal forecast combinations under general loss functions and forecast error distributions. Journal of Econometrics 122, 47–79.

Engelberg, Joseph, Manski, Charles F., Williams, Jared, 2009. Comparing the point predictions and subjective probability distributions of professional forecasters. Journal of Business and Economic Statistics 27, 30–41.

Engelberg, Joseph, Manski, Charles F., Williams, Jared, 2011. Assessing the temporal variation of macroeconomic forecasts by a panel of changing composition. Journal of Applied Econometrics 26, 1059–1078.

Engle, Robert F., 1982. Autoregressive conditional heteroskedasticity with estimates of the variance of United Kingdom inflation. Econometrica 50, 987–1007.

Epstein, Edward S., 1969. A scoring system for probability forecasts of ranked categories. Journal of Applied Meteorology 8, 985–987.

Faust, Jon, Wright, Jonathan H., 2009. Comparing greenbook and reduced form forecasts using a large realtime dataset. Journal of Business and Economic Statistics 27 (4), 468–479.

Faust, Jon, Wright, Jonathan H., 2013. Forecasting inflation. In: Elliott, Graham, Granger, Clive, Timmermann, Allan (Eds.), Handbook of Economic Forecasting, vol 2A. Elsevier Science, North-Holland, pp. 2–56.

Favara, Giovanni, Song, Zheng, 2014. House price dynamics with dispersed information. Journal of Economic Theory 149, 350–382.

Figlewski, Stephen, Wachtel, Paul, 1981. The formation of inflationary expectations. Review of Economics and Statistics 63, 1–10.

Figlewski, Stephen, Wachtel, Paul, 1983. Rational expectations, informational efficiency, and tests using survey data: a reply. Review of Economics and Statistics 65, 529–531.

Ganics, Gergely, Rossi, Barbara, Sekhposyan, Tatevik, 2020. From Fixed-Event to Fixed-Horizon Density Forecasts: Obtaining Measures of Multi-Horizon Uncertainty from Survey Density Forecasts. CEPR Discussion Paper No. DP14267.

Garcia, Juan A., 2003. An Introduction to the ECB's Survey of Professional Forecasters. ECB Occasional Paper No 8. European Central Bank.

Geanakoplos, John, 2010. The leverage cycle. In: NBER Macroeconomics Annual 2009. University of Chicago Press, Chicago and London, pp. 1–65.

Genre, Veronique, Kenny, Geoff, Meyler, Adian, Timmermann, Allan, 2013. Combining expert forecasts: can anything beat the simple average? International Journal of Forecasting 29, 108–121.

Giordani, Paolo, Söderlind, Paul, 2003. Inflation forecast uncertainty. European Economic Review 47, 1037–1059.

Giordani, Paolo, Söderlind, Paul, 2006. Is there evidence of pessimism and doubt in subjective distributions? Implications for the equity premium puzzle. Journal of Economic Dynamics and Control 30, 1027–1043.

Glas, Alexander, 2020. Five dimensions of the uncertainty-disagreement linkage. International Journal of Forecasting 36, 607–627.

Glas, Alexander, Hartmann, Matthias, 2016. Inflation uncertainty, disagreement and monetary policy: evidence from the ECB survey of professional forecasters. Journal of Empirical Finance 39, 215–228.

Glas, Alexander, Hartmann, Matthias, 2022. Uncertainty measures from partially rounded probabilistic forecast surveys. Quantitative Economics 13, 979–1022.

Granger, Clive W., 1969. Prediction with a generalized cost of error function. Operations Research Quarterly 20, 199–207.

Granger, Clive W., Machina, Mark J., 2006. Forecasting and decision theory. In: Elliott, Graham, Granger, Clive, Timmermann, Allan (Eds.), Handbook of Economic Forecasting, vol. 1. Elsevier Science, North Holland, pp. 81–98.

Granger, Clive W., Ramanathan, Ramu, 1984. Improved methods of combining forecasts. Journal of Forecasting 3, 197–204.

Grothe, Magdalena, Meyler, Aidan, 2018. Inflation forecasts: are market-based and survey-based measures informative? International Journal of Financial Research 9 (1), 171–188.

Handley, Kyle, Limao, Nuno, 2015. Trade and investment under policy uncertainty: theory and firm evidence. American Economic Journal: Economic Policy 7, 189–222.

Handley, Kyle, Limao, Nuno, 2017. Policy uncertainty, trade, and welfare: theory and evidence for China and the United States. The American Economic Review 107, 2731–2783.

Keane, Michael F., Runkle, David E., 1990. Testing the rationality of price forecasts: new evidence from panel data. The American Economic Review 80, 714–735.

Kenny, Geoff, Kostka, Thomas, Masera, Federico, 2014. How informative are the subjective density forecasts of macroeconomists? Journal of Forecasting 33, 163–185.

Kenny, Geoff, Kostka, Thomas, Masera, Federico, 2015. Density characteristics and density forecast performance: a panel analysis. Empirical Economics 48, 1203–1231.

Knüppel, Malte, 2015. Evaluating the calibration of multi-step-ahead density forecasts using raw moments. Journal of Business and Economic Statistics 33 (2), 270–281.

Knüppel, Malte, Schultefrankenfeld, Guido, 2019. Assessing the uncertainty in central banks' inflation outlooks. International Journal of Forecasting 35, 1748–1769.

Knüppel, Malte, Vladu, Stefan, 2016. Approximating Fixed-Horizon Forecasts Using Fixed-Event Forecasts. Discussion Paper 28-2016. Deutsche Bundesbank, Research Centre.

Krüger, Fabian, 2017. Survey-based forecast distributions for euro area growth and inflation. Empirical Economics 53, 234–246.

Lahiri, Kajal, Liu, Fushang, 2006. Modelling multi-period inflation uncertainty using a panel of density forecasts. Journal of Applied Econometrics 21, 1199–1219.

Lahiri, Kajal, Sheng, Xuguang, 2010. Measuring forecast uncertainty by disagreement: the missing link. Journal of Applied Econometrics 25, 514–538.

Leahy, John V., Whited, Toni M., 1996. The effects of uncertainty on investment: some stylized facts. Journal of Money, Credit, and Banking 28, 64–83.

Liu, Yang, Sheng, Simon, 2019. The measurement and transmission of macroeconomic uncertainty: evidence from the U.S. and BRICC countries. International Journal of Forecasting 35, 967–979.

Lorenzoni, Guido, 2009. A theory of demand shocks. The American Economic Review 99, 2050–2084.

Mankiw, Gregory N., Reis, Ricardo, 2002. Sticky information versus sticky prices: a proposal to replace the new Keynesian Phillips curve. The Quarterly Journal of Economics 117, 1295–1328.

Mankiw, Gregory N., Shapiro, Matthew D., 1986. News or noise: an analysis of GNP revisions - survey of current business. Survey of Current Business 66, 20–25.

Manski, Charles F., 2007. Identification for Prediction and Decision. Harvard University Press, Cambridge, MA.

Manski, Charles F., 2011. Interpreting and combining heterogeneous survey forecasts. In: Clements, Michael P., Hendry, D.F. (Eds.), Oxford Handbook of Economic Forecasting. Oxford University Press, Oxford, pp. 457–472.

Manski, Charles F., Molinari, Francesca, 2010. Rounding probabilistic expectations in surveys. Journal of Business and Economic Statistics 28 (2), 219–231.

Manzan, Sebastiano, 2011. Differential interpretation in the survey of professional forecasters. Journal of Money, Credit, and Banking 43 (530), 993–1017.

Meyler, Aidan, 2020. Forecast Performance in the ECB SPF: Ability or Chance? Working Paper Series. European Central Bank.

Mincer, Jacob A., Zarnowitz, Victor, 1969. The evaluation of economic forecasts. In: Mincer, Jacob A. (Ed.), Economic Forecasts and Expectations: Analysis of Forecasting Behavior and Performance. National Bureau of Economic Research, New York, pp. 3–46.

Morris, Stephen, Shin, Hyun Song, 2002. Social value of public information. The American Economic Review 92, 1521–1534.

Muth, John F., 1961. Rational expectations and the theory of price movements. Econometrica 29, 315–335.

Nordhaus, William D., 1987. Forecasting efficiency: concepts and applications. Review of Economics and Statistics 69, 667–674.

Novy, Dennis, Taylor, Alan M., 2020. Trade and uncertainty. Review of Economics and Statistics 102, 749–765.

O'Hagan, Anthony, Buck, Caitlin E., Daneshkhah, Alireza, Eiser, J. Richard, Garthwaite, Paul H., Jenkinson, David J., Oakley, Jeremey E., Rakow, Tim, 2006. Uncertain Judgements: Eliciting Experts' Probabilities. John Wiley and Sons, Ltd.

Patton, Andrew J., Timmermann, Allan, 2007. Testing forecast optimality under unknown loss. Journal of the American Statistical Association 102, 1172–1184.

Patton, Andrew J., Timmermann, Allan, 2010. Why do forecasters disagree? Lessons from the term structure of cross-sectional dispersion. Journal of Monetary Economics 57, 803–820.

Patton, Andrew J., Timmermann, Allan, 2012. Forecast rationality tests based on multi-horizon bounds. Journal of Business and Economic Statistics 30 (1), 36–40.

Pesaran, M. Hashem, 1987. The Limits to Rational Expectations. Basil Blackwell, Oxford.

Poncela, Pilar, Senra, Eva, 2017. Measuring uncertainty and assessing its predictive power in the euro area. Empirical Economics 53, 165–182.

Rich, Robert W., Tracy, Joseph, 2010. The relationships among expected inflation, disagreement, and uncertainty: evidence from matched point and density forecasts. Review of Economics and Statistics 92, 200–207.

Rich, Robert W., Tracy, Joseph, 2021a. All Forecasters Are Not the Same: Time-Varying Predictive Ability Across Forecast Environments. Working Paper WP 21-06. Federal Reserve Bank of Cleveland.

Rich, Robert W., Tracy, Joseph, 2021b. A closer look at the behavior of uncertainty and disagreement: micro evidence from the euro area. Journal of Money, Credit, and Banking 53, 233–253.

Rosenblatt, Murray, 1952. Remarks on a multivariate transformation. The Annals of Mathematical Statistics 23 (3), 470–472.

Rossi, Barbara, Sekhposyan, Tatevik, 2016. Forecast rationality tests in the presence of instabilities with application to federal reserve and survey forecasts. Journal of Applied Econometrics 31, 507–532.

Schaal, Edouard, 2017. Uncertainty and unemployment. Econometrica 85, 1675–1721.

Sims, Christopher A., 2009. Inflation Expectations, Uncertainty and Monetary Policy. Working Paper 275. Bank for International Settlements.

Smets, Frank, Warne, Anders, Wouters, Rafael, 2014. Professional forecasters and real-time forecasting with a DSGE model. International Journal of Forecasting 30, 981–995.

Snowberg, Erik, Wolfers, Justin, Zitzewitz, Eric, 2013. Prediction markets for economic forecasting. In: Elliott, Graham, Granger, Clive, Timmermann, Allan (Eds.), Handbook of Economic Forecasting, vol. 2. Elsevier Science, North Holland, pp. 657–687.

Söderlind, Paul, 2011. Inflation risk premia and survey evidence on macroeconomic uncertainty. International Journal of Central Banking 7, 113–133.

Stark, Tom, 2013. SPF Panelists' Forecasting Methods: a Note on the Aggregate Results of a November 2009 Special Survey. Research Department, Federal Reserve Bank of Philadelphia.

Stekler, H.O., 1987. Who forecasts better? Journal of Business and Economic Statistics 5, 155–158.

Tian, Weidong, Yan, Hong, 2009. Heterogeneous Beliefs, Imitation, and the Viability of Financial Innovation. Working Paper. University of North Carolina at Charlotte.

Tomura, Hajime, 2013. Heterogeneous beliefs and housing-market boom–bust cycles. Journal of Economic Dynamics and Control 37, 735–755.

Turnovsky, Stephen J., Wachter, Michael L., 1972. A test of the 'expectations hypothesis' using directly observed wage and price expectations. Review of Economics and Statistics 54, 47–54.

Wallis, Kenneth F., 2005. Combining density and interval forecasts: a modest proposal. Oxford Bulletin of Economics and Statistics 67, 983–994.

Woodford, Michael, 2003. Imperfect common knowledge and the effects of monetary policy. In: Aghion, Philippe, Frydman, Roman, Stiglitz, Joseph, Woodford, Michael (Eds.), Knowledge, Information, and Expectations in Modern Macroeconomics: In Honor of Edmund S. Phelps. Princeton University Press, Princeton.

Zarnowitz, Victor, 1969. The new ASA-NBER survey of forecasts by economic statisticians. American Statistician 23, 12–16.

Zarnowitz, Victor, Lambros, Louis A., 1987. Consensus and uncertainty in economic predictions. Journal of Political Economy 95, 591–621.

Zellner, Arnold, 1986. Biased predictors, rationality and the evaluation of forecasts. Economics Letters 21 (1), 45–48.

Survey experiments on economic expectations[☆]

Andreas Fuster[a,b] **and Basit Zafar**[c,d]

[a]*EPFL, Swiss Finance Institute, Lausanne, Switzerland*
[b]*CEPR, London, United Kingdom*
[c]*University of Michigan, Ann Arbor, MI, United States*
[d]*NBER, Cambridge, MA, United States*

4.1 Introduction

In recent years, there has been increased interest in subjective expectations as a driver of economic behaviors, as is reflected by the publication of this *Handbook*. A first key step to understand the role of expectations is the ability to measure expectations, as is commonly done in surveys. Such data then allow the researcher to estimate models of decision-making by relaxing standard assumptions (such as full information rational expectations). While such an approach does not require the researcher to observe the respondent's information set and to understand how expectations are formed, doing so is necessary for counterfactuals, when the researcher wants to understand how behavior and expectations may change in different scenarios. This typically requires some plausibly exogenous variation in expectations. An increasingly popular way to obtain such exogenous variation is via experiments in surveys, which we will review in this chapter.

We begin by outlining the conceptual arguments for why experimentally induced variation in expectations is useful to understand decision-making, and also to understand expectation formation itself. Next, we review the most commonly used experimental paradigm, so-called information provision experiments. Here, we complement a comprehensive recent review paper by Haaland et al. (2021), who show that the number of published papers in top economics journals that use such experiments has strongly increased in recent years. Rather than discussing the wide variety of applications of the paradigm, which will also be covered in other chapters in this Handbook, we restrict ourselves to a few examples in the areas that we have worked in, namely human capital investments and macroeconomics/finance. We also provide an overview of selected methodological issues related to this paradigm.

We then turn to extensions of and alternatives to randomized information provision. One extension is to move beyond exogenously providing a given piece of information and instead allowing survey respondents to choose which information (if any) they want to see. Incorporating this aspect arguably brings the experimental setting closer to everyday decision situations. An alternative approach we

---

[☆] We thank the editors and participants at the Handbook conference for helpful comments and suggestions.

discuss is the elicitation of conditional expectations in a number of assumed states of the world (or "vignettes"). This approach can allow researchers to collect much richer data, though may not be equally suitable for all settings. Finally, we provide some directions for future work.

4.2 Why (field) experiments on expectations?

Survey experiments on expectations are primarily useful for two purposes: one, for understanding decision-making under uncertainty; second, for understanding the process of expectation formation. In this section, we outline each of these identification issues, in turn.

4.2.1 Understanding decision-making

Researchers in economics are typically interested in understanding determinants of choices. Specifically, the researcher is interested in recovering the preference parameters and factors of the economic environment that can explain choices. For the sake of exposition, we focus on the choice of college major here; the same arguments apply to any choice under uncertainty. The arguments presented here are a simplified version of those presented in Wiswall and Zafar (2015a); interested readers should refer to the paper for a more in-depth discussion.

Going back to Freeman (1971), economists have been interested in understanding how sensitive educational choices are to potential earnings. Take the following reduced-form model:

$$(\ln \pi_{k,i} - \ln \pi_{\tilde{k},i}) = \beta_0 + \beta_1(\ln w_{k,i} - \ln w_{\tilde{k},i}) + C_i'\delta + v_k + \psi_{k,i}, \tag{4.1}$$

where $\pi_{k,i}$ is individual i's subjective probability of graduating with major k, $w_{k,i}$ are the earnings for individual i in major k, C_i is a vector of individual-specific characteristics, v_k is a major k fixed effect, and $\tilde{k}$ is the reference major. The residual error $\psi_{k,i}$ equals $\gamma_{k,i} - \gamma_{\tilde{k},i} + \varepsilon_{k,i}$, that is, it consists of unobserved relative taste differences $(\gamma_{k,i} - \gamma_{\tilde{k},i})$ and a component $\varepsilon_{k,i}$ which reflects all other residual components. The goal is to recover β_1, which tells us how sensitive major choice is to the earnings (note that the log–log form of the regression means that β_1 has an "elasticity" interpretation). Without data on subjective expectations, identification requires three additional layers of assumptions:

1. An assumed mapping between revealed or actual earnings in the individual's chosen major to beliefs;
2. An assumed model for counterfactual beliefs about earnings in majors not chosen by the individual; and
3. An assumed distribution of tastes for all majors.

Cross-sectional data on expectations allows the researcher to relax the first two assumptions. In that case, Eq. (4.1) becomes

$$(\ln \pi_{k,i} - \ln \pi_{\tilde{k},i}) = \beta_0 + \beta_1(\ln \hat{w}_{k,i} - \ln \hat{w}_{\tilde{k},i}) + C_i'\delta + v_k + \psi_{k,i}, \tag{4.2}$$

where $\hat{w}_{k,i}$ is i's beliefs about earnings in major k. Using beliefs and choice data at *only* one point in time, a cross-sectional OLS estimation of Eq. (4.2) is unbiased only if the residual term—which includes individual components reflecting individual variation in tastes for each of the majors in this example—is uncorrelated with beliefs about earnings, an assumption that is unlikely to hold in reality. In the absence of data on beliefs and choices at multiple points in time, there is little else that a researcher can do. Now, if the researcher had data on choices and beliefs at another point in time, then she could estimate Eq. (4.2) in differences and net out the individual taste components $(\gamma_{k,i} - \gamma_{\bar{k},i})$, that is,

$$[(\ln \pi'_{k,i} - \ln \pi'_{\bar{k},i}) - (\ln \pi_{k,i} - \ln \pi_{\bar{k},i})] = \beta_0 + \beta_1 [(\ln \hat{w}'_{k,i} - \ln \hat{w}'_{\bar{k},i}) - (\ln \hat{w}_{k,i} - \ln \hat{w}_{\bar{k},i})]$$
$$+ \epsilon'_{k,i} - \epsilon_{k,i},$$

where $\pi'_{k,i}$ and $\hat{w}'_{k,i}$ are the stated probabilistic choices and earnings beliefs at a second point in time. The estimates of this model are equivalent to adding individual fixed effects (FE) as individual dummy variable indicators to Eq. (4.2).

So how does one get data on probabilistic choices and earnings at multiple points in time? One obvious approach is to track individuals over time and collect panel data on beliefs and choices. However, identification requires that the *change* in beliefs about unobserved events or measurement error, given by $\epsilon'_{k,i} - \epsilon_{k,i}$, is mean-independent of the *changes* in observed beliefs about earnings. The issue with longitudinal information on beliefs collected over several months or years is that the individual and major-specific taste parameters $\gamma_{k,i}$ may change. Instead, if the researcher is able to experimentally perturb beliefs and choices *within* a survey, one can credibly claim that the identification arguments hold (that is, tastes are likely to be truly time invariant over the horizon of a survey). Violations of the assumption would occur if the experimental perturbation also changes beliefs about outcomes that the researcher does not ask about. This is not directly testable, but the researcher could collect data on other major-related outcomes both before and after the experimental intervention. This is the approach that Wiswall and Zafar (2015a) use to estimate the sensitivity of college major choice to earnings. An added advantage of a stylized information experiment embedded in a survey is that the shock to the individual's information set is truly exogenous, and hence the identifying variation is "clean."

An alternative approach to generate arguably exogenous variation in expectations and choices is to rely on "natural experiments." For example, researchers have leveraged cross-sectional variation across counties in the ideological predisposition of constituents to use election outcomes as an exogenous shifter of expectations and sentiment (Mian et al., 2015; Conlon and Zafar, 2017; Benhabib and Spiegel, 2018; De Stefani, 2021). Likewise, surprise monetary policy announcements have been shown to impact consumers' confidence in the state of the economy (Lewis et al., 2019). These studies show a strong immediate impact on sentiment. The impact on expectations, though, generally tends to be weaker. It is also not clear *which* expectations are really affected by such shocks. Hence, it is not surprising that many of these studies find only limited impact on behavior.

Herein lies the trade-off between stylized survey-based information experiments and natural experiments. Stylized experiments are powerful in the sense that, by design, the information is salient and hence likely to impact expectations. Natural experiments accord less control to the researcher. In addition, few individuals may have been attentive to the event. However, natural settings are arguably more reflective of how individuals go about acquiring information in the real world, and are less susceptible to an experimenter demand effect. Later in the chapter, we discuss how survey experiments may incorporate some of this realism.

4.2.2 Understanding expectation formation

A more common use of information experiments to date has been to study the process of expectation formation. This is relevant not only for policy, in the sense of inferring whether individuals have accurate expectations, but also for informing the modeling of expectations. Returning to the example above, let $i's$ earnings expectations in major k be given by

$$\hat{w}_{k,i} = f(\Omega_i),$$

where Ω_i is i's information set at a given point in time that she uses to form earnings expectations. The researcher's goal is to say something about the function f and about what the possible components of the information set are, but neither are easily observable. The researcher may have a prior about the elements of the information set. Suppose the researcher thinks that the individual may base her earnings beliefs in major k, in part, on her beliefs about what college graduates earn (let us denote this as z) and that i's beliefs about z may be biased, that is, $\hat{z}_i \neq z$. To test this, the researcher can provide objective information about z to the individual, and reelicit her earnings expectations $\hat{w}'_{k,i}$. If $\hat{w}'_{k,i}$ differs from the preinformation expectations $\hat{w}_{k,i}$, that tells us that in fact z is an element of the individual's information set *and* that she had biased beliefs about it.

Now, if the reelicited expectations are exactly the same as baseline expectations, that could imply one of two things: (1) z is not an element of i's information set, or (2) z is in fact an element of i's information set but i has correct beliefs about z. To tell apart these two very different implications, the researcher needs to elicit i's beliefs about z *before* the information is given to her.[1]

4.3 Information provision experiments

The most common experimental paradigm within surveys has been the randomized provision of information. Expectations can then also be linked to (intended or actual) economic behaviors. In this section, we describe the basic ingredients of this paradigm, and then discuss a few examples from different areas. We focus our discussion mainly on details of the design, less on results (since those will be discussed in later chapters in this Handbook).

4.3.1 Design basics

Most information provision experiments in the literature consist of three main stages:

1. Measurement of respondents' prior expectations about the variable(s) of interest, y, and/or the variable(s) about which information will be provided, x. We denote i's prior expectations by $\hat{y}_{i,prior}$ and $\hat{x}_{i,prior}$.
2. One of K possible pieces of information, or signals, is randomly provided to respondents. We denote the signal received by respondent i as x_i.

---

[1] There is another possibility: it could be that z is in individual i's information set, and i is misinformed about z but does not find the provided information credible/trustworthy. Empirical work, to date, has not systematically investigated this possibility. We return to this issue in Section 4.4.4.

3. Respondents' posteriors $\hat{y}_{i,post}$ are measured, as well as potentially (intended or actual) behaviors that $\hat{y}_i$ should plausibly influence.

Various different implementations of the three steps above can be found in the literature. For example:

- Expectations about the variable of interest y are measured either as full subjective distributions, as prominently advocated by Manski (2004), or as point forecasts (but often with a qualitative question about the respondents' confidence in their forecast). The measurement method can also differ between steps 1 and 3.
- Variable x is often information about past realized y (sometimes provided over different past horizons across respondents), some factual information, or expert forecast(s).
- In some cases, all respondents are provided with some piece of information (varying across respondents) while in other cases, only some respondents receive information while a control group does not.
- It is also possible to provide a group of respondents with more than one signal, and compare them to respondents who receive only one or the other signal.
- In addition to respondents' own expectations, higher-order beliefs (beliefs about the expectations of others) can be elicited (Coibion et al., 2021b).

Since information x_i is randomized across respondents, one can in principle directly estimate the treatment effect of a given piece of information on posterior beliefs:

$$\hat{y}_{i,post} = \alpha + \sum_{k=1}^{K} \beta_k I(x_i = x^k) + \varepsilon_i, \tag{4.3}$$

where $I(x_i = x^k)$ is a dummy variable indicating that respondent i received signal k.

Although this regression allows one to cleanly estimate the effect of a signal k on average posterior expectations, it is not necessarily informative about the effects on individual expectations. To see why, imagine that different respondents' priors are symmetrically distributed around a signal. Then, even if respondents' fully align their posteriors with the signal if they receive it, the average posterior would be unaffected, as those with priors above the signal revised their beliefs downwards, and vice versa for those with priors below the signal.

To better capture how receiving a given signal k affects beliefs, it is therefore common to relate a respondent's posterior belief to the difference between the signal and the respondent's prior *about the signal*, often called the "perception gap":

$$\hat{y}_{i,post} = \alpha + \sum_{k=1}^{K} \beta_k \underbrace{I(x_i = x^k)}_{\substack{\text{Treatment} \\ \text{Indicator}}} \underbrace{(x^k - \hat{x}_{i,prior}^k)}_{\substack{\text{Perception} \\ \text{Gap}}} + \varepsilon_i. \tag{4.4}$$

Furthermore, when the prior about the outcome was measured, researchers often directly use the belief *update* (= posterior minus prior) as the dependent variable:

$$(\hat{y}_{i,post} - \hat{y}_{i,prior}) = \alpha + \sum_{k=1}^{K} \beta_k I(x_i = x^k)(x^k - \hat{x}_{i,prior}^k) + \varepsilon_i. \tag{4.5}$$

A nice feature of this formulation is that it can naturally be linked to a Bayesian learning model with Gaussian distributions, where the posterior is the weighted average of a person's prior, with weight $1 - \omega$, and a signal received, with weight ω. This weight ω in this case corresponds to the coefficient β_k. Theoretically, β_k should then decrease in the dispersion of a respondent's prior (somebody who is already very confident in their forecast will update little in response to a signal). Furthermore, it should increase in the (perceived) precision of the signal. See, e.g., Cavallo et al. (2017) for additional discussion.

In practice, Eq. (4.5) above is estimated including not only the interaction between the treatment indicator and the perception gap, but also the two terms separately.[2] Simplifying to the case of a single signal x that randomly gets shown to only some respondents, the regression would then be specified as

$$(\hat{y}_{i,post} - \hat{y}_{i,prior}) = \alpha + \beta I(x_i = x)(x - \hat{x}_{i,prior}) + \gamma_1 I(x_i = x) + \gamma_2(x - \hat{x}_{i,prior}) + \varepsilon_i. \tag{4.6}$$

The coefficient of interest is still β, but the two additional coefficients are useful in their own right: γ_1 allows testing whether receiving a signal that does not differ from a respondent's prior about the signal has a systematic effect on updating (or on posterior beliefs), while γ_2, which is estimated off of the control group, accounts for the possibility that respondents' revisions may be correlated with their priors, for instance due to "noise" in the answers in the prior stage.

In addition to individual updating, researchers also often study how receiving a given signal affects the dispersion of posterior expectations within a group that receives the same signal or across groups that receive different signals.

Finally, the basic design is often augmented by a fourth stage, where expectations are again elicited in a follow-up survey that is run a few weeks (or sometimes a few months) after the original survey. One can then repeat the regressions above using $\hat{y}_{i,followup}$ instead of $\hat{y}_{i,posterior}$ as dependent variable. Such follow-up data is useful to measure the persistence of the effects of the information, and is often used to dismiss demand effects or simple numerical anchoring to the provided information as drivers of effects within the main survey.[3]

---

[2] One can also estimate a version of Eq. (4.5) where the dependent variable is the posterior, instead of the update. In that case, $\hat{y}_{i,prior}$ is included on the right-hand-side. This specification is more flexible. However, most work uses revisions as the dependent variable since the estimates are easier to interpret.

[3] An alternative way to assess the strength of numerical anchoring is to feature a placebo treatment in which a number on an unrelated topic is provided. Coibion et al. (2022) do so in their study of inflation expectations, providing one group with information on population growth. They find only very small effects of this treatment, suggesting that numerical anchoring is not a big concern in such studies.

4.3.2 Expectations and behavior

To the extent that the randomized information provision shifts respondents' expectations, this exogenous shift can then be used to study the effect of expectations on economic behaviors that, according to theory, should be driven by expectations. This, of course, requires data on behavior, which is not always readily available. We discuss this issue in the next subsection.

If the randomized information provision differentially affected respondents' beliefs, and denoting by a_i some action by respondent i that is taken after the posterior stage, one can estimate the following model:

$$a_i = \delta + \kappa \widehat{y_{i,post}} + \Gamma Z_i + v_i, \tag{4.7}$$

where the posterior expectation $\widehat{y_{i,post}}$ is instrumented using some variation of Eqs. (4.4) or (4.6).[4] Further, Z_i is a vector of other individual characteristics that could also influence the action a_i. Including these controls can help with estimating κ more precisely, though it is not strictly necessary if the provided information was successfully randomized so that it is orthogonal to all relevant individual characteristics.

Estimating Eq. (4.7) using the instrumented expectations, rather than just with OLS based on the actual measured expectations, has two advantages. First, it reduces concerns about omitted variables that affect both behaviors and expectations and therefore could lead to a spurious correlation. Second, the instrumental variable strategy can help with measurement error in expectations, which in a standard OLS regression would tend to attenuate the coefficient κ toward zero.

Nevertheless, the exogenous information provision is not a panacea to learn about the causal effect of expectations about a given economic variable on behavior, because to allow for such an interpretation, the exclusion restriction also needs to be satisfied. In other words, the provided information should only affect action a through its effect on expectations about the specific variable y. As we discuss below, this can be challenging especially when asking macroeconomic questions, where expectations about different types of variables are likely correlated and affect many decisions jointly. However, even in cases where a singular interpretation is difficult, the "reduced form" effect of the experimental treatment on behavior is of course still of interest.

4.3.3 Examples

Human capital investments

Information frictions have been well-documented in the context of educational choices and health behaviors. Our goal here is not to cover the large literature—here, we summarize a few papers, with a focus on methodology. Chapters 7 and 9 in this Handbook provide more extensive overviews of studies in this area.

While several information-based randomized controlled trials have shown significant effects on educational and health outcomes, few of these papers tend to collect data on both expectations and behaviors. One of the most influential information experiments in this area is the study by Jensen

---

[4] One would generally want to instrument for the level of expectations after the experimental intervention, rather than the change between prior and posterior stage as in Eq. (4.6). This can be done for instance by simply adding the prior expectation(s) to the vector of controls Z_i.

(2010). His study design closely follows the paradigm mentioned above: that is, elicitation of priors at the baseline, randomized provision of information about schooling returns to a treatment group, and reelicitation of beliefs in the short-term as well as data on choices in the long-term. In this particular context, since there were no public data on the relationship between schooling and returns, the author himself collected such data—these formed the basis of the information intervention. He then first documents that eighth-graders in the Dominican Republic underestimate returns to secondary schooling. Next, he shows that a treated group of students who are provided with measured returns (which are simply the average earnings conditional on different years of schooling) have higher perceived returns to schooling four to six months after the intervention, and attain 0.2–0.3 more years of schooling over the next four years, compared to a control group.[5] A nice feature of this study is that it documents systematically biased baseline expectations, provides direct evidence on information impacting beliefs, and shows meaningful impacts on actual choices (which is only possible because longer-term data were collected).

Beliefs about returns is only one side of the picture. Perceived costs, especially at the post-secondary level, are likely a factor in schooling decisions, especially in the US. Bleemer and Zafar (2018) find that households' perceptions of college costs and benefits tend to be systematically biased, with larger biases among lower-income and noncollege households. They embed a randomized information experiment within the survey where respondents are randomly exposed to objective information about either average college "returns" or costs. The "returns" experiment leads to an increase in the intended likelihood of college attendance, with the impacts being larger for disadvantaged households (since they tend to be more misinformed ex-ante). The impacts persist in a follow-up survey two months later. On the other hand, they find no impact of the cost information treatment. Their results generally suggest that information frictions might be larger for more disadvantaged households.

The studies above only provided information about average earnings. However, there is a fair amount of dispersion in earnings, even conditional on the level/kind of human capital choice. This (perceived) uncertainty could play a role in individuals' decisions. Wiswall and Zafar (2015a) conduct a multistage information experiment on undergraduate students at New York University and collect beliefs about their *self* earnings—both average earnings and earnings uncertainty—at various points in the life cycle. Specifically, for earnings uncertainty, they ask respondents about the likelihood of earning more than certain thresholds if they were to graduate with different majors. They collect beliefs data on not only earnings but also several other outcomes (such as marriage, fertility, spousal earnings). Importantly, at the baseline, they also elicit *population* beliefs (that is, the students' beliefs about the earnings and other outcomes of current college graduates). After the baseline elicitation, students are provided with detailed objective information about the earnings distribution by college major and employment likelihood of current college graduates. Self beliefs are subsequently reelicited. In this design, since population beliefs were elicited prior to the revelation of the objective information, it is possible to assess the nature of the errors at the individual level. This rich panel of beliefs (all elicited within one survey) reveals that students have biased beliefs about population earnings and there is considerable heterogeneity in errors, which is uncorrelated with observable characteristics. Unique to their setup, the authors are able to study how students revise their self beliefs, and find substantial heterogeneity

---

[5] Importantly, the impacts of actual schooling are observed only for students from higher-income households, suggesting that information frictions are not the only binding constraint in this context.

in the students' updating heuristics (Wiswall and Zafar, 2015b). They also find large impacts on intended major choice, with the intervention nudging students towards higher-paying majors. This study is somewhat underpowered to investigate impacts on actual major choice.[6]

While these papers provide information about population earnings or costs, there are also field interventions that provide personalized information to students or their parents about the student's (relative) ability (Bobba and Frisancho, 2016; Dizon-Ross, 2019; Franco, 2019). The typical set-up in these papers is as follows: (1) the researcher elicits baseline expectations about relative ability and observes either actual human capital investments or intended choices; (2) a randomized group is provided with a signal about ability; and (3) data on updated beliefs and intended/actual choices are collected. These papers tend to find that individuals are quite misinformed about their ability and that providing such information generally leads to an improvement in the match between students and choices/investments, although impacts are quite heterogeneous.[7]

Macroeconomics and finance

The use of information experiments in the context of macroeconomics has exploded in recent years. Initial survey experiments in this area focused on households' or firms' expectations of future inflation, which play a key role in standard macroeconomic models and had also been highlighted by policymakers as an area where more empirical work would be valuable (Bernanke, 2007).

Focusing on households, Armantier et al. (2016) directly follow the basic design above, providing respondents with information either about past price changes (for food and beverages), or about the predictions of professional forecasters. They then study respondents' updating of expected inflation as a function of a respondent's perception gap (i.e., the difference between the signal a respondent received and their prior about the signal). Cavallo et al. (2017) implement similar experiments, comparing estimated treatment effects from the low-inflation US context to those found in Argentina, where inflation is much higher, and also comparing the effects of showing either price changes on selected goods, official statistics, or both. Binder and Rodrigue (2018) study how longer-term inflation expectations are affected when respondents are either informed about the Fed's inflation target or shown a time series (and summary statistics) of past inflation.[8]

More recent work by Coibion et al. (2022) compares effects on inflation expectations of eight different treatments, using a sample of nearly 20,000 individuals.[9] These authors are also able to link the survey responses to spending data measured by Nielsen, which allows the study of actual (not reported) spending effects of exogenous changes in inflation expectations. A related study, Coibion et al. (2021a),

---

[6] Conlon (2019), in a field experiment at a public university, finds that students, on average, tend to underestimate mean salaries by majors. Importantly, he finds that students who are treated with earnings information about a given field are significantly more likely to major in it. The importance of information frictions has also been studied by complementing experimental variation with large scale surveys (Hastings et al., 2015).

[7] For example, Franco (2019) finds that feedback discourages low-performing students; Bobba and Frisancho (2016) find that information is processed more efficiently by higher-socioeconomic students; Dizon-Ross (2019) finds that poorer, less-educated parents tend to have less accurate baseline beliefs, and that their beliefs/investments respond more to information, relative to richer parents.

[8] Binder and Rodrigue (2018) do not feature a control group and furthermore show both signals to all respondents, but in randomized order and eliciting beliefs after both treatments.

[9] The large sample size further makes it possible to run follow-up surveys with meaningful sample sizes 3 and 6 months after the initial survey.

presents information about past inflation to a subset of survey respondents and then measures effects on inflation expectations and on subsequent self-reported spending. These authors provide a thorough discussion of the issue raised above regarding the interpretation of the estimated effects on behavior: providing information about recent inflation may affect subsequent spending not just through the effects on future expected inflation, but also because survey respondents update their perceptions and expectations about other variables.[10]

Armona et al. (2019) apply an information-provision experiment to the study of individuals' expectations of future house price growth. Respondents receive information about either past 1-year or past 5-year local house price growth (or no information, in the control group), and expectations are similarly measured over the 1-year and 5-year horizon. These different horizons are studied because empirically, house price growth exhibits strong momentum (positive autocorrelation) over the 1–2 year horizon, but mean reversion over longer horizons such as 5 years, and this design allows studying to what extent people's updating after learning about past growth is consistent with these patterns.[11] The exogenous variation in expectations generated by the information provision is then also used to study the effects of expectations on investment behavior within a stylized incentivized experiment, where respondents could allocate some funds either to a risk-free account or to a fund that pays a return equal to local house price growth. Bottan and Perez-Truglia (2020) apply similar information provision to study real-world home selling behavior, detecting substantial effects.[12] See Chapter 6 in this Handbook for further discussion of work in this area.

Roth and Wohlfart (2020) study how beliefs about the likelihood of a recession affect people's expectations of personal unemployment, and how this in turn may affect behavior. After eliciting priors, these authors generate variation in recession expectations by providing a forecast from the Survey of Professional Forecasters—half the respondents randomly get the most optimistic forecaster (lowest recession probability), the others the most pessimistic forecaster (highest probability). This means there is no need for a control group. Qian (2020) uses a similar design to study the effect of expected house price growth on intended spending.

In addition, information provision experiments have also been used to study beliefs about the stock market and effects on investment behavior (Hanspal et al., 2021; Laudenbach et al., 2021), or to study effects of interest rate expectations (Coibion et al., 2020a; Link et al., 2021). Beutel et al. (2021) study how randomized provision of a central bank's warnings about financial stability risks affects risk perceptions and investment behavior in a stylized setting.

The examples mentioned above in the context of human capital investments typically (though not always) elicit expectations about outcomes that the individual has full or partial control over. For instance,

---

[10] Another recent study that experimentally manipulates expectations and studies effects on (credit-card) spending is Galashin et al. (2020). Other work has used similar information provision experiments to study the expectations and behaviors of firms (Coibion et al., 2018, 2019). We refer to Chapters 5 and 11 in this Handbook for more detailed discussion of work in this area.

[11] A methodological feature of this study is that respondents are randomly asked all questions either in terms of levels (the price of a typical house in USD) or in growth rates (the percent change in the price of a typical house), based on earlier evidence suggesting that framing could affect inference about extrapolation vs. mean reversion in beliefs (Glaser et al., 2007). In Armona et al. (2019), results are consistent across the two frames.

[12] This study directly measures the effects of random information provision on real-world behavior, without being able to measure expectations of the home sellers directly. However, to still obtain measures of the elasticity of behavior with respect to expectations, the authors run an auxiliary survey study to measure the effects of the same information provision on expectations only.

the individual chooses whether to attend college or not, and can at least influence future earnings (e.g., via labor supply choices). This is in contrast to most applications in the area of macroeconomics and finance where expectations are generally elicited about events that the individual has no control over (such as the rate of inflation). In this case, heterogeneity in expectations depends on individual-specific beliefs regarding the underlying processes and information sets. This distinction matters for how such data should be incorporated in choice models. For example, if the model includes an expectation over a variable that the individual has control over, then such expectations have to be jointly modeled with the main choice outcome.[13]

It is also worth noting that, while the link between expectations and behavior has been studied quite extensively in the context of human capital investments, fewer survey experiments in the macro area study impacts on actual behavior. This is largely due to data limitations and is gradually changing. In addition, evidence to date suggests that impacts of macro-related expectations on behaviors (stylized or actual) are generally modest. This could be due to several factors. First, macroeconomic expectations are likely not the first-order determinant for certain behaviors—for example, it is plausible that household spending responds primarily to financial constraints and personal income uncertainty rather than inflation expectations. Second, most papers in this area focus on inflation, which has been largely stable and fairly low in the US and other developed economies until recently. That may make households less sensitive to changes in inflation.[14] Third, individuals may simply be more responsive to factors that are somewhat in their own control. These explanations are largely speculative, and merit further investigation.

Other applications

Information experiments are increasingly being used in other subfields, including labor economics (for example, to understand the role of information barriers in job search), public economics (for example, to understand drivers of support for various public policies including redistribution), health economics, political behavior, and so on. In addition, information experiments have also been used to explore the role of social norms or social pressure in affecting individual behavior (for example, Bursztyn and Jensen, 2015, and Bursztyn et al., 2020). Interested readers are referred to Section 2 in the recent review article by Haaland et al. (2021), which provides a detailed overview of areas within economics where information experiments have been used, and to other chapters in this Handbook.

4.4 **Methodological issues**

This section discusses various methodological issues related to the design of information experiments.

---

[13] For illustration, consider a model of university choice which incorporates the subjective likelihood of dropping out as one factor. Dropping out of a given school is likely going to be a function of some of the parameters that directly affect the utility of attending that school. Thus, the dropping out likelihood has to be jointly modeled with the choice of enrolling in that school; readers are referred to Delavande and Zafar (2019) for a discussion of this issue.

[14] Studies that do find effects in experimental or nonexperimental settings include Armantier et al. (2015), Bachmann et al. (2015), Coibion et al. (2022), or Crump et al. (2022). See Chapter 5 in this Handbook for further discussion.

4.4.1 **Within-subject or between-subject design?**

The identification argument laid out above in Section 4.2.1 should make it clear that for recovering preference parameters, it is important to have a within-individual design. That is, a setup where expectations and choices are elicited from the *same* individual before and after the provision of information. On the other hand, a between-subject design—where expectations and choices are measured only after different groups have received some information, potentially with one control group not receiving any information—may suffice to shed some light on the expectation formation process, or simply study the treatment effect of a given piece of information on posterior beliefs or choices. However, a within-subject design is still more powerful since it allows the researcher to more extensively study heterogeneity in belief formation. More specifically, while a between-subject design allows one to investigate heterogeneity in belief updating based on observables (for example, by gender, one could simply compare the reported expectations for the treated and control group), it does not allow controlling for heterogeneity based on unobservables. The panel data that is collected through a within-subject design allows the researcher to include an individual fixed effect and, hence, enables the researcher to conduct a more detailed investigation of heterogeneity.

A within-subject design entails the elicitation of expectations twice, once before the information provision and once afterwards. A concern with eliciting the expectation using the same question twice is that responses may be biased due to an experimenter demand effect. That is, the respondent, upon seeing the same question again after the information provision, may be inclined to answer in a way that is consistent with the provided information only to please the researcher. This would bias the impacts upwards (relative to a between-subject design, where demand effects should, in general, be weaker). While this is hard to rule out entirely, existing evidence suggests that typical experimenter demand effects in surveys tend to be modest (De Quidt et al., 2018).[15] Conversely, respondents may want to appear consistent and not change their posterior due to this bias. This would attenuate the effects of the information downwards. Roth and Wohlfart (2020) find no significant difference in updating of expectations in a robustness check where respondents are randomized to a between- or within-subject design. More work undertaking such comparisons would be useful to determine whether and when one should be concerned about such biases.

Some researchers, in order to avoid asking the respondent the same question twice, instead elicit the prior and posterior expectation using different wordings. For example, Coibion et al. (2022) use a within-subject design to study how different kinds of inflation-related information impact consumers' inflation expectations. They elicit the prior expectation as a subjective density forecast and the post-information expectation as a point estimate. While such an approach likely reduces consistency bias and survey fatigue, it implicitly assumes that *all* respondents report the same statistic of their subjective density forecast when asked for a point estimate. Unfortunately, this may not be a great assumption—Engelberg et al. (2009) show that there is a lot of variation across forecasters in what percentile of the subjective distribution the point estimate corresponds to. Thus, here again, researchers face potential trade-offs, and it is not clear (yet) what the best approach is.

---

[15] It is worth noting that the best-known examples of demand effects come from social-psychology experiments in which students received class credits from participating in experiments and might have been informed about the psychological theories their instructors wanted to test. In the case of online surveys of the general population, it is much less plausible that subjects align their behavior with the hypotheses to be tested, since (i) they are less likely to correctly guess the hypotheses to be tested, (ii) they mostly just receive a fixed monetary payment for participation, and (iii) the experimenters are anonymous to them.

Since within-subject designs (which are the most common approach to date in the literature) rely on within-individual changes in expectations, the issue of measurement error is further exacerbated when using belief revisions to study impact on behaviors. Under classical measurement error, this would then yield a lower bound on the role of beliefs in explaining behavior. While an instrumental variables strategy may partially mitigate some of these concerns (as discussed in Section 4.3.2), more work is needed to understand the nature and extent of measurement error—it is likely that measurement error in certain instances may be non-classical. In fact, Chapter 26 in this Handbook flags the issue of rounding and imprecise probabilities as an important open research question.

4.4.2 Eliciting perceptions about the provided information

In order to study heterogeneity in belief updating, it is important that researchers elicit perceptions about the information they will eventually provide in the experiment before the information is given to the respondent. This is usually rather straightforward. Take, for example, the set-up in Wiswall and Zafar (2015a). They provide respondents with labor market information of current 30-year-olds with a college degree by major. Before they do so, they ask their respondents about their perceptions about these—this is what they refer to as "population beliefs," i.e., these are respondents' beliefs/perceptions about how much individuals in the population earn.[16]

This raises two issues. First, the mere act of asking people to think about a fact may prime them to factor that information into their beliefs and expectations, and may affect their subsequent behavior (Zwane et al., 2011; Crossley et al., 2017). Absent the survey, the respondent would not have acted in the same way. To bound such effects the researcher would need three groups: a pure control which is not surveyed, a control which is surveyed, and a treatment group. This, of course, imposes demands on the sample size and the researcher's budget. The extent to which one should be concerned about this issue likely depends on the application at hand. But, at the minimum, researchers should be aware of this potential bias and seriously think about how much to survey respondents.

The second issue is related to whether the elicitation of perceptions (or beliefs that can be validated) should be incentivized. As a researcher, the goal is to recover the belief the respondent holds and uses when making decisions in the real-world. Incentives may increase the effort the respondent exerts in the survey, but it is far from clear that incentives increase the likelihood of recovering the true belief. Some researchers strongly argue for the necessity of incentives for belief elicitation and have provided some evidence of differences in beliefs elicited with and without incentives (Harrison and Phillips, 2014). On the other hand, Grewenig et al. (2020) show that incentivizing beliefs can impact the distribution of stated beliefs (relative to an unincentivized group). Their analysis of the data indicates that the incentive effects may be related to the usage of online search engines.[17] Providing incentives, as a result, leads to respondents having more accurate beliefs. But, in most instances, that is *not* the goal—instead the researcher is interested in recovering the true beliefs, whether biased or not, of the respondent.

---

[16] In other settings, eliciting priors about the information to be provided is not easily possible. For instance, in the Coibion et al. (2022) paper discussed above, some treatments consist of newspaper articles or official statements. Also, to the extent that there are several possible signals, one would have to elicit every subjects' priors about all of these signals, which would be tedious.

[17] They, in fact, conduct a treatment that explicitly encourages online-search activity without providing incentives. They find that this encouragement treatment produces effects that are similar to the incentive treatment, suggesting that altered online-search behavior is responsible for the impacts in the incentive treatment.

In line with this, Haaland et al. (2021) also conclude that incentives have little effect on beliefs in nonpolitical domains and when responses cannot be readily looked up. Finally, it is worth noting that incentivized elicitation mechanisms can generate biases when respondents are not risk neutral (Murphy and Winkler, 1970). Even if respondents are risk neutral, incentivized belief elicitation techniques are not incentive-compatible when the respondent has a stake in the event that they are predicting (the "no stake" condition in Karni and Safra, 1995). Armantier and Treich (2013) also show that beliefs are less biased (but noisier) in the absence of incentives.

4.4.3 Eliciting higher-order moments

As mentioned in Section 4.3.1, it is common to elicit the full subjective distribution from respondents. Not only does this allow the respondent to express uncertainty, it also provides a richer analysis of belief updating. For example, under Bayesian updating, respondents with more uncertain priors should be more responsive to the provided information.[18] Having information on baseline uncertainty allows the researcher to investigate this directly.

Methodologically, there are multiple ways of eliciting subjective densities (see Chapter 1 in this Handbook for further discussion). One way entails providing respondents with predetermined bins, asking them to assign probabilities (on a 0–100 scale) to the bins such that they sum to 100. The density questions in the NY Fed's Survey of Consumer Expectations (SCE), for example, use this approach. Alternatively, since respondents are typically first asked for a point estimate in many surveys, one could make the bins individual-specific, by anchoring the variation around the individual's point estimate. For example, this approach is used by Armona et al. (2019), who provide bins that are anchored to the respondent's baseline expectation.

A potential shortcoming with the former approach is that the point estimate may lie outside the support of the bins which are presented to the respondent, and hence the researcher will not have quantitative measures of respondent uncertainty in such a case. The SCE provides bins that go from -12 to $+12$ percent for year-ahead inflation and home price changes. Using the individual-level publicly available SCE data since 2020, we find that the point forecasts for inflation and housing price changes are outside this interval for more than 15% percent of the respondents.

An alternative approach has been to use a qualitative measure of uncertainty, where respondents are asked for the certainty in their response on a Likert-scale. While there are well-known issues with the interpretation of such data, especially for comparisons across individuals and groups, such data are easier to elicit, and may still be useful to document descriptive patterns of heterogeneity in belief-updating.

4.4.4 Information content and presentation

While information provision experiments routinely vary the quantitative content of the information that is provided—indeed, that is usually the purpose of the randomization—not very much is known about how other "dimensions" of the provided information matter. For instance, does it matter who provides the information, meaning what source for a given piece of information is shown to respondents? There

---

[18] Note that this is only true if prior uncertainty is not systematically correlated with other information-processing preferences/costs of the respondent. See Fuster et al. (2020b) for a detailed discussion.

is some work that shows that the identity of the messenger has an impact on how different groups of respondents incorporate the same information, and what information they choose (D'Acunto et al., 2021). Likewise, different ways of communicating similar information can have differential impact on expectations: for example, Coibion et al. (2022) find that an intervention that provides respondents with a news article about the most recent Federal Open Market Committee (FOMC) meeting leads to an impact on expectations that is only half as strong as reading the FOMC statement itself. These two pieces of information differ in terms of their technicality, content, and credibility, and so it is difficult to fully disentangle what leads to these differential impacts. For example, to assess the role of the source, the ideal experiment would entail providing the same identical information but with different sources.[19] That, of course, is generally not feasible.

Related to this, there is so far limited evidence on how credible and relevant respondents find the information to be, and to our knowledge there have not been studies that exogenously vary the credibility of the information source to study how that affects the extent to which it is incorporated into subjective beliefs.[20]

Researchers also have to decide how complex and detailed the provided information is. There is a trade-off: one wants the information to be as comprehensible and simple as possible for the respondent, without it being misleading. For example, most experiments give respondents information about the average of a variable (for example, average earnings of college graduates in the population, or the average inflation forecast of experts). But, of course, these are just averages and there is a confidence interval around these estimates. Should the researcher just provide a point estimate or convey some sense of the distribution (or the uncertainty in the estimate)? While the former is easier to communicate, there is a risk that doing so may inadvertently make the respondent think of the outcome as being deterministic.

Finally, one may ask whether respondents could be provided with false (made-up) information, either out of convenience (in order to get more variation in the provided information) or to study whether people are able to distinguish false from true information. However, it is important to keep in mind that in experimental economics, there is a strong norm against using deception (although there are different opinions on what constitutes deception; see Charness et al., 2021 for discussion). Thus, we advise to only use factual information.

In short, more systematic work is needed to understand the most effective way of presenting information. We suspect the answer will depend on the application and context.

4.4.5 Where and how to run these surveys?

Most of the studies that use information provision experiments are run online. The most commonly used platform to run surveys is Qualtrics, although some survey panels have separate dedicated platforms. Aside from the platform on which the survey is run, one then needs access to a subject pool. Haaland et al. (2021) provide an overview of different types of samples: (i) probability-based samples (e.g.,

---

[19] Coibion et al. (2022) show that respondents tend to assign lower credibility to newspapers as a source of information about the economy than, e.g., to the government or social media, making it likely that differential credibility played a role in their results.

[20] Similarly, to our knowledge, it is an open question whether information provided by one person (one forecaster) versus (the average from) a group of forecasters has differential effects.

RAND American Life Panel); (ii) representative online samples (based on certain observable characteristics; e.g., Dynata, Lucid, Prolific, or Qualtrics); or (iii) online labor markets (Amazon MTurk). The representativeness declines across these options, but so does the cost.

Especially for relatively low-cost options like Amazon MTurk, it is important to have a few attention checks/screens in the survey, as the data can otherwise be quite noisy.[21] However, one has to be careful not to exaggerate the number of such checks, as this could otherwise introduce selection (with experienced survey takers being better at spotting such checks) or alienate respondents. Reading comprehension checks, recall questions or open-ended questions can also be useful.

A very useful reference on such implementation issues is Bergman et al. (2020). They highlight, for instance, the need to think carefully about question wording and survey length, and the best practice of running a small-scale pilot survey before launching the full study, in order to detect any potential issues that would compromise the usefulness of the data.[22] They also provide example Qualtrics files.

Some central banks and other public institutions maintain high-quality probability-based samples (often with a panel dimension), which have been used for many of the studies discussed in this chapter. To the extent possible, it is desirable for such institutions to allow outside researchers to add their own questions to their surveys, e.g., via a "call for proposals" as was done by the Bundesbank when launching their online pilot survey on consumer expectations (see Beckmann and Schmidt, 2020).

4.5 Extensions and alternative approaches

4.5.1 Moving beyond exogenously provided information

There are two important limitations to the information provision experiments discussed in Section 4.3. The first is that the signals provided to respondents are picked by the researcher, while, of course, in reality there is a very large number of signals that an economic agent could consult when forming expectations about a given variable.

The second limitation is that signals are simply "dropped" exogenously on survey respondents, often in a way that makes the signals quite salient and ensures that respondents are paying attention to them. However, in their everyday lives, respondents would themselves choose whether to pay attention to any signal, which they generally have to expend some effort to obtain (e.g., by searching for information online), and they would choose which of the many possible signals to look for.

A few recent studies have extended the survey-experimental paradigm to better understand the information acquisition decision. While the set of available signals is still chosen ex-ante by the researchers, this allows studying which signals respondents with different characteristics or priors tend to prefer, and how much they value the information.

Fuster et al. (2020b) study information acquisition within the context of home price expectations. Their experimental design has four stages. First, prior expectations about the future national median home price are elicited. Second, in a later part of the survey, respondents are informed that they will

---

[21] In some cases it is easy to spot noisy responses—e.g., if a respondent always chooses the first option in multiple choice answers or is extremely fast in completing the survey—but it is also possible that some respondents effectively respond "randomly."

[22] A more powerful but also expensive type of pilot is to have a few respondents recorded as they take the survey and "think aloud" as they go through each question.

again be asked for their forecast, but that (i) they can now win a monetary reward if their forecast turns out to be accurate[23]; and (ii) that they have the option to choose among different pieces of information that they could consult and that could be useful for their forecast. Respondents were then asked to express their preference over the following four signals: the national home price change over the past 1 year, the change over the past 10 years, the average expert forecast of future home prices, or seeing no information at all. Third, respondents' willingness to pay for their most preferred signal is elicited (unless they stated they preferred not seeing any information), using an incentive-compatible "multiple price list" method. Then, depending on the willingness to pay and randomness, some respondents are shown their preferred piece of information. Finally, in the fourth stage, posterior expectations are elicited.

Thus, the first and last stage are as in a standard information-provision experiment, but in-between, additional information is collected that allows studying respondent preferences across signals, as well as the valuation of information. Results indicate substantial heterogeneity in respondents' rankings of the available signals, and more sophisticated respondents (measured by education or numeracy) are more likely to select the arguably more informative signals (the expert forecast or past 1-year growth). Respondents display high valuation for the signals (when compared to the possible prizes from a successful forecast) and incorporate the information, if they receive it, into their beliefs.

The heterogeneity in preferences across signals has an important implication: as the price of information is lowered, the cross-sectional dispersion in posterior beliefs does not necessarily decrease. This is because a decrease in dispersion *within* a group that sees a certain signal—which is a typical result obtained in standard information provision experiments—is offset by an increase in dispersion *across* groups that chose different signals.[24] This second channel would be missed by standard information provision experiments.

Roth et al. (2022) also focus on information acquisition. This study tests whether people become more likely to select a given piece of information (in this case, a professional forecast about future recession risk) when their (perceived) personal benefit from the information is higher. To manipulate this personal benefit, the authors use variation in the unemployment rates from a past recession measured across different official statistics. The main result is that indeed, exogenously increased perceived exposure to macroeconomic risk leads respondents to become more likely to want to be informed about recession risk (relative to other macro variables such as inflation).

Other recent studies that consider endogenous information acquisition within surveys are Faia et al. (2021), who let respondents choose between different newspaper headlines about topics related to the COVID-19 pandemic, and D'Acunto et al. (2021), who study how the choice of newspaper articles about the Federal Reserve is affected by identity of the Fed policymaker that is featured in the article, and how these effects differ across demographic groups. Capozza et al. (2021) review the broader literature on information acquisition in field settings.

---

[23] This reward was randomized to be either $10 or $100 (in each case with probability 10% of being eligible for the reward), in order to study whether incentives matter for the choice, valuation, and use of information.

[24] This result continues to hold in an extension of the survey experiment where respondents can obtain more than one signal, which of course would also be the case in reality.

4.5.2 **Alternatives to information provision experiments**

An attractive feature of information experiments is that they allow the researcher to generate shocks to an individual's information set in order to study resulting effects on expectations and behavior. An alternative approach to generate within-individual variation in the economic environment is to elicit *conditional* expectations and/or planned behaviors in so-called vignettes, i.e., hypothetical scenarios.

To illustrate the usefulness of such data, let us go back to the example of college major choice from Section 4.2.1. The ideas presented here are a condensed version of those in Wiswall and Zafar (2021). Consider an individual i who at time τ is deciding which college major to choose. Individual i's perception of the expected utility from major k is given by

$$E_{i,\tau}(V_k) = \sum_{t=\tau+1}^{T} \beta^{t-\tau} \int u_t(X)\, dG_{i,\tau}(X|k,t),$$

where $\beta \in (0,1)$ is the discount rate, $u(X)$ is the postgraduation utility function that provides the mapping from the finite vector of postgraduation events X to utility, and $G_{i,\tau}(X|k,t)$ is the individual's *beliefs* at period τ about the probability of the vector of future outcomes X occurring in all future periods $t > \tau$ *if* she were to complete major k. Given her beliefs at period τ, individual i chooses the major that provides the highest expected present discounted utility.

Surveys that collect data on subjective expectations directly elicit individual's beliefs $G_{i,\tau}(X|k,t)$. For example, Wiswall and Zafar (2021) ask each individual what they believe the distribution of X would be in some future period t *if* they were to complete different majors. That is, students are asked their expectations about postgraduation events *conditional* on different majors. In their case, X includes a wide range of events such as earnings, labor supply, marriage, and spousal earnings.

From the collection of self beliefs data, one can analyze *individual-level* differences in belief distributions:

$$\Delta_{G,i\tau}(k,k') = G_{i,\tau}(X|k,t) - G_{i,\tau}(X|k',t),$$

where $\Delta_{G,i\tau}(k,k')$ can be viewed as the *ex-ante* (i.e., prior to the choice of major) "treatment effect" on the distribution of future events X. Specifically, it reflects the "causal effect" individual i expects if she chooses major k rather than k'. As an example, consider beliefs about future earnings at age $t = 30$, where earnings w would be one element of the X vector, $w \subset X$. By eliciting each individual's beliefs about their expected future earnings at age $t = 30$ *if* they were to complete major k, and if they were to complete major k', one can compute the difference in the individual's point forecast of expected earnings:

$$\delta_i = E_i(w|k, 30) - E_i(w|k', 30).$$

Wiswall and Zafar (2021) extend this idea to many other potential outcomes beyond expected earnings, including earnings uncertainty, marriage, fertility, spousal characteristics, and labor supply. Arcidiacono et al. (2020) use the same approach to study the causal impact of majors on perceived returns to occupations. Similarly, by collecting data on conditional probabilities of work given health, Giustinelli and Shapiro (2019) estimate the subjective ex ante treatment effect of health on retirement.[25] Chapters 10 and 21 in this Handbook provide additional discussion and references.

---

[25] Note that the concept of ex-ante treatment effects is distinct from ex-post treatment effects of choices. In the case of ex-post treatment effects, the alternative outcomes are counterfactual and unobserved. A large econometrics and statistics literature

The studies above measure both conditional expectations and actions in a given hypothetical state of the world, but it is also possible to measure only expectations or only actions. An example of the former in the context of macroeconomics is Andre et al. (2021). These authors present respondents (both a representative sample from the general population and a sample of experts) with vignettes in which respondents are asked to predict future unemployment and inflation under different hypothetical macroeconomic shocks, for instance about the monetary policy rate or government spending.[26] The resulting data allow them to study heterogeneity in respondents' "subjective models" of how the economy responds to such shocks, and the source of such heterogeneity (which they link to personal experiences).[27]

Other work uses vignettes to study conditional intended behaviors only, without measuring conditional expectations.[28] For instance, in Fuster et al. (2020a), respondents are presented with scenarios that provide hypothetical one-time income gains or losses of different sizes. Respondents are then asked for their propensity to spend. This allows the authors to estimate, for example, how the size of a one-time cash transfer causally impacts the intended marginal propensity to spend, an object that is of policy relevance (see also Jappelli and Pistaferri, 2014; Christelis et al., 2019). In a different context, Fuster and Zafar (2021) use vignettes to study survey respondents' willingness-to-pay for a home under different configurations of financing conditions (interest rate, downpayment requirement).

The elicitation of conditional expectations hinges on two implicit assumptions. First, that individuals have well-formed expectations about the outcomes conditional on the state of the world that they are being asked about. This is not directly testable and is really at the discretion at the researchers. For example, it is hard to argue that this assumption is not satisfied in the case of asking college students about outcomes conditional on college major—a decision that the students are actively thinking about. Second, that there is no systematic bias in the reporting of expectations. This is an assumption that is implicitly made when using any survey data, and is not specific to (conditional) expectations data.

When eliciting choices in hypothetical scenarios, likewise, an implicit assumption is that stated choices are reflective of what respondents would do in actual scenarios. Although there has historically been concern about the plausibility of this assumption (Diamond and Hausman, 1994), there is growing evidence that the two approaches of using stated choices or actual choices yield similar preference estimates (see Fuster et al., 2020a, and references therein), and that the stated approach yields meaningful responses when the counterfactual scenarios presented to respondents are realistic and relevant for them.

---

studies how to identify these potential outcomes and moments of the potential outcomes (such as average treatment effects) from realized choice data (Heckman and Vytlacil, 2005).

[26] They are explicitly providing information about the assumed source of the shocks, in order to make respondents think of them as truly "exogenous" (as opposed to an endogenous response to other economic developments).

[27] Other examples of conditional expectation elicitation in macro are Coibion et al. (2020b), where respondents are asked about expected paths for the economy depending on the outcome of the presidential election, and Dibiasi et al. (2021), where firm managers are asked how their expected investment, employment and production would change in the face of a (mean zero) uncertainty shock, in this case linked to a popular vote.

[28] There is also work that elicits intended behaviors in different conditional states, but expectations in only one state of the world. This then requires the researcher to also model how expectations may change in counterfactual states. For example, Delavande and Zafar (2019) use such data to estimate the causal impact of credit constraints and pecuniary and non-pecuniary factors on the choice of type of higher education institution.

A challenge with the vignette approach is that the researcher has to decide how much information to include in each scenario. Should the scenarios be fully specified or incomplete? The results may depend on these decisions because respondents may "fill the blanks" for unspecified features. The answer really depends on what the goal is. If the goal is to use the vignette to estimate a specific model, then fully specifying the model assumptions (obviously, in a comprehensible way) makes sense. This, for example, is the approach used by Ameriks et al. (2020) to estimate preferences for motives for late-in-life saving in a lifecycle model with incomplete markets. Such an approach could make the vignettes cognitively demanding for respondents, who may perceive the questions to be artificial, but allows the researcher to nicely map the vignette to the model framework.

In short, vignettes appear to be a promising method to obtain richer information than is possible with information provision alone.

4.6 Directions for future work

The arguments in this chapter have hopefully made it clear that survey experiments are a powerful tool to help researchers understand decision-making and belief formation. Empirical evidence overwhelmingly suggests that, across domains, individuals are quite misinformed and that simple information provision is often effective at nudging expectations and, in some cases, behaviors.

We end by providing a discussion of possible directions for future work. First, the fact that information experiments—which largely provide information that is readily available in the public domain—shift individuals' expectations is rather puzzling. That individuals respond to such information implies that they find such information useful. Then *why* are individuals choosing to stay misinformed? Several models in the literature have attempted to explain this, either based on barriers to information selection or information acquisition (see the references in Fuster et al., 2020b). With the exception of a few empirical studies mentioned in Section 4.5.1, most information experiments to date have little to tell us about heterogeneity in information selection and information acquisition. Instead, they primarily focus on heterogeneity in information processing. A natural extension of prevalent information experiments is to bring in these dimensions.

Second, as alluded to earlier in Section 4.3.3, the literature that investigates the link between macroeconomic expectations and behavior has mostly relied on elicited intended behaviors or stylized behaviors within incentivized decision situations. Only in rare cases do researchers have access to actual behaviors as reported in follow-up surveys or direct measures of behavior (for instance, in administrative data) from the same individuals from whom expectations data are elicited. With increasing ease of collecting data and ability to link to administrative data (on behaviors), we expect this data limitation to relax over time. The few papers in the macro space that have such rich data typically find modest impacts of expectations on behavior. Work that sheds light on why that may be the case would be useful.

Third, information experiments have been quite useful in documenting heterogeneity in updating rules or mental models. Going forward, it will be useful for theory and experimental evidence to evolve interactively—with new theories being proposed based on this heterogeneity, and then being tested again more systematically in new settings.

Fourth, beyond heterogeneity based on observables, there is also evidence that individuals process information in a biased manner, especially when updating over variables that they have control over or that can impact utility directly, such as ability (see Benjamin, 2019 for an overview of biases in the belief-updating literature). In the context of ability updating, the tendency of people to be conservative in updating is fairly common. On the other hand, evidence on whether individuals tend to update more in response to "good" news versus "bad news"—a bias referred to as "asymmetric updating" (Mobius et al., 2014) or the "good news-bad news effect" (Eil and Rao, 2011)—is quite mixed (see the discussion in Benjamin, 2019). In addition, we know even less about the dynamics of motivated beliefs (Zimmermann, 2020). More work is needed to better understand these biases and the circumstances in which particular biases may emerge. Much of the existing evidence comes from lab studies, but incorporating the analysis of such motivated-belief biases in the context of larger-scale survey experiments also seems a fruitful avenue for future research to us.

Finally, as mentioned in Section 4.4.4, there has been little systematic work on how to design the content and presentation of information interventions. While we do not expect a unified theory of how information should be presented and communicated, and the answer likely depends on the context and application at hand, work that sheds further light on these issues would certainly be useful.

References

Ameriks, J., Briggs, J., Caplin, A., Shapiro, M.D., Tonetti, C., 2020. Long-term-care utility and late-in-life saving. Journal of Political Economy 128, 2375–2451.

Andre, P., Pizzinelli, C., Roth, C., Wohlfart, J., 2021. Subjective models of the macroeconomy: evidence from experts and representative samples. The Review of Economic Studies. Forthcoming.

Arcidiacono, P., Hotz, V.J., Maurel, A., Romano, T., 2020. Ex ante returns and occupational choice. Journal of Political Economy 128, 4475–4522.

Armantier, O., Bruine de Bruin, W., Topa, G., Klaauw, W., Zafar, B., 2015. Inflation expectations and behavior: do survey respondents act on their beliefs? International Economic Review 56, 505–536.

Armantier, O., Nelson, S., Topa, G., Van der Klaauw, W., Zafar, B., 2016. The price is right: updating inflation expectations in a randomized price information experiment. Review of Economics and Statistics 98, 503–523.

Armantier, O., Treich, N., 2013. Eliciting beliefs: proper scoring rules, incentives, stakes and hedging. European Economic Review 62, 17–40.

Armona, L., Fuster, A., Zafar, B., 2019. Home price expectations and behaviour: evidence from a randomized information experiment. The Review of Economic Studies 86, 1371–1410.

Bachmann, R., Berg, T.O., Sims, E.R., 2015. Inflation expectations and readiness to spend: cross-sectional evidence. American Economic Journal: Economic Policy 7, 1–35.

Beckmann, E., Schmidt, T., 2020. Bundesbank online pilot survey on consumer expectations. Technical Paper 01/2020. Deutsche Bundesbank.

Benhabib, J., Spiegel, M.M., 2018. Sentiments and economic activity: evidence from US states. The Economic Journal 129, 715–733.

Benjamin, D.J., 2019. Chapter 2 – errors in probabilistic reasoning and judgment biases. In: Bernheim, B.D., DellaVigna, S., Laibson, D. (Eds.), Handbook of Behavioral Economics – Foundations and Applications, vol. 2. North-Holland, pp. 69–186.

Bergman, A., Chinco, A., Hartzmark, S.M., Sussman, A.B., 2020. Survey Curious? Start-up Guide and Best Practices for Running Surveys and Experiments Online. Working Paper. University of Chicago – Booth School of Business.

Bernanke, B.S., 2007. Inflation Expectations and Inflation Forecasting. Speech at the Monetary Economics Workshop of the NBER Summer Institute, Cambridge, MA.

Beutel, J., Metiu, N., Stockerl, V., 2021. Toothless tiger with claws? Financial stability communication, expectations, and risk-taking. Journal of Monetary Economics 120, 53–69.

Binder, C., Rodrigue, A., 2018. Household informedness and long-run inflation expectations: experimental evidence. Southern Economic Journal 85, 580–598.

Bleemer, Z., Zafar, B., 2018. Intended college attendance: evidence from an experiment on college returns and costs. Journal of Public Economics 157, 184–211.

Bobba, M., Frisancho, V., 2016. Perceived Ability and School Choices. TSE Working Papers 16-660. Toulouse School of Economics (TSE).

Bottan, N.L., Perez-Truglia, R., 2020. Betting on the House: Subjective Expectations and Market Choices. Working Paper 27412. National Bureau of Economic Research.

Bursztyn, L., González, A.L., Yanagizawa-Drott, D., 2020. Misperceived social norms: women working outside the home in Saudi Arabia. The American Economic Review 110, 2997–3029.

Bursztyn, L., Jensen, R., 2015. How does peer pressure affect educational investments? The Quarterly Journal of Economics 130, 1329–1367.

Capozza, F., Haaland, I., Roth, C., Wohlfart, J., 2021. Studying Information Acquisition in the Field: a Practical Guide and Review. CEBI working paper series 21-15. University of Copenhagen.

Cavallo, A., Cruces, G., Perez-Truglia, R., 2017. Inflation expectations, learning and supermarket prices: evidence from survey experiments. American Economic Journal: Macroeconomics 9, 1–35.

Charness, G., Samek, A., van de Ven, J., 2021. What is considered deception in experimental economics? Experimental Economics.

Christelis, D., Georgarakos, D., Jappelli, T., Pistaferri, L., van Rooij, M., 2019. Asymmetric consumption effects of transitory income shocks. The Economic Journal 129, 2322–2341.

Coibion, O., Georgarakos, D., Gorodnichenko, Y., van Rooij, M., 2021a. How Does Consumption Respond to News about Inflation? Field Evidence from a Randomized Control Trial. Working Paper.

Coibion, O., Georgarakos, D., Gorodnichenko, Y., Weber, M., 2020a. Forward Guidance and Household Expectations. Working Paper 26778. National Bureau of Economic Research.

Coibion, O., Gorodnichenko, Y., Kumar, S., 2018. How do firms form their expectations? New survey evidence. The American Economic Review 108, 2671–2713.

Coibion, O., Gorodnichenko, Y., Kumar, S., Ryngaert, J., 2021b. Do you know that I know that you know...? Higher-order beliefs in survey data. The Quarterly Journal of Economics 136, 1387–1446.

Coibion, O., Gorodnichenko, Y., Ropele, T., 2019. Inflation expectations and firm decisions: new causal evidence. The Quarterly Journal of Economics 135, 165–219.

Coibion, O., Gorodnichenko, Y., Weber, M., 2020b. Political Polarization and Expected Economic Outcomes. Working Paper 28044. National Bureau of Economic Research.

Coibion, O., Gorodnichenko, Y., Weber, M., 2022. Monetary policy communications and their effects on household inflation expectations. Journal of Political Economy 130 (6), 1537–1584.

Conlon, J., Zafar, B., 2017. Measuring Americans' Expectations Following the 2016 Election. Federal Reserve Bank of New York Liberty Street Economics Blog.

Conlon, J.J., 2019. Major malfunction: a field experiment correcting undergraduates' beliefs about salaries. The Journal of Human Resources. 0317-8599R2.

Crossley, T.F., de Bresser, J., Delaney, L., Winter, J., 2017. Can survey participation alter household saving behaviour? The Economic Journal 127, 2332–2357.

Crump, R.K., Eusepi, S., Tambalotti, A., Topa, G., 2022. Subjective intertemporal substitution. Journal of Monetary Economics 126, 118–133.

D'Acunto, F., Fuster, A., Weber, M., 2021. Diverse Policy Committees Can Reach Underrepresented Groups. Working Paper 2021-95. University of Chicago Becker-Friedman Institute.

De Quidt, J., Haushofer, J., Roth, C., 2018. Measuring and bounding experimenter demand. The American Economic Review 108, 3266–3302.

De Stefani, A., 2021. House price history, biased expectations and credit cycles: the role of housing investors. Real Estate Economics 49 (1), 1238–1266.

Delavande, A., Zafar, B., 2019. University choice: the role of expected earnings, nonpecuniary outcomes, and financial constraints. Journal of Political Economy 127, 2343–2393.

Diamond, P.A., Hausman, J.A., 1994. Contingent valuation: is some number better than no number? The Journal of Economic Perspectives 8, 45–64.

Dibiasi, A., Mikosch, H., Sarferaz, S., 2021. Uncertainty Shocks, Adjustment Costs and Firm Beliefs: Evidence from a Representative Survey. Working Paper. KOF, ETH Zurich.

Dizon-Ross, R., 2019. Parents' beliefs about their children's academic ability: implications for educational investments. The American Economic Review 109, 2728–2765.

Eil, D., Rao, J.M., 2011. The good news–bad news effect: asymmetric processing of objective information about yourself. American Economic Journal: Microeconomics 3, 114–138.

Engelberg, J., Manski, C.F., Williams, J., 2009. Comparing the point predictions and subjective probability distributions of professional forecasters. Journal of Business & Economic Statistics 27, 30–41.

Faia, E., Fuster, A., Pezone, V., Zafar, B., 2021. Biases in information selection and processing: survey evidence from the pandemic. Review of Economics and Statistics. Forthcoming.

Franco, C., 2019. How does relative performance feedback affect beliefs and academic decisions? Working paper.

Freeman, R., 1971. The market for college trained manpower. Harvard University Press. Outstanding Books in Industrial Relations and Labor Economics, 1970–1979. Chapter 6 reprinted in In: Burton, J., Benham, L., Vaughn, W., Flanagan, R. (Eds.), Labor Market Analysis, 1971.

Fuster, A., Kaplan, G., Zafar, B., 2020a. What would you do with $500? Spending responses to gains, losses, news, and loans. The Review of Economic Studies 88, 1760–1795.

Fuster, A., Perez-Truglia, R., Wiederholt, M., Zafar, B., 2020b. Expectations with endogenous information acquisition: an experimental investigation. Review of Economics and Statistics. Forthcoming.

Fuster, A., Zafar, B., 2021. The sensitivity of housing demand to financing conditions: evidence from a survey. American Economic Journal: Economic Policy 13, 231–265.

Galashin, M., Kanz, M., Perez-Truglia, R., 2020. Macroeconomic Expectations and Credit Card Spending. Working Paper 28281. National Bureau of Economic Research.

Giustinelli, P., Shapiro, M.D., 2019. SeaTE: Subjective ex ante Treatment Effect of Health on Retirement. Working Paper 26087. National Bureau of Economic Research.

Glaser, M., Langer, T., Reynders, J., Weber, M., 2007. Framing effects in stock market forecasts: the difference between asking for prices and asking for returns. Review of Finance 11, 325–357.

Grewenig, E., Lergetporer, P., Werner, K., Woessmann, L., 2020. Incentives, search engines, and the elicitation of subjective beliefs: evidence from representative online survey experiments. Journal of Econometrics. Forthcoming.

Haaland, I., Roth, C., Wohlfart, J., 2021. Designing information provision experiments. Journal of Economic Literature. Forthcoming.

Hanspal, T., Weber, A., Wohlfart, J., 2021. Exposure to the COVID-19 stock market crash and its effect on household expectations. Review of Economics and Statistics 103 (5), 994–1010.

Harrison, G.W., Phillips, R.D., 2014. Subjective Beliefs and Statistical Forecasts of Financial Risks: The Chief Risk Officer Project. Palgrave Macmillan UK, London, pp. 163–202.

Hastings, J., Neilson, C.A., Zimmerman, S.D., 2015. The effects of earnings disclosure on college enrollment decisions. Working Paper 21300. National Bureau of Economic Research.

Heckman, J.J., Vytlacil, E., 2005. Structural equations, treatment effects, and econometric policy evaluation. Econometrica 73, 669–738.

Jappelli, T., Pistaferri, L., 2014. Fiscal policy and MPC heterogeneity. American Economic Journal: Macroeconomics 6, 107–136.

Jensen, R., 2010. The (perceived) returns to education and the demand for schooling. The Quarterly Journal of Economics 125, 515–548.

Karni, E., Safra, Z., 1995. The impossibility of experimental elicitation of subjective probabilities. Theory and Decision 38, 313–320.

Laudenbach, C., Weber, A., Wohlfart, J., 2021. Beliefs About the Stock Market and Investment Choices: Evidence from a Field Experiment. Working Paper.

Lewis, D.J., Makridis, C., Mertens, K., 2019. Do Monetary Policy Announcements Shift Household Expectations? Working Papers 1906. Federal Reserve Bank of Dallas.

Link, S., Peichl, A., Roth, C., Wohlfart, J., 2021. Information Frictions among Firms and Households. Working paper.

Manski, C.F., 2004. Measuring expectations. Econometrica 72, 1329–1376.

Mian, A., Sufi, A., Khoshkhou, N., 2015. Government Economic Policy, Sentiments, and Consumption. Working Paper 21316. National Bureau of Economic Research.

Mobius, M., Niederle, M., Niehaus, P., Rosenblat, T., 2014. Managing Self-Confidence. Working paper.

Murphy, A.H., Winkler, R.L., 1970. Scoring rules in probability assessment and evaluation. Acta Psychologica 34, 273–286.

Qian, W., 2020. House Price Expectations and Consumption – a Survey-based Experiment. Working Paper. University of Notre Dame.

Roth, C., Settele, S., Wohlfart, J., 2022. Risk exposure and acquisition of macroeconomic information. American Economic Review: Insights 4 (1), 34–53.

Roth, C., Wohlfart, J., 2020. How do expectations about the macroeconomy affect personal expectations and behavior? Review of Economics and Statistics 102, 731–748.

Wiswall, M., Zafar, B., 2015a. Determinants of college major choice: identification using an information experiment. The Review of Economic Studies 82, 791–824.

Wiswall, M., Zafar, B., 2015b. How do college students respond to public information about earnings? Journal of Human Capital 9, 117–169.

Wiswall, M., Zafar, B., 2021. Human capital investments and expectations about career and family. Journal of Political Economy 129, 1361–1424.

Zimmermann, F., 2020. The dynamics of motivated beliefs. The American Economic Review 110, 337–361.

Zwane, A.P., Zinman, J., Van Dusen, E., Pariente, W., Null, C., Miguel, E., Kremer, M., Karlan, D.S., Hornbeck, R., Giné, X., et al., 2011. Being surveyed can change later behavior and related parameter estimates. Proceedings of the National Academy of Sciences 108, 1821–1826.

Expectations as data

What do the data tell us about inflation expectations?[☆]

Francesco D'Acunto[a], **Ulrike Malmendier**[b,c,d], **and Michael Weber**[e,c,d]

[a]*Georgetown University, Washington, DC, United States*
[b]*University of California at Berkeley, Berkeley, CA, United States*
[c]*CEPR, London, United Kingdom*
[d]*NBER, Cambridge, MA, United States*
[e]*University of Chicago, Chicago, IL, United States*

5.1 Introduction

Subjective expectations are a key determinant of virtually all forward-looking decisions households and firms make. Within the set of subjective expectations, inflation expectations play a special role because they determine households' savings and consumption decisions via the consumption Euler equation, which describes the relationship between perceived real interest rates and consumption. Inflation expectations also drive agents' wage bargaining, durable investment including housing and mortgage choices, and portfolio choices (Bernanke, 2007). Because inflation expectations affect the decisions and actions of many economic actors, they also affect aggregate economic outcomes. The New Keynesian Phillips curve—a leading theory that explains the determination of realized inflation—attributes an important role to inflation expectations.

Central banks around the world actively try to manage inflation expectations. In normal times, when no constraints on nominal policy rates bind, many central banks operate under the assumption that inflation expectations are well anchored and that changes in nominal policy rates transmit one-for-one to perceived real interest rates based on the Fisher equation. In times when an effective lower bound on nominal policy rate binds, the management of inflation expectations becomes especially important because it remains one of the only tools available to central banks to affect agents' perceived real interest rates and hence their consumption, savings, debt, and investment decisions.

Given the important role of inflation expectations for households' economic choices and aggregate outcomes, we might expect economists and central bankers to have a deep understanding of the properties of households' inflation expectations, their formation process, and how expectations transmit into economic decisions. And yet, after the rational-expectations revolution of the 1970s, economists seemingly lost interest in studying the actual expectations formation process. Instead, most of the literature adhered to the postulate that in a rational-expectations setting, the economic model implies the repre-

[☆] We thank Rudi Bachmann, Giorgio Topa, and Wilbert van der Klaauw. Weber gratefully acknowledges financial support from the University of Chicago Booth School of Business and the Fama Research Fund.

Handbook of Economic Expectations. https://doi.org/10.1016/B978-0-12-822927-9.00012-4

133

sentative agent's expectations directly. Moreover, full information rational expectations (FIRE) models predict no dispersion in the subjective expectations of economic agents.

These theoretical predictions stand in stark contrast to a growing literature documenting systematic deviations from the FIRE paradigm. For instance, households' inflation expectations are upward biased relative to ex-post outcomes and the inflation rates central banks target. Forecast errors are predictable by publicly available data. And, the dispersion in inflation expectations across households is substantial.

This chapter summarizes and discusses critically the body of knowledge about subjective inflation expectations the recent literature has produced based on micro-level survey data.

In the first part, we provide an overview of commonly used sources of survey-based data on inflation expectations. We discuss the pros and cons of their designs and argue that, ultimately, the nature of the economic questions researchers want to ask dictates which source is most appropriate to use.

In the second part, we present a set of facts about households' inflation expectations—the time series, the cross section, and the term structure of inflation expectations. We also compare the most salient features of households' inflation expectations with those of professional forecasters, who are arguably among the most sophisticated agents on which micro-level information about inflation expectations is available. This comparison allows us to assess which features of households' inflation expectations are peculiar to the household sector and which are more general regularities.

The most salient regularity in households' inflation expectations is the substantial cross-sectional dispersion, which is systematically correlated with demographic characteristics. Based on this premise, in the third part of this chapter we overview the recent body of work on the determinants of households' inflation expectations. We highlight four sets of findings. First, we discuss the significant role of everyday price signals. Households focus on the price changes of goods they purchase frequently, such as grocery items, rather than the price changes of a representative consumption bundle when forming their inflation expectations. Moreover, households put a higher weight on positive relative to negative price changes when forming inflation expectations, which helps explain the persistent upward bias.

Second, the accumulation of those personal experiences over individuals' lifetimes has a significant long-run effect. Personal past inflation experiences, such as the high inflation in the 1970s, affect inflation expectations of those who experienced it for years. The influence of personal exposure and past experiences is present even among the most sophisticated professionals, such as the members of the Federal Open Market Committee (FOMC). This role of personal experiences goes beyond mere overextrapolation from recent observations and explains persistent differences across cohorts.

These two sets of findings suggest agents use the prices they directly observe in their daily lives to form expectations about aggregate inflation, exactly as posited by Lucas (1972, 1973) in his seminal islands model. It turns out that Lucas provided a more literal description of reality than he probably intended.

Third, we discuss the role of cognition in explaining the accuracy of individual-level subjective expectations, their cross-sectional variation, and the time-series properties. We also discuss recent research that documents and quantifies how heterogeneous cognitive abilities have aggregate effects by muting the transmission of monetary and fiscal policies because limited cognition results in biased expectations formation and sub-optimal economic choices.

Fourth, we review research on how individuals gather and process economic information, how information feeds into their beliefs, and how the transmission of economic policies could be enhanced by using communication to the general public as a policy tool on the part of central banks and governments.

In the last part of the chapter, we provide an overview of how households' inflation expectations relate to their economic choices based on micro-level data. We discuss evidence on the effects of inflation expectations on intertemporal consumption choices and on the financing of such decisions—mortgages and debt to finance housing and other current consumption as well as financial investments to finance future consumption through current savings. We stress that understanding how inflation expectations affect choices in the field begets substantial follow-up empirical and theoretical research.

We conclude the chapter with a review of open questions in the area of households' subjective expectations and how researchers can lever existing data sets as well as new ad-hoc surveys. We argue that further research might also inform advances in models with heterogeneous beliefs and novel models of expectations formation.

5.2 **Data sources**

In this section, we introduce the most common data sources on households' inflation expectations. We emphasize the differences in terms of sample periods, the surveyed populations, the design of survey questions, and the availability of cross-linked information.

5.2.1 **Michigan Survey of Consumers**

The Michigan Surveys of Consumers (*MSC*) is one of the longest-running household surveys in the world. It is conducted by the Survey Research Center at the University of Michigan since 1946, initially three times per year, then quarterly (1960–1977), and finally monthly (since 1978; see Curtin (1982)). Each wave contains about 50 core questions and has around 500 survey participants representative of the US population. It has a rotating panel component: each month about 60 percent of interviewees are first-time respondents, whereas 40 percent were interviewed six months prior.

Data on inflation expectations are available since 1953.[1] The survey elicits inflation expectations through a two-step procedure. First, it asks respondents whether they think *prices in general* will increase, decrease, or stay the same over the next 12 months. Second, the survey asks those who answered "increase" or "decrease" "By about what percent do you expect prices to go (up/down) on average?" (The early survey waves only contain the categorical questions.) In many periods, the survey includes the same set of questions for a longer, five-to-ten year horizon. Since March 1982, the survey includes a follow-up question to those responding "stay the same" in the first step as the administrators of the survey had found that such respondents often meant to say that the inflation rate stays the same. The *MSC* elicits a broad set of motivations underlying households' reported inflation expectations. The wealth of belief elicitations and demographic information in combination with the long time series allows researchers to assess the effects of aggregate shocks on households' inflation expectations.

---

[1] The 1953–1977 surveys are available from the Inter-University Consortium for Political and Social Research (*ICPSR*) at the University of Michigan. From 1959 to 1971, the winter-quarter Survey of Consumer Attitudes were administered as part of the Survey of Consumer Finances (*SCF*), also available at the *ICPSR*. The data from 1978 onward are available via the University of Michigan Survey Research Center.

On the negative side, responses larger than 5% are probed, that is, interviewers ask respondents whether the response is correct. This probing might alert households to think that their answers are incorrect, possibly biasing the resulting distribution of numerical inflation expectations. Moreover, by asking about changes in prices in general, rather than inflation rates, the survey might induce individuals to think about grocery prices, which are not representative of the overall consumption bundle (see van der Klaauw et al. (2008); de Bruin et al. (2011)). Finally, the *MSC* has a smaller number of households than other surveys and only a small panel component, which limits the scope to analyze demographic and spatial heterogeneity.

5.2.2 New York Fed Survey of Consumer Expectations

The Survey of Consumer Expectations (*SCE*) by the Federal Reserve Bank of New York is a more recent widely used data source. The *SCE* is a nationally representative monthly rotating panel, which started in June 2013; in it, 1300 household heads participate up to 12 times. The core module elicits subjective expectations about personal and aggregate outcomes such as income, inflation, and unemployment. The survey also contains special modules that are either fully ad-hoc or repeated regularly (such as modules on credit access, labor markets, and spending). The *SCE* elicits numerical expectations as well as full subjective probability distributions. Chapter 1 in this Handbook contains a detailed description of these data.

The SCE uses two elicitation methods. First, it asks households whether they think that there will be inflation or deflation and elicits a point estimate. Second, it elicits a subjective probability distribution for inflation by asking for the percent chance that inflation might take values in each of a set of predefined nonoverlapping bins centered around zero. The bin width is larger for bins farther from zero, up to open intervals of ± 12% or more. Warning messages alert respondents if the sum of the probabilities differs from 100.

The relatively short time series currently available is arguably the SCE's main shortcoming. Answers' anchoring is limited to the preset symmetric bins around 0 and the narrower bin width for smaller values of inflation. Moreover, an increase in average inflation expectations due to a spike in expected inflation rates of more than 12% cannot be detected.

5.2.3 European Commission Consumer Survey

Internationally, the European Commission (EC) has pioneered the elicitation of households' inflation and other macroeconomic expectations from representative samples across different countries. Since 1972, the Directorate General for Economic and Financial Affairs (DG ECFIN) coordinates the *EC Consumer Survey* with harmonized questions translated into national languages. The monthly survey consists of repeated cross sections. The sample size is currently 31,810 household heads and ranges from 600 participants in Cyprus to 2000 in Germany, Italy, Spain, and Belgium. Data are collected by national institutions, which have to approve access to their country-level micro-data for research purposes.

The EC Consumer Survey provides a long time series and a large cross-section of households. One disadvantage is that not all countries participated throughout the sample period. Moreover, quantitative expectations were not elicited until 2003. As with the *MSC*, researchers have proposed approaches to leverage the qualitative responses. For instance, D'Acunto et al. (2022a) show that the share of households who expect inflation to increase approximates subsequent realized inflation much more closely than average quantitative point estimates and with less noise and is a strong predictor of households' consumption choices.

5.2.4 Ad-hoc surveys

Other recent surveys have been fielded on an "ad hoc" basis, both in the US and internationally. These surveys are typically designed with the purpose of matching the responses to existing micro-level data about the same households and their economic choices in the field.

The *Chicago Booth Expectations and Attitudes Survey* (*CBEAS*), for instance, was first fielded in July 2015 on about 60,000 households from the Kilts Nielsen Consumer Panel (*KNCP*). The *KNCP* records the nondurable consumption bundles of these households through itemized scanner data. The *CBEAS* was originally designed to test whether price changes of nondurable goods help explain households' inflation expectations and economic choices in other domains, such as durable spending, investment, and labor supply. The survey includes 44 questions and obtained responses from 92,511 individuals across two waves. It elicits demographic information such as education levels, employment status, occupation, rent, mortgages, and other expenses. It then elicits numerical perceived inflation (over the previous 12 months) and expected inflation (over the next 12 months), in terms of both point estimates and probability distributions. To avoid framing effects, the *CBEAS* randomizes between an *MSC*-inspired question about the prices of things on which respondents spend money and the *SCE* question about general consumer inflation.

Since 2018, quarterly waves have been fielded to allow for information-provision experimental treatments on the effects of monetary and fiscal policy communication on households' inflation expectations (Coibion et al., 2022a, 2020a, 2021b). Later waves assess households' expectations during the COVID-19 crisis, the effectiveness of policy communication during a pandemic, and the use of stimulus payments (Coibion et al., 2020c, 2022b, 2020d,e).

Other ad hoc surveys have targeted single cross sections and often include randomized information treatments. For instance, Andre et al. (2019) access a representative US cross section through *Lucid* to assess how households process economic information and think about the relationship between macroeconomic expectations and economic decision-making. D'Acunto et al. (2021a) run a one-wave expectations-elicitation survey through *Qualtrics* on a representative US cross-section to assess the effects of FOMC diversity (or lack thereof) on consumers' macroeconomic expectations and trust in the Fed. Coibion et al. (2020f) also run a survey through *Qualtrics* to study how political polarization shapes macroeconomic beliefs and how the provision of polling data shapes expected election outcomes and macroeconomic beliefs in the days leading to the 2020 US presidential election. D'Acunto et al. (2020a) paired up with *Statistics Finland* to elicit Finnish households' inflation expectations and the effect of different types of communication about the ECB's interventions during the COVID-19 pandemic.

Online platforms such as Amazon Mechanical Turk (*mTurk*) have also become standard platforms for ad hoc surveys. This approach allows garnering just-in-time information around or immediately after specific economic shocks. For instance, Binder (2020) provides a timely assessment of how the COVID-19 pandemic affected US households' macroeconomic expectations right at the time of the shock. These platforms offer great flexibility and immediate fielding although the lack of representativeness and the presence of bots on the platform are caveats. Best practices to reduce these concerns include using *mTurk*-provided filters of the respondent pool as well as including attention-verification and typing questions to identify potential bots (for instance, see D'Acunto (2018)). Online platforms have also been used to provide ancillary analyses of specific effects and economic channels when reaccessing the main survey population would be impractical (for instance, see Cavallo et al. (2017), D'Acunto et al. (2019c), and D'Acunto et al. (2021a)).

5.2.5 Comparing elicited inflation expectations across surveys

Varying survey features—eliciting point estimates vs. probability distributions, asking about different prices, or adding probing follow-up questions after unusual answers—are likely to generate differences in responses. The differences between eliciting point estimates or probability distributions have attracted attention. Point estimates leave households free to report any level of inflation expectations they deem likely. Probability distributions, instead, impose more structure on the elicitation process along at least four dimensions. First, researchers choose upper- and lower-bounds for expected levels of inflation between which they partition the distribution in intervals. Households are likely to infer that levels of inflation in the open intervals above and below the limits are deemed implausible by the researchers. Second, researchers choose the intervals between the bounds, which are usually symmetric around zero. In response, households might be more likely to anchor their expectations closer to zero, which would reduce the cross-sectional dispersion in elicited expectations. Third, the widths of the intervals are typically narrower for values around 0, possibly resulting in participants inferring that values close to zero are more plausible. And, some of the surveys provide examples of how to fill probability distributions which might anchor answers.[2] Fig. 5.1 shows evidence consistent with these conjectures using the responses elicited using the point-estimate and the probability-distribution questions of the *SCE*.

The average inflation expectations implied by the point-estimate question are systematically higher by about 2 percentage points (pp) than those implied by the probability distributions (Panel A). The dynamics of average inflation expectations are quite similar across elicitation methods, although the higher volatility of point estimates hints at the possibility of higher cross-sectional variation for this type of question. Panel B indeed reveals a standard deviation about 5 pp higher each month for point estimates. A few salient facts about household expectations' dispersion are common across elicitation methods. For instance, in March 2020 disagreement about inflation expectations surged in both cases, with the spike in point estimates being noticeably larger.[3]

Turning to the role of "probing" follow-up questions, we compare average point estimates of expected inflation in the *MSC* and the *SCE* in Fig. 5.2. The two series display similar variation over time and imply a substantial upward bias relative to ex-post realized inflation, but average expected inflation in the *SCE* is consistently above that in the *MSC*. This systematic level difference likely arises because of two features of the *MSC*, that is, follow-up probing and truncation of answers above 95%.[4]

---

[2] Note also that the probability-distribution question requires a set of assumptions to obtain point estimates and within-individual uncertainty measures, especially in case respondents assign the whole probability to one interval or provide disconnected distributions. For detailed discussions, see Armantier et al. (2013); Krüger and Pavlova (2019).

[3] An alternative explanations for the difference in average expectations across the two elicitation methods are that respondents report minimum-loss estimates when answering the point estimates, see discussion in Chapters 1 and 3 in this Handbook.

[4] Chapter 8 in this Handbook discusses additional details on the possible role of survey question wording, nudging, and other design features on respondents' answers.

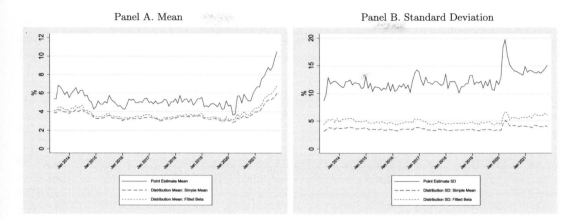

FIGURE 5.1 Households' Inflation Expectations: Point Estimates vs. Probability Distributions

Panel A(B) compares the monthly mean (standard deviation) of households' inflation expectations over time across survey question designs in the New York Fed Survey of Consumer Expectations (SCE). Specifically, we compare the mean from the point estimate question for inflation over the next twelve months (after dropping households that report inflation expectations larger than 100%) to the simple mean from the distribution question and the implied mean from fitting a beta distribution to the distribution question following De Bruin et al. (2011). In the distribution question, each household is asked to provide probability mass to prespecified bins of possible inflation rates over the next twelve months that has to add up to 100. The bins range from +12% to −12%. To calculate the simple average expected inflation over the next 12 months, we calculate the weighted average of the distribution question using the center of each bin and ±14% for the extreme bins. The sample period is from June 2013 to November 2021.

Ultimately, the choice of question format depends on the economic questions researchers tackle. Without a probability distribution, no questions about subjective uncertainty can be answered. Moreover, eliciting probability distributions reduces the noise in the data on quantitative inflation expectations. At the same time, if respondents do not understand probabilities they might report values that do not correspond to their actual expectations, which is especially problematic if respondents' understanding of probabilities correlates with demographic characteristics that also predict inflation expectations. The guiding role of preset intervals might also hinder respondents from reporting extreme values they might deem likely.[5]

We conclude this section by comparing households' inflation expectations in the US (*SCE*) and internationally (EC Consumer Survey). Fig. 5.3 compares the average expected inflation rates at the quarterly level to harmonize survey frequencies. Two facts are noticeable. First, average expected one-year-ahead inflation is consistently above realized inflation in each of the two monetary areas (around or below 2% before the COVID-19 pandemic). Second, US average inflation expectations are less volatile than EU ones. Also, contrary to US expectations, EU expectations have consistently increased from

---

[5] Chapters 1 and 9 in this Handbook discuss the issue of bin selection on subsequent responses.

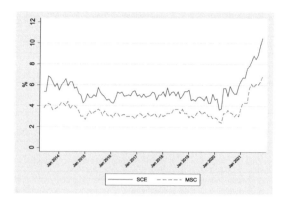

FIGURE 5.2 Households' Inflation Expectations: SCE vs. MSC

This figure compares the monthly mean of households' inflation expectations from the New York Fed Survey of Consumer Expectations (SCE) and the Michigan Survey of Consumers (MSC) over time. The MSC elicits point estimates for monthly expected changes in prices in general over the next 12 months. For the SCE, we use the point estimate question for inflation over the next twelve months after dropping households that report inflation expectations larger than 100%. The sample period is from June 2013 to November 2021.

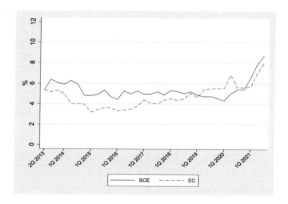

FIGURE 5.3 Households' Inflation Expectations: US vs. EU

This figure compares the quarterly mean of households' inflation expectations from the New York Fed Survey of Consumer Expectations (SCE) and European Commission Consumer Survey (EC) over time. The EC elicits point estimates for monthly expected inflation rates over the next twelve months at the quarterly frequency for households in all European Union member countries and several applicant countries. For the SCE, we use the point estimate question for inflation over the next 12 months after dropping households that report inflation expectations larger than 100%. The sample period is from Q2 2013 to Q3 2021.

2015 until the end of 2019 and hence before the COVID-19 pandemic started. The changing composition of countries included in the EC Consumer Survey complicates the interpretation of this drift. This last set of facts is important in light of the often US-centered discussion of beliefs formation. In the next section, we will provide such US-based stylized facts about households' inflation expectations keeping in mind that, internationally, baseline features are similar but their extent might differ.

5.3 Stylized facts

In this section, we discuss the main facts economists have learned from data on the inflation expectations of households and experts. We focus on households in the *SCE* to maintain consistency across samples.

5.3.1 Time-series facts

Fig. 5.4 plots the distribution of the mean of US households' 12-month-ahead numerical inflation expectations from subjective distributions.[6] In Panel A, we report the average numerical expectation, as well as the 25th, 50th, and 75th percentiles. Panel B compares households' mean with a proxy for the 12-month-ahead market participants' inflation expectations based on data on inflation swaps.

First, households' inflation expectations are systematically higher than the inflation expectations of financial market participants (Panel B), and this phenomenon is not driven by outliers who report implausibly high values (Panel A). Rather, most of the distribution of households' inflation expectations lies above market participants' expectations. Only households at or below the 25th percentile hold numerical inflation expectations that are consistent with those of market participants.

Second, the distribution of households' inflation expectations is systematically skewed with the mean monthly expected inflation rate being about 1 pp higher than the median. This skewness stresses the importance of understanding whether specific demographic characteristics correlate with systematically higher inflation expectations.

A third feature relates to disagreement over time (Mankiw et al. (2003)). In times of relatively stable economic conditions (between June 2013 and early 2020), households across the distribution report changes in inflation expectations that are directionally similar from one month to the other. In times of large negative economic shocks such as the onset of the COVID-19 pandemic in February and March 2020, though, disagreement arises: the 25th and 75th percentiles move in opposite directions. Higher disagreement did not fully revert by September 2020. Households at the 25th percentile behave similarly to financial market participants and display deflationary expectations in March 2020, but revert to the pre-COVID-19 levels immediately afterwards. By contrast, households at the 75th percentile (and to a lower extent median households) increase their inflation expectations and do not revert them for several months.[7]

---

[6] We calculate the implied mean of the distribution, assigning values of $+14\%$ and -14% to the extreme bins.

[7] These facts are consistent with Armantier et al. (2021) and Weber et al. (2022a). Weber et al. (2022b) show that realized inflation at the household level also increased substantially at the onset of the pandemic.

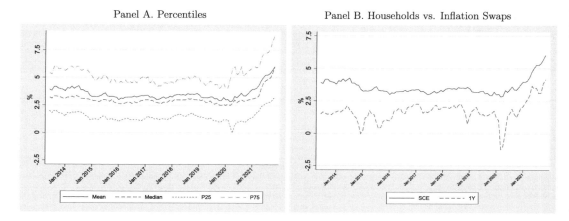

FIGURE 5.4 Households' and Financial Markets' Inflation Expectations

Panel A plots the mean and the 25th, 50th, and 75th percentiles of households' inflation expectations over time. We use the distribution question in the New York Fed Survey of Consumer Expectations (SCE) to measure inflation expectations over the next 12 months. In this question, each household is asked to provide probability mass to prespecified bins of possible inflation rates over the next twelve months that has to add up to 100. The bins range from +12% to −12%. To calculate the average expected inflation over the next 12 months, we calculate the weighted average of the distribution question using the center of each bin and ±14% for the extreme bins. Panel B compares average expected inflation from the SCE with breakeven inflation rates obtained from inflation swaps. Month-end prices of zero-coupon US dollar inflation swaps for a 1-year duration are obtained from Bloomberg. The sample period is from June 2013 to November 2021.

5.3.2 Cross-sectional facts

Fig. 5.4 reveals substantial cross-sectional heterogeneity and dispersion in households' inflation expectations: The interquartile range of 12-month-ahead expectations is consistently around 3 pp, even though realized annual inflation has been at or below the Fed inflation target of 2% until the onset of the COVID-19 pandemic. To dig deeper into this cross-sectional heterogeneity, we consider the role of different demographic groups.[8]

In Fig. 5.5, the top left panel compares respondents of different genders and confirms a fact about inflation expectations that has been documented consistently across data sets and time periods at least since Jonung (1981): Women hold systematically higher inflation expectations than men. We discuss explanations in Section 5.4.

The middle top panel of Fig. 5.5 considers three age groups—below 40, between 40 and 60, and above 60. Younger respondents tend to have lower average inflation expectations than older respondents.

In the right top panel, we consider three racial groups—Blacks, Whites, and Asian Americans. The number of Black and Asian-American respondents in the *SCE* is substantially lower than the number

---

[8] See also Bruine de Bruin et al. (2010) and Weber et al. (2022b) for demographic differences in inflation expectations.

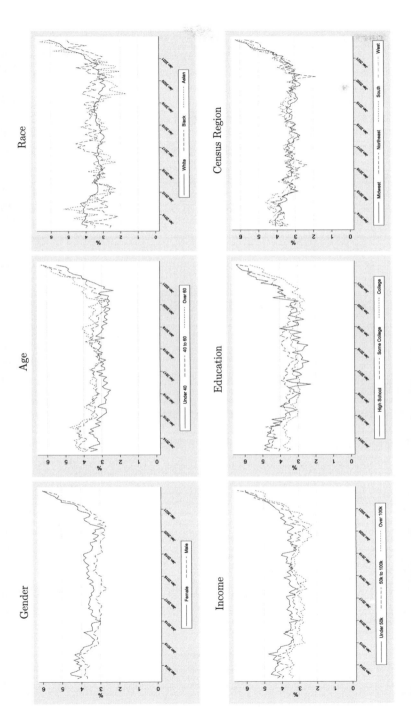

FIGURE 5.5 Households' Inflation Expectations by Demographic Characteristics

This figure plots households' average inflation expectations over time for several subsamples of socioeconomic characteristics indicated on top of each subplot. We use the distribution question in the New York Fed Survey of Consumer Expectations (SCE) to measure inflation expectations over the next 12 months. In this question, each household is asked to provide probability mass to prespecified bins of possible inflation rates over the next 12 months that has to add up to 100. The bins range from +12% to −12%. To calculate the average expected inflation over the next 12 months, we calculate the weighted average of the distribution question using the center of each bin and ±14% for the extreme bins. The sample period is from June 2013 to November 2021.

of White respondents, hampering the interpretation of differences in the time-series volatility across racial groups. We can, however, assess differences in average inflation expectations: The average 12-month-ahead inflation expectations of Blacks tend to be above those of Whites and Asian-Americans with notable exceptions at the beginning and end of the sample.

The panels in the bottom part of Fig. 5.5 consider univariate sample splits based on respondents' income (bottom left), education levels (bottom center), and the region of residence (bottom right).

For income, we see a clear negative correlation: the lower is income, the higher are inflation expectations. Average inflation expectations of respondents who earn less than $50K per year are about 1 pp higher than for respondents who earn more than $100k. In terms of education levels, college-educated respondents differ from others: Their inflation expectations are about 3% before the COVID-19 pandemic, whereas respondents who never attended college expect inflation around 4% in most months. The latter groups also display more volatile expectations, even if the smaller size of this subsample might at least in part explain this feature. We then consider US Census regions—the Midwest, Northeast, South, and West—to capture local business-cycle-driven inflation dynamics (Beraja et al., 2019). Respondents in the US West have higher average inflation expectations than others in most, though not in all months.

Overall, the cross-sectional facts highlight the importance of individual-level drivers of inflation expectations,[9] and suggest that traditional models of beliefs formation, which target the mean, median, or otherwise representative household expectations, fail to account for the most notable empirical features of inflation expectations.

5.3.3 Term-structure facts

So far, our evidence has focused on households' 12-month-ahead inflation expectations, but several surveys also elicit medium-term inflation expectations.

Arguably, the most salient fact here is that barely any term structure exists—short- and long-run expectations are consistently close to each other (see Fig. 5.6). The COVID-19 pandemic stands out as an exception: households expected higher short-run than long-run inflation. As we saw when discussing the time series of households' expectations, March 2020 was a time of substantial disagreement about short-run inflation and, on average, of spiking short-run inflation expectations, which explains the negative term structure whose gap builds over time.

5.3.4 Households versus professional forecasters

In the last part of this section, we compare households' inflation expectations to those of professional forecasters from the *Survey of Professional Forecasters*, who likely display the highest level of sophistication in the formation of inflation expectations.

---

[9] Indeed, using panel data from the Netherlands, Vellekoop and Wiederholt (2019) provide direct evidence that individual fixed effects strongly determine individuals' inflation expectations in the cross-section.

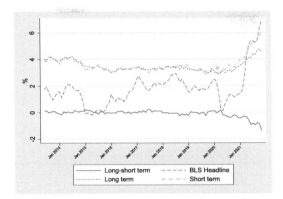

FIGURE 5.6 The Term Structure of US Households' Inflation Expectations

This figure plots the monthly mean difference of households' inflation expectations over the 12 months starting in 24 months and the next 12 months over time and the realized CPI inflation rate over the last 12 months. We use the distribution question in the New York Fed Survey of Consumer Expectations (SCE) to measure inflation expectations. In this question, each household is asked to provide probability mass to prespecified bins of possible inflation rates over the next twelve months that has to add up to 100. The bins range from +12% to −12%. To calculate the average expected inflation, we calculate the weighted average of the distribution question using the center of each bin and ±14% for the extreme bins. The sample period is from June 2013 to November 2021.

Panel A of Fig. 5.7 reports the inflation expectations of professional forecasters over time. To be consistent with the plot for households, we report the average numerical expectations in each quarterly sample as well as the 25th, 50th, and 75th percentiles.[10]

Professionals' expectations differ from those of households. First, professionals expect inflation below 2.5% before the COVID-19 pandemic, whereas only the bottom quarter of households does. To appreciate this difference, we compute the average quarterly (rather than monthly) expected inflation rate for households. We see in Panel B of Fig. 5.7 that the mean expected inflation rate fluctuates around 4% for households, whereas it varies around 2% for professional forecasters—a value that is close to realized inflation rates during most of our sample period.

Second, we detect no skewness in the expectations of professional forecasters: the cross-sectional distribution is rather symmetric, with the mean and the median overlapping throughout the sample period.

Third, the distribution of professional forecasters' inflation expectations is tight. The interquartile range is typically below 0.5 pp, and thus substantially less dispersed around the mean than for households.

Lastly, professional forecasters reacted to the onset of the COVID-19 pandemic differently than households. In the second and third quarters of 2020, virtually all professional forecasters revised their

---

[10] Note that the frequency of the *Survey of Professional Forecasters* is quarterly and hence we do not observe monthly cross-sections as we do for the households in the *SCE*.

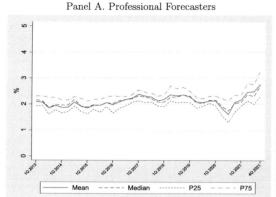

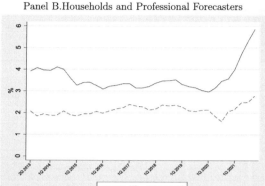

FIGURE 5.7 Households vs. Professional Forecasters

Panel A plots the monthly mean and the 25th, 50th, and 75th percentiles of professional forecasters' inflation expectations over time. We use the micro data underlying the official Philadelphia Fed Survey of Professional Forecasters (SPF) to measure inflation expectations. Professional forecasters are asked to give point estimates for the expected quarter-on-quarter inflation rate for the current and the next 4 quarters. Using these quarter-on-quarter inflation rates, we calculate the expected inflation rate over the next 4 quarters for each forecaster. The sample period is from Q1 2013 to Q4 2021. Panel B compares the mean inflation expectations of professional forecasters and households over time. We use the distribution question in the New York Fed Survey of Consumer Expectations (SCE) to measure inflation expectations over the next 12 months. In this question, each household is asked to provide probability mass to prespecified bins of possible inflation rates over the next twelve months that has to add up to 100. The bins range from +12% to −12%. To calculate the average expected inflation over the next 12 months, we calculate the weighted average of the distribution question using the center of each bin and ±14% for the extreme bins. The sample period is from Q2 2013 to Q3 2021.

12-month-ahead inflation expectations downwards, including those at the 75th percentile of the distribution.

The comparison of household and professional forecasters' inflation expectations over time suggests a set of interesting directions to consider for future research. To begin with, only a fraction of households—those whose level of expectations is up to the 25th percentile of the distribution—have expectations that are consistent with those of sophisticated agents. Proxies for sophistication are thus likely to help explain the cross-sectional variation in households' inflation expectations at each point in time. Moreover, the high dispersion of households' inflation expectations suggests that the sources of information households use to form their expectations might differ from those used by forecasters. Even more interestingly, the disagreement in households' but not forecasters' reaction to major economic shocks suggests heterogeneous processing of economic news by households. We return to this observation when discussing how exposure to selected price signals drives households' belief-formation process in Section 5.4.

5.4 Determinants of inflation expectations

We now discuss how existing research informed by the facts documented in Section 5.3 has dug deeper into understanding the determinants of households' inflation expectations.

5.4.1 Exposure to price signals

Lucas (1975) might have provided a closer description of reality than he anticipated when writing that "the history of prices [...] observed by an individual is his source of information on the current state of the economy and [...] of information on future price." Indeed, Lucas (1975) is often cited as a foundation for models of information frictions, such as rational inattention, which play an important role in our understanding of the real effects and transmission of monetary policy (Sims, 2003). Recent research has provided empirical support for models of sticky information (Mankiw and Reis, 2002), in which agents update their information infrequently and noisy information models (Mackowiak and Wiederholt, 2009), in which agents receive noisy signals (Coibion and Gorodnichenko, 2015a).[11]

As it turns out, the prices consumers observe when shopping indeed are their main source of information to form expectations about aggregate inflation rather than simply looking up inflation statistics. A powerful example is the "gender expectations gap." Since Jonung (1981), one of the longest-standing puzzles in individuals' inflation expectations has been the difference in inflation expectations across genders. Although both men and women's average inflation expectations are upward biased, those of women are systematically higher. This stylized fact is a robust feature of inflation expectations across time periods, surveys, and countries. While prior literature had relied on surveying participants from different households, D'Acunto et al. (2021c) establish these gender differences within members of the same household. Hence, systematic differences across households such as family structures, wealth, income, or financial choices cannot drive this difference.

To establish this fact, D'Acunto et al. (2021c) exploit a unique feature of the CBEAS, which we discussed in Section 5.2: researchers can observe all grocery purchases of participating households, including product categories, shopping outlets, and per-unit prices, alongside the expectations of general inflation of several household members. Using this unique empirical setting, D'Acunto et al. (2021c) show that the gender expectations gap is robust to a host of observable characteristics such as income, education, and occupation, but also preference parameters such as patience and risk aversion, which they elicit in the CBEAS.

So what explains the gender expectations gap? D'Acunto et al. (2021c) find the gap only arises within households in which women are solely responsible for grocery shopping. In households in which both male and female household heads partake in grocery chores, the gap entirely disappears. In other words, exposure to systematically different price signals (grocery versus nongrocery) appears to strongly predict beliefs about the aggregate inflation rate.

But why does exposure to grocery prices bias inflation expectations systematically upwards? Grocery prices are more volatile than other prices and price changes typically revert more quickly. These features are one reason why many central banks focus on measures of core inflation, which exclude the price changes of groceries (and gas and energy), to analyze inflationary pressures in the economy. By

---

[11] See also the discussion in Chapter 11 in this Handbook.

doing so, though, central banks miss the powerful influence of daily price stimuli on inflation expectations.

In a related study, D'Acunto et al. (2021b) provide details on the underlying mechanism. Via the *CBEAS*, they run two customized surveys on the *KNCP* in June 2015 and 2016 to elicit inflation expectations as well as to create measures of realized inflation at the household level following Kaplan and Schulhofer-Wohl (2017). They find households that witnessed the highest realized inflation in their grocery bundle have the highest inflation expectations and this relationship is monotonic.

Furthermore, measures of realized inflation that overweigh frequently-purchased goods or positive price changes drive the baseline association between realized inflation and inflation expectations at the individual level. Other determinants of price changes such as their volatility, recency, or alternative weighting schemes do not add explanatory power. These associations are likely causal because they hold up in analyses exploiting changes in realized inflation and inflation expectations within individual across the two survey waves. The within-individual analysis also rules out that time-invariant individual characteristics, such as cognitive abilities or financial sophistication, might explain the findings.

These results suggest that the salience of observed price signals, including the frequency of exposure, exerts a strong influence on individual expectations. Related work confirms this insight. For example, Brachinger (2008) shows in aggregate time series that overweighing the inflation of goods consumers purchase frequently helps explain the aggregate perceived inflation of German households. Coibion and Gorodnichenko (2015b) show that the surge of gas prices can explain the missing disinflation during the Financial Crisis of 2007 to 2009 because of the large resulting spike in average inflation expectations. And, Cavallo et al. (2017) show that the price changes of specific grocery goods consumers purchase influence their inflation expectations.

In summary, both the high average level of inflation expectations and the dispersion across genders are tightly linked to the heterogeneous price signals individuals observe in their daily lives. And, this influence is not eliminated by financial sophistication, education levels, income, or other time invariant and time-varying individual characteristics.

5.4.2 The role of the lifetime experiences and neuroplasticity

Turning from gender to another demographic characteristic, age, Section 5.3 showed fluctuations in the relative positions of older and younger cohorts' inflation expectations over time. Understanding this heterogeneity is of first-order importance given the vastly different consumption and saving decisions agents make at different stages of their life cycles and the systematically different roles of younger and older cohorts on the borrowing and lending side of financial markets.

It turns out that cohorts' personal lifetime exposures to price signals ("experience effects") can explain the magnitude of these age differences, cohorts' relative position, and its evolution over time. Malmendier and Nagel (2016) find that a (weighted) average of personal inflation experiences over individuals' lives strongly predicts individual inflation expectations. Their model of experience-based learning also helps to understand the differential reaction of younger and older cohorts to the stark increase in inflation in 2020-21.

How does experience-based learning work? The authors build on adaptive learning by assuming that individuals form expectations based on historical data (Marcet and Sargent, 1989; Evans and Honkapohja, 2001). Individuals try to estimate an AR(1) process as the perceived law of motion (e.g., Orphanides and Williams (2004)) recursively from past data. Malmendier and Nagel (2016) depart from prior models by allowing individuals to put more weight on data experienced during their lives than on other

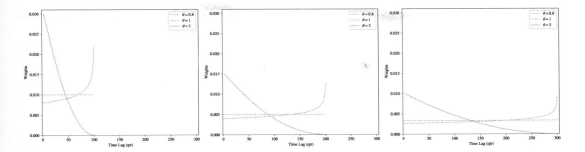

FIGURE 5.8 The Implied Weighting of Experienced Data

The figure shows the implied weights on past inflation rates for a young (25 years, left), mid-aged (50 years, middle), and old (75, right) individual for different values of θ, which modulates a differential weighting across time periods.

historical data. Fig. 5.8 illustrates the effects of making the implied weight individuals assign to recent news dependent on age for a hypothetical 25-, 50-, and 75-year-old person.[12] We see the difference in the lengths of the past time series that obtains additional weights, and that recent realizations obtain higher weights from younger than older generations. The figure shows that if $\theta = 1$ then individuals equally weigh all lifetime experiences; if instead $\theta > 1$, a recency bias emerges. In either case, beliefs do not converge. The weights on historical realizations diminish over time and perpetual disagreement arises.

Empirically, Malmendier and Nagel (2016) use data from the *MSC* and estimate θ to be 3.044, implying recency-biased weights (see Fig. 5.8). Moreover, they find a strong relationship between past experiences and current expectations: for each 1 pp difference in learning-from-experience forecast, the model predicts a 0.672 pp difference in one-year inflation expectations.

The experience-effect estimates capture much of the fluctuating relative positions of older and younger cohorts (see Fig. 5.9, updated from Malmendier and Nagel (2016)). The figure reports both the raw data and fitted values based on the model estimates for young (below 40), mid-aged (between 40 and 60), and old individuals (above 60), but expressed as deviations from the cross-sectional mean expectations (across all ages) in each period. The data reveal not only the disagreement and fluctuating relative positions of different generations, but also large dispersion across age groups, up to almost 3 pp during the high-inflation years of the 1970s and early 1980s.

The fitted lines reveal that learning-from-experience explains a large degree of the differences in inflation expectations, such as the sizable difference in the late 1970s and early 1980s, including the double-spike. It also captures all the low-frequency reversals in the expectations gap across cohorts.

One key implication of experience-based learning is thus that, at any point in time, older individuals are affected by a longer lifetime history of inflation realizations than younger individuals, and hence the different age groups will disagree about future inflation paths. For example, before the increase in inflation during the COVID-19 pandemic, younger generations in the US had never experienced

---

[12] The weights are also a function of the parameter θ, which modulates a differential weighting across time periods.

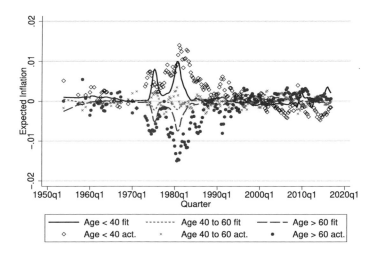

FIGURE 5.9 Fitted Experience-based Expectations

The figure shows both the raw MSC data and the fitted values based on the model estimates for the four-quarter moving averages of mean 12 months inflation expectations of young individuals (below 40), mid-aged individuals (between 40 and 60), and old individuals (above 60), expressed as deviations from the cross-sectional mean expectation across all age groups in each period.

high inflation, whereas older generations did in the 1970s and 1980s. And, indeed, those aged 60 and above had persistently higher inflation expectations over the last decade. If the high levels of inflation persist, experience-based learning predicts that the expectations of younger cohorts will approach and ultimately cross those of the older generations. For the most recent data, this reversal has already happened for the middle-aged group. For the younger cohorts, the reversal is slowed down by the second key component of experience-based learning, perceived persistence. Because the persistence parameter is around 0 for younger cohorts but higher for older cohorts (around 0.2 at the end of the time series in Malmendier and Nagel (2016)), older cohorts do update more strongly immediately after an increase in inflation sets in.

Overall, lifetime experiences appear to be powerful predictors of expectations because individuals assign extra weight to personal past experiences, with an embedded recency bias (higher weights on the more recent experiences).

Personal experiences affect not only the expectations of households, but also those of sophisticated professionals. For example, Malmendier et al. (2021) document that members of the FOMC who have personally experienced higher inflation during their lifetime are more likely to indicate higher inflation expectations in their semiannual Monetary Policy Reports to Congress. These differences in beliefs feed into actual votes: those with experience of higher inflation are more likely to dissent from the chairperson's proposal, and their dissent is more likely to be hawkish.

The findings on lifetime experiences are just examples from a growing body of work on experience-based learning that suggests that the effect of prolonged exposure to certain price stimuli might be best thought as inducing a "rewiring" of the brain's hardware rather than information processing via the brain's (unbiased or biased) software. As discussed in Malmendier (2021a,b), the excess weight assigned to personally experienced outcomes mirrors the underlying neurological process of synapse formation and reflects the modern understanding of neuroplasticity, that is, of the brain's lifelong ability to change and adapt as a result of experience. The brain forms stronger connections between neurons that are used more frequently, while those that are not used eventually die over time.

5.4.3 The role of cognition and human frictions

But how can we reconcile the large differences between households' and professional forecasters' expectations? Forecasters' expectations, as we discussed in Section 5.3, are much closer to actual realizations and less dispersed than households' expectations.

One route is noting that forming expectations and beliefs is a cognitively demanding task.[13] Agents have to think about various future inflation scenarios and assign probabilities to each. Professional forecasters are used to this task, but consumers are not. Thinking about the potential price changes of frequently-purchased goods might help consumers assess future states of the world, but does not help with assessing the probabilities of each state.[14]

To assess if and how the cognitive burden of the expectations-formation process plays a role that is quantitatively relevant, D'Acunto et al. (2019a,c) relate individuals' cognitive abilities to the formation of inflation expectations in uniquely rich Finnish micro-data, which combine administrative information on individual cognitive abilities, income, wealth, as well as individuals' actual consumption and saving choices and survey-based economic expectations and plans. They find that cognitive abilities (IQ) predict individuals' inflation expectations above and beyond the direct effects of income, education levels, wealth, and other proxies for economic sophistication: forecast errors for inflation are monotonically declining in IQ. Moreover, high-IQ individuals form inflation expectations in line with existing models of beliefs formation—in particular, extrapolative beliefs best explain their expectations-formation process—whereas the expectations-formation of low-IQ individuals is inconsistent with extant theoretical models.

The authors also find that the direct effect of cognitive abilities on the accuracy of inflation expectations feeds into actual and planned consumption and saving choices, because high-IQ individuals behave in line with the consumer Euler equation, whereas those below the median of the population by IQ, even when not facing any financial or liquidity constraints, do not behave in line with any standard model of intertemporal consumption optimization.

The role of cognitive abilities in driving inflation expectations and hence economic choices is not only important to our understanding of microeconomic mechanisms, but has also important aggregate implications. D'Acunto et al. (2019b) show that the aggregate effects of fiscal and monetary policies are substantially reduced by the fact that many households, due to heterogeneous cognitive abilities, do not form expectations and plans in line with economic incentives. These understudied frictions to the

---

[13] Trust in central banks might increase individuals' willingness to anchor their expectations to the official figures and avoid the need to form expectations on their own (D'Acunto et al., 2021a). Evidence for the US, though, where inflation was low for decades, shows that many households do not have well-anchored inflation expectations: Coibion et al. (2022a) find that 40% of a large sample of Americans think the Fed inflation target is higher than 10%.

[14] Note that agents do not need a formal knowledge of the concept of probability to form beliefs. They only need to assess, even qualitatively, how likely they expect different future scenarios.

transmission of economic policies, which the authors label "human frictions," have effects of similar magnitude as financial frictions and other supply-side forces that a large body of work in economics and finance has been studying for decades.

In addition to deepening our understanding of how human frictions affect beliefs formation, economic choices, and the effectiveness of policy interventions, a big open question is how such frictions could be overcome by policy makers to increase the effectiveness of their actions. Cognitive abilities are for the most part an endowment of individuals that can only marginally be improved over time. Rather than aiming at reducing these frictions, a promising avenue is the design of simple policies as well as simple and targeted communication about policies. D'Acunto et al. (2022a) and D'Acunto et al. (2020a) provide observational and experimental evidence that scratches the surface of our understanding of which types of policies and which forms of policy communication can effectively influence the beliefs and choices of all consumers in the economy.

5.4.4 **The role of the media and communication**

A third dimension that matters for individuals' beliefs formation is the availability of information about the economy, which they might gather from the media or the communication of central banks and governments. In fact, researchers consistently find that individuals do not gather and/or process readily available information that would be relevant to their beliefs and choices. For instance, Dräger (2015) shows that media reports on inflation have a small role in explaining the average inflation expectations of a nordic population. Coibion et al. (2020b) document that one of the most dramatic policy announcements in recent decades, the 2020 Federal Reserve's change in policy framework, was entirely unnoticed by most US households. Moreover, Lamla and Vinogradov (2019) show that less salient FOMC announcements do not change individuals' inflation expectations either (see also De Fiore et al. (2021)). The muted role of official communication is consistent with households focusing on their own shopping experiences when forming inflation expectations, as demonstrated by D'Acunto et al. (2021b).

A recent line of research investigates the roots of this lack of response to news through "information-provision experiments" (Haaland et al. (2021)). Such experiments elicit prior inflation expectations, then provide pieces of economic information to different subsets of respondents, and finally elicit posterior beliefs. The updating in inflation expectations relative to the control group that does not receive any (relevant) information shows the causal effect of the information provision. Several experiments have documented that information can affect inflation expectations when it reaches individuals. For example, Armantier et al. (2016) and Cavallo et al. (2017) find that individuals update their expectations to information about past inflation or professional inflation forecasts. Coibion et al. (2022a) provide information in three different formats: (1) simple summary statistics of inflation, (2) full FOMC press releases, and (3) media coverage of FOMC releases in the USA Today. They find that formats (1) and (2) generate large average revisions of inflation expectations of 1 to 1.5 pp, while the effect of (3) is smaller. Traditional news media (including USA Today) rank low in terms of credibility and trust, which might explain the differential effects. Although trust in central banks is generally high (Ehrmann et al., 2013; Christelis et al., 2020), many consumers do not know who runs the central bank (Kumar et al., 2015) and 40% of Americans think the Federal Reserve aims to target an inflation rate of more than 10% (Coibion et al., 2022a).

Why the information provided by trusted institutions is ignored by decision-makers is an open puzzle, especially given the powerful role such communication plays in standard macroeconomic models

(Del Negro et al., 2012). Recent work suggests that information is ignored when policies are hard to understand by consumers. D'Acunto et al. (2022a), for instance, show that German households sharply increased their average inflation expectations following the preannouncement of a future increase of the value added tax (*unconventional fiscal policy*, see D'Acunto et al. (2018)), whose effect on future prices is obvious. Instead, the same households' inflation expectations did not adjust to any forward guidance announcements by the European Central Bank, whose implications for future inflation are obscure to anybody who is not sophisticated in economic matters. Moreover, D'Acunto et al. (2021a) show that a diverse monetary policy committee in terms of gender and race increases the effectiveness of policy communication and consumers' willingness to acquire information about monetary policy. These findings could be driven by the principle that the experiences of others "similar to me," including role models, affect belief formation (D'Acunto et al., 2019d; Malmendier and Veldkamp, 2022).

Understanding how innovative and engaging communication formats such as the reggae songs by the Central Bank of Jamaica or the use of Twitter as a policy tool might increase policy effectiveness is an exciting open area of research (D'Acunto et al., 2020a).

5.5 Inflation expectations and economic choices

The patterns of expectations formation and underlying mechanisms documented above have relevant implications only if agents' inflation expectations help explain their economic decisions. Despite recent disagreement on the interpretation of such patterns (Rudd, 2021), a growing body of work using high-quality micro-data convincingly shows that inflation expectations do guide the economic choices of households and firms.

Below, we discuss the empirical research that has documented a direct role of inflation expectations in shaping consumption, financing, and savings decisions.

5.5.1 Intertemporal consumption and saving choices

Virtually all modern models of the intertemporal consumption decision attribute a fundamental role to subjective inflation expectations. Inflation expectations can affect the consumption–savings nexus through various channels. On the one hand, higher subjective inflation expectations reduce perceived real interest rates (via the Fisher equation) and hence the incentives to save, which increases current consumption (via the consumer Euler equation). On the other hand, higher inflation is a tax on nominal assets, and a negative wealth effect in addition to negative income effects can counteract the positive influence of inflation expectations on current consumption. Some households might also expect nominal policy rates to increase more than one for one (via the Taylor rule) when their inflation expectations increase (Carvalho and Nechio, 2014), again implying a decrease rather than an increase in current consumption. Moreover, if the second moment of subjective inflation expectations, that is, inflation uncertainty, increases, agents' precautionary-saving motive increases (Ben-David et al., 2018), which further reduces current consumption (D'Acunto et al., 2020b; Coibion et al., 2021a). Finally, individuals might have a supply-side view of the economy and associate higher inflation with bad economic times (Kamdar et al., 2019; Andre et al., 2019; Coibion et al., 2020a).

Empirically, researchers find evidence consistent with these different mechanisms. Bachmann et al. (2015) find no significant relationship between inflation expectations and consumption for participants in the *MSC*, except for those whose expectations lie within 1 pp of the ex-post realized inflation rate. For the latter subset, higher inflation expectations predict higher current consumption, which corroborates the predictions of the Euler equation. Burke and Ozdagli (2021) confirm these results for nondurable spending. Similarly, using micro-data on inflation expectations, spending plans, and individuals' cognitive abilities, D'Acunto et al. (2019c) show that only high-cognition consumers, who form inflation expectations closer to ex-post realized inflation rates, behave in line with the consumer Euler equation. Binder and Brunet (2020) and Ichiue and Nishiguchi (2015) also find a positive association between inflation expectations and consumption spending during the beginning of the Korean War and in Japan, two episodes in which nominal rates were held constant.

The lack of empirical evidence in support of the consumer Euler equation for agents whose inflation expectations are inaccurate might indicate that the large cross-sectional dispersion in quantitative inflation expectations obfuscates the relationship between inflation expectations and consumption. In fact, when using qualitative expectations data and spending plans from the EC Consumer Survey, D'Acunto et al. (2018, 2022a) find strong economic and statistical evidence that households who expect higher inflation over the following 12 months have a higher current propensity to purchase durable goods. Using customized survey data from Germany, Dräger and Nghiem (2021) confirm the positive association between inflation expectations and current spending. Crump et al. (2022) also find a positive relation in the SCE data.

More recently, researchers have turned to assessing whether the relation between inflation expectations and current consumption is causal. To this aim, D'Acunto et al. (2022a) exploit a natural experiment in Germany: In November 2005, a newly-elected government preannounced an increase in the value added tax to be effective in 2007. The announcement increased German consumers' inflation expectations independent of their levels of income or education. Using a difference-in-differences strategy, the authors document a contemporaneous increase in consumers' readiness to purchase durable goods immediately after the announcement, compared to their willingness before and to the change in the willingness to spend of observationally similar households in France, Sweden, and the UK and show a large positive treatment effect of the announcement on spending. Bachmann et al. (2021) exploit an unexpected temporary cut in the value added tax combined with customized surveys and household scanner data to show large effects on household spending via intertemporal substitution, that is, individuals' inflation expectations.

Another path to establish causality is the design of randomized information-provision experiments. After the random provision of information about inflation, Coibion et al. (2022a, 2020a) find a positive effect of inflation expectations on nondurable spending in survey and household scanner data that lasts up to six months, though they do not detect a positive effect for durables. Coibion et al. (2019) estimate a small effect of inducing higher inflation expectations on nondurable spending among Dutch households and a *negative* effect on durable spending. They rationalize this result with a sharp decrease in real income and aggregate demand expectations for households who update upwards their inflation expectations, which is consistent with the findings of Kamdar et al. (2019) and Andre et al. (2019).

5.5.2 Financing current consumption: mortgages and borrowing

Inflation expectations are also a key determinant of financing decisions, especially for larger durable goods such as housing.

Empirically, Coibion et al. (2020a) show that households revise their inflation and interest rate expectations jointly. Hence, we can trace interest rate expectations to inflation expectations, which are

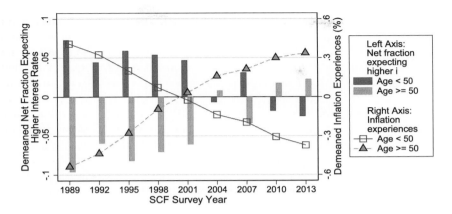

FIGURE 5.10 Interest-Rate Expectations and Inflation Experiences

The figure illustrates the cohort-specific time series of answers to the *SCF* question "Five years from now, do you think interest rates will be higher, lower, or about the same as today?" from 1989 to 2013. Cohorts are split into "older" and "younger" based on the sample median of age. The graph shows each group's deviations from the survey-year mean (average across implicates) of the net fraction of respondents expecting interest rates to rise (fraction answering "higher" minus the fraction answering "lower").

in turn determined by lifetime inflation experiences as discussed in Section 5.4. Fig. 5.10, replicated from Botsch and Malmendier (2021), illustrates this result using qualitative interest-rate expectations from the Survey of Consumer Finances (*SCF*).[15] A higher net fraction of the younger cohorts (red (dark gray in print version) bars) than the older cohorts (blue (gray in print version) bars) expected higher interest rates during the early *SCF* waves (1989, 1992, etc.), but the relative positions switched in the mid-2000s, precisely when the lifetime inflation experiences of younger cohorts (red (dark gray in print version) squares) switched from higher to lower than those of older cohorts (blue (gray in print version) triangles). The reversal reflects young households without Great-Inflation experience coming in and the fading memory of Great Inflation among older cohorts (see Fig. 5.8).

Turning to households' financial choices, the most prominent borrowing decision pertains to the financing of housing—whether to take up a mortgage, how much to borrow, and the choice between a fixed- and adjustable-rate contract (FRM versus ARM). Higher inflation expectations tilt the decision towards fixed-rate borrowing as consumers who expect higher nominal interest rates discount the sum of fixed payment obligations by more, lowering its present value. Under an ARM, instead, borrowers with high inflation- and interest-rate expectations expect both higher nominal ARM payments and using a higher discount rate. These two effects offset. As a result, borrowers who expect higher future interest rates perceive FRMs to be relatively cheaper.

Malmendier and Nagel (2016) provide evidence consistent with this channel: *SCF* borrowers with higher past inflation experiences also have a greater inclination to choose an FRM. Botsch and Mal-

---

[15] The figure is based on the following SCF question: *"Five years from now, do you think interest rates will be higher, lower, or about the same as today?"*

mendier (2021) confirm these results in multivariate analyses, and are the first to show directly the inflation-experience–interest-rate channel and its influence on the ARM-versus-FRM choice using the Census Bureau's Residential Finance Surveys (*RFS*). The RFS surveys households as well as mortgage servicers, thus providing both demographic information and mortgage contract terms. Botsch and Malmendier (2021) estimate that a 1 pp increase in experienced inflation increases a borrower's willingness to pay for a FRM by 6–14 basis points.

Exposure to high past inflation also affects the decision to become homeowner in the first place, as consumers aim to shield against inflation with real assets. For example, in a survey of 700 homeowners across European countries, Malmendier and Steiny Wellsjo (2020) find that 72% select concerns about price increases (*protection against inflation* and *protection against rent price increases*) as their motives for homeownership, dominating all other motives such as tax benefits, higher quality of homes to buy, low mortgage rates, and even increasing house prices. Moreover, a third of all respondents, mostly those who experience high inflation, say that inflation concerns directly impacted their personal decision to buy a house. Hence, regardless of whether real estate is a suitable inflation hedge, or not, the inflation-hedge motive is important to homeowners.

Malmendier and Steiny Wellsjo (2020) utilize the vast cross-sectional differences in past inflation experiences across European countries as well as within-country differences (by cohort) to explain the substantial differences in homeownership rates across and within countries. Experience-based forecasts of future inflation, including the "national memory" of past inflationary periods, thus appear to play a significant role in shaping housing markets both across and within countries.

5.5.3 Investment and savings decisions

The implications of inflation expectations for investment and savings decisions are less explored, and the existing evidence is weaker. Malmendier and Nagel (2016), for instance, test the prediction that investors with higher inflation expectations shy away from fixed-rate bonds in the *SCF*. Their estimations yield a negative albeit insignificant relationship. Armantier et al. (2015) find clearer evidence in an incentivized survey experiment, albeit using hypothetical investment choices. Here, respondents participate more in inflation-indexed savings vehicles when they expect higher inflation. Survey participants with lower numeracy and financial and economic literacy, instead, make choices that cannot be rationalized by standard economic theory. Overall, these findings complement Leombroni et al. (2020), who show that disagreement about future inflation between younger and older households in the late 1970s helps understand household borrowing, lending, and portfolio choices. Advancement on this question requires observational data on individual portfolios and fixed-rate investment opportunities.

Better data would also allow testing the effects of inflation expectations on other economic choices, such as business-to-business contracting, price setting, wage negotiations, and labor-supply decisions. All of these arenas are lacking direct evidence of their relation to inflation expectations, largely due to the lack of viable data sources.

5.6 Conclusion and outlook

Inflation expectations determine the effectiveness of fiscal and monetary policy and shape realized inflation (Bernanke, 2007; Galí, 2015; Sims, 2009). Households' inflation expectations are especially important because they determine consumption, financing, and investment choices (Weber et al., 2022a). And yet, until recently, our understanding of how individuals form inflation expectations was in a state of "relative ignorance" (Armantier et al., 2013).

Over the last decade, departures from the rational-expectations paradigm revived the interest in how subjective expectations of inflation are formed. We now know that agents' inflation expectations are upward biased, dispersed, and volatile. They differ systematically across demographic groups—gender, race, age, income, and other characteristics—and reflect the specific price changes individuals observe in their daily lives. Personal experiences and cognition mediate the role of abstract knowledge and information and are the best predictors of actual, decision-relevant expectations.

The wealth of new facts in the domains of inflation expectations and other economic and financial expectations indicate a pervasive deviation of subjective expectations from the FIRE paradigm. These facts can help discriminate across existing models of beliefs formation but also inform new models and approaches. New-generation behavioral macro models should not only match salient features of average expectations over time but also depart from the representative-agent modeling framework to be consistent with the substantial sources of heterogeneity documented in the literature (D'Acunto et al. (2019c)). Models accounting for heterogeneous past experiences, memory, and context-specific retrieval such as Wachter and Kahana (2019, 2020); Bordalo et al. (2020); Malmendier et al. (2020a) (see the overview in Malmendier and Wachter (2021)) represent a promising avenue because of the recent supporting evidence from the field (D'Acunto and Weber (2022)).

More research is also needed on the impact of inflation expectations on economic choices—a line of inquiry that becomes especially important in times of rising inflation. More data-construction projects that combine survey-based expectations and economic plans with the contemporaneous economic decisions of households and registry-based income and wealth information, such as in D'Acunto et al. (2019b), will be crucial to advance on this front. For instance, how do inflation expectations shape agents' wage expectations, their wage bargaining decisions, and their labor supply? We also know little about how inflation expectations shape portfolio choice decisions due to return expectations and the perceived inflation hedging properties of alternative assets. The possibility of reaching consumers directly with surveys at the time they engage in spending and financial transactions through FinTech apps is a promising direction to obtain rich micro data in a logistically viable fashion (for instance, see D'Acunto et al. (2020b) and D'Acunto et al. (2022b)).

The mechanisms we discuss in this chapter apply beyond the context of inflation. For example, personal experiences have a long-lasting effect on stock-market participation (Malmendier and Nagel, 2011), on the dynamics of stock-market trading (Malmendier et al., 2020a), and on patterns of international capital flows such as home bias, fickleness, and retrenchment (Malmendier et al., 2020b). Malmendier and Shen (2020) find that unemployment experiences predict lasting consumer pessimism as well as consumption and saving choices.[16] More individual-level data on previous exposure to price signals and other macroeconomic variables are needed to deepen this area of research.

---

[16] See the overviews of economic and financial applications in Malmendier (2021b) and Malmendier (2021a), respectively.

References

Andre, P., Pizzinelli, C., Roth, C., Wohlfart, J., 2019. Subjective models of the macroeconomy: Evidence from experts and a representative sample. Available at SSRN 3355356.

Armantier, O., Bruine de Bruin, W., Potter, S., Topa, G., van der Klaauw, W., Zafar, B., 2013. Measuring inflation expectations. Annual Review of Economics 5 (1), 273–301.

Armantier, O., Bruine de Bruin, W., Topa, G., van der Klaauw, W., Zafar, B., 2015. Inflation expectations and behavior: do survey respondents act on their beliefs? International Economic Review 56 (2), 505–536.

Armantier, O., Koşar, G., Pomerantz, R., Skandalis, D., Smith, K., Topa, G., van der Klaauw, W., 2021. How economic crises affect inflation beliefs: evidence from the COVID-19 pandemic. Journal of Economic Behavior & Organization 189, 443–469.

Armantier, O., Nelson, S., Topa, G., van der Klaauw, W., Zafar, B., 2016. The price is right: updating inflation expectations in a randomized price information experiment. Review of Economics and Statistics 98 (3), 503–523.

Bachmann, R., Berg, T.O., Sims, E., 2015. Inflation expectations and readiness to spend: cross-sectional evidence. American Economic Journal: Economic Policy 7 (1), 1–35.

Bachmann, R., Born, B., Goldfayn-Frank, O., Kocharkov, G., Luetticke, R., Weber, M., 2021. A temporary VAT cut as unconventional fiscal policy. Technical report. National Bureau of Economic Research.

Beraja, M., Hurst, E., Ospina, J., 2019. The aggregate implications of regional business cycles. Econometrica 87 (6), 1789–1833.

Ben-David, I., Fermand, E., Kuhnen, C., Li, G., 2018. Expectations uncertainty and household economic behavior. National Bureau of Economic Research.

Bernanke, B., 2007. Inflation expectations and inflation forecasting. Technical report. Board of Governors of the Federal Reserve System (US).

Binder, C., 2020. Coronavirus fears and macroeconomic expectations. Working Paper.

Binder, C., Brunet, G., 2020. Inflation expectations and consumption: Evidence from 1951. Available at SSRN 3594809.

Bordalo, P., Coffman, K., Gennaioli, N., Schwerter, F., Shleifer, A., 2020. Memory and representativeness. Psychological Review.

Botsch, M.J., Malmendier, U., 2021. The long shadows of the great inflation: Evidence from residential mortgages. Available at SSRN 3888762.

Brachinger, H.W., 2008. A new index of perceived inflation: assumptions, method, and application to Germany. Journal of Economic Psychology 29 (4), 433–457.

Bruine de Bruin, W., van der Klaauw, W., Downs, J.S., Fischhoff, B., Topa, G., Armantier, O., 2010. Expectations of inflation: the role of demographic variables, expectation formation, and financial literacy. The Journal of Consumer Affairs 44 (2), 381–402.

Burke, M.A., Ozdagli, A.K., 2021. Household inflation expectations and consumer spending: Evidence from panel data.

Carvalho, C., Nechio, F., 2014. Do people understand monetary policy? Journal of Monetary Economics 66, 108–123.

Cavallo, A., Cruces, G., Perez-Truglia, R., 2017. Inflation expectations, learning, and supermarket prices: evidence from survey experiments. American Economic Journal: Macroeconomics 9 (3), 1–35.

Christelis, D., Georgarakos, D., Jappelli, T., Van Rooij, M., 2020. Trust in the central bank and inflation expectations. International Journal of Central Banking 16 (6), 1–37.

Coibion, O., Georgarakos, D., Gorodnichenko, Y., Kenny, G., Weber, M., 2021a. The effect of macroeconomic uncertainty on household spending. Technical report. National Bureau of Economic Research.

Coibion, O., Georgarakos, D., Gorodnichenko, Y., van Rooij, M., 2019. How does consumption respond to news about inflation? Field evidence from a randomized control trial. Technical report. National Bureau of Economic Research.

Coibion, O., Georgarakos, D., Gorodnichenko, Y., Weber, M., 2020a. Forward guidance and household expectations. Technical report. National Bureau of Economic Research.

Coibion, O., Gorodnichenko, Y., 2015a. Information rigidity and the expectations formation process: a simple framework and new facts. The American Economic Review 105 (8), 2644–2678.

Coibion, O., Gorodnichenko, Y., 2015b. Is the Phillips curve alive and well after all? Inflation expectations and the missing disinflation. American Economic Journal: Macroeconomics 7 (1), 197–232.

Coibion, O., Gorodnichenko, Y., Knotek II, E.S., Schoenle, R., 2020b. Average inflation targeting and household expectations. Technical report. National Bureau of Economic Research.

Coibion, O., Gorodnichenko, Y., Weber, M., 2020c. The cost of the COVID-19 crisis: Lockdowns, macroeconomic expectations, and consumer spending. Technical report. National Bureau of Economic Research.

Coibion, O., Gorodnichenko, Y., Weber, M., 2020d. How did us consumers use their stimulus payments? Technical report. National Bureau of Economic Research.

Coibion, O., Gorodnichenko, Y., Weber, M., 2020e. Labor markets during the COVID-19 crisis: a preliminary view. Technical report. National Bureau of Economic Research.

Coibion, O., Gorodnichenko, Y., Weber, M., 2020f. Political polarization and expected economic outcomes. Technical report. National Bureau of Economic Research.

Coibion, O., Gorodnichenko, Y., Weber, M., 2021b. Fiscal policy and households' inflation expectations: Evidence from a randomized control trial. Technical report. National Bureau of Economic Research.

Coibion, O., Gorodnichenko, Y., Weber, M., 2022a. Monetary policy communications and their effects on household inflation expectations. Journal of Political Economy 130 (6), 1537–1584.

Coibion, O., Gorodnichenko, Y., Weber, M., 2022b. Does policy communication during COVID work? International Journal of Central Banking 18 (1), 3–39.

Crump, R.K., Eusepi, S., Tambalotti, A., Topa, G., 2022. Subjective intertemporal substitution. FRB of New York Staff Report (734).

Curtin, R.T., 1982. Indicators of consumer behavior: the university of Michigan surveys of consumers. Public Opinion Quarterly 46 (3), 340–352.

D'Acunto, F., 2018. Identity and choice under risk. Available at SSRN 3263787.

D'Acunto, F., Fuster, A., Weber, M., 2021a. Diverse policy committees can reach underrepresented groups. University of Chicago, Becker Friedman Institute for Economics Working Paper (2021-95).

D'Acunto, F., Hoang, D., Paloviita, M., Weber, M., 2019a. Cognitive abilities and inflation expectations. In: AEA Papers and Proceedings, vol. 109, pp. 562–566.

D'Acunto, F., Hoang, D., Paloviita, M., Weber, M., 2019b. Human frictions in the transmission of economic policy. Chicago Booth Research Paper. pp. 19–21.

D'Acunto, F., Hoang, D., Paloviita, M., Weber, M., 2019c. IQ, expectations, and choice. Working Paper, No. 25496. National Bureau of Economic Research.

D'Acunto, F., Hoang, D., Paloviita, M., Weber, M., 2020a. Effective policy communication: Targets versus instruments. Bank of Finland Research Discussion Paper (17).

D'Acunto, F., Hoang, D., Weber, M., 2018. Unconventional fiscal policy. In: AEA Papers and Proceedings, vol. 108, pp. 519–523.

D'Acunto, F., Hoang, D., Weber, M., 2022a. Managing households' expectations with unconventional policies. The Review of Financial Studies 35 (4), 1597–1642.

D'Acunto, F., Malmendier, U., Ospina, J., Weber, M., 2021b. Exposure to grocery prices and inflation expectations. Journal of Political Economy 129 (5), 1615–1639.

D'Acunto, F., Malmendier, U., Weber, M., 2021c. Gender roles produce divergent economic expectations. Proceedings of the National Academy of Sciences 118 (21).

D'Acunto, F., Rauter, T., Scheuch, C.K., Weber, M., 2020b. Perceived precautionary savings motives: Evidence from FinTech. Technical report. National Bureau of Economic Research.

D'Acunto, F., Rossi, A.G., Weber, M., 2019d. Crowdsourcing peer information to change spending behavior. CESifo Working Paper.

D'Acunto, F., Weber, M., 2022. Memory and beliefs: Evidence from the field. Working Paper.

D'Acunto, F., Weber, M., Yin, X., 2022b. Microfounding household debt cycles with diagnostic expectations. Working Paper.

De Bruin, W.B., Manski, C.F., Topa, G., van der Klaauw, W., 2011. Measuring consumer uncertainty about future inflation. Journal of Applied Econometrics 26 (3), 454–478.

de Bruin, W.B., van der Klaauw, W., Topa, G., 2011. Expectations of inflation: the biasing effect of thoughts about specific prices. Journal of Economic Psychology 32 (5), 834–845.

De Fiore, F., Lombardi, M.J., Schuffels, J., et al., 2021. Are households indifferent to monetary policy announcements? Technical report. Bank for International Settlements.

Del Negro, M., Giannoni, M.P., Patterson, C., 2012. The forward guidance puzzle. FRB of New York Staff Report (574).

Dräger, L., 2015. Inflation perceptions and expectations in Sweden – are media reports the missing link? Oxford Bulletin of Economics and Statistics 77 (5), 681–700.

Dräger, L., Nghiem, G., 2021. Are consumers' spending decisions in line with an Euler equation? Review of Economics and Statistics 103 (3), 580–596.

Ehrmann, M., Soudan, M., Stracca, L., 2013. Explaining European Union citizens' trust in the European Central Bank in normal and crisis times. Scandinavian Journal of Economics 115 (3), 781–807.

Evans, G.W., Honkapohja, S., 2001. Learning and Expectations in Macroeconomics. Princeton University Press, Princeton, NJ.

Galí, J., 2015. Monetary Policy, Inflation, and the Business Cycle: An Introduction to the New Keynesian Framework and Its Applications. Princeton University Press.

Haaland, I., Roth, C., Wohlfart, J., 2021. Designing information provision experiments. Journal of Economic Literature. Forthcoming.

Ichiue, H., Nishiguchi, S., 2015. Inflation expectations and consumer spending at the zero bound: micro evidence. Economic Inquiry 53 (2), 1086–1107.

Jonung, L., 1981. Perceived and expected rates of inflation in Sweden. The American Economic Review 71 (5), 961–968.

Kamdar, R., et al., 2019. The inattentive consumer: Sentiment and expectations. Manuscript. https://rupalkamdar.github.io/pdfs/Inattentive_Consumer.pdf.

Kaplan, G., Schulhofer-Wohl, S., 2017. Understanding the long-run decline in interstate migration. International Economic Review 58 (1), 57–94.

Krüger, F., Pavlova, L., 2019. Quantifying subjective uncertainty in survey expectations. Technical report, Discussion Paper Series.

Kumar, S., Afrouzi, H., Coibion, O., Gorodnichenko, Y., 2015. Inflation targeting does not anchor inflation expectations: Evidence from firms in New Zealand. Technical report. National Bureau of Economic Research.

Lamla, M.J., Vinogradov, D.V., 2019. Central bank announcements: big news for little people? Journal of Monetary Economics 108, 21–38.

Leombroni, M., Piazzesi, M., Schneider, M., Rogers, C., 2020. Inflation and the price of real assets. Technical report. National Bureau of Economic Research.

Lucas, R.E., 1972. Expectations and the neutrality of money. Journal of Economic Theory 4 (2), 103–124.

Lucas, R.E., 1973. Some international evidence on output-inflation tradeoffs. The American Economic Review 63 (3), 326–334.

Lucas, R.E., 1975. An equilibrium model of the business cycle. Journal of Political Economy 83 (6), 1113–1144.

Mackowiak, B., Wiederholt, M., 2009. Optimal sticky prices under rational inattention. The American Economic Review 99 (3), 769–803.

Malmendier, U., 2021a. Experience effects in finance: foundations, applications, and future directions. Review of Finance 25 (5), 1339–1363.

Malmendier, U., 2021b. *FBBVA Lecture 2020* Exposure, experience, and expertise: why personal histories matter in economics. Journal of the European Economic Association 19 (6), 2857–2894.

Malmendier, U., Nagel, S., 2011. Depression babies: do macroeconomic experiences affect risk-taking? The Quarterly Journal of Economics 126, 373–416.

Malmendier, U., Nagel, S., 2016. Learning from inflation experiences. The Quarterly Journal of Economics 131 (1), 53–87.

Malmendier, U., Nagel, S., Yan, Z., 2021. The making of hawks and doves. Journal of Monetary Economics 117, 19–42.

Malmendier, U., Pouzo, D., Vanasco, V., 2020a. Investor experiences and financial market dynamics. Journal of Financial Economics 136 (3), 597–622.

Malmendier, U., Pouzo, D., Vanasco, V., 2020b. Investor experiences and international capital flows. Journal of International Economics 124, 103302.

Malmendier, U., Shen, L.S., 2020. Scarred consumption. Working paper. UC-Berkeley.

Malmendier, U., Steiny Wellsjo, A., 2020. Rent or buy? Inflation experiences and homeownership within and across countries. Technical report. National Bureau of Economic Research.

Malmendier, U., Veldkamp, L., 2022. Information resonance. Working Paper.

Malmendier, U., Wachter, J., 2021. Memory of past experiences and economic decisions. Working Paper.

Mankiw, N.G., Reis, R., 2002. Sticky information versus sticky prices: a proposal to replace the new Keynesian Phillips curve. The Quarterly Journal of Economics 117 (4), 1295–1328.

Mankiw, N.G., Reis, R., Wolfers, J., 2003. Disagreement about inflation expectations. NBER Macroeconomics Annual 18, 209–248.

Marcet, A., Sargent, Thomas J., 1989. Convergence of least squares learning mechanisms in self-referential linear stochastic models. Journal of Economic Theory 48, 337–368.

Orphanides, A., Williams, J.C., 2004. Imperfect knowledge, inflation expectations and monetary policy. In: Bernanke, B.S., Woodford, M. (Eds.), The Inflation Targeting Debate. University of Chicago Press, Chicago, IL.

Rudd, J.B., 2021. Why do we think that inflation expectations matter for inflation? (And should we?).

Sims, C.A., 2003. Implications of rational inattention. Journal of Monetary Economics 50 (3), 665–690.

Sims, C.A., 2009. Inflation expectations, uncertainty and monetary policy.

van der Klaauw, W., Bruine de Bruin, W., Topa, G., Potter, S., Bryan, M.F., 2008. Rethinking the measurement of household inflation expectations: Preliminary findings. FRB of New York Staff Report (359).

Vellekoop, N., Wiederholt, M., 2019. Inflation expectations and choices of households.

Wachter, J.A., Kahana, M.J., 2019. A retrieved-context theory of financial decisions. Technical report. National Bureau of Economic Research.

Wachter, J.A., Kahana, M.J., 2020. Associative learning and representativeness. Available at SSRN 3602327.

Weber, M., D'Acunto, F., Gorodnichenko, Y., Coibion, O., 2022a. The subjective inflation expectations of households and firms: measurement, determinants, and implications. The Journal of Economic Perspectives. Forthcoming.

Weber, M., Gorodnichenko, Y., Coibion, O., 2022b. The expected, perceived, and realized inflation of US households before and during the COVID19 pandemic. IMF Economic Review.

Housing market expectations[☆]

Theresa Kuchler[a,b,c], **Monika Piazzesi**[d,b,c], **and Johannes Stroebel**[a,b,c]

[a]*New York University, New York, NY, United States*
[b]*NBER, Cambridge, MA, United States*
[c]*CEPR, London, United Kingdom*
[d]*Stanford University, Stanford, CA, United States*

The 2008 Global Financial Crisis was the culmination of a large boom–bust cycle in U.S. house prices. Observers quickly proposed overly optimistic house price expectations as a key factor in explaining the run-up and subsequent fall of house prices.[1] Expectations are a natural candidate as a key determinant of aggregate market outcomes since they are an important factor in intertemporal decision making in the presence of uncertainty. Many decisions in housing and mortgage markets—for example, whether to buy or sell a home and whether to default on a mortgage—are in part determined by individual expectations about future market conditions. Individual beliefs therefore have the potential to influence market-level outcomes and the aggregate economy. Following the Global Financial Crisis, researchers have focused on better understanding how individuals form housing market expectations, how these expectations determine individual decisions, and, ultimately, how those decisions influence aggregate outcomes. In this chapter, we review the existing literature on each step of the way from individual expectation formation to aggregate outcomes and propose promising avenues for future work.

To empirically study the determinants and effects of housing market expectations, researchers first need to be able to credibly measure expectations. Since people's expectations are not directly observable, researchers mostly rely on survey elicitation. We start by providing an overview of existing surveys of U.S. households' expectations of national or local housing markets as well as planned housing investments. We also highlight surveys of U.S. housing market expectations of professionals and industry experts. We conclude our overview of existing surveys by describing a number of surveys from outside the United States. We also briefly discuss alternative non-survey-based measures of expectations used by researchers, and end with a "wish list" of key elements that we would like to see included in future housing market expectation surveys.

We next use data from the Michigan Surveys of Consumers and the New York Fed Survey of Consumer Expectations to document a number of salient facts about the time-series and cross-sectional

---

[☆] We thank Sara Gong for outstanding research assistance, and Shifrah Aron-Dine, Rudi Bachmann, Andreas Fuster, Adam Guren, Brian Higgins, Wilbert van der Klaauw, Giorgio Topa, and participants at the "Handbook of Economic Expectations" conference for helpful feedback.
[1] For instance, Shiller (2007) described house price growth fueled by "public observations of price increases and public expectations of future price increases."

variation in U.S. house price expectations. We show that house price beliefs vary substantially over time and in the cross-section. We also document that only a small part of the cross-sectional variation in house price beliefs at any given point in time can be explained by basic demographic characteristics.

We then review a large literature that has used survey data to study how individuals form housing market expectations. Prior work has found that, across a range of settings such as the stock market, individuals rely on recently observed price changes when forming expectations about future prices. Similar forces appear to be at work in the housing market. We summarize work that has documented that recent house price changes affect house price expectations.[2] Since house price changes are known to be autocorrelated, it is a quantitative question whether the observed extrapolation by individuals when forming beliefs represents an optimal use of past information. Recent work suggests that individuals appear to underextrapolate from recent price changes when forming short-run expectations and overextrapolate when forming long-run expectations.

The observed extrapolation from past price changes suggests that households rely on information from recent episodes of price change when forming their expectations. We also summarize work that documents that people forming housing market expectations disproportionately rely on information from their recent personal experiences, their geographically local experiences, and the experiences of those in their social networks. Since individuals differ in terms of their experiences, locations, and social networks, their reliance on these factors when forming local and aggregate housing market expectations helps explain the very heterogeneous expectations observed in the data.

The same factors that influence individuals' average expected house price changes—own experiences, local experiences, and friend experiences—also influence higher moments of individuals' belief distributions. For example, we describe evidence that the dispersion of house price changes experienced within an individual's social network affects the variance of that individuals belief distribution.

Current ownership of housing also matters for the formation of house price expectations. In particular, a key difference between housing and other assets is that nonowners in the housing market (i.e., renters) have good information about the dividend stream of the asset, because they pay rent each month. This information may provide useful signals about the value of the asset itself, which owner-occupiers do not receive. We discuss evidence that suggests that, on average, renters indeed make better forecasts of future house prices during a housing boom than owners, but also that renter forecasts are more dispersed. While evidence from other asset markets suggests the presence of endowment effects, whereby owners become more optimistic than non-owners when they receive positive signals about their assets, the existing evidence on housing markets suggests the opposite effect.

Having explored some of the determinants of individuals' housing market expectations, we next summarize work that analyzes the effects of these beliefs on individuals' housing decisions. Identifying the effect of expectations on actual decisions is challenging, since few data sets contain information linking housing expectations to housing market decisions. Even if available, concerns about unobservable factors influencing both expectations and housing market decisions make it difficult to identify a causal effect. Using a variety of empirical approaches—including lab and field experiments—researchers have documented that housing market expectations indeed affect individual's housing investments, such as whether or not to buy or sell a home, how large of a home to buy,

---

[2] Throughout this chapter, we use the term house price expectations to refer to expected price changes for residential real estate more broadly, instead of referring more narrowly to expectations relating to houses or single-family residences.

and how much to pay or charge for a given home. In addition, expectations about future house prices, inflation, and interest rates affect individuals' decisions about how to finance their homes, such as how much leverage to take on and whether to choose fixed or variable rate mortgages.

In our final section, we describe work that analyzes the effects of individuals' housing market expectations on market-level and aggregate economic outcomes. Specifically, we explore the role of various expectations in explaining different housing market episodes, including the U.S. housing cycles of the 1970s and the 2000s, as well as the more recent house price increases during the 2010s. Some of the theoretical frameworks assume rational expectations and introduce preference shocks for housing that persistently increase the weight on housing consumption in the utility function. The dynamics of the preference shocks are then disciplined using survey evidence. More recent work abandons the rational expectations assumption and adopts models of belief formation that more directly aim to match the survey evidence, including the heterogeneity of beliefs observed in the survey responses.

6.1 **Measuring expectations**

To study the determinants and effects of housing market expectations, researchers need to be able to measure people's expectations. Unlike many other variables of interests (e.g., housing transactions, house prices, or mortgage decisions), these expectations are not easily observable.

Faced with the challenge of being unable to directly observe expectations, economists have traditionally focused on inferring expectations from individuals' observable actions. In most settings, however, observed choices are consistent with many possible combinations of preferences and expectations, requiring researchers to make strong assumptions on the structure of preferences or the exact process of forming expectations (see Manski, 2004, for a review). Over the past decades, researchers have therefore increasingly turned to surveys to directly elicit expectations. Indeed, we believe that if we want to learn what different agents are expecting house prices to look like in the future, the natural approach is to go and ask them.

6.1.1 **Surveys about housing market expectations**

We next describe a number of existing surveys of housing market expectations (see Chapter 1 in this Handbook for a detailed discussion of household surveys more generally). Table 6.2 summarizes the questions, sample periods, frequencies, and access modalities of these surveys.

The longest-running survey eliciting housing market expectations is the Michigan Surveys of Consumers. Founded in 1946 and fielded monthly to at least 500 households in the contiguous U.S., the core survey includes questions on current perceptions and expectations for the housing market: for instance, whether it is a good or bad time for buying and selling a house (and why), and whether (and by how much) prices of local homes will increase or decrease.[3] Another early survey effort focusing explicitly on housing market expectations was undertaken by Case and Shiller (1988), who surveyed a random sample of recent homebuyers in four U.S. metropolitan areas in 1988. The survey was fielded annually from 2003 to 2014 to a wider geographic area (Case et al., 2012).

---

[3] The questions on sentiments regarding current conditions for buying and selling go back to 1960, but those asking for point estimates of house price changes were added later in 2007.

As interest in better understanding housing market expectations grew during the housing boom and bust of the 2000s, more housing surveys emerged, many of them incorporating new knowledge about how to elicit various aspects of expectations in surveys. For example, the RAND American Life Panel (ALP) was one of the first surveys to elicit expectations in probabilistic form when, in 2009, it added questions about respondents' expectations about the price development of their own homes into its Financial Crisis Surveys (these surveys were fielded until 2016). From 2011 to 2013, the RAND ALP Asset Price Expectations Surveys also included questions about local house price expectations.

In 2013, the Federal Reserve Bank of New York launched the Survey of Consumer Expectations (SCE), fielded monthly to a rotating panel of about 1300 households. The main monthly module includes questions about respondents' expectations of aggregate house prices, eliciting both point estimates and probabilistic estimates via density forecasts. In addition to the main monthly module, the SCE fields an annual submodule on housing—the SCE Housing Survey—which includes questions on perceived past, present, and future conditions in the local housing market (see Zafar et al., 2014).[4] Researchers using SCE data have conducted several studies showing that participants' expressed expectations correlate with their incentivized choices across a range of settings (Armantier et al., 2015, 2016; Armona et al., 2019). These findings contribute to alleviating potential concerns about the reliability of unincentivized survey data of beliefs.

Fannie Mae's National Housing Survey (NHS) has surveyed U.S. households since 2010 on current conditions and expectations about housing markets "in general," as well as respondents' plans for purchasing a home. Based on the survey, key indicators such as the Home Purchase Sentiment Indicator are made publicly available. Similarly, since 2014, Pulsenomics has constructed and published various indicators for different local housing markets based on its U.S. Housing Confidence Survey (HCS), which asks about current local housing market conditions, expectations about future local housing market conditions, and plans for purchasing a home.

With the exception of the early Case–Shiller surveys focusing on recent homebuyers, all surveys described above aim to obtain responses from a representative sample of U.S. households. But housing market expectations are also elicited in surveys focusing on specific subsets of the population. The University of Michigan's Health and Retirement Survey (HRS) focuses on respondents aged 50 and above, and has included questions about housing market expectations since 2010. The National Survey of Mortgage Originations (NSMO) surveys households who hold a recently originated mortgage contained in the National Mortgage Database (a 5% sample of U.S. residential mortgages), and elicits perceived past housing market conditions, local house price expectations, and the respondents' perceived likelihood of selling and moving in the future.

In addition to these household surveys, several surveys focus on the expectations of industry professionals and experts. The National Association of Home Builders (NAHB) together with Wells Fargo has surveyed its members since 1985 about housing market demand conditions (e.g., the interests of prospective buyers). Fannie Mae's Mortgage Lender Sentiment Survey (MLSS) has surveyed lenders since 2014 about their expectations for home prices and mortgage demand. Since 2010, Zillow and Pulsenomics have asked around 100 industry professionals and economists each quarter to predict house price growth. Similarly, the Wall Street Journal has been asking around 70 academic, business, and financial economists to predict house prices twice a year since 1980 and monthly since 2003.

---

[4] The NY Fed's internal version of the SCE includes the zip codes of respondents, allowing researchers to match SCE expectations data with external data on actual local outcomes (see Kuchler and Zafar, 2019).

Outside the U.S., surveys about housing market expectations have mainly been conducted by central banks. In Europe, the following surveys include questions about housing market expectations: the European Central Bank's Household Finance and Consumption Survey (HFCS) and its Consumer Expectation Survey (CES); the Deutsche Bundesbank's Survey on Consumer Expectations; the Bank of Spain's Survey of Household Finances; the Bank of Italy's Survey of Household Income and Wealth; Tilburg University's DNB Household Survey; and the English Longitudinal Study on Ageing (ELSA). Beyond Europe, the Reserve Bank of New Zealand's Household Expectations Survey and the Bank of Canada's Survey of Consumer Expectations ask participants about housing market expectations.

Dimensions for the Development of Future Surveys. We close this section by compiling a "wish list" of features to be included in future surveys that would further advance our understanding of the determinants and effects of housing market beliefs. As with most "wish lists," not all of these will be feasible within the scope and constraints of every survey, but each of the elements would expand the set of insights that can be generated. With this in mind, we recommend that future surveys:

- Include a panel dimension to the survey population to better understand the variation in individual beliefs over time.
- Include both qualitative questions (e.g., "Do you think buying a house is a good investment?") and quantitative questions (e.g., "By how much do you think house prices will grow over the coming year?"). While qualitative questions may be easier to understand for some people, quantitative questions are more useful to discipline economic models, and have been shown to be predictive of behavior in economically meaningful ways (Giglio et al., 2021a,b).
- Include questions that elicit beliefs over different horizons, and questions that elicit higher moments of the belief distribution (for example, by asking individuals to assign subjective probabilities to different possible house price realizations).
- Elicit expectations about both house price growth and rent growth. Understanding cross-sectional and time-series variation in beliefs about both prices and rents ("dividends") can be helpful to distinguish between different explanations for house price movements.
- Elicit expectations about other macroeconomic quantities that are relevant determinants of home purchasing and financing decisions in quantitative models (e.g., inflation, interest rates, stock returns, and GDP growth).
- Collect households' expectations about their future housing consumption needs, such as "How long do you plan to stay in your current residence?" and "What is your target family size?". Unlike buying stocks or other financial assets, purchasing a house is both an investment and a consumption decision, and such questions will allow researchers to better understand the interactions between those two factors.
- Collect information (either in the survey, or from matched administrative data) on individuals' housing and mortgage market choices that would allow researchers to better understand how expressed beliefs align with actual behavior.
- Collect information on individuals' other investments to allow researchers to consider housing investments as part of a portfolio choice problem.
- Exploit the potential of information experiments that allow for a more causal exploration of the determinants of housing market beliefs (see Chapter 4 in this Handbook).
- Exploit the potential of incentivized investment games within surveys that allow for a more detailed exploration of the effects of housing market beliefs on real decisions.

- Exploit the potential for "free-text" questions to allow respondents to communicate how they are thinking about specific housing market trade-offs (see Bailey et al., 2019a), or to provide details such as their key sources of information on housing markets (see Kindermann et al., 2021).
- Consider surveying a population that oversamples housing market investors and landlords. These individuals play an important role in the housing market, yet their behavior is not well understood.

6.1.2 Nonsurvey measures of housing market expectations

While surveys have been the most widely used tool to measure housing market expectations, researchers have also proposed alternative ways of capturing housing expectations or sentiment.

Soo (2018) constructs indicators of sentiment in 34 urban housing markets using textual analysis of the tone of local newspaper articles about housing. This housing sentiment index, validated against data from the Michigan and Case–Shiller surveys, is strongly predictive of future growth in house prices. Ben-David et al. (2019) use a structural VAR model with sign restrictions to infer price expectation shocks from vacancy data. They argue that analyzing vacancy data can help distinguish whether prices are high due to an underlying increase in demand for housing (associated with low vacancy rates as people are eager to live in the purchased homes), or whether prices are high due to shocks to expectations (leading to high vacancies as agents amass empty homes in the anticipation of future price increases). Using this approach, the paper argues that expectations shocks are the most important factor explaining the boom in house prices in the early 2000s.

Landvoigt (2017) uses predictions from a consumption-portfolio choice model with housing to estimate belief parameters. In the model, the extensive margin—the decision whether to rent or own a house—is largely driven by households' expected house price appreciation. Meanwhile, the intensive margin—how much housing to buy—is mostly determined by downpayment constraints. Landvoigt (2017) finds that the mean expected house price appreciation was only slightly elevated at the beginning of the boom, an estimate that is within reasonable confidence bounds of the survey evidence in Case and Shiller (2003). Thus, many households chose to buy during the boom years mostly because mortgage rates and the perceived house price volatility were low; these factors also explain the higher loan-to-value ratios during these years. Landvoigt (2017) also concludes that households did not foresee the bust in housing markets: at the peak of the boom, households' inferred expectations of future house price growth were in line with long-run average house price appreciation.

6.2 Determinants of expectations and expectations heterogeneity

Using data from the surveys described in the previous section, a large literature tries to understand how housing market beliefs vary both over time and across individuals. To highlight some representative patterns that have motivated this research, Panel A of Fig. 6.1 shows the time series of expected house price increases over the coming year, as collected by the Michigan Surveys of Consumers; it also plots annual changes in the Zillow Home Value Index as a representative measure of house price movements.

There is substantial time-series variation in house price expectations, a pattern that is replicated across most expectation surveys. The particular expectation series from the Michigan Survey starts in January 2007, near the peak of the 2000s housing boom, with individuals expecting house prices to increase by 2%, on average, going forward. Over the following months and years, as house prices fell

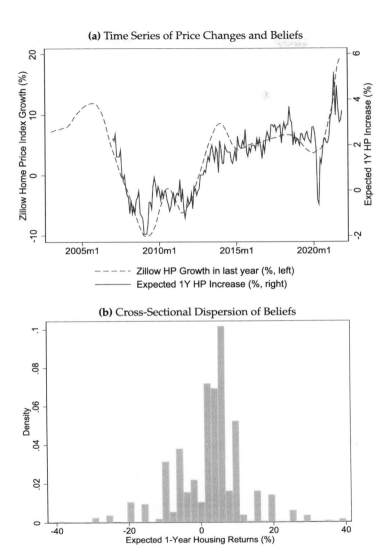

FIGURE 6.1 Patterns of Expectations

Note: Figure presents representative patterns of U.S. housing market expectations. Panel A shows monthly data on the average expected 1-year house price increase, as reported by the Michigan Surveys of Consumers (solid line). The exact question is "By about what percent do you expect prices of homes like yours in your community to go (up/down), on average, over the next 12 months?". Panel A also plots 1-year changes of the Zillow Home Value Index (dashed line). Panel B shows a histogram of 1-year expected house price increases, as reported by the New York Fed Survey of Consumer Expectations, pooling across all responses from survey waves in 2020, excluding responses with absolute values in excess of 40% ($N = 14,794$). The exact question is "Over the next 12 months, what do you expect will happen to the average home price nationwide? By about what percent do you expect the average home price to increase/decrease? Please give your best guess."

precipitously, expected 1-year house price increases declined to about 0%. From mid-2012, as house prices began to recover and increase steadily for the rest of the decade, expected 1-year house price gains also increased, at first rapidly to about 1.5% by mid-2013, and then gradually further to 2% by about late 2016. Expected house price increases have stayed relatively flat since, with the salient exception of the period at the start of the COVID-19 pandemic, when they fell to below 0% before recovering almost immediately to above 3%.[5] Overall, two salient patterns emerge: house price expectations are more optimistic following recent price increases, and the time-series variation in expectations is smaller than the time-series variation in price changes. In the following sections—and in particular in Section 6.2.1—we review research that explores some of the determinants of this time-series variation in house price beliefs, and its relationship with house prices.

Panel B of Fig. 6.1 shows the heterogeneity of house price expectations across individuals from the 2020 waves of the New York Fed SCE. There is a wide dispersion of house price beliefs across individuals. While some individuals expected house prices to decrease by 20% over the coming year, others expected them to increase by 20%. Similar to beliefs about other asset returns, such as beliefs about expected stock returns (see Giglio et al., 2021a), the observed cross-sectional dispersion is much larger than the observed time-series variation in average expected house price increases.

Why do people disagree so much about expected house price changes? In Table 6.1, we show results from a regression of house price expectations on a number of explanatory variables. (Again, the sample consists of respondents in the 2020 waves of the New York Fed SCE.) In columns 1–3 of Table 6.1, we assess national house price expectations over the coming year. In column 1, we only control for month-of-wave fixed effects. This is to ensure that the dispersion in beliefs is not primarily driven by common time-series variation during 2020, a year of unprecedented time-series variation in house price beliefs, with expected average expectations of 1-year house price growth ranging from 5.8% in February 2020 to −2.7% in April 2020 (see Panel A of Fig. 6.1). This time-series variation, although large, only accounts for 6.4% of the variation in beliefs across responses collected in 2020.

In column 2 of Table 6.1, we include controls for a range of demographic characteristics. In 2020, older respondents were more optimistic about future house price growth, while more-educated and higher-numeracy respondents were more pessimistic. These differences are statistically significant and economically large: for example, individuals above the age of 60 had a 2 percentage point higher house price expectation than those below the age of 40. Conditional on the other controls, we find no large differences in house price expectations across individuals with different incomes.

In column 3 of Table 6.1, we add fixed effects for the state of residence of individuals. The R-squared of the regression—the share of variation in our data that is explained by the control variables—increases somewhat, suggesting that there are systematic geographic differences in beliefs about national house price movements.

Despite these systematic and statistically significant patterns, controls for time, location, and demographics jointly explain only about 10% of the cross-sectional dispersion in house price expectations

---

[5] The Michigan Survey also reports average 5-year expected house price increases, which are significantly less volatile, and, for example, do not parallel the substantial drop in 1-year expectations during the initial months of the COVID-19 pandemic. Since the start of the NY Fed Survey of Consumer Expectations in June 2013, the expectations measured by the NY Fed survey have shown similar patterns to those in the Michigan Survey. In terms of levels, average expected 1-year returns are usually around 2 percentage points higher in the NY Fed SCE, though differences in the question and object elicited complicate any direct comparison.

Table 6.1 Correlates of Individual-Level House Price Beliefs.

	1Y Expected HP Growth (Now)			1Y Expected HP Growth (In 2 Years)		
	(1)	(2)	(3)	(4)	(5)	(6)
Age: 40-60 Years		0.261	0.233		0.191	0.174
		(0.187)	(0.189)		(0.176)	(0.178)
Age: 60+ Years		1.918***	2.023***		1.278***	1.281***
		(0.194)	(0.196)		(0.182)	(0.185)
		.	.		.	.
Some College		−1.271***	−1.145***		−0.723**	−0.701**
		(0.272)	(0.275)		(0.256)	(0.260)
College		−2.177***	−2.058***		−1.453***	−1.423***
		(0.270)	(0.273)		(0.254)	(0.258)
		.	.		.	.
Income $50k–$100k		−0.005	0.008		−0.348*	−0.384*
		(0.185)	(0.185)		(0.173)	(0.174)
Income >$100k		−0.037	0.189		−0.176	−0.084
		(0.205)	(0.207)		(0.192)	(0.195)
		.	.		.	.
High Numeracy		−1.399***	−1.370***		−1.339***	−1.302***
		(0.175)	(0.176)		−(0.165)	−(0.166)
Survey Month FE	Y	Y	Y	Y	Y	Y
State FE			Y			Y
N	14,794	14,794	14,794	12,862	12,862	12,862
R-Squared	0.064	0.087	0.101	0.006	0.025	0.037

Note: Table shows results from a regression of 1-year expected house price changes on various respondent characteristics. We pool all responses to 2020 waves from the NY Fed Survey of Consumer Expectations, pooling across all responses from survey waves in 2020, but dropping responses with absolute values in excess of 40%. The exact question in columns 1–3 is "Over the next 12 months, what do you expect will happen to the average home price nationwide? By about what percent do you expect the average home price to increase/decrease? Please give your best guess." The exact question in columns 4–6 is "Over the 12-month period between [24 months from survey date] and [36 months from survey date], what do you expect will happen to the average home price nationwide? By about what percent do you expect the average home price to increase/decrease over that period?" All columns include month-of-survey fixed effects; columns 3 and 6 also include fixed effects for the state in which the respondent is located. Standard errors in parentheses: ***, $p < 0.001$; **, $p < 0.01$; *, $p < 0.05$.

visible in Panel B of Fig. 6.1. (Giglio et al., 2021a, show a similarly low predictive power of demographics for stock market expectations).

Columns 4–6 of Table 6.1 assess expectations about house price changes over the 1-year period that starts two years into the future. Directionally, demographics affect these expectations the same way as we saw in columns 1–3 for more immediate expectations, though the overall explanatory power of the various observable characteristics is even smaller.

We have documented substantial variation in house price expectations over time and across individuals, much of which is not explained by individual demographics. What drives this observed variation in house price expectations? More generally, how do individuals form expectations about the housing market? In the following sections, we review recent research efforts attempting to understand belief formation.

6.2.1 Extrapolation

A large literature studying expectation formation across a variety of settings has found that individuals extrapolate from recent information when forming expectations (e.g., Fuster et al., 2010; Greenwood and Shleifer, 2014; Barberis et al., 2015; Liu and Palmer, 2021; Giglio et al., 2021a,b). Several papers, including early work by Case and Shiller (1988) and follow-up work by Case et al. (2012), show that measured housing market expectations are also strongly related to recent house price developments (see also Panel A of Fig. 6.1).

To explore the causal relationship between past realized house prices and expected future house prices, Armona et al. (2019) conduct an information experiment in which housing market expectations are elicited before and after a random subset of individuals receive information about actual past house price changes (see Chapter 4 in this Handbook for a detailed discussion of such information experiments in surveys). The authors find that both short- and long-term expectations are revised based on this information, highlighting that individuals do indeed extrapolate from information about the recent past when forming house price forecasts.

To what extent does the observed extrapolation represent an optimal use of information? Early work studying stock market expectations argued that any extrapolation from recent price changes would correspond to a deviation from rational expectations, since stock prices are serially uncorrelated. In housing markets, evaluating whether extrapolation from recent price changes is a violation of rational expectations is more complicated, since house prices are serially correlated in the short-run, but exhibit mean reversion in the long-run (e.g., Case and Shiller, 1989; Cutler et al., 1991; Guren, 2018). A rational forecaster therefore should "extrapolate" from recent house price changes when forming expectations about near-term price changes, but not when forming medium- to long-term expectations. To assess whether the extent of extrapolation from past prices observed is consistent with rational expectation formation therefore requires comparing the extent of extrapolation to the extent of serial correlation in the underlying data.

Case et al. (2012) and Armona et al. (2019) show that, in the short-run, individuals underreact to recent house prices changes, while in the long-run they overreact relative to the actual predictiveness of past house price changes in the data. Similarly, De Stefani (2020) shows that recent local house price developments systematically affect the house price expectations of respondents in the Michigan Survey, and that individuals systematically underestimate the extent of both short-run momentum and long-term mean reversion in housing markets.

Overall, these findings are consistent with individuals naively extrapolating from recent local house price changes when forming expectations about future price changes. This extrapolation underestimates the serial correlation in house prices in the short-run and overestimates it in the long-run.

Additional evidence that households rely on information from past house price changes when forming expectations about the future comes from Fuster et al. (2018). In this work, the authors show that when individuals are given the opportunity to pick among different sources of information to help predict future house price changes, about half pick forward-looking information (45.5% chose the forecast of housing experts), while the other half pick backward-looking information (28% chose the past one-year home price change, 22% chose the past ten-year home price change). This finding suggest that many individuals perceive past price changes as informative of future price changes, explaining why their forecasts appear to vary with this information in the data.

Glaeser and Nathanson (2017) specify a micro-foundation for extrapolative house price expectations. In their model, buyers assume that past prices reflect only contemporaneous demand and neglect that they are also influenced by market participants' beliefs. Buyers also do not take into account that prior buyers may have made similar simplifying assumptions when inferring demand from prices. This leads individuals to extrapolate from recent price changes when forming their house price expectations. Consistent with the empirical evidence described above, individuals in the model underextrapolate in the short-run and overextrapolate in the long-run since they underestimate the long-term mean reversion relative to a rational benchmark. Glaeser and Nathanson (2017) show that their model leads house prices to display three features present in the data but usually missing from rational expectations models: momentum at one-year horizons, mean reversion at five-year horizons, and excess longer-term volatility relative to fundamentals.

Other authors have proposed alternative micro-foundations of belief formation that also generate belief dynamics consistent with the evidence that households become more optimistic about future price changes after observing recent price increases. For example, Chodorow-Reich et al. (2021) show how diagnostic expectations in the spirit of Bordalo et al. (2019) can lead to temporary overoptimism during a housing boom: when dividends increase unexpectedly, diagnostic agents overweight the likelihood of high trend growth going forward, thereby making them excessively optimistic. Chodorow-Reich et al. (2021) highlight that this model of belief formation fits a number of features of the 2000s housing cycle, including the overshooting of expectations during the housing boom and the absence of substantial overshooting of expectations during the housing bust. (The model in Chodorow-Reich et al., 2021, instead generates an overshooting of prices during the housing bust as the result of a price-default spiral and foreclosure externalities).

6.2.2 Personal experiences

In addition to the evidence above that recent information plays an important role when households form expectations, a related literature suggests that individuals put substantial weight on *personal* experiences in belief formation. For instance, Malmendier and Nagel (2016) argue that individuals overweight information about events that happened during their lifetimes compared to information about events that occurred before they were born. But the overweighting of personal experiences is not unique to the time dimension. Rather, this can also include experiences that happened to the individual personally (such as returns earned on a prior housing investment) or events that are closer geographically (local versus national house price movements).[6] A number of papers provide evidence for a range of such forces in determining expectations about the housing market.

Kuchler and Zafar (2019) analyze data from the New York Fed SCE to show that when individuals form expectations about aggregate housing market outcomes, they overweight recent information that is geographically local to them. Specifically, larger recent local house price gains lead respondents to

---

[6] Extrapolation and the overweighting of personal experiences are not mutually exclusive forces: individuals might overweight local relative to aggregate house price changes (personal experiences) and at the same time, overweight recent local house prices compared to local house price changes further in the past (extrapolation).

expect larger increases in national house prices.[7] The authors also find that the expectations of less educated and less numerate respondents are more heavily influenced by personal local experiences.

Both extrapolation from the recent past and the overweighting of personal experiences involve focusing on some information that is close—either in time or personally—when forming expectations. Extrapolation alone, however, does not lead to heterogeneous expectations among individuals who share the same information set and form expectations in the same extrapolative way (unless people differ in the extent to which they extrapolate, as suggested by Armona et al., 2019). On the other hand, since personal experiences differ across individuals, the overweighting of personal experiences naturally leads to heterogeneous expectations across individuals at any given point in time, even when the process of belief formation is the same among them. The extrapolation from person experiences thus contributes to the large differences in expectations across individuals at the same point in time (which we documented in Panel B of Fig. 6.1).

As with extrapolation from the recent past, judging whether the overweighting of personal experiences is consistent with rational expectations is challenging. Under the assumption of full information—i.e., that all individuals share the same information set—it would violate rationality to overweight personal experiences in forming beliefs about a common object such as national house prices. However, without the assumption of full information, the observed behavior could arise from a variety of underlying factors, some of which do not constitute a violation of rational expectations. For instance, it could be that the availability and cost (monetary or cognitive) of accessing different information varies across individuals, perhaps because it is cheaper to learn about past local house prices than about prices in other parts of the country. This would naturally lead different information to receive varying weights in the expectation formation process of different individuals. Whether the implied information acquisition costs are plausible is an open question.

6.2.3 Social interactions

So far, we have described research that documents how individuals overweight recent information and personal experience. We next discuss the growing evidence that housing market expectations are also affected by information from their *social network*.

Robert Shiller has long argued that house prices are driven largely by belief fluctuations resulting from social interactions. For example, Shiller (2007) wrote that "many people seem to be accepting that the recent home price experience is at least in part the result of a social epidemic of optimism for real estate." In this narrative, some individuals become more optimistic about national house price growth (for example, because they observe substantial recent local house price increases). Borrowing language from the epidemiology literature, these individuals then "infect" their friends and acquaintances with their optimism, allowing the optimism to spread across society.

We agree with Shiller that in settings such as the housing market, where there are substantial information and search frictions and individuals transact only infrequently (Piazzesi and Schneider, 2009;

---

[7] Similar to the work on extrapolation described above, Kuchler and Zafar (2019) also find that expectations of future *local* house price changes underreact to past local price changes in the short-run and overreact in the long-run. The authors also find evidence for the overweighting of geographically close information in other domains. In particular, personal transitions to (and from) unemployment lead respondents to be more (or less) pessimistic about national unemployment rates. See also the discussion of labor market expectations in Chapter 22 in this Handbook.

Kurlat and Stroebel, 2015; Stroebel, 2016; Piazzesi et al., 2020), it is indeed natural to expect individuals to rely on their social networks when forming beliefs.[8] However, while the idea of social dynamics in housing markets has a long history, it is only recently that researchers have been able to document that house price beliefs are truly socially "contagious" in the way proposed by Shiller and others.

Bailey et al. (2018b) were the first to provide direct empirical evidence for belief contagion in the housing market. Specifically, they document that individuals whose geographically distant friends experienced higher recent house price growth are indeed more optimistic about future local house price growth. To measure social networks, Bailey et al. (2018b) collaborate with Facebook, the world's largest online social networking service. The authors begin their empirical analysis by documenting that, at any point in time, different people in the same local housing market have friends who have experienced vastly different recent house price movements. This variation is driven by heterogeneity in the locations of peoples' friends and heterogeneity in regional house price changes.

Bailey et al. (2018b) then provide evidence for an important effect of social interactions on an individual's assessment of the attractiveness of local property investments. To conduct this analysis, they field a housing expectations survey among Los Angeles-based Facebook users. Over half of the survey respondents report that they regularly talk to their friends about investing in the housing market, providing strong evidence that social dynamics could end up being important.[9] The survey in Bailey et al. (2018b) also asked respondents to assess the attractiveness of property investments in their own zip codes. The authors find a strong positive relationship between the recent house price experiences of a respondent's friends and whether that respondent believes that local real estate is a good investment. Importantly, this relationship is stronger for individuals who report that they regularly talk with their friends about investing in real estate. For individuals who report to never talk to their friends about investing in the housing market, there is no relationship between friends' house price experiences and their own evaluations of the attractiveness of local housing investments.

These results suggest that social interactions provide a natural link between friends' house price experiences and an individual's own housing market expectations (and indeed, as we discuss below, their housing investment behavior). Since social networks differ across individuals, the overweighting of the experiences in a person's social network also generates heterogeneity in expectations, even among individuals living in the same location, contributing to the large observed belief dispersion.

Much exciting research remains to be done in our quest to better understand the role of social dynamics in the belief formation process, both in general and specifically with respect to housing market beliefs. For example, it would be interesting to explore whether some types of friends—work friends, college friends, better-educated friends, or closer friends—have particularly strong effects on individuals' beliefs, as suggested by Bailey et al. (2019b) in other settings. Readers interested in this question should make sure to read Chapter 25 in this Handbook, which provides detailed discussion of various epidemiological models of belief formation. We believe that many of these models have the potential

---

[8] Kuchler and Stroebel (2021) provide a survey of the role of social interactions in determining household financial decisions more broadly. Social interactions have also been shown to affect beliefs and behaviors across a wide range of other settings, from labor markets (Topa, 2001, 2011; Gee et al., 2017), to trade flows (Rauch, 2001; Bailey et al., 2021), to investment behaviors (Ouimet and Tate, 2020; Kuchler et al., 2020), to social distancing behavior during the COVID-19 pandemic (Bailey et al., 2020).

[9] Consistent with the findings by Bailey et al. (2018b), Kindermann et al. (2021) document that more than 50% of survey respondents in Germany report that talking to family members and friends is an important source of information when forming expectations about the housing market.

to provide accurate description of beliefs dynamics, and expect the associated models to become more prominent over time.

A related area for future research is to better understand the economic mechanisms that explain why individuals rely on their social networks when forming expectations. One possible reason is that it is cheaper to acquire information through friends than through other channels. A second possible explanation is that individuals are more likely to trust information obtained through their social networks, perhaps because friends—unlike, for example, real estate agents or mortgage brokers—are not perceived to have potential conflicts of interest (see Bailey et al., 2020, for evidence of such a "trust"-based channel) Third, it is possible that information obtained through friends is more likely to "resonate" with individuals. This mechanism is described in a recent paper by Malmendier and Veldkamp (2022): *"[Information resonance] is not a question of 'limited attention' or cognitive limitations, as frequently modeled in economics. Recipients did not 'miss' the information in question, and might be able to reproduce and recite it even it does not resonate with them. Instead, they simply do not identify with the person conveying the information and, as a result, put less weight on it in terms of its relevance to their own decision-making."*

6.2.4 Ownership status

The process of forming beliefs about future housing market outcomes also depends on individuals' current ownership status. One reason is that a key difference between housing and other assets is that nonowners of the asset who almost always rent can more easily observe the cash flows of the asset—they are, after all, paying rent every month—while owner-occupiers simply consume housing services and do not need to pay attention to the value of their consumption (see Kindermann et al., 2021).

Kindermann et al. (2021) find that survey data during the recent German house price boom reveal sizable differences in house price forecasts between renters and owners that are consistent with such an information environment. While all households were, on average, underpredicting the strength of the house price boom, the average renter had higher house price growth forecasts than owners, especially in areas where house prices grew the most.[10] However, while renters had more accurate house price expectations on average, their forecasts were also more dispersed than those of owners. Combining these two effects, renters had forecasts with higher average mean squared errors than owners.

An explanation based purely on common experiences of renters may account for their higher average forecast, but cannot account for their worse overall forecasting performance. Instead, Kindermann et al. (2021) show that Bayesian learning with ownership status-dependent information can quantitatively account for these stylized facts (see Chapter 23 in this Handbook for a discussion of learning models). More specifically, agents learn about the determinants of house price growth from signals that differ in their precision depending on whether they rent or own. Renters receive signals about rent that are more precise, while they get noisier signals about house prices than owners. The noisier signals about house prices generate the larger dispersion of renter forecasts.

---

[10] Some households own their primary residence but also other houses that they rent out to other households. These landlord households should have forecasts that are more similar to those of renters, because they receive more precise signals about rents—after all, they charge rent to their tenants. The survey data shows that this is indeed the case. Demographics such as age, income, wealth, risk aversion, other economic forecasts (growth), and financial literacy play minor roles.

Another mechanism through which ownership status could affect belief formation is through an endowment effect. For example, Hatzmark et al. (2021) argue that stock owners overreact to signals about stock prices: owners overpredict future stock prices in response to positive signals about their stocks compared to nonowners (see also Anagol et al., 2018, 2021). In contrast, the evidence in Kindermann et al. (2021) point to a period with positive signals about house prices, in which owners of houses make *lower* house price forecasts than nonowners (renters). This is the opposite from what an endowment effect would predict. An interesting question for future research is to understand these differences in belief formation across asset markets.

6.2.5 Determinants of higher moments of belief distribution

The research described above has focused on the determinants of the expectations of average future house prices. But recent information and personal experiences can also affect other moments of their belief distributions, such as variance and skewness, which have important implications for households' housing and mortgage choices.

To explore the determinants of higher moments of individuals' belief distributions, Kuchler and Zafar (2019) exploit that the New York Fed SCE not only elicits a point estimate for beliefs, but also asks respondents to assign probabilities to different ranges of possible future house price changes. The authors relate the volatility of recent local house prices changes to the variance of each respondents' expected house price distribution. More volatile local house price changes are associated with a wider distribution of expected national house price changes. This finding highlights that the effect of recent local experiences on aggregate expectations works through both the first and second moments of the locally experienced price changes.

Ben-David et al. (2018) also use the New York Fed SCE to measure uncertainty in respondents' expectations. They first show that uncertainty about inflation, own income growth, and U.S. house price growth is correlated within individuals. They also show that uncertainty about these outcomes is higher for respondents with lower incomes, lower educations, and more precarious finances, as well as those living in counties with higher unemployment rates. These results suggest that individuals facing more economic adversity are more uncertain in their economic forecasts, potentially due to their experienced uncertainty affecting the uncertainty in their expectations in what the authors call "an effect akin to extrapolation in the second moment of beliefs."

Adelino et al. (2018) use data from the Fannie Mae National Housing Survey, which includes a question about how risky individuals perceive an investment in housing to be. The authors first document that 66% of respondents perceive housing as a relatively safe investment, while only 18% feel similarly about stock investments. Renters are more likely to perceive housing as a risky investment compared to owners. In addition, the share of households who perceive housing as risky correlates with past local house price changes and, importantly, measures of the volatility of local house price changes. As such, the authors interpret their findings as showing that "beliefs about house price risk extrapolate from recent experience."

Bailey et al. (2019a) show that individuals with friends from counties with a wider variety of house price experiences—that is, individuals with a higher second moment of house price experiences across individuals in their social network—report wider distributions of expected house price changes. This result suggests that social dynamics do not only affect the first moment of individuals' beliefs, as documented in Bailey et al. (2018b) and described above, but also higher moments of the belief distribution.

6.3 **The effects of expectations on individual housing market behavior**

There are a number of reasons why it is challenging to explore how differences in housing expectations translate into differences in housing market behaviors. First, there are few data sets that contain information on both individuals' house price beliefs and their actual behaviors in the housing market. Second, even when such data sets exist, one needs to worry about the ability to cleanly identify a causal link from expectations to behavior, since factors that lead individuals to be more optimistic about house price growth may also affect their housing market behavior through channels other than their expectations. For instance, a large past increase in local house prices could make individuals more optimistic about future house prices, but could also directly affect their housing market behaviors by increasing the equity of current homeowners. A local housing boom may also coincide with a general local economic boom, leaving prospective home buyers with higher incomes and more money to invest in the housing market. Hence, causally estimating the effect of housing market expectations on housing market investments requires plausibly exogenous variation in expectations.

6.3.1 **Homeownership decisions**

We begin this discussion by reviewing several research papers that study the effects of housing market expectations on the decision of whether to buy and rent, as well as related decisions in the home purchasing process, such as how large of a home to buy and how much to pay for a house.

After showing that friends' house price experiences affect an individual's housing market expectations (see Section 6.2.3), Bailey et al. (2018b) document that friends' house price experiences also affect that individual's actual housing market investments. The authors argue that this effect occurs through friends influencing the individual's expectations. To do so, the authors combine de-identified social network data from Facebook with anonymized information on individuals' housing transactions from public deeds data. Friends' house price experiences affect both the intensive and extensive margins of individuals' housing market investments: renters with friends who have experienced more positive local house price growth are more likely to become homeowners, while homeowners with social networks that experienced more positive local house price growth are less likely to sell their homes. Conditional on buying a home, those with more positive friend experiences buy larger homes and pay more for a given home. The economic magnitudes of these effects are substantial. Bailey et al. (2018b) then provide evidence that the relationships between the house price experiences in an individual's social network and that individual's housing market behavior are explained by the effect of friends' house price experiences on the individual's own housing market expectations.

Bottan and Perez-Truglia (2020) estimate the role of house price expectations on homeowners' decisions to sell their homes. To causally identify the effect of differences in expectations, homeowners who recently listed their homes for sale were mailed information about past local home price changes. The authors randomize the horizon, time frame, and source of this information across homeowners, leading some respondents to randomly receive more positive, albeit non-deceptive, signals about local house prices. A supplemental survey exposing subjects to the same information that was mailed to potential home sellers shows that receiving more positive information about past local house price changes indeed leads individuals to be more optimistic about future house price growth, consistent with the evidence in Section 6.2. The authors then use administrative data to observe subsequent home sales. Receiving more positive information about past local house price changes caused potential sellers to delay selling their homes, suggesting that differences in expected future house prices (induced by differences in the information received) are reflected in differences in selling behaviors.

There is also evidence that house price beliefs affect the housing search process. Gargano et al. (2020) focus on the effects of home buyers' expectations on their housing search. The authors show that individuals experiencing higher past house price growth in their postcode of residence search more broadly across locations and house characteristics, without changing attention devoted to individual sales listings. They also have shorter search durations. The authors argue that at least part of this effect comes from individuals extrapolating from their locally experienced house price growth when forming housing market expectations. In particular for renters, higher experienced house price growth increases future expected house price growth and thus the returns to finding a matching house quickly, before ownership becomes less affordable. Using the model of Piazzesi et al. (2020), Gargano et al. (2020) show that the expansion of search breadth in response to locally experienced house price growth translates into spillovers onto house sales prices and inventories of listings across postcodes within a metropolitan area.

Housing investment decisions are also affected by individuals' uncertainty about future house price movements. Ben-David et al. (2018) argue that individuals with more uncertain expectations about income growth, inflation and home price changes are more cautious in their consumption and investment behaviors. Similarly, Adelino et al. (2018) point to the role of beliefs about house price risk in explaining homeownership decisions. They find that individuals who perceive housing as risky are about 12% more likely to be renters than homeowners. Similarly, individuals perceiving housing as risky are much more likely to say they would rent rather than buy the next time they move to a new home. There are no differences in renters and owners in risk perceptions of the stock market, suggesting that housing decisions are driven specifically by perceived house price risk.

Malmendier and Steiny (2017) argue that macroeconomic conditions beyond the housing market can also affect homeownership decisions. In particular, they show that individuals who have experienced higher inflation during their lifetimes expect higher inflation going forward, making owning a home—traditionally seen as an inflation hedge—more attractive. The authors argue that, through this channel, differences in lifetime macroeconomic experiences can help explain the vastly different rates of homeownership across European countries.

6.3.2 Mortgage choice

In addition to affecting housing market investments, house price expectations also influence how a home purchase is financed, including choices about the type of mortgage and the overall leverage.

Bailey et al. (2019a) study the effect of home buyers' house price expectations on their mortgage leverage choices, asking whether households that are more concerned about large house price drops make larger or smaller downpayments. The authors highlight that, from a theoretical perspective, the relationship is ambiguous and depends on the ability of households to directly adjust their exposure to the housing market by renting or purchasing a smaller home. Intuitively, if such an adjustment is comparably easy, relatively pessimistic households will choose to purchase smaller homes with less leverage. However, households' ability to rent or buy a smaller home might be restricted by a variety of constraints, such as the desire for a certain amount of space due to family size. In the extreme case, households' home sizes are completely determined by their consumption preferences. In this case, the only way for relatively pessimistic homeowners to reduce their exposure to future house price declines is by levering up more and investing fewer own resources into the purchase, allowing them to limit their losses through defaulting in the case of large prices decline. This ability to "insure" against house price drops by making smaller downpayments and defaulting on the loan in case of large house price declines ("risk shifting") is higher when default is less costly, for example, when there is no recourse to the nonhousing assets of defaulting borrowers. Importantly, both the first and second moment of the belief distribution affect leverage choices through this channel, since both lower expected house price increases and higher expected house price volatilities are associated with larger probabilities of the very large house price drops that might induce a household to default.

In addition to highlighting these novel insights into the relationship between beliefs and leverage choices, Bailey et al. (2019a) explore which force dominates in the U.S. housing market. Their identification relies on the finding that geographically-distant friends' house price experiences affect individuals' expectations, but should not directly affect their behaviors (see above). The authors then show empirically that individuals choose higher leverage when their friends have recently seen house price declines and have experienced more dispersed housing market outcomes, both of which increase individuals' subjective expectations of a large house price drop. Consistent with the theoretical framework, the overall effect is driven by households living in U.S. states where default costs are relatively low; the effect of beliefs on leverage is also larger in housing markets with few rental options, where even relatively pessimistic households may be forced to owner-occupy to live there.

De Stefani (2020) similarly links home price expectations to the mortgage choices of housing investors. While Bailey et al. (2019a) find that optimistic house price beliefs are associated with *lower* leverage for owner-occupied homes, De Stefani (2020) finds that when buying investment properties, more optimistic borrowers take on more leverage. This difference between owner-occupied properties and investment properties is consistent with the model in Bailey et al. (2019a). As described above, the sign of the relationship depends on the ability of pessimistic households to reduce their exposures to the housing market by means other than reducing their downpayment. While owner-occupiers often have consumption motives for buying a specific home, this is not the case for buyers of investment properties. Investors who are pessimistic about housing as an asset can choose other asset classes and abstain from owning investment property altogether (see also Geanakoplos, 2010; Simsek, 2013). As such, more optimistic investment property buyers will choose higher leverage to finance larger purchases, while more pessimistic investors will abstain from housing market investments altogether.

Other important determinants of mortgage choice are a household's expectations of future inflation and interest rates. Malmendier and Nagel (2016) argue that the inflation experienced during an individual's lifetime disproportionately affects her inflation expectations.[11] They also show that differences in inflation expectations due to variation in experienced inflation affect household borrowing and lending behaviors, including the choice between fixed-rate and variable-rate mortgages. Botsch and Malmendier (2020) build on this earlier work and incorporate inflation expectations shaped by lifetime inflation experiences into a structural model of mortgage choice, focusing on the decision between fixed-rate and adjustable-rate mortgages. They find that for every percentage point increase in experienced inflation, households are willing to pay between 6 and 14 basis points more in interest for a fixed-rate mortgage.

---

[11] See Chapter 5 in this Handbook for a discussion of the literature studying the determinants of inflation expectations.

6.4 **House price expectations and aggregate economic outcomes**

Households' expectations of future house prices can be important drivers of aggregate trends and volatility in house prices. If households expect to sell their homes at higher prices in the future, they will be willing to pay higher prices for those homes today. Although households generally hold their homes for a long time after purchase—in the U.S., more than a decade, on average—the expected resale value remains important in determining the expected overall return on the investment. Survey evidence of house price expectations allows researchers to quantify the importance of changes in those expectations in driving boom–bust episodes in housing markets and, thus, in driving house price volatility. In this section, we review some of the work in this direction.

During the postwar period, the U.S. experienced two national boom–bust episodes in house prices. These episodes stand out because house prices climbed to historically high levels relative to rents not only in the U.S., but also in many other countries (for the international evidence, see Piazzesi and Schneider, 2008). The first postwar housing boom occurred during the Great Inflation of the 1970s: many countries experienced extraordinary inflation in consumption good prices following the oil price shocks. During this high-inflation episode, many households considered housing to be a particularly attractive real asset that hedges against inflation. The second boom was in the early 2000s (see Fig. 6.1), a period when banks in many countries relaxed their mortgage lending standards.

As we are writing this chapter, we are in the middle of the COVID-19 pandemic. At the start of the pandemic, U.S. housing market activity came to a screeching halt, as uncertainty spiked and emergency measures made it difficult for real estate agents to organize open houses. As highlighted in Fig. 6.1, while house prices remained relatively steady, housing market expectations collapsed during the early months of the pandemic. Later, the desire for social distancing combined with the rising feasibility of remote work increased the demand for housing, including in cheaper areas outside of crowded cities like San Francisco and New York. As a result, the pandemic ignited a third national house price boom (again paralleled in many other countries); very quickly, house price expectations recovered, and data from the February 2021 Survey of Consumer Expectations indicates that households were expecting house prices to appreciate by more than 5% over the subsequent year.

There is a vibrant debate in the research community about the relative importance of different potential causes of these national house price boom and bust episodes. Some researchers believe that exuberant house price expectations are important for explaining house price booms, while others emphasize the relevance of inflation expectations (especially in the 1970s, but also now again in the 2020s), changing credit conditions (particularly in the early 2000s), as well as other fundamental demand-side factors, such as a stronger preference for housing during the pandemic. Naturally, these different mechanisms can interact and are therefore hard to disentangle. For example, higher inflation expectations may convince households that real borrowing rates are lower and thus that credit is cheaper; alternatively, more optimistic house price expectations by loan officers could lead to a reduction in downpayment requirements and other easing of access to credit. These forces increase housing demand and drive up house prices today. If they are expected to persist, or if households extrapolate from recent price changes, households may also form higher expectations of future house prices.

To argue that high house price expectations cause a house price boom today, researchers would ideally like to identify an exogenous shift in house price expectations. But while some of the research described above has been able to isolate exogenous shifts in individual-level beliefs to explore their effects on individual housing market decisions (Bailey et al., 2018b, 2019a; Bottan and Perez-Truglia, 2020), identifying exogenous shifts in beliefs held by many households is a daunting challenge.

Researchers have therefore focused on other testable implications of their preferred explanations of boom–bust episodes. For example, many models of aggregate price movements also make important predictions for the cross-section of house prices and capital gains, both across space and segments within a location. In the language of empirical asset pricing, the cross-section of house prices is thus a useful set of "test assets" for these models and their alternative explanations of aggregate patterns.

In the following, we describe some of the progress in the housing literature to understand the quantitative importance of house price expectations as well as expectations of other variables such as inflation, nominal interest rates, earnings growth, and credit conditions. A key feature of the past booms and busts in housing markets is that they do not look alike. In some booms, houses in lower-quality segments appreciate much more than houses in higher-quality segments, while in other booms the opposite is true. Moreover, some booms witness a large increase in mortgage debt by households, while other booms do not. Some booms affect the entire country, while others are more concentrated in some geographies. Finally, disagreement among households about the future path of inflation or house prices is strong in some booms, while other booms are characterized by broad agreement about future economic conditions. These differences across boom–bust episodes are helpful to understand the quantitative importance of various channels. Survey evidence on household expectations is therefore an important piece of data that models in this literature should want to match.

6.4.1 The housing boom of the late 1970s

The Great Inflation of the 1970s witnessed a huge shift in U.S. household portfolios out of equity into housing (Leombroni et al., 2020). House prices and price–rent ratios increased nationwide in the U.S. and many other countries during this time (Piazzesi and Schneider, 2008). In the U.S., expensive homes appreciated more than cheaper homes (Poterba, 1991).

Researchers have argued that these patterns are consistent with an important role of inflation levels and expectations in driving the 1970s housing boom. Since households borrow at the nominal interest rate, beliefs about expected inflation determine beliefs about the prevailing real interest rate (Leombroni et al., 2020). When inflation expectations are high, the perceived real cost of credit is thus low. In addition, several features of the tax code makes housing a more attractive asset during times of high expected inflation. First, mortgage interest is tax deductible, and this homeowner subsidy increased dramatically during the Great Inflation (Poterba, 1984). Second, capital gains on housing are easier to shelter from taxes than capital gains on other assets like stocks. With higher expected inflation, this difference in tax treatment implies larger differences in expected after-tax capital gains across assets (since the tax is on nominal capital gains.) Third, dividends from owner-occupied housing are not taxed (Floetotto et al., 2016), which also matters more when expected inflation is high. Poterba (1991) documents that through these channels, the tax code made housing particularly attractive for households in higher tax brackets. Correspondingly, housing demand increased more in those segments of the housing market in which higher income households buy compared to segments in which lower income households buy. Increasing inflation expectations can therefore explain why house prices appreciated the most in the more expensive segments of the housing market.

Inflation expectations can explain another important cross-sectional feature of the 1970s housing boom. In household surveys, we observe that young households were expecting much higher inflation rates than older households during this episode.[12] Leombroni et al. (2020) show that this disagreement about expected inflation is important to quantitatively account for the aggregate portfolio shift towards housing in an overlapping-generations model with incomplete markets. In the model, households choose between three broad asset classes: bonds, houses and stocks. A key prediction of this lifecycle model is that younger households build riskier portfolios than older households in the form of a leveraged position in housing, because they own more human wealth which is a relatively safe asset. When inflation expectations of the different generations are chosen to match the Michigan survey data, the model explains the observed overall portfolio shift towards housing and away from stocks. Younger households had higher inflation expectations and therefore perceived housing to be a particularly attractive asset because of the tax code. Moreover, younger households perceived the real (borrowing) rate to be low, which further increased the attractiveness of a leveraged position in housing from their perspective, while older households perceived real rates to be high and were happy to hold bonds. The higher aggregate demand for housing matches the higher price–rent ratios and increased mortgage borrowing that we observe in the data.

6.4.2 The housing boom of the early 2000s

The two most prominent explanations of the large increase in house prices during the early 2000s are high house price expectations and easier access to credit. Landvoigt et al. (2015) put both of these channels in an assignment model of the housing market with heterogeneous households. While lower interest rates increased house prices in all segments of the housing market, relaxations of credit constraints are required to account for the higher capital gains observed in low quality segments, since lower downpayments enabled poorer households to borrow more. However, changes in credit constraints cannot fully explain the observed patterns. To quantitatively account for the overall increase in house prices during the 2000s, Landvoigt et al. (2015) show that it is important that homebuyers at the peak of the boom did not expect house prices to decline, which is a key feature of the survey evidence in Case et al. (2012) on recent homebuyers. If instead homebuyers expected house prices to continue growing at historical trend (which is within reasonable confidence bands of the survey evidence), the model can account for the house price increase of the early 2000s. Both forces—optimistic house price expectations and easier access to credit—are thus important to explain the housing boom of the 2000s.

　　While the Case et al. (2012) evidence shows that recent homebuyers had high house price expectations during the housing boom, the broader population was much less optimistic. Based on the Michigan survey, Piazzesi and Schneider (2009) find that the overall enthusiasm among households about housing purchases cooled early on during the 2000s housing boom. The fraction of enthusiastic households who believed that now is a "good time to buy" was initially high (above 80%). The overwhelming majority of these enthusiastic households justified this belief citing good credit conditions: credit is either perceived to be cheap or easy to get in the very early years of the 2000s. The fraction of enthusiastic households then declined to less than 60%, lower than at any time during the entire previous decade. The paper also identifies a small group of households who believed that now is a good time to buy

---

[12] Malmendier and Nagel (2016) attribute these differences in inflation expectations to differences in lifetime experiences: older households in the 1970s based their expectations in a long record of low inflation rates, while the early inflation spikes after the oil price shocks received a bigger weight in the shorter record of younger households.

because house prices will rise further. This group of "momentum" households made up only 10% of households at the beginning of the boom but had doubled in size by the time the market started to turn.

In a liquid market like the stock market, few optimists or optimism that is not backed by a sufficient amount of wealth to buy the entire market are not enough to support high valuations. But while every stock trades at least once a year, a house trades only once every decade. Market illiquidity amplifies the effect of optimistic beliefs and a few optimists can indeed be sufficient to support high transaction prices. Piazzesi and Schneider (2009) formalize this intuition in a search model of the housing market with heterogeneous households. The housing search process takes time; some houses sit on the market for many weeks and few houses transact. When a small fraction of renters becomes optimistic about house price fundamentals, they look for a house, get matched with a seller after a while, and pay a high transaction price. Over some time, all housing transactions therefore feature high house prices until all optimists are matched with a house.

Building on this model of housing as an illiquid asset, Burnside et al. (2016) introduce waves of optimism and pessimism among households that capture several features of the survey data during the 2000s housing boom–bust cycle. Their approach specifies "social dynamics" of beliefs about housing based on an epidemiological model consistent with the empirical evidence in Bailey et al. (2018b, 2019a). The model's central ingredient is that households change their housing market expectations as a result of social dynamics: they meet randomly, and those with tighter priors are more likely to convert other households. Through this mechanism, optimists can "infect" their peers with their beliefs. The model can generate a "fad": that is, the fraction of the population with a particular view can rise and fall. During a housing boom, these belief dynamics imply a higher difference between the mean and median house price expectation of households, because there are few optimists initially who drive up the mean but not the median. This difference disappears as the boom unfolds and more households are infected, consistent with the Case et al. (2012) survey evidence from the early 2000s.

In an alternative framework in which housing is modeled as a capital stock, Kaplan et al. (2020) introduce news shocks about future housing preferences. News shocks are immediately reflected in house prices, but since current preferences for housing are still the same, the marginal rate of substitution between housing consumption and other consumption is unaffected. Therefore, house prices rise relative to rents. When parameter values for the Markov chain that describes the dynamics of housing preference shocks are matched to (i) data on the length of housing booms and busts, and (ii) expected house price growth by recent homebuyers in the Case et al. (2012) survey assuming that *all* households share the same strong optimism during the boom, the model explains the 2000s housing boom.[13]

Taken together these papers provide robust evidence for the importance of beliefs in driving aggregate behavior. Recent work by Chodorow-Reich et al. (2021) documents that areas with the strongest house price booms in the early 2000s not only experienced the largest busts in the late 2000s but also the strongest rebounds during the 2010s. The authors argue that the cycle was in part due to overoptimism about long-run fundamental growth at the city level. In their model, a single improvement in fundamentals in the early 2000s triggers a boom–bust–rebound that quantitatively matches the experience of the cross-section of cities. Agents who infer long-run growth from observing the dividend to living in a city become overoptimistic due to diagnostic expectations. Eventually, agents realize their

---

[13] The model implies that all houses experience the same capital gains during a boom. The reason is that, in a model of housing capital, houses only differ by the units of capital that they represent. Unless these units somehow change from one period to the next, the capital gains on all houses are identical.

error, triggering a bust that is exacerbated by a wave of foreclosures that cause prices to overshoot in the bust. Foreclosures then subside and prices converge to a higher-growth path, resulting in a rebound. The authors point out that while a number of different formulations of non-rational expectations could cause initial overoptimism during a boom that subsequently corrects, diagnostic expectations help to quantitatively match several features of the data: expectations do not overshoot in the bust and cities have boom–bust–rebound cycles of different size but similar length.

6.5 Conclusion

Housing is the largest asset held by U.S. households, and understanding the determinants of housing market expectations is therefore of central importance. In this chapter, we discussed active research efforts to (i) better measure housing market expectations and understand their determinants, and (ii) better understand the role of housing market expectations in driving individual housing market choices and aggregate housing market outcomes. Along the way, we have highlighted a number of exciting avenues for researchers to further advance our understanding. In this concluding section, we want to expand upon our discussion of these future areas of focus.

On the measurement side, we believe that developing surveys that incorporate more of the elements described in Section 6.1.1 offers a valuable direction for future work, in particular for researchers at central banks and other institutions with the resources to field large-scale surveys over extended periods of time. Expanding the availability of better survey data beyond the U.S. also holds promise for generalizing our understanding of the determinants and effects of housing market expectations.

On the determinants side, it is clear that, despite the advances described in Section 6.2, much of the cross-sectional variation in house price beliefs remains unexplained. This realization generates substantial scope for additional research. We believe that it is unlikely that researchers will eventually discover a single factor that explains a dominant share of the observed cross-sectional dispersion of beliefs. Instead, it is more likely that researchers will continue to discover new factors that might each only explain a relatively small part of the observed belief heterogeneity, and that will thus contribute to an understanding of beliefs as formed through a complex amalgamation of forces. In this light, we expect that the increasing availability of electronic trace data, such as GPS and social network data, will allow researchers to refine the measurement of some of the most plausible factors, including social interactions (see Bailey et al., 2018a; Kuchler and Stroebel, 2022).

The realization that belief formation is neither rational nor easily explained by a few simple factors provides challenges for researchers hoping to create models that accurately capture how beliefs are formed. Indeed, when there are many factors that each explain an important but ultimately small part of the overall dispersion of beliefs, it is complicated to develop canonical models to compete with the rational expectations framework—after all, is it worth moving away from the tractability of rational expectations if the proposed alternative has low explanatory power in the cross-section? We believe that the ideal competing model will depend on the specific question, and expect that not all applications will require researchers to match both the observed time-series and cross-sectional variation in beliefs. In any case, much work remains to be done to translate the growing list of factors that have been shown to influence beliefs into new models of belief formation.

We believe that there is also substantial scope for additional work studying the joint determination of beliefs about different aspects of the economy. House prices are clearly influenced by beliefs about other economic variables (inflation, interest rates, etc.), and house price beliefs are formed jointly with beliefs about these other outcomes. Therefore, rather than studying beliefs about house prices, inflation, growth, and unemployment in isolation, we believe that much empirical and theoretical progress can be made by exploring their joint determination.

Finally, most work studying the determinants and effects of house price expectations has focused on the first moment of the belief distribution. We believe that expanding on the research efforts described in Section 6.2.5 to better understand the determinants and effects of higher moments of the belief distribution holds much promise. Related to this, it may be worth studying individuals' confidence in their own beliefs, as Giglio et al. (2021a) do in the context of the stock market.

Table 6.2 Surveys of housing expectations.

	Description	History	Access	Relevant Question Topics
Surveys of U.S. consumers				
University of Michigan Surveys of Consumers	Rotating panel Fielded monthly >500 U.S. households (excl. AK + HI)	1946–present[a]	Data available online[b]	Expectations for the local housing market Perceptions of past housing prices, current general market conditions
New York Fed Survey of Consumer Expectations (SCE): Core Questions	Rotating panel Fielded monthly ~1300 U.S. households	2013–present	Data available online	Expectations for the general housing market Plans to move
New York Fed SCE Housing Survey	Cross-sectional Fielded annually as a special module of the NY Fed SCE ~1300 U.S. households	2014–present	Data available online	Expectations for the price of own home, local housing market Perceptions of past housing prices, current local market conditions Plans to buy, sell, move
Fannie Mae National Housing Survey (NHS)	Cross-sectional Fielded monthly 1000 U.S. households	2010–present	Data on key indicators is available online	Expectations for the general housing market Perceptions of current market conditions Plans to move
Pulsenomics U.S. Housing Confidence Survey (HCS)	Cross-sectional Fielded twice a year >15500 U.S. households	2014–present	Limited time series data available online; microdata must be requested	Expectations for the price of own home, local housing market Perceptions of past housing prices, current general market conditions Plans to buy
Case–Shiller Homebuyer Surveys	Cross-sectional Fielded annually ~5000 U.S. recent homebuyers in total across all waves	1988; 2003–2012	Private	Expectations for the price of own home, local housing market Perceptions of past housing prices, current market conditions Plans to buy
RAND American Life Panel (ALP): Financial Crisis Surveys	Unbalanced panel Fielded monthly (short version) and quarterly (long version) ~3000 U.S. internet users	2009–2016	Limited data available online; restricted data available at a cost	Expectations for the price of own home, local housing market, general housing market Perceptions of past housing prices, current market conditions

continued on next page

Table 6.2 (*continued*)

	Description	History	Access	Relevant Question Topics
RAND American Life Panel (ALP): Asset Price Expectations Surveys	Unbalanced panel Fielded monthly ~3000 U.S. internet users	2011–2013	Limited data available online; restricted data available at a cost	Expectations for the local housing market Perceptions of current market conditions
National Survey of Mortgage Originations (NSMO)	Cross-sectional Fielded quarterly 6000 U.S. borrowers with newly originated mortgages that are part of the NMDB	2014–present	Data available online	Expectations for the local housing market Perceptions of past housing prices Plans to sell, move
University of Michigan Health and Retirement Survey (HRS)	Unbalanced panel Fielded once a year (1992–1995) or once every two years (1996–2020) ~20,000 U.S. households with ≥ 1 individual over age 50	1992–present[c]	Limited data available online; restricted data upon request	Expectations for the price of own home
Surveys of U.S. industry professionals and experts				
National Association of Home Builders (NAHB) / Wells Fargo Housing Market Index (HMI)	Fielded monthly NAHB members (homebuilders)	1985–present	Data for the HMI and its component indices is available online	Expectations for the single-family housing market Perceptions of current market conditions
Fannie Mae Mortgage Lender Sentiment Survey (MLSS)	Cross-sectional Fielded quarterly >200 Fannie Mae partner lenders	2014–present	Limited data on key indicators is available online	Expectations for the general housing market
Zillow / Pulsenomics Home Price Expectations Survey	Fielded quarterly >100 industry professionals and economists	2010–present	Limited data available online	Expectations for the general housing market
The Wall Street Journal Economic Forecasting Survey	Fielded twice a year (1980s–2002), monthly (2003–2021), and quarterly (2021–present) > 70 academic, business, and financial economists	1980s–present[d]	Data available online	Expectations for the general housing market
Surveys of non-U.S. consumers				
European Central Bank Household Finance and Consumption Survey (HFCS)[e]	Cross-sectional with a panel subset[f] Fielded once every three years 60,000–90,000 households in Eurozone countries, as well as Croatia, Hungary and Poland (as of the 2017 wave)	2010, 2014, 2017	Data can be requested from the ECB	Expectations for the price of own home, general housing market[g]

continued on next page

Table 6.2 (*continued*)

	Description	History	Access	Relevant Question Topics
Deutsche Bundesbank Survey on Consumer Expectations	Cross-sectional with a panel subset Fielded monthly ~2000 German households	2019–present	Data can be requested from the Bundesbank	Expectations for the local housing market
Banco de España Survey of Household Finances (EFF)	Cross-sectional with a panel subset Fielded once every three years ~6000 Spanish households	2002–present[h]	Data can be requested from the Bank of Spain	Expectations for the price of own home Plans to move
Tilburg University CentERdata Institute DNB Household Survey	Panel Fielded annually >1500 Dutch households	1993–present	Data can be requested from CentERdata	Expectations for the price of own home, general housing market Perceptions of past housing prices
Banca d'Italia Survey of Household Income and Wealth	Cross-sectional with a panel subset (about 50%) Fielded annually (before 1987) or ~ every two years (since 1987) ~8000 Italian households (most recently)	1960s–present	Data available online	Expectations for the price of own home
European Central Bank Consumer Expectations Survey	10,000 households in Belgium, France, Germany, Italy, the Netherlands, and Spain total (in 2020 pilot)	Piloted in 2020; still under development as of Jan 2022	As of Jan 2022, available to ECB researchers; external access unclear	Expectations for the price of own home, local housing market Plans to buy
English Longitudinal Study on Ageing (ELSA)	Unbalanced panel Fielded once every two years >18,000 individuals over age 50 in England	2002–present	Data can be requested from the UK Data Service	Expectations for the price of own home
Reserve Bank of New Zealand Household Expectations Survey	Cross-sectional Fielded quarterly ~750–1000 New Zealand households	1995–present[i]	Limited time series data available online	Expectations for the general housing market
Bank of Canada Survey of Consumer Expectations	Rotating panel Fielded quarterly ~2000 Canadian households	2014–present	Data available online	Expectations for the local housing market

[a] *Questions eliciting point estimates were not introduced until the 2000s.*
[b] *Annual and quarterly data is available for 1960 onward; monthly data is available for 1978 onward.*
[c] *Questions on house price expectations asked since 2010.*
[d] *Question on housing expectations asked since 2006*
[e] *Independently administered by participating countries according to a central blueprint*
[f] *Panel data has been collected in the surveys administered by Belgium, Germany, Spain, Italy, Cyprus, Malta, the Netherlands, Estonia, France, Latvia, Poland, Slovakia and Finland.*
[g] *Own home price expectations was a core variable in the 2017 wave; own and general house prices were non-core variables in the 2014 wave.*
[h] *Question on housing expectations asked since 2011.*
[i] *Questions on house price expectations asked since 2011.*

References

Adelino, Manuel, Schoar, Antoinette, Severino, Felipe, 2018. Perception of house price risk and homeownership. National Bureau of Economic Research Working Paper Series.

Anagol, Santosh, Balasubramaniam, Vimal, Ramadorai, Tarun, 2018. Endowment effects in the field: evidence from India's IPO lotteries. The Review of Economic Studies 85 (4), 1971–2004.

Anagol, Santosh, Balasubramaniam, Vimal, Ramadorai, Tarun, 2021. Learning from noise: evidence from India's IPO lotteries. Journal of Financial Economics 140 (3), 965–986.

Armantier, Olivier, Bruine de Bruin, Wändi, van der Klaauw, Wilbert, Topa, Giorgio, Zafar, Basit, 2015. Inflation expectations and behavior: do survey respondents act on their beliefs? International Economic Review 56 (2), 505–536.

Armantier, Olivier, Nelson, Scott, Topa, Giorgio, van der Klaauw, Wilbert, Zafar, Basit, 2016. The price is right: updating of inflation expectations in a randomized price information experiment. Review of Economics and Statistics 98 (3), 503–523.

Armona, Luis, Fuster, Andreas, Zafar, Basit, 2019. Home price expectations and behaviour: evidence from a randomized information experiment. The Review of Economic Studies 86 (4), 1371–1410.

Bailey, Michael, Cao, Rachel, Kuchler, Theresa, Stroebel, Johannes, Wong, Arlene, 2018a. Social connectedness: measurement, determinants, and effects. The Journal of Economic Perspectives 32 (3), 259–280.

Bailey, Michael, Cao, Ruiqing, Kuchler, Theresa, Stroebel, Johannes, 2018b. The economic effects of social networks: evidence from the housing market. Journal of Political Economy 126 (6), 2224–2276.

Bailey, Michael, Dávila, Eduardo, Kuchler, Theresa, Stroebel, Johannes, 2019a. House price beliefs and mortgage leverage choice. The Review of Economic Studies 86 (6), 2403–2452.

Bailey, Michael, Gupta, Abhinav, Hillenbrand, Sebastian, Kuchler, Theresa, Richmond, Robert, Stroebel, Johannes, 2021. International trade and social connectedness. Journal of International Economics 129, 103418.

Bailey, Michael, Johnston, Drew M., Koenen, Martin, Kuchler, Theresa, Russel, Dominic, Stroebel, Johannes, 2020. Social networks shape beliefs and behavior: Evidence from social distancing during the COVID-19 pandemic. National Bureau of Economic Research.

Bailey, Michael, Johnston, Drew M., Kuchler, Theresa, Stroebel, Johannes, Wong, Arlene, 2019b. Peer effects in product adoption. National Bureau of Economic Research.

Barberis, Nicholas, Greenwood, Robin, Jin, Lawrence, Shleifer, Andrei, 2015. X-CAPM: an extrapolative capital asset pricing model. Journal of Financial Economics 115 (1), 1–24.

Ben-David, Itzhak, Fermand, Elyas, Kuhnen, Camelia M., Li, Geng, 2018. Expectations uncertainty and household economic behavior. National Bureau of Economic Research Working Paper Series.

Ben-David, Itzhak, Towbin, Pascal, Weber, Sebastian, 2019. Inferring Expectations from Observables: Evidence from the Housing Market. National Bureau of Economic Research Working Paper Series.

Bordalo, Pedro, Gennaioli, Nicola, La Porta, Rafael, Shleifer, Andrei, 2019. Diagnostic expectations and stock returns. The Journal of Finance 74 (6), 2839–2874.

Botsch, Matthew J., Malmendier, Ulrike, 2020. The Long Shadows of the Great Inflation: Evidence from Residential Mortgages.

Bottan, Nicolas L., Perez-Truglia, Ricardo, 2020. Betting on the house: Subjective expectations and market choices. National Bureau of Economic Research Working Paper Series.

Burnside, Craig, Eichenbaum, Martin, Rebelo, Sergio, 2016. Understanding booms and busts in housing markets. Journal of Political Economy 124 (4), 1088–1147.

Case, Karl E., Shiller, Robert J., 1988. The Behavior of Home Buyers in Boom and Post-Boom Markets. NBER Working Paper, (w2748).

Case, Karl E., Shiller, Robert J., 1989. The efficiency of the market for single-family homes. The American Economic Review 79 (1), 125.

Case, Karl E., Shiller, Robert J., 2003. Is there a bubble in the housing market? Brookings Papers on Economic Activity 2, 299–362.

Case, Karl E., Shiller, Robert J., Thompson, Anne K., 2012. What have they been thinking? Homebuyer behavior in hot and cold markets. Brookings Papers on Economic Activity.

Chodorow-Reich, Gabriel, Guren, Adam M., McQuade, Timothy J., 2021. The 2000s Housing Cycle with 2020 Hindsight: a Neo-Kindlebergerian View. National Bureau of Economic Research Working Paper Series.

Cutler, David M., Poterba, James M., Summers, Lawrence H., 1991. Speculative dynamics. The Review of Economic Studies 58 (3), 529–546.

De Stefani, Alessia, 2020. House price history, biased expectations, and credit cycles: the role of housing investors. Real Estate Economics.

Floetotto, Max, Kirker, Michael, Stroebel, Johannes, 2016. Government intervention in the housing market: who wins, who loses? Journal of Monetary Economics 80, 106–123.

Fuster, Andreas, Laibson, David, Mendel, Brock, 2010. Natural expectations and macroeconomic fluctuations. The Journal of Economic Perspectives 24 (4), 67–84.

Fuster, Andreas, Perez-Truglia, Ricardo, Wiederholt, Mirko, Zafar, Basit, 2018. Expectations with endogenous information acquisition: an experimental investigation. Review of Economics and Statistics, 1–54.

Gargano, Antonio, Giacoletti, Marco, Jarnecic, Elvis, 2020. Local Experiences, Attention and Spillovers in the Housing Market.

Geanakoplos, John, 2010. The leverage cycle. NBER Macroeconomics Annual 24 (1), 1–66.

Gee, Laura K., Jones, Jason, Burke, Moira, 2017. Social networks and labor markets: how strong ties relate to job finding on Facebook's social network. Journal of Labor Economics 35 (2), 485–518.

Giglio, Stefano, Maggiori, Matteo, Stroebel, Johannes, Utkus, Stephen, 2021a. Five facts about beliefs and portfolios. The American Economic Review 111 (5), 1481–1522.

Giglio, Stefano, Maggiori, Matteo, Stroebel, Johannes, Utkus, Stephen, 2021b. The joint dynamics of investor beliefs and trading during the COVID-19 crash. Proceedings of the National Academy of Sciences 118 (4).

Glaeser, Edward L., Nathanson, Charles G., 2017. An extrapolative model of house price dynamics. Journal of Financial Economics 126 (1), 147–170.

Greenwood, Robin, Shleifer, Andrei, 2014. Expectations of returns and expected returns. The Review of Financial Studies 27 (3), 714–746.

Guren, Adam M., 2018. House price momentum and strategic complementarity. Journal of Political Economy 126 (3), 1172–1218.

Hatzmark, Sam, Hirshman, Sam, Imas, Alex, 2021. Ownership, learning, and beliefs. The Quarterly Journal of Economics 136 (3), 1665–1717.

Kaplan, Greg, Mitman, Kurt, Violante, Giovanni, 2020. The housing boom and bust: model meets evidence. Journal of Political Economy 128 (9), 3285–3345.

Kindermann, Fabian, Le Blanc, Julia, Piazzesi, Monika, Schneider, Martin, 2021. Learning about housing cost: Survey evidence from the German house price boom. National Bureau of Economic Research Working Paper Series.

Kuchler, Theresa, Li, Yan, Peng, Lin, Stroebel, Johannes, Zhou, Dexin, 2020. Social proximity to capital: Implications for investors and firms. National Bureau of Economic Research.

Kuchler, Theresa, Stroebel, Johannes, 2021. Social finance. Annual Review of Financial Economics 13.

Kuchler, Theresa, Stroebel, Johannes, 2022. Social interactions, resilience, and access to economic opportunity: a research agenda for the field of computational social science.

Kuchler, Theresa, Zafar, Basit, 2019. Personal experiences and expectations about aggregate outcomes. The Journal of Finance 74 (5), 2491–2542.

Kurlat, Pablo, Stroebel, Johannes, 2015. Testing for information asymmetries in real estate markets. The Review of Financial Studies 28 (8), 2429–2461.

Landvoigt, Tim, 2017. Housing demand during the boom: the role of expectations and credit constraints. The Review of Financial Studies 30 (6), 1865–1902.

Landvoigt, Tim, Piazzesi, Monika, Schneider, Martin, 2015. The housing market(s) of San Diego. The American Economic Review 105 (4), 1371–1407.

Leombroni, Matteo, Piazzesi, Monika, Rogers, Ciaran, Schneider, Martin, 2020. Inflation and the Price of Real Assets.

Liu, Haoyang, Palmer, Christopher, 2021. Are stated expectations actual beliefs? New evidence for the beliefs channel of investment demand. National Bureau of Economic Research Working Paper Series.

Malmendier, Ulrike, Nagel, Stefan, 2016. Learning from inflation experiences. The Quarterly Journal of Economics 131 (1), 53–87.

Malmendier, Ulrike, Steiny, Alexandra, 2017. Rent or buy? The role of lifetime experiences of macroeconomic shocks within and across countries.

Malmendier, Ulrike, Veldkamp, Laura, 2022. Information Resonance.

Manski, Charles F., 2004. Measuring expectations. Econometrica 72 (5), 1329–1376.

Ouimet, Paige, Tate, Geoffrey, 2020. Learning from coworkers: peer effects on individual investment decisions. The Journal of Finance 75 (1), 133–172.

Piazzesi, Monika, Schneider, Martin, 2008. Inflation illusion, credit, and asset pricing. In: Campbell, John Y. (Ed.), Asset Pricing and Monetary Policy. Chicago University Press, Chicago, IL, pp. 147–181.

Piazzesi, Monika, Schneider, Martin, 2009. Momentum traders in the housing market: survey evidence and a search model. The American Economic Review 99 (2), 406–411.

Piazzesi, Monika, Schneider, Martin, Stroebel, Johannes, 2020. Segmented housing search. The American Economic Review 110 (3), 720–759.

Poterba, Jim, 1984. Tax subsidies to owner-occupied housing: an asset-market approach. The Quarterly Journal of Economics 99 (4), 729–752.

Poterba, Jim, 1991. House price dynamics: the role of tax policy and demography. Brookings Papers on Economic Activity 2, 143–202.

Rauch, James E., 2001. Business and social networks in international trade. Journal of Economic Literature 39 (4), 1177–1203.

Shiller, Robert J., 2007. Understanding recent trends in house prices and home ownership.

Simsek, Alp, 2013. Belief disagreements and collateral constraints. Econometrica 81 (1), 1–53.

Soo, Cindy K., 2018. Quantifying sentiment with news media across local housing markets. The Review of Financial Studies 31 (10), 3689–3719.

Stroebel, Johannes, 2016. Asymmetric information about collateral values. The Journal of Finance 71 (3), 1071–1112.

Topa, Giorgio, 2001. Social interactions, local spillovers and unemployment. The Review of Economic Studies 68 (2), 261–295.

Topa, Giorgio, 2011. Labor markets and referrals. In: Handbook of Social Economics, vol. 1. Elsevier, pp. 1193–1221.

Zafar, Bais, Fuster, Andreas, van der Klaauw, Wilbert, Cocci, Matthew, 2014. Introducing the SCE housing survey. Liberty Street Economics.

Expectations in education☆

Pamela Giustinelli
Bocconi University, Milan, Italy

7.1 Introduction

Subjective expectations have long been important primitives in microeconomic models of decision-making under uncertainty and intertemporal behavior, including but not limited to educational choices and other forms of human capital investment and accumulation.[1] Nowadays, the expression "subjective expectations" is also commonly used to refer to an increasingly available and popular type of survey data meant to measure those primitives. This chapter reviews the economic literature on *subjective expectations as data in* the domain of *education*, with a focus on high-income countries.[2]

There was a time when survey data on subjective expectations related to education and its consequences for the individual were scant and when the sole idea of eliciting subjective expectations about the returns to schooling from subjects involved in making educational choices was largely considered radical and unfeasible among economists.[3]

In a seminal paper titled "*Adolescent Econometricians: How Do Youth Infer the Returns to Schooling?*", Manski (1993) examines the implications for contemporary human capital research of the scarcity of interpretable data on youth's perceptions of the returns to schooling. This lack of data had caused two fundamental and interrelated identification problems. "*The first problem is that, not knowing how youth perceive the returns to schooling, one cannot infer their decision processes from*

☆ This chapter is based on a longer working paper titled "Expectations in Education: Framework, elicitation, and evidence", available at my research webpage. The Norwegian Research Council supported this research under project no. 275906. Jacopo Lunghi provided invaluable research assistance. I am grateful to the Editors and to Todd Stinebrickner for generously providing many constructive comments. I have benefited from insightful conversations with Massimo Anelli, Timm Gries, and Stefano Rossi and received helpful feedback from Peter Arcidiacono, Teodora Boneva, John Conlon, Luis Diaz-Serrano, Inês Gonçalves Raposo, Nick Huntington-Klein, Francesca Leombroni, Jacopo Lunghi, Carlos Madeira, Maria Menon Eliophotou, Frauke Peter, Gregor Pfeifer, Chris Rauh, Stefano Rossi, Ali Vergili, Stefan Wolter, Basit Zafar, and participants at the virtual Conference for the Handbook of Economic Expectations. I dedicate this work to the memory of Gábor Kézdi, Alberto Mezzanini, and Virginia Pinardi, who greatly contributed to the education of many, and to the six cohorts of PhD students whom I have had the privilege to meet, teach, and learn from since joining Bocconi.

[1] For a historical introduction to expectations in microeconomics, see Carter and Maddock (1984). For early models of human capital decisions under uncertainty, see Weiss (1972), Levhari and Weiss (1974), Groot and Oosterbeek (1992)'s extension of the Becker–Mincer model, and Altonji (1993).

[2] See Chapter 9 in this Handbook for evidence on low and middle income countries.

[3] Scholars in other social sciences have a longer tradition of collecting and analyzing subjective data. Dominitz and Manski (1999) review the different cultures of research on subjective expectations.

their schooling choices. (...) The most one can do is infer the decision rule conditional on maintained assumptions on expectations. (...) The second problem is that, not knowing youth's decision processes, one cannot infer the objective returns to schooling from data on realized outcomes. (...) Hence, one can only infer the objective returns to schooling conditional on the validity of expectations assumptions." (Manski (1993), pp. 44–45).[4]

The paper concludes that the question posed in the title could not be answered at the time of writing and that progress would be possible only if economists opened up to the possibility of collecting interpretable subjective data on expectations and/or preferences. While recognizing that the enterprise may be especially challenging in the education context – as it would require elicitation of choice-conditioned forecasts from adolescent respondents – the paper closes unequivocally: *"We shall not know whether this is feasible until we try."* (Manski (1993), p. 56).

Shortly after, Dominitz and Manski (1996) developed a computer-assisted self-administered interview protocol for survey elicitation of subjective expectations and used it to measure subjective earnings expectations, schooling expectations, and population earnings beliefs from high school students and college undergraduates in Madison, Wisconsin.

The survey featured a number of important innovations over earlier studies of students' expectations. Because a primary goal of the study was to characterize students' perceived uncertainty, the survey measured respondents' *subjective distributions* about own and population earnings by eliciting the probability that earnings exceed multiple thresholds, rather than eliciting a single moment (say, expected mean earnings). Because another important goal was to learn how students perceive the returns to schooling, the survey asked respondents their earnings expectations *under hypothetical scenarios* about their school attainment, in addition to their unconditional expectations. Because the study also aimed at collecting expectations that could be compared both within and between students, the survey elicited respondents' subjective probabilities on a *numerical scale of percent chance*, instead of a nominal probability scale.

Finding that respondents' were willing and able to give meaningful answers, the authors concluded that measuring youth's perceptions of the returns to schooling was both feasible and promising. Many more studies of students' expectations followed as a result.

A remarkable example is the Berea Panel Study (BPS), launched by Ralph and Todd Stinebrickner shortly after the Dominitz and Manski (1996)'s study. By following two cohorts of Berea College freshmen for up to 14 years, and by collecting rich information on the expectations and realizations of participants' education and labor market outcomes during and after college, the BPS has become a landmark among existing surveys of students' expectations.

---

[4] The first problem refers to the difficulty of performing empirical revealed preference analysis when the available data consists of a single distribution of choices within a population of heterogeneous individuals; observing one choice per individual does not reveal the distribution of underlying primitives, since multiple configurations of preferences and expectations may be consistent with a given choice. The identification problem gets harder with intra-family decision-making, peer interactions, or heterogeneous choice sets, all of which are relevant concerns in models of schooling decisions (Giustinelli and Manski, 2018). The second problem is a direct consequence of selection; it *"arises because the youth who choose to enroll in school are those who expect schooling to have favorable outcomes for them. If the expected outcomes are related to the objective ones, then the outcomes experienced by youth who choose to enroll in school differ from those that nonenrollees would experience if they were to enroll. (...) [Any] effort to infer the objective returns to schooling from observations of realized outcomes requires at least some knowledge of the way youth make their schooling decisions."* (Manski (1993), p. 45).

Over the years, different studies have experimented with different survey modes and question formats, have elicited percent-chance expectations from youth of varying ages and backgrounds in different countries, and have expanded the scope of the outcomes and scenarios posed. Expectations for nonmonetary benefits and costs of schooling have been increasingly collected and analyzed along with those for monetary returns and costs. Most studies have collected expectations at one point in time from a single group of respondents, usually college students and less frequently younger students. Occasionally, expectations have been collected longitudinally, as in the Berea Panel Study (BPS) and in Zafar (2011b, 2013)'s survey of Northwestern University (NU)'s undergraduates, or within field experiments, as in Wiswall and Zafar (2015b,a)'s survey of New York University (NYU)'s undergraduates. Sporadically, they have been elicited from multiple subjects, as in Giustinelli (2016)'s survey of Italian 9th-graders and their parents.

These data have been used to study the perceived monetary and nonmonetary returns to schooling of youth and their families, to estimate random utility models of schooling decisions under uncertainty, and to investigate how students form expectations and update them to arrival of new information.[5]

The present chapter surveys this literature, while complementing in scope and content earlier reviews addressing the role of expectations for human capital.[6] The chapter focuses on the vast empirical evidence accumulated since Dominitz and Manski (1996). The working paper version (Giustinelli, 2022) additionally provides a motivating analytical framework, information and discussions about survey elicitation, and further empirical evidence for each section. It also collects a list of nearly 50 surveys of expectations related to education in its Supplementary Appendix.[7]

Section 7.2 deals with expectations of monetary returns, risks, and costs of schooling. Section 7.3 covers expectations of nonmonetary outcomes and educational expectations. Section 7.4 reviews studies of schooling decisions with expectations data. Section 7.5 covers studies of expectations formation and updating in education. Section 7.6 summarizes key findings and discusses avenues for future research.

7.2 Survey expectations about monetary outcomes of schooling
7.2.1 Are elicited earnings expectations meaningful?

Early expectations studies have evaluated the informativeness and quality of survey expectations by investigating the prevalence and predictors of item nonresponse, by checking the coherence of expectations reports with respect to probability rules, by comparing expectations with realizations for the

---

[5] The economic literature on survey expectations related to education and labor earnings (e.g., Dominitz and Manski (1996, 1997), Dominitz (1998, 2001), Fischhoff et al. (2000), Dominitz et al. (2001)) has been the cradle of the broader expectations literature reviewed by Manski (2004, 2018) and multiple chapters in this Handbook. The former has especially contributed to the transition from a first phase of largely exploratory and descriptive studies to a still ongoing second phase where survey expectations have been used to test economic theories, estimate formal models of decision-making and/or learning, and perform counterfactual analyses (e.g., van der Klaauw (2012), Arcidiacono et al. (2012, 2020), Stinebrickner and Stinebrickner (2012, 2014a,b), Zafar (2012, 2013), Wiswall and Zafar (2015b,a), Giustinelli (2016), Kapor et al. (2020)).

[6] These include Heckman et al. (2006), Hartog and Diaz-Serrano (2014), Altonji et al. (2016), Giustinelli and Manski (2018), and Patnaik et al. (2020b).

[7] For further evidence and discussions on elicitation and measurement of expectations not specific to education, see Chapters 1, 4, and 26 in this Handbook. For use of survey expectations in microstructural models not specific to education, see Chapter 21 in this Handbook.

same or comparable individuals, and by investigating whether expectations covary with respondents' characteristics and other observables as do realizations (Manski, 2004).

Early quality assessments are sometimes performed in the survey pretest phase. For example, Dominitz and Manski (1996) held multiple debriefing sessions with pretest respondents. These sessions revealed that students generally understood the questions well, could articulate meaningful answers, and greatly enjoyed the interactive features of the software. At the same time, these preliminary discussions also revealed some critical issues with the interpretation of specific questions. For example, when reporting expectations of their own future earnings, pretest respondents tended to condition on being employed full-time even though the scenario did not specify future employment. Dominitz and Manski addressed these issues during the design phase by appropriately revising the text and wording of the relevant questions.

The consistency checks and error screens embedded in Dominitz and Manski (1996)'s CASI protocol did ensure that students' final responses were logically consistent. Nevertheless, the authors took advantage of their software capturing the entire sequence of responses and revisions given by each student to investigate the internal coherence of the students' initial responses. They focused on three types of errors: (1) reporting a probability outside the unit interval; (2) reporting a sequence of probabilities violating monotonicity of the cumulative distribution; (3) reporting a probability inconsistent with the previously reported median. None of the respondents made the first type of error, but some made errors of the second or third type. The analysis reveals three main patterns. First, (3) errors were more common than (2) errors. Second, the error rates in the early sections of the survey were higher than the error rates in later sections, suggesting that respondents tend to learn. Third, investigation of person-specific patterns of responses across questions revealed that some respondents are more error-prone than others. Additionally, Dominitz and Manski (1996) find little bunching of responses.[8]

Wiswall and Zafar (2015a) quantify the extent of measurement error in the earnings expectations of NYU students and assess the impact of measurement error on inference. Under the maintained assumption of classical measurement error, they estimate a reliability ratio of 0.984 (equal to 1 minus the noise-to-signal ratio), implying a minimal attenuation bias in their estimates of about 1.6%.

The majority of surveys eliciting earnings expectations from students has focused on college-going or older students. A smaller but increasing number of studies has elicited earnings expectations from high school students.[9] A natural question is whether elicitation from younger students presents special challenges. Wolter (2000) appears to be the only study, after Dominitz and Manski (1996), to have elicited earnings expectations from both high school and university students and finds no systematic differences by age or type of school attended.

Using a similar survey instrument fielded online among high school Dutch students, Mazza and Hartog (2011) document a high prevalence of early quitters, which they attribute to the online mode. Conditional on not quitting in the early part of the survey, the authors do not find differential nonre-

---

[8] Bunching of probability reports at 0% and at multiples of 5% or 10% may be an indication of rounding, a nonclassical form of measurement error. For evidence and methods on rounded probabilities, see Manski and Molinari (2010), de Bresser and van Soest (2013), Kleinjans and van Soest (2014), Gong et al. (2019, 2020), Giustinelli et al. (2020, 2022), and Chapter 26 in this Handbook.

[9] See Menon Eliophotou (1997b,a), Wolter (2000), Menon Eliophotou (2008a,b), Mazza and Hartog (2011), Hastings et al. (2015, 2016), Huntington-Klein (2015, 2016), Belfield et al. (2020), Boneva and Rauh (2021), Boneva et al. (2022a), and Briel et al. (2022).

sponse rates to the questions eliciting earnings expectations vis-à-vis other questions. When investigating response mistakes, the authors find that, *ceteris paribus*, male students, immigrant students, and students with a low-education background are more likely to be early quitters and make significantly more mistakes.

In a sample of Italian 14-year-olds and their parents, Giustinelli (2016) finds that the majority of survey participants were unable or unwilling to report their expectations about the student's future earnings under alternative schooling scenarios, but they were able and willing to provide subjective probabilities about other track-specific outcomes.[10] On the other hand, Belfield et al. (2020) and Boneva and Rauh (2021) do not report of any particular issue with elicitation from younger respondents in the UK.

7.2.2 Patterns and heterogeneity of earnings expectations

Dominitz and Manski (1996) analyze the empirical distributions of the median and interquartile range (IQR) of respondents' subjective belief distributions about their future earnings at ages 30 and 40 under three attainment scenarios: (1) unconditional on schooling, (2) conditional on obtaining a high school diploma (for high school respondents) or terminating school after the current semester (for college respondents), and (3) conditional on obtaining at least a bachelor's degree. They find limited variation in the median and IQR by gender and schooling, but substantial heterogeneity within groups. Furthermore, the authors find that students expect their earnings to increase with age, especially under the scenario of obtaining a bachelor's degree.

Among US college seniors enrolled in a randomly selected set of courses at the College of Business of Florida International University in Miami, Carvajal et al. (2000) find that female students expect lower mean earnings than their male peers.

Brunello et al. (2004) analyze the earnings expectations of students specializing in Economics or Business from 26 universities across Europe, spanning Austria, Finland, Germany, Greece, Italy, Portugal, Sweden, Switzerland, and the UK. Like Carvajal et al. (2000), they focus on expected mean earnings. Like Dominitz and Manski (1996), they elicit expectations about students' own future earnings at two points in time (at labor market entry and after 10 years on the job) and under two attainment scenarios (the student obtains a college degree and the counterfactual in which the student had not continued onto college after high school). The authors find that female students expect significantly lower college and high-school earnings than male students, *ceteris paribus*. The implied gender difference widens when expectations about earnings after 10 years on the job are considered, consistent with females expecting to enter jobs with lower relative earnings growth. Students in their second and third year of college expect lower college wages at labor market entry than freshman students, but these differences shrink when considering expectations for earnings after 10 years on the job. Students who expect to take longer than required to complete college have lower expected college wages than their counterparts, but similar expected high school wages, for both horizons. Students with a more educated mother have higher expected earnings after college and high school. Students who rank themselves

---

[10] The majority of students reported being clueless about the order of magnitude of monthly salaries, while a minority gave estimates based on their parents' earnings. Some parents left written notes, expressing their perceived difficulty of providing meaningful earnings forecasts and stating that they did not regard future earnings as an important factor for the choice of high school track.

above the average in their class and those who report having acquired information about earnings from personal sources or from the daily or weekly press have higher expected college earnings. On the other hand, students who report having chosen their university based on costs or by an external assignment have lower earnings expectations. Finally, students from countries that have higher wages and those enrolled in more selective universities have higher expectations.

Moving to younger students, Mazza and Hartog (2011) uncover five main patterns in their data on expected median earnings of Dutch high school students. First, earnings expectations display higher variation within groups than between groups, as in Dominitz and Manski (1996). Second, female students expect significantly lower median earnings than male students, consistent with findings of most expectations studies except Dominitz and Manski (1996). Third, for the scenario in which the student does not continue to university, the expected median varies by attended high school tracks. Fourth, expected median earnings following university are generally higher than those from going to work right after high school. Fifth, the subjective earnings distributions shift upward with hypothesized work experience, suggesting that respondents are aware of the increasing wage profile over the life cycle.

Other studies have elicited earnings expectations under hypothetical scenarios specifying alternative fields of study (e.g., college majors), rather than attainment levels. For example, Arcidiacono et al. (2012) elicit expectations about earnings 10 years after graduation under alternative major-career combinations in a sample of male undergraduates attending Duke University. First, the way in which students' subjective probabilities of entering each career vary across majors suggests that some careers are perceived to be tied to certain majors (e.g., Science), whereas other careers less so (e.g., Business). Second, also students' earnings expectations vary systematically across majors. For example, majoring in Science or Engineering is perceived to lead to higher earnings in Science and Health careers, while majoring in Economics is perceived to lead to higher earnings in Business. Third, students in later years tend to report lower earnings expectations than students in earlier years, irrespective of their major. The authors attribute this to students learning over time. Fifth, students' earnings expectations are consistent with income sorting in choice of majors.

Reuben et al. (2017) document a large, and increasing with age, gender gap in expected future earnings of NYU undergraduates, amounting to 31% lower expected earnings at age 30 and 39% lower expected earnings at age 45. These figures are partly attributable to gender differences in major/career choices, since male students are more likely to select high-earning majors such as Business and less likely to select low-earning majors such as Humanities than female students. However, the authors also show that a large gap remains when analyzing students' earnings expectations for all majors, including the unchosen ones. On average across all majors, female students expect to earn 19% less than men at age 30 and 23% less at age 45.[11]

7.2.3 Perceived monetary returns to schooling

Earnings differentials across schooling levels and fields of study are large and well documented.[12] What do youth believe about the monetary returns to schooling?

---

[11] Using experimental measures of competitiveness, overconfidence, and economic preferences, the authors show that, conditional on the chosen major, gender differences in competitiveness and overconfidence explain nearly 20% of the gender gap in earnings expectations.

[12] For example, Card (1999), Heckman et al. (2006), Altonji et al. (2016), and Psacharopoulos and Patrinos (2018).

Dominitz and Manski (1996) show that students share a common belief that the monetary returns to a college education are positive and heterogeneous in magnitude, for example, increasing with age.[13] These results have been repeatedly confirmed by subsequent studies (e.g., Menon Eliophotou (1997b,a), Wolter (2000), Botelho and Costa Pinto (2004), Brunello et al. (2004), Webbink and Hartog (2004), Mazza and Hartog (2011), Schweri et al. (2011), Belfield et al. (2020), Boneva and Rauh (2021), Boneva et al. (2022b)).

Botelho and Costa Pinto (2004) find that, *ceteris paribus*, female students expect significantly lower monetary returns to a college education than male students and that, irrespective of gender, senior students expect lower returns than freshman students. Moreover, the authors find that students expect for themselves returns that are above average, with this tendency being stronger among male and freshman students.

Brunello et al. (2004), too, find that female students expect lower college wage premia at both labor market entry and after 10 years, but the difference is statistically significant only for the latter case. The authors additionally find that older students have lower expected college wage premia, conditional on year of enrollment. Students from countries that have higher college wage premia have higher perceived college wage premia, but only based on their subjective expectations about earnings after 10 years on the job.

Among younger UK students, Belfield et al. (2020) find that female and low socioeconomic (low-SES) students report, on average, lower expected earnings across all schooling scenarios (high school, sixth form, and university). However, in multivariate regressions both female and low-SES students hold significantly higher perceived monetary returns to university and insignificantly higher perceived monetary returns to sixth form. In a separate analysis of UK students aged 13–18, Boneva and Rauh (2021) find that low-SES students expect a lower earnings premium from going to university than high-SES students.

7.2.4 **Perceived earnings risk**

A smaller set of studies have investigated the spread of individuals' subjective earnings distributions. Dominitz and Manski (1996) analyze the interquartile ranges (IQRs) of students' fitted subjective earnings distributions and show that most students perceive substantial uncertainty, with the IQRs being of the same order of magnitude as the reported subjective medians. The authors additionally show that students tend to be more uncertain about their future earnings with a bachelor's degree than with a lower attainment level. On the other hand, students tend to be equally uncertain about their future earnings at ages 30 and 40, conditional on attainment.

Mazza and Hartog (2011) find similar results in their sample of Dutch high school students, which the authors interpret as an indication that students have a high perceived wage risk. Perceived wage risk does not vary systematically across hypothetical schooling levels, but does vary by gender, with females perceiving higher wage risk than males. Irrespective of gender, students' expectations imply a perceived decreasing wage variance over time, between entry wage and wage after 10 years.

Schweri et al. (2011) also find that students' belief distributions about post-schooling earnings are highly dispersed. However, unlike Mazza and Hartog (2011), they find that the variance tend to be

---

[13] A person's perceived return to a college education is defined as the person-specific difference in subjective earnings expectations between the scenario in which the person obtains a college degree and that in which the person does not.

higher in high-age and high-education scenarios (age 40 vs. 30 and tertiary vs. secondary education). As predicted by theory, higher perceived risk (variance) significantly increases expected median wage and higher skewness reduces it. The authors show that the risk elasticities implied by their expectation-based estimates are comparable to those estimated using risk-augmented Mincer earnings equations with realizations data. The authors further show that these effects are not mechanically due to the fact that students' subjective earnings distributions are lognormal, as they are not.

Schweri et al. (2011) show that students expect median earnings to increase with both age and education and that males expect significantly higher median earnings than females, but find no differences by family background or by ability. The authors view these patterns in students' subjective belief distributions as being consistent with observable labor market patterns, but inconsistent with students having/using private information when reporting their earnings expectations. Yet, as noted by Gong et al. (2019), the uncertainty-reducing effect of the greater or better information that high-ability or high-SES students may well be counterbalanced by the uncertainty-enhancing effect of their having greater access to job opportunities. Gong et al. (2019), too, find no difference by American College Testing (ACT) score in the extent of uncertainty held by Berea students at college entrance about their future labor market earnings. They do find differences by race, though. Specifically, black students have significantly larger earnings uncertainty when they enter college, but resolve more uncertainty than the other students during college. So, the race gap in earnings uncertainty is closed by the end of college.

7.2.5 Beliefs about population earnings

Beliefs (or expectations) about population earnings and expectations about own earnings are different concepts. Hence, respondents' reports about them may differ. First, respondents may think that future earnings distributions will differ from current ones. Second, respondents should form expectations about own outcomes conditional on the information available to them; such information may include personal attributes and other factors that distinguish the respondent from the relevant population. At the same time, it is possible that when forming expectations about own future earnings respondents take into account what they know about current earnings in a relevant population, as hypothesized by Manski (1993). This provides a rationale for collecting both sets of data and investigating their relationship.

Betts (1996) finds that undergraduate students at the University of California, San Diego (UCSD) are aware that wage profiles are positively sloped, but their estimates of population earnings vary greatly across personal characteristics and wage subpopulations. For example, students in later study years and students from lower income families provide systematically lower earnings estimates than other students.[14] Moreover, students give higher estimates of the average starting salary of graduates in their own field than in other fields. Betts (1996) shows that this is due to students underestimating population earnings in fields other than their own, while holding more accurate beliefs about starting salaries following graduation in their field. Accuracy of students' beliefs starting salaries in their own field, however, does not carry over to salaries of more experienced workers. Betts (1996) further documents that students in later years of study make smaller mistakes, consistently with learning over time; students from poorer families make larger errors when estimating salaries of college graduates; and higher GPA students make smaller errors when estimating starting salaries.

---

[14] Betts (1996) hypothesizes that this may be because young people form beliefs about the returns to education by observing workers in their neighborhood.

In a sample of community college students in California, Baker et al. (2018) find that less than 15% of students can rank broad categories of majors accurately in terms of labor market outcomes and that students believe that salaries are, on average, 13% higher than they actually are. In contrast, Conlon (2021) finds that Ohio State University (OSU)'s freshmen underestimate the average salaries of workers from most fields by about $15K (19% of the average true value) or more, on average. Additionally, the author shows that students are significantly misinformed about the differences in average salary between fields. Across all pairs of fields, the mean error in the difference in average salary is close to $20K (84% of the average true difference).

Dominitz and Manski (1996) and Wiswall and Zafar (2015a) are, to my knowledge, the only two studies to have elicited both population earnings beliefs and own earnings expectations from the same students.[15] Dominitz and Manski (1996) find that both sets of beliefs follow a similar pattern: limited variation across genders and schooling levels, but substantial variation within those groups. The median male respondent has accurate perceptions of the current median earnings of males, whereas the median female respondent overestimates the median earnings in the female population. The authors speculate that this may be due to a tendency of respondents to report their beliefs about full-time, year-round workers. When examining the IQRs, the authors find that students are aware that the spread of the earnings distribution among college graduates is larger than that among high school graduates, but tend to overestimate the degree of earnings inequality.[16] Finally, the authors find that the subjective medians of the two distributions are highly correlated with each other, suggesting that students take their knowledge of the distributions of current earnings into account when forming expectations about own future earnings.

Wiswall and Zafar (2015a) find that their respondents – despite their being high-ability undergraduates at New York University (NYU), a selective private university – significantly underpredict annual average earnings of male workers with no college degree and overpredict average earnings of male graduates in Economics/Business, on average. While errors in students' beliefs vary widely across respondents, these errors are only weakly correlated with students' observables. Using an experimental design that randomly gives students information about population earnings, the authors show that students' expectations about own earnings are causally linked to students' beliefs about the population earnings. However, the latter do not fully explain the former, indicating that students form their expectations about own earnings also based on other factors.

Outside of the U.S., Botelho and Costa Pinto (2004) find that on average Portuguese university students tend to overestimate the actual returns, but female and senior students have significantly more accurate beliefs than male students and students in earlier years of university.[17] Among Chilean college applicants, Hastings et al. (2015) find that high-achieving students hold nearly correct beliefs on average, while low-income and low-achieving students who apply to low-earning programs overestimate earnings for past graduates by over 100%.

---

[15] Briel et al. (2022) did that as well, but only the first moment.

[16] Wolter (2000), instead, finds that Swiss students tend to underestimate the extent of the spread in wages.

[17] Botelho and Costa Pinto (2004)'s elicitation uses a scoring rule providing a random subsample of respondents with financial incentives for accurate reporting. The authors find no significant effects of incentives on accuracy.

7.2.6 **Are elicited earnings expectations rational?**

A number of studies has compared students' earnings expectations with earnings realizations. Early analyses have focused on the means of the expectations and realizations distributions. More recent analyses have also looked at higher moments of the two distributions. Sometimes, elicited expectations have been compared with subsequent realizations in a relevant population; whenever possible, they have been compared within the same sample.

For example, Webbink and Hartog (2004) cannot reject the null hypothesis of equality of means between expected and realized earnings in their sample of Dutch students. They further show that this finding does not vary by respondent's characteristics. More recently, D'Haultfoeuille et al. (2021) and Crossley et al. (2021) have developed a series of new tests of rational expectations that take into account the information on higher moments, contained in survey expectations of continuous variables whenever these expectations are elicited as multiple points on the respondent's subjective belief distribution. Crossley et al. (2021) find that earnings expectations become more accurate as BPS students progress through college, and especially after they leave college. Their analysis almost always rejects the null hypothesis of rational expectations based on the data collected in the in-school period, but the evidence against rationality is much weaker on basis of the data collected in the post-college period (see also Crossley et al. (2022)).

7.2.7 **Other labor market outcomes**

Some studies have also elicited students' expectations for employment status, unemployment risk, and labor supply, finding that these expectations follow empirical patterns that are similar to or consistent with those documented for earnings expectations, for example, in terms of how expectations vary by students' characteristics (e.g., Carvajal et al. (2000), Fischhoff et al. (2000), Brunello et al. (2004), Zafar (2011b, 2012, 2013), Huntington-Klein (2015, 2016), Wiswall and Zafar (2015b,a, 2020), Giustinelli (2016), Baker et al. (2018), Gong et al. (2019), Gong et al. (2020), Belfield et al. (2020), Delavande et al. (2020), Boneva and Rauh (2021), and Boneva et al. (2022b)).

7.2.8 **Monetary costs**

Measurement of expectations about the monetary costs of education, financing opportunities, and student debt is highly topical, as they have the potential to shed light on the unsettled debate regarding the importance and role of credit constraints in human capital investment and educational choices (see Lochner and Monge-Naranjo (2012, 2016)'s reviews on credit constraints in education).

Hastings et al. (2015, 2016) find that Chilean college applicants have correctly centered but noisy expectations about the costs of college. Nearly 40% of students report not knowing the costs of their stated first-choice degree program, with this proportion varying by students' socioeconomic status (SES) and performance in the college admission exam (*Prueba Seleccion Universitaria* or PSU). Low-SES students are almost 11 percentage points more likely than high-SES students to report not knowing program costs, and low-PSU students are 19 percentage points more likely than high-PSU students to report not knowing them. Overall, 50% of students have cost expectations that are approximately within 11% of the cost value observed in the administrative data, but again low-SES and low-PSU students have significantly noisier expectations.

Huntington-Klein (2016) finds that high school students in King County, Washington overestimate costs at their first-choice institution by about 41% at the median, and that low-SES students are more likely to skip the tuition question and exhibit larger IQR of the error distribution.

Using the Survey of Consumer Expectations (SCE), Bleemer and Zafar (2018) find that about 60% of their respondents overestimate average college net costs in the U.S., with no significant differences by education or income.

Using UK data, Belfield et al. (2020) document a mean cost belief of £7.3K per year and a modal cost belief of £9K, consistently with the transition of most universities to the maximum fee of £9K. The authors also find that the response distribution is similar across gender and socioeconomic groups, with responses bunching at £5–6K and £9–10K and a few outliers above £10K. However, high-SES students expect somewhat higher costs than low-SES students. Boneva et al. (2022b) find that female university students report a higher average probability of struggling financially than their male peers, and that high-SES students who attended a state school perceive a significantly larger difference in the probability of struggling financially if they were to pursue postgraduate education relative to not pursuing it than students who attended a private school, despite giving lower subjective estimates of the immediate costs of postgraduate education. Boneva and Rauh (2021) find that, on average, students report a higher probability of struggling financially, a lower probability of having enough money, and a higher probability of receiving financial support from their parents, in the university enrollment scenario than otherwise. Again, beliefs vary significantly across SES groups, with low-SES students reporting significantly higher probabilities of struggling financially and lower probabilities of having enough money and receiving financial support from their parents than high-SES students.

7.3 Survey expectations about nonmonetary outcomes of schooling
7.3.1 Are elicited probabilities meaningful? Rational?

Similarly to studies of earnings expectations, early studies of expectations about nonmonetary outcomes have focused on evaluating the informativeness and quality of survey expectations. Fischhoff et al. (2000) evaluate the probability reports of teen respondents aged 16–17 in the National Longitudinal Study of Youth 1997 (NLSY97) to 18 questions eliciting percent-chance expectations for significant life events, including "Be a student in a regular school one year from now," "Have received a high school diploma by the time you turn 20," and "Have a 4-year college degree by the time you turn 30." Students' responses to the first question match favorably with the figure that 95% of the sample teens report being currently in school and with teens not in school giving lower probabilities (46% vs. 95%), whereas the responses to the other two questions seem too optimistic. The average subjective probability of achieving a high school diploma by age 20 exceeds the completion rate of 20-year olds (93% vs. 84%). Even more optimistic are the expectations of earning a 4-year college degree by age 30 (73% vs. 30%).[18]

---

[18] The authors' overall assessment of the expectations module is that the relative accuracy of most aggregate estimates, the lack of stable individual-difference tendency to give high or low probabilities, the sensible correlations between probability responses and responses to related NLSY97 questions, the respondents' use of the entire response scale, and the between-group differences reflecting social realities provide confidence in the ability of the instrument to capture respondents' beliefs.

Cowan (2017) finds that NLSY97 teens' expectations are highly predictive of their future college completion and concludes that youths take the expectations question seriously. At the same time, his analysis confirms Fischhoff et al. (2000)'s earlier finding that teens' college expectations are overly optimistic. This is also consistent with earlier evidence based on nonprobabilistic expectations (e.g., Reynolds and Pemberton (2001) and Jacob and Wilder (2010)) and subsequent evidence based on probabilistic expectations in other samples (e.g., Zafar (2011b) and Stinebrickner and Stinebrickner (2012)). Cowan (2017) further shows that the expectation bias is highly negatively correlated with youths' scholastic aptitude (AFQT) and that, once AFQT test scores are accounted for, other variables such as gender, race/ethnicity, parental education, and family income have little or no predictive power. Moreover, the empirical relationship between youths' expectations and family income tracks closely that between actual college completion and family income. The author interprets these results as suggesting that while teenagers seem to properly anticipate the role of family income in college outcomes, they tend to have a poor understanding of the importance of academic preparation for college success. Using a regression test, Cowan (2017) formally rejects the null hypothesis of rational expectations and confirms that youths' college expectations are overly optimistic, although the degree of bias shrinks as the AFQT percentile increases.

Subsequent studies perform additional analyses assessing the quality of students' probability judgements about nonmonetary education outcomes. Zafar (2011a) rejects cognitive dissonance (the concern that respondents may report beliefs that rationalize their choices). Boneva and Rauh (2021) validate their measures by showing that test-retest correlations are high and do not vary by socioeconomic background. Stinebrickner and Stinebrickner (2012) show that, at the end of the first year of college, both past grades (a stock variable) and expectations about future grades (a flow variable) are related to college drop out, implying that subjective expectations data outperform standard assumptions (e.g., rational expectations) in satisfying a basic theoretical implication of their model. Analyses of this type can be highly valuable for assessing the credibility of subjective expectations data vis-à-vis traditional economic assumptions.

7.3.2 Academic performance, study effort, and ability

Studies of college students find a similar optimism about own academic achievement to that previously documented among NLSY97 respondents with regard to their educational attainment. For example, Zafar (2011b) find that NU undergraduates are on average overoptimistic about their likelihood of graduating with a GPA of at least 3.5. Using the same data, Zafar (2012, 2013) further show that, even though students are largely aware of the relative difficulty of different majors, their expectations about academic performance vary widely by respondent characteristics and major. Zafar (2013) finds that about 60% of male students hold a subjective probability of graduating with a GPA of at least 3.5 in Engineering greater than 50%, while only 30% of female students do so; whereas the gender differences for Literature and Fine Arts are much smaller. Zafar (2012) finds that double-major students report a higher probability of graduating with a GPA of at least 3.5 and lower expected hours per week spent on coursework than single-major students for most majors, consistently with a positive selection of double-major students, who indeed have a higher GPA than single-major students.

Stinebrickner and Stinebrickner (2012) show that also Berea students are too optimistic about grade performance, especially at college entrance. Overoptimism is concentrated among students with a high school GPA in the bottom third of the sample (students with a high school GPA in the top-third have instead accurate beliefs) and among male students (female students are also overoptimistic but less so). Overoptimism about academic performance is driven by overoptimism about ability (about 70%), not effort. Gender differences in overoptimism about ability are similar to those about grade performance. Boneva et al. (2022b) report similar findings for UK university students.

Belfield et al. (2020) examine the subjective probability of obtaining in 11th grade the necessary grades to go to sixth form, and of obtaining in sixth form the necessary grades to go to university, among UK 9th-graders. They document a strong positive association between these subjective probabilities and students' standardized test scores in grade 6 and household's income quartile. They also find evidence that students exert more effort in school to achieve higher grades if they believe that by getting the required grades they can pursue further education from which they derive a high consumption value. Boneva and Rauh (2021) confirm that low-SES students have, on average, a significantly lower subjective probability of obtaining the required grades to go to university (67% vs. 73%), of graduating from university if they enroll (82% vs. 85%), and of obtaining high grades if they graduate (65% vs. 71%) relative to high-SES students.

7.3.3 "Enjoying" education and other nonmonetary outcomes

Belfield et al. (2020) document that female and high-SES students have higher enjoyment probabilities for both sixth form and university than male and low-SES students, respectively. They also find low correlations between the perceived consumption values of education and the perceived monetary returns to education.[19]

Boneva and Rauh (2021) find that students from different SES backgrounds share the beliefs that they would be more likely to enjoy the content, find the material interesting, find the material hard, enjoy social life, meet people they easily get along with, lose contact with their family/friends, and feel stressed, and that they would be less likely to feel lonely, if they were to attend university instead of working. However, low-SES students display smaller perceived returns of positive outcomes (e.g., enjoying the content, the material, and social life), and larger perceived returns of negative outcomes (e.g., feeling stressed or lonely) relative to high-SES students. Boneva et al. (2022b) report broadly similar findings among university students with respect to the possibility of continuing to postgraduate education vis-à-vis starting to work.

Gong et al. (2021) estimate an average annual consumption value of college as high as $15K with considerable heterogeneity across students using the Euler equation, expectations data, and other measures collected in the BPS.

7.3.4 Nonmonetary outcomes in the labor and marriage markets

Zafar (2012) shows that the belief distribution about the prospects of being able to reconcile family and work at the available jobs following graduation for Natural Sciences is first order stochastically dominated by that for Literature and Fine Arts, consistent with the general perception that the typical jobs in the pure science and medical profession entered by NU graduates with a major in Natural

---

[19] These findings are consistent with those of Baker et al. (2018), who find that salary beliefs are uncorrelated with enjoyment beliefs, but in contrast with those of Wiswall and Zafar (2015b), who find that salary expectations are correlated with taste for majors.

Sciences have hectic work schedules. Zafar (2013) further shows that the belief distributions of male and female students are similar for Economics and Mathematical Methods in the Social Sciences, but dramatically different for Engineering, where the belief distribution of males first order stochastically dominates that of females.

Wiswall and Zafar (2020) find that male and female students share the belief that the marriage return to completing a college degree is positive, but their average perceived returns differ, with female students believing that their likelihood of being married at age 30 would be nearly 13% higher on average if they completed a college degree and men believing that their likelihood would be over 35% higher. Furthermore, unlike males, female students believe that there is a marriage market penalty of about 15 points on the percent chance scale to completing a degree in Science or Business relative to that in the Humanities or Social Sciences. Using earnings expectations, the authors also find that students believe that investing in human capital will not only lead to higher earnings for themselves but also to a match with a higher-earning spouse. With respect to fertility, students expect that by age 30 they would have fewer children following a major in Science or Business than in the Humanities. However, these same expectations are halved when asked for age 45, suggesting that students anticipate that human capital investments will also have an effect on the timing of fertility, not only on its level.

Among UK students, Boneva et al. (2022b) document higher likelihoods of career and life satisfaction conditional on hypothetical attainment of a postgraduate degree and find no statistically significant differences in average perceived returns across SES groups. Boneva and Rauh (2021) further find that students from all SES groups share the belief that they are more likely to meet their life partner if they go to university than if they start working, but the perceived marriage premium from attending university is significantly larger among high-SES students on average.

7.3.5 Attainment and dropout

Comparing NLSY79 with NLSY97, Reynolds and Pemberton (2001) show that in 1979 less than 40% of respondents expected to achieve 16 or more years of education; by 1997, over 70% of respondents reported they had more than a 50% chance of completing college by age 30 and over 50% believed their chances were greater than 75%. The authors further find that in 1979 racial/ethnic minorities have significantly higher college attainment expectations than non-Hispanic Whites, *ceteris paribus*. College attainment expectations are also significantly positively associated to parental education, parental income, the percentage of the county population with a college degree, and the county's unemployment rate, but not to gender. On the other hand, youth in two-parent families where only one parent is related to the youth through birth or adoption have significantly lower college attainment expectations than youth living with both biological parents. Similarly, youth with more siblings have lower college expectations. By 1997, the associations with race/ethnicity, family resources, and county context become weaker and those with family size remain unchanged relative to 1979. The most noticeable differences are the growing gaps between male and female youths and among family arrangements. In 1997, high school girls have significantly higher college attainment expectations than their male peers and, according to enrollment data, are significantly more likely to attend college. Similarly, high school youth living with both biological parents have significantly higher college expectations than youth with any other type of family arrangement. For 1997, the authors further find that grades received in 8th grade, having good teachers who are interested in their students, and having peers who plan to go to college all have a strong positive impact on expectations.

Stinebrickner and Stinebrickner (2012) show that Berea students' overoptimism about GPA and ability translates into overoptimism about completion. Stinebrickner and Stinebrickner (2014a) provide additional evidence that students are substantially overoptimistic about graduation at entrance. BPS respondents assign an average probability of about 13% to the possibility that they will drop out of college and only 5% of them believe that dropping out is their most likely outcome, whereas over 35% of Berea students actually drops out. In a high-ability sample of NYU undergraduates, Wiswall and Zafar (2015b) document similar degrees of optimism.

Boneva et al. (2022b) find that UK students believe they have an 89% chance of completing university. This estimate does not vary significantly by students socioeconomic background and compares favorably with UK statistics. On the other hand, low-SES students report significantly lower probability of graduating from a postgraduate degree than high-SES students.

Kunz and Staub (2020) show that German respondents aged 16–17 tend to be overly optimistic about their medium run graduation prospects; yet, students' subjective probabilities have a comparable information content to that of standard econometric models with perfect foresight. Furthermore, the authors find that the most important predictors of students' completion expectations are their academic ability and personality traits, whereas the most important predictors of actual enrollment and completion are measures of family background (parental education and household income) and local labor market conditions (youth unemployment and education demand and supply).

7.3.6 Education plans

Stinebrickner and Stinebrickner (2014a) document that at college entrance BPS students are highly uncertain about their college major, e.g., students assign a probability of only 31% to choosing the major they actually choose. The authors show that this partly occurs because initially 20% of students indicate Science as their most likely major, but only 7% end up majoring in Science. The reasons are overoptimism about own probability of graduating from college, overoptimism about remaining in Science, and overoptimism about switching to Science.

Wiswall and Zafar (2015b) show that for most university fields the cross-sectional distribution of NYU students' choice probabilities is bimodal, due to a considerable mass of students reporting a zero-to-small probability of majoring in each field and another mass reporting a large-to-one probability of doing so. Using the same data, Patnaik et al. (2020b) find that female students report a significantly higher probability of majoring in Humanities than their male peers (49.9% vs. 31.4%) and a significantly lower probability of majoring in Economics/Business (23.8% vs. 36.7%) or Engineering (5.6% vs. 8.7%).

Belfield et al. (2020) document that UK high school students aged 13–14 have an average probability of continuing to sixth form that compares favorably to UK enrollment statistics. Female students, students who have at least one parent with a university degree, and students in the top income quartile report higher probabilities of going to sixth form and of going to university than other students. Among older UK students, Boneva et al. (2022b) show that university students whose parents never went to university report a lower average probability of enrolling in postgraduate education than other students.

7.3.7 Parental approval and parental beliefs

Zafar (2012) document that the mean subjective probability of gaining parental approval varies across majors (from a low of 59% for Literature and Fine Arts to a high of 87% for Natural Sciences), which they interpret as suggestive that students believe parents to be more likely to approve of majors associated with higher status and returns in the labor market.

In the context of postgraduate enrollment choice in the UK, Boneva et al. (2022b) find that the mean subjective probability of gaining nonmonetary parental support is similar across schooling scenarios (79% for both stopping with an undergraduate degree and pursuing a postgraduate degree). Parents with a postgraduate degree are perceived as more likely to support pursuing a postgraduate degree relative to stopping with an undergraduate degree, whereas the opposite is true for parents who never went to university.

Only a handful of studies to date has separately elicited percent-chance expectations from students and their parents and have compared the two sets of expectations. Using NLSY97 data, Fischhoff et al. (2000) document that parents share their teens' generally high expectations for educational attainment, with no significant child–parent difference in the mean probabilities of being in school in a year and of having a diploma by age 20. At the family level, the authors document high correlations between the judgments of paired teens and parents, declining slightly as the time period increases. Dominitz et al. (2001) further document that most youths and parents see no chance of an adverse schooling outcome, with the parents being more optimistic than the students on average. They also find that the within-family differences between parent and child is significantly lower for female relative to male youth. Furthermore, in families where the child report unfavorable past experiences such as school suspension, grade repetition, sexual intercourse, and cigarette or marijuana smoking, both child and parents report lower subjective probabilities that the child will receive a diploma by age 20.

Giustinelli (2016) similarly finds that Italian students and parents hold broadly similar beliefs about the chances of a variety of outcomes at the time of high school track choice. The within-family differences in beliefs between child and parent are generally small on average, especially for outcomes such as school enjoyment, but display substantial heterogeneity across families. Based on a Wilcoxon matched-pairs signed-ranks test, the null hypothesis of expectations equality between the child–parent matched pairs is rejected for the majority of choice alternatives and outcomes. Consistently with Dominitz et al. (2001)'s evidence from the NLSY97, also Italian parents appear to be more optimistic about the student's performance than students are. Moreover, parents expect on average smaller differences in the student's study effort and academic performance across high school tracks than students do.

7.4 Analysis of schooling decisions with survey expectations

7.4.1 Monetary returns and risks

Observational studies have typically found modest effects of expected earnings on schooling decisions.[20] How about studies of schooling decisions using survey expectations?

Zafar (2013) finds a positive but small and insignificant effect of subjective expectations of income at age 30 on college major choices of NU undergraduates, irrespective of gender and other stratifications. Arcidiacono et al. (2012) find somewhat larger and statistically significant effects among male

---

[20] For example, see Arcidiacono (2004) and Beffy et al. (2012) for evidence on the postsecondary field of study in the U.S. and France, respectively. See also Altonji et al. (2016)'s review.

Duke undergraduates (e.g., a one standard deviation increase in expected earnings in a business career increases the fraction of students majoring in economics from 19.7% to 22.9%). Wiswall and Zafar (2015b), too, find that expectations about future earnings are a significant determinant of major choice among NYU undergraduates, although their estimated average elasticities are modest (between 0.03 and 0.07). They provide evidence that younger students display higher responsiveness to changes in future earnings than older students, presumably because older students have a higher cost of switching major.

Wiswall and Zafar (2015b) show that the estimated elasticities shrink substantially once the correlation between unobserved tastes for majors and expected earnings has been taken into account, and that it is also important to account for students' subjective uncertainty about future earnings. They estimate a large degree of risk and find that unaccounted-for risk aversion tends to inflate the estimated responsiveness of major choice to changes in expected earnings. In follow-up work, Patnaik et al. (2020a) show that ignoring heterogeneity in risk and time preferences also overstates the importance of expected earnings for major choice.

Some studies investigate whether differences in schooling decisions across demographic or socioeconomic groups can be explained by differences in students' subjective expectations or are due to differences in preferences. Zafar (2013) finds that the gender gaps in college majors among NU undergraduates, whereby females are significantly less likely than males to pursue majors such as Engineering or Computer Science and more likely to pursue majors such as Education or Health, cannot be explained by gender differences in either expectations or preferences for future earnings. Patnaik et al. (2020a) similarly find that, while male students are less risk averse and patient than female students, gender differences in expectations about future earnings, risk aversion, and patience cannot explain gender gaps in major choice among NYU undergraduates.

Hastings et al. (2015) evaluate a large-scale randomized disclosure policy, giving information about program-specific earnings and costs to college applicants in Chile and find that the intervention decreases the demand for degree programs in the bottom tercile of the returns distribution, especially among low-income students, while leaving college enrollment unaffected. To understand why disclosure does not completely eliminate the demand for low-return programs, the authors estimate a model of college demand with belief uncertainty and learning about earnings and costs and show that the intervention reduces the uncertainty in earnings beliefs, but the latter's effect on program demand is dampened by students' preferences for nonmonetary attributes.

Among UK students aged 13–14, Belfield et al. (2020) find that the perceived monetary returns to further education are statistically associated with students' plans to continue in full-time education, but can only explain a small share of the latter's variation relative to other perceived benefits of schooling. Boneva et al. (2022b) further document that, on average, low-SES students perceive significantly lower monetary returns to postgraduate education and assign a lower probability to continuing to postgraduate education than high-SES students.[21] Yet, differences in beliefs about nonmonetary factors have greater explanatory power on the observed socioeconomic gap in postgraduate education plans and enrollment than do differences in earnings expectations.

---

[21] The authors find substantial differences also within high-SES students, with students who have at least one parent holding a postgraduate degree reporting an 8 percentage points higher probability of enrolling in a postgraduate degree than students whose parents are college educated but have no postgraduate degree.

7.4.2 **Monetary costs**

Recent decades have been characterized by increasing monetary returns, labor market risk, and monetary costs of postsecondary education, especially in the U.S. These trends have increased the demand for credit, simultaneously raising the question of whether college students can borrow enough or are credit constrained, and the concern that some students may be actually taking on too much college debt (Lochner and Monge-Naranjo, 2016). Recent evidence on the high degree of complementarity between early and late human capital investments has further generated a concern that postsecondary aid policies may simply come too late to be effective in helping disadvantaged youth (Lochner and Monge-Naranjo, 2012).

Given the ongoing debate, it would seem natural to ask whether students' expectations about tuition and other monetary costs of postsecondary education and their beliefs about borrowing opportunities and terms play a role in college decisions and outcomes such as enrollment, dropout, and major. In practice, the evidence for the U.S. is scarce.[22] Based on a randomized experiment providing information about the monetary costs of college or the monetary returns to college in a sample of SCE respondents, Bleemer and Zafar (2018) find that the cost treatment has no significant impact on college attendance expectations, whereas the return treatment has a significant impact on them. Respondents' subjective probability of sending their own child to college increases by about 5 percentage points on average and that of recommending college for a friend's child by 2.3 points. The effects are larger for disadvantaged respondents. In the short run, the return treatment closes the education and income gaps in college attendance expectations by around 30% and in college recommendation expectations by about 15%. These effects were still persistent two months after the treatment.

Hastings et al. (2015) too find that the cost disclosure intervention does not cause Chilean college applicants to choose lower-cost programs. Thus, both Hastings et al. (2015)'s and Bleemer and Zafar (2018)'s findings suggest that information provision about the monetary returns to college can significantly affect college decisions and plans, whereas information provision about monetary costs does not.

Combining the same data with an informal model of college enrollment,[23] Hastings et al. (2016) show that students who overestimate costs are less likely to matriculate in any degree program and more likely to drop out; whereas students who overestimate earnings matriculate at similar rates as other students, but choose degree programs where past students have performed poorly (less likely to graduate, earned less in starting jobs, and more likely to default on student loans). Students with a stated preference for degree characteristics related to the labor market are less likely to overestimate earnings and to choose degree programs whose past graduates have earned more on the labor market, while the opposite is true for students with a stated preference for curriculum enjoyment.[24]

---

[22] Altonji et al. (2016) review the studies examining the impact of financial aid and tuition fees on college attendance, and note that very little is known about their impact on college major choice.

[23] In the model, college applicants face uncertainty about costs and earnings for different degree programs, decide whether to engage in costly degree-specific search, and can further learn about the chosen degree after enrollment. The model has five main predictions: (1) students facing higher search costs have less accurate beliefs about program attributes such as monetary costs and returns; (2) students who place low value on costs or earnings when making the enrollment decision have less accurate beliefs about those outcomes; (3) students know more about programs in their consideration set; (4) students with less accurate expectations about costs or earnings are more likely to enroll in degrees where past students have performed poorly in those dimensions and more likely to drop out when the uncertainty is resolved.

[24] Huntington-Klein (2016) replicates Hastings et al. (2016)'s analysis and selected findings in the U.S.

Belfield et al. (2020) find no significant role of UK students' expectations about tuition costs in sixth-form and college enrollment plans. The authors view this result as being consistent with the failed drop of enrollment in higher education after the recent increase in university tuition fees. Conversely, Boneva et al. (2022b) find that financial considerations do play a role in students' postgraduate plans. The authors estimate that students would be willing to trade off £0.38 in immediate costs for a £1 increase in earnings at age 35. However, nonmonetary factors are found to play a larger role. Boneva and Rauh (2021) find similar results with regard to younger students' college enrollment plans. Financial considerations related to the possibility of struggling financially during college and receiving financial support from parents play a greater role than earnings expectations, but a smaller role than other nonmonetary factors.

7.4.3 Nonmonetary factors: ability, taste, and beyond

Due to the failure of expected monetary returns and costs to explain schooling decisions and related differences across demographic and socioeconomic groups, the literature has turned to investigating the explanatory power of expectations for nonmonetary factors, leading to the robust finding that these are indeed predominant drivers of schooling decisions and plans, although their importance vary across settings and groups.

Two factors whose importance has been long emphasized in the human capital literature are students' abilities and tastes, as they capture key dimensions of the quality of the match between a student and each of the educational alternatives available to him or her (Arcidiacono, 2004). Indeed, Arcidiacono et al. (2012) find that major-specific abilities are important determinants of major choice among Duke undergraduates, above and beyond expected earnings, and that students prefer majors at which they are good. The authors show that equalizing student abilities across majors would drop the fraction of humanities majors from 9.3% to 5.9%, while increasing the fraction of economics majors to 23.8%. Similarly, Baker et al. (2018) find that students' beliefs about course enjoyment and grades are the main determinants of major choice among community college students in California.

Wiswall and Zafar (2015b) identify the residual unobserved taste-for-major component as the dominant factor driving major choice among NYU undergraduates, especially among older students, consistent with a large and increasing cost of switching majors as students progress through college.[25]

Zafar (2013) finds that enjoying the coursework, enjoying the work at potential jobs, and gaining parental approval are the most important factors driving major choice of NU undergraduates, and that nonmonetary factors explain over 50% of the variation in college major choices among male students and over 80% among female students. Zafar (2013) shows that this is due to gender differences in preferences for workplace attributes, with females valuing nonmonetary aspects such as reconciling work and family substantially more than males. Using his model, Zafar (2013) shows that replacing females' expectations about enjoying the major-specific coursework with those of males would reduce the choice gap in Engineering by 50%, whereas replacing females' expectations about ability and future earnings with those of males would reduce the gap by only 15%, implying that policies aiming at sensitizing females' preferences for STEM fields may be more promising than policies providing information about the monetary returns to STEM fields.

---

[25] Wiswall and Zafar (2015b) discuss the implications of these results for modeling of tastes in choice models with subjective expectations. See also Giustinelli (2022) and Chapter 21 in this Handbook.

Wiswall and Zafar (2020) complement this evidence by showing that students sort into college majors partly based on their perceived returns in terms of potential spouse's earnings and fertility, and that family expectations are particularly important for the major choices of NYU female students.

In the context of high school track choice, Giustinelli (2016) finds that enjoying track-specific subjects is by far the most valued attribute by both students and parents, irrespective of the family decision-making process (solo choice by the student, student choice with parental input, child-parent joint decision). The importance of other short-term outcomes (e.g., academic performance and study effort) relative to longer-term ones (e.g., facing flexible college and work choices after graduation) is instead highly heterogeneous across family members and decision processes. Using her model to perform a number of policy counterfactuals, the author finds that a "math sensitization" campaign increasing students' perceived likelihood of enjoying math in the general track by 10 points on the 0–100 percent chance scale, a relatively small movement in expectations, can have a large impact on the distribution of choices due to the large utility weight that students and parents attach to coursework enjoyment. Subjecting university access to graduation from one of the general curricula – a policy tightening curricular specialization – would also have a significant impact on choices. Instead, providing information about population graduation rates or college enrollment rates by track would have little-to-no impact on choices, due to the modest associated utility weights and to respondents' expectations being already on target for these outcomes.

The findings of Belfield et al. (2020), Boneva et al. (2022b), and Boneva and Rauh (2021) for the UK also point to a predominant importance of nonmonetary factors in driving students' education plans and in accounting for observed demographic and socioeconomic differences in them. Belfield et al. (2020) find that students' perceived consumption value alone explains up to 43% (51%) of the variation in students' subjective probability of going to sixth form (university). Boneva et al. (2022b) find that 91% of the SES gap estimated by their model of postgraduate enrollment can be explained by SES differences in expectations and only 9% by SES differences in preferences, with expectations about the returns to postgraduate education accounting for approximately 70% of the gap. Among younger students, Boneva and Rauh (2021) find that differences in perceived returns across SES groups explain 35% of the SES gap in students' subjective probability of enrolling in university. Students' expectations about receiving parental approval, enjoying studying, and job satisfaction play a major role, whereas monetary factors and parental wealth play a minor role.

7.4.4 **Parents and family decision-making**

Economic models of school choice have traditionally assumed that parents make schooling decisions for their children while children are minors and that students become solo decision makers when they come of age.[26] Accordingly, demand models of postsecondary schooling have typically taken the student as the main decision maker or have implicitly viewed the family as a unitary entity.[27] Yet, Zafar (2013)'s and Boneva and Rauh (2021)'s findings on the importance of gaining parental approval in college major choices of NU undergraduates and university enrollment plans of UK high school students,

---

[26] Only limited attention has been devoted to the roles of agency acquisition by children, child–parent interactions, and family decision-making in schooling decisions. Giustinelli and Manski (2018) and Giustinelli (2022) review existing works.

[27] Kalenkoski (2008) and Attanasio and Kaufmann (2014) are notable exceptions.

respectively, suggest that parents may play a more active role in postsecondary schooling decisions than previously assumed.[28]

Giustinelli (2016) addresses the roles of student vis-à-vis parents in the choice of high school track in Italy. The author documents that in nearly 59% of the sample families the actual choice does not coincide with the stated-preferred choice of at least one member, and that in the majority of these cases (about 33% of the whole sample) the actual choice coincides with the stated-preferred choice of the student but not of the parents. This figure is substantially higher among students making a unilateral choice (40%) and lower among families where child and parents make a joint decision (29%).[29] Giustinelli (2016) estimates a model that explicitly allows for the documented heterogeneity in family decision processes and in the ways in which student and parent expectations and preferences over track-specific outcomes affect high school track choice. The analysis uncovers significant differences in preferences over track-specific outcomes between students and parents and, within each group, across decision processes. For example, students value outcomes such as experiencing a regular path in high school and being in school with one's friends more than their parents. Among students, those from PR1 families have a higher disutility of study effort and assign a greater utility to pleasing one's parent than students from other families. Among PR2 families, parental expectations have differential influence on the student's choice through different outcomes. For example, parental expectations about the child's academic performance in high school matters more than the child's own expectations, whereas the opposite is true about postgraduation choice flexibility. Among PR3 families, parents have a greater influence on the final choice than their children, with an estimated decision weight of about two-thirds. Counterfactual simulations further confirm the importance of accounting for students' and parents' expectations and decision roles. Mistakenly taking the parent to be the main (or representative) decision maker in all families is found to overestimate the enrollment response to a simulated math sensitization campaign. On the other hand, taking process heterogeneity into account shows that a disclosure policy publishing population statistics on graduation rates would have the largest impact on the choices of solo-choice students. It also shows that if parents alone were made aware of an institutional policy making curricular tracking more rigid, the policy impact would be smaller than if children too were made aware.

7.4.5 Peer effects

Giustinelli (2016)'s estimates suggest that students prefer high school tracks in which they expect their best friends to enroll. In her setting, the mechanism underlying this preference is that students value the possibility of attending the same high school as their best friends and of sharing with them the following five years of their school lives. An alternative but not mutually exclusive possibility is that students value choice alternatives that they expect to be chosen by many of their peers because of the implied "popularity" of these alternatives. Garbin (2021) investigates this possibility by estimating a model of high school track choice, where students' subjective expected utility depends on their expectations about the high school track choices made by the students in their network. The author finds that stu-

---

[28] See also recent evidence by Hotz et al. (2021) on the role of American parents in financing college enrollment and completion of their children.

[29] In about 20% of families, the student chooses unilaterally with respect to his/her parents (PR1); in about 30%, the student chooses with parental input (PR2); in the remaining 42%, student and parents make a joint decision (PR3).

dents' expectations about the choices of one's peers matter more for own choice than the expectations over important academic outcomes such as the coursework enjoyment and study effort.

7.4.6 Centralized school choice

In many places around the world, school choices are determined within centralized choice systems matching students to schools on the basis of families' self-reported preferences over schools, schools' capacity, and other constraints. Different matching mechanisms can have different properties in terms of matching stability, allocation efficiency, and strategy proofness (see Hakimov and Kübler (2021)). However, these theoretical properties hold under the strong and often unrealistic assumptions that the canonical version of the mechanism is actually implemented and that applicants are fully informed, hold rational expectations, and make rational choices. In practice, students and families may not be fully familiar with the application-and-admission rules, may not hold accurate beliefs about the student's chances of being admitted to different schools, and may consequently make application mistakes. These problems may disproportionally affect disadvantaged youth and lead to individually suboptimal outcomes and undesirable distributional properties.[30]

Kapor et al. (2020) study the application behavior of families of rising 9th-graders in New Haven, Connecticut. The authors find that many families engage in strategic reporting behavior, but do so on the basis of an inaccurate understanding on the rules and inaccurate beliefs about the admission chances, leading to application mistakes. Indeed, a lower fraction of respondents correctly describe key features of the assignment mechanism than that implied by random guessing. Moreover, respondents report subjective beliefs about admission probabilities that differ from a rational expectations benchmark constructed by the authors by a large mean (absolute) value of 37 percentage points. As a consequence, families end up underestimating the extent to which ranking a school higher or lower on their application affects the admission chances. Using a model of centralized school choice that incorporates these patterns, the authors show that switching to a strategy-proof deferred acceptance (DA) mechanism, where applicants do not need to understand assignment probabilities to play an optimal strategy, would yield welfare improvements over the status quo, but the opposite conclusion would be reached if families were assumed to have accurate beliefs.

In follow-up work, Larroucau et al. (2021) investigate the role of beliefs about admissions chances in centralized choice settings with strategy-proof mechanisms and show that beliefs still matter, as they influence applicants' search behavior over schools. Combining a model where applicants engage in costly school search with data from a large-scale survey of school applicants in Chile, the analysis provides evidence that learning about schools is costly, beliefs about admissions chances affect searching, and applicants underestimate the risk of not being placed by the system. Using randomized and regression discontinuity designs, the authors evaluate policies that give live feedback about admission chances to applicants within the Chilean and New Haven choice systems. They find that 22% of applicants submitting applications where nonplacement risk is high respond to the feedback by adding schools to their lists and that this reduces nonplacement risk by 58%.

In companion research, Arteaga et al. (2022) analyze the prevalence and relevance of application mistakes in the Chilean strategy-proof centralized college admissions system, with a focus on admissibility mistakes which consist in applying to programs without meeting all requirements. The authors

---

[30] For example, see Sattin-Bajaj (2014), Calsamiglia and Güell (2018), Son (2020), and references therein.

find that 2%–4% of students do not list their true most preferred program, that only a fraction of this behavior can be rationalized by belief biases, and that students tend to underestimate the probability of extreme events and to underpredict the risk of not being placed. The authors additionally show that providing personalized information about admission probabilities significantly reduces the risk of not being placed and the incidence of admissibility mistakes.

7.5 Analysis of expectation formation and learning
7.5.1 Earnings

Manski (1993)'s question about what information students condition on when forming their expectations about future earnings and related perceptions about the monetary returns to schooling underlies many of the analyses of survey-elicited earnings expectations reviewed above. Notably, Wiswall and Zafar (2015a) establish that college students' expectations about own future earnings are causally linked to their beliefs about the distribution of earnings in relevant populations; thus, the former are formed at least partially based on the latter. Taking advantage of their experimental design, the authors document a positive relationship between students' revisions in own earnings expectations and population errors. Treated students who discover that they underestimated (overestimated) population earnings revise their earnings expectations upward (downward). The estimated mean response is inelastic, with larger revisions occurring in response to major-specific information. In the full sample, 20% of students do not update their expectations. Among those who do, the most common heuristic is unit updater (28% of the sample), followed by alarmist (19%), contrary and conservative (12% each), and undefined (9%).[31] Students who have been in college longer are less likely to revise their expectations and to react excessively to information relative to the quasi-Bayesian benchmark (unit updater). Students whose prior population beliefs exceed actual population earnings are more likely to update conservatively. No difference across genders is found. The information treatment also induces revisions in choice probabilities over majors, implying a switch in the modal major for about 12% of the students.

Gong et al. (2019) take advantage of the longitudinal structure of the BPS to investigate the extent and evolution of perceived uncertainty about future earnings among Berea students. The authors document that at college entrance, the cross-sectional average of the standard deviation of students' subjective belief distributions about future own earnings at age 28 ranges between $9.6K and $14.1K a year. While the importance of this initial earnings uncertainty relative to that of heterogeneity is well below 50%, the uncertainty itself is quite persistent, as about 65% of it is still present at the end of college. The authors show that 15%–18% of the variance representing the uncertainty about earnings at age 28 perceived at college entrance can be attributed to uncertainty about grade performance and 11%–17% to uncertainty about college major. The uncertainty about these two factors combined accounts for about 18%–24% of the initial overall uncertainty about future income, suggesting that uncertainty resolution during college reflects students' learning about their academic ability and college

---

[31] A student is classified as (1) a unit updater, if his/her posterior is within a certain band around the benchmark posterior; (2) an alarmist, if his/her response is more exaggerated than implied by the benchmark; (3) a conservative, if the respondent updates in the right direction but less than the benchmark; (4) a contrary, if the updating is in the opposite direction than prescribed by the benchmark model; and (5) a nonupdater, if there is no response to the information.

major. The authors provide further evidence that transitory factors, including search frictions, play an important role in accounting for the remaining uncertainty.

7.5.2 Academic performance

Zafar (2011b) studies expectations about academic performance, defined as the probability of graduating with a GPA of at least 3.5, and uses students' GPA realizations to construct an "information metric" that identifies new information about own academic ability the students receive between survey waves. The author finds that students are initially overconfident about their academic performance in all majors, but they adjust their short-term predictions in response to the new information sensibly: upward upon receiving very positive news, downward upon receiving very negative news, no adjustment for news in the intermediate range. No significant adjustments are observed in long-term GPA expectations. The information metric and the revisions in expectations about weekly hours spent on coursework are negatively related, suggesting that students view ability and effort as substitutes. A comparison of the updating patterns between GPA expectations in the student's own major and GPA expectations in nonpursued majors shows that the two are statistically indistinguishable, suggesting that learning has a general component. That is, by learning about match quality in one's own major, students learn also about their match quality in other majors. Despite the substantial cross-sectional heterogeneity in information-processing rules, a number of empirical patterns suggests that students revise their expectations in ways that are broadly consistent with Bayesian learning.

Stinebrickner and Stinebrickner (2014a) develop a model to understand the reasons behind Berea students' overoptimistic initial expectations about completing a degree in science relative to their final outcomes.[32] The model explicitly accounts for the fact that before making a final decision about one's future major, students will have the opportunity to resolve some of their initial uncertainty about major-specific factors.[33] The authors find that students' initial overoptimism about completing a degree in science is largely due to their initial misperception about their likelihood of performing well in science. Science is special relative to other majors, in that students learn about their ability in science primarily by taking science classes (specific learning), whereas substantial learning about one's ability in other majors occurs by taking classes outside those majors (general learning).

Motivated by the inability of financial factors and credit constraints to explain the educational attainment of low-income students and by existing differences in dropout rates within low-income students (e.g., by gender), Stinebrickner and Stinebrickner (2012, 2014b) investigate the role of learning about academic ability through grade performance in college dropout. Stinebrickner and Stinebrickner (2012) find that dropout would be reduced by 41% if no learning occurred about grade performance. Moreover, the substantial gender difference in dropout is predicted almost entirely by academic differences by gender, as measured by both first-year grades and students' expectations about future grades, with males holding significantly more overoptimistic grade beliefs than females. Because students tend to remain overoptimistic about their future performance due to their not understating the importance of permanent

---

[32] Recall that while about 20% of entering students views science as their most likely outcome (a higher proportion than for any other major), and students' average perceived likelihood of completing a science degree is 16% (similar to that of other majors), only 7% of students complete a degree in science.

[33] At college entrance, Berea students are highly uncertain about their final major. On average, they have a subjective probability of graduating from the major from which they eventually graduate of about 30%.

factors in determining grades, the authors conclude that their evidence mitigates the widespread policy concern that students may be leaving college prematurely.

Stinebrickner and Stinebrickner (2014b) develop a dynamic model of college dropout to quantify the overall importance of students' learning about grade performance for dropout and to assess the empirical relevance of three mechanisms why low-performing students may dropout, i.e., (1) they are forced out of college by grade requirements even though they would prefer to stay, (2) they leave because getting low grades lowers their financial returns to staying in college, (3) they leave because getting low grades reduces enjoyability of college. The authors show that, if students held initially correct expectations about future grade performance, about 45% (36%) of dropout in the first two (three) years would disappear, and that the dropouts observed in early years of college are primarily due to students' learning about their academic performance. The analysis further shows that students who perform poorly in the first years leave mainly because staying is not sufficiently valuable (2 and 3), rather than because they are at risk of failing (1), and that students are more likely to drop out relative to females because of academic issues rather than because of inherent taste factors.

Giustinelli and Pavoni (2017) investigate the evolution of students' choice set awareness and belief ambiguity[34] about the likelihood of experiencing a regular path in high school, during the process of high school track choice in Italy.[35] At the beginning of 8th grade, students display incomplete awareness and ambiguous expectations, especially with regard to low-ranked and newly-introduced alternatives. By the time of preenrollment in high school, students' learning is still incomplete. Moreover, learning itself tends to be concentrated on specific alternatives, this time those most highly ranked by students. The authors identify five main patterns of heterogeneity as a function of students' gender, 8th-grade GPA, mother's education (high SES), father's occupation (low SES), and country of birth. High-SES students display an intensive learning pattern differentiated across high school tracks. Conversely, low-SES students display a more focused learning pattern concentrated on curricula of the technical and vocational tracks. Foreign-born students start 8th grade with lower choice awareness and higher belief ambiguity relative to native students and follow a biased learning pattern, whereby their level of ambiguity for curricula of the general track tends to increase over time. One-fourth of students change their preference ranking over choice alternatives over the survey period, suggesting that the learning process may be crucial for the choice of a sizable fraction of students. The "selective learner" may become stuck with a coarse view of the world that associates a high degree of ambiguity to initially unattractive options, thus reinforcing undesirability of the latter in later periods.

7.6 Conclusion

The economic literature on survey-elicited probabilistic expectations in education was put in motion nearly 30 years ago by a question lacking empirical answer, *"How do youth infer the returns to schooling?"* (Manski, 1993), and by a small set of pioneering studies such as Dominitz–Manski's study and Stinebrickner–Stinebrickner's BPS, which paved the way for subsequent surveys ad analyses of

---

[34] See Chapter 24 in this Handbook on uncertainty as ambiguity. See Manski and Molinari (2010) and Giustinelli et al. (2022) for elicitation and analyses of ambiguous probabilities outside education.

[35] Giustinelli and Pavoni (2019) carry out a parallel analysis using parents' responses.

subjective expectations, both within and outside education. The amounts and varieties of survey measurements, analytic tools, and empirical evidence accumulated since have been extraordinary. Having taken stock of them, it is natural to ask what they have taught us about Manski (1993)'s initial question. Upon careful review, it appears that they have generated a number of important answers. And yet, in the process of doing so, they have also expanded the scope of the initial question and raised important new ones.

We have learned that students' expectations about own future earnings are causally linked to students' beliefs about population earnings, but only partially determined by them. We have further learned that students form expectations about own future earnings and about the monetary returns, risks, and costs of schooling heterogeneously, but only a part of this heterogeneity can be accounted for by observable factors such as students' characteristics and institutional or market conditions.

In fact, the latter have received much less attention than the former. For example, Arcidiacono et al. (2020) find that a larger share of their study participants ended up in a business occupation than respondents themselves had predicted when they were still Duke undergraduates, while smaller shares ended up in government and law occupations. The authors hypothesize that these differences may be the result of an aggregate shock to the labor market, especially as the Great Recession began in December 2007 and their study surveyed Duke undergraduates in early 2009.[36] This suggests an interesting avenue for future research investigating how expectations of the college premium and of college attendance respond to the business cycle. This may be addressed by collecting expectations longitudinally over the business cycle or by eliciting expectations under alternative business cycle scenarios.

Systematic investigation of earnings expectations across alternative schooling scenarios has shown that students do believe that higher levels of education, or specific fields of study, are more remunerative and, in some cases, more risky than others. Yet, these perceived monetary returns and risks of schooling do not seem to be the major determinants of students' schooling plans and decisions, as nonmonetary returns, risks, and costs are often more or equally important.

An underinvestigated issue concerns the perceived sources of individuals' subjective returns to schooling; namely, the main causal models underlying students' and families' perceived monetary returns to schooling.[37]

We have learned that students form expectations about the nonmonetary consequences of schooling partly on the basis of their personal experiences and socioeconomic circumstances. Students and their families tend to be overly optimistic about the student's educational attainment, with this tendency being more prominent among male students and low-ability students. Among the latter, substantial learning and uncertainty resolution occurs during school, especially about own ability and monetary labor market returns. However, the learning process remains often incomplete, partly due to students'

---

[36] Existing evidence points to a post-Great Recession negative shock, which affected entry into the legal profession and was likely not fully anticipated by prospective graduates.

[37] The two main explanations put forward by economic theory are the human capital theory, positing that education increases individuals' labor market productivity and earnings through skill acquisition (e.g., Becker (1962), Schultz (1963), Mincer (1974)), and the signaling theory, positing that education serves as a mere signaling device enabling employers to identify high-ability workers (e.g., Spence (1973), Stiglitz and Weiss (1990)). A third hypothesis emphasizes the screening or selection role of (higher) education, whereby premia arise because university attendance induces students to resolve the uncertainty about their returns (e.g., Chiswick (1973), Lange and Topel (2006)). To my knowledge, the only analysis investigating this issue is Ehrmantraut et al. (2020), which finds evidence consistent with the signaling hypothesis and inconsistent with the screening or selection hypothesis using German data.

unobserved tastes for programs and their preferences for nonmonetary aspects of schooling. Similar learning patterns have started to emerge also in settings where the information is exogenously provided to students rather than endogenously acquired by them.

Last but not least, we have just began to learn about the dangers of ignoring family interactions, peer interactions, and the role of teachers in expectations formation and related schooling decisions and paths.

The experience and evidence accumulated so far suggest that measurement-wise we need more longitudinal surveys capable of tracking the evolution of expectations and realizations for multiple related outcomes over a long period of time, like Stinebrickner–Stinebrickner's BPS. We need more surveys embedding randomized field-experimental components, like Wiswall–Zafar NYU study and the Chilean studies by Hastings, Neilson, and collaborators. We need more surveys linkable to administrative schooling data, like the BPS and the Chilean studies. We need more multiactor surveys of probabilistic expectations enabling the linking of responses across students and parents within families and across students within networks of peers, like the NLSY97 and Giustinelli's studies in Northern Italy. We also need probabilistic measures of expectations from teachers that are linkable to students' and parents' expectations. We need more studies willing to experiment with elicitation formats that enable respondents to express deep uncertainty, like Giustinelli–Pavoni's study. Eventually, we need studies that can combine a number of these features on a larger scale.[38]

We should also not discount the already large and continuously increasing number of surveys that have collected the same or largely overlapping sets of expectations related to education in different populations or using different survey mediums. Systematizing the survey instruments and expectations data already collected and making them more visible and accessible could lead to novel analyses and new findings.

On the modeling and estimation fronts, we need extensions of the current analytical tools that will enable us to employ more systematically survey-elicited expectations to investigate settings with dynamics, interacting decision makers, and deep uncertainty.

On substantive grounds, there are still many fruitful avenues to explore. We have very limited evidence about when, where (from whom), and how individuals involved in making or counseling schooling decisions acquire information; what information they acquire; and how they incorporate the information in their expectations and decision process. We have very limited evidence about who are the relevant actors for different schooling decisions, who are the main decision makers, whether these are the same as those who acquire choice-relevant information or shape students' choice set, and whether/how these aspects vary across groups.[39] We have even less evidence about teachers' information, expectations, and objectives when counseling schooling decisions. And we have close to no evidence on the precise or ambiguous nature of the expectations held by the relevant actors and on how

---

[38] A potential challenge comes from the tension between the opposing strengths and weaknesses of small researcher-led studies and larger-scale multipurpose studies. The former can afford greater richness of data to study a specific topic in depth, but must pay the price of smaller samples, lower representativeness, and more limited scope and focus, and vice versa. A potential solution may be the pursuit of larger and more representative studies, but with embedded innovation tools such as the experimental modules included in the U.S. Health and Retirement Study (HRS) or the rotating-panel structure of the NYFed's Survey of Consumer Expectations (SCE).

[39] The mismatch between the "normative model" of family decision-making assumed by the NYC Department of Education and school administrators and the quite distinct and heterogeneous decision-making processes followed by actual NYC families documented by Sattin-Bajaj (2014)'s ethnographic work is eye-opening.

all these aspects interact with one another in determining observed schooling decisions and subsequent outcomes.

Similarly to 30 years ago, the path ahead looks both exciting and challenging. But perhaps differently from 30 years ago, the accumulated experience and progress provide some confidence that the enterprise is again feasible and rewarding.

References

Altonji, J.G., 1993. The demand for and return to education when education outcomes are uncertain. Journal of Labor Economics 11 (1), 48–83.

Altonji, J.G., Arcidiacono, P., Maurel, A., 2016. The analysis of field choice in college and graduate school: determinants and wage effects. In: Hanushek, E., Machin, S., Woessmann, L. (Eds.), Handbook of Economics of Education, vol. 5. Elsevier B.V., pp. 305–396. Chapter 7.

Arcidiacono, P., 2004. Ability sorting and the returns to college major. Journal of Econometrics 121 (1–2), 343–375.

Arcidiacono, P., Hotz, V.J., Kang, S., 2012. Modeling college choices using elicited measures of expectations and counterfactual. Journal of Econometrics 166 (1), 3–16.

Arcidiacono, P., Hotz, V.J., Maurel, A., Romano, T., 2020. Ex ante returns and occupational choice. Journal of Political Economy 128, 4475–4522.

Arteaga, F., Kapor, A.J., Neilson, C.A., Zimmerman, S.D., 2022. Smart matching platforms and heterogeneous beliefs in centralized school choice. The Quarterly Journal of Economics 137 (3), 1791–1848.

Attanasio, O., Kaufmann, K.M., 2014. Education choices and returns to schooling: intrahousehold decision making, gender and subjective expectations. Journal of Development Economics 109, 203–216.

Baker, R., Bettinger, E., Jacob, B., Marinescu, I., 2018. The effect of labor market information on community college students' major choice. Economics of Education Review 65, 18–30.

Becker, S.G., 1962. Investment in human capital: a theoretical analysis. Journal of Political Economy 70, 9–49.

Beffy, M., Fougere, D., Maurel, A., 2012. Choosing the field of study in postsecondary education: do expected earnings matter? Review of Economics and Statistics 94, 334–347.

Belfield, C., Boneva, T., Rauh, C., Shaw, J., 2020. What drives enrollment gaps in further education? The role of beliefs in sequential schooling decisions. Economica 87, 490–529.

Betts, J.R., 1996. What do students know about wages? Evidence from a survey of undergraduates. The Journal of Human Resources 31, 27–56.

Bleemer, Z., Zafar, B., 2018. Intended college attendance: evidence from an experiment on college returns and costs. Journal of Public Economics 157, 184–211.

Boneva, T., Buser, T., Falk, A., Kosse, F., 2022a. The Origins of Gender Differences in Competitiveness and Earnings Expectations: Causal evidence from a mentoring intervention. Discussion Paper 17008. CEPR.

Boneva, T., Golin, M., Rauh, C., 2022b. Can perceived returns explain enrollment gaps in postgraduate education? Labour Economics 77 (101998), 1–17.

Boneva, T., Rauh, C., 2021. Socio-economic Gaps in University Enrollment: the Role of Perceived Pecuniary and Non-Pecuniary Returns. Working paper.

Botelho, A., Costa Pinto, L., 2004. Students' expectations of the economic returns to college education: results of a controlled experiment. Economics of Education Review 23, 645–653.

Briel, S., Osikominu, A., Pfeifer, G., Reutter, M., Satlukal, S., 2022. Gender differences in wage expectations: the role of biased beliefs. Empirical Economics 62, 187–212.

Brunello, G., Lucifora, C., Winter-Ebmer, R., 2004. The wage expectations of European business and economics students. The Journal of Human Resources 39, 1116–1142.

Calsamiglia, C., Güell, M., 2018. Priorities in school choice: the case of the Boston mechanism in Barcelona. Journal of Public Economics 163, 20–36.

Card, D., 1999. The causal effects of education on earnings. In: Ashenfelter, O., Card, D. (Eds.), Handbook of Economics of Labor Economics, vol. 3. Elsevier B.V., pp. 1801–1863. Chapter 30.

Carter, M., Maddock, R., 1984. Expectations in economics. In: Rational Expectations. Macroeconomics for the 1980s?. Palgrave Macmillan, pp. 12–42. Chapter 2.

Carvajal, M.J., Bendana, D., Bozorgmanesh, A., Castillo, M.A., Pourmasiha, K., Rao, P., Torres, J.A., 2000. Inter-gender differentials between college students' earnings expectations and the experience of recent graduates. Economics of Education Review 19, 229–243.

Chiswick, B., 1973. Schooling, screening, and income. In: Does College Matter?. Academic Press, New York, pp. 151–158.

Conlon, J.J., 2021. Major malfunction: a field experiment correcting undergraduates' beliefs about salaries. The Journal of Human Resources 56 (3), 922–939.

Cowan, B.W., 2017. Sources of bias in teenagers' college expectations. Social Science Quarterly 99 (1), 136–153.

Crossley, T., Gong, Y., Stinebrickner, T., Stinebrickner, R., 2021. Examining Income Expectations in the College and Early Post-college Periods: New Distributional Tests of Rational Expectations. Working Paper 01. Institute for Fiscal Studies.

Crossley, T., Gong, Y., Stinebrickner, T., Stinebrickner, R., 2022. The ex post accuracy of subjective beliefs: a new measure and decomposition. Economics Letters 210, 110160.

de Bresser, J.R., van Soest, A.H.O., 2013. Survey response in probabilistic questions and its impact on inference. Journal of Economic Behavior & Organization 96, 65–84.

Delavande, A., Del Bono, E., Holford, A., 2020. Academic and non-academic investments at university: the role of expectations, preferences and constraints. Journal of Econometrics. In press.

D'Haultfoeuille, X., Gaillac, C., Maurel, A., 2021. Rationalizing rational expectations: characterizations and tests. Quantitative Economics 12 (3), 817–842.

Dominitz, J., 1998. Earning expectations, revisions, and realizations. Review of Economics and Statistics 80, 374–388.

Dominitz, J., 2001. Estimation of income expectations models using expectations and realization data. Journal of Econometrics 102, 165–195.

Dominitz, J., Manski, C.F., 1996. Eliciting student expectations of the return to schooling. The Journal of Human Resources 31, 1–26.

Dominitz, J., Manski, C.F., 1997. Using expectations data to study subjective income distribution. Journal of the American Statistical Association 87, 855–867.

Dominitz, J., Manski, C.F., 1999. The several cultures of research on subjective expectations. In: Smith, J., Willis, R. (Eds.), Wealth, Work and Health: Innovations in Measurement in the Social Sciences. The University of Michigan Press, pp. 15–33. Chapter 1.

Dominitz, J., Manski, C.F., Fischhoff, B., 2001. Who are the youth "at risk"? Expectations evidence in the NLSY97 In: Michael, R. (Ed.), Social Awakening, Sixth World Congress 8. Russell Sage Foundation, New York, pp. 230–257.

Ehrmantraut, L., Pinger, P., Stans, R., 2020. The Expected (Signaling) Value of Higher Education. Discussion Paper 12522. IZA.

Fischhoff, B., Parker, A.M., Bruine de Bruin, W., Downs, J., Palmgren, C., Dawes, R., Manski, C.F., 2000. Teen expectations for significant life events. Public Opinion Quarterly 64, 189–205.

Garbin, F., 2021. The Role of Expectations on Peers in Educational Choices. PhD thesis chapter. Bocconi University.

Giustinelli, P., 2016. Group decision making with uncertain outcomes: unpacking child–parent choice of the high school track. International Economic Review 57, 573–602.

Giustinelli, P., 2022. Expectations in Education: Framework, elicitation, and evidence. Working paper.

Giustinelli, P., Manski, C.F., 2018. Survey measures of family decision processes for econometric analysis of schooling decisions. Economic Inquiry 56 (1), 81–99.

Giustinelli, P., Manski, C.F., Molinari, F., 2020. Tail and center rounding of probabilistic expectations in the health and retirement study. Journal of Econometrics. In press.

Giustinelli, P., Manski, C.F., Molinari, F., 2022. Precise or imprecise probabilities? Evidence from survey response related to late-onset dementia. Journal of the European Economic Association 20 (1), 187–221.

Giustinelli, P., Pavoni, N., 2017. The evolution of awareness and belief ambiguity in the process of high school track choice. Review of Economic Dynamics 25, 93–120.

Giustinelli, P., Pavoni, N., 2019. Skill Mismatch, Family Information, and High School Track Choice in Italy. Policy report. JPMorgan.

Gong, Y., Lochner, L., Stinebrickner, T., Stinebrickner, R., 2021. The Consumption Value of College. Working paper.

Gong, Y., Stinebrickner, T., Stinebrickner, R., 2019. Uncertainty about future income: initial beliefs and resolution during college. Quantitative Economics 10 (2), 607–641.

Gong, Y., Stinebrickner, T., Stinebrickner, R., 2020. Marriage, children, and labor supply: beliefs and outcomes. Journal of Econometrics. In press.

Groot, W., Oosterbeek, H., 1992. Optimal investment in human capital under uncertainty. Economics of Education Review 11 (I), 41–49.

Hakimov, R., Kübler, D., 2021. Experiments on centralized school choice and college admissions: a survey. Experimental Economics 24, 434–488.

Hartog, J., Diaz-Serrano, L., 2014. Schooling as a risky investment. a survey of theory and evidence. Foundations and Trends in Microeconomics 9 (3–4), 1–176.

Hastings, J., Neilson, C., Zimmerman, S., 2015. The Effects Earnings Disclosure on College Enrollment Decisions. Working Paper 21300. NBER.

Hastings, J.S., Neilson, C.A., Ramirez, A., Zimmerman, S.D., 2016. (Un)information, college and major choice: evidence from linked survey and survey. Economics of Education Review 51, 136–151.

Heckman, J.J., Lochner, L., Todd, P.E., 2006. Earnings functions, rates of return and treatment effects: the mincer equation and beyond. In: Hanushek, E., Welch, F. (Eds.), Handbook of Economics of Education, vol. 1. Elsevier B.V., pp. 307–458. Chapter 7.

Hotz, V.J., Wiemers, E., Rasmussen, J., Maxwell Koegel, K., 2021. The role of parental wealth and income in financing children's college attendance and its consequences. The Journal of Human Resources. In press.

Huntington-Klein, N., 2015. Subjective and projected returns to education. Journal of Economic Behavior & Organization 117, 10–25.

Huntington-Klein, N., 2016. "(Un)informed college and major choice": verification in an alternate setting. Economics of Education Review 53, 159–163.

Jacob, B., Wilder, T., 2010. Educational Expectation and Attainment. Working Paper 15683. NBER.

Kalenkoski, C., 2008. Parent–child bargaining, parental transfers, and the post-secondary education decision. Applied Economics 40 (4), 413–436.

Kapor, A.J., Neilson, C.A., Zimmerman, S.D., 2020. Heterogeneous beliefs and school choice mechanisms. The American Economic Review 110, 1274–1315.

Kleinjans, K.J., van Soest, A.H.O., 2014. Rounding, focal point answers and nonresponse to subjective probability questions. Journal of Applied Econometrics 29, 567–585.

Kunz, J.S., Staub, K.E., 2020. Early subjective completion beliefs and the demand for post-secondary education. Journal of Economic Behavior & Organization 177, 34–55.

Lange, F., Topel, R., 2006. The social value of education and human capital. In: Hanushek, E., Welch, F. (Eds.), Handbook of Economics of Education, vol. 1. Elsevier B.V., pp. 459–509. Chapter 8.

Larroucau, T., Martinez, M., Neilson, C., Rios, I., 2021. Application Mistakes and Information Frictions in College Admissions. Working paper. Princeton University.

Levhari, D., Weiss, Y., 1974. The effect of risk on the investment in human capital. The American Economic Review 64, 950–963.

Lochner, L., Monge-Naranjo, A., 2012. Credit constraints in education. Annual Review of Economics 4, 225–256.

Lochner, L., Monge-Naranjo, A., 2016. Student loans and repayment: theory, evidence and policy. In: Hanushek, E., Machin, S., Woessmann, L. (Eds.), Handbook of Education Economics, vol. 5. Elsevier B.V., pp. 397–478. Chapter 8.

Manski, C.F., 1993. Adolescent econometricians: how do youth infer the returns to schooling? In: Clotfelter, C.T., Rothschild, M. (Eds.), Studies of Supply and Demand in Higher Education. University of Chicago Press, pp. 43–60.

Manski, C.F., 2004. Measuring expectations. Econometrica 72 (5), 1329–1376.

Manski, C.F., 2018. Survey measurement of probabilistic macroeconomic expectations: progress and promise. NBER Macroeconomics Annual 32, 411–471.

Manski, C.F., Molinari, F., 2010. Rounding probabilistic expectations in surveys. Journal of Business and Economic Statistics 28 (2), 219–231.

Mazza, J., Hartog, J., 2011. Do They Understand the Benefits from Education? Evidence on Dutch High School Students' Earnings Expectations. Discussion Paper 5714. IZA.

Menon Eliophotou, M., 1997a. Perceived economic benefits of higher education: the case of Cyprus. Education Economics 5, 53–61.

Menon Eliophotou, M., 1997b. Perceived rates of return to higher education in Cyprus. Economics of Education Review 16, 425–430.

Menon Eliophotou, M., 2008a. Perceived rates of return to higher education: further evidence from Cyprus. Economics of Education Review 27, 39–47.

Menon Eliophotou, M., 2008b. The economic benefits of higher education in Cyprus: the expectations of prospective students. International Journal of Educational Development 28, 259–267.

Mincer, J., 1974. Schooling, Experience and Earnings. Columbia University Press.

Patnaik, A., Venator, J., Wiswall, M.J., Zafar, B., 2020a. The role of heterogeneous risk preferences, discount rates, and earnings expectations in college major choice. Journal of Econometrics. In press.

Patnaik, A., Wiswall, M.J., Zafar, B., 2020b. Working paper. College Majors.

Psacharopoulos, G., Patrinos, H.A., 2018. Returns to investment in education: a decennial review of the global literature. Education Economics 26 (5), 445–458.

Reuben, E., Wiswall, M.J., Zafar, B., 2017. Preferences and biases in education choices and labor market expectations: shrinking the black box of gender. The Economic Journal 604, 2153–2186.

Reynolds, J.R., Pemberton, J., 2001. Rising college expectations among youth in the United States. A comparison of the 1979 and 1997 NLSY. The Journal of Human Resources 36, 703–726.

Sattin-Bajaj, C., 2014. Unaccompanied Minors: Immigrant Youth, School Choice, and the Pursuit of Equity. Harvard Education Press.

Schultz, T., 1963. The Economic Value of Education. Columbia University Press.

Schweri, J., Hartog, J., Wolter, S.C., 2011. Do students expect compensation for wage risk? Economics of Education Review 30, 215–227.

Son, S.J., 2020. Distributional Impacts of Centralized School Choice. Job market paper. Yale University.

Spence, M., 1973. Job market signalling. The Quarterly Journal of Economics 87, 355–374.

Stiglitz, J., Weiss, A., 1990. Sorting out the differences between signalling and screening models. In: Bacharach, M., Dempster, M., Enos, J. (Eds.), Mathematical Models in Economics. University of Oxford, pp. 1–34. Chapter 4.

Stinebrickner, T., Stinebrickner, R., 2012. Learning about academic ability and the college drop-out decision. Journal of Labor Economics 30 (4), 707–748.

Stinebrickner, T., Stinebrickner, R., 2014a. A major in science? Initial beliefs and final outcomes for college major and dropout. The Review of Economic Studies 81 (1), 426–472.

Stinebrickner, T., Stinebrickner, R., 2014b. Academic performance and college dropout: using longitudinal expectations data to estimate a learning model. Journal of Labor Economics 32 (3), 601–644.

van der Klaauw, W., 2012. On the use of expectations data in estimating structural dynamic models. Journal of Labor Economics 30 (3), 521–554.

Webbink, D., Hartog, J., 2004. Can students predict starting salaries? Yes! Economics of Education Review 23, 103–113.

Weiss, Y., 1972. The risk element in occupational and educational choices. Journal of Political Economy 80, 1203–1213.

Wiswall, M.J., Zafar, B., 2015a. Belief updating among college students: evidence from experimental variation in information. Journal of Human Capital 9 (2), 117–169.

Wiswall, M.J., Zafar, B., 2015b. Determinants of college major choice: identification using an information experiment. The Review of Economic Studies 82 (2), 791–824.

Wiswall, M.J., Zafar, B., 2020. Human capital and expectations about career and family. Journal of Political Economy 129 (5), 1361–1424.

Wolter, S.C., 2000. Wage expectations: a comparison of Swiss and US students. Kyklos 53, 51–69.

Zafar, B., 2011a. Can subjective expectations data be used in choice models? Evidence on cognitive biases. Journal of Applied Econometrics 26 (3), 520–544.

Zafar, B., 2011b. How do college students form expectations? Journal of Labor Economics 29 (2), 301–348.

Zafar, B., 2012. Double majors: one for me, one for the parents? Economic Inquiry 50 (2), 287–308.

Zafar, B., 2013. College major choice and the gender gap. The Journal of Human Resources 48 (3), 545–595.

Mortality and health expectations[☆]

Péter Hudomiet[a], **Michael D. Hurd**[a,b,c], **and Susann Rohwedder**[a,c]

[a]*RAND, Santa Monica, CA, United States*
[b]*NBER, Cambridge, MA, United States*
[c]*NETSPAR, Tilburg, the Netherlands*

8.1 Introduction

Expectations about future health play an important role in many economic decisions. Life expectancy is an important determinant of consumption, savings, and labor supply decisions in standard life cycle models. Those who expect to live longer should retire at later ages, consume less and save more to maintain their standard of living at advanced ages. Upon retirement, these individuals have a greater incentive to annuitize their private pensions to benefit from their longer expected life spans. Similarly, the risk of developing serious health conditions has financial implications for which households should be prepared. A long stay in a nursing home, for example, is costly, and it is not covered by Medicare in the U.S. (the universal federal health insurance program for 65+-year-olds). The treatment costs of many chronic conditions, such as cancer or diabetes, are also substantial, although health insurance can mitigate some of these costs. Expectations about longevity and health have important implications for life cycle decisions or the demand for various insurance products, among others.

This chapter provides an overview of the state of research on the expectations of individuals in the domain of longevity and health as elicited in household surveys. This literature is vast, so we narrow our focus in several ways. First, we focus on the expectations of individuals collected in general-purpose household surveys. Health expectations of professional forecasters, businesses, or other institutions are not considered. Second, we focus on the main ideas in the literature rather than summarizing individual papers. Third, we mainly focus on quantitative expectations measures rather than qualitative scales. Qualitative elicitation asks respondents to express the likelihood of an event with verbal descriptors such as "very likely" or "not likely at all." Numerically scaled subjective probabilities have several advantages compared to qualitative measures: they can be used directly in life cycle models; they can be aggregated to population forecasts that can be compared quantitively to eventual outcomes, and their scaling has the same meaning across individuals, whereas the meaning of "likely" may differ across individuals.

The pioneering studies by Hamermesh and Hamermesh (1983) and Hamermesh (1985) reported about probabilistic expectations to survive to age 60 and 80. They showed that these data passed several

---

[☆] This research was supported by a grant from the National Institute on Aging (P01AG008291). Kelsey O'Hollaren provided excellent research assistance.

consistency checks. For example, the averages lined up closely with life-table survival probabilities, and survival expectations of smokers were significantly below those of non-smokers.

The Health and Retirement Study (HRS) was launched a few years later in 1992. The HRS was the first major survey to devote an entire section to probabilistic questions. Since 1992 it has asked about many health-related expectations: survival, nursing home entry, out-of-pocket (OOP) medical expenditures, cognition and dementia, health, disability, and the future of the Medicare system (See Table 8.7 in the appendix). The success of the HRS inspired other countries that later launched surveys following the HRS design (see Chapter 1 in this Handbook). These surveys are sometimes called the HRS sister studies. They also include many expectation questions, especially survival expectations, and sometimes disability, health, and nursing home expectations. Survival expectations have also been asked in other U.S. surveys such as the American Life Panel, the National Longitudinal Survey of Youth, the Panel Study of Income Dynamic, and the Understanding America Study. In the last few decades, many other U.S. and international surveys have adopted similar questions on other health-related topics that are not included in the HRS, such as expectations about the harmful effects of smoking, HIV infections, vaccinations, and contraception use.

Standard survey measures of health, such as self-reported health or the presence of various chronic conditions, are useful to measure individuals' current health status but less so for characterizing the risk of developing new health conditions in the future. Traditionally, researchers have used observable risk factors to characterize health risks, such as socio-economic status (SES), smoking, and dietary habits that predict future health problems. Individuals, however, hold private information about their health and about the future course of their health that may go beyond such observable risks. Subjective expectations aim to measure this private information. For example, some people may expect to develop certain conditions in the future based on what they know about their families or early symptoms. Private information about health risks may affect their decisions, such as demand for health and life insurance, health behaviors, or savings decisions. This private information has implications for the efficiency of insurance markets: indeed, some studies have used subjective expectations data to learn about adverse selection in insurance markets.

Subjective expectations can be used to test if individuals' beliefs are in line with more objective measures of health risks. Expectations and beliefs may or may not be accurate, and discrepancies in beliefs may have implications for individuals' decision quality and welfare, such as the adequacy of their financial resources in old age. While traditional economic models assume individuals are fully rational, psychologists and behavioral economists have robustly documented systematic deviations. Because of their numerical scales, subjective probabilities can quantify the deviations from the rational benchmarks. We summarize research studies that related discrepancies in beliefs to various puzzles such as under saving, underusing medical screenings, or inadequately controlled hypertension.

While most studies find that expectations line up well with objective risks, numerous discrepancies have been identified, which we discuss along with our best explanations. For example, it has been found that survival expectations are too sensitive to parents' and grandparents' survival status, perhaps due to the saliency of these events. Another discrepancy is the relatively shallow slope of survival expectations with respect to age, shallower than lifetable survival, which, as we will argue, is, at least partially, the consequence of the way most surveys collect this information.

Subjective probabilities capture individual variation in risks, in contrast with objective risk measures that are only available in groups, such as life-table probabilities of survival or the age-specific prevalence of dementia. Researchers can use more robust estimation methods on models involving subjective probabilities such as fixed effects.

Expectations provide an opportunity to examine the determinants of future health behaviors without waiting until the future behavior has materialized. Future health behaviors such as smoking cessation may be impacted by an income, economic, or information shock in the present. Instead of estimating the effect of the shock on actual behavior, which may occur with a considerable lag, one can estimate the effect of the shock on the subjective probability of future behavior. Expectations also offer the possibility to study the (expected) effects of interventions and produce population forecasts of health trends.

The chapter first discusses methodological problems frequently observed in health expectations, such as measurement error, focal responses and rounding, and overreporting small probabilities. By far, the most well-studied health expectation measure is survival, and we devote an entire section to it. We pay particular attention to open questions and gaps in the literature. Section 8.4 discusses other health expectation measures, including moving to a nursing home, medical expenditures, substance use, dementia, health, and HIV infections. The last section summarizes our main points.

8.2 Methods

This section discusses key methodological issues that researchers commonly encounter when analyzing health and survival expectations, though many of them apply to expectation questions in other domains.

8.2.1 Measurement error, focal answers, and rounding

Measurement error is a common problem to all survey data, but it tends to be more pronounced in questions that are more difficult for respondents to understand and require individuals to process complex information to arrive at an answer (Tourangeau et al., 2000). The concept of probabilities may be challenging for some respondents. Even those who are familiar with the concept may find it hard to apply it to their own lives, which may result in errors and focal answers, such as 50% (Bruine de Bruin et al., 2000; Fischhoff and Bruine De Bruin, 1999; Chapter 1 in this Handbook). Measurement error in health and survival expectations is likely less prevalent than in many other expectation questions because health expectations pertain to topics that are highly salient for everyone, especially older individuals.

Bago d'Uva et al. (2020) characterized the extent of measurement error in survival expectations in the HRS using various methodologies. They consistently found measurement error, especially among low educated individuals and those with lower levels of cognition, possibly because on average these individuals have a less developed understanding of probabilities.

It is expected that group averages of reported probabilities are more accurate than individuals' reports because they average out a substantial fraction of the errors. Motivated by these observations, Zhao (2014) suggested using the predicted values of survival expectations based on a regression model with many predictors. He found that this approach substantially increased the signal-to-noise ratio in survival expectations. This is an interesting approach. However, it likely takes out too much variation from the data: anything that is not explained by the predictor variables is lost by this transformation. There is strong evidence that expectations data predict future mortality even when many predictor variables are controlled (Section 8.3.1). Therefore, it would seem desirable to model measurement error directly instead of using simple transformations. Researchers who collect their own data could ask multiple questions on the same outcome to be able to estimate the moments of measurement error.

Rounding is another form of error. Surveys typically allow respondents to use the entire 0–100% scale, but most answers are rounded (Manski and Molinari, 2010; Chapter 1 in this Handbook). There is extensive research on rounding in survival expectations (Bissonnette et al., 2017; Bissonnette and de Bresser, 2018; Hudomiet and Willis, 2013; Kleinjans and van Soest, 2014). The most frequent answer is typically 50%, but 0% and 100% answers also tend to be very common. These three answers are sometimes called "focal responses." The rest of the responses are typically multiples of 10% and 25%.

Manski and Molinari (2010) offered a nonparametric approach to account for these rounding patterns based on a partial identification estimation strategy (Manski, 2003). Because rounding is very common in expectations data, this method tends to find quite wide (possibly uninformative) bounds for most coefficients. In the survival context, both Manski and Molinari and Bissonnette and de Bresser (2018) found that this method yielded very wide bounds. Bissonnette and de Bresser (2018) also showed that by using further logical restrictions on the data, such as various monotonicity requirements, the bounds could be made considerably sharper.

A parametric alternative was derived by Kleinjans and van Soest (2014) using six expectation questions, including survival expectations. They assumed that true beliefs were unobserved (latent); only the intervals they belonged to were observed. They specified a parametric model of expectations, rounding, focal answers, and item non-response and estimated it with Maximum Simulated Likelihood. Their model used stronger parametric assumptions than Bissonnette and de Bresser (2018), but we believe this approach works well in most applications. These types of rounding error models can replicate the observed distributions of subjective survival probabilities well.

Why do we observe heaping on 50%? Bruine de Bruin et al. (2000), Fischhoff and Bruine De Bruin (1999), and other papers from psychology argued that many 50% answers are due to ignorance rather than precisely formulated probabilities. That is, many respondents use 50% as a synonym for "God only knows." Motivated by this reasoning, Hudomiet and Willis (2013) suggested a model of survival expectations, in which individuals are born with a flat prior about their survival chances. Those with a flat prior answer 50% to any question about survival. As the individuals observe more and more signals over time, they update their priors and start providing more refined answers.

8.2.2 Biases in small and large probabilities

Reports of extreme probabilities (close to 0% and 100%) are frequently biased towards the middle of the probability scale. This observation goes back at least to Tversky and Kahneman (1974), who argued that some individuals may use 50% as an anchor and "*insufficiently adjust their answers away from 50%.*" In the context of survival, Lichtenstein et al. (1978) showed evidence that individuals tended to overestimate substantially the small probabilities of dying from various causes.

We illustrated this bias in Hudomiet et al. (2018): We asked survey participants about the probability of drawing a white ball from an urn that contained ten red balls and zero white balls. The average response was 6.9% (vs. the actual 0%). We also asked about the probability of drawing a red ball from the same urn, and the average response was 91.9% (vs. 100%). Both averages, thus, were significantly biased toward 50%. About half of the bias was due to reporting "50%" focal answers, and the other half was due to reporting other incorrect values.

This reporting bias in extreme probabilities is critical in the study of health expectations because many health conditions have low prevalence in the population. For example, Carman and Kooreman (2014) found that for multiple health conditions, for which the population prevalence was less than 1%, such as dying from influenza or getting breast cancer, the average reports were orders of magnitudes larger than the objective value. Similarly, Fischhoff et al. (2000) found that teenagers, on average, substantially overreported the probabilities of certain low-probability events, such as becoming pregnant, becoming the victim of a violent crime, or dying in the next year. If these reports reflected teenagers' actual beliefs, the results would imply that teenagers substantially overestimate the risks of these significant life events. Fischhoff et al. discussed some caveats in taking these reports at face values, such as the high frequency of 50% answers and the insensitivity of some answers to the time frames used in the questions. We add to this list that low-probability events tend to be overreported in surveys in general.

We believe three phenomena play important roles in explaining the bias in extreme probabilities:

1. Because extreme probabilities are close to the boundaries of the probability scale, measurement error is asymmetric and naturally biases the means away from the boundaries.
2. Some individuals use 50%, the middle of the scale, as an anchor, which biases some responses toward 50%.
3. Individuals who are uncertain about the distribution of an outcome tend to overestimate the variance and thus report values biased towards the "uninformed" 50%.

The first "measurement error" argument is intuitive. However, when we tried to calibrate reasonable noise models (such as adding a classical measurement error term to the probit of an event), we found that, while the error led to some bias toward 50%, the bias was never large enough to explain all the bias.

The second "anchoring" argument is likely relevant, because the 50% answer is by far the most frequent answer to most probability questions, and it seems natural that some use it as an anchor (Tversky and Kahneman, 1974).

Perhaps the most interesting is the third "excess uncertainty" explanation. By excess uncertainty, we mean that individuals may have a good idea of the central tendency of some outcome such as survival, but they overestimate its variance and therefore overestimate the probability mass in the tails. Fig. 8.1 illustrates this in a survival context. It shows the objective and subjective probability density functions of the age of death conditional on surviving to age 80. In the excess uncertainty scenario, individuals' subjective beliefs have greater variance. If these individuals were asked about their probability of surviving to age 90, they would respond with a probability close to the objective value, about 50%. However, if asked about the likelihood of surviving to age 100, for which the objective value is close to 0%, the subjective reports would be substantially biased toward 50%. Thus, excess uncertainty leads to a bias toward the middle of the probability scale.

8.2.3 Jointly modeling objective and subjective expectations

Subjective probability data may suffer from noise and biases, but it offers several advantages compared to objective data, such as providing individual variation (objective data are always group-specific) and the ability to directly characterize individuals' beliefs. A growing number of articles model objective and subjective data jointly to get the best out of both approaches. In a joint model, the population

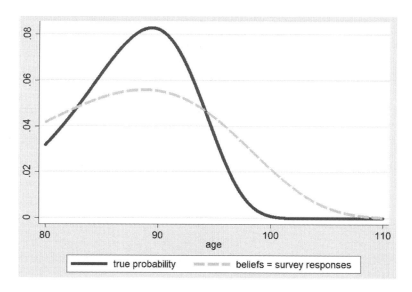

FIGURE 8.1 Illustration of the effect of excess uncertainty about mortality on subjective survival expectations. Probability density functions of mortality, actual and believed.

Note: The figure shows hypothetical probability density functions of ages at death conditional on survival to age 80. "True probability" refers to the objective distribution, and "beliefs = survey responses" refers to the subjective distribution with excess uncertainty.

risk is usually identified by the objective data and the individual-level risks are based on subjective expectations.

Mueller et al. (2021) used this approach to model unemployment duration and unemployment expectations, and Hudomiet et al. (2022) used this approach to model retirement expectations and realizations. Gan et al. (2005), and more recently, Bissonnette et al. (2017) used joint models of survival expectations and actual survival.

Bissonnette, Hurd, and Michaud used HRS data to study the relationships between actual mortality, and subjective survival. They modeled "objective" mortality using a Gompertz framework, permitting the shape parameter to depend on respondent characteristics such as education, race/ethnicity, sex, and cohort. Subjective survival was also modeled as Gompertz with the same specification but with an unobserved frailty term to account for individual differences between actual mortality (conditional on observed characteristics) and subjective survival. To account for focal responses and rounding, they used a response model based on an individual propensity to report focal or precise survival probabilities. The median of the subjective survival curves was quite close to the objective survival curve. The model produced individual subjective survival curves with considerable variation: those at the 10th percentile of the frailty index had a median survival age about 20 years less than those at the 90th percentile. They demonstrated that the heterogeneity in survival curves mattered from an economic perspective by calculating the welfare loss resulting from using potentially inaccurate subjective survival curves, and they found it large, especially in the absence of Social Security, because pessimistic persons (expecting to die early) consumed too much early in retirement.

8.3 Survival expectations
8.3.1 Properties

Hamermesh and Hamermesh (1983) and Hamermesh (1985) analyzed survey data they collected on subjective survival expectations. These early papers already laid out many important questions researchers have addressed since then. The papers argued that rational consumers' retirement and savings decisions over the life cycle crucially depended on their subjective (as opposed to objective) longevity beliefs; subjective longevity affects individuals' decisions to annuitize pension wealth after retirement; and the accuracy of expectations has important implications for the welfare of individuals and the optimal design of the Social Security system.

The authors collected probabilistic survival expectations as:

What is your subjective probability of living to at least age [60/80]?

which we call P60 and P80. They found that the subjective expectations aligned reasonably well with life-table values in subgroups by gender and age, despite some discrepancies. For example, they found that individuals placed too much weight on their parents' and grandparents' life expectancy when they formed beliefs about their own. They found that both smokers' and nonsmokers' expectations are reasonably accurate. As we shall see, this result is somewhat controversial in follow-up studies (Section 8.3.3.1).

They also noted that while P60 was slightly pessimistic compared to objective values, P80 was moderately optimistic, implying a mortality distribution that is too flat compared to the actual. We call this the "flatness bias" of survival expectations which we discuss in detail below.

After the inception of the HRS in 1992, the first papers documented the accuracy of its survival expectations measures by comparing them to "objective values" and testing if they covaried with known risk factors of mortality such as SES and health measures. What constitutes the objective survival risk varied by study. The most straightforward method is to compare the expectations of individuals to future realizations observed in later panel waves. Many early studies, however, did not yet have a long enough observation period for such an analysis, and they used period or cohort life tables to proxy the objective risk.

Studies documented that average subjective probabilities lined up closely with objective mortality risk (variously defined),[1] and they covaried with demographic and health predictors similarly to objective mortality. Hurd and McGarry (2002) and Siegel et al. (2003) used the panel information in the HRS and showed that individuals revised their expectations reasonably after the onset of a new disease condition, and expectations predicted future mortality, observed in the panel, even after a large set of mortality risk factors were controlled. (See also Hudomiet and Willis, 2013.)

The positive HRS results were confirmed in other U.S. datasets, such as the Aging, Status, and the Sense of Control survey (Mirowsky, 1999; Mirowsky and Ross, 2000), and in international datasets.[2]

Overall, the early studies were optimistic about the performance of survival probabilities. Perhaps the most optimistic was the study by Perozek (2008). She constructed cohort life tables that used subjective survival probabilities. The tables showed that the discrepancies between HRS expectations data

---

[1] Hurd and McGarry (1995, 2002), Hurd et al. (1999), Perozek (2008), Schoenbaum (1997), Siegel et al. (2003).
[2] Bell et al. (2020), Delavande and Rohwedder (2011), Delavande et al. (2017), Liu et al. (2007), Kim and Kim (2017), Kotter-Gruhn et al. (2010), Kutlu-Koc and Kalwij (2017), Philipov and Scherbov (2020).

and published cohort life tables by Social Security in the early 1990s predicted later revisions of the cohort life tables. It would be interesting to extend this type of analysis to cohort trends and turning points in subjective expectations and study how they predict cohort trends and turning points in actual mortality. Simply extrapolating past trends in mortality cannot discover turning points, while subjective probabilities, being forward-looking measures, may have the capacity to do so.

8.3.2 Flatness bias in survival expectations

Hamermesh (1985) reported that subjective survival expectations implied a mortality distribution that is too flat compared to the actual: P80 (subjective probability to live to 80) was considerably higher than the objective risk based on life tables. Hamermesh discussed how such biases in beliefs may affect the predictions of life cycle models of savings and other outcomes.

The flatness bias has been verified in several papers, such as Hudomiet and Willis (2013), Hurd et al. (1999), Ludwig and Zimper (2013), and Elder (2013). Elder argued that "*SSFs predict in-sample survival rates that compare poorly with population life tables [...] stems largely from 'flatness bias,' the tendency for individuals to understate the likelihood of living to relatively young ages while overstating the likelihood of living to ages beyond 80.*"

In the HRS, the probability of survival is lower than lifetable values among younger respondents and greater than lifetable values among older respondents. Still, we believe the reason is not systematic bias related to age, but rather the flatness bias is primarily the result of a tendency of individuals to report probabilities that are biased toward 50% when compared with objective frequencies (Section 8.2.2). The HRS asks about the probabilities of surviving to a target age, which is calibrated to be about 10–15-years ahead of individuals' age. For example, 65–69-year-old individuals are asked about the probability of living to age 80, while 86–89-year-olds are asked about surviving to 100. Many surveys use the same or similar question formats. Thus, the objective survival probabilities are considerably smaller for older persons in the HRS. For example, according to the 2016 SSA actuarial life tables, the probability of surviving from age 65 to 80 is 63.5% for men and 73.2% for women; while the probability of surviving from age 85 to 100 is 2.8% for men and 5.6% for women. If responses are biased toward 50%, then the probability of survival to age 80 will be understated relative to life tables, and the likelihood of survival to age 100 will be overstated. Because the objective survival probabilities in the HRS get closer and closer to zero with age, this bias also increases with age, leading to flatness bias.

To separate pessimism or optimism associated with age from flatness bias related to the distance from 50% probability, we designed an experimental module administered in the 2014 HRS. The module asked three survival expectation questions from almost everyone older than 65 (those above 85 only received two questions). The target ages used in the three questions were calibrated to correspond to similar objective survival probabilities in all age and gender groups. Thus, the objective value was about 60% in the first question, 30% in the second question, and 10% in the third one. We expected that the questions would be reasonably well-calibrated (i.e., not much affected by the bias toward 50%) for the question with 60% objective risk, but they would be biased upward for the other two questions, especially the one with 10% objective risk.

Fig. 8.2 illustrates our main findings. Panel A shows the standard core HRS responses. The x-axis refers to life-table survival probabilities, and the y-axis refers to survival expectations. Each marker corresponds to the means by 5-year age and gender groups. If the subjective probabilities were accurate,

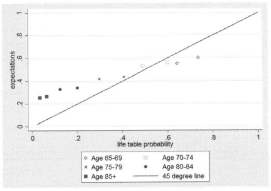

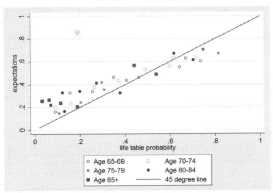

Panel A: The core HRS survival expectations   Panel B: Experimental module expectations

FIGURE 8.2 Life table and subjective survival probabilities by age, gender, and varying target ages.

Notes: Panel A is based on 2014 HRS core data; Panel B is based on a 2014 HRS experimental module.

each marker would be on the 45-degree line shown on the graph. Instead, the responses are above the line at older ages (too optimistic) and below the line at younger ages (too pessimistic): this is the flatness bias. Panel A also nicely illustrates that all responses appear to be biased toward 50%. It is not clear if the bias is truly age-related (as often suspected in the literature) or due to a general bias toward 50%.

Panel B strongly suggests the latter interpretation. It shows the mean responses in our experimental module, in which each group answers multiple questions. Now each age and gender group appears to be well-calibrated when asked about probabilities close to 50%, but almost all appear to be overly optimistic when reporting probabilities for which the objective value is closer to 0%.

To formally decompose the bias, Table 8.1 reports regression models of the group-specific biases (average subjective reports minus lifetable values by age and gender) on age and the distance of the lifetable value from 50%. The regression has 38 observations containing the group-specific means of each core and module question.

Column 3 shows that the questions further away from 50% are more strongly biased, but once this distance is accounted for, the bias does not vary with age. In other words, the test implies that all of the flatness bias is due to the general bias towards 50%, and none is a real age effect. This interpretation is also supported by the partial R-squared values in the last two rows of the table.

Moreover, column 1 shows that the constant term is not statistically significant, meaning that subjective expectations are well-calibrated at 50%: the mean subjective survival reports are unbiased when the target age has an objective survival probability of 50%.

These results imply that the flatness bias in the HRS and other surveys is not primarily an age-effect in survival optimism but a general bias in subjective probabilities toward 50%. Because the HRS experimental module had a relatively small sample, we cannot rule out the presence of some age effect, but it is unlikely to be strong. We replicated the HRS experimental module in an ALP survey and found similar results. Moreover, Jarnebrant and Myrseth (2013) and Wu et al. (2015) reported similar results using different data sources: one using German university students, one using Amazon Turk,

Table 8.1 Linear regressions of the bias in expectations.

	Bias in expectations		
	[1]	[2]	[3]
$p_x^{lifetab} - 0.5$	0.3227		0.3158
	[0.0376]***		[0.0399]***
Age		0.0042	0.0008
		[0.0022]*	[0.0014]
Constant	0.0044	−0.2766	−0.055
	[0.0102]	[0.1679]	[0.1058]
N	38	38	38
R-squared	0.672	0.093	0.675
Partial R-squared (lifetable - 50%)		0.641	
Partial R-squared (Age)		0.009	

Notes: Based on 2014 HRS core and experimental module data.

and one from Australia. These findings align with a long list of articles showing that small and large probabilities tend to be biased toward 50% (Section 8.2.2).

Several recent studies attempted to explain various economic puzzles by the flatness bias in survival expectations, such as anomalies in life-cycle savings behavior (Heimer et al., 2019; Ludwig and Zimper, 2013; Nicholls and Zimper, 2015), and the annuitization puzzle (O'Dea and Sturrock, 2020; Wu et al., 2015). Most papers attributed the observed flatness bias in survival probabilities to age-specific bias in individuals' subjective life expectancies; they interpreted the data as if younger individuals were overly pessimistic and older individuals were overly optimistic about survival. But as we just discussed, the flatness bias in survival probabilities is primarily due to the 50% bias, and mean life expectancies do not show a strong bias at any age group. An exception is Wu et al. (2015), who used a rich model that allowed the bias to vary by the target age. Heimer et al. (2019) showed evidence of some flatness bias in non-probabilistic survival expectations (which are immune to the 50% bias), though they used the probabilistic questions for estimation.

Research studying economic decision-making based on data that exhibit flatness bias needs to consider the source of that bias carefully. In Section 8.2.2, we mentioned three reasons that can explain biases toward 50% in subjective probabilities. The flatness bias in reported survival probabilities, for example, may be due to individuals being very uncertain about their survival chances (excess uncertainty) or because of measurement error. It is not currently known what the underlying mechanism is.

A related but separate topic from excess uncertainty is survival ambiguity, which is having imprecise knowledge of survival probabilities. A few papers have studied the role of survival ambiguity in life cycle models (Caliendo et al., 2020; Groneck et al., 2016) and find that survival ambiguity may lead to suboptimal saving decisions and welfare loss.

8.3.3 Determinants of survival expectations

8.3.3.1 Health and health behaviors

There is extensive literature on how health and health-related behaviors, such as exercising, smoking, and obesity, covary with survival expectations and how the relationship compares to objective survival. Holding age constant, subjective survival is lower among those with health conditions such as cancer or a heart condition, and longitudinally subjective survival declines after the onset of a health condition. Most articles find that the gradient of subjective mortality is not as steep in these factors as the gradient of objective mortality. For example, several researchers have found that smokers have lower subjective survival chances than nonsmokers, but they are not as low as their actual survival chances (Arpino et al., 2018; Schoenbaum, 1997). Balia (2014), however, found that former smokers were the most overly optimistic (compared with current smokers and those who never smoked). Khwaja et al. (2007) and Kutlu-Koc and Kalwij (2017) found that the effect of smoking was relatively muted on expected survival. Falba and Busch (2005) found the same pattern for BMI. Hudomiet and Willis (2013) found weaker effects on subjective survival of several health behaviors (exercising, drinking, and smoking). In the model of Hudomiet and Willis (2013), individuals update their survival beliefs based on relevant observed events. They argued that the effects of many of these health behaviors on mortality are not very salient, and they receive smaller weights in survival expectations compared to objective mortality.

We are not aware of any paper that systemically analyzed how health behaviors are related to response styles, such as missing data, focal answers, and the flatness bias. It is possible, for example, that smokers appear overly optimistic about survival because their objective survival rates are smaller than those of nonsmokers, possibly making their survival expectations more vulnerable to flatness bias.

8.3.3.2 The vital status of parents and other relatives

There is robust evidence in the literature that subjective expectations strongly covary with parents' and grandparents' vital status.[3] The relationships are particularly strong when the child and parent are of the same sex. Only a few papers compared the gradient of survival expectations to that of actual mortality, but those who did found that parental mortality predicted subjective survival considerably stronger than actual survival (Hamermesh and Hamermesh, 1983; Hudomiet and Willis, 2013). Hudomiet and Willis (2013) interpreted this finding in the context of their Bayesian learning model: the death of parents is one of the most salient factors affecting mortality, and it may receive a comparatively large weight in expectations.

Very few papers analyzed the effect of the vital status of other relatives. Donnelly et al. (2020) found that the mortality status of siblings and children also strongly affects survival expectations. Not much is known about the effects of cousins, uncles, other relatives, or friends. It would be interesting to test if these effects vary by the genetic distance of the relatives. It would also be interesting to study how the vital status of friends and non-blood-relatives affect survival expectations.

The vital status of relatives might have a stronger effect on survival expectations if the relative lived a similar lifestyle to the respondent, though little is known about this in the literature. Griffin et al. (2013) found that the effects of parental longevity were weaker among those who lived healthy lifestyles. However, the authors did not have direct information about the prior lifestyle of the parents.

---

[3] Bloom et al. (2006), Donnelly et al. (2020), Dormont et al. (2018), Griffin et al. (2013), Hamermesh and Hamermesh (1983), Hudomiet and Willis (2013), Hurd and McGarry (2002), Liu et al. (2007), O'Donnell et al. (2008).

Observing the strong predictive power of parental longevity, many research studies used parents' survival status as an instrumental variable for survival probabilities (1) to mitigate the effect of measurement error in expectations and (2) to deal with the endogeneity of expectations. We believe argument (1) is relatively solid with the caveat that measurement error in expectations is not classical, which is assumed by the typically used correction methods. We believe, however, that argument (2) is problematic because the mortality status of parents has direct effects on many economic outcomes through a variety of channels, such as bequests, financial and emotional support (or lack thereof), stress and anxiety, etc. This approach would need a reasonable justification for why the exclusion restriction holds for a particular outcome.

8.3.3.3 *Expectations of minority groups*

The literature finds more significant discrepancies between subjective and objective survival among respondents from racial and ethnic minorities compared to non-Hispanic white respondents. Hurd and McGarry (1995) and Mirowsky (1999) reported that African American individuals expected to live longer on average than white individuals even though their actual life expectancy was lower. Bulanda and Zhang (2009) found that Mexican American respondents expected a lower chance of living to ages 75 and 85 than white respondents, even though their actual life expectancy was higher. Hudomiet and Willis (2013) reported similar patterns among Hispanic study participants.

One possible explanation for these differences is that the "objective" mortality risk used as yardstick in these papers (typically period life tables) is less accurate for minorities than for non-Hispanic white subgroups. This would be the case, for example, if there are more pronounced cohort trends among minorities, or the composition of a subgroup rapidly changes due to immigration.

A second explanation centers on survey response differences rather than actual beliefs. Lee and Smith (2016) investigated whether response styles differed by race and ethnicity, and they found substantial variation: Hispanic study participants who completed the interview in Spanish answered "I don't know" significantly more often than any other group. Those saying "I don't know" had significantly higher mortality rates by the next HRS wave. In the total sample, nearly half of the respondents chose 0, 50, or 100 "focal point" answers, and the frequency of the different types differed by race. The 50% responses were most prevalent among white respondents, the 100% answers were most frequent among Black participants, and the 0% answers most common among Hispanic interviewees who completed the interview in Spanish. These patterns likely contributed to racial differences in the documented survival bias, but the study did not quantify their role. Overall, it seems plausible that cultural differences among racial and ethnic groups affect how individuals express uncertainties about survival.

8.3.4 **The effect of survival expectations on economic and health outcomes**

An important goal of collecting subjective probabilities is to understand how perceived longevity affects individuals' economic decisions and welfare. Many papers found evidence that survival expectations predicted various economic and health outcomes in line with prior theories, but it is less obvious if we can interpret the estimated relationships in causal ways. For example, under the life-cycle model people who expect long lives should consume less than people who expect short lives. But their expectations have determinants that may affect consumption independently from their operation through expectations: bad health reduces survival expectations and may independently cause increased health care spending. Randomized controlled trials are not feasible in this research, and the proposed quasi-experimental methods (such as using IVs, see Section 8.3.3.2) rely on strong assumptions. Using survival expectations in structural models is promising, provided the issue of endogeneity is addressed. An important line of research is how to retain the individual variation in expectations while addressing the issue of causality.

Hamermesh (1985) suggested that individuals' survival expectations have direct implications for life cycle models. For example, those who expect to live longer than average should save more, retire later, start collecting Social Security benefits later, and annuitize their private pension plans. Many research papers have been written on these topics over the last thirty years. Papers have analyzed how survival expectations predict consumption and savings decisions,[4] retirement decisions,[5] the propensity to annuitize pension wealth,[6] and portfolio choice.[7]

Puri and Robinson (2007) derived a measure of "optimism" by subtracting life-table survival probabilities from subjective survival expectations. They showed that this optimism measure predicted several outcomes: More optimistic people worked harder, expected to retire later, were more likely to remarry, invested more in individual stocks, and saved more. They also found that moderate optimists displayed the best financial behavior, while extreme optimists displayed less prudent financial habits and behavior.

Various articles analyzed the effect of mortality beliefs on health decisions. Picone et al. (2004) studied the impact of survival expectations on demand for means of early detection of breast and cervical cancer: regular breast self-exams, mammograms, and Pap smears. They hypothesized that those with longer expected life spans would be more worried about cancer risks, and they would more likely undergo medical testing. They found support for this hypothesis.

Lou and Carr (2020) found evidence that survival expectations predicted advance care planning, such as having a will, a durable power of attorney for health care designations, and whether they had any discussions with their families: lower survival probabilities made it more likely that individuals would prepare for death.

Hypertension is a widespread medical condition in the older population, but treatment options can effectively keep individuals' blood pressure in the normal range. It has been shown that many individuals who live with hypertension are not aware of their condition, and many do not control it adequately. Less is known about why this is the case. Do individuals know the importance of testing themselves for hypertension? Do those with a prior diagnosis see the importance of controlling it? Zacher et al. (2021) showed that self-reported hypertension and hypertension control measures are far stronger predictors of survival expectations than objective hypertension measures (measured at the interviews). Their interpretation was that most individuals are aware of the importance of controlling blood pressure, but somehow many fail to do so.

Survival expectations have also been used to forecast future mortality trends. In Hudomiet et al. (2021), we documented trends in survival expectations and other health outcomes of 54–60-year-olds in the HRS. Our investigation was motivated by three recent observations: 1) life-expectancies have been increasing throughout the 20th century, but the rate of increase recently slowed and possibly halted;

---

[4] Bíró (2013), Bloom et al. (2006), Cocco and Gomes (2012), Gan et al. (2015), Groneck et al. (2016), Heimer et al. (2019), Nicholls and Zimper (2015), Salm (2010) van der Klaauw and Wolpin (2008).

[5] Bloom et al. (2006), Hurd et al. (2004), O'Donnell et al. (2008), van der Klaauw and Wolpin (2008), van Solinge and Henkens (2010), Zhao (2014).

[6] Chen et al. (2020), O'Dea and Sturrock (2020), Teppa (2011), Wu et al. (2015).

[7] Spaenjers and Spira (2015).

2) some health outcomes, such as obesity and diabetes, have significantly worsened in recent decades; and 3) health and mortality inequalities have substantially grown measured by trends in health and mortality by various SES measures. Using HRS data, we found that average survival expectations of individuals were lower in 2016 than in 1992, in line with observation (2). We have also found evidence that inequalities in survival probabilities have substantially increased across SES groups (measured by Social Security wealth quintile) in line with (3). Together with other health measures, we used these patterns to forecast the life expectancies of the HRS cohorts. Our preferred specification predicted that average life expectancies would continue to grow in the U.S., but mortality inequalities across Social Security wealth groups would also grow substantially.

The great majority of studies do not embed survival probabilities in structural models, such as a life-cycle model of spending where subjective mortality risk affects spending decisions (see Chapters 25 and 21 in this Handbook and Gan et al., 2015, for an example of an application involving subjective expectations in a structural model). Yet, such use was the primary motive for their initial introduction because they could provide an alternative to rational expectations. The payoff from future research that uses them in this manner seems high.

8.4 Health expectations

8.4.1 Moving to a nursing home

The lifetime risk of entering a nursing home was estimated at 56% in the U.S. (Hurd et al., 2017). More than half of these stays are used for rehabilitation and are relatively short. Still, the lifetime risk of entering a nursing home for an episode of at least 100 days was estimated at 27% by the same authors. The cost of nursing homes is very high and is not covered by general health insurance (Medicare) in the U.S. Therefore, nursing homes pose a very significant financial risk to households.

Do individuals know of the high lifetime risk of entering nursing homes and the associated costs? Are adverse selection and other market failures present in the long-term care insurance market? Subjective expectations offer the opportunity to study these questions.

Nursing home expectation questions have been available in the HRS since the first wave in 1992. Those above age 65 have been asked

What is the percent chance that you will move to a nursing home in the next five years?

Those below 65 are asked about the chances of "ever moving to a nursing home."

The early papers using HRS data documented the measurement properties of these questions. Holden et al. (1997) compared average reports of ever moving to a nursing home of 51–62-year old participants to published objective lifetime risk measures. They found that the HRS subjective average was 40%, and it lined up closely with objective risks. They also found that the risk varied reasonably with gender, race, and family characteristics, such as being married and having children, who could provide informal care to substitute the need for nursing home care. Lindrooth et al. (2000) conducted a similar study using the older half of the HRS sample, and they reported similarly favorable results.

Taylor et al. (2005) used 70+-year-old participants in the HRS and analyzed the relationship between reported expectations of moving to a nursing home in the next five years and actually doing so, observed in follow-up panel waves. They found evidence that expectations strongly predicted future nursing home use, but expectations were significantly higher than the actual probability, namely 14%

vs. 8%. However, because the objective rate is less than 10%, the bias may be due to the same extreme probability bias that we observed in survival expectation, i.e., flatness bias. In fact, the authors reported that expectations were well-calibrated among 85+ individuals for whom the objective rate was higher (19% expected vs. 21% actual), and the bias was entirely driven by the younger sample members for whom the objective rate was meager, such as 50–74-year-olds (12% expected vs. 3% actual) and 75–84-year-olds (15% expected vs. 10% actual). It appears that expectations data about nursing home use are highly consistent with the actual nursing home risk, except for a bias away from 0%.

Ayyagari and Wang (2020), using HRS data, found that individuals revised their nursing home expectations when they developed new health conditions (such as ADL and IADL limitations) and that expectations predicted future nursing home use, but they did not find evidence that individuals with higher expectations prepared themselves financially for these future costs by increasing savings. However, the incentives to save for covering these costs vary by economic position. Individuals at the low end of the income and asset distribution do not need to save for their future nursing home stays, because Medicaid would cover them. Those not eligible for Medicaid in the middle of the wealth distribution may even want to dissave to become eligible sooner. The relationship between nursing home expectations and saving is complex and possibly not even monotonic. Several papers have investigated whether subjective probabilities of future nursing home use predict asset spend down, coming to mixed conclusions.[8]

Several articles analyzed the relationship between nursing home expectations and demand for long-term care insurance (LTCI). Brown et al. (2012) found that the demand for LTCI was significantly higher among those with higher nursing home expectations and those who had fewer alternative options to get care, such as family members. Coe et al. (2015) found that those who had a parent or parent-in-law who entered a nursing home revised their expectations and increased their demand for LTCI.

Finkelstein and McGarry (2006) analyzed adverse selection on the LTCI market in an influential paper. In principle, those with a higher risk of entering a nursing home are more likely to purchase LTCI. Because the risk is not observable for insurance companies, this asymmetric information may lead to adverse selection. Finkelstein and McGarry showed that, indeed, other things equal, higher expected risk implied increased demand for LTCI. However, individuals who preferred being insured were also more likely to purchase LTCI. These two factors were positively correlated, mitigating the effect of adverse selection. Overall, they found that adverse selection was not a major concern in the LTCI market.

The Finkelstein and McGarry (2006) methodology could be used to study asymmetric information and adverse selection in various other markets, such as life insurance, health insurance, etc. The study by Kettlewell (2020), for example, uses a similar methodology to study the health insurance market in Australia. This is an interesting and productive way of using expectations data.

8.4.2 Expectations about medical expenditures

The HRS collects information about individuals' expectations about future out-of-pocket medical expenditures. Between 2004 and 2008, HRS used the question

---

[8] See Bassett (2007), Ayyagari and He (2018), Liu and Mukherjee (2021), and Baird et al. (2021).

What do you think are the chances that medical expenses will use up all your savings in the next five years?

Because the outcome involves the distribution of health care expenses interacted with insurance and assets, it is not related simply to observable characteristics, and it resists ex-ante analysis. In 2010 the HRS changed to a series of questions aimed at directly quantifying medical expenditure risk. The first question asks

Please think about what you might spend out-of-pocket for your own medical expenses over the next year, including expenses such as doctor and dentist expenses, hospitals, nursing homes, prescription drugs and any others. Please include expenses that you would pay yourself (or a family member for you), but do not include what is covered by insurance. On a scale from 0 to 100 (where 0 means absolutely no chance and 100 means absolutely certain), what are the chances that you will spend more than $1500 during the coming year?

The question asks about the probability of spending more than $1500 out-of-pocket in the next year to cover medical expenses. Similar to the survey questions about actual medical spending in the HRS, individuals are asked to consider any medical expenditure that was not covered by health insurance, including spending paid by family members, credit cards, or health care accounts.

Depending on the answer, individuals get one or two additional questions with the targets of $500, $3000, and $8000. These values were calibrated to cover most parts of the objective distribution to permit the quantification of the entire distribution of expected expenditures, but possibly excluding the tail risk of very high spending, which may result from a nursing home entry or other reasons.

We estimated basic statistics about OOP expectations and actual spending using the 2010–2018 HRS waves. We restricted the sample to 55-years and older individuals, and our analytic sample included 74,482 nonmissing person-year observations. In Table 8.2, we compare medical expenditure expectations to actual spending. Actual OOP spending is based on the RAND–HRS public-use data files (RAND HRS Data, 2021). All statistics are weighted, and when expectations and realizations are compared, the samples are restricted to nonmissing observations in both variables. Actual OOP spending is annualized to be on the same scale as expectations (individuals in the HRS report on spending since the previous HRS interview). The table shows the average subjective probability of spending more than three different targets ($1500, $3000, and $8000) and the percent of persons who actually spent more. For example, the average subjective probability of spending more than $1500 was 44.0% among women, and the actual frequency was 31.1%. The table shows that the subjective probability of exceeding the targets declines sharply with the targets (row "all") but the gap between expectations and actual is about ten percentage points. There is little difference between men and women. The variation by age shows a puzzle: while actual OOP spending increases modestly with age, OOP expectations weakly fall with age. For example, the fraction of women who spend more than $1500 is 31.4% among 55–64-year-olds and 35.9% among those 85-years and older. The corresponding expectations are 46.7% in the younger and 35.8% in the older groups. These qualitative patterns also hold among men and in the other threshold values. We found the same patterns when comparing expectations to past (vs. future) spending (not shown in the table). The level of expectations appears to be calibrated reasonably well in the oldest groups, but spending expectations are significantly above actual spending in the younger groups. Expectations of spending more than $8000 also significantly exceed realizations in all groups, but that is likely affected by the extreme probability bias (flatness bias) we discussed earlier since the objective values are close to zero.

Table 8.2 Average subjective probability OOP spending will exceed the target and actual frequency.

Women Age	OOP>$1500		OOP>$3000		OOP>$8000	
	Expect	Actual	Expect	Actual	Expect	Actual
55–64	46.7	31.4	28.1	15.2	13.4	2.8
65–74	43.8	29.8	26.1	13.0	13.3	2.4
75–84	39.1	30.9	24.0	14.4	12.7	3.4
85+	35.8	35.9	22.5	21.1	13.1	8.4
Total	44.0	31.1	26.5	14.7	13.2	3.1

Men Age	OOP>$1500		OOP>$3000		OOP>$8000	
	Expect	Actual	Expect	Actual	Expect	Actual
55–64	45.9	26.1	26.5	12.3	11.6	2.6
65–74	44.4	28.2	25.5	12.5	11.7	2.2
75–84	42.8	32.8	24.7	15.7	11.9	3.2
85+	40.1	34.0	24.1	20.1	13.0	6.1
Total	44.8	28.0	25.9	13.1	11.7	2.7

HRS 2010-2018. Weighted statistics. Actual OOP refers to spending in the next year. The sample is restricted to nonmissing expectations and OOP spending in the next wave.

It is not obvious why younger individuals expect to spend more on medical expenses than they actually do. The expectation questions used the same language as the questions about actual spending. One possible explanation is that some individuals include cost elements in their expectations that actual spending excluded, such as insurance premia, which are specifically excluded in the questions about OOP spending. A learning model could explain the decline with age in the difference between expectations and realizations: it is widely known that health care costs are high and increase sharply with age, but those over the age of 65 are relatively well insured so that OOP spending does not similarly increase (except for spending on long-term care). Further, Medicare likely reduces variance in spending, making it more forecastable. Perhaps some experience with actual spending in a reduced variance setting is required to form more accurate expectations.

Table 8.3 shows for each target spending amounts average subjective probabilities for spending next year, classified by actual spending before the HRS interview (last year) and by actual spending after the HRS interview (next year). For example, among those whose actual spending in the previous 12 months was less than $1500, the average subjective probability that spending would be greater than $1500 in the coming 12 months was 36.1%, whereas it was 65.6% among those whose actual spending was greater than $1500, thus showing that respondents use past spending as a guide to predict future spending. The right three columns show the average subjective probability of spending classified by spending in the following 12 months. The table shows a powerful correspondence between expectations and realizations. We found evidence that expectations line up with past values a little bit stronger than with future values. Table 8.3 provides good evidence that the OOP expectations data in the HRS can be used to discriminate *ex-ante* who is likely to have high OOP spending.

Yilma et al. (2018) used similar questions from an Ethiopian survey to find that expectations strongly varied with past medical expenditures, implying persistence in beliefs similar to what we found. Ex-

Table 8.3 Average subjective probability OOP spending will exceed the target.

Target	Last year actual was ...			Next year actual was ...		
	below target	above target	all	below target	above target	all
$1500	36.1	65.6	44.5	37.6	60.3	44.3
$3000	22.9	51.0	26.6	23.3	44.2	26.2
$8000	12.3	35.1	12.9	12.1	27.9	12.6

HRS 2010–2018. Weighted statistics. Actual OOP spending is annualized to be on the same scale as expectations. "Last year actual" refers to spending in the year before the HRS interview, and "next year actual" refers to spending in the year following the survey, which was determined from the HRS survey two years later. The samples for last year actual and next year actual differ slightly because of missing values.

pectations varied moderately strongly with future expenditures, while there was no correlation with demand for health insurance.

8.4.3 Substance use

Even though the harmful effects of smoking are now widely known, many teenagers and young adults still take up smoking, and many smokers who would like to quit fail. An important question is whether current and future smokers are aware of the harmful effects of smoking. Subjective expectations provide an opportunity to quantify individuals' beliefs.

Khwaja et al. (2007) analyzed the expectations of smokers and nonsmokers to develop lung diseases, heart problems, stroke, and survival. Overall, they found that smokers' beliefs were fairly well-calibrated, and that they understood the most critical health risks associated with smoking. According to Viscusi and Hakes (2008) smokers even overestimate the health risks associated with it. Similarly, Skinner et al. (1998) found that smokers overestimated the risk of developing breast cancer. Lundborg and Lindgren (2004) documented that both smokers and nonsmokers overestimated the risk of lung cancer. Overall, most of the available evidence suggests that the majority of the population is aware of the adverse health effects of smoking.

Still, about 14% of U.S. adults smoke (Cornelius et al., 2020), and the prevalence is higher in many other countries. Teenagers and young adults may misperceive how addictive nicotine is and how difficult it is to successfully quit. Gerking and Khaddaria (2012), though using nonprobabilistic expectations, showed evidence that teenagers who thought it was easier to quit, were more likely to start smoking.

There are a few papers about the health effects of alcohol consumption. Sanchez-Ramirez et al. (2018), using nonprobabilistic question formats, found that binge drinkers were less likely to believe that alcohol use leads to health problems. Thus, the harmful effects of alcohol consumption may be less well known in the population compared to smoking. However, Lundborg and Lindgren (2002) found that people, on average, overestimated the risk of alcoholism.

There are several articles about the perceived risks of using marijuana and other drugs, though most of these papers used qualitative (nonprobabilistic) question formats. The main conclusion of these papers is that the fraction of Americans who consider the use of marijuana a significant risk substantially

Table 8.4 Mean expectations of developing problems with thinking, reasoning, and remembering things in the next 10–15-years.

Age	Men	Women	Total
65–69	51.6	48.3	49.8
70–74	52.7	49.8	51.1
75–79	60.3	57.7	58.8
80–84	65.7	63.8	64.6
85+	69.4	69.8	69.6
Total	56.2	54.2	55.1

HRS   2006–2008,   and   2012–2018. Weighted statistics.

fell over time, and a majority is not considering it a great risk nowadays.[9] It would be interesting to complement this research using probability-based expectations measures.

8.4.4 Expectations about cognitive decline and dementia

The prevalence of Alzheimer's and related dementias rapidly increases with age, and it is expected that population prevalence will increase with the aging population. The cost of dementia is high, mainly because many individuals who live with this condition need expensive nursing care. It is essential to know if people are aware of the risk of dementia.

The HRS has asked one related question since the 2006 wave (Table 8.7):

> Assuming that you are still living at [Target Age], what are the chances that you will be free of serious problems in thinking, reasoning or remembering things that would interfere with your ability to manage your own affairs?

The target age varied between 85 and 100 depending on the age of the person, similarly to the survival expectation question. This question does not directly ask about the risk of dementia; it asks about its most common symptoms, namely the loss of short-term memory and developing problems with thinking and reasoning.

We have not found any published articles using these measures. Table 8.4 shows the means of these expectations by age and gender. To simplify interpretation, we reverse-coded the answers so that higher values correspond to a large likelihood of having memory problems. The mean of the variable is 55% among those 65-years and older. We find relatively modest gender differences: men are slightly more pessimistic about their future mental health than women. We also found a strong age gradient: older individuals gave a significantly higher chance of developing memory problems, which is in line with age patterns in dementia. The level of these expectations appears a little higher than the objective risk, though we could not find good comparisons of the actual risks for the same time frame. Estimates for

---

[9] Merrill (2015), Okaneku et al. (2015), Pacek et al. (2015).

the lifetime risk of dementia range from about 27% to 41% depending on the methodology (Fishman, 2017; Hudomiet et al., 2019), but the HRS subjective probability reports exceed even the high end of those estimates. Although the HRS question does not directly ask about the lifetime risk, the values seem high. One likely explanation is that many individuals considered a broader set of conditions as a "problem with thinking and reasoning," including dementia and milder cognitive problems. It would be interesting for future research to estimate the relationship between these expectations and more objectively measured cognition markers. Another possible explanation is that the question conditions on survival. In querying the older population, it is advantageous to explicitly tell respondents whether they should condition on survival.

Giustinelli et al. (2019) used data from an HRS experimental module that asked a more direct question about Alzheimer's disease and other dementias from a subsample of the HRS. The module asked about lifetime risks as opposed to the risk in the next 10–15 years, and it directly asked about the risk of dementia as opposed to having some of its symptoms. Their module allowed respondents to report point probabilities and probability intervals. They documented widespread use of relatively wide interval responses. Using empirical models that accounted for these response types, the authors found that the mean subjective probabilities were reasonable and in line with objective values.

8.4.5 Other health expectations

The HRS does not ask expectation questions about specific health conditions, such as cancer risk, stroke, heart problems, but some other surveys do. The risk of developing cancer, in particular, received some attention in the literature. This is an important topic because the perceived risk may influence individuals to seek out cancer screening regularly or engage in activities that mitigate the risk of cancer. The main conclusion of this literature is that the perceived risk of cancer is high, and the subjective risk covaries with known risk factors, such as smoking.[10] Chalian et al. (2018) found that some cancer risk factors were not calibrated well, though. For example, physical exercise and being overweight were not related to the perceived risk of cancer even though they predict the actual risk. All of the cited papers about cancer risk used qualitative question formats that make it difficult to quantify individuals' perceived risks. Future research should collect and analyze probability-based cancer risk data.

Some studies investigated how probabilistic expectations about HIV infections are related to sexual behavior and contraception use in African countries with high infection rates and found strong relationships.[11] A reoccurring theme in these papers is that individuals overestimate, on average, the HIV infection rates. However, these results are likely affected by the extreme probability bias we discussed earlier since the objective risks of HIV infections are relatively low.

A significant share of the population is reluctant to vaccinate against flu, COVID-19, and other diseases, and beliefs about the effectiveness of vaccines and their side effects likely play a role. Recent literature has investigated how individuals form such beliefs. Chapman and Coups (1999) showed that the perceived effectiveness and side effects of flu vaccines affect their acceptance. Brewer et al. (2007) found that risk perceptions affected individuals' vaccination behavior. Bruine de Bruin et al. (2017)

---

[10] Chalian et al. (2018), Honda and Neugut (2004), Lipkus et al. (2000), Skinner et al. (1998).

[11] Anglewicz and Kohler (2009), Bignami-Van Assche et al. (2007), Delavande (2008), Delavande and Kohler (2012), Kerwin (2018), Shapira (2017), and Chapter 9 in this Handbook.

showed that pro- and anti-vaccine narratives significantly affected individuals' beliefs about their effectiveness, and these effects were considerably stronger among low-numeracy individuals. In follow-up work, Bruine de Bruin et al. (2019, 2020) found that beliefs about vaccinations in individuals' social networks and the general population have strong effects on individuals' vaccination plans (elicited as expectations). More recently, research has begun investigating beliefs and expectations about COVID vaccinations (Felten et al., 2021; Motta, 2021).

8.5 Conclusion

This chapter summarized and discussed research studies on health and survival expectations reported in household surveys. It first discussed methodological issues that researchers commonly encounter when analyzing these data, such as measurement error, rounding, focal responses, and overreporting small probabilities. Most of these issues are relevant for expectation questions broadly, but many nuances are present for health and survival expectations. For example, extreme probabilities (i.e., close to 0% and 100%) tend to be biased toward 50%, which is particularly relevant for health expectations because the probabilities of many health conditions are relatively low in the general population (such as dying of flu or getting lung cancer in the next ten years). More generally, the bias toward 50% leads to "flatness." Flatness bias in survival probabilities with respect to age (i.e., overpessimism at younger ages and overoptimism at older ages) received a fair amount of attention in the literature. Some researchers argued that this flatness bias might explain under saving at younger ages and insufficient pension annuitization after retirement. However, we showed that the flatness bias is primarily the result of the specifics of the elicitation interacted with response behaviors. Thus, insufficient savings or lack of annuitization should not be attributed to systematic misapprehension in subjective average life expectancies with respect to age unless the measurement model accounts for these biases.

We argued that it is not currently known what causes the 50% bias. It can be that individuals are very uncertain about their survival chances (excess uncertainty), which pushes probability responses toward the uninformed 50%; and it can also be due to measurement error and anchoring bias; or other reasons. Research on understanding the sources of this 50% bias in survival expectations would be beneficial, as would studies about whether it leads to suboptimal life decisions and whether it has welfare consequences. Progress could be made by considering the difference between what people believe and what they report. An approach would be to study the survey responses of doctors, medical researchers, or other professionals who likely have relatively accurate beliefs about mortality probabilities. Another approach would be to test how modes of elicitation affect measurement error, such as the telephone mode versus Internet, or whether question designs reduce flatness bias such as Bins and Balls (Delavande and Rohwedder, 2008) versus stated probabilities. It would also be interesting to study whether survey respondents can be incentivized to provide more accurate responses in surveys.

We see a need for more research on the implications of excess uncertainty. For example, what do life cycle models imply about savings, retirement, and annuitization patterns if individuals are highly uncertain about their survival (compared to objective risks)? What is the welfare loss of such biases in beliefs? More research should be done on subgroup variation in these biases. For example, do low SES individuals hold less certain beliefs? If so, what do the models imply for their economic behavior and welfare?

While there are extensive literatures on survival and nursing home expectations, as well as about substance use, cancer, and some other health condition, we identified multiple areas that have received surprisingly little attention in the literature so far, even though there are high quality, available data. For example, the HRS has been collecting longitudinal data about out-of-pocket medical expenditures expectations since 2010 and cognitive problems since 2006. We have shown some basic properties of these data and identified some puzzles. For example, out-of-pocket medical expenditure expectations appear to be overestimated on average among individuals in their 50s and 60s, while they are fairly accurate at older ages. While we offered some speculative explanations, more work is needed to understand those patterns.

The first wave of research studies in the 1990s primarily focused on documenting the measurement properties of health and survival expectations. They tested if averages lined up with objective values (variously defined), tested if expectations varied with known risk factors of health and survival, and tested the predictive power of expectations in later waves of panel surveys. Most papers found that expectations data aligned reasonably well with these benchmarks. However, numerous discrepancies have been identified. For example, people's survival expectations are overly sensitive to the survival status of their parents, grandparents, and possibly other relatives; and they are less sensitive to other known risk factors such as smoking, exercising, or being obese (though these latter results are debated). We also found that racial minorities hold less accurate beliefs than non-Hispanic, white respondents, although there are questions about the accuracy of the objective probabilities with respect to racial minorities.

We discussed articles that used survival expectations in economic models, such as life cycle models of labor supply, consumption, and savings. Future research could extend these models with other expectations data. Survival expectations have been used to study health behaviors and health outcomes, such as why the prevalence of smoking is still high in the population, why many do not use medical screenings more regularly, and why many hypertensive individuals do not treat their conditions appropriately. Survival and health expectations have also been used to forecast trends in health and survival.

Subjective expectations can be used to characterize how much private information individuals have about their health and survival chances. Such private information may affect their demand for various insurance products, affecting the extent of adverse selection in these markets. We cited studies that analyzed this question, and we urge more research in this area.

Despite some measurement problems, subjective health and survival expectations have been used productively over the past 40 years in several domains. Looking forward, we expect substantial advances in understanding expectation formation, in the use of subjective probabilities in formal models, in the measurement and understanding of heterogeneity both in domains and in subpopulations, and in the elicitation of ambiguity in beliefs to better understand its role in individual decision making.

Appendix 8.A **Estimation of a rounding model of survival expectations**

The model is estimated on survival expectations collected at high frequency in the ALP Financial Crisis surveys. We used one of the questions that asked about the probability of surviving to various target ages:

> What is the percent chance that you will live to be [Target age] or more? Remember "0" means there is absolutely no chance and "100" means that you are absolutely certain.

The logic of the target ages followed the HRS design by taking values between 75 and 105 depending on peoples' age. Those below 65 were asked about ages 75 and 85, and those above received the value that was 10–15-years ahead of their ages. For example, 68-year-olds were asked about surviving to age 80. This question was asked every three months in the survey between waves 38 and 61. We used data from 55–94-year old individuals; and we had 18,851 nonmissing person-year observations in our final dataset from 1708 individuals for a maximum of 16 times.[12]

We fit a flexible panel probit model on survival expectations. We assumed that true survival beliefs are

$$p_{it}^{belief} = \Phi\left(\beta x_{it} + u_{it}\right). \tag{8.1}$$

The probit link function is somewhat nonstandard in survival models, but we wanted to use a general modeling framework. The model can be modified to use other link functions based on a parametric survival model. The unobserved heterogeneity term is modeled as a random walk,

$$u_{it} = u_{i,t-1} + \eta_{it}. \tag{8.2}$$

We assumed all error terms are mean zero and normally distributed, and the variance of u_{i0} and η_{it} are estimated by the model.

In the survey, individuals report a noisy and rounded version of their true beliefs,

$$p_{it}^{report} = R_{it}\left[\Phi\left(\beta x_{it} + u_{it} + m_{it}\right)\right]. \tag{8.3}$$

Here m_{it} is a normally distributed measurement error term, and the $R_{it}\left(\cdot\right)$ is a rounding function. We saw evidence that certain population groups provided noisier answers, so we allowed the noise variance to vary by observable characteristics,

$$\ln\sigma_i^m = \kappa x_{it}. \tag{8.4}$$

We used an ordered probit type rounding model, in which, depending on the value of a latent variable, r_{it}, individuals round their answers to the closest multiple of 1%, 5%, 10%, 25%, or 50%. For example, if the latent rounding value implies rounding to the closest multiple of 25%, then an individual will report 0% if his noisy belief is in interval 0–12.5%, he reports 25% if his noisy belief is in interval 12.5–37.5%, etc. The latent rounding value is modeled with a random effect,

$$r_{it}^{rounding} = \delta x_{it} + \omega_i + v_{it}. \tag{8.5}$$

The random effects term, ω_i, captures individuals' tendency to round in certain ways; in addition, the model allows random deviations from this individual tendency to round across survey waves.

We estimated the model by Markov Chain Monte Carlo. We used rich demographic and health predictors in all equations, including gender, age, race, education, citizenship status, number series test score, probability numeracy, self-assessed health, CESD depression, parental survival status, smoking, drinking, exercising, BMI, and various chronic medical conditions (such as diabetes or heart problems). Appendix Table 8.5 shows the outcome of the model, which exhibits statistically significant effects of the expected sign for various controls in line with previous findings in the literature.

---

[12] For those less than 65 we used data for the target age of 85.

Table 8.5 Outcome of the survival model with flexible rounding patterns, ALP Financial Crisis Surveys.

	Beliefs	Rounding	Log std of error
Constant	−0.076	2.528***	−1.229***
	[0.120]	[0.188]	[0.050]
Female	0.151***	−0.197**	0.040*
	[0.055]	[0.085]	[0.022]
Age 55–64		reference	
Age 65–69	0.568***	−0.369***	−0.092***
	[0.038]	[0.083]	[0.032]
Age 70–74	0.408***	−0.434***	−0.119***
	[0.053]	[0.108]	[0.037]
Age 75–79	−0.199***	0.002	0.129***
	[0.071]	[0.134]	[0.041]
Age 80–84	−0.480***	0.397**	0.121*
	[0.103]	[0.192]	[0.070]
Age 85–89	−0.849***	1.082***	0.439***
	[0.178]	[0.322]	[0.104]
Age 90–94	−0.682	−0.012	0.769***
	[0.495]	[0.644]	[0.198]
Age 65–69 × female	−0.056	0.062	−0.074*
	[0.051]	[0.108]	[0.043]
Age 70–74 × female	−0.017	0.209	−0.052
	[0.072]	[0.143]	[0.050]
Age 75–79 × female	0.224**	−0.159	−0.074
	[0.097]	[0.181]	[0.058]
Age 80–84 × female	−0.024	−0.710***	0.021
	[0.145]	[0.260]	[0.094]
Age 85–89 × female	−0.075	−0.888*	0.061
	[0.263]	[0.465]	[0.147]
Age 90–94 × female	−0.458	−0.139	−0.393
	[0.603]	[0.825]	[0.270]
Black	0.605***	0.045	0.114***
	[0.093]	[0.129]	[0.036]
Other race	0.028	−0.053	0.126***
	[0.121]	[0.169]	[0.048]
Hispanic	−0.089	0.234*	0.012
	[0.096]	[0.137]	[0.037]
Born abroad	0.153	0.071	−0.053
	[0.110]	[0.159]	[0.040]
Not US citizen	0.418*	−0.232	0.499***
	[0.243]	[0.332]	[0.095]

continued on next page

Table 8.5 (*continued*)

	Beliefs	Rounding	Log std of error
Less than HS	−0.165	−0.057	0.398***
	[0.143]	[0.196]	[0.053]
High school		reference	
Some College	0.103	−0.086	0.068***
	[0.070]	[0.098]	[0.025]
College or more	0.199***	0.162	0.012
	[0.073]	[0.103]	[0.025]
Number series, best tertile		reference	
Number series, 2nd tertile	−0.045	−0.136	0.064***
	[0.064]	[0.091]	[0.021]
Number series, worst tertile	−0.032	−0.184*	0.185***
	[0.070]	[0.098]	[0.023]
Number series, missing	0.036	−0.248	−0.085
	[0.137]	[0.203]	[0.070]
Probabilistic literacy, best quintile		reference	
Probabilistic literacy, 2nd quintile	−0.016	−0.095	0.104***
	[0.083]	[0.118]	[0.026]
Probabilistic literacy, 3rd quintile	0.042	−0.128	0.119***
	[0.083]	[0.118]	[0.026]
Probabilistic literacy, 4th quintile	0.226***	−0.193	0.145***
	[0.086]	[0.121]	[0.027]
Probabilistic literacy, worst quintile	0.023	−0.171	0.407***
	[0.091]	[0.128]	[0.030]
Probabilistic literacy, missing	0.020	−0.189	0.228***
	[0.089]	[0.130]	[0.037]
Health excellent		reference	
Health very good	−0.053**	−0.176**	0.091***
	[0.026]	[0.080]	[0.034]
Health good	−0.151***	−0.180**	0.076**
	[0.029]	[0.089]	[0.035]
Health fair	−0.266***	−0.175*	0.066
	[0.035]	[0.100]	[0.042]
Health poor	−0.546***	−0.175	0.105*
	[0.054]	[0.133]	[0.058]
Depression, lowest quintile		reference	
Depression, 2nd quintile	−0.041***	0.044	0.031
	[0.014]	[0.044]	[0.026]
Depression, 3rd quintile	−0.047***	−0.017	−0.028
	[0.016]	[0.046]	[0.024]

continued on next page

Table 8.5 (*continued*)

	Beliefs	Rounding	Log std of error
Depression, 4th quintile	−0.082***	0.077	−0.043
	[0.019]	[0.055]	[0.027]
Depression, highest quintile	−0.141***	0.157**	0.094***
	[0.024]	[0.065]	[0.028]
Mother alive	−0.010	−0.298***	−0.049**
	[0.060]	[0.086]	[0.020]
Father alive	0.222***	0.198*	0.064**
	[0.078]	[0.111]	[0.026]
No info on parents	−0.159	−0.147	0.062
	[0.104]	[0.150]	[0.039]
Never smoked	reference		
Used to smoke	−0.134**	−0.050	0.034*
	[0.054]	[0.076]	[0.018]
Smokes less than half pack	−0.492***	−0.284	−0.059
	[0.140]	[0.195]	[0.054]
Smokes 0.5–1 pack	−0.374***	−0.110	0.045
	[0.087]	[0.122]	[0.030]
Smokes more than a pack	−0.499**	−0.036	0.160**
	[0.200]	[0.278]	[0.073]
Never drinks	reference		
Infrequently drinks	0.044	0.026	0.046**
	[0.060]	[0.084]	[0.021]
Frequently drinks	−0.024	−0.032	−0.026
	[0.073]	[0.103]	[0.024]
Binge drinker	−0.341***	0.312*	−0.054
	[0.116]	[0.167]	[0.042]
Regular vigorous exercising	reference		
Some vigorous exercising	−0.016	−0.061	−0.022
	[0.063]	[0.089]	[0.022]
Only moderate exercising	−0.109*	−0.021	0.004
	[0.063]	[0.090]	[0.022]
Only mild exercising	−0.177**	−0.036	−0.026
	[0.087]	[0.124]	[0.031]
No exercising at all	−0.050	0.078	0.088*
	[0.144]	[0.203]	[0.052]
Ever had hypertension	−0.034	0.009	−0.067***
	[0.052]	[0.074]	[0.018]
Ever had diabetes	−0.034	−0.154	0.034
	[0.067]	[0.095]	[0.023]

continued on next page

Table 8.5 (*continued*)

	Beliefs	Rounding	Log std of error
Ever had cancer	−0.006	0.014	0.028
	[0.074]	[0.104]	[0.025]
Ever had lung disease	−0.419***	0.145	0.013
	[0.099]	[0.139]	[0.037]
Ever had heart condition	−0.099	−0.035	0.036
	[0.070]	[0.098]	[0.023]
Ever had stroke	−0.004	0.063	0.064*
	[0.112]	[0.158]	[0.038]
Ever had psychiatric problems	0.031	−0.003	−0.019
	[0.067]	[0.095]	[0.023]
Ever had arthritis	−0.018	0.162**	−0.034**
	[0.051]	[0.071]	[0.017]
Not overweight	reference		
Overweight	−0.042	−0.126	0.011
	[0.060]	[0.084]	[0.020]
Obese	−0.063	−0.023	0.115***
	[0.066]	[0.093]	[0.022]
Sd of permanent	0.878***		
	[0.019]		
Sd of random walk	0.126***		
	[0.005]		
Sd of rounding	1.210***		
	[0.035]		
Rounding cutoff 1	1.058***		
	[0.048]		
Rounding cutoff 2	2.089***		
	[0.066]		
Rounding cutoff 3	4.193***		
	[0.079]		
Observations	18,851		

Standard errors in brackets. *, **, *and* *** *indicate statistical significance at 10%, 5%, and 1%, respectively.*

Fig. 8.3 compares the observed histograms to simulated ones based on our model and on a simpler one that does not model the detailed response patterns. Panel A shows the histogram of survival expectations as observed in the data. Panel B shows a simulated histogram based on a standard linear regression model where the outcome variable is defined as the sum of the predicted value of the regression (using the same predictor variables as in our model) and a normally distributed noise term with the appropriate variance. The means and variances of the outcome variables in Panel A and B are the same, but the shape of the histograms are very different: Panel A exhibits many focal responses

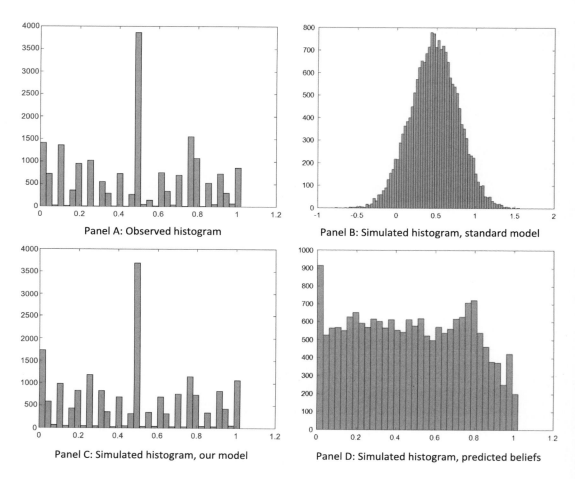

FIGURE 8.3 Observed and simulated histogram of survival probabilities in the ALP Financial Crisis Surveys.

(0%, 50%, 100%) and rounding, while Panel B has a bell shape. Panel C shows the histogram of a simulated outcome based on our model: the predicted value of the model, an added noise term, and applying the estimated rounding rules for each person. Though the two histograms are not exactly the same due to noise, the model successfully replicated the main features of the observed histogram: the excess heaping on the 50% answers, and the prevalence of rounding to multiples of 10% and 25%. There is only one feature of the data that this model did not accurately predict: answers that are not multiples of 5% (such as 1% or 37%) are typically only reported close to 0% and 100%, but very rarely in the middle of the probability scale. Our model did not model this property and so such answers are uniformly distributed across the scale in the simulated histogram. Finally, Panel D shows the histogram of true beliefs based on our model without the noise term and rounding. This predicted histogram has nice support in the 0–1 interval; its mean is the same as that of the raw data, and the variance is slightly smaller due to less noise.

Appendix 8.B Additional tables

Table 8.6 Subjective and life table survival probabilities, by age and gender in the 2014 HRS core and in the experimental module.

Core HRS	Males				Females			
Age	N	Target Age	Life table	Subjective	N	Target Age	Life table	Subjective
65–69	870	80	64.3	54.3	1245	80	73.6	60.8
70–74	930	85	48.6	52.2	1333	85	59.7	56.1
75–79	911	90	29.8	42.8	1235	90	40.6	43.1
80–84	569	95	12.4	32.5	811	95	20.0	33.7
85–90	306	100	3.3	25.9	435	100	6.4	27.0

Module 1	Males				Females			
Age	N	# years	Life table	HRS	N	# years	Life table	HRS
65–69	55	10	73.6	69.0	79	15	65.3	63.1
70–74	91	10	62.6	63.8	111	10	72.7	62.7
75–79	66	5	75.3	73.2	102	5	81.6	68.5
80–84	42	5	60.4	66.3	49	5	69.8	64.2
85–90	–	–	–	–	–	–	–	–

Module 2	Males				Females			
Age	N	# years	Life table	HRS	N	# years	Life table	HRS
65–69	55	20	32.7	42.8	79	25	23.2	34.4
70–74	90	15	38.7	44.3	108	20	28.5	37.3
75–79	68	10	47.0	47.5	105	15	31.2	34.5
80–84	43	10	26.0	42.2	51	10	37.2	35.7
85–90	36	5	43.4	57.1	45	5	52.7	50.9

Module 3	Males				Females			
Age	N	# years	Life table	HRS	N	# years	Life table	HRS
65–69	55	25	13.9	30.7	79	30	7.6	17.2
70–74	89	20	17.0	23.7	109	25	10.3	17.9
75–79	65	15	21.0	25.6	105	20	11.0	14.2
80–84	43	15	6.6	23.2	51	15	12.8	17.6
85–90	38	10	11.1	26.4	47	10	18.0	21.1

The core HRS uses the question: "What is the percent chance that you will live to be [Target age] or more." Our experimental module used the question: "What is the percent chance that you will live at least [X] more years?" The used target ages values and the X values are shown in the table.

Table 8.7 Availability of health expectation questions in the core HRS by wave.

Question	92	94	96	98	00	02	04	06	08	10	12	14	16	18	20
Survival															
Live to be 75 or more	Y	Y	Y	Y	Y	Y	Y	Y	Y	Y	Y	Y	Y	Y	Y
Live to be age X or more	Y	Y	Y	Y	Y	Y	Y	Y	Y	Y	Y	Y	Y	Y	Y
Nursing home															
Move to nursing home	Y	Y	Y	Y	Y	Y	Y	Y	Y	Y	Y	Y	Y	Y	Y
Disability															
Health limits work	Y	Y	Y	Y	Y	Y	–	–	–	–	–	–	–	–	–
Medical expenditures															
OOP medical expense >$1500	–	–	–	–	–	–	–	–	–	Y	Y	Y	Y	Y	Y
OOP medical expense >$500	–	–	–	–	–	–	–	–	–	Y	Y	Y	Y	Y	Y
OOP medical expense >$3000	–	–	–	–	–	–	–	–	–	Y	Y	Y	Y	Y	Y
OOP medical expense >$8000	–	–	–	–	–	–	–	–	–	Y	Y	Y	Y	Y	Y
High medical expenses	–	–	–	–	–	–	Y	Y	Y	–	–	–	–	–	–
Cognition															
Live independently at 75	–	–	–	–	–	–	–	Y	Y	–	–	–	–	–	–
No mental problems at 75	–	–	–	–	–	–	–	Y	Y	–	–	–	–	–	–
Live independently at X	–	–	–	–	–	–	–	Y	Y	–	–	–	–	–	–
No mental problems at X	–	–	–	–	–	–	–	Y	Y	–	Y	Y	Y	Y	Y
Future health															
Same health in 4 years	–	–	–	–	–	–	–	Y	Y	–	–	–	–	–	–
Worse health in 4 years	–	–	–	–	–	–	–	Y	Y	–	–	–	–	–	–
Medicare															
Medicare less generous	–	–	–	–	–	–	–	–	–	–	Y	Y	Y	Y	Y
Bioterrorism															
Victim of bio-terrorism	–	–	–	–	–	Y	–	–	–	–	–	–	–	–	–

Note: OOP means "out of pocket."

References

Anglewicz, P., Kohler, H.P., 2009. Overestimating HIV infection: the construction and accuracy of subjective probabilities of HIV infection in rural Malawi. Demographic Research 20 (6), 65–96. https://doi.org/10.4054/DemRes.2009.20.6.

Arpino, B., Bordone, V., Scherbov, S., 2018. Smoking, education and the ability to predict own survival probabilities. Advances in Life Course Research 37, 23–30. https://doi.org/10.1016/j.alcr.2018.06.001.

Ayyagari, P., He, D., 2018. Means-tested social insurance and strategic asset spend-down: evidence from medicaid asset look-back policies. Available at http://wmpeople.wm.edu/asset/index/dhe/assettransfer. Assessed February 13, 2021.

Ayyagari, P., Wang, Y., 2020. Nursing home use expectations and wealth accumulation among older adults. Center for Financial Security, University of Wisconsin-Madison Working Paper.

Bago d'Uva, T., O'Donnell, O., van Doorslaer, E., 2020. Who can predict their own demise? Heterogeneity in the accuracy and value of longevity expectations. The Journal of the Economics of Ageing 17 (C).

Baird, M., Hurd, M.D., Rohwedder, S., 2021. Transferring assets to attain eligibility for Medicaid reimbursement of nursing home expenses. RAND Working Paper.

Balia, S., 2014. Survival expectations, subjective health and smoking: evidence from SHARE. Empirical Economics 47 (2), 753–780. https://doi.org/10.1007/s00181-013-0750-1.

Bassett, W.F., 2007. Medicaid's nursing home coverage and asset transfers. Public Finance Review 35 (3), 414–439.

Bell, D.N.F., Comerford, D.A., Douglas, E., 2020. How do subjective life expectancies compare with mortality tables? Similarities and differences in three national samples. The Journal of the Economics of Ageing 16 (C).

Bignami-Van Assche, S., Chao, L.W., Anglewicz, P., Chilongozi, D., Bula, A., 2007. The validity of self-reported likelihood of HIV infection among the general population in rural Malawi. Sexually Transmitted Infections 83 (1), 35–40.

Bíró, A., 2013. Subjective mortality hazard shocks and the adjustment of consumption expenditures. Journal of Population Economics 26, 1379–1408. https://doi.org/10.1007/s00148-012-0461-5.

Bissonnette, L., de Bresser, J., 2018. Eliciting subjective survival curves: lessons from partial identification. Journal of Business & Economic Statistics 36 (3), 505–515. https://doi.org/10.1080/07350015.2016.1213635.

Bissonnette, L., Hurd, M.D., Michaud, P.C., 2017. Individual survival curves comparing subjective and observed mortality risks. Health Economics 26 (12), 285–303.

Bloom, D.E., Canning, D., Moore, M., Song, Y., 2006. The effect of subjective survival probabilities on retirement and wealth in the United States. PGDA Working Papers 1706, Program on the Global Demography of Aging.

Brewer, N.T., Chapman, G.B., Gibbons, F.R., Gerard, M., McCaul, K., Weinstein, N.D., 2007. A meta-analysis of the relationship between risk perception and vaccination behavior. Health Psychology 26 (2), 136–145.

Brown, J.R., Goda, G.S., McGarry, K., 2012. Long-term care insurance demand limited by beliefs about needs, concerns about insurers, and care available from family. Health Affairs 31 (6), 1294–1302. https://doi.org/10.1377/hlthaff.2011.1307.

Bruine de Bruin, W., Fischhoff, B., Millstein, S.G., Halpern-Felsher, B.L., 2000. Verbal and numerical expressions of probability: "it's a fifty–fifty chance". Organizational Behavior and Human Decision Processes 81 (1), 115–131. https://doi.org/10.1006/obhd.1999.2868.

Bruine de Bruin, W., Galesic, M., Parker, A.M., Vardavas, R., 2020. The role of social circle perceptions in 'false consensus' about population statistics: evidence from a national flu survey. Medical Decision Making 40 (2), 235–241.

Bruine de Bruin, W., Parker, A.M., Galesic, M., Vardavas, R., 2019. Reports of social circles' and own vaccination behavior: a national longitudinal survey. Health Psychology 38 (11), 975–983.

Bruine de Bruin, W., Wallin, A., Parker, A.M., Strough, J., Hanmer, J., 2017. Effects of anti- versus pro-vaccine narratives on responses by recipients varying in numeracy: a cross-sectional survey-based experiment. Medical Decision Making 37 (8), 860–870. https://doi.org/10.1177/0272989X17704858.

Bulanda, J.R., Zhang, Z., 2009. Racial-ethnic differences in subjective survival expectations for the retirement years. Research on Aging 31 (6), 688–709. https://doi.org/10.1177/0164027509343533.

Caliendo, F.N., Gorry, A., Slavov, S., 2020. Survival ambiguity and welfare. Journal of Economic Behavior & Organization 170 (C), 20–42.

Carman, K.G., Kooreman, P., 2014. Probability perceptions and preventive health care. Journal of Risk and Uncertainty 49, 43–71. https://doi.org/10.1007/s11166-014-9196-x.

Chalian, H., Khoshpouri, P., Assari, S., 2018. Demographic, social, and behavioral determinants of lung cancer perceived risk and worries in a national sample of American adults; does lung cancer risk matter? Medicina 54 (6), 97. https://doi.org/10.3390/medicina54060097.

Chapman, G., Coups, E.J., 1999. Predictors of influenza vaccine acceptance among healthy adults. Preventive Medicine 29, 249–262.

Chen, A., Hieber, P., Rach, M., 2020. Optimal retirement products under subjective mortality beliefs. Insurance. Mathematics & Economics.

Cocco, J.F., Gomes, F.J., 2012. Longevity risk, retirement savings, and financial innovation. Journal of Financial Economics 103, 507–529.

Coe, N.B., Skira, M.M., van Houtven, C.H., 2015. Long-term care insurance: does experience matter? Journal of Health Economics 40, 122–131. https://doi.org/10.1016/j.jhealeco.2015.01.001.

Cornelius, M.E., Wang, T.W., Jamal, A., Loretan, C., Neff, L., 2020. Tobacco product use among adults – United States, 2019. Morbidity and Mortality Weekly Report 69 (46), 1736–1742.

Delavande, A., 2008. Pill, patch, or shot? Subjective expectations and birth control choice. International Economic Review 49 (3), 999–1042.

Delavande, A., Kohler, H.P., 2012. The impact of HIV testing on subjective expectations and risky behavior in Malawi. Demography 49 (3), 1011–1036. https://doi.org/10.1007/s13524-012-0119-7.

Delavande, A., Lee, J., Menon, S., 2017. Eliciting survival expectations of the elderly in low-income countries: evidence from India. Demography 54, 673–699.

Delavande, A., Rohwedder, S., 2008. Eliciting subjective probabilities in internet surveys. Public Opinion Quarterly 72 (5), 866–891. https://doi.org/10.1093/poq/nfn062.

Delavande, A., Rohwedder, S., 2011. Differential survival in Europe and the United States: estimates based on subjective probabilities of survival. Demography 48 (4), 1377–1400. https://doi.org/10.1007/s13524-011-0066-8.

Donnelly, R., Umberson, D., Pudrovska, T., 2020. Family member death and subjective life expectancy among black and white older adults. Journal of Aging and Health 32 (3–4), 143–153. https://doi.org/10.1177/0898264318809798.

Dormont, B., Samson, A.L., Fleurbaey, M., Luchini, S., Schokkaert, E., 2018. Individual uncertainty about longevity. Demography 55 (5), 1829–1854.

Elder, T.E., 2013. The predictive validity of subjective mortality expectations: evidence from the Health and Retirement Study. Demography 50 (2), 569–589. https://doi.org/10.1007/s13524-012-0164-2.

Falba, T.A., Busch, S.H., 2005. Survival expectations of the obese: is excess mortality reflected in perceptions? Obesity Research 13 (4), 754–761. https://doi.org/10.1038/oby.2005.85.

Felten, R., Dubois, M., Ugarte-Gil, M.F., Chaudier, A., Kawka, L., Bergier, et al., 2021. Vaccination against COVID-19: expectations and concerns of patients with autoimmune and rheumatic diseases. Lancet Rheumatology 3 (4), e243–e245. https://doi.org/10.1016/S2665-9913(21)00039-4.

Finkelstein, A., McGarry, K., 2006. Multiple dimensions of private information: evidence from the long-term care insurance market. The American Economic Review 96 (4), 938–958.

Fischhoff, B., Bruine De Bruin, W., 1999. Fifty–fifty = 50%? Journal of Behavioral Decision Making 12 (2), 149–163. https://doi.org/10.1002/(SICI)1099-0771(199906)12:2<149::AID-BDM314>3.0.CO;2-J.

Fischhoff, B., Parker, A.M., Bruine de Bruin, W., Downs, J., Palmgren, C., Dawes, R., Manski, C.F., 2000. Teen expectations for significant life events. Public Opinion Quarterly 64 (2), 189–205. https://doi.org/10.1086/317762.

Fishman, E., 2017. Risk of developing dementia at older ages in the United States. Demography 54 (5), 1897–1919.

Gan, L., Gong, G., Hurd, M.D., McFadden, D.L., 2015. Subjective mortality risk and bequests. Journal of Econometrics 188 (2), 514–525.

Gan, L., Hurd, M.D., McFadden, D.L., 2005. Individual subjective survival curves. In: Analyses in the Economics of Aging. University of Chicago Press, pp. 377–412.

Gerking, S., Khaddaria, R., 2012. Perceptions of health risk and smoking decisions of young people. Health Economics 21 (7), 865–877. https://doi.org/10.1002/hec.1760.

Giustinelli, P., Manski, C.F., Molinari, F., 2019. Precise or Imprecise Probabilities? Evidence from Survey Response on Late-onset Dementia. NBER Working Papers 26125. National Bureau of Economic Research, Inc.

Griffin, B., Loh, V., Hesketh, B., 2013. A mental model of factors associated with subjective life expectancy. Social Science & Medicine 82, 79–86. https://doi.org/10.1016/j.socscimed.2013.01.026.

Groneck, M., Ludwig, A., Zimper, A., 2016. A life-cycle model with ambiguous survival beliefs. Journal of Economic Theory 162 (C), 137–180.

Hamermesh, D.S., 1985. Expectations, life expectancy, and economic behavior. The Quarterly Journal of Economics 100, 389–408.

Hamermesh, D.S., Hamermesh, F.W., 1983. Does perception of life expectancy reflect health knowledge? American Journal of Public Health 73, 911–914.

Heimer, R.Z., Myrseth, K.O.R., Schoenle, R.S., 2019. YOLO: mortality beliefs and household finance puzzles. The Journal of Finance 74 (6), 2957–2996.

Holden, K., McBride, T., Perozek, M., 1997. Expectations of nursing home use in the Health and Retirement Study: the role of gender, health, and family characteristics. The Journals of Gerontology. Series B, Psychological Sciences and Social Sciences 52 (5), S240–S251. https://doi.org/10.1093/geronb/52b.5.s240.

Honda, K., Neugut, A.I., 2004. Associations between perceived cancer risk and established risk factors in a national community sample. Cancer Detection and Prevention 28 (1), 1–7. https://doi.org/10.1016/j.cdp.2003.12.001.

Hudomiet, P., Hurd, M.D., Rohwedder, S., 2018. Measuring probability numeracy. RAND Working Papers WR-1270.

Hudomiet, P., Hurd, M.D., Rohwedder, S., 2019. The relationship between lifetime out-of-pocket medical expenditures, dementia, and socioeconomic status in the U.S. Journal of the Economics of Ageing 14, 100181. https://doi.org/10.1016/j.jeoa.2018.11.006.

Hudomiet, P., Hurd, M.D., Rohwedder, S., 2021. Forecasting mortality inequalities in the U.S. based on trends in midlife health. Journal of Health Economics 80, 102540.

Hudomiet, P., Hurd, M.D., Rohwedder, S., 2022. The causal effects of wages, wealth, and health on retirement: Estimates based on subjective conditional probabilities. Working Paper.

Hudomiet, P., Willis, R.J., 2013. Estimating second order probability beliefs from subjective survival data. Decision Analysis 10 (2), 152–170.

Hurd, M.D., McFadden, D.L., Merrill, A., 1999. Predictors of mortality among the elderly. Working Paper 7440. National Bureau of Economic Research.

Hurd, M.D., McGarry, K., 1995. Evaluation of the subjective probabilities of survival in the health and retirement study. The Journal of Human Resources 30, S268–S292.

Hurd, M.D., McGarry, K., 2002. The predictive validity of subjective probabilities of survival. The Economic Journal 112 (482), 966–985.

Hurd, M.D., Michaud, P.C., Rohwedder, S., 2017. Distribution of lifetime nursing home use and of out-of-pocket spending. Proceedings of the National Academy of Sciences of the United States of America 114 (37), 9838–9842. https://doi.org/10.1073/pnas.1700618114.

Hurd, M.D., Smith, J.P., Zissimopoulos, J.M., 2004. The effects of subjective survival on retirement and social security claiming. Journal of Applied Econometrics 19 (6), 761–775.

Jarnebrant, P., Myrseth, K.O.R., 2013. Mortality beliefs distorted: Magnifying the risk of dying young. ESMT Research Working Papers ESMT-13-03. ESMT European School of Management and Technology.

Kerwin, J., 2018. Scared straight or scared to death? The effect of risk beliefs on risky behaviors. Working Paper. University of Minnesota.

Kettlewell, N., 2020. Subjective expectations for health service use and consequences for health insurance behavior. IZA Discussion Papers 13445. Institute of Labor Economics (IZA).

Khwaja, A., Sloan, F., Chung, S., 2007. The relationship between individual expectations and behaviors: mortality expectations and smoking decisions. Journal of Risk and Uncertainty 35 (2), 179–201. https://doi.org/10.1007/s11166-007-9019-4.

Kim, J.H., Kim, J.M., 2017. Subjective life expectancy is a risk factor for perceived health status and mortality. Health and Quality of Life Outcomes 15, 190. https://doi.org/10.1186/s12955-017-0763-0.

Kleinjans, K., van Soest, A., 2014. Rounding, focal point answers and nonresponse to subjective probability questions. Journal of Applied Econometrics 29, 567–585.

Kotter-Gruhn, D., Gruhn, D., Smith, J., 2010. Predicting one's own death: the relationship between subjective and objective nearness to death in very old age. European Journal of Ageing 7 (4), 293e300.

Kutlu-Koc, V., Kalwij, A., 2017. Individual survival expectations and actual mortality: evidence from Dutch survey and administrative data. European Journal of Population 33, 509–532.

Lee, S., Smith, J., 2016. Methodological aspects of subjective life expectancy: effects of culture-specific reporting heterogeneity among older adults in the United States. The Journals of Gerontology. Series B, Psychological Sciences and Social Sciences 71 (3), 558–568. https://doi.org/10.1093/geronb/gbv048.

Lichtenstein, S., Slovic, P., Fischoff, B., Layman, M., Combs, B., 1978. Judged frequency of events. Journal of Experimental Psychology. Human Learning and Memory 4 (6), 551–578.

Lindrooth, R.C., Hoerger, T.J., Norton, E.C., 2000. Expectations among the elderly about nursing home entry. Health Services Research 35 (5 Pt 2), 1181–1202.

Lipkus, I.M., Kuchibhatla, M., McBride, C.M., Bosworth, H.B., Pollak, K.I., Siegler, I.C., Rimer, B.K., 2000. Relationships among breast cancer perceived absolute risk, comparative risk, and worries. Cancer Epidemiology Biomarkers & Prevention 9 (9), 973–975.

Liu, J., Mukherjee, A., 2021. Medicaid and long-term care: the effects of penalizing strategic asset transfers. The Journal of Risk and Insurance 88 (1), 53–77.

Liu, J.-T., Tsou, M.-W., Hammitt, J.K., 2007. Health information and subjective survival probability: evidence from Taiwan. Journal of Risk Research 10 (2), 149–175.

Lou, Y., Carr, D., 2020. Racial differences in the impact of subjective life expectancy on advance care planning. Innovation in Aging 4 (Suppl 1), 903. https://doi.org/10.1093/geroni/igaa057.3325.

Ludwig, A., Zimper, A., 2013. A parsimonious model of subjective life expectancy. Theory and Decision 75 (4), 519–541.

Lundborg, P., Lindgren, B., 2002. Risk perceptions and alcohol consumption among young people. Journal of Risk and Uncertainty 25 (2), 165–183.

Lundborg, P., Lindgren, B., 2004. Do they know what they are doing? Risk perceptions and smoking behaviour among Swedish teenagers. Journal of Risk and Uncertainty 28 (3), 261–286.

Manski, C.F., 2003. Partial Identification of Probability Distributions. Springer Series in Statistics. Springer, New York.

Manski, C.F., Molinari, F., 2010. Rounding probabilistic expectations in surveys. Journal of Business and Economic Statistics 28 (2), 219–231. https://doi.org/10.1198/jbes.2009.08098.

Merrill, R.M., 2015. Use of marijuana and changing risk perceptions. American Journal of Health Behavior 39 (3), 308–317. https://doi.org/10.5993/AJHB.39.3.3.

Mirowsky, J., 1999. Subjective life expectancy in the US: correspondence to actuarial estimates by age, sex and race. Social Science & Medicine 49, 967–979.

Mirowsky, J., Ross, C., 2000. Socioeconomic status and subjective life expectancy. Social Psychology Quarterly 363 (2), 133–151.

Motta, M., 2021. Can a COVID-19 vaccine live up to Americans' expectations? A conjoint analysis of how vaccine characteristics influence vaccination intentions. Social Science & Medicine 272. https://doi.org/10.31235/osf.io/kxmw7.

Mueller, A.I., Spinnewijn, J., Topa, G., 2021. Job seekers' perceptions and employment prospects: heterogeneity, duration dependence, and bias. The American Economic Review 111 (1), 324–363.

Nicholls, N., Zimper, A., 2015. Subjective life expectancy. In: Krauss Whitbourne, Susan (Ed.), Encyclopedia of Adulthood and Aging. Wiley-Blackwell.

O'Dea, C., Sturrock, D., 2020. Survival pessimism and the demand for annuities. NBER Working Papers 27677. National Bureau of Economic Research, Inc.

O'Donnell, O., Teppa, F., Doorslaer, E., 2008. Can subjective survival expectations explain retirement behaviour? DNB Working Paper#188.

Okaneku, J., Vearrier, D., McKeever, R.G., LaSala, G.S., Greenberg, M.I., 2015. Change in perceived risk associated with marijuana use in the United States from 2002 to 2012. Clinical Toxicology 53 (3), 151–155. https://doi.org/10.3109/15563650.2015.1004581.

Pacek, L.R., Mauro, P.M., Martins, S.S., 2015. Perceived risk of regular cannabis use in the United States from 2002 to 2012: differences by sex, age, and race/ethnicity. Drug and Alcohol Dependence 149, 232–244. https://doi.org/10.1016/j.drugalcdep.2015.02.009.

Perozek, M., 2008. Using subjective expectations to forecast longevity: do survey respondents know something we don't know? Demography 45, 95–113.

Philipov, D., Scherbov, S., 2020. Subjective length of life of European individuals at older ages: temporal and gender distinctions. PLoS ONE 15 (3), e0229975. https://doi.org/10.1371/journal.pone.0229975.

Picone, G., Sloan, F., Taylor, D., 2004. Effects of risk and time preference and expected longevity on demand for medical tests. Journal of Risk and Uncertainty 28, 39–53.

Puri, M., Robinson, D.T., 2007. Optimism and economic choice. Journal of Financial Economics 86 (1), 71–99.

RAND HRS Data, 2021. Version 1992-2018. Produced by the RAND Center for the study of aging, with funding from the National Institute on Aging and the Social Security Administration. Santa Monica, CA.

Salm, M., 2010. Subjective mortality expectations and consumption and saving behaviours among the elderly. Canadian Journal of Economics 43 (3), 1040–1057.

Sanchez-Ramirez, D.C., Franklin, R.C., Voaklander, D., 2018. Perceptions about alcohol harm and alcohol-control strategies among people with high risk of alcohol consumption in Alberta, Canada and Queensland, Australia. Journal of Preventive Medicine and Public Health 51 (1), 41–50. https://doi.org/10.3961/jpmph.17.112.

Schoenbaum, M., 1997. Do smokers understand the mortality effects of smoking? Evidence from the Health and Retirement Survey. American Journal of Public Health 87 (5), 755–759.

Shapira, G., 2017. How subjective beliefs about HIV infection affect life-cycle fertility: evidence from rural Malawi. The Journal of Human Resources 52 (3), 680–718.

Siegel, M., Bradley, E.H., Kasl, S.V., 2003. Self-rated life expectancy as a predictor of mortality: evidence from the HRS and AHEAD surveys. Gerontology 49, 265e271.

Skinner, C.S., Kreuter, M.W., Kobrin, S., Strecher, V.J., 1998. Perceived and actual breast cancer risk: optimistic and pessimistic biases. Journal of Health Psychology 3 (2), 181–193. https://doi.org/10.1177/135910539800300203.

Spaenjers, C., Spira, S.M., 2015. Subjective life horizon and portfolio choice. Journal of Economic Behavior & Organization 116 (C), 94–106.

Taylor, D.H., Osterman, J., Will Acuff, S., Ostbye, T., 2005. Do seniors understand their risk of moving to a nursing home? Health Services Research 40 (3), 811–828. https://doi.org/10.1111/j.1475-6773.2005.00386.x.

Teppa, F., 2011. Can the longevity risk alleviate the annuitization puzzle? Empirical evidence from Dutch data. Working Papers 223. ECINEQ, Society for the Study of Economic Inequality.

Tourangeau, R., Rips, L.J., Rasinski, K. (Eds.), 2000. The Psychology of Survey Response. Cambridge University Press.

Tversky, A., Kahneman, D., 1974. Judgment under uncertainty: heuristics and biases. Science 185 (4157), 1124–1131.

van der Klaauw, W., Wolpin, K.I., 2008. Social security and the retirement and savings behavior of low-income households. Journal of Econometrics 145, 21–42.

van Solinge, H., Henkens, K., 2010. Living longer, working longer? The impact of subjective life expectancy on retirement intentions and behavior. European Journal of Public Health 20, 47e51.

Viscusi, W.K., Hakes, J.K., 2008. Risk beliefs and smoking behavior. Economic Inquiry 46 (1), 45–59.

Wu, S., Stevens, R., Thorp, S., 2015. Cohort and target age effects on subjective survival probabilities: implications for models of the retirement phase. Journal of Economic Dynamics and Control 55, 39–56.

Yilma, Z., O'Donnell, O., Mebratie, A., Alemu, G., Bedi, A.S., 2018. Subjective expectations of medical expenditures and insurance in rural Ethiopia. Health Econometrics 294, 23–55.

Zacher, M., Wang, J., Short, S.E., 2021. The contributions of hypertension diagnosis and blood pressure control to subjective life expectancy in a representative sample of older U.S. adults. The Journals of Gerontology. Series B, Psychological Sciences and Social Sciences gbab022. https://doi.org/10.1093/geronb/gbab022.

Zhao, Z., 2014. The effect of longevity on retirement and unretirement. Working paper.

Expectations in development economics☆

9

Adeline Delavande[a,b]
[a]*University of Technology Sydney, Broadway, NSW, Australia*
[b]*Nova School of Business and Economics, Carcavelos, Portugal*

9.1 Introduction

Measuring expectations in low- and middle-income countries (LMICs) is particularly relevant because individuals there face numerous sources of uncertainty, including those related to disease burden, input and output prices, weather, and political stability. The expansion of high-quality household surveys has made possible the elicitation of probabilistic expectations, notwithstanding respondents' low literacy and numeracy.

There has been early skepticism about the feasibility of eliciting expectations from respondents with low literacy and numeracy. In this chapter, I begin by reviewing how probabilistic expectations have been measured in LMICs. I then discuss typical patterns of answers that can give researchers confidence that respondents are able and willing to report their beliefs in a probabilistic format. Moreover, I emphasize the substantial heterogeneity detected in measured expectations, which underscores the need to collect such data rather than making assumptions about them. The evidence on the feasibility of obtaining high-quality data is positive, and suggests that collecting expectations in LMICs is a useful endeavor.

Underinvestment in high-return opportunities is a key puzzle in development economics (Kremer et al., 2019). Why do people in LMICs fail to invest in preventive, life-saving health technologies? Why do children drop out from school despite the returns to schooling being high? Why do farmers fail to adopt productive modern inputs? A lack of well-functioning institutions and markets may explain some of these behaviors, but misperceptions about the returns to these opportunities are another potentially important factor. They are likely so in contexts where people may not have access to relevant information, lack opportunities to experiment, and may not be able to consult with experts. Our understanding of the role of (mis)information as a contributing factor in underinvestment can be improved by careful elicitation of expectations in surveys. I cover recent substantive applications in several important domains which show that expectations are a key driver of behavior.

Development economics has been transformed since the 1990s, in part due to the expansion of randomized control trials. Promoting development by providing information to the public has been

☆ I acknowledge funding from the Research Centre on Micro-Social Change (MiSoC), award number ES/S012486/1. I am grateful for the comments received from the editors, Emily Beam, Tilman Brück, Xavier Gine, Edward Jones, Jason Kerwin, David McKenzie, Ricardo Santos, Rebecca Thornton, and Ali Vergili. I thank Sonkurt Sen for his excellent research assistance.

Handbook of Economic Expectations. **https://doi.org/10.1016/B978-0-12-822927-9.00016-1**

an important area of research. I review several recent studies highlighting the usefulness of collecting expectations data when conducting randomized information interventions for obtaining a better understanding of the mechanisms behind their (non-)effectiveness. In particular, expectations data are crucial in testing whether the provision of information has been successful in changing beliefs in an intended direction, or has instead made a particular behavior salient.

This chapter builds on three earlier literature reviews on expectations in developing countries (Attanasio, 2009; Delavande et al., 2011a, and Delavande, 2014), and expands their remit to more recent elicitation methods and areas of research. The geographical focus is limited to LMICs as defined by the World Bank classification (World Bank, 2021).

9.2 Measuring probabilistic expectations in surveys in developing countries

9.2.1 Percent chance format

In developed country surveys, the standard method of eliciting subjective probabilities is to use a percent chance format (see Chapter 1 in this Handbook). A similar question wording has been used in developing countries with literate respondents, such as high school or university students. For example, Delavande and Zafar (2019) asked university students in Pakistan "*What do you think is the percent chance (or chances out of 100) that you would have a job at the age of 30?*" Other examples include Attanasio and Kaufmann (2014, 2017), who elicited the employment and income expectations of high school students in Mexico, and McKenzie et al. (2013), who asked Tongans with an average of 12.4 years of education their income expectations if they were to migrate to New Zealand. Among these educated samples, patterns of answers are similar to those observed in developed countries, with low item nonresponse rates (e.g., below 2% in Delavande and Zafar, 2019).

9.2.2 Physical objects as visual aid

Many existing studies involving less literate respondents have used physical objects as a visual aid to help respondents express a probability. This commonly entails asking respondents to allocate 10 or 20 stones, peanuts, or beans. Delavande and Kohler (2009) present results from the Malawi Longitudinal Study of Families and Health (MLSFH), one of the first large-scale surveys eliciting probabilistic expectations in an LMIC. They asked respondents to choose up to 10 beans to express the likelihood of an event happening ("*I will ask you several questions about the chance or likelihood that certain events are going to happen. I would like you to choose some beans out of these 10 beans and put them in the plate to express what you think the likelihood or chance is of a specific event happening. One bean represents one chance out of 10.*"). It is important to explain to respondents that one physical object represents one chance out of 10 (or 20), to ensure that their answers can be interpreted as probabilities. Other examples include Delavande et al. (2011b) and Delavande et al. (2017).

The main advantage of using such objects is that it reduces the burden on respondents and helps them convey probabilistic beliefs in a less abstract way. This is confirmed by the negligible item nonresponse rate for surveys using a visual aid (e.g., under 2% in the MLSFH, Delavande and Kohler, 2009), and by the regularity of answer patterns documented in Section 9.3, such as those conforming to the basic properties of probabilities. This elicitation format requires face-to-face interviews and some logistics, such as ensuring interviewers provide respondents with a complete set of physical objects. The latter issue has been resolved in some studies through use of a card with a bar chart, as in Bhalotra et al. (2020) in Pakistan.

Some researchers may be concerned about the coarseness of responses. Note, however, that rounding probabilities to the nearest 5 and 10 is common when respondents are given the opportunity to report their answers on a 0–100% scale (e.g., Manski and Molinari, 2010; Chapter 1 in this Handbook). Hence, forcing respondents to round answers by using a small set of physical objects may not be overly problematic, and needs to be balanced against the burden and comprehension of respondents. The coarseness of answers may be more relevant with very low probability events. Since 2017, the MLSFH has replaced beans with peanuts, which can be split in half, allowing respondents to express subjective probabilities in 5 percentage point increments, while maintaining the longitudinal design of 10 physical objects. Fewer than 2% of respondents opt to split the peanuts.

9.2.3 Interactive touchscreen

Data collection in developing countries increasingly involves hand-held devices, which present new avenues for eliciting beliefs. Maffioli and Mohanan (2018) discuss findings from a touchscreen-based application developed to elicit probabilistic expectations in India. Respondents could indicate a probability by moving the position of the slider from 0% at the extreme left to 100% at the extreme right. The application features dynamic images that change size relative to the probability reported by a respondent, while the slider's position also reveals the corresponding numerical probability. Maffioli and Mohanan (2018) randomly allocated respondents to this new touchscreen-based application or to a format with 20 beans. Reassuringly, the two formats generated a very similar distribution of beliefs for a wide range of outcomes, and required comparable data collection times, with respondents reporting a lower difficulty rating for the touchscreen. Noting the discussion above, this format also has the advantage of not forcing respondents to round their answers, since it gives them a scale from 0% to 100%. It also eliminates data entry errors. However, we should bear in mind that it has the potential to introduce user errors. While it is promising, more evidence is required to evaluate this type of method.

9.2.4 Proportion of people (like you)

In some studies, respondents are asked questions based on numbers of other people, or of people like themselves (sometimes in combination with physical objects). Such wordings may be appealing, since findings from psychology suggest that people can better apply probability theory when statistics are presented in the form of natural frequencies (Gigerenzer, 1991). For example, Chinkhumba et al. (2014), Godlonton et al. (2016), and Kerwin (2021) asked questions such as "*If 100 men, who do not have HIV, each sleep with a woman who is HIV-positive tonight and do not use a condom, how many of them do you think will have HIV after the night?*", and Delavande et al. (2017) asked "*Think about 10 people like you (same age, gender, income, etc.). Pick the number of beans to reflect how many will be alive in 5 years.*"

Conceptually, we need to remember that such questions elicit expectations of *population* risk, rather than *individual-specific* risk. In some contexts, researchers are interested in population risk. In others, they are interested in individual-specific risk but still elicit population risk. The two may, of course, not be identical, since (i) respondents may make various assumptions about the unspecified characteristics of those hypothetical other people, and (ii) respondents may have private information about themselves.

Indeed, when respondents in the Longitudinal Aging Study in India (LASI) were asked to give both population and individual-specific mortality expectations, more than half provided different answers, with a median difference of 20 percentage points (Delavande et al., 2017). Moreover, the difference was larger for respondents who reported being in poorer health.

In principle, if a researcher is interested in the beliefs pertaining to the individual respondent (to explain decision-making, for example), then individual-specific risk is the most desirable format. However, researchers may elicit population instead of individual-specific risk for any of the following reasons. First, it may increase response rates in some contexts. For example, respondents may feel uneasy talking about their own mortality (Delavande et al., 2017), or about an unborn child (Bhalotra et al., 2020), or they may be subject to desirability bias (Adams and Andrew, 2019; Galesic et al., 2018). In LASI, the response rate was marginally higher for population mortality expectations than for own mortality expectations, although they are not statistically different (Delavande et al., 2017). Second, researchers may believe it will help respondents to think about the concept in a less abstract way (see discussion in Delavande et al., 2011a). Finally, researchers interested in analyzing how expectations shape decisions may be concerned with the issue of endogeneity, which may be somewhat mitigated by using population risk since it is less likely to be correlated with unobserved individual characteristics (see discussion in Delavande and Kohler, 2016, and Attanasio et al., 2019).

9.2.5 Phone interviews

While face-to-face surveys have traditionally been used in LMICs, the increasing availability of inexpensive phones and the rapidly growing network coverage in many developing countries since the mid-2000s mean that mobile phones can be a useful tool for collecting data. More than three out of four people in LMICs own a phone, and about one in three have internet access (Fabregas et al., 2019). In terms of eliciting probabilistic expectations, use of phones does mean that interviewers cannot deploy physical objects or visual aids, unless participants own a smartphone, which is still not very common.

The existing evidence on phone surveys eliciting subjective probabilities in LMICs is very limited. Dillon (2012, 2017) and Jones et al. (2020) both conducted a face-to-face baseline survey and follow-up phone surveys. In the first study, respondents were provided with a laminated packet of visual aids for use during the follow-up phone interviews, and were given extensive training. This has probably resulted in high quality data, although the author does not specifically discuss differences between answers in face-to-face versus phone interviews.

In the 2020 MLSFH COVID-19 phone survey, most respondents had been exposed to probabilistic questions with a visual format in the past. Indeed, we began by asking respondents if they remembered using peanuts to respond to questions during our last visit, which 93% of 2261 people affirmed. We then asked them to imagine they were using peanuts to answer our new questions. The questions focused on Covid-19 and were therefore not directly comparable to earlier surveys. Nevertheless, the proportion of "don't knows" was low (under 1%) and similar to that in the 2019 face-to-face interviews. Some questions jointly tested knowledge of COVID−19 and understanding of probabilities. For example, respondents were asked to report the chance of a man contracting Covid-19 in the next 3 months, firstly while practicing rigorous social distancing and secondly while behaving similarly to before the pandemic. The average answers to these two questions were 16% and 74%, respectively. At the individual level, only 1.2% of respondents provided a strictly higher probability with social distancing than without.

While this is somewhat reassuring, more evidence is needed from samples who have not been previously exposed to probabilistic questions.

9.2.6 Eliciting subjective distribution of beliefs

So far, our focus has been on, and examples have been given of, eliciting beliefs about binary events. Often, researchers are interested in eliciting the full distribution of beliefs about a continuous outcome, such as income or price (see discussion in Chapter 1 in this Handbook). One option is to ask respondents to report multiple points in their cumulative distribution function of beliefs, meaning each question equates to asking about a binary event. For example, Delavande and Kohler (2009) asked respondents to report the likelihood of them dying within one year, 5 years and 10 years. However, this format can lead to violation of the monotonicity property of cumulative distribution functions. Interviewers can either prompt respondents to ensure that answers are non-decreasing, or the answers can be checked ex-post to see whether respondents understand probability. When the likelihood of dying in Malawi is elicited, the beans representing the 1-year horizon are left on the plate, and respondents are asked to *add* additional beans for a longer time horizon.

Another option is to ask respondents to allocate probability mass into several intervals to provide information on the density function. The use of physical objects such as beans, as in Delavande et al. (2011b), is particularly well suited to eliciting distributions, as respondents construct their own histograms. Other methods include asking respondents to think about people like themselves, as in De Mel et al. (2008) (think "*about 20 businesses that are just like yours. The owners have the same age, education, experience, skill level, commitment, and similar locations to you*"), or using a ruler, as in Attanasio and Augsburg (2016).

I am not aware of any studies in LMICs that compare distributions elicited by means of the two options above. However, Delavande and Rohwedder (2008) randomly allocated respondents to one of the two formats in the Internet survey of the US Health and Retirement Study. Distributions elicited by the two formats were very similar. The main advantage of the visual format eliciting a density is that it generates usable answers for virtually all respondents, while in the percent chance format a significant fraction (about 20%) of responses is lost due to violation of the monotonicity of a cumulative distribution. The same likely applies in LMICs.

Regardless of format, an important design issue is specification of intervals. One possibility is to use a common, predetermined support for all respondents. Preexisting data or prior knowledge is used to define the support, and a relatively large number of intervals is often given within this support. Another possibility is to ask respondents preliminary questions, such as their perceived maximum and minimum or a point estimate, and then use their answers to define a small number of individual-specific intervals (Kaufmann, 2014; Attanasio and Augsburg, 2016). One advantage of an individual-specific support is that it may enhance accuracy if the subjective distributions are heterogeneous, while a predetermined support may lead to excessively coarse intervals for many respondents. However, eliciting the support usually involves some real-time calculations. Enumerators using paper and pencil methods are less likely to make mistakes with a predetermined support. For example, in Yilma et al. (2015), 15% of households interviewed in Ethiopia featured an enumerator mistake in the threshold computations (reduced to 6% the following year). Tablet-based surveys may considerably reduce this risk.

As with a binary event, researchers also need to choose the number of physical objects. Ten and 20 stones appear to be the most common choices in the literature. Exceptions are Luseno et al. (2003) and

Lybbert et al. (2007), who both use 12 stones, with three states of nature. The advantage of 12 stones in their settings is that they allow respondents to answer with a uniform distribution, which would not be possible with 10 stones. Using a greater number of physical objects allows respondents to express their beliefs in a more refined way.

Delavande et al. (2011b) randomly allocated different elicitation formats to boat owners in India in order to test the sensitivity of expectations about future fish catches to several variations in elicitation design. They found that the spread of elicited distribution was slightly smaller under a 20-bean format than under a 10-bean format. One possible interpretation is that respondents have relatively concentrated beliefs around the mean of the distribution, but the availability of fewer beans may constrain their answers. In addition, respondents were asked about the distribution of the value of future catches, using both a predetermined support with many intervals and an individual-specific support with four intervals, and randomizing the order in which these were used. Reassuringly, the results showed that the distributions elicited with the two supports were remarkably consistent, suggesting that the subjective distribution elicited was quite robust to modifications in the elicitation design. In this context, the most accurate forecast is obtained using 20 beans (rather than 10) and a predetermined support.

These methods deliver probabilistic measures of certain percentiles of the subjective distribution. To move from these percentiles to means, medians, standard deviations, and other moments of interest requires the imposition of further assumptions. For example, McKenzie et al. (2013) and Dillon (2017) fit a log-normal distribution to the percentiles elicited, Attanasio and Augsburg (2016) assume a piecewise uniform probability distribution, and Delavande and Zafar (2019) fit respondents' answers to a beta distribution. See discussions relating to fitting distributions in Chapters 3 and 15 in this Handbook. Researchers might consider whether to use minimum and maximum from the preliminary questions to design the support in this fitting; however, the evidence suggests caution should be exercised (see discussion in Delavande et al. (2011a) and Chapter 1 in this Handbook).

9.2.7 Point expectations

Nonprobabilistic expectations such as *"At what age do you expect to receive benefits from a pension?"* in the China Health and Retirement Longitudinal Study and *"What is the highest education level you expect?"* in the Indonesian Family Life Survey are more commonly sought than probabilistic expectations. Although these questions are simple and straightforward to pose and answer, a common critique is that it is unclear whether people respond with the mean, mode, median, or other features of their subjective distribution of beliefs (see Chapter 1 in this Handbook). Delavande et al. (2011a) use data from De Mel et al. (2008) to compare point expectations (*"How much do you expect the profit of your business to be in December?"*) with the features of the fitted subjective distribution of beliefs. Although the point expectation is strongly correlated with the subjective mean and median, in more than half of cases the point expectation is closer to both the median and the mode than to the mean. Moreover, when assessing their predictive power for future outcomes, point expectations perform worse, and in this context there is considerable accuracy gain from eliciting the distribution (in particular because this elicitation format is less prone to outliers). This suggests some caution should be exercised in interpreting and using point expectations.

9.2.8 Piloting, interviewers' training and other considerations

The discussion so far has presented a few options for researchers interested in eliciting probabilistic expectations in developing countries. Ultimately, no settings are equal, and extensive piloting is crucial for evaluating which elicitation format is likely to deliver high-quality data. The education level of participants and the extent to which local games of chance can provide contextual knowledge are important factors. From my own experience based on small pilots, sliders appear to work well in peri-urban areas of Ghana, but leave respondents in rural Malawi confused. Unfortunately, with one exception (Aguila et al., 2014), the piloting process is rarely documented. Researchers should therefore allow sufficient time to pilot the methods and tailor them to the local context.

Another essential element is interviewer quality and training. Interviewers need to be, as a minimum, high school graduates, with an understanding of the concept of probability. This is not a challenging requirement, since interviewers are typically educated, but a refresher of probabilistic concepts may be useful. For example, from my own experience, some may fail to remember certain properties of probabilities, such as the monotonicity of a cumulative distribution function. It is evident that some interviewers are better at explaining these issues than others. There is, however, only limited evidence from systematic analysis of the effect of interviewers on subjective expectations. In an interesting recent study, Kerwin and Ordaz Reynoso (2021) document how elicited beliefs are significantly shifted by interviewers' knowledge about the events considered. The context is an interviewer-delivered randomized information experiment on HIV transmission risks in Malawi, where people tend to overestimate such risks. Respondents who were interviewed at baseline by interviewers who had already been trained to deliver the information treatment reported *lower* HIV transmission risks prior to the intervention. This is likely the result of the interviewer priming respondents, or encouraging guesses. Also, as discussed in Delavande et al. (2011a), some interviewers may be better at identifying and double-checking less credible answers.

Survey time is another key consideration when designing a questionnaire. Eliciting a probability may take between one and five minutes, while eliciting a full distribution can take up to 10 minutes if the support also needs to be elicited. Note that, because there is a fixed cost of initially explaining the question, subsequent elicitations can be obtained much more quickly. Maffioli and Mohanan (2018) report an overall completion time of 32 minutes for a survey that included various examples, 16 probabilistic questions about binary events, and basic demographic characteristics. Overall, this is not prohibitively high. Anecdotal evidence from the field also suggests that respondents welcome the change of pace that a visual aid injects within a lengthy interview.

As with any survey questions that entail some complexity, it is useful to start the questionnaire with some simple practice questions. These can pertain to expectations about events that are conceptually simple, and they can be used to evaluate whether individual respondents have difficulty with the concept of probabilities, as discussed in Section 9.3.2. Finally, as with any questionnaire design, it is important to be mindful of the potential role of framing, anchoring, and question ordering. For example, Delavande et al. (2017) document a framing effect in the elicitation of survival probabilities, with higher survival expectations reported with a survival format (chance of being alive in 10 years) than with a mortality format (chance of dying within a 10-year period). The differences are quite significant for longer time horizons, when uncertainty is likely to be greater. Brañas-Garza et al. (2020) find that collecting data on parental education before eliciting parental educational expectations for their children results in less optimistic expectations, as parental education may anchor respondents' answers.

9.3 Patterns of answers

Initial concerns relating to the elicitation of probabilistic expectations in both developed and developing countries included whether many individuals (especially nonliterate people) might not understand the concept of probability. There is now a large body of evidence demonstrating that this particular concern is unfounded, and that respondents are willing and able to express their beliefs in a probabilistic format. As a basic assessment of data quality, item nonresponse rates are typically very low in studies eliciting such data in LMICs (see also Delavande, 2014). In addition, elicited probabilistic expectations appear to be coherent and meaningful, according to various criteria: (i) the vast majority of respondents follow basic properties of probabilities, (ii) expectations vary with respondents' characteristics in the same way that actual outcomes vary with those characteristics, (iii) expectations are correlated with past and future outcomes in the expected direction, and, most importantly, (iv) expectations are important predictors of behavior, as discussed at length in the applications explored in Section 9.4. Another noteworthy feature is the vast heterogeneity in elicited expectations.

9.3.1 Respect of basic properties of probabilities

Researchers have used various types of preliminary questions to investigate whether respondents respect basic properties of probabilities.

Nested events: Delavande and Kohler (2009) investigated whether respondents in rural Malawi respected basic properties of probabilities by asking about two nested events: going to the market within (a) two days, and (b) two weeks. If respondents understood the concept of probability, their answer for the two-week period ought to have been larger than or equal to that for the two-day period. Only 1% violated the monotonicity property of the probability of nested events. This high consistency rate was not driven by respondents providing the same answers to both questions (only 6% of respondents did so). Asking about nested events has become a relatively standard check, and other studies have documented similarly low rates of violation of monotonicity (e.g., 0% among Indian fishermen in Delavande et al., 2011b; 0% in Bangladesh in Tarozzi et al., 2009; less than 1% in India in Attanasio and Augsburg, 2016; between 1% and 9% in India in Maffioli and Mohanan, 2018; and 3% of expectant Pakistani mothers in Bhalotra et al., 2020). Older respondents, though, may experience more difficulty: in LASI, 21% violated the monotonicity property (Delavande et al., 2017).

Certain events: Practice questions about certain events are sometimes posed in order to assess whether people are able to express the likelihood of events occurring with probability zero or one. Typically, all (or the vast majority of) respondents report a certain probability (e.g., Delavande et al., 2011b; Maffioli and Mohanan, 2018).

Known probability: Some practice questions may refer to known probabilities in order to assess respondents' numeracy and their ability to express known probabilities with a visual aid (e.g., "*Imagine I have five fishes, one of which is red and four of which are blue. If you pick one of these fishes without looking, how likely it is that you will pick the red fish?*", as in Delavande et al., 2011b). All but one respondent in Delavande et al. (2011b) gave the correct answer of a probability of one-fifth, while average answers were close to the known probabilities in Maffioli and Mohanan (2018).

Complement events: Another validation exercise is to test whether the sum of the probability of complement events is equal to one (e.g., Attanasio, 2009). In LASI, respondents were asked about the probability of winning and losing a game. Just over half answered that the sum was equal to one, or +/-10% of one.

9.3.2 Expectations and respondents' characteristics

Expectations are found to vary with characteristics in the same way that actual outcomes vary with those characteristics, at least qualitatively. This is an important validation exercise, as we expect individuals to infer what will happen to them based in part on what they observe in others. Delavande and Kohler (2009) provide a detailed description of the relationship between a wide range of subjective beliefs and respondents' characteristics. Despite substantial heterogeneity in beliefs, the mean and percentiles of the distribution of beliefs vary with observable characteristics in the *a priori* expected direction. For example, respondents' subjective probabilities of experiencing food shortages in the next 12 months vary meaningfully with respondents' socioeconomic status such as education, land ownership or having any savings. Attanasio and Augsburg (2016) find that Indian households headed by a person with formal education, or by married individuals, or by people from a higher caste expect a higher income in the coming year. In the context of the expected returns to schooling, several studies find an association between expected earnings and gender, socio-economic status, and test score (see Table 9.1 and discussion in Section 9.4.2). When investigating the relationship between survival probabilities and biomarkers, Delavande et al. (2017) find a positive association with height (a powerful indicator of health), and a negative association with hemoglobin concentration in men (low hemoglobin concentration being an indicator of anemia and a predictor of mortality).

9.3.3 Accuracy of elicited expectations

Manski (2004) describes three ways in which researchers have evaluated the accuracy of elicited expectations in developed countries. Similar comparisons have been made in LMICs.

Individual Expectations and Realizations: The most direct way of assessing accuracy is to follow respondents over time and compare the events that they experience with the expectations elicited from them. This requires longitudinal data or some form of follow-up data collection. Delavande et al. (2011b) find that Indian boat owners have accurate perceptions about the quantity of fish they are going to catch in the next month, although a few are overly optimistic about large catch values. In a similar sample, Delavande et al. (2011a) find that accuracy is improved when the time horizon for the prediction is shorter. Ciancio et al. (2020) find that respondents who reported a lower probability in 2010 of surviving the next 5 years are more likely to be dead by 2017.

Mean Expectations and Realizations: With repeated cross-sectional surveys, one can compare the expectations elicited at one point in time with later realizations in a different sample. McKenzie et al. (2013) compare the expectations of potential migrants (immigration ballot losers) with the income realized by similar migrants (immigration ballot winners) at the same point in time, allowing them to assess accuracy even in the presence of aggregate shocks. They find significant underestimation of labor earnings for men, possibly due to migrants reporting lower earnings to ease remittance pressures, but relatively accurate expectations for women.

Mean Expectations and Historical Realizations: Such comparisons assume that successive cohorts of individuals have the same distribution of realizations for the event considered. Attanasio and Augsburg

(2016) find a positive and large correlation in India between actual income in the past year and expected income in the next year, although the two are statistically different. Santos and Barrett (2011) elicit a year ahead expectations of rainfall and herd size from Ethiopian pastoralists. Herd size expectations vary with rainfall in a way that matches the nonstationary herd dynamics suggested by historical data. Giné et al. (2015) compare farmers' expectations and historical realizations about the onset of the monsoon in India. About a quarter of respondents report a subjective distribution that is significantly different from the historical distribution. Farmers whose income is more dependent on the monsoon are more accurate.

These methods enable evaluation of accuracy at the group level (see, e.g., discussion in Chapter 22 in this Handbook). An important question is how to interpret the lack of accuracy. First, aggregate shocks need to be ruled out, or taken into consideration if they are observable and measurable. Second, it is key to bear in mind that, when undertaking the comparisons discussed above, what is being tested is effectively the joint hypothesis of respondents understanding the question and having accurate expectations. If expectations are inaccurate, it is necessary to establish whether respondents have understood the questions and concepts. The evidence discussed so far is encouraging, and comprehension for a given sample can be assessed using basic questions such as the ones discussed in Section 9.3.1. Finally, the examples mentioned above suggest some general patterns in the deviation from accuracy. Respondents are less accurate in relation to events about which they have limited scope of learning (e.g., own death), when the event is far in time, when there are reasons for information frictions (e.g., remittance pressures), or when there is less incentive to learn (e.g., less critical to income). In addition to having limited access to information, individuals may use heterogeneous updating rules (Benjamin, 2019).

9.3.4 Heterogeneity in beliefs

Despite the regularity in the data presented so far, it should be stressed that there is substantial heterogeneity in beliefs, irrespective of the events considered (e.g., Delavande and Kohler, 2009). Moreover, a substantial part of the variation in beliefs is not explained by variation in observable characteristics. In least square regressions of expectations on characteristics, R-squares are typically low. This underscores the usefulness of eliciting expectations data instead of making assumptions about them.

A common pattern of expectation surveys is focal answers at 50, as well as 0 and 100, although this is less frequent with visual aids (Bruine de Bruin and Carman, 2018). Focal answers are discussed in Chapter 1 in this Handbook.

9.4 Applications

I now review the recent but growing literature in LMICs that focuses on how individuals' expectations shape their behavior, whether and why there are systematic misperceptions in some subgroups, and whether information provision can help people make better decisions. The papers are organized by substantive topics, but I discuss other innovations where applicable.

9.4.1 **Health**

Subjective expectations are an important determinant of health-related behaviors in LMICs, where individuals face substantial uncertainty about their own and others' health status, the local burden of disease, and the relationship between health inputs and outcomes. However, there is evidence that individuals hold inaccurate beliefs in some contexts. These misperceptions may be a significant driver of underinvestment in health; in particular, the low demand for preventive health (Dupas and Miguel, 2017; Kremer et al., 2019).

Survival: There is growing evidence that many individuals in LMICs are overly pessimistic about survival risk compared with life tables. In Malawi, Delavande and Kohler (2009) find that the median perceived five-year mortality risk exceeds the corresponding life table estimate by a factor of 3.2 for males and 4.1 for females. Similar patterns of pessimistic survival expectations have been documented in India and among migrants in Nepal (Delavande et al., 2017; Shrestha, 2020). This pessimism may be influenced by radical changes in objective survival probabilities in some contexts (Ciancio et al., 2021), by uncertainty about the objective risks, and by anchoring toward 50% (see Chapter 8 in this Handbook). It may dampen people's motivation to engage in healthy behaviors since they perceive that they will reap the returns only for a short period. Note that, at least in Malawi, this pessimism is less common when it comes to infant mortality. For example, the most common answer for the under-one-year mortality rate is 10% (which is close to the 9.8% infant mortality rate for rural areas in Malawi), with about 60% of respondents reporting a chance of 20% or less (Delavande and Kohler, 2009).

Despite this pessimism, individuals' survival expectations are responsive to technological advances that can alter the disease burden. Baranov and Kohler (2018) and Baranov et al. (2015) investigate the impact of the roll-out of antiretroviral therapy (ART) in Malawi on survival expectations and lifecycle decisions. Using a difference-in-difference identification strategy, they find that ART availability substantially reduces subjective mortality risk, including among HIV-negative respondents. They also find that ART has a significant impact on savings and human capital investment. However, in the context of noncommunicable diseases but still in Malawi, Ciancio et al. (2021) find that a referral letter for elevated blood pressure had no effect on survival expectations.

Individuals are also aware of the impact of health status on mortality risk. For example, respondents aged 45+ in Malawi expect a hypothetical healthy individual of their age and gender to have a 70% chance of surviving the next 5 years, compared with 62% for a person who is HIV+ and 49% for a person who is sick with AIDS (Ciancio et al., 2020).

Health status: Expectations about an individual's current health status are also likely to be an important determinant of health behavior. With HIV remaining a global health priority, HIV/AIDS-related expectations have been explored in some depth.

Perceptions relating to HIV status are important as they are likely related to demand for testing and adoption of safe-sex strategies. Evidence from qualitative beliefs tends to suggest that people overestimate the likelihood of being infected in high HIV-prevalence environments (e.g., Anglewicz and Kohler, 2009; Maughan-Brown and Venkataramani, 2018). However, the subjective probabilities of being currently infected with HIV described in Delavande and Kohler (2009) are relatively low. On average, respondents expect a 12% chance of being HIV+, compared to a sample HIV prevalence of 7%. Moreover, the distribution of subjective probabilities is relatively skewed, with a median belief of zero. The higher mean results from a subset of individuals viewing themselves as being at risk. Consistent with the pattern of observed HIV prevalence, divorced/separated/widowed respondents report the highest perceived probability of being HIV-positive; similarly, respondents with more sexual partners report a higher probability of being infected. This sample is somewhat atypical as respondents have had access to HIV testing as part of the MLSFH data collection. However, with increasing access to testing across Africa, it probably represents a picture closer to the current situation. For example, in 2014–2015 in Malawi, nearly 80% of individuals had been tested for HIV at least once (National Statistical Office/Malawi and ICF, 2017), compared with the 80% testing rate in the 2006 MLSFH (Delavande and Kohler, 2016). Adolescents' risk perceptions tend to be less accurate than those of adults in many contexts. In Malawi, adolescents overestimate their HIV status despite their limited sexual experience, possibly due to peer effects (Kim, 2016).

Several papers investigate the role of subjective probability of being HIV+ on health and lifecycle choices. Shapira (2017) develops a dynamic discrete-choice life-cycle fertility model in which expectations about life horizon and child survival depend on a perceived infection hazard. In counterfactual simulations, the presence of HIV is found to reduce the number of births, while HIV testing reduces the fertility of infected women.

Delavande and Kohler (2016) and de Paula et al. (2014) investigate the causal impact of HIV/AIDS-related beliefs on the decision to engage in risky sex. One concern relevant when analyzing the effect of beliefs about HIV status on behavior is the potential endogeneity of beliefs arising from the way current beliefs depend on past sexual behaviors. Unobserved heterogeneity capturing time-invariant preferences for risky sex may be correlated with beliefs about own HIV status if, for example, individuals revise their beliefs about the chance of being infected with HIV upwards after engaging in risky sex, or if this unobserved heterogeneity also influences the decision to get tested for HIV. De Paula et al. (2014) use a panel data estimator which accommodates unobserved heterogeneity as well as belief endogeneity arising from the dependence of current beliefs on lagged behaviors. They find that downward revisions in the subjective probability of being HIV-positive increase risky behavior while upward revisions decrease it.

Delavande and Kohler (2016) find that the decision to have multiple partners is influenced by expectations about survival and future HIV status (which in turn depend on the perceived impact of HIV/AIDS on survival, expectations about a person's own and their partner's current HIV status, and expectations about HIV transmission rates). They deal with the potential endogeneity of beliefs by estimating a system of equations that considers outcomes related to the propensity to engage in risky sex (e.g., learning HIV status) and relying on exclusion restrictions. Note that, despite their concern, the empirical results suggest that, in this context, there is no endogeneity issue when estimating the impact of HIV-related expectations on the number of sexual partners. Policy simulations indicate that information campaigns on HIV transmission risks, which are currently overestimated, would have a perverse effect, increasing the probability of multiple partners. However, information on mortality risk would reduce it.

Testing: In many contexts, individuals may have access to a testing technology that reveals information about their health status. Current beliefs about health status may influence the uptake of a testing technology. The results in Delavande and Kohler (2012) suggest that HIV testing is selective, in that individuals who believe they have a higher chance of being infected with HIV are less likely to attend a clinic to learn their test result. Maffioli et al. (2021) find a limited effect of beliefs about having malaria on malaria testing uptake in Kenya.

Testing can then lead to a revision of beliefs about health status and to behavioral changes. Due to the selection into testing, different empirical strategies have been used to study this question. Gong

(2015) uses a random assignment to HIV testing, and finds behavioral responses when test results provide unexpected information. Individuals who receive an unexpected HIV-positive (HIV-negative) test increase (decrease) their risky sexual behavior.

Delavande and Kohler (2012) and Eriksson and Sovero (2016) investigate the causal impact on health expectations and behavior of a person learning their own (and potentially their spouse's) HIV status. The authors rely on a randomized experiment in which respondents receive no, or a small, financial incentive to learn their HIV test result (Thornton, 2008). Delavande and Kohler (2012) find that receiving an HIV-negative test results in a higher subjective probability of being infected with HIV, although the effect disappears in HIV-negative couples who also learn their spouse's status. This is consistent with the observed effect of testing on behavior. In married couples where both people are HIV-negative, an individual learning only their own status is associated with a decrease in consistent condom use with at least one partner, while learning both theirs and their partner's status is associated with an increase in condom use.

With a focus on testing of couples, Angelucci and Bennett (2021) find that, in the context of a randomized, high-frequency, "opt-out" HIV testing intervention, women whose partners underwent multiple HIV tests became more confident that their partner was HIV-negative, while those whose partners had one or no tests became less confident. This intervention also increased marriage and pregnancy rates. This is consistent with asymmetric information in the marriage market causing adverse selection and delay in marriage if partner quality (sexual safety) is hard to observe.

Note that learning one's own or others' health status may also lead to the revision of other relevant health expectations. For example, Godlonton and Thornton (2013), again relying on Thornton's (2008) randomized experiment for identification, find that as more people in a village learn their HIV results, individuals revise their beliefs downwards about people they suspect to have died from AIDS, which is consistent with a perceived decrease in HIV prevalence at the village level (and leads to a reduction in condom use). Delavande and Kohler (2012) find that, among HIV-positive respondents, learning their status resulted in lower perceptions of HIV transmission risk, presumably because some also learnt that their partners were HIV-negative.

Testing hence has ramifications for health status beliefs about oneself and others, as well as for a wide range of health-related expectations and health behaviors.

Subjective health returns to behavior: Another important focus has been on the expected health returns to health behavior (i.e., the relationship between health inputs and outcomes), and on how they shape choices. These are typically elicited by asking respondents their expected health outcomes in hypothetical scenarios. These health returns to behavior are sometimes called individual subjective treatment effects, whereby the potential "treatment" is the adoption of health behavior and the potential "outcomes" are the health outcomes.

In the context of HIV, there is evidence that individuals overestimate HIV transmission risk conditional on some behaviors. For example, respondents in Malawi report, on average, a 93% chance of becoming HIV+ within 12 months if married to an HIV-positive spouse, compared with seroconversion rates in Uganda of between 5% and 11% (Delavande and Kohler, 2016). Individuals also vastly overestimate the transmission risk of one unprotected sexual act (Sterck, 2014). Note that this suggests that respondents would engage in *more* risk-taking behavior if they became aware that actual transmission risks were significantly lower (Delavande and Kohler, 2016), except where fatalistic behavior is common (Sterck, 2014; Kerwin, 2021). People in Africa also appear to be unaware of the reduced transmission risk associated with being on ART (Bor et al., 2021; Derksen et al., 2021). For example, students in South Africa perceive, on average, a 73% annual risk of HIV transmission with virally suppressive ART, whereas the objective risk is below 1%. They also perceive that, on average, ART reduces the annual transmission risk by 17%, while the objective reduction is above 96% (Bor et al., 2021). Individuals also seem unaware of the benefits of certain other HIV risk-mitigating technologies, such as circumcision, which may restrict their adoption (Godlonton et al., 2016).

Indoor air pollution is a global health threat. Chattopadhyay et al. (2021) asked households in India about the expected likelihood of a hypothetical individual becoming sick given two different cooking fuel options. Respondents recognized the possible health benefits from clean fuel usage, and this was associated with actual usage. Other interesting examples eliciting subjective health returns include Miller et al. (2020), focusing on contraception choice in Mozambique, and Mahajan et al. (2020), on the adoption of insecticide-treated nets in India.

9.4.2 Education

Many children in LMICs do not attend school or drop out early despite high returns. There are several explanations for this, including credit constraint, lack of access to schools, and high discount rates. Another important factor may be that parents and youth are misinformed about the returns to schooling. This has prompted a growing body of research measuring expectations about the returns to schooling. See also Chapter 7 in this Handbook for a broader overview of the literature.

Labor market returns to education: Following the pioneering work of Dominitz and Manski (1996), various studies describe students' (and/or parents') expectations about the returns to schooling, typically in terms of future earnings (sometimes employment), by asking expectations conditional on several levels of schooling. Although some elicit a point estimate ("*How much do you expect to earn at age 30 if you complete primary school?*", "*How much do you expect to earn at age 30 if you complete high school?*"), many elicit conditional subjective distributions of future earnings, which in addition permit measurement of the variance in earnings. While the question wording is not identical across settings, there is now evidence from various LMICs on expectations about the returns to schooling.

Table 9.1 presents a summary of studies on the expected returns to schooling in different LMICs. Some of these studies contain interesting analysis of the correlates of expectations, with associations between expected earnings and gender, socio-economic status, and test scores found across various contexts. Other studies provide comparisons with actual earnings data. Most compare the expectations that students currently hold about their earnings in the future (e.g., when they are aged 30) with the earnings of 30-year-olds. These comparisons are informative about the accuracy of expectations only if one assumes that successive cohorts have the same distribution of realized earnings, which may be a strong assumption. An alternative way to assess accuracy in cross-section is to also ask respondents their perceptions of current earnings of 30-year-olds, which can then be compared with population earnings (see, e.g., Jensen, 2010, and Delavande and Zafar, 2019). Eliciting expectations both about own future earnings and perceived current population earnings is also useful for understanding whether heterogeneity in expectations is driven by inaccurate information on prevailing wages in the labor market or private information about oneself. The evidence suggests that, in several contexts, students or parents hold expectations about earnings conditional on a university degree that are above the earnings of people with a degree. However, their expectations of earnings conditional on primary- or secondary-school education tend to be lower than observed earnings (Table 9.1).

Table 9.1 Summary of studies on expected returns to schooling.

Study	Country	Participants	Correlates of expectations of future earnings	Comparisons with population earnings	If yes, do participants over-estimate/underestimate/have accurate expectations compared to population earnings
Gamboa and Rodríguez-lesmes (2018)	Colombia	High school students	Age, gender, socio-economic background, school characteristics	Yes	Relatively accurate for the average earnings with high school or vocational school completion/Overestimate the earnings with university completion
Bonilla-Mejía et al. (2019)	Colombia	High school students	N/A	Yes	Overestimate the earnings with university completion
Jensen (2010)	Dominican Republic	Primary school students (8th grade boys)	N/A	Yes	Underestimate the earnings with primary education/Overestimate the earnings with secondary and tertiary education
Maertens (2011)	India	Household decision-makers	Number of people known outside of village with such degree, caste, child's gender, child's age	No	N/A
Chari and Maertens (2014)	India	Parents	Child's gender	No	N/A
Armand et al. (2019)	Macedonia	Parents	Local labor market characteristics	No	N/A
Nguyen (2008)	Madagascar	Parents of primary school students	Wealth	Yes	Median perceptions of population returns to schooling are well aligned with estimated average returns, but with large dispersion in perceived returns
Attanasio and Kaufmann (2014)	Mexico	High school students/mothers of high school students	Child's gender and age, having a father who is an employer, family income, parental education	Yes	Roughly accurate
Estrada and Gignoux (2017)	Mexico	High school students	Test score, private junior high school, parental education, parental occupation, asset, gender	No	N/A
Avitabile and de Hoyos (2018)	Mexico	High school students	N/A	Yes	Underestimate the average earnings with high school completion/Overestimate the earnings with university completion
Gradín et al. (2020)	Mozambique	University students	Age, course duration, performance at job, university, subject	No	N/A

continued on next page

Table 9.1 (*continued*)

Study	Country	Participants	Correlates of expectations of future earnings	Comparisons with population earnings	If yes, do participants overestimate/underestimate/have accurate expectations compared to population earnings
Jones et al. (2020)	Mozambique	University students	Gender, subject, previous work experience	Comparison of students expectations with their realized earnings	Overestimate the earnings with university completion
Delavande and Zafar (2019)	Pakistan	Male university students	University type	No	N/A
Favara et al. (2021)	Peru	High school students	Gender, living in a poorer household, numeric skills, self-efficacy	Yes	Relatively accurate for the average earnings with high school completion/Overestimate the earnings with university completion
Prakhov (2021)	Russia	High school students	Full-time study, tuition-free study, subject, gender, average salary in the university region	No	N/A
Nikolov and Jimi (2018)	Tanzania	Household members	Experience, gender, education	Yes	Underestimate the earnings with primary and secondary school level education

One of the primary reasons for eliciting expectations about the returns to schooling is to better understand educational investment. There is now widespread evidence that expectations about future earnings predict educational choices (see Chapter 7 in this Handbook), including in LMICs. For example, Attanasio and Kaufmann (2014) examine the role of expected earnings and unemployment risk in Mexico in the decision to continue into further education. Boys' expectations predict their decision to enter college, but not to enter senior high school. While girls' expectations do not predict their educational decisions, mothers' expectations are strong predictors of their daughters' decisions. See also Favara et al. (2021) for the case of Peru and Kaufmann (2014), who finds that less well-off individuals in Mexico require higher expected returns in order to be induced to attend college than individuals from rich families, which is consistent with the former being credit-constrained.

Nonpecuniary returns to education: Psychic costs or nonpecuniary outcomes are also thought to be important determinants of educational choices. Delavande and Zafar (2019) investigate the role of expected monetary returns, nonpecuniary factors enjoyed at school, and financial constraints in university choice in Pakistan, conditional on participation in higher education. They find that labor market prospects play only a small role. Instead, nonpecuniary outcomes, such as a school's ideology, are the major determinants. Financial constraints are also important. Three methodological innovations are worth noting. First, the authors use stated instead of actual university choice of university students to ensure that the expectations measured are those held at the time of the (stated) choice, which is used as an outcome variable. Second, the probability of dropout from university is explicitly modeled and depends on the same structural parameters as those relevant to university choice. Hence, the authors use both stated choice and the subjective probability of dropout as outcomes to identify and estimate the model using a generalized method of moments (GMM) procedure. Third, when conducting policy simulations, they allow expectations to vary with the policy considered (for example, expectations of dropout are assumed to depend on school fees, which vary by policy).

Another example is marriage market returns to education. Attanasio and Kaufmann (2017) find that youths in Mexico expect their spouses to have close to 30% higher earnings if they themselves have a college degree instead of a high school degree. Adams and Andrew (2019) measure Indian parents' beliefs about how the quality of marriage offers varies with a young woman's age and education. Those are beliefs over a large state space. Thus, instead of being directly elicited using the methods discussed so far, average beliefs are inferred from a series of discrete choices in hypothetical vignettes. Note that this method recovers sample average beliefs rather than individual-specific beliefs. Conditional on a marriage match, parents place little intrinsic value on a daughter's education.

Source of information friction in education: It is important to understand why misperceptions exist and persist. One possibility is that students and parents live in segregated neighborhoods, and individuals with low education tend to live in poor neighborhoods. Jensen (2010) presents some suggestive evidence for the Dominican Republic. Using longitudinal data, Armand et al. (2019) show that contemporaneous variations in local labor markets affect the way parents from poor households in Macedonia update their expectations. Mismatch between the profiles of jobs expected and realized may be another explanation, as discussed by Jones et al. (2020) for university students in Mozambique. Another possibility might be a lack of information about an individual's own academic ability, although the existing evidence does not seem to support this hypothesis (Estrada and Gignoux, 2017; Sequeira et al., 2016).

9.4.3 Parental investment in children

Gaps in children's development by socio-economic status emerge early in childhood (World Bank, 2015). Differences in parental behaviors are likely an important factor in the emergence of unequal capabilities in children. This has prompted recent work measuring parental beliefs about the technology of skill production in developed countries (Cunha et al., 2020) and, more recently, in LMICs, to assess whether heterogeneity in beliefs is responsible for the heterogeneity in parental behavior. These beliefs are typically elicited by asking parents about the expected outcomes of a hypothetical child in different scenarios of parental investment, sometimes coupled with different scenarios of child endowment.

Bhalotra et al. (2020) focus on the very early years in Pakistan, a context where maternal depression is common. They elicit maternal beliefs about the benefits of breastfeeding and stimulation, as well as the expected cost of these investments. There is heterogeneity across mothers in expected effort costs (in particular, by depression status) and expected returns, which contributes to explaining heterogeneity in investments. They find no significant heterogeneity in preferences for child developmental outcomes by socio-economic and depression status. Attanasio et al. (2019) elicit parental beliefs in the context of a follow-up of a randomized stimulation intervention in Colombia. They find that mothers tend to underestimate the productivity of parental investments, compared with the objective production function estimated from panel data. Nonetheless, parents who expect higher returns invest more in their children. Giannola (2020) is interested in intra-household inequality in child development in India, and finds that parents allocate more resources to children with high endowment.

9.4.4 **Migration, income, and the labor market**

Income and labor market expectations are relevant for a wide range of decisions, including migration, occupation choices, and job search (see Chapter 22 in this Handbook).

While there is a general concern that potential migrants are overoptimistic about economic prospects abroad, McKenzie et al. (2013) in Tonga and Baseler (2021) in rural Kenya find that individuals underestimate earnings in New Zealand and Kenyan big cities, respectively. This underestimation may be sustained by income hiding from migrants who try to mitigate the pressure to send remittances. In McKenzie et al. (2013), income expectations are positively associated with the decision to apply to a migration lottery.

Employment expectations are also relevant for job search behavior, performance in recruiter-administered test, and occupational choices (Beam, 2021; Godlonton, 2020; Keats, 2012). For example, Beam (2021) finds that higher perceived probability of finding a job abroad increases participation in a job fair for overseas work in the Philippines, as well as in job applications. Despite their importance, beliefs about job prospects appear optimistic in Uganda (Bandiera et al., 2021), Ethiopia (Abebe et al., 2021), and South Africa (Banerjee and Sequeira, 2020). Interestingly, in a rare survey of firms in LMICs, Abebe et al. (2021) document that firms likewise have unrealistically high expectations about job-seeker quality, highlighting misperceptions on both sides of the labor market.

Labor market expectations are also affected by training opportunities. In Uganda, Bandiera et al. (2021) find that youth offered vocational training become more optimistic about their job prospects and search for jobs more intensively. However, perhaps counterintuitively, youth who are additionally offered matching to firms revise their expectations downwards, possibly because of low callback rates. This leads the latter group having worse labor market outcomes in the long run. See also Banerjee and Sequeira (2020).

9.4.5 **Agricultural inputs and outputs**

Rural households living off agricultural production face substantial income fluctuations due to input and output price variation, input quality, weather shock and land tenure insecurity. Inaccurate beliefs may be one cause of suboptimal decision-making that reduces food and income security. I discuss work pointing to the difficulty in learning from one's environment.

For example, Giné et al. (2015) find that Indian farmers whose income is more dependent on the monsoon hold more accurate beliefs about the monsoon's timing. Moreover, farmers with inaccurate beliefs are more likely to make planting errors. In Malawi, Maertens et al. (2021) find a positive correlation between farmers' baseline expectations about yields and their knowledge score after receiving a demonstration of a new product. The results of both papers are consistent with learning being a choice, constrained by factors such as time, credit and cognitive resources.

Adoption of modern agricultural technologies, such as fertilizers and hybrid seeds, remains puzzlingly low in many LMICs, especially in Sub-Saharan Africa. A series of papers investigates whether low input quality, and difficulty in learning about input quality, may explain this. Bold et al. (2017) establish that inputs are of poor and heterogeneous quality in Ugandan markets, yielding low average returns. Farmers' expectations reveal that they are aware, on average, of this poor quality; however, the substantial variations in expectations suggest their ability to infer quality is limited. Farmers also expect low-quality input to result in lower yield. Taken together, these factors may explain why farmers do not adopt modern inputs. They calibrate a learning model emphasizing that the ability to learn about quality is limited because agricultural yields are noisy, explaining the low-quality equilibrium observed in the data. See also Ashour et al. (2019), Michelson et al. (2021), and Hoel et al. (2021).

Output price uncertainty also influences farmers' decisions. Hill (2009, 2010) focuses on Ugandan coffee farmers, and finds that perceived coffee price risk is substantial and highly heterogeneous across households. Coffee prices received in past seasons and the salience of particular prices explain a significant portion of this variation. Importantly, the perceived probability of a negative return to producing coffee is negatively associated with labor allocation to coffee production.

Expectations data about tenurial insecurity have also been used to shed light on contracting decisions in LMICs, in particular sharecropping (Bellemare, 2009a,b, 2012), as well as the absence of insurance markets for crops (Dillon, 2017).

9.4.6 Conflicts and natural disasters

Surprisingly, there is little evidence to date on expectations of conflicts, political instability and natural disasters. Moreover, we know little about how these negative events influence expectation formation in other domains. Some notable expectations include Bozzoli et al. (2011), who report that higher exposure to violent conflict in northern Uganda depresses individual expectations about the future economic situation, and Brück et al. (2011), who find that natural disasters and terrorist attacks influence individual perceptions of the reward to entrepreneurialism.

9.4.7 Information experiments

Our discussion so far suggests that lack of knowledge and information frictions are potential barriers to welfare-enhancing investments. As a result, a large body of research has studied the effect of information provision, which is generally a cost-effective policy. Existing reviews include Dupas and Miguel (2017) for health choices, Fabregas et al. (2019) for agricultural decisions, and Kremer et al. (2019) for behaviors pertinent to development economics.

While information interventions have large effects in some settings, and small or no effects in others, we still have limited understanding of these overall mixed findings. Many factors come into play, such as whether informational gaps – as opposed to other institutional or financial constraints – are really binding constraints for behavioral change; whether the information is easily accessible to those for whom it is relevant; whether individuals trust the source of information, and how information is disseminated. One difficulty is that beliefs are rarely measured in studies investigating the role of information on behavior, meaning researchers cannot test directly whether beliefs were inaccurate prior to the information, and whether the information provision was effective in changing the targeted beliefs in the intended direction, or whether it operated through another channel (such as making a behavior more salient). I review here some work that has specifically elicited beliefs as part of a randomized information experiment. See Chapter 4 in this Handbook and Haaland et al. (forthcoming) for a discussion on the rationale and design of these types of experiments.

Health: A few studies investigate the impact of information on HIV transmission risk on beliefs, HIV testing, and risky sex. For example, Chinkhumba et al. (2014) investigate whether information provision on how medical male circumcision reduces the likelihood of men contracting HIV, and also price subsidies, increase the demand for male circumcision in urban Malawi. They find overall very low demand for male circumcision, with a small positive effect of information and price intervention. The main barriers to male circumcision (cultural norms and fear of pain) do not seem to be affected by price and information. See also Godlonton et al. (2016). In a related study, Maughan-Brown et al. (2015) show that men who correctly internalize the protective benefits of male circumcision in response to randomly assigned information also incorrectly infer that it directly reduces a woman's HIV infection risk, despite a lack of information or discussion about female risk in the intervention. This emphasizes that information can spill over into different beliefs, sometimes erroneously.

Also related to HIV transmission risk, Derksen et al. (2021) delivered information about ART considerably reducing that risk via community health meetings in Malawi. The intervention led to a large downward shift in expectations about transmission risk when on ART, and an increase in testing. In the context of an information about the (low) average risk of HIV transmission, Kerwin (2021) finds evidence of fatalism in Malawi, with those with high transmission risk beliefs engaging in more risk-taking because the high perceived chance of being already infected decreases the marginal cost of such behavior.

Still in the same context, Ciancio et al. (2021) investigate the impact of information about population mortality risk on risky sexual behavior by mature Malawians, a context in which people are pessimistic about their survival. The intervention had a positive treatment effect on safe sex practices. The mechanism behind this behavioral change included an upward revision of the perceived HIV transmission risk associated with multiple partners, which was not targeted but is consistent with the positive treatment effect on the survival expectations of HIV-positive people. There were, however, limited effects on individuals' own survival risk.

In another domain, Brown et al. (2017) provided information on household water quality in Cambodia. The information changed households' beliefs – especially those of low-SES households – about the health risks posed by their source of water, with a waning effect over time. Low-SES households were also more likely to purchase a treatment product, but consistency of use was low. Higher-SES households were more pessimistic to begin with, and did not change their (higher) hygiene-improving behavior as a result of the information.

These results are encouraging but there are a few important lessons. These are that other constraints may prevent people from acting on newly acquired information, that not all expectations are equally malleable and effects may fade over time, and that information interventions can have ramifications for a wide range of health beliefs.

Education: The misinformation about the returns to schooling discussed in Section 9.4.2 suggests that providing information about future earnings conditional on educational outcomes might be a successful avenue for increasing educational attainment. In a pioneering study, Jensen (2010) is motivated by the returns to secondary schooling perceived by primary school boys in the Dominican Republic being extremely low compared to measured returns. Students from randomly selected schools were informed about the returns, estimated from earnings data. The perceived returns of all students increased when they were reinterviewed 6 months later, regardless of parental wealth. Four years later, those from the least poor households had completed significantly more schooling, suggesting that both lack of information and credit constraints are important. See also Nguyen (2008) for a similar approach in Madagascar.

Section 9.4.2 also emphasizes that, in some contexts, high school and university students seem to hold expectations about future earnings that are above current population earnings, e.g., Bonilla-Mejía et al. (2019) in Colombia, and Jones and Santos (2020) in Mozambique. In both studies, beliefs are persistent with no, or only a moderate, response to information about college earnings. Jones and Santos (2020) find larger effects for more tailored information.

The evidence to date suggests that information interventions in education in LMICs might be more successful in primary and secondary school contexts for modifying beliefs and promoting education. It is less clear in relation to university enrollment, since beliefs appear to be more persistent. Note that credit constraints may blunt the effect of such interventions, and these constraints may be starker at the tertiary level.

Information interventions related to individual skills and ability are another potential avenue for correcting information frictions in education (e.g., Bobba and Frisancho, 2020; Dizon-Ross, 2019; Franco, 2019). See Chapter 4 in this Handbook for discussion of these papers. Related interventions include providing information about school quality, as in Andrabi et al. (2017) in India.

Agricultural Input: We discuss in Section 9.4.5 prevalent misinformation about input quality, and the limited opportunity for learning by doing in agriculture. This has led to the design of interventions to tackle these issues.

Gars et al. (2020) study the impact of information provision on soil quality in India combined with fertilizer recommendations, while measuring beliefs about the optimal quantity of fertilizers. On average, the recommendations increased the application of some inputs, while the precision of prior beliefs affected the demand for and responsiveness to information. Tjernström et al. (2021), focusing on fertilizer adoption by maize farmers in western Kenya, implemented an interactive, "gamified" information intervention designed to overcome the limited opportunities for farmers to learn about the effectiveness of fertilizers. The game was played on a researcher-provided tablet and allowed farmers to experiment with different fertilizers. Farmers revised their beliefs about input returns upwards after using the games.

Migration and job search: A few recent studies seek to investigate the impact of information on the decision to migrate, in contexts where mobility is low despite being welfare-enhancing. Beam (2016) examines the effect on labor market outcomes and expectations in the Philippines of providing overseas wage information, information about minimum qualifications for overseas work, and a voucher for job fair attendance. Wage information increased the likelihood of people having a current passport (a prerequisite for migration), while the job fair voucher increased the likelihood of them working in the formal sector. Each of the three interventions had a different effect on labor market expectations, suggesting that they filled different knowledge gaps. Baseler (2021) finds that providing information about urban earnings to rural Kenyans increased migration to the capital city. Shrestha (2020) focuses on misinformation about earnings returns and the mortality risks of migrating from Nepal. Information on death rates abroad lowered expected mortality rates for potential migrants who had never worked abroad (making migration more attractive), while information on earnings lowered their expected earnings (making migration less attractive). These changes in expectations led to changes in migration decisions by inexperienced potential migrants. See also Bah et al. (2020).

Policy: The information that government officials use to make decisions determines the effectiveness of public policy. Hjort et al. (2021) find that mayors in Brazil update their beliefs about policy effectiveness when informed of research findings, and that information increases the probability of policy implementation. See also Rogger and Somani (2018).

Design considerations in LMICs: In the same way that visual aids are important for belief elicitation, they can be useful for conveying information in ways that can be easily understood. Some studies also present narratives or qualitative evidence together with quantitative information (e.g., Ciancio et al., 2021, Bah et al., 2020). In Ciancio et al. (2021), the narratives delivered by video seemed more effective than precise statistical information in changing beliefs, with a significant effect on beliefs one year after the intervention. Such narratives may be more important in LMICs, although more research is required to confirm this.

Most of the studies described here include a control group which receives no information. This design is well suited to answering policy-relevant questions, such as whether an information campaign would impact behavior. Another option is to give information unrelated to the main treatment to the control group, as in Bah et al. (2020). Motives for doing so include ensuring that respondents' time and exposure to the study are similar across treatment arms, to maximize comparability. A third option is to give different information about the main outcome to different groups, as in Shrestha (2020). Through a random choice of different districts in Nepal about which to give information, some respondents in this study received information about high death rate districts and others about low death rate districts. This design has the advantage of creating variation in belief among individuals with different sets of priors. See the discussion in Haaland et al. (forthcoming).

9.5 Datasets

Although most of the researchers whose work has been mentioned above have purposefully collected their own data, there are growing opportunities to use existing surveys with (some) public access. Table 9.2 presents a list of selected datasets from LMICs which collected expectations data, with information on countries, sample size, participants, and topics.

9.6 Conclusions

Overall, the evidence from existing work eliciting probabilistic expectations in LMICs is positive and encouraging. As shown for high-income countries, respondents in LMICs are able and willing to express their beliefs in probabilistic formats, and these data are useful for drawing inferences on decision-making under uncertainty.

The elicitation methods developed for LMICs that use physical objects as visual aids may be useful with other populations that may be less literate and numerate, such as children, teenagers, and underprivileged groups in high-income countries. These methods lead to high response rates, elicit answers that are consistent with probabilities, are particularly well suited for eliciting distributions, and typically engage respondents. Physical objects can be adapted for use in online surveys, as in Delavande and Rohwedder (2008). More generally, visual aids are likely to help all types of respondents. I thus encourage researchers to consider the methods described here in settings beyond LMICs.

While the early work in development economics had a large focus on survey design, recent work has centered more on applications of relevance to LMICs. Both areas are vital and should continue to be a focus of research efforts. In particular, an understanding of how to elicit imprecise probabilities or ambiguity in LMICs would be beneficial (see Chapter 26 in this Handbook). In addition, researchers should strive to document their efforts (successes or failures) in the field, as this can only benefit the scientific community.

Table 9.2 Dataset collecting expectations data in LMICs.

Datasets	Country	Start date	Topics	Point or Probabilistic Expectations	Waves	Sample Size
Argentina Inflation Expectations Survey	Argentina	2006	Inflation	Point	Monthly	~1200
Belarus Expectations of the Population	Belarus	2017	Inflation	Point	Quarterly since November 2017	~1000 until May 2018, ~2000 afterwards
Brazilian Longitudinal Study of Aging	Brazil	2015	Pension	Yes/No	Wave 1	~9400
China Family Panel Study	China	2010	Parental expectations about child's academic achievement	Point	Baseline, Follow-ups 1, 2, 3, and 4	~16,000 households
China Health and Retirement Study	China	2011	Employment, Unemployment, Earnings, Pension	Point	Every 2 to 3 years	~17,500
Costa Rican Longevity and Healthy Ageing Study	Costa Rica	2005 (pre-1945 cohort), 2010 (1945-195 retirement cohort)	Mortality, Pension, Income, Expenditure	Point and Probabilistic	Waves 1–3 for both cohorts (biennial)	~2800 per cohort
Young Lives	Ethiopia, India, Peru, Vietnam	2002	Education, Employment Marriage and Parenthood	Point and Probabilistic Point	Round 5 Young Child Cohort (Age 15)	~12,000 (1000 in Older Cohort and 2000 in Younger Cohort, per country)
			Education, Migration	Point	Round 4, Older Child Cohort (Age 19)	
Longitudinal Aging Study in India	India	Pilot: 2010, 2017/18	Earnings, Inflation Heath and Survival	Point Probabilistic	Pilot, Wave 1	~1600 in pilot, ~72,250 at wave 1
Reserve Bank of India Inflation Expectations of Households	India	2016	Inflation	Point	Quarterly	~6000 households
Indonesia Family Life Survey	Indonesia	1993/94	Retirement, Employment, Health	Point	2,3,4,5	~22,000
Malaysia Aging and Retirement Survey	Malaysia	2018	Employment	Point	Wave 1	~5600
Malawi Longitudinal Study of Families and Health	Malawi	1998	HIV/AIDS-related outcomes, Survival, Economic shocks	Probabilistic	From 2006	~4000
Mexican Health and Aging Study	Mexico	2001	Pension	Point	2001, 2003, 2012, 2015, 2018	15,000

continued on next page

Table 9.2 (*continued*)

Datasets	Country	Start date	Topics	Point or Probabilistic Expectations	Waves	Sample Size
Programa de Educacion, Salud y Alimentacion (PROGRESA)	Mexico	2005	Education	Point and Probabilistic	2005	23,000
Philippines Consumer Expectations Survey	Philippines	2004	Inflation, Unemployment	Point	Quarterly	~2400
Trajectories in Education and Careers	Russia	2011	Expected Scores, Salary, Cost of University, Effort	Point	Wave 3	~3800
			STEM choice, Enrollment, University admission,	Probabilistic	Wave 3	
			Earnings, Profession	Point	Wave 4	
			Earnings	Point	Waves 5 and 6	
South Africa Bureau for Economic Research Inflation Expectation Survey	South Africa	2000	Inflation	Point	Quarterly	~2000
Panel Survey and Study on Health, Aging, and Retirement in Thailand	Thailand	2015	Employment, Mortality, Personal Finance, Inheritance	Probabilistic	Wave 1 and 2 (Annual)	~5600 households
Demographic and Health Surveys	90 countries	1984	Future childbearing intentions	Point	400 surveys	Between 5000 and 30,000 households per country, typically every 5 years

To facilitate international comparisons, it would be useful if researchers designing surveys were to use, if appropriate, question wording that has been used elsewhere. I describe research on the expected returns to schooling, and while the wording tends to be similar across studies, the results are not always comparable. In some cases, large-scale surveys, such as the Health and Retirement Study and its sister surveys, can be useful models in this respect. Of course, there is a tradeoff between innovation and ensuring comparability with other studies.

In terms of specific areas, health, education and the labor market, and agriculture have attracted the lion's share of research to date. Other topics merit further investigation. These include expectations about inflation, for which some data in LMICs exist, and which have received considerable attention in high-income countries (see Chapter 5 in this Handbook), together with expectations about the economy more broadly. There are also important topics for which there is a dearth of data in LMICs, such as firm expectations (as described in Chapters 11 and 12 in this Handbook for high-income countries), and expectations about political instability, conflicts, and climate change.

Misinformation in various domains has been documented, with potential causes that include neighborhood segregation reducing information flow, limited governmental resources for collecting and diffusing information, incentives not to share relevant information, lack of opportunity for learning, and cognitive and time barriers. Information provision may help individuals to make more informed decisions, and the spread of mobile phone coverage opens a new avenue for sharing information in a very cost-effective way, with the potential to roll out individual-specific information via phone messaging. As with any intervention, care needs to be taken to ensure such interventions are acceptable in a specific local cultural context.

The existing evidence on information provision reveals some positive impacts on beliefs and, sometimes, behaviors. It is, however, important to bear in mind that other constraints (e.g., financial, cultural) may be binding, and possibly more so in LMICs, implying that the behavioral effects may be small or limited to subgroups. A key lesson learnt from studies in LMICs is that information provision can have an effect on a wide set of beliefs, including some not specifically targeted by the intervention. With the growing prominence of RCTs in development economics, I encourage researchers to complement their data collection with a careful and, crucially, a comprehensive elicitation of expectations, to obtain deeper knowledge of the mechanisms underlying why programs succeed or fail. This is particularly relevant to information interventions, but would be beneficial to many types of program evaluation.

References

Abebe, Girum, Caria, Stefano, Fafchamps, Marcel, Falco, Paolo, Franklin, Simon, Quinn, Simon, Shilpi, Forhad, 2021. Matching Frictions and Distorted Beliefs: Evidence from a Job Fair Experiment. Mimeo.

Adams, Abigail, Andrew, Alison, 2019. Preferences and Beliefs in the Marriage Market for Young Brides. CEPR Discussion Papers. pp. 1–74.

Aguila, E., Borges, A., Castillejos, C.M., Pierson, A., Weimer, B., 2014. Mortality Expectations of Older Mexicans: Development and Testing of Survey Measures. RAND Technical Report TR-1288/6-SOY-NIA.

Andrabi, Tahir, Das, Jishnu, Khwaja, Asim Ijaz, 2017. Report cards: the impact of providing school and child test scores on educational markets. The American Economic Review 107 (6), 1535–1563. https://doi.org/10.1257/aer.20140774.

Angelucci, Manuela, Bennett, Daniel, 2021. Adverse selection in the marriage market: HIV testing and marriage in rural Malawi. The Review of Economic Studies 88 (5), 2119–2148. https://doi.org/10.1093/restud/rdaa088.

Anglewicz, Philip, Kohler, Hans-Peter, 2009. Overestimating HIV infection: the construction and accuracy of subjective probabilities of HIV infection in rural Malawi. Demographic Research 20 (6), 65.

Armand, Alex, Carneiro, Pedro, Toppeta, Alessandro, 2019. Local Labor Market Shocks and Learning about the Returns To Schooling. Mimeo.

Ashour, Maha, Gilligan, Daniel Orth, Hoel, Jessica Blumer, Karachiwalla, Naureen Iqbal, 2019. Do beliefs about herbicide quality correspond with actual quality in local markets? Evidence from Uganda. Journal of Development Studies 55 (6), 1285–1306. https://doi.org/10.1080/00220388.2018.1464143.

Attanasio, Orazio P., 2009. Expectations and perceptions in developing countries: their measurement and their use. The American Economic Review: Papers and Proceedings 99 (2), 87–92. https://doi.org/10.1257/aer.99.2.87.

Attanasio, Orazio P., Augsburg, Britta, 2016. Subjective expectations and income processes in rural India. Economica 83 (331), 416–442. https://doi.org/10.1111/ecca.12190.

Attanasio, Orazio P., Cunha, Flávio, Jervis, Pamela, 2019. Subjective Parental Beliefs. Their Measurement and Role. NBER Working Paper, No. 26516.

Attanasio, Orazio P., Kaufmann, Katja M., 2014. Education choices and returns to schooling: intrahousehold decision making, gender and subjective expectations. Journal of Development Economics.

Attanasio, Orazio P., Kaufmann, Katja M., 2017. Education choices and returns on the labor and marriage markets: evidence from data on subjective expectations. Journal of Economic Behavior & Organization 140, 35–55. https://doi.org/10.1016/j.jebo.2017.05.002.

Avitabile, Ciro, de Hoyos, Rafael, 2018. The heterogeneous effect of information on student performance: evidence from a randomized control trial in Mexico. Journal of Development Economics 135, 318–348. https://doi.org/10.1016/j.jdeveco.2018.07.008.

Bah, Tijan L., Batista, Catia, Gubert, Flore, Mckenzie, David, 2020. Can information and alternatives to irregular migration reduce 'backway' migration from the Gambia? Journal of Development Economics Registered Report Stage 1.

Bandiera, Oriana, Bassi, Vittorio, Burgess, Robin, Rasul, Imran, Sulaiman, Munshi, Vitali, Anna, 2021. The search for good jobs: evidence from a six-year field experiment in Uganda. SSRN Electronic Journal. https://doi.org/10.2139/ssrn.3910330.

Banerjee, Abhijit V., Sequeira, Sandra, 2020. Spatial Mismatches and Imperfect Information in the Job Search. CEPR Discussion Paper No. DP14414.

Baranov, Victoria, Bennett, Daniel, Kohler, Hans Peter, 2015. The indirect impact of antiretroviral therapy: mortality risk, mental health, and HIV-negative labor supply. Journal of Health Economics 44, 195–211. https://doi.org/10.1016/j.jhealeco.2015.07.008.

Baranov, Victoria, Kohler, Hans Peter, 2018. The impact of AIDS treatment on savings and human capital investment in Malawi. American Economic Journal: Applied Economics 10 (1), 266–306. https://doi.org/10.1257/app.20150369.

Baseler, Travis, 2021. Hidden income and the perceived returns to migration: experimental evidence from Kenya. SSRN Electronic Journal (September), 1–40. https://doi.org/10.2139/ssrn.3534715.

Beam, Emily A., 2016. Do job fairs matter? Experimental evidence on the impact of job-fair attendance. Journal of Development Economics 120, 32–40. https://doi.org/10.1016/j.jdeveco.2015.11.004.

Beam, Emily A., 2021. Search costs and the determinants of job search. Labour Economics 69, 101968. https://doi.org/10.1016/j.labeco.2021.101968.

Bellemare, Marc F., 2009a. When perception is reality: subjective expectations and contracting. American Journal of Agricultural Economics 91 (5), 1377–1381. https://doi.org/10.1111/j.1467-8276.2009.01351.x.

Bellemare, Marc F., 2009b. Sharecropping, insecure land rights and land titling policies: a case study of Lac Alaotra, Madagascar. Development Policy Review 27 (1), 87–106. https://doi.org/10.1111/j.1467-7679.2009.00437.x.

Bellemare, Marc F., 2012. Insecure land rights and share tenancy: evidence from Madagascar. Land Economics 88 (1), 155–180. https://doi.org/10.3368/le.88.1.155.

Benjamin, Daniel J., 2019. Errors in probabilistic reasoning and judgment biases. In: Bernheim, Doug, DellaVigna, Stefano, Laibson, David (Eds.), Handbook of Behavioral Economics. Elsevier Press.

Bhalotra, Sonia, Delavande, Adeline, Font-Gilabert, Paulino, Maselko, Joanna, 2020. Maternal Investments in Children: the Role of Expected Effort and Returns. IZA Discussion Paper, no. 13056.

Bobba, Matteo, Frisancho, Veronica, 2020. Self-perceptions about academic achievement: evidence from Mexico city. Journal of Econometrics. https://doi.org/10.1016/j.jeconom.2020.06.009.

Bold, Tessa, Kaizzi, Kayuki C., Svensson, Jakob, Yanagizawa-Drott, David, 2017. Lemon technologies and adoption: measurement, theory and evidence from agricultural markets in Uganda. The Quarterly Journal of Economics 132 (3), 1055–1100.

Bonilla-Mejía, Leonardo, Bottan, Nicolas L., Ham, Andrés, 2019. Information policies and higher education choices experimental evidence from Colombia. Journal of Behavioral and Experimental Economics 83, 101468. https://doi.org/10.1016/j.socec.2019.101468.

Bor, Jacob, Musakwa, Nozipho, Onoya, Dorina, Evans, Denise, 2021. Perceived efficacy of HIV treatment-as-prevention among university students in Johannesburg, South Africa. Sexually Transmitted Infections. https://doi.org/10.1136/sextrans-2021-055031.

Bozzoli, Carlos, Brück, Tilman, Muhumuza, Tony, 2011. Does war influence individual expectations? Economics Letters 113 (3), 288–291.

Brañas-Garza, Pablo, Ciacci, Riccardo, Rascon-Ramirez, Ericka, 2020. Order Matters: Eliciting Maternal Beliefs on Educational Choices. Munich Personal RePEc Archive no. 100391.

Brown, Joe, Hamoudi, Amar, Jeuland, Marc, Turrini, Gina, 2017. Seeing, believing, and behaving: heterogeneous effects of an information intervention on household water treatment. Journal of Environmental Economics and Management 86, 141–159. https://doi.org/10.1016/j.jeem.2016.08.005.

Brück, Tilman, Llussá, Fernanda, Tavares, José A., 2011. Entrepreneurship: the role of extreme events. European Journal of Political Economy 27, S78–S88.

Bruine de Bruin, W., Carman, K.G., 2018. Measuring subjective probabilities: the effect of response mode on the use of focal responses, validity, and respondents' evaluations. Risk Analysis 38 (10), 2128–2143. https://doi.org/10.1111/risa.13138.

Chari, A.V., Maertens, Annemie, 2014. Gender, productive ability and the perceived returns to education: evidence from rural India. Economics Letters 122 (2), 253–257. https://doi.org/10.1016/j.econlet.2013.10.029.

Chattopadhyay, Mriduchhanda, Arimura, Toshi H., Katayama, Hajime, Sakudo, Mari, Yokoo, Hide-Fumi, 2021. Subjective probabilistic expectations, household air pollution, and health: evidence from cooking fuel use patterns in West Bengal, India. Resource and Energy Economics 66, 101262. https://doi.org/10.1016/j.reseneeco.2021.101262.

Chinkhumba, Jobiba, Godlonton, Susan, Thornton, Rebecca, 2014. The demand for medical male circumcision. American Economic Journal: Applied Economics 6 (2), 152–177. https://doi.org/10.1257/app.6.2.152.

Ciancio, Alberto, Delavande, Adeline, Kohler, Hans-Peter, Kohler, Iliana V., 2020. Mortality Risk Information, Survival Expectations and Sexual Behaviors. Mimeo.

Ciancio, Alberto, Kämpfen, Fabrice, Kohler, Hans Peter, Kohler, Iliana V., 2021. Health screening for emerging non-communicable disease burdens among the global poor: evidence from sub-Saharan Africa. Journal of Health Economics 75. https://doi.org/10.1016/j.jhealeco.2020.102388.

Cunha, Flavio, Elo, Irma, Culhane, Jennifer, 2020. Maternal subjective expectations about the technology of skill formation predict investments in children one year later. Journal of Econometrics. https://doi.org/10.1016/j.jeconom.2020.07.044.

De Mel, Suresh, McKenzie, David, Woodruff, Christopher, 2008. Returns to capital: results from a randomized experiment. The Quarterly Journal of Economics 123 (4), 1329–1372.

Delavande, Adeline, 2014. Probabilistic expectations in developing countries. Annual Review of Economics 6, 1–20. https://doi.org/10.1146/annurev-economics-072413-105148.

Delavande, Adeline, Giné, Xavier, McKenzie, David, 2011a. Measuring subjective expectations in developing countries: a critical review and new evidence. Journal of Development Economics 94 (2), 151–163. https://doi.org/10.1016/j.jdeveco.2010.01.008.

Delavande, Adeline, Giné, Xavier, McKenzie, David, 2011b. Eliciting probabilistic expectations with visual aids in developing countries: how sensitive are answers to variations in elicitation design. Journal of Applied Econometrics 26 (3), 479–497. https://doi.org/10.1002/jae.1233.

Delavande, Adeline, Kohler, Hans-Peter, 2012. The impact of HIV testing on subjective expectations and risky behavior in Malawi. Demography 49 (3), 1011–1036.

Delavande, Adeline, Kohler, Hans Peter, 2009. Subjective expectations in the context of HIV/AIDS in Malawi. Demographic Research 20, 817–867. https://doi.org/10.4054/DemRes.2009.20.31.

Delavande, Adeline, Kohler, Hans Peter, 2016. HIV/AIDS-related expectations and risky sexual behaviour in Malawi. The Review of Economic Studies 83 (1), 118–164. https://doi.org/10.1093/restud/rdv028.

Delavande, Adeline, Lee, Jinkook, Menon, Seetha, 2017. Eliciting survival expectations of the elderly in low-income countries: evidence from India. Demography 54 (2), 673–699. https://doi.org/10.1007/s13524-017-0560-8.

Delavande, Adeline, Rohwedder, Susann, 2008. Eliciting subjective probabilities in Internet surveys. Public Opinion Quarterly 72 (5), 866–891.

Delavande, Adeline, Zafar, Basit, 2019. University choice: the role of expected earnings, nonpecuniary outcomes, and financial constraints. Journal of Political Economy 127 (5), 2343–2393. https://doi.org/10.1086/701808.

Derksen, Laura, Muula, Adamson, van Oosterhout, Joep, 2021. Love in the Time of HIV: How Beliefs about Externalities Impact Health Behavior. Mimeo.

Dillon, Brian, 2012. Using mobile phones to collect panel data in developing countries. Journal of International Development 24 (4). https://doi.org/10.1002/jid.1771.

Dillon, Brian, 2017. Private Information and Dynamic Risk. Mimeo.

Dizon-Ross, Rebecca, 2019. Parents' beliefs about their children's academic ability: implications for educational investments. The American Economic Review 109 (8), 2728–2765.

Dominitz, Jeff, Manski, Charles F., 1996. Eliciting student expectations of the returns to schooling. The Journal of Human Resources 31, 1–26. https://doi.org/10.2307/146041.

Dupas, P., Miguel, E., 2017. Impacts and Determinants of Health Levels in Low-Income Countries. Handbook of Economic Field Experiments, vol. 2. Elsevier Ltd.

Eriksson, Katherine, Sovero, Veronica, 2016. The impact of HIV testing on subjective mortality and investments in children: experimental evidence from Malawi. Economics Letters 149, 90–93. https://doi.org/10.1016/j.econlet.2016.10.017.

Estrada, Ricardo, Gignoux, Jérémie, 2017. Benefits to elite schools and the expected returns to education: evidence from Mexico city. European Economic Review 95, 168–194. https://doi.org/10.1016/j.euroecorev.2017.03.007.

Fabregas, Raissa, Kremer, Michael, Schilbach, Frank, 2019. Realizing the potential of digital development: the case of agricultural advice. Science 366 (6471). https://doi.org/10.1126/science.aay3038.

Favara, Marta, Glewwe, Paul, Porter, Catherine, Sanchez, Alan, 2021. Expecting Better? How Young People Form Their Earnings Expectations. IZA Discussion Paper, no. 14289.

Franco, Catalina, 2019. How Does Relative Performance Feedback Affect Beliefs and Academic Decisions? Evidence from a Field Experiment. Working Paper. pp. 1–77.

Galesic, M., Bruine De Bruin, W., Dumas, M., Kapteyn, A., Darling, J.E., Meijer, E., 2018. Asking about social circles improves election predictions. Nature Human Behaviour 2 (3), 187–193. https://doi.org/10.1038/s41562-018-0302-y.

Gamboa, Luis Fernando, Rodríguez-lesmes, Paul Andrés, 2018. Subjective earnings and academic expectations of tertiary education in Colombia. Ensayos sobre política económica 36 (86), 159. https://doi.org/10.32468/espe.8601.

Gars, Jared, Fishman, Ram, Gars, Jared, Kishore, Avinash, Rothler, Yoav, Ward, Patrick, 2020. Confidence and Information Usage: Evidence from Soil Testing in India. Mimeo.

Giannola, Michele, 2020. Parental Investments and Intra-Household Inequality in Child Development: Theory, Measurement, and Evidence from a Lab-in-the-Field Experiment. Mimeo.

Gigerenzer, Gerd, 1991. How to make cognitive illusions disappear: beyond "heuristics and biases". European Review of Social Psychology 2. https://doi.org/10.1080/14792779143000033.

Giné, Xavier, Townsend, Robert M., Vickery, James, 2015. Forecasting when It Matters: Evidence from Semi-Arid India. Mimeo.

Godlonton, Susan, 2020. Employment risk and job-seeker performance. The Journal of Human Resources 55 (1), 194–239. https://doi.org/10.3368/jhr.55.1.0317-8662R2.

Godlonton, Susan, Munthali, Alister, Thornton, Rebecca, 2016. Responding to risk: circumcision, information, and HIV prevention. Review of Economics and Statistics 98 (2), 333–349. https://doi.org/10.1162/REST_a_00516.

Godlonton, Susan, Thornton, Rebecca L., 2013. Learning from others' HIV testing: updating beliefs and responding to risk. The American Economic Review: Papers and Proceedings 103 (3), 439–444. https://doi.org/10.1257/aer.103.3.439.

Gong, Erick, 2015. HIV testing and risky sexual behaviour. The Economic Journal 125 (582), 32–60.

Gradín, Carlos, Mambo, Felix, Paris, Yonesse, 2020. Unequal Expectations Gender Inequality in the Salary Expectations of University Students. WIDER Working Paper 2020/78.

Haaland, Ingar, Roth, Christopher, Wohlfart, Johannes, forthcoming. Designing Information Provision Experiments. Journal of Economic Literature.

Hill, Ruth Vargas, 2009. Using stated preferences and beliefs to identify the impact of risk on poor households. Journal of Development Studies 45 (2), 151–171. https://doi.org/10.1080/00220380802553065.

Hill, Ruth Vargas, 2010. Liberalisation and producer price risk: examining subjective expectations in the Ugandan coffee market. Journal of African Economies 19 (4), 433–458. https://doi.org/10.1093/jae/ejq010.

Hjort, Jonas, Moreira, Diana, Rao, Gautam, Santini, Juan Francisco, 2021. How research affects policy: experimental evidence from 2,150 Brazilian municipalities. The American Economic Review 111 (5), 1442–1480. https://doi.org/10.1257/AER.20190830.

Hoel, Jessica B., Michelson, Hope, Norton, Ben, Manyong, Victor, 2021. Misattribution and Uncertainty about Beliefs Prevent Learning. Mimeo.

Jensen, Robert, 2010. The (perceived) returns to education and the demand for schooling. The Quarterly Journal of Economics 125 (2), 515–548.

Jones, Sam, Santos, Ricardo, 2020. Updating Great Expectations the Effect of Peer Salary Information on Own-Earnings Forecasts Sam Jones and Ricardo Santos. WIDER Working Paper 2020/138.

Jones, Sam, Santos, Ricardo, Xirinda, Gimelgo, 2020. Misinformed, Mismatched, or Misled? Explaining the Gap between Expected and Realized Graduate Earnings in Mozambique. WIDER Working Paper 2020/47.

Kaufmann, Katja Maria, 2014. Understanding the income gradient in college attendance in Mexico: the role of heterogeneity in expected returns. Quantitative Economics 5 (3), 583–630. https://doi.org/10.3982/qe259.

Keats, Anthony, 2012. Occupational Choice in Rural Kenya: Using Subjective Expectations Data to Measure Credit and Insurance. UCLA Working Paper. pp. 1–42.

Kerwin, Jason T., 2021. Scared Straight or Scared to Death? Fatalism in Response to Disease Risks. Working Paper.

Kerwin, Jason T., Reynoso, Natalia Ordaz, 2021. You know what I know: interviewer knowledge effect in subjective expectation elicitation. Demography 58 (1), 1–29. https://doi.org/10.1215/00703370-8932274.

Kim, Jinho, 2016. The effect of peers on HIV infection expectations among Malawian adolescents: using an instrumental variables/school fixed effect approach. Social Science & Medicine 152, 61–69. https://doi.org/10.1016/j.socscimed.2016.01.036.

Kremer, Michael, Rao, Gautam, Schilbach, Frank, 2019. Behavioral development economics. In: Bernheim, Douglas, DellaVigna, Stefano, Laibson, David (Eds.), Handbook of Behavioral Economics: Applications and Foundations, vol. 2. North-Holland, pp. 345–458. Chapter 5.

Luseno, Winnie K., McPeak, John G., Barrett, Christopher B., Little, Peter D., Gebru, Getachew, 2003. Assessing the value of climate forecast information for pastoralists: evidence from southern Ethiopia and northern Kenya. World Development 31 (9), 1477–1494. https://doi.org/10.1016/S0305-750X(03)00113-X.

Lybbert, Travis J., Barrett, Christopher B., McPeak, John G., Luseno, Winnie K., 2007. Bayesian herders: updating of rainfall beliefs in response to external forecasts. World Development 35 (3), 480–497.

Maertens, Annemie, 2011. Does education pay off? Subjective expectations on education in rural India. Economic and Political Weekly 46 (9), 58–63.

Maertens, Annemie, Michelson, Hope, Nourani, Vesall, 2021. How do farmers learn from extension services? Evidence from Malawi. American Journal of Agricultural Economics 103 (2), 569–595. https://doi.org/10.1111/ajae.12135.

Maffioli, Elisa M., Mohanan, Manoj, 2018. Touching beliefs: using touchscreen technology to elicit subjective expectations in survey research. PLoS ONE 13 (11), 1–15. https://doi.org/10.1371/journal.pone.0207484.

Maffioli, Elisa Maria, O'Meara, Wendy Prudhomme, Turner, Elizabeth L., Mohanan, Manoj, 2021. Can individuals' beliefs help us understand nonadherence to malaria test results? Evidence from rural Kenya. Review of Development Economics 25 (1), 163–182. https://doi.org/10.1111/rode.12708.

Mahajan, Aprajit, Michel, Christian, Tarozzi, Alessandro, 2020. Identification of Time-Inconsistent Models: the Case of Insecticide Treated Nets. National Bureau of Economic Research WP 27198.

Manski, Charles F., 2004. Measuring expectations. Econometrica 72 (5), 1329–1376.

Manski, Charles F., Molinari, Francesca, 2010. Rounding probabilistic expectations in surveys. Journal of Business and Economic Statistics 28 (2), 219–231. https://doi.org/10.1198/jbes.2009.08098.

Maughan-Brown, Brendan, Godlonton, Susan, Thornton, Rebecca, Venkataramani, Atheendar S., 2015. What do people actually learn from public health campaigns? Incorrect inferences about male circumcision and female HIV infection risk among men and women in Malawi. AIDS and Behavior 19 (7), 1170–1177.

Maughan-Brown, Brendan, Venkataramani, Atheendar S., 2018. Accuracy and determinants of perceived HIV risk among young women in South Africa. BMC Public Health 18 (1), 1–9. https://doi.org/10.1186/s12889-017-4593-0.

McKenzie, David, Gibson, John, Stillman, Steven, 2013. A land of milk and honey with streets paved with gold: do emigrants have over-optimistic expectations about incomes abroad? Journal of Development Economics 102, 116–127. https://doi.org/10.1016/j.jdeveco.2012.01.001.

Michelson, Hope, Fairbairn, Anna, Ellison, Brenna, Maertens, Annemie, Manyong, Victor, 2021. Misperceived quality: fertilizer in Tanzania. Journal of Development Economics 148, 102579. https://doi.org/10.1016/j.jdeveco.2020.102579.

Miller, Grant, de Paula, Aureo, Valente, Christine, 2020. Subjective Expectations and Demand for Contraception Subjective Expectations and Demand for Contraception. Mimeo.

National Statistical Office/Malawi and ICF, 2017. Malawi Demographic and Health Survey 2015-16. National Statistical Office and ICF, Zomba, Malawi. Available at http://dhsprogram.com/pubs/pdf/FR319/FR319.pdf.

Nguyen, Trang, 2008. Information, Role Models and Perceived Returns to Education: Experimental Evidence from Madagascar. Mimeo.

Nikolov, Plamen, Jimi, Nusrat, 2018. What factors drive individual misperceptions of the returns to schooling in Tanzania? Some lessons for education policy. Applied Economics 50 (44), 4705–4723. https://doi.org/10.1080/00036846.2018.1466991.

Paula, Áureo De, Shapira, Gil, Todd, Petra E., 2014. How beliefs about HIV status affect risky behaviors: evidence from Malawi. Journal of Applied Econometrics 29 (6), 944–964.

Prakhov, Ilya, 2021. The determinants of expected returns on higher education in Russia: a human capital theory approach. Higher Education Quarterly 75 (2), 302–320. https://doi.org/10.1111/hequ.12281.

Rogger, Daniel, Somani, Ravi, 2018. Hierarchy and Information. World Bank Policy Research Working Paper No. 8644.

Santos, Paulo, Barrett, Christopher B., 2011. Persistent poverty and informal credit. Journal of Development Economics 96 (2), 337–347. https://doi.org/10.1016/j.jdeveco.2010.08.017.

Sequeira, Sandra, Spinnewijn, Johannes, Xu, Guo, 2016. Rewarding schooling success and perceived returns to education: evidence from India. Journal of Economic Behavior & Organization 131, 373–392. https://doi.org/10.1016/j.jebo.2016.08.015.

Shapira, Gil, 2017. How subjective beliefs about HIV infection affect life-cycle fertility: evidence from rural Malawi. The Journal of Human Resources 52 (3), 680–718. https://doi.org/10.3368/jhr.52.3.0314-6263R1.

Shrestha, Maheshwor, 2020. Get rich or die tryin': perceived earnings, perceived mortality rate and the value of a statistical life of potential work-migrants from Nepal. World Bank Economic Review 34 (1), 1–27. https://doi.org/10.1093/wber/lhz023.

Sterck, Olivier, 2014. HIV/AIDS and fatalism: should prevention campaigns disclose the transmission rate of HIV? Journal of African Economies 23 (1), 53–104.

Tarozzi, A., Bennear, L., Balasubramanya, S., Pfaff, A., Matin, A.K., van Geen, L., 2009. Subjective Risk Assessment and Reactions to Health-related Information: Evidence from Bangladesh. UPF Working Paper.

Thornton, Rebecca L., 2008. The demand for, and impact of, learning HIV status. The American Economic Review 98 (5), 1829–1863.

Tjernström, Emilia, Lybbert, Travis J., Hernández, Rachel Frattarola, Correa, Juan Sebastian, 2021. Learning by (virtually) doing: experimentation and belief updating in smallholder agriculture. Journal of Economic Behavior & Organization 189, 28–50. https://doi.org/10.1016/j.jebo.2021.03.001.

World Bank, 2015. Early childhood intervention. In: Mind, Society and Behaviour, World Development Report 2015. World Bank Group. Chapter 5.

World Bank, 2021. World bank country and lending groups. Available online at https://datahelpdesk.worldbank. org/knowledgebase/articles/906519-world-bank-country-and-lending-groups.

Yilma, Zelalem, O'Donnell, Owen, Mebratie, Anagaw, Alemu, Getnet, Bedi, Arjun S., 2015. Subjective expectations of medical expenditures and insurance in rural Ethiopia. SSRN Electronic Journal. https://doi.org/10.2139/ ssrn.2680129.

Retirement expectations[☆]

Gábor Kézdi[†] **and Matthew D. Shapiro**
University of Michigan, Ann Arbor, MI, United States

10.1 Introduction

When to retire is a key decision made by working individuals. The retirement decision is closely tied to many decisions and outcomes bearing on later life—how much to save and consume, how to spend time, where to live. Retirement is affected by health, and might affect health outcomes itself. Retirement is an important component to explicit and implicit labor contracts. Retirement is regulated by public policy and social insurance. Because of the complex, intertemporal decision-making surrounding retirement, and because it is affected by so many factors, both internal and external to the individual, modeling retirement decisions is challenging.

In this chapter, we will argue that retirement expectations are a valuable complement to both reduced-form and structural modeling of retirement. People's decision about when to retire is likely affected by a host of factors and preferences that are at best partially observable to outsiders. Moreover, even when they are observed, their effects are likely to be heterogeneous. To take into account unobservable individual heterogeneity in these factors and their effects, a substantial and growing literature uses people's reported expectations of when they would retire to answer these questions. It is important to note that retirement is something that most people think about after a certain age, so it may very well be that their own predictions are informative. We indeed show that expectations are reliable predictors of behavior and that they reflect much of what affects retirement decisions. Analysis of the expectations about when to retire also serves as a methodological template for analyzing expectations about other decisions, especially those with an intertemporal dimension.

This chapter will evaluate the value of retirement expectations. It uses a simple discrete-choice model to clarify what is being elicited in standard survey questions concerning retirement expectations. Moreover, it presents evidence on the predictive performance of retirement expectations elicited in the Health and Retirement Study (HRS), implements a machine learning procedure to assess the predictive content of retirement expectations, and surveys the wide literature using retirement expectations for prediction and analysis.

☆ Acknowledgment: Gábor Kézdi was Research Associate Professor, Survey Research Center at the University of Michigan. Matthew D. Shapiro is Director and Research Professor, Survey Research Center and Lawrence R. Klein Collegiate Professor of Economics at the University of Michigan and Research Associate at the NBER. We are grateful for comments from Pamela Giustinelli and the editors and to Meifeng Yang for assistance.
† Deceased.

10.2 Theoretical framework

To provide context for the findings of the literature and identify open questions, we first consider a general theoretical framework and what it implies for the measurement strategies of retirement age expectations. We define retirement as the transition from full-time work to not working full-time. This definition is one of the several potential definitions of retirement, but it is simple and clear, and it corresponds to the way many people think about retirement. For example, as we will see, when asked if they have a plan for retirement, more than half of the people who do have some plan would reduce hours when retiring, and less than half would stop working altogether. In addition, and perhaps for the same reason, the most widely used measure of retirement age expectations also uses this definition.

For analytic convenience, we assume that retirement is an absorbing state: Once retired, an individual is assumed not to resume full-time work.[1] They may switch back and forth between no work and part-time work. Retirement is a forward-looking decision: one weighs the benefits of working and nonworking now as well as in the future. With these assumptions, retirement can be modeled as an optimal stopping problem. An individual who works full-time compares the value of continuing to work full-time to the value of retiring now. If the difference declines monotonically over time (but not necessarily smoothly), at one point in time the individual decides to stop working full-time and never resumes full-time work.

While the main purpose of the theoretical framework discussed here is to assist in the interpretation of survey questions, the framework equally applies to modeling retirement decisions. van der Klaauw and Wolpin (2008) show how to incorporate expectations data into the moment restrictions of a dynamic programming model of household retirement and saving, and then implement the procedure using the HRS. The procedure combines unconditional working and longevity expectations with observed realizations of respondents' labor supply, health, and the other variables to increase estimation precision. van der Klaauw (2012) discusses this approach generally with an application to career decisions. See also Wiswall and Zafar (2015, 2021). Chapter 21 in this Handbook discusses incorporating expectations into structural models. See also Giustinelli and Shapiro (2019) for structural interpretation of probabilistic expectation questions. These structural approaches complement the reduced form approaches discussed in Section 10.10 of this chapter.

Consider individual i who at age t thinks about retiring. Let the set Ω_{it} include everything that goes into that decision: the individual's perceptions of the relevant state variables, their current preferences, and their beliefs about the future path of the state variables, and their own preferences. See Lumsdaine et al. (1992) for a discussion of embedding retirement models in a statistical framework. The set Ω_{it} is heterogeneous across individuals and it evolves with time. Let the binary variable w denote working full-time, and let D denote the difference of the value of continuing to work full-time and the value of retiring now, the optimal decision is

$$w_{it} = 1 \; iff \; D_{it}\,(\Omega_{it}) > 0, \tag{10.1}$$

where w_{it} is an indicator for working full-time.

---

[1] Late-in-life labor supply decisions are more complex and fluid than a permanent transition from working full-time to complete retirement. For example, individuals may move from lifetime to bridge jobs, may return to work after a period of retirement, and so on. Hence, though our analytic framework is well-defined, the alternate to full-time continuing work reflects many possibilities. See Maestas (2010) for analysis of expectations of work after retirement. We return to this issue in Sections 10.4 and 10.7.

The question analyzed in this section is expectations about when that stopping would occur in the future. Time is measured in terms of age, and for convenience is assumed to be discrete with integer values only. Individual i who is of age a looks into the future and forms beliefs about when the individual would retire. There are alternative ways to characterize these beliefs.

One way to characterize these beliefs is to specify a series of probabilities of whether the individual would work full-time past each subsequent age t. Importantly, at age a, the individual cannot know with certainty the relevant future set Ω_{it}, for any $t > a$, which provides the basis for each subsequent optimal decision. Instead, what they have available at age a is Ω_{ia}, which contains their preferences and perception of the state at age a as well as their beliefs about future states and preferences. Denote the probability that individual i would work full-time past age t as they perceive it at age a, $a < t$, as

$$p^t_{ia} = \Pr[w_{it} = 1|\Omega_{ia}].$$ (10.2)

From a statistical point of view, the optimal stopping problem of retirement is a duration problem. The series of the p^t_{ia} probabilities is the survival curve as of age a: they show the probability of working full-time at least to age t for each age t based on age a information. Another representation of the same problem is the probability distribution of the retirement age. Let r^t_{ia} be the joint probability of working full-time at age $t - 1$ and retiring at age t,

$$r^t_{ia} = \Pr\left[w_{i(t-1)} = 1 \ \& \ w_{it} = 0|\Omega_{ia}\right].$$ (10.3)

It is also the change in the survival curve,

$$r^t_{ia} = p^{t-1}_{ia} - p^t_{ia}.$$ (10.4)

Note that the probability distribution of the retirement age is closely related to the hazard function, which is a more standard statistical representation of the same distribution. The hazard function is the probability of retiring conditional on not having retired by that age. Thus the hazard function renormalizes the probability of the retirement age at each year of age. For our purposes, the hazard function is less intuitive than the distribution of the unconditional probability of the retirement age, so we don't consider the hazard representation. Importantly, each of the three objects—the survival curve, the probability distribution of the retirement age or the hazard function—fully characterizes the same retirement age expectations.

Fig. 10.1 shows a hypothetical example, though it is a realistic one for the U.S. where retirement at 62 and 65 is common. In this example, the probabilistic path to retirement is viewed from age 55 when the individual works full-time, and the individual is retired with a probability of one by age 75. The left panel is the survival curve of full-time work; the right panel is the corresponding probability of the retirement age. The survival curve shows a gradual decline in the probability of full-time work until age 62 where a larger drop occurs so that the probability of working past age 62 is 70%. Then some gradual decline again and an even larger drop age 65 to 30%. Finally, a gradual decline until age 75 when the probability of full-time work becomes zero. (Ages 62 and 65 correspond to eligibility for early claiming of Social Security and to eligibility for Medicare, respectively.) The right panel shows the probability of the retirement age at specific years of age. These probabilities are the change in the survival curve so they show a spike at ages 62 and 65, with values of 0.2 and 0.36, respectively. The gradual decline phases show up as uniform distributions within the appropriate age intervals.

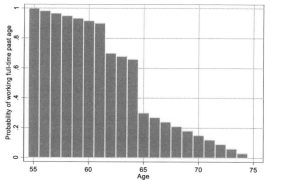
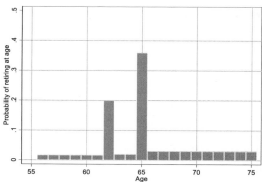

The probability of working past the age threshold (survival curve of full-time work)

The probability of the retirement age

FIGURE 10.1 Two representations of the same retirement age expectations: An example.

10.3 Measuring retirement age expectations

To characterize fully an individual's retirement age expectations, we would need to elicit the individual's entire probability distribution of working past age thresholds or the entire probability distribution of the retirement age. However, in most survey situations it is impractical to elicit entire distributions. Instead, surveys tend to follow one of two approaches: elicit a statistic about the probability distribution of the retirement age, such as an expected value, or elicit subjective probability predictions of working past certain target ages. Neither of these approaches can completely characterize individuals' retirement expectations. This is not a problem as long as the elicited statistic is exactly what the analyst needs. But it is a problem when the analyst needs some other statistic or the entire distribution. In such cases, analysts need to make additional assumptions on the survival curve or the probability distribution of the retirement age, and then use interpolation and extrapolation.

Let's return to our hypothetical example of Fig. 10.1. Suppose that a survey elicits two points of the survival curve: the probabilities of full-time work past age 62 and 65; these are 0.7 and 0.3 here, respectively. Knowing these two numbers would not identify the entire distribution because there are infinitely many survival curves that would fit these two points. Without a complete survival curve, we would not be able to identify the distribution of the probability of the retirement age, and thus we would not be able to compute statistics such as the expected age of retirement. In practice, we would need to make assumptions to interpolate and extrapolate from the two points to fit a survival curve and use that fitted curve for additional computations. It is an empirical question how many cut-points provide a reasonable approximation of the distribution. The choice of age 62 and 65 in the HRS (see below) is a judicious one given U.S. institutions.

Similarly, eliciting a statistic about the probability of the retirement age would not identify the probability distribution and would not identify points on the survival curve either. Candidate statistics include the expected value or the mode (the most likely retirement age). Denoting the age when individual i retires as $ageret_i$, and assuming that there is a terminal age T after which the individual would work with zero probability, the corresponding formulae are

$$E\left[ageret_i | \Omega_{ia}\right] = \sum_{t=a}^{T} t \times r_{ia}^t,$$ (10.5)

$$\text{mode}\left[ageret_i | \Omega_{ia}\right] = \arg\max_t \left\{r_{ia}^t\right\}_{t=a}^{T}.$$ (10.6)

In our hypothetical example in Fig. 10.1, the expected retirement age is 65.3 and the modal age is 65. Knowing either or both of these numbers would be informative, but it would not identify the probability distributions without additional assumptions, and we would not be able to compute statistics such as the probability that the individual would work full-time past age 65.

10.4 Eliciting a planned or expected retirement age

Let's now turn to establishing the measurement properties of the two different elicitation strategies of subjective retirement age expectations. We start with the direct elicitation of a retirement age and turn to subjective probability predictions after that. We analyze the Health and Retirement Study, which includes both elicitations. Given that the HRS is a longitudinal study, we will also be able to compare these elicitations to realizations.[2] Since its very beginning, the HRS has included questions about planning for and thinking about retirement. The first question in the sequence asks,

> When you retire, do you plan to stop working altogether or reduce work hours at a particular date or age, have you not given it much thought, or what?

Multiple response categories are allowed, including stop working altogether, reducing hours, no plans to retire, or will never retire. Depending on the response, several follow-up questions elicit a retirement age; we call this the planned or expected retirement age. Not all retirement plan responses lead to an elicitation of the planned or expected retirement in the HRS before 2002.

In this chapter, we define retirement as the transition from working full-time to not working full-time. We construct a sample of HRS respondents accordingly to analyze the planned or expected retirement age. In particular, we include respondents in HRS 2002 through 2018 who were younger than 64 and worked full-time when the retirement planning questions were asked. Table 10.1 shows the distribution of responses to the retirement planning question (last column) and statistics of the distribution of planned or expected retirement age (previous columns).

---

[2] While the discussion in this chapter will focus on the questions in the HRS, there are similar questions in the HRS International Family of Studies including the ELSA (England), SHARE (multiple European countries), KLoSSA (Korea), and LASI (India) studies. See Delavande et al. (2012) for a comparison of the questions, which use questions similar to the HRS, though sometimes different ages based on national institutional arrangements. See also the Gateway to Global Aging Data (https://g2aging.org/). The HRS interviews both respondents and their spouses. The Federal Reserve Bank of New York's Survey of Consumer Expectation includes both probabilistic expectations (ages 62 and 67) and retirement age expectations similar to the HRS. See Federal Reserve Bank of New York (2022). The PSID uses a somewhat different questions from the HRS and its sister studies. PSID first asks, "What is the usual retirement age for people who sore with you or have the same kind of job?" [P39AGE] and then asks, "At what age do you plan to stop working?" [P40AGE]. See Panel Study of Income Dynamics Wave 41 Questionnaire (2019).

Table 10.1 Retirement plan and age when plans or thinks will retire.

Retirement plan	Age when plans to retire or thinks will retire									Distribution of retirement plan %
	Avg.	Median	Percentage of specific age bins							
			<62	62	63–64	65	>65	never	missing	total	
Stop working altogether	63.8	65	17	22	7	26	26	0	2	100	22
Reduce hours	63.9	65	18	20	7	27	23	1	4	100	31
No plans	66.7	65	4	8	2	24	37	1	23	100	39
Will never stop working	-	-	0	0	0	0	0	100[a]	0	100	4
Other or missing	-	-	0	0	0	0	0	0	100[a]	100	4
Total	64.9	65	11	14	5	23	27	4	16	100	100

Notes. Data: HRS 2002–2018, age 51–64, working full-time, retirement plans asked. N = 30,155.
[a] Inferred, not elicited.

Table 10.2   Actual retirement age compared to planned/expected retirement age.

Plan for retirement	Actual retirement age (%)			
	Lower	Same	Higher	Total
Stop working altogether	46	33	21	100
Reduce hours	46	23	31	100
No plans	67	19	14	100
Will never stop working	-	-	-	-
Other	-	-	-	-
Total	54	24	22	100

Notes. Actual retirement age is the year after the last year respondent worked full-time.

Same means within a 3-year bin; lower and higher mean outside this bin. Data: HRS 2002–2018, age < 65, working full-time, nonmissing planned/expected retirement age. N = 24,196.

Let's start with distribution of plans in the last column. In this sample of full-time workers aged 64 or less, 22% plan to stop working altogether when retired, 31% plan to reduce hours, and 39% have no plans. Four percent say they will never retire. The item nonresponse rate is 4%. The average planned or expected retirement age is 64.9 overall (first column), practically the same as the median of 65; it is higher among respondents with no plans. Across all plans, it is "never" or missing for 20% of the observations. The vast majority of "other or missing" values is among respondents with no retirement plans, and because of this high proportion, the overall item nonresponse rate is quite high.

As a first check on the information contained by the elicited planned or expected retirement age, we can compare the responses to the age the individuals actually retire from full-time work. Table 10.2 shows, for different retirement plans, whether the actual retirement age turns out to be lower, the same, or higher than expected. To allow for noisy responses with respect to the retirement window, we define the two to be equal using a 3-year window (the difference is −1, 0, or 1 years). The results show large deviations, with only 24% retiring at their planned or expected age, 54% ending up retiring younger, and 22% ending up retiring older. The deviations are only slightly smaller among respondents with an explicit plan, but again almost half of them end up retiring earlier. Hence, there is a bias toward reporting a later than realized age of retirement. Perhaps more striking is the size of the variability of realizations compared to expectations. Note that this is what we would expect with a lot of uncertainty (large spread of the probability distribution of retiring at certain ages). Hence, with this large spread, a single statistic of central tendency of retirement age has relatively little information.

In addition to these measurement issues, eliciting expected retirement age has a problem of interpretation. Recall that retirement age expectations are completely characterized by either the survival curve of working or the distribution of the probability of retiring at certain ages. This measurement strategy elicits a single statistic derived from the probability distribution of retiring at certain ages. It is unclear, however, what that statistic is. It may be any statistic of central tendency, including the expected age or the modal age. Arguably, it is more likely that respondents report the mode of the distribution (the age with the highest retirement probability) than some other statistic. Bernheim (1989) indeed finds that excepted retirement age is the mode based on data from the Retirement History Survey, a precursor of the HRS that was fielded between 1969 and 1979.

In summary, the combination of issues with interpretation and measurement makes the expected age measure challenging to use. Nevertheless, there are applications in which the planned or expected retirement age is the measure of interest despite its limitations. Such applications need to address the conceptual and measurement issues.

10.5 Subjective retirement probability

The alternative strategy elicits the probability of working past certain age thresholds. This measurement strategy aims at eliciting points of the survival curve, so it has a conceptually clear interpretation. In this subsection, we analyze the measurement properties of this elicitation using the HRS data. Since its start in 1992, the HRS has asked its respondents about the subjective probability of working full-time past age 62 and, in a separate question, past age 65. The question is the following:

What do you think the chances are that you will be working full-time after you reach age 62 [65]?

The response scale is a percent chance on a scale of 0 to 100 (in 1992 it was a 0 to 10 scale). The HRS now includes six similar questions in total (age thresholds 62, 65, and 70, working at all and working full-time). The question asking about full-time work after ages 62 and 65 has been fielded consistently since 1994, so we focus on those two questions. Specifically, let p_{ia}^{62} denote the response of individual i, who is age a, to the question about the probability of working after age 62, and let p_{ia}^{65} denote the response to working after age 65. When referring to these two probabilities we use $t = b$ in the upper index p_{ia}^{b} where $b = 62$ or $b = 65$.

In line with our focus on retirement from full-time work, we restricted the analysis to respondents who worked full-time when asked the subjective probability question, had a nonzero survey weight, who were asked the probability question (or whose p_{ia}^{65} response we filled in), and who were 3 to 8 years younger than the age in the working probability question (54 to 59 years old for p_{ia}^{62} and 57 to

Table 10.3 Subjective probability predictions and realizations among full-time workers.

	Average subjective probability prediction	Proportion working full-time	N	Percent missing
Working full-time past age 62	0.58	0.55	15,469	1%
Working full-time past age 65	0.41	0.41	12,922	1%

Notes. Percent missing is the proportion of don't know or refused probability responses. Data: HRS 1994–2018. Pooled cross-section of full-time workers at the time of the elicited subjective probability prediction; whether working full-time observed 3 to 8 years after the subjective probability elicitation.

62 years old for p_{ia}^{65}).[3] For p_{ia}^{62}, there are $N = 24,958$ observations for 12,872 respondents; for p_{ia}^{65}, $N = 21,042$ observations for 11,122 respondents. The proportion of don't know or refused responses is below 1% for both questions.

While respondents make broad use of the scale 0 to 100 scale with its 101 potential responses, almost all responses are rounded to a number ending in zero or five. Additionally, there is heaping at 0, 0.5, and 1. See Chapters 1 and 26 in this Handbook and Giustinelli et al. (2022a,b) for discussion of these ubiquitous features of elicited probabilities.

To investigate how biased or unbiased the subjective probability responses are, we compared subjective probability predictions with actual work decisions later. For this exercise, we record whether each individual worked after the age threshold 62 or 65. When defining working full-time after age b, we included respondents who were recorded to work full-time any time between ages b and $b + 5$ (changing this time window has no effect on our main conclusions). The sample sizes are smaller because we require realizations to be observed. Table 10.3 shows the average subjective probability predictions and the corresponding realized rates, together with the number of observations and the proportion of don't know or refused answers for these samples.

The subjective probability predictions made 3 to 8 years before the respective age thresholds are essentially unbiased. On average, full-time workers' predictions of the probability of their full-time working past the two age thresholds is close to the proportion of their full-time working past those thresholds. The last column shows that the proportion of don't know and refused answers (item-nonresponse) is negligible. Hence, the elicited retirement probability predictions are potentially high-quality measures. Importantly, the bias in predicting retirement age shown above is absent for the subjective probability elicitations.

We investigate unbiasedness further by conditioning on observable personal characteristics. We regress the difference between subjective probability predictions and realizations, $p_{ia}^{b} - w_{ib}$ on some important observable personal characteristics, including age, race, education, self-reported health, and

---

[3] This focuses on the retirement expectations among those currently working also fits the structure of the questions as originally asked in the HRS. It allows us to pool over all waves of the HRS and interpret the results consistent with the theoretical framework developed above. The implementation of the HRS questions have evolved over time—reflecting both the evolution of use of probability questions and the aims to pose the questions in situations reflecting the complexity of late-in-life labor supply decisions (see also Footnote 1). The HRS initially asked the P62 and P65 questions in the Current Job section (e.g., Section F of HRS 1992), so it was asked of those working. Starting in 2002, these questions and other expectations questions moved to the Expectations section (Section P). Section P also asks versions of work expectation of those not with current jobs. See Health and Retirement Study (2022). The FRBNY SCE asks the retirement expectations questions unconditionally on current labor force participation.

Table 10.4 Prediction error regressions.

	(1) $p^{62}-w^{62}$	(2) $p^{65}-w^{65}$
Female	−0.010	0.016
	(0.015)	(0.018)
Couple	−0.095**	−0.044*
	(0.018)	(0.020)
Age	−0.001	−0.005*
	(0.003)	(0.003)
African American	−0.099**	−0.132**
	(0.023)	(0.025)
Hispanic	−0.051	−0.053
	(0.031)	(0.034)
Years of education	−0.001	−0.000
	(0.003)	(0.003)
Cognitive score	−0.002	−0.014
	(0.007)	(0.008)
Self-rated health very good	0.002	0.015
	(0.016)	(0.019)
Self-rated health good	0.038*	0.054**
	(0.018)	(0.021)
Self-rated health fair	0.105**	0.080**
	(0.025)	(0.027)
Self-rated health poor	0.167**	0.164**
	(0.054)	(0.053)
Constant	0.185	0.326
	(0.157)	(0.168)
Observations	13,403	11,363
R-squared	0.015	0.011

Notes. The dependent variable is the difference between the subjective probability of working full-time at age b and a dummy variable that is one for realized working full-time at that age or later. The cognitive score variable is standardized. Robust standard errors clustered at the individual and household level are in parentheses. ** $p < 0.01$, * $p < 0.05$.

the 27-item cognitive score (see, e.g., Crimmins et al., 2011). All conditioning variables are measured at the time the subjective probability predictions are made. The sample used for this analysis is somewhat smaller because of missing cognitive score values. Table 10.4 shows the results.

The results are remarkable. Except for race and couple status, none of the standard demographics is associated with the direction of the prediction error. In fact, the coefficient estimates on years of education and cognitive score are relatively precise zeros. At the same time, subjective health is strongly associated with the prediction error: respondents in worse health are more likely to err on the positive

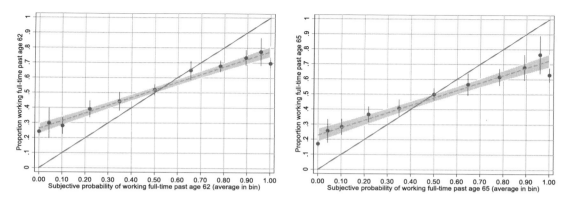

FIGURE 10.2 Calibration curves for the subjective probability predictions p^{62} and p^{65}.

side than respondents in better health. We can conclude that respondents' subjective probability predictions are close to being unbiased except for negative biases among respondents who are members of a couple or are African Americans and a positive bias among respondents with low health.

Absence of biases in prediction does not imply free from any error. To investigate the error of the elicited predictions in more detail, we carried out a calibration exercise. A calibration exercise compares realizations against probability predictions at different levels of the probability prediction. In this case, it means estimating the actual proportion of respondents with $w_{ib} = 1$ for various values of p_{ia}^b. Calibration is perfect if $\Pr\left(w_{ib} = 1 | p_{ia}^b = p\right) = p$, $\forall p \in [0, 1]$; that is, among people with the same subjective probability prediction, the proportion who end up working at the target age is equal to the subjective probability prediction for all values of that subjective probability prediction.

The original response scale allows for 101 values so we need to group the responses to avoid too much noise at certain points of the calibration curve. We created bins and plotted the actual proportion of $w = 1$ observations against the average subjective probability prediction within each bin. Due to their high prevalence and potential substantive importance, we created separate bins for exact 0%, 50%, and 100% responses. We put the remaining responses into bins of $[1, 9]$, $[10, 19]$, $[20, 29]$, $[30, 49]$, $[51, 70]$, $[71, 80]$, $[81, 90]$, and $[91, 99]$.

Fig. 10.2 shows the results of the calibration exercise with 95% confidence intervals around the estimated proportion of working full-time for the two age thresholds. The standard errors allow for clustering due to repeated observations of individuals and intra-household correlations. The figure includes the linear approximation to the calibration curve and the 95% confidence interval around that regression (dashed line and shaded area), and a 45-degree line denoting perfect calibration (solid line).

The calibration curves suggest strong attenuation. These figures add several important conclusions to our previous results on unbiasedness. First, the calibration curves for the two age thresholds (62 and 65) are similar. Recall that the two samples are similar in terms of the time distance between the subjective probability predictions and actual realizations. Second, the calibration curves are flatter than the 45-degree line. Third, the calibration curves appear approximately linear except for lower values for exact 100% responses $\Pr(w_{ib} = 1 | p_{ia}^b = 1)$. Fourth, the calibration of the 50% responses is remarkably good: very close to 50% of them end up being working full-time, that is, $P(w_{ib} = 1 | p_{ia}^b = 0.5) \approx 0.5$.

What can be the reason for the attenuation? To investigate this question let's ignore the nonlinearity of the calibration curve at exact 100%, and let's consider its linear regression approximation

$$P\left[w_{ib} = 1 | p_{ia}^b\right] = E\left[w_{ib} | p_{ia}^b\right] = \alpha_b + \beta_b p_{ia}^b. \tag{10.7}$$

The probability limit of the OLS estimator for $\hat{\beta}_b$ is

$$\text{plim}\,\hat{\beta}_b = \frac{Cov\left(w_{ib}, p_{ia}^b\right)}{V\left(p_{ia}^b\right)}. \tag{10.8}$$

We estimate $\hat{\beta}$ to be around 0.5 for both age thresholds (see the more detailed regression results later). With a perfect 45-degree calibration line we would have $\text{plim}\,\hat{\beta} = 1$ and $Cov\left(w_{ib}, p_{ia}^b\right) = V\left(p_{ia}^b\right)$. It is with $Cov\left(w_{ib}, p_{ia}^b\right) < V\left(p_{ia}^b\right)$ that the linear regression approximation shows a flatter calibration curve, so $\text{plim}\,\hat{\beta} < 1$.

Why would we have $Cov\left(w_{ib}, p_{ia}^b\right) < V\left(p_{ia}^b\right)$? Based on simple econometrics intuition, classical additive measurement error in the subjective probability variables is an explanation. Note that measurement error cannot be entire classical here because the variable is bounded: It has to be negatively correlated with the error-free measure. Errors in responses that correspond to low error-free probabilities are more likely positive, and errors in responses that correspond to high error-free probabilities are more likely negative. That negative correlation leads to attenuation in itself due to a smaller positive $Cov\left(w_{ib}, p_{ia}^b\right)$, reenforcing the effect of a larger $V\left(p_{ia}^b\right)$.

One source of measurement error is survey noise, which is likely present both for theoretical reasons and based on evidence. We have argued that people in this age group often think about when they would retire, and this is why eliciting their beliefs in surveys can lead to informative variables. Respondents are asked, however, about probabilities, even though most people do not carry around probabilities in their heads when they think about when they would retire. Thus, when answering the survey question they have to transform what they think into probabilities. That transformation may involve randomness so that the same beliefs may result in different probability responses.

Besides a theoretical plausibility, there is empirical evidence for survey noise in subjective probability responses and its attenuation effect. It was identified in stock market expectations from test-retest evidence by Kézdi and Willis (2011) and from differences in stated averages and averages implied by stated probabilities by Ameriks et al. (2020). Both papers found that taking survey noise into account for estimation leads to stronger estimates of the associations. Kimball et al. (2008) make the same point in the context of eliciting preference parameters in surveys.

It turns out that we can use test-retest evidence to identify survey noise with respect to retirement expectations, too, although not in terms of p[62] or p[65]. In 2018, in an experimental module fielded on a random subsample of its respondents to investigate their intentions to work longer, the HRS asked 753 respondents of age 64 or younger about their subjective probability of doing any work for pay after age 70. It turns out that this question has been part of the HRS core questionnaire, too, since 2012. Thus, in 2018, this same question was asked from 753 respondents twice during the same survey, separated by about 30 minutes and many other survey questions. We restrict the sample to respondents of ages 55 through 64 who worked at the time of the interview (n = 444) and estimate a regression of one subjective probability prediction on the other. Table 10.5 shows these test-retest results.

Table 10.5 Test–retest regression of the probability of working past age 70: Responses in the experimental module regressed on responses in the core survey.

	Response in experimental module
Response in core survey	0.81^{**}
	(0.065)
Constant	0.07**
	(0.014)
Observations	444
R-squared	0.576

Data: HRS 2018 experimental module on working longer; respondents of age 55 through 64.

Robust standard errors in parentheses. $^{**}p < 0.01,\, ^{*}p < 0.05.$

While not a perfect test for p^{62} and p^{65}, this result suggests that survey noise in itself leads to a substantial attenuation in those, too, possibly as much as a third of the total attenuation. The slope coefficient estimate is approximately 0.8 for the subjective probability prediction of working at all after age 70. There is high, but not perfect, test–retest validity. Treating deviations in the responses as classical errors in variables, the 0.8 regressions coefficient in Table 10.5 corresponds to a signal-to-noise ratio of 4. One would need a more complete model of retirement—including a quantification of the variance of the shocks affecting outcomes—in order to establish how much measurement error accounts for the attenuation shown in Fig. 10.2. Nonetheless, the finding that about 20% of the variance of the elicited probabilities is survey response error goes a long way in explaining the attenuated response work outcomes to the probabilities of work. In the next section, we show how accounting for this attenuation is critical when using subjective probabilities to model outcomes.

Apart from any biases or errors in survey responses, a fundamental source of prediction error is—at the time of the prediction—that there is less or different information available to the individuals than at the time of the outcome, that is, $\Omega_{ia} \neq \Omega_{ib}$, b = 62 or b = 65 and a < b. If respondents integrated out all uncertainty in a rational way and formed their responses based on optimal predictions, absent survey response error the subjective probability should be an unbiased predictor of outcomes. That we see attenuation that not fully explained by survey noise is indirect evidence of departures from probabilistic thinking. For example, Ω_{ia}, the information used when making the subjective probability prediction at age a, Ω_{ia} may contain additional elements that would not be in Ω_{ib}, the information used when the actual decision is made—for example, whether one's older peers did at the time the prediction is elicited. In general, individuals get news about their own circumstances and desires.

As noted, there is likely some evidence from the calibration curve findings of more attenuation than can be explained by survey response error. Respondents may not apply probability laws accurately, for example, they may attach disproportionately large weights to elements in the information set that are salient at the time of elicitation, but are less relevant for the actual decision or outcome. Alternatively, there may be systematic departures from systematic probabilistic thinking.[4] To shed more light on why

---

[4] Chapter 8 in this Handbook indeed makes such arguments in evaluating the predictive power of mortality expectations. It finds calibration curves for mortality expectations that are very similar to those we find for retirement (see Fig. 10.2). It, however,

Table 10.6 Calibration regressions including interactions with p^{65}.

	(1)	(2)	(3)	(4)
	w^{65}	w^{65}	w^{65}	w^{65}
p^{65}	0.49**	0.48**	0.48**	0.48**
	(0.018)	(0.018)	(0.018)	(0.019)
p^{65} interacted with time to age 65		−0.03**		
		(0.007)		
p^{65} interacted with years of education			0.04**	
			(0.007)	
p^{65} interacted with cognitive score				0.06**
				(0.016)
Constant	0.21**	0.21**	0.21**	0.22**
	(0.009)	(0.009)	(0.009)	(0.010)
Observations	12,922	12,922	12,895	11,390
R-squared	0.14	0.14	0.14	0.14

*Notes. w^{65} is whether the individual worked full-time after age 65; $w^{65} = 0$ or 1; p^{65} is the subjective probability prediction of working full-time after age 65. Time to age 65 is 3 to 8 years; years of education ranges from 0 to 17; cognitive score is the standardized 27-item score combining immediate word recall (10 pts), delayed word recall (10pts), counting backward from 20 (2pts), sequentially subtracting 7 from 100 (5 pts). All three variables are mean-differenced. Each of columns (2)–(4) includes the interaction variable as well (coefficients not shown). All regressions are weighted by respondent survey weights. Data: Health and Retirement Study, pooled survey years 1994–2018, valid responses to p65 and known w65, age 57–62. Standard errors are clustered at the household level. ** $p < 0.01$, * $p < 0.05$.*

the calibrations of p^{62} and p^{65} are imperfect we investigated how the slope of the calibration curve varies with observable covariates that are potentially related to the magnitude of prediction error. Note that this question is different from whether the covariates are associated with the direction of the error, which we investigated above.

Table 10.6 shows results from calibration curve regressions that include interactions with the covariates. The covariates are measured at the time of the elicitation of the probabilities. We show the results for p^{65} text; corresponding results p^{62} are similar. The regressions have the same binary left-hand-side variable, actually working past age 65, w_i^{65}, and the same main right-hand-side variable, the subjective probability response, p_{ia}^{65}. They are estimated on the pooled cross-sectional sample as for the calibration exercise (Fig. 10.2): full-time workers 3 to 8 years prior to age 65. Column (1) does not include anything else and replicates the linear approximation of the calibration curve on Fig. 10.2; column (2) includes the interaction of p_{ia}^{65} with the time between the interview and age 65 (range is 3 to 8 years); column (3) includes the interaction of p_{ia}^{65} with years of education; column (4) includes the interaction of p_{ia}^{65} with a standardized score of cognitive capacity. For easier interpretation we mean-differenced

---

discounts measurement response error as the sole explanation for the attenuation—pointing to biases in the probability reports including heaping at the extremes and at 50–50. More generally, it points to the possibility that the distribution of subjective mortality is flatter than that of objective mortality for reasons in addition to measurement error. See Fig. 8.1 for an illustration of this point. We return to the issue of attenuation in Section 10.6.

the interaction variables. Columns (2)–(4) include the interaction variable in itself as well. Their coefficients are not shown in the table for brevity. Standard errors are clustered at the household level to account for repeated individuals in the pooled cross-section and potential intra-household correlations.

Column (1) documents the result from Fig. 10.2 that the calibration coefficient is estimated to be 0.5, which is an attenuation by one-half of what perfect calibration would imply. The interaction results (columns (2)–(4)) show that the slope is flatter the further away the prediction from the target age, and it is steeper the higher the level of education or the higher the cognitive score. These findings are in line with our intuition about the sources of the prediction error: The error should be smaller at shorter forecast horizons and for respondents with more education and higher cognitive capacity who are arguably better equipped for and more used to think about complex decision problems ahead of time. The estimated variation in the slope by the covariates is substantial. For example, five years closer to the target age results in a slope that is steeper by 0.13; respondents with four more years more education, such as college versus high school have a slope that is steeper by 0.15. Thus the magnitude of the error varies systematically across individuals.

Taking the results together, we find that full-time workers' subjective probability predictions of whether they would work full-time at target ages 62 and 65 that are 3 to 8 years in the future have high quality, but they are imperfect. Subjective probability predictions are conceptually clean, and they have good measurement properties. In particular, the subjective probability predictions are essentially unbiased both overall and along important personal characteristics. While we have found some systematic heterogeneity in the direction of the prediction error by couple, race and health, but there is no such relationship with education, cognitive capacity or other demographic characteristics. In addition, the variables have negligible item nonresponse.

At the same time, the subjective probability predictions contain substantial error that makes them attenuated predictors of future retirement. The magnitude of the attenuation is about 50%, which means that respondents who, for example, give a 10 percentage point higher prediction of working full-time at age 65 tend to be not 10% but 20% more likely to be working full-time then. The magnitude of the prediction error, and thus the attenuation, is related to the forecast horizon, respondents' education and cognitive capacity in intuitive ways. Part of the attenuation is due to survey noise, which likely arises because the survey question requires a transformation of respondents' expectations into probabilities, and there appears to be random deviations in that transformation. A methodologically important finding is that the calibration curve is approximately linear, with somewhat larger prediction error for exact 100% responses.

10.6 Predicting retirement: subjective probability predictions and predictive analytics

Subjective retirement probability predictions can be used as either substitutes or complements to statistical models or structural models using observable characteristics to predict the retirement of currently working people. See Chapter 21 in this Handbook for an overview of the use of expectations in structural models. There are multiple reasons why using subjective probability predictions may be advantageous. First, subjective retirement predictions are a single variable that is cheaper to measure in a survey than the many predictor variables that may go into the decision. Second, subjective retirement predictions may include information that is not measured by other predictor variables as no dataset

Table 10.7 Details of the four predictive models.

Model	Formula or method	Variables used
p^{65}	$\hat{p}_i = p_i^{65}$	p^{65}
Adjusted p^{65}	$\hat{p}_i = 0.2 + 0.5 p_i^{65}$	p^{65}
RF(x)	Random Forest	x = {age, race, ethnicity, education, detailed marital status, veteran status, earnings, total household income, total household wealth, whether the respondent has a DB pension plan, a DC pension plan, total balance of the DC pension plans, total balance of the IRA accounts in the household, self-rated health status, whether the respondent has a spouse, and the age, education, work status, earnings, pensions, and self-rated health of the spouse}
RF(x,p^{65})	Random Forest	p^{65}, x

Notes. The Random Forest predictive models use the ranger package in R with default settings, treating the target variable (w^{65}) as numeric so the prediction is a probability.

can measure all potential predictors. Third, subjective retirement predictions may also reflect how re-spondents use that information to make decisions based on their preferences and cognitive functioning. People might not behave according to the statistical or structural models used for prediction. Indeed, subjective retirement prediction may be better predictors of shifts in retirement across birth cohorts than predictive models based on other variables. The potential disadvantages of using subjective retirement predictions include its substantial prediction error that varies by the respondents' characteristics as we documented above, and the fact that the individual subjective retirement predictions cannot properly reflect the realization of the macro environment.

To get a better understanding of how subjective retirement probability predictions perform in actual predictions, we have run a horse race between four predictive models of the actual future probability of working full-time past age 65 among people of ages 57–62 working full-time. We use the same forecast horizon of 3 to 8 years and the same sample that we used in our previous analysis. Model 1 includes the response to the subjective work probability predictions as they are ($\hat{p}_i = p_i^{65}$). Model 2 includes an adjustment to the subjective work probability predictions to recalibrate them from the noise. In par-ticular, Model 2 uses the rounded values of the simple OLS linear regression parameters from column (1) in Table 10.6, that is, $\hat{p}_i = 0.2 + 0.5 p_i^{65}$. Model 3 is a cross-validated random forest probability prediction model using a large set of predictor variables. Model 4 is the same as Model 3 except it adds the subjective probability predictions to the other predictor variables. Table 10.7 summarizes the details of the four predictive models.

We used these competing models to predict whether the individual worked full-time at or after age 65 in years 2014 through 2018. For each target year we used the variables that were measured up to three years earlier and the sample of respondents who were 57 to 62 years old then (up to four years in case there was no survey three years earlier). For example, we used data from waves 2006 through 2012 and respondents who were 57 to 62 years old in each survey wave to predict working full-time past age 65 in year 2014 (it is 2006 to 2012 and not 2011 because a few people who were 62 in 2012 turned 65 by the 2014 survey wave as some interviews are conducted in 2015).

In the language of predictive analytics (also known as machine learning), years 2014–2018 are the five test sets, where each test set has a corresponding training set of data from three to eight years earlier, and our comparison of the various models is a five-fold cross-validation. In cross-sectional data test sets tend to be drawn randomly. The longitudinal nature of this data warrants another approach,

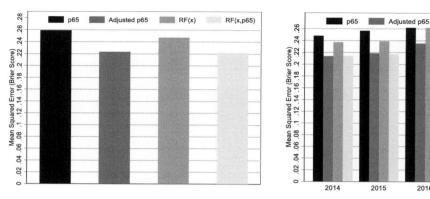

Average of test years 2014–2018 | Test years 2014–2018 separately

FIGURE 10.3 Predictive performance of the four models.

that is, to select specific years as test sets so we can further investigate the predictive performance of the different models in different years corresponding to potentially different macro environments. To evaluate the performance of the four models we compare the predicted probabilities to the realized 0–1 variable of working full-time in the test years. The measure we use is the mean squared error (MSE) of the prediction (the square of the difference of the 0–1 realization and the predicted probability), which is also known as the Brier score (see, e.g., Békés and Kézdi, 2021). The lower the MSE the better the prediction. Fig. 10.3 shows the results. The left panel shows the average MSE across the five test years; the right panel shows the MSE for each test year separately.

Perhaps not surprisingly, the raw subjective probability predictions perform the worst. More surprisingly, the random forest with a rich set of predictor variables performs only slightly better. In contrast, the adjusted subjective probability predictions perform substantially better than either the unadjusted subjective probability or the random forest based on the rich set of predictors. Moreover, when the random forest prediction is based on the subjective probability plus the rich set of predictors, there is little further improvement compared to using the adjusted subjective probability predictions alone. All of this is true not only as the average over the five test years, but in each test year separately. These results are especially remarkable because the adjustment here is very simple, using the same intercept and slope coefficients for all respondents in all years. As we have shown in Table 10.6, these parameters vary by education, cognitive score, and how far they are from the target year. The adjustment here has not used any of those differences.

Thus, we can conclude that subjective probability predictions, if adjusted in a simple way for attenuation bias, are well-performing predictors of future retirement at age 65 among full-time workers. Additional variables and more sophisticated modeling does not produce significantly better predictions. Because using adjusted subjective probability predictions is substantially less burdensome in terms of data requirements and modeling than building predictive models with many variables, this finding is important in practice.

Note that the near-sufficiency of the attenuation-adjusted retirement probability strongly supports our contention that the attenuation arises from measurement error in survey responses. If the atten-

Table 10.8 Working full-time past ages 62 and 65: Subjective probability predictions and realizations.

Labor force status at the time of the subjective probability prediction	Working full-time past age 62			Working full-time past age 65		
	p^{62}	w^{62}	N	p^{65}	w^{65}	N
Works full-time	0.58	0.55	15,469	0.41	0.41	12,922
Works part-time	0.41	0.20	2928	0.29	0.14	2477
Unemployed	0.50	0.20	673	0.31	0.11	500
Partly retired	0.20	0.09	1366	0.13	0.06	2059
Retired	0.06	0.02	3596	0.04	0.01	5624
Disabled	0.05	0.02	1061	0.02	0.02	1017
Not in the labor force	0.13	0.06	1502	0.06	0.04	1703
Total	0.43	0.37	26,595	0.26	0.24	26,302

Notes. p^{62} and p^{65} are the average subjective probability predictions; w^{62} and w^{65} are the proportions of the corresponding realizations; p^{62} and p^{65} are measured 3 to 8 years younger than the target age. Data: HRS 1994–2018 pooled cross-section.

uation arises instead from differences between subjective and objective probabilities as suggested by Chapter 8 in this Handbook, other variables related to the objective probability should be helpful in predicting realized outcomes. There certainly could be omitted factors in the set x that predict retirement. Leading candidates would include macroeconomic shocks, though the year-by-year near-sufficiency of retirement probabilities suggest that they were not factors in the period studied.[5]

10.7 Subjective work probability predictions among non-full-time worker respondents

Before moving on to summarizing the results of the research that uses retirement age expectations, let us take a detour examining the subjective predictions of non-full-time workers. While our main focus is retirement from full-time work to some other state, the HRS asks these questions from a wider set of respondents. In particular, all respondents who worked for pay at the time of the interview are asked the p^{62} and p^{65} questions. Respondents not working for pay at the time of the interview are asked about the percent chance that they would work for pay at some time in the future. If their response is a nonzero percent chance, they, too, are asked the p^{62} and p^{65} questions. If their response is zero, don't know, or refuse, they are skipped out of the subsequent questions. We imputed $p_{ia}^{62} = 0$ and $p_{ia}^{65} = 0$ if the response to the working-at-all question was 0%.

Table 10.8 shows the average subjective probability predictions and the proportion of realizations by labor force status at the time of the interview. Similar to our previous analysis, we restricted the

---

[5] Of course, unexpected macro shocks, e.g., a dramatic change in Social Security, could lead to systematic deviations of expectations from outcomes. This would not be a violation of rational expectations, but simply an illustration of the fact that aggregated shocks do not average to zero in a cross-section.

sample to respondents who were 3 to 8 years younger than the target age when their predictions were elicited, but we include all respondents regardless of their labor force status.

The first row in Table 10.8 repeats the information in Table 10.3, showing that the subjective probability predictions of full-time work past the two age thresholds are essentially unbiased among current full-time workers. At the same time, respondents in all other current labor force status tend to overpredict substantially their future full-time work chances, with two or three times as high probabilities on average. For example, respondents who work part-time tend to overpredict their probability of working full-time past each of the age thresholds, by a factor of two (0.41 instead of 0.20 for age 62; 0.29 instead of 0.14 for age 65). The same is true for the similar category of respondents who considered themselves partially retired. The relatively few unemployed respondents in the sample tend to overpredict their likelihood of their full-time working past the age thresholds by a factor of three. Respondents in the remaining labor force status have very low full-time work chances, but they, too, tend to overpredict those low probabilities.

These results have important consequences for research uses of the subjective probability predictions. Pooling full-time workers with other groups, including part-time workers or partially retired respondents, reduces the quality of the measurement and may introduce stronger noise or bias in the results. The problem may not be very severe if the non-full-time-workers make up a small fraction of the overall sample (for example, part-time workers are only about 16% of the group working for pay in our sample), but the cleaner empirical strategy is to focus on full-time workers.

10.8 Research on the quality of retirement age expectations

The first analysis of the subjective probability predictions that we know of is by Hurd (1999). He analyzed the quality of the subjective probability predictions of working full-time past age 62 (p^{62}) in the first two waves of the HRS. His results show that p^{62} is a strong predictor of actual full-time work past age 62 two years later, it contains information beyond important variables that predict retirement, and it varies with important variables very similarly to the actual full-time work probabilities. Most studies that use the subjective probability predictions of future work to investigate substantial economic questions tend to contain some analysis of the quality of those variables, too (for example, Honig, 1996; Chan and Stevens, 2004). Their general conclusion is similar to Hurd's (1999) initial assessment and the conclusions of our own analysis: The subjective probability predictions contain a lot of information, some of which is otherwise unmeasured, and they can be used to predict actual future retirement.[6]

As for the other approach, Benitez-Silva and Dwyer (2005) use HRS data from 1992 to 2000 to examine the elicited planned or expected retirement age on a restricted sample of respondents who report to have a retirement plan. (In our sample of full-time workers, 40% did not have such a plan.) They test whether, conditional on observables, the expected retirement age follows a random walk, which is a test of rational expectation formation in their theoretical framework. They address measurement error in the responses by an instrumental variables strategy, and they augment it with a Heckman-type selection model to correct for selection into giving a valid answer (with longevity expectations and smoking

---

[6] See Chapter 22 in this Handbook for a similar favorable assessment of the predictive power of expectations of job finding and Chapter 8 in this Handbook for a more mixed assessment of the predictive power of expectations of health and longevity.

behavior as instruments for measurement error and age of the respondent and whether the parents of the respondent reached retirement age as instruments for selection). They cannot reject the null hypothesis of planned retirement age following a random walk. They do reject a stronger, perfect foresight version, so retirement expectations appear to be rational, but they are not perfect predictors.

Papers that use this variable for investigating substantive questions tend to include some assessment of the quality of the variable (for example, Haider and Stephens, 2007). They find that the variable has a lot of useful and otherwise unmeasured information about actual future retirement, but its measurement issues require more sophisticated analysis.

Our reading of this literature reinforces the conclusion of our own analyses. Eliciting the planned or expected retirement age may be the good strategy for the substantive research question, but this variable has its issues of interpretation and high and selective item nonresponse. There is very valuable information in this variable, but using it requires a lot of work and additional assumptions. Subjective retirement probabilities are good although imperfect predictors that contain information not fully captured by other observables. That is great news if the research question can use this variable.

10.9 **Potential uses of retirement age expectations**

After having discussed the quality of the different approaches to elicit retirement age expectations, let us discuss how such data can be used in research and policy analysis. First and most obviously, having inexpensive and good predictions of future work probabilities for various cohorts and social groups can directly help policy analysis. For example, the U.S. Social Security Administration, and its counterparts in other countries, regularly forecast the actuarial status and financial conditions of their funds. These forecasts typically use complex models with many parts using many parameters, of which the rate at which various groups retire is only one small subset (see, e.g., Social Security Administration, 2019). Using a statistic of a single variable from available surveys, potentially adjusted in a simple way, can be used as a parameter in an appropriate model in a relatively simple way. To do so relying on our findings, the model should be about the medium run because our results establish the good properties of the (adjusted) subjective probability predictions up to 8 years from the time of the measurement of the variable.

Second, the good predictive performance of subjective probability predictions of retirement opens up the possibility to use them to evaluate the effects of various state variables and interventions on future retirement.

Third, it also allows for analyzing the effect of retirement age expectations, or deviations from such expectations, on economic behavior and outcomes. In the next section, we summarize results in the literature that use retirement expectations as a left-hand-side variable or as a right-hand-side variable. Before doing so, let's reflect on what our results imply for such applications.

We have shown that subjective probability predictions are imperfect, and the simplest way to rationalize the imperfection is as if it were a mean-zero additive measurement error to the hypothetical error-free probability prediction, with several features. This measurement error increases the variance of the error-free variable. Moreover, it is negatively correlated with the error-free variable because of its bounded nature. We found systematic heterogeneity in the magnitude of the measurement error, most importantly with respect to education and cognitive capacity. We also found that some systematic heterogeneity in the direction of the error, by race, being in a couple, and health.

When on the left-hand-side of a regression, this measurement error does not necessarily induce bias in the coefficients of interest, but it increases estimation uncertainty. The caveat here is that the measurement error should not be correlated with the right-hand-side variable of interest. For example, the correlation of the measurement error with health can have consequences for estimating the effect of health on the probability of working past an age threshold. The potential for such correlations needs to be addressed in each application separately.

10.10 Research with retirement age expectations as the left-hand-side variable

What leads people to retire at certain ages has been the subject of a large literature. The most researched potential causes include health, financial incentives in the pension formula, and availability of health care (this last one in the U.S. context). In this subsection, we review the literature that attempts to estimate these effects by having the retirement age expectations as the left-hand-side variable. Having expectations on the left-hand-side instead of realized retirement allows not only for estimating effects ahead of time, but it also allows for using within-person variation in the retirement age that would be impossible to analyze using realizations. The advantage of the ability to restrict variation to within-person is that can mitigate potential biases to the effect estimates due to unmeasured and endogenous heterogeneity. Most papers use the subjective probability predictions in the HRS data, but some use other data sources and/or the direct elicitation of the expected retirement age.

McGarry (2004) uses the subjective probability predictions as a left-hand-side variable to estimate the effect of health on retirement. She uses the first two waves of the HRS, 1992 and 1994, to examine how self-rated health and its change are associated with the subjective probability prediction of working full-time past age 62 (p^{62}) and its change. The sample consists of working people younger than 62 in 1994 (wave 2). She argues that, by focusing on working people and their expectations instead of realized retirement, one can mitigate a potential justification bias that would make people who retire for other reasons report worse or worsening health. Recall that we have found that the level of health is negatively correlated with the measurement error in p^{62}, which in this case would lead to an additional bias of cross-sectional estimates. For those reasons, we focus on her results from the specification with change in p^{62} regressed on whether the respondent reported that they had the same, better, or worse health in wave 2 than in wave 1.

The main finding is that respondents who reported deteriorating health revised their p^{62} downwards from the previous wave—by 4 percentage points (McGarry, 2004, Table 6). What do the measurement properties of p^{62} that we learned in this chapter imply for this result? We do not know whether the first difference of the prediction is correlated with self-rated change in health, so we do not know if that would result in a bias. What we know is that the measurement error itself would lead to estimation uncertainty. That uncertainty is likely particularly strong here both because taking the difference magnifies the role of noise and because the sample includes the non-full-time workers with lower quality p^{62} variables. This estimation uncertainty shows up in the relatively wide 95% confidence interval that nevertheless does not contain zero. Hence, McGarry's result provides reasonably strong evidence for the negative effect of deteriorating health on working past age 62, but with an effect size smaller than what cross-sectional estimates would imply.

Chan and Stevens (2004) use HRS data from 1992 through 1998 to analyze the effect of retirement incentives on the subjective probability prediction p^{62}. They measure retirement incentives based on respondents' self-reported pension information, as opposed to matched objective pension plan characteristics, arguing that it is what people know about the incentives that should matter for their behavior. They summarize incentives in a pension gain variable: how much people would gain by retiring after age 62 instead of before age 62. They estimate a moderate effect in pooled cross-sectional regressions, and a more modest effect in regressions that within-person variation only. Such within-person analysis is possible because they use longitudinal data on subjective probability predictions. Note that such within-person analysis would be impossible with data using realized retirement. With p^{62} on the left-hand-side, measurement error in this variable is unlikely to lead to biased estimates. They argue that measurement error in their causal variable is also unlikely to account for the fact that restricting to within-person variation decreases the effects to be modest. They conclude that, while financial incentives for retiring early matter, that affect may be more modest than what the previous literature suggested that analyzed realized retirement and could not condition on unobserved individual heterogeneity.

Bottazzi et al. (2006) investigate the combined effect of three pension reforms in Italy in the 1990s that reduced pension benefits for some groups on savings, the expected retirement age and expectations about future pension benefits. Here we summarize their results on retirement age expectations. The authors use the Survey of Household Income and Wealth conducted by the Bank of Italy from 1989 through 2002 that elicited the expected retirement age. In a difference-in-differences analysis making use of control groups whose benefits were not affected by the reforms, they show that the pension reforms increased the expected retirement age by one to four years in various groups.

Okumura and Usui (2014) use data from the Japanese Study of Aging and Retirement (JSTAR) to estimate the effect of a gradual increase in the age eligibility of employee pensions on the expected age of pension claiming and retirement, as well as the expected pension benefits. The survey elicited the expected age of claiming. The authors document substantial item-nonresponse to both the expected pension claiming age and the expected retirement age. Their results show that, in the subsample that gave valid age responses, the increase in the age eligibility of pensions lead to a substantial increase in the expected age of pension claiming and retirement. Our conclusion from these studies is that large policy changes tend to result in revised retirement age expectations (the Italian and Japanese studies), but people tend to be modestly responsive to the incentives in complex pension plans as those in the United States (Chan and Stevens, 2004).

The effect of health care availability on the timing of retirement is addressed by several papers in the U.S. context. Mermin et al. (2007) compare subjective retirement probability predictions among 51 to 56 year-old people across two birth cohorts: those born in 1936–1941 versus 1948–1953. They use the subjective probability predictions p^{62} and p^{65} from two waves of the HRS apart from each other by 12 years, 1992 and 2004. Their sample consists of people who worked for pay at the time of the interview. They show significantly higher reported probability of working full-time both past 62 and 65 in the younger birth cohort, both among men and women. They argue that the result is due to the fact that the younger generation plans to retire later. In an Oaxaca-type decomposition, they find that the substantial decrease in defined benefit pensions and employee-sponsored retiree health insurance can explain as much as two thirds of the increase in the likelihood of working full-time past age 62 and one third of the increase in working past 65.

Ayyagari (2019) uses HRS data to estimate the effect of the Affordable Care Act (ACA) in the USA on p^{62}. In pooled cross-sectional difference-in-differences specification, she compares p^{62} responses from before ACA to after ACA for people without employer-sponsored retiree health insurance coverage (the treatment group) to people with retiree coverage (the control group). Without retiree coverage, those who retire at age 62 would not have employer-sponsored health insurance, and they would not be qualified for Medicare until age 65. The effect of ACA here is that it could provide affordable health insurance for these years even for people who retire. People without retiree coverage are 6 percentage points less likely to work past age 62 because of the availability of health insurance through ACA (Table 10.1). The conclusion of these papers is that the availability of affordable health insurance in retirement is an important cause of whether people retire before age 65 in the USA.

10.11 Research with retirement age expectations as the right-hand-side variable

Let's start this part of the review with a note. When retirement age expectations are a right-hand-side variable of a behavioral relationship, they may be of interest even if the expectations are not unbiased predictors of retirement. As long as people behave differently if they have different expectations, learning about those effects is interesting on its own right. At the same time, aspects of measurement quality still play a role here, such as item nonresponse or measurement error due to survey noise. The former needs to be treated if it is a significant problem; the latter implies a moderate measurement error that is close to being classical.

Haider and Stephens (2007) use data from the HRS from 1992 through 2002 as well as data from its predecessor, the Retirement History Survey (RHS) from 1969 through 1977, to investigate the extent to which retirement results in a decline of consumption. More specifically, their question is whether expected retirement leads to the same reduction in food expenditures as unexpected retirement. They measure consumption by expenditures on food, and they use the elicited planned or expected retirement age and compare it to the actual retirement age to differentiate expected retirement from unexpected retirement. They find that expected retirement results in a substantially smaller reduction than unexpected retirement, which suggests that it may not be retirement itself but potentially other changes that are responsible for the decline in food expenditures with retirement. Using the elicited planned or expected retirement age brings about the problem of item-nonresponse, but the authors carry out a robustness check by transforming this variable to whether the respondent expects to retire by the subsequent survey wave and find similar results. Note that for this analysis, expected retirement age is the variable of interest; using the probability predictions instead would require functional form assumptions to estimate that statistic. Besides its substantive results, this study highlights the methodological issues and potential solutions with using the planned or expected retirement age variable.

Romm (2015) uses data from the HRS from 1992 through 2004 to investigate the relationship between the expected time of retirement and preretirement wealth accumulation, and how that varies with the distribution of bargaining power between members of a couple. Later expected retirement should call for less wealth to be accumulated, ceteris paribus, but retirement plans are inherently endogenous to wealth accumulation through unobserved heterogeneity in preferences and constraints. The author uses the change of the subjective probability predictions p^{62} to condition on the time-invariant component of such unobserved heterogeneity and augments it with an instrumental variable strategy with self-reports of the usual retirement age at the job as an instrument. Both the noninstrumented and instrumented results indicate a strong effect in households with the husband being the sole earner, but no significant effect of married women's retirement age expectations whether or not they were the sole earners or dual earners.

Clarke et al. (2012) use the HRS data from 1998 through 2008 to investigate the effect of unexpected retirement on life satisfaction. They use the subjective probability prediction p^{62}, observed repeatedly for individuals, and they use a generalized growth mixture modeling to classify respondents into low, moderate, and high work expectation categories. They find that men with less job stability but high expectations to work full-time past age 62 experienced substantial lower life satisfaction when those expectations were not met and, instead, they retired earlier.

Another literature investigates whether and to what extent working couples coordinate retirement or take into account their spouses' resources and characteristics. Retirement expectations data have been used in some of this research. Pienta and Hayward (2002) use the first wave of HRS subjective probability predictions p^{62} and p^{65} to investigate the extent to which expectations of members of working couples are related to their own, their spouses', and household characteristics. They find that all three matter for both husbands and wives, but they also find a stronger influence of husbands on wives' retirement expectations than vice versa.

Benitez-Silva and Dwyer (2006) extend their analysis of whether the planned or expected retirement age conforms the rational expectation hypothesis (Benitez-Silva and Dwyer, 2005, discussed above), by focusing on couples and including the spouse's expected retirement age as a conditioning variable. They find that couples do take spousal retirement age into account and they form rational expectations accordingly.

Ho and Raymo (2009) use a sample of couples in the HRS observed from 1992 through 2004 to examine how their actual retirement timing is related to their retirement age expectations. They make use of responses to a question that directly asks if couples plan to retire together. This question follows the retirement plan and planned retirement age elicitations that we discussed earlier. The authors exclude couples with one or two members reporting not to have plans for retirement, and they find that, in the remaining subsample, couples who report to plan to retire together are three times more likely to retire within 12 months than couples who do not plan to retire together.

Michaud et al. (2020) estimate a structural model of the joint retirement decision of spouses that combines stated preference and retirement plans elicited in an internet supplement to the HRS. Their approach is designed to disentangle the effects of preferences and expectation, and in particular, points to husbands' misperception of wives' disutility of work.

Overall, the conclusion from these studies is that many couples plan to retire jointly, and they tend to realize these plans.

10.12 Using conditional subjective work probability predictions to estimate effects on retirement

Recent research on retirement age expectations as the left-hand-side variable builds on fielding conditional subjective probability questions instead of the unconditional subjective probability predictions. The idea is to control variation in the conditioning event by asking multiple questions. In practice, this amounts to asking the probability of working in one state of the world (good health, for example) followed by asking the probability of working in another state of the world (bad health). These are direct elicitations of the probabilities of potential outcomes from the same individuals. Under ideal circumstances, the difference between the two reported probabilities identifies the effect of one state versus the other (bad health versus good health) on the probability of the outcome (working), for each individual. This strategy has multiple potential uses. First, it may identify the effect without observing the various states of the world, and second, it may identify not only the average effect, but the entire distribution of the heterogeneous effects. See also Chapters 1 and 4 in this Handbook for general discussion of the used of hypothetical and conditional expectations questions.

Giustinelli and Shapiro (2019) define this effect as the Subjective ex ante Average Treatment Effect, abbreviated as SeaTE. It is subjective because it is stated by the individuals themselves, it is ex ante because the effect is measured without observing any change in the state variable, and it is a treatment effect at the level of the individual. They investigate the effect of bad health versus good health on the probability of working for pay in two- and four-years ahead. They field the questions as part of the fourth wave of the Vanguard Research Initiative (VRI), a longitudinal survey of Vanguard account holders, on a sample consisting of working respondents aged 57 to 81 who are in good health and were still working at the time of the survey.[7]

The questions elicit subjective probability predictions of working (unconditional), the conditioning events (bad or good health), and working conditional on health (working if in bad health, working if in good health). The SeaTE of bad health for each of individual is the difference between the two conditional probabilities. The results show a substantial average effect. The average SeaTE is −28.5% at a two-year horizon and −25.7% at a four-year horizon. There is substantial heterogeneity in the effect, with zero effect for close to 30% of the respondents. The authors carry out a validation exercise making use of the detailed sequence of probability questions. In particular, they compute the unconditional probability of work implied by the responses to the conditional probability questions and the probabilities of the conditioning events, and then they compare this to the directly elicited unconditional probability responses. They find a remarkable accordance with a correlation coefficient of 0.93. They also show that the subjective probabilities predict retirement decisions in the VRI panel though there are limited adverse health shocks realized.

The conditional expectations framework is helpful for controlling for endogeneity and selectivity in empirical analysis. For example, a regression of the retirement outcomes on health shocks will not produce an unbiased estimate of the treatment effect of health on retirement if health is related to unobserved taste for work. Using as simulation based on the distribution of taste for work elicited from the VRI respondents, Giustinelli and Shapiro (2019) show that such biases would emerge in estimates based on data on health and retirement outcomes.

Hudomiet et al. (2020) report results from similar conditional probability questions fielded on the RAND American Life Panel survey on a sample of 51 to 69 year-old respondents. In particular, a series of questions asked about the probability of working past age 70 conditional on various states of the world, including good health versus bad health, a hypothetical policy change that would increase wage for workers who are over 70 years old, a large inheritance, increased longevity, and various work characteristics. Similar to Giustinelli and Shapiro (2019), they find substantial positive average effect of good health on the probability of future work (here the effect is calculated as good health versus bad health). In addition, they find a moderate average positive effect of higher wages, a large negative effect of inheritance, a small positive effect of increased longevity, and small effects of work characteristics.

---

[7] They also report results for a nearly identical survey fielded as experimental module in the HRS 2016.

Using health as the conditioning state of the world the authors carry out the validation exercise of comparing the probability of work elicited directly with the probability of work computed from the conditional probabilities and the probabilities of the conditioning events. As in Giustinelli and Shapiro (2019), they find remarkable accordance of the two. As a methodologically interesting point, Hudomiet et al. (2020) show that the same accordance is not true if joint probabilities are elicited (for example, working and in bad health) instead of conditional probabilities (working if in bad health). They also assess whether respondents answer ceteris paribus in scenarios with low degrees of specification (what they call the "filling-in problem"). They find no evidence of filling-in, which supports interpreting the conditional probabilities as causal.

10.12.1 Conditioning versus subjectivity in general

This section's consideration of the conditional expectation relates to a general issue in eliciting unconditional expectations: What do respondents have in mind when they provide a point response to a probabilistic question? Formally, if they are thinking probabilistically, what states are they integrating over when they give a response? Informally, what are they thinking about and what are they not thinking about? See Dominitz (1997), Chapters 1, 26, and 8 in this Handbook, and Giustinelli and Shapiro (2019) for discussion of this issue.

The issue of implicit conditioning may be important for retirement expectations. For example, there is an ambiguity of whether people's retirement age expectations are conditional on certain circumstances, such whether they are alive at age t, whether their employer wants them to retire at a certain age, or the state of the labor market at age t. Because of limitations on the length of a survey question and the desire not to prime the answer by specifying conditions, survey questions leave such conditioning implicit. Therefore, when they interpret the responses, researchers need to be careful about implicit assumptions about what circumstances respondents condition on and what they integrate out.

Conditional expectations questions, by being specific about conditioning events, may be a step toward addressing these ambiguities. By being explicit about a dimension, conditional probabilities are a route to grappling with the incomplete scenario problem (Manski, 1999). Vignettes discussed in Chapter 4 in this Handbook likewise have promise for addressing this problem.

10.13 Conclusions

Retirement and retirement expectations are of keen interest to social scientists and policymakers. Predicting the effect of changes to policies or in circumstances requires evaluating how people's decisions would change as a result. Predicting how the retirement rate will evolve in the future requires predictions of not only how those circumstances would evolve but also how those would affect people's decisions. Retirement expectations are a key tool for analysis. This chapter demonstrates the usefulness of these measures—both by describing their statistical properties and by surveying their wide use in research and policy analysis.

Retirement expectations—measured as expected retirement age or the probability of being retired at a particular age—are among the most common expectational variables in longitudinal household surveys. Both measures have been included in the Health and Retirement Study since its inception in

1992. Similar measures are included in the international sister studies of the HRS, the Panel Study of Income Dynamics, and the Survey of Consumer Expectations.

This chapter analyzes retirement expectations in the context of a simple discrete choice model of late-in-life labor supply. It then evaluates measures using the data from the HRS. Several findings emerge. When measured in terms of expected age of retirement, expectations are a somewhat biased predictor of actual retirement age, with a tendency to retire earlier than the expected age. In contrast, probabilistic expectations, specifically the percent chance of working full-time past the age of 62 or 65, is an unbiased predictor of actual behavior on average. The fraction of respondents who actually work beyond those ages is almost identical to the average subjective probability of working past those ages at horizons of 3 to 8 years. Additionally, the subjective probabilities are close to being conditionally unbiased predictors of retirement in the cross section. Though a few covariates (current poor health and race) have significant point estimates in a prediction error regression, the magnitude of predictable forecast errors is very small (R^2 of 1% or 2%).

Across individuals, however, subjective probabilities give an attenuated predictor of retirement behavior. Recalibrating the subjective probability p^b of working after age b with the linear relation $\hat{p}^b = E\left[w_b|p^b\right] = \alpha + \beta p^b$ where w_b is an indicator for working at age b robustly yields unbiased predictors of working with a value of β equal to 0.5. The value of the attenuation parameter β is remarkably consistent with what one would expect from classical measurement error where the variance of the measurement error is identified using repeated elicitations of the probabilities within a single survey, i.e., test-retest error.

The recalibrated subjective probability of retirement carries very substantial information for understanding retirement outcomes. This chapter presents a novel, machine learning (ML) model for predicting retirement. A random forest predictor of continuing to work at age 65 based on age, education, demographics, family status, earnings, pension plan, health, and spousal variables at time of elicitation of the subjective probability does less well than the recalibrated subjective probability at predicting retirement outcomes 3 to 8 years ahead. Moreover, the ML predictor has little predictive power incremental to the recalibrated subjective probability. Hence, conditional on a large set of information relevant for retirement, the recalibrated subjective probability is close to a sufficient statistic. Of course, the subjective probability will not fully account for outcomes since there is substantial news about individuals, their workplaces, economic policy, and macroeconomic conditions that affect realizations.

Subjective probability of retirement has been widely used to study retirement outcomes and economic decisions involving late-in-life work. These uses are supported by the wide availability of retirement expectations in longitudinal studies, and by the reliability of these measures as documented in this chapter. These uses include predicting retirement (subjective probability on the "left-hand side") and analyzing retirement or retirement surprises (subjective probability on the "right-hand side"). This chapter surveys a variety of these applications including the retirement income puzzle, joint labor supply decisions of spouses, and the effect of health on retirement. Additionally, this chapter discusses recent advances in eliciting and using conditional probabilities.

Because retirement is such a complex problem—involving the dynamics of income, wealth, health, joint decisions within couples, and complex interactions with private and public pension and insurance arrangements—subjective expectations are a powerful tool for analysis. Their implementation in longitudinal studies allows them to be studied as predictors of retirement and for research on the dynamics of late-in-life work. The value of retirement expectations for structural or policy analysis is underscored by the near sufficiency of probabilistic expectations for predicting retirement.

References

Ameriks, John, Kézdi, Gábor, Lee, Minjoon, Shapiro, Matthew D., 2020. Heterogeneity in expectations, risk tolerance, and household stock shares: the attenuation puzzle. Journal of Business and Economic Statistics 38 (3), 633–646.

Ayyagari, Padmaja, 2019. Health insurance and early retirement plans: evidence from the affordable care act. American Journal of Health Economics 5 (4), 533–560.

Békés, Gábor, Kézdi, Gábor, 2021. Data Analysis for Business, Economics, and Policy. Cambridge University Press.

Benitez-Silva, Hugo, Dwyer, Debra S., 2005. The rationality of retirement expectations and the role of new information. Review of Economics and Statistics 87 (3), 587–592.

Benitez-Silva, Hugo, Dwyer, Debra S., 2006. Expectation formation of older married couples and the rational expectations hypothesis. Labour Economics 13 (2), 191–218.

Bernheim, Douglas B., 1989. The timing of retirement: a comparison of expectations and realizations. In: Wise, David A. (Ed.), The Economics of Aging. University of Chicago Press, Chicago.

Bottazzi, Renata, Jappelli, Tullio, Padula, Mario, 2006. Retirement expectations, pension reforms, and their impact on private wealth accumulation. Journal of Public Economics 90 (12), 2187–2212.

Chan, Sewin, Stevens, Ann Huff, 2004. Do changes in pension incentives affect retirement? A longitudinal study of subjective retirement expectations. Journal of Public Economics 88 (7–8), 1307–1333.

Clarke, Philippa, Marshall, Victor W., Weir, David, 2012. Unexpected retirement from full time work after age 62: consequences for life satisfaction in older Americans. European Journal of Ageing 9 (3), 207–219.

Crimmins, E.M., Kim, J.K., Langa, K.M., Weir, D.R., 2011. Assessment of cognition using surveys and neuropsychological assessment: the health and retirement study and the aging, demographics, and memory study. The Journals of Gerontology. Series B, Psychological Sciences and Social Sciences 66 (suppl_1), i162–i171.

Delavande, Adeline, Lee, Jinkook, Yoong, Joanne, 2012. Harmonization of Cross-National Studies of Aging to the Health and Retirement Study Expectations. No. WR-861/3. RAND Corporation.

Dominitz, Jeff, 1997. The Role of Conditioning Information in Reports of Subjective Phenomena. Unpublished paper. California Institute of Technology.

Federal Reserve Bank of New York, 2022. Survey of consumer expectations labor market survey. https://www.newyorkfed.org/medialibrary/media/research/microeconomics/interactive/downloads/sce-labor-questionnaire.pdf.

Giustinelli, Pamela, Manski, Charles F., Molinari, Francesca, 2022a. Tail and center rounding of probabilistic expectations in the health and retirement study. Journal of Econometrics 231 (1), 265–281.

Giustinelli, Pamela, Manski, Charles F., Molinari, Francesca, 2022b. Precise or imprecise probabilities? Evidence from survey response related to late-onset dementia. Journal of the European Economic Association 20 (1), 187–221.

Giustinelli, Pamela, Shapiro, Matthew D., 2019. SeaTE: Subjective ex ante Treatment Effect of Health on Retirement. National Bureau of Economic Research Working Paper 26087.

Haider, Steven J., Stephens Jr., Melvin, 2007. Is there a retirement-consumption puzzle? Evidence using subjective retirement expectations. Review of Economics and Statistics 89 (2), 247–264.

Health and Retirement Study, 2022. Questionnaires. https://hrs.isr.umich.edu/documentation/questionnaires.

Ho, Jeong-Hwa, Raymo, James M., 2009. Expectations and realization of joint retirement among dual-worker couples. Research on Aging 31 (2), 153–179.

Honig, Marjorie, 1996. Retirement expectations: differences by race, ethnicity, and gender. The Gerontologist 36 (3), 373–382.

Hudomiet, Peter, Hurd, Michael D., Rohwedder, Susann, 2020. The Causal Effects of Economic Incentives, Health and Job Characteristics on Retirement: Estimates Based on Subjective Conditional Probabilities. Unpublished working paper presented at the AEA meetings, January 2021.

Hurd, Michael, 1999. Labor market transitions in the HRS: effects of the subjective probability of retirement and of pension eligibility. In: Smith, J.P., Willis, R.J. (Eds.), Wealth, Work and Health: Innovations in Measurement in the Social Sciences. University of Michigan Press, Ann Arbor, MI.

Kézdi, Gábor, Willis, Robert J., 2011. Household Stock Market Beliefs and Learning. National Bureau of Economic Research Working Paper 17614.

Kimball, Miles S., Sahm, Claudia R., Shapiro, Matthew D., 2008. Imputing risk tolerance from survey responses. Journal of the American Statistical Association 103 (483), 1028–1038.

Lumsdaine, Robin L., Stock, James H., Wise, David A., 1992. Three models of retirement: computational complexity versus predictive validity. In: Wise, David A. (Ed.), Topics in the Economics of Aging. University of Chicago Press, Chicago.

Maestas, Nicole, 2010. Back to work: expectations and realizations of work after retirement. The Journal of Human Resources 4 (3), 718–747.

Manski, Charles F., 1999. Analysis of choice expectations in incomplete scenarios. Journal of Risk and Uncertainty 19, 49–66.

McGarry, Kathleen, 2004. Health and retirement: do changes in health affect retirement expectations? The Journal of Human Resources 39 (3), 624–648.

Mermin, Gordon B.T., Johnson, Richard W., Murphy, Dan P., 2007. Why do boomers plan to work longer? The Journals of Gerontology. Series B, Psychological Sciences and Social Sciences 62 (5), S286–S294.

Michaud, Pierre-Carl, Van Soest, Arthur, Bissonnette, Luc, 2020. Understanding joint retirement. Journal of Economic Behavior & Organization 173, 386–401.

Okumura, Tsunao, Usui, Emiko, 2014. The effect of pension reform on pension-benefit expectations and savings decisions in Japan. Applied Economics 46 (14), 1677–1691.

Panel Study of Income Dynamics, 2019. Questionnaire. https://psidonline.isr.umich.edu/guide/documents.aspx.

Pienta, Amy M., Hayward, Mark D., 2002. Who expects to continue working after age 62? The retirement plans of couples. The Journals of Gerontology. Series B, Psychological Sciences and Social Sciences 57 (1), S199–S208.

Romm, Aylit Tina, 2015. The effect of retirement date expectations on pre-retirement wealth accumulation: the role of gender and bargaining power in married US households. Journal of Family and Economic Issues 36 (4), 593–605.

Social Security Administration, 2019. The 2019 Annual Report of the Board of Trustees of the Federal Old-Age and Survivors Insurance and Federal Disability Insurance Trust Funds. https://www.ssa.gov/OACT/TR/2019/.

van der Klaauw, Wilbert, 2012. On the use of expectations data in estimating structural dynamic choice models. Journal of Labor Economics 30 (3), 521–554.

van der Klaauw, Wilbert, Wolpin, Kenneth I., 2008. Social security and the retirement and savings behavior of low-income households. Journal of Econometrics 145 (1–2), 21–42.

Wiswall, Matthew, Zafar, Basit, 2015. Determinants of college major choice: identification using an information experiment. The Review of Economic Studies 82 (2), 791–824.

Wiswall, Matthew, Zafar, Basit, 2021. Human capital investments and expectations about career and family. Journal of Political Economy 129 (5), 1361–1424.

The macroeconomic expectations of firms☆

Bernardo Candia[a], Olivier Coibion[b,c], and Yuriy Gorodnichenko[a,c]

[a]*University of California at Berkeley, Berkeley, CA, United States*
[b]*University of Texas at Austin, Austin, TX, United States*
[c]*NBER, Cambridge, MA, United States*

11.1 Introduction

How do firms think about the aggregate economy and how do those beliefs affect their decisions? A growing literature is investigating the formation of firms' expectations about the overall economic outlook as well as the role that these expectations may play in shaping firms' economic choices. We review some of these findings and provide new evidence using a broader collection of firm-level surveys from a wide range of countries. Because of data constraints, we focus on inflation expectations, but our conclusions extend to other macroeconomic expectations.

We emphasize several key features of firms' macroeconomic expectations. First, the macroeconomic expectations of firms typically differ from those of both households and professional forecasters. Although professional forecasters have been often used as a proxy for firm managers, surveys of professional forecasters are no substitute for representative survey evidence coming from firms. For example, the average expectations for firms often deviate discernably from the average expectations for professional forecasters. Furthermore, firms' average expectations can be close to households' average expectations, a pattern that is particularly evident for inflation expectations but can be found for the expectations of other macroeconomic variables as well.

Second, there is pervasive disagreement among firms about macroeconomic conditions. This disagreement dwarfs what is seen among professional forecasters. Qualitatively, the amount of disagreement across firms is generally similar to or slightly smaller than what is observed in surveys of households.

Third, there is typically a high correlation between firms' long- and short-run inflation expectations. In principle, to the extent that many shocks to inflation are transitory, short- and long-run inflation expectations should not be strongly correlated if expectations are "well-anchored": long-run expectations

☆ Acknowledgment: This research was funded in part by National Science Foundation grants 1919307 and 1530467. We thank the editors (Rüdiger Bachmann, Wilbert van der Klaauw, Giorgio Topa) for their comments. We are grateful to Zhaosheng Li, Jake Lyons and Yizhong Zhang for excellent research assistance. We thank George Kershoff, Javier Turén, Rodrigo Lluberas, Serafín Frache, Pär Österholm, Jens Iversen, Ulf Söderström, Gustaf Lundgren, Knut Are Aastveit, Jorgovanka Tabaković, Vesna Martin, Karen Vignisdóttir, Ásgeir Daníelsson, Michela Coppola, Péter Gábriel, Jaime Ruiz-Tagle, Lorena Flores, Ignacio Sarmiento, Gonzalo Marivil, and Martín Caruso for sharing data. Online appendix material is available at https://eml.berkeley.edu/~ygorodni/CCG_handbook_appendix.pdf.

should be pinned down by the inflation target of the central bank. Instead, we find strong correlations between revisions in short- and long-run inflation forecasts of firms. Combined with the previous stylized facts, this indicates that firms' inflation forecasts, at least in countries with a history of low and stable inflation, cannot be characterized as well-anchored.

Fourth, firms seem to form expectations of the future as a combination of their beliefs about recent events as well as their views about very long-run "natural" levels. But both beliefs can be quite far from actual values. For example, inattention on the part of firms about recent macroeconomic dynamics implies they often have very inaccurate beliefs about recent inflation, misconceptions that then extend into their views about the future. Firms also can have a poor understanding about long-run policy objectives, such as the central bank's inflation target, which also shapes their views about future economic outcomes. The degree of inattention, however, varies with the level of inflation. Using cross-country firm survey data, we show that, when countries experience higher inflation rates, the forecasts of firms are closer to those of professional forecasters, i.e., more informed, than when inflation rates are low. We observe a similar pattern for households. How inattentive agents are to macroeconomic conditions, and inflation in particular, depends on the economic environment.

Fifth, firms seem to form distributions across macroeconomic variables jointly. In other words, revisions in their beliefs about one macroeconomic variable are generally correlated with their revisions in beliefs about other macroeconomic variables. We provide a variety of evidence for this fact. For example, we show that the unconditional correlation between firms' expectations of future inflation and future real economic activity is nonzero. In many countries, firms associate inflation with low levels of economic activity, consistent with a stagflationary view of the world, whereas in other countries they seem to take a more demand-side view. We also show that when firms are asked to provide a joint distribution over future wage inflation and unemployment, their answers incorporate a strong negative covariance between the two.

Jointly, these stylized facts regarding firms' macroeconomic expectations can be helpful to policy-making, where expectations are central, as well as to inform theory. We provide one example of the latter by assessing the extent to which observing firms' inflation expectations can help explain the inflation history across countries through the lens of an expectations-augmented Phillips curve. Macroeconomic models with nominal or information rigidities typically imply that inflation is positively related to the level of economic activity after conditioning on the inflation expectations of firms. We show using cross-country firm surveys that this prediction is confirmed in the data: once one conditions on firms' historical inflation expectations, a clear positive relationship between inflation and economic activity is visible. This is consistent with theories in which firms' macroeconomic expectations matter for economic dynamics and policy.

Another approach to assessing the potential importance of firms' expectations is through randomized control trials that generate exogenous variation in those beliefs to determine whether they have any causal effect on firm decisions. We review recent work using surveys of firms in New Zealand and Italy that use this strategy to assess whether the inflation expectations of firms affect their decisions. This recent work provides direct causal evidence that exogenous changes in the inflation expectations of firms do indeed affect their subsequent decisions, particularly for employment and investment. The way in which they do so, however, seems to depend on the interpretation that firms take about the source of the change in inflation.

We describe how different surveys measure firms' macroeconomic expectations in Section 11.2. Section 11.3 presents stylized facts about firms' macroeconomic beliefs. Section 11.4 documents the fact that firms' macroeconomic expectations affect their decisions and economic outcomes. Section 11.5 concludes.

11.2 Surveys of firms' macroeconomic expectations

Implementing a survey of firms poses many challenges. First, one needs to be able to contact the desired respondent within a firm. For larger firms, reaching a top executive requires bypassing a cadre of staff who carefully protect their manager's time and accessibility. Second, one needs to convince the respondent to participate in the survey. Household surveys commonly rely on nominal amounts to induce participation in short surveys, but these nominal amounts are generally insufficient for senior executives. In addition, executives may worry about sharing confidential information or helping the competition by unilaterally sharing knowledge. Third, given the time constraints on managers' time, surveys must be short and easy to complete, or risk being discarded. As a result, few surveys ask for quantitative measures of expectations or, when they do so, they focus only on variables specific to the firm. Given these challenges, even mandatory government-managed surveys like the Annual Survey of Manufacturers run by the U.S. Census Bureau achieve response rates of only around 50%.[1] Surveys that are neither mandatory nor supported by a governmental authority typically struggle to develop a large pool of willing respondents to participate in a survey. As a result, many surveys of firms are either not representative of the broader population of firms or pose only qualitative questions that are of limited value for economic analysis.

Tables 11.1 and 11.2 present a nonexhaustive list of surveys of firms' macroeconomic expectations across countries.[2] Table 11.1 focuses on how quantitative inflation expectations of firms are measured in these surveys, as inflation expectations are the most commonly measured aggregate expectations. Even for a specific variable like inflation, there is a lot of variation in how expectations are measured across surveys. Firms may be asked about "prices in general," "inflation" or even specific measures of inflation (e.g., CPI inflation rate). They may be asked for point estimates or to assign probabilities to different possible outcomes. They may be asked about inflation over different horizons. Some may have the option of saying "I don't know" while others do not. Even small differences in the formulation of questions can have discernible effects on survey results (e.g., Haldane and McMahon, 2018; Haldane et al., 2020; Savignac et al., 2021; Chapter 1 in this Handbook).

Table 11.2 focuses on the broader implementation of the survey and whether each survey meets several desired characteristics identified in Coibion et al. (2020). For example, a survey should be

---

[1] Response rates in the ASM are described here: https://www.census.gov/programs-surveys/asm/technical-documentation/methodology.html.

[2] There are a number of prominent firm surveys that we omit from Table 11.1. Some are omitted because they do not include quantitative macroeconomic forecasts. This includes for example the ifo survey of manufacturers in Germany described in Bachmann (2019) and Enders et al. (2019) as it elicits qualitative macroeconomic forecasts. Another qualitative survey is the French Quarterly Survey of Economic Conditions in Industry studied in Andrade et al. (2022). We also omit some very high-quality firm surveys that focus on expectations about firm-specific outcomes and uncertainty, such as the U.K. Decision Maker Panel described in Bloom et al. (2019), the U.S. Survey of Business Uncertainty described in Altig et al. (2020) or the Atlanta Fed's Business Inflation Expectations survey. Another omitted group are very new surveys that do not yet provide time series data, such as the German Business Panel described in Bischof et al. (2021) or the French survey of firms described in Savignac et al. (2021). Finally, we also do not explicitly discuss surveys with annual frequency. One notable example is the Japanese Annual Survey of Corporate Behavior, which includes firm-level forecasts of GDP growth studied in Tanaka et al. (2019).

Table 11.1 Selected Surveys and Firms' Inflation Expectations.

Country	Institution	Respondents	Price Definition	Sampling	Freq.	Start date	Bins	Horizon	Question
Canada	Conf. Board of Canada	Firms	Prices in general	Convenience	Quarterly	1993	9	6 months	Do you expect prices, in general, in Canada to increase over the next six months at an annual rate of
Canada	Central bank	Firms	Inflation (CPI)	Quota	Quarterly	1997	4	2 years	Over the next two years, what do you expect the annual rate of inflation to be, based on the consumer price index?
Colombia	Centra bank	Firms	Inflation (CPI)	Quota	Quarterly	2000	open	3, 6 and 9 months, 1 and 2 years	The last month, the annual inflation rate was equal to X%. What do you expect the annual inflation rate to be at the end of: (also range with max and min value)
Colombia	Delgado et al. (2021)	Firms	Inflation (CPI)	Representative (Mnfg.; retail)	Monthly	2019	open	1 year	By what percentage do you think the economy's prices, as measured by the Consumer Price Index (CPI), will increase, or decrease in Colombia over the next 12 months?
Czech Republic	Central bank	Firms	Inflation (CPI)	Representative	Quarterly	1999	open	1 and 3 years	What year-on-year consumer price change in per cent do you expect in the next 12 months?
EU Members	European Commission	Firms	Prices for consumers	Probabilistic sample	Monthly	1985	(up/down/same)	1 year	By what percentage you would say that prices will increase for the consumer in the next 12 months?
Hungary	Central bank	Firms	Inflation (CPI)	Representative	Quarterly	2007	open	1 year	During the next 12 months, do you think that prices in general will go up, or go down, or stay where they are now? By how many percent do you expect consumer prices to go up/down in the next 12 months?
Iceland	Central bank	Firms	Inflation	Convenience	Quarterly	2003	open	1, 2 and 5 years	What do you think inflation will measure over the next twelve months?
Iran	Central bank	Mnfg. Firms, ≥100 workers	Inflation	Probabilistic Sample	Quarterly	2016	open	1 year	What do you think the [yearly] inflation will be during the next year?
Israel	Ungar and Zilberfarb (1993)	Firms	Inflation (CPI)	Representative	Quarterly	1980	open	1-4 quarters	The cumulative inflation rate (not monthly average), in %, which is expected for the following periods is as follows: The next 12 months
Italy	Central bank	Firms	Inflation	Probabilistic sample	Quarterly	1999	open	1 year	The last [month] consumer price inflation, measured by the 12-month change in the harmonized index of consumer prices was equal to [IT] in Italy and to [EA] in the euro area. What do you think it will be in Italy.
Jamaica	Central bank	Firms	Inflation (CPI)	n.a.	Bimonthly	2012	open	1 year	What do you expect the rate of inflation to be over the next 12 months?

continued on next page

Table 11.1 (*continued*)

Country	Institution	Respondents	Price Definition	Sampling	Freq.	Start date	Bins	Horizon	Question
Japan	Central bank	Firms	Prices in general (CPI)	Probabilistic sample	Quarterly	2014	10	1, 3, and 5 years	What are your institution's expectations of the annual % change in general prices (as measured by the CPI) for one year ahead, three years ahead, and five years ahead, respectively?
New Zealand	Central bank	Firms and professionals	Inflation (CPI)	Convenience	Quarterly	1987	open	1, 2, 5 and 10 years	What annual % change do you expect in the CPI for the:
New Zealand	ANZ Economics	Firms	Inflation (CPI)	Representative	Monthly	1983	open	1 year	What do you think the annual Inflation Rate (as measured by the Consumer Price Index) will be in 12 months' time?
Norway	Central bank	Firms, ≥20 workers	Inflation (CPI)	Representative	Quarterly	2002	open	1 and 2 years	What do you think the general rise in prices for goods and services will be in 12 months and 2 years, measured by the 12-month change in the CPI?
Poland	Central bank	Firms	Prices	Sector representation	Quarterly	2008	5	1 year	In ... [month with the latest data is available] of the current year, the CPI (inflation) was equal to x% in annual terms. In the enterprise's opinion, during the next 12 months prices:
Serbia	Central bank	Firms	Inflation (CPI)	Random	Monthly	2009	open	1 and 2 years	c stands for current month. What year-on-year rate of inflation do you expect in c+12 (consumer price growth in c+12 relative to c)?
South Africa	Central bank	Firms and consumers	Inflation (CPI)	Convenience	Quarterly	2000	open	Current+following 2 years and, 5 years	What do you expect the average headline inflation rate (as measured by the % change in the CPI) to be during the year
Sweden	Central bank	Firms with ≥200 workers	Inflation (CPI)	Random	Quarterly	2000	open	1 year	What do you think the annual CPI inflation in Sweden will be the next coming year (12 months forward), measured as the percentage change in the CPI
UK	Confed. of British Industry	Firms	Prices of competition	Convenience	Quarterly	2008	4	1 year	What has been the % change over the past 12 months in the general level of output prices in the UK markets that your firm competes in, and what is expected to occur over the next twelve months?
Ukraine	Central bank	Firms	Inflation	Random	Quarterly	2006	8	1 year	How do you think the level of consumer prices will change in the next 12 months?
USA	Livingston, Philly Fed	Large Firms	Inflation (CPI)	Convenience	Semi-Annual	1946	open	1 year	n.a.

continued on next page

Table 11.1 (*continued*)

Country	Institution	Respondents	Price Definition	Sampling	Freq.	Start date	Bins	Horizon	Question
USA	SoFIE	Firms	Inflation (CPI)	Representative	Quarterly	2018	open	1 and 5 years	What do you think will be the inflation rate (for the Consumer Price Index) over the next 12 months? Please provide an answer in an annual percentage rate.
Uruguay	Central bank	Firms	Inflation (CPI)	Representative	Monthly	2009	open	Current year, 1 and 2 years	What do you believe is going to be the change in the CPI?
Uruguay	Deloitte	Firms	Inflation CPI	Non-probability	Biannual	2010	open	Current and, following year, 3 or 4 years	What do you expect the rate of inflation to be during the year:
Turkey	Central Bank	Manufacturing Firms	Inflation (PPI)	Sector representation	Monthly	1987	open	1 year	What is your expectation for inflation (producer prices) rate over the next 12 months (as an annual percentage)?

Table 11.2 Selected Surveys and Firms' Inflation Expectations.

Country	Institution	Representative Sample	Heterogeneous sample	Monthly or Quarterly Frequency	Large Sample Size (>350)	No Priming	Quantitative Question	Many/wide bins	Distributional question	Aggregate Inflation
Canada	Conference Board of Canada	X	✓	✓	✓	✓	X	✓	X	✓
Canada	Central bank	X	✓	✓	X	X	X	X	X	✓
Colombia	Central bank	X	X	✓	X	X	✓	–	X	✓
Colombia	Delgado et al. (2021)	✓	X	✓	✓	✓	✓	–	X	✓
Czech Republic	Central bank	✓	✓	✓	X	✓	✓	–	X	✓
EU Members	European Commission	✓	✓	✓	✓	✓	X	X	✓	✓
Hungary	Central bank	✓	✓	✓	✓	✓	✓	✓	X	✓
Iceland	Central bank	X	X	✓	✓	✓	✓	–	X	✓
Iran	Central bank	✓	X	✓	✓	✓	✓	–	X	✓

continued on next page

Table 11.2 (*continued*)

Country	Institution	Representative Sample	Heterogeneous sample	Monthly or Quarterly Frequency	Large Sample Size (>350)	No Priming	Quantitative Question	Many/wide bins	Distributional question	Aggregate Inflation
Israel	Ungar and Zilberfarb (1993)	✓	✗	✗	✗	✗	✓	–	✗	✓
Italy	Central bank	✓	✗	✓	✓	✗*	✓	–	✗	✓
Jamaica	Central bank	n.a.	n.a.	✓	✗	✓	✓	–	✗	✓
Japan	Central bank	✓	✓	✓	✓	✓	✗	✓	✗	✓
New Zealand	Central bank	✗	✗	✓	✗	✓	✓	–	✗	✓
New Zealand	ANZ Economics	✓	✓	✓	✓	✓	✓	–	✗	✓
Norway	Central bank	✓	✓	✓	✓	✓	✓	–	✗	✓
Poland	Central bank	✗	✓	✓	✗	✗	✗	✗	✗	✓
Serbia	Central bank	✗	✗	✓	✗	✓	✓	–	✗	✓
South Africa	Central bank	✗	✓	✓	✓	✓	✓	–	✗	✓
Sweden	Central bank	✗	✗	✓	✗	✓	✓	–	✗	✓
UK	Confederation of British Industry	✗	✓	✓	✓	✓	✓	–	✗	✗
Ukraine	Central bank	✓	✓	✓	✓	✓	✗	✓	✗	✓
USA	Livingston, Philadelphia Fed	✗	✗	✗	✗	✓	✓	–	✗	✓
USA	SoFIE	✓	✓	✓	✓	✓	✓	–	✓	✓
Uruguay	Central bank	✓	✗	✓	✗	✓	✓	–	✗	✓
Uruguay	Deloitte	✓	✗	✗	✗	✓	✓	–	✗	✓
Turkey	Central bank	✓	✗	✓	✓	✓	✓	–	✗	✓

Notes: Column "Representative sample" indicates whether firms in a survey are representative of the group that is being surveyed. Column "Heterogeneous sample" indicates if a sample of firms covers various types (size, sector, etc.) of firms so that the resulting sample represents or resembles the population of firms in the economy. Column "Large Sample Size" indicates if a survey has more than 350 firms with nonmissing responses. Column "No priming" indicates whether a survey does not provide information to firms before eliciting expectations, does not restrict the sample in any particular way (e.g., does not exclude firms that do not understand the concept of inflation), and does not restrict possible responses (e.g., does not present firms with a limited set of possible responses). Column "Quantitative question" indicates if firms are free to report an unrestricted inflation forecast (i.e., responses are not restricted to a binned/range/multiple-choice menu). Column "Many/wide bins" indicates whether a survey allows firms to choose from a wide and detailed range of possible responses if quantitative response are not available. Column "Distributional question" indicates whether a survey elicits a probability distribution for future inflation. Column "Aggregate Inflation" indicates whether a survey asks firms to report an aggregate measure of inflation, changes in prices overall, etc. (rather than firm's unit costs or prices). * last month annual inflation is given up to 2/3 of the firms and firms are not allowed to report "extreme" values.

broadly representative of the economy, which means covering a range of industries and firm sizes. Table 11.2 indicates that many surveys focus on specific sectors or geographic areas and therefore fail to be representative of the broader distribution of firms. For a survey to be useful for research or policy, it should be high-frequency (e.g., monthly or quarterly), which some surveys are not (e.g., Livingston survey). Sample sizes should be sufficiently high, which we define as exceeding 350 responses on average. Very few surveys satisfy this restriction. Another desired characteristic is that surveys do not "prime" responses, i.e., push responses in specific ways either through the formulation of the question or by providing other information to the firm. For example, some surveys offer very few bins for possible inflation outcomes, and those bins are very close to 2%, leading all responses to look "anchored." Other surveys provide information about recent inflation prior to asking about firms' inflation forecasts. As shown in Coibion et al. (2020) as well as Savignac et al. (2021), this kind of information provision significantly affects reported forecasts.

Table 11.2 documents that most available surveys of firms suffer from several severe shortcomings as defined here. However, there are several surveys that stand out in their quality, those from Norway, Hungary, Uruguay, and Ukraine. Each country has been running a large-scale, representative and quantitative survey of firms since the early to late 2000s.[3] More recently, the Survey of Firm Inflation Expectations (SoFIE) has measured the inflation expectations of U.S. firms in a large scale, representative and quantitative way since 2018.[4] These data are described and utilized in Candia et al. (2021) and Binder and Kim (2020). The Bank of Italy's survey of firms' inflation expectations has historically provided information about recent inflation to participants, but since 2012, a randomly selected subset has not been provided any additional information. We view this subset of the survey as also satisfying most criteria for being representative, large scale, and quantitative. Finally, an intermittent survey of firms in New Zealand also satisfies many of the criteria, albeit at lower frequency than these other surveys just described. Given the availability of micro-level data from these high-quality surveys, our results will focus primarily on these specific cases, but we will illustrate how not satisfying the criteria of high-quality surveys can lead to dramatically different results.[5] In Tables 11.3–11.7, we also consider the extent to which these surveys cover noninflation expectations. Similar issues arise in the measurement of expectations about real GDP and unemployment in terms of potential priming, size of bins, etc., as discussed in Chapter 2 in this Handbook. These tables indicate that coverage for noninflation questions is even more limited than for inflation.

11.3 Properties of firms' macroeconomic expectations

We now consider the properties of firms' macroeconomic expectations that can be seen in available surveys.[6] Many of these properties can directly shed light on the extent to which inflation expectations are anchored (see Kumar et al., 2015 for a detailed discussion).

---

[3] Unfortunately, the National Bank of Hungary stopped collecting survey data (both households and firms) in 2015.

[4] Detailed information about the survey as well as updated survey results can be found at http://www.firm-expectations.org/.

[5] Sometimes we supplement our results with surveys of firms in Sweden and South Africa.

[6] There are other ways of measuring firms' expectations that are not survey based. For example, Hassan et al. (2019) and Gallermore et al. (2021) rely on the content of discussions during firms' earnings calls. However, these measures are not direct quantitative forecasts per se, so we do not include them here.

Table 11.3 Selected Surveys and Firms' GDP (economic activity) Expectations.

Country	Institution	Question	Quantitative Question	Many/wide bins	Distributional question	Aggregate output
Canada	Conf. Board of Canada	Do you expect overall economic conditions in Canada six months from now to be: (better/same/worse)	✕	✕	✕	✓
Colombia	Central bank	What do you expect the annual economic growth rate to be during the year: (also range with minimum and maximum value)	✓	–	✕	✓
Germany	ifo Institute	According to your assessment, by how much percent will the real gross domestic product in Germany change in the year X relative to the previous year? (special question in 2018 and 2019)	✓	–	✕	✓
Italy	Central bank	What do you think is the probability of an improvement in Italy's general economic situation in the next 3	✕	✕	✕	✓
Japan	Cabinet Office, ESRI	Please enter a figure up to one decimal place in each of the boxes below as your rough forecast of Japan's nominal and real economic growth rates for: next 1, 3, and 5 years	✓	–	✕	✓
New Zealand	Central bank	What is your expectation of the annual % change in real production-based GDP for the: 1 and 2 years	✓	–	✕	✓
New Zealand	ANZ Economics	With regard to the New Zealand Economy. Do you believe that General Business Conditions in 12 months' time will have? (Improved, Remain the same, Deteriorated)	✕	✕	✕	✓
South Africa	Central bank	What do you expect the average economic growth rate (as measured by the percentage change in the real GDP) to be during the year: current and following year	✓	–	✕	✓
Sweden	Central bank	What GDP-growth, in percentage terms, do you think Sweden will have; -the next coming year, counting from now and 12 months forward? -the second year (12–24 months forward) -the fifth year (48–60 months forward)	✓	–	✕	✓
Ukraine	Central bank	How do you think the level of Ukrainian goods and services will change over the next 12 months? (increase/decrease/unchanged)	✕	✕	✕	✓
USA	Livingston, Philly Fed	The value of the real GDP/GNP in the current quarter, two and four quarters beyond, two annual-average forecasts (current and following year)	✓	–	✕	✓
USA	CFO, Duke/Richmond/Atlanta	Please indicate what probabilities you would attach to the various possible year-ahead percentage changes in U.S. economic output (Real Gross Domestic Product) Results should sum to 100%	✓	–	✓	✓
Uruguay	Deloitte	What do you expect the GDP growth rate to be during the year: current and following year	✓	–	✕	✓

Notes: The table reports the types of questions about expected GDP (or economic activity generally) in the set of surveys covered in Table 11.1.

Table 11.4 Selected Surveys and Firms' Unemployment Rate Expectations.

Country	Institution	Question	Quantitative Question	Many/wide bins	Distributional question	Aggregate unemployment
New Zealand	Central bank	What is your expectation of the official HLFS unemployment rate for the: 1 and 2 years	✓	–	✗	✓
New Zealand	ANZ Economics	How do you expect the unemployment rate to has changed in 12 months' time? (Increased, Remain the same, Decreased)	✗	✗	✗	✓

Notes: The table reports the types of questions about expected unemployment rate in the set of surveys covered in Tables 11.1 and 11.2. See notes to these tables for more details.

Table 11.5 Selected Surveys and Firms' Exchange Rate Expectations.

Country	Institution	Question	Quantitative Question	Many/wide bins	Distributional question
Colombia	Central bank	What do you think the exchange rate (Pesos/USD) will be for the following time periods ahead: 3, 6, 9, and 12 months (also range with minimum and maximum value)	✓	–	✗
Colombia	Delgado et al. (2021)	If in twelve months you were to buy dollars in the financial sector, at what exchange rate do you think you could get them?	✓	–	✗
Jamaica	Central bank	In MMYYYY the exchange rate was J$X=US$ Y. What do you think the rate will be for the following time periods ahead: 3, 6, and 12 months.	✓	–	✗
New Zealand	Central bank	Relative to the following currencies (US Dollar and Australian Dollar), what spot exchange rate do you expect for the NZ Dollar at the end of: 6 and 12 months.	✓	–	✗
South Africa	Central bank	What do you expect the rand/US dollar exchange rate to be at the end of: current and following year	✓	–	✗
Ukraine	Central bank	What do you think the UAH/USD will be in the next 12 months?	✓	–	✗
Uruguay	Deloitte	What do you expect the pesos/US dollar exchange rate to be in the next 12 months	✓	–	✗

Notes: The table reports the types of questions about expected exchange rate (local currency vs the US dollar) in the set of surveys covered in Tables 11.1 and 11.2. See notes to these tables for more details.

11.3.1 Mean inflation forecasts

Since most surveys of firms' macroeconomic forecasts are focused primarily on their inflation expectations, we first focus on the nature of these beliefs and return to firms' forecasts about other variables in Section 11.3.5. In Fig. 11.1, we plot the time series of the average 12-month-ahead inflation forecasts of firms for each of the seven countries for which we have a large-scale, representative, and quantitative survey as described in Section 11.2. For comparison, we also include the time series of actual

Country	Institution	Question	Quantitative Question	Many/wide bins	Distributional question	Aggregate interest rates
Colombia	Central bank	What do you think the interest rate (DTF: 90-day annual effective interest rate) will be for the following time periods ahead: 3, 6, 9, and 12 months (also range with minimum and maximum value)	✓	–	✗	✓
Jamaica	Central bank	In MM YYYY the 180-day T-bill rate was X%. What do you think the rate will be for the next 3 months? In MM YYYY, the Bank of Jamaica's 30-day rate was X%. What do you think this rate will be for the next 3 months?	✓	–	✗	✓
New Zealand	Central bank	What do you expect the Official Cash Rate (OCR) to be at the end of: 1 and 2 years. What do you expect the 10-year government bond market yield to be at the end of: 1 and 2 years	✓	–	✗	✓
New Zealand	ANZ Economics	How do you expect the interest rates to have change in 12 months' time? Increased, Remain the same, Decreased	✗	✗	✗	✓
South Africa	Central bank	What do you expect the prime overdraft rate to be at the end of: current and following year.	✓	–	✗	✓
Sweden	Central bank	Interest rate (Repo rate: the Riksbank's borrowing/lending rate from/to banks for seven days' money) for 3, 6, 12, and 24 months ahead.	✓	–	✗	✓

Table 11.6 Selected Surveys and Firms' Interest Rate Expectations.

Notes: The table reports the types of questions about expected nominal interest rate in the set of surveys covered in Tables 11.1 and 11.2. See notes to these tables for more details.

(CPI) inflation in each country, as well as the 12-month-ahead inflation expectations for professional forecasters (from Consensus Economics for most countries) and household surveys (when available).

Panel A of Fig. 11.1 plots U.S. firms' inflation expectations from SoFIE, as previously shown in Candia et al. (2021), available for 2018Q2–2021Q3. Firms' inflation expectations were high at the start of the survey sample, well above 3% in 2018. At the time, professional forecasters were predicting inflation of just over 2% while households (from the Michigan Survey of Consumers) were predicting inflation of about 3.5%. Thus, firms' beliefs were initially quite close to those of households. In 2019, however, firms' inflation forecasts fell sharply to around 2% and remained there through 2020, close to those of professional forecasts for much of this time period. In 2021, firms' inflation expectations rose sharply, reaching 4.7% in 2021Q3, the last available wave of the survey.

The results from SoFIE suggest that the inflation expectations of firms can differ significantly from those of both households and professional forecasters. This result for U.S. firms is not limited to SoFIE however. The Federal Reserve Bank of Atlanta runs a survey of firms known as the Business Inflation

Table 11.7 Selected Surveys and Firms' Wage Expectations.

Country	Institution	Question	Quantitative Question	Many/wide bins	Distributional question	Aggregate wages
New Zealand	Central bank	What is your expectation of the annual % change in QES average hourly (ordinary time, private sector)	✓	–	✕	✓
Norway	Central bank	What do you think the average annual wage growth will be this year? Next year?	✓	–	✕	✓
South Africa	Central bank	What do you expect the average salary and wage increase to be during the year: current and following	✓	–	✕	✓
Sweden	Central bank	Wage increase (the percentage increase in wages/salaries as measured over all sectors in the economy)	✓	–	✕	✓

Notes: The table reports the types of questions about expected nominal wages in the set of surveys covered in Tables 11.1 and 11.2. See notes to these tables for more details.

Expectations (BIE) survey, in which firms from the Southeastern region of the U.S. are surveyed about their costs (see Chapter 12 in this Handbook for a discussion of how firms form expectations about their own prices and production). Occasionally, the survey has also asked questions about aggregate inflation. These occasional waves are described in Meyer et al. (2021) and are also shown in Panel A of Fig. 11.1. For the two waves in 2014 and 2015, the average inflation forecasts from the BIE were close to those of U.S. households. For the two other waves run in 2019, the results were either very close to those from SoFIE or point to even higher inflation expectations.

Evidence from other countries for which high-quality surveys of firms' inflation expectations is available confirm that the inflation expectations of firms are generally distinct from those of either households or professional forecasts (see Chapters 3 and 5 in this Handbook for systematic overviews of the inflation expectations of professional forecasters and households, respectively). Panel B of Fig. 11.1, for example, plots the inflation expectations of firms in Italy (specifically those firms who were *not* provided with information about recent inflation as part of the survey) against corresponding forecasts from professionals and households (whenever available). Clear differences across agents are again visible. For example, as inflation fell sharply in 2013 and 2014, the inflation forecasts of professionals responded more rapidly than those of firms. In the case of Hungary (Panel C, Fig. 11.1) and Norway (Panel D, Fig. 11.1), we again observe that the inflation forecasts of firms were generally above those of professionals and below those of households, periodically moving closer to one or the other such that neither would have presented a clear substitute for a separate measure of firms' inflation expectations. Panel E of Fig. 11.1 plots equivalent results for New Zealand. Firms' inflation forecasts in New Zealand were either higher than (in 2013–2014) or very similar to (in 2016–2020) to those of households and persistently well above those of professional forecasters.[7]

---

[7] In its survey of households, the Reserve Bank of New Zealand first asks respondents to define inflation and only measures the inflation expectations of those who correctly respond (approximately 50% of respondents), see Kumar et al. (2015). Due to this unusual selection within the survey, the inflation expectations of households in New Zealand are likely underestimated.

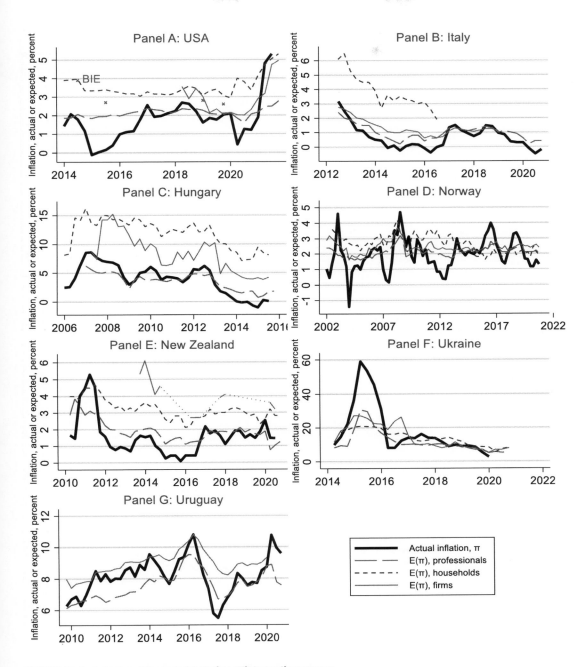

FIGURE 11.1 Actual and Expected Inflation, High-quality surveys

Notes: Each panel plots one-year ahead inflation expectations for professional forecasters, firms, and households, depending on data availability, as well as actual inflation. See Section 11.3.1 for details.

Panels F and G of Fig. 11.1 present equivalent results for Ukraine and Uruguay, respectively. Note that relative to the previous five countries, Ukraine and Uruguay both experienced significantly higher and more volatile inflation over this time period (as well as in earlier years). As a result, these countries are more indicative of firms' inflation expectations in high-inflation environments. Firms' inflation expectations in Ukraine, while initially higher than those of households during the inflation spike of 2015, fell sharply thereafter and subsequently remained close to those of professional forecasters. In Uruguay, we can observe that firms' inflation expectations were quite volatile and closely followed even transitory changes in inflation. This high correlation with actual inflation suggests firms were paying a lot of attention to recent inflation dynamics.

Jointly, these results make clear that firms' inflation expectations often deviate significantly from those of both professional forecasters as well as households. To the extent that firms' inflation expectations are important to economic dynamics, this pattern indicates that *high-quality* surveys of firms' inflation expectations are crucial to properly understanding their beliefs. The importance of focusing on high-quality surveys can be seen by comparing the results of these surveys to those available for other countries, for which firm surveys suffer from some of the limitations described in Section 11.2. Fig. 11.2 plots the resulting measures of inflation expectations of firms from these surveys, as well as forecasts from professionals and households when available. In each case, we can see that firm forecasts appear to closely track those of professional forecasters.

Why are these firm forecasts so different from those in Fig. 11.1? In the case of Japan, the survey proposes a set of bins that are centered on 2% and whose extremes are $>+6\%$ and $<-2\%$. This kind of "guidance" in terms of what are reasonable expectations unduly pushes responses toward the 2% level. This is also in sharp contrast to the much wider bins offered firms for other questions (which range from $+20\%$ to -20%). Similarly, the use of nonrepresentative samples and reliance on convenience sampling (which selects on firms that are particularly interested in inflation and monetary policy) in other countries similarly yields firm forecast series that track those of professionals. The differences between Figs. 11.1 and 11.2 are stark and highlight the importance of survey design.[8]

11.3.2 Disagreement about inflation

An additional important characteristic of expectations that has been emphasized (see in particular Mankiw et al., 2003) is the amount and behavior of disagreement across agents over time. Disagreement across agents indicates a departure from full-information rational expectations, and its dynamics can be informative about the nature of those deviations from FIRE (e.g., Coibion and Gorodnichenko, 2012; Reis, 2021). Fig. 11.3 therefore plots the cross-sectional standard deviation of firms' 12-month-ahead inflation expectations for those same countries as in Fig. 11.1 for which we have high-quality surveys.

---

[8] The properties of inflation expectations also vary by who is being surveyed within firms. For example, since 2015, Deloitte has conducted the European CFO survey, collecting European Chief Financial Officers' sentiments and expectations for investments and hiring. The survey covers senior financial executives in manufacturing, services, retail, construction, and the public sector. Each wave includes responses from around 1500 CFOs based in 19 European countries. Even though this survey does not meet the desired characteristics of a high-quality survey mentioned above—it covers only very large firms and respondents are contacted using Deloitte's internal lists of clients—it is the only cross-country survey of firms' expectations in major advanced economies. In 2018, this biannual survey added a quantitative question about 12-month-ahead CPI inflation expectations. Online Appendix Fig. 5 documents that inflation expectations of large firms' CFOs are close to professional forecasters'.

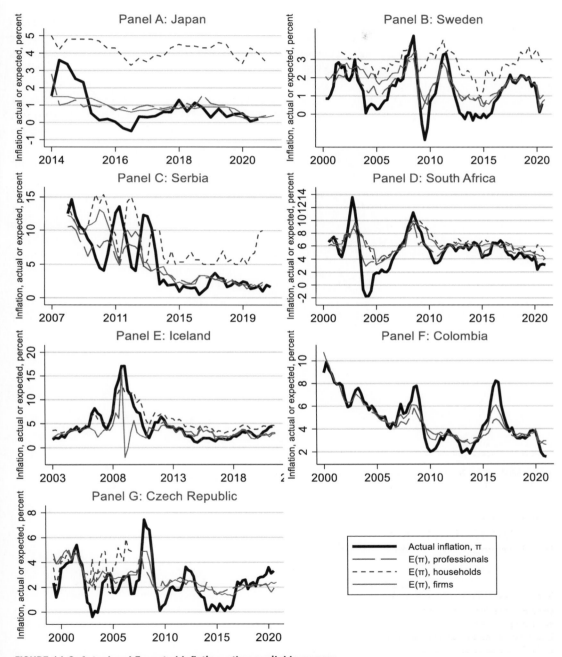

FIGURE 11.2 Actual and Expected Inflation, other available surveys

Notes: Each panel plots one-year ahead inflation expectations for professional forecasters, firms, and households, depending on data availability, as well as actual inflation. See Section 11.3.1 for details.

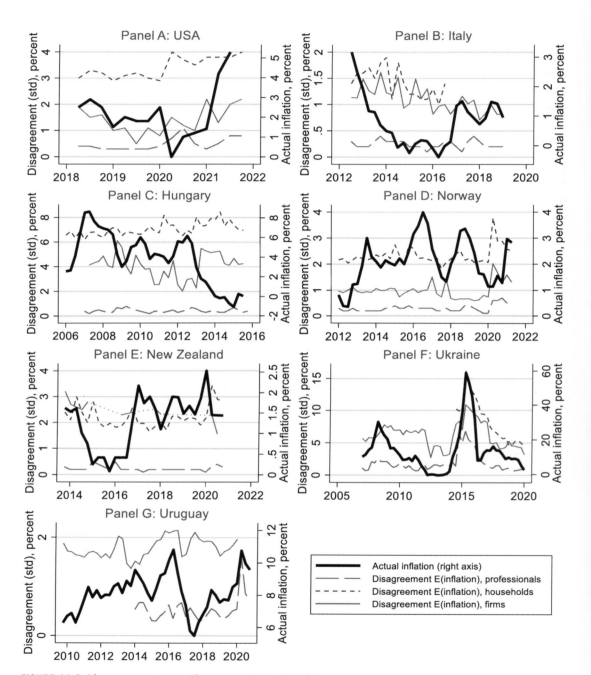

FIGURE 11.3 Disagreement among Firms about Future Inflation

Notes: Each panel plots the cross-sectional standard deviation of one-year ahead inflation expectations for professional forecasters, firms, and households, depending on data availability, as well as actual inflation. See Section 11.3.2 for details.

Panel A of Fig. 11.3 plots the time series of disagreement about inflation for firms in the U.S., as well as corresponding measures for households and professional forecasters. As emphasized in Mankiw et al. (2003), disagreement among households is an order of magnitude larger than disagreement across professional forecasters. Results from SoFIE indicate that disagreement about inflation among U.S. firms is approximately midway between the two, with the cross-sectional standard deviation staying around 1 to 2 percentage points. There is a mild positive correlation between firm disagreement and the level of inflation, with disagreement falling mildly with inflation from 2018 to 2020 and rising somewhat thereafter.

Panels B–G of Fig. 11.3 suggest that similar findings hold in other countries.[9] The level of disagreement for firms is consistently higher than that among professional forecasters and generally below or at a similar level as households. We can also observe a positive correlation between the level of inflation and the amount of disagreement across countries. For example, the large spike in inflation in Ukraine in 2015 is accompanied by a large increase in disagreement among firms.

Where does disagreement among firms come from? "Island" models in the spirit of Lucas (1972) posit that firms observe noisy signals about local and aggregate economic conditions. As a result, firms may have different expectations because they observe different signals. Consistent with this hypothesis, Andrade et al. (2022) document that French firms revise their aggregate inflation expectations in response to industry-level ("idiosyncratic") variation in prices that has no bearing on the macroeconomy. In a similar spirit, Kumar et al. (2015) interview managers in New Zealand to identify sources of their information about prices and find that managers often rely on their own shopping experience to form inflation expectations. This behavior suggests that, similar to households' expectations (D'Acunto et al., 2021), managers' expectations may be sensitive to salient price changes for homogeneous, frequently-purchased goods like food or gasoline for advanced economies or to variation in the exchange rate for countries with a history of dollarization or chronically high inflation (e.g., Coibion and Gorodnichenko, 2015b). Because the shopping experience may be different across managers, one may observe high disagreement in managers' inflation expectation, which could be similar to the disagreement observed for households' inflation expectations. Finally, Candia et al. (2021) show that some of the disagreement is systematically related to some firm characteristics. While few differences in expectations can be explained by the size of the firm, there are some notable differences across industries. For example, firms in the Telecommunications industry and in the Food and Drinks industry report systematically higher inflation expectations.

11.3.3 Short and long-run expectations

A separate dimension of inflation expectations that has received attention in the literature is the correlation between changes in short-run vs. long-run inflation expectations (e.g., Kumar et al., 2015). This correlation is often interpreted as the degree to which inflation expectations are "anchored." If expectations are well-anchored, long-run inflation expectations should be pinned down by the inflation target and changes in beliefs about the long-run should be largely unrelated to the transitory shocks that

---

[9] Online Appendix Fig. 11.3 shows the time series of countries with other surveys. Even for firm surveys with potential problems, we find that disagreement in firms' inflation expectations is much greater than disagreement in professional forecasters' expectations.

affect inflation in the short-run. In other words, the correlation between revisions in short- and long-run inflation expectations should be close to zero if expectations are well-anchored.

Following Candia et al. (2021), Fig. 11.4 presents some evidence on the extent of inflation anchoring for firms in the United States. Panel A plots a bin-scatter of average revisions in U.S. firms' short-run expectations vs revisions in their long-run (5-year ahead) inflation expectations. There is a very strong positive correlation between the two. The slope coefficient is close to 1 (0.71), indicating that when households revise their short-run expectations upward, they tend to raise their long-run inflation expectations upward by almost as much. The R^2 of this specification is very high (0.62), indicating that much of the variation in firms' beliefs about long-run inflation can be accounted for by the same source as those that shape their short-run inflation expectations, a finding strikingly at odds with the zero correlation expected under perfectly anchored expectations.

For comparison, Panels B and C plot equivalent figures for households (from the SCE) as well as professional forecasters (SPF) over the same period and are constructed in the same way. In each case, we observe a positive correlation between revisions in short-run inflation expectations and long-run inflation expectations, calling into question the extent to which one can characterize any agents' expectations as well-anchored in the U.S. However, firms display even stronger correlations than either households or professionals, indicating that the lack of anchoring is particularly pronounced for them.[10]

11.3.4 Inattention to inflation and monetary policy

What lies behind the disagreement displayed by firms? One natural source of disagreement about inflation in the future is if firms disagree about what inflation has been in the past. Beliefs about recent inflation rates have long been found to be a strong predictor of household expectations about future inflation (Jonung, 1981) and similar evidence has been documented for firms in New Zealand (Coibion et al., 2018). Another reason why firms might disagree about future inflation is if they disagree about the long-run objectives of the central bank. Inattention to recent inflation or monetary policy can therefore each provide one potential rationale to help account for the widespread disagreement in beliefs about future inflation by firms.

How inattentive are firms to monetary policy and recent inflation? In terms of the former, we can assess how informed firms are about long-run monetary policy by asking them to identify their central bank's inflation target. This question was asked of firms in SoFIE as well as in surveys of firms in New Zealand and Uruguay. The distributions of answers are presented in Fig. 11.5. Over 50% of U.S. firms responded that they did not know the Fed's inflation target and did not want to provide a quantitative answer. Only about 25% of respondents correctly identified the 2% inflation target, with many providing answers significantly higher. This suggests that inattention to monetary policy is pervasive among firms in the United States. Results for New Zealand are similar. Despite a long-run history of inflation targeting, only about one-third of New Zealand firms could correctly identify the Reserve Bank of New Zealand's 2% inflation target. More than 40% provided answers of 4% or above. Firms in New Zealand appear no more informed about monetary policy than those in the United States.

Fig. 11.5 also plots corresponding results based on a survey of firms in Uruguay (Frache and Lluberas, 2019; Borraz et al., 2020). The inflation target in Uruguay ranges from 3% to 7%. Forty-five

---

[10] Online Appendix Fig. 4 shows that similar findings hold for Sweden and South Africa.

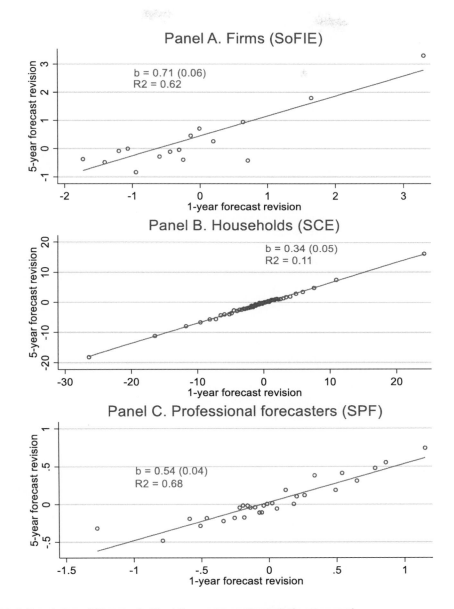

FIGURE 11.4 Correlation of Changes in Short-Run and Long-Run Inflation Expectations

Notes: Each panel shows the relationship (binscatter) between revisions in 1-year-ahead and 5-year-ahead inflation forecasts. Firms in SoFIE 2019Q4 and 2020Q4, households in the SCE 2017Q1–2020Q4, and professional forecasters from SPF 2018Q1–2021Q3. Each specification uses Huber robust regression to downweight the importance of outliers and influential observations.

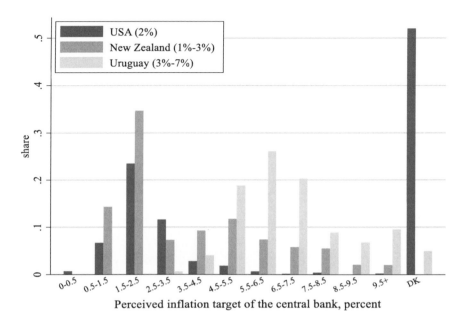

FIGURE 11.5 Perceived Inflation Target of the Central Bank

Notes: The panel plots the distribution of responses to questions about firms' perceptions of their central bank's inflation target in the U.S., New Zealand, and Uruguay. "DK" stands for "Don't Know".

percent of respondents said that the inflation target was 5% or 6% and the share reporting a number from 3% to 7% was approximately 70%. This is a much larger fraction of firms able to correctly identify their central bank's inflation target than in the U.S. or New Zealand. Hence, while inattention to monetary policy appears to be symptomatic of firms in New Zealand or the U.S., it is at odds with what we observe in Uruguay, where firms appear attentive to the central bank's objectives.[11]

Inattention to recent inflation presents another possible source of disagreement in expectations. The surveys of firms in the U.S., New Zealand, and Uruguay all included questions asking firms about what they thought the most recent 12-month inflation rate had been. The distributions of responses in each country are plotted in Panels A, B, and C of Fig. 11.6 for the U.S., New Zealand, and Uruguay, respectively. In 2018Q2, when U.S. firms in SoFIE were asked about the recent inflation rate, the latest CPI inflation number was unusually high, at just around 3%. Less than 20% of respondents said that inflation had been 3%, while close to 50% answered 2%, with another 15% answering 0% or 1%, leaving about 25% of respondents answering 4% or more. Despite the widespread availability of data on inflation, we can, nonetheless, observe significant dispersion in beliefs about recent inflation in the

---

[11] Similar to Uruguay, firms in Russia, a country with a history of high and volatile inflation, are quite informed about the central bank's inflation target. Using a one-time survey in 2018, Karlova et al. (2019) find that, although approximately a third of respondents had "no idea" about the inflation target (Russia adopted inflation targeting in 2014), respondents who provided quantitative responses overwhelmingly picked 4%, the official inflation target.

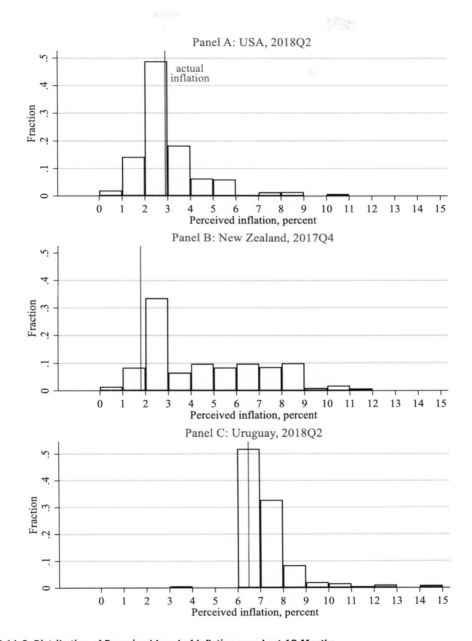

FIGURE 11.6 Distribution of Perceived Level of Inflation over Last 12 Months

Notes: Each panel plots the distribution of perceived inflation rates over the previous 12 months for firms in each country's survey. The vertical red line in each panel indicates the actual inflation rate.

United States. The same question was asked of firms in New Zealand in 2013Q4, when inflation was around 1.5%. Less than 40% of firms reported that inflation was either 1% or 2%. Around 50% of firms responded that inflation had been running at 4% or more. As in the U.S., firms in New Zealand also display remarkable inattention to recent inflation with a wide variety of views about what those recent rates have been.

Corresponding results for Uruguay are for a survey wave in 2018Q2, when the same question about recent inflation was asked. At the time, the most recent inflation rate was 6.5%. Strikingly, around 85% of firms responded that inflation had been either 6% or 7% and only 15% of firms were off by more than 1 percentage point. Unlike what we see with firms in the U.S. and New Zealand, this result indicates that firms in Uruguay are much more attentive to aggregate inflation.

Jointly, these results yield a striking contrast. Firms in the U.S. and New Zealand are very inattentive to both inflation and monetary policy. Firms in Uruguay, on the other hand, are much better informed about both. One possible explanation for this contrast is their respective histories of inflation and the incentive that firms face in terms of staying informed about inflation. Both the U.S. and New Zealand have had low and stable inflation since the 1990s. During this period, inflation has rarely moved far from the 2% target of both central banks, and when it has, these deviations have been very transitory. The success of the U.S. Federal Reserve and the Reserve Bank of New Zealand in stabilizing inflation has therefore created an environment in which firms have little incentive to remain attentive to either inflation or monetary policy. In contrast, Uruguay has a history of higher and more volatile inflation, an environment in which firms must pay attention to inflation and monetary policy to stay afloat. As a result, we observe little sign of inattention to either inflation or monetary policy on the part of Uruguayan firms. Afrouzi et al. (2020) document a similar finding for firms in Iran.

More generally, to what extent do economic agents in volatile environments stay more informed than agents in stable environments? Cavallo et al. (2017) documented a similar result for households in Argentina who, facing an environment of high and volatile inflation, were well-informed about recent inflation and monetary policy, whereas U.S. households, who were living in an environment of low and stable inflation, were very inattentive. Similarly, there is variation in the degree of informedness of households in the U.S. over time. Their forecasts were very close to those of professionals through the 1970s and early 1980s when inflation in the U.S. was high and volatile, but household forecasts began to deviate from professional forecasts in persistent swings starting in the 1990s, as inflation fell to the lower levels experienced since. This suggests that households, like firms, likely adapt how they allocate their attention to their economic environment.

To assess this predicted relationship, we first measure the degree of attention to economic conditions by firms and households across countries. We do so by constructing a measure of the difference between their inflation forecasts from those of professional forecasters at the quarterly frequency. Specifically, for country i and period t, we measure the absolute value of the difference between the average 12-month-ahead inflation forecast of firms and the average 12-month-ahead inflation forecast of professionals. We then take the average over time of each country's series, which yields an average absolute distance from professional forecasts. Finally, we normalize this by the standard deviation of 12-month-ahead inflation forecast errors of professional forecasters over the corresponding period. Equivalently,

our measure for country c is: $MAD^c = \left| E_t^{firms,c} \pi_{t+4} - E_t^{spf,c} \pi_{t+4} \right| / std \left(\pi_{t+4}^c - E_t^{spf,c} \pi_{t+4} \right)$ where

$E_t^{firms,c} \pi_{t+4}$ is the average 12-month-ahead inflation forecast of firms in country c and period t, $E_t^{spf,c} \pi_{t+4}$ is the average 12-month-ahead inflation forecast of professionals, π_{t+4}^c is the annual in-

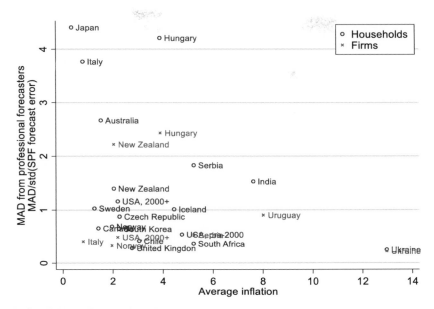

FIGURE 11.7 Inattention and Average Inflation

Notes: The figure plots average inflation rates against average deviations of firm or household forecasts from professional forecasts. Blue circles indicate household forecasts while red x's indicate firm forecasts. US sample for households is separated into pre-2000 and post-2000 observations. See Section 11.3.4 for construction of y-axis variable measuring average distance of households/firms' forecasts from professional forecasts.

flation rate at time $t + 4$, and both the average $(\overline{|\cdot|})$ and std operators apply across time. We then construct equivalent measures for households in countries for which we have appropriate time samples.

We plot in Fig. 11.7 the average annual inflation rate for each country over the corresponding time period (x-axis) versus the distance from professional forecasts of firm and household forecasts in that country over that same period (y-axis). Our MAD measure is normalized by the volatility of inflation, because the fact that higher inflation tends to be more volatile inflation would naturally lead to larger differences in forecast levels. This scale effect would tend to induce an artificial positive correlation. Instead, what we observe in Fig. 11.7 is that there tends to be a negative correlation between the level of inflation and the distance of both firm and household forecasts from those of professional forecasters. In high inflation environments like India, Uruguay, or Ukraine, the inflation forecasts of both firms and households are relatively close to those of professionals, with average differences of less than one percentage point. As we consider countries with lower inflation, however, we tend to see rising differences between firm or household forecasts and those of professionals, indicating more inattention on the part of the former.

This evidence is of course meant to be only suggestive due to data limitations.[12] We have few firm-level surveys, for example, and some of these surveys have very limited time samples. In addition, the

---

[12] An alternative route is to use structural models and indirect inference to relate the degree of inattention to macroeconomic or firm-specific factors. For example, Yang (2019), Pasten and Schoenle (2016), Bhattarai and Schoenle (2014) examine whether

inflation rate in the relevant samples may not necessarily be representative of that country's historical experience. Household surveys are not necessarily constructed in the same way across countries, and different countries often apply different thresholds for identifying outliers. Despite these shortcomings, we view the cross-country experience as broadly consistent with rational inattention: households and firms allocate more attention to inflation when not knowing about inflation would become more costly.

11.3.5 The joint formation of beliefs

While we have so far focused exclusively on the inflation expectations of firms, some surveys also consider firms' expectations about other macroeconomic variables as well, although this is a restricted subset of surveys described before. Surveys of New Zealand firms, for example, sometimes asked firms about their expectations of future output growth. The Italian survey of firms regularly asks firms about future business conditions, although responses are only qualitative in nature. Firms in Ukraine are also asked about future output growth. Surveys of firms in Sweden and South Africa ask quantitative questions about GDP growth expectations. Jointly, these surveys allow us to assess how firms perceive the relationship between inflation and output, at least unconditionally.

Building on Candia et al. (2020), Fig. 11.8 plots the unconditional correlation between firms' inflation forecasts and their expectations about future output growth. In the case of firms in New Zealand and Sweden (keep in mind that the survey of Sweden is not representative), we see a strong positive correlation between their expectations of growth and inflation, consistent with demand-side shocks moving the economy along a Phillips curve. In Italy, we observe very little correlation between firms' expectations of output growth and their expectations of inflation prior to the effective lower bound period on interest rates, but a much stronger positive correlation during the ELB period. This is consistent with the idea that even supply shocks inherit demand-side characteristics at the ZLB, as in New Keynesian models. Firms in Ukraine and South Africa, in contrast, exhibit a very negative correlation between their expectations of output growth and inflation, as if they perceived the economy to be primarily driven by supply-side shocks. These results suggest that firms generally do form expectations of inflation and output growth jointly, although the resulting joint distributions can look quite different across countries.[13] For comparison, professional forecasters systematically expect a positive correlation between the real economy and inflation (Online Appendix Fig. 1).[14] Households (Online Appendix Fig. 2), in contrast, systematically expect a negative correlation between the real economy and inflation, as emphasized in Kamdar (2018) for the United States. Thus, firms once again appear to hold economic views that are somewhere between those of professionals and households.

While unconditional correlations are suggestive of a joint formation of beliefs across macroeconomic variables, such correlations do not imply that firms necessarily see a connection between the level of economic activity and inflation. To get at this, the survey of firms in New Zealand considered a

---

multiproduct firms are more attentive than single-product firms. Mackowiak et al. (2009) examine sectoral variation in the sensitivity of prices to shocks and relate the estimated sensitivity to incentives to pay attention to aggregate shocks. This type of evidence is consistent with the direct evidence in firm surveys.

[13] For Sweden, South Africa and New Zealand, we can link firms across survey waves and hence explore if the same relationships hold for forecast revisions. We find the same patterns for correlations when we use revisions.

[14] Except for Ukraine and South Africa, countries with a history of high and volatile inflation. However, the negative correlation between output growth and inflation expectations for both countries is more robust for firms than for professional forecasters.

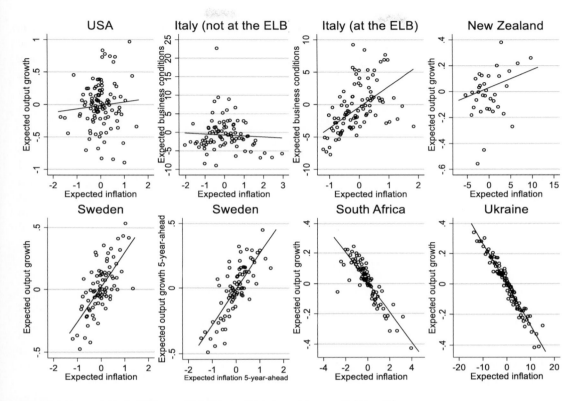

FIGURE 11.8 Joint Distribution of Inflation and Output Growth Expectations, Firms

Notes: Each panel plots a binscatter for the joint distribution of expectations for output growth rate and inflation in the next calendar year. For each variable, we take out the time×country fixed effect so that all variables are mean zero. Inflation expectations are for the one-year-ahead horizon. United States: output expectations are one-year-ahead predictions for real GDP growth rate. The Livingston survey is the source of the data. The sample is restricted to nonfinancial corporations. The sample period is 1992–2019. Italy: output expectations are responses to a multiple-choice question ("What do you think is the probability of an improvement in Italy's general economic situation in the next 3 months?") with size options: zero, 1–25%, 26–50%, 51–75%, 76–99%, 100%. For each option, we code responses as midpoints of the chosen ranges. Coibion et al. (2020) is the source of the data. The sample period is 2012–2019. New Zealand: output expectations measure one-year-ahead projections for GDP growth. Coibion et al. (2018) is the source of the data. The sample period is 2014–2017. Sweden: inflation and GDP growth rate expectations are elicited as point predictions. The sample period is 2000–2020. The source is Sveriges Riksbank. South Africa: inflation and GDP growth rate expectations are elicited as point predictions. The sample period is 2000–2020. The source is South African Reserve Bank. Ukraine: inflation expectations are reported as answers to multiple-choice questions (typically 7–9 options; e.g., the bins could be "less than 5%," "5–10%," "10–15%," ..., "more than 40%"). Output expectations are responses to a multiple-choice question ("What changes do you expect in the dynamics for output of goods and services in Ukraine over the next 12 months?") with three options: "increase" (coded as "+1"), "same" (coded as "0"), "decrease" (coded as "-1"). The sample period is 2007–2020. The National Bank of Ukraine is the source of the data.

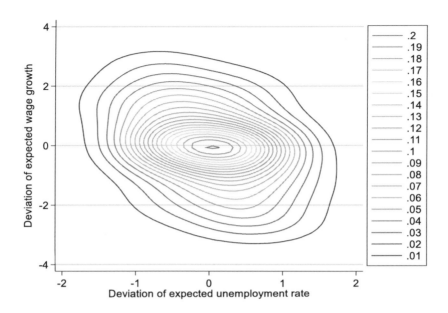

FIGURE 11.9 Joint Expectations of Wage Growth and Unemployment Rate for Firms in New Zealand

Notes: The figure shows negative correlation in the within-firm joint distribution of subjective expectations for future wage growth and unemployment rate in a survey of firm managers in New Zealand. The figure shows contour maps for the average joint distribution (kernel density) of expected wage growth and unemployment rate. The joint distribution is elicited by asking managers to assign probabilities to each cell in a table of wage-growth and unemployment-rate outcomes (each dimension of the table has a series of bins with a range of possible outcomes). To aggregate distributions across managers, we demean each manager's distribution using his/her implied mean for future wage growth and unemployment rate and then we take an average across managers. The horizontal axis measures deviation of manager i's expectation from his/her mean forecast for unemployment rate over the next 12 months. The vertical axis measures deviation of manager i's expectation from his/her mean forecast for wage growth over the next 12 months. This figure was initially published in Candia et al. (2020).

unique question that described the formation of beliefs about unemployment and wage inflation *jointly*. Specifically, firms were first asked to assign probabilities to different possible future unemployment rates. Then, for *each* unemployment rate that they assigned a positive probability to, they were asked to assign probabilities to different aggregate wage inflation outcomes. This question therefore allows us to assess how firms revise probabilities across future wage inflation rates as they consider different unemployment rates, i.e., this provides a complete joint distribution over unemployment and wage inflation expectations.

The average distribution reported by firms in the New Zealand survey is plotted in Fig. 11.9, as previously shown in Candia et al. (2020), after normalizing by each firm's mean forecast of unemployment and wage inflation. The *x*-axis shows different values of unemployment above or below each firm's average unemployment forecast, while the *y*-axis shows the deviations of wage growth from each firm's mean forecast. The figure is a heat map, so the lines in the figure reflect the average probability that firms assigned to this combination of wage inflation and unemployment deviations from the mean. The key finding is the downward sloping nature of the heat map: when considering values of unemployment lower than their mean forecast, firms tend to think that wage inflation will be higher than their mean forecast, and vice versa when considering higher values of unemployment. This shape is consistent with a wage Phillips curve: high unemployment is associated with lower wage inflation while a tight labor market is associated with higher wage inflation.

One can also consider the way in which firms revise their beliefs about real and nominal variables after acquiring information. For example, in the Italian survey of firms, a significant number of (randomly selected) firms were provided with information about recent inflation each quarter ("treatment group") while others were not ("control group"). This information treatment led those treated firms to have different inflation expectations than those of the control group, as shown in Coibion et al. (2018). But inflation expectations were *not* the only macroeconomic beliefs that changed. Over the entire sample, firms who revised their inflation expectations upward due to the treatment tended to become more pessimistic about the economic outlook. But during the effective lower bound period, this pattern reversed and treated firms that raised their inflation expectations tended to become optimistic about the real economy. Hence, joint revisions in expectations of different variables exist conditional on information treatments, as well as unconditionally as shown in Figs. 11.8 and 11.9.

Jointly, we view this evidence as consistent with the idea that firms form expectations about macroeconomic variables jointly. However, there is much to learn about how they form these views. For example, it is not clear why in some countries firms seem to have a supply-side view of the world whereas in others their expectations are more in line with demand shocks moving the economy along a Phillips curve. One possibility is that this reflects the historical experience of each country. For example, the historical correlation between inflation and output growth in the U.S., Sweden, and New Zealand during the Great Moderation era has been mildly positive and in these countries firms perceive a positive correlation. In contrast, inflation and output growth have been much less weakly correlated, or even negatively correlated, historically in South Africa and Ukraine, and firms in these countries perceive a negative correlation. News coverage could also affect how firms view the interaction of different macroeconomic variables, as could different policy responses. The fact that the perceived correlation between inflation and output growth changes so dramatically before and the ELB period in Italy, for example, is consistent with firms incorporating monetary policy responses into their expectations. To the extent that these macroeconomic expectations matter for economic decisions and outcomes, better understanding the joint formation of economic expectations should be a priority for firm surveys.

11.4 Do firms' macroeconomic expectations matter?

The measurement of firms' expectations is perceived as important to the extent that these expectations should matter for economic outcomes and policy. But is it in fact the case that firms act on their macroeconomic expectations? In this section we consider two pieces of evidence that support the notion that firms' aggregate expectations matter.

11.4.1 Firms' inflation expectations and the expectations-augmented Phillips curve

Since Friedman (1968) and Phelps (1968), many macroeconomic models have featured expectations-augmented Phillips curves: structural relationships linking inflation and the real side of the economy that condition on firms' aggregate inflation expectations. This role for inflation expectations arises naturally in models with either nominal or information frictions. Previous work has documented that an expectations-augmented Phillips curve fits U.S. data quite well (Coibion and Gorodnichenko, 2015a).

Given the cross-country firm-level data compiled here, we can assess whether an expectations-augmented Phillips curve works more generally across countries. Coibion et al. (2019) did so using inflation expectations for firms and (mostly) households, but here we focus on firm surveys more specifically. The first step is to create a measure of an inflation gap for each country, the deviation between inflation and firms' one-year inflation expectations. The second is to create an unemployment gap for each country, a measure of the cyclical variation in the real economy. We do so by taking the difference between the unemployment rate and the HP-filtered unemployment rate with a smoothing parameter of one million, a simple way of measuring the natural rate of unemployment. We then demean both measures for each country (i.e., we control for country fixed effects) to make them comparable.

The left Panel A of Fig. 11.10 plots the resulting correlation between inflation gaps and unemployment rates using the USA, Norway, Italy, New Zealand, Hungary, Uruguay, Japan, Sweden, South Africa, Serbia, Colombia, and Czech Republic.[15] There is a clear and strong negative relationship between the two: periods when unemployment is above the natural rate are periods when countries are experiencing inflation below expectations of future inflation. Conditioning on firms' inflation expectations is crucial for recovering this strong negative relationship between real and nominal variables. The right Panel A of Fig. 11.10 shows the corresponding relationship when lagged inflation is used in place of expected inflation: the correlation between the inflation gap and unemployment is close to zero across countries. But just as predicted by Friedman (1968) and Phelps (1968), taking into account firms' inflation expectations helps uncover the enduring (short-run) tradeoff between inflation and unemployment in the data. Panels B and C of Fig. 11.10 show that these results are maintained when we split the sample in low-inflation countries (USA, Italy, New Zealand, Norway, Sweden, and Japan) and high-inflation countries (Hungary, Uruguay, South Africa, Serbia, Colombia, and Czech Republic). We also find similar results if we use longer-run inflation expectations rather than one-year ahead inflation expectations.

11.4.2 Randomized control trials

Another way to determine if firms' macroeconomic expectations affect their decisions is through randomized control trials (RCT) as discussed in Chapter 4 in this Handbook. The idea is to generate exogenous variation in the macroeconomic beliefs of a randomly selected subset of firms then assess whether these firms end up behaving differently than non-treated firms (the control group). A random-

---

[15] The countries with the best firm surveys have only short time samples available, so we augment the range of countries to include some whose firm surveys are not as ideal as those emphasized in Fig. 11.1. Ukraine is not included because of the dramatic spike in inflation in 2015, which was a clear shock due to the war, the associated elimination of energy subsidies and the currency depreciation.

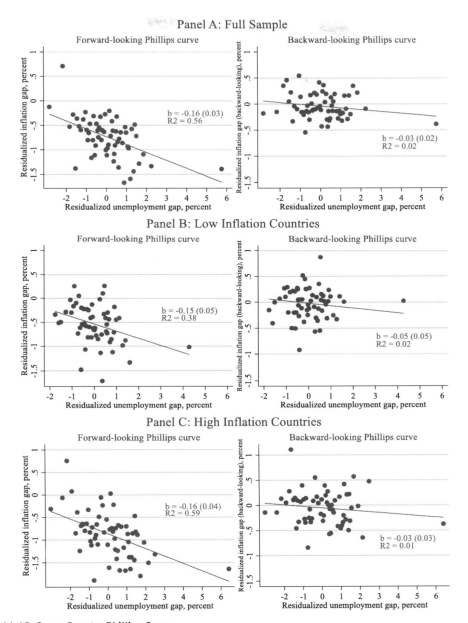

FIGURE 11.10 Cross-Country Phillips Curve

Notes: This figure shows a binscatter plot for inflation gap (left panel: actual inflation minus one-year-ahead expected inflation; right panel: actual current inflation minus actual lagged inflation) and unemployment gap (the cyclical component in unemployment rate after applying the HP filter with a smoothing parameter of one million). Panel A (full sample) includes the following countries: USA, Norway, Italy, New Zealand, Uruguay, Japan, Sweden, South Africa, Serbia, Colombia, Hungary, and Czech Republic. Panel B (low inflation countries) includes USA, Norway, Italy, New Zealand, Japan, and Sweden. Panel C (high inflation countries) includes Uruguay, South Africa, Serbia, Colombia, Hungary, and Czech Republic. Ukraine is excluded because the sample for Ukraine is dominated by a very large spike in inflation. The series cover the sample period shown in Figs. 11.1 and 11.2, except for Norway (the survey is representative since 2009). Country fixed effects are controlled for.

ized control trial can provide direct *causal* evidence that changes in firms' expectations affect their economic decisions.

One such RCT was conducted using the survey of firms in New Zealand and is described in detail in Coibion et al. (2018). Two surveys of firms were run, separated by six months. In the first wave, firms were asked several questions about their expectations, both at the aggregate level as well as for their firm's planned actions over the next six months, such as recruiting plans, pricing plans, investment plans and wage plans. A randomly selected subset of these firms was then told about the inflation target of the Reserve Bank of New Zealand. As discussed in Section 11.3.4, firms in New Zealand are largely unaware of the RBNZ's inflation target so this treatment provided many of them with new information. In light of this information, initially uninformed firms significantly and immediately changed their inflation expectations in the direction of the target. Other firms in the survey, on the other hand, were not provided with any additional information. Six months later, these firms were surveyed again and asked about how they changed prices, employment, and wages over the previous six months, as well as the amount of investment they had done. Comparing this to their planned levels from six months before provides a measure of the surprise in their actions over this time period. The key finding of CGK was that uninformed firms in the treatment group significantly revised downward their inflation expectations after the information treatment and subsequently lowered their employment and investment relative to other firms but did not deviate from their price or wage plans in any systematic way relative to other firms. Coibion et al. (2021) subsequently replicated and expanded on this experiment and found a similar response by firms to exogenous changes in their inflation expectations arising from different sources. Hence, exogenous shocks to firms' inflation expectations in New Zealand are followed by significant adjustments along the employment and investment margins of firms, indicating that macroeconomic expectations do seem to play a role in firm decision-making.

More evidence comes from another "experiment" applied to firms in Italy. As explained in Section 11.2, starting in 2012, some firms in the Italian survey were repeatedly and systematically given information about recent inflation while other firms in the Italian survey were not. Much like the one-time information treatment provided to firms in New Zealand, the provision of information about recent inflation led firms to change their expectations in a significant fashion relative to those who were not provided this information. But unlike the one-time New Zealand experiment, the information treatment in Italy was applied to the same firms repeatedly over the course of years, leading to long-lived differences in the inflation expectations across firms. Since many firm decisions were observable from the repeated surveys (e.g., prices) and many others were also observable from external administrative sources (e.g., employment, investment, financial situation), Coibion et al. (2020) are able to study how the exogenous variation in inflation expectations induced by the repeated information treatment led firms to adjust differentially along these margins.

Over the entire sample, firms with exogenously higher inflation expectations were found to reduce their investment and employment persistently over the next year, with little change in prices taking place. A potential explanation for this contractionary effect of expected inflation on firm decisions is that as firms in Italy raise their inflation expectations, they generally become more pessimistic about the broader economic outlook as well as the economic outlook for their firm. When looking specifically at the effective lower bound on interest rates period, this negative association with inflation is reversed and firms with higher inflation expectations become more optimistic about the economic outlook. This leads them to raise their prices and increase their employment when their inflation expectations rise. These results indicate that macroeconomic expectations clearly affect the decisions made by firms, but the manner in which they do so seems to depend on how they interpret the source of these revisions in beliefs, e.g., if they stem from demand or supply shocks. Understanding the joint formation of expectations across variables, and how they relate to perceived underlying shocks, is therefore an important avenue for future surveys to pursue.

11.5 Conclusion

Firms' expectations about the broader economy translate into their decisions. For macroeconomists, understanding how these expectations are formed should therefore be a central area for future research. One limitation to this line of work is the paucity of high-quality surveys of firms. Indeed, Bernanke (2007) observed, "Do we need new measures of expectations or new surveys? Information on the price expectations of businesses–who are, after all, the price setters in the first instance–as well as information on nominal wage expectations is particularly scarce." This state of affairs is slowly changing as new surveys of firms gradually arise. This paper describes some of these new surveys, but others are also in the works. For example, the Bank of France is designing a new quantitative survey of firms' expectations, as described in Savignac et al. (2021). This growing list of high-quality surveys of firms' macroeconomic expectations, covering not just inflation but increasingly also other macroeconomic variables such as output growth, interest rates, and financial market conditions, is promising for future work.

The expanding list of firm surveys will also be a boon to policymakers. Understanding the inflation outlook hinges in part on knowing what firms expect, and this can only be done with real-time high-quality quantitative surveys. As surveys such as SoFIE become more common across advanced economies, this real-time measurement and tracking will simplify the work of policymakers who are otherwise often forced to guess or presume what economic agents are anticipating (as discussed in Reis (2022), the rise of the Great Inflation in the 1970s is a grim reminder of the cost of lacking measurement of inflation expectations). These surveys will also allow policymakers to assess how well their policies are working, since many new policies like forward guidance or the announcement of average inflation targeting are supposed to operate via the inflation expectations of firms and households.

References

Afrouzi, Hassan, Bayat, Saeed, Ghaderi, Omid, Madanizadeh, Ali, 2020. Inflation Expectations under High Inflation: Evidence from Iran. Manuscript.

Altig, David, Barrero, Jose Maria, Bloom, Nicholas, Davis, Steven J., Meyer, Brent, Parker, Nicholas, 2020. Surveying business uncertainty. Journal of Econometrics. Forthcoming.

Andrade, Philippe, Coibion, Olivier, Gautier, Erwan, Gorodnichenko, Yuriy, 2022. No firm is an island? How industry conditions shape firms' expectations. Journal of Monetary Economics 125, 40–56.

Bachmann, Rudiger, 2019. Comments on 'monetary policy announcements and expectations: evidence from German firms'. Journal of Monetary Economics 108, 64–68.

Bernanke, Ben S., 2007. Inflation expectations and inflation forecasting. Speech at the Monetary Economics Workshop of the National Bureau of Economic Research Summer Institute, Cambridge, Massachusetts, July 10, 2007. Available at https://www.federalreserve.gov/newsevents/speech/bernanke20070710a.htm.

Bhattarai, Saroj, Schoenle, Raphael, 2014. Multi-product firms and price-setting: theory and evidence from U.S. producers prices. Journal of Monetary Economics 66, 178–192.

Binder, Carola, Kim, GwangMin, 2020. Learning-Through-Survey in Inflation Expectations. Manuscript.

Bischof, Jannis, Doerrenberg, Philipp, Rostam-Afschar, Davud, Simons, Dirk, Voget, Johannes, 2021. The German Business Panel: Insights on Corporate Taxation and Accounting during the COVID-19 Pandemic. Manuscript.

Bloom, Nicholas, Bunn, Philip, Chen, Scarlet, Mizen, Paul, Smietanka, Pawel, Thwaites, Gregory, 2019. The Impact of Brexit on UK Firms. NBER Working Paper 26218.

Borraz, Fernando, Mello, Miguel, Zacheo, Laura, 2020. Communication, Information and Inflation Expectations. BIS CCA Research Network.

Candia, Bernardo, Coibion, Olivier, Gorodnichenko, Yuriy, 2020. Communication and the Beliefs of Economic Agents. NBER Working Paper 27800.

Candia, Bernardo, Coibion, Olivier, Gorodnichenko, Yuriy, 2021. The Inflation Expectations of U.S. Firms: Evidence from a new survey. NBER Working Paper 28836.

Cavallo, Alberto, Cruces, Guillermo, Perez-Truglia, Ricardo, 2017. Inflation expectations, learning, and supermarket prices: evidence from survey experiments. American Economic Journal: Macroeconomics 9 (3), 1–35.

Coibion, Olivier, Gorodnichenko, Yuriy, 2012. What can survey forecasts tell us about informational rigidities? Journal of Political Economy 120, 116–159.

Coibion, Olivier, Gorodnichenko, Yuriy, 2015a. Is the Phillips curve alive and well after all? Inflation expectations and the missing disinflation. AEJ Macroeconomics 7 (1), 197–232.

Coibion, Olivier, Gorodnichenko, Yuriy, 2015b. Inflation expectations in Ukraine: a long path to anchoring? Visnyk of the National Bank of Ukraine 233, 6–23.

Coibion, Olivier, Gorodnichenko, Yuriy, Kumar, Saten, 2018. How do firms form their expectations? New survey evidence. The American Economic Review 108, 2671–2713.

Coibion, Olivier, Gorodnichenko, Yuriy, Ulate, Mauricio, 2019. Is inflation just around the corner? The Phillips curve and global inflationary pressures. AEA Papers and Proceedings 109 (1), 465–469.

Coibion, Olivier, Gorodnichenko, Yuriy, Kumar, Saten, Ryngaert, Jane, 2021. Do you know that I know that you know...? Higher-order beliefs in survey data. The Quarterly Journal of Economics 136 (3), 1387–1446.

Coibion, Olivier, Gorodnichenko, Yuriy, Ropele, Tiziano, 2020. Inflation expectations and firm decisions: new causal evidence. The Quarterly Journal of Economics 135 (1), 165–219.

D'Acunto, Francesco, Malmendier, Ulrike M., Ospina, Juan, Weber, Michael, 2021. Exposure to daily price changes and inflation expectations. Journal of Political Economy 129 (5), 1615–1639.

Delgado, Martha E., Herreño, Juan, Hofstetter, Marc, Pedemonte, Mathieu, 2021. Inflation and Exchange Rate Expectations of Colombian Firms: a new survey. Manuscript.

Enders, Zeno, Hunnekes, Franziska, Muller, Gernot, 2019. Monetary policy announcements and expectations: evidence from German firms. Journal of Monetary Economics 108, 45–63.

Frache, Serafin, Lluberas, Rodrigo, 2019. New Information and Inflation Expectations among Firms. BIS Working Paper 781.

Friedman, Milton, 1968. The role of monetary policy. The American Economic Review 58, 1–17.

Gallermore, John, Hollander, Stephan, Jacob, Martin, Zheng, Xiang, 2021. Tax Policy Beliefs and Investment: Evidence from the 2016 U.S. Election and the Tax Cuts and Jobs Act. Manuscript.

Haldane, Andrew, Macaulay, Alistair, McMahon, Michael, 2020. The 3 E's of Central Bank Communication with the Public. Bank of England Working Paper No. 847.

Haldane, Andrew, McMahon, Michael, 2018. Central bank communications and the general public. American Economic Association Papers and Proceedings 108, 578–583.

Hassan, Tarek, Hollander, Stephan, van Lent, Laurence, Tahoun, Ahmed, 2019. Firm-level political risk: measurement and effects. The Quarterly Journal of Economics 134, 2135–2202.

Jonung, Lars, 1981. Perceived and expected rates of inflation in Sweden. The American Economic Review 71 (5), 961–968.

Kamdar, Rupal, 2018. The Inattentive Consumer: Sentiment and Expectations. Manuscript.

Karlova, Natalia, Puzanova, Elena, Bogacheva, Irina, Morozov, Alexandr, 2019. The Nature of Companies' Inflation Expectations: Survey Results. Bank of Russia Research Note.

Kumar, Saten, Afrouzi, Hassan, Coibion, Olivier, Gorodnichenko, Yuriy, 2015. Inflation targeting does not anchor inflation expectations: evidence from New Zealand. Brookings Papers on Economic Activity 2015 (Fall), 151–225.

Lucas Jr., Robert, 1972. Expectations and the neutrality of money. Journal of Economic Theory 4 (2), 103–124.

Mackowiak, Bartosz, Moench, Emanuel, Wiederholt, Mirko, 2009. Sectoral price data and models of price setting. Journal of Monetary Economics 56 (S), 78–99.

Mankiw, N. Gregory, Reis, Ricardo, Wolfers, Justin, 2003. Disagreement about inflation expectations. NBER Macroeconomics Annual 2003 (18), 209–248.

Meyer, Brent H., Parker, Nicholas B., Sheng, Xuguang Simon, 2021. Unit Cost Expectations and Uncertainty: Firms' Perspectives on Inflation. Federal Reserve Bank of Atlanta Working Paper 2021.

Pasten, Ernesto, Schoenle, Raphael, 2016. Rational inattention, multi-product firms and the neutrality of money. Journal of Monetary Economics 80 (C), 1–16.

Phelps, Edmund, 1968. Money-wage dynamics and labor-market equilibrium. Journal of Political Economy 76 (4), 678–711.

Reis, Ricardo, 2021. Comment on 'imperfect macroeconomic expectations:' yes, but we disagree. NBER Macroeconomics Annual 35 (1), 99–111.

Reis, Ricardo, 2022. Losing the inflation anchor. Brookings Papers on Economic Activity 2021 (2), 307–379.

Savignac, Frederique, Gautier, Erwan, Gorodnichenko, Yuriy, Coibion, Olivier, 2021. Firms' Inflation Expectations: New Evidence from France. Manuscript.

Tanaka, Mari, Bloom, Nicholas, David, Joel M., Koga, Maiko, 2019. Firm performance and macro forecast accuracy. Journal of Monetary Economics 114, 26–41.

Ungar, Meyer, Zilberfarb, Ben-Zion, 1993. Inflation and its unpredictability- theory and empirical evidence. Journal of Money, Credit, and Banking 25 (4), 709–720.

Yang, Choongryul, 2019. Rational Inattention, Menu Costs, and Multi-Product Firms: Micro Evidence and Aggregate Implications. Manuscript.

Firm expectations about production and prices: facts, determinants, and effects[☆]

12

Benjamin Born[a,b,c,d], **Zeno Enders**[e,c], **Gernot J. Müller**[f,b,c], **and Knut Niemann**[f]

[a]*Frankfurt School of Finance and Management, Frankfurt am Main, Germany*
[b]*CEPR, London, United Kingdom*
[c]*CESifo, Munich, Germany*
[d]*ifo, Munich, Germany*
[e]*Heidelberg University, Heidelberg, Germany*
[f]*University of Tübingen, Tübingen, Germany*

12.1 Introduction

In this chapter, we review recent work which uses survey data to analyze firm expectations—with a particular focus on firms' production and price expectations. These matter a great deal for actual firm decisions. To see this, consider the responses to a brief survey among German firms about their production and pricing decisions. As illustrated by Fig. 12.1, firm-specific developments are as important for these decisions as the developments of the aggregate economy and a firm's market segment (see also Freuding et al., 2021). At the same time, forecasting their own variables is potentially hard for firms and perhaps even harder than forecasting the aggregate economy (Bloom et al., 2021).[1]

We revisit the evidence based on various surveys from different countries. Because the existing literature on the issue is still in a somewhat early stage, we complement our discussion of existing work with new evidence based on the ifo Survey of German firms. The ifo Survey is one of the oldest and largest surveys of firms currently available. It is based on a firm survey which has been conducted since 1949 and whose design has since then been adopted by other surveys as well (Becker and Wohlrabe, 2008). We provide details about this survey and introduce basic concepts in Section 12.2.[2]

In Section 12.3, we use the ifo Survey to establish—on the basis of a common data set—five stylized facts which emerge robustly across various studies and surveys. First, firms' expectation errors are unconditionally unbiased, that is, mostly not significantly different from zero. Second, survey re-

---

[☆] An online appendix with additional material is available at https://www.benjaminborn.de/files/BEMN2022_handbook_webappendix.pdf. We thank Manuel Menkhoff and various seminar audiences for useful comments and discussions and the team of the LMU-ifo Economics & Business Data Center (EBDC) in Munich for technical support. The usual disclaimer applies. This research has received financial support by the German Science Foundation (DFG) under Priority Program 1859.

[1] Chapters 5 and 11 in this Handbook consider inflation expectations of households and firms, respectively.
[2] The ifo Survey is also one of the surveys discussed in greater detail in Chapter 2 in this Handbook.

Handbook of Economic Expectations. https://doi.org/10.1016/B978-0-12-822927-9.00019-7

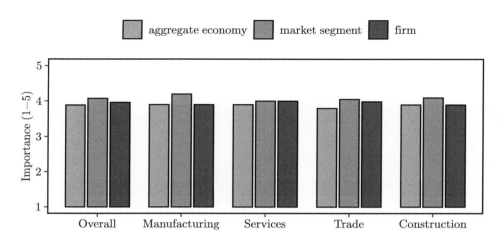

FIGURE 12.1 What matters for firm decisions?

Notes: Responses to special question in the October 2020 wave of the ifo survey of German firms. "How important are the following domains for your production and/or pricing decisions?", with answer scale 1 to 5. Categories: recent developments in the aggregate economy, the firm's market segment, and within the firm. No. of responses: 1666. Left bars show results for all firms, the other blocks results for specific sectors.

sponses are informative in that they outperform static and adaptive expectations in terms of forecasting firm-specific developments. Third, larger and older firms tend to do even better in terms of forecasting. Fourth, we find that firms make predictable forecast errors. Past information about firms' own variables, in particular, predict expectation errors. Fifth, the dispersion and volatility of expectations and expectation errors is countercyclical, in line with the notion that uncertainty increases during recessions. In addition to those stylized facts, we present a sixth observation which has not been made in the survey literature so far: firm expectations are sticky, that is, they are adjusted only infrequently.

In the second part of the chapter, we seek to shed light on both, expectation formation (Section 12.4) and the effects of expectations on firm actions (Section 12.5). We stick to our strategy and revisit for our sample results established in earlier work. As we do so, we focus on the main results in the literature but also offer some additional findings. A first important result concerning the expectation-formation process is that firm-specific variables account for almost all the variation in firm expectations regarding their own output and prices. Next, we consider the responsiveness of firm expectations to news. Here we discuss some recent results which pertain mostly to professional forecasters (Coibion and Gorodnichenko, 2015; Bordalo et al., 2020; Chapter 3 in this Handbook). As a noteworthy exception, Born et al. (2022) study the response of firms' forecast errors about their own variables to forecast revisions (news): firms tend to overreact to firm-specific news, but underreact to news about the aggregate economy.

Eventually, we care about firm expectations to the extent that they matter for actual outcomes—an issue we revisit last, following earlier work by Enders et al. (2022). Here two results are key. First, firm expectations about future production significantly impact current production and pricing decisions. Second, this also holds for expectations that turn out to be incorrect from an ex-post point of view. This suggests that expectations not only operate as a transmission channel of news but also as a genuine source of shocks. There is also evidence that expectations are key for firms' investment decisions.

Before getting started, we note that rather than relying on surveys, one may measure expectations or, relatedly, confidence through proxies extracted from observable behavior (e.g., Malmendier and Tate, 2005a,b; Hirshleifer et al., 2012). Also, in our analysis, we treat firms and firm expectations as the primitives and abstract from within-firm dynamics and management practices and personality traits of CEOs (e.g., Bloom and Reenen, 2007; Kaplan et al., 2012).

12.2 Surveying firm expectations

By now there is a sizeable number of firm surveys which collect direct evidence on firm expectations about their own variables, such as production and prices. In what follows we provide an overview. We then zoom in on the ifo Business Expectations Panel (BEP), which we will use throughout the chapter to replicate the most importing findings in the literature and to generate some new results based on a single data set.

12.2.1 Background

Several surveys were initiated in the 1950s–1970s in order to provide early and additional information about the current state of the (national or regional) economy when official statistics were incomplete and available with a considerable lag only (INSEE, 2007; Nerb and Sauer, 2020; Bank of Japan, 2020; Trebing and Fenske, 2018).[3] In these surveys, firms are typically asked only qualitative questions. They may respond that they expect, say, prices or production to increase, stay the same, or decrease, likewise for their business situation or related variables.[4]

Questions regarding realized values are typically structured analogously to those about expectations. For instance, firms report if production had risen, fallen, or stayed the same. Nerb and Sauer (2020) document that this format was adopted in order to increase the return rate of the survey. Moreover, the format is considered adequate because the surveys feature several questions which require subjective evaluations. Responding qualitatively to questions about, say, the current business situation or the adequateness of inventories, allows firms to weigh different aspects depending on current circumstances in a flexible manner. These types of questions also constitute the so-called "Judgement" part of the Tankan Survey (Bank of Japan, 2020).[5] Rosewell (1987) adds, referring to the CBI Industrial Trends Survey, that the qualitative format increases chances that senior management answers the questionnaires (which is confirmed in Glynn, 1969) and that questions about actual outcomes and expectations can be easily asked in the same context. By aggregating answers regarding current and expected firm-specific variables (most often by forming balances of positive and negative answers), the surveys turn out to have a high predictive value for sector-wide or even national economic developments, see Abberger and Wohlrabe (2006), Henzel and Rast (2013), and Lehmann (2020) for the ifo

---

[3] See also Chapter 2 in this Handbook for further details on individual firm surveys.

[4] See Table A.2 in the online appendix for examples of qualitative questions from the ifo Survey. Note that throughout this chapter, material in the online appendix will be marked with an "A." prefix.

[5] The predecessor of the Tankan started in 1951, following the methodology of the ifo Survey (Bank of Japan, 2022).

Survey, Trebing and Fenske (2018) for the Manufacturing Business Outlook Survey of the Philadelphia Fed, and Glynn (1969) for capital expenditure elicited in the CBI Industrial Trends Survey. Note that this result lends credibility to the choice of aggregating qualitative answers by calculating balances of positive and negative answers.

The large potential of business surveys for rigorous empirical analysis became more apparent over time (see, e.g., Nerb, 1987; Seiler and Wohlrabe, 2013, for the ifo Survey).[6] To increase the scope further still, quantitative questions have been added in several surveys.[7] In this case, respondents are asked to provide a specific number or to choose from predefined ranges when responding to questions about, say, expected sales growth. Providing predefined ranges to elicit point estimates involves potential pitfalls, as the provision of ranges may have a bearing on the elicited answers (Schwarz et al., 1985). Even more recently, following Bloom (2009) and others, business-cycle research highlighted the role of uncertainty for economic developments and, as a consequence, several firm surveys now ask for probability distributions in addition to point forecasts to measure uncertainty.[8] Specifically, survey participants are asked to assign probabilities to either several bins that cover predefined ranges for the future realizations of the variable of interest (e.g., Business Inflation Expectations Survey) or to freely selected bins (Survey of Business Uncertainty, SBU).[9] However, in order to evaluate the answers to these questions additional assumptions need to be made regarding, for instance, probability-mass distribution inside the bins or the underlying models (formal or not) used by survey participants (Krüger and Pavlova, 2020; Glas and Hartmann, 2022).[10]

We provide an overview of existing firm surveys in Table 12.1, panels (a) and (b). Here we focus on those surveys that are available for economic research on firm expectations about firms' own variables.[11]

12.2.2 Example: the ifo Business Expectations Panel

Below we survey the existing literature on firm expectations and, in doing so, we replicate the most important findings on the basis of a single data set. Because of its large coverage in terms of firms, firm-specific variables, and its time dimension, we choose the Business Expectations Panel of the LMU-ifo Economics and Business Data Center (BEP or ifo Survey from now on). It is based on the ifo

---

[6] This is not necessarily true for the underlying micro data, that is, the individual responses. They were often, after aggregation, not kept for later use.

[7] For instance, the ifo Survey and the CBI Industrial Trends Survey introduced quantitative questions in 2005 and 2008, respectively. There is some evidence that using qualitative (elicited via visual analog scales) and quantitative expectation data yields similar results (Enders et al., 2022). Similarly, we stress that the facts established in Section 12.3 hold for qualitative and quantitative data. Nevertheless, a systematic investigation of differences induced by choosing qualitative or quantitative answer possibilities, e.g., by randomizing this choice, seems fruitful.

[8] See Chapter 1 in this Handbook for the use of probabilistic questions in household surveys.

[9] Bloom et al. (2020) analyze business expectations that are surveyed as part of the Census Bureau's Management and Organizational Practices Survey. For selected years, it elicits point estimates for current-year outcomes and five-point probability distributions for the next. Bloom et al. (2020) find that 85% of respondents provide logically sensible responses to the five-point distribution questions, suggesting that most managers can form and express detailed subjective probability distributions.

[10] See also Chapter 3 in this Handbook for issues relating to constructing measures of disagreement and uncertainty in the context of surveys of professionals.

[11] We only consider those surveys that include questions about firm expectations about their own variables and whose firm-level answers are generally provided to researchers. These criteria eliminate a moderate number of firm surveys.

Table 12.1 Surveys with firm expectations about firm-specific developments.

(a) General information

Name	Country	Expectation Variables	From	Freq.	Format	Maintained by
ifo Business Climate Survey	Germany	output, prices, employment, business situation	1949	m	ql, qt 2005+ d 2013+	ifo
Tankan Survey	Japan	sales, exports, profits, investment	1951	q	ql, qt	METI
CBI Industrial Trends Survey	UK	wages, sales prices, employment, unit costs, new orders	1958	q	ql, qt 2008+	Confederation of British Industry
Monthly Outlook Survey in Industry	France	sales, prices, employment	1962	m	ql, qt	INSEE
Survey of Industrial Trends	Australia	output, employment, prices, stocks, overtime	1966	m	ql	Australian Chamber of Commerce
Survey of Production Forecasts	Japan	production	1971	m	qt	METI
Survey on Industrial and Service Firms	Italy	investment, production, turnover, prices, costs	1972	a	qt	Banca d'Italia
ifo Investment Survey	Germany	investment	1973	s	qt	ifo
Basic Survey on Overseas Business Activities	Japan	sales	1995	a	qt	METI
CFO Survey	US	revenue, wages, unit costs, employment	1996	q	qt	FRB Richmond and FRB Atlanta
Survey on Inflation and Growth Expectations	Italy	economic situation, prices, demand, investment, empl.	1999	q	ql, qt	Banca d'Italia
Business Outlook Survey	Japan	sales, operating profits	2004	q	qt	Ministry of Finance of Japan
Monitoraggio Economia e Territorio Survey	Italy	sales, prices	2008	a	ql, qt	MET Research Center
Management and Organizational Practices Survey	US	production, capital expenditures, employment, costs	2010	5a	ql	U.S. Census Bureau
Business Inflation Expectations Survey	US	unit costs	2011	m	qt, d	FRB Atlanta
Survey of Business Uncertainty	US	employment, sales, capital expenditures (investment rate)	2014	m	d	FRB Atlanta
Bundesbank Online Panel - Firms	Germany	employment, sales, inputs, finances, inventories	2020	i	ql, qt, d	Bundesbank

Notes: Frequencies (Freq.) are monthly (m), quarterly (q), semi-annually (s), annually (a), every 5 years (5a), and irregular (i). Formats are qualitative (ql), quantitative (qt), and distributional (d). METI is the Ministry of Economy, Trade, and Industry in Japan. Surveys ordered by their inception date, although the quality and scope of the initial waves may be much reduced (if they are available at all) relative to subsequent waves, e.g., data from the ifo Business Climate Survey is available for research since 1980. Only those surveys are listed whose firm-level data about firms' expectations about own variables are generally provided to researchers. For this reason, the surveys of some central banks and regional Federal Reserve Banks (mostly <250 participants/month) are not included, e.g., the Business Outlook Surveys run by the Bank of Canada and the FRB Philadelphia. Similarly, the Joint Harmonised EU Programme of Business and Consumer Surveys consists of a number of national surveys but does not provide firm-level data.

continued on next page

Table 12.1 (*continued*)

(b) Additional information

Name	Selected Literature	Sectors	Resp.[*]	Firm Size	Documentation
ifo Business Climate Survey	Nerlove (1983), Kawasaki and Zimmermann (1986), Bachmann et al. (2013), Bachmann and Elstner (2015), Massenot and Pettinicchi (2018), Enders et al. (2019), Enders et al. (2022), Born et al. (2022)	man	2000	nr	https://bit.ly/doc-ifo
Tankan Survey	Morikawa (2016)	nr	11,000	20m.+ yen	https://bit.ly/doc-tankan
CBI Industrial Trends Survey	Bennett (1984), McIntosh et al. (1989), Thomas (1995), Lui et al. (2010), Boneva et al. (2020)	man	500	nr	https://bit.ly/doc-cbi
Monthly Outlook Survey in Industry	König et al. (1981), Nerlove (1983), Andrade et al. (2022)	man, extr	1600	20+ empl	https://bit.ly/doc-mos-ind
Survey of Industrial Trends	Smith and McAleer (1995)	man	250	nr	https://bit.ly/doc-sit
Survey of Production Forecasts	Morikawa (2019)	man			https://bit.ly/doc-spf
Survey on Industrial and Service Firms	Guiso and Parigi (1999), Ma et al. (2020)	man, con, serv	5000	20+ empl	https://bit.ly/doc-sisf
ifo Investment Survey	Bachmann et al. (2017)	man, trade	2000	nr	https://bit.ly/doc-ifo
Basic Survey on Overseas Business Activities	Chen et al. (2020)	nr	8700	mult.nat.	https://bit.ly/doc-bsoba
CFO Survey	Gennaioli et al. (2015)	nr	1,00	nr	https://bit.ly/doc-cfos
Survey on Inflation and Growth Expectations	Coibion et al. (2020)	ind, serv	1000	50+ empl	https://bit.ly/doc-sige
Business Outlook Survey	Chen et al. (2021)	nr	11,500	nr	https://bit.ly/doc-bos
Monitoraggio Economia e Territorio Survey	Balduzzi et al. (2020)	man	25,000	nr	https://bit.ly/doc-met
Management and Organizational Practices Survey	Bloom et al. (2020)	man	37,000	nr	https://bit.ly/doc-mops
Business Inflation Expectations Survey	Meyer et al. (2021)	nr	300	nr	https://bit.ly/doc-bies
Survey of Business Uncertainty	Altig et al. (2020b), Barrero (2021)	nr	1300	nr	https://bit.ly/doc-sbu
Bundesbank Online Panel - Firms	Balleer et al. (2020)	nr	10,000	nr	https://bit.ly/doc-bopf

Notes: [*]Resp. refers to current respondents per wave. The ifo Business Climate Survey was initially launched for the manufacturing sector. Similar surveys were later added for the construction, trade, services, and insurance sectors. Sector refers to sectoral coverage: not restricted (nr), manufacturing (man), extraction (extr), construction (con), non-financials private services (serv), industry (ind), and trade. Firm size gives restrictions on target firms: not restricted (nr), minimum number of employees (empl), mult.nat. (multinationals). The Tankan Survey targets firms with capital of at least 20 million Yen (Bank of Japan, 2020).

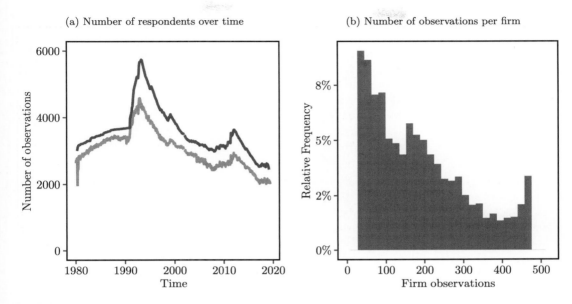

(a) Number of respondents over time (b) Number of observations per firm

FIGURE 12.2 BEP observations across both panel dimensions

Notes: Observations of the ifo Business Expectations Panel (BEP) across time and firms. Left panel: number of actual (light blue (light gray in print version)) and target observations (dark blue (dark gray in print version)). The number of actual observations is the number of firms that respond in a given month. Target observations equal the number of firms that are in the survey during a given month. Due to the harmonization of survey periods introduced by the European Union, no survey was conducted in December 2001. We set the value to missing in this plot.

Business Climate Survey, one of the oldest firm surveys in existence. Specifically, the BEP combines survey data from the Business Climate Survey and balance sheet data from the Amadeus and Hoppenstedt databases (EBDC-BEP, 2019). Because the wording of the questions and possible answers differs somewhat across sectors, we focus on firms in the manufacturing sector for our analysis, the sector with the largest number of firms and the longest time dimension. Since the BEP combines annual balance-sheet data with the monthly survey data, we use the most recent balance-sheet data at a given point in time to avoid using information that is not yet available when firms report expectations. The BEP starts in January 1980; the last observation available to us is for June 2019. The survey questions (regarding prices, production, etc.) refer to a specific product.[12]

In the following, we produce a set of descriptive statistics for the BEP sample. Panel (a) of Fig. 12.2 displays the actual number of responses per month (light blue (light gray in print version) line) and the target observations (dark blue (dark gray in print version) line), i.e., the number of firms that are in principle in the survey during a given month but did not return the questionnaire, over time. The differ-

---

[12] Some firms, hence, respond to several questionnaires each month. In our sample, however, this is the case for less than 10% of firms. In our analysis below, we refer to the individual observation as a "firm" in order to ease the exposition.

ence between the two is usually small, that is, the average monthly response rate of 85% is quite high.[13] Furthermore, the median firm responds in 92% of the months they are in the panel. The ifo institute enlarged the panel significantly at various points in time, for example, after the German reunification in 1990. The right panel of Fig. 12.2 shows the number of responses per firm. While there are many firms that participate only a few times in the survey, there is still a relatively high number of firms that answer the survey more than 100 and up to almost 500 times.

12.3 Stylized facts

The literature has established a number of facts about firm expectations—they emerge consistently across surveys and for both qualitative and quantitative measures. In this section, we offer a synthesis of these facts with a focus on firms' expectations (and expectation errors) about their own production and prices. We consolidate five facts that we illustrate using one consistent, mostly qualitative data set: the ifo Business Expectations Panel (BEP), introduced in the previous section. Afterwards, we present a new, sixth fact that—to the best of our knowledge—has not been documented in the literature so far.

Given that we not only look at firm expectations but also at expectation errors, we first have to define expectation errors. There are different ways to do this for qualitative business surveys. However, Table A.1 and the discussion in Section A.1 show that these yield very similar outcomes for the ifo Survey. In what follows, we employ the widely-used definition of Bachmann et al. (2013). It is based on firms' reported realized monthly changes $x^i_{t+j,1}$ of production or prices over a 3-month period, $x^i_{t,3} = \sum^h_{j=1} x^i_{t+j,1}$, and their 3-months ahead expectations, $x^i_{t,3|t}$.[14] The expectation error is then defined as

$$e^i_{t,3} = \begin{cases} 0 & \text{if } \operatorname{sgn}(x^i_{t,3}) = \operatorname{sgn}(x^i_{t,3|t}), \\ \frac{1}{3}(x^i_{t,3} - x^i_{t,3|t}) & \text{else.} \end{cases} \tag{12.1}$$

When the sign of the summed-up realizations is equal to the expectation, no error is assigned. In all other cases, the error is equal to the sum of the realizations minus the expectation, standardized by the forecasting horizon $h = 3$.

Fact 1 (Unbiasedness). *Unconditionally, firms' expectation errors are small and almost always insignificant.*

This fact emerges robustly from a number of studies. Evaluating a quantitative supplement to the ifo Business Climate Survey, Bachmann and Elstner (2015) find that more than two-thirds of firms in their sample of German manufacturing firms do not systematically over- or underpredict their production

---

[13] Firms do not receive any compensation for participating in the survey, except the aggregate and sectoral results of the survey itself. Andrade et al. (2022) report a response rate of 60% for the quarterly INSEE survey. Banca d'Italia (2019) indicate a response rate of 40–50% for its Survey of Inflation and Growth Expectations, similar to the monthly response rate of 45% for the SBU (FRB Atlanta, 2021). Note, however, that our reported response rate refers to firms which have already answered at least once. Out of all firms that were contacted in mid 2021 for the first time, around 2/3 returned at least two surveys. For the SBU, around 1/3 of firms responded at least once after the initial contact (FRB Atlanta, 2021).

[14] See Table A.2 for the exact wording in the ifo Survey.

Table 12.2 Average unconditional expectation errors.

Grouped by	Group	Production			Prices		
		N	Median	% insig.	N	Median	% insig.
Overall		5122	−0.0183	77.59	5074	−0.0097	79.96
Number of Employees	Fewer than 50	801	−0.0128	76.40	779	−0.0056	81.51
	50–199	881	−0.0143	76.73	865	−0.0078	81.73
	200–499	410	−0.0097	81.22	410	−0.0048	84.88
	500–999	131	−0.0324	78.63	129	−0.0013	77.52
	More than 1000	95	−0.0041	77.89	93	−0.0051	75.27
Employees (Quartile)	First Quartile	566	−0.0115	77.56	548	−0.0048	81.02
	Second Quartile	588	−0.0172	76.19	578	−0.0085	82.87
	Third Quartile	582	−0.0154	77.15	569	−0.0076	81.20
	Fourth Quartile	582	−0.0097	79.38	581	−0.0039	81.76
Sales (Quartile)	First Quartile	566	−0.0191	74.56	546	−0.0046	82.97
	Second Quartile	576	−0.0147	77.08	557	−0.0071	81.33
	Third Quartile	562	−0.0169	80.25	564	−0.0058	82.27
	Fourth Quartile	571	−0.0159	78.98	574	−0.0063	79.27
Total Assets (Quartile)	First Quartile	672	−0.0159	75.60	652	−0.0070	82.82
	Second Quartile	673	−0.0113	77.86	655	−0.0065	81.07
	Third Quartile	666	−0.0193	78.53	668	−0.0079	83.98
	Fourth Quartile	676	−0.0153	79.29	677	−0.0056	79.03
Location	Eastern Germany	527	−0.0215	79.70	497	−0.0040	89.13
	Western Germany	1050	−0.0123	79.81	1052	−0.0041	82.60

Notes: Firm-level average expectation errors (computed by regressing a firm's expectation error on a constant); table entries provide number of firms in each subgroup (N), the median of their average expectation errors (Median) and share of insignificant average expectation errors (% insig.), based on Newey–West standard errors. When grouping by location, we only consider firms that joined the ifo Survey after the German reunification.

growth one quarter ahead. Using qualitative and quantitative questions from the same survey, Massenot and Pettinicchi (2018) also find that, on average, firms do not make unconditional expectations errors about their business situation. Altig et al. (2020b) and Barrero (2021) again find little evidence of an unconditional bias in expected firm-level sales growth rates, using qualitative and quantitative data from the Survey of Business Uncertainty. Chen et al. (2020) document for a panel of Japanese firms small quantitative forecast errors on average. Andrade et al. (2022), in turn, show in a quantitative French firm survey that there is a strong positive relationship between firms' anticipated and ex-post price changes. To illustrate Fact 1 further, Table 12.2 reports average expectation errors of individual firms for production, panel (a), and prices, panel (b), based on the BEP. For the full sample and across various classification schemes, we find robustly that the median forecast error is close to zero and the share of insignificant expectations errors is consistently above 75%. Table A.3 provides additional sectoral evidence in support of Fact 1.

Fact 2 (Information content). *Firm expectations outperform static and adaptive expectations.*

Firm expectations have significant information content because they help predicting future developments. To see this formally, we compute the root mean squared expectation error (RMSE), based

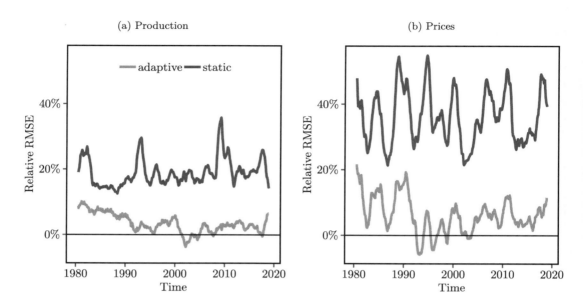

FIGURE 12.3 Performance of firm expectations relative to benchmark models

Notes: Relative RMSE for production, panel (a), and price expectations, panel (b), both for adaptive (light blue (light gray in print version) line) and static expectations (dark blue (dark gray in print version) line). Values above (below) zero mean that the respective benchmark model does not (does) beat the actual survey-based expectations. All series are plotted as moving averages over the previous and the next six months. All values expressed in percent.

on the actual expectations reported in the BEP, and compare it to two alternative models of expectation formation. The first assumes *adaptive* expectations: here, we simply carry forward as expectation the most recent realization (increase, no change, decrease) of either production or prices. The second model assumes *static* expectations: here we simply assume that no further change for either production or prices is expected. Fig. 12.3 compares the RMSE of the benchmark models to reported production and price expectations. It shows that for almost all months, the benchmark models are less precise, that is, have larger RMSEs, than the reported expectations.

This observation is consistent with earlier work. Kawasaki and Zimmermann (1986) also find that ifo Survey-based qualitative price expectations beat adaptive expectations. Using the Confederation of Australian Industries (CAI)/Westpac Survey of Industrial Trends, Smith and McAleer (1995) also document the high information content of qualitative survey expectations about firms' output, prices, employment, stocks, and overtime relative to static expectations, and relative to a number of univariate/multivariate time-series models. Using quantitative survey questions, Chen et al. (2020) show for Japanese firms that a large majority of firms do not just use their realized sales to forecast next periods sales.

Fact 3 (Experience). *Larger and older firms are better at forecasting their own variables.*

While firm expectations generally reflect meaningful information (Facts 1 and 2), this is even more the case as firms get older and/or larger: experience, according to Fact 3, matters for the accuracy of firm expectations about their own variables. Massenot and Pettinicchi (2018), for instance, show, based on qualitative and quantitative questions in the ifo Survey, that older and larger firms make smaller expectation errors. Bachmann and Elstner (2015) for German firms in the ifo Business Climate Survey and Morikawa (2019) for Japanese firms in the Survey of Production Forecast document that larger firms make smaller quantitative expectation errors, presumably because they are able to spend more resources on forecasting than smaller firms. Experience also matters: Triebs and Tumlinson (2013) find that firms located in eastern Germany did worse, relative to their western peers, in predicting business conditions early after German reunification, but improved their forecasting performance over time. Similarly, Chen et al. (2020) show for a panel of Japanese firms that forecast precision increases with age. Related, there is also evidence that better-managed firms make smaller forecasting errors (Bloom et al., 2021).

We complement the existing work with new evidence based on the BEP and present it in Table 12.3. Panel (a) shows that mean squared expectation errors (MSEs) tend to be smaller for older firms and consistently so across decades. One exception are the 2000s: here older firms did worse. This result may be caused by the global financial crisis and deserves some future research. Panel (b) of Table 12.3 reports firm-level mean and median SEs for different firm sizes. In line with the literature, we observe that larger firms tend to make smaller MSEs.

Fact 4 (Predictability). *Firms make predictable expectation errors.*

Under rational expectations (RE), expectation errors should not be predictable on the basis of information that is available at the time when expectations are formed. The RE hypothesis can be framed in a regression setup as

$$e_{t,h}^i = x_t^i \beta + v_t^i, \tag{12.2}$$

where the forecast error $e_{t,h}^i$, at horizon $h = 3$ in our case, is the dependent variable and x_t^i contains candidate predictors. The β-coefficients should not be different from zero under the null of RE.[15] We estimate the equation using the observations for the BEP and report results in Table A.8. While macroeconomic variables turn out to be mostly insignificant as predictors, many firm-specific variables—such as the order backlog, changes in demand, or past expectations—help in predicting expectation errors for production and prices. Overall, about 17% of the variance in expectations errors can be explained in our regressions.

Consistent with our results, Massenot and Pettinicchi (2018) find that firms extrapolate from past experience too much and end up making predictable expectation errors. Similarly, Barrero (2021), using distributional questions from the Survey of Business Uncertainty (SBU), documents that firm managers overextrapolate: their forecasts are too optimistic after positive shocks and too pessimistic after negative shocks. Ma et al. (2020) analyze expectation errors of Italian firms about their sales

---

[15] An alternative test for rationality is based on the regression $x_{t,h}^i = \beta_0 + \beta_1 x_{t,h|t}^i + v_t^i$, where $\beta_0 = 0$ and $\beta_1 = 1$ under the null of RE. This test is discussed in Chapter 3 in this Handbook.

Table 12.3 Experience and expectation errors.

(a) Experience by age

Decade	Production				Prices			
	MSE_{old}	MSE_{young}	Difference	p-value	MSE_{old}	MSE_{young}	Difference	p-value
1980–1989	0.1058	0.1121	−0.0064	0.00	0.0447	0.0498	−0.0051	0.00
1990–1999	0.1185	0.1343	−0.0158	0.00	0.0533	0.0556	−0.0022	0.01
2000–2009	0.1415	0.1405	0.0010	0.53	0.0674	0.0637	0.0037	0.00
2010–2019	0.1303	0.1414	−0.0110	0.00	0.0607	0.0658	−0.0051	0.01

(b) Experience by size

Grouped by	Group	Production			Prices		
		N	Mean	Median	N	Mean	Median
Overall		5122	0.1278	0.1170	5074	0.0594	0.0372
Number of Employees	Fewer than 50	801	0.1319	0.1197	779	0.0617	0.0363
	50–199	881	0.1299	0.1217	865	0.0615	0.0386
	200–499	410	0.1233	0.1184	410	0.0556	0.0358
	500–999	131	0.1209	0.1052	129	0.0500	0.0372
	More than 1000	95	0.1088	0.0988	93	0.0615	0.0422
Employees (Quartile)	First Quartile	566	0.1312	0.1165	548	0.0622	0.0370
	Second Quartile	588	0.1323	0.1262	578	0.0579	0.0359
	Third Quartile	582	0.1302	0.1216	569	0.0645	0.0406
	Fourth Quartile	582	0.1187	0.1078	581	0.0549	0.0363
Sales (Quartile)	First Quartile	566	0.1348	0.1220	546	0.0587	0.0360
	Second Quartile	576	0.1326	0.1248	557	0.0655	0.0391
	Third Quartile	562	0.1240	0.1147	564	0.0558	0.0375
	Fourth Quartile	571	0.1199	0.1074	574	0.0615	0.0355
Total Assets (Quartile)	First Quartile	672	0.1310	0.1197	652	0.0611	0.0375
	Second Quartile	673	0.1326	0.1209	655	0.0624	0.0375
	Third Quartile	666	0.1284	0.1187	668	0.0589	0.0370
	Fourth Quartile	676	0.1188	0.1082	677	0.0586	0.0361

Notes: Panel (a) shows the difference of mean squared expectation errors (MSE) between young and old firms. At the time of being surveyed, a firm is considered young when it was founded at most 10 years ago. For each decade, we pool observations by age and estimate the difference in the MSE between old and young firms. Panel (b) shows firm-level mean and median squared expectation errors; table entries provide summary statistics for different firm sizes. We measure size in terms of the absolute number of employees, as well as firms' location in the distributions of employees, sales, and total assets; N denotes the number of firms in each group.

and detect significant autocorrelation. Boneva et al. (2020) show that UK firms tend to have rational expectations of quantity variables, such as their own employment and new orders, but deviate from rational expectations when it comes to prices, wages, and unit costs. Hence, Fact 4.

At first sight, this fact is hard to reconcile with Fact 1. Note, however, that while Fact 1 is about the unconditional accuracy of expectations, Fact 4 shows that forecast errors are predictable conditional on specific information. As such, the two facts are not contradictory but raise challenges that need to be addressed in future research. At an empirical level, a more systematic investigation into the two facts

Table 12.4 Dispersion and volatility measures.

(a) Definitions

Domain	Measure	Definition
firm & time	Absolute forecast error	$\text{absfe}_{i,t} = abs(e^i_{t,h})$
	Rolling window standard deviation	$\text{stdef}_{i,t} = \sqrt{\frac{1}{3}\sum_{k\in\{-3,0,3\}}(e^i_{t+k,h} - \overline{e}^i_{t,h})^2}$
time	Forecast dispersion	$\text{fdisp}_t = \sqrt{\text{frac}^+_t + \text{frac}^-_t - (\text{frac}^+_t - \text{frac}^-_t)^2}$
	Forecast error dispersion	$\text{fedisp}_t = \sqrt{Var(e_{t,h,i|t})}$
	Mean absolute forecast error	$\text{mae}_t = \frac{1}{n_t}\sum_i \text{absfe}_{i,t}$
	Avg. rolling window standard deviation	$\text{stdfe}_t = \frac{1}{n_t}\sum_i \text{stdef}_{i,t}$

(b) Business cycle properties

Variable	Production				Prices			
	fdisp	fedisp	mae	stdfe	fdisp	fedisp	mae	stdfe
Correlation within measures								
fdisp	1.00	0.69***	0.56***	0.58***	1.00	0.40***	0.60***	0.46***
fedisp		1.00	0.93***	0.73***		1.00	0.94***	0.88***
mae			1.00	0.82***			1.00	0.87***
stdfe				1.00				1.00
Correlation with aggregates								
Δ log Production	−0.12***	−0.04	−0.12***	−0.15***	0.06	−0.07	−0.07	−0.03
Δ log Hours	−0.02	−0.08*	−0.18***	−0.14***	−0.01	−0.03	−0.04	−0.03
Δ log Employment	−0.20***	−0.30***	−0.44***	−0.44***	−0.04	−0.21***	−0.22***	−0.20***
Recession Dummies								
Recession	0.019***	0.016**	0.043***	0.029***	0.024*	0.061***	0.114***	0.094***
Recession 2008/09	0.083***	0.084***	0.128***	0.140***	0.088***	0.154***	0.246***	0.243***

Notes: Panel (a): $e^i_{t,h}$ is the forecast error of Bachmann et al. (2013) defined in Eq. (12.1) and $\overline{e}^i_{t,h}$ is the average forecast error of the current value, its third lag, and its third lead; $\text{frac}^+_t = \sum_i \mathbf{1}(x^i_{t,h|t} = +1)/n_t$ and $\text{frac}^-_t = \sum_i \mathbf{1}(x^i_{t,h|t} = -1)/n_t$ are the shares of expected increases and decreases at time t; fdisp_t, fedisp_t, and mae_t based on Bachmann et al. (2013); stdfe_t on Bachmann et al. (2019). Panel (b) shows Spearman rank correlation among dispersion measures first, Spearman rank correlation with aggregate business cycle measures second, and regression results using recession dummies third. After standardizing each time series by its nonrecession mean, we report coefficients for a general recession dummy and a dummy for the 2008/09 recession. One, two, and three stars (*) correspond to significance at the 10, 5, and 1 percent significance levels.

seems warranted. At a conceptual level, one may explore models of learning and/or limited attention which can rationalize the patterns in the data.

Fact 5 (Countercyclical second moments). *The dispersion and volatility of expectations and expectation errors are countercyclical.*

This fact has been observed for a variety of survey-based measures (e.g., Bachmann et al., 2013, 2017, 2019; Enders et al., 2019; Morikawa, 2016, 2019), based both on qualitative and quantitative survey questions. As before we corroborate these findings. While panel (a) of Table 12.4 lists dispersion and volatility measures, panel (b) reports their time-series properties based on BEP data. The first subpanel shows correlation coefficients between the measures for production (left) and prices (right). The correlation is generally quite high, in particular for the error-based measures.

The countercyclicality of the dispersion and volatility measures can be read off the second subpanel where we report correlation coefficients vis-à-vis monthly measures of economic activity: the growth rates of industrial production, hours worked, and employment. Across the board, the signs of the correlation coefficients are negative and mostly significantly so. We also regress the measures on recession dummies—as dated by the German Council of Economic Experts—and again find a significant increase in dispersion and volatility in economic downturns. Especially so in the Great Recession of 2008/09, where our measures increase by between 8.3% and 25%.

Fact 6 (Stickiness). *Firm expectations are updated infrequently; updates for production and prices often happen at the same time and in the same direction.*

This fact has not been documented in the literature. This is surprising in light of influential work which models firms' sticky information, that is, infrequent updating as key friction for business cycle dynamics (Mankiw and Reis, 2002). As a first pass towards assessing the stickiness of expectations in the BEP, we compute mean and median spells of expectations, that is, the number of consecutive months for which expectations remain unchanged. Panel (a) of Table 12.5 shows results, both for production (left) and prices (right). For the whole sample, expectations are quite sticky: we observe, for instance, that production expectations are not adjusted for more than 3 months on average. The panel also offers a breakdown into the stickiness of the three different response categories. Here, we observe the largest degree of stickiness for the "no change" category. Overall, price expectations tend to be more sticky than production expectations. Panel (b) of Table 12.5 shows that firms in the BEP tend to update expectations across variables at the same time. Specifically, observing an update in price expectations increases the probability of observing an update (upwards or downwards) in production expectations by 10 percentage points or 39%. A production expectation update increases the probability of observing a price expectation update by 9 percentage points or 46%. This is consistent with the findings for firms' macroeconomic expectations discussed in Chapter 11 in this Handbook. Calibrating sticky information models to capture the evidence put forward in Table 12.5 seems a promising venue for future research. Moreover, Panel (c) of Table 12.5 shows, that for the majority of cases, price and production expectations change in the same direction. In particular, if we observe a change in either production or price expectations, we find that the other variable is updated in the same direction at least twice as often as in the opposite direction. This pattern in the data suggests an important role for demand shocks for firm expectations and calls for further investigation.

12.4 Expectation formation

In this section, we turn to the expectation formation process of firms with a focus on recent survey evidence. This evidence often points to departures from the full information rational expectations (FIRE) benchmark. For instance, Fact 4 shows that firms make predictable forecast errors. At this point, however, there is no consensus about an alternative to FIRE. At a very basic level, there is a long tradition of noisy information models. Here, information processing is rational but information is incomplete. In the classic contributions by Lucas (1973), Woodford (2002), Sims (2003), or Maćkowiak and Wiederholt (2009), economic actors—and notably firms—process information and update expectations in a rational way. This goes some way to account for the evidence presented above. Likewise, more recent

Table 12.5 Stickiness of firm expectations.

(a) Spell lengths

Spell type	Production			Prices		
	Share in %	Mean	Median	Share in %	Mean	Median
overall		3.38	2		4.85	2
decrease	24.73	2.17	1	18.25	2.21	1
no change	48.36	4.67	2	51.00	7.23	4
increase	26.91	2.15	1	30.74	2.45	2

(b) Conditional updating frequencies

	Production		Prices	
	Updating freq. conditional on	Value	Updating freq. conditional on	Value
Frequencies				
	Update in price exp.: yes	36.58%	Update in prod. exp.: yes	24.74%
	Update in price exp.: no	26.32%	Update in prod. exp.: no	16.91%
Difference				
in percentage points		10.26pp		8.83pp
in percent		38.98%		46.30%

(c) Conditional distribution of expectation updates

$P(Y = y \mid X = x)$	Production			Prices		
	$Y =$ Prod. update $\mid X =$ Price update			$Y =$ Price update $\mid X =$ Prod. updates		
$y =$	downwards	no update	upwards	downwards	no update	upwards
$x =$ downwards	25.63	63.64	10.73	17.17	75.47	7.37
no update	13.35	73.68	12.97	8.51	83.09	8.40
upwards	11.05	63.19	25.76	7.36	75.05	17.58

Notes: Panel (a) shows summary statistics for spell length of qualitative expectations for prices and production. Given qualitative expectations (increase, no change, decrease), we calculate the lengths of sequences with identical expectations (spells). We compute their average and median length in months both across spell types (overall) and for each spell type separately. Panel (b) shows relative frequencies of expectation updates (changes in the reported qualitative expectations) for production (prices) conditional whether a firm reported update for price (production) expectations. Observations are pooled across time and firms. Panel (c) shows distribution of expectation updates for production conditional on price-expectation updates (left) and vice versa (right). Entries in the table are conditional probabilities of observing an update, as in the column labels, conditional on observing an update of the other variable, as in the row labels. Each row for production and prices sums to 100. Computation based on full ifo sample (manufacturing, 2002–2019)

contributions emphasize that a (rational) focus on certain sectors/media distorts the information formation process (Chahrour et al., 2021; Kohlhas and Walther, 2021). Other models, by contrast, allow for behavioral aspects in the expectation formation process (for instance, Shiller, 2017; Bordalo et al., 2019), where, under certain conditions, behavioral models and incomplete information models give rise to equivalent equilibrium effects (Angeletos and Huo, 2021).

In what follows, we seek to inform this discussion by first surveying the evidence on the determinants of expectations. In the second part of this section, we zoom in on the expectation formation process as we discuss recent evidence regarding the response of firms to news, both at the firm level and the aggregate level. As in the previous section, we revisit key findings on the basis of the BEP.

12.4.1 Determinants of expectations

We aim to provide a simple empirical characterization of the determinants of firm expectations. We first focus on the mean forecast (first moment). Afterwards, we also consider briefly the determinants of firm uncertainty (second moment).

12.4.1.1 *Firm expectations*

In terms of expectations, we focus, as before, on firm expectations about production and prices. To set the stage, we perform an analysis based on the ifo Survey which builds on earlier work by Enders et al. (2022). Because firm answers regarding production and price expectations are qualitative in the ifo Survey, we estimate an ordered probit model. Specifically, using $j = \{-1, 0, 1\}$ to index the reported expectations $x^i_{t,h|t}$ about firms' prices or production, we estimate

$$
\begin{aligned}
Pr(x^i_{t,h|t} = j) &= Pr(a_{j-1} < x^{i*}_{t,h|t} \leq a_j) \\
&= \Phi(\alpha_j - X'_{it}\beta) - \Phi(\alpha_{j-1} - X'_{it}\beta),
\end{aligned}
\tag{12.3}
$$

where X_{it} contains the variables which may influence firm expectations, $x^{i*}_{t,h|t}$ is the latent variable, and α_{j-1} and α_j are threshold parameters. Since the set of potential variables is large, we consider different groups of variables and summarize their impact by focusing on the model fit, namely on the pseudo-R^2 as defined by McFadden (1974).[16] In terms of explanatory variables X_{it}, we distinguish three sets of variables. The first set contains variables that describe a firm's own condition as reported in the survey, such as, for instance, the current state of business, orders, and capacity utilization. In addition, it includes lags of expected production and prices. It also contains interaction terms that we include on the basis of a log-likelihood test. The second set consists of firm fundamentals as reported in the most recent balance sheet, such as, for instance, the debt share. Here our selection of variables follows Enders et al. (2022). A third set of variables contains macro variables as observable by firms in real time, notably the unemployment rate in the previous month as well as industrial production. Table A.5 provides a full list of variables for each of the three sets. In addition, we always include sector fixed effects and the average reported state of business, both on a two-digit level.

We estimate model (12.3) using all combinations of the three sets of variables and show results in Table 12.6. Results are clear cut. The survey responses account for a fairly large share of the variation in firm expectations, with a pseudo-R^2 of 25% and 32% for production and prices, respectively. The contributions of balance-sheet fundamentals and macro variables, on the other hand, appear negligible. We should stress, however, that balance sheet data ("fundamentals") is available only at annual frequency and may therefore not matter much for changes in the short-term outlook of firms over the next three months. In addition to using the R^2 to judge the contribution of each group of variables, we also checked by how much the share of correctly predicted expectations increases when we include each group one-by-one. We find that the first set of variables helps to increase the performance of the model most strongly also in this case.

The result that firm-specific information, as reflected in survey responses, is a key determinant of firm expectations echoes early work based on the ifo Survey in the 1950s. Pioneering work by Anderson

---

[16] Formally, we consider $R^2_{mf} = 1 - \ln L_M / \ln L_0$, where R^2_{mf} is the pseudo-R^2, L_M is the likelihood of the model, and L_0 is the likelihood of a constant-only model.

Table 12.6 Determinants of production and price expectations.

Variables	Production		Prices	
	Observations	Pseudo-R^2	Observations	Pseudo-R^2
Survey	181,329	0.2523	181,276	0.3204
Fundamentals	271,498	0.0002	277,890	0.0001
Macro	337,028	0.0057	345,828	0.0074
Survey + Fundamentals	180,686	0.2524	180,633	0.3204
Survey + Macro	172,428	0.2524	172,374	0.3244
Fundamentals + Macro	254,624	0.0064	260,988	0.0075
Survey + Fundamentals + Macro	172,327	0.2525	171,731	0.3244

Notes: Summary statistics for ordered probit models using expectations about a firm's own production and price as dependent variables. Explanatory variables are combinations of variables from the survey (business situation, orders, etc., with up to three lags and interaction terms), firm fundamentals from their balance sheet (debt share, financing coefficient) and macro variables (monthly growth rates of PPI, CPI, and IP and the unemployment rate, each with their publication lag). See Table A.5 for more details on the variables.

et al. (1956a), Anderson et al. (1956b), and somewhat later by Anderson and Strigel (1960), showed that unexpected changes in demand lead to changes in firms' production and pricing plans. This early work already established that production plans are more responsive to surprise demand changes than price plans. For the latter, cost changes are important. More recently, Carlsson and Skans (2012) document an influence of both current and expected future marginal cost on firms' price-setting behavior, while Meyer et al. (2021) find that firms' year-ahead unit-cost expectations covary strongly with year-ahead price expectations.[17] Massenot and Pettinicchi (2018), in turn, find for the ifo Survey that business expectations are responsive to past business developments. Similarly, Boneva et al. (2020) show for UK firms that past orders are important when it comes to accounting for price and wage expectations. Financial factors, too, matter for expectations: Balduzzi et al. (2020) study Italian firms during the Corona crisis and find that financially constrained firms expect to charge higher prices relative to their unconstrained counterparts.

Our results above suggest that firm-specific developments are considerably more important than macroeconomic developments when it comes to accounting for firm expectations. But there is also evidence that firm expectations are responsive to macroeconomic developments. Enders et al. (2019), for instance, find that firm expectations respond to monetary policy shocks. Similarly, Eminidou and Zachariadis (2022) document effects of monetary policy shocks on firm expectations for a panel of euro area countries. For this purpose, they rely on the Joint Harmonised EU Programme of Business and Consumer Surveys (BCS). Strasser (2013) uses the ifo Survey and investigates to what extent firms' export expectations respond to exchange-rate movements.

Several studies use survey data to explore the impact of the COVID-19 pandemic on firm expectations. Meyer et al. (2022) rely on the Business Inflation Expectations Survey run by the Federal Reserve Bank of Atlanta. Balleer et al. (2020) and Deutsche Bundesbank (2021) look at German firms, using ifo

---

[17] The former use Swedish firm-level data and the latter the Atlanta Fed's Business Inflation Expectations Survey. Meyer et al. (2021) also demonstrate that information treatments about aggregate inflation and policymakers' forecasts have a negligible effect on firms' unit-cost expectations.

data and the Bundesbank Online Panel – Firms, respectively. These studies find consistently that firms' price expectations have decreased in the early phase of the pandemic. In addition, there is evidence that lockdown measures matter for firm expectations. Buchheim et al. (2022), using ifo data for Germany, show that the announcement of nationwide school closures on March 13, 2020 in response to the first wave of Corona infections was followed by the largest change in business perceptions by far.

Finally, there is evidence that the developments of the sectors or regions in which firms operate influence their expectations. Andrade et al. (2022) stress the importance of industry-level shocks, as distinct from aggregate and firm-specific shocks, for both firm actions and expectations. Their analysis is based on a survey of French firms. Kukuvec and Oberhofer (2020) use input-output tables and establish on the basis of the BCS that firms' business expectations are also influenced by expectations of other firms, in particular of those located upstream. Dovern et al. (2020) find for the ifo Survey that firms extrapolate from local economic conditions to aggregate growth expectations.

12.4.1.2 *Firm uncertainty*

So far, we have focused on the determinants of the first moment of firm expectations, that is, the mean forecast. But firm surveys also shed light on the determinants of the second moment of firm expectations, that is, into firm-level uncertainty. Altig et al. (2020b) survey business executives about firm outcomes with a particular focus on business uncertainty. They find, among other things, that subjective uncertainty is higher when firms' have grown faster and when they have revised their growth expectations. Similarly, Bachmann et al. (2021), using data for German firms, show that firms' subjective uncertainty of future sales growth increases in the aftermath of unusual, in particular negative, growth experiences. In the cross section of firms, large and fast-growing firms display, for a given shock volatility, lower subjective uncertainty than unsuccessful ones.

Dovern et al. (2020) document a negative relationship between firms' uncertainty about their own business outlook and expectations about GDP growth. There is also survey evidence that specific events raise uncertainty at the firm level, notably in the context of Brexit and Covid-19 (Bloom et al., 2019; Altig et al., 2020a). Finally, we note that measuring firm uncertainty remains challenging from a methodological point of view. Bachmann et al. (2020), for instance, find that a majority of firms use an interval of probabilities instead of a single number at least once in their sample period. The authors interpret this behavior as reflecting Knightian uncertainty.

12.4.2 Over- and underreaction to news

How do firms form expectations? In an influential study, Coibion and Gorodnichenko (2015) propose a simple diagnostic in order to shed light on the expectation-formation process. Specifically, using the Survey of Professional Forecasters (SPF), they regress the upcoming forecast error on the current forecast revision. It turns out that forecast revisions predict forecast errors in the same direction. An upward revision, say, is followed by an underprediction of the same variable—forecasters seem to underreact to news, as reflected in the revision. This finding is in line with rational expectations models featuring noisy information. Yet, it has given rise to an intensive debate about the expectation-formation process and motivated new explorations, both empirically and in terms of theory.

In their original contribution, Coibion and Gorodnichenko (2015) study the response of the average forecast error in the SPF to the average forecast revision in the SPF. Against this background, Bordalo et al. (2020) stress that results change—from underreaction to overreaction—once one studies the relationship between forecast errors and forecast revisions *at the level of individual forecasters*. Other work, some of which we discuss below, establishes that whether there is over- or underreaction depends on the nature of the news which forecasters receive. Most of the evidence to date, however, is based on the SPF.

In what follows, we broaden the discussion and follow Born et al. (2022) in turning to firms' forecasts and their expectation formation process. We estimate a simplified version of their empirical model on our BEP sample[18]:

$$e_{t,h}^i = \beta_0^i + \beta_1^i FR_{t,h}^i + v_{t+h}^i, \tag{12.4}$$

where index i denotes a specific firm, $e_{t,h}^i$ is the forecast error (as defined in Eq. (12.1)), $FR_{t,h}^i$ is the forecast revision defined as $\text{sgn}(x_{t+h|t}^i - x_{t-1+h|t-1}^i) \in \{+1, 0, -1\}$, and v_{t+h}^i is a zero-mean error. A positive β_1^i-coefficient implies underreaction to the news that is reflected in the forecast revision. We estimate this equation separately for each firm, for both price and production expectations.[19]

Fig. 12.4 shows the distribution of the estimates for β_1^i across firms for production and price expectations. The mass of firms is characterized by negative betas, of which 32% are significant for production and 41% for prices. The overall mean estimate for production is -0.112 and -0.107 for prices. The overall result is in line with Born et al. (2022) and clear cut: firms tend to overreact to news.[20] This is particularly noteworthy because, in our analysis, news and forecast errors pertain to firms' expectations about their own production and prices rather than the aggregate economy and rational expectations models with noisy information have a hard time rationalizing overreactions. A number of behavioral models have been put forward to account for overreaction in other contexts. Azeredo da Silveira and Woodford (2019), for instance, show that if memory is noisy, current realizations are extrapolated into the future disproportionally. Bordalo et al. (2020), instead, rely on diagnostic expectations to rationalize overreaction. Here, forecasters overweigh the probability of certain states in the light of recent signals.

Table A.6 shows that the coefficients are robustly below zero across different measures of firm size and location. The same holds if we consider distinct sectors. We conclude that overreaction of firm expectations to news is a robust and pervasive feature of the data, not driven by a particular group of firms.

Born et al. (2022) also estimate Eq. (12.4) on pooled data while allowing for firm and time-fixed effects. For this specification, the estimate of β_1^i is significantly negative as well. They further distinguish the response to "macro news" (measured by unexpected changes in the aggregate ifo index or manufacturing orders) from the response to firm-specific micro news (as reflected in the revision of a firms' own production expectation net of time-fixed effects) and still find that firms overreact to micro news, but also that they underreact to macro news.[21]

---

[18] In the context of the qualitative ifo Survey data, there are a number of noteworthy conceptual issues and limitations that are discussed in Born et al. (2022).

[19] For a firm to be considered in the estimation we require it to provide us with at least 30 observations and a nonzero variance of forecast errors and forecast revisions, that is, a firm must have revised its expectation at least once.

[20] Figure A.1 shows that estimates for the intercept in Eq. (12.4) are generally well-behaved in the sense that they are scattered evenly around zero. Moreover, there is no systematic pattern which would suggest a specific relationship between the estimate for the slope and the intercept.

[21] Similarly, Kučinskas and Peters (2021) document for professional forecasters that their inflation forecasts underreact to aggregate shocks but overreact to idiosyncratic shocks. Using the ifo Survey, Massenot and Pettinicchi (2018) regress, in turn,

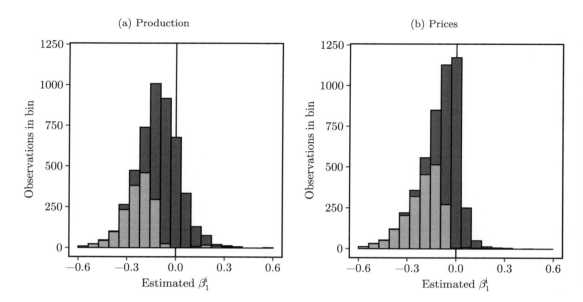

FIGURE 12.4 Response of forecast error to forecast revision

Notes: Histograms of estimated β_1^i-coefficients in firm-level regressions for production and price expectations, see Eq. (12.4); sample restricted to firms that initially report no expected change. Coefficients outside of the 1% and 99% quantiles (pooled over all subfigures) are dropped. Dark blue (dark gray in print version) is for estimates that are insignificant at the 5%-level, light blue (light gray in print version) is for significant estimates.

Born et al. (2022) rationalize their findings in a general equilibrium model that allows for noisy information and 'island illusion'. The key feature of their model is that firms overestimate the importance of firm-specific relative to aggregate developments for their own future output. In line with additional model predictions, firms with a larger 'island illusion' empirically display larger production and forecast-error volatility, as well as lower profits. These systematic differences demonstrate that the measured bias is not the result of random forecast fluctuations. Broer and Kohlhas (2022) put forward a related mechanism. They stress that what they call "overrevision" of individual forecasts may mask both over- and underreactions to salient public signals, as documented for inflation expectations in the SPF.[22]

---

expectations and forecast errors on past changes of the business situation (rather than on forecast revisions). They find that the regression coefficient is positive and significant, and robustly so, across a number of specifications. They refer to this result as "over-extrapolation."

[22] They extend a model of noisy rational expectations by allowing forecasters to be overconfident about the precision of their own information. In this account, absolute overconfidence (perceiving own information as more informative than it actually is) makes forecasters overreact to private information while relative overconfidence (perceiving own information as more informative than information of others) makes forecasters underreact to public signals which, in turn, are understood to reflect the response of others to their own forecasts.

In sum, recent survey evidence shows that firm expectations are responsive to information. Firm-specific information turns out to be more important and impacts expectations more strongly than information about the aggregate economy. This finding emerges from a number of recent contributions and is confirmed once we estimate models (12.3) and (12.4) on our BEP sample. When it comes to the details of the expectation-formation process, the recent literature has put forward a number of promising alternatives to the FIRE benchmark. They go some way to account for the evidence. But further work is required for the profession to be able to settle on a new consensus model.

12.5 Firm expectations and firm decisions

One reason why we care about firm expectations is that they matter for firm decisions—at least according to theory. For the longest time, the link from economic expectations to actions has been taken for granted. At an empirical level, models featuring a key role for expectations that lay the foundation for, e.g., the New Keynesian Phillips curve, have been shown to describe the data reasonably well (e.g., Galí and Gertler, 1999). There are also numerous purely empirical studies which suggest that, in general, expectations of economic agents are key for the business cycle (see, for instance, Beaudry and Portier, 2006; Born et al., 2019; Enders et al., 2021). These studies, however, do not directly rely on expectations data at the firm level. Only recently has the literature started to explore these data to study the effect of firm decisions on firm actions.

12.5.1 The effect of firm expectations

We revisit some of this work in what follows, with a particular focus on Enders et al. (2022) since their analysis is also based on the BEP. The basic idea of the study is to compare the behavior of firms that report that they expect either an increase or a decrease of production to otherwise very similar firms that expect production to remain unchanged. Because the responses regarding expected production are qualitative, one may think of expectations as a kind of "treatment": firms may either expect an increase, no change, or a decrease. Of course, expectations are not literally assigned in a random way. By comparing firms that display the same fundamentals but different expectations, however, the assignment can be interpreted as random.

In terms of identification, two features of the ifo Survey are crucial. First, the survey features a fairly large set of control variables, including balance-sheet data and received orders of firms. One may thus approximate the set of fundamentals which matter for firm decisions fairly accurately. Second, the timing of survey responses is key: because the large majority of responses to the survey is filed early in the month, they represent expectations about future periods (namely, for the three months following the current one) at a time when production plans for the current month may be formed but actual demand has not yet been observed.[23] Enders et al. (2022) investigate how production expectations impact both production and pricing decisions in the current month. In what follows, we modify the original analysis in three ways. First, for the matching exercise we use data from 1991–2019, that is, three more years

---

[23] About 50% of firms answer within the first eight days and another 25% answer in the following week. These figures are calculated for those firms that answer the survey electronically, which is the majority by now.

of data. Second, to control for fundamentals we compute the propensity score, that is, the likelihood, of a treatment for a given firm-month observation on the basis of model (12.3). In this way, we directly build on the estimates reported in Section 12.4, which allows for macroeconomic control variables, rather than for time-fixed effects as in Enders et al. We use the propensity score to match treated and untreated observations and, eventually, to compute the average treatment effect on the treated (ATT), both for production and pricing decisions. Third, we also report results for various subsets of firms.

Table 12.7 reports the results, separately for firms which report an "increase" and a "decrease" of production expectations. The top row shows the results for the full sample. We observe that expectations of a production increase impact current production and prices positively. Quantitatively our results are very similar to those reported by Enders et al. (2022).[24] The effect of an expected production decrease on production and prices is negative and quantitatively comparable to that of an expected production increase. Table 12.7 also reports results for a detailed break-down for different subsets of firms that turn out to be quite similar.

Importantly, expectations may impact current decisions for two reasons. First, expectations may reflect *news* that are not yet incorporated into current fundamentals. According to this interpretation, firm expectations operate as a transmission channel through which future fundamentals impact current decisions. Second, expectations might be fundamentally unwarranted and as such are genuine *noise*. Enders et al. assess the distinct role of news and noise for firm decisions on the basis of forecast errors. Specifically, taking an ex-post perspective, they ask whether firms that expect a change in production behave differently vis-à-vis firms which correctly expect production to remain unchanged, once for firms whose expectations turn out to be correct and once for firms with, in hindsight, incorrect expectations. They find that the treatment effect is present for both correct and incorrect expectations. This finding suggests that expectations impact current firm decisions for both fundamental (news) and nonfundamental reasons (noise).

Other work has also looked into how firm expectations shape firm behavior based on survey evidence. Boneva et al. (2020) study a survey of UK firms and estimate Phillips-curve relationships to capture the effect of firm expectations on firm decisions. Similar to the findings above, they also find an effect on firms' pricing decisions. Other papers have established a link between firm expectations and firms' investment decisions. Bachmann and Zorn (2020) do so on the basis of the ifo Investment Survey. Gennaioli et al. (2015), instead, rely on the Duke University Quarterly Survey of Chief Financial Officers. They stress, in particular, that while CFOs' expectations matter for investment decisions, these expectations cannot be easily accounted for by conventional variables. Ma et al. (2020) establish a relation between capital investment and sales forecasts using a business survey of Italian firms run by the Bank of Italy.

12.5.2 Firm-level uncertainty and firm decisions

In theory, not only the first moment of firm expectations matters for firm decisions. The second moment, that is, uncertainty, is important, too. In an influential study, Bloom (2009) emphasized the real option value of delaying an (irreversible) investment decision in the face of increased uncertainty. Whether

---

[24] This positive effect may reflect a stronger tendency among treated firms to raise production and prices or a reduced tendency to lower production and prices, or both. As they disentangle the two effects, Enders et al. (2022) find that the overall effect is dominated by the increased tendency to raise production and prices.

Table 12.7 Effects of increased and decreased production expectations.

Grouped by	Group	Production		Prices	
		increase	decrease	increase	decrease
Full sample		0.152***	−0.193***	0.012***	−0.034***
Number of Employees	Fewer than 50	0.140***	−0.175***	0.025***	−0.040***
	50–199	0.154***	−0.207***	0.003	−0.029***
	200–499	0.183***	−0.149***	0.026**	−0.052***
	500–999	0.186***	−0.245***	−0.009	−0.048*
	More than 1000	0.150***	−0.242***	0.092***	0.006
Employees	First Quartile	0.162***	−0.160***	0.033***	−0.051***
	Second Quartile	0.143***	−0.179***	0.015	−0.017
	Third Quartile	0.140***	−0.229***	−0.005	−0.044***
	Fourth Quartile	0.177***	−0.176***	0.030***	−0.035***
Sales	First Quartile	0.159***	−0.159***	0.038***	−0.028**
	Second Quartile	0.128***	−0.191***	0.005	−0.038***
	Third Quartile	0.139***	−0.163***	−0.002	−0.053***
	Fourth Quartile	0.163***	−0.217***	0.013*	−0.024***
Total Assets	First Quartile	0.153***	−0.151***	0.034***	−0.034***
	Second Quartile	0.132***	−0.225***	0.007	−0.028***
	Third Quartile	0.160***	−0.169***	−0.001	−0.048***
	Fourth Quartile	0.159***	−0.211***	0.016**	−0.029***
Location	Eastern Germany	0.146***	−0.149***	−0.002	−0.025**
	Western Germany	0.144***	−0.183***	0.013**	−0.040***
Sector	Chemical	0.145***	−0.120***	0.011	−0.054***
	Electrical	0.157***	−0.184***	−0.005	−0.052***
	Food	0.154***	−0.224***	−0.002	0.037*
	Furniture	0.114***	−0.160***	−0.018	−0.039**
	Glass	0.122***	−0.192***	0.016	−0.024
	Leather	0.294***	−0.294***	−0.033	0.020
	Machine	0.174***	−0.231***	0.029***	−0.035***
	Metal	0.143***	−0.181***	0.030***	−0.043***
	Oil	0.166*	−0.241*	−0.014	−0.133
	Paper	0.133***	−0.152***	−0.006	−0.065***
	Rubber	0.116***	−0.193***	−0.018	0.015
	Textile	0.247***	−0.223***	0.096***	−0.038
	Vehicle	0.197***	−0.244***	0.004	−0.043*
	Wood	0.147***	−0.197***	0.050*	−0.025

Notes: Treatment effect of increased and decreased production expectations. Independent of the sample split, all available observations are used for the matching. The treatment effect is then computed using all observations in a given group. Instead of including time-fixed effects, we use the macro variables introduced in Section 12.4. When grouping by location, we only consider firms that joined the ifo Survey after the German reunification. One, two, and three stars (*) correspond to significance at the 10, 5, and 1 percent significance levels, respectively.

this matters a lot for aggregate dynamics and the business cycle remains controversial (Bachmann and Bayer, 2013, 2014; Bloom et al., 2018). A direct empirical assessment of the effect of uncertainty on firm decisions is thus called for in order to advance our understanding of how firm-level expectations influence firm decisions.

A study by Bachmann et al. (2013) uses the ifo Survey to construct empirical proxies for time-varying business-level uncertainty. They estimate a VAR model to identify uncertainty shocks and find that they induce a temporary contraction of aggregate production in the manufacturing sector as well as of employment and hours—consistent with the notion that uncertainty drives firm decisions. Also, they obtain similar results for the US based on the Business Outlook Survey maintained by the Federal Reserve Bank of Philadelphia. Bachmann et al. (2019), in turn, zoom in on the decisions at the firm level. They find that idiosyncratic firm-level volatility raises the probability of a decision to reset prices (upwards or downwards). This may reflect the fact that firms are exposed to larger shocks as uncertainty (volatility) increases and suggests that the "volatility effect" dominates the "wait-and-see" effect, according to which one would expect a reduced probability to adjust prices. They also establish a fall in the aggregate price level following a shock to average firm-specific volatility.[25] Lastly, we note that misperceptions of the extent of uncertainty may also impact firms' decisions. Ben-David et al. (2013) find for CFOs in the US that more "miscalibrated" (realized returns lie often outside the reported confidence intervals) managers invest more and tolerate higher leverage.

In sum, recent evidence based on survey data suggests that firm expectations matter for firm decisions—as economic theory would suggest. Yet the evidence to date is limited and more research is called for, not least with a view towards assessing the importance of expectations—both its first and its second moment—for firm decisions from a quantitative view. It would be particularly desirable to compare the evidence against predictions from quantitative models which also allow for departures from FIRE in order to account simultaneously for the expectation-formation process (as discussed in Section 12.4 above) and the effect of expectations on firm decisions.

12.6 Conclusion

As more and more survey data on firms' expectations has become available, the literature has started to explore this data systematically from various angles over the last decade or so. In surveying this work, we have focused on firm expectations about firm-specific developments. We have identified a number of stylized facts and revisited a number of noteworthy insights into the expectation-formation process. Lastly, we have also discussed evidence which illustrates the importance of firm expectations for firm behavior.

More research on firm expectations is called for. The following items feature prominently on our non-exhaustive wish list. First, we need more evidence on firms' forecast errors. While they are not biased unconditionally (Fact 1), they are predictable conditional on some firm-specific variables (Fact 4). Models which account simultaneously for both observations would be important advances. Second, regarding the expectation-formation process of firms, we need to develop a better understanding of how often and how strongly firms update their expectations and what role behavioral features play in this

---

[25] See also Vavra (2014) for a model-based analysis of how volatility impacts pricing behavior.

process. Third, we are currently lacking a comprehensive theory which ties together the expectation-formation and decision process of firms. Any advances in these directions are highly welcome. Fourth, while we have made an effort to assemble observations from many countries and surveys, a systematic cross-country comparison of firm-level data on firm expectations is bound to deliver additional valuable insights. While there has been efforts to harmonize firm surveys in the EU, the firm-level data is not available on a common platform. Lastly, we also consider a systematic comparison of qualitative and quantitative survey responses a promising venue for future research.

References

Abberger, Klaus, Wohlrabe, Klaus, 2006. Einige Prognoseigenschaften des ifo Geschäftsklimas – Ein Überblick über die neuere wissenschaftliche Literatur. Ifo-Schnelldienst 59, 19–26.

Altig, Dave, Baker, Scott, Barrero, Jose Maria, Bloom, Nicholas, Bunn, Philip, Chen, Scarlet, Davis, Steven J., Leather, Julia, Meyer, Brent H., Mihaylov, Emil, Mizen, Paul, Parker, Nicholas, Renault, Thomas, Smietanka, Pawel, Thwaites, Gregory, 2020a. Economic uncertainty before and during the COVID-19 pandemic. Journal of Public Economics 191, 104274.

Altig, David, Barrero, Jose Maria, Bloom, Nicholas, Davis, Steven J., Meyer, Brent H., Parker, Nicholas, 2020b. Surveying business uncertainty. Journal of Econometrics. Forthcoming.

Anderson, Oskar, Bauer, Rainald K., Führer, Hellmuth, Petersen, Jens-Peter, 1956a. Ursachen und Typen kurzfristiger Produktions- und Preisplanrevisionen der Unternehmer. Ifo-Studien 2, 1–26.

Anderson, Oskar, Fürst, Hildegard, Schulte, Willi, 1956b. Zur Analyse der unternehmerischen Reaktionsweise. Ifo-Studien 2, 129–156.

Anderson, Oskar, Strigel, Werner H., 1960. Empirische Untersuchungen des Unternehmerverhaltens an Hand von Konjunkturtest-Daten. Ifo-Studien 6, 143–156.

Andrade, Philippe, Coibion, Olivier, Gautier, Erwan, Gorodnichenko, Yuriy, 2022. No firm is an island? How industry conditions shape firms' expectations. Journal of Monetary Economics 125, 40–56.

Angeletos, George-Marios, Huo, Zhen, 2021. Myopia and anchoring. The American Economic Review 111 (4), 1166–1200.

Azeredo da Silveira, Rava, Woodford, Michael, 2019. Noisy memory and over-reaction to news. AEA Papers and Proceedings 109, 557–561.

Bachmann, Rüdiger, Bayer, Christian, 2013. 'Wait-and-see' business cycles? Journal of Monetary Economics 60 (6), 704–719.

Bachmann, Rüdiger, Bayer, Christian, 2014. Investment dispersion and the business cycle. The American Economic Review 104 (4), 1392–1416.

Bachmann, Rüdiger, Born, Benjamin, Elstner, Steffen, Grimme, Christian, 2019. Time-varying business volatility and the price setting of firms. Journal of Monetary Economics 101, 82–99.

Bachmann, Rüdiger, Carstensen, Kai, Lautenbacher, Stefan, Schneider, Martin, 2020. Uncertainty is more than risk - Survey evidence on Knightian and Bayesian firms. Mimeo. Stanford University.

Bachmann, Rüdiger, Carstensen, Kai, Lautenbacher, Stefan, Schneider, Martin, 2021. Uncertainty and change: Survey evidence of firms' subjective beliefs. NBER Working Paper 29430.

Bachmann, Rüdiger, Elstner, Steffen, 2015. Firm optimism and pessimism. European Economic Review 79, 297–325.

Bachmann, Rüdiger, Elstner, Steffen, Hristov, Atanas, 2017. Surprise, surprise - measuring firm-level investment innovations. Journal of Economic Dynamics and Control 83, 107–148.

Bachmann, Rüdiger, Elstner, Steffen, Sims, Eric R., 2013. Uncertainty and economic activity: evidence from business survey data. American Economic Journal: Macroeconomics 5 (2), 217–249.

Bachmann, Rüdiger, Zorn, Peter, 2020. What drives aggregate investment? Evidence from German survey data. Journal of Economic Dynamics and Control 115, 103873.

Balduzzi, Pierluigi, Brancati, Emanuele, Brianti, Marco, Schiantarelli, Fabio, 2020. The economic effects of COVID-19 and credit constraints: evidence from Italian firms' expectations and plans. IZA Discussion Paper 13629.

Balleer, Almut, Link, Sebastian, Menkhoff, Manuel, Zorn, Peter, 2020. Demand or supply? Price adjustment during the Covid-19 pandemic. Covid Economics: Vetted and Real-Time Papers 31, 59–102.

Banca d'Italia, 2019. Survey on inflation and growth expectations. In: Methods and Sources: Methodological Notes.

Bank of Japan, Research and Statistics Department, 2020. Tankan (short-term economic survey of enterprises in Japan) explanation. Mimeo. Bank of Japan.

Bank of Japan, Research and Statistics Department, 2022. Frequently asked questions on Tankan (short-term economic survey of enterprises in Japan). http://www.boj.or.jp/en/statistics/outline/exp/tk/faqtk02.htm/#p0106. (Accessed 1 December 2022).

Barrero, Jose Maria, 2021. The micro and macro of managerial beliefs. Journal of Financial Economics 143 (2), 640–667.

Beaudry, Paul, Portier, Franck, 2006. Stock prices, news, and economic fluctuations. The American Economic Review 96 (4), 1293–1307.

Becker, Sasha O., Wohlrabe, Klaus, 2008. Micro data at the Ifo Institute for Economic Research - the 'ifo business survey' usage and access. Schmollers Jahrbuch-Zeitschrift für Wirtschafts- und Sozialwissenschaften 182 (2), 307–319.

Ben-David, Itzhak, Graham, John R., Harvey, Campbell R., 2013. Managerial miscalibration. The Quarterly Journal of Economics 128 (4), 1547–1584.

Bennett, Adam, 1984. Output expectations of manufacturing industry. Applied Economics 16 (6), 869–879.

Bloom, Nicholas, 2009. The impact of uncertainty shocks. Econometrica 77 (3), 623–685.

Bloom, Nicholas, Bunn, Philip, Chen, Scarlet, Mizen, Paul, Smietanka, Pawel, Thwaites, Gregory, 2019. The impact of Brexit on UK firms. Staff Working Paper 818. Bank of England.

Bloom, Nicholas, Davis, Steven J., Foster, Lucia, Lucking, Brian, Ohlmacher, Scott, Saporta Eksten, Itay, 2020. Business-level expectations and uncertainty. NBER Working Paper 28259.

Bloom, Nicholas, Floetotto, Max, Jaimovich, Nir, Saporta-Eksten, Itay, Terry, Stephen J., 2018. Really uncertain business cycles. Econometrica 86 (3), 1031–1065.

Bloom, Nicholas, Kawakubo, Takafumi, Meng, Charlotte, Mizen, Paul, Riley, Rebecca, Senga, Tatsuro, Reenen, John Van, 2021. Do well managed firms make better forecasts? NBER Working Paper 29591.

Bloom, Nicholas, Reenen, John Van, 2007. Measuring and explaining management practices across firms and countries. The Quarterly Journal of Economics 122, 1351–1408.

Boneva, Lena, Cloyne, James, Weale, Martin, Wieladek, Tomasz, 2020. Firms' price, cost and activity expectations: evidence from micro data. The Economic Journal 130 (627), 555–586.

Bordalo, Pedro, Gennaioli, Nicola, La Porta, Rafael, Shleifer, Andrei, 2019. Diagnostic expectations and stock returns. The Journal of Finance 74 (6), 2839–2874.

Bordalo, Pedro, Gennaioli, Nicola, Ma, Yueran, Shleifer, Andrei, 2020. Overreaction in macroeconomic expectations. The American Economic Review 110 (9), 2748–2782.

Born, Benjamin, Enders, Zeno, Menkhoff, Manuel, Müller, Gernot J., Niemann, Knut, 2022. Firm expectations and news: micro vs. macro. Mimeo. Frankfurt School.

Born, Benjamin, Müller, Gernot J., Schularick, Moritz, Sedláček, Petr, 2019. The costs of economic nationalism: evidence from the Brexit experiment. The Economic Journal 129 (623), 2722–2744.

Broer, Tobias, Kohlhas, Alexandre N., 2022. Forecaster (mis-)behavior. Review of Economics and Statistics. Forthcoming.

Buchheim, Lukas, Krolage, Carla, Link, Sebastian, 2022. Sudden stop: when did firms anticipate the potential consequences of COVID-19? German Economic Review 23 (1), 79–119.

Carlsson, Mikael, Skans, Oskar N., 2012. Evaluating microfoundations for aggregate price rigidities: evidence from matched firm-level data on product prices and unit labor cost. The American Economic Review 102 (4), 1571–1595.

Chahrour, Ryan, Nimark, Kristoffer, Pitschner, Stefan, 2021. Sectoral media focus and aggregate fluctuations. The American Economic Review 111 (12), 3872–3922.

Chen, Cheng, Hattori, Takahiro, Luo, Yulei, 2021. Information rigidity and elastic inattention: evidence from Japan. CREPE Discussion Paper 96.

Chen, Cheng, Senga, Tatsuro, Sun, Chang, Zhang, Hongyong, 2020. Uncertainty, imperfect information, and expectation formation over the firm's life cycle. CESifo Working Paper 8468.

Coibion, Olivier, Gorodnichenko, Yuriy, 2015. Information rigidity and the expectations formation process: a simple framework and new facts. The American Economic Review 105 (8), 2644–2678.

Coibion, Olivier, Gorodnichenko, Yuriy, Ropele, Tiziano, 2020. Inflation expectations and firm decisions: new causal evidence. The Quarterly Journal of Economics 135 (1), 165–219.

Deutsche Bundesbank, 2021. Assessments and expectations of firms in the pandemic: findings from the Bundesbank Online Panel Firms. Monthly report, April.

Dovern, Jonas, Müller, Lena, Wohlrabe, Klaus, 2020. How do firms form expectations of aggregate growth? New evidence from a large-scale business survey. CESifo Working Paper 8179.

EBDC-BEP, 2019. Business Expectations Panel 01/1980 – 06/2019, LMU-ifo Economics & Business Data Center, Munich.

Eminidou, Snezana, Zachariadis, Marios, 2022. Firms' expectations and monetary policy shocks in the eurozone. Journal of International Money and Finance 122, 102556.

Enders, Zeno, Hünnekes, Franziska, Müller, Gernot J., 2019. Monetary policy announcements and expectations: evidence from German firms. Journal of Monetary Economics 108, 45–63.

Enders, Zeno, Hünnekes, Franziska, Müller, Gernot J., 2022. Firm expectations and economic activity. Journal of the European Economic Association. Forthcoming.

Enders, Zeno, Kleemann, Michael, Müller, Gernot J., 2021. Growth expectations, undue optimism, and short-run fluctuations. Review of Economics and Statistics 103 (5), 905–921.

FRB Atlanta, 2021. Survey of Business Uncertainty - Methodology.

Freuding, Julia, Seitz, Raffaela, Wohlrabe, Klaus, 2021. Was steckt hinter dem ifo Geschäftsklima? Einschätzungen der Unternehmen zu ihrer aktuellen Lage und Erwartungen. Ifo-Schnelldienst 74 (08), 40–45.

Galí, Jordi, Gertler, Mark, 1999. Inflation dynamics: a structural econometric analysis. Journal of Monetary Economics 44 (2), 195–222.

Gennaioli, Nicola, Ma, Yueran, Shleifer, Andrei, 2015. Expectations and investment. In: NBER Macroeconomics Annual 2015, Volume 30. In: NBER Chapters. National Bureau of Economic Research, pp. 379–431.

Glas, Alexander, Hartmann, Matthias, 2022. Uncertainty measures from partially rounded probabilistic forecast surveys. Quantitative Economics 13 (3), 979–1022.

Glynn, D.R., 1969. The CBI industrial trends survey. Applied Economics 1 (3), 183–196.

Guiso, Luigi, Parigi, Giuseppe, 1999. Investment and demand uncertainty. The Quarterly Journal of Economics 114 (1), 185–227.

Henzel, Steffen R., Rast, Sebastian, 2013. Prognoseeigenschaften von Indikatoren zur Vorhersage des Bruttoinlandsprodukts in Deutschland. Ifo-Schnelldienst 66, 39–46.

Hirshleifer, David, Low, Anieg, Teoh, Siew Hong, 2012. Are overconfident CEOs better innovators? The Journal of Finance 67 (4), 1457–1498.

INSEE, 2007. The French business survey on the situation and outlook in industry: methodology. Insee Méthodes 117.

Kaplan, Steven N., Klebanov, Mark M., Sorensen, Morten, 2012. Which CEO characteristics and abilities matter? The Journal of Finance 67, 973–1007.

Kawasaki, Seiichi, Zimmermann, Klaus F., 1986. Testing the rationality of price expectations for manufacturing firms. Applied Economics 18 (12), 1335–1347.

Kohlhas, Alexandre N., Walther, Ansgar, 2021. Asymmetric attention. The American Economic Review 111 (9), 2879–2925.

König, Heinz, Nerlove, Marc, Oudiz, Gilles, 1981. On the formation of price expectations. European Economic Review 16 (1), 103–138.

Krüger, Fabian, Pavlova, Lora, 2020. Quantifying subjective uncertainty in survey expectations. KIT Working Paper in Economics 139.

Kučinskas, Simas, Peters, Florian S., 2021. Measuring under- and overreaction in expectation formation. Mimeo. Humboldt-University Berlin.

Kukuvec, Anja, Oberhofer, Harald, 2020. The propagation of business expectations within the European Union. CESifo Working Paper Series 8198. CESifo Group Munich.

Lehmann, Robert, 2020. The forecasting power of the ifo business survey. CESifo Working Paper 8291.

Lucas, Robert E., 1973. Some international evidence on output-inflation tradeoffs. The American Economic Review 63 (3), 326–334.

Lui, Silvia, Mitchell, James, Weale, Martin, 2010. Qualitative business surveys: signal or noise? Journal of the Royal Statistical Society. Series A. Statistics in Society 174 (2), 327–348.

Ma, Yueran, Ropele, Tiziano, Sraer, David, Thesmar, David, 2020. A quantitative analysis of distortions in managerial forecasts. NBER Working Paper 26830.

Maćkowiak, Bartosz, Wiederholt, Mirko, 2009. Optimal sticky prices under rational inattention. The American Economic Review 99 (3), 769–803.

Malmendier, Ulrike, Tate, Geoffrey, 2005a. CEO overconfidence and corporate investment. The Journal of Finance 60 (6), 2661–2700.

Malmendier, Ulrike, Tate, Geoffrey, 2005b. Does overconfidence affect corporate investment? CEO overconfidence measures revisited. European Financial Management 60 (11), 649–659.

Mankiw, N. Gregory, Reis, Ricardo, 2002. Sticky information versus sticky prices: a proposal to replace the new Keynesian Phillips curve. The Quarterly Journal of Economics 117 (4), 1295–1328.

Massenot, Baptiste, Pettinicchi, Yuri, 2018. Can firms see into the future? Survey evidence from Germany. Journal of Economic Behavior & Organization 145, 66–79.

McFadden, Daniel, 1974. Conditional logit analysis of qualitative choice behavior. Frontiers in Econometrics.

McIntosh, James, Schiantarelli, Fabio, Low, William, 1989. A qualitative response analysis of UK firms' employment and output decisions. Journal of Applied Econometrics 4 (3), 251–264.

Meyer, Brent H., Parker, Nicholas B., Sheng, Xuguang S., 2021. Unit Cost Expectations and Uncertainty: Firms' Perspectives on Inflation. FRB Atlanta Working Paper 2021-12a.

Meyer, Brent H., Prescott, Brian, Sheng, Xuguang S., 2022. The impact of the COVID-19 pandemic on business expectations. International Journal of Forecasting 38 (2), 529–544.

Morikawa, Masayuki, 2016. Business uncertainty and investment: evidence from Japanese companies. Journal of Macroeconomics 49, 224–236.

Morikawa, Masayuki, 2019. Uncertainty over production forecasts: an empirical analysis using monthly quantitative survey data. Journal of Macroeconomics 60, 163–179.

Nerb, Gernot, 1987. Der Konjunkturtest im Lichte neuerer wirtschaftstheoretischer Ansätze. Ifo-Studien 32, 27–40.

Nerb, Gernot, Sauer, Stefan, 2020. Einführung in die ifo Umfragen. In: Sauer, Stefan, Wohlrabe, Klaus (Eds.), Handbuch der umfragebasierten konjunkturforschung. In: ifo Beiträge zur Wirtschaftsforschung, vol. 88. ifo Institut für Wirtschaftsforschung, pp. 1–8. Chapter 200.

Nerlove, Marc, 1983. Expectations, plans, and realizations in theory and practice. Econometrica 51 (5), 1251–1279.

Rosewell, B.C., 1987. The CBI industrial trends survey and capacity working. In: Bosworth, Derek, Heathfield, David F. (Eds.), Working Below Capacity. Palgrave Macmillan UK, London, pp. 3–22.

Schwarz, Norbert, Hippler, Hans-J., Deutsch, Brigitte, Strack, Fritz, 1985. Effects of category range on reported behavior and comparative judgments. Public Opinion Quarterly 49 (3), 388–395.

Seiler, Christian, Wohlrabe, Klaus, 2013. Das ifo Geschäftsklima und die deutsche Konjunktur. Ifo-Schnelldienst 66 (18), 17–21.

Shiller, Robert J., 2017. Narrative economics. The American Economic Review 107 (4), 967–1004.

Sims, Christopher A., 2003. Implications of rational inattention. In: Swiss National Bank/Study Center Gerzensee Conference on Monetary Policy Under Incomplete Information. Journal of Monetary Economics 50 (3), 665–690.

Smith, Jeremy, McAleer, Michael, 1995. Alternative procedures for converting qualitative response data to quantitative expectations: an application to Australian manufacturing. Journal of Applied Econometrics 10 (2), 165–185.

Strasser, Georg, 2013. Exchange rate pass-through and credit constraints. In: Carnegie-NYU-Rochester Conference. Journal of Monetary Economics 60 (1), 25–38.

Thomas, David G., 1995. Output expectations within manufacturing industry. Applied Economics 27 (5), 403–408.

Trebing, Michael, Fenske, Caroline B., 2018. The "Philly Fed Index" turns 50 with steadfast success. Economic Insights 3 (4).

Triebs, Thomas P., Tumlinson, Justin, 2013. Learning to forecast the hard way—evidence from German reunification. NBER Working Paper 19209.

Vavra, Joseph, 2014. Inflation dynamics and time-varying volatility: new evidence and an Ss interpretation. The Quarterly Journal of Economics 129 (1), 215–258.

Woodford, Michael, 2002. Imperfect Common Knowledge and the Effects of Monetary Policy. Princeton University Press, Princeton, pp. 25–58.

Expectations of financial market participants[☆]

13

Anthony M. Diercks[a] **and Haitham Jendoubi**[b]

[a]Federal Reserve Board, Washington, DC, United States
[b]Federal Reserve Bank of New York, New York, NY, United States

13.1 Introduction

When economic agents face uncertainty, they must adopt a view regarding unknown future or latent conditions in the economy and financial markets. Some agents may form an outlook on the basis of model outputs while others may use their own judgmental forecasts; however, many find value in canvassing the views of a range of market participants.[1] For instance, surveys are of particular interest to investors and policymakers—especially those at central banks—because they provide valuable information about market expectations for future economic outcomes, financial conditions, and policy actions. This information is useful for many reasons, including as a measure of the degree to which market participants expect (or do not expect) various potential policy interventions—an important input into the deliberations of forward-looking policymakers.

Surveys usually complement other sources of information—such as market pricing data or anecdotal information from market participants—but the rigor and structure of periodic surveys, as well as the absence of risk premiums, make them a valuable input into research, analysis, and decision-making. They are methodical, periodic snapshots of expectations elicited from a range of respondents over a set period of time. They can also minimize subjective differences by using explicitly defined terms (compared to, say, anecdotal information or published commentary). The most appropriate survey population depends largely on the intended application of the data, and the views of households, academic forecasters, and nonfinancial corporate actors are highly relevant for various purposes.[2] In this chapter, we focus on surveys of financial market participants in particular, as the views of entities that themselves transact in financial markets constitute an important input for many researchers and policymakers with an interest in the evolution of those markets.

[☆] We thank Rudi Bachmann, Ryan Bush, Christopher Carroll, Olivier Coibion, Marco Del Negro, Andrew Meldrum, Matthew Raskin, Alex Thorp, Giorgio Topa, and Wilbert van der Klaauw for helpful comments and suggestions. All errors remain our sole responsibility. The views expressed herein are those of the authors and not necessarily those of the Board of Governors of the Federal Reserve System or the Federal Reserve Bank of New York.

[1] There is a large literature documenting the benefits in terms of forecast accuracy in constructing a consensus or average of respondents' views, e.g., see Bauer et al. (2003).

[2] For the views of households, see Chapter 1 in this Handbook. For academic and nonfinancial forecasters, see Chapter 3 in this Handbook.

Despite these advantages, surveys are also subject to potential drawbacks—as we will see, some of these drawbacks include sample bias and biases arising from the behavior of respondents themselves such as forecast smoothing. As with any tool, researchers and practitioners must understand the limitations of surveys and exercise caution in their use; as a result, surveys are likely to be most effective when combined with other tools as appropriate.

The structure of this chapter is as follows. Section 13.2 details formal dimensions along which surveys of financial market participants can differ. Section 13.3 introduces and describes a range of surveys that target market participants both in the United States and other jurisdictions. Section 13.4 focuses on the advantages of using surveys while Section 13.5 discusses the potential drawbacks. Section 13.6 concludes.

13.2 Distinctions across surveys

While surveys have many commonalities, they differ in important ways that allow them to elicit information according to their purpose or idiosyncrasies of a given economic environment. This section describes some of the formal dimensions along which surveys of financial market participants can differ.

Target jurisdiction

Surveys are usually focused on a specific jurisdiction—generally the one in which the survey administrator is located. (See Section 13.3 for examples across various jurisdictions.) However, in some cases (e.g., Blue Chip), surveys are designed to cover a range of major jurisdictions.

Target respondents

Surveys of market participants may focus on a specific population, such as banks, broker-dealers, or fund managers. Within each of these institutions, surveys may be completed by individuals in various roles, such as economists, strategists, traders, or asset managers. In addition, some surveys also poll academic researchers, economic consultancies, industry groups, and/or corporate officers. The number of respondents varies widely across surveys as well, though the respondent pool for a given survey often remains roughly stable over time given the lack of rapid changes in the major institutions active in a given jurisdiction. Surveys of market participants also generally tend to poll a smaller number of respondents than most surveys of households or firms—often fewer than 100, and sometimes only a few dozen.

The views of households can sometimes diverge from those of economic forecasters or market participants, which also represents useful information to survey users. For example, following the onset of the COVID-19 pandemic, median expectations for inflation over the next several years among consumers polled by the University of Michigan increased somewhat earlier than expectations among primary dealers surveyed in the New York Fed's Survey of Primary Dealers (Fig. 13.1).

Frequency

Surveys can be conducted at a range of periodicities, such as monthly or quarterly frequencies or a frequency tied to the deliberations of a policy body such as the monetary policy committee of a central

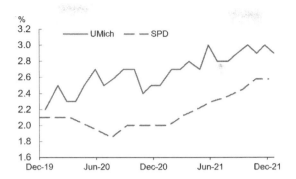

FIGURE 13.1 Expectations for Changes in Prices over the Next Several Years

Source: FRBNY Survey of Primary Dealers median response to the question: "Please provide your point estimate for the most likely outcome [for annual average CPI inflation over the next five years]), University of Michigan Surveys of Consumers median response to the question: "By about what percent per year do you expect prices to go up or down, on the average, during the next 5 to 10 years?"

bank. On occasion, surveys may be conducted on an ad-hoc basis, in response to a particular political or economic development.

Subject matter

Surveys can cover a wide swath of potential topics, though certain areas are particularly common. One such area is economic indicators, particularly economic growth, inflation, and measures of unemployment. Another area is expectations for market prices, including policy interest rates; short-, medium-, and long-term sovereign bond yields; risky borrowing rates such as mortgage rates or corporate bond yields; and foreign exchange rates. Other areas include fiscal or monetary policy, such as expected government securities issuance or central bank asset purchases. Some surveys may also occasionally ask normative questions regarding economic policy, rather than descriptive—that is, what respondents believe is the best course of action, rather than what they expect is the most likely outcome.

Forecast horizon

Survey questions that ask about future outcomes can vary widely in their forecast horizon, with horizons as short as several days or as long as a decade or more. For example, a question may relate to expectations for the outcome of a central bank policy meeting in the coming days; another may ask for expectations for economic growth in the next several quarters; and others might ask for expectations for government borrowing costs or the unemployment rate on the scale of several years. Some surveys also ask questions that relate to expectations up to about a decade, or "longer-run" expectations under conditions that are expected to prevail in equilibrium. The number of horizons over which a survey elicits expectations is necessarily limited, making market data (which can be more flexible and reflect expectations over a wider range of horizons) a useful complement. (Note that some surveys also ask about current conditions or past events, e.g., eliciting views on the unobserved drivers of observed changes in market prices.)

Anonymity

Some surveys (such as those conducted by Bloomberg or Blue Chip) make individual survey responses available, while others (such as the European Central Bank's [ECB] Survey of Monetary Analysts and the New York Fed's Survey of Primary Dealers [SPD] and Survey of Market Participants [SMP]) publish the names of their respondents but maintain the anonymity of individual respondents' answers. In addition, certain surveys (such as the Philadelphia Fed's Survey of Professional Forecasters) include some anonymous respondents, and as such do not disclose their full list of participants.

Survey format

Finally, surveys can elicit expectations over uncertain outcomes in a variety of ways. The most common data elicited are modal expectations (i.e., the most likely outcome) and probability distributions (i.e., assigning probabilities to each of a range of potential outcomes). Often, surveys do not indicate whether they elicit modal or probability-weighted expectations; this can complicate the interpretation of the results, as described below in Section 13.5. Other types of survey questions include Likert rating scale and qualitative, open-ended questions.

i. Modal expectations

When specified, the most common type of survey question asks for the most likely value of a particular quantity—also known as the modal expectation. This has the advantage of being a salient property of most respondents' views and is the most common way in which market participants communicate their views anecdotally or in written commentary.

ii. Probabilistic questions

Probabilistic questions are those that elicit the range of respondents' subjective distribution of potential outcomes, as opposed to point estimates such as modal estimates.[3] In other words, for these questions, respondents are asked to describe their views on the likelihood of a range of (usually exhaustive) outcomes for a given policy, macroeconomic, or financial indicator—not just the most likely outcome. (For continuous variables, respondents are generally asked to assign probabilities to the variable falling into various bins.) For example, a question may ask for the probability that the inflation rate will fall into each of several bins. These probabilistic questions have been employed by a range of surveys, such as the ECB's SMA and New York Fed's SPD and SMP. They elicit expectations for various rates of inflation, growth, Treasury yields, policy rates and other indicators (for example, see Figs. 13.2 and 13.3).

There are several benefits to using probabilistic questions, such as the ability to elicit the likelihood attached to nonmodal outcomes in addition to the modal outcome, and to obtain various quantitative measures of interest, such as uncertainty or skewness.[4] In addition, eliciting a probability distribution enables the estimation of an implied probability-weighted mean estimate, which in some cases can be useful in a comparison to market prices (which in theory reflect a probability-weighted average of expectations among market participants).

---

[3] For an in-depth discussion on probabilistic survey questions, see Potter et al. (2017).

[4] Indeed, this measure of uncertainty can only be elicited from a probabilistic question. The disagreement among respondents' point estimates is sometimes substituted but this is a distinct and in general unrelated concept. For example, see https://libertystreeteconomics.newyorkfed.org/2015/01/what-does-disagreement-tell-us-about-uncertainty.html.

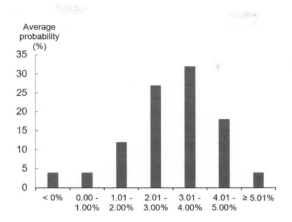

FIGURE 13.2 Average Probability Distribution for U.S. Real GDP Growth in 2022 (Q4/Q4)

Source: December 2021 FRBNY Survey of Primary Dealers. Question: "Please provide the percent chance you attach to the following outcomes for U.S. real GDP growth in 2021 and 2022 (Q4/Q4)."

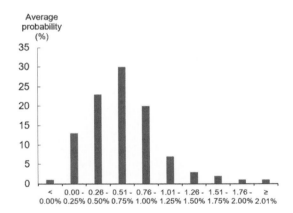

FIGURE 13.3 Year-End 2022 Federal Funds Target

Source: December 2021 FRBNY Survey of Market Participants. Question: "Please indicate the percent chance that you attach to the target federal funds rate or range falling in each of the following ranges at the end of 2021, 2022, 2023, and 2024. If you expect a target range, please use the midpoint of that range in providing your response."

Finally, we note that probabilistic questions can reveal patterns or shifts in respondents' subjective distributions that may not be apparent when only asking for point estimates. For example, according to the New York Fed's SPD, median modal outcomes for the target range for the federal funds rate at the end of 2022 remained at the effective lower bound from April 2020 through September 2021, but the distribution of potential outcomes shifted downward, then upward, over the same timeframe.

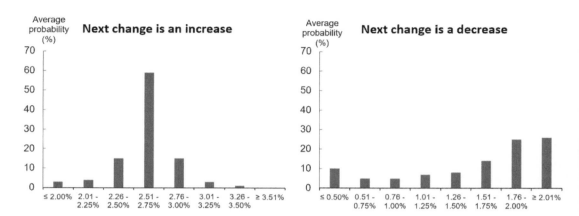

FIGURE 13.4 Conditional Year-End 2019 Federal Funds Target Expectations

Source: April/May 2019 FRBNY Survey of Market Participants. Question: "Please indicate the percent chance that you attach to the target federal funds rate or range falling in each of the following ranges at the end of 2019, conditional on the following possible scenarios for the direction of the Committee's next policy action between now and the end of 2019. Only fill out the conditional probability distributions for which you assigned a nonzero probability to the conditioning event occurring. If you expect a target range, please use the midpoint of that range in providing your response."

iii. Conditional questions

Some surveys, including the New York Fed's SPD and SMP, sometimes ask conditional questions. These questions ask respondents to provide their views conditional on a given state of the world or policy outcome. For example, the SPD and SMP have included questions that ask for respondents' subjective distribution for the target range for the federal funds rate conditional on the next change being an increase or a decrease in the range (Fig. 13.4) as well as views on the most likely target range conditional on various hypothetical combinations of inflation and unemployment rate outcomes (Fig. 13.5). These types of questions can generate data of greater granularity and answer questions that similar unconditional questions cannot.[5] It is also possible to elicit conditional probabilities for one variable across a range of outcomes for another variable (the conditioning variable), as well as marginal probabilities for outcomes of the conditioning variable. This allows researchers to construct a joint probability distribution (e.g., question 8 in the June 2013 SPD). At the same time, however, conditional questions may require more time and effort to answer compared to more commonly expressed modal expectations, particularly as respondents may not independently maintain these conditional forecasts.

---

[5] Note that even though they sometimes include questions that are conditional on a particular outcome or action, the SPD and SMP never presume any particular policy action. Accordingly, the conditioning scenarios are generally symmetrical, e.g., a symmetrical upward or downward perturbation to inflation or unemployment, or the next change in the target range being an increase or a decrease.

The following matrix lays out hypothetical scenarios in which the realized levels of the 2020 unemployment rate (Q4 average level) and 2020 core PCE inflation (Q4/Q4 growth) are either 50 basis points above, below, or equal to the medians of FOMC participants' projections for these indicators in the December Summary of Economic Projections (SEP). For example, the upper left box represents a scenario in which the unemployment rate and core PCE inflation are both 50 basis points below the current SEP medians. The upper right box represents a scenario in which the unemployment rate is 50 basis points above the current SEP median, while core PCE inflation is 50 basis points below the current median.

For each of the following scenarios, please indicate the level of the target federal funds rate or range that you expect would prevail <u>at the end of Q1 2021</u>. If you expect a target range, please indicate the midpoint of that range in providing your response.

Median Responses		2020 Unemployment rate (Q4 average level)		
		Current SEP median 3.5%		
		- 50 bps	median 3.5%	+ 50 bps
2020 Core PCE inflation (Q4/Q4)	- 50 bps	1.61%	1.25%	0.75%
	Current SEP median 1.9%	1.63%	1.63%	1.13%
	+ 50 bps	2.13%	1.63%	1.63%

FIGURE 13.5 Q1 2021 Federal Funds Target Rate Under Hypothetical Scenarios

Source: January 2020 FRBNY Survey of Primary Dealers.

12) How do you characterize the policy adjustments made by the BOJ after its March review? (Multiple answers OK)	
Response Count:	52 responses from 44 economists
A dialing back of stimulus	1
A strengthening of stimulus framework	23
A step toward policy normalization	18
A step toward further easing	1
Hard to tell	9

FIGURE 13.6 Question on Interpretation of Bank of Japan Policy Adjustments in April 2021 Survey

Source: Bloomberg.

iv. Nonquantitative and rating questions

Some questions may ask respondents to select one or more unordered responses that do not lie on a continuum, whereby nonnumerical views can be aggregated and analyzed quantitatively (Figs. 13.6 and 13.7).

In addition, surveys may also employ rating questions, particularly those that use a Likert scale (e.g., a rating from one to five). These questions are useful in assigning a numerical value to an attribute or normative view that does not correspond to an observable quantity, such as the unobserved drivers of

5   a. Does the balance of risks to your inflation forecasts lie to the upside?

	Yes	No
	97%	3%

   b. If yes, what is the main source of those upside risks?

A stronger than expected recovery	42%
Commodity price pressures	18%
Looser monetary policy	12%
Looser fiscal policy	18%
A weaker US dollar	0%
Other factors	9%

FIGURE 13.7 Questions on Upside Risks to Inflation Forecasts and Source of Risks

Source: May 2021 Blue Chip Financial Forecasts.

Factors Explaining the Change in the 10-Year Treasury Yield					
	Changes To Expectations for Fiscal Policy	Changes to Expectations for the Course of the Pandemic	Changes to Perceptions of the FOMC's Reaction Function	Changes in Uncertainty Around Interest Rates	Changes in Actual or Expected Treasury Supply and Treasury Liquidity	Other (Please Explain)
1-Not Important	0	0	3	0	1	0
2	0	2	6	10	5	0
3	1	5	9	10	8	4
4	13	8	3	4	7	1
5-Very Important	10	9	3	0	3	1
# of Responses	24	24	24	24	24	6

FIGURE 13.8 Importance of Various Factors in Explaining Change in 10-Year Nominal Treasury Yield Since the January 2021 FOMC Meeting

Source: March 2021 FRBNY Survey of Primary Dealers. Question: "[P]lease rate the importance of the following factors in explaining changes in the 10-year Treasury yield since the January FOMC meeting (5=very important, 1=not important)."

observed changes in market prices (Fig. 13.8). This enables quantitative comparisons between respondents and over successive surveys.

v. Qualitative questions

Many surveys of market participants employ qualitative (or open-ended) questions that elicit written responses. While these responses are necessarily less structured than those of numerical questions, they nonetheless provide useful information—particularly in cases where more conceptual views are desired and where a more structured question is difficult to formulate because possible answers cannot readily be categorized or there is not a strong prior view on the range of potential answers (see Fig. 13.9).

1a)   Provide below your expectations for **changes**, if any, to the language referencing each of the following
topics in the March FOMC statement. **Please write N/A if you do not expect any changes.**

Current economic conditions:

> **Many respondents indicated that they expected the Committee to
> upgrade its assessment of current economic conditions, including
> several who expected the Committee to note a faster pace of
> recovery for economic activity and/or employment. Several
> respondents also indicated that they expected the Committee to
> note an improvement in recent economic data, while several
> indicated that they did not expect material changes to the
> Committee's characterization of current economic conditions.**

**FIGURE 13.9 Expectations for Changes to Language Referencing Current Economic Conditions in March 2021
FOMC Statement**

Source: March 2021 FRBNY Survey of Market Participants.

13.3 Examples of surveys of financial market participants

In this section, we briefly introduce a range of expectational surveys that target market participants both
in the United States and in other jurisdictions. For an overview of selected surveys, see Table 13.1.

13.3.1 Survey of Primary Dealers and Survey of Market Participants

Among official sector surveys that elicit market expectations for monetary policy and the economic
outlook, two important surveys in the United States are the New York Fed's Survey of Primary Dealers
(SPD),[6] which has been published since 2011, and its companion the Survey of Market Participants
(SMP),[7] published since 2014. These surveys are conducted in advance of each Federal Open Market
Committee (FOMC) meeting by the New York Fed's Open Market Trading Desk, polling primary
dealers and active investment decision-makers (such as asset managers and funds) on economic and
financial market topics that have been widely discussed in public venues. FOMC participants are not
consulted in the formulation of survey questions. The combination of the depth and the breadth of
these surveys makes them a valuable tool to understand expectations for how policy will evolve in
the context of changing economic conditions. Findings from the surveys are often cited in the FOMC
meeting minutes, indicating that they are considered a pertinent source of information for understanding
market participants' expectations for the evolution of the economy and for domestic monetary policy
decisions.

The objective of these surveys is to gain insight into the expectations of respondents on a range of
topics. For instance, in the past, respondents have been asked about their expectations on the future
level of the federal funds rate and the future size of the Federal Reserve's balance sheet, as well as
their forecasts of economic indicators. Part of the versatility of the SPD and SMP lies in their ability to

---

[6] See https://www.newyorkfed.org/markets/primarydealer_survey_questions.html.

[7] See https://www.newyorkfed.org/markets/survey_market_participants.

Table 13.1 Selected Surveys of Financial Market Participants.

Survey	Publisher	Target Respondents	Main Topics Covered	Website
Survey of Primary Dealers (SPD)	FRBNY	FRBNY's primary dealers	"Economic and financial market topics that have been widely discussed in public venues"	https://www.newyorkfed.org/markets/primarydealer_survey_questions
Survey of Market Participants (SMP)	FRBNY	Active investment decision-makers, with initial eligibility limited to a subset of firms associated with certain New York Fed advisory and sponsored groups	"Economic and financial market topics that have been widely discussed in public venues"	https://www.newyorkfed.org/markets/survey_market_participants
Blue Chip Economic Indicators and Blue Chip Financial Forecasts	Wolters Kluwer	"Economists employed by some of America's largest and most respected manufacturers, banks, insurance companies, and brokerage firms"	Forecasts for various real economy-focused and financial market indicators and special questions	https://www.wolterskluwer.com/en/solutions/vitallaw-law-firms/blue-chip
The Wall Street Journal Economic Forecasting Survey	The Wall Street Journal	"academic, business, and financial economists"	"Range of economic indicators" and "questions related to current events"	https://www.wsj.com/articles/economic-forecasting-survey-archive-11617814998
Shadow Survey of Market Participants	MacroPolicy Perspectives	Portfolio/risk managers, market makers, traders, economists, strategists, etc.	Expectations for economic and financial conditions, Fed policy, and related questions	https://www.macropolicyperspectives.com/shadow-survey
Senior Loan Officer Opinion Survey on Bank Lending Practices (SLOOS)	Federal Reserve Board of Governors	Domestically chartered commercial banks and U.S. branches and agencies of foreign banks	"questions designed to measure changes in credit standards and terms on bank loans and perceived changes in the demand for bank credit" and "special questions about developments in banking practices"	https://www.federalreserve.gov/data/sloos.htm
Senior Financial Officer Survey (SFOS)	Federal Reserve Board of Governors; FRBNY	Domestic banks and foreign banking organizations	"a limited number of questions directed at topics of timely interest"; [in March 2021] "expectations for reserve and balance sheet management in the months ahead"	https://www.federalreserve.gov/data/sfos/sfos.htm

continued on next page

Table 13.1 (*continued*)

Survey	Publisher	Target Respondents	Main Topics Covered	Website
The CFO Survey	Duke University's Fuqua School of Business, Federal Reserve Bank of Richmond, Federal Reserve Bank of Atlanta	"Respondents include chief financial officers, owner-operators, vice presidents and directors of finance, accountants, controllers, treasurers, and others with financial decision-making roles"	"financial outlook for their firms, the challenges they face, and their expectations for the U.S. economy"	https://www.richmondfed.org/cfosurvey
Bloomberg economic and monetary policy surveys	Bloomberg LP	Economists at financial and academic institutions and consultancies	Expectations for economic and financial indicators, monetary policy, and related questions in the United States and other jurisdictions	E.g., https://www.bloomberg.com/news/articles/2021-09-17/fed-seen-announcing-bond-taper-in-november-rate-liftoff-in-2023
Consensus Forecasts	Consensus Economics	Economists at financial and academic institutions and consultancies	"Country economic forecasts and topical analyses covering the G-7 industrialized nations, Asia Pacific, Eastern Europe and Latin America"	https://www.consensuseconomics.com/
Action Economics (formerly known as Money Market Services Survey)	Action Economics	Dealers of securities	Forecasts for various real economy-focused and financial market indicators	http://actioneconomics.com

ask special questions regarding current events or market phenomena that have been widely discussed publicly—for example, the impact of the coronavirus pandemic on economic growth, or the drivers of a pronounced decline in long-dated Treasury yields over a given period—which can provide more detailed and relevant data on topics of interest. Survey questions are published on the New York Fed's website before they are distributed to respondents—ahead of each FOMC meeting—and summaries of the results are published about three weeks after each FOMC meeting, following the release of the corresponding FOMC meeting minutes.

The New York Fed's SPD and SMP generally ask substantially the same questions across both the Federal Reserve's primary dealers and the institutional investors that comprise the SMP panel. The SMP was launched in 2014 as a way to expand the survey sample and probe whether the investor community might hold different views from the dealer community.[8] Though responses from primary

---

[8] Speaking in 2016, then-Executive Vice President Simon Potter describes some of the rationale behind expanding the New York Fed's policy survey beyond primary dealers following the so-called "taper tantrum" of 2013. "Importantly, it is possible that the size of future asset purchases was seen as smaller by primary dealer respondents than by the marginal investor. Following this experience, we introduced the Survey of Market Participants to better capture the diversity of views in the market." https://www.newyorkfed.org/newsevents/speeches/2016/pot160519.

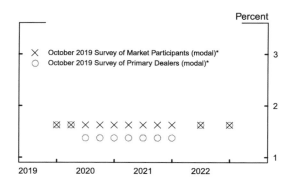

FIGURE 13.10 Median Modal Expectations for the Federal Funds Target Rate or Range

Source: October 2019 FRBNY Surveys of Primary Dealers and Market Participants. Question: "Provide your estimate of the most likely outcome (i.e., the mode) for the target federal funds rate or range, as applicable, immediately following the FOMC meetings and at the end of each of the following quarters and half-years below. For the time periods at which you expect a target range, please indicate the midpoint of that range in providing your response."

dealers and institutional investors have not revealed systematic, long-term differences, these groups of respondents have, at times, held differing views on specific questions. For instance, in October 2019, median responses to the Survey of Primary Dealers were consistent with a decrease in the target range for the federal funds rate in 2020, while median responses to the Survey of Market Participants were consistent with no change to the target range (Fig. 13.10). Over a longer timeframe, Fig. 13.11 provides a comparison of the SPD and SMP median of modal one-year ahead projections for the target federal funds rate, as documented in Diercks et al. (2021).

The SPD and SMP are a rich source of detailed information on market expectations for a range of U.S. economic and financial market indicators, but they offer particularly granular and varied questions regarding expectations for U.S. monetary policy, many of which are not asked in other surveys. This affords the users of these surveys the ability to draw various useful conclusions regarding the evolution of policy expectations. For example, one common pattern observed is that with the passage of time and in response to communications from monetary authorities, expectations for the magnitude or timing of various policy actions show a decline in uncertainty and disagreement as consensus builds (Fig. 13.12).

The SPD and SMP are notable in a few ways, both in form and substance.[9] With respect to the organization of the surveys, while some other surveys have retained many of the same questions and formats over time, the SPD and SMP have evolved with time in response to financial and economic conditions as well as the monetary policy context. For example, during periods in which the policy rate was at the effective lower bound, the surveys asked questions regarding the timing of the first increase in the target range for the federal funds rate ("liftoff") and economic conditions at liftoff. At other times,

---

[9] Another way in which the SPD is notable is that primary dealers' relationship with the Federal Reserve helps to ensure high response rates and continuity in the sample over time (Correia-Golay et al. (2013)).

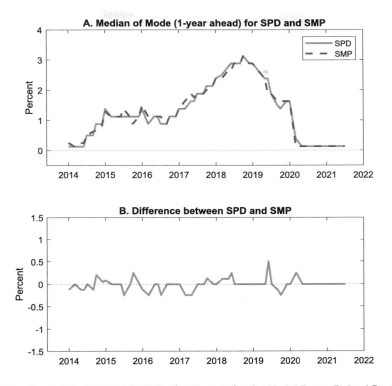

FIGURE 13.11 Comparison of the SPD and SMP Median Expectation for Modal Target Federal Funds Rate

Source: Federal Reserve Bank of New York and Diercks et al. (2021). Note: Panel A shows the median of each respondent's modal forecast of the approximately 1-year ahead federal funds rate from the SPD and the SMP. Panel B shows the difference between the two series.

the surveys introduced other types of questions (for example, the probability of increases or decreases in the target range).

Similarly, during periods in which the FOMC has been engaged in the purchase of securities—such as the Large Scale Asset Purchase programs in response to the Global Financial Crisis or purchases following the onset of the global pandemic in 2020—the surveys have included questions related to the timing and amount of these purchases. The surveys also sometimes introduce topical questions related to recent events in financial markets, such as bouts of market volatility, developments in specific asset markets such as foreign exchange or oil, or market functioning.

13.3.2 Blue Chip Survey

Two important surveys that are produced by the firm Wolters Kluwer are the Blue Chip Economic Indicators and the Blue Chip Financial Forecasts. Each of these surveys are conducted monthly and cover a broad range of economic and financial variables. There are about 40 to 50 respondents that

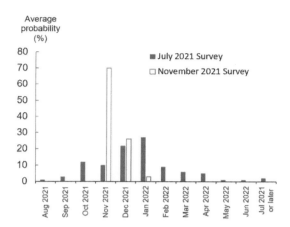

FIGURE 13.12 Probability of First Reduction in Asset Purchases Occurring in Each Period

Source: July and November 2021 FRBNY Survey of Primary Dealers. Question: "Please indicate the percent chance that you attach to the first reduction in the pace of asset purchases occurring in each of the following periods."

come from a wide range of backgrounds such as professional economists (many of whom are associated with firms that are active in financial markets) and academics.

13.3.2.1 *Blue Chip Economic Indicators*

The Blue Chip Economic Indicators monthly survey has been conducted since 1976. The survey results are released to the public around the middle of each month and the forecasts are typically submitted three business days before publication. The forecasts cover a wide range of economic indicators including the components of GDP, unemployment, housing, auto sales, inflation, as well as financial variables such as the 3-month Treasury bill. Forecasts are provided at the quarterly and annual forecast horizon for most variables. The survey also asks about five key economic variables for 15 of the U.S.'s largest trading partners.

Similar to the SPD and SMP, special questions are asked that help provide insight into more qualitative forecasts or topical developments. For instance, in the April 2021 survey, respondents were asked if they perceive inflation risks to be temporary or likely to linger. In the May 2021 survey, respondents were asked whether they see the size of the U.S. federal fiscal deficit supporting growth. In addition to these special questions, long-range forecasts are provided twice a year for horizons of 1 to 5 years, plus an average of the five years after that. In all months, the survey features near- and medium-term forecasts at the annual and quarterly frequency.

13.3.2.2 *Blue Chip Financial Forecasts*

The Blue Chip Financial Forecasts monthly survey has been conducted since 1982. In this survey, forecasts are more focused on U.S. interest rates. The forecasts extend across the entire yield curve and also to other interest rates such as those on corporate and municipal bonds. The horizons of interest include the next five quarters. Several respondents also forecast international interest rates and foreign exchange rates. Similar to the Blue Chip Economic Indicators survey, long-range forecasts are provided twice a year.

13.3.3 Consensus Economics

Consensus Economics publishes Consensus Forecasts and covers a broad range of economic and financial indicators. The survey is conducted on a monthly basis and forecasts are available since 1989. It typically polls over 20 financial market participants and other forecasters. Forecasts are provided for the next two years at both quarterly and annual horizons. Each month, a special set of questions is introduced that garners responses on a topical issue. This survey has a greater international focus, with forecasts provided for over 15 other countries in addition to the United States.

13.3.4 Surveys administered in other jurisdictions

Among other jurisdictions, public-sector surveys of financial market participants are often conducted by the fiscal or monetary authorities, and private-sector surveys are often conducted by international or local information services companies or the financial press. For example, the European Central Bank and the Bank of England conduct surveys of market participants, and central banks in many other developed and emerging economies also conduct surveys of this kind.

The target respondents for each of these surveys are usually tailored to the jurisdiction in question; for example, the respondents to the ECB's Survey of Monetary Analysts include "financial institutions participating in the ECB Market Contact Groups (i.e., the Money Market, Bond Market, and Foreign Exchange Contact Groups)", while the respondents to the Bank of Japan's Bond Market Survey are "eligible institutions for the Bank of Japan's outright purchases and sales of JGBs and major insurance companies, asset management companies, etc.". Eliciting expectations from institutions that are active in each jurisdiction can help ensure that survey responses are informed and representative of participants in the markets in question.

In many jurisdictions, data companies or financial journalists also conduct surveys, either at a fixed frequency or matching the meeting schedule of the policy body of the monetary authority. For example, Bloomberg LP conducts monthly surveys of economists to gather expectations for a range of macroeconomic indicators in major economies. In addition, the firm conducts surveys on expectations for major central banks; for example, in recent years it has polled economists ahead of monetary policy meetings of the Federal Reserve's FOMC, the Policy Board of the Bank of Japan, and the ECB's Governing Council to elicit expectations for any changes to communications or policy actions. Similarly, Bloomberg and Thomson Reuters have conducted regular surveys in which they elicit expectations for the People's Bank of China's (PBOC) Loan Prime Rate, its benchmark lending rate.

The subject matter of surveys also differs according to the structure and unique characteristics of financial markets and institutions in the relevant jurisdiction. For example, the monthly Survey of Expectations conducted by the Central Bank of the Republic of Turkey (CBRT) has recently asked about the CBRT one-week repo auction rate, while Banco Central do Brasil's (BCB) Focus Survey has asked about the Selic, an overnight interbank borrowing rate that serves as the BCB's policy rate. Meanwhile, in jurisdictions with an ongoing asset purchase program, surveys will often ask respondents questions relating to potential changes to these purchases.

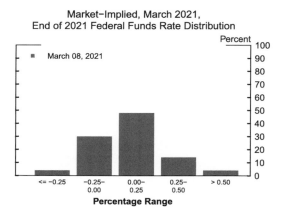

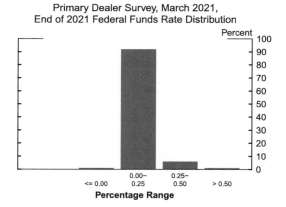

FIGURE 13.13 Market- and Survey-Based Probability Distributions for Federal Funds Rate

Source: Author's calculations based on CME Group Inc., DataMine, FRBNY. The left panel shows the option-implied probability distribution of the December 2021 Federal Funds Futures contract according to CME. The right panel shows the aggregate probability distribution of the expected target range for the federal funds rate at the end of 2021 in the March 2021 Survey of Primary Dealers.

13.4 Some advantages and uses of surveys

This section covers some of the advantages of using surveys to back out expectations versus asset prices. It also touches upon the questions that can be uniquely addressed by surveys and how surveys are often incorporated into economic modeling.

13.4.1 Risk premiums

There is a large literature documenting the presence of risk premiums[10] in financial markets, as highlighted by Fama and Bliss (1987) and Campbell and Shiller (1991). Thus, a major benefit of using surveys over relying on financial market asset prices is the absence of risk premiums, which provides a measure of expectations undistorted by risk preferences (for further discussion of market-based measures, see Chapter 14 in this Handbook). To get a better sense of the important differences when using surveys versus financial markets to back out expectations, one can compare market-implied and survey-based probability distributions for the federal funds rate at the end of 2021 (Fig. 13.13). On the left is the federal funds futures options-implied probability distribution that is calculated based on Chicago Mercantile Exchange (CME) options quotes. On the right is the average probability distribution as asked in the March 2021 Survey of Primary Dealers.

---

[10] In the context of bonds, risk premiums capture the difference between the yield investors require for holding longer-term securities—whose realized returns are more sensitive to risks from future inflation or volatility in interest rates than shorter-term securities—and the expected yield from rolling over shorter-dated ones.

One notable difference between the two data sources is the weight being placed on negative rate scenarios. The options-implied probability density function (PDF) places a weight close to 0.3 on negative rates, while the survey-based measure places a weight of just 0.01. This is a dramatic difference, as the options-implied distribution is putting an economically significant weight on the chance of negative rates. In contrast, the surveys indicate virtually no expectations for negative rates by the end of 2021.[11]

The difference could potentially be explained by the possibility of a large premium being placed on states of the world in which the Federal Reserve decides to cut rates into negative territory. These are likely to be very bad states of the world—e.g., a severe recession—in which a range of investible assets drop sharply in value. Consequently, investors may require a high risk premium to engage in a trade involving that potential outcome, which pushes up its risk-neutral probability. In addition, the federal funds futures options exhibit very low trading volume and open interest, which is another issue that surveys can avoid. In contrast, the average distribution arising from the SPD places nearly all of its weight on no rate changes through the end of the year, which is more consistent with expectations expressed in published commentary by market participants.

One can also see how the gap between survey-based expectations and expectations derived from asset prices have evolved over time. Below is a plot showing a six-month ahead forward rate derived from overnight index swap (OIS) rates minus the six-month-ahead survey-implied expectation of the federal funds rate from the Blue Chip (Fig. 13.14).

One can see that during the most recent rate hiking cycle, OIS rates were below the survey-implied rates for quite some time, which is consistent with a negative risk premium. It turned out that over this specific window (2015–2018), the survey forecasts came closer to the realized federal funds rate than the expectations based on OIS rates.[12]

13.4.2 Types of questions that are best answered by surveys

In some cases, market expectations easily lend themselves to observation through market prices, such as for outcomes for which a useful (though imperfect) proxy might exist. For example, expectations for inflation are an important component of the pricing of inflation swaps or inflation-protected securities, and expectations for a given jurisdiction's policy rate are largely reflected in its overnight indexed swaps (OIS) as well as various short-term interest rate derivatives markets, if available.

However, in many instances, expectations cannot be straightforwardly recovered from market prices because observable market prices do not bear a direct, one-to-one relationship with the outcome in question. For example, expectations for the issuance of government or corporate debt, or asset purchases by the monetary authority, are only part of the range of information embedded in market prices for these securities. Accordingly, it can be valuable to ask directly about outcomes such as policies related to asset purchases (Fig. 13.15).

In addition, surveys are a useful way to elicit respondents' judgments of "unobservable" quantities, such as a measure of the equilibrium policy rate (so-called r^*) (see Laubach and Williams (2003)) or

---

[11] Note that the federal funds rate options are for effective federal funds rate outcomes while the SPD elicits expectations for the midpoint of the target range.

[12] However, there is some evidence to suggest that OIS rates can at times forecast relatively well compared to surveys in other circumstances (see Diercks and Munir (2020)). This will be further discussed in the limitations of surveys section.

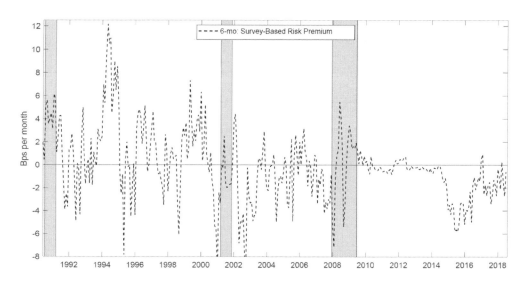

FIGURE 13.14 Six-Month-Ahead Survey-Based Risk Premium

Source: Bloomberg Finance LP; Wolters Kluwer Legal and Regulatory Solutions, U.S. Blue Chip Financial Forecasts. This plot shows the overnight index swap (OIS) rate minus the Blue Chip Financial Forecast consensus expectation of the federal funds rate 6 months ahead. The units are in basis points per month. The gray bars denote recessions as defined by NBER.

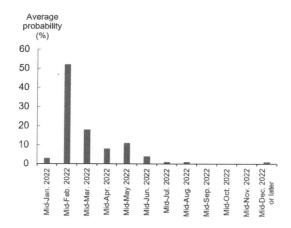

FIGURE 13.15 Expectations for the Timing of the End of Positive Net Purchases of Treasury Securities and Agency Mortgage-Backed Securities

Source: December 2021 FRBNY Survey of Primary Dealers. Question: "Please indicate the percent chance that you attach to each of the following monthly purchase periods beginning mid-month being the last period in which there are positive net purchases of Treasury securities and agency mortgage-backed securities."

3. Minutes from the Fed's Nov. 4-5 meeting indicated most FOMC members favored updating their guidance on asset purchases "fairly soon," and implementing "qualitative outcome-based guidance" that links the time horizon for purchases to economic conditions. When is the FOMC most likely to take such a step?

Response Count: 47	No. Responses	Percentage
Dec 16	26	55%
Jan. 27	9	19%
March 17	6	13%
April 28 or later	6	13%

4. New qualitative outcome-based guidance is most likely to link the time horizon for asset purchases to:

Response Count: 45	No. Responses	Percentage
Progress toward maximum employment	11	24%
Progress toward achieving average inflation of 2% over time	3	7%
Progress toward both employment and inflation goals	31	69%

FIGURE 13.16 Questions on Federal Reserve Asset Purchases in December 2020 Survey

Source: Bloomberg.

the equilibrium unemployment rate (u^*) (see Laubach (2001)).[13] These values can differ from model outputs, providing valuable information regarding where market views might differ from theoretical values.

Surveys are also particularly well suited to views regarding conceptual or causal relationships, as well as qualitative expectations for future events (which do not correspond to numerical outcomes). For example, surveys can ask respondents for their views on the drivers of changes in asset prices over a particular horizon, such as the relative importance of a range of different potential drivers of an increase or decrease in interest rates since a specific date. Similarly, surveys can elicit expectations for the content of certain events, such as communications around monetary policy meetings (Fig. 13.16).

Finally, surveys can be a useful way to gather normative (rather than descriptive) information from respondents; that is, to elicit views on whether a given past or hypothetical action is good or bad, or provide views on the best course of action in their view. For example, the SPD and SMP regularly ask respondents to rate the effectiveness of the Federal Reserve's communications with the markets and with the public (Fig. 13.17).

13.4.3 Surveys as model inputs

An important area where surveys have frequently been used as inputs is term structure models, which are often used by practitioners and policymakers to extract market expectations from asset prices.[14] Term structure models tend to rely on the historical time-series dynamics of interest rates to back out physical expectations (i.e., expectations that are not distorted by risk premiums). As pointed out in Wright (2017), this can lead to several econometric issues such as downward bias in persistence estimates due to the parameter uncertainty (i.e., flat likelihood) and small-sample bias (see Bauer et al. (2012) and Wright (2014)). To address these issues, Kim and Orphanides (2012) incorporate Blue Chip

---

[13] Joergensen and Meldrum (2019) compare survey-based measures of r^* to market-based measures.

[14] For additional discussion on extracting market expectations from asset prices, see Chapter 14 in this Handbook.

How would you grade the Federal Reserve System's communication with the markets and with the public since the last policy survey? Please provide a rating between 1 and 5, with 1 indicating ineffectiveness and 5 indicating effectiveness.

	Number of Respondents
1 - Ineffective	0
2	0
3	6
4	15
5 - Effective	3
# of Responses	24

FIGURE 13.17 Rating of Federal Reserve System Communication

Source: April 2021 FRBNY Survey of Primary Dealers.

surveys[15] along with measurement error and find greater success in generating sensible physical expectations. Chun (2011) similarly finds success incorporating Blue Chip forecasts as observable factors. Priebsch (2017) also includes Blue Chip forecasts while taking into account the effective lower bound.

In contrast to the studies above which combine information from surveys with historical dynamics of interest rates to construct expectations, some studies have computed risk premiums based solely on the gaps between expectations in surveys and forward rates.[16] Durham (2003), Peacock (2004), Gameiro (2006), Durham (2015) and Crump et al. (2018) have each taken this approach along with Piazzesi et al. (2009) and Buraschi et al. (2018), who refer to them as subjective bond risk premia (for additional discussion on survey-based risk premiums, see Chapter 17 in this Handbook). The common finding from these studies is that risk premiums based on this approach tend to be smaller, less volatile, and more acyclical than risk premiums computed from predictive regression-based measures using realized excess returns. Diercks et al. (2021) also compute survey-based risk premiums, but in contrast to the previous studies, they use probability-weighted means from the Survey of Primary Dealers and find this leads to better forecast performance relative to modal-based forecasts, consistent with economic theory.

An alternative approach to directly using the survey-forward rate gap is to extract relevant movements in the gap that are related to economic fundamentals. This approach is adopted by Diercks et al. (2021a) by model averaging over regressions of the survey-OIS gaps at various horizons onto covariances between real and nominal activity. This helps address some of the challenges associated with surveys that are highlighted in the following section and also leads to superior out-of-sample forecasting compared to surveys and OIS rates by themselves.

Other studies such as d'Amico et al. (2018) have used 10-year inflation forecasts from the Survey of Professional Forecasters to help decompose differences in nominal and TIPS yields into inflation expec-

---

[15] The model uses monthly data on the 6-month and 12-month-ahead forecasts of the 3-month Treasury bill yield and semiannual data on the average expected three-month Treasury bill yield from 6 to 11 years hence from Blue Chip Financial Forecasts.

[16] This approach requires no econometrics or historical dynamics of interest rates to form expectations.

tations and liquidity premiums.[17] Ang et al. (2007) also examine inflation forecasts and determine that survey-based measures provide better performance than models estimated with yields only. Likewise, Chernov and Mueller (2012) use survey-based forecasts of inflation to uncover a hidden factor in the nominal yield curve that helps improve forecasting of inflation and yields. In addition, Grishchenko et al. (2019) build a term structure model of surveys that takes raw survey forecasts as given and provides an estimated synthetic measure of inflation forecasts consistent with various surveys and horizons.

13.5 **Drawbacks of surveys**

Surveys are not without their limitations and sometimes there can be challenges associated with their interpretation. A large academic literature has been devoted to better understanding these issues and is the focus of the remainder of this chapter.[18]

13.5.1 **Distributional inconsistencies**

While market-based measures of expectations typically provide signal on mean-based expectations, the signal from surveys can be less clear, depending on the choice of question language. For instance, it is not clear whether respondents to certain surveys provide means or modes for their forecasts. In contrast, other surveys such as the SPD and SMP formally distinguish between questions associated with modal expectations and those that elicit subjective probabilities across a range of outcomes from which a probability-weighted mean can be derived. On that note, Potter et al. (2017) document that consensus modal forecasts have, at times, deviated from the associated probability-weighted means. This disparity becomes an issue any time there are notable upside or downside risks to the outlook. While the probability-weighted mean expectation should in theory be impacted by changes in risks to the outlook, expectations based on the modal outcome may be less likely to react. Alternatively, changes in modal outcomes may be less informative if the underlying distribution is flat or there is multimodality. For additional discussion on the merits of soliciting probability-weighted responses, see Chapter 1 in this Handbook.

Diercks et al. (2021) attempt to clarify whether respondents provide means or modes for their forecasts of the target range for the federal funds rate. They extract modal paths and probability-weighted means derived from the SPD and compare them to consensus forecasts from Blue Chip Financial Forecasts. In addition to finding economically significant quantities of skewness in these forecasts, they also find evidence suggesting that the Blue Chip survey responses line up with modal outcomes and not the probability-weighted means.

13.5.2 **Sample**

Another potential issue is that surveys may not come from a representative sample of market participants. Consensus beliefs (whether measured as the mean, median, etc.) coming from surveys are

---

[17] Alternatively, Abrahams et al. (2016) adjusts TIPS yields using an observable measure of liquidity and does not use surveys.
[18] We focus on drawbacks most relevant to the ways that policymakers are most likely to use survey data, though other challenges also exist.

representative of "true" market expectations only if they reflect the broader market population. Moreover, the consensus belief may also not coincide with the views of the marginal investor, which is key for the determination of asset prices. On that note, several studies argue that the marginal investor is unlikely to hold consensus beliefs. For instance, Hong et al. (2017) argue that optimistic investors (those expecting low inflation) will be the marginal investor in long-term bonds when there is large inflation disagreement and there are constraints on short-selling (which prevents pessimists who expect inflation to rise from participating). Likewise, Xiong and Yan (2010) argue that bond pricing is determined by investors' wealth-weighted average beliefs about future interest rates (not the consensus based on equal weights). This suggests the identity of the marginal investor will change as wealth shifts. It should also be acknowledged that in general, the specific individuals filling out the surveys are not necessarily the same individuals who are actively trading in financial markets.

13.5.3 Rationality and rigidities

Rationality of survey-based measures of expectations for interest rates has also been widely studied. Expectations coming from surveys are considered rational if their forecast errors are unbiased (mean of zero) and efficient (unpredictable) in the context of a symmetric quadratic loss function. Researchers care about this because assuming that agents exhibit rational expectations is the most common approach for macroeconomic simulations coming from dynamic stochastic general equilibrium models. Froot (1989), Ferrero and Nobili (2009), Bacchetta et al. (2009) and Cieslak (2018) each demonstrate inefficient forecast errors, showing that expectational errors for Treasury yields coming from surveys can be predicted with proxies of real activity. Other studies that have rejected notions of rationality for surveys include Friedman (1980), Jongen and Verschoor (2008), Chun (2012), and Miah et al. (2016).

Rigidities in surveys are also frequently noted by researchers. Placing an excessive weight on an easily observable prior value is known as an anchoring bias. This gives rise to predictable errors because of the underweighting of new information. Campbell and Sharpe (2009) emphasize anchoring bias in survey expectations of monthly macroeconomic data releases and find that bond yields are less susceptible to this bias. Nakazono (2012) finds evidence of anchoring in forecasting Japanese company stock prices while Tzu-Pu Chang and Chou (2018) find evidence in U.S. macroeconomic forecasts. Ichiue and Yuyama (2009) find that Blue Chip consensus forecasts of the U.S. federal funds rate are significantly anchored by one- and two-quarters-behind consensus forecasts. Likewise, Gallo et al. (2002) find that forecasters place a significant weight on the previous period's consensus forecast when updating their individual forecast.

13.5.4 Forecast/revision smoothing

The literature has also found evidence of a departure from rational expectations through forecast/revision smoothing in surveys. Nordhaus (1987) posits that forecasters smooth their estimates because a more accurate but erratic forecast would irritate investors who would have to reverse decisions about investment plans too often. He finds evidence of serial correlation of forecast revisions, meaning that current forecast revisions are anchored by previous forecast revisions. Isiklar et al. (2006) find additional evidence of inefficiency (i.e., predictability) in forecast revisions of real GDP growth across 18 countries.

Scotese (1994) argues a similar point, in that if a forecast is subject to large and frequent revisions, it becomes difficult to rely on a current forecast for future actions. For example, the end-user may fear today's forecast for positive growth could be revised next period to predict a modest downturn, which inhibits planning. She finds evidence of smoothing or underutilization of current information in Federal Reserve staff forecasts of economic growth and inflation. Tillmann (2011) also documents evidence of forecast revision smoothing for individual FOMC members.

From a more theoretical perspective, Ehrbeck and Waldmann (1996) develop a model to show that less-able professional forecasters would rationally choose to change their forecasts by smaller amounts than the changes in their beliefs, since able forecasters do not have to change their forecasts by large amounts as their forecasts are relatively accurate. Peterson (2001) finds evidence of this "rational stubbornness" in Blue Chip surveys for shorter maturities that have relatively higher yield volatility. Deschamps and Ioannidis (2013) confirm similar results across a panel of G7 countries as professional forecasters, on average, underreact to new information. Kirchgässner and Müller (2006) examine surveys of forecasts for Germany's economy and suggest revisions of past forecasts are costly as people may be reluctant to admit mistakes.

Batchelor and Dua (1992), based on Blue Chip surveys, also posit that demand for economic forecasts may be related to factors other than accuracy. Users may mistrust forecasts that are very different from the consensus or forecasts that frequently change. Profit-maximizing forecasters therefore will have to trade off expected accuracy against stability and credibility. The study finds evidence of "conservatism," in which Blue Chip panel members could improve their forecasts if they put less weight on their past forecasts in making revisions regarding short-term interest rates. Jain (2014, 2018) also finds evidence of "conservativism" for U.S. inflation forecasts and in the Survey of Professional Forecasters.[19] Other studies such as Lamont (2002) find that the behavior of forecasters who establish their own firm changes dramatically and they begin to produce bolder forecasts that turn out to be less accurate. Likewise Laster et al. (1999) develop a model in which forecasters' wages are based on their accuracy and ability to generate publicity for their firms, which could lead to extreme forecasts.

Lastly, timing differences and other disparities can make comparisons across surveys difficult. Surveys are only updated relatively infrequently and can become stale almost immediately after publication, making the predictions less able to take into account the most up-to-date information.[20] A clear example for this involved the situation surrounding the 2020 global pandemic, in which forecasts taken at a specific point in time quickly became outdated amid fast-moving developments.

13.6 Conclusion

This chapter has provided an overview of expectational surveys of financial market participants conducted by the official sector and private organizations relating to economic and financial indicators. Surveys can provide a standardized, periodic signal from a predetermined set of informed respondents on a range of forecast variables and other views of interest, and they are often a key input into a range of

---

[19] Underreaction to new information is also documented in Coibion and Gorodnichenko (2015) and Bordalo et al. (2018), both in the consensus forecast and individual forecasts for various interest rates using Blue Chip surveys. Dovern et al. (2015) expand this analysis to 36 countries and finds the degree of information rigidity in average forecasts is substantially higher than in individual forecasts.

[20] Of course, there are many economic variables which are less volatile and updated infrequently (e.g., GDP, inflation) so staleness is less of a concern.

economic choices such as investment decisions as well as policy actions by fiscal and monetary authorities. Surveys are a useful complement to other sources of information, such as anecdotal views from market participants as well as market-based measures; they can confirm anecdotal views in a more systematic way, and can provide helpful clues about market risk premiums. Practitioners and researchers may benefit from exploring the universe of available surveys and identifying those with useful properties for their aims. Surveys of market participants will continue to evolve over time in response to economic and financial conditions as well as the needs of their audience. For example, the content of surveys is likely to reflect the rise of new asset classes over time, and the link between various economic or policy outcomes and market reactions could be explored further.

However, surveys are not without drawbacks; users of surveys should bear in mind that survey data are potentially subject to various sample and behavioral biases that (to varying degrees) may limit their ability to elicit the true expectations of the market or even of the survey respondents. Nevertheless, surveys are a useful and widely-used tool to gain insight into otherwise-opaque expectations and beliefs about the future.

References

Abrahams, M., Adrian, T., Crump, R.K., Moench, E., Yu, R., 2016. Decomposing real and nominal yield curves. Journal of Monetary Economics 84, 182–200.

Ang, A., Bekaert, G., Wei, M., 2007. Do macro variables, asset markets, or surveys forecast inflation better? Journal of Monetary Economics 54 (4), 1163–1212.

Bacchetta, P., Mertens, E., Van Wincoop, E., 2009. Predictability in financial markets: what do survey expectations tell us? Journal of International Money and Finance 28 (3), 406–426.

Batchelor, R., Dua, P., 1992. Conservatism and consensus-seeking among economic forecasters. Journal of Forecasting 11 (2), 169–181.

Bauer, A., Eisenbeis, R.A., Waggoner, D.F., Zha, T., 2003. Forecast evaluation with cross-sectional data: the blue chip surveys. Economic Review (Atlanta, Ga.) 88 (2), 17–33.

Bauer, M.D., Rudebusch, G.D., Wu, J.C., 2012. Correcting estimation bias in dynamic term structure models. Journal of Business & Economic Statistics 30 (3), 454–467.

Bordalo, P., Gennaioli, N., Shleifer, A., 2018. Diagnostic expectations and credit cycles. The Journal of Finance 73 (1), 199–227.

Buraschi, A., Piatti, I., Whelan, P., 2018. Rationality and subjective bond risk premia. Said Business School Research Papers 36.

Campbell, J.Y., Shiller, R.J., 1991. Yield spreads and interest rate movements: a bird's eye view. The Review of Economic Studies 58 (3), 495–514.

Campbell, S.D., Sharpe, S.A., 2009. Anchoring bias in consensus forecasts and its effect on market prices. Journal of Financial and Quantitative Analysis 44 (2), 369–390.

Chernov, M., Mueller, P., 2012. The term structure of inflation expectations. Journal of Financial Economics 106 (2), 367–394.

Chun, A.L., 2011. Expectations, bond yields, and monetary policy. The Review of Financial Studies 24 (1), 208–247.

Chun, A.L., 2012. Forecasting interest rates and inflation: blue chip clairvoyants or econometrics? In: EFA 2009 Bergen Meetings Paper.

Cieslak, A., 2018. Short-rate expectations and unexpected returns in treasury bonds. The Review of Financial Studies 31 (9), 3265–3306.

Coibion, O., Gorodnichenko, Y., 2015. Information rigidity and the expectations formation process: a simple framework and new facts. The American Economic Review 105 (8), 2644–2678.

Correia-Golay, E., Friedman, S., McMorrow, M., 2013. Understanding the New York Fed's Survey of Primary Dealers. Current Issues in Economics and Finance 19 (6).

Crump, R.K., Eusepi, S., Moench, E., 2018. The term structure of expectations and bond yields.

d'Amico, S., Kim, D.H., Wei, M., 2018. Tips from TIPS: the informational content of Treasury Inflation-Protected Security prices. Journal of Financial and Quantitative Analysis 53 (1), 395–436.

Deschamps, B., Ioannidis, C., 2013. Can rational stubbornness explain forecast biases? Journal of Economic Behavior & Organization 92, 141–151.

Diercks, A.M., Munir, I., 2020. Conflicting Signals: Implications of Divergence in Surveys and Market-Based Measures of Policy Expectations. Discussion paper. Board of Governors of the Federal Reserve System (US).

Diercks, A.M., Munir, I., Carl, U., 2021a. A Macro-Finance Risk-Adjustment to Near-term Policy Expectations. FEDS Working Paper.

Diercks, A.M., Tanaka, H., Cordova, P., 2021. Asymmetric Monetary Policy Expectations. Available at SSRN 3930267.

Dovern, J., Fritsche, U., Loungani, P., Tamirisa, N., 2015. Information rigidities: comparing average and individual forecasts for a large international panel. International Journal of Forecasting 31 (1), 144–154.

Durham, J.B., 2003. Estimates of the term premium on near-dated federal funds futures contracts. Available at SSRN 419703.

Durham, J.B., 2015. Another view on US Treasury term premiums. The Journal of Fixed Income 24 (4), 5–21.

Ehrbeck, T., Waldmann, R., 1996. Why are professional forecasters biased? Agency versus behavioral explanations. The Quarterly Journal of Economics 111 (1), 21–40.

Fama, E.F., Bliss, R.R., 1987. The information in long-maturity forward rates. The American Economic Review 77 (4), 680–692.

Ferrero, G., Nobili, A., 2009. Futures contract rates as monetary policy forecasts. International Journal of Central Banking.

Friedman, B.M., 1980. Survey evidence on the 'rationality' of interest rate expectations. Journal of Monetary Economics 6 (4), 453–465.

Froot, K.A., 1989. New hope for the expectations hypothesis of the term structure of interest rates. The Journal of Finance 44 (2), 283–305.

Gallo, G.M., Granger, C.W., Jeon, Y., 2002. Copycats and common swings: the impact of the use of forecasts in information sets. IMF Economic Review 49 (1), 4.

Gameiro, I., 2006. Estimating Forward Premia of Short-Term Interest Rates Based on Survey Results. Economic Bulletin and Financial Stability Report Articles and Banco de Portugal Economic Studies.

Grishchenko, O., Mouabbi, S., Renne, J.-P., 2019. Measuring inflation anchoring and uncertainty: a US and euro area comparison. Journal of Money, Credit, and Banking 51 (5), 1053–1096.

Hong, H., Sraer, D., Yu, J., 2017. Inflation bets on the long bond. The Review of Financial Studies 30 (3), 900–947.

Ichiue, H., Yuyama, T., 2009. Using survey data to correct the bias in policy expectations extracted from fed funds futures. Journal of Money, Credit, and Banking 41 (8), 1631–1647.

Isiklar, G., Lahiri, K., Loungani, P., 2006. How quickly do forecasters incorporate news? Evidence from cross-country surveys. Journal of Applied Econometrics 21 (6), 703–725.

Jain, M., 2014. Conservatism in inflation forecasts. Manuscript of the Bank of Canada.

Jain, M., 2018. Sluggish forecasts. Discussion paper, Bank of Canada Staff Working Paper.

Joergensen, K., Meldrum, A., 2019. Expectations about the Federal Funds Rate in the Long Run. FEDS Notes 2019 (10), 09.

Jongen, R., Verschoor, W.F., 2008. Further evidence on the rationality of interest rate expectations. Journal of International Financial Markets, Institutions & Money 18 (5), 438–448.

Kim, D.H., Orphanides, A., 2012. Term structure estimation with survey data on interest rate forecasts. Journal of Financial and Quantitative Analysis 47 (1), 241–272.

Kirchgässner, G., Müller, U.K., 2006. Are forecasters reluctant to revise their predictions? Some German evidence. Journal of Forecasting 25 (6), 401–413.

Lamont, O.A., 2002. Macroeconomic forecasts and microeconomic forecasters. Journal of Economic Behavior & Organization 48 (3), 265–280.

Laster, D., Bennett, P., Geoum, I.S., 1999. Rational bias in macroeconomic forecasts. The Quarterly Journal of Economics 114 (1), 293–318.

Laubach, T., 2001. Measuring the NAIRU: evidence from seven economies. Review of Economics and Statistics 83 (2), 218–231.

Laubach, T., Williams, J.C., 2003. Measuring the natural rate of interest. Review of Economics and Statistics 85 (4), 1063–1070.

Miah, F., Rahman, M.S., Albinali, K., 2016. Rationality of survey based inflation expectations: a study of 18 emerging economies' inflation forecasts. Research in International Business and Finance 36, 158–166.

Nakazono, Y., 2012. Heterogeneity and anchoring in financial markets. Applied Financial Economics 22 (21), 1821–1826.

Nordhaus, W.D., 1987. Forecasting efficiency: concepts and applications. Review of Economics and Statistics, 667–674.

Peacock, C., 2004. Deriving a market-based measure of interest rate expectations. Bank of England Quarterly Bulletin, Summer.

Peterson, S.P., 2001. Rational bias in yield curve forecasts. Review of Economics and Statistics 83 (3), 457–464.

Piazzesi, M., Schneider, M., et al., 2009. Trend and Cycle in Bond Premia, vol. 424. Citeseer.

Potter, S., Del Negro, M., Topa, G., van der Klaauw, W., 2017. The advantages of probabilistic survey questions. Review of Economic Analysis 9 (1), 1–32.

Priebsch, M.A., 2017. A shadow rate model of intermediate-term policy rate expectations. Discussion paper. Board of Governors of the Federal Reserve System (US).

Scotese, C.A., 1994. Forecast smoothing and the optimal under-utilization of information at the Federal Reserve. Journal of Macroeconomics 16 (4), 653–670.

Tillmann, P., 2011. Reputation and forecast revisions: Evidence from the FOMC. Discussion paper, MAGKS Joint Discussion Paper Series in Economics.

Tzu-Pu Chang, R.Y.C., Chou, R.Y., 2018. Anchoring effect on macroeconomic forecasts: a heterogeneity approach. Journal for Economic Forecasting 4, 134–147.

Wright, J.H., 2014. Term premia and inflation uncertainty: empirical evidence from an international panel dataset: reply. The American Economic Review 104 (1), 338–341.

Wright, J.H., 2017. Forward-looking estimates of interest-rate distributions. Annual Review of Financial Economics 9, 333–351.

Xiong, W., Yan, H., 2010. Heterogeneous expectations and bond markets. The Review of Financial Studies 23 (4), 1433–1466.

Expectations and economic theory

Measuring market expectations[☆]

Christiane Baumeister[a,b,c,d]

[a]*University of Notre Dame, Notre Dame, IN, United States*
[b]*University of Pretoria, Pretoria, South Africa*
[c]*NBER, Cambridge, MA, United States*
[d]*CEPR, London, United Kingdom*

14.1 Introduction

Expectations about future economic outcomes play a key role in decision-making under uncertainty and form a building block for a wide range of forward-looking models in macroeconomics and finance. For example, expectations about future inflation will influence the price- and wage-setting behavior of firms and the consumption and storage decisions of households. Similarly, expectations about commodity price developments will affect production and investment plans as well as economic policy interventions.

A popular way to obtain measures of people's expectations is to use surveys of the public or economic forecasters; however, they are often conducted at relatively low frequencies or on an ad-hoc basis and offer only a limited range of forecast horizons. It is also not always clear whether stated beliefs by survey participants lead to actions in accordance with their stated beliefs. A valuable alternative is to use market prices of assets traded in financial and futures markets to infer investor's expectations of future macroeconomic outcomes such as inflation, monetary policy, and commodity prices. The market population tends to be composed of households, firms, professional forecasters, and institutional investors, among others, which makes market-based expectations an inclusive measure of different groups of economic agents. Even agents who do not actively trade in financial markets often turn to asset prices to see "what the market thinks" when forming their own expectations. In that sense the market is often perceived to convey the collective wisdom of people willing to put money on their beliefs about different aspects of the economy. This chapter surveys the literature on extracting market expectations from asset prices and summarizes existing empirical methods.

Section 14.2 reviews the asset pricing theory that forms the basis for the empirical analysis. In particular, it highlights the problem that financial instruments not only incorporate the rational expectation of market participants but also a compensation for undiversifiable risk. I revisit empirical efforts to uncover the presence of time-varying risk premia and provide an overview of modeling techniques

[☆] I am grateful to Anthony Diercks, Jim Hamilton, Emanuel Moench, Stefan Nagel, and the editors, Rüdiger Bachmann, Wilbert van der Klaauw, and Giorgio Topa for helpful suggestions. Additional material to this chapter is provided in an online appendix at https://sites.google.com/site/cjsbaumeister/research.

Handbook of Economic Expectations. https://doi.org/10.1016/B978-0-12-822927-9.00022-7

used to separate out risk factors from the expectation component considering two classes of models for estimating time-varying risk premia, return regressions and Gaussian affine term structure models.

Section 14.3 addresses the question of which information set should be used for estimating the risk premium and introduces a general approach that allows to discriminate among different estimates. Using the oil futures market for illustration, I document the substantial disagreement on the magnitude and sign of the time-varying risk premium across predictor variables and discuss a methodology to identify the optimal estimate of the risk premium that allows to construct a unique and reliable measure of market expectations which can be used as input in economic decision problems. Specifically, I show how standard forecasting tools can be applied to obtain the most credible estimate of the market price of risk and thus the implied market expectation.

Section 14.4 focuses on the universe of financial instruments that are useful for obtaining monetary policy expectations and inflation expectations. It discusses the difficulties that certain institutional features and trading frictions entail in accurately measuring these expectations.

Section 14.5 presents a number of economic applications where market-based expectation measures have been used to address important policy questions. I provide a retrospective analysis of the oil market that ties the selected price expectation measure to historical events and changes in economic conditions to externally validate this market-based measure. I then consider a variety of contexts in which market expectations can be used as inputs for empirical exercises and theoretical models to test hypotheses, model decision problems, and inform policymakers. In discussing these various applications, I offer some suggestions for promising directions for future research.

Section 14.6 briefly concludes.

14.2 Market expectations and the price of risk

It is common practice for central banks, international organizations, the private sector, and the financial press to treat the prices of futures, forwards, and other financial instruments as measures of market expectations. For example, Bernanke (2008) stresses that "policymakers and other analysts have often relied on quotes from commodity futures markets to derive forecasts of the prices of key commodities." This practice finds its origin in the notion that the price of a futures contract F_t^h with maturity h purchased at time t equals the expected value of the spot price S at expiry: $F_t^h = E_t(S_{t+h})$ where E_t denotes the expectations operator conditional on information available at time t. Thus, under the expectations hypothesis, the expected payoff of holding a futures contract until maturity is zero since, in efficient and rational financial markets, it is impossible to devise a trading strategy based on all relevant information that leads to making economic profits. This is equivalent to postulating that the prices of futures or forward contracts are unbiased predictors of future spot prices.

14.2.1 Testable implications

This proposition can be tested using forecast efficiency regressions of the form

$$\frac{(S_{t+h} - S_t)}{S_t} = \alpha + \beta \frac{(F_t^h - S_t)}{S_t} + \varepsilon_{t+h} \tag{14.1}$$

where the dependent variable is the realized percent change in the spot price between t and $t + h$, the independent variable is the current futures–spot spread expressed in percent changes, and ε_{t+h} denotes the error term.[1] If futures prices are rational expectations of the future spot price, then we would expect the joint hypothesis $H_0 : \alpha = 0, \beta = 1$ to hold. There are several other hypotheses of interest that can be tested based on these regressions. The null that the slope coefficient $\beta = 1$ implies that the futures price is an unbiased predictor of the future spot price, whereas the null that $\beta = 0$ implies that the futures–spot spread has no predictive content for future price changes. Deviations from the null of $\alpha = 0$ indicate that forecast errors contain a systematic component on average. The joint hypothesis $\alpha = 0$ and $\beta = 0$ means that any price changes are unpredictable.

We can test the validity of these hypotheses using commodity futures prices for a set of energy products and base metals with maturities $h = 3$ and 12 months. I use futures prices on maturing contracts to measure spot prices as in Dusak (1973), Fama and French (1987), Hamilton (1992), and Chinn and Coibion (2014). Futures prices are sampled on the last trading day of month t.[2]

The coefficients $\widehat{\alpha}$ and $\widehat{\beta}$ from estimating Eq. (14.1) by OLS are summarized in Table 14.1 together with the p-values associated with the various hypotheses. I also report the R^2 to gauge the explanatory power of the futures–spot spread for the variation of future price changes.

For the energy commodities, the slope coefficients are all positive and statistically different from zero which indicates that there is useful information in the slope of the futures curve. While the slope coefficients are all less than 1 except for gasoline, we cannot reject the null that the futures price is an unbiased predictor of the future spot price. The joint hypothesis of no predictability is decisively rejected for all energy products. Among the base metals, copper, lead, and tin yield negative slope coefficients which are statistically indistinguishable from zero, while the slope coefficients for zinc are well above 1. What is noteworthy is that even though we fail to reject the hypothesis that $\beta = 1$ for most metals, the point estimates are actually quite far from one in most cases, suggesting that future price changes do vary with the futures–spot spread. There is no statistical evidence of predictability of future price changes except for zinc where we can reject the joint hypothesis that $\alpha = 0$ and $\beta = 0$. The joint hypothesis of market efficiency is rejected for seven out of the ten commodities and there is overwhelming evidence for a predictable component in energy and zinc futures. The futures–spot price differential only explains a small proportion of subsequent price changes for most commodities, in particular for base metals.

This evidence is in line with previous findings in other contexts where the unbiased expectations hypothesis has also been consistently rejected. For evidence on forward interest rates, refer to Fama and Bliss (1987), Froot (1989), Campbell and Shiller (1991), Chernenko et al. (2004), Cochrane and Piazzesi (2005), Ludvigson and Ng (2009), and Gürkaynak and Wright (2012); for federal funds futures, to Sack (2004), Piazzesi and Swanson (2008), Ferrero and Nobili (2009), Hamilton (2009), and Hamilton and Okimoto (2011); for foreign exchange, to Hansen and Hodrick (1980), Fama (1984), Korajczyk (1985), Froot and Frankel (1989), Bekaert and Hodrick (1993), and Chernenko et al. (2004);

---

[1] Much of the literature on forecast efficiency regressions uses log changes which are a good approximation if price changes are relatively small. However, some of the commodity prices considered in the empirical analysis below exhibit large fluctuations which makes the use of percent changes more appropriate.

[2] Table 1A in the online appendix provides details on the commodity- and horizon-specific start dates, the exchange where each commodity is traded, and the futures ticker used by Bloomberg.

Table 14.1 Forecast Efficiency Regressions.

Monthly horizon	$\hat{\alpha}$	$\hat{\beta}$	$H_0 : \beta = 1$	$H_0 : \alpha = 0, \beta = 0$	$H_0 : \alpha = 0, \beta = 1$	Adj R^2
Panel A: Energy Products						
WTI crude oil						
3	0.017*	0.838***	0.570	0.010	0.087	0.023
12	0.094**	0.808**	0.560	0.005	0.068	0.067
Brent crude oil						
3	0.020*	0.743**	0.458	0.054	0.037	0.012
12	0.117**	0.800*	0.625	0.034	0.049	0.049
Gasoline						
3	0.034***	1.184***	0.193	0.000	0.001	0.221
12	0.140***	1.343***	0.198	0.000	0.014	0.178
Heating oil						
3	0.020**	0.800***	0.198	0.000	0.010	0.061
12	0.092**	0.977***	0.943	0.002	0.136	0.094
Natural gas						
3	−0.006	0.984***	0.877	0.000	0.864	0.207
12	0.033	0.738***	0.166	0.000	0.374	0.103
Panel B: Base Metals						
Copper						
3	0.015	−0.377	0.025	0.322	0.050	−0.029
12	0.085*	−1.202	0.122	0.206	0.099	−0.037
Lead						
3	0.016*	−0.602	0.002	0.173	0.005	−0.004
12	0.118**	−0.951	0.027	0.141	0.049	0.010
Nickel						
3	0.014	0.059	0.292	0.508	0.317	−0.017
12	0.141*	0.889	0.912	0.215	0.222	−0.088
Tin						
3	0.015*	0.270	0.345	0.199	0.172	−0.007
12	0.094	−0.911	0.224	0.129	0.045	−0.002
Zinc						
3	−0.002	1.750**	0.370	0.056	0.620	0.020
12	0.077	1.284	0.823	0.053	0.332	−0.029

NOTES: One, two, and three asterisks indicate whether α and β are significantly different from zero at the 10%, 5%, and 1% levels, respectively. All t-tests and Wald tests have been computed based on Newey–West heteroskedasticity- and autocorrelation-consistent (HAC) standard errors with lag truncation parameter set equal to the number of overlapping observations. For the three null hypotheses, we report asymptotic p-values; Adj R^2 stands for adjusted R^2. The end date is 2018.12 and is common across all specifications. The start date is specific to the commodity and the horizon (see Table 1A in the online appendix).

and for agricultural commodities and precious metals, to Fama and French (1987, 1988) and Chinn and Coibion (2014), among others.

14.2.2 Some asset pricing basics

The theoretical justification for unbiased expectations is the presumption that risk-neutral market participants price any asset only based on the expected payoff without factoring in the uncertainty related to the randomness of the outcome and that any nonzero expected profits are arbitraged away. This assumption does not seem to hold in the data according to the results presented above.

One possible explanation is that financial market participants are risk averse. Chernenko et al. (2004) discuss several other potential explanations such as rational learning behavior, irrational expectations, and "peso problems," but conclude that risk aversion is the most plausible one. Adam and Nagel (see Chapter 16 in this Handbook) make the case that expectational errors contribute substantially to excess return predictability and call for moving away from rational expectations which is the conventional paradigm in asset pricing models. The idea is to allow for subjective beliefs of investors by drawing on direct survey evidence to discipline expectations. The existing evidence for the role of expectational errors hinges on the premise that survey data accurately measure the market's unobserved expectation (Froot, 1989). This assumption might not hold.[3] For example, Bianchi et al. (2022) show that time-varying systematic expectational errors are a pervasive feature of surveys and that these belief distortions apply to survey respondents of all types including professional forecasters, corporate executives, and households.

Also in the case of risk aversion, the pricing of assets has to ensure the absence of profitable arbitrage opportunities which implies that there exists a strictly positive random variable M_{t+h} called the stochastic discount factor or pricing kernel that prices any asset at time $t < t + h$ with a stochastic payoff X_{t+h} at time $t + h$ accounting for variations in economic risk. For example, let $S_{t+h} - F_t^h$ be the random payoff of taking a long position in a forward or futures contract at time t for delivery h periods later and S_{t+h} the realized price at time $t + h$ for immediate delivery of the asset, then the equilibrium pricing condition is given by

$$E_t(M_{t+h}(S_{t+h} - F_t^h)) = 0 \qquad (14.2)$$

where E_t denotes the expectations operator conditional on time-t information. Solving for the forward or futures price F_t^h results in

$$F_t^h = \frac{E_t(M_{t+h}S_{t+h})}{E_t(M_{t+h})} = \frac{E_t(M_{t+h})E_t(S_{t+h}) + cov_t(M_{t+h}S_{t+h})}{E_t(M_{t+h})} = E_t(S_{t+h}) + \frac{cov_t(M_{t+h}S_{t+h})}{E_t(M_{t+h})},$$
$$(14.3)$$

which shows that under risk aversion the observed futures price equals the conditional expectation of the future spot price plus a risk premium that investors demand as compensation for taking on risky positions. This means that the evidence on predictability in future price changes and the rejection of forecast efficiency documented in Table 14.1 is consistent with the existence of risk premia that arise from the exposure to nondiversifiable systematic risk factors. Time variation in risk premia can be explained by changes in both the risks and the investors' willingness to bear those risks over time.[4]

---

[3] Other complications are how to aggregate survey expectations given that different survey respondents have different beliefs and how to ensure that surveys are representative of the population who is actively trading in financial markets (see also Chapter 13 in this Handbook).

[4] Söderlind and Svensson (1997) provide an illustration of what determines econometrically whether the slope coefficient β in Eq. (14.1) is different from unity (see online appendix A).

This discussion highlights that testing for market efficiency or unbiasedness only makes sense in conjunction with specifying an asset pricing model which in the case of Eq. (14.3) amounts to postulating an economic model for the risk premium.[5] The decomposition in Eq. (14.3) makes it clear that if we had a direct measure of the risk premium or knew the process generating it, we could adjust the futures price and use it to infer the market's expected price. In fact, Dai and Singleton (2002) show that projections of risk-adjusted returns on the slope of the term structure of interest rates yields a β coefficient of unity, but only if the asset pricing model accurately captures the dynamic behavior of risk premia. This begs the question of how best to model risk premia.

14.2.3 Modeling risk premia

One of the key questions in empirical finance is what determines the risk premium and how to estimate it. There are two broad classes of models that have been developed for this purpose. The first class is return regressions which relate the ex-post risk premium to a set of observable factors that capture the investors' risk tolerance. The second class is dynamic term structure models that ensure the absence of arbitrage by imposing cross-equation restrictions and allow us to obtain an estimate of the risk premium based on the structural parameters of the model. I introduce both model frameworks, provide an illustration of their basic features, and show how they are related.

14.2.3.1 Return regressions

This approach models the realized payoff or excess return as a linear function of possibly multiple, observable proxies for risk factors. For example, the final payoff on a long position in an h-period futures contract entered into at time t at rate F_t^h can be measured at the time of expiry $t + h$ as $(S_{t+h} - F_t^h)$ with the spot price S_{t+h} again being represented by the maturing contract F_{t+h-1}^1 and changes expressed in percentage terms,

$$\frac{F_{t+h-1}^1 - F_t^h}{F_t^h} = a_h + \sum_{k=1}^{K} b_{k,h} \, X_{k,t} + \epsilon_{t+h}, \tag{14.4}$$

where a_h and b_h are horizon-specific regression coefficients, $\mathbf{X}_t$ is a vector containing up to K predictor variables available to market participants at time t, and ϵ_{t+h} is a mean-zero prediction error. The fitted value from this regression is an estimate of the time-varying risk premium.

In theory, in the absence of trading frictions or liquidity factors, there should exist a single stochastic discount factor M_{t+h} that characterizes the risk premium in every financial asset as in (14.2). The theoretical value of M_{t+h} is a function of a postulated state vector that determines everything that could possibly happen in all aspects of the economy. In practice, for a particular class of assets, researchers focus on a small subset of variables thought to be most important in that market. Several risk factors are considered common across asset classes, while others are asset-specific and vary across markets and financial instruments.

A standard common factor derived from the capital asset pricing model is the overall return of the market portfolio, which is often measured by the CRSP value-weighted equity index (Bessembinder,

---

[5] See Timmermann and Granger (2004) and Fama (2014) for a discussion of the joint hypothesis problem.

1992) or the S&P 500 stock price index (De Roon et al., 2000). Another common factor is a measure of the overall level of economic activity (Campbell and Cochrane, 1999; Ferson and Harvey, 1991). Popular proxies for cyclical risk factors are employment growth (Piazzesi and Swanson, 2008), unexpected changes in industrial production (Bessembinder, 1992), the degree of capacity utilization in manufacturing (Pagano and Pisani, 2009), and indicators of U.S. real activity and global economic conditions (Hong and Yogo, 2012; Pagano and Pisani, 2009; Baumeister et al., 2022), among others. Unexpected inflation is also considered a source of economic risk to the extent that inflation has real effects (Bessembinder, 1992). Financial indicators of the business cycle such as interest rates and yield spreads are also often used (Hong and Yogo, 2012; Pagano and Pisani, 2009; Piazzesi and Swanson, 2008), along with corporate bond spreads that measure changes in the default risk (Bessembinder and Chan, 1992; Piazzesi and Swanson, 2008) and measures of stock market volatility that proxy for economic uncertainty (Casiraghi and Miccoli, 2019).

In commodity futures markets, one of the most widely used predictor variables is the slope of the futures curve (Fama and French, 1987). In bond markets, the analogous measure is the spread between long-term and short-term yields (Campbell and Shiller, 1991).[6] Asset-specific risks often arise from the different types of traders who participate in a market such as commodity producers (e.g., farmers, oil producers, miners), primary buyers (e.g., the food industry, airline companies, steel producers), and investor clienteles (e.g., exchange-traded funds, hedge funds, pension funds). Empirical measures to capture risk pricing include the relative size of positions taken by traders with commercial and noncommerical interests (De Roon et al., 2000; Piazzesi and Swanson, 2008; Hamilton and Wu, 2015), overall trading activity (Hong and Yogo, 2012), and risk-bearing capacity (Adrian and Shin, 2010; Acharya et al., 2013; Etula, 2013). Another market-specific friction for which investors demand compensation is liquidity risk. Proxies for market liquidity include relative transaction volume (Bessembinder and Seguin, 1993; Gürkaynak et al., 2010b; Pflueger and Viceira, 2016) and asset–swap spreads to infer financing costs (Pflueger and Viceira, 2016). A fundamental determinant of risk for financial instruments that reference storable commodities such as oil, gasoline, and industrial metals, are inventory levels and dynamics motivated by the convenience yield implicit in the theory of storage (Acharya et al., 2013; Gorton et al., 2013; Pindyck, 2001).

This provides an illustration of the type of risk factors that have been proposed in the literature and their corresponding empirical measures. These risk factors are not all equally successful at predicting returns. I explore the usefulness of a subset of these risk factors for modeling risk premia in oil futures markets in Section 14.3.

14.2.3.2 *Gaussian affine term structure models*

The idea underlying this class of models is that a small set of m latent or observed factors x_t jointly determine all asset prices in the economy in an internally-consistent way whose dynamics can be described as a Gaussian first-order vector autoregression (VAR)

$$x_{t+1} = c + \rho x_t + \Sigma u_{t+1}, \quad u_{t+1} \sim N(0, I_m). \tag{14.5}$$

---

[6] Return regressions with the slope of the futures or yield curve as the only predictor are often treated as a separate class of models referred to as "basis regressions."

Since all assets are priced in the same way, we can focus on a single asset class without loss of generality to illustrate the basic principles underlying this modeling framework.[7] For example, log oil futures prices $f_t^h \equiv \ln F_t^h$ for a contract entered into at time t that matures h periods later are assumed to be affine functions of these factors in the following way:

$$f_t^h = \alpha_h + \beta_h' x_t, \qquad (14.6)$$

with the factor loadings given by

$$\alpha_h = \alpha_{h-1} + \beta_{h-1}'(c - \lambda) + \frac{1}{2}\beta_{h-1}' \Sigma \Sigma' \beta_{h-1}, \qquad (14.7)$$

$$\beta_h' = \beta_{h-1}'(\rho - \Lambda), \qquad (14.8)$$

where $\lambda_t = \lambda + \Lambda x_t$ are the market prices of risk that summarize the investor's attitudes toward risk and are also affine functions of the fundamental factors x_t that make them vary over time. These expressions are derived from the first-order condition of an investor who cares about the mean and variance of his portfolio.[8] The recursions implied by Eqs. (14.7) and (14.8) have to hold for every h and are the cornerstone of all affine term structure models since they allow pricing all the assets in the economy ruling out arbitrage possibilities (see, e.g., Piazzesi, 2010; Gürkaynak and Wright, 2012). Specifically, the restriction that the cross-sectional factor loadings are functions of the parameters describing the state dynamics ensures dynamic consistency.

If investors were risk neutral, the same recursions would still apply and assets would still be priced according to (14.6) but under a modified law of motion for the factors,

$$x_{t+1} = c^Q + \rho^Q x_t + \Sigma u_{t+1}^Q, \quad u_{t+1}^Q \sim N(0, I_m),$$

where the adjustments $c^Q = c - \lambda$ and $\rho^Q = \rho - \Lambda$ result from risk aversion. This means that in a risky environment investors behave as if the asset offers a lower expected payoff than it effectively does. What the pricing kernel M_{t+1} does is describe the mapping between the true data-generating process, also known as the P-measure, and the risk-neutral distribution, also known as the Q-measure.[9] Intuitively, the pricing kernel reweights the objective probabilities implied by the true distribution such that some outcomes have a higher probability than they objectively do which implies that investors require some compensation in that state of the world. Time-varying risk premia are then obtained as the difference between observed futures prices and the rational expectation of futures prices implied by the estimated term structure model when setting $\lambda = \Lambda = 0$.

---

[7] The majority of papers in this literature study one asset or market at the time. Exceptions are, for example, Hamilton and Wu (2014) who consider an arbitrageur who takes positions in a range of different assets, and Christensen et al. (2010) and D'Amico et al. (2018) who jointly model investments in real and nominal bonds.

[8] The derivations can be found in online appendix B. For details on the empirical implementation and estimation that the results in Section 14.3 are based on, the reader is referred to Hamilton and Wu (2014). Their code is available at http://econweb.ucsd.edu/~jhamilto/hw4_code.zip.

[9] Most papers in this literature postulate a particular functional form for the pricing kernel. For more details, the reader is referred to Ang and Piazzesi (2003) and Gürkaynak and Wright (2012). For a more technical treatment of affine term structure models, see Piazzesi (2010).

14.2.3.3 *An integrative view*

Hamilton and Wu (2015) use equation (B2) in online appendix B to provide a unifying perspective by illustrating how the term structure framework relates to the return regression approach. Specifically, substituting Eqs. (14.5) and (14.6) into (B2), they show

$$f_{t+1}^{h-1} - f_t^h = \kappa_{h-1} + \delta'_{h-1} x_t + \varepsilon_{t+1}^{h-1}, \tag{14.9}$$

with $\kappa_{h-1} = \beta'_{h-1} \lambda - \frac{1}{2} \beta'_{h-1} \Sigma \Sigma' \beta_{h-1}$, $\delta'_{h-1} = \beta'_{h-1} \Lambda$, and $\varepsilon_{t+1}^{h-1} = \beta'_{h-1} \Sigma u_{t+1}$. Dai and Singleton (2002) draw a similar parallel for affine models of the yield curve in their equation (21), where they show that risk premia formulations resulting from Gaussian dynamic term structure models imply the same structure as the excess return regressions in Fama (1984) and Fama and Bliss (1987) (see also Adrian et al., 2013, 2015). A key difference between these two modeling frameworks is that affine term structure models impose cross-equation restrictions that rule out arbitrage strategies which means that at all horizons h the coefficients depend on the same set of structural parameters that describe the state dynamics and risk premia, while the coefficients in return regressions are obtained from unrestricted least-squares regressions estimated separately for each maturity h. Another difference is that return regressions rely on observed proxies for relevant risk factors, whereas in affine term structure models the unobserved factors are commonly inferred from the behavior of asset prices themselves. While often a small set of factors is sufficient to describe the term structure dynamics, many variants of empirical term structure models exist and have evolved over time to incorporate additional observable determinants beyond the information contained in the cross-section of asset prices. For example, Ang and Piazzesi (2003) include factors extracted from a panel of inflation and real activity measures in addition to three latent yield curve factors (typically referred to as level, slope, and curvature). Instead, Bernanke et al. (2004) only rely on a set of observed macroeconomic variables within a standard term structure model of interest rates.[10] Affine term structure models are flexible and can be tailored to account for different market characteristics (e.g., liquidity, segmentation) and specific institutional features (e.g., calendar irregularities) without having to resort to observed proxies. At the same time, the advantage of using observed variables to model risk premia is that we can pinpoint the source(s) of risk, whereas giving economic content to the latent factors in term structure models is often more difficult.[11]

While these modeling frameworks enable us to separate risk premia from market expectations, the previous discussion makes it clear that different models will produce different estimates of time-varying risk premia which imply different expectation measures. This raises the important question of how to choose among different measures of market expectations which I turn to next.

---

[10] While this practice helps with the interpretability of the fundamental drivers in affine term structure models and establishes a link between asset price movements and macroeconomic dynamics (albeit often only unidirectional), it raises the question whether macroeconomic variables are truly factors for the purpose of yield curve modeling, often referred to as the "spanning hypothesis" (see, e.g., Rudebusch and Wu, 2008; Ludvigson and Ng, 2009; Bauer and Hamilton, 2018).

[11] An active strand of this literature concerned with macrofinance term structure models links the factor dynamics more explicitly to structural macroeconomic models and/or derives the pricing kernel from utility maximization which greatly enhances economic interpretability (see Gürkaynak and Wright (2012) for an overview of such models).

14.3 Extracting measures of market expectations from asset prices

Using Eq. (14.4) which has the same basic structure as the generalized version of Eq. (14.9) that nests both modeling frameworks, we solve for the futures price at expiry to obtain

$$F^1_{t+h-1} = F^h_t(1 + a_h + \mathbf{b}'_h\mathbf{x}_t + \epsilon_{t+h}),$$

where $\mathbf{x}_t$ refers to a $(K \times 1)$ vector of observable proxies or latent risk factors. Taking expectations on both sides and using the approximation $F^1_{t+h-1} \approx S_{t+h}$ yields the market's current expectation of the h-period-ahead spot price as the risk-premium-adjusted futures price,

$$E_t(S_{t+h}) = F^h_t(1 + a_h + \mathbf{b}'_h\mathbf{x}_t),$$

where the risk premium in dollars is $RP^h_t = F^h_t - E_t(S_{t+h})$. It is evident that there will be as many implied price expectation measures as there are risk premium estimates which can differ substantially across model specifications and which cannot all be equally valid. The key challenge is to select the most credible estimate of the market expectation for a given set of candidate risk premium models.

14.3.1 A general approach to identifying market expectations

Baumeister and Kilian (2017) propose a systematic approach to evaluating the plausibility of different estimates of time-varying risk premia drawing on insights from the forecasting literature. A conventional metric in assessing the accuracy of price expectations is their mean-squared prediction error (MSPE), defined as $E[S_{t+h} - E_t(S_{t+h})]^2$. The central idea is that the conditional expectation minimizes the MSPE under quadratic loss which is a well-known result in statistics (see, e.g., Granger, 1969; Granger and Newbold, 1986). This theoretical result allows us to rank alternative model specifications based on their MSPE and resolve the model uncertainty that arises from the multiplicity of candidate risk factors. The most accurate measure of the implied market expectation will be the one that delivers the largest MSPE reduction.

14.3.2 An illustration based on the oil market

I illustrate the usefulness of this approach for identifying the best possible, unique measure of the market's expectation about the future path of the spot price of crude oil along the lines of Baumeister and Kilian (2017), but for a larger universe of risk premium models and an updated sample that includes the 2014–2016 oil price decline. Consistent with the existing literature on estimating the oil risk premium, my analysis focuses on the WTI price of crude oil.[12] To obtain estimates of the time-varying risk premium for horizons $h = 3, 6, 9$, and 12 months, I rely on (*i*) basis regressions as in Fama and French (1987), (*ii*) payoff regressions for a selected set of prominent risk factors applied to commodity markets, which are summarized in Table 2A in the online appendix, and (*iii*) the Hamilton and

---

[12] I use monthly averages of WTI futures prices for consistency with the predictor variables in the payoff regressions whose reference period is the month. Data for variables available at a higher than monthly frequency are also averaged.

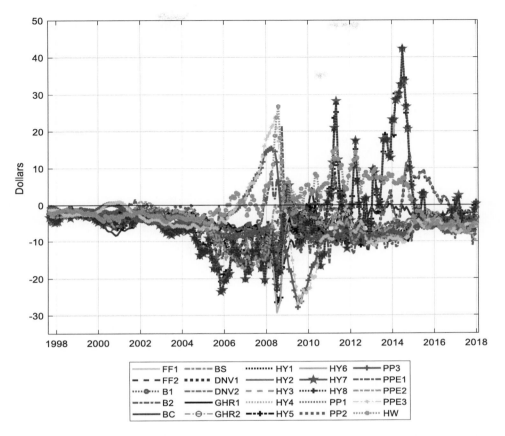

FIGURE 14.1 Alternative Monthly Estimates of the Time-Varying Risk Premium in the WTI Oil Futures Market at the 12-Month Horizon 1997.8–2017.12

NOTES: The graph shows 25 alternative estimates of the time-varying risk premium based on the models summarized in Table 2A in the online appendix. Qualitatively similar results are obtained for other horizons.

Wu (2014), henceforth HW, term structure model for the oil futures market.[13] The evaluation period is 1997.8–2018.12.

Fig. 14.1 shows the resulting estimates for the risk premium at the 12-month horizon across all 25 model specifications. Given the definition of the risk premium, a value of −$3 indicates that the price expected by market participants was $3 higher than the quoted futures price. While there is broad

---

[13] HW (2014) conduct their analysis on two subsamples with the first ending in 2004.12 and the second starting in 2005.1 to allow the structural parameters to change in response to the increased participation of index-fund traders in commodity markets after 2004. I impose the same break in estimation to account for changes in oil futures price dynamics. The model is estimated at weekly frequency and the risk premium estimates are averaged over the month.

agreement across models that the risk premium was small, negative on average, and relatively stable before 2004, there is a notable increase in volatility thereafter. The most striking feature in the evolution of risk premia after 2005 is the substantial heterogeneity in magnitude and sign. Alternative estimates can differ as much as $55 in a given month. The two episodes with the largest disagreement in risk compensation across model specifications are July 2008 and June 2014 where the estimated premia range from −$28 to $27 and from −$10 to $43, respectively. Mapping these risk-premium estimates into market expectations by adjusting the futures price would result in an equally dispersed set of price expectations that cannot all be representative of the market's assessment of the future course of oil prices. Thus, Fig. 14.1 provides a graphical illustration of the problem highlighted above that I am now going to resolve by evaluating the predictive success of the price expectations implied by the various models.

Table 14.2 presents the ratio of the MSPE of the model-implied price expectation to the MSPE of the monthly no-change prediction. This normalization is standard in forecasting and facilitates the implementation of statistical tests for improvements in accuracy (see, e.g., Baumeister et al., 2022). A ratio below 1 indicates that the model does better than a random walk, while a value above 1 indicates that it does worse.

The first row of Table 14.2 reports the results for the unadjusted futures price which is the relevant benchmark against which to evaluate the price expectation estimates derived from the given set of risk premium models. The futures price outperforms the no-change prediction at each horizon with statistically significant gains in forecast accuracy that increase as the horizon lengthens. The two basis regressions only beat the no-change prediction at the 12-month horizon but do not imply competitive expectation measures since their MSPE ratios exceed those of the unadjusted futures price. Among the payoff regressions, a larger set of predictor variables is useful at short horizons than at longer horizons. The most promising model specifications across all horizons include financial and macroeconomic indicators of the business cycle and measures of hedging pressure and trading activity. The implied price expectations yield additional reductions in MSPE ratios relative to the non-risk-adjusted futures price. The most successful model is the HW term structure model which attains the smallest MSPE ratios with impressive improvements on the futures price of 14 percentage points on average. Only at horizon 3 is the HW model tied with two specifications proposed by Hong and Yogo (2012), while it outperforms them by a large margin at all other horizons. Based on the selection criterion, the oil price expectation implied by the HW model is the most credible measure of market expectations overall.

In addition to the statistical evidence, Baumeister and Kilian (2017) suggest to check the plausibility of the preferred market-based measure of oil price expectations based on economic criteria which might be particularly useful if the MSPE ratios are tied. They make the case that longer-term oil price expectations should not shift abruptly but rather evolve smoothly over time except in times of major market turmoil. More specifically, they should be less volatile than the unadjusted futures prices. This is indeed the case. The standard deviation of the expected price 1-year-ahead recovered from the HW model is 15% lower than that for the corresponding futures price. Instead, the price expectation measure that is ranked second according to the statistical criterion (HY7) is just as volatile as the futures price. Another useful check is to examine whether the expected price developments align with the historical narrative. I will provide a retrospective analysis of the evolution of market participants' oil price expectations in Section 14.5.1.

Table 14.2 Predictive Accuracy of Risk-Adjusted Futures Prices for WTI Crude Oil MSPE Ratios for Evaluation Period: 1997.8–2018.12.

Models	Monthly horizon h			
	3	6	9	12
F_t^h	**0.976***	**0.965****	**0.923****	**0.859****
Basis Regressions				
FF1	1.013	1.037	1.027	**0.985***
FF2	1.015	1.036	1.029	**0.987***
Payoff Regressions				
B1	**0.984***	1.022	1.017	**0.975***
B2	**0.899***	**0.930****	**0.931****	**0.865****
BC	**0.994**	1.020	1.005	**0.959***
BS	1.003	1.004	1.055	1.016
DNV1	**0.925****	**0.978**	**0.938***	**0.853****
DNV2	**0.925****	**0.969**	**0.939***	**0.850****
GHR1	**0.957****	**0.989***	1.031	**0.994***
GHR2	1.011	1.037	1.015	**0.980***
HY1	**0.977****	**0.992**	**0.989**	**0.938***
HY2	**0.975***	**0.995**	**0.993**	**0.947***
HY3	**0.909****	**0.955****	**0.963****	**0.915****
HY4	**0.912****	**0.954****	**0.963****	**0.926****
HY5	**0.970***	**0.954**	**0.906***	**0.848****
HY6	**0.972***	**0.957**	**0.908***	**0.861****
HY7	**0.887****	**0.894****	**0.849****	**0.794****
HY8	**0.892****	**0.888****	**0.838****	**0.801****
PP1	1.003	1.031	1.032	**0.997***
PP2	**0.979***	**0.989***	**0.981***	**0.960***
PP3	1.012	1.013	**0.949****	**0.865****
PPE1	**0.953***	**0.995***	**0.986***	**0.942****
PPE2	**0.926****	**0.945****	**0.943****	**0.930****
PPE3	**0.954***	**0.973****	**0.907****	**0.825****
Term Structure Model				
HW	**0.896***	**0.829****	**0.762****	**0.697****

NOTES: *All MSPE ratios have been normalized relative to the monthly no-change forecast. Boldface indicates an improvement on the monthly no-change forecast. Statistically significant MSPE reductions are denoted ** at the 5% level and * at the 10% level based on the tests of Diebold and Mariano (1995) and Clark and West (2007), as appropriate. The underlying risk-premium estimates are based on the full sample which provides the most efficient estimate of the price expected by the market at each point in time. HW refers to Hamilton and Wu (2014) and the other labels correspond to the model specifications listed in Table 2A in the online appendix. Gray shades indicate the model with the lowest MSPE ratio at each horizon.*

14.4 Existing empirical evidence for selected markets

There exists a long list of assets traded on financial, forward, and futures markets whose prices incorporate expectations about key macroeconomic variables such as inflation, house prices, freight costs, commodity prices, interest and exchange rates. The same general methodology for selecting the most plausible market-based expectation measure can be applied to the set of price expectation estimates derived for each variable of interest based on the broad model classes discussed in Section 14.2. Care must be exercised in accounting for specific features of each market in determining the relevant set of expectations for evaluation. To illustrate this point, I focus on monetary policy expectations and inflation expectations.

14.4.1 Monetary policy expectations

The futures market for federal funds has long been the primary source for gauging the future course of monetary policy given that the payoff at maturity is directly tied to the actual average Fed funds rate, the policy instrument of the Federal Reserve, realized over the delivery month (see, e.g., Kuttner, 2001; Faust et al., 2004; Sack, 2004; Piazzesi and Swanson, 2008; Hamilton and Okimoto, 2011). In contrast to oil and other commodities, futures contracts for federal funds are not the only financial instruments whose rates are influenced by traders' views about near-term changes in Fed policy and thus can be used to extract monetary policy expectations. There exists a range of alternative securities available for this purpose like Treasury bills, eurodollar deposits and futures, commercial paper, and term federal funds loans that differ in their credit quality and trading activity.[14] Thus, it is not obvious a priori which financial instrument delivers the best market-based measure of the expected value of the future policy rate.

The general approach described earlier can be used to shed light on this question by ranking the various models according to their forecasting performance where the multiplicity now arises from the multitude of financial instruments (i.e., the left-hand-side variable in Eq. (14.9)). In fact, Gürkaynak et al. (2007) apply exactly this principle and perform a forecasting horserace to identify the security with the highest predictive power for the federal funds rate. They find that federal funds futures outperform all other instruments for horizons up to six months which they interpret to mean that futures rates provide the best measure for monetary policy expectations; however, they do not account for time-varying risk premia.[15]

Several studies have documented the existence of time-varying risk premia in Fed funds futures and their role in distorting the market's assessment of the expected path of monetary policy (see Sack, 2004; Piazzesi and Swanson, 2008; Ferrero and Nobili, 2009).[16] For example, Piazzesi and Swanson (2008) show that Fed funds (and eurodollar) futures adjusted for a cyclical risk factor produce smaller forecast errors than unadjusted futures, making the risk-adjusted futures the preferred measure of monetary

---

[14] Gürkaynak et al. (2007) provide a detailed description of the market characteristics and available maturities for each financial instrument.

[15] They do examine the presence of constant risk premia and find that for many instruments the estimated average risk premia are fairly large; this is consistent with evidence provided in Chernenko et al. (2004).

[16] Hamilton (2009) shows that time-varying risk premia are less of a concern in very short-horizon futures contracts and thus, daily changes in near-dated Fed funds futures do primarily reflect the market's expectation of very near-term changes in Fed policy.

policy expectations. It is likely that time-varying risk premia are an even more relevant component in the other financial market instruments given their different safety and liquidity characteristics which affect the measurement of target rate expectations. Therefore, to derive the most accurate market-based measure of monetary policy expectations a comprehensive analysis is needed that controls for risk premia contained in these different securities and explores additional risk factors.

Inferring market participants' expectations concerning the path of monetary policy poses additional challenges when nominal interest rates are close to or at the zero lower bound (ZLB). For example, the fact that in standard Gaussian affine term structure models nothing prevents the short-term rate from turning negative impairs the accuracy of model-implied monetary policy expectations. Bauer and Rudebusch (2016) propose to resort to shadow-rate models that enforce the ZLB constraint to recover monetary policy expectations embedded in the yield curve. Their modeling framework produces market-based expectation measures about the path of monetary policy that can be used to determine the timing of policy-rate liftoff and subsequent pace of tightening. They show that including macroeconomic variables as additional risk factors in their shadow-rate model is particularly useful to characterize monetary policy expectations during the ZLB period since yields at the short end lose much of their information content.

Another feature that can influence the size and variation of risk-premium estimates are heterogeneous beliefs. For example, Kelly and Pruitt (2013) make the case that exploiting the rich cross-sectional information about individual investors' perceptions of future prices can result in superior estimates of market expectations. Barillas and Nimark (2017, 2019) build a model of the term structure of interest rates in which traders have rational but heterogeneous expectations about future bond prices, in particular the resale value of a bond. They show that the speculative behavior, resulting from the fact that individual traders form expectations based on different subsets of available information, changes the magnitude of historical estimates of time-varying risk premia and expectations about future short rates. In Cao et al. (2020), heterogeneity derives from investors' disagreement about the expected path of the policy rate which triggers speculative trading. Crump et al. (see Chapter 17 in this Handbook) provide a detailed account of how dispersion in interest rate forecasts, especially in the long run, affects the pricing of risk in bond markets. They conclude that differences in beliefs about the long-run evolution of rates play an important role in measuring risk premia which impact the market's overall expectation of monetary policy.[17]

14.4.2 Inflation expectations

Another interesting case is the derivation of market-based inflation expectations. It might seem that the existence of inflation-linked assets is a precondition for uncovering financial market expectations of inflation. This is not the case. There exist several market-based approaches that have been used to estimate investors' inflation expectations in historical periods that predate the introduction of financial instruments tied to inflation. As long as some market prices incorporate inflation expectations, it is possible to exploit the relationship between observed variables to infer the rates of inflation market participants were anticipating. For example, Hamilton (1985) and Burmeister et al. (1986) obtain estimates of market expectations of inflation by modeling the joint dynamics of nominal interest rates and

---

[17] For a general treatment of how different models impose different assumptions about beliefs and how this affects asset pricing outcomes, the reader is referred to Adam and Nagel (see Chapter 16 in this Handbook).

realized inflation using a state-space framework where expected inflation and real rates are unobserved states. Hamilton (1992) proposes to use the prices of several agricultural commodities traded on futures exchanges to derive expectations about changes in the general price level. The idea is that if there is a stable relationship between commodity prices and consumer prices, then price changes expected by futures markets can be mapped into overall inflation expectations.

While there have been several unsuccessful attempts to establish trading in futures contracts written on the U.S. Consumer Price Index (CPI),[18] other markets for inflation-linked assets have developed during the past two decades, the inflation-indexed bond market and the inflation swap market, both of which convey high-frequency information about investors' views on future inflation.[19] One closely followed indicator is the difference between yields on nominal Treasury securities and Treasury inflation-protected securities (TIPS) for a given maturity, also known as breakeven inflation given that it is the level of inflation that makes investors indifferent between both kinds of securities. The standard practice of treating breakeven inflation rates as pure measures of inflation expectations is problematic, however, since they contain several other components. A salient aspect of breakeven inflation rates is that they involve two securities whose markets differ in important characteristics. It is therefore essential to account for institutional factors that affect nominal and inflation-indexed bonds differently when trying to infer inflation expectations. One major difference is the lower liquidity of TIPS relative to nominal government debt, particularly in periods of financial market stress. Liquidity risks may arise from multiple market frictions, such as limited investor participation, transaction costs, the composition of market participants, funding constraints, and net supply imbalances between the two types of securities, for which TIPS investors demand compensation (see Pflueger and Viceira, 2011; D'Amico et al., 2018; Andreasen et al., 2020).[20] For example, Pflueger and Viceira (2016) provide empirical evidence for the presence of liquidity premia in inflation-indexed bonds that are economically significant and vary substantially over time. Liquidity issues and other risk factors likely influence the pricing of inflation swaps as well (Campbell et al., 2009; Christensen and Gillan, 2011; Faust and Wright, 2013).

Different empirical strategies have been developed to separate risk factors from the expectation component. Abrahams et al. (2016), D'Amico et al. (2018), Andreasen et al. (2020), among others, use a no-arbitrage pricing framework that jointly models nominal and real yield curves to decompose breakeven inflation rates into expected inflation, inflation risk premia, and liquidity premia. To separately identify these latent components, studies in this literature rely on a variety of pricing factors and modeling choices. For example, D'Amico et al. (2018) model the unobserved liquidity factor as the spread between TIPS yields and the model-implied frictionless real yields and include information on nominal yields, TIPS yields, CPI inflation, and survey-based inflation expectations in the estimation. In contrast, Abrahams et al. (2016) dispense with survey data but use an observable liquidity indicator to adjust TIPS yields for their relative illiquidity. Like D'Amico et al. (2018), Haubrich et al. (2012) use survey forecasts of inflation but replace TIPS yields with inflation swap rates leading them to discard

---

[18] CPI futures contracts were first introduced in June 1985 but trading was suspended in April 1987 due to the lack of investor interest. They were reintroduced in February 2004, restructured in June 2006, and delisted in November 2006. The most recent attempt in 2013 failed even before the contracts were launched.

[19] Campbell et al. (2009) provide a detailed description and analysis of the evolution of both markets.

[20] Other features that influence TIPS pricing include tax treatment, seasonality of CPI, indexation lags, and the embedded deflation protection; see Pflueger and Viceira (2011, 2016), and Christensen and Gillan (2011) for more details. D'Amico et al. (2018) conclude that these factors only play a minor role.

the liquidity factor. Gospodinov and Wei (2018) further explore the promise of financial derivatives as additional sources of market information on expected inflation by integrating not only inflation swaps but also inflation options and oil futures into an affine term structure framework. Christensen et al. (2010) propose a "yields-only" model with separate level factors for nominal and real yields but common slope and curvature factors. They ignore the liquidity disadvantage of TIPS given that their sample is limited to a period when distortions from liquidity premia were of lesser concern. Andreasen et al. (2020) use the same basic dynamic factor structure as Christensen et al. (2010) but correct for liquidity risk by exploiting price differentials in the cross-section of individual TIPS that arise from the relatively less liquid older securities within the same maturity segment. While the dominant modeling framework for extracting inflation expectations are term structure models, there are also a few studies that have used return regressions with various liquidity proxies and risk factors to generate liquidity-adjusted breakeven inflation rates (Gürkaynak et al., 2010a; Bauer, 2015; Pflueger and Viceira, 2016) and risk-adjusted inflation swap rates (Casiraghi and Miccoli, 2019).

Again, this results in a situation where there is an abundance of market-based measures of inflation expectations, often with the assertion that a particular measure is better than others with little formal evidence offered in support. While some of these studies show that risk- and liquidity-adjusted breakeven rates improve inflation forecasts compared to unadjusted rates or standard benchmarks like no-change and survey-based forecasts, there is no comparison across different model-implied measures of inflation expectations. To resolve any disagreement between alternative models, it is useful to systematically evaluate the merit of each of these market-based measures by applying the principles laid out in Baumeister and Kilian (2017) to identify the most reliable measure of inflation expectations. While this is straightforward for short- and medium-term inflation expectations, one limitation for long-term inflation expectations is that the available sample might not be long enough yet to evaluate the forecasting performance accurately, as noted by Faust and Wright (2013). To safeguard the selection against spurious forecasting success (until more data accumulate), it seems prudent to pursue a conservative approach that considers the range of implied estimates for market-based measures of long-term inflation expectations across models to obtain lower and upper bounds that can guide monetary policymakers as discussed in Section 14.5.3 (see Christensen and Gillan (2011) for a similar approach).

14.5 Economic applications of market-based expectation measures
14.5.1 Evaluation of economic models

Reliable measures of historical price expectations are a precondition for evaluating the empirical content of forward-looking economic models. As pointed out in Section 14.3.2, it is useful to supplement the statistical model selection with narrative evidence on price developments to increase our confidence in market-based expectation measures. I illustrate this by conducting a retrospective analysis of oil price expectations derived from the preferred risk premium model.[21]

Panel A of Fig. 14.2 presents the change in the oil price expected over the next year, computed as $E_t(S_{t+12}) - S_t$, where the price expectation is obtained from the HW model for the period 1989.2–2019.6. For example, in the summer of 2008 market participants anticipated the oil price to

---

[21] The oil price expectation measures can be downloaded from https://sites.google.com/site/cjsbaumeister/research.

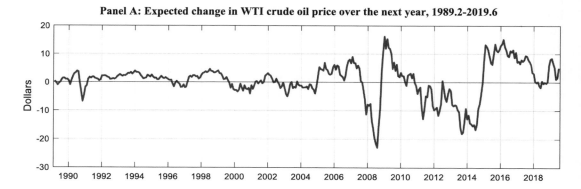

Panel A: Expected change in WTI crude oil price over the next year, 1989.2-2019.6

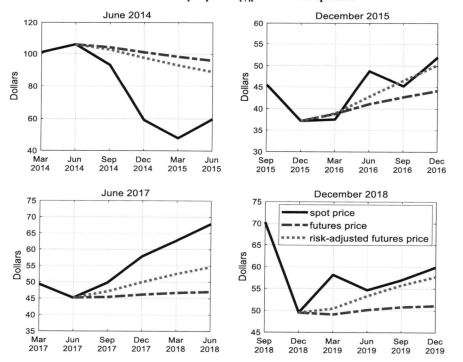

Panel B: Trajectories of the WTI futures price F_t^h, the risk-adjusted futures price $F_t^h - RP_t^{HW}$ and the realized spot price S_{t+h} for selected episodes

FIGURE 14.2 Historical Oil Price Expectations

fall by $22 from its peak of $133 when a year later it had dropped by half. A strong rebound of more than $16 to a level of close to $60 was expected in December 2008 with the realized value one year later a little over $70. When WTI passed the $100 mark again in early 2011, the market expected a continuous downward correction over the next 12 months of $10 on average up until the end of 2014. While the price had been more sluggish to come down relative to what was expected over this period, when its decline accelerated in 2015 the market was optimistic and expected a relatively swift reversal and recovery to about $60 in 2016/17 which was only reached in early 2018. This illustrates that the market mostly got the direction of change right, but it did not always anticipate the severity of major events.

Panel B of Fig. 14.2 reports the term structure of futures prices and price expectations of market participants together with the subsequent realized path of the spot oil price at four different points in time, each 18 months apart from the previous one, starting with June 2014. It shows that accounting for the risk premium narrows the gap between what the market expected the price to be and what it turned out to be. However, for some episodes there are still some substantial prediction errors, a question I will turn to in Section 14.5.2. Overall, the expected price paths are reasonable and in line with historical events lending further credence to the market-based measure.

Next I discuss several settings in which this and other market-based expectation measures can be directly used as inputs for empirical exercises or theoretical models.

Testing model hypotheses. Information about price expectations is useful for testing hypotheses. For example, Pavlidis et al. (2018) rely on the measure of oil price expectations of Baumeister and Kilian (2017) as an input to test for periodically collapsing speculative bubbles in oil futures markets. The advantage of using market-based expectations is that one does not have to take a stand on how to measure market fundamentals. Their proposed test only requires data on the current and expected price. They find no evidence for the existence of bubbles. Studying the evolution of market-based expectations is also helpful to assess the role of rational learning and peso problems in futures markets (Timmermann, 1993; Leduc et al., 2021). Risk-premium estimates across commodity markets can also be informative to test the hypothesis of financialization. For example, Baumeister et al. (2017) assess the degree of integration among the futures markets for crude oil, motor gasoline, and ethanol based on the correlation of risk premia derived from the HW term structure model for each market. If the increased inflow of index-fund investors achieved full market integration, this would be reflected in risk premia being perfectly correlated across markets. Their results do not support the financialization hypothesis.

Model validation. Expectation measures also serve as an independent source of information to validate modeling assumptions. For example, implicit in the vector autoregressive model used by Wieland (2019) is the assumption that news of oil demand arrives within the period but that oil producers do not respond simultaneously. If oil demand shocks for the next month were known, producers could adjust production at the time of the change in demand. In that case, the model would attribute forecastable demand shocks to oil supply shocks. Wieland tests if supply shocks are forecastable based on past changes in oil price expectations derived in Baumeister and Kilian (2017). He finds no evidence of predictability which supports the validity of his identification strategy. Reis (2020) exploits the discrepancy between inflation expectations by the public, measured using household surveys, and by financial market participants, measured using inflation swaps, to validate models of expectation formation for macroeconomic variables. He shows, for example, that this discrepancy affects inflation dynamics by changing both the effective real interest rate in savings decisions and the nominal interest rate the central bank chooses to set. He also provides estimates of the underlying expected inflation anchor and illustrates the trade-off that central banks face when deciding how strongly to respond to this discrepancy.

Modeling storage demand. The economic theory of storage implies that price spreads are the main determinant of stockpiling (Fama and French, 1987, 1988; Pindyck, 2001). Thus, expected price changes can guide inventory decisions. Baumeister and Kilian (2017) illustrate this for storage in oil markets. When long-term price expectations exceed the current price, traders have an incentive to accumulate inventories as long as this differential is larger than the cost of storage. Instead, when the expected price is below the current price, traders have an incentive to run down inventories to deal with the implied temporary shortage. For example, there was a constant incentive to hold inventories in the 1990s except for the period following the invasion of Kuwait in August 1990 which called for a drawdown of oil stocks (see Fig. 14.2, panel A). A positive price spread also incentivized the built-up of oil inventories from the mid-2000s until the Great Recession, during which there was a strong incentive to destock. Using information about price expectations to gauge incentives for storage is even more useful for commodities for which no inventory data exist. For example, Baumeister et al. (2017) extract information about market expectations from ethanol futures prices to test whether storage demand increased in response to changes in biofuel policies.

Modeling agents' decisions. Households' purchase decisions of durables and firms' production and investment decisions are forward-looking and thus depend on expected price developments. For example, Kahn (1986), Busse et al. (2013), and Allcott and Wozny (2014) analyze how consumers trade off future gasoline costs with the sales price of vehicles with different fuel economy ratings when making car-buying decisions. Kahn (1986) and Allcott and Wozny (2014) show that the choice of the measure for gasoline price expectations matters for determining whether the market values energy efficiency. To assess the sensitivity of vehicle prices to changes in gasoline price expectations, these studies rely on unadjusted crude oil futures prices and survey data to proxy consumers' forecasts of gasoline prices. Baumeister et al. (2017) show that risk-adjusted gasoline futures prices outperform both the no-change forecast implied by surveys and "pure" futures prices which would make them a preferred choice to represent gasoline price expectations in these models. In light of the policy consequences of potential undervaluation of energy costs, in particular the implications for the design of climate policies, it would be interesting to revisit the evidence derived from these models using a superior measure of price expectations. This measure can also be used to estimate how sensitive consumers are to expected operating costs when purchasing other energy-using durables. Similarly, market-based commodity price expectations can replace simpler measures when studying resource owners' decisions to extract nonrenewable resources and invest in the development of new reserves of raw materials (Anderson et al., 2018; Gilje et al., 2020).

14.5.2 Deriving shock measures

Monetary policy shocks. Kuttner (2001) forcefully argues that distinguishing between expected and unexpected Federal Reserve policy actions is essential to correctly estimate the impact of policy surprises on the yield curve and other asset prices. Key for successfully separating out the unanticipated component of policy decisions is an accurate measure of what the market expected the policy rate to be.

Having identified the single, most accurate measure of near-term target rate expectations, we can apply Rudebusch's (1998) definition of a monetary policy shock as the difference between the realized

Fed funds rate target and the market-based expectation to obtain the surprise measure. Piazzesi and Swanson (2008) provide an illustration of the difference that risk adjustment of policy expectations makes for the computation of monetary policy shocks. When the measurement of policy surprises is tied to FOMC meetings, as suggested by Kuttner (2001), the timing of policy announcements within the month impacts the derivation of shocks to the immediate policy setting. Therefore, Gürkaynak et al. (2007) advocate constructing policy shocks using expectations with slightly longer horizons to capture changes in the expected near-term policy path which is less affected by shifts in the dates of policy decisions (see also Nakamura and Steinsson, 2018). In the case of using changes in the Fed funds futures rate on the day of an FOMC announcement as the policy surprise, risk adjustment might be of lesser importance since risk premia are unlikely to change much at higher frequencies (see Kuttner, 2001; Faust et al., 2004; Piazzesi and Swanson, 2008; Hamilton, 2009).

Oil price shocks. The oil market is another setting where understanding whether markets expected oil price changes or were surprised by these changes is of immediate interest to policymakers and economists seeking to understand the determinants and economic impact of oil price fluctuations. As in the case of monetary policy, percent deviations of oil price expectations from the realized price can be interpreted as market-based oil price shocks. For example, Baumeister and Kilian (2016a) examine quarterly expectational shocks to the WTI price for several historical episodes to assess how forward-looking market participants are relative to policymakers and consumers. Comparing oil price expectations, derived from Brent oil futures using the HW model, to subsequent outcomes from June to December 2014, Baumeister and Kilian (2016b) conclude that investors failed to anticipate the sharp decline in the Brent price over this period, resulting in a large negative oil price shock.

Panel A of Fig. 14.3 plots the time series of oil price surprises computed as the log difference between the realized price of WTI and what market participants expected that price to be last month for the period 1986.1–2020.4. Using surprises defined on monthly intervals makes this market-based shock measure comparable to oil market shocks derived from structural vector autoregressions (see, e.g., Baumeister and Hamilton, 2019). The figure shows that the largest oil price shocks tend to coincide with well-known historical episodes of political and economic turmoil that caught market participants by surprise.[22] For example, the market seems to have underestimated the price effects of additional oil supply from Saudi Arabia in early 1986 being surprised by the sharp drop in oil prices within a few months. While traders expected higher oil prices in August 1990, they were surprised on the upside by the magnitude of the price increase as a result of the invasion of Kuwait. In the months after this event, the price reversal happened faster than the market had expected, leading to a series of oil price surprises on the downside. Over the 2014–2016 period, traders were repeatedly surprised by developments in global oil markets both on the upside and the downside, indicating that expectations adapted only gradually. The largest market-based oil price shock took place in early 2020 when news about the spread of COVID-19 made oil prices tumble beyond expectations.

The previous discussion highlights that shocks to market participants' expectations are often related to events that cause shifts in oil supply and oil demand. To gain a better understanding of these shocks, I filter out the "pure" expectation component by regressing the market-based surprises on fundamental oil supply and demand shocks.[23] Panel B of Fig. 14.3 presents the orthogonalized expectational shocks

---

[22] Baumeister and Kilian (2016a) provide a detailed account of the history of oil markets.

[23] Specifically, I use the time series of the four structural oil market shocks of Baumeister and Hamilton (2019), namely oil supply shocks, oil consumption demand shocks, oil inventory demand shocks, and global economic activity shocks. These fun-

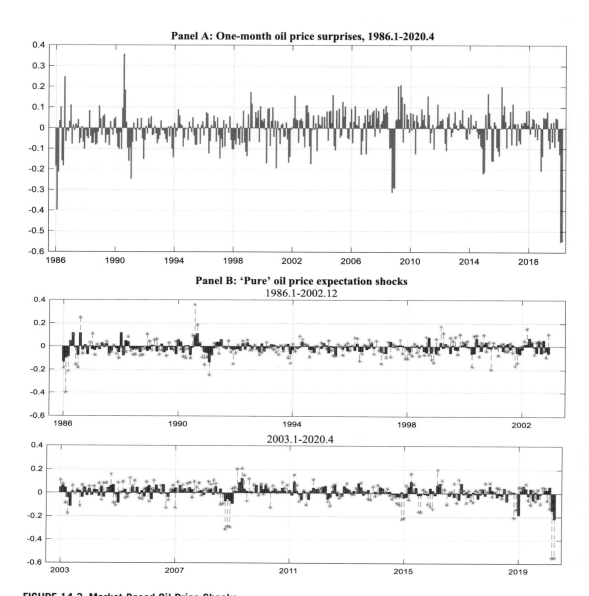

FIGURE 14.3 Market-Based Oil Price Shocks

NOTES: The red (mid gray in print version) bars in panel A and the red (mid gray in print version) dashed lines with a star in panel B are the log difference between the realized WTI price and the oil price that was expected last month. The blue (dark gray in print version) bars in panel B are "pure" expectational shocks orthogonal to the four fundamental oil market shocks in Baumeister and Hamilton (2019).

along with the original oil price surprises to get a sense of the relative importance of "pure" expectation shocks that are driven by market beliefs distinct from new information about fundamentals. Overall, these shocks account for a nontrivial fraction of market-based oil price surprises. It would be interesting to examine the macroeconomic dynamics of "pure" oil price expectation shocks to learn more about their nature. Another possibility would be to include oil price expectation measures directly as an observable in a vector autoregressive (VAR) model and isolate the shock component by applying existing identification strategies. For example, Barsky and Sims (2012), D'Amico and King (2017), Levchenko and Pandalai-Nayar (2020), Clements and Galvão (2021), and Lukmanova and Rabitsch (2021) augment standard VARs with survey expectations and study the role of innovations to expectations for business cycle fluctuations and/or the conduct of policy.

So far I have focused on month-to-month oil price surprises. In other contexts, it might be useful to consider shocks to oil price expectations at longer horizons. For example, López-Salido and Loria (2021) use 3-month and 6-month oil price surprises constructed based on the market-based oil price expectation measures of Baumeister and Kilian (2017) to assess the role of oil price shocks for their market-based measure of inflation risks. They show that their options-implied inflation probabilities exhibit a strong correlation with oil price surprises.

14.5.3 Policy analysis

Expectations about future price developments play a key role in assessing the effectiveness of public policies, designing appropriate policy instruments, and guiding policy decisions given that they influence the behavior of economic agents.

Regulations and government policies. To identify the policy instrument most suitable to achieve a certain policy goal, it is necessary to ensure that consumers or firms respond to incentives intended by the instrument. For example, knowing to what extent consumers factor future fuel costs into their purchase decisions of vehicles is critical for deciding whether fuel-economy regulations (CAFE standards) or price-based policies (gasoline or carbon taxes) are more efficient to curb greenhouse gas emissions (Busse et al., 2013; Allcott and Wozny, 2014). It is also important to know how environmental and other policies affect individual markets. For example, Baumeister et al. (2017) study the implications of the creation of the Renewable Fuel Standard (RFS) for the ethanol market. With the help of market-based price expectations for oil and gasoline, they design a counterfactual of how ethanol prices would have evolved in the absence of the policy where the difference between the actual and counterfactual price paths provides an estimate of the causal effects of the RFS. Market-based expectation measures can also be used to inform specific policy interventions. For example, the difference between the market's expected oil price and the current price carries valuable information for the government about when and how much oil to release from or add to the U.S. Strategic Petroleum Reserve (Newell and Prest, 2017).

Monetary policy. Central banks closely monitor inflation expectations. Among the indicators used to gauge the future path of inflation, market-based measures of expected inflation have gained popularity among policymakers given that they are available at higher frequencies and for a wider range of time

---

damental shocks together with the market-based oil price surprises and the orthogonalized expectational shocks can be found at https://sites.google.com/site/cjsbaumeister/research.

horizons compared to more traditional survey measures. Being able to assess in real time at which horizons relevant changes in the market's inflation outlook take place provides valuable information for conducting monetary policy. The higher-frequency nature of market-based inflation expectations is also useful for the purpose of assessing the reaction of expected inflation to conventional and unconventional monetary policy actions using the event study methodology (see Abrahams et al., 2016; Nakamura and Steinsson, 2018).

Policymakers also pay close attention to long-term inflation expectations to get a sense of the market's confidence in the central bank's ability to achieve its mandate of price stability. Stable levels of long-term inflation expectations are an indication of a central bank's commitment to fight inflation since short-run inflationary pressures due to cyclical factors do not change market participants' expectations about the rate of inflation over the longer run (see, e.g., Gürkaynak et al., 2010b; Chapter 17 in this Handbook). Söderlind and Svensson (1997) suggest to use the difference between long-term inflation expectations and a central bank's inflation target as an indicator of investors' perception of the credibility of the monetary policy regime. Knowing whether inflation expectations are well anchored to a central bank's inflation target is also important to obtain a more favorable trade-off between inflation and growth. For example, Gürkaynak et al. (2010a) rely on market-based measures of long-run inflation expectations to show that an explicit inflation target helps to more firmly anchor the private sector's expected level of inflation at long horizons which improves economic performance. Other economic benefits of stable and well-anchored inflation expectations include lower variability of long-term nominal interest rates and reduced uncertainty about future inflation (see, e.g., Bauer, 2015).

Market-based real rate expectations can be used to gauge the stance of monetary policy (see, e.g., Christensen and Rudebusch, 2019). This not only allows assessing whether financial market participants perceive current monetary policy as expansionary or contractionary, but also examining historical episodes; for example, whether the market thought monetary policy was too accommodative during the run-up of house prices in the early-to-mid 2000s.

14.5.4 Implications for out-of-sample forecasts

So far the focus has been on historical market-based price expectations which rely on the information contained in the entire sample. Insofar as risk premia are predictable, an interesting question is whether risk-adjusting asset prices in a real-time out-of-sample forecasting setting would achieve similar gains in accuracy compared to unadjusted asset prices. It is well known that even if the model is correct, predictive success based on the full sample does not necessarily imply good out-of-sample performance, given the bias–variance trade-off in estimating forecasting models.

As noted earlier, market prices are a popular choice by central banks and international organizations to gauge the future paths of inflation and commodity prices which often feed into macroeconomic projections and policy decisions. For example, Abrahams et al. (2016) conduct an out-of-sample evaluation of inflation forecasts and show that breakeven inflation rates adjusted for liquidity and risk premia beat unadjusted breakeven rates. D'Amico et al. (2018) provide further evidence that the liquidity correction yields model-implied inflation forecasts that improve upon the forecast accuracy of the Michigan survey and are tied with two professional surveys (Blue Chip and SPF). With regard to commodities, Pagano and Pisani (2009) study the promise of risk adjustment of oil futures prices for forecasting purposes. They infer the risk premium based on a U.S. business cycle indicator and show that risk-adjusted futures prices consistently outperform unadjusted futures prices. Baumeister and Kilian (2017) evaluate the out-of-sample forecast accuracy of the HW term structure model since it produced the most reliable measure of market expectations based on the full-sample selection criterion. They conclude that this new approach to oil price forecasting looks promising and recommend monitoring the evolution of its performance as more data become available given their short evaluation period. In online appendix C, I revisit the evidence for an evaluation period that now spans a decade. This exercise highlights that the out-of-sample forecasting performance of futures prices varies considerably over time and might depend on changes in the size of time-varying risk premia. One useful way forward would be to examine the benefits of adding the HW model to the suite of models used for pooling oil price forecasts (see Baumeister, 2014; Baumeister and Kilian, 2015). In this regard, Altavilla et al. (2014) show that incorporating market expectations extracted from Fed funds futures into model-based forecasts of bond returns yields sizeable improvements in forecast accuracy and profitable investment strategies for investors. More generally, the usefulness of risk-adjusting asset prices for the purposes of out-of-sample forecasting and optimal portfolio choice has not been explored much to date in other contexts and thus offers fruitful avenues for future research.

14.6 Conclusions

Asset prices are a valuable source of information since they incorporate market participants' expectations about the future. However, they also contain a time-varying risk premium that is unobservable. Thus, to extract information about expectations we need to purge risk premia from asset prices. In this chapter, I illustrated a general approach for recovering market expectations from asset prices and its usefulness in a number of economic settings.

References

Abrahams, Michael, Adrian, Tobias, Crump, Richard K., Moench, Emanuel, Yu, Rui, 2016. Decomposing real and nominal yield curves. Journal of Monetary Economics 84, 182–200.

Acharya, Viral V., Lochstoer, Lars A., Ramadorai, Tarun, 2013. Limits to arbitrage and hedging: evidence from commodity markets. Journal of Financial Economics 109, 441–465.

Adrian, Tobias, Crump, Richard K., Moench, Emanuel, 2013. Pricing the term structure with linear regressions. Journal of Financial Economics 110 (1), 110–138.

Adrian, Tobias, Crump, Richard K., Moench, Emanuel, 2015. Regression-based estimation of dynamic asset pricing models. Journal of Financial Economics 118 (2), 211–244.

Adrian, Tobias, Shin, Hyun Song, 2010. Liquidity and leverage. Journal of Financial Intermediation 19 (3), 418–437.

Allcott, Hunt, Wozny, Nathan, 2014. Gasoline prices, fuel economy, and the energy paradox. Review of Economics and Statistics 96, 779–795.

Altavilla, Carlo, Giacomini, Raffaella, Costantini, Riccardo, 2014. Bond returns and market expectations. Journal of Financial Econometrics 12 (4), 708–729.

Anderson, Soren, Kellogg, Ryan, Salant, Stephen, 2018. Hotelling under pressure. Journal of Political Economy 126, 984–1026.

Andreasen, Martin, Christensen, Jens H.E., Riddell, Simon, 2020. The TIPS Liquidity Premium. FRBSF Working Paper 2017-11.

Ang, Andrew, Piazzesi, Monika, 2003. A no-arbitrage vector autoregression of term structure dynamics with macroeconomic and latent variables. Journal of Monetary Economics 50, 745–787.

Barillas, Francisco, Nimark, Kristoffer, 2017. Speculation and the term structure of interest rates. The Review of Financial Studies 30 (11), 4003–4037.

Barillas, Francisco, Nimark, Kristoffer, 2019. Speculation and the bond market: an empirical no-arbitrage framework. Management Science 65 (9), 4179–4203.

Barsky, Robert, Sims, Eric, 2012. Information, animal spirits, and the meaning of innovations in consumer confidence. The American Economic Review 102 (4), 1343–1377.

Bauer, Michael D., 2015. Inflation expectations and the news. International Journal of Central Banking 11 (2), 1–40.

Bauer, Michael D., Hamilton, James D., 2018. Robust bond risk premia. The Review of Financial Studies 31, 399–448.

Bauer, Michael D., Rudebusch, Glenn D., 2016. Monetary policy expectations at the zero lower bound. Journal of Money, Credit, and Banking 48 (7), 1439–1465.

Baumeister, Christiane, 2014. The art and science of forecasting the real price of oil. Bank of Canada Review, Spring, 21–31.

Baumeister, Christiane, Ellwanger, Reinhard, Kilian, Lutz, 2017. Did the Renewable Fuel Standard Shift Market Expectations of the Price of Ethanol? NBER Working Paper 23752.

Baumeister, Christiane, Hamilton, James D., 2019. Structural interpretation of vector autoregressions with incomplete identification: revisiting the role of oil supply and demand shocks. The American Economic Review 109 (5), 1873–1910.

Baumeister, Christiane, Kilian, Lutz, 2015. Forecasting the real price of oil in a changing world: a forecast combination approach. Journal of Business and Economic Statistics 33 (3), 338–351.

Baumeister, Christiane, Kilian, Lutz, 2016a. Forty years of oil price fluctuations: why the price of oil may still surprise us. The Journal of Economic Perspectives 30 (1), 139–160.

Baumeister, Christiane, Kilian, Lutz, 2016b. Understanding the decline in the price of oil since June 2014. Journal of the Association of Environmental and Resource Economists 3 (1), 131–158.

Baumeister, Christiane, Kilian, Lutz, 2017. A General Approach to Recovering Market Expectations from Futures Prices with an Application to Crude Oil. CEPR Discussion Paper 10162.

Baumeister, Christiane, Korobilis, Dimitris, Lee, Thomas K., 2022. Energy markets and global economic conditions. Review of Economics and Statistics 104 (4), 828–844.

Bekaert, Geert, Hodrick, Robert J., 1993. On biases in the measurement of foreign exchange risk premiums. Journal of International Money and Finance 12, 115–138.

Bernanke, Ben S., 2008. Outstanding Issues in the Analysis of Inflation. Speech at the Federal Reserve Bank of Boston's 53rd Annual Economic Conference, Chatham, Massachusetts, June 9.

Bernanke, Ben S., Sack, Brian P., Reinhart, Vincent R., 2004. Monetary policy alternatives at the zero bound: an empirical assessment. Brookings Papers on Economic Activity 2, 1–100.

Bessembinder, Hendrik, 1992. Systematic risk, hedging pressure, and risk premiums in futures markets. The Review of Financial Studies 5, 637–667.

Bessembinder, Hendrik, Chan, Kalok, 1992. Time-varying risk premia and forecastable returns in futures markets. Journal of Financial Economics 32, 169–193.

Bessembinder, Hendrik, Seguin, Paul, 1993. Price volatility, trading volume and market depth: evidence from futures markets. Journal of Financial and Quantitative Analysis 28 (1), 21–39.

Bianchi, Francesco, Ludvigson, Sydney C., Ma, Sai, 2022. Belief distortions and macroeconomic fluctuations. The American Economic Review 112 (7), 2269–2315.

Burmeister, Edwin, Wall, Kent D., Hamilton, James D., 1986. Estimation of unobserved expected monthly inflation using Kalman filtering. Journal of Business and Economic Statistics 4 (2), 147–160.

Busse, Meghan, Knittel, Christopher R., Zettelmeyer, Florian, 2013. Are consumers myopic? Evidence from new and used car purchases. The American Economic Review 103, 220–256.

Campbell, John Y., Cochrane, John H., 1999. By force of habit: a consumption-based explanation of aggregate stock market behavior. Journal of Political Economy 107 (2), 205–251.

Campbell, John Y., Shiller, Robert J., 1991. Yield spreads and interest rate movements: a bird's eye view. The Review of Economic Studies 58, 495–514.

Campbell, John Y., Shiller, Robert J., Viceira, Luis M., 2009. Understanding inflation-indexed bond market. Brookings Papers on Economic Activity, Spring, 79–120.

Cao, Shuo, Crump, Richard K., Eusepi, Stefano, Moench, Emanuel, 2020. Fundamental Disagreement about Monetary Policy and the Term Structure of Interest Rates. CEPR Discussion Paper 15122.

Casiraghi, Marco, Miccoli, Marcello, 2019. Inflation risk premia and risk-adjusted expectations of inflation. Economics Letters 175, 36–39.

Chernenko, Sergey, Schwarz, Krista, Wright, Jonathan H., 2004. The Information Content of Forward and Futures Prices: Market Expectations and the Price of Risk. Federal Reserve Board. Mimeo.

Chinn, Menzie, Coibion, Olivier, 2014. The predictive content of commodity futures. The Journal of Futures Markets 34 (7), 607–636.

Christensen, Jens H.E., Gillan, James, 2011. TIPS liquidity, breakeven inflation, and inflation expectations. FRBSF Economic Letter 2011 (19).

Christensen, Jens H.E., Lopez, Jose A., Rudebusch, Glenn D., 2010. Inflation expectations and risk premiums in an arbitrage-free model of nominal and real bond yields. Journal of Money, Credit, and Banking 42 (6), 143–178.

Christensen, Jens H.E., Rudebusch, Glenn D., 2019. A new normal for interest rates? Evidence from inflation-indexed debt. Review of Economics and Statistics 101 (5), 933–949.

Clark, Todd E., West, Kenneth D., 2007. Approximately normal tests for equal predictive accuracy in nested models. Journal of Econometrics 138, 291–311.

Clements, Michael P., Galvão, Ana Beatriz, 2021. Measuring the effects of expectations shocks. Journal of Economic Dynamics and Control 124, 104075.

Cochrane, John H., Piazzesi, Monika, 2005. Bond risk premia. The American Economic Review 95 (1), 138–160.

Dai, Qiang, Singleton, Kenneth J., 2002. Expectation puzzles, time-varying risk premia, and affine models of the term structure. Journal of Financial Economics 63 (3), 415–441.

D'Amico, Stefania, Kim, Don H., Wei, Min, 2018. Tips from TIPS: the informational content of treasury inflation-protected security prices. Journal of Financial and Quantitative Analysis 53 (1), 395–436.

D'Amico, Stefania, King, Thomas, 2017. What Does Anticipated Monetary Policy do? FRB Chicago. Mimeo.

De Roon, Frans A., Nijman, Theo E., Veld, Chris, 2000. Hedging pressure effects in futures markets. The Journal of Finance 55, 1437–1456.

Diebold, Francis X., Mariano, Roberto S., 1995. Comparing predictive accuracy. Journal of Business and Economic Statistics 13, 253–263.

Dusak, Katherine, 1973. Futures trading and investor returns: an investigation of commodity market risk premiums. Journal of Political Economy 81 (6), 1387–1406.

Etula, Erkko, 2013. Broker-dealer risk appetite and commodity returns. Journal of Financial Econometrics 11, 486–521.

Fama, Eugene F., 1984. Forward and spot exchange rates. Journal of Monetary Economics 14, 319–338.

Fama, Eugene F., 2014. Two pillars of asset pricing. The American Economic Review 104 (6), 1467–1485.

Fama, Eugene F., Bliss, Robert R., 1987. The information in long-maturity forward rates. The American Economic Review 77 (4), 680–692.

Fama, Eugene F., French, Kenneth R., 1987. Commodity futures prices: some evidence on forecast power, premiums, and the theory of storage. Journal of Business 60, 55–73.

Fama, Eugene F., French, Kenneth R., 1988. Business cycles and the behavior of metals prices. The Journal of Finance 43, 1075–1093.

Faust, Jon, Swanson, Eric T., Wright, Jonathan H., 2004. Identifying VARS based on high frequency futures data. Journal of Monetary Economics 51, 1107–1131.

Faust, Jon, Wright, Jonathan H., 2013. Forecasting inflation. In: Elliott, G., Timmermann, A. (Eds.), Handbook of Economic Forecasting, vol. 2A. North-Holland, Amsterdam, pp. 3–56.

Ferrero, Giuseppe, Nobili, Andrea, 2009. Futures contract rates as monetary policy forecasts. International Journal of Central Banking 5 (2), 109–146.

Ferson, Wayne E., Harvey, Campbell R., 1991. The variation of economic risk premiums. Journal of Political Economy 99 (2), 385–415.

Froot, Kenneth A., 1989. New hope for the expectations hypothesis of the term structure of interest rates. The Journal of Finance 44 (2), 283–305.

Froot, Kenneth A., Frankel, Jeffrey A., 1989. Forward discount bias: is it an exchange risk premium? The Quarterly Journal of Economics 104 (1), 139–161.

Gilje, Erik, Loutskina, Elena, Murphy, Daniel, 2020. Drilling and debt. The Journal of Finance 75 (3), 1287–1325.

Gorton, Gary B., Hayashi, Fumio, Rouwenhorst, K. Geert, 2013. The fundamentals of commodity futures returns. Review of Finance 17, 35–105.

Gospodinov, Nikolay, Wei, Bin, 2018. Forecasts of Inflation and Interest Rates in No-Arbitrage Affine Models. FRB Atlanta. Mimeo.

Granger, Clive W.J., 1969. Prediction with a generalized cost of error function. Operations Research Quarterly 20, 199–207.

Granger, Clive W.J., Newbold, Paul, 1986. Forecasting Economic Time Series, 2nd ed. Academic Press, San Diego.

Gürkaynak, Refet S., Levin, Andrew, Swanson, Eric T., 2010a. Does inflation targeting anchor long-run inflation expectations? Evidence from long-term bond yields in the U.S., U.K., and Sweden. Journal of the European Economic Association 8 (6), 1208–1242.

Gürkaynak, Refet S., Sack, Brian, Swanson, Eric T., 2007. Market-based measures of monetary policy expectations. Journal of Business and Economic Statistics 25 (2), 201–212.

Gürkaynak, Refet S., Sack, Brian, Wright, Jonathan H., 2010b. The TIPS yield curve and inflation compensation. American Economic Journal: Macroeconomics 2 (1), 70–92.

Gürkaynak, Refet S., Wright, Jonathan H., 2012. Macroeconomics and the term structure. Journal of Economic Literature 50 (2), 331–367.

Hamilton, James D., 1985. Uncovering financial market expectations of inflation. Journal of Political Economy 93 (6), 1224–1241.

Hamilton, James D., 1992. Was the deflation during the great depression anticipated? Evidence from the commodity futures market. The American Economic Review 82 (1), 157–178.

Hamilton, James D., 2009. Daily changes in fed funds futures prices. Journal of Money, Credit, and Banking 41 (4), 567–582.

Hamilton, James D., Okimoto, Tatsuyoshi, 2011. Sources of variation in holding returns for fed funds futures contracts. The Journal of Futures Markets 31 (3), 205–229.

Hamilton, James D., Wu, Cynthia, 2014. Risk premia in crude oil futures prices. Journal of International Money and Finance 42, 9–37.

Hamilton, James D., Wu, Cynthia, 2015. Effects of index-fund investing on commodity futures prices. International Economic Review 56, 187–205.

Hansen, Lars P., Hodrick, Robert J., 1980. Forward exchange rates as optimal predictors of future spot rates: an econometric analysis. Journal of Political Economy 88 (5), 829–853.

Haubrich, Joseph, Pennacchi, George, Ritchken, Peter, 2012. Inflation expectations, real rates, and risk premia: evidence from inflation swaps. The Review of Financial Studies 25 (5), 1588–1629.

Hong, Harrison, Yogo, Motohiro, 2012. What does futures market interest tell us about the macroeconomy and asset prices? Journal of Financial Economics 105, 473–490.

Kahn, James A., 1986. Gasoline prices and the used automobile market: a rational expectations asset price approach. The Quarterly Journal of Economics 101, 323–339.

Kelly, Bryan, Pruitt, Seth, 2013. Market expectations in the cross-section of present value. The Journal of Finance 68 (5), 1721–1756.

Korajczyk, Robert, 1985. The pricing of forward contracts for foreign exchange. Journal of Political Economy 93 (2), 346–368.

Kuttner, Kenneth, 2001. Monetary policy surprises and interest rates: evidence from the federal funds futures market. Journal of Monetary Economics 47, 523–544.

Leduc, Sylvain, Moran, Kevin, Vigfusson, Robert J., 2021. Learning in the oil futures markets: evidence and macroeconomic implications. Review of Economics and Statistics. Forthcoming.

Levchenko, Andrei A., Pandalai-Nayar, Nitya, 2020. TFP, news, and "sentiments:" the international transmission of business cycles. Journal of the European Economic Association 18 (1), 302–341.

López-Salido, David, Loria, Francesca, 2021. Inflation at Risk. Federal Reserve Board. Mimeo.

Ludvigson, Sydney C., Ng, Serena, 2009. Macro factors in bond risk premia. The Review of Financial Studies 22 (12), 5027–5067.

Lukmanova, Elizaveta, Rabitsch, Katrin, 2021. New Evidence on Monetary Transmission: Interest Rate versus Inflation Target Shocks. KU Leuven. Mimeo.

Nakamura, Emi, Steinsson, Jón, 2018. High-frequency identification of monetary non-neutrality: the information effect. The Quarterly Journal of Economics 133 (3), 1283–1330.

Newell, Richard, Prest, Brian, 2017. Informing SPR Policy through Futures and Inventory Dynamics. NBER Working Paper 23974.

Pagano, Patrizio, Pisani, Massimiliano, 2009. Risk-adjusted forecasts of oil prices. The B.E. Journal of Macroeconomics 9 (1), 1–25.

Pavlidis, Efthymios, Paya, Ivan, Peel, David, 2018. Using market expectations to test for speculative bubbles in the crude oil market. Journal of Money, Credit, and Banking 50 (5), 833–856.

Pflueger, Carolin, Viceira, Luis, 2011. Inflation-indexed bonds and the expectations hypothesis. Annual Review of Financial Economics 3 (1), 139–158.

Pflueger, Carolin, Viceira, Luis, 2016. Return predictability in the treasury market: real rates, inflation, and liquidity. In: Veronesi, P. (Ed.), Handbook of Fixed-Income Securities. Wiley, NJ. Chapter 10.

Piazzesi, Monika, 2010. Affine term structure models. In: Aït-Sahalia, Y., Hansen, L. (Eds.), Handbook of Financial Econometrics: Tools and Techniques, vol. 1. North-Holland, pp. 691–766.

Piazzesi, Monika, Swanson, Eric T., 2008. Futures prices as risk-adjusted forecasts of monetary policy. Journal of Monetary Economics 55, 677–691.

Pindyck, Robert, 2001. The dynamics of commodity spot and futures markets: a primer. Energy Journal 22 (3), 1–29.

Reis, Ricardo, 2020. The People versus the Markets: a Parsimonious Model of Inflation Expectations. LSE. Mimeo.

Rudebusch, Glenn D., 1998. Do measures of monetary policy in a VAR make sense? International Economic Review 39, 907–931.

Rudebusch, Glenn D., Wu, Tao, 2008. A macro-finance model of the term structure, monetary policy and the economy. The Economic Journal 118 (530), 906–926.

Sack, Brian, 2004. Extracting the expected path of monetary policy from futures rates. The Journal of Futures Markets 24 (8), 733–754.

Söderlind, Paul, Svensson, Lars, 1997. New techniques to extract market expectations from financial instruments. Journal of Monetary Economics 40, 383–429.

Timmermann, Allan, 1993. How learning in financial markets generates excess volatility and predictability in stock prices. The Quarterly Journal of Economics 108, 1135–1145.

Timmermann, Allan, Granger, Clive W.J., 2004. Efficient market hypothesis and forecasting. International Journal of Forecasting 20, 15–27.

Wieland, Johannes, 2019. Are negative supply shocks expansionary at the zero lower bound? Journal of Political Economy 127 (3), 973–1007.

Inference on probabilistic surveys in macroeconomics with an application to the evolution of uncertainty in the survey of professional forecasters during the COVID pandemic

Federico Bassetti[a], **Roberto Casarin**[b], and **Marco Del Negro**[c,d]

[a] Polytechnic University of Milan, Milan, Italy
[b] Ca' Foscari University of Venice, Venice, Italy
[c] Federal Reserve Bank of New York, New York, NY, United States

15.1 Introduction

Manski (2004) made economists appreciate the advantages of probabilistic surveys relative to surveys that simply ask respondents for their point projections. Probabilistic surveys provide information about the entire predictive distribution, which can in principle be used to extract subjective measures of mean predictions, uncertainty, and tail risks. Partly following Manski (2004)'s lead, and partly because of the growing interest in studying uncertainty in the aftermath of the Great Recession, a large number of probabilistic surveys in macroeconomics have emerged over the last decade or so, which elicit predictive probabilities on macroeconomic variables from professional forecasters, financial market participants, consumers, and firms, in the US and other countries. Examples are the NY Fed's Survey of Consumer Expectations (see Armantier et al., 2017), the NY Fed's Survey of Primary Dealers and Market Participants, the Atlanta Fed's Survey of Business Uncertainty and Business Inflation Expectations Survey (see Altig et al., 2020), the ECB's Survey of Professional Forecasters and the Bank of England's Survey of External Forecasters (see Boero et al., 2008), in addition to the already established Philadelphia Fed's U.S. Survey of Professional Forecasters (henceforth, SPF).

Yet, respondents to probabilistic surveys do not generally provide macroeconomists with direct information on the objects they are interested in, such as various moments (e.g., mean, variance, skewness) and quantiles of their forecast distribution. Instead they provide probabilities associated with

---

[d] The views expressed in this paper do not necessarily reflect those of the Federal Reserve Bank of New York or the Federal Reserve System.

Handbook of Economic Expectations. **https://doi.org/10.1016/B978-0-12-822927-9.00023-9**

generally prespecified (by the survey designer) bins. Extracting and using the information provided by respondents is not a trivial task. This chapter discusses the challenges involved in this task, and the approaches used so far in the literature for conducting inference on probabilistic surveys. While the focus of the chapter is on the inference problem, it also discusses some of the literature that made use of probabilistic surveys in macroeconomics—although we keep this review to a minimum given that some of this literature is already covered in Chapter 3 in this Handbook.

Finally, the chapter also provides an application of some of these inference methods using the SPF. In particular, it investigates the evolution of uncertainty and tail risk for both output growth and inflation during the COVID pandemic.

The structure of the chapter is as follows. Section 15.2 discusses the approaches used in conducting inference on probabilistic surveys and some related econometric issues that arise. In particular, Section 15.2.1 describes the inference problem posed by probabilistic forecasts, while Section 15.2.2 reviews existing approaches and their limitations. Section 15.2.3 describes a Bayesian nonparametric approach based on Del Negro et al. (2022) which tries to address some of the issues mentioned in Section 15.2.2, with a particular emphasis on inference for measures of uncertainty and tail risk. This section also includes a comparisons between the different approaches in a real data application. Section 15.3 discusses some of the challenges in assessing the uncertainty of forecasters, while Section 15.4 documents the heterogeneity in density predictions across forecasters, again focusing on uncertainty. Section 15.5 gives an overview of some of the existing approaches for aggregating individual responses (opinion pools). Finally, the Bayesian nonparametric method discussed in Section 15.2.3 is used in Section 15.6 to analyze the evolution of US SPF density forecasts for GDP growth and inflation during the COVID pandemic. The analysis focuses on how the COVID pandemic affected the consensus forecast, average measures of subjective uncertainty, as well as heterogeneity in mean projections, uncertainty, and tail probabilities.

15.2 Inference on probabilistic surveys

This section reviews current approaches used for inference on probabilistic surveys. It discusses some challenges these approaches face, while attempting to address some of them based on recent work by Del Negro et al. (2022).

15.2.1 The inference problem

Probabilistic forecasts take the form of probabilities assigned to bins: the percent chance that the variable of interest, such as inflation or GDP growth, falls within different contiguous ranges. In most of the surveys, the bins are prespecified by the survey designer (e.g., the Philadelphia Fed's SPF), although some recent surveys only specify the number of bins and let the respondents determine their boundaries (e.g., the Atlanta Fed's Survey of Business Uncertainty, where a 5-point probability is provided by each survey respondent). The bins are mutually exclusive and contiguous, and generally cover the entire real line whenever the variable being forecast, y, is continuous and can take values in the interval $(-\infty, +\infty)$. In what follows, $(y_{j-1}, y_j]$, $j = 1, \ldots, J$ will be a set of bins such that $y_0 < y_1 < \cdots < y_J$, where y_0 and y_J are equal to $-\infty$ (left-open bin) and $+\infty$ (right-open bin), respectively. For each forecaster $i = 1, \ldots, n$, the available data consists of a vector of probabilities $\mathbf{z}_i = (z_{i,1}, \ldots, z_{i,J})$, with

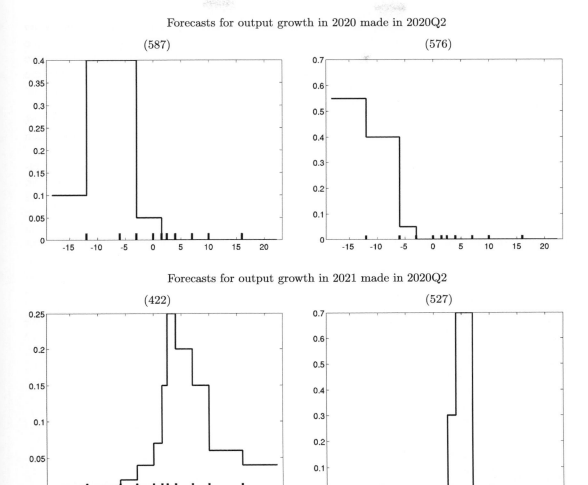

FIGURE 15.1 Probability Forecasts for Selected Examples from the 2020Q2 SPF

Note: Each panel displays the forecast probabilities $z_{i,j}$, $j = 1, \ldots, 11$ (stepwise solid lines) for a given fore-caster (forecaster number shown in parentheses) and the bin bounds (black ticks, horizontal axis).

$z_{i,j} \geq 0$ and $z_{i,1} + z_{i,2} + \cdots + z_{i,J} = 1$, measuring the predictive likelihood that y falls within the re-spective bins.

Fig. 15.1 shows the probabilities that the 2020 (first row) and the 2021 (second row) real GDP growth falls within the bins (horizontal axis) as provided by four respondents in the US SPF conducted in the second quarter of 2020, specifically in mid-May (from now on, we will use the notation XQY to denote the survey made in quarter Y of year X). These probabilities are displayed as histograms, while the black ticks on the horizontal axis mark the boundaries of the bins. In 2020Q2 the survey histogram has 11 bins with bounds $-12, -6, -3, 0, 1.5, 2.5, 4, 7, 10$, and 16, with left- and right-open bins. In the SPF the bins have been changing over time. Stark (2013) discusses at length some of the features of the SPF survey, and the Philadelphia Fed's site provides a manual for interpreting the data that includes the history up to the present of bin boundaries for the various variables being forecast. The fact that the bin boundaries change over time needs to be borne in mind when comparing surveys for different years.

These four examples illustrate a few common features of the SPF data: potential asymmetry, the presence of probability mass on open bins (forecaster 576 assigns most probability mass to the left open bin), the fact that some forecasters assign positive probability to most if not all bins (forecaster 422) while for others most bins have zero probability (forecaster 527), and rounding (almost all probabilities in Fig. 15.1 are round numbers, with some bins for forecaster 422 being the only exception). The econometrician's problem is to use those few points given by the elements of the survey probability vector $\mathbf{z}_i$ of the ith forecaster to address a number of questions of interest: What is the mean prediction for forecaster i? How uncertain are they? What probability do they place on tail events, e.g., output growth in 2020 or 2021 being below 10%? The next section describes how the literature has gone after this problem, considering the survey features mentioned above.

15.2.2 Current approaches

This section describes the approaches used so far for translating the information provided by the respondents into the objects of interest mentioned above. The general approach for macroeconomic surveys has been to postulate that forecasters $i = 1, \ldots, n$ have in mind a given predictive probability distribution $F_i(y)$ over the variable being forecast, which they use to assign the bin probabilities $\mathbf{z}_i$. The name of the game for the econometrician is then to conduct inference on $F_i(y)$ based on the data $\mathbf{z}_i$, and then use the estimated $F_i(y)$ to answer the questions of interest.

To our knowledge, all existing literature has accomplished this task by fitting a given *parametric distribution* to the Cumulative Distribution Function (CDF) implied by the bin probabilities, respondent by respondent, that is fitting $Z_{ij} = z_{i,1} + \cdots + z_{i,j}$ $j = 1, \ldots, J, i = 1, \ldots, n$ using a parametric family of distributions $\{F(y|\boldsymbol{\theta}) : \boldsymbol{\theta} \in \Theta\}$. The type of the parametric distribution varies across studies, from a mixture of uniforms/piecewise linear CDF (that is, assuming that the probability is uniformly distributed within each bin; Zarnowitz and Lambros, 1987), to a Gaussian (Giordani and Soderlind, 2003), a skew-normal (Garcia and Manzanares, 2007), a generalized beta (Engelberg et al., 2009)[1] and a skew-t distribution (e.g., Ganics et al., 2020). The Gaussian and the generalized beta assumptions have been the most popular approaches in academic research, as discussed in Chapter 3 in this Handbook, although in applied work at central banks the mixture of uniforms approach is often followed. The parameters of each distribution are usually estimated using nonlinear least squares, respondent by respondent; that is, $F_i(y) = F(y|\boldsymbol{\theta}_i^*)$, where

$$\boldsymbol{\theta}_i^* = \underset{\boldsymbol{\theta}_i}{\arg\min} \sum_{j=1}^{J} \left| Z_{ij} - F(y_j|\boldsymbol{\theta}_i) \right|^2. \tag{15.1}$$

---

[1] Whenever the number of (adjacent) bins with positive probability is two or fewer, Engelberg et al. (2009) uses a triangular distribution.

These approaches have been popular but have some limitations, which are generally well known in the literature and which we discuss in the remainder of this section using the examples of Fig. 15.1, focusing on the generalized beta and Gaussian cases.[2] A first limitation is that the assumed parametric distribution may be misspecified, in the sense that it may not fit the individual responses very well. For instance, the right column panels of Fig. 15.2 show that for respondents 587 and 422 neither the normal nor the beta distributions fit all the observed Z_{ij}'s. Second, the width of the bins can be large, as is the case for real output growth in 2020Q2, implying that even if the distributions fit the Z_{ij}'s well, the inference results on moments and quantiles can be sensitive to the distributional assumption.

Another issue is that bounded distributions such as the beta or the mixture of uniforms take literally the z_{ij} that are zero, in that they place no probability mass on bins where the respondents place no mass (see respondents 587, 576, and 527). Since y is a continuous variable, one suspects that $z_{ij} = 0$ may not literally mean that $F_i(y)$ places no mass on that interval, but that the mass is relatively small so that the respondent felt comfortable reporting zero. More generally, for all assumed $F(\cdot)$'s the approach outlined in expression (15.1) ignores the issue of rounding, in that it takes all the Z_{ij}'s literally even though, as mentioned before, they are all round numbers suggesting that the respondent reported approximate probabilities (Dominitz and Manski, 1996; D'Amico and Orphanides, 2008; Boero et al., 2008, 2014; Engelberg et al., 2009; Manski and Molinari, 2010; Manski, 2011; Giustinelli et al., 2020, among others, discuss the issue of rounding; Binder, 2017 uses rounding to measure uncertainty).[3]

Finally, and very importantly, existing approaches do not capture inference uncertainty. Because of the limited information available, the econometrician cannot be sure about the inferred CDF $F_i(\cdot)$. Yet, most if not all existing approaches completely ignore this inference uncertainty, even that concerning θ_i for a given parametric assumption, let alone the uncertainty about the shape of $F_i(\cdot)$. For respondent 527 in Fig. 15.2, there are arguably many Gaussians with a fit very close to that of the one implied by θ_i^*.[4] This omission implies that confidence bands and hypothesis testing procedures cannot be derived.

As mentioned, these limitations are well known in the literature. There have been attempts to address some of these issues, in particular the potential misspecification, by choosing more flexible families of distributions such as the skew-normal or the skew-Student-t distribution (e.g., Garcia and Manzanares, 2007; Ganics et al., 2020). But the risk of misspecification obviously remains; for example, some forecasters display multimodal histograms (see Del Negro et al., 2022). Most importantly, if the econometrician does not account for inference uncertainty, this flexibility comes at the price of possible overparamterization. Again, respondent 527 has a histogram with only two bins, and one can hardly dis-

---

[2] In what follows, when showing results using the beta assumption we follow Engelberg et al. (2009) quite literally. We also followed the literature in terms of closing the open bins for both the generalized beta and the stepwise uniform.

[3] Manski and Molinari (2010) and Giustinelli et al. (2020) propose to treat the issue of rounding by considering interval data and using a person's response pattern across different questions to infer her or his rounding practice. It is important to note that the inferential approach based on interval data followed by these researchers is very different from the one described at the beginning of this section.

[4] Researchers recognize the emergence of an inference issue especially when the information provided by the respondent is very limited, but the proposed solution mostly amounts to either choosing less parameterized distributions or discarding the respondent. For instance, some researchers simply discard histograms with fewer than three bins Clements (2010), others (Engelberg et al., 2009; Clements, 2014b,a; Clements and Galvão, 2017) use a triangle distribution in these cases, as mentioned above. Liu and Sheng (2019), however, make an attempt to account for parameter uncertainty for given parametric assumptions. They propose maximum likelihood estimation of parametric distributions on artificial data generated from the histogram.

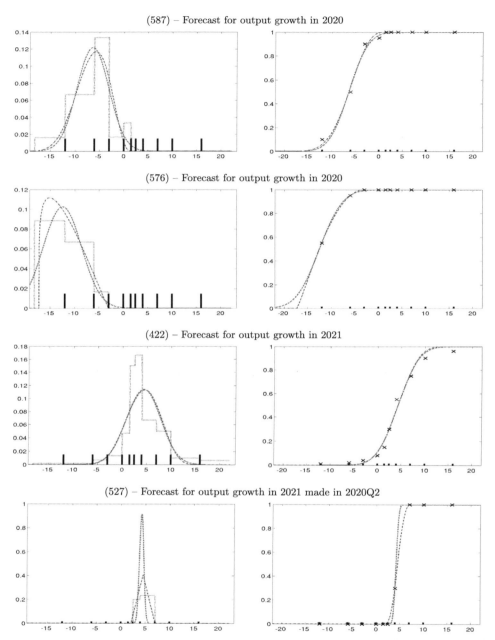

FIGURE 15.2 Inference Using the Uniform, Beta, and Gaussian Distributions: PDFs and CDFs for Selected Examples from the 2020Q2 SPF

Note: Nonlinear least squares estimation of the subjective PDF (left) and CDF (right) using the normal (gray, dashed line) or beta (black, dashed–dotted line) parametric assumptions. In addition, the left column shows the stepwise uniform PDF (dotted lines) obtained from stepwise uniform PDF (dotted lines) implied by the histogram probabilities z_{ij}, $j = 1, \ldots, J$. The right column displays the observed cumulated histogram probabilities Z_{ij} $j = 1, \ldots, J$ (crosses).

criminate between normal and Student-t distributions. The next section discusses an inference method that attempts to overcome some of the limitations of the current approaches.

15.2.3 **A Bayesian nonparametric alternative**

The Bayesian method developed in Del Negro et al. (2022) relies on a probabilistic model for the forecaster's subjective probabilities and a flexible (nonparametric) modeling approach. We will refer to this method as BNP. It differs from existing methods in four important dimensions. First, it is robust to misspecification regarding the parametric assumption for predictive CDF $F_i(\cdot)$. Second, the method allows for full-fledged inference regarding the mapping between data and objects of interest (e.g., the quantiles of the predictive density), thereby providing posterior probabilities that reflect inference uncertainty. Third, it conducts inference *jointly* across survey respondents, that is, using the entire cross-section instead of being applied to each respondent separately. The joint inference allows for partial information pooling across forecasters and exploits commonalities across forecasters to improve our inference for the aggregate and individual CDFs. This implies that when the number of forecasters grows posterior estimates become more precise, making it possible to obtain some consistency results, as discussed later. Fourth, it explicitly accounts for noise (including rounding toward zero) in the survey responses.

This section offers a mostly verbal description of the approach, keeping the analytical expressions to a minimum. Del Negro et al. (2022) provides any missing detail and contains formal derivations of the results mentioned in this section. The model description works as follows. We first describe a *parametric* model. This model follows the literature in that it assumes that forecasters have in mind a specific predictive distribution $F(\cdot)$ which they use to assign probabilities v to the bins. It is different from the literature in that it explicitly postulates that the data $\mathbf{z}$ are noise-ridden versions of the v's, where again the noise is assumed to have some parametric form. We then depart from this parametric framework by embedding it into a more general Bayesian *nonparametric* approach, thereby amending the potential misspecification associated with the parametric assumptions.

A parametric probabilistic model

The probabilities $\mathbf{z}_i$ reported by the forecaster are imperfect representations of the respondent forecast uncertainty (see Boero et al., 2008 and the discussion in Chapter 3 in this Handbook), and can be considered noise-ridden measurements of an unobserved vector of subjective probabilities over the J bins $\mathbf{v}_i = (v_{i1}, \dots, v_{iJ})$ with $v_{ij} \geq 0$ and $v_{i1} + \cdots + v_{iJ} = 1$. The uncertainty in the vector of probabilities $\mathbf{z}_i$ is encoded into a probability distribution $h(\cdot)$,

$$\mathbf{z}_i = (z_{i,1}, \dots, z_{i,J}) \sim h(\mathbf{z}_i | \mathbf{v}_i; \boldsymbol{\theta}_i), \tag{15.2}$$

which captures the noise due to approximations or to actual mistakes in reporting. In choosing $h(\cdot)$, one needs to account for the fact that $\mathbf{z}_i$ belongs to the simplex; that is, the elements of $\mathbf{z}_i$ are positive and sum up to one. A natural choice for random variables on the simplex is the Dirichlet distribution. A drawback of the standard Dirichlet distribution is that its PDF is null for $\mathbf{z}_i$'s that have some elements equal to zero, when in fact forecasters often assign zero probability to one or more bins. Del Negro et al. (2022) therefore use the Zadora distribution (see Zadora et al. (2010); Scealy and Welsh (2011)), which allows for values of the random vector that are zeros.

The vector of probabilities over the J bins can be reparameterized with a family of subjective probability functions $F(y|\boldsymbol{\theta})$:

$$v_{ij}(\boldsymbol{\theta}_i) = F(y_j|\boldsymbol{\theta}_i) - F(y_{j-1}|\boldsymbol{\theta}_i), \quad j = 1, \ldots, J. \tag{15.3}$$

This leads us to write $h(\mathbf{z}_i|\mathbf{v}_i; \boldsymbol{\theta}_i)$ as $h(\mathbf{z}_i|\boldsymbol{\theta}_i)$, where $\boldsymbol{\theta}_i \in \Theta$ includes both the parameters describing the CDF $F(\cdot)$ and those needed to specify $h(\cdot)$ in (15.2). In the application below, we follow Del Negro et al. (2022) and assume $F(\cdot)$ is a mixture of two normal distributions.[5]

A Bayesian nonparametric approach

The Bayesian nonparametric approach amounts to a flexible hierarchical setup where each respondent is described by a potentially infinite mixture of the parametric probability distribution described so far. These mixtures can be seen as forecaster "types" (for concreteness, let us think of low and high uncertainty; low and high mean; left-skewed and right-skewed; low and high reporting noise, etc.). Assume that the population of forecasters has K different types, and recall that $h(\mathbf{z}_i|\boldsymbol{\theta}_i)$ subsumes differences in the parameterization of both the $h(\cdot)$ and the $F(\cdot)$ functions. At the first stage of the hierarchy of distributions, the ith forecaster's response is characterized by $h(\mathbf{z}_i|\boldsymbol{\theta}_i)$, where the parameters $\boldsymbol{\theta}_i$ are distributed according to

$$\boldsymbol{\theta}_i \overset{iid}{\sim} \begin{cases} \boldsymbol{\theta}_1^* & \text{with probability } p_1, \\ \vdots \\ \boldsymbol{\theta}_K^* & \text{with probability } p_K, \end{cases} \tag{15.4}$$

or, equivalently, $\boldsymbol{\theta}_i \sim G$ i.i.d. for

$$G(\boldsymbol{\theta}) = \sum_{k=1}^{K} p_k \delta(\boldsymbol{\theta} - \boldsymbol{\theta}_k^*) \tag{15.5}$$

with $\delta(x)$ a point mass distribution located at 0, $p_k > 0$ and $p_1 + \cdots + p_K = 1$. At the second stage of the hierarchy, it is assumed that the unknown parameter types are sampled from a common distribution

---

[5] The mixture is parametrized as $F(y|\boldsymbol{\theta}) = (1 - \omega)\Phi(y|\mu, \sigma_1^2) + \omega\Phi(y|\mu + \mu_\delta, \sigma_2^2)$, where $\Phi(y|\mu, \sigma^2)$ denotes the normal CDF with location μ and variance σ^2. The Zadora distribution is parameterized as

$$h(\mathbf{z}|\boldsymbol{\theta}) \propto \left(\prod_{j=1}^{J} \alpha_j(\boldsymbol{\theta})^{\xi_j} (1 - \alpha_j(\boldsymbol{\theta}))^{1-\xi_j} \right) \frac{\Gamma\left(\sum_{j \in \mathcal{J}^*} \phi v_j(\boldsymbol{\theta})\right)}{\prod_{j \in \mathcal{J}^*} \Gamma(\phi v_j(\boldsymbol{\theta}))} \prod_{j \in \mathcal{J}^*} z_j^{\phi v_j(\boldsymbol{\theta})-1},$$

where the auxiliary variable ξ_j is equal to 1 if $z_j = 0$ and 0 otherwise, $\mathcal{J}^* = \{j = 1, \ldots, J; \xi_j = 0\}$ indicates the bins with nonzero probabilities, $(\alpha_1(\boldsymbol{\theta}), \ldots, \alpha_J(\boldsymbol{\theta}))$ are the probabilities that a forecaster will report a zero on the J bins, and

$$\alpha_j(\boldsymbol{\theta}) = \int_0^\epsilon g(x|v_j(\boldsymbol{\theta}), r)dx,$$

where $g(x|m, r)$ denotes the PDF of a beta distribution $\mathcal{B}e(m, 100)$ with mean m and precision 100.

$\theta_k^* \overset{iid}{\sim} G_0(\boldsymbol{\theta})$, $k = 1, \ldots, K$, and the type probabilities have prior distribution

$$(p_1, \ldots, p_K) \sim \text{Dir}\left(\frac{\psi_0}{K}, \ldots, \frac{\psi_0}{K}\right), \tag{15.6}$$

where ψ_0 is a concentration parameter and $\text{Dir}(a_1, \ldots, a_K)$ a Dirichlet distribution of parameters $(a_1, \ldots, a_K)$.

When K goes to infinity, one obtains

$$G(\boldsymbol{\theta}) = \sum_{k=1}^{\infty} p_k \delta(\boldsymbol{\theta} - \boldsymbol{\theta}_k^*), \tag{15.7}$$

where $\boldsymbol{\theta}_k^* \overset{iid}{\sim} G_0$ and p_ks is a sequence of random weights with stick breaking representation $SB(\psi_0)$ described, for example, in Pitman (2006). This hierarchical model is known as a Dirichlet process prior:

$$\boldsymbol{\theta}_i \overset{iid}{\sim} G, \quad G \sim \mathcal{DP}(\psi_0, G_0),$$

where the random probability measure G is a Dirichlet process with law $\mathcal{DP}(\psi, G_0)$ (see Ferguson, 1973). The base measure G_0 has the interpretation of mean type distribution, and the precision parameter ψ_0 measures the concentration of G around G_0, so that when $\psi_0 \to 0$ all forecasters are assumed to be of the same type and when $\psi_0 \to +\infty$ the inference is done forecaster by forecaster (using the same prior).

The intuition behind Bayesian nonparametrics is that each forecaster can be described by a prior distribution over a sufficiently rich parameter space. Bayesian nonparametrics allows for some degree of pooling: the approach allocates forecasters whose predictive distributions are similar to one another into groups and allows the number of groups to grow naturally as more data becomes available. This pooling mitigates overfitting and produces sharper inference. At the same time, the nonparametric nature of the prior overcomes the inherent misspecification implied by the use of a specific parametric distribution and thereby delivers some consistency results when n goes to infinity which we briefly mention below.[6]

Some asymptotic properties

Asymptotic properties of the proposed Bayesian model can be studied in two settings: large n and large J. The first asymptotic scenario concerns the consistency of the posterior distribution of the Bayesian model for the inference on the z's, while the second concerns the inference on the underlying probability distribution $F(\cdot)$. When the number of forecasters n grows to infinity, the posterior distribution concentrates around the process that is generating the data $\mathbf{z}_1, \mathbf{z}_2, \ldots$ (Ghosh and Ramamoorthi, 2003). Very loosely speaking, this implies that whatever the data generating process for the $\mathbf{z}_1, \mathbf{z}_2, \ldots$, the

---

[6] The Dirichlet process prior is an example of a Bayesian nonparametric model and it has been applied in many fields, including econometrics (e.g., see Hirano, 2002; Griffin and Steel, 2011; Bassetti et al., 2014, 2018; Griffin and Kalli, 2018; Billio et al., 2019) and psychometrics (e.g., see Navarro et al., 2006; Karabatsos and Walker, 2009; Li et al., 2019). In econometrics, Bayesian nonparametrics has been used to build robust models that account for heavy tails, skewness, and multimodality. In psychometrics, Bayesian nonparametrics has been successfully employed to accommodate heterogeneity in experimental responses within models for cognitive processes.

posterior will recover it. When, in addition, the number of bins J goes to infinity, the bin size goes to zero and the rounding disappears, the random histogram model $\mathbf{z}_i$ converges to an infinite dimensional model where each forecaster's response is modeled by a (random) CDF $Z_{i,\infty}$ with mean $F(\cdot|\boldsymbol{\theta}_i)$. Del Negro et al. (2022) provide a much more formal treatment.

Finite sample properties and caveats

Given a finite sample of forecasters, the posterior distribution can be easily approximated by Monte Carlo sampling (see Del Negro et al., 2022, for further details). This method generates random draws from the posterior distribution of $\boldsymbol{\theta}_i$ and of the subjective CDF $F(y|\boldsymbol{\theta}_i)$. For each posterior draw, the quantity of interest is computed, whether it involves individual forecasters or the cross-sectional distribution of forecasters. Point estimates, whenever used, and posterior credible intervals for any such object are obtained from this simulated posterior distribution.

The choice of the probabilistic model and of the prior distribution can have an impact on the results given that n is far from infinity (it hovers around 30 for the SPF) and especially because the number of bins J and of observations for forecasters are small (e.g., $J = 10$ in the US SPF on GDP in 2020). Therefore the choice of the probability density $h(\cdot)$, and in particular the distribution family $F(\cdot)$, does matter. When the number of bins decreases and/or the bin width increases, the amount of information available to reconstruct the subjective CDF diminishes, and model assumptions can have a more significant impact on the empirical results. An advantage of the Bayesian approach is that it accounts for the lack of information returning wider credible intervals, as we will see below. In general, the approach provides a measure of the level of estimation uncertainty for all objects of interest. Nevertheless, a robustness check with respect to the specification of the prior distribution and the distribution family should be considered in all applications of this method.

A comparison with existing approaches

We conclude this section with some comparisons between the different approaches in our application.[7] Fig. 15.3 shows the inference results for the four SPF respondents shown in Fig. 15.1. For each forecaster we show posterior draws (thin gray lines) from the BNP model for the subjective CDFs (top) and their quantiles (bottom), and compare it with the beta (black, dashed–dotted lines for the CDF, and squares for the quintiles) and Gaussian (gray, dashed lines for the CDF, and circles for the quintiles) approaches. The CDF plots also show the observed cumulated histogram Z_{ij} (crosses), as in Fig. 15.2. The quantiles shown in the bottom panels are the 5th, 10th, 25th, 50th, 75th, 90th, and 95th, with colors becoming lighter the farther away the quantile is from the median.

For the BNP approach, the bars represent the posterior means for each quantile and, for each quantile, the (5, 95) posterior coverage intervals are shown using triangles. Fig. 15.4 shows posterior draws from the BNP model for the subjective PDFs for the same forecasters, along with the stepwise uniform PDF obtained from histogram probabilities z_{ij}, $j = 1, \ldots, J$ (dotted lines).

---

[7] The prior distribution on the parameters μ, μ_δ, σ_1, σ_2, ω, ϕ, and ϵ is a Dirichlet process with concentration $\psi_0 = 1$ and base measure G_0 given by $\mu \sim \mathcal{N}(2, 5^2)$ (normal); $\sigma_j \sim \mathcal{IGa}(a_\sigma, b_\sigma)\mathcal{I}(\sigma_j)_{(0,10)}$ $j = 1, 2$ (inverse gamma), $E[\sigma_j] = 2$ and $V[\sigma_j] = 4$; $\mu_\delta \sim \mathcal{N}(0, 2.5^2)$ (normal); $\omega \sim \mathcal{Be}(0.5, 3)$ (beta); $\phi \sim \mathcal{Ga}(a_\phi, b_\phi)\mathcal{I}(\sigma_j)_{(0,10)}$ (gamma) such that $E[\phi] = 25$ and $V[\phi] = 100$; $\epsilon \sim \mathcal{Ga}(a_\epsilon, b_\epsilon)$ (gamma) such that α_j is close to one for $\nu_j < 0.01$, very small for any $\nu_j > 0.05$, and virtually zero when $\nu_j > 0.1$.

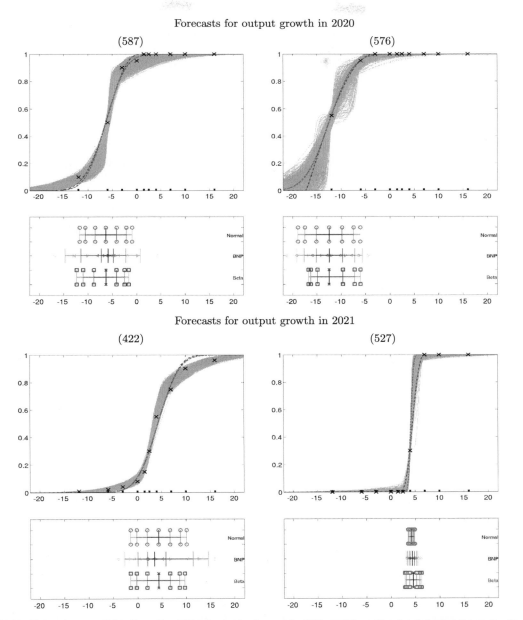

FIGURE 15.3 Inference Using Bayesian Nonparametric Approach: CDFs and Quantiles for Selected Examples from the 2020Q2 SPF

Note: In each panel: the subjective CDFs (top panels) and selected quantiles (bottom panels). Top panels: subjective CDF using least-squares approach with normal (gray, dashed line) or beta (black, dashed–dotted line) assumption; subjective CDF using BNP approach (posterior random draws in light gray); and observed cumulated histogram probabilities Z_{ij} $j = 1, \ldots, J$ (crosses). Bottom panels: quantiles of the predictive distribution computed using the normal (gray circles) or beta (black squares), and the BNP approach. The quantiles shown are the 5th, 10th, 25th, 50th, 75th, 90th, and 95th, with colors becoming lighter the farther away the quantile is from the median. For the BNP approach the bars represent the posterior means for each quantile and, for each quantile, the (5, 95) posterior coverage intervals are shown using triangles.

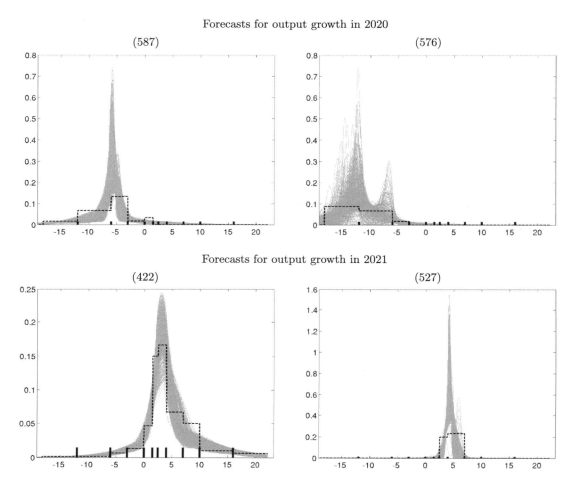

FIGURE 15.4 Inference Using Bayesian Nonparametric Approach: PDFs for Selected Examples from the 2020Q2 SPF

Note: In each panel: subjective PDF using BNP approach (posterior random draws in gray); and stepwise uniform PDF (dotted lines) implied by the histogram probabilities z_{ij}, $j = 1, \ldots, J$.

Fig. 15.3 is helpful in illustrating a few points about the BNP approach. First, the observed cumulative histogram (the Z_{ij}'s; crosses) belongs to the high posterior density region for all respondents. In contrast, as noted in discussing Fig. 15.2, the beta and the normal approaches do not always fit the Z_{ij}'s well, and in these cases their CDFs do not belong to the high posterior density region obtained from the BNP approach. This implies that there can be significant differences in the quantiles implied by the different approaches (see, for instance, forecaster 587 or 422). Both the beta and the normal distributions miss the fat-tails of the distribution (e.g., see the left tails in the CDF chart, which are apparent also from Fig. 15.4), and the interquartile range is much wider than that implied by the BNP approach.

Fig. 15.3 also shows that whenever there is less information from the respondent, the BNP approach delivers wider posterior coverage intervals reflecting the higher degree of uncertainty. The case of respondent 576 is exemplary. This respondent places 55% probability on the left open bin (see Fig. 15.1), implying that we know very little about the left-tail behavior of this forecaster. The posterior coverage intervals for both the BNP CDF and PDF reflect this uncertainty, as evidenced by the fact that the gray lines for both the CDF and the PDF are far less concentrated for forecaster 576 in the left tail than for other forecasters (e.g., 587). Moreover, the gray lines for the left tails are less concentrated than for the right tails, where we have more information. The posterior distribution for the quantiles (especially for the left tail) also reflects this lack of information.

While Figs. 15.2, 15.3, and 15.4 looked at a few examples, Fig. 15.5 compares all participants across different parametric assumptions and estimation approaches, for the forecasts for 2021 made in 2020Q1 and 2020Q2.[8] In the comparison we use the interquantile distances (IQD) of the subjective CDF. Let F denote a CDF; its IQD(q, r) is defined as

$$IQD(q, r) = F^{-1}(r/100) - F^{-1}(q/100) \tag{15.8}$$

with $q \leq r$ and $q, r \in [0, 100]$. The interquartile range (IQR), a measure widely used to measure uncertainty in probability forecasts (see Chapter 3 in this Handbook), is a special case of the IQD(q, r) for $q = 25$ and $r = 75$.

Each plot shows the IQDs computed according to BNP on the x-axis versus the IQDs computed using the normal (left column; gray circles) or beta (right column; black squares) approaches on the y-axis. The dot reports the BNP posterior mean while the thin horizontal lines provide the 95% posterior credible intervals. The 45-degree line indicates BNP and least-squares estimates are equal. While some of the points lie not too far from the 45-degree line, there are several deviations. For many forecasters, the BNP estimates of the IQD$(10, 90)$ are smaller than the least-square estimates (dots below the 45-degree line), suggesting that the subjective CDF BNP estimates' tails have a slower decay rate than one of the other models. Note that this is the case both before and after COVID, although the range of the x-axis is very different. For the IQRs (not shown), differences between BNP and alternative approaches are smaller—most points lie not far from the 45-degree line. Still, if we compute the ratio of the IQRs computed using the different approaches, we find that the posterior mean of these ratios varies from below 0.5 to above 1.5, suggesting that different approaches can lead to a different assessment of uncertainty.

15.3 Challenges in measuring uncertainty

Assessing uncertainty plays an important role in macroeconomics analysis (Bloom, 2009, and Jurado et al., 2015, are two notable examples, and Bloom, 2014, provides a survey). Density predictions have the advantage over point predictions in that they provide information about the forecasters' subjective

---

[8] Note that beginning with the 2020:Q2 SPF, changes were made to the definition of the bins for real GDP growth. Prior to 2020Q2, there were 11 bins with bounds −3, −2, −1, 0, 1, 2, 3, 4, 5, and 6 with left- and right-open bins.

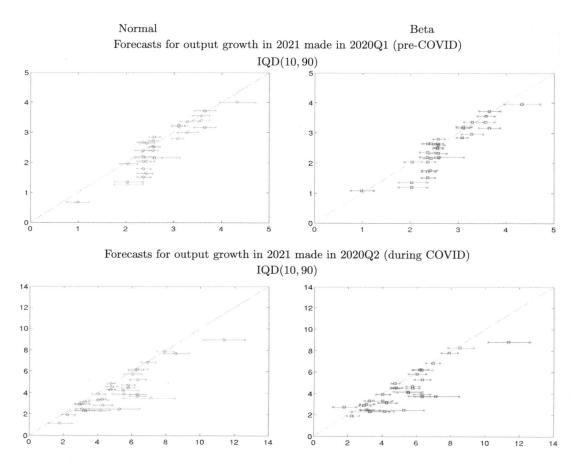

FIGURE 15.5 Inter-quantile Ranges: Implications from Alternative Approaches

Note: In each plot, the dot coordinates represent the IQDs (or IQR) computed according to the BNP (horizontal axis) and the least-squares (vertical axis) approaches for the normal (left, gray circles) or beta (right, black squares) distributions.

view on uncertainty. A large body of literature, much of it reviewed in Chapter 3 in this Handbook, makes use of uncertainty measures based on surveys of forecasters and investigates their properties.[9]

Measuring uncertainty in the context of density forecasts is not a trivial task, and this section reviews the approaches that have been used in the literature and the extent to which they may lead to different

---

[9] Zarnowitz and Lambros (1987) and Giordani and Soderlind (2003) find that forecasters underestimate uncertainty. Boero et al. (2008), Daniel and Hirshleifer (2015), Kenny et al. (2014), Malmendier and Taylor (2015) also find that forecasters are overconfident and discuss various strategy to measure overconfidence. Some researchers (e.g., Liu and Sheng, 2019) explore the impact of subjective uncertainty on macroeconomic activity or discuss its evolution over time (e.g., Campbell, 2007).

answers (see also Manski, 2018, for an insightful discussion). The variance (or the standard deviation) is a natural measure of uncertainty, but it is sensitive to assumptions on the tail behavior of the PDF. Cognizant of its current limitations (e.g., the fact that the beta chops off the tails altogether, or that the Gaussian does not capture possible fat tails), the literature has often relied on measures of uncertainty based on the IQR or other IQDs (e.g., Engelberg et al., 2011; Manski, 2018; Bruine De Bruin et al., 2011, among many others). If one ignores issues of rounding, IQRs are particularly robust because the bins' edges can provide a nonparametric boundary for the quartiles. Since in normal circumstances it is quite rare for respondents to place more than 25% probability on the open bins, if $F(y_j) < 0.25$ and $F(y_{j+1}) > 0.25$, then it had better be that $y_j < F^{-1}(0.25) < y_{j+1}$.

A number of challenges remain, however. First, rounding may make nonparametric boundaries less reliable. Second, it is not clear what to do in the event that the given parametric distribution does not fit the points in the CDF well, such that $F^{-1}(0.25)$ or $F^{-1}(0.75)$ and the nonparametric boundaries are at odds—the beta for forecaster 422 in Fig. 15.2 being one example. Third, there are cases, as we have seen, where respondents place more than 25% probability on the outer bins, and these cases are more frequent precisely when the uncertainty increases, that is, when monitoring it becomes most important. Fourth, when the gap between bins is wide, the IQR remains dependent on the assumed parametric distribution, as is the case for output forecasts during COVID. For instance, $F^{-1}(0.25)$ could be anywhere between -6% and -12% percent for respondent 587 in Fig. 15.2.

Perhaps the most important issue is that only under Gaussianity are the IQR, other IQDs, and the standard deviation proportional to one another and provide the same assessment of uncertainty. In the presence of skewness or kurtosis these various measures can provide quite different answers. We have seen above examples of distributions that appear to be far from Gaussian. How general is this situation? In the remainder of the section, we use the SPF dataset to provide an illustration of this issue.

Fig. 15.6 considers two sets of forecasts: forecasts for 2020 made before (2020Q1, left column) and after (2020Q2, right column) COVID. The first row plots show, for each respondent in the survey, the ratio (vertical axis) between the IQR and the IQD(10, 90) (BNP estimates), divided by the theoretical value of this ratio under Gaussianity versus the mean IQR (horizontal axis). In other words, if the distributions were all Gaussian, all the points should be equal to 1 (horizontal dashed line). We see that under standard circumstances (left column) when uncertainty is small, most observations are fairly close to 1 with only a handful of exceptions. When uncertainty becomes very large, however (right column), deviations from Gaussianity become both larger (a ratio of 2 means that the IQD(10, 90) is twice as large as that implied by the IQR under normality) and more common. The last two rows perform the same analysis for IQD(5, 95) and for the standard deviation. Not surprisingly, the deviations from Gaussianity are even larger when looking at these two statistics and quantitatively striking for forecasts made in 2020Q2: for several forecasters, uncertainty is at least 50% larger when measured using the IQD(5, 95) or the standard deviation relative to the IQR. The bottom line from this section is that one measure of uncertainty is probably not sufficient, particularly in periods when uncertainty is high. For this reason, when assessing the evolution of uncertainty over time in Section 15.6 we look at a variety of measures.

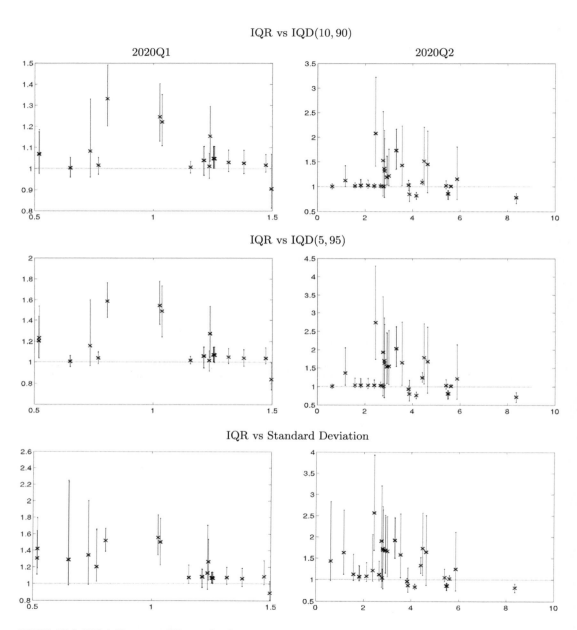

FIGURE 15.6 Which Measure of Uncertainty?

Note: In each plot: dots coordinates are the ratio between the BNP IQR/IQD ratio and the theoretical value of the ratio under Gaussianity (vertical axis) and the mean IQR (horizontal axis); vertical lines represent credible intervals.

15.4 **Heterogeneity in density forecasts**

Subjective density forecasts can be very different from one another. The probabilistic predictions for output growth in 2021 made by forecasters 422 and 527 in Fig. 15.1 are a shining example of this phenomenon. This section discusses heterogeneity in both the first and the second moments of the forecast distributions, using the SPF surveys during the pandemic as an illustration.

It was established long ago—at least since Wachtel (1977) and Bomberger and Frazer (1981)—that forecasters disagree about point forecasts, and a large literature has documented and tried to explain this phenomenon for macroeconomic surveys (see, for instance, Mankiw et al., 2003; Carroll, 2003; Capistrán and Timmermann, 2009; Patton and Timmermann, 2010, 2011; Andrade and Le Bihan, 2013; Andrade et al., 2016 and other papers surveyed in Chapter 3 in this Handbook). While much of the early literature focused on point projections, some studies documented the fact that forecasters disagree about uncertainty (e.g., Lahiri and Liu, 2006, D'Amico and Orphanides, 2008 and Manski, 2018).[10] A number of papers provide evidence of persistent heterogeneity in subjective uncertainty (Bruine De Bruin et al., 2011; Boero et al., 2014) and interpret this fact as suggesting that the degree of uncertainty is a forecaster-specific characteristic akin to the individual optimism and pessimism established in the literature on point forecasts. While the papers mentioned above provide quantitative evidence on forecasters' heterogeneity by focusing on the variance of first- or second-order moments, other work discusses higher moments (e.g., Mirkov and Steinhauer, 2018) or uses measures of discrepancy based on entire predictive distribution (e.g., Shoja and Soofi, 2017, Cumings-Menon et al., 2021, and Rich and Tracy, 2021). In particular, Rich and Tracy (2021) propose a measure of heterogeneity based on the Wasserstein distance, which they computed assuming that individual PDFs are stepwise Uniform distributions; see also Chapter 3 in this Handbook for further references.

In the remainder of the section we document the fact that SPF forecasters do indeed significantly disagree about the uncertainty in the economy and that the extent of their disagreement increases in high-volatility periods such as COVID. Fig. 15.7 shows the quantiles for the individual output growth density forecasts for 2020 made in 2020Q1 (left panel), right before the COVID pandemic reached the US, and the following quarter, 2020Q2 (right panel). For each forecaster the quantiles of the distribution are depicted using different shades of gray: light gray for the segment connecting the 5th and 95th quantiles, slightly darker gray for that connecting the 10th and 90th quantiles, and black for the 25th–75th range. The median is denoted using a single vertical black bar and the mean by a cross. For each object (quantiles and mean) we report only the posterior mean, because visualizing posterior uncertainty as in Fig. 15.3 becomes challenging. In each panel the forecasters are sorted from 1 to n, where n is the total number of forecasters in each survey, on the basis of their (posterior mean) IQR.

Since the survey composition changes from survey to survey the figure does not allow for comparing the change in uncertainty for the same individual (some of the results shown later in Section 15.6 are more suited for this purpose). The point of Fig. 15.7 is instead twofold. First, it provides a bird's-eye

---

[10] Lahiri and Liu (2006) measure the uncertainty by fitting a Gaussian CDF to each forecaster's histogram and using the "whisker plots" (that is, plotting some key quantiles of the distribution). D'Amico and Orphanides (2008) measure the individual variance under the Normal parametric assumption, assume a Gamma distribution for the cross-section of individual variances, and use the variance of this Gamma to measure disagreement about uncertainty. Still in the context of the SPF, Manski (2018) plots the median versus the IQR for a cross-section of SPF forecasters and thereby documents the heterogeneity in both the central tendencies and uncertainty. A few papers (Clements, 2014b; Manzan, 2021, among others) discuss the updating of density forecasts and in particular uncertainty in light of new information.

Forecasts for 2020 made in 2020Q1

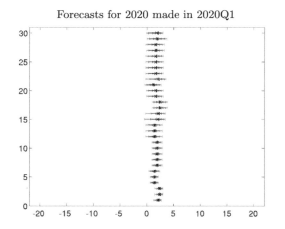

Forecasts for 2020 made in 2020Q2

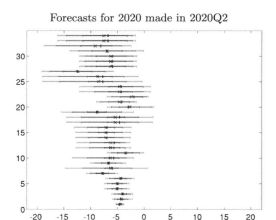

FIGURE 15.7 Quantiles and Mean of Individual Density Forecasts for Output Growth

Note: For each object (quantiles and mean), we report the posterior mean.

view of the dramatic differences in uncertainty between the two surveys, even though their temporal distance is only one quarter (the x-axis is the same in both panels to emphasize this point). In 2020Q1 essentially all IQD(5, 95) are between 0 and 4, while in 2020Q2, for many of the participants, they are several times as large. Second, it shows that heterogeneity in both central tendencies and subjective uncertainty is sizeable. Some forecasters remain quite confident about their predictions even during COVID, while for others the IQD(5, 95) is almost as large as 20%. While the fact that the location of the bins changed from 2020Q1 to Q2 may explain part of the increase in average uncertainty across surveys, it is less clear that it has an effect on the increase in heterogeneity.

Fig. 15.8 provides evidence on the heterogeneity in central tendencies and uncertainty, as well as its evolution with COVID. The left column in Fig. 15.8 shows the means (light gray, squares) for all respondents, sorted in increasing order, and expressed in difference from the cross-sectional median (of the means). The black line with crosses does the same for the median. The right column uses the same approach to quantify heterogeneity in uncertainty, as measured by the IQR (black, crosses), the IQD(95, 5) (gray, diamonds), and the standard deviation (light gray, squares). Full homogeneity implies that each line is vertical at zero. The flatter the curve, the higher the level of disagreement among forecasters. The top and bottom row concern predictions made in 2020Q1 and 2020Q2, respectively.

That the scale of the x-axis is almost one order of magnitude larger for 2020Q2 than 2020Q1 for both heterogeneity in central tendencies and uncertainty is quite telling. Differences in means or medians between more and less optimistic forecasters are on the order of about 1% in 2020Q1. They become about 10% in 2020Q2. Heterogeneity in uncertainty is more sensitive to how it is measured. In 2020Q1 the difference in IQRs between the least and the most uncertain respondent is on the order of 1%, while the difference in IQD(5, 95) and standard deviations is about 1.5% and 2%, respectively. In 2020Q2, as the COVID pandemic hit the US, the difference in IQRs between the least and the most uncertain respondent is about 7%, while that in IQD(5, 95) is almost a staggering 20%. This suggests that the assessment of tail events is far more different in 2020Q2 than before COVID. The different behavior

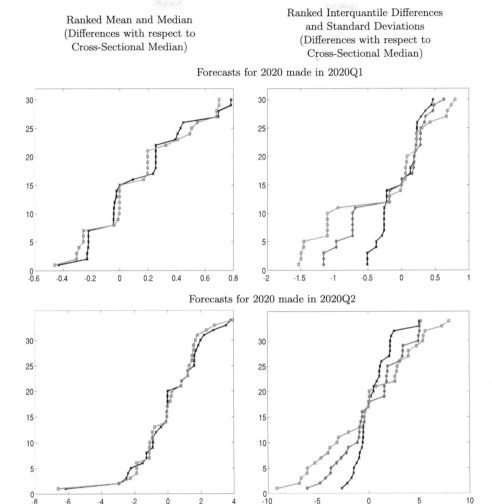

FIGURE 15.8 Disagreement About Mean, Median, and Uncertainty for Output Growth

Note: Left: ranked differences in the mean (light gray, squares) and the median (black, crosses). Right: ranked differences in the IQR (black, crosses), IQD(5, 95) (gray, diamonds), and standard deviation (light gray, squares). The reported values are the posterior means of the quantities of interest.

of the IQRs and IQD(5, 95) confirms the departure from Gaussianity discussed in the previous section. The difference in standard deviations in 2020Q2 is smaller, however, and closer to that of IQRs.

An interesting feature of Fig. 15.8 is that the clustering of the CDF forecasters in terms of both means and uncertainty is quite evident from the staircase-like behavior of the curves for the pre-COVID density predictions, with three or more forecasters having very similar central tendencies or degrees of uncertainty. In 2020Q2 the curves are more continuous, although there is still some amount of clustering. This also indicates that the amount of heterogeneity increases together with uncertainty during COVID.

15.5 Pooling and consensus forecasts

It is common practice to aggregate forecasters, if only to simplify the presentation of the analysis and avoid reporting all the individual responses. The goal of forecast combination is to reduce the information of a pool of forecasts to a single combined forecast (e.g., see Timmermann, 2006). Combination may occur at two different levels: point forecasts or probability forecasts. For example, the Philadelphia Fed reports the SPF data aggregated across forecasters in two ways: the median of the point forecasts and the average probability mass in each bin for the probability forecasts. In the remainder of the section we focus on combining probabilistic forecasts.

The simplest possible combination formula for histograms, densities, and CDF is the linear combination, also known as linear pooling (se, e.g., Genest and Zidek, 1986). The linear pooling of subjective PDFs and CDFs is defined as

$$\bar{f}^w(y) = \sum_{i=1}^n w_i f(y|\boldsymbol{\theta}_i), \quad \bar{F}^w(y) = \sum_{i=1}^n w_i F(y|\boldsymbol{\theta}_i), \tag{15.9}$$

where $w_i \geq 0$, $i = 1, \ldots, n$, $\sum_{i=1}^n w_i = 1$, and $f(y|\boldsymbol{\theta}_i)$ is the PDF associated with the subjective CDF $F(y|\boldsymbol{\theta}_i)$. The equally weighted linear pooling, also known as "consensus density forecast," is obtained for $w_i = 1/n$. In what follows, we denote with $\bar{f}(y)$ and $\bar{F}(y)$ the consensus PDF and CDF, respectively. Analogous definitions can be given for equally weighted linear pooling of histograms and cumulated histograms, that is, $\bar{z}_j = (z_{1j} + \cdots + z_{nj})/n$ and $\bar{Z}_j = (Z_{1j} + \cdots + Z_{nj})/n$. Empirical studies have shown that consensus performs relatively well in practice and usually outperforms more sophisticated pooling schemes (e.g., Zarnowitz, 1967, and more recently Genre et al., 2013, and Conflitti et al., 2015).

Fig. 15.9 provides examples of consensus density forecasts. The top-row panels show the stepwise uniform PDF implied by the pooling probabilities $\bar{z}_j$, $j = 1, \ldots, J$, for output growth in 2020 (left) and 2021 (right) from the 2020Q2 SPF survey (stepwise dotted lines). They also show the estimated consensus PDF obtained using the BNP approach (posterior draws in gray). The middle-row panels show the cumulated histogram pooling probabilities $\bar{Z}_j$ $j = 1, \ldots, J$ (crosses) and the consensus CDF (posterior draws in gray). The bottom panels display selected quantiles of the consensus distribution computed using the BNP approach, with the bars representing the posterior means for each quantile and the triangles representing the $(5, 95)$ percent posterior coverage intervals. Fig. 15.9 shows that the level of estimation uncertainty for the consensus PDF or CDF is generally much smaller than that for individual forecasters (recall Fig. 15.3). This reduction in the inference uncertainty is an effect of both averaging and the fact that pooling favors posterior concentration. Fig. 15.9 also suggests that estimation uncertainty for the consensus distribution in 2020 (left) is larger than that for 2021 (right), partly because in 2020 respondents assign substantial mass to the left-open bin and to the very wide bin $(-12, -6]$.

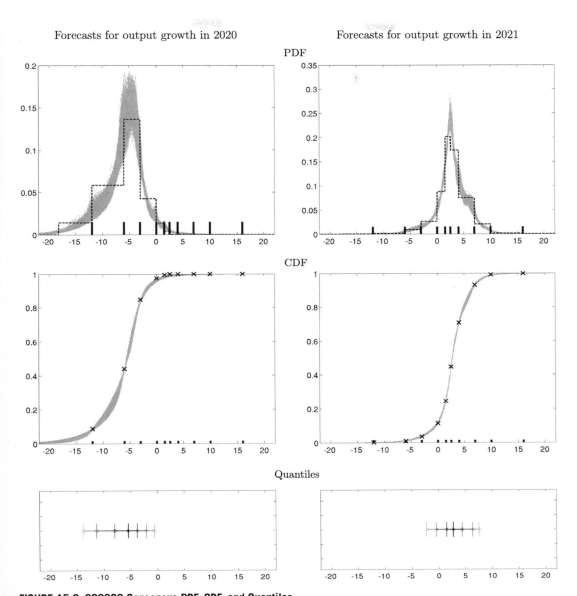

FIGURE 15.9 2020Q2 Consensus PDF, CDF, and Quantiles

Note: Top row: stepwise uniform PDF (dotted lines) implied by the pooling probabilities $\bar{z}_j$, $j = 1, \ldots, J$ and consensus PDF using BNP (posterior random draws in light gray). Middle row: cumulated histogram pooling probabilities $\bar{Z}_j$ $j = 1, \ldots, J$ (crosses) and consensus CDF using BNP (posterior random draws in gray). Bottom row: quantile ranges of the consensus distribution. Bottom panels: selected quantiles of the consensus distribution computed using the BNP approach. The quantiles shown are the 5th, 10th, 25th, 50th, 75th, 90th, and 95th, with colors becoming lighter the farther away the quantile is from the median. The bars represent the posterior means for each quantile and, for each quantile, the $(5, 95)$ percent posterior coverage intervals are shown using triangles.

After the seminal paper by Stone (1961), pooling of densities has been extensively applied in the empirical literature (see, e.g., DeGroot and Mortera, 1991; DeGroot et al., 1995) and extended along different directions including nonlinear pooling (e.g., see Genest and Zidek, 1986; DeGroot and Mortera, 1991; Clements and Harvey, 2011), calibrated linear pooling (e.g., Ranjan and Gneiting, 2010), and generalized pooling (see, e.g., Kapetanios et al., 2015; Bassetti et al., 2018). In this literature, a parametric family of aggregation functions C_{η} from $[0, 1]^n$ to $[0, 1]$, with $\eta \in E$, is used to pool together the CDFs:

$$\bar{F}^{\eta}(y) = C_{\eta}(F(y|\boldsymbol{\theta}_1), \ldots, F(y|\boldsymbol{\theta}_n)). \tag{15.10}$$

The linear pooling is a special case of these general frameworks, which can be obtained choosing $C_{\eta}(x_1, \ldots, x_n) = \eta_1 x_1 + \cdots + \eta_n x_n$ and $\eta_j = w_j$. Optimal pooling has been introduced to take advantage of the heterogeneous forecast abilities of the respondents (see, e.g., Hall and Mitchell, 2007; Geweke and Amisano, 2011; Clements and Harvey, 2011). In this framework the weights w_j, $j = 1, \ldots, n$, of the linear pooling or the parameters η of the generalized pooling are either specified as a function of the relative performances of the forecasters, or chosen following some statistical criteria. In both frameworks, forecast performances are taken into account and usually obtained from previous forecasting exercises. The literature has also recognized that relative forecasting performance may change over time and has proposed time-varying pooling schemes (see, e.g., Billio et al., 2013; Del Negro et al., 2016; McAlinn and West, 2019).

The pooling techniques reviewed above make it possible to partly summarize the information content of the individual predictive densities. In the case of linear pooling it is possible to establish a relationship between the first and second moments of the pooled distribution and the cross-sectional distribution of the moments of the individual CDFs. For instance, the uncertainty in the linear pooling distribution can be related to the uncertainty in the individual forecasts. The variance of the consensus CDF, sometimes refereed to as *aggregate uncertainty*, is the sum of the *average (individual) uncertainty* $\bar{\sigma}^2$ and the *disagreement* among forecasters $\mathbb{V}(\mu)$, defined as

$$\bar{\sigma}^2 = \sum_{i=1}^{n} w_i \sigma_i^2, \quad \mathbb{V}(\mu) = \sum_{i=1}^{n} w_i (\mu_i - \bar{\mu})^2, \tag{15.11}$$

where μ_i and σ_i^2 are the mean and variance, respectively, of the ith forecaster CDF, $i = 1, \ldots, n$, and $\bar{\mu} = w_1 \mu_1 + \cdots + w_n \mu_n$ is the mean of the linear pooling. These indicators have been used in macroeconomic analysis, to capture different aspects of the aggregate uncertainty (see, e.g., Giordani and Soderlind, 2003); see also Chapter 3 in this Handbook for more details on the uncertainty and disagreement decomposition and for a review of the literature.

15.6 The evolution of professional forecasters' density forecasts during the COVID pandemic

This section describes the evolution of SPF density forecasts for GDP growth and inflation during the COVID pandemic. We discuss the change in the consensus forecast, in average measures of subjective uncertainty, as well as heterogeneity in both mean projections and subjective confidence in such projections. We show the time series for these various objects of interest from 2007 to 2021, where the starting date is chosen so that the analysis includes the Great Recession for comparison. We will focus on the surveys for both the current and the following year made in Q2 of each year, keeping constant the quarter in which the survey is taken so that the forecast horizon is comparable across the time series. We choose Q2 because we have observations in 2020 after the pandemic had begun as well as for 2021, but the general conclusions are broadly similar regardless of the quarter chosen.

15.6.1 GDP growth

The two panels in the top row of Fig. 15.10 display the mean and selected quantiles of the consensus forecast PDF $\bar{f}(y)$ defined in Eq. (15.9) for the current and the following year. Specifically, in each panel the black solid line in each panel shows the mean of the consensus distribution, while the 5th, 10th, 25th, 75th, 90th, and 95th quantiles of the distribution are displayed using different shades of gray (for all objects in the top panels we show the BNP posterior means).

The panels on the bottom row show the variance of the consensus forecast (solid black line) together with its decomposition between average uncertainty across forecasters $\bar{\sigma}^2$ (dashed gray line) and disagreement $\mathbb{V}(\mu)$ (dashed–dotted black line). For each object the line represents the posterior BNP mean, while the shaded areas display the 90% posterior credible intervals.

Focusing on the projections for the current year (left column), we see that the consensus forecast distribution goes deep into negative territory in 2020, and its variance increases to unprecedented levels.[11] While disagreement also rises notably in 2020, most of the increase in the variance of the consensus distribution is due to the increase in the average variance across individuals. In 2021 the variance of the consensus forecasts, the average variance, and disagreement all fall to about one-third of their 2020 respective levels, but remain elevated compared to historical standards. The bottom panels also display the 90% credible intervals for each object of interest (shaded areas) and show that the increases in both uncertainty and disagreement during COVID are very significant even if one takes inference uncertainty into account.

Moving on to the forecasts for the following year (right column), the variance of the consensus forecast also rises to unprecedented levels in 2020, although it is smaller by about one-third than the variance for the current year. A key difference relative to the current-year projections is that disagreement is as important a driver for this increase as the average variance across individuals. In 2021 the average variance declines a bit, but remains very high, while disagreement falls by more than half, but remains quantitatively important. The only two episodes where disagreement plays a nonnegligible role are the COVID crisis and the Great Recession.

Fig. 15.10 showed that average subjective uncertainty for GDP growth predictions, as measured by the variance, rose dramatically during the COVID pandemic. Was this rise common to all forecasters? Is it robust to different measures of uncertainty? (Recall from previous sections that different measures can result in different answers as density forecasts are sometimes far from Gaussian.) Was it due to compositional effects? Fig. 15.11 addresses these questions.

The top panels of Fig. 15.11 use the IQR as a measure of uncertainty (results for the IQD(10, 90) are qualitatively similar). Each panel displays the IQR for individual forecasters (thin gray lines with crosses), the mean of the cross-sectional IQR distribution (solid line; the median is very similar and

---

[11] It is important to recall that the survey design, and in particular the location of the bin edges y_j, changed in 2009 and then again, dramatically, in 2020. This may have impacted the reported subjective uncertainty.

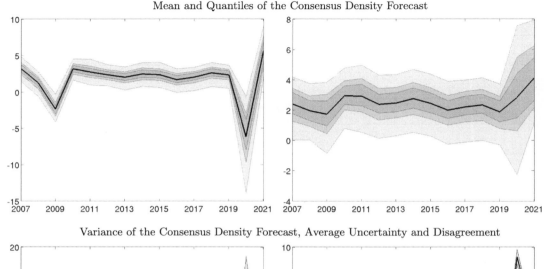

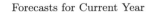

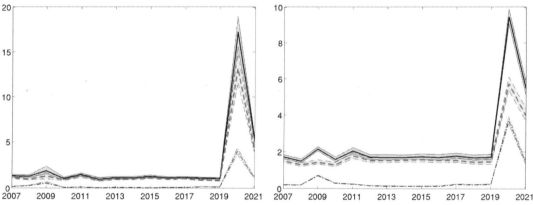

FIGURE 15.10 GDP Growth Uncertainty during COVID

Note: Left column: current year; right column: next year. Top row: mean of the consensus distribution (black solid line); the 5th, 10th, 25th, 75th, 90th, and 95th quantiles of the consensus distribution are displayed using different shades of gray. Bottom row: variance of the consensus forecast (solid black line), average uncertainty across forecasters $\bar{\sigma}^2$ (dashed gray line); disagreement $\mathbb{V}(\mu)$ (dashed–dotted black line). For each object the shaded areas display the 90% posterior credible intervals.

therefore not reported), and the IQR for the consensus forecast (dashed line). We show individual measures of uncertainty so that one can informally assess the extent to which changes in the composition of the panel affect summary measures of uncertainty such as the mean (Manski, 2018, stresses the extent to which the literature has often ignored compositional changes when discussing the evolution of consensus measures). The bottom panels of Fig. 15.11 provide summary measures of heterogeneity

Forecasts for Current Year   Forecasts for the Following Year

Individual, Mean, and Consensus Density Forecast IQR

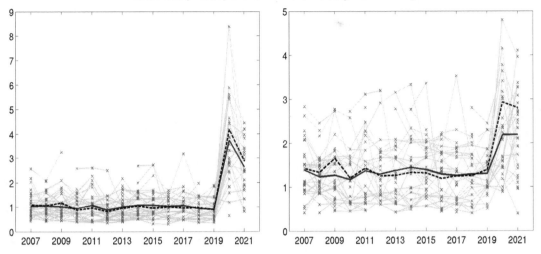

Heterogeneity in Uncertainty for GDP Density Forecasts

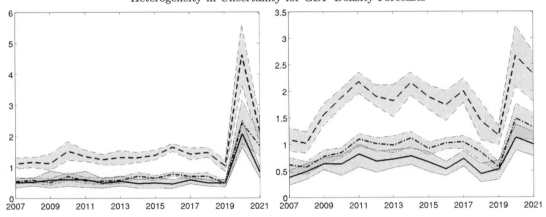

FIGURE 15.11 Average and Individual GDP Growth Uncertainty during COVID

Note: Top panels: Individual (light gray with crosses), mean (solid black), and consensus density forecast (dashed black) IQRs. Left column: current year; right column: next year. Bottom panels: Cross-sectional IQR for individual IQD(10, 90)'s (dashed), IQRs (dashed–dotted), and standard deviation (solid). For each object, the shaded areas display the 90% posterior credible intervals. Left column: current year; right column: next year.

in uncertainty across respondents. Specifically, they display the cross-sectional IQR of different measures of individual uncertainty: the IQR, the IQD(10, 90), and the standard deviation. The left and right columns show the results for projections concerning the current and following year, respectively.

The left column of Fig. 15.11 shows that the increase in the uncertainty for the current year is (almost) universal: the IQR rises for all but one forecaster. The mean of the ranges and the range of the consensus forecast increase approximately by the same amount, highlighting that disagreement, while important in absolute terms, is, in relative terms, swamped quantitatively by the increase in uncertainty. The change in uncertainty for current-year projections differs widely across respondents, however. This is shown by the fact that the cross-sectional IQRs of various measures of uncertainty all rise substantially in 2020 (bottom-left panel). For instance the IQR for both standard deviations and IQR rises from about 0.5 to 2 in 2020, while the IQR for IQD(10, 90) increases from 1 to almost 5.

The situation is very different for the year-ahead forecasts. The increase in volatility in 2020 for the following-year forecast is less noticeable, as observed before. It is also far from homogeneous, with a sizable rise in uncertainty for some forecasters and a decline for others (top-right panel). The increase in disagreement is also evident, as the IQR for the consensus rises more than the average individual IQR. Another difference with the current-year forecasts is that uncertainty remains on average as elevated in 2021 as in 2020. Heterogeneity in uncertainty for year-ahead forecasts also rises in 2020 (bottom-right panel). Partly because the increase in uncertainty is not as pronounced as for current-year projections, the rise in heterogeneity is also less sizable.

Last, we discuss "growth at risk" as measured by the 10th quantiles of the forecast distribution (results for the 5th quantile are similar, if a bit more extreme). The notion of "growth at risk" has become popular following the seminal work of Adrian et al., 2019; see also Kozlowski et al., 2020b, 2019, 2020a for a discussion of the macroeconomic implications of tail risks. In 2020 there is much dispersion in growth at risk across respondents, with the 10th quantiles ranging from -5% to about -18%. All quantiles are much lower relative to pre-COVID years, however, indicating that growth at risk in the short run increased dramatically relative to previous years. The picture is quite different for year-ahead forecasts, where growth at risk increases noticeably for some forecasters but declines for others, so that the 10th quantile of the consensus forecast falls in 2020 but the mean declines only slightly. See Fig. 15.12.

15.6.2 **Inflation**

Turning to density forecasts for GDP deflator inflation, Fig. 15.13 documents that the mean of the consensus distribution, which of course coincides with the average mean projection across forecasters, fell in the period from 2019 to 2020 but then increased noticeably in 2021, especially for the current year. In sharp contrast with the GDP growth projections, the variance of the consensus forecast for inflation remains well below pre-Great Recession levels for both current-year and year-ahead predictions, although it increased a bit during COVID for current-year forecasts. In fact, much of the increase in the variance of the consensus distribution for current-year projections from 2019 to 2020 is due to an increase in disagreement, as average uncertainty across forecasters rose only modestly. From 2020 to 2021, average uncertainty remained essentially flat for the current year, after accounting for estimation uncertainty, but disagreement declined.

Fig. 15.14 confirms that average inflation uncertainty remains low by historical standards during the COVID period, no matter how it is measured. In fact, for most individuals, uncertainty barely changes

Forecasts for Current Year   Forecasts for the Following Year

10th Quantile for Individual and Consensus Density Forecasts

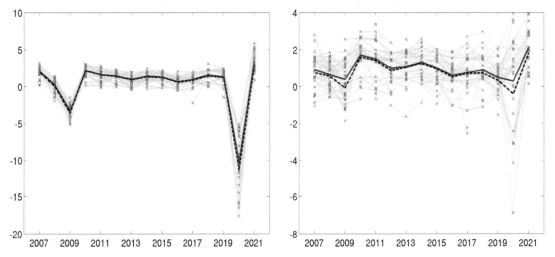

FIGURE 15.12 GDP Growth at Risk during COVID

Note: 10th quantile for individual (light gray with crosses) and consensus density forecast (dashed black); the solid black line depicts the average across individuals. Left column: current year; right column: next year.

from 2019 to 2020. Heterogeneity in uncertainty, as measured by the cross-sectional IQRs also does not rise during the pandemic. Indeed, both average uncertainty and heterogeneity in uncertainty appear to be on a downward trend since the Great Recession—a trend that is barely affected by the COVID period. This trend seems to be driven by high uncertainty forecasters who either changed their view and became more confident about their inflation projections, or disappeared from the sample.

Fig. 15.15 shows that "inflation at risk," as measured by the 90th quantile of the distribution, fell on average from 2019 to 2020 but rose noticeably in 2021 (results for the 95th quantile are similar; to our knowledge, Andrade et al., 2012, coined the term "inflation at risk" and were the first to measure it for SPF forecasters). However, in Q2 this measure was close to or slightly below the levels reached in 2007, before the Great Recession. The dispersion in inflation at risk across forecasters in 2021 is much less pronounced than it was in 2007 or even in 2011, when oil prices rose following the so-called Arab Spring.

15.7 Conclusions

The past two decades witnessed the emergence of a large number of probabilistic surveys in macroeconomics eliciting predictive probabilities from professional forecasters, financial market participants, consumers, and firms, in the US and other countries. These surveys provide a wealth of information to

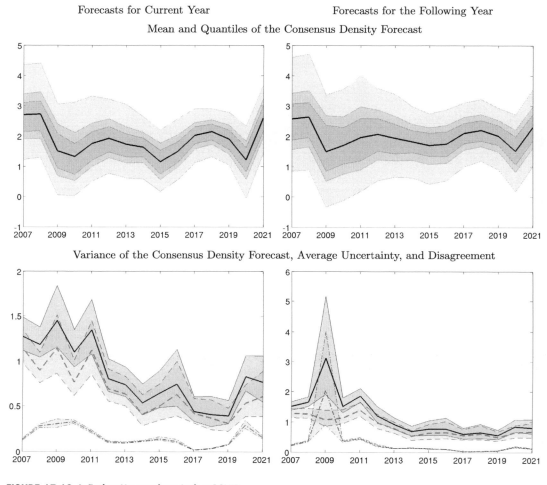

FIGURE 15.13 Inflation Uncertainty during COVID

Note: Left column: current year; right column: next year. Top row: mean of the consensus distribution (black solid line); the 5th, 10th, 25th, 75th, 90th, and 95th quantiles of the consensus distribution are displayed using different shades of gray. Bottom row: variance of the consensus forecast (solid black line), average uncertainty across forecasters $\bar{\sigma}^2$ (dashed gray line), disagreement $\mathbb{V}(\mu)$ (dashed–dotted black line). For each object, the shaded areas display the 90% posterior credible intervals.

researchers, who have enthusiastically used them to study several questions, such as the evolution of uncertainty over time.

This chapter reviewed this growing literature, with a particular emphasis on the approaches employed to translate the information provided by forecasters into objects of interest for macroeconomists. It also discussed the substantial inference challenges that this task entails and presented a novel

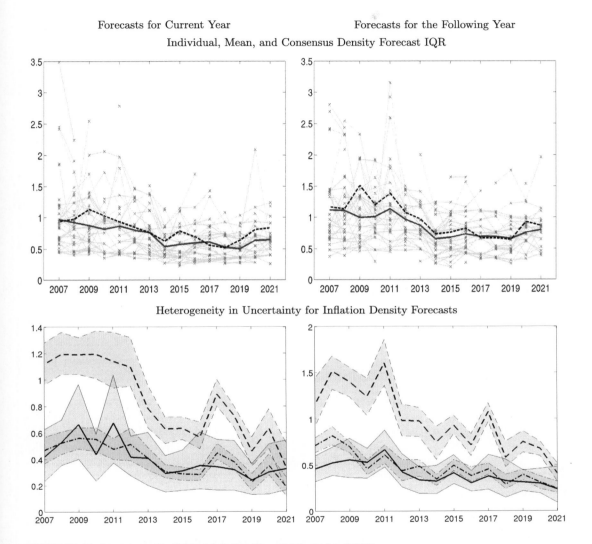

FIGURE 15.14 Average and Individual Inflation Uncertainty during COVID

Note: Top panels: Individual (light gray with crosses), mean (solid black), and consensus density forecast (dashed black) IQRs (top row) and IQD(10, 90) (bottom row). Left column: current year; right column: next year. Bottom panels: Cross-sectional IQR for individual IQD(10, 90)'s (dashed), IQRs (dashed–dotted), and standard deviation (solid). For each object, the shaded areas display the 90% posterior credible intervals. Left column: current year; right column: next year.

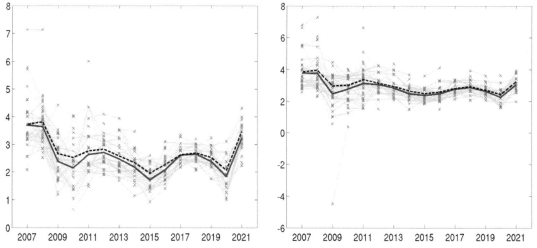

FIGURE 15.15 Inflation at Risk during COVID

Note: 90th quantile for individual (light gray with crosses) and consensus density forecast (dashed black); the solid black line depicts the average across individuals.

Bayesian nonparametric approach proposed by Del Negro et al. (2022) that tries to address some of these challenges.

Many questions concerning the proposed approach remain. One question pertains to the robustness with respect to the choice of priors and the base function—e.g., using a mixture of three as opposed to two normals. Another question relates to the robustness of the inference to the survey design and in particular to the location of the bin edges. We performed two experiments using the 2020Q2 real GDP survey. In the first experiment we merged the left open bin $(-\infty, -12]$ with the adjacent closed bin $(-12, -6]$, while in the second we merged the two closed bins $(-12, -6]$ and $(-6, -3]$. This preliminary investigation indicates, not surprisingly, that inference is much sharper when more information is provided—that is, when the bins are not merged. For most of the objects considered, the $(5, 95)$ percent posterior credible intervals from BNP obtained when less information is available (when the bins are merged) include the much narrower $(5, 95)$ percent intervals obtained using all the information from the survey. This suggests that the procedure may adequately reflect the loss of information, although a much more thorough investigation is needed.

Finally, for the time being the BNP approach deals with one survey (one cross-section) and one forecast variable at the time. It would be interesting to extend the approach to a panel context, which would permit joint inference across surveys for any object of interest (e.g., one could test the significance of changes over time for the average uncertainty across forecasters). Similarly, it would be interesting to extend the approach to a multivariable context, although at the moment we are not aware of any survey that systematically asks probabilistic questions for joint distributions (say, GDP growth and inflation).

As more and more probabilistic surveys are being conducted, it is clear that much more research is needed in order to make progress on the econometric challenges discussed in this chapter—ideally using a variety of diverse approaches, both frequentist and Bayesian. We hope that this review will help spur interest in such research.

References

Adrian, Tobias, Boyarchenko, Nina, Giannone, Domenico, 2019. Vulnerable growth. The American Economic Review 109 (4), 1263–1289.

Altig, David, Barrero, Jose Maria, Bloom, Nicholas, Davis, Steven J., Meyer, Brent, Parker, Nicholas, 2020. Surveying business uncertainty. Journal of Econometrics.

Andrade, Philippe, Crump, Richard K., Eusepi, Stefano, Moench, Emanuel, 2016. Fundamental disagreement. Journal of Monetary Economics 83, 106–128.

Andrade, Philippe, Ghysels, Eric, Idier, Julien, 2012. Tails of inflation forecasts and tales of monetary policy. Available at SSRN 2185958.

Andrade, Philippe, Le Bihan, Hervé, 2013. Inattentive professional forecasters. Journal of Monetary Economics 60 (8), 967–982.

Armantier, Olivier, Topa, Giorgio, Van der Klaauw, Wilbert, Zafar, Basit, 2017. An overview of the survey of consumer expectations. Economic Policy Review 23-2, 51–72.

Bassetti, Federico, Casarin, Roberto, Leisen, Fabrizio, 2014. Beta-product dependent Pitman–Yor processes for Bayesian inference. Journal of Econometrics 180 (1), 49–72.

Bassetti, Federico, Casarin, Roberto, Ravazzolo, Francesco, 2018. Bayesian nonparametric calibration and combination of predictive distributions. Journal of the American Statistical Association 113 (522), 675–685.

Billio, Monica, Casarin, Roberto, Ravazzolo, Francesco, Van Dijk, Herman K., 2013. Time-varying combinations of predictive densities using nonlinear filtering. Journal of Econometrics 177, 213–232.

Billio, Monica, Casarin, Roberto, Rossini, Luca, 2019. Bayesian nonparametric sparse VAR models. Journal of Econometrics 212, 97–115.

Binder, Carola C., 2017. Measuring uncertainty based on rounding: new method and application to inflation expectations. Journal of Monetary Economics 90, 1–12.

Bloom, Nicholas, 2009. The impact of uncertainty shocks. Econometrica 77 (3), 623–685.

Bloom, Nicholas, 2014. Fluctuations in uncertainty. The Journal of Economic Perspectives 28 (2), 153–176.

Boero, G., Smith, Jeremy, Wallis, Kenneth F., 2014. The measurement and charateristics of professional forecasts' uncertainty. Journal of Applied Econometrics 7 (30), 1029–1046.

Boero, Gianna, Smith, Jeremy, Wallis, Kenneth F., 2008. Uncertainty and disagreement in economic prediction: the Bank of England Survey of External Forecasters. The Economic Journal 118 (530), 1107–1127.

Bomberger, William A., Frazer, William J., 1981. Interest rates, uncertainty and the Livingston data. The Journal of Finance 36 (3), 661–675.

Bruine De Bruin, Wändi, Manski, Charles F., Topa, Giorgio, Van Der Klaauw, Wilbert, 2011. Measuring consumer uncertainty about future inflation. Journal of Applied Econometrics 26 (3), 454–478.

Campbell, Sean D., 2007. Macroeconomic volatility, predictability, and uncertainty in the great moderation: evidence from the Survey of Professional Forecasters. Journal of Business & Economic Statistics 25 (2), 191–200.

Capistrán, Carlos, Timmermann, Allan, 2009. Disagreement and biases in inflation expectations. Journal of Money, Credit, and Banking 41 (2–3), 365–396.

Carroll, Christopher D., 2003. Macroeconomic expectations of households and professional forecasters. The Quarterly Journal of Economics 118 (1), 269–298.

Clements, Michael P., 2010. Explanations of the inconsistencies in survey respondents' forecasts. European Economic Review 54 (4), 536–549.

Clements, Michael P., 2014a. Forecast uncertainty—ex ante and ex post: US inflation and output growth. Journal of Business & Economic Statistics 32 (2), 206–216.

Clements, Michael P., 2014b. Probability distributions or point predictions? Survey forecasts of US output growth and inflation. International Journal of Forecasting 30 (1), 99–117.

Clements, Michael P., Galvão, Ana Beatriz, 2017. Model and survey estimates of the term structure of US macroeconomic uncertainty. International Journal of Forecasting 33 (3), 591–604.

Clements, Michael P., Harvey, David I., 2011. Combining probability forecasts. International Journal of Forecasting 27 (2), 208–223.

Conflitti, Cristina, De Mol, Christine, Giannone, Domenico, 2015. Optimal combination of survey forecasts. International Journal of Forecasting 31 (4), 1096–1103.

Cumings-Menon, Ryan, Shin, Minchul, Sill, Keith, 2021. Measuring Disagreement in Probabilistic and Density Forecasts. Technical Report. Federal Reserve Bank of Philadelphia.

D'Amico, Stefania, Orphanides, Athanasios, 2008. Uncertainty and disagreement in economic forecasting. Technical Report. Board of Governors of the Federal Reserve System (US).

Daniel, Kent, Hirshleifer, David, 2015. Overconfident investors, predictable returns, and excessive trading. The Journal of Economic Perspectives 29 (4), 61–88.

DeGroot, Morris H., Dawid, Philip, Mortera, Julia, 1995. Coherent combination of experts' opinions. Test 4, 263–313.

DeGroot, Morris H., Mortera, Julia, 1991. Optimal linear opinion pools. Management Science 37 (5), 546–558.

Del Negro, Marco, Casarin, Roberto, Bassetti, Federico, 2022. A Bayesian Approach for Inference on Probabilistic Surveys. Staff Report 1025. Federal Reserve Bank of New York.

Del Negro, Marco, Hasegawa, Raiden B., Schorfheide, Frank, 2016. Dynamic prediction pools: an investigation of financial frictions and forecasting performance. Journal of Econometrics 192 (2), 391–405.

Dominitz, Jeff, Manski, Charles F., 1996. Eliciting student expectations of the returns to schooling. The Journal of Human Resources, 1–26.

Engelberg, Joseph, Manski, Charles F., Williams, Jared, 2009. Comparing the point predictions and subjective probability distributions of professional forecasters. Journal of Business & Economic Statistics 27 (1), 30–41.

Engelberg, Joseph, Manski, Charles F., Williams, Jared, 2011. Assessing the temporal variation of macroeconomic forecasts by a panel of changing composition. Journal of Applied Econometrics 26 (7), 1059–1078.

Ferguson, T.S., 1973. A Bayesian analysis of some nonparametric problems. The Annals of Statistics 1, 209–230.

Ganics, Gergely, Rossi, Barbara, Sekhposyan, Tatevik, 2020. From fixed-event to fixed-horizon density forecasts: obtaining measures of multi-horizon uncertainty from survey density forecasts.

Garcia, Juan A., Manzanares, Andrés, 2007. What can probability forecasts tell us about inflation risks?.

Genest, Christian, Zidek, James V., 1986. Combining probability distributions: a critique and an annotated bibliography. Statistical Science 1 (1), 114–135.

Genre, Véronique, Kenny, Geoff, Meyler, Aidan, Timmermann, Allan, 2013. Combining expert forecasts: can anything beat the simple average? International Journal of Forecasting 29 (1), 108–121.

Geweke, J., Amisano, G., 2011. Optimal prediction pools. Journal of Econometrics 164, 130–141.

Ghosh, J.K., Ramamoorthi, R.V., 2003. Bayesian Nonparametrics. Springer Series in Statistics. Springer, New York.

Giordani, Paolo, Soderlind, Paul, 2003. Inflation forecast uncertainty. European Economic Review 47, 1037–1059.

Giustinelli, Pamela, Manski, Charles F., Molinari, Francesca, 2020. Tail and center rounding of probabilistic expectations in the health and retirement study. Journal of Econometrics.

Griffin, Jim E., Kalli, Maria, 2018. Bayesian nonparametric vector autoregressive models. Journal of Econometrics 203, 267–282.

Griffin, J.E., Steel, M.F.J., 2011. Stick-breaking autoregressive processes. Journal of Econometrics 162, 383–396.

Hall, Stephen G., Mitchell, James, 2007. Combining density forecasts. International Journal of Forecasting 23 (1), 1–13.

Hirano, Keisuke, 2002. Semiparametric Bayesian inference in autoregressive panel data models. Econometrica 70, 781–799.

Jurado, Kyle, Ludvigson, Sydney C., Ng, Serena, 2015. Measuring uncertainty. The American Economic Review 105 (3), 1177–1216.

Kapetanios, George, Mitchell, James, Price, Simon, Fawcett, Nicholas, 2015. Generalised density forecast combinations. Journal of Econometrics 188, 150–165.

Karabatsos, George, Walker, Stephen G., 2009. Coherent psychometric modelling with Bayesian nonparametrics. British Journal of Mathematical & Statistical Psychology 62 (1), 1–20.

Kenny, Geoff, Kostka, Thomas, Masera, Federico, 2014. How informative are the subjective density forecasts of macroeconomists? Journal of Forecasting 33 (3), 163–185.

Kozlowski, Julian, Veldkamp, Laura, Venkateswaran, Venky, 2019. The tail that keeps the riskless rate low. NBER Macroeconomics Annual 33 (1), 253–283.

Kozlowski, Julian, Veldkamp, Laura, Venkateswaran, Venky, 2020a. Scarring body and mind: the long-term belief-scarring effects of COVID-19. Technical Report. National Bureau of Economic Research.

Kozlowski, Julian, Veldkamp, Laura, Venkateswaran, Venky, 2020b. The tail that wags the economy: beliefs and persistent stagnation. Journal of Political Economy 128 (8), 2839–2879.

Lahiri, Kajal, Liu, Fushang, 2006. Modelling multi-period inflation uncertainty using a panel of density forecasts. Journal of Applied Econometrics 21 (8), 1199–1219.

Li, Yuelin, Schofield, Elizabeth, Gönen, Mithat, 2019. A tutorial on Dirichlet process mixture modeling. Journal of Mathematical Psychology 91, 128–144.

Liu, Yang, Sheng, Xuguang Simon, 2019. The measurement and transmission of macroeconomic uncertainty: evidence from the U.S. and BRIC countries. International Journal of Forecasting 35 (3), 967–979.

Malmendier, Ulrike, Taylor, Timothy, 2015. On the verges of overconfidence. The Journal of Economic Perspectives 29 (4), 3–8.

Mankiw, N. Gregory, Reis, Ricardo, Wolfers, Justin, 2003. Disagreement about inflation expectations. NBER Macroeconomics Annual 18, 209–248.

Manski, Charles F., 2004. Measuring expectations. Econometrica 72 (5), 1329–1376.

Manski, Charles F., 2011. Interpreting and combining heterogeneous survey forecasts. In: Clements, M.P., Hendry, D.F. (Eds.), Oxford Handbook of Economic Forecasting, vol. 85. Oxford University Press, pp. 457–472.

Manski, Charles F., 2018. Survey measurement of probabilistic macroeconomic expectations: progress and promise. NBER Macroeconomics Annual 32 (1), 411–471.

Manski, Charles F., Molinari, Francesca, 2010. Rounding probabilistic expectations in surveys. Journal of Business & Economic Statistics 28 (2), 219–231.

Manzan, Sebastiano, 2021. Are professional forecasters Bayesian? Journal of Economic Dynamics and Control 123, 104045.

McAlinn, Kenichiro, West, Mike, 2019. Dynamic Bayesian predictive synthesis in time series forecasting. Journal of Econometrics 210 (1), 155–169.

Mirkov, Nikola, Steinhauer, Andreas, 2018. Asymmetry of individual and aggregate inflation expectations: a survey. Manchester School 86 (4), 446–467.

Navarro, Daniel J., Griffiths, Thomas L., Steyvers, Mark, Lee, Michael D., 2006. Modeling individual differences using Dirichlet processes. Journal of Mathematical Psychology 50 (2), 101–122.

Patton, Andrew J., Timmermann, Allan, 2010. Why do forecasters disagree? Lessons from the term structure of cross-sectional dispersion. Journal of Monetary Economics 57 (7), 803–820.

Patton, Andrew J., Timmermann, Allan, 2011. Predictability of output growth and inflation: a multi-horizon survey approach. Journal of Business & Economic Statistics 29 (3), 397–410.

Pitman, Jim, 2006. Combinatorial Stochastic Processes, vol. 1875. Springer.

Ranjan, Roopesh, Gneiting, Tilmann, 2010. Combining probability forecasts. Journal of the Royal Statistical Society, Series B, Statistical Methodology 72 (1), 71–91.

Rich, Robert, Tracy, Joseph, 2021. A closer look at the behavior of uncertainty and disagreement: micro evidence from the euro area. Journal of Money, Credit, and Banking 53 (1), 233–253.

Scealy, Janice L., Welsh, Alan H., 2011. Regression for compositional data by using distributions defined on the hypersphere. Journal of the Royal Statistical Society, Series B 73 (3), 351–375.

Shoja, Mehdi, Soofi, Ehsan S., 2017. Uncertainty, information, and disagreement of economic forecasters. Econometric Reviews 36 (6–9), 796–817.

Stark, Tom, 2013. SPF panelists' forecasting methods: a note on the aggregate results of a November 2009 special survey. Federal Reserve Bank of Philadelphia.

Stone, Mervyn, 1961. The opinion pool. The Annals of Mathematical Statistics 32, 1339–1342.

Timmermann, Allan, 2006. Forecast combinations. In: Elliott, Graham, Granger, Clive, Timmermann, Allan (Eds.), Handbook of Economic Forecasting, vol. 1. In: Handbooks in Economics, vol. 24. North Holland, Amsterdam, pp. 135–196.

Wachtel, Paul, 1977. Survey measures of expected inflation and their potential usefulness. Technical Report. National Bureau of Economic Research.

Zadora, Grzegorz, Neocleous, Tereza, Aitken, Colin, 2010. A two-level model for evidence evaluation in the presence of zeros. Journal of Forensic Sciences 55 (2), 371–384.

Zarnowitz, Victor, Lambros, Louis A., 1987. Consensus and uncertainty in economic prediction. Journal of Political Economy 95, 591–621.

Zarnowitz, Victor, 1967. Front matter: 'an appraisal of short-term economic forecasts'. In: An Appraisal of Short-Term Economic Forecasts. NBER, p. 14.

Expectations data in asset pricing

16

Klaus Adam[a,b,c,f] **and Stefan Nagel**[d,e,b,c]

[a]*University of Mannheim, Mannheim, Germany*
[b]*CEPR, London, United Kingdom*
[c]*CESIfo, Munich, Germany*
[d]*University of Chicago, Chicago, IL, United States*
[e]*NBER, Cambridge, MA, United States*

16.1 Introduction

Asset prices are inherently forward looking. The willingness to pay for an asset today depends on investors' expectations about the asset's future payouts and the future price at which the asset can be sold again. The market price of assets therefore reflects investors' price and payout expectations, as well as the risk-adjustments associated with discounting future payouts and sale prices.

Understanding the temporal behavior of asset prices thus requires understanding how price and payout expectations move over time. The traditional approach to this problem is to assume rational expectations (RE). Under RE, investors' expectations are objective in the sense that they reflect the true underlying law of motion that generates asset payoffs. With investor expectation tied down in this way, much of the large observed swings in asset prices over time are then attributed to changes in risk premia rather than changing expectations of future payouts and prices. Consequently, much of the asset pricing literature has focused on searching for specifications of preferences or technology that produce sufficiently volatile risk premia.

While analytically convenient, RE is a strong assumption. Whether or not it is a plausible one is ultimately an empirical question. A growing recent literature examines whether some of the empirical difficulties of RE asset pricing models could be addressed by allowing subjective beliefs of investors to deviate from RE.

Developing models in which investors price assets based on their subjective beliefs about future payouts and prices then requires taking a stand on how these subjective beliefs are formed. Without the tight link of beliefs to some underlying model of objective reality that RE entails, there are many possibilities. Reverse-engineering subjective beliefs from asset prices seems unattractive. Presumably, there are many different belief formation mechanisms that are observationally equivalent in terms of their predictions for asset price movements seen in historical asset price.

Expectations data therefore play an important role. Mechanisms of subjective belief formation in asset pricing models should not only produce empirically realistic asset price behavior, but they should

---

[f] Funding by the German Research Foundation (DFG) through CRC TR 224 (Project C02) is gratefully acknowledged.

477

also be plausible in light of observable data on investor expectations. With increasing availability of survey data, the study of investor expectations has become a very active area of research. In this chapter, we review this work. We start with a basic asset pricing framework that clarifies the role that different types of expectations play in asset pricing. We then discuss existing empirical evidence on the dynamics of investor expectations, followed by a review of work that aims to build asset pricing models with subjective beliefs that are consistent with this empirical evidence. We conclude with some thoughts on the outlook for future research in this area.

16.2 A general asset pricing framework

We consider a general asset pricing setup allowing for heterogeneity across agents in their beliefs and preferences. The setup nests many structural asset pricing models as special cases. It allows us to illustrate how different assumptions about beliefs in these models affects asset pricing outcomes.

Let us consider a particular asset with a (potentially) stochastic payout stream D_t and let P_t denote the (ex-dividend) price of the asset in period $t \geq 0$. The asset may have payouts over a finite time horizon only, as is typically the case with bonds, or it can be infinitely lived, as is the case with stocks.

To price the asset, structural economic models must determine—at a minimum—the following three elements: (1) the stochastic process determining the set of marginal agents $\{\mathcal{M}_t\}_{t=0}^{\infty}$ pricing the asset in all periods and contingencies, (2) the one-step-ahead stochastic discount factor (SDF) $\{M_{t+1}^m\}_{t=0}^{\infty}$ that discounts period $t + 1$ payouts into period t of at least one marginal agent, and (3) this marginal agent's (subjective) probability measures $\mathcal{P}_t^m$, which provides in each period t the perceived probability distribution over the next period's asset price P_{t+1} and payout D_{t+1}.

The probability measure $\mathcal{P}_t^m$ is part of a probability space $(\Omega, \mathcal{S}, \mathcal{P}_t^m)$, where the space of outcomes Ω contains (among other things) the infinite sequence of price and payout outcomes $(P_0, D_0, P_1, D_1, \ldots)$ and where $\mathcal{S}$ is the sigma-algebra of all Borel subsets of Ω. The probability measure is a model primitive under subjective beliefs that needs to be specified by the modeler. In a setting with dynamically consistent beliefs, we have $P_t^m = P^m$, even in the presence of learning. We allow here for belief specifications where the probability measure varies over time. Such time dependence arises, for instance, when agents forget about old data or face memory constraints.

Element (1) allows for the possibility that not all agents are marginal at all points time or in all contingencies. This is the case whenever agents are constrained in their portfolio choices. Whether or not an agent is constrained depends also on the agent's beliefs. Optimistic agents, for instance, would perhaps prefer taking a levered position in the asset, but a leverage constraint may prevent them from doing so. Conversely, pessimistic agents would perhaps like to take a short position, but a short-selling constraint may prevent them from doing so. Belief heterogeneity thus interacts with portfolio constraints to determine the set of marginal agents $\mathcal{M}_t$.

Element (2), which captures marginal agents' stochastic discount factor, allows for heterogeneity in investor preferences and in the optimal consumption plans. The agents' optimal consumption plan also depends on the agent's beliefs.

Beliefs are captured by element (3). For asset pricing with subjective beliefs, this element is of particular importance. Unlike in RE models, the true law of motion that generates payouts does not pin down beliefs about future payouts and prices. From a theoretical viewpoint, this requires taking a stand on the mechanism by which investors form beliefs. Empirically, the lack of a tight link to the true law of motion raises the question whether an assumed belief specification is plausible. Expectations data from surveys can help answer this question.

Given the three elements introduced above, one can price the asset. Let m be an index for marginal agents $m \in \mathcal{M}_t$ and let E_t^m denote the expectation of marginal agent m, as determined by her beliefs $\mathcal{P}_t^m$. The asset price P_t then satisfies in each period $t \geq 0$ the first-order necessary condition for optimality of marginal agent m, i.e.,

$$P_t = E_t^m[M_{t+1}^m(P_{t+1} + D_{t+1})]. \tag{16.1}$$

Economic models differ in the way they determine who is marginal, in the way they model the marginal agents' discount factor M_{t+1}^m, and in the way they assign beliefs $\mathcal{P}_t^m$ to marginal agents. Nevertheless, they have a common core in terms of Eq. (16.1), which we will use as the starting point of our discussion.

Without loss of generality, we can write marginal agent m's SDF as

$$M_{t+1}^m = \delta_t^m \xi_{t+1}^m, \qquad \text{where} \quad E_t^m[\xi_{t+1}^m] = 1 \tag{16.2}$$

and hence δ_t^m controls the conditional mean of the SDF under agent m beliefs while ξ_{t+1}^m captures the variation of the SDF across states of the world. The pricing equation (16.1) then becomes

$$P_t = \delta_t^m E_t^m[D_{t+1} + P_{t+1}] - \delta_t^m \operatorname{cov}_t^m(D_{t+1} + P_{t+1}, \xi_{t+1}^m). \tag{16.3}$$

Suppose there also exists a risk-free asset with unit payoff at $t+1$ that all agents that are marginal for the risky asset have access to.[1] Let $R_{f,t}$ denote the gross return of this risk-free asset. The pricing equation for this risk-free asset then implies

$$\frac{1}{R_{f,t}} = \delta_t^m \tag{16.4}$$

for each agent m. This means that the agents must adjust their portfolios—by trading in the risk-free and/or the risky asset—such that the δ_t^m are equalized for all marginal agents m,

$$\delta_t^m = \delta_t. \tag{16.5}$$

Eq. (16.3) thus simplifies further to

$$P_t = \delta_t E_t^m[D_{t+1} + P_{t+1}] + \delta_t \operatorname{cov}_t^m(D_{t+1} + P_{t+1}, \xi_{t+1}^m). \tag{16.6}$$

The first term captures the agent's subjective payoff and price expectations, discounted with the conditional mean of the SDF. The second term represents a subjective risk premium. Lower covariance of payoffs and prices with ξ_{t+1}^m implies a higher required risk premium and hence a lower price. Defining the gross return of the risky asset as $R_{t+1} = (P_{t+1} + D_{t+1})/P_t$, Eqs. (16.4) and (16.6) yield an expression for the subjectively expected excess return

$$E_t^m[R_{t+1}] - R_{f,t} = -\operatorname{cov}_t^m(R_{t+1}, \xi_{t+1}^m). \tag{16.7}$$

---

[1] We also assume that all agents understand that this asset has a unit payoff.

16.2.1 Rational expectations

The vast majority of asset pricing models in the literature assumes that investors hold RE. The RE assumption is stronger than the assumption of individual rationality in belief formation. Individual rationality implies that agents update subjective beliefs using Bayes' rule and that they make optimal decisions given their subjective beliefs about variables beyond their control. RE additionally requires that all subjective distributions coincide with the objective distributions implied by the asset pricing model in equilibrium (Sargent, 2008). With RE, the expectations that show up in our pricing equation (16.6) become

$$E_t^m[D_{t+1} + P_{t+1}] = E[D_{t+1} + P_{t+1}|\mathcal{J}_t] \text{ for all } t \geq 0, \tag{16.8}$$

where $E[\cdot|\mathcal{J}_t]$ denotes objective expectations given the information set $\mathcal{J}_t$ available to agents at time t. More precisely, agents are endowed with knowledge on how to calculate the density of the payoff D_{t+1} conditional on $\mathcal{J}_t$, which means that they know the functional form and parameters of this density. They also know the function that maps agents' beliefs about future payoffs into the equilibrium price, which allows them to form objective conditional expectations of P_{t+1} (Adam and Marcet, 2011).

Under RE, Eq. (16.7) then implies

$$E[R_{t+1}|\mathcal{J}_t] - R_{f,t} = -\text{cov}(R_{t+1}, \xi_{t+1}^m|\mathcal{J}_t), \tag{16.9}$$

which shows that the risk premium must be the same for all marginal agents.

The RE assumption is convenient in several ways. First, RE greatly simplifies asset pricing by removing the need to separately specify how agents form beliefs. There is no need to study subjective expectations data to understand the belief formation mechanism. Given a model of the economy, the model-consistency requirement of RE pins down agents beliefs.[2] Whether the assumed beliefs are empirically plausible is a different question.

Second, RE is convenient for econometric evaluation. While an econometrician outside the model may not be able to observe $E[\cdot|\mathcal{J}_t]$, simply because the econometrician's information set $\mathcal{A}_t$ is smaller than the agents', the econometrician can make use of the fact that with $\mathcal{A}_t \subseteq \mathcal{J}_t$ the law of iterated expectations (LIE) holds, i.e., $E[E[\cdot|\mathcal{J}_t]|\mathcal{A}_t] = E[\cdot|\mathcal{A}_t]$. Taking conditional expectations of Eq. (16.9), the econometrician can approximate the risk-premium as[3]

$$\text{cov}(R_{t+1}, \xi_{t+1}^m|\mathcal{A}_t) = E[R_{t+1}|\mathcal{A}_t] - R_{f,t}. \tag{16.10}$$

Since these expectations are consistent with the underlying economy generating the data, a sufficiently large sample of empirical data will allow the econometrician to use empirical moments to approximate the population moments on both sides of this equation. The econometrician can then test statistically whether the equality implied by (16.10) holds.

While RE offers these convenient simplifications, the RE assumption is rather strong and generates empirically unattractive features. For instance, RE implies that expectations are homogeneous and conditionally unbiased. As we will discuss, these predictions are difficult to square with empirical evidence

---

[2] This assumes that the model does not allow for the presence of rational bubbles. In such cases, the RE assumption does not uniquely pin down expectations.

[3] To see this, note that $\text{cov}(R_{t+1}, \xi_{t+1}^m|\mathcal{J}_t) = E[R_{t+1}\xi_{t+1}^m|\mathcal{J}_t]$ because $E[\xi_{t+1}^m|\mathcal{J}_t] = 0$. Therefore, $E[\text{cov}(R_{t+1}, \xi_{t+1}^m|\mathcal{J}_t)|\mathcal{A}_t] = \text{cov}(R_{t+1}, \xi_{t+1}^m|\mathcal{A}_t)$.

on beliefs. Therefore, we now turn to approaches that allow subjective beliefs to differ from RE. But this means giving up on some of the convenient properties of RE. Expectations data then becomes a crucial input for implementation and evaluation of these asset pricing models.

16.2.2 Subjective beliefs in a single-period setting

To highlight some key relationships in subjective beliefs models in the simplest possible setting, we start with a risky asset with a maturity of one period that pays a single cash flow of D_{t+1} in $t + 1$. The asset pricing equation (16.6) then simplifies to[4]

$$P_t = \delta_t E_t^m [D_{t+1}] + \delta_t \operatorname{cov}_t^m (D_{t+1}, \xi_{t+1}^m). \tag{16.11}$$

The first term captures the agent's subjective payoff expectations, discounted with the conditional mean of the SDF. The second term represents a subjective risk premium. From these simple equations, one can derive several equilibrium relations that must hold in asset-pricing models with subjective beliefs for one-period assets with a single payoff.

16.2.2.1 *Homogeneous subjective beliefs*

We first consider the case of belief homogeneity among marginal investors. Eq. (16.11) tells us that homogeneity in $E_t^m [D_{t+1}]$ implies homogeneity in the subjectively required risk premium $- \operatorname{cov}_t^m (D_{t+1}, \xi_{t+1}^m)$ among marginal investors. All marginal agents must thus have adjusted their portfolios and consequently their SDFs such that the subjectively required risk premia are the same.[5]

With pricing under investors' subjective beliefs, the interpretation of empirical data can then be very different compared to a setting where the econometrician assumes investors have RE. In particular, there is a difference between *subjective risk premia*, perceived by the agents pricing the assets, and *objective risk premia* extracted by an econometrician studying empirical data ex post. Consider an econometrician who uses data on realized returns $R_{t+1} = D_{t+1}/P_t$ and a statistical model to approximate $E[R_{t+1}|\mathcal{A}_t]$. Taking expectations of the return definition under the econometrician's and the agents' beliefs, and comparing these expectations, we obtain

$$E[R_{t+1}|\mathcal{A}_t] - R_{f,t} = E_t^m [R_{t+1}] - R_{f,t} + \frac{E[D_{t+1}|\mathcal{A}_t] - E_t^m [D_{t+1}]}{P_t}. \tag{16.12}$$

Therefore, if the econometrician observes, for example, a high objective risk premium $E[R_{t+1}|\mathcal{A}_t] - R_{f,t}$, this does not imply that agents necessarily demanded a high subjective risk premium $E_t^m [R_{t+1}] - R_{f,t}$ when they priced the asset. The high objective risk premium could, instead, be a manifestation of agent pessimism about the future payoffs, which gives rise to a positive belief wedge $E[D_{t+1}|\mathcal{A}_t] - E_t^m [D_{t+1}]$, as, e.g., in Cogley and Sargent (2008b). To disentangle the effects of risk aversion, perceived risk, and beliefs about payoffs on the objective risk premia, researchers thus need direct measurements of payoff expectations from survey data. Econometric analysis of asset price data alone cannot provide such a decomposition.

---

[4] This assumes that investors understand that $P_{t+1} = 0$, which is the case in the absence of pure bubbles.

[5] If the asset market is complete, agents' SDFs must be equal state by state.

The pricing equation under subjective beliefs (16.11), in conjunction with the expression for expected returns (16.7), also reveals several fundamental properties of the relation between payoff and return expectations in a homogeneous beliefs equilibrium. While it may seem intuitive that more optimistic subjective expectations of terminal payoffs would also imply higher subjective return expectations, this is not true unless high $E_t^m[D_{t+1}]$ is also accompanied by higher perceived risk or risk aversion, and hence greater magnitude of the subjective risk premium term in (16.7): Optimistic payoff expectations at time t will lead to higher prices P_t, but, according to (16.7), not in itself to higher return expectations. Equilibrium requires that the asset will be priced such that $E_t^m[R_{t+1}] - R_{f,t}$ is equal to the risk premium that investors demand to hold the supply of the asset given their risk aversion and subjective perception of risk.

This is already a hint that it is not entirely straightforward to devise equilibrium models in which subjective return expectations vary a lot over time. Any such variation would have to be associated with time-variation in perceived risk and/or risk aversion.

16.2.2.2 *Heterogeneous subjective beliefs*

We now allow for heterogeneity in beliefs about D_{t+1}. Eq. (16.11) then again delivers important restrictions. It tells us that heterogeneity in beliefs about payoffs must be accompanied by heterogeneity in subjective risk premia. For example, if we pick two marginal agents, A and B, with payoff expectations $E_t^A[D_{t+1}] > E_t^B[D_{t+1}]$, Eq. (16.11) tells us that agent A must also demand a higher subjective risk premium than B such that both agents can agree on the same price P_t. One way in which this can play out in equilibrium is that agent A would devote a larger share of her portfolio to the risky asset than B, which generates a higher required risk premium that then coincides with the subjectively perceived risk premium (Martin and Papadimitriou, 2021).

If agents' differences in payout beliefs vary over time, their risky asset exposures, and consequently their subjective risk premia vary over time as well. This opens up a channel for time-varying beliefs about payouts to generate time-varying expectations of excess returns.

This also means that in a heterogeneous belief setting, with a cross-section of agents, there is a tight *cross-sectional* relationship between cash flow expectations and return expectations. Disagreement about $E_t^m[D_{t+1}]$ is reflected one for one in disagreement about future returns. This is very different from the absence of a *time-series* relation between $E_t^m[D_{t+1}]$ and return expectations that we noted above in the homogeneous belief setting.

Since a heterogeneous beliefs equilibrium may require that agents hold heterogeneous portfolios, it may also happen that some agents' desired portfolio is not feasible due to portfolio constraints. Especially in models with risk-neutral agents, portfolio constraints play a crucial role for a heterogeneous-belief equilibrium to exist. Without such constraints, risk-neutral agents with heterogeneous payoff expectations would want to take infinitely sized bets against each other. Another way to see the nonexistence issue is to recognize that the SDF in this case is conditionally deterministic, $M_{t+1}^m = \delta_t$, and hence the pricing equation (16.11) simplifies to $P_t = \delta_t E_t^m[D_{t+1}]$. Since the left-hand side is the same for all agents, the right-hand side must be the same as well. This leaves no room for differences in $E_t^m[D_{t+1}]$ between marginal agents. The only way for equilibrium to exist is that all but a subset of agents with homogeneous beliefs are not marginal because they are stuck at constraints, e.g., on leverage for optimists and short-selling for pessimists (Geanakoplos, 2009).

16.2.3 Subjective beliefs in a multiperiod setting

We now turn to assets that offer a payout stream D_t over multiple periods, potentially extending to infinity. The key difference to the case with a single-period assets is that agents can now buy or sell the asset at market prices in intermediate periods. This causes expectations about future market prices to become relevant for equilibrium pricing outcomes.

Defining capital gains as

$$\beta_{t+1}^P \equiv P_{t+1}/P_t \tag{16.13}$$

and using Eq. (16.4), we can express subjectively expected excess returns as

$$E_t^m \left[\frac{P_{t+1} + D_{t+1}}{P_t} \right] - R_{f,t} = E_t^m[\beta_{t+1}^P] + \frac{E_t^m[D_{t+1}]}{P_t} - \frac{1}{\delta_t}. \tag{16.14}$$

Expected excess returns now have three components: (i) contributions from expected capital gains; (ii) contributions from next-period's payouts; and (iii) the risk-free interest rate, which depends on the expected value of the discount factor.

Using Eq. (16.7), we can replace the left-hand side of Eq. (16.14) with $-\text{cov}_t^m(\xi_{t+1}^m, R_{t+1})$ and solve for P_t, which yields

$$P_t = \frac{E_t^m[D_{t+1}]}{\frac{1}{\delta_t} - \text{cov}_t^m(\xi_{t+1}^m, R_{t+1}) - E_t^m[\beta_{t+1}^P]}. \tag{16.15}$$

Naturally, the equilibrium asset price depends positively on expected payouts, $E_t^m[D_{t+1}]$, and negatively on the subjective risk premium, namely $-\text{cov}_t^m(\xi_{t+1}^m, R_{t+1})$, and the risk-free rate $\frac{1}{\delta_t}$. In addition, expectations about future capital gains can now potentially affect the current price level in this multiperiod setting.

Suppose, for example, that $E_t^m[D_{t+1}]$, δ_t, and the subjective risk premium $-\text{cov}_t^m(\xi_{t+1}^m, R_{t+1})$ stay unchanged, but investors revise upward their view of $E_t^m[\beta_{t+1}^P]$. Eq. (16.15) tells us that P_t will rise in this case. Intuitively, since $\text{cov}_t^m(\xi_{t+1}^m, R_{t+1})$ and δ_t stay fixed, the total expected return $E_t^m[R_{t+1}]$ must stay fixed, too. For this unchanged $E_t^m[R_{t+1}]$ to be consistent with a rise in expected capital gains, P_t must rise sufficiently such that a decline in the expected payout yield $E^m[D_{t+1}]/P_t$ exactly offsets the rise in expected capital gains.

Clearly, there is a limit to how much capital gain expectations can rise in this example. As the dividend cannot be negative, it must be that $E_t^m[\beta_{t+1}^P] < E_t^m[R_{t+1}]$, otherwise an equilibrium does not exist. In general, however, $\text{cov}_t^m(\xi_{t+1}^m, R_{t+1})$ and δ_t, and hence $E_t^m[R_{t+1}]$, may also respond in equilibrium to a change in expected capital gains, ensuring existence. How much P_t moves in response to changing capital gains expectations, and how the subjective risk premium and the discount factor respond depends on the specifics of the model (preferences, technology, and belief dynamics).

While the multiperiod setting thus opens room for capital gains expectations as a source of variation in asset prices aside from payout expectations, subjective risk premium, and the discount factor, this does not uncouple subjective expected excess returns from perceived risk and risk aversion. Eq. (16.7) always holds, which makes subjective expected excess return to be exactly equal to $\text{cov}_t^m(\xi_{t+1}^m, R_{t+1})$ in equilibrium. Time series variation in expected capital gains $E_t^m[\beta_{t+1}^P]$ thus can only affect subjective excess return expectations if they also generate time series variation in perceived risk or risk aversion.

Intuitively, when subjective expected excess returns are high (and perhaps higher than objectively justified), it must be that perceived risk and/or risk aversion is high, otherwise the high expected excess returns would be an unexploited investment opportunity, which can not be an equilibrium outcome.

16.2.3.1 *Common knowledge*

Whether price expectations play an independent role as a source of asset price variation in addition to payout expectations depends on the assumptions about how investors form beliefs. Specifically, the crucial question is whether it is common knowledge among agents (i.e., they know, and they know that other agents know, and they know that other agents know that other agents know, etc.) that each period t the asset is price is determined according to Eq. (16.1) and that the discount factor is given by Eq. (16.5).

To simplify the exposition and to focus on the key differences to the setting with a single payoff, we consider a setting with risk-neutral marginal agents, which have the same constant SDF at all times:

$$M_{t+1}^m = \delta \in (0, 1) \text{ for all } t \geq 0. \tag{16.16}$$

Equipped with common knowledge, the marginal agent can iterate forward on the market-pricing equation (16.1) and express the equilibrium asset price as a generalized discounted sum of subjectively expected payouts[6]:

$$P_t = \delta E_t^m[D_{t+1}] + \delta^2 E_t^m[E_{t+1}^m[D_{t+2}]] + \delta^3 E_t^m[E_{t+1}^m[E_{t+2}^m[D_{t+3}]]] \ldots \tag{16.17}$$

Eq. (16.17) involves the marginal agent's (first-order) expectation about the payout in the next period and higher-order expectations of future payouts, i.e., expectations of future marginal agents' payout expectations, expectations of future marginal agents' expectations of future marginal agents' expectations, and so on.

Eq. (16.17) implies that subjective price expectations in Eq. (16.1) reflect higher-order payout expectations, i.e.,

$$E_t^m[P_{t+1}] = \delta E_t^m[E_{t+1}^m[D_{t+2}]] + \delta^2 E_t^m[E_{t+1}^m[E_{t+2}^m[D_{t+3}]]] \ldots \tag{16.18}$$

Without further assumptions on what agents know or believe about other agents' expectations, the higher-order payout expectations remain undetermined and the same holds true for the subjective price expectations $E_t^m[P_{t+1}]$. In particular, absent further assumptions, the marginal agents' *first-order expectations* about future payouts ($E_t^m[D_{t+j}]$, $j \geq 1$) generally fail to determine the marginal agents' *higher-order expectations* about future payouts and thus also fail to determine the subjective price expectations ($E_t^m[P_{t+1}]$), see Adam and Marcet (2011).

When beliefs are homogeneous and dynamically consistent and it is common knowledge that agents share the same subjective payout expectations, the Law of Iterated Expectations (LIE) holds also *across* agents, despite expectations being subjective. For instance, we then have[7]

---

[6] For the terminal price to disappear, it must also be common knowledge that the expected discounted terminal price is equal to zero under all agents' beliefs.

[7] Recall, $E_{t+1}^m[\cdot]$ denotes the expectations operator that uses the beliefs of an agent that is marginal in time $t + 1$. This agent can differ from the one that is marginal in time t, whose expectations are given by $E_t^m[\cdot]$.

$$E_t^m[E_{t+1}^m[D_{t+2}]] = E_t^m[D_{t+2}].$$

The general pricing equation (16.17) then again greatly simplifies to

$$P_t = \delta E_t^m[D_{t+1} + \delta D_{t+2} + \delta^2 D_{t+3} + \cdots]. \tag{16.19}$$

Price fluctuations are now driven by fluctuations in the marginal agents' *subjective* (first-order) payout expectations. Under the stated assumptions, an asset-pricing model requires a specification of the dynamics of individual agents' own first-order payout expectations, but there is no need for a separate modeling of agents' higher-order expectations and price expectations, as common knowledge and the LIE implicitly determine them from first-order payout expectations.

An example of an asset pricing setup that fits into this framework is a Bayesian learning model with common priors and common knowledge in which agents learn about the properties of an exogenous payout process, possibly coupled with constraints on portfolios that lead to changes in the set of marginal agents in different contingencies.

However, once we entertain belief dynamics that deviate from Bayesian rationality, it is not obvious that subjective beliefs necessarily obey the LIE. For example, if agents update beliefs like a Bayesian, but their memory of past data fades over time, the LIE no longer holds (Nagel and Xu, 2022). When agents form diagnostic expectations as in Bordalo et al. (2021), whether the LIE holds depends on parameter values (see Bianchi et al., 2021). In this case, even with homogeneous beliefs and common knowledge, higher-order payout expectations cannot be eliminated from the pricing equation (16.17) without further assumptions.

Asset pricing then requires taking a stand on how agents' think about the beliefs of future marginal agents, i.e., how $E_t^m[E_{t+1}^m[D_{t+2}]]$ and other expectations in Eq. (16.17) are determined. One possibility, as in Nagel and Xu (2022), is to assume that in period t agents form expectations about time $t + 1$ beliefs of agents in a rational Bayesian fashion and that future agents will do the same. For example, in the case of fading memory, this would imply that time t agents rationally anticipate that time $t + 1$ will have experienced some loss of memory of the data that is known to time t agents. This leads to a specific version of the pricing equation (16.17) with a chain of nested expectations.

Another possibility is to assume that agents at t believe that future agents' expectations are formed in a way that LIE applies. In the fading memory model, this would mean assuming that agents at t believe that for this point in time onwards, agents' memory will not fade further, and hence the LIE can be applied to future agents' expectations. Under either interpretation higher-order expectations collapse to first-order expectations. For example, we get $E_t^m[E_{t+1}^m[D_{t+2}]] = E_t^m[D_{t+2}]$, so that the pricing equation collapses to one like in (16.19) where only first-order expectations of future payouts appear. Bordalo et al. (2021) take this route with diagnostic expectations.

Our discussion showed that theory restricts higher-order expectations tightly in this homogeneous beliefs, common knowledge setting. We need to make an assumption whether agents are sophisticated about their behavioral limitation and anticipate that future selves will have them, too, or whether they naively anticipate that future agents will not have them.[8] But once this choice is made, the law of motion for first-order expectations also pins down agents' higher-order expectations. Which of these assumptions is a better description of agents' expectations formation is ultimately an empirical question. In

---

[8] O'Donoghue and Rabin (1999) discuss a similar choice between sophistication and naivete about the behavior of future selves in the context of self-control problems.

particular, it remains to be explored to what extent agents' first-order dividend expectations are in fact tightly linked to agents' expectations about the future asset price, as implied by these approaches.

The asset pricing literature also studied settings in which agents hold heterogeneous subjective first-order expectations about payouts and "agree to disagree" about future payouts. Differences in payout beliefs can arise from differences in subjective prior beliefs Harrison and Kreps (1978) or differences in the they way incoming information is interpreted (Dumas et al., 2009).

With risk averse agents that do not face portfolio constraints, all agents are marginal at all times, even in a heterogeneous belief setting. In this case, if the LIE holds for individual beliefs, higher-order expectations of stochastically discounted payouts collapse to first-order expectations. As a consequence, heterogeneity affects asset prices through uncertainty about agents' future portfolio positions and hence their SDFs, but not through higher-order expectations (Martin and Papadimitriou, 2021).

With risk-neutral agents, as in our illustrative example here, portfolio constraints or specific forms of market incompleteness are required to ensure existence of equilibrium. In this case, the identity of the marginal agent can change over time and higher-order payout expectations do not collapse to first-order expectations.

To insure tractability, models where agents agree-to-disagree assume identical conditioning information (even if information signals are interpreted differently by agents) and common knowledge of expectations. These assumptions imply that agents possess the same information about their own and other agents' beliefs, so that higher-order expectations do not depend on the identity of the marginal agent (e.g., Harrison and Kreps, 1978). The general pricing equation (16.17) then simplifies to

$$P_t = \delta E_t^m[D_{t+1}] + \delta^2(E[E_{t+1}^m[D_{t+2}]|\mathcal{J}_t] + \delta^3(E[E_{t+2}^m[D_{t+3}]]|\mathcal{J}_t] + \cdots, \tag{16.20}$$

where $E[\cdot|\mathcal{J}_t]$ denotes agents' common and rational expectation based on time t information. Asset prices now depend on the marginal agents' subjective one-step-ahead payout expectations and on rational expectations of future marginal agents' first-order payout expectations.

Harrison and Kreps (1978) show that the equilibrium asset price can then exceed (in the presence of short-sale constraints) the subjectively expected discounted value of future payout of all agents in the economy, i.e., we have

$$P_t \geq E_t^i[\delta D_{t+1} + \delta^2 D_{t+2} + \delta^3 D_{t+3} + \cdots]$$

for all investors i, unlike in the case with common subjective payout expectations in Eq. (16.19).

16.2.3.2 *Lack of common knowledge*

Common knowledge about a high-dimensional object such as all other investors' (first-order) payout expectations is a somewhat implausible starting point in terms of descriptive realism. How could investors possibly be sure about how other investors form beliefs about payoffs and about what other investors believe, etc.?

If we abandon the assumption that (first-order) payout expectations are common knowledge, asset pricing looks quite different. The higher-order payout expectations in (16.17) are then no longer determined by first-order payout expectations (or rational expectations thereof).

One approach to asset pricing without common knowledge is to explicitly model the (high-dimensional) process of higher-order payout expectations. An alternative approach is to directly model the process for subjective (first-order) capital gains expectations that appear in Eq. (16.15), which sidesteps the need to specify how higher-order expectations are formed. Under lack of common knowledge, the latter approach is consistent with individual rationality and rational belief formation (Adam and Marcet, 2011; Adam et al., 2017). From a modeling perspective, there are some advantages of this approach. First-order capital gains expectations are a considerably more tractable object than higher-order payout expectations. In addition, while higher-order payout expectations are very hard to observe empirically,[9] first-order capital gains expectations are regularly included in investor surveys. Therefore, subjective capital gain expectations in asset pricing models can be disciplined by survey data.

Models with subjective beliefs about prices can generate strong belief-based amplification of asset price volatility. As we highlighted in our discussion of Eq. (16.15), a rise in capital gain expectations can generate a rise in asset prices. Therefore, if subjective capital gain expectations are positively influenced by observed past capital gains, as suggested by survey data that we discuss in the next section, then past price increases generate optimism about future capital gains and thus a further rise in asset prices. The resulting propagation over time allows models without common knowledge about payout beliefs to replicate the observed large volatility of stock prices, even in a setting with standard time-separable utility functions (Adam et al., 2016).

This dynamic feedback from past price changes to future prices is absent in setups in which agents hold subjective beliefs only about exogenous objects, e.g., exogenous payouts D_t that are independent of agents' beliefs. This absence of feedback effects makes it considerably harder to generate the empirically observed high volatility of stock prices.

Abandoning the assumption of common knowledge of (first-order) payout expectations provides economic models with additional degrees of freedom in specifying subjective capital gains expectations. While these an be disciplined with the help of investor survey data, the specification of subjective capital gains beliefs, and their relation to beliefs about payouts, is also subject to a set of restrictions generated from theory.

First, subjective beliefs must be consistent with agents' own optimality conditions, so as to have a well-defined agent problem. Adam and Marcet (2011) refer to such beliefs as internally rational beliefs. In some special cases, internal rationality implies that capital gain beliefs cannot be specified independently of payout beliefs. For instance, when agents are risk-neutral and *know* to be marginal at all times, then the individual optimality condition, $P_t = \beta E_t^m[P_{t+1} + D_{t+1}]$, holds in all periods and all contingencies. If the LIE holds for individual agent beliefs, the agent can then forward-iterate on her *own* first-order condition to arrive at the asset pricing equation (16.19), without relying on common knowledge assumptions. Specifying price beliefs that differ from the ones implied by Eq. (16.19) would then lead to a situation where agents' first-order conditions are violated. More generally, however, when agents are risk-averse, subjective price beliefs cease to be determined by first-order payout beliefs, even when agents know to be marginal at all times (Adam et al., 2017). This is the case because the stochastic discount factor is then endogenous to price beliefs, unlike in the special case with risk-neutrality.

Second, independently specifying subjective beliefs for returns and payouts, instead of specifying them for capital gains and payouts sharpens the non-existence problem we discussed following equation (16.15). To ensure existence, $\frac{1}{\delta_t} - \text{cov}_t^m(\xi_{t+1}^m, R_{t+1})$ may have to adjust. However, using Eq. (16.7) we see that fixing return expectations directly fixes $\frac{1}{\delta_t} - \text{cov}_t^m(\xi_{t+1}^m, R_{t+1})$, so this adjustment mechanism

---

[9] One exception is recent work by Coibion et al. (2021) that provides survey data on higher-order macroeconomic expectations of firm managers.

is not available. For this reason, one should formulate beliefs as subjective probability distributions over prices and payouts and refrain from formulating them over returns and payouts.

Third, since Eq. (16.7) ties subjective expected excess returns to a covariance with the SDF, the subjective expected excess returns can only change if subjectively perceived risk and/or risk aversion changes. Such changes in risk can arise when the SDF responds endogenously to a change in capital gains expectations.

16.3 Empirical dynamics of investor expectations

The asset pricing models with subjective beliefs that we sketched in the previous section require assumptions about belief formation. Unlike in RE models, the objective law of motion of the variables driving payoffs and the SDF does not pin down investors' subjective beliefs. Researchers must therefore make additional assumptions about how agents form beliefs. These assumptions in turn should be informed by empirical evidence on the dynamics of investors' subjective expectations about future prices or returns, asset cash flows, future interest rates, and beliefs about risks and higher moments. We now provide a brief overview of existing empirical evidence on the dynamics of investor expectations. The appendix at the end of this chapter lists the data sources for most of the empirical studies we discuss in this section.

16.3.1 Return and price expectations

Most empirical studies of investor subjective beliefs have focused on expectations of future returns and prices, and especially on expectations of returns and price levels of aggregate stock market indices.

For individual retail investors, expectations of stock market returns over the next year appear strongly related to past returns that these investors have experienced. Using the UBS/Gallup survey, Vissing-Jorgensen (2003) finds a positive relation between expected returns and the (self-reported) returns of investors' own portfolios in the past. Using the same survey, Malmendier and Nagel (2011) show that at the cohort level, subjective expectations of future stock market returns are positively related to a weighted average of the life-time stock market returns experienced by an individual's birth-cohort.

As we discussed in the previous section of this chapter, such a cross-sectional relationship between investors' experienced past returns and their expected returns indicates either that subjective expected cash flow expectations are positively related to past returns, or that, in absence of common knowledge, price expectations decoupled from cash flow expectations are related to experienced past returns.

From an equilibrium asset pricing perspective, the aggregate dynamics of subjective return expectations over time are more important than these cross-sectional relationships. Yet, it is not obvious that the apparent extrapolation from past returns in the cross-section of survey respondents also translates into a positive time-series relation between past returns when expectations are averaged across individuals. As we discussed in the earlier sections, if investors are generally optimistic about future cash-flows or the level of future prices, this generates high current prices and does not necessarily lead to high subjective expected returns.

Empirically, however, past returns and return expectations are positively related at the aggregate level, too. Using the UBS/Gallup survey and several other surveys, Greenwood and Shleifer (2014) find a positive relation between the average return expectation of individuals and returns over the most recent 12 months and the log price–dividend ratio of the stock market portfolio.

Total return expectations can change over time due to movements in the dividend yield or the expected capital gain. Similarly, a change in the total expected return can reflect changes in the risk-free rate or changes in the subjective risk premium perceived by investors. To relate the expectations data to asset pricing models, it is important to understand the behavior of these different components.

Adam et al. (2017) focus on capital gains expectations. They show, using econometric tests that account for small-sample biases, that there is a positive relation between expected stock market capital gains and the price–dividend ratio and that this is inconsistent with the RE hypothesis. Using the UBS/Gallup survey, the Yale/ICF survey of individual investors, and the Graham–Harvey survey of Chief Financial Officers, they find that the relation between the price–dividend ratio and future realized capital gains is considerably more negative than the relation between the price–dividend ratio and survey expectations of capital gains at all forecast horizons, ranging from one to ten years ahead.

Other work focuses on the subjective risk premium. A positive relationship between the price–dividend ratio and total subjective expected returns does not necessarily imply that the subjective risk premium is positively related to the price–dividend ratio. To understand whether perceived risk or risk aversion is changing with the price–dividend ratio one must isolate the subjective risk premium component. Bacchetta et al. (2009) and Nagel and Xu (2022) show, when return expectations are measured in excess of Treasury yields, i.e., as a subjective risk premium, they exhibit only a weak positive relationship with variables like the price–dividend ratio that capture slow-moving valuation cycles in the stock market. The reason is that interest rates tend to be procyclical so that part of the positive relationship between the price–dividend ratio and subjectively expected total returns is due to the risk-free rate. In contrast, as Nagel and Xu (2022) document, the relationship of total expected returns with the past 12-month return works mainly through the subjective risk premium channel.

While it is not entirely clear to what extent individual investors' subjective excess return expectations are procyclical, it is clear that they fail to be countercyclical. Irrespective of whether they are expressed in terms of total returns, excess returns, or capital gains, the dynamics of subjective expectations do not match the countercyclical dynamics implied by predictive regressions of stock returns on valuation ratios and by RE models that are reverse-engineered to fit this predictive regression evidence. As a consequence, individual investors' forecast errors are strongly countercyclical and thus not unpredictable, as the RE hypothesis would imply.

To map the expectations evidence from investor surveys into asset pricing models, one must also take a stand on who the individual investors in these surveys represent. Is the average belief of individual investors a good approximation of the subjective expectations of a representative agent? Then a representative agent model that targets the average individual investor belief will provide a good match with the survey data. Or do investor groups that are excluded from individual investor surveys have systematically different expectations? Then perhaps a heterogeneous-agent approach, or a representative agent approach that targets an aggregate of beliefs across these different investor groups, would be more suitable.

Broadly, the group not covered in the individual investor surveys are professional investors. The available evidence on the dynamic properties of professional investor expectations is mixed. Andonov and Rauh (2020) find that pension funds tend to extrapolate past returns: those with higher past performance expect higher risk premia on risky assets. Yet, this is again a cross-sectional result. Using the Yale/ICF survey of U.S. institutional investors, Bacchetta et al. (2009) find that subjective expected excess returns are acyclical. Wu (2018) uses return expectations aggregated from analyst price targets and forecasts from the Livingston survey and finds countercyclicality (see, also, Wang, 2021). Dahlquist and Ibert (2021) examine year stock equity premium expectations of asset managers, CFOs, and professional forecasters. They find countercyclical subjective risk premia for expectations at a one-year horizon. They also find that one-year expectations are not countercyclical enough relative to the RE benchmark, because forecast errors are still countercyclical, although for professional forecasters the forecast error predictability is not statistically significant. For 10-year expectations, they find countercyclicality only for asset manager expectations, but not the others. What is not clear yet is how much of the countercyclicality of professionals' subjective risk premia is driven by a contrarian effect of recent past returns that are correlated with valuation ratios, i.e., whether it is the mirror image of individuals' apparent extrapolation from recent past returns, or whether it is due to lower-frequency variation.

Overall, the cyclical properties of individual investor subjective expected (excess) returns deviate sharply from the countercyclicality implied by ex-post predictive regressions and RE models. Professionals' expectations may be closer to the RE benchmark, but quantitatively it is not clear at this point whether the countercyclicality is strong enough, and the variation at the right frequency, to be consistent with RE. In any case, if market equilibrium reflects an average of beliefs that gives both groups substantial weight, the idea that countercyclical risk premia are a main driver of asset price booms and busts cannot be reconciled with the evidence on individual investor expectations.

16.3.2 Cash flow expectations

Return expectations alone carry only limited information about the link between subjective expectations of investors and asset prices. For example, asset prices could fluctuate wildly in response to volatile subjective expectations of future cash-flow growth or future prices, but, at the same time, subjective return expectations could be constant. Studying return expectations in this case would not reveal the extent to which asset prices are driven by subjective belief dynamics. Data on cash-flow expectations can provide another important piece of the picture how subjective belief dynamics generate asset price volatility.

The number of existing research studying directly subjective cash flow expectations of investors is relatively small, compared to the number of papers that examine return expectations. Moreover, the available evidence at this point is based exclusively on data from surveys of professional forecasters and from aggregated firm-level earnings or dividend forecasts of equity analysts. Existing individual investor surveys do not ask respondents for cash flow forecasts. The cash flow expectations also tend to be relatively crude in the sense that they are provided only for a few forecast horizons rather than a full term structure.

Chen et al. (2013) and De La O and Myers (2021) use aggregated equity analyst earnings forecasts to measure subjective cash flow expectations. While their methods differ, they come to broadly similar conclusions. Chen et al. (2013) work with a valuation model with a constant discount rate (implied cost of capital). They show that changes in these earnings forecasts go a long way toward explaining the observed movements in aggregate stock prices. De La O and Myers (2021) work with a log-linearized approximate present value identity framework which allows decomposing the variance of the log price–dividend (or price–earnings) ratio into the covariance of these valuation ratios with subjective expected dividend (or earnings) growth and the covariance with subjective expected returns. This is the equivalent to the variance decomposition in Campbell and Shiller (1988), but under subjective expectations instead of objective expectations implied by predictive regressions. De La O and Myers (2021) find that about two thirds of the variation in the price–earnings ratio is attributable to subjective earnings growth expectations. Using a shorter sample of analyst dividend forecasts, they find that almost all variation in the price–dividend ratio is explained by subjective dividend growth expectations.

Perhaps surprisingly, De La O and Myers (2021) find that variation in expectations of short-term cash flow growth seem to explain much of the variation in the price–earnings ratio. In contrast, Bordalo et al. (2020), working with a similar Campbell–Shiller framework and similar data, come to the conclusion that long-term expectations are an important source of variation in the aggregate stock price level. The fact that likely reconciles these seemingly conflicting findings is that a substantial amount of variation in the price–earnings ratio comes from earnings rather than prices. For example, during the financial crisis, aggregate earnings plunged dramatically and, unlike the price–dividend ratio, the price–earnings ratio spiked up. In the depth of the crisis, analysts expected a strong reversal of this earnings drop, resulting in rise in forecasted earnings growth that coincided with a high price–earnings ratio. A lot of the short-term movements of earnings that affect the price–earnings ratio are largely offset, in terms of valuation implications, by a predictable near-term reversal of these earnings shocks. For this reason, the sources of variation in the price–earnings ratio (that De La O and Myers examine) are quite different from the sources of variation in the price level (that Bordalo et al. examine).[10] For asset pricing, the variation of the price level is the main question of interest, not the effect of short-term earnings dynamics on the price–earnings ratio.

Furthermore, Bordalo et al. (2020) find that variation in subjective long-term expectations is the main source of predictable forecast errors and predictable returns. Relatedly, Nagel and Xu (2022) find their "experienced dividend growth" variable—a slow moving exponentially weighted average of past aggregate dividend growth that predicts stock market excess returns—is positively related to analysts' long-term aggregate earnings forecasts in a way that is consistent with subjective cash flow expectations as the source of asset price variation and predictable returns. Overall, for understanding the wedge between rational expectations forecasts and subjective cash flow growth expectations, the long-term component of these expectations seems to be important.

In summary, the evidence on subjective cash flow growth expectations is broadly consistent with the view that asset price fluctuations reflect, to a large extent, variation in investors' subjective cash flow growth expectations. This fits well with the evidence from subjective return expectations that countercyclical movements in subjective risk premia cannot be the reason why asset prices are volatile. Taken together, the evidence suggest that high current prices, for example, are not associated with low subjective expectations of future returns, but rather with expectations of high future cash flows and high future prices. That said, the available data on cash flow expectations at this point is still rather limited. While it is reasonable to assume that analysts' and investors' forecasts may be closely related, it is unclear to what extent analyst forecasts are representative of investors' forecasts. Additional data on cash flow expectations of market participants would thus be valuable to analyze this issue further.

16.3.3 Interest rate expectations

In a multiperiod setting, the current price of an asset reflects not only expectations of future prices and cash flows, but also expectations of future discount factors of marginal agents. For default-free bonds with certain cash flows, uncertainty about future discount factors is the only uncertainty that matters for

---

[10] This is also why, to focus on movements of the price level, Shiller (2005) uses a 10-year trailing moving average of earnings rather than current earnings to form a valuation ratio.

pricing. To see this, consider a zero-coupon bond with a sure payoff of $1 at time $t + 2$. Iterating once on (16.1), we obtain

$$P_t = E_t^m \left[M_{t+1}^m E_{t+1}^m M_{t+2}^m \right]. \tag{16.21}$$

Since $1/R_{f,t} = E_t^m[M_{t+1}^m]$, we obtain

$$P_t = \frac{1}{R_{f,t}} E_{t+1}^m \left[\frac{1}{R_{f,t+1}} \right]. \tag{16.22}$$

Thus, the price of the bond reflects expectations of future short-term interest rates (or yields).

Analogous to stock return predictability with valuation ratios such as the dividend–price ratio, there is evidence in the bond pricing literature that returns on long-term bonds in excess of short-term interest rates are predictable with the spread of yields between long- and short-term bonds. Rational expectations models explain this predictability of excess returns with time-varying risk or risk aversion. However, just as for stocks, bond return predictability could also be the consequence of predictable forecast errors due to deviations from rational expectations.

Using bond yield expectations of professional forecasters to measure subjective interest-rate expectations, Froot (1989) finds that expectational errors contribute substantially to excess return predictability of U.S. Treasury bonds. Cieslak (2018) and Piazzesi et al. (2015) find similar results in data that includes more recent decades. In particular, Piazzesi et al. find that subjective expected excess returns implied by the yield forecasts of professional forecasters are substantially less volatile than the forecasts from predictive regressions and do not show much cyclicality. Thus, similar to stocks, much of the bond price variation that is associated with predictable future returns seems to be driven by subjective expectations, yet in this case not payoff expectations but discount factor or interest rate expectations.

16.3.4 Subjective risk perceptions

Our discussion of empirical work on expectations data in asset pricing so far focused on first moments. But subjective perceptions of second and higher moments are also relevant for asset pricing. For example, if there is time-variation in subjective risk premia, the economic reason for this variation may be that subjective perceptions of risk are time-varying. Moreover, empirically observed time-variation in risk premia on options and other derivatives—such as the variance risk premium, for example—could potentially reflect predictable forecast errors for asset return variances and higher moments rather than a subjective risk premium that investors priced in ex ante. In other words, similar to the case of the time-varying equity premium that we mostly focused on so far, subjective belief dynamics could be the driver of empirically observed time-varying risk premia. Data on subjective risk perceptions of investors can help disentangle these competing explanations.

The available evidence is rather limited at this point. Lochstoer and Muir (2022) recently took a first look at this. They use survey data from the Graham and Harvey CFO survey in which respondents are asked to state the 10th and 90th percentile of stock returns over the next year and the Yale/ICF survey in which respondents provide subjective probabilities of a stock market crash over the next 6 months. Lochstoer and Muir (2022) find that investors' subjective stock market risk perceptions seems to be slowly moving, with initial underreaction to volatility shocks and subsequent delayed overreaction. They show that these dynamics in forecast errors provide a potential explanation of the empirical dynamic response of the variance risk premium to volatility shocks. Claims that provide insurance against future volatility appear underpriced immediately following a rise in volatility, which matches the initial underreaction in survey data, and then overpriced later on, which is consistent with the delayed overreaction of subjective risk perceptions.

The elicitation of entire subjective distributions has been introduced recently in other contexts, e.g., in the Survey of Primary Dealers and the Survey of Market Participants of the Federal Reserve Bank of New York. The Survey of Professional Forecasters, as discussed in Chapter 15 in this Handbook, also provides density forecasts of macro variables. Eliciting similar density forecasts in the context of investor survey would allow for a further and more detailed analysis of the role of risk perceptions.

16.4 Mapping survey expectations into asset pricing models

The mapping between investors' beliefs in an asset pricing model and the expectations data described in the previous section is often difficult to establish. In particular, the subjective expectations or distributions elicited in surveys may not always provide information about the beliefs of the relevant set of investors inside the model. The remainder of this section discusses the main issues that arise, focusing on the elicitation of expected values. Much of the discussion also applies to surveys that elicit other moments or probability distributions.

We use $\mathcal{E}^i[\cdot]$ to denote individual i's expectation measured in the survey, which could be distinct from the expectation $E^i[\cdot]$ that the individual truly holds. We focus mostly on household survey data and thus abstract from the strategic considerations and career concerns that may distort reported expectations of professional forecasters. There exists a substantial body of literature dealing with these concern, which is reviewed by Marinovic et al. (2013).

16.4.1 Are survey expectations risk adjusted?

When respondents are asked to report an expected value or a probability assessment in a survey, the intention of the survey administrators is to elicit individuals' assessment of physical probabilities, i.e., their assessment of empirical frequencies that are not distorted by risk preference effects. In line with this intention, researchers typically interpret beliefs elicited in surveys as physical measure beliefs.

However, it is at least a theoretical possibility that risk preference effects could distort individuals responses to expectations questions in surveys. For example, an individual who is highly risk averse might put more weight on "bad" outcomes in high marginal utility states, reporting more pessimistic expectations than warranted under her subjective assessment of physical probabilities, as also discussed in Chapter 26 in this Handbook.

Along these lines, Cochrane (2011) suggests that individuals might report expectations under the risk-neutral measure and that this could help explain the large wedges between survey expectations and investor expectations implied by rational expectations asset pricing models. This risk-neutral expectations hypothesis states that when individual i reports an expected value in a survey, say the expectation of an asset return R_{t+1}, then this expectation incorporates a risk-adjustment based on the individual's SDF

$$\mathcal{E}_t^i[R_{t+1}] = E_t^i\left[\frac{M_{t+1}^i}{E_t^i[M_{t+1}^i]} R_{t+1}\right] \tag{16.23}$$

where the ratio premultiplying R_{t+1} inside the expectations operator transforms the physical probability of future states, which enter the computation of the expectation $E^i[\cdot]$ into a risk-neutral, or marginal-utility weighted probability. Under this hypothesis, holding $E_t^i[R_{t+1}]$ fixed, greater risk aversion or greater risk of bad outcomes, would induce more pessimistic reported expectations $\mathcal{E}_t^i[R_{t+1}]$.

Whether individuals report physical expectations, risk-neutral expectations, or otherwise risk-adjusted expectations is an empirical question. Adam et al. (2021) examine the evidence for stock market return expectations from various surveys of individual and professional investors. They first note that if investors have access to trading in the asset that delivers the return R_{t+1} and the risk-free asset with return $R_{f,t}$, then, for such a marginal investor m, their first-order conditions imply

$$E_t^m[M_{t+1}^m R_{t+1}] = 1, \qquad E_t^m[M_{t+1}^m R_{f,t}] = 1, \qquad (16.24)$$

which, together with (16.23) for $i = m$ implies that the risk-neutral expectation of asset returns equals the risk-free rate,

$$\mathcal{E}_t^m[R_{t+1}] = R_{f,t}. \qquad (16.25)$$

This is a testable hypothesis and Adam et al. (2021) show that it is strongly rejected in all survey data sets they examine. On average, reported return expectations are much higher than risk-free rate proxies.

A less extreme version of the risk-adjustment hypothesis would imply that individuals reported expectations that are tilted pessimistically towards risk-neutral expectations, but not necessarily all the way. Adam et al. (2021) do not find empirical support for such pessimistic tilts. Comparing survey stock market return expectations to subsequently realized stock market returns, they find that unconditionally, survey expectations are close to unbiased, not pessimistically biased.

Overall, the evidence does not provide support for the notion that individuals report risk-adjusted return expectations in surveys. We therefore proceed under the assumption that when individuals respond to expectations questions in a survey, they are reporting $E_t^i[\cdot]$ without risk-adjustments.

16.4.2 **Measurement error and cognitive uncertainty**

Even if individuals are attempting to report their expectation under the physical measure, it is still not necessarily true that $\mathcal{E}_t^m[R_{t+1}]$ can be interpreted as a direct measurement of the physical expectation. The expectation that respondents provide in a survey may not be the expectation that individuals would truly hold if they had the time to reflect more carefully on their response and if they had to make decisions based on these expectations in a high-stakes environment. As a consequence, there may be an error component, ε_{t+1}^i, in measured expectations of individual i,

$$\mathcal{E}_t^i[R_{t+1}] = E_t^i[R_{t+1}] + \varepsilon_{t+1}^i. \qquad (16.26)$$

For example, as with any variable elicited in a survey, there is the possibility that survey expectations are subject to measurement error. Such measurement error could be the consequence of misunderstanding of the survey question or insufficient deliberation before providing a response; see also the discussion in Chapter 21 in this Handbook.

The existing evidence indicates that survey return expectations contain useful information about individuals' $E_t^i[R_{t+1}]$, but at the same time the error ε_{t+1}^i is not negligible. In data from the UBS/Gallup survey, Vissing-Jorgensen (2003) finds a positive cross-sectional correlation between individual retail investors' expected stock returns and the percentage of their portfolio that they report to hold in stocks. Adam et al. (2015) show that the cross-sectional dispersion in expected returns correlates with trading volume over time, i.e., periods with high measured disagreement are periods with more active stock trading, which suggests that beliefs dispersion in surveys is unlikely driven by measurement error alone.

However, using survey data on stock return expectations combined with administrative data on portfolio holdings, Ameriks et al. (2020) and Giglio et al. (2021) show that the portfolio share of stocks in individuals' portfolios is substantially less sensitive to individuals' stock market return expectations than implied by standard portfolio choice models under plausible values for relative risk aversion.

Measurement error seems to be part of the reason for this low sensitivity. Using instrumental variable techniques that assume measurement error is uncorrelated across different survey questions that elicit return expectations and perceived probability distributions of stock market returns, Ameriks et al. (2020) and Giglio et al. (2021) find a stronger sensitivity of portfolio shares to expected returns, but it is still weaker than implied by standard models. There seem to be components of ε_{t+1}^i that are common across survey questions and which may not be interpretable as classical measurement error.

One possibility for the low sensitivity, suggested by Drerup et al. (2017), is that individuals have a lack of confidence in their own stated beliefs. Along these lines, Enke and Graeber (2019) show that if individuals perceive cognitive uncertainty about what the optimal action is, they may behave as if they shrink probabilities toward a cognitive default. However, it remains unclear whether this shrinkage only affects actions or also the expectations reported in surveys. Would individuals facing cognitive uncertainty respond with these shrunk probabilities or would they report their subjective assessment prior to shrinkage? The fact that Giglio et al. (2021) find the sensitivity of portfolio shares to expectations to be stronger for investors who are active, confident in their beliefs, and pay attention is consistent with agents reporting their expectations prior to shrinkage.

Low sensitivity of decisions to expectations at the individual investor level does not necessarily imply low sensitivity at the aggregate level. The identification of sensitivity in Giglio et al. (2021) rests on cross-sectional differences in expectations and actions between individuals. It is possible that the effects of measurement error, cognitive uncertainty, and other frictions largely cancel out when expectations and actions are aggregated. The fact, documented in Greenwood and Shleifer (2014), that individuals' stock market return expectations are strongly correlated with aggregate flows into equity mutual funds would be consistent with this latter interpretation.

16.4.3 Heterogeneity and beliefs aggregation

Heterogeneity of reported expectations is a pervasive feature of survey data.[11] This raises the question how researchers should deal with this dispersion when they want to map survey expectations into the expectations of agents in an asset pricing model.

For tractability reasons, many asset pricing models are set up as representative agent models. So which individual beliefs in the survey data should be mapped into the representative agent's beliefs? A typical approach is to take an equally-weighted mean or median of some observed set of expectations. Even if the survey data captured expectations of all investors in the economy, this approach would be subject to some approximation error. Jouini and Napp (2007) construct a representative agent in an

---

[11] See Chapter 17 in this Handbook, which provides evidence on disagreement about output growth, inflation and interest rates over various forecast horizons.

economy with heterogeneous beliefs and heterogeneous risk tolerance. They show that the representative agent's beliefs are a risk tolerance-weighted average of individual agent beliefs (belief dispersion also has an effect on the representative agent's discount factor and hence the risk-free rate).

In practice, without comprehensive data on risk tolerance and beliefs of the investor population, it is difficult to empirically implement such a weighting scheme. Moreover, additional complications may come into play. Participation constraints keep some individuals out of the market. Lack of attention may render some investors effectively nonparticipating for certain time intervals. It remains to be seen whether weighting schemes based on observable proxies for risk tolerance and likelihood of market participation can improve the fit between representative-agent asset pricing models and survey data.

For aggregating professional forecasters beliefs is also potentially important to consider that professional forecasters are not directly investing themselves, but their forecast may influence investment decisions of professional investors (who pay for these forecasts). How much influence they have on investors may differ between forecasters and it may depend on their past forecast performance. Accordingly, Buraschi et al. (2018) construct an aggregated subjective bond risk premium measure that gives more weight to professional forecasters that were more accurate in the past.

An alternative approach is to move away from representative agent models to explicitly specify belief heterogeneity. David (2008), for example, calibrates an asset pricing model with heterogeneous beliefs to earnings forecast data from the Survey of Professional Forecasters. Likewise, in models in which belief heterogeneity is tied to some observable agent characteristics, researchers can aim for a more detailed comparison of model implied beliefs and survey data beyond broad measures of dispersion. For example, in the model of Collin-Dufresne et al. (2017) agents' beliefs are heterogeneous between age cohorts and they can be compared with cohort-aggregated survey data. Another observable dimension is professional vs. individual investors. Given the heterogeneity in return expectations that we discussed in Section 16.3.1, it may make sense to consider models that specify different belief dynamics for these two groups of participants.

Clearly, aggregating survey expectations within groups such as age-cohorts or among professionals and individuals, one again encounters the issue of how to weigh the empirically heterogeneous beliefs within each group to approximate the beliefs of each group's representative agent. Moreover, due to the technical difficulty of solving models with heterogeneous agents, representative agent models will likely continue to play an important role. For these reasons, the need to implement some aggregation scheme for survey expectations data is difficult to avoid.

16.5 Models of expectations formation

A growing body of work develops asset pricing models in which investors' subjective beliefs deviate from RE. Many of these papers aim not only to reproduce the key empirical properties of asset prices, but also the stylized facts about investor beliefs in survey data that we presented in Section 16.3. The belief specifications differ, but many involve some form of learning where investors use observed data to form expectations about future payouts or prices. Most use a homogeneous-beliefs setup, but we also discuss a few papers that explore the effects of belief heterogeneity.

16.5.1 **Learning about payouts**

Learning about dividend payouts can generate volatile asset prices and high risk premia. Belief revisions about the parameters of the payout process contribute to variations in expected payouts and hence to asset price volatility, unlike in full information RE models where the parameters governing the payout process are assumed to be known. Risk premia can be high because parameter uncertainty contributes to perceived consumption uncertainty in a way that covaries with payouts. Both features help achieve a better fit with asset price data. The belief dynamics also help match data on the dynamics of subjective payout expectations.

Early work in this literature, e.g., Timmermann (1993, 1996), shows that excess volatility and return predictability can emerge from learning about the payout process. This literature follows Kreps (1998) in using an anticipated-utility framework in which the agents pricing assets ignore posterior uncertainty about payout process parameters and the fact that their beliefs will be revised in the future. This means that the additional subjective uncertainty (relative to the case of RE) that investors face in these models is not priced and therefore does not contribute to risk premia.

In Collin-Dufresne et al. (2016), Bayesian investors learn about the mean of an i.i.d. log endowment growth process

$$\Delta d_t = \mu + \varepsilon_t, \qquad \eta_t \sim N(0, \sigma^2), \tag{16.27}$$

and they price a consumption claim that has the endowment $D_t = \exp(d_t)$ as payout. As they show, switching to the assumption that investors fully take into account posterior uncertainty when they price assets actually has only very small effects when investors have constant relative risk aversion (CRRA) utility. In other words, for the CRRA case, anticipated utility is a good approximation (see, also, Cogley and Sargent, 2008a). However, when investors have Epstein–Zin utility, the result can be drastically different. With Epstein–Zin utility, investors demand a large risk premium for uncertainty about long-run endowment growth. As long as investors have not seen enough data to have precise beliefs about long-run growth, risk premia can therefore be very high.

When the parameters of the endowment process are time-invariant and investors prior beliefs reflect this, Bayesian learning has the perhaps unrealistic implication that the learning effects disappear in the long run: asymptotically, the model predictions approach the predictions of an RE model.

Models with perpetual learning avoid this outcome. Perpetual learning can arise for a number of reasons. For example, if investors believe, based on their prior, that there is time-variation in the payout process parameters, this may lead them to discount observations in the distant past as seem of little relevance for current parameter values. For example, if μ in Eq. (16.27) is not constant, but instead follows a random walk, a Bayesian investor's posterior mean would be an exponentially-weighted average, with fixed weights, of past endowment growth rates. As a consequence, the posterior mean would continue to drift forever and subjective uncertainty about μ would never disappear.

In Nagel and Xu (2022) learning is perpetual because agents have slowly fading memory of past growth rate observations. This also gives rise to persistently high uncertainty about endowment growth. Nagel and Xu (2022) also show that the pricing implications of the fading memory model are similar to one in which investors have full memory and they believe that μ follows a random walk, but only if the true μ is in fact constant. The wedge between investors' time-varying posterior mean of μ and the true constant μ are needed for the model to produce excess return predictability and return expectations forecast error predictability that is in line with the data. Using aggregate earnings growth as a proxy for payout growth, Nagel and Xu (2022) also show that analysts' long-run earnings growth forecast errors are predictable with an exponentially-weighted average of past observed payout growth observations, which is in line model predictions and consistent with the evidence discussed in Section 16.3.2 that long-term payout growth expectations appear to be an important source of variation in the aggregate stock price level.

Models in which investors are uncertain about long-run growth can have a built-in fragility. It is important to keep this in mind, because this fragility may not be apparent in log-linearized or numerically solved versions of these models. To illustrate this issue, consider first the simplest case with risk-neutrality as in Eq. (16.19), where we had

$$
P_t = E_t^m \left[\lim_{T \to \infty} \sum_{j=1}^T \delta^j D_{t+j} \right]. \tag{16.28}
$$

Suppose log dividends are generated as $d_t = d_{t-1} + \mu + \eta_{t+1}$ where $\eta_t > 0$ is i.i.d. with $E[\eta_t] = 0$ and $\mu > 0$ is an unknown parameter. If investors' prior beliefs about μ assign arbitrarily small but positive probability mass to growth rates above δ^{-1}, then the asset price (16.28) diverges to infinity. When prior beliefs about μ are bounded strictly below δ^{-1}, arbitrarily small prior mass sufficiently close to δ^{-1} gives rise to arbitrarily large (albeit finite) equilibrium price levels. This shows how a small amount of uncertainty can make a large difference for the asset price predictions.

Geweke (2001) shows that the blow-up problem becomes even starker with CRRA preferences. When the endowment is log-normal as in (16.27) with uncertainty about μ, then expected utility ceases to exist under conjugate Bayesian prior beliefs, unless the intertemporal substitution elasticity is exactly equal to one or unless one restricts the support of prior beliefs.[12] Weitzman (2007) shows the restrictions in prior beliefs can then dominate the model's asset pricing implications. The divergence problem also arises with Epstein–Zin preferences, whenever the inter-temporal elasticity of substitution differs from a value of exactly one (Collin-Dufresne et al., 2016; Nagel and Xu, 2022).

As a result, Collin-Dufresne et al. (2016) truncate the state space to insure finite outcomes. Pástor and Veronesi (2003, 2006) assume that uncertainty about growth rates disappears after some time period T, which can be stochastic. Nagel and Xu (2022) specify informative prior beliefs that pull long-run growth expectations toward a prior mean. In their perpetual learning model, the persistent pull toward this prior mean applies to beliefs of all future agents, which is sufficient to ensure finite valuations in with Epstein–Zin utility even if the intertemporal elasticity of substitution is different from one.

There are a number of alternative views about the economic relevance of the blow-up problem. One view is that it would be simply unreasonable for investors to entertain the possibility of long-run growth rates that imply very high valuations or valuations that are extremely sensitive to growth rate uncertainty. An alternative view is that it will be very difficult to empirically discipline present value models using survey data, as the asset pricing implications can be driven by small amounts of uncertainty that are empirically hard to determine. Yet another view is that it is ultimately just an empirical question whether or not measured payout expectations from survey data are able to explain asset price behavior.

---

[12] Further results about the existence of present value relationships under Baysian learning are derived in Pesaran et al. (2007) and Adam and Marcet (2011).

16.5.2 **Learning about prices**

A number of asset pricing models introduce learning directly about price behavior, as discussed in Section 16.2.3.2. Price learning can generate stronger endogenous propagation of fundamental disturbances than payout learning, due to the "self-referential" nature of price learning: price beliefs affect price outcomes and price outcome future revisions in price beliefs. This feedback loop, which is absent when learning is about exogenous fundamentals, say payouts, can generate plausible asset price volatility, even with time-separable preference specifications. Models of price learning can also explain the strong positive comovement between recent past returns and investors' return expectations observed in survey data, which is an empirical fact that models featuring payout learning struggle to explain. Models specifying learning about prices rely on the one-step ahead asset pricing equation (16.1), rather than the discounted sum formula (16.28), therefore also do not face the kind of large sensitivity of the asset price predications to small changes in subjective price beliefs.

Early models of learning about prices, e.g., Timmermann (1996), studied learning about the *level* of next period's asset price. Such learning specifications generated only modest amounts of additional asset price volatility, despite the feedback between price beliefs and price outcomes. The reason is that the strength of the feedback tends to be weak under price *level* learning. This is so because the expected *future* price level affects the *current* price level approximately one-to-one, see Eq. (16.3). In the vicinity of rational price beliefs, outcomes and beliefs will thus move virtually in the same way. The weak divergence between outcomes and beliefs causes learning-induced belief revisions to be weak, so that learning adds little asset price volatility.

As a result, subsequent models studied learning about capital gains, i.e., learning about the *change* in the price level from one period to the next. As should be clear from Eq. (16.15), realized asset prices and thus realized capital gains are rather sensitive to revisions in capital gain expectations $E_t^m[\beta_{t+1}^P]$, as $\beta_t^m = 1/R_{f,t}$ tends to be close to one. Adam et al. (2016) show how many forms of learning about capital gains impart momentum and long-horizon mean-reversion into asset price dynamics, thereby generating large and persistent swings in the price–dividend ratio. This allows simple asset pricing models with time-separable preferences to generate realistic amounts of stock price volatility, even if they struggle to fully replicate the equity premium.

Learning-induced variations in subjective capital gain expectations also generate positive comovement of the price–dividend ratio and subjective expected excess returns. As we discussed in Section 16.2.3.2, such time-variation in subjective expected excess returns requires that the SDF adjusts in response to a change capital gains expectations. In Adam et al. (2017), in a setting with CRRA utility and with wage income as a source of wealth outside of the stock market, an agent optimistic about future capital gains anticipates that a greater share of future wealth is exposed to stock market risk. As a consequence, perceived risk rises. Specifically, under the agent's subjective beliefs, the SDF is more volatile when with capital gains expectations are higher. In equilibrium, optimism about capital gains therefore produces not only a high price–dividend ratio, but also a high subjective risk premium. Price growth expectations in their model are a function of an exponentially-weighted average of past price growth, similar to models of fading memory or perceived parameter drift.

Jin and Sui (2022) pursue an alternative approach that retains the assumption of common knowledge. In their model, investors forecast future prices, but they implicitly form payout growth expectations that justify their expectation of the future price such that a discounted sum valuation like (16.28) holds under subjective beliefs. This brings the model quite close to models of payout learning. It also allows the model to match the evidence on time-varying subjective cash flow expectations that we discussed in Section 16.3.2.

Overall, models of payout learning and price learning share a common thrust in that they explain cycles in asset price valuations with waves of optimism and pessimism about future levels of stock prices. They differ in what data agents use to form these expectations and how agents reason about the justification for these beliefs about future prices. In the end, elements from both classes of models may be needed.

16.5.3 Learning biases

The models we discussed so far employ forms of belief formation that can broadly be motivated by Bayesian learning, albeit with some additional tweaks, such as fading memory or a prior belief that parameters are drifting and hence data far in the past has become irrelevant. A different strand of the literature starts instead with an assumption, motivated by psychological experimental evidence, that agents use certain heuristics in belief formation. Reliance on these heuristics generates biases in updating of beliefs in response to incoming information.

One heuristic that seems to be particularly suitable for explaining cyclical asset price behavior is the representativeness heuristic of Kahneman and Tversky (1972). An early example is the model presented by Barberis et al. (1998) where a string of positive or negative earnings change leads an investor to view this repeat performance as representative and adopt a forecasting model that extrapolates the past performance too far into the future. In this model, this extrapolation has no grounding in reality as the true process does not have any persistence.

In the diagnostic expectations approach of Bordalo et al. (2018), agents apply the representativeness heuristic in a way that is closer to Bayesian learning. In their setup, agents observe a signal that has predictive information for the variable that they want to forecast. In line with the representativeness heuristic, however, they overweight outcomes that have become more likely in light of recently incoming information. As a consequence, agents exaggerate true predictability patterns in the data. Bordalo et al. (2019) apply this approach to stock valuation and show that it can explain a number of interesting financial market regularities, for instance, why the returns on stocks with the most optimistic analyst long-term earnings growth forecasts are lower than those on stocks with the most pessimistic forecasts.

One tension in the diagnostic expectations approach is that agents observe (and overreact to) objective news, that is, the realization of variables relative to an undistorted Bayesian forecast from the previous period. And the news reaction is added to the previous period's Bayesian forecast. Thus, while their actual forecast in the previous period was distorted by the representativeness heuristic, agents are able, in the current period, to calculate the innovation relative to the previous period's Bayesian forecast and adjust this Bayesian forecast in the direction of the innovation. This raises the question where the knowledge of the Bayesian forecast comes from.

Rather than assuming that agents exaggerate true predictability patterns, or see predictability where there is none, an alternative approach to biased learning is to assume that agents use simplified models that do not capture the full complexity of the true predictability that exists in the data. Fuster et al. (2011) call this approach "natural expectations." For example, the true data-generating process may be a high-order ARMA process, while agents estimate a forecasting model that allows only for a small number of lags. In this case, agents may fail to fully perceive the degree of mean reversion inherent in fundamental dynamics, which can also lead to overreaction that generates asset price cycles with procyclical optimism in investors' subjective beliefs.

The difference between these biased-learning approaches and Bayesian learning is smaller than it may seem. Updating that deviates from Bayesian learning with priors grounded in objective reality can often be rationalized as Bayesian learning under a particular subjective prior belief. To illustrate, consider the natural expectations approach and suppose the true data-generating process is an AR(5), but the agent estimates a simplified AR(1) model to construct forecasts. The agent's approach could be rationalized by giving the agent a dogmatic subjective prior that the data-generating process is an AR(1). Given this prior, the agent's updating of beliefs is in accordance with Bayes' law. In this sense, there often exists an equivalent Bayesian belief formulation, so that it becomes difficult to identify whether updating bias arises due to a deviation from Bayes' law or simply due to an application of Bayes' law under a particular subjective prior. The distinction between both views is more of a philosophical nature. What matters for model predictions is the sequence of subjective beliefs that updating gives rise to.

16.5.4 **Heterogeneity**

Motivated by the fact that survey measures of expectations typically display a large degree of heterogeneity, a number of papers study asset pricing setups in which agents hold different beliefs. Giglio et al. (2021) show that belief heterogeneity has predictive power for the composition of individual portfolios and for trading behavior. Belief heterogeneity also appears relevant for understanding the large volume of assets traded on financial markets, as arguably these volumes are difficult to square with risk-sharing motives alone. Heterogeneity also allows studying the redistributive effects associated with subjective belief dynamics.

In Barberis et al. (2015) some investors form price growth expectations by extrapolating from past price growth, while other investors have rational expectations. The extrapolators are assumed to hold implicit subjective payout expectations that support their beliefs about future prices under a discounted sum valuation as in Eq. (16.28). Following a string of price increases, extrapolators are therefore effectively more optimistic about future payouts than rational investors and therefore hold a greater share of the outstanding supply of stocks. Due to their resulting greater exposure to stock market risk, they demand a higher subjective risk premium, which allows high past price growth to coincide with optimistic return expectations of the extrapolators in equilibrium. In contrast, rational investors have counter-cyclical return expectations. One potential interpretation is that the extrapolators represent individual investors while the rational investors represent more sophisticated professional investors. For tractability in the presence of heterogeneity, investors in the model have CARA preferences. But this has the consequence that the model does not produce realistic asset pricing predictions on a number of dimensions, such as the equity premium, the volatility of the price–dividend ratio, and the long-run behavior in the presence of economic growth.

Collin-Dufresne et al. (2017) explore heterogeneity of a different kind. Motivated by the empirical evidence in Malmendier and Nagel (2011) and Malmendier and Nagel (2016) that investors learn from life-time experiences, they assume that overlapping cohorts of investors learn about the dividend process from the dividend history observed during their life times. The model does well on a number of standard asset pricing moments and in matching the learning-from-experience evidence in microdata and surveys, but the dynamics of asset prices and beliefs are somewhat difficult to evaluate quantitatively as there are only two overlapping cohorts and subjective risk premia jump every 20 years when there is a generational shift.

Adam et al. (2015) consider a model in which agents are heterogeneous in their tendency to extrapolate past capital gains. The heterogeneity is motivated by the empirical observation that the capital gain expectations of investors with more years of stock market experience react significantly weaker to past capital gains than the expectations of less experienced investors. Working with the one-step ahead asset pricing equation (16.1) for all investors allows the use of CRRA preferences without losing tractability. The model produces quantitatively realistic asset price dynamics, can replicate patterns of trading volume and generates significant amounts of wealth redistribution over stock price boom and bust cycles.

Overall, the literature that incorporates belief heterogeneity in asset pricing in a way that is disciplined by survey evidence is still in its infancy. In many settings, lack of tractability makes it difficult to entertain empirically realistic belief heterogeneity and, at the same time, produce quantitatively plausible asset price behavior.

16.6 **Future research directions**

During the past decade, researchers have made substantial progress in linking investor expectations data with asset pricing theory. We conclude by highlighting several areas in which further advances would be desirable:

- We need more evidence on the links between expectations and investor portfolio decisions. Does low sensitivity of actions to expectations at the individual level translate into low sensitivity at more aggregated levels (e.g., cohorts, investor category, market-wide)? Which are the investors influenced by professional forecasters' expectations, and how strong is the influence?
- Subjective risk perceptions may be as important as the perceived first moments of returns and payoffs. So far, however, the available empirical evidence on the dynamics of subjective risk perceptions is rather limited. We need more work that explores how investors form beliefs about asset risks and how these risk perceptions are linked to the subjective risk premia that they demand to hold risky assets.
- There is substantial heterogeneity in the subjective beliefs of different groups of market participants, e.g., between professional forecasters and individual investors. Is it important for asset pricing to account for this heterogeneity? How should the belief formation be modeled for these groups?
- More generally, it would be desirable to make progress on the question of how to best aggregate the heterogeneous expectations of different investors, with the objective of identifying the marginal agents' beliefs. While this will prove difficult because survey responses are contaminated by response errors and tend to be measured infrequently, it is an important question that needs to be tackled.
- Subjective belief dynamics may not only be a major source of asset price volatility, but they may also play an important role as a source of macroeconomic fluctuations. Expectations about asset payoffs should be linked to the expectations that shape the decisions of consumers and firms about investment, production, and consumption. Therefore, there is much to be learned from integrating asset pricing based on subjective belief dynamics into macroeconomic models. Relatedly, expectations of financial intermediaries may affect credit supply, macroeconomic outcomes, and asset prices. Study-

ing intermediaries' expectations, as done recently in Ma et al. (2021), may provide new insights for macrofinance models with intermediary sectors.

- Analysis of policy in models with subjective beliefs brings up special challenges. On the theory side, the challenge is modeling how subjective beliefs react to changes in the policy environment, e.g., as in Adam and Woodford (2021). This may in turn provide new insights about asset price reactions to policy announcements. On the empirical side, we need more evidence on how expectations change in response to policy interventions. Such evidence can be obtained through information experiments, e.g., as in Coibion et al. (2019) that induce changes in participants perceptions about actual policy. Chapter 4 in this Handbook provides an overview of this line of research. One open question is whether participants' responses in survey experiments could differ from real-world responses because the experiment forces individuals to pay attention to stimuli that they would have ignored in a real-world setting.

Appendix 16.A Data sources for investor expectations

Table 16.1 Investor Survey Data Sets.

Survey	Population	Repository
Panel A: Stock market return or capital gain expectations		
UBS/Gallup	Individuals	Roper Center[a]
Yale/ICF	Wealthy individuals	Yale ICF[b]
Yale/ICF	Institutional investors	Yale ICF[b]
Michigan Survey of Consumers	Individuals	UM Survey Research Center[c]
Graham-Harvey CFO	Financial managers	FRB of Richmond[d]
Livingston	Professional forecasters	FRB of Philadelphia[e]
Panel B: Stock market cash flow expectations		
IBES	Equity Analysts	WRDS[f]
Survey of Professional Forecasters	Professional forecasters	FRB of Philadelphia[g]
Panel C: Interest rate expectations		
Survey of Professional Forecasters	Professional forecasters	FRB of Philadelphia[g]
Bluechip Financial Forecasts	Professional forecasters	Wolters Kluwer[h]

[a] *https://ropercenter.cornell.edu.*
[b] *https://som.yale.edu/centers/international-center-for-finance/data.*
[c] *https://data.sca.isr.umich.edu.*
[d] *https://www.richmondfed.org/cfosurvey.*
[e] *https://www.philadelphiafed.org/surveys-and-data/real-time-data-research/livingston-survey.*
[f] *https://wrds-www.wharton.upenn.edu.*
[g] *https://www.philadelphiafed.org/surveys-and-data/real-time-data-research/survey-of-professional-forecasters.*
[h] *https://www.wolterskluwer.com/en/solutions/vitallaw-law-firms/blue-chip.*

References

Adam, K., Beutel, J., Marcet, A., Merkel, S., 2015. Can a financial transaction tax prevent stock price booms? Journal of Monetary Economics 76, S90–S109.

Adam, K., Marcet, A., 2011. Internal rationality, imperfect market knowledge and asset prices. Journal of Economic Theory 146 (3), 1224–1252.

Adam, K., Marcet, A., Beutel, J., 2017. Stock price booms and expected capital gains. The American Economic Review 107 (8), 2352–2408.

Adam, K., Marcet, A., Nicolini, J.P., 2016. Stock market volatility and learning. The Journal of Finance 71 (1), 33–82.

Adam, K., Matveev, D., Nagel, S., 2021. Do survey expectations of stock returns reflect risk adjustments? Journal of Monetary Economics 117, 723–740.

Adam, K., Woodford, M., 2021. Robustly optimal monetary policy in a new Keynesian model with housing. Journal of Economic Theory, 105–352.

Ameriks, J., Kézdi, G., Lee, M., Shapiro, M.D., 2020. Heterogeneity in expectations, risk tolerance, and household stock shares. Journal of Business & Economic Statistics 38 (3), 633–646.

Andonov, A., Rauh, J., 2020. The Return Expectations of Institutional Investors. Discussion paper. Stanford University.

Bacchetta, P., Mertens, E., Van Wincoop, E., 2009. Predictability in financial markets: what do survey expectations tell us? Journal of International Money and Finance 28 (3), 406–426.

Barberis, N., Greenwood, R., Jin, L., Shleifer, A., 2015. X-CAPM: an extrapolative capital asset pricing model. Journal of Financial Economics 115, 1–24.

Barberis, N., Shleifer, A., Vishny, R., 1998. A model of investor sentiment. Journal of Financial Economics 49, 307–343.

Bianchi, F., Ilut, C., Saijo, H., 2021. Diagnostic Business Cycles. Discussion paper. Duke University.

Bordalo, P., Gennaioli, N., Kwon, S.Y., Shleifer, A., 2021. Diagnostic bubbles. Journal of Financial Economics 141 (3), 1060–1077.

Bordalo, P., Gennaioli, N., La Porta, R., Shleifer, A., 2020. Expectations of Fundamentals and Stock Market Puzzles. Discussion paper. National Bureau of Economic Research.

Bordalo, P., Gennaioli, N., Porta, R.L., Shleifer, A., 2019. Diagnostic expectations and stock returns. The Journal of Finance 74 (6), 2839–2874.

Bordalo, P., Gennaioli, N., Shleifer, A., 2018. Diagnostic expectations and credit cycles. The Journal of Finance 73, 199–227.

Buraschi, A., Piatti, I., Whelan, P., 2018. Rationality and Subjective Bond Risk Premia. Imperial College.

Campbell, J.Y., Shiller, R.J., 1988. The dividend–price ratio and expectations of future dividends and discount factors. The Review of Financial Studies 1, 195–228.

Chen, L., Da, Z., Zhao, X., 2013. What drives stock price movements? The Review of Financial Studies 26 (4), 841–876.

Cieslak, A., 2018. Short-rate expectations and unexpected returns in treasury bonds. The Review of Financial Studies 31 (9), 3265–3306.

Cochrane, J.H., 2011. Presidential address: discount rates. The Journal of Finance 66 (4), 1047–1108.

Cogley, T., Sargent, T.J., 2008a. Anticipated utility and rational expectations as approximations of Bayesian decision making. International Economic Review 49 (1), 185–221.

Cogley, T., Sargent, T.J., 2008b. The market price of risk and the equity premium: a legacy of the great depression? Journal of Monetary Economics 55, 454–476.

Coibion, O., Gorodnichenko, Y., Kumar, S., Ryngaert, J., 2021. Do you know that I know that you know...? Higher-order beliefs in survey data. The Quarterly Journal of Economics 136 (3), 1387–1446.

Coibion, O., Gorodnichenko, Y., Weber, M., 2019. Monetary Policy Communications and their Effects on Household Inflation Expectations. Discussion paper. National Bureau of Economic Research.

Collin-Dufresne, P., Johannes, M., Lochstoer, L.A., 2016. Parameter learning in general equilibrium: the asset pricing implications. The American Economic Review 106 (3), 664–698.

Collin-Dufresne, P., Johannes, M., Lochstoer, L.A., 2017. Asset pricing when 'this time is different'. The Review of Financial Studies 30 (2), 505–535.

Dahlquist, M., Ibert, M., 2021. How Cyclical Are Stock Market Return Expectations? Evidence from Capital Market Assumptions. Discussion paper. Stockholm School of Economics.

David, A., 2008. Heterogeneous beliefs, speculation, and the equity premium. The Journal of Finance 63 (1), 41–83.

De La O, R., Myers, S., 2021. Subjective cash flows and discount rates. The Journal of Finance 76 (3), 1339–1387.

Drerup, T., Enke, B., Von Gaudecker, H.-M., 2017. The precision of subjective data and the explanatory power of economic models. Journal of Econometrics 200 (2), 378–389.

Dumas, B., Kurshev, A., Uppal, R., 2009. Equilibrium portfolio strategies in the presence of sentiment risk and excess volatility. The Journal of Finance 64, 579–629.

Enke, B., Graeber, T., 2019. Cognitive Uncertainty. Discussion paper. National Bureau of Economic Research.

Froot, K.A., 1989. New hope for the expectations hypothesis of the term structure of interest rates. The Journal of Finance 44 (2), 283–305.

Fuster, A., Hebert, B., Laibson, D., 2011. Natural expectations, macroeconomic dynamics and asset pricing. In: Acemoglu, D., Woodford, M. (Eds.), NBER Macroeconomics Annual 2011. University of Chicago Press, Chicago, IL.

Geanakoplos, J., 2009. The leverage cycle. In: Acemoglu, D., Rogoff, K., Woodford, M. (Eds.), NBER Macroeconomics Annual.

Geweke, J., 2001. A note on some limitations of CRRA utility. Economics Letters 71 (3), 341–345.

Giglio, S., Maggiori, M., Stroebel, J., Utkus, S., 2021. Five facts about beliefs and portfolios. The American Economic Review 111 (5), 1481–1522.

Greenwood, R., Shleifer, A., 2014. Expectations of returns and expected returns. The Review of Financial Studies 27 (3), 714–746.

Harrison, J.M., Kreps, D.M., 1978. Speculative investor behavior in a stock market with heterogeneous expectations. The Quarterly Journal of Economics 92 (2), 323–336.

Jin, L.J., Sui, P., 2022. Asset pricing with return extrapolation. Journal of Financial Economics 145 (2, Part A), 273–295.

Jouini, E., Napp, C., 2007. Consensus consumer and intertemporal asset pricing with heterogeneous beliefs. The Review of Economic Studies 74 (4), 1149–1174.

Kahneman, D., Tversky, A., 1972. Subjective probability: a judgment of representativeness. Cognitive Psychology 3 (3), 430–454.

Kreps, D., 1998. Anticipated utility and dynamic choice. In: Jacobs, E.K.D.P., Kamien, M. (Eds.), Frontiers of Research in Economic Theory. Cambridge University Press, Cambridge, England.

Lochstoer, L.A., Muir, T., 2022. Volatility expectations and returns. The Journal of Finance 77 (2), 1055–1096.

Ma, Y., Paligorova, T., Peydro, J.-L., 2021. Expectations and Bank Lending. Discussion paper. University of Chicago.

Malmendier, U., Nagel, S., 2011. Depression babies: do macroeconomic experiences affect risk-taking? The Quarterly Journal of Economics 126, 373–416.

Malmendier, U., Nagel, S., 2016. Learning from inflation experiences. The Quarterly Journal of Economics 131 (1), 53–87.

Marinovic, I., Ottaviani, M., Sorensen, P., 2013. Forecasters' objectives and strategies. In: Elliott, G., Timmermann, A. (Eds.), Handbook of Economic Forecasting, vol. 2. Elsevier, pp. 690–720.

Martin, I., Papadimitriou, D., 2021. Sentiment and Speculation in a Market with Heterogeneous Beliefs. Discussion paper. London School of Economics.

Nagel, S., Xu, Z., 2022. Asset pricing with fading memory. The Review of Financial Studies 35 (5), 2190–2245.

O'Donoghue, T., Rabin, M., 1999. Doing it now or later. The American Economic Review 89 (1), 103–124.

Pástor, Ľ., Veronesi, P., 2003. Stock valuation and learning about profitability. The Journal of Finance 58 (5), 1749–1790.

Pástor, Ľ., Veronesi, P., 2006. Was there a NASDAQ bubble in the late 1990s? Journal of Financial Economics 81 (1), 61–100.

Pesaran, H., Pettenuzzo, D., Timmermann, A., 2007. Learning, structural instability, and present value calculations. Econometric Reviews 26, 253–288.

Piazzesi, M., Salomao, J., Schneider, M., 2015. Trend and Cycle in Bond Premia. Discussion paper. Stanford University.

Sargent, T.J., 2008. Evolution and intelligent design. The American Economic Review 98 (1), 5–37.

Shiller, R.J., 2005. Irrational Exuberance, second edn. Princeton University Press, Princeton, NJ.

Timmermann, A., 1996. Excess volatility and predictability of stock prices in autoregressive dividend models with learning. The Review of Economic Studies 63, 523–557.

Timmermann, A.G., 1993. How learning in financial markets generates excess volatility and predictability in stock prices. The Quarterly Journal of Economics, 1135–1145.

Vissing-Jorgensen, A., 2003. Perspectives on behavioral finance: does 'irrationality' disappear with wealth? Evidence from expectations and actions. NBER Macroeconomics Annual 18 (1), 139–194.

Wang, R., 2021. Subjective Return Expectations. Discussion paper. Columbia University.

Weitzman, M.L., 2007. Subjective expectations and asset-return puzzles. The American Economic Review 97 (4), 1102–1130.

Wu, L., 2018. Estimating risk–return relations with analysts price targets. Journal of Banking & Finance 93, 183–197.

The term structure of expectations[☆]

17

Richard K. Crump[a]**, Stefano Eusepi**[b]**, Emanuel Moench**[c,d]**, and Bruce Preston**[e]

[a]*Federal Reserve Bank of New York, New York, NY, United States*
[b]*University of Texas at Austin, Austin, TX, United States*
[c]*Frankfurt School of Finance and Management, Frankfurt am Main, Germany*
[d]*CEPR, London, United Kingdom*
[e]*University of Melbourne, Parkville, VIC, Australia*

17.1 Introduction

Economic theory predicts that intertemporal decisions critically depend on expectations about future outcomes. Over the past two decades, a concerted research program has aimed to measure household, firm, and policymaker beliefs using numerous data sources, including surveys, asset prices, and controlled experiments. By dint of this effort, we now have invaluable data that can be used to evaluate alternative theories of expectations formation and their implications for macroeconomics and finance.

Yet the vast majority of this work has focused on expectations about *short-term* economic developments. This choice is partly driven by what data are available, as there is substantially less information on long-run forecasts. But it also reflects the common assumption in macroeconomic models that economic agents operate in a stationary environment and, consequently, that they can quickly and efficiently come to understand the long-run behavior of the economy. In these models, any information frictions that might be relevant to the expectations formation process, are only relevant to short-run economic dynamics.

These assumptions, however, belie the considerable uncertainty that confronts decision makers in practice. Indeed, direct survey evidence clearly reveals that expectations about the *long-run* values of economic and financial variables vary over time. For example, the Survey of Professional Forecasters annually queries respondents on their estimate of the nonaccelerating inflation rate of unemployment, the Federal Reserve Bank of New York's Survey of Primary Dealers includes questions on "longer-run" values of economic variables such as output, inflation, and the target interest rate, and the FOMC members themselves report, in the Survey of Economic Projections, the value that key macroeconomic variables would be expected to converge to under appropriate monetary policy and in the absence of further shocks to the economy. All of these long-run forecasts display substantial variation over time.

☆ Oliver Kim and Nick Ritter provided excellent research assistance. Preston acknowledges research support from the Australian Research Council, under the grant DP210103427. The views expressed in this paper are those of the authors and do not necessarily reflect the position of the Federal Reserve Bank of New York or the Federal Reserve System.

Handbook of Economic Expectations. https://doi.org/10.1016/B978-0-12-822927-9.00025-2

Movements in long-term expectations are not without consequence. Prominent debates in macroeconomics and finance rest on the long-term behavior of the economy. The seminal contribution of Lucas (2003) argued that the economic costs of short-term fluctuations pale in comparison to the implications of long-run growth, underscoring the need to study long-term expectations and their impact on economic decisions. Among academics and policymakers there is widespread agreement that the ability of central banks and fiscal authorities to manage business cycles depends on the maintenance of long-term fiscal sustainability and stable long-run inflation expectations. And a growing literature in finance understands movements in asset prices by linking them to changes in perceived long-run risk, again highlighting the need to understand market participants' shifting views about the long run.

In this chapter we use survey measures of U.S. professional forecasters to study the term structure of expectations including long horizons. One key advantage of using professional forecasts is the wealth of available data in the U.S. and other countries. Multiple surveys covering a wide range of forecast horizons spanning "nowcasts" to the very long run are available. And unlike the growing number of new surveys of households and firms that have become available to researchers only in recent years, data on professional forecasts have been collected since at least the mid-1950s. Using these data we document the evolution of the entire term structure of expectations since the 1980s and propose a simple expectations formation mechanism that rationalizes their behavior. Armed with this framework, we evaluate some implications in a standard New Keynesian dynamic general equilibrium model.

We emphasize that professional forecasts display two important stylized facts. First, long-run expectations about economic variables such as output growth, inflation and short-term nominal interest rates fluctuate significantly over time, tracking perceived slow-moving changes in the economy such as the long-run mean of inflation or the natural rate of interest. Second, the individual components of the term structure of expectations display a clear pattern of comovement across different variables and forecast horizons. Changes in long-term expectations are tied to short-term forecast errors, consistent with an expectations formation mechanism where agents estimate unobserved trend and cycle components from available data. At the same time, agents appear to form expectations about macroeconomic variables jointly, so that, for example, policy rate forecasts are tightly linked to inflation and output growth forecasts.

Throughout the chapter we use a model of expectations formation that is consistent with these observations. While we discuss the literature on the term structure of expectations throughout the chapter, our primary aim is not to provide an exhaustive summary of existing work. Recent research covers a wide range of theories that can potentially account for some of the empirical regularities in survey data. Here we focus on a specific class of information frictions, and, therefore, a specific modeling approach, and discuss its implications for different aspects of the data.

This chapter is structured in four broad sections. Section 17.2 introduces our workhorse model of the expectations formation mechanism and the information frictions at its foundations. This is an unobserved components model of the trend and cycle which agents estimate using standard filtering methods. The model captures the key aspects of our theory and accounts for the joint term structure of expectations of output growth, inflation and the policy rate. The forecast data are based on the universe of professional forecasts for the United States in the post-war era. We argue that a drifting long-run mean is essential to capture the low-frequency adjustment in long-run beliefs. Moreover, the multivariate model provides a far superior fit when compared to a univariate model specification for each variable. This underscores that the dynamic behavior of survey forecasts of different macroeconomic variables need to be modeled jointly. Existing studies often focus on expectations about an individual variable.

Section 17.3 focuses specifically on the term structure of interest rates, the linchpin of the monetary policy transmission mechanism. We use our measure of expectations to evaluate the expectations hypothesis, stating that yields on government bonds reflect the average short rate that investors expect to prevail over the life of the bond. We compare the behavior of the term structure of consensus expectations with the U.S. Treasury yield curve. Despite the observed volatility of expectations, there remains substantial unexplained variation at the long end of the yield curve. We obtain the subjective term premium as the residual between observed yields and average expected future short rates. The survey-based measure of the term premium does not comove in any meaningful way with expected short rates, suggesting that a large share of movements in longer-maturity interest rates remains unaccounted for by changes in expectations.

The first parts of this chapter are motivated by a reduced-form model of the expectations formation process. This has the advantage of sidestepping detailed assumptions about information frictions and, in particular, taking a stand on the rationality of expectations. There are notable advantages, however, to a more structural approach. Section 17.4 presents a dynamic structural general equilibrium model where agents are boundedly rational and have to learn about a possibly changing economic environment. Subjective beliefs of households and firms are consistent with our reduced-form forecasting model based on survey evidence. However, the structural model assumes a specific deviation from the full information rational expectations setup: subjective and objective (model consistent) forecasting models differ. We discuss the implications for monetary and fiscal policy design under different assumptions about how expectations are formed. Finally, Section 17.5 concludes and provides suggestions for future directions of research.

17.2 Joint behavior of short- and long-term forecasts

In this section, we present a simple model of expectations formation. The key insight of the model—which will resonate throughout the chapter—is that agents revise their beliefs about both the trend and the cyclical components of macroeconomic variables in response to short-term forecast errors. As a result, unanticipated short-term innovations may drive the entire term structure of macroeconomic expectations.[1]

17.2.1 Motivation: a simple model of long-term drift

Market participants observe a wealth of data about the current state of the economy. These data provide signals both about short-term economic developments as well as longer-run trends. Forming expectations about economic variables at different horizons into the future therefore requires decomposing the data into transitory and persistent components. Such decompositions have a long tradition in theoretical and empirical macroeconomic research. For instance, the seminal real-business-cycle model in Kydland and Prescott (1982) assumes agents cannot perfectly observe the short- and long-term components of

---

[1] For a more detailed discussion of this mechanism along with additional empirical evidence, see Crump et al. (2021).

technical progress. Stock and Watson (1989) and Stock and Watson (2007) model inflation as having a trend and a transitory component. This approach has also been incorporated in countless structural models of inflation dynamics of which Cogley et al. (2010) is a prominent example. Various studies apply trend-cycle decompositions to other macroeconomic variables, showing that models which embed slow-moving time-varying drifts capture the dynamic properties of real GDP growth (Stock and Watson, 1989; Cogley and Sargent, 2005 and Laubach and Williams, 2003) and the federal funds rate (Kozicki and Tinsley, 2001 and Gürkaynak et al., 2005) well.

17.2.1.1 *Modeling a drift in the long-run mean*

Consider forecasting the observable variable z_t using the model

$$z_t = \omega_t + x_t \tag{17.1}$$

where

$$\omega_t = \omega_{t-1} + \epsilon_t^{\omega}, \tag{17.2}$$

$$x_t = \phi x_{t-1} + \epsilon_t^x, \tag{17.3}$$

with $0 < \phi < 1$, and ϵ_t^x and ϵ_t^{ω} are mutually independent *i.i.d.* Gaussian innovations. The variables x_t and ω_t are *unobserved* by the forecaster. While x_t captures a stationary cyclical or business-cycle component of z_t, ω_t represents a slow-moving trend or drift. For example, ω_t could represent the underlying productivity trend of the economy, the implicit or explicit inflation target of the central bank, or the long-term drift in the natural rate of interest. This trend is assumed to be nonstationary, but a sufficiently persistent process would deliver essentially the same dynamics. Kozicki and Tinsley (2001) labeled the nonstationary case a "shifting endpoint" model.

Observing z_t at time t, agents estimate the trend and cycle components, $\omega_{t|t}$ and $x_{t|t}$, using the Kalman filter. The expected value of z_t for any horizon $T > t$ is then

$$E_t z_T \equiv z_{T|t} = \omega_{t|t} + \phi^{T-t} x_{t|t},$$

where the persistent and cyclical components satisfy

$$\omega_{T|t} = \omega_{t|t} = \omega_{t-1|t-1} + \eta_t, \tag{17.4}$$

$$x_{T|t} = \phi^{T-t} x_{t|t} = \phi^{T-t} \times [\phi x_{t-1|t-1} + v_t], \tag{17.5}$$

where $\eta_t = \kappa_\omega \left(z_t - z_{t|t-1} \right)$ and $v_t = \kappa_x \left(z_t - z_{t|t-1} \right)$ are innovations measuring the forecast "surprises." These surprises are given by the one-step-ahead or short-term forecast error scaled by the Kalman gain coefficients κ_ω and κ_x. The size of the Kalman gains depends on the relative volatility of the innovations in the trend component and the persistence of the stationary process (e.g., Hamilton, 1994). Given the slow-moving nature of the trend component, κ_ω is assumed to be relatively small.

We explore three implications of this model in the data. First, the model parameters forge a tight connection among forecasts at different horizons. For example, we show that the term structure of inflation forecasts is consistent with random-walk behavior, i.e., $\phi \approx 0$. The entire term structure of inflation expectations shifts in response to revisions in the estimate $\omega_{t|t}$. In contrast, interest rate forecasts at short horizons largely reflect a persistent cyclical component, while long-term forecasts are tied to the drift component.

Second, the model implies a tight connection between long-run forecasts and short-term forecast errors. To see this, for a forecast horizon $T^* > t$ sufficiently large that the cyclical component becomes unimportant, that is $\phi^{T^*-t} \approx 0$, so that we have

$$E_t z_{T^*} \approx \omega_{t|t}.$$

Using the law of motion for the estimated trend component in Eq. (17.4), the change in longer-term forecasts is tied to short-term forecast errors or surprises

$$E_t z_{T^*} - E_{t-1} z_{T^*} \approx \omega_{t|t} - \omega_{t|t-1} = \kappa_\omega \left(z_t - z_{t|t-1} \right).$$

A forecaster who underpredicts z_t for a few periods should revise upwards their long-term forecast, reflecting a perceived increase in the estimated unobserved drift component.

Third, the model predicts a strong, in this simple example a perfect, correlation between the updates to the trend and cycle components, as they both depend on the same forecast error: $z_t - z_{t|t-1}$. This property holds in more general models albeit with a nonzero, but not necessarily perfect, correlation (see, for example, Crump et al., 2022a and Crump et al., 2022b). Crump et al. (2022b), using a novel panel of individual professional forecasts at short and long horizons, provide evidence in favor of such a relation in the data.

17.2.2 **A model to fit the term structure of expectations**

Based on the theoretical framework discussed in the previous section, we now present a parsimonious reduced-form model of the term structure of expectations for three key U.S. macroeconomic variables: output growth, inflation and the short-term nominal interest rate. The model and the analysis are based on Crump et al. (2022a). The model serves three purposes. First, it permits evaluating whether our simple theory of expectations formation can account for the observed dynamics of expectations across a range of forecast horizons. Second, the model matches different surveys and different types of forecasts (i.e., fixed-horizon and fixed-event) in a coherent way. It also provides consistent proxies for missing survey observations. As a result, the model enables us to construct *a consensus measure of expectations at all horizons* that avoids unduly overweighting a particular survey. Third, since we observe fewer forecasts for short-term interest rates than we do for output and inflation, the multivariate nature of the model allows us to exploit the correlation structure across variables and time horizons to inform the term structure of expectations of the short-term interest rate.

17.2.2.1 *Baseline multivariate model*

The state of the macroeconomy is defined by the vector $z_t = (g_t, \pi_t, i_t)'$ representing monthly real output growth, inflation and the short-term nominal interest rate, respectively. They evolve as

$$z_t = \hat{\omega}_t + \hat{x}_t \tag{17.6}$$

where

$$\hat{\omega}_t = \hat{\omega}_{t-1} + \eta_t, \tag{17.7}$$
$$\hat{x}_t = \Phi \hat{x}_{t-1} + \nu_t, \tag{17.8}$$

and the variables $\hat{x}_t \equiv x_{t|t}$ and $\hat{\omega}_t \equiv \omega_{t|t}$ are 3×1 vectors capturing agents' estimates about the underlying unobserved states. To keep the model simple, the innovations $\varepsilon_t = \left(\eta_t', \nu_t' \right)'$ are assumed to be *i.i.d.* across time and normally distributed with variance-covariance matrix Σ_ε. Consistent with the model presented in Section 17.2.1, innovations in the drift are potentially correlated with innovations in the cyclical components of the model. The matrix Φ measures the autocorrelation properties of the stationary component $\hat{x}_t$ and consequently has eigenvalues in the unit circle. The model is defined at the monthly frequency which is the highest frequency observed across the range of surveys of professional forecasts to which we fit the model.

17.2.2.2 *Data overview*

We utilize the universe of professional forecasts for the United States in the post-war era, obtained from nine different survey sources: (1) Blue Chip Financial Forecasts (BCFF); (2) Blue Chip Economic Indicators (BCEI); (3) Consensus Economics (CE); (4) Decision Makers' Poll (DMP); (5) Economic Forecasts: A Worldwide Survey (EF); (6) Goldsmith–Nagan (GN); (7) Livingston Survey (Liv.); (8) Survey of Primary Dealers (SPD); (9) Survey of Professional Forecasters (SPF). Further details about each survey are available in Crump et al. (2022a) (see also Chapter 3 in this Handbook). We focus on three sets of forecasts. For output growth, we use forecasts of real GNP growth prior to 1992 and forecasts of real GDP growth thereafter. For inflation, we use forecasts of growth in the consumer price index (CPI). We choose the CPI over alternative inflation measures such as the GDP deflator because CPI forecasts are available more frequently and for a longer history than alternative inflation measures. Finally, we use the 3-month Treasury bill (secondary market) rate as our measure of a short-term interest rate as it is by far the most frequently surveyed short-term interest rate available.[2]

Combined, these surveys provide a rich portrait of professional forecasters' macroeconomic expectations. Our results are based on 627 variable-horizon pairs spanning the period 1955 to 2019. The survey data differ in frequency, forecast timing, target series, sample availability and forecast horizons. As we make clear below, we are careful to ensure consistency between model-implied and observed forecasts with respect to variable definition and forecast horizon. Table 17.1 summarizes the survey data we use in the paper. Near-term survey forecasts (target period is up to two years ahead) are available for the longest sample with CPI forecasts from the Livingston Survey beginning in the mid-1940s. Medium- and long-term forecasts (target period includes three-years ahead and longer) are available for real output growth and inflation starting in the late 1970s. However, a more comprehensive set of long-term forecasts (a target period of five or more years ahead) for all three variables is available only starting in the mid-1980s. At all horizons there are relatively fewer forecasts for the 3-month Treasury bill than for output growth and inflation.

In the discussion of our results we focus on the period from the early 1980s through 2019, covering the Great Moderation, the Great Recession following the Global Financial Crisis, up to the pre-COVID period. This period includes the majority of the available survey forecasts with over 75% of the total number of series used available in this 35 year time span.

---

[2] For example, forecasts of the Federal Funds rate, the target rate of U.S. monetary policy are only available in two of the eight surveys we consider (BCFF and SPD).

Table 17.1 Summary of Surveys.

	BCFF	BCEI	CE	DMP	EF	GN	Liv.	SPD	SPF
Survey Sample (full)									
Frequency	*Monthly*	*Monthly*	*Monthly*	*Irregular*	*Monthly*	*Quarterly*	*Biannually*	*8 per year*	*Quarterly*
RGDP:	1984–present	1978–present	1989–present	n/a	1984–1995	n/a	1971–present	2011–present	1968–present
CPI:	1984–present	1980–present	1989–present	1978–1987	n/a	n/a	1946–present	2011–present	1981–present
TBILL:	1982–present	1982–present	1989–present	n/a	1984–1995	1969–1986	1992–present	n/a	1981–present
Survey Sample (LT)									
Frequency	*Biannually*	*Biannually*	*Quarterly*	*n/a*	*n/a*	*n/a*	*n/a*	*8 per year*	*Quarterly*
RGDP:	1984–present	1979–present	1989–present	n/a	n/a	n/a	1990–present	2012–present	1992–present
CPI:	1984–present	1984–present	1989–present	1978–1987	n/a	n/a	1990–present	2011–present	1991–present
TBILL:	1983–present	1983–present	1998–present	n/a	n/a	n/a	n/a	n/a	1992–Present
Horizons (NT)									
RGDP:	Q0-Q6, Y2, Y1-5, Y2-6	Q0-Q7, Y2, Y0-4, Y1-5, Y2-6, Y1-10	Q0-Q8, Y1, Y2	n/a	Q1-Q4	n/a	Q1-2, Q3-4, Y2, Y0-9	Q0-Q2, Y1, Y2	Q0-Q4, Y2, Y0-9
CPI:	Q0-Q6, Y2, Y1-5, Y2-6	Q1-Q7, Y2, Y1-5, Y2-6	Q2-Q8, Y1, Y2	Y1-10	n/a	n/a	Q3-4, Y2, Y0-9	n/a	Q2-Q4, Y1, Y2, Y0-4, Y0-9
TBILL:	Q0-Q6, Y1, Y2, Y1-5, Y2-6	Q1-Q7, Y1, Y2, Y1-5, Y2-6	M3, M12, Y1, Y2	n/a	Q1-Q4, Y0, Y1	M3	Q0, Q2, Q4, Y1, Y2	n/a	Q1-Q4, Y1, Y2, Y0-9
Horizons (LT)									
RGDP:	Y3, Y4, Y5, Y6, Y6-10, Y7-11	Y3, Y4, Y5, Y6, Y5-9, Y6-10, Y7-11	Y3-Y10	n/a	n/a	n/a	Y0-9	Y3, LR	Y3, Y0-9
CPI:	Y3, Y4, Y5, Y6, Y6-10, Y7-11	Y3, Y4, Y5, Y6, Y5-9, Y6-10, Y7-11	Y3-Y10	Y1-10	n/a	n/a	Y0-9	Y5-10	Y0-4, Y0-9
TBILL:	Y3, Y4, Y5, Y6, Y6-10, Y7-11	Y3, Y4, Y5, Y6, Y6-10, Y7-11	Y3-Y10	n/a	n/a	n/a	n/a	n/a	Y3, Y0-9

This table provides a summary of the forecast data available from each survey: Blue Chip Financial Forecasts (BCFF), Blue Chip Economic Indicators (BCEI), Consensus Economics (CE), Decision Makers' Poll (DMP), Goldsmith-Nagan Survey (GN), Economic Forecasts: A Worldwide Survey (EF), Livingston Survey (Liv.), Survey of Primary Dealers (SPD), and the Survey of Professional Forecasters (SPF). NT refers to horizons of two years or less while LT refers to horizons including more than two years in the future. Forecasts for output growth (RGDP) are based on real GNP growth prior to 1992 and real GDP growth thereafter. M3 and M12 signify forecasts of 3-months and 12-months ahead, respectively. Q1 represents a one-quarter ahead forecast, Q2 represents a two-quarter ahead forecast and so on. Y1 represents a one-year ahead forecast, e.g., a forecast for the year 2014 made at any time in 2013. Y2 represents a two-year ahead forecast and so on. Y0-5 represents a forecast for the average value over the years ranging from the current year to five years ahead, e.g., a forecast for the average annual growth rate of GDP from 2014 through 2019 made at any time in 2014. Y1-6, Y2-7 and so on are defined similarly. Y6-10 represents a forecast for the average value over the years ranging from six years ahead to 10 years ahead, e.g., a forecast for the average annual growth rate of GDP from 2020 through 2024, made at any time in 2014. Finally, "–" indicates sequential horizons, e.g., entries of the form Q0-Q6 imply that horizons Q1, Q2, Q3, Q4, Q5, and Q6 are available.

17.2.3 Mapping the model to survey forecasts

The model defined by Eqs. (17.6)–(17.8) has the state-space representation

$$Z_t = F(\Phi) Z_{t-1} + V \varepsilon_t$$

where $Z_t = \left(z_t, z_{t-1}, z_{t-2}, z_{t-3}, z_{t-4}, \hat{x}_t, \hat{\omega}_t \right)'$. The presence of four lags in z_t facilitates mapping data definitions to model concepts, as discussed further below. The heterogeneity of available forecasts makes this a nontrivial task. Start with a simple example. Suppose each month we only observe survey forecasts at monthly horizons. For example, we might measure a forecast for the n-month-ahead inflation rate at time t. Using the model, the n-step-ahead forecast of all model variables is given by

$$E_t z_{t+n} = \hat{\omega}_t + \Phi^n \hat{x}_t,$$

where the model forecast of inflation would be the second element of the vector z_t. The larger state vector satisfies

$$E_t Z_{t+n} = F(\Phi)^n Z_t$$

and provides the observation equation. The mapping between data and model is then straightforward.

In practice, however, survey participants are rarely asked to provide monthly forecasts. Rather they are queried about different types of forecasts, which involve quarterly averages, year-over-year growth rates, and so on. When estimating our model we take care to match as closely as possible the observed forecasts with the correct model representation. The following examples help clarify how we do this. Consider the short-term interest rate. Forecasts for the three-month Treasury bill rate are either a simple average over a period or end of period. For the latter, we assign these forecasts to the last month in the period. For real output growth and inflation, survey forecasts come in three possible forms: quarter-over-quarter annualized growth, annual average growth, and Q4/Q4 growth. Let G_{2019Q1} and G_{2019Q2} be the level of real GDP in billions of chained dollars in the first and second quarter of 2019, respectively. Then, the quarterly average annualized growth rate is defined as $100 \cdot ((G_{2019Q2}/G_{2019Q1})^4 - 1)$. Our model variables define a month-over-month (annualized) real GDP growth rate series. To map the monthly series into this specific measured quarterly growth rate, we follow Crump et al. (2014) and use

$$100 \cdot ((G_{2019Q2}/G_{2019Q1})^4 - 1) \approx \frac{1}{9} \left(g_{2019m2} + 2 \cdot g_{2019m3} + 3 \cdot g_{2019m4} + 2 \cdot g_{2019m5} + g_{2019m6} \right),$$

where, for example, g_{2019m2} represents the model-based month-over-month annualized real output growth in February 2019. This notation makes clear why lagged values of z_t appear in the state vector Z_t. Annual average growth rates follow a similar pattern. For example, let G_{2018} and G_{2019} be the average level of real GDP in billions of chained dollars in the years 2018 and 2019. The annual average growth rate is $100 \cdot (G_{2019}/G_{2018} - 1)$ which we approximate via

$$100 \cdot (G_{2019}/G_{2018} - 1) \approx \frac{1}{144} \left(g_{2018m2} + 2 \cdot g_{2018m3} + 3 \cdot g_{2018m4} + \cdots + 12 \cdot g_{2019m1} \right.$$
$$\left. + 11 \cdot g_{2019m2} + 10 \cdot g_{2019m3} + \cdots + 2 \cdot g_{2019m11} + g_{2019m12} \right).$$

Finally, Q4/Q4 growth rates are calculated, for example, by $100 \cdot (G_{2019Q4}/G_{2018Q4} - 1)$ and approximated via

$$100 \cdot (G_{2019Q4}/G_{2018Q4} - 1) \approx \frac{1}{12} \left(g_{2019m1} + g_{2019m2} + g_{2019m3} + \cdots + g_{2019m12} \right).$$

The above shows that certain short-term survey forecast horizons will implicitly include time periods which have already occurred. To avoid taking a stand on how forecasters treat past data (e.g., do forecasters use realized data, filtered versions, or another measure?), we exclude all survey forecast horizons that include past months' values of z_t. The only exception we make is to include current quarter (Q0) and one-quarter ahead (Q1) forecasts for real output growth which extend back, at most, four months and one month, respectively. We do so to help pin down monthly real output growth since the actual series is only available at the quarterly frequency. Finally, for simplicity, forecasts which involve averages over multiple years are mapped as simple averages over the corresponding horizons.

The mapping between unobserved states and observed forecasts is then given by the observation equation

$$\mathcal{Y}_t = H_t(\Phi) \times Z_t + o_t,$$

where $\mathcal{Y}_t$ includes the survey forecasts. The observation matrix depends nonlinearly on Φ and is time-varying, reflecting missing observations in the survey forecasts series. The vector o_t denotes measurement errors. We assume individual observation errors for each survey to be mean-zero, i.i.d. and mutually independent Gaussian innovations. To ensure a parsimonious model we impose equal variances for each target variable at similar forecast horizons (but not by the specific survey). We group forecast horizons by: very short term—up to two-quarters ahead; short term—up to two-years ahead; medium term—from three-to-four-years ahead; and long term—five or more years ahead.

17.2.4 Discussion

The model is designed around the central mechanism driving changes in the term structure of expectations introduced in the previous section. The time-varying long-run mean captures the observed drift in survey-based forecasts. This model feature has been exploited in the previous literature with a tight focus on inflation expectations. Kozicki and Tinsley (2012), a precursor of this approach, show this class of models fits professional forecasters' inflation expectations at different horizons, including the long-run. Chan et al. (2018) conduct a similar exercise for a wide set of countries. Aruoba (2020) fits the term structure of survey-based inflation expectations by adapting the structure of the Nelson–Siegel (NS) model of the yield curve, which summarizes the yield curve with three factors (level, slope, and curvature). In contrast to the existing literature, in our model forecasters form *joint* expectations about different macroeconomic variables.

However, for the sake of simplicity the model ignores some possibly important features of the expectations formation mechanism. First, the model parameters are time invariant. Shifts in the volatility of forecast errors might have an impact on the updating of expectations by affecting the sensitivity to forecast errors via the Kalman gain. While it has been widely documented that economic volatility has changed in the post-war U.S., this is likely less of a concern for our baseline estimation period. Other sources of structural change such as regime shifts in monetary or fiscal policy can also impact the expectations formation process that the model aims to capture. Mertens and Nason (2020) extend the framework by introducing time-varying persistence and volatility in their model of inflation expectations.[3] Carvalho et al. (2021) and Eusepi et al. (2020) allow for structural changes in the expectations formation process in general equilibrium frameworks. We revisit these ideas in Section 17.4.

Second, to what degree is the model used by our representative forecaster close to the correct data generating process? Under the common assumption of rational expectations agents use the correct model. This implies the updating equations (17.4) and (17.5) are based on the optimal filter.[4] Macroeconomic models embedding these assumptions have been used to study the response of the economy to changes in long-run productivity (Tambalotti, 2003; Edge et al., 2007); shifts in the long-run mean of inflation (Erceg and Levin, 2003); or movements in asset prices in response to long-run dividend growth (Timmermann, 1993). However, a growing literature assumes agents form expectations under bounded rationality. These models produce a wedge between subjective expectations and the model-consistent data generating process. Agents' inference and expectations updating is then no longer optimal. This literature includes models of adaptive learning (Marcet and Sargent, 1989; Evans and Honkapohja, 2001 and Eusepi and Preston, 2011), or models where expectations exhibit extrapolation bias (Fuster et al., 2010; Bordalo et al., 2020 and Angeletos et al., 2020).[5] We discuss these additional frictions in Section 17.4, where we study the term structure of expectations in a structural general equilibrium model.

17.2.5 Results

17.2.5.1 *Model fit*

The model is estimated over the period January 1983 to December 2019 using Bayesian methods and provides an excellent fit of the 627 times series, especially for the short-term nominal rate. In particular, Crump et al. (2022a) show that it strongly outperforms univariate versions of the unobserved components model for each variable. The superior fit of the multivariate model suggests that market participants form expectations about the short rate jointly with those of output and inflation.

Given the large number of series involved in the estimation, it is not straightforward to illustrate the fit of our model comprehensively in the time series domain. Fig. 17.1 offers a subset of this information, detailing three forecast horizons for each variable: the short term (two-quarters ahead); the medium term (two-years ahead); and the long term (five-years ahead and beyond). In each panel, we show a collection of survey forecasts from different sources that approximately match the appropriate forecast horizon (we use about sixty time series in total). The model does a remarkable job. Perhaps not surprisingly given the vast number of survey forecasts available for this time period, the gray areas capturing the 95% coverage interval are very tight. Moreover, the model-implied forecast values closely track the data, with a few exceptions for real GDP long-term forecasts during the late 1980s and the 2009 recession.

---

[3] Grishchenko et al. (2019) go beyond consensus inflation forecasts and use probability distributions of future inflation rates from several U.S. and euro-area surveys of professional forecasters to estimate a dynamic factor model featuring time-varying uncertainty.

[4] Under this assumption the surprises measured by $z_t - z_{t|t-1}$ are uncorrelated with information available at $t-1$, as we assume here for convenience. In particular, the Kalman filter produces innovations to trend (η_t) and cycle (ν_t) that are *i.i.d.* across time.

[5] See Angeletos et al. (2020) which offers a comprehensive discussion on the literature and introduces a model featuring both disperse information and extrapolation bias. This model reproduces the observed response of survey-based forecasts to an identified business cycle shock.

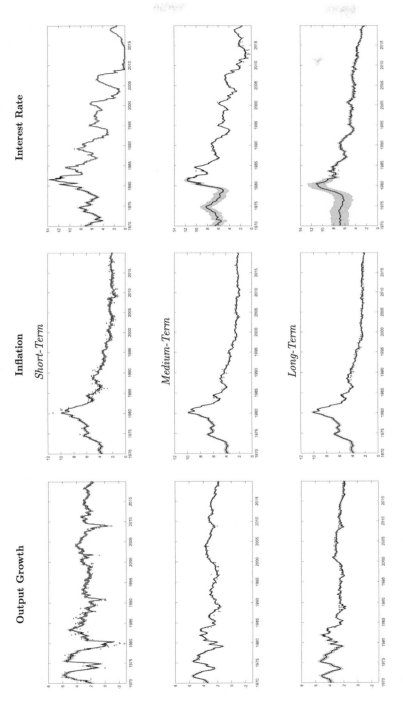

FIGURE 17.1 Fitting the Term Structure of Expectations

The panels contrast model predictions with survey data at different forecast horizons. The solid line shows median predictions and the gray shade shows the 95% coverage interval. The squares represent survey-based forecasts at short-term (two quarters ahead), medium-term (two years ahead) and long-term (five years ahead and beyond) horizons from different surveys.

In addition to fitting the observed survey forecasts over the estimation period 1983–2019, we back-cast the individual model-implied forecast series and report smoothed estimates of expectations going back to 1970. Over this earlier period the availability of survey forecasts is scarce and, for longer-range forecasts, nonexistent. Therefore, there is considerable uncertainty about the term structure of forecasts. One additional caveat with this exercise is that the expectations formation mechanism has most likely undergone structural change across the full sample. As discussed in Section 17.4, the evolution of the perceived drifts has changed and has become less responsive to short-term developments over time. Also, economic volatility and, possibly, the perceived policy regime could have shifted over time.[6]

These caveats notwithstanding, the model also fits the few observed survey forecasts for output growth and inflation that are available before 1983 reasonably well. Not surprisingly, the uncertainty around the estimates increases as we move backwards in time. However, model predictions accord with conventional wisdom, with an increase in inflation and interest rate expectations over the mid-1970s, peaking in the early 1980s. While predicted long-term forecasts for real GDP are possibly too volatile, they capture the higher growth rate during that period. Overall, this simple and highly parsimonious model fits the term structure of survey-based expectations, especially after the mid-1980s, exceptionally well.

Beyond consensus expectations

Here we focus on a representative forecaster and disregard the forecast disagreement widely documented in surveys. Researchers have introduced a rich set of informational frictions that can generate plausible degrees of forecast dispersion. Models of sticky (Mankiw and Reis, 2002) or noisy information (Woodford, 2003) and models of rational inattention (Sims, 2003 and Maćkowiak and Wiederholt, 2009) assume that individual forecasters endogenously have different information sets regarding the current state of the economy. As such, they disagree in their forecasts about future economic outcomes. Coibion and Gorodnichenko (2012) show that forecast dispersion can affect the dynamic properties of consensus measures of expectations.

A few recent papers incorporate this theoretical framework to explain observed forecaster disagreement. Andrade and Le Bihan (2013) employ a multivariate setup and assume forecasters are subject to sticky *and* noisy information. Mertens and Nason (2020) capture a wider set of information frictions by allowing for infrequent forecast updating of inflation expectations by individual forecasters. This prior literature has largely focused on individual target variables, such as inflation, and shorter-term forecast horizons. However, as shown in Andrade et al. (2016) and Crump et al. (2022b), individual *long-term* forecasts show a high degree of dispersion for all variables considered and for all forecasting horizons. This is consistent with economic agents facing uncertainty about the long-run behavior of the economy. Andrade et al. (2016) show that the nature of disagreement is fundamentally different across macroeconomic variables: the term structure of disagreement is upward-sloping only for short-rate forecasts while it is flat across horizons for inflation and downward-sloping for output growth. While the primary focus here is on the consensus (mean) forecast, this model can also explain the behavior of the term

---

[6] A potential extension to the framework involves explicitly incorporating time variation in both the systematic and stochastic components of the model. For example, Garnier et al. (2015) estimate a model for trend inflation on different countries and allow time variation in the volatility of the trend. Primiceri (2005) and Bianchi and Ilut (2017) estimate VARs with time-varying coefficients on U.S. data in order to account for structural change.

structure of disagreement. In particular, Andrade et al. (2016) show that models of dispersed information, such as noisy and sticky information models, must be endowed with a multivariate setup along with a drifting long-run mean to match the observed behavior of forecast disagreement. Taken together, this shows that the model introduced in Section 17.2.2.1 is able match the evolution of both the first and second moments of professional forecast data.

17.2.5.2 *Evolution of the term structure of expectations*

The estimated model allows us to study the fitted expected paths of the three variables at any specific point in time. Fig. 17.2 shows a number of "hair charts" which are a convenient way to summarize the evolution of these forecast paths. The top panel displays real GDP growth whereas the middle panels show the nominal interest rate and the underlying rate of CPI inflation.[7] The black solid lines show the actual realized data while the gray lines show the expected paths of the variable over the next 10 years once every 12 months.

The forecast paths display substantial volatility over time, typically flattening (and often inverting) at the end of economic expansions and steepening in the aftermath of recessions. This pattern is starker for nominal (and real) interest rates, as professional forecasters respond to the predictable component of monetary tightening and easing cycles. For example, the term structure of short-rate expectations inverts in early 1989 when short rates reached their local peak leading into the 1990–1991 recession. A flattening and slight inversion is also observed at the end of the 2004–2006 tightening cycle. Importantly, these estimated measures of short-rate expectations based on survey forecasts, in contrast to many model-based expected short-rate paths, are consistent with a perceived zero lower bound (ZLB) on nominal interest rates. After the short rate reached the ZLB in 2008, the term structure first flattened and then steepened again as forecasters continued to expect an eventual lift-off. This "overoptimism" about lift-off that is apparent in the short-rate expectations is mirrored by overoptimistic real GDP forecasts during the same period.

While expected nominal short rates display a significant degree of volatility, the shape of the expected path of inflation (third panel) exhibits far less variation, remaining mostly flat around the prevailing level of inflation. Professional forecasters perceive the persistent component of inflation to approximately follow a random walk. An important implication is that movements in expected nominal short rates translate almost one-to-one to expected real short rates, consistent with nominal rigidities preventing prices from adjusting in the short term.

The expected ten-year paths of short rates and inflation converge to each variable's time-varying long-run mean extracted from all available surveys of professional forecasters. These long-run projections reflect forecasters' perceptions of macroeconomic fundamentals rather than cyclical variation. Long-run forecasts have all varied substantially over the past thirty years. The long-run expected nominal short rate has gradually fallen from about 8% in the mid-1980s to about 2.5% in 2019. Much of this decline is accounted for by a secular decline in the expected long-run level of inflation, which dropped from about 6% in the early 1980s to a level of around 2.5% in the late 1990s. Since then, the perceived inflation target has remained quite stable, only showing a small dip around the Great Recession and over the last two years in our sample.

---

[7] In order to smooth the high volatility in this series we plot the model-based measure of underlying CPI inflation which does not include transitory shocks which are captured by an observation error.

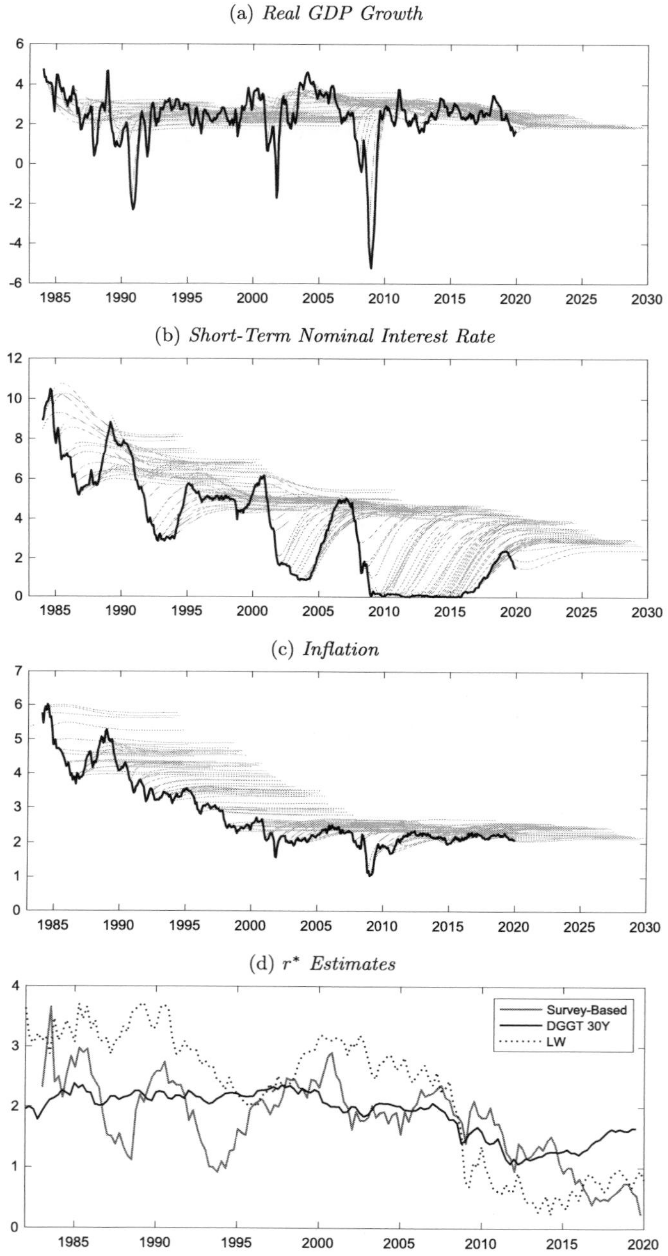

(a) *Real GDP Growth*

(b) *Short-Term Nominal Interest Rate*

(c) *Inflation*

(d) *r* Estimates*

FIGURE 17.2 Estimated Forecast Paths

The figure shows fitted survey-based expectations for real output growth, the short-term nominal interest rate, inflation, and the short-term real interest rate. The top three panels show the actual variable along with the fitted survey-based forecast path up to the ten-year horizon. The bottom panel shows the long-term forecast of the real short rate (i.e., the perceived natural rate of interest) along with r* estimates from Del Negro et al. (2018) and Laubach and Williams (2003).

Using the survey-implied term structures of expectations for the nominal short rate and inflation, the final panel shows the evolution of the long-term forecast of the real short rate (i.e., the perceived natural rate of interest).[8] The long-term expected real short rate has remained fairly stable around 2% over the 30 year period starting in 1983, but has begun to decline after 2010, falling below 1% by the end of 2014. This is consistent with long-run real GDP growth forecasts which have fallen modestly over the past 10 or so years, reaching slightly below 2% by the end of the sample. It is also in line with recent evidence on the decline of the natural real rate of interest. Summers (2014), Johannsen and Mertens (2021), Holston et al. (2017), Del Negro et al. (2018), Crump et al. (2022a) among others, have argued that long-run equilibrium real rates in the U.S. have seen a secular decline over the past decades. This chart also compares the perceived natural rate of interest based on survey data with two other estimates – those of Laubach and Williams (2003) and Del Negro et al. (2018).[9] All three estimates share a similar broad pattern – a fairly stable natural rate around 2% up until the financial crisis followed by a marked decline.

17.3 Expectations and the term structure of interest rates

Monetary policy affects the aggregate economy primarily via the term structure of interest rates. While central banks have tight control over short-term rates, the efficacy of monetary policy depends on the ability to affect longer-maturity interest rates which drive the saving and investment decisions of households and firms. Standard macroeconomic models assume that the transmission mechanism of monetary policy is given by the expectations hypothesis: yields on longer-term government bonds reflect the average short rate that investors expect to prevail over the life of the bond.

We now use the fitted term structure of expectations to evaluate how well movements in future short rate expectations explain long-term yields. We do this by decomposing observed government bond yields into an expectations hypothesis component and a residual component which we interpret as a measure of the subjective term premium perceived by professional forecasters. Because our survey-based term premiums represent the residual between yields and expected short rates, we can remain agnostic about what specifically they represent. For example, they might reflect shifts in investor risk attitudes leading to time variation in expected excess bond returns, differences between the expectations of the marginal investor and consensus expectations, or frictions in the bond market which prevent the elimination of arbitrage opportunities. Hereafter we will refer to this measure as the "term premium" for simplicity.

17.3.1 Decomposing the term structure of interest rates

We obtain zero coupon U.S. Treasury yields from the Gurkaynak et al. (2007) dataset available on the Board of Governors of the Federal Reserve's research data page.[10] The sample period is March

---

[8] In particular, since our model is at the monthly frequency we define the real rate as the current interest rate less the one-month ahead forecast of inflation.

[9] Data available at https://www.newyorkfed.org/research/policy/rstar and https://github.com/FRBNY-DSGE/rstarBrookings2017.

[10] See https://www.federalreserve.gov/pubs/feds/2006/200628/200628abs.html.

1983–December 2019. Let $y_t(n)$ be the continuously compounded yield on an n-month discount bond and i_t the risk-free nominal short rate at time t. To separate longer-term from short-term expectations, we conduct our analyses in terms of *forward rates*, defined as the current yield of an n-month bond maturing in $n + m$ months:

$$f_t(n, m) = \frac{1}{n}[(n + m)y_t(n + m) - my_t(m)].$$ (17.9)

Because our empirical model of expectations is estimated at the monthly frequency, we construct annual forward rates as the annual average of monthly forward rates. For example, a 4Y1Y forward would set $n = 12$ and $m = 48$. We then define forward term premiums as the difference between $f_t(n, m)$ and the expected nominal short-term rate over the n months from m months hence, which we can further decompose into the expected real short rate and expected inflation:

$$
\begin{aligned}
tp_t^{fwd}(n, m) &= f_t(n, m) - \frac{1}{n} \sum_{h=m+1}^{n+m} \mathbb{E}_t[i_{t+h}] \\
&= f_t(n, m) - \frac{1}{n} \sum_{h=m+1}^{n+m} \mathbb{E}_t[r_{t+h} + \pi_{t+h+1}].
\end{aligned}
$$ (17.10)

In other words, the forward term premium is the difference between observed forwards and what would be the yield predicted by the expectations hypothesis, i.e., the average expected future short rate over the n months beginning in m months. Note that this is an identity: there are no implicit assumptions about the rationality or bias of expectations or the data generating process for yields, expectations, or term premiums.

Fig. 17.3 uses Eq. (17.10) to decompose nominal Treasury forward rates into expected future real short rates, expected future inflation, as well as the forward term premium. The figure displays the 1Y1Y, 4Y1Y, and 9Y1Y forward horizons in the top, middle, and bottom panel, respectively. All three components of bond yields contribute to the secular decline in Treasury yields observed over the past several decades, albeit to different degrees and with different timing. At the 1Y1Y horizon, the term premium declined from about 3% in the early 1980s and stabilized around zero in the early 2000s, mimicking the path of expected inflation. At longer maturities, forward term premiums display a similar pattern, falling over the 1980s and 1990s and stabilizing in the 2000s. Since about 2010, however, longer-maturity forward term premiums again declined together with the expected real short rate. Term premiums have remained at negative levels since 2010, except for a brief uptick around the "taper tantrum" episode of 2013.

Overall, forward term premiums account for more than half of the secular decline in longer-maturity forwards. This finding of a secular decline in term premiums is consistent with the evidence in Wright (2011) who uses an affine term structure model to show that term premiums in the U.S. and in other developed economies have experienced sizable and persistent declines between 1990 and mid-2009. He attributes this decline to a broad-based reduction of inflation uncertainty. Our survey-based decomposition shows that even when one takes full account of the expected short rate path of well-informed economic agents (professional forecasters), there is a secular decline of term premiums. Cao et al. (2021) offer one potential explanation based on heterogeneous beliefs about short rates.

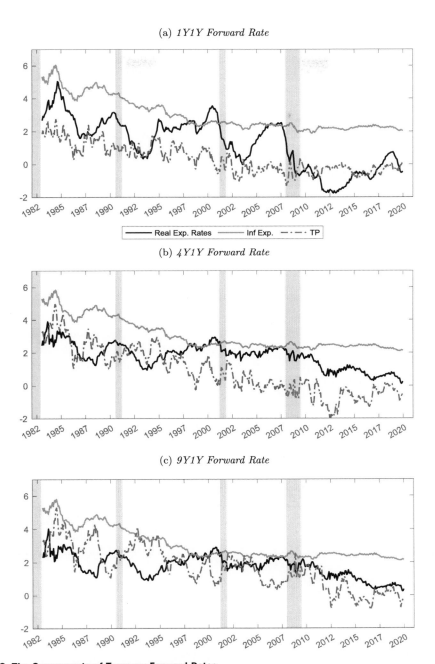

(a) *1Y1Y Forward Rate*

(b) *4Y1Y Forward Rate*

(c) *9Y1Y Forward Rate*

FIGURE 17.3 The Components of Treasury Forward Rates

This figure shows the decomposition of Treasury forwards into the expected short-term real interest rates ("Real exp. rates"), expected inflation ("Infl Exp.") and the nominal forward term premium ("TP"). The top panel reports results for the 1Y1Y forward rate, the middle panel for the 4Y1Y forward rate, and the bottom panel for the 9Y1Y forward rate. Treasury forwards are based on the zero coupon bond yields from Gurkaynak et al. (2007). The sample period is March 1983–December 2019.

Term premiums and survey forecasts: existing literature

Our measure of the term premium is model-free, in the sense that we simply obtain it as a residual from observed yields and observed or tightly fitted expected short rates. A few other studies have estimated term premiums using information from surveys of professional forecasters. However, they all obtain term premium estimates from no-arbitrage term structure models, fitted using observed yields and some survey forecasts of interest rates. For example, Kim and Wright (2005) and Kim and Orphanides (2012) employ survey forecasts of the nominal short rate at select horizons to discipline their estimates. Similarly, Piazzesi et al. (2015) combine survey forecasts of the short rate, inflation, and of longer-term Treasuries to distinguish subjective beliefs (i.e., surveyed forecasters), objective beliefs (i.e., those of a statistician endowed with full-sample information) and subjective risk premiums. All these models assume a small-scale stationary VAR governing the dynamics of short rates and term premiums and, therefore, do not explicitly allow for low-frequency variation in expected short-rate paths which we have shown is a key element of actual short-rate expectations. In more recent work, Cieslak and Povala (2015), Bauer and Rudebusch (2020), and Feunou and Fontaine (2021) incorporate shifting endpoints for macroeconomic variables into models of the term structure of interest rates.

Variance decomposition of forwards

Fig. 17.3 shows that at higher frequencies, forward term premiums and expected real rates feature significant variability across all maturities. Crump et al. (2022a) perform a variance decomposition of the components to quantify their relative contributions. They highlight the pivotal role of term premiums in accounting for yield variation. Expected real rates explain about 60% of the variance of the one-year yield while expected inflation and the term premium account for about 30% and 10%, respectively. Expected real rates also explain just shy of 50% and 30% of forward rates at the one- and two-year maturity. However, their importance then declines sharply at longer maturities, accounting for less than 20% at forward horizons beyond four years. In contrast, term premiums only explain a small amount of variation at the very short end, but account for about 50% of the variation in forward rates at intermediate and longer maturities. The share of variance explained by expected inflation is relatively stable at around 30% across the maturity spectrum.

Since yields and forward rates are quite persistent, it is instructive to investigate the decomposition of their *changes*. The contribution of term premiums to the variation of monthly changes in forward rates is substantial at all horizons and increases from 75% at the one-year forward horizon to over 90% at longer forward horizons. In contrast, expected real short rates only account for 20% of the month-to-month variation at the one-year forward horizon, and this contribution quickly drops to zero at longer maturities. Expected inflation also accounts for a negligible share of the variance of forward rate changes across maturities.

Given the considerable volatility of expected short rates, how can we explain the dominant role of term premiums in accounting for the variability of longer-maturity bond yields? Crump et al. (2022a) show that this is driven by the fact that changes in expectations *co-move very little* with changes in yields, except at short forecast horizons.

Short-run forecast errors and the components of yields

To gain further intuition about the determinants of longer-term interest rates we return to the simple model of Section 17.2.1. Revisions in long-term expectations should be positively related to short-term forecast errors. The top two panels in Fig. 17.4 show this is indeed the case for both nominal

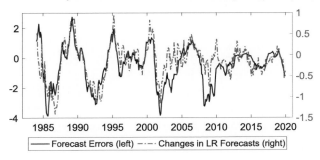

(a) *Nominal short rate forecast errors vs. Revisions in Long-run (9Y1Y) Forecasts*

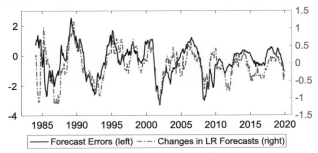

(b) *Real short rate forecast errors vs. Revisions in Long-run (9Y1Y) Forecasts*

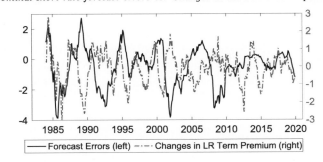

(c) *Nominal short rate forecast errors vs. Changes in the 9Y1Y Term premium*

FIGURE 17.4 Short Rate Forecast Errors vs. Changes in Long-Run Forecasts

This figure compares forecast errors with changes in long-run expectations and term premiums. Nominal and real short-rate forecast errors are calculated as the 12-month ahead forecast error. Revisions to long-run forecasts and changes in term premiums are defined as changes relative to 12 months ago. The sample period is January 1984–December 2019.

and real short rates. The comovement is striking with correlations of 74% and 63%, respectively. This implies that market participants update their views about the long-term mean of the nominal and real short rate in response to new information captured by forecast surprises. In contrast, the bottom panel showing both short-term forecast revisions and our measure of the term premium shows no discernible relation; furthermore, the correlation of only −15% clearly indicates that forces other than forecast errors determine the behavior of term premiums.

Cross-sectional comovement of the components of yields

We have discussed the weak comovement of expected short rates and forward rates in the time dimension. Next, we uncover another important difference by looking across bond maturities. A long literature in finance has documented that government bond yields feature substantial comovement across maturities (e.g., Garbade, 1996; Scheinkman and Litterman, 1991). This is also true in our sample: the first two principal components extracted from one-year forward rates, from zero-to-nine-years ahead, explain 97% and 3% of their joint variation. The loadings of these principal components confirm the common interpretation as level and slope of the yield curve.

Based on our decomposition of forwards into expected short rate and term premium components, we can parse out the sources of the strong cross-sectional correlation. Almost half of the variance of the level factor is explained by term premiums, one third by expected inflation and the remaining 20% by expected real short rates. Also consistent with the variance decompositions for individual forwards, almost 90% of the month-to-month variation in the level factor and more than three quarters of the year-over-year variation are explained by term premiums. The expectations components are somewhat more important for the slope factor: 85% of its variation is accounted for by expected real short rates, about 10% by expected inflation, and the remainder by term premiums. However, more than two-thirds of the month-to-month variation of the slope factor is explained by term premiums, in line with the above finding that only a small share of the yield curve variation at higher frequencies is driven by expectations.

Fig. 17.5 visualizes the importance of term premiums for the strong comovement across maturities. It shows 12-month changes in short- and long-maturity forward rates (top panel), expected rates (middle panel), and forward term premiums (bottom panel) for the 1Y1Y and 9Y1Y forward maturities. The figure documents that across maturities survey-based term premiums comove much more strongly than survey-based expected future short rates or even forwards themselves. Twelve month changes in expected rates at short and long horizons are only weakly correlated, whereas changes in forward term premiums comove in lockstep, at least until the mid to late 2000s.

Note that the strong comovement of term premiums is a feature of the data and is not imposed in any way in our analysis as term premiums are obtained as residuals between observed forwards and expected average short rates. Term premiums equal average expected short-term excess holding period returns over the life of a bond, see, for example, Cochrane and Piazzesi (2008). Hence, our finding of a strong comovement of term premiums across maturities is consistent with a strong factor structure in expected excess returns as also documented by Cochrane and Piazzesi (2005). Interestingly, we observe a break in this comovement around the financial crisis. This might be capturing the unconventional monetary policy actions undertaken during that period, with particularly strong effects on term premiums of longer-term bonds.

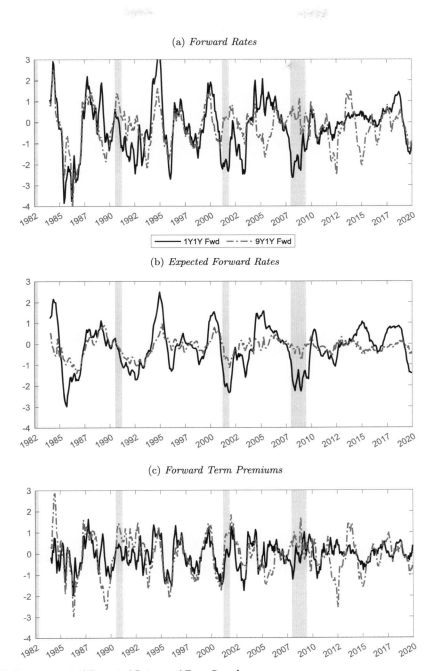

(a) *Forward Rates*

(b) *Expected Forward Rates*

(c) *Forward Term Premiums*

FIGURE 17.5 Comovement of Expected Rates and Term Premiums

This figure shows 12-month changes in forward rates (top chart), expected forward nominal short-term rates (middle chart) and the forward term premium (bottom chart) for the 1Y1Y and 9Y1Y forward maturities. The sample period is January 1984–December 2019.

Forecast accuracy

The previous results based on the decomposition of longer-term interest rates into expected short rate paths and term premiums rely on the quality of survey-based short-rate forecasts as representative measures of expectations. While a formal forecast evaluation is beyond the scope of this chapter, we illustrate the precision of survey-based short-rate expectations by visually comparing them with the expected short rates implied by the forward curve.[11] As discussed above, these expected short-rate paths are consistent with the expectations hypothesis in the absence of any term premiums.

In fact, forward rates are often interpreted as market-based (or risk-neutral) expectations and used as an alternative to professional surveys. Cochrane (2017) argues that "risk-neutral probabilities are a good sufficient statistic to make decisions." Crump et al. (2022a) show that forward-based short-rate paths display very different dynamics compared to survey-based short-rate expectations. They are typically steeper and lie above those of surveys, in line with the notion of a time-varying term premium that is positive on average. Fig. 17.6 compares the forecast performance, as measured by the difference of squared errors over time for different forward horizons. The main takeaway is that our survey-based measure of short-rate expectations has on average performed substantially better in predicting short rates than the forward curve, and the performance gap widens with the forecast horizon. This finding is consistent with the notion that forecasters do not simply report risk-neutral expectations extracted from the forward curve when being surveyed about short rates, a conclusion also shared by Adam et al. (2021) and Chapter 16 in this Handbook. At the same time both measures have come closer in the past 20 or so years, reflecting the overall decline of term premiums. In addition, forward rates appear to have performed somewhat better at intermediate horizons since around 2010: this is consistent with the notion that professional forecasters were more optimistic about the normalization process at that time, while terms premiums where compressed. For a more general discussion of forecasts based on market prices, see Chapter 14 in this Handbook.

Summing up, we offer two conclusions. First, we document that the term structure of short-rate expectations is fairly volatile and its behavior is consistent with market participants frequently updating their beliefs about the medium- to long-term evolution of the policy rate. Second, we show that the term structure of interest rates is only partly driven by short-rate expectations. The residual component, the term premium, plays a key role in determining the evolution of interest rates at longer maturities. This component is often left unaccounted for in standard macroeconomic models used for monetary policy analysis.

17.4 **The term structure of expectations in structural models**

So far, our analysis of the term structure of expectations has yet to take a stand on the rationality of expectations. We now develop a dynamic structural general equilibrium model in which the subjective

---

[11] Crump et al. (2011) study the forecast accuracy of professional forecasts for the federal funds rate based on BCFF data. They show that forecast accuracy is negatively correlated with the variation in the federal funds rate (i.e., forecast accuracy is generally worse during easing and tightening cycles). Moreover, they show that forecast accuracy has been consistently improving across tightening cycles over their sample period (1982 through mid-2011). In contrast, there is no such improvement when the forecast evaluation is restricted to easing cycles. Cieslak (2018) and Schmeling et al. (2021) investigate the relationship between short-rate forecast errors and the dynamics of returns on fixed-income assets.

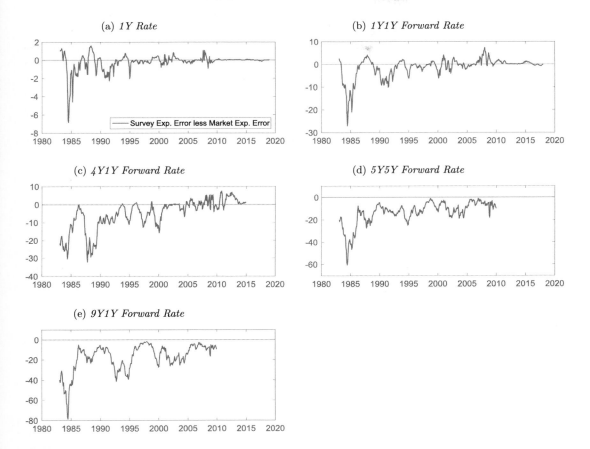

FIGURE 17.6 Forecast Errors

This figure shows the difference between the mean-square forecast error (MSFE) of survey expectations and the MSFE of market expectations. Values below zero indicate that survey expectations have a lower MSFE. The sample period is January 1983–December 2019.

beliefs of households and firms are consistent with our reduced-form forecasting model. The structural model has the equilibrium property that subjective beliefs are more persistent than the true data generating process. Household and firm expectations exhibit extrapolation bias, consistent with empirical and laboratory evidence. That subjective and objective forecasting models differ represents a departure from full-information rational expectations.

An advantage of a structural model is that we can estimate how different economic shocks determine forecast errors and the term structure of expectations. In principle, this permits addressing some earlier questions—such as the determinants of real neutral rates and inflation expectations—left unanswered by the reduced-form model. Having a structural theory of long-term expectations allows the analysis of important practical policy questions that rational expectations models cannot answer. For example, we argue that our framework provides a coherent definition of expectations anchoring, and clear predictions of the economic conditions in which expectations will be anchored or un-anchored. We show this has important implications for monetary and fiscal policy.

17.4.1 A general structural model

Dynamic stochastic general equilibrium (DSGE) models describe the behavior of economic agents solving infinite-horizon intertemporal decision problems in a market economy.[12] The equilibrium behavior of the economy therefore depends on the expected future path of aggregate variables such as prices, quantities and policy variables. The log-linear solution of a typical DSGE model can be expressed as

$$A_0 z_t = \sum_{s=1}^{n} A_n \left(E_t \sum_{T=t}^{\infty} \lambda_s^{T-t} z_{T+1} \right) + A_{n+1} z_{t-1} + A_{n+2} \varepsilon_t,$$

where the vector z_t collects all model variables in deviation from their nonstochastic steady-state values; the vector ε_t collects exogenous innovations; $\lambda_s \in 1, \ldots, n$ are discount factors resulting from the agents' decisions rules; A_i for $i \in 1, \ldots, n+2$ coefficient matrices; and

$$E_t = \int_0^1 E_t^i \, di$$

average beliefs across agents. This representation holds for arbitrary beliefs, including rational expectations.[13] Under rational expectations, the model has the equilibrium solution

$$z_t = \Psi z_{t-1} + \Psi_\varepsilon \varepsilon_t.$$

The matrix Ψ measures the transitional dynamics around the steady state, and Ψ_ε captures the economy's impact response to innovations. Agents are fully informed about the economy's steady-state; they face no information frictions leading to fluctuating long-run beliefs.

Now introduce an information friction to this full information benchmark. Consistent with our simple model in Sections 17.2.1 and 17.2.2 agents are uncertain about the long run. Expectations are then formed using the forecasting model

$$z_t = S\omega_t + \Psi z_{t-1} + v_t, \tag{17.11}$$

$$\omega_t = \omega_{t-1} + \eta_t, \tag{17.12}$$

where both the drift ω_t and the innovations v_t are unobserved by agents.[14] Reflecting the perceived slow-moving drift we further assume agents' priors imply $E\left[\eta_t \eta_t'\right] = \kappa_\omega^2 \times E\left[v_t v_t'\right]$ where $0 < \kappa_\omega \ll 1$.

---

[12] For a discussion of using survey data to help estimate DSGE models, see Chapter 18 in this Handbook.

[13] See Eusepi et al. (2020) for a detailed example and derivations. For an analysis of real-business-cycle theory, see Eusepi and Preston (2011).

[14] For simplicity we assume the matrix Ψ which governs short-run dynamics is known to agents.

The matrix S is a selection matrix which maps the set of drifts to a larger vector with the same dimension as z_t.[15] This signal extraction problem delivers the now familiar Kalman filter updating

$$\hat{\omega}_{t+1} = \hat{\omega}_t + \kappa_\omega S' \left(z_t - S\hat{\omega}_t - \Psi z_{t-1} \right)$$
$$= \hat{\omega}_t + \kappa_\omega S' \left(z_t - z_{t|t-1} \right), \tag{17.13}$$

where $z_t - z_{t|t-1}$ denotes the short-term forecast error. Given the estimate $\hat{\omega}_t$, forecasts at any horizon $T > t$ are determined as

$$E_t z_T = \Psi^{T-t} z_t + \sum_{j=0}^{T-t} \Psi^j S\hat{\omega}_t \tag{17.14}$$

while their estimate of the time-varying mean is

$$\lim_{T \to \infty} E_t z_T = (I - \Psi)^{-1} S\hat{\omega}_t. \tag{17.15}$$

As before, beliefs are characterized by a "shifting end-point" model.

Evaluating expectations in the structural equations and combining with the belief updating equation gives the true data-generating process:

$$z_t = \Gamma(\Psi)S\hat{\omega}_t + \Psi z_{t-1} + \Psi_\varepsilon \varepsilon_t, \tag{17.16}$$
$$\hat{\omega}_{t+1} = \left[I + \kappa_\omega S' \left(\Gamma(\Psi) - I \right) S \right] \hat{\omega}_t + \kappa_\omega S' \Psi_\varepsilon \varepsilon_t, \tag{17.17}$$
$$z_t - z_{t|t-1} = (\Gamma(\Psi) - I)S\hat{\omega}_t + \Psi_\varepsilon \varepsilon_t, \tag{17.18}$$

where the matrix $\Gamma(\Psi)$ is a composite of structural parameters Ψ. Provided $\hat{\omega}_t$ is stationary, the rational expectations equilibrium represents a limiting case of this model with $\kappa_\omega \to 0$.[16]

Comparison with the reduced-form model of earlier sections reveals three new properties of structural models. First, forecast errors are determined by long-run drifts and model innovations. This permits giving a structural interpretation to the economic determinants of the term structure of expectations. Second, because economic decisions depend on the estimated drifts, dynamics exhibit self-referentiality. Beliefs affect realized data, and the data in turn affect beliefs. The matrix $\Gamma(\Psi)$ determines the extent to which equilibrium outcomes depend on beliefs.[17] Third, and related, the model displays *extrapolation bias* as an equilibrium property.[18] Subjective beliefs have a unit root, while the true data-generating process implies beliefs evolve as a stationary vector autoregressive process, with eigenvalues determined by the matrix

$$I + \kappa_\omega S' \left(\Gamma(\Psi) - I \right) S.$$

---

[15] For example, if agents observe purely exogenous shocks, these elements of z_t will have no drift.

[16] That is, the eigenvalues of $I + \kappa_\omega S' (\Gamma(\Psi) - I) S$ are inside the unit circle.

[17] In the case that $\Gamma(\Psi) = I$, the model would have a self-confirming equilibrium (see Sargent 1999). In general, $\|\Gamma(\Psi)\| < 1$ so that beliefs are only partially self-fulfilling. This implies beliefs in equilibrium are stationary variables.

[18] See Fuster et al. (2010), Piazzesi et al. (2015), and Bordalo et al. (2020) along with the discussion in Section 17.2.4.

The wedge between subjective and objective beliefs provides a metric of the importance of the information friction from belief formation. The use of a structural model permits understanding how structural shocks and economic policy affect this wedge.

17.4.2 The New Keynesian model

To give some context for these properties, consider the simple New Keynesian model given by the aggregate demand and supply equations:

$$x_t = E_t \sum_{T=t}^{\infty} \beta^{T-t} \left[(1 - \beta) x_{T+1} - \left(i_T - \pi_{T+1} - r_T^n \right) \right], \tag{17.19}$$

$$\pi_t = E_t \sum_{T=t}^{\infty} (\xi\beta)^{T-t} \left[\kappa x_T + (1 - \xi) \beta \pi_{T+1} \right], \tag{17.20}$$

where π_t is inflation, x_t the output gap, i_t is the one-period nominal interest rate, the instrument of monetary policy, and r_t^n the natural rate of output, an exogenous first-order autoregressive process. The parameters $0 < \beta, \xi < 1$ are the household discount factor and the probability that the firm cannot re-optimize their price in any given period. These parameters determine the slope of the aggregate supply curve as $\kappa \equiv (1 - \xi\beta)(1 - \xi)/\xi > 0$. The model is closed with the assumption that the central bank adopts the simple rule

$$i_t = \varphi\pi_t, \tag{17.21}$$

where $\varphi > 1$ is a policy parameter.

Under rational expectations, there is a unique bounded equilibrium of the form

$$z_t = \Psi r_{t-1}^n + \Psi_\epsilon \epsilon_t^n,$$

where $z_t = (\pi_t, x_t, i_t)'$ and ϵ_t^n the innovation to the natural rate of interest. Under imperfect information beliefs are given by Eqs. (17.11) and (17.12) with $\omega_t = (\omega^\pi, \omega^x, \omega^i)$, S an identity matrix, and lagged state vector replaced by the natural rate of interest, so that $z_{t-1} \equiv r_{t-1}^n$. With this replacement, Eq. (17.13) continues to determine the updating of beliefs and Eqs. (17.16), (17.17) and (17.18) the true data-generating process.

Extrapolation bias

Extrapolation bias is an equilibrium property of the model driving a wedge between subjective and objective beliefs. To illustrate in the case of interest rates, consider an economy where prices are nearly flexible, that is $\xi \to 0$, and monetary policy is understood to be implemented using the simple rule so that beliefs satisfy $\omega^i = \varphi\omega^\pi$. Long-term interest rate forecasts are revised in response to short-term forecast errors according to

$$\begin{aligned} \hat{\omega}_{t+1}^i &= \hat{\omega}_t^i + \kappa_{\omega_i} \left(i_t - \hat{\omega}_t^i - \Psi_i r_{t-1}^n \right) \\ &= \hat{\omega}_t^i + \kappa_{\omega_i} \left(i_t - i_{t|t-1} \right), \end{aligned} \tag{17.22}$$

where Ψ_i is the element of Ψ corresponding to the rational expectations solution for the interest rate. Shocks to the natural rate of interest induce interest rate surprises leading to shifts in long-term beliefs—indeed, the whole term structure of expectations.

Taking the difference between subjective interest-rate forecasts, $\hat{E}_t$, and model-consistent projections under the true data-generating process, E_t, gives the wedge in any future period $T > t$

$$
\begin{aligned}
\hat{E}_t i_T - E_t i_T &= \left(1 - \frac{\varphi^{-1} - \beta}{1 - \beta} \right) \hat{\omega}_t^i \\
&= \kappa_{\omega_i} \left(1 - \frac{\varphi^{-1} - \beta}{1 - \beta} \right) \sum_{j=0}^{\infty} \left(1 - \kappa_{\omega_i} \frac{1 - \varphi^{-1}}{1 - \beta} \right)^j \epsilon_{t-1-j}^n,
\end{aligned}
\tag{17.23}
$$

where the second equality follows from writing current interest rate beliefs as a function of the entire past history of natural rate innovations. Both the size of the learning gain and monetary policy regulate the degree of extrapolation bias. Depending on the expectations formation mechanism and monetary policy, transitory natural-rate shocks may have long-lived effects. For example, a sequence of positive shocks to the natural rate leads to an increase in the wedge, leading to a steeper path of the interest rate compared to that path which would be expected under the true data-generating process. This wedge has empirical and policy implications.

Implications for aggregate dynamics

Eusepi et al. (2020) explore the empirical and policy implications of extrapolation bias in general equilibrium. They estimate a medium-sized DSGE model using U.S. macroeconomic data, including the term structure of interest rate and inflation expectations from professional forecasters. The wedge between subjective and objective beliefs is central to understanding the evolution of macroeconomic data and therefore U.S. monetary history and to understanding the ability of the Federal Reserve to pursue active stabilization policy.[19]

Fig. 17.7 summarizes some relevant results. The top and middle panel plot the model-implied five-to-ten (black solid line) and one-to-ten year (blue dashed–dotted line) expectations for both inflation and nominal short-term interest rates along with survey measures of long-term expectations from Blue Chip Financial Forecasts and Blue Chip Economic Indicators (red dots and blue squares, respectively). The gray solid lines show the actual quarterly realizations of inflation and short-term interest rates. The DSGE model matches the behavior of long-term expectations well, while at the same time also fitting shorter-term survey forecasts (not shown).[20] Low frequency movements in long-term expectations provide a compelling theory of trend inflation. At higher frequencies, long-term expectations display cyclical variation and are clearly correlated with inflation and short-term interest rates. The estimates reveal that monetary policy shocks explain the sustained rise in long-term inflation and interest rate expectations over the 1970s.

The bottom panel plots the *subjective* one-to-ten-year-ahead expectation for the short-term nominal rate (black solid line) together with the *model-consistent* expectation (blue dashed line) held by an

---

[19] See Giannoni and Woodford (2004).

[20] See Eusepi et al. (2020) for further details. The estimation allows a structural break in the learning gain at the end of the 1990s.

Long-Term Inflation Expectations

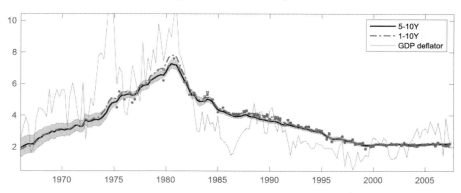

Long-Term Expectations of the Short Rate

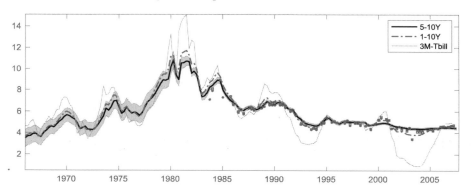

Subjective and Model-Consistent Expectations

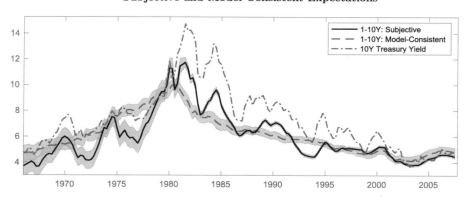

FIGURE 17.7 Long-Term Expectations from a DSGE model

The top and middle panels show the evolution of long-term survey expectations data for inflation and the short-term nominal rate of interest. Actual variable (gray), survey expectations for 5 to 10 year average and 1 to 10 year average (red dots and blue squares, respectively),
the model implied 1–10 year average expectations (the blue dashed–dotted line), and the model implied 5–10 year average expectations
with 95% coverage interval (black solid line and gray shaded area). The bottom panel shows the subjective (black solid) and model
consistent expectations (blue dashed) with 95% coverage interval (gray shaded area). Then red dashed–dotted line defines the 10-year
Treasury yield.

outside observer knowing the true data-generating process. Because of extrapolation bias subjective expectations display weaker mean reversion and higher volatility compared to objective expectations. This wedge has economic content. Model consistent expectations would correctly predict short-term rates to fall more quickly from the peak of the Great Inflation over the subsequent Great Moderation period: a lower expected path of the short-term rate in turn would deliver lower equilibrium long-term interest rates. Similarly, at the beginning of the sample, loose monetary policy flattens the term structure of interest rates and forecasters systematically under-predicted the significantly higher interest rates observed over the 1970s. These discrepancies result in excessive stimulus to real activity in the 1970s and excessive restraint in the 1980s.

The figure also illustrates that the wedge between subjective and objective expectations varies over time: over the last decade of the sample this wedge shrinks significantly as long-term expectations stabilize. Furthermore, ten-year Treasury yields (red dash-dotted line) move together with yields implied by subjective expectations, but still leave a significant residual, consistent with the reduced-form model of Section 17.3. Finally, note that the new Keynesian model satisfies the expectations hypothesis of the yield curve. The fact that subjective yields differ markedly from objective yields represents a strong rejection of the expectations hypothesis under rational expectations. As shown by Sinha (2016), learning models can explain rejections of the expectations hypothesis of the yield curve identified by Campbell and Shiller (1991). Econometric tests that assume rational expectations are misspecified when financial market participants are Bayesian, learning about the long-run.

17.4.3 Implications for monetary and fiscal policy

The previous example adduces further evidence that long-term movements in expectations of inflation and interest rates are tied to short-term forecast errors. Eusepi et al. (2020) show that these properties of long-term expectations have implications for monetary policy. In contrast to a full-information rational expectations model, a central bank cannot fully stabilize the macroeconomy, even in the case of demand shocks. The degree to which stabilization policy is compromised depends on how sensitive long-term expectations are to short-run forecast errors. As long-term expectations become less stable, aggressive aggregate demand management becomes infeasible: large movements in policy rates translate into volatility in long rates and therefore aggregate demand. However, when long-term expectations are quite stable, model predictions are much closer to those of a rational expectations analysis. The constraint posed by the term structure of interest rate expectations is quantitatively important.

That activist stabilization policy is undesirable contrasts with earlier papers by Ferrero (2007), Orphanides and Williams (2007), and Molnar and Santoro (2013). These papers emphasize how departures from rational expectations can alter the short-run trade-off in the new Keynesian Phillips curve and conclude that optimal policy should be more aggressive than a rational expectations analysis. However, this literature makes the assumption that the central bank can directly control aggregate demand. Accounting for the transmission mechanism of monetary policy turns this result on its head, because aggressive adjustment of overnight rates creates volatility in the term structure of interest rate expectations.

These papers assume a single constant gain. Building on work by Marcet and Nicolini (2003), Milani (2014), and Cho and Kasa (2015), Carvalho et al. (2021) develop a theory in which the sensitivity of long-run inflation expectations to short-run inflation surprises depends on recent forecasting performance. Firms do not know the inflation target and must learn it from observed inflation data. In response to large and persistent forecast errors, firms doubt the central bank's commitment to the inflation target. They switch from a decreasing gain algorithm to a constant gain algorithm to better track changes in the inflation target. Because the forecasting model is endogenous, the sensitivity of long-term expectations to forecast errors depends on historical forecasting performance. The relationship between short-run forecast errors and long-run expectations is time varying. In this way the model gives a coherent definition of "anchored" inflation expectations as a situation in which expectations display declining sensitivity to forecast errors. The model fits professional forecast data exceptionally well both in the United States and a range of other countries. Importantly, the empirical model predicts various periods of poorly anchored expectations. Gáti (2021) considers optimal monetary policy in this environment, confirming the insights of Eusepi et al. (2020): better anchored expectations permit aggressive monetary policy.

Building on Eusepi et al. (2020), Eusepi et al. (2021) explore the implications for optimal monetary policy at the zero lower bound. Their model addresses the common practical concern that long-term inflation expectations might become un-anchored and drift downwards in response to a large negative demand shock. They show learning about the long run complicates monetary policy requiring an extended period of zero interest policy because expectations themselves, if sufficiently pessimistic, can cause the zero lower bound to be a constraint on policy actions. The optimal forward guidance policy is front-loaded and displays an insurance principle: aggressive responses to a negative demand shock are required to support inflation expectations in the case of a persistent deterioration in economic conditions. However, policy is too stimulative in the case of transitory disturbances. These policy implications are strikingly different to Eggertsson and Woodford's (2003) rational expectations analysis.

Introducing fiscal and debt management policy further complicates inflation control in this class of models. Eusepi and Preston (2012) and Eusepi and Preston (2018) show that when households are uncertain about their long-run tax obligations, modeled in the same way as uncertainty about long-run inflation or interest rates, then Ricardian equivalence fails to hold, even when the fiscal authority has access to lump-sum taxation. Movements in expectations about taxes, inflation, and interest rates generate shifting valuations of the public debt and the expected tax burden attached to that debt. The resulting wealth effects on aggregate demand complicate stabilization policy, fundamentally changing the economy's response to different kinds of disturbances. These effects are larger for higher levels of debt and for moderate debt maturities, and quantitatively important for debt levels observed for the United States and other countries since the Great Recession. These results are relevant for analyzing inflation policy over the coming decade, given the substantial debt-financed stimulus packages in response to the global pandemic.

17.5 Conclusions and further directions

This chapter has provided a simple expectations formation mechanism to fit and study the term structure of expectations. Observed survey-based measures of expectations are consistent with forecasters frequently revising their long-term outlook. In particular, these revisions are partly associated with their short-term forecast errors, as predicted by standard statistical models of trend and cycle decomposition. This holds not only for the consensus term structure of expectations but also for individual forecasts. In addition to fitting consensus expectations, the proposed model provides valuable insights into the sources of forecast dispersion from short to long horizons.

In the final section, we consider the implications of this expectations formation mechanism in DSGE models. Here additional information frictions are imposed. In particular, economic agents are boundedly rational and do not know the correct data generating process: consistent with much empirical evidence, they tend to overextrapolate from recent developments. Having estimated the models using the term structure of expectations, we show that the proposed expectations formation mechanism has profound implications for monetary and fiscal policy design when compared with the benchmark of rational expectations.

The work explored also suggests interesting future avenues of investigation. First, both reduced-form and structural models should allow for time-varying components in the expectations formation process. As discussed in the last section, agents' model validation process can lead to state-dependent sensitivity of revisions of long-term expectations to short-term forecast errors. But time- and state-dependence of information frictions can be more general. For example, the agents' ability or willingness to process information likely depends on the associated costs and benefits which may change with the state of the economy.

Second, while models of information frictions with dispersed information are now ubiquitous in macroeconomics, these models mostly focus on forecast dispersion over the short-term. Incorporating learning about the long run in structural models of dispersed information could deliver important implications for both business cycle analysis and policy design.

Third, our measure of consensus expectations suggests that the term structure of interest rates is driven only partly by the term structure of policy rate expectations. An overwhelming majority of monetary models used for policy analysis instead assumes that the only transmission channel of monetary policy is via short rate expectations. The results in this chapter help better quantify the importance of this channel but also highlight the importance of additional channels, including variation in term premiums, forecast dispersion or failure of equilibrium asset pricing restrictions grounded on the assumption of perfect information and rational expectations.

Finally, while the reduced-form framework we have introduced offers a fairly flexible specification that is able to provide a tight fit to the observed survey data, when incorporating the expectations formation mechanism in a DSGE setup we made specific assumptions about information frictions. While the literature has made remarkable progress in using survey data to select among competing theories of expectations formation, the jury is still out. The properties of the term structure of expectations that this chapter summarizes can be used to make further gains in selecting the models that best describe the data, for example, by studying the dynamic response of the term structure of expectations to specific macroeconomic shocks.

References

Adam, K., Matveev, D., Nagel, S., 2021. Do survey expectations of stock returns reflect risk adjustments? Journal of Monetary Economics 117, 723–740.

Andrade, P., Crump, R.K., Eusepi, S., Moench, E., 2016. Fundamental disagreement. Journal of Monetary Economics 83, 106–128.

Andrade, P., Le Bihan, H., 2013. Inattentive professional forecasters. Journal of Monetary Economics 60, 967–982.

Angeletos, G.-M., Huo, Z., Sastry, K.A., 2020. Imperfect macroeconomic expectations: evidence and theory. In: NBER Macroeconomics Annual 2020. In: National Bureau of Economic Research, vol. 35, pp. 1–86.

Aruoba, S.B., 2020. Term structures of inflation expectations and real interest rates. Journal of Business and Economic Statistics 38, 542–553.

Bauer, M.D., Rudebusch, G.D., 2020. Interest rates under falling stars. The American Economic Review 110, 1316–1354.

Bianchi, F., Ilut, C., 2017. Monetary/fiscal policy mix and agents' beliefs. Review of Economic Dynamics 26, 113–139.

Bordalo, P., Gennaioli, N., Ma, Y., Shleifer, A., 2020. Overreaction in macroeconomic expectations. The American Economic Review 110, 2748–2782.

Campbell, J.Y., Shiller, R.J., 1991. Yield spreads and interest rate movements: a bird's eye view. The Review of Economic Studies 58, 495–514.

Cao, S., Crump, R.K., Eusepi, S., Moench, E., 2021. Fundamental disagreement about monetary policy and the term structure of interest rates. Staff Report 934. Federal Reserve Bank of New York.

Carvalho, C., Eusepi, S., Moench, E., Preston, B., 2021. Anchored inflation expectations. American Economic Journal: Macroeconomics. Forthcoming.

Chan, J., Clark, T., Koop, G., 2018. A new model of inflation, trend inflation, and long-run inflation expectations. Journal of Money, Credit, and Banking 50, 5–53.

Cho, I.-K., Kasa, K., 2015. Learning and model validation. The Review of Economic Studies 82, 45–82.

Cieslak, A., 2018. Short-rate expectations and unexpected returns in Treasury bonds. The Review of Financial Studies 931, 3265–3308.

Cieslak, A., Povala, P., 2015. Expected returns in Treasury bonds. The Review of Financial Studies 28, 2859–2901.

Cochrane, J., Piazzesi, M., 2005. Bond risk premia. The American Economic Review 95, 138–160.

Cochrane, J., Piazzesi, M., 2008. Decomposing the yield curve. Working paper.

Cochrane, J.H., 2017. Macro-finance. Review of Finance 21, 945–985.

Cogley, T., Primiceri, G.E., Sargent, T.J., 2010. Inflation-gap persistence in the US. American Economic Journal: Macroeconomics 2, 43–69.

Cogley, T., Sargent, T.J., 2005. Drift and volatilities: monetary policies and outcomes in the post WWII U.S. Review of Economic Dynamics 8, 262–302.

Coibion, O., Gorodnichenko, Y., 2012. What can survey forecasts tell us about informational rigidities? Journal of Political Economy 120, 116–159.

Crump, R.K., Eusepi, S., Lucca, D., Moench, E., 2014. Which growth rate? It's a weighty subject. Liberty Street Economics Blog.

Crump, R.K., Eusepi, S., Moench, E., 2011. A look at the accuracy of policy expectations. Liberty Street Economics Blog.

Crump, R.K., Eusepi, S., Moench, E., 2022a. The term structure of expectations and bond yields. Staff Report 775. Federal Reserve Bank of New York.

Crump, R.K., Eusepi, S., Moench, E., Preston, B., 2021. The term structure of expectations. Staff Report 992. Federal Reserve Bank of New York.

Crump, R.K., Eusepi, S., Moench, E., Preston, B., 2022b. Fundamental revisions: Short-term forecast errors and updates to long-term expectations. Working paper.

Del Negro, M., Giannone, D., Giannoni, M.P., Tambalotti, A., 2018. Safety, liquidity, and the natural rate of interest. Brookings Papers on Economic Activity 49, 235–294.

Edge, R.M., Laubach, T., Williams, J.C., 2007. Learning and shifts in long-run productivity growth. Journal of Monetary Economics 54, 2421–2438.

Eggertsson, G.B., Woodford, M., 2003. The zero bound on interest rates and optimal monetary policy. Brookings Papers on Economic Activity 34, 139–235.

Erceg, C.J., Levin, A.T., 2003. Imperfect credibility and inflation persistence. Journal of Monetary Economics 50, 915–944.

Eusepi, S., Giannoni, M., Preston, B., 2020. On the limits of monetary policy. Working paper.

Eusepi, S., Gibbs, C., Preston, B., 2021. Forward guidance with unanchored expectations. Working paper.

Eusepi, S., Preston, B., 2011. Expectations, learning and business cycle fluctuations. The American Economic Review 101, 2844–2872.

Eusepi, S., Preston, B., 2012. Debt, policy uncertainty and expectations stabilization. Journal of the European Economics Association 10, 860–886.

Eusepi, S., Preston, B., 2018. Fiscal foundations of inflation: imperfect knowledge. The American Economic Review 108, 2551–2589.

Evans, G.W., Honkapohja, S., 2001. Learning and Expectations in Macroeconomics. Princeton University Press, Princeton, NJ.

Ferrero, G., 2007. Monetary policy, learning and the speed of convergence. Journal of Economic Dynamics and Control 39, 3006–3041.

Feunou, B., Fontaine, J.-S., 2021. Secular economic changes and bond yields. Review of Economics and Statistics. Forthcoming.

Fuster, A., Laibson, D., Mendel, B., 2010. Natural expectations and macroeconomic fluctuations. The Journal of Economic Perspectives 24, 67–84.

Garbade, K., 1996. Fixed Income Analytics. MIT Press, Cambridge.

Garnier, C., Mertens, E., Nelson, E., 2015. Trend inflation in advanced economies. International Journal of Central Banking 11, 65–136.

Gáti, L., 2021. Monetary policy & anchored expectations: an endogenous gain learning model. Working paper.

Giannoni, M., Woodford, M., 2004. Optimal inflation-targeting rules. In: The Inflation-Targeting Debate. In: NBER Chapters. National Bureau of Economic Research.

Grishchenko, O., Mouabbi, S., Renne, J.-P., 2019. Measuring inflation anchoring and uncertainty: a U.S. and Euro area comparison. Journal of Money, Credit, and Banking 51, 1053–1096.

Gürkaynak, R., Sack, B., Swanson, E.T., 2005. The sensitivity of long-term interest rates to economic news: evidence and implications for macroeconomic models. The American Economic Review 95, 425–436.

Gurkaynak, R.S., Sack, B., Wright, J.H., 2007. The U.S. Treasury yield curve: 1961 to the present. Journal of Monetary Economics 54, 2291–2304.

Hamilton, J.D., 1994. Time Series Analysis. Princeton University Press, Princeton, NJ.

Holston, K., Laubach, T., Williams, J.C., 2017. Measuring the natural rate of interest: international trends and determinants. Journal of International Economics 108, S59–S75.

Johannsen, B.K., Mertens, E., 2021. A time series model of interest rates with the effective lower bound. Journal of Money, Credit, and Banking 53, 1005–1046.

Kim, D.H., Orphanides, A., 2012. Term structure estimation with survey data on interest rate forecasts. Journal of Financial and Quantitative Analysis 47, 241–272.

Kim, D.H., Wright, J.H., 2005. An arbitrage-free three-factor term structure model and the recent behavior of long-term yields and distant-horizon forward rates. Finance and Economics Discussion Series 2005-33. Federal Reserve Board.

Kozicki, S., Tinsley, P.A., 2001. Shifting endpoints in the term structure of interest rates. Journal of Monetary Economics 47, 613–652.

Kozicki, S., Tinsley, P.A., 2012. Effective use of survey information in estimating the evolution of expected inflation. Journal of Money, Credit, and Banking 44, 145–169.

Kydland, F.E., Prescott, E.C., 1982. Time to build and aggregate fluctuations. Econometrica 50, 1345–1370.

Laubach, T., Williams, J.C., 2003. Measuring the natural rate of interest. Review of Economics and Statistics 85, 1063–1070.

Lucas Jr., Robert E., 2003. Macroeconomic priorities. The American Economic Review 93, 1–14.

Maćkowiak, B., Wiederholt, M., 2009. Optimal sticky prices under rational inattention. The American Economic Review 99, 769–803.

Mankiw, N.G., Reis, R., 2002. Sticky information versus sticky prices: a proposal to replace the new Keynesian Phillips curve. The Quarterly Journal of Economics 117, 1295–1328.

Marcet, A., Nicolini, J.P., 2003. Recurrent hyperinflations and learning. The American Economic Review 93, 1476–1498.

Marcet, A., Sargent, T.J., 1989. Convergence of least squares learning mechanisms in self-referential linear stochastic models. Journal of Economic Theory 48, 337–368.

Mertens, E., Nason, J., 2020. Inflation and professional forecast dynamics: an evaluation of stickiness, persistence, and volatility. Quantitative Economics 11, 1485–1520.

Milani, F., 2014. Learning and time-varying macroeconomic volatility. Journal of Economic Dynamics and Control 47, 94–114.

Molnar, K., Santoro, S., 2013. Optimal monetary policy when agents are learning. European Economic Review 66, 39–62.

Orphanides, A., Williams, J.C., 2007. Robust monetary policy with imperfect knowledge. Journal of Monetary Economics 54, 1406–1435.

Piazzesi, M., Salomao, J., Schneider, M., 2015. Trend and cycle in bond premia. Working paper.

Primiceri, G.E., 2005. Time varying structural vector autoregressions and monetary policy. The Review of Economic Studies 72, 821–852.

Scheinkman, J.A., Litterman, R., 1991. Common factors affecting bond returns. The Journal of Fixed Income 1, 54–61.

Schmeling, M., Schrimpf, A., Steffensen, S.A.M., 2021. Monetary policy expectation errors. Working paper.

Sims, C.A., 2003. Implications of rational inattention. Journal of Monetary Economics 50, 665–690.

Sinha, A., 2016. Learning and the yield curve. Journal of Money, Credit, and Banking 48, 513–547.

Stock, J.H., Watson, M.W., 1989. New indexes of coincident and leading economic indicators. In: NBER Macroeconomics Annual 1989. In: National Bureau of Economic Research, vol. 4, pp. 351–409.

Stock, J.H., Watson, M.W., 2007. Why has U.S. inflation become harder to forecast? Journal of Money, Credit, and Banking 39, 3–33.

Summers, L.H., 2014. Reflections on the 'new secular stagnation hypothesis'. Secular stagnation: Facts, causes and cures, pp. 27–38.

Tambalotti, A., 2003. Inflation, productivity and monetary policy: from the great stagflation to the new economy. Working paper.

Timmermann, A.G., 1993. How learning in financial markets generates excess volatility and predictability in stock prices. The Quarterly Journal of Economics 108, 1135–1145.

Woodford, M., 2003. Interest and Prices: Foundations of a Theory of Monetary Policy. Princeton University Press.

Wright, J.H., 2011. Term premia and inflation uncertainty: empirical evidence from an international panel dataset. The American Economic Review 101, 1514–1534.

Expectational data in DSGE models

18

Fabio Milani[a]

University of California at Irvine, Irvine, CA, United States

18.1 Introduction

One of the main developments in the field of macroeconomics in recent years has been its increased reliance on empirical work to guide and evaluate theories. Structural models, built from microfoundations, are now routinely and meticulously tested against the data: if necessary, the models are revised to include additional frictions or mechanisms that can improve their fit. State-of-the-art macroeconomic DGSE models, as those built on the works by Christiano et al. (2005) and Smets and Wouters (2003, 2007), can successfully match a large set of observable time series. This approach marks a clear shift with respect to previous decades in which model evaluation was based on a more indirect strategy: first, the models were calibrated using some accepted parameter values, and, then, a range of moments from simulated series were informally compared to those obtained in the data.

In both theoretical and empirical work in macroeconomics, expectations play a central role. Optimizing decisions by households and firms are, in large part, influenced by expectations about future economic conditions, future inflation rates, and future policies. In the vast majority of cases, DSGE models are estimated under the assumption that all economic agents' expectations are formed according to the rational expectations hypothesis. Economic agents in the model form expectations that are, therefore, model-consistent, being formed from a mathematical conditional expectation based on the same model that is assumed to be generating the data, and using all the available information.

When estimating the models, researchers conventionally use data on realized macroeconomic variables (real output, consumption, investment, inflation, interest rates, and so forth). But it has been far less common to use direct data on expectations, which can be obtained from surveys, or extracted from market prices. Expectations are treated, instead, more dogmatically, as they are simply assumed to be equal to the values implied by rational expectations.

Many mechanisms of interest in the model, however, heavily rely on the response of expectations. Monetary policy acts largely through its effects on expectations: this channel has become even more important with the shift of central banks toward transparency and increased communication. Consumers' and firms' decisions are driven by expectations of future real interest rates, future inflation rates, and marginal costs. The effects of fiscal policy depend on the anticipated responses of wages and interest

[a] I would like to thank the Handbook Editors Rüdiger Bachmann, Giorgio Topa, and Wilbert van der Klaauw, as well as Marco Del Negro, Stefano Eusepi, and Cosmin Ilut, for comments and suggestions on this chapter.

Handbook of Economic Expectations. **https://doi.org/10.1016/B978-0-12-822927-9.00026-4**

rates. Any misspecification in the modeling of expectations would, therefore, severely taint the conclusions that can be obtained from a model.

Given how widespread the assumption of rational expectations has been, it is natural to ask whether rational-expectations DSGE models produce expectation series that can accurately approximate observed expectations from surveys. One way to answer the question is to directly incorporate information from survey expectations in the estimation of DSGE models. Data on expectations should be used not only as a means of external validation; rather, they should be routinely included as observable variables that estimations have to match. The importance of incorporating survey expectations has been similarly emphasized in Coibion et al. (2018).

First, expectational data can be useful to discriminate among competing theories, to evaluate alternative assumptions, and to test the importance of different frictions. When responses to shocks in the model hinge on behaviors of expectations that are found to be unrealistic in the data, the models can be revised accordingly.

Observed expectations can also provide useful information about latent states, which are unobservable for the econometrician, yet play a key role in many economic theories. For example, expectations, particularly for long-horizon variables, can be used to infer economic agents' perceptions about low-frequency movements in the economy (such as movements in the inflation target, in the long-term growth rate of the economy, or in the natural rate of interest).

In this chapter, I discuss the research to date that uses expectational data in DSGE models. First, I present models that retain the assumption of rational expectations. Later, I move to research that examines deviations from rational expectations. In the latter case, observed expectations can be particularly valuable to put structure on the forms of non-rationality that should be inserted in the models.

18.2 Expectational data in rational expectations DSGE models

18.2.1 Do DSGE models generate expectations that fit observed data?

A major step forward in the empirical macroeconomics literature in recent years has been to show that general equilibrium models, based on microfoundations, and including various frictions and a menu of different shocks, can fit macroeconomic data well, often outperforming reduced-form alternatives such as VARs and Bayesian VARs.

The DSGE models under rational expectations that have been built on the frameworks of Christiano et al. (2005) and Smets and Wouters (2003, 2007) have been particularly successful. They match very closely the responses of endogenous variables to identified monetary policy shocks, as obtained from structural VARs. Moreover, they are able to capture a variety of empirical moments, leading to autocorrelation and cross-correlation profiles that track closely those in the data.

To facilitate their analysis and estimation, log-linearized DSGE models are typically cast in state-space form. The state transition equation is then given by the model solution under rational expectations

$$\xi_t = F(\theta)\xi_{t-1} + G(\theta)\epsilon_t, \tag{18.1}$$

where the vector $\xi_t = [Y_t, E_t Y_{t+1}, w_t]'$ includes the model's endogenous variables Y_t (some observed and some potentially unobserved), the corresponding expectations terms $E_t Y_{t+1}$, and the exogenous disturbances w_t, the vector ϵ_t contains the exogenous *i.i.d.* innovations, and $F(\theta)$, $G(\theta)$, are coefficient matrices of appropriate dimensions, which are functions of the vector of structural parameters θ. The variables ξ_t in the model are then linked to the available data series through a set of observation equations, given by

$$Y_t^{obs} = H_0 + H\xi_t \ (+ \ o_t). \tag{18.2}$$

The observation equations typically select a subset of the endogenous state variables in Y_t, through the selection matrix H, and matches them to a vector of observables Y_t^{obs}; the vector H_0 can contain, instead, steady-state values. Observation equations in the DSGE literature usually abstract from measurement error terms, but those can be easily added through o_t if necessary. Under the assumption that the exogenous innovations ϵ_t are normally distributed, the state-space system (18.1)–(18.2) is both linear and Gaussian, and its likelihood function can be conveniently evaluated using the Kalman filter.

DSGE models are often estimated using sets of observables in Y_t^{obs} that include the growth rates of real output, consumption, investment, wages, levels of hours worked, inflation, and nominal interest rates. In larger models, the set of observables is expanded to include financial variables, such as credit spreads and stock price indexes, labor variables, as the unemployment rate, fiscal variables, related to government debt, deficits, and taxes, and many others. Expectations, on the other hand, are almost universally modeled as rational, that is, $E_t Y_{t+1}$ simply equals the implied rational expectations value. Unlike other parts of the model, they are treated dogmatically and typically not required to conform to available time series observations, even though those are potentially available and easy to incorporate in the estimation. This would simply require extending the set of observation equations to include observed expectations, denoted by $E_t^{obs} Y_{t+1}$, as follows:

$$\begin{bmatrix} Y_t^{obs} \\ E_t^{obs} Y_{t+1} \end{bmatrix} = H_0 + H\xi_t \ (+ \ o_t). \tag{18.3}$$

For example, inflation expectations $E_t \pi_{t+1}$ in the model can be related to observations on survey inflation expectations $E_t^{obs} \pi_{t+1}$, through the relation $E_t^{obs} \pi_{t+1} = \pi^* + E_t \pi_{t+1} \ (+ \ o_t)$, where π^* can denote the value of inflation in steady-state. The addition of *i.i.d.* measurement error recognizes that survey expectations can be noisy measures of actual expectations in the economy. In lieu of measurement error, researchers can alternatively add a new structural shock to the original model, such as a time-varying inflation target. A potential pitfall, however, is that the shock may not be fully structural, since it can spuriously embody deviations between survey and model-consistent expectations.

Recently, a number of papers are making efforts to move beyond the neglect of expectational data in the literature, as they start to explicitly test whether model-implied expectations are consistent with observations from surveys.

Most of the interest in the literature so far has, perhaps unsurprisingly, fallen on inflation expectations. Survey inflation expectations were already used in the context of single-equation estimations in the past. Roberts (1997), Brissimis and Magginas (2008), and Adam and Padula (2011), for example, use survey forecasts as proxies for the expectation term in the New Keynesian Phillips curve, and they find that the equation with this modification can fit inflation dynamics well. More recently, Coibion and Gorodnichenko (2015a) use an expectations-augmented Phillips curve, with household inflation expectations from the Michigan Survey, and show that this specification can account for the missing drop in inflation in 2009 and beyond.

Moving to DSGE settings, Del Negro and Eusepi (2011) include (one-year ahead) inflation expectations as an observable in the estimation of the New Keynesian model, in addition to conventional variables related to output growth, hours worked, labor share, inflation, and the interest rate. They consider different variants of the model, depending on whether agents know or have to learn about the inflation target.

First, they find that, without expectations data, it is hard to disentangle the perfect versus imperfect information versions of their model. The four-quarter-ahead expected inflation series generated from the different model specifications remain all far from the median four-quarter-ahead survey forecast. The survey indicates higher expected inflation in the 1980s until the early 1990s (with model-implied expectations that are sometimes half of the survey value), and much lower expected inflation than the model during the dot-com boom in the second half of the 1990s. The correlations between survey and model-implied expectations are modest, ranging around 0.25 and less. With the addition of inflation expectations, the new information is, instead, useful to discriminate among the different specifications.

Moreover, the use of inflation expectations matters also for inference regarding latent variables. When information on expectations is omitted, the estimates for the time-varying inflation target look almost identical between the perfect and imperfect information cases. When expectations are included, the inferred targets are different: under perfect information, the target estimates increase toward the values reached by inflation expectations. The model is unable to match the new observable; therefore, the unobserved variable moves to capture the unexplained difference. Overall, it's possible to conclude that none of the model versions are able to capture the dynamics of observed inflation expectations. That suggests a misspecification that needs to be resolved in the model. Inflation expectations contain extra information, not present in realized series, that can be exploited to revise some of the modeling assumptions.

Earlier work by Schorfheide (2005) also compares inflation expectations from two versions of the New Keynesian model (full information and learning about the monetary policy regime, which can be subject to switches in the inflation target) with survey estimates for average one-year-ahead and ten-year-ahead inflation expectations. Those are not included as observables in the estimation, though, but only used as external validation for the model predictions, an approach that has been probably more common in the literature to date. The inflation expectation series generated from different versions of the model resemble each other, but are not always close to the survey measures. The model-implied short-run expectations are more volatile than the corresponding survey expectations, whereas model-implied long-run expectations are even more sluggish than the survey forecast.

Data on inflation expectations are also used in a paper by Del Negro et al. (2015), which aims to analyze the performance of a DSGE model with financial frictions around the Great Recession and shed light on the behavior of inflation during this period. Many interpret the missing deflation in those years as a failure of models based on the Phillips curve. Del Negro et al. use ten-year inflation expectations from the Blue Chip Economic Indicators survey and from the Survey of Professional Forecasters as observables in the estimation, to better capture low-frequency movements in inflation. The behavior of inflation predicted by the model is reasonable, although it misses higher-frequency movements as the deflation in 2009. They do not include, however, a broader comparison between the implied rational expectation series and the survey evidence. A larger set of forecasts is analyzed in Del Negro and Schorfheide (2013). Their main focus is not on whether the model can generate expectations that match those from surveys. Instead, they show that adding external information, incorporating survey forecasts by professional forecasters for example, into conventional DSGE models, can significantly improve their out-of-sample forecasting performance. The standard set of observables in the estimation is augmented to include long-run inflation expectations (the average CPI inflation rate expected over the next ten years, obtained using data from both the Blue Chip Economic Indicators survey and the Survey of Professional Forecasters), long-run output growth expectations (expected ten-year average, from the Blue Chip Economic Indicators survey), and k-quarters-ahead Federal funds rate forecasts (from the Blue Chip Financial Forecasts survey), as well as a number of nowcasts. To avoid singularity, the model requires additional structural shocks that can account for the discrepancies between expectations in the model and the data: here, this is achieved by adding time-varying inflation target shocks, technology growth shocks, and anticipated monetary policy shocks. The strong forecasting performance of survey forecasts is already well known in the literature (e.g., Ang et al., 2007). Adding expectational data can help DSGE models benefit from their informational advantages. The results in the paper indicate that long-run survey inflation forecasts are particularly useful in improving forecasting accuracy, while output growth forecasts are less effective. The forecasting performance is also analyzed in Monti (2010), who presents an alternative way to combine judgmental forecasts from surveys with model-based forecasts: the survey forecasts can be seen as an optimal estimate of a variable, which is possibly produced using a different, richer, information set than the one available in the model.

The role of expectations data in enhancing the models' forecasting performance is not limited to the academic literature, but it has proven valuable to policymaking institutions as well. The Federal Reserve Bank of New York's DSGE model (see Del Negro et al., 2013), for example, is estimated using Bayesian methods and including data on ten-year-horizon survey inflation expectations and on future Federal Funds rate expectations based on Overnight Index Swap (OIS) rates. Model-based forecasts are routinely disseminated and compared with professional forecasts. Therefore, innovations in the theoretical modeling of expectations, tested against the data, can now rapidly spill over into policy models used by central banks. They can prove useful for forecasting applications and help policymakers more accurately simulate the economy's response to different policy paths.

Other papers explore the option of directly replacing rational expectations with expectations measured from surveys (without adding expectations to the observation equation). Hence, expectations are no longer model-consistent. Instead, they are assumed to equate the values from the survey at each point in time (with the measured value $E_t^{meas} Y_{t+1}$ entering the model equations directly, in place of RE). This approach, therefore, generalizes similar exercises in a single-equation context (e.g., Roberts, 1997; Adam and Padula, 2011) to a system setting, and it is used, for example, in Paloviita (2007). In some cases, expectations are allowed to be a weighted average of the survey forecast and the rational expectation (Kortelainen et al., 2016; Nunes, 2010). It would be an important drawback, however, to assume that survey expectations can be simply taken as exogenous. Fuhrer (2017) employs a semistructural model and, in fact, endogenizes expectations by iterating the model equations forward, and replacing infinite sequences of expected terms with long-run expectations from the Survey of Professional Forecasters. The system estimation reveals that the use of direct expectations reduces the need for lagged endogenous variables in the model equations. Inertia hence arises from the sluggishness of expectations, not from intrinsic features of the economy. The paper also performs a horse race between the rational expectations and survey expectations versions. The results are stark, with rational expectations receiving a weight that is not significantly different from zero and survey expectations receiving a weight of one. Interestingly, the estimates show a significant degree of partial adjustment of survey expectations compared to rational expectations: this seems to indicate that individual forecasters adjust their expectations to the mean value of forecasters' expectations in the previous period, as also documented in Fuhrer (2015).

Finally, the information from expectational data is of obvious importance also in the macro-finance literature. De Graeve et al. (2009) consider a macrofinance DSGE model, which includes information on the term structure of interest rates. The predictions for inflation from the model are compared, again as an external validation tool, with survey inflation expectations. As some of the previous papers, they conclude that an inflation target shock is essential to match observed expectations, as well as longer-term yields. Expectations in relation to the term structure of interest rates are also discussed in Chapter 17 in this Handbook.

18.2.2 Survey expectations to evaluate alternative frictions

DSGE models assume optimizing behavior by agents, who also have perfect information about their environment, and form rational expectations. In their stripped-down versions, the models have trouble fitting the data because they imply exceedingly rapid adjustments to shocks, which are at odds with real-world observations. Therefore, researchers need to introduce various frictions to generate persistence: habit formation in consumption, adjustment costs in investment, indexation to past inflation in price setting, and so forth. Using only a subset of available data, it is difficult to identify whether agents' decisions may be due to alternative preferences, frictions, or to beliefs. Data on expectations can be used to reject assumptions that are imposed about expectations, and to better identify whether empirical observations can be attributed to specific preferences or expectation formation models. The role of data on expectations has been recognized for some time also outside the macroeconomic literature, see, for example, Manski (2004).

We have already discussed the works by Del Negro and Eusepi (2011) and Schorfheide (2005), who use inflation expectations to compare model versions with perfect or imperfect information (about the inflation target). A number of papers exploit additional information contained in survey expectations to test a number of alternative, more pervasive, frictions, spanning from monetary frictions, to dispersed information, learning, inattention, and ambiguity aversion.

Aruoba and Schorfheide (2011) develop a DSGE model that allows them to merge monetary frictions (based on search theory models) and New Keynesian frictions, such as price stickiness, and to measure their relative importance. The model has a two-sector structure and is composed by a decentralized and a centralized market. In the decentralized market, agents meet and engage in bilateral trades; the double coincidence problem and their anonymity create a motive for holding money and using it as a medium of exchange in equilibrium. When agents leave the decentralized market, they move to a centralized market, which resembles a standard New Keynesian model, with price rigidities à la Calvo. The authors treat the inflation target in the model as observable and assume that it can be interpreted as the agents' long-run inflation expectations. They combine three different inflation measures: bandpass-filtered GDP deflator, one-year- and ten-year-ahead inflation expectations; a common factor across the series is extracted using the Kalman filter. The target joins output, inflation, the interest rate, and the velocity of money, as variables to be matched in the estimation. The data used to identify the inflation target play an important role, since the paper studies, among other things, the effects of changes in the target on welfare. The results indicate that for some target inflation rates, distortions caused by monetary frictions may be as important as distortions due to price stickiness.

Melosi (2017) develops a DSGE model with dispersed information among price-setting firms. Firms have noisy private signals about aggregate conditions. The model includes a signaling channel of monetary policy: a change in the policy rate signals to the private sector the views that the central bank holds on the state of the economy. For example, an increase in the short-term rate might signal that the central bank has knowledge about higher than expected inflation; therefore, the information may influence private sector's beliefs and it may counteract the contractionary effects of the initial policy decision. Melosi estimates the model using a Bayesian approach. The observables include data on one-quarter-ahead and four-quarters-ahead inflation expectations from the SPF, along with the real-time output gap, and real-time inflation from the Federal Reserve's Greenbook. As benchmark, Melosi considers a monetary VAR. The VAR impulse responses show that inflation expectations barely respond on impact after a monetary policy shock, while actual inflation adjusts more rapidly. The resulting inflation forecast errors are, therefore, very persistent and can last for around five years, meaning that inflation expectations can remain unanchored for a long time. Turning to the DSGE model, the paper shows that conventional models with perfect information fail to match these facts: the conditional forecast errors are zero by construction. The Smets and Wouters model, under almost any possible parameterization, does not come close to matching the response of inflation expectations to a monetary shock that is found in the VAR. The model with dispersed information and signaling, instead, matches the responses of inflation expectations and forecast errors quite well. Moreover, the model matches much more closely the run-up of inflation rates in the 1970s.

Nimark (2014), instead, investigates the business cycle implications of "man-bites-dog" news, that is, signals that are likely to be observed in correspondence of extraordinary, tail, events. He estimates the model using the entire cross-section of individual survey responses from the SPF, in addition to standard macro variables. The cross-sectional dispersion can help identify man-bites-dog episodes in the sample. He finds that the model with man-bites-dog events fits the data better than a baseline specification that omits public signals. These papers well exemplify the importance of incorporating information from expectations: empirical evidence on the response of aggregate or individual expectations, and of the corresponding forecast errors, to shocks is used to help decide among alternative theoretical frameworks.

Milani (2017) estimates a model that includes both econometric learning by economic agents and endogenous sources of persistence, such as habit formation, inflation and wage indexation, adjustment costs in investments, as well as a number of serially-correlated disturbances. Data on expectations are used in the estimation to evaluate, among other things, whether macroeconomic persistence is driven by endogenous features, or by the sluggishness of agents' beliefs. The results suggest that learning can match survey expectations closely. Moreover, the empirical importance of the structural sources of persistence and the degree of autocorrelation that are estimated for structural disturbances are considerably reduced under learning. The paper by Fuhrer (2017) discussed in the previous section points in the same direction: replacing rational expectations with survey expectations reduces the need for lagged variables in the model equations and simplifies the properties of exogenous disturbances.

Acuña Armenta (2021) integrates survey forecasts in the estimation of a model that merges different expectational frictions: irrational expectations based on learning models and sticky information. She finds that both frictions improve the model's fit to the data compared with the rational expectations version. However, the estimated level of information stickiness is sensitive to the modeling of expectations: it is substantially reduced when learning replaces rational expectations. Hajdini (2020) tests an expectation formation process based on misspecified forecasting rules and myopia against rational expectations. The model's testable implications are evaluated using survey inflation expectations. Again, departures from rational expectations improve fit and reduce the need for real rigidities as sources of persistence.

Survey data can also be used to evaluate alternative preference structures. The literature on ambiguity, for example, implies a sizable departure from conventional assumptions about expected utility preferences in macroeconomic models. They assume households, who are averse to ambiguity, or Knightian uncertainty. Agents behave as if they maximize utility under worst-case beliefs. A number of papers in this literature (that will be discussed in detail in Chapter 24 in this Handbook) exploit survey expectations, including measures of their dispersion, to discipline agents' beliefs and identify confidence or ambiguity shocks (Ilut and Schneider, 2014; Ilut and Saijo, 2021; Bianchi et al., 2018; Bhandari et al., 2016; Rossi et al., 2016).

18.2.3 Survey expectations & news shocks

Beaudry and Portier (2006) estimate a bivariate SVAR that includes a measure of total factor productivity and a stock price index, as an example of a variable that contains forward-looking information about the economy. They consider two identification schemes: one that imposes a short-run restriction, often used to identify demand shocks, and one that imposes long-run restrictions, often used to disentangle demand versus supply, or technology, shocks. Their results reveal a correlation close to one between the two shocks identified under the different strategies. This finding motivates them to offer a news-based interpretation: one shock is a conventional technology shock, with long-run effects, while the other represents news shocks about future technology. The news is reflected into stock prices, before it can materialize into actual TFP. Barsky and Sims (2011) employ a different strategy to identify news shocks about future productivity. The news shock is assumed to be orthogonal to the TFP innovation, and it is obtained as the shock that can explain the largest share of the TFP's forecast error variance. The resulting news shock is responsible for a significant fraction of medium-term output fluctuations. Barsky and Sims (2012), instead, test whether innovations in consumer confidence reflect the action of "animal spirits" or news about future productivity. They conclude that the relationship between confidence and economic activity can be mostly attributed to news.

Similar ideas are inserted in DSGE settings, which imply that news about the future can cause macroeconomic fluctuations. In the earlier papers (Beaudry and Portier, 2004; Jaimovich and Rebelo, 2009), news relates to future technology and is embedded in neoclassical models. The approach has later expanded to consider news about a wide variety of disturbances besides technology, and within different modeling frameworks.[1]

In the DSGE literature, fluctuations are usually attributed to shocks that are entirely unanticipated by economic agents. The news view literature extends the shock structure to include both anticipated, the "news," and unanticipated, or surprise, components. Anticipated components are indeed pervasive in the economy. They can capture monetary policy announcements, which have become progressively more important with the growing reliance on communication and forward guidance by central banks. They are also essential to understand the impact of fiscal policies: tax changes are legislated, announced, and incorporated into private-sector's expectations many quarters before they become official. News may also incorporate expectations by economic agents that may or may not materialize later on: for example,

---

[1] Chapter 19 in this Handbook, covers the response of the economy to news shocks in HANK set-ups with search and matching in the labor market.

anticipations about future productivity, or demand, improvements may be immediately expansionary, but become recessionary in the future when the actual improvement is smaller than expected.

Therefore, the news literature assigns a central role to shifts in expectations, possibly due to optimism and pessimism, while keeping expectations rooted in the rational expectations hypothesis.

The paper by Schmitt-Grohé and Uribe (2012) estimates a DSGE model with real rigidities and news shocks, but they do not use expectational data. The standard deviations of news shocks are well identified, in their case, even if the number of shocks far exceeds the number of observable variables. One of the reasons is that they use extra variables that provide information on the disturbances themselves: their observable list includes the relative price of investment, which in the model is related to the inverse of the investment-specific technology shock, and total factor productivity, which corresponds to the neutral technology shock in the model. Their exercise consists in comparing the shares of output fluctuations that are due to news versus unanticipated shocks. They find that news shocks can explain almost half of business cycle fluctuations, but news about technology is quite unimportant. Sims (2016) delves deeper into the results to separate news about future fundamentals that has yet to materialize and news that has already materialized in the past. He finds that the quantitative importance of news is mostly due to the latter.

In general, however, the results on the empirical contribution of news shocks in the papers that estimate DSGE models without expectational data remain mixed. Fujiwara et al. (2011) find that technology news explains less than 10% of output fluctuations, Khan and Tsoukalas (2012) find that news shocks explain less than 15%, with non-technology news playing a role, but technology news accounting for an almost nil share. These papers differ in their model choice from Schmitt-Grohé and Uribe (2012), as they use a sticky-price/sticky-wage framework.[2]

The identification of news in a microfounded model is entirely driven by its impact on forward-looking expectations, which, in turn influences economic agents' optimal choices of consumption, investment, and labor supply. Unanticipated shocks are, instead, by construction, unforecastable. While possible in theory, the identification is complicated in practice. Structural shocks are unobserved to the econometrician: with news, these unobserved variables contain multiple terms, some unanticipated, some anticipated, that are all equally unobserved. Disentangling them often relies on a very limited number of observables (with shocks outnumbering observables by many factors). The use of expectation data can, therefore, be crucial for the identification of news shocks.

The papers by Hirose and Kurozumi (2021) and Milani and Rajbhandari (2020) take this route and add a large set of survey expectations, about different variables and at different horizons, as observables; the number of shocks and observables can now coincide (which is not necessary, but can help identification). Hirose and Kurozumi estimate a small-scale New Keynesian model, using forecasts on output growth, inflation, and the nominal interest rate from the Survey of Professional Forecasters. The paper finds that news shocks about technology represent the main source of U.S. output fluctuations. When expectations data are not used, unanticipated shocks are predominant, mirroring the results in Fujiwara et al. (2011) and Khan and Tsoukalas (2012). They show that the model estimated with expectational data is much more successful in replicating the existing cross-correlations between output growth and inflation expectations than the estimation that omits survey expectations. The estimates of

---

[2] Milani and Treadwell (2012) also estimate a New Keynesian model with news, and focus on the importance of surprise versus news monetary policy shocks; Gomes et al. (2017) also document the importance of monetary policy news shocks in a medium-scale model. Born et al. (2013) focus, instead, on anticipated tax shocks.

news shocks and other structural parameters also become more precise, judging by the tighter posterior probability intervals. Milani and Rajbhandari (2020) consider, instead, a medium-scale DSGE model, based on Smets and Wouters (2007). To the original observable series, they add information from the term structure of survey expectations, including SPF forecasts about output growth, consumption growth, investment growth, government spending growth, inflation, and interest rates, at horizons ranging from one-quarter to five-quarters ahead. In total, the set of observables has eight realized variables and 30 expectation series. The link between expectation series and expectations in the model is provided by observation equations, which allow for *i.i.d.* measurement error terms. The paper evaluates the strength of identification using the tests proposed by Iskrev (2010). The parameters related to news shocks are shown to be poorly identified or nonidentified when the model is estimated using the same observable variables as in Smets and Wouters, without expectations. In many cases, the priors for news standard deviations are not updated in light of the data, or slightly updated toward zero (Gamma priors with equal mean and standard deviation are used to assign higher probability to zero and progressively lower probability to larger values). Moreover, news plays a limited role, again as in Fujiwara et al. (2011) and Khan and Tsoukalas (2012). When the model is instead estimated by exploiting data on expectations, news shocks are more clearly identified. The estimates of other parameters also change: for example, the importance of real frictions, such as habits and adjustment costs, and nominal frictions, as price and wage stickiness, are reduced in the model with observed expectations and news shocks. The news series thus obtained largely differ from their counterparts that are estimated using only data on realized variables. The identified news shocks explain roughly 40% of business cycle fluctuations, with news about investment-specific technology and risk premium shocks accounting for the largest share.

Miyamoto and Nguyen (2020) also estimate a medium-scale New Keynesian model, augmented with news referring to horizons from one-quarter to eight-quarters ahead. Their empirical results indicate that longer-horizon news plays a more limited role for fluctuations, while short-horizon news shocks are confirmed as an important determinant of business cycles.

All the papers that use expectations data demonstrate that they are helpful in improving the identification of news. Overall, they also suggest that the implied role of news over business cycles increases.

One possible drawback, on the other hand, is that observed expectations may reflect biases that are not reflected in the assumption of rational expectations. In that case, news may spuriously incorporate the effects of these biases, in addition to actual anticipations. Hirose and Kurozumi (2021), however, consider this possibility in a robustness exercise and conclude that, even though the model with biased expectations provides a better fit, the main conclusions remain unchanged.

18.2.4 **Survey expectations & sunspots**

A long-standing literature in macroeconomics views economic systems as inherently unstable, potentially characterized by multiple equilibria, and subject to sunspot-driven fluctuations. Benhabib and Farmer (1999) and Farmer (2019) review the early and the more recent literature. The first phase in the literature shows how equilibrium indeterminacy can arise in real business cycle models when production functions exhibit increasing returns to scale or external effects, and in New Keynesian models, typically as a result of passive monetary policies, or, in extended environments, of coordination failures between monetary and fiscal policies. In these cases, the models retain the assumptions of market clearing and rational expectations. In the most recent, second phase, the model, instead, is revised to include a belief function, which is modeled separately and represents a departure from rational expectations.

For example, in Farmer and Nicoló (2018), it is assumed that expectations for nominal output growth equal contemporaneous nominal output growth plus a random shock. The literature provides one possible approach to model the idea of "animal spirits" popularized by Keynes in the *General Theory*. When the equilibrium is not determinate, forecast errors are no longer simply a function of fundamental innovations, but they are also influenced by a nonfundamental sunspot shock (the animal spirit). Models with indeterminacy, therefore, often exhibit extra volatility and they can solve some of the propagation and persistence issues that characterize models relying on a unique equilibrium.

The existence of indeterminacy, however, has for a long time rendered full-information estimation of the corresponding models more challenging. Lubik and Schorfheide (2004) developed the techniques to estimate a New Keynesian model, in which parameter draws can be allowed to fall either in regions characterized by determinacy or indeterminacy. They can then test whether particular samples of data (for example, U.S. time series before and after Volcker's appointment as Federal Reserve's Chairman) are better explained by a determinate or indeterminate system. In their empirical application, they find that pre-1979 data are consistent with a passive monetary policy and indeterminate equilibria, while post-1982 data are characterized by active monetary policy, which is conducive to a determinate equilibrium. Lubik and Schorfheide's approach has been used in Benati and Surico (2009), Hirose (2008), Hirose et al. (2020), and others. Recently, Farmer et al. (2015) and Bianchi and Nicoló (2021) have provided alternative approaches that can substantially reduce the estimation burden. Farmer and Nicoló (2018), using those techniques, run a horse race of the three-equation New Keynesian model, either closed using a standard Phillips curve or the proposed autonomous belief function. Cuba-Borda and Singh (2019), Ilabaca et al. (2020), Ilabaca and Milani (2021), Dai et al. (2020) estimate models with determinacy and indeterminacy using Bianchi and Nicolò's approach.

With its emphasis on forecast errors and on fluctuations in beliefs that can be triggered by sunspots, the indeterminacy literature places the dynamics of expectations decidedly in a central role. So far, however, estimations have resorted to conventional sets of observable variables. It is possible, and probably natural, to start exploiting the extra information contained in observed expectations to inform the estimation of DSGE models with indeterminacy as well.

The study of interactions between expectations and sunspots can be inspired, for instance, by related work by Canova and Gambetti (2010). They use theoretical restrictions from the New Keynesian model, which they test using expectations data and including them in a VAR. Expectations would be a new state variable under indeterminacy: under the commonly accepted story of a policy switch from indeterminacy to determinacy in the early 1980s, there should be structural breaks in the predictive power of expectations. Canova and Gambetti employ different measures of expectations, obtained from survey data, Greenbook forecasts, and from bond markets. They find that the role of expectations is unchanged over time, casting doubts on the switch from indeterminacy to determinacy narrative. However, in their case, they do not run a full estimation of the New Keynesian model. Here, we are not taking a stand on the indeterminacy versus determinacy debate, but simply argue that there is a clear direction for the literature to use expectational data more regularly to assess the empirical importance of sunspots. Ilabaca et al. (2020) do estimate, in one of their cases, the model with indeterminacy using survey inflation expectations as observable, but fitting expectations is not a main focus of the paper. They find that the evidence supports determinacy rather than indeterminacy even before 1979, in a Behavioral New Keynesian model with myopic agents.

18.2.5 **Misspecification of expectations**

One of the possible uses of expectational data is to uncover misspecification in DSGE models. The DSGE-VAR approach, proposed by Del Negro and Schorfheide (2004), provides a powerful tool to detect where the sources of misspecification lie in a model. DSGE-VARs allow researchers to entertain all models in a continuum spanning between two extremes: the rational expectations DSGE model, with all the resulting cross-equation restrictions, and an unrestricted VAR, where no DSGE restrictions are imposed. A key parameter in this approach is given by λ, which measures the tightness of the DSGE-restrictions prior used in the VAR estimation. The coefficient λ can be estimated: if it is close to zero, it means that DSGE restrictions are better ignored; if it is large, it suggests that DSGE restrictions carry useful information that improve over VARs. In general, the techniques are applied to models that impose rational expectations. Hence, conditional on expectations being formed according to the rational expectations hypothesis, they can reveal whether misspecification is due to the modeling of inflation, consumption, or other variables, by comparing the corresponding impulse responses when the DSGE restrictions are imposed, to those obtained in a best-fitting specification that partially relaxes those restrictions. Discrepancies in the impulse responses may indicate to researchers that modifications are needed in the Phillips curve, the Euler equation, or in other relationships, for the model to become consistent with the data.

But misspecification may also arise from the expectation formation side of New Keynesian DSGE models. Del Negro and Eusepi (2011) compare the fit for inflation expectations obtained by the DSGE model with the fit from a VAR, following Del Negro and Schorfheide's (2004) DSGE-VAR approach. They find that all model versions are inferior to VARs in capturing the dynamics of inflation expectations: when the tight DSGE cross-equation restrictions are loosened, the fit for inflation expectations gets better.

Cole and Milani (2019) investigate the ability of New Keynesian models to match the dynamic interactions between macroeconomic variables and the corresponding expectations that are observed in the data. The interactions between macroeconomic realizations and expectations represent a central channel for monetary policy transmission, which is largely based on the "management of expectations." The paper estimates a DSGE-VAR on output growth, inflation, interest rate, as well as expectations about one-period-ahead real output growth, two-period-ahead real output growth, and one-period-ahead inflation. The results reveal serious misspecification in the modeling of expectations in the New Keynesian model. When the model is estimated under rational expectations, and including expectational data, the posterior estimate for the prior tightness parameter λ declines closer to zero, indicating that the data are more favorable toward the unrestricted VAR version. The impulse responses of the model-implied expectations often show the wrong sign and magnitude compared with the responses of expectation series in the data. The DSGE restrictions achieve, instead, a higher weight when the model with rational expectations is spared the requirement to match the data on expectations. The paper then proposes alternative models of expectation formation that relax rational expectations, including models that resemble agents' laws of motion under learning, or forecasting rules that are heterogeneous and consistent with the evidence from the experimental literature. The latter are based on the results in Hommes (2011) and model expectations by grouping them in three clusters: trend-following expectations, adaptive expectations, and anchor-and-adjustment expectations. The DSGE-VAR estimations show an overall fit that improves under the alternative expectation formation mechanisms: DSGE restrictions are now more valuable, with estimates for λ that increase significantly compared with rational expectations. The fit of the DSGE model, however, still remain far from that of the best-fitting DSGE-VAR specification.

These results suggest that expectational data should be used more frequently to uncover the main sources of misspecification in DSGE models, particularly when they relate to the key interaction between macroeconomic expectations and outcomes. The findings also point researchers to rethink the modeling of expectations, in favor of models that are able to match the available observations. In the next sections, we will discuss papers that take this route by introducing deviations from rational expectations.

18.3 Expectational data and deviations from rational expectations

There is a long tradition of research that uses survey expectations to test the rational expectations hypothesis using micro-level data from surveys (see Pesaran and Weale, 2006). In most cases, the tests lead to rejection of rational expectations. Coibion and Gorodnichenko (2012, 2015b), Bordalo et al. (2020), and Angeletos et al. (2020), present ample, updated, evidence documenting the existence of frictions and incomplete information in the formation of expectations. In what follows, we consider papers that depart from rational expectations and use survey expectations in structural models.

18.3.1 Adaptive learning

Probably the main alternative to the dominant paradigm of rational expectations has been offered over the years by the literature on adaptive learning in macroeconomics (e.g., Sargent, 1999; Evans and Honkapohja, 2001). Initially, agents' learning was introduced to justify the plausibility of rational expectations: agents were learning during a transition period, but, under some conditions, the system would converge to the same equilibrium that would exist under rational expectations (Lucas, 1986). A large literature subsequently studied the conditions under which convergence to the Rational Expectations Equilibrium could take place, in a variety of model settings. Researchers, however, also started to propose learning as an alternative model of expectation formation, which could replace rational expectations. In an economy potentially subject to large degrees of structural change (due to fundamental factors, such as changes in technology, political institutions, globalization, or due to shifts in monetary policy or exchange rate regimes, and so forth), economic agents may live almost permanently in a period of transition and, as a result, they need to continuously engage in learning about their economic environment.

The first papers to estimate DSGE models with adaptive learning did so by matching the same observable variables that were used under rational expectations. Milani (2007) estimates a New Keynesian model, augmented to include endogenous sources of persistence, such as habit formation in consumption and price indexation to past inflation. The model with adaptive learning fits the data better than the model with rational expectations does, according to marginal likelihood comparisons. Learning introduces additional inertia in the system and it provides a parsimonious way to account for time-variation in the formation of beliefs. Several other papers insert learning in versions of the benchmark New Keynesian model and estimate them.[3] In such estimations, the best-fitting learning process is extracted to

---

[3] For example, Milani (2008, 2009, 2014, 2020), Berardi and Galimberti (2017), Chevillon et al. (2010), Gaus and Ramamurthy (2019), Best (2017), Meggiorini and Milani (2021).

allow the model to match as closely as possible the dynamics of realized inflation, output gap, and interest rate. The learning process in these cases is not required to match empirical counterparts for the expectations themselves. Slobodyan and Wouters (2012) extend the analysis to a medium-scale DSGE models based on Smets and Wouters (2003, 2007).[4] Again, they select similar sets of variables as the original papers as observables.

More recently, the literature has started to incorporate expectational data to impose more discipline in the estimation of the learning process. Previous evidence, based on minimum-distance exercises, already suggested that survey expectations were closely matched by constant-gain learning models. Orphanides and Williams (2005) calibrate constant gains to the values that minimize the distance between the learning expectations and those obtained from the Survey of Professional Forecasters. Branch and Evans (2006) show that constant-gain learning provides the best fit of SPF expectations for output growth and inflation, among a set of competing models, outperforming also Kalman-filter learning.

A new strand of papers estimate DSGE models with adaptive learning, which are now required to match both realized macroeconomic series and observed expectations from surveys. Ormeño and Molnár (2015) start by adding survey data on inflation expectations to estimate the Smets and Wouters' model. They compare its performance under rational expectations and learning. They find that adaptive learning does substantially better than rational expectations in fitting, at the same time, realized macro series and the corresponding survey expectations.

A larger number of expectation series are incorporated in Milani (2011, 2017) to help infer the best-fitting learning process. The first paper assumes a small-scale New Keynesian model, estimated on observables for output growth, inflation, nominal interest rate, and on the corresponding one-period-ahead expectations for the same three variables. The second extends the analysis to the Smets and Wouters' model: the observable list is augmented to include expectations about consumption, investment, and inflation, from the Survey of Professional Forecasters (mean of expectations across forecasters, about the $t + 1$ value of the variable). Given that the paper tries to identify the learning process of economic agents in real-time, it becomes essential to match as closely as possible the information set that was actually available to agents at each point in time. Therefore, it uses real-time data in the estimation. Real-time data are available through the *Real Time Data Set for Macroeconomists*, provided by the Federal Reserve Bank of Philadelphia. The data consist of different vintages of macroeconomic variables, which capture the information that would have been available to researchers, policymakers, and the public, at each point in the past (see Croushore and Stark, 2001, for more discussion of the data set).

Carvalho et al. (2020) estimate a New Keynesian model using data on inflation and the following short-term inflation expectations: one- and two-quarter-ahead CPI inflation forecasts from the SPF, and two measures from the Livingston Survey, based on the expected CPI inflation six months ahead. The model aims to explain low-frequency movements in inflation expectations and relate them to the short-term forecasting performance. They assume a state-dependent learning rule, which follows Marcet and Nicolini (2003). Even though the model is estimated only using short-term expectations, they show that it can explain long-term survey inflation expectations very well. Those are again explained through an endogenous learning process, rather than resorting to an exogenous target shock. Chapter 17 in this Handbook expands on models that can explain the joint dynamics of short- and long-term forecasts.

---

[4] Medium and larger-scale DSGE models with learning are also estimated in Milani (2017), Vázquez and Aguilar (2021), Rychalovska (2016), Bassanin and Maldonado (2021), among others.

Gáti (2020) presents a model in which the degree of expectations unanchoring depends on a continuously time-varying endogenous gain function. She estimates the functional form of the gain using a Simulated Method of Moments approach, targeting the autocovariance properties of a set of observables that include the 12-month-ahead CPI inflation forecast from the SPF. Her results, along with those in Carvalho et al. (2020) and Milani (2014), suggest that the sensitivity of expectations to new information, as measured by the value of gain coefficients, increases when forecast errors are larger by historical standards.

Finally, turning to the literature studying issues at the intersection between macro and finance, the paper by Dewachter and Lyrio (2008) integrates information on the term structure of interest rates, average inflation expectations over the next year, and over the next ten years (as the full the term structure of inflation expectations is unavailable) in their observation equations. The microfounded macrofinance model, extended with learning, successfully explains both variations in the yield curve and the dynamics of inflation expectations.

Given the central role that the adaptive learning literature devotes to expectations, we can expect that in the future it will become more popular, and perhaps standard, to use expectational data in empirical work. In addition to comparisons with rational expectations, the data can be fruitfully used to discriminate among different perceived laws of motion that agents might use, and to refine the algorithms used to describe their updating of beliefs.

18.3.2 Survey expectations and sentiment

Many of the papers that include information about expectations and that we have discussed so far adopt a similar approach. They relate expectations obtained from the model to the corresponding survey data, up to some exogenous measurement errors, which need to be introduced in the observation equation to avoid stochastic singularity. The measurement errors do not receive any structural interpretation.

In systems under rational expectations, expectational errors are obtained entirely as a function of fundamental shocks: they can be solved out and removed from the system as independent sources of fluctuations. There is no role for excesses of optimism or pessimism that go beyond the actions of structural innovations.

With the addition of expectational data, however, such assumptions can be relaxed. This permits researchers to reassign a role to psychological factors, which were seen as central in the writings of Pigou (1927), Keynes (1936), and Haberler (1937). When data on expectations are used, expectations in the model should still be treated as endogenous. Under learning, for example, they can be assumed to be formed from a near-rational perceived model of the economy (the Perceived Law of Motion, or PLM), given by

$$Y_t = a_{t-1} + b_{t-1}Y_{t-1} + c_{t-1}w_t + \varepsilon_t. \tag{18.4}$$

Agents adopt the PLM to form their forecasts (here shown for a $t+1$ horizon), as

$$\widehat{E}_t^{obs} Y_{t+1} = \left(I + \widehat{b}_{t-1} \right) \widehat{a}_{t-1} + \widehat{b}_{t-1}^2 Y_{t-1} + \left(\widehat{c}_{t-1}\rho + \widehat{b}_{t-1}\widehat{c}_{t-1} \right) w_t + s_t \tag{18.5}$$

$$= \widehat{E}_t^{PLM} Y_{t+1} + s_t. \tag{18.6}$$

Milani (2011, 2017) follows this approach to model sentiment in DSGE models and to investigate the role that sentiment shocks play over the business cycle. The observed expectations are assumed to be formed, on average, as the outcome of the learning model that agents are using. The agents' perceived model is linear and is assumed to have the same structural form of the system solution under rational expectations (that is, it shares the same variables). Expectations are hence formed in reaction to values assumed by past endogenous variables Y_{t-1} (assuming information on those up to $t-1$ rather than t), the contemporaneous realization of exogenous disturbances w_t (if assumed to be observed), with the most recently updated beliefs by agents denoted by $\widehat{a}_{t-1}$, $\widehat{b}_{t-1}$, and $\widehat{c}_{t-1}$ (ρ refers instead to the disturbances' persistence parameters). This represents the endogenous component of expectations that arises from the learning model, and can be more compactly written as $\widehat{E}_t^{PLM} Y_{t+1}$. However, agents can, in every period, form expectations that deviate from the point forecasts arising from the learning model. It is these deviations of actual, observed, expectations from the expectations that can be rationalized by the learning model that define the "sentiment" terms in the model, denoted above by the vector s_t. Sentiments are meant to capture exogenous waves of undue optimism or undue pessimism, which are not justified based on the state of contemporaneous and past fundamentals. In the estimation, it is the dynamic interactions among observed expectations and realized macroeconomic time series that are exploited to extract sentiment shocks.

The estimation is performed using realized macroeconomic series and survey expectations. Real-time data are used to increase the credibility of the identification of endogenous learning versus exogenous sentiment in each period.

The results show that the expectations from the learning model can closely approximate the survey expectations. Moreover, the empirical evidence shows that sentiment shocks, typically omitted in DSGE models with rational expectations, explain a sizable portion (about half) of U.S. business cycle fluctuations. Different sentiments can be identified: excess optimism/pessimism related to consumption, investment, or inflationary pressures.

The resulting sentiment series are obtained without using any data on consumer or investor confidence, only expectations. The papers, however, show that the identified sentiment is strongly correlated with purified measures (purified by regressing them on a vector of contemporaneous and lagged macro variables) from popular surveys, such as the University of Michigan Consumer Sentiment Index, the Business Confidence Indicator obtained from the OECD's Business Tendency Surveys for Manufacturing, and the Duke Fuqua School of Business' CFO Expectations Index, which computes the shares of respondents feeling more optimistic or more pessimistic about the U.S. economy. Sentiments, on the other hand, do not appear to spuriously reflect extraneous factors, such as credit spreads, oil prices, total factor productivity, or news shocks.

The approach used in these papers treats the modeling of expectations more symmetrically with respect to the way other variables are treated. In modeling consumption, for example, the dynamics of the variable is governed by the Euler equation; unexplained deviations are captured by exogenous disturbances, which are given a structural interpretation, as preference disturbances, or sometimes disturbances to bonds' risk-premia. Along the same lines, expectations are obtained endogenously based on a model (in this case, a near-rational perceived law of motion with learning), and the deviations are interpreted as an exogenous disturbance, here denoted as "sentiment."

The work on sentiment in learning models has points of connection with other recent studies, which have introduced sentiment, although modeled in a variety of ways. For example, in Benhabib et al. (2015), sentiment arises because of imperfect information about expected demand and it can lead to self-fulfilling fluctuations. Angeletos et al. (2018) introduce a belief shock, interpreted as a shift in confidence, which can emerge as a result of coordination frictions based on Angeletos and La'O (2013).

Chapter 20 in this Handbook surveys this line of research in more depth. They discuss specifications that relax the assumption of common knowledge, but maintain rational expectations, and specifications that replace rational expectations with Level-k Thinking. In all cases, they show that general equilibrium effects are attenuated. A key testable implication is that expectations should underreact to shocks, a feature that appears consistent with survey evidence. Various other papers have investigated the impact of confidence in more empirical frameworks (e.g., Barsky and Sims, 2012; Bachmann and Sims, 2012; Enders et al., 2021; Bianchi et al., 2022).

18.3.3 First moment vs. second moment shocks

The information contained in observed expectations allows empirical researchers to more credibly measure the transmission mechanisms of interest, and to better identify the properties of structural shocks. The simplest, and most common, approach is to use mean or median forecasts from surveys. Higher moments, instead, generally don't enter the model or the formation of expectations.

An even more ambitious direction, however, would be to also exploit those higher moments available from the surveys. Some surveys (the Survey of Professional Forecasters, for example) also provide data that reflect the forecasters' whole subjective probability distributions. Forecasters are asked to communicate their probability assessments for inflation, output growth, and other variables, falling within specified intervals.[5]

Subjective probability distributions can be used to extract forecasters' real-time beliefs about second moments, for example, to gauge their degree of uncertainty toward future inflation or output developments. Typically, uncertainty is included in DSGE models through the assumption of stochastic volatility: the exogenous shocks have a variance that changes, exogenously, over time. The innovation to the variance is treated as an uncertainty shock, and, when the model is solved using third-order or higher-order approximations, it affects consumers and firms' optimizing decisions.

Chatterjee and Milani (2020) offer a different approach to study the importance of first and second moments in the context of a microfounded model, and to estimate the importance of uncertainty over the business cycle. The paper uses information from the Subjective Probability Density forecasts about inflation and the GDP growth rate that are contained in the Survey of Professional Forecasters. Uncertainty is extracted from the subjective distributions using the approach by D'Amico and Orphanides (2008). It represents here the expected future variance of output and inflation by economic agents.

The model includes several behavioral features. Agents are allowed to form nonfully rational expectations, they have finite, rather than infinite, horizons, and they are learning over time. In forecasting, they have a potentially asymmetric loss function, which allows them to weigh differently positive and negative forecast errors and which creates a direct channel for expected variances to enter the model equations. As a result of finite horizons, expectations up to L-periods ahead matter for current dynamics in the Euler equation and in the New Keynesian Phillips curve. Agents' beliefs are also subject to excesses in optimism and pessimism and they may be affected by perceptions about future uncertainty. The estimation uses 12 observed survey expectation series (mean across forecasters): expected growth rates of real GDP at horizons from $t+1$ to $t+4$, expected inflation from $t+1$ to $t+4$, and

---

[5] The value of probabilistic questions is discussed in Manski (2017) and Potter et al. (2017). Chapter 15 in this Handbook, discusses the challenges and approaches connected with extracting information from probabilistic surveys on macroeconomic variables.

expected nominal interest rates from $t + 1$ to $t + 4$. In addition, the list of observables includes also the perceived uncertainty series, given by the approximate $t + 4$ uncertainty (expected variance) for output growth and the approximate $t + 4$ uncertainty for inflation. The use of a large set of expectation series, allows the identification of sentiment related to the short-run, longer-run (up to $t + 4$ in the main exercise of the paper), and perceived uncertainty (at $t + 4$ horizon).

The empirical results show that private sector's beliefs are impacted by uncertainty: higher perceived uncertainty about output leads to lower output expectations, whereas higher uncertainty about inflation leads to higher inflation expectations. Through such confidence channel, perceived uncertainty shocks have recessionary effects on output, which are comparable to the effects estimated in models with stochastic volatility. However, it is first-moment, sentiment, shocks, particularly those at longer horizons, that are responsible for the largest share of business cycle fluctuations.

In principle, the same subjective density forecasts can be used to assess tail risk (Andrade et al., 2015) and possibly integrated with DSGE models that give a role to beliefs about rare events and disasters (example of DSGE models that consider tail risks are Kozlowski et al., 2019; Orlik and Veldkamp, 2014; Gourio, 2012). On the negative side, it can be argued that estimates of tail risk by forecasters are potentially less accurate than estimates of first moments, as they require computation of probabilities related to events that happen extremely rarely.

A related literature has emphasized the role of disagreement, a concept that is usually discussed in relation to uncertainty, but which is distinct. Mankiw et al. (2004) document substantial disagreement among survey respondents about expected future inflation. Novel stylized facts about disagreement from survey data are reported in Andrade et al. (2016). The construction of measures of disagreement and uncertainty, and their relationship, is discussed in more depth in Chapter 3 in this Handbook.

The disagreement that can be extrapolated from surveys can also, in principle, be used as an observable in an estimation of a model that allows for significant heterogeneity. We discuss in the next section papers that deal with heterogeneity, but the use of disagreement as an observable has not become customary, yet.

Measures of uncertainty extracted from surveys could also be used in the estimation of DSGE models with stochastic volatility (the literature is reviewed in Fernández-Villaverde and Guerrón-Quintana, 2020, but it does not use expectational data). Treating subjective uncertainty as an observable can provide additional restrictions that can help the identification of the volatility series. A potential issue is that uncertainty modeled as stochastic volatility and obtained from particle filter estimations looks quite different from the perceived uncertainty series from the SPF. The discrepancies may be due to data limitations, or, possibly to behavioral biases by forecasters in their estimates of uncertainty.

18.4 Heterogeneity in survey expectations

The majority of papers in the DSGE literature assume expectations that are homogeneous: all consumers and firms share exactly the same expectation formation model as everybody else.

A growing literature in macroeconomics is, however, documenting the substantial heterogeneity that exists in observed survey expectations. Branch (2004) analyzes inflation expectations data at the individual level from the Michigan Survey of Consumers and finds different shares of consumers that form expectations from models of varying degrees of complexity. Several other studies (e.g., Mankiw et al., 2004; Coibion and Gorodnichenko, 2012; Andrade et al., 2016; Pesaran and Weale, 2006; Dovern et al.,

2012; Cole and Milani, 2021) similarly reveal large degrees of heterogeneity in microlevel survey data. Heterogeneity also consistently arises as an outcome of laboratory experiments focused on forecasting behavior. Hommes (2011, 2013), for example, demonstrate that expectations can be approximated by different types of forecasting behaviors: some are adaptive, others are trend-following, or based on anchor-and-adjustment heuristic.

Branch and McGough (2009) models expectation heterogeneity in a New Keynesian setting and analyzes the corresponding microfoundations. In the simplest case, a fraction of agents are assumed to form rational expectations, while the remaining agents form backward-looking expectations based on lagged endogenous variables, which can be either adaptive (mean-reverting), naïve, or extrapolative (trend-chasing). The literatures on heterogeneous expectations are reviewed in detail in Hommes (2021) and Branch and McGough (2018).

A number of papers take the Heterogeneous Expectations New Keynesian (HENK) model to the data. Massaro (2013) estimates a model that includes long-horizon expectations, Beqiraj et al. (2018) estimate shares of agents that depart from rational expectations that vary and can reach up to almost half of the forecasters. Ilabaca and Milani (2021) estimate the HENK model using rolling windows. They find even larger shares of agents who depart from rational expectations. Moreover, the model with heterogeneous expectations is preferred by the data at each point in the sample. Elias (2022) also estimates a New Keynesian model with heterogeneous expectations: agents in his model, however, use either a correctly-specified or an underspecified learning model. A large share of agents employ the simpler model, suggesting significant deviations from rational expectations.

The heterogeneity can arise from different sources. The previous papers typically rest it on the existence of rational versus backward-looking forecasters. More generally, heterogeneity may originate from model uncertainty, with agents using a set of models and possibly switching among them based on past performance, as in Brock and Hommes (1997) and Branch (2004). Alternatively, agents can have different priors or initial beliefs (introduced as in Suda, 2018, for example), which may also arise as a result of different ages or life experiences (Malmendier and Nagel, 2016). In Cole and Milani (2021), instead, the heterogeneity stems from different degrees of recency bias, captured by different constant-gain values across forecasters. Chapter 25 in this Handbook offers another explanation for heterogeneity, focusing on how beliefs spread in the society, using an epidemiological framework. The initial papers in the heterogeneous expectations literature made consistent use of survey data on expectations. Those, however, have not been used in DSGE estimations to the same extent yet. Ilabaca and Milani (2021), in one of the robustness exercises, add inflation and output expectations from the Survey of Professional Forecasters to the set of observables that need to be matched, with the addition of measurement errors. They find that model-implied expectations are close to the corresponding survey data in the pre-1979 sample, whereas the model has difficulties in fitting expectation series in the 1990s. In the latter case, they appear to excessively track lagged inflation rather than the survey series.

Expectational data should ideally be used to test the ability of DSGE models to match not only mean expectations, but also the dispersion of forecasts that exists in survey data. In this respect, models with heterogeneous expectations are promising, although it remains to be seen which particular form of heterogeneity is more consistent with survey data. Identifying the main sources of heterogeneity should definitely represent a priority for future work.

Finally, expectations data can be used in models with a different kind of heterogeneity: Heterogeneous Agents New Keynesian (HANK) models (Kaplan et al., 2018). In such settings, the existence of incomplete markets and uninsurable idiosyncratic risk affects the sensitivity of the economy to expectation-driven fluctuations. Chapter 19 in this Handbook discusses in detail the role of expectations in HANK models. Incomplete markets induce two changes: first, they introduce extra discounting in the Euler equation, with agents becoming less forward-looking; second, they can lead to amplification of shocks. Survey forecasts can, therefore, be exploited to evaluate the responses of expectations to shocks, and to identify the relative strength of the amplification versus myopia channels. Moreover, since the models are suitable to study wealth and income inequality, the literature could incorporate and analyze differences in the responses of expectations across the income distribution. Overall, the estimation of HANK models using survey expectations data is an important need for future research.

18.5 Issues and limitations

This chapter argues in favor of a drastic increase in the use of expectational data in the estimation of DSGE models. However, we recognize here some possible limitations.

First, how representative are the surveys that are used to measure expectations? It is well known that expectations differ based on income, education levels, demographic variables, and geography. Using a limited sample of respondents may not capture all these variations. In the Survey of Professional Forecasters, central tendency measures may be affected by the entry and exit of respondents, as emphasized by Manski (2011). One potential solution is to reduce the sample to retain only those forecasters who remain in the survey for at least several quarters, but still some issues persist. For example, it is not clear that the same individuals actually remain in the SPF; sometimes the codes that they are assigned may refer to the companies employing them and may be shared by the future employees.

Researchers working with expectations data need to deal with discrepancies between the timing of information in the surveys versus the timing typically assumed in the models. Surveys are typically mailed at the beginning or at the middle of a quarter, and respondents are asked for their forecasts for the same quarter and for subsequent ones. Assuming in the model that they have time-t information is inaccurate, since they report their forecasts almost two months before the quarter is over. Assuming information up to $t-1$, on the other hand, underestimates their knowledge when completing the survey.

The use of expectational data renders natural the use of real-time, rather than fully-revised, data in the estimation. Observed expectations are produced by forecasters based on information sets that were available to them in real time: the estimation should, therefore, try to match such information sets as accurately as possible. If the literature moves toward a more consistent use of expectations data, it should therefore become the norm to incorporate real-time data. The use of revised data, instead, may distort the inference about best-fitting expectation formation models, learning processes, and sentiment terms. On the other hand, real-time observations bring complications connected with the treatment of data revisions. It is not obvious what vintage of data forecasters are trying to predict: it can be the first release that they encounter, the final revised data many years later (which seems highly unlikely), or one of the releases, after the first one, when many of the revisions have already been incorporated.

Many of the papers that we discussed assume that expectations in the model can be well approximated by the expectations of professional forecasters. But there is no consensus on whose expectations we should measure. Based on DSGE models, it would be natural to measure consumer and firm expectations. The most popular sources of consumer expectations data for the U.S. have been the Michigan Survey of Consumers and from the New York Fed Survey of Consumer Expectations. The elicitation of firm expectations and new related surveys are discussed instead in Chapter 11 in this Handbook.

Expectations derived from surveys of professional forecasters, however, have been far more common. Chapter 3 in this Handbook discusses some of their advantages and a number of related issues.

Coibion et al. (2018) argue that household expectations are better proxies not only for consumers in the model, but even for firm expectations, than professional forecasts. They discuss the incentives that professional forecasters may have when reporting their answers (for example, they may be averse to having their forecast fall too far from the consensus), which may skew the measurement of aggregate expectations.

On the other hand, consumer and household expectations may be affected by limitations in cognition that are quite significant (D'Acunto et al., 2019). An argument in favor of the use of professional forecasters expectations is provided by Carroll (2003). He shows evidence that household expectations are significantly affected by the expectations of "experts." Another advantage is availability: professional forecasts are available for a large number of series, for a long sample, for different horizons, and for different countries. The types of forecasts are more limited for surveys at the household level, and the definitions of variable sometimes more qualitative and less immediately useful for research, due to their need of being more easily understandable.

Other measures of expectations are possible and have been used, even if more sporadically. At least for inflation and interest rates, it is possible to use market-based expectations. For inflation, expectations can be derived as the spread between yields on nominal Treasury bonds and yields on Treasury Inflation-Protected Securities (TIPS), after some possible adjustments. Expectations about policy rates can be obtained from future and option contracts. However, such market expectations are likely to be closer to professional forecasters' expectations than to households' expectations. They may also be affected by shifts in liquidity and risk premia that are unobserved to the researcher. Finally, they can be more responsive than household expectations to asset purchases by the Federal Reserve, which may severely skew them, at least, in the most recent part of the sample.

Many of the existing issues will be solved with a better measurement of different types of expectations, which ideally would be obtained both at the household and at the firm level, to match the main sets of economic agents that populate our macroeconomic models. For the DSGE literature, ideal data on expectations should move beyond the main focus on inflation and the short term. Empirical work will benefit from expectations at a multitude of horizons, including a bigger focus on the long-run, and for a multitude of variables, including future monetary policy decisions, wages, taxes, asset returns, and so forth. A broader set of data would permit to infer the perceived models that respondents are implicitly using to form their forecasts. Forecasts data should be numerical, whenever possible, rather than qualitative. Fixed-horizon forecasts are easier to work with in macroeconomic models than fixed-event forecasts (such as the popular current year/next year forecasts), which often require arbitrary transformations. In applied work, it would be useful to have a better understanding of forecasters' real-time perceptions about trends and cycles, about developments that they perceive as transitory versus persistent or permanent. Professional forecasters' data already provide a lot of high-quality information, but it will be important to collect similar observations for consumers and firms. Ideally, the same respondents should be tracked over time, to provide researchers with panel data sets on expectations. Finally, surveys should more often try to elicit information about higher moments, capturing respondents' full subjective distributions. In this case, survey questions should be carefully crafted in ways that do not unduly influence the responses, for example, by avoiding limiting forecasters to strict prespecified bin choices, and maybe providing them with more flexible graphical interfaces.

18.6 Conclusions and future directions

This chapter has reviewed existing and potential uses of expectational data in the estimation of DSGE models.

At this stage, it seems reasonable to predict that survey data on expectations will become more popular in the future and more routinely used to test the restrictions imposed by our theoretical models. Many papers have already used mean and median expectations, particularly those generated by professional forecasters, which are widely available. In the future, information at the micro level can be more often exploited, for example, to assess the models' ability to generate levels of disagreement that match those in reality. Expectational data can provide information on economic agents' perceptions about higher moments, such as their perceived uncertainty of economic conditions, or their estimates of tail risk. To this scope, surveys should incorporate more broadly questions that report the full subjective probability distribution that forecasters have in mind.

As in the past, data on expectations can be used to test whether rational expectations succeed or fail in matching the evidence. But different strands of the literature are recognizing that to explain observed expectations, it may be necessary to model departures from rational expectations (or at least, substantial refinements to the rational expectations assumption that still have strong behavioral connotations). The behavioral elements that are added to macroeconomic models should not be taken for granted, but they should be similarly evaluated based on their ability to jointly match both realizations and expectations.

References

Acuña Armenta, L.C., 2021. Information frictions: Learning and Inattention in an Estimated New Keynesian Model. Mimeo. UC Irvine.

Adam, K., Padula, M., 2011. Inflation dynamics and subjective expectations in the United States. Economic Inquiry 49 (1), 13–25.

Andrade, P., Crump, R.K., Eusepi, S., Moench, E., 2016. Fundamental disagreement. Journal of Monetary Economics 83 (C), 106–128.

Andrade, P., Ghysels, E., Idier, J., 2015. Tails of Inflation Forecasts and Tales of Monetary Policy. Mimeo.

Ang, A., Bekaert, G., Wei, M., 2007. Do macro variables, asset markets, or surveys forecast inflation better? Journal of Monetary Economics 54 (4), 1163–1212.

Angeletos, G.M., Collard, F., Dellas, H., 2018. Quantifying confidence. Econometrica 86 (5), 1689–1726.

Angeletos, G.M., Huo, Z., Sastry, K.A., 2020. Imperfect macroeconomic expectations: evidence and theory. In: NBER Macroeconomics Annual, vol. 35. NBER, pp. 1–86.

Angeletos, G.M., La'O, J., 2013. Sentiments. Econometrica 81 (2), 739–779.

Aruoba, S.B., Schorfheide, F., 2011. Sticky prices versus monetary frictions: an estimation of policy trade-offs. American Economic Journal: Macroeconomics 3 (1), 60–90.

Bachmann, R., Sims, E.R., 2012. Confidence and the transmission of government spending shocks. Journal of Monetary Economics 59 (3), 235–249.

Barsky, R.B., Sims, E.R., 2011. News shocks and business cycles. Journal of Monetary Economics 58 (3), 273–289.

Barsky, R.B., Sims, E.R., 2012. Information, animal spirits, and the meaning of innovations in consumer confidence. The American Economic Review 102 (4), 1343–1377.

Bassanin, M., Maldonado, L., 2021. Housing Price Bubbles and Macroprudential Policies, an Adaptive Learning Approach. Mimeo. Bank of England.

Beaudry, P., Portier, F., 2004. An exploration into Pigou's theory of cycles. Journal of Monetary Economics 51 (6), 1183–1216.

Beaudry, P., Portier, F., 2006. Stock prices, news, and economic fluctuations. The American Economic Review 96 (4), 1293–1307.

Benati, L., Surico, P., 2009. VAR analysis and the great moderation. The American Economic Review 99 (4), 1636–1652.

Benhabib, J., Farmer, R.E.A., 1999. Indeterminacy and sunspots in macroeconomics. In: Taylor, J.B., Woodford, M. (Eds.), Handbook of Macroeconomics, vol. 1, Part 1. Elsevier, Amsterdam, pp. 387–448.

Benhabib, J., Wang, P., Wen, Y., 2015. Sentiments and aggregate demand fluctuations. Econometrica 83 (2), 549–585.

Beqiraj, E., Di Bartolomeo, G., Di Pietro, M., Serpieri, C., 2018. Bounded-rationality and heterogeneous agents: Long or short forecasters? JRC Working Papers JRC111392. Joint Research Centre.

Berardi, M., Galimberti, J.K., 2017. On the initialization of adaptive learning in macroeconomic models. Journal of Economic Dynamics and Control 78, 26–53.

Best, G., 2017. Policy preferences and policy makers' beliefs: the great inflation. Macroeconomic Dynamics 21 (8), 1957–1995.

Bhandari, A., Borovicka, J., Ho, P., 2016. Identifying ambiguity shocks in business cycle models using survey data. Working paper. New York University.

Bianchi, F., Ilut, C., Schneider, M., 2018. Uncertainty shocks, asset supply and pricing over the business cycle. The Review of Economic Studies 85, 810–854.

Bianchi, F., Ludvigson, S.C., Ma, S., 2022. Belief distortions and macroeconomic fluctuations. The American Economic Review 112 (7), 2269–2315.

Bianchi, F., Nicoló, G., 2021. A generalized approach to indeterminacy in linear rational expectations models. Quantitative Economics 12 (3), 843–868.

Bordalo, P., Gennaioli, N., Ma, Y., Shleifer, A., 2020. Overreaction in macroeconomic expectations. The American Economic Review 110 (9), 2748–2782.

Born, B., Peter, A., Pfeifer, J., 2013. Fiscal news and macroeconomic volatility. Journal of Economic Dynamics and Control 37 (12), 2582–2601.

Branch, W.A., 2004. The theory of rationally heterogeneous expectations: evidence from survey data on inflation expectations. The Economic Journal 114 (497), 592–621.

Branch, W.A., Evans, G.W., 2006. A simple recursive forecasting model. Economics Letters 91 (2), 158–166.

Branch, W.A., McGough, B., 2009. A new Keynesian model with heterogeneous expectations. Journal of Economic Dynamics and Control 33 (5), 1036–1051.

Branch, W.A., McGough, B., 2018. Heterogeneous expectations and micro-foundations in macroeconomics. In: Schmedders, K., Judd, K.L. (Eds.), Handbook of Computational Economics, vol. 4. Elsevier Science, North-Holland.

Brissimis, N.S., Magginas, N., 2008. Inflation forecasts and the new Keynesian Phillips curve. International Journal of Central Banking 4 (2), 1–22.

Brock, W.A., Hommes, C.H., 1997. A rational route to randomness. Econometrica, 1059–1095.

Canova, F., Gambetti, L., 2010. Do expectations matter? The great moderation revisited. American Economic Journal: Macroeconomics 2 (3), 183–205.

Carroll, C.D., 2003. Macroeconomic expectations of households and professional forecasters. The Quarterly Journal of Economics 118 (1), 269–298.

Carvalho, C., Eusepi, S., Moench, E., Preston, B., 2020. Anchored inflation expectations. CAMA Working Papers 2020-25. The Australian National University.

Chatterjee, P., Milani, F., 2020. Perceived uncertainty shocks, excess optimism-pessimism, and learning in the business cycle. Journal of Economic Behavior & Organization 179, 342–360.

Chevillon, G., Massmann, M., Mavroeidis, S., 2010. Inference in models with adaptive learning. Journal of Monetary Economics 57 (3), 341–351.

Christiano, L.J., Eichenbaum, M., Evans, C.L., 2005. Nominal rigidities and the dynamic effects of a shock to monetary policy. Journal of Political Economy 113, 1–45.

Coibion, O., Gorodnichenko, Y., 2012. What can survey forecasts tell us about information rigidities? Journal of Political Economy 120 (1), 116–159.

Coibion, O., Gorodnichenko, Y., 2015a. Is the Phillips curve alive and well after all? Inflation expectations and the missing disinflation. American Economic Journal: Macroeconomics 7 (1), 197–232.

Coibion, O., Gorodnichenko, Y., 2015b. Information rigidity and the expectations formation process: a simple framework and new facts. The American Economic Review 105, 2644–2678.

Coibion, O., Gorodnichenko, Y., Kamdar, R., 2018. The formation of expectations, inflation, and the Phillips curve. Journal of Economic Literature 56 (4), 1447–1491.

Cole, S., Milani, F., 2019. The misspecification of expectations in new Keynesian models: a DSGE-VAR approach. Macroeconomic Dynamics 23 (3), 974–1007.

Cole, S., Milani, F., 2021. Heterogeneity in individual expectations, sentiment, and constant-gain learning. Journal of Economic Behavior & Organization 188, 627–650.

Croushore, D., Stark, T., 2001. A real-time data set for macroeconomists. Journal of Econometrics 105, 111–130.

Cuba-Borda, P.A., Singh, S.R., 2019. Understanding Persistent Stagnation. IF Discussion Papers 1243. Board of Governors of the Federal Reserve System.

D'Acunto, F., Hoang, D., Paloviita, M., Weber, M., 2019. Cognitive abilities and inflation expectations. AEA Papers and Proceedings 109, 562–566.

Dai, W., Weder, M., Zhang, B., 2020. Animal spirits, financial markets, and aggregate instability. Journal of Money, Credit, and Banking 52 (8), 2053–2083.

D'Amico, S., Orphanides, A., 2008. Uncertainty and disagreement in economic forecasting. Finance and Economics Discussion Series 2008-56. Board of Governors of the Federal Reserve System.

De Graeve, F., Emiris, M., Wouters, R., 2009. A structural decomposition of the US yield curve. Journal of Monetary Economics 56 (4), 545–559.

Del Negro, M., et al., 2013. The FRBNY DSGE Model. FRBNY Staff Reports, no. 647. p. 647.

Del Negro, M., Eusepi, S., 2011. Fitting observed inflation expectations. Journal of Economic Dynamics and Control 35 (12), 2105–2131.

Del Negro, M., Giannoni, M., Schorfheide, F., 2015. Inflation in the great recession and new Keynesian models. American Economic Journal: Macroeconomics 7 (1), 168–196.

Del Negro, M., Schorfheide, F., 2004. Priors from general equilibrium models for VARS. International Economic Review 45 (2), 643–673.

Del Negro, M., Schorfheide, F., 2013. DSGE model-based forecasting. In: Elliott, G., Granger, C., Timmermann, A. (Eds.), Handbook of Economic Forecasting, vol. 2, 1st edition. Elsevier, pp. 57–140. Chapter 0.

Dewachter, H., Lyrio, M., 2008. Learning, macroeconomic dynamics and the term structure of interest rates. In: Asset Prices and Monetary Policy. In: NBER Chapters. NBER, pp. 191–245.

Dovern, J., Fritsche, U., Slacalek, J., 2012. Disagreement among forecasters in G7 countries. Review of Economics and Statistics 94 (4), 1081–1096.

Elias, C.J., 2022. Bayesian estimation of a small-scale new Keynesian model with heterogeneous expectations. Macroeconomic Dynamics 26 (4), 920–944.

Enders, Z., Kleemann, M., Muller, G.J., 2021. Growth expectations, undue optimism, and short-run fluctuations. Review of Economics and Statistics 103 (5), 905–921.

Evans, G.W., Honkapohja, S., 2001. Learning and Expectations in Macroeconomics. Princeton University Press, Princeton, NJ.

Farmer, R.E.A., 2019. The Indeterminacy School in Macroeconomics. NBER Working Papers 25879.

Farmer, R.E.A., Khramov, V., Nicoló, G., 2015. Solving and estimating indeterminate DSGE models. Journal of Economic Dynamics and Control 54, 17–36.

Farmer, R.E.A., Nicoló, G., 2018. Keynesian economics without the Phillips curve. Journal of Economic Dynamics and Control 89 (C), 137–150.

Fernández-Villaverde, J., Guerrón-Quintana, P.A., 2020. Uncertainty shocks and business cycle research. Review of Economic Dynamics 37, S118–S146.

Fuhrer, J., 2015. Expectations as a source of macroeconomic persistence: an exploration of firms' and households' expectations. FRB Boston Working paper 15-5.

Fuhrer, J., 2017. Expectations as a source of macroeconomic persistence: evidence from survey expectations in a dynamic macro model. Journal of Monetary Economics 86 (C), 22–35.

Fujiwara, I., Hirose, Y., Shintani, M., 2011. Can news be a major source of aggregate fluctuations? A Bayesian DSGE approach. Journal of Money, Credit, and Banking 43 (1), 1–29.

Gáti, L., 2020. Monetary Policy & Anchored Expectations. An Endogenous Gain Learning Model. Mimeo. Boston College.

Gaus, E., Ramamurthy, S., 2019. A new approach to modeling endogenous gain learning. Advances in Econometrics 40A, 203–227.

Gomes, S., Iskrev, N., Mendicino, C., 2017. Monetary policy shocks: we got news! Journal of Economic Dynamics and Control 74 (C), 108–128.

Gourio, F., 2012. Disaster risk and business cycles. The American Economic Review 102 (6), 2734–2766.

Haberler, G., 1937. Prosperity and Depression: a theoretical analysis of cyclical movements. League of Nations, Geneva.

Hajdini, H., 2020. Misspecified Forecasts and Myopia in an Estimated New Keynesian Model. Mimeo. Drexel University.

Hirose, Y., 2008. Equilibrium indeterminacy and asset price fluctuation in Japan: a Bayesian investigation. Journal of Money, Credit, and Banking 40 (5), 967–999.

Hirose, Y., Kurozumi, T., 2021. Identifying news shocks with forecast data. Macroeconomic Dynamics 25 (6), 1442–1471.

Hirose, Y., Kurozumi, T., Van Zandweghe, W., 2020. Monetary policy and macroeconomic stability revisited. Review of Economic Dynamics 37, 255–274.

Hommes, C., 2011. The heterogeneous expectations hypothesis: some evidence from the lab. Journal of Economic Dynamics & Control 35 (1), 1–24.

Hommes, C., 2021. Behavioral & experimental macroeconomics and policy analysis: a complex systems approach. Journal of Economic Literature 59 (1), 149–219.

Hommes, C.H., 2013. Behavioral Rationality and Heterogeneous Expectations in Complex Economic Systems. Cambridge University Press.

Ilabaca, F., Meggiorini, G., Milani, F., 2020. Bounded rationality, monetary policy, and macroeconomic stability. Economics Letters 186, 108522.

Ilabaca, F., Milani, F., 2021. Heterogeneous expectations, indeterminacy, and postwar US business cycles. Journal of Macroeconomics 68, 103307.

Ilut, C., Saijo, H., 2021. Learning, confidence, and business cycles. Journal of Monetary Economics 117 (C), 354–376.

Ilut, C., Schneider, M., 2014. Ambiguous business cycles. The American Economic Review 104, 2368–2399.

Iskrev, N., 2010. Local identification in DSGE models. Journal of Monetary Economics 57, 189–202.

Jaimovich, N., Rebelo, S., 2009. Can news about the future drive the business cycle? The American Economic Review 99 (4), 1097–1118.

Kaplan, G., Moll, B., Violante, G.L., 2018. Monetary policy according to HANK. The American Economic Review 108 (3), 697–743.

Keynes, J.M., 1936. The General Theory of Employment, Interest and Money. MacMillan and Co., London.

Khan, H.U., Tsoukalas, J., 2012. The quantitative importance of news shocks in estimated DSGE models. Journal of Money, Credit, and Banking 44 (8), 1535–1561.

Kortelainen, M., Paloviita, M., Viren, M., 2016. How useful are measured expectations in estimation and simulation of a conventional small New Keynesian macro model? Economic Modelling 52 (PB), 540–550.

Kozlowski, J., Veldkamp, L., Venkateswaran, V., 2019. The tail that keeps the riskless rate low. NBER Macroeconomics Annual 33, 253–283.

Lubik, T.A., Schorfheide, F., 2004. Testing for indeterminacy: an application to U.S. monetary policy. The American Economic Review 94, 190–219.

Lucas, R.E., 1986. Adaptive behaviour and economic theory. In: Hogarth, R.M., Reder, M.W. (Eds.), Rational Choice: The Contrast Between Economics and Psychology. University of Chicago Press, Chicago and London, pp. 217–242.

Malmendier, U., Nagel, S., 2016. Learning from inflation experiences. The Quarterly Journal of Economics 131 (1), 53–87.

Mankiw, N.G., Reis, R., Wolfers, J., 2004. Disagreement about inflation expectations. In: NBER Macroeconomics Annual, vol. 18. In: NBER Chapters, pp. 209–270.

Manski, C.F., 2004. Measuring expectations. Econometrica 72, 1329–1376.

Manski, C.F., 2011. Interpreting and combining heterogeneous survey forecasts. In: Clements, M., Hendry, D. (Eds.), Oxford Handbook on Economic Forecasting. Oxford University Press, Oxford, pp. 457–472. Chapter 16.

Manski, C.F., 2017. Survey measurement of probabilistic macroeconomic expectations: progress and promise. NBER Working Paper No. 23418.

Marcet, A., Nicolini, J.P., 2003. Recurrent hyperinflations and learning. The American Economic Review 93 (5), 1476–1498.

Massaro, D., 2013. Heterogeneous expectations in monetary DSGE models. Journal of Economic Dynamics and Control 37, 680–692.

Meggiorini, G., Milani, F., 2021. Behavioral New Keynesian Models: Learning vs. Cognitive Discounting. Mimeo. UC Irvine.

Melosi, L., 2017. Signalling effects of monetary policy. The Review of Economic Studies 84 (2), 853–884.

Milani, F., 2007. Expectations, learning and macroeconomic persistence. Journal of Monetary Economics 54 (7), 2065–2082.

Milani, F., 2008. Learning, monetary policy rules, and macroeconomic stability. Journal of Economic Dynamics and Control 32 (10), 3148–3165.

Milani, F., 2009. Adaptive learning and macroeconomic inertia in the Euro area. Journal of Common Market Studies 47 (3), 579–599.

Milani, F., 2011. Expectation shocks and learning as drivers of the business cycle. The Economic Journal 121 (552), 379–401.

Milani, F., 2014. Learning and time-varying macroeconomic volatility. Journal of Economic Dynamics and Control 47, 94–114.

Milani, F., 2017. Sentiment and the U.S. business cycle. Journal of Economic Dynamics and Control 82, 289–311.

Milani, F., 2020. Learning and the evolution of the Fed's inflation target. Macroeconomic Dynamics 24 (8), 1904–1923.

Milani, F., Rajbhandari, A., 2020. Observed expectations, news shocks, and the business cycle. Research in Economics 74 (2), 95–118.

Milani, F., Treadwell, J., 2012. The effects of monetary policy 'news' and 'surprises'. Journal of Money, Credit, and Banking 44 (8), 1667–1692.

Miyamoto, W., Nguyen, T.L., 2020. The expectational effects of news in business cycles: evidence from forecast data. Journal of Monetary Economics 116 (C), 184–200.

Monti, F., 2010. Combining judgment and models. Journal of Money, Credit, and Banking 42 (8), 1641–1662.

Nimark, K.P., 2014. Man-bites-dog business cycles. The American Economic Review 104 (8), 2320–2367.

Nunes, R., 2010. Inflation dynamics: the role of expectations. Journal of Money, Credit, and Banking 42 (6), 1161–1172.

Orlik, A., Veldkamp, L., 2014. Understanding Uncertainty Shocks and the Role of Black Swans. NBER Working Paper 20445, August.

Ormeño, A., Molnár, K., 2015. Using survey data of inflation expectations in the estimation of learning and rational expectations models. Journal of Money, Credit, and Banking 47, 673–699.

Orphanides, A., Williams, J.C., 2005. Imperfect knowledge, inflation expectations and monetary policy. In: Bernanke, Ben S., Woodford, Michael (Eds.), Inflation Targeting. University of Chicago Press.

Paloviita, M., 2007. Estimating a small DSGE model under rational and measured expectations: some comparisons. Bank of Finland Discussion Papers 14/2007.

Pesaran, M.H., Weale, M., 2006. Survey expectations. In: Elliott, G., Granger, C., Timmermann, A. (Eds.), Handbook of Economic Forecasting, vol. 1, 1st edition, pp. 715–776. Chapter 14.

Pigou, A.C., 1927. Industrial Fluctuations. MacMillan, London.

Potter, S., Del Negro, M., Topa, G., van der Klaauw, H.W., 2017. The advantages of probabilistic survey questions. Review of Economic Analysis 9 (1), 1–32.

Roberts, J.M., 1997. Is inflation sticky? Journal of Monetary Economics 39 (2), 173–196.

Rossi, B., Sekhposyany, T., Soupre, M., 2016. Understanding the Sources of Macroeconomic Uncertainty. Economic Working Paper Series 1531. UPF.

Rychalovska, Y., 2016. The implications of financial frictions and imperfect knowledge in the estimated DSGE model of the U.S. economy. Journal of Economic Dynamics and Control 73 (C), 259–282.

Sargent, T.J., 1999. The Conquest of American Inflation. Princeton University Press, Princeton.

Schmitt-Grohé, S., Uribe, M., 2012. What's news in business cycles? Econometrica 80 (6), 2733–2764.

Schorfheide, F., 2005. Learning and monetary policy shifts. Review of Economic Dynamics 8 (2), 392–419.

Sims, E., 2016. What's news in News? A cautionary note on using a variance decomposition to assess the quantitative importance of news shocks. Journal of Economic Dynamics and Control 73 (C), 41–60.

Slobodyan, S., Wouters, R., 2012. Learning in a medium-scale DSGE model with expectations based on small forecasting models. American Economic Journal: Macroeconomics 4 (2), 65–101.

Smets, F., Wouters, R., 2003. An estimated dynamic stochastic general equilibrium model of the Euro area. Journal of the European Economic Association 1 (5), 1123–1175.

Smets, F., Wouters, R., 2007. Shocks and frictions in US business cycles: a Bayesian DSGE approach. The American Economic Review 97 (3), 586–606.

Suda, J., 2018. Belief-twisting shocks and the macroeconomy. Macroeconomic Dynamics 22 (7), 1844–1858.

Vázquez, J., Aguilar, P., 2021. Adaptive learning with term structure information. European Economic Review 134 (C).

Expectations and incomplete markets[☆]

Evi Pappa[a,b], Morten O. Ravn[c,b], and Vincent Sterk[c,b]

[a] Universidad Carlos III de Madrid, Madrid, Spain
[b] CEPR, London, United Kingdom
[c] University College London, London, United Kingdom

19.1 Introduction

In this chapter, we analyze how the introduction of incomplete markets and idiosyncratic risk matter for three issues regarding the role of expectations in macroeconomics. We do so within a HANK&SAM (heterogeneous agents New Keynesian model with search and matching) economy.[1]

In our analysis, existing firm–worker relationships face exogenous separation risk and there are frictions in the matching between households looking for jobs, and firms with job vacancies searching for new hires. Households are unable to insure themselves against two sources of earning risk: Changes in real wages, and job loss. Due to incomplete markets, these features introduce a precautionary savings motive amongst employed households which modifies the standard Euler equation that dictates intertemporal choices, a main channel through which expectations matter for aggregate outcomes. First, under incomplete markets, the (log-linearized) Euler equation involves discounting which tilts the consumption stream towards current consumption. This feature, by itself, makes households less forward looking introducing a source of "myopia" in the sense of Angeletos and Huo (2021). We show that the strength of this discounting is determined by the amount of idiosyncratic risk faced by agents. Secondly, variations in real wages and in job finding rates affect employed agents' precautionary savings motives. In line with Ravn and Sterk (2021), we show that this latter feature may either increase or reduce the economy's sensitivity to aggregate shocks depending on whether earning risk is dominated by job loss risk or by real wage cyclicality. In the former of these cases, which we refer to as countercyclical earnings risk, employed households increase their precautionary savings in recessions which introduces an amplification mechanism. The latter case instead, which we refer to as procyclical earnings risk, introduces a stabilization mechanism.

In combination these features have implications for how incomplete markets affect aggregate outcomes and for a number of issues relating to the role of expectations in macroeconomics. We analyze

---

[☆] We are grateful to comments received at the Handbook of Economic Expectations Conference. Ravn acknowledges financial support from ERC Project BUCCAC - DLV 8845598. Pappa acknowledges financial support from MCIN/ AEI /10.13039/501100011033 for project PGC2018-094321-B-I00.

[1] Our framework builds on Ravn and Sterk (2017) and Ravn and Sterk (2021). See Gornemann et al. (2016), McKay and Reis (2016a), Kaplan et al. (2018), or Bayer et al. (2019) for other contributions to the HANK literature.

three issues: (i) the response of the economy to news shocks; (ii) the impact of expectational shocks deriving from noisy information; (iii) the sensitivity of the economy to pure expectational shocks that we model as fluctuations of household sentiments deriving from stochastic sunspots. We argue that incomplete markets tend to make the economy more sensitive to aggregate shocks because job loss risk dominates amongst the sources of income risk faced by households. We relate our analysis to other contributions to the literature such as McKay et al. (2016) and McKay et al. (2017) who have considered the role of incomplete markets for forward guidance. In line with Werning (2015), we argue that incomplete markets may worsen or resolve the forward guidance puzzle because of a trade-off between a discounting effect and an amplification mechanism. We add to the literature a characterization of the underlying structural parameters that determine whether incomplete markets resolve the forward guidance or not.[2] We also argue that incomplete markets features provide amplification of "noise" shocks deriving from incomplete information about fundamental shocks. Finally, we show how the economy may be susceptible to purely expectations driven fluctuations between periods of high and low unemployment when endogenous earnings risk is "sufficiently" countercyclical.

Our setup combines in a transparent way three major frictions that are often studied in isolation in macroeconomics: frictions in price setting, incomplete markets, and labor market frictions. The three frictions combine to produce an interesting interplay between the demand and supply sides of the economy. An issue that we do not examine but which is of considerable interest is heterogeneity in the formation of expectations across agents, see also Chapters 21 and 22 in this Handbook. Survey evidence on expectations indicate a substantial discrepancy between the formation of households' and professional forecasters' expectations, but also substantial heterogeneity across households, see, e.g., Reis (2020). In a very interesting contribution, Broer et al. (2020a) study the information acquisition in a heterogeneous agents set-up and show that their model can account for the dispersion in expectations observed across households in surveys. In their setting, differences in the incentive to acquire information amplify the impact of incomplete markets on wealth dispersion and also increase the economy's sensitivity to aggregate shocks.

Our analysis focuses on a rational expectations framework. Farhi and Werning (2019) instead introduce level-k thinking into an incomplete markets framework and analyze the implications of bounded rationality for forward guidance. Angeletos and Huo (2021) introduce heterogeneity in MPCs with incomplete information and higher order beliefs and study the propagation of expectational shocks. Angeletos and Lian (2022) and Chapter 20 in this Handbook combine bounded rationality with intertemporal substitution on the supply side and show that in such framework demand shocks are amplified, but supply shocks are possibly dampened. One might also want to explore settings with learning, see Chapter 18 in this Handbook, to further explore deviations from the rational expectations hypothesis.

The rest of this chapter is organized as follows. The next section lays out the economy and discusses some of the model's properties. Section 19.3 examines the impact of news shocks related to productivity and monetary policy. Section 19.4 studies expectational shocks modeled as noise shocks, while Section 19.5 analyzes expectational shocks in a setting with multiple steady-states.

---

[2] The incomplete markets framework also provides an interesting setup to think about fiscal policy and fiscal news, see, e.g., Rendahl (2020) or Auclert et al. (2019).

19.2 The general setup

We study an HANK model with labor market frictions building on Ravn and Sterk (2017) and Ravn and Sterk (2021). The key forces that make this an interesting laboratory for thinking about expectations is (a) interaction between the demand and supply side of the economy (due to sticky prices), (b) precautionary savings (due to incomplete markets), and (c) *endogenous* income risk due to labor market matching. In this section we present the general setup and discuss some of its properties.

Households. There is a continuum of measure $1 - \varphi$ of infinitely-lived households indexed by i who maximize expected discounted utility. Agents live in single-member households, consume a bundle of goods, $\mathbf{c}_i$, and face uninsurable unemployment risk.

Preferences are given as

$$
\mathbf{U}_{i,s}^w = \widehat{\mathbb{E}}_s \sum_{h=0}^{\infty} \beta_w^h \frac{\mathbf{c}_{w,i,s+h}^{1-\mu} - 1}{1 - \mu},
\tag{19.1}
$$

where $\widehat{\mathbb{E}}_s x_{s+h}$ is the date s expectation of the stochastic variable x_{s+h} given the information set available[3]; β_w is households' intertemporal discount factor; $\mathbf{c}$ is a constant elasticity of substitution (CES) aggregate over individual goods varieties,

$$
\mathbf{c}_{w,i,s} = \left(\int_j \left(\mathbf{c}_{w,i,s}^j \right)^{1-1/\gamma} dj \right)^{1/(1-1/\gamma)},
\tag{19.2}
$$

where $\mathbf{c}_{w,i,s}^j$ denotes household i's consumption of goods variety j, and $\gamma > 1$ is the elasticity of substitution between varieties.

Household i's employment status is given by the binary variable, $\mathbf{n}_{i,s}$, namely

$$
\mathbf{n}_{i,s} = \begin{cases} 0 & \text{if unemployed at date } s, \\ 1 & \text{if employed at date } s, \end{cases}
\tag{19.3}
$$

so that workers are either employed and working full-time or unemployed. Employed workers earn a real wage $\mathbf{w}_s$ while unemployed workers receive an endowment of the consumption basket, $\xi > 0$. The fact that all employed workers earn the same real wage anticipates an assumption about wage determination that we make below.

Labor markets are characterized by search and matching frictions. We assume that a currently searching worker finds a new job opportunity with probability $\eta_s \in (0, 1)$ which she takes as exogenously given. The risk of unemployment is the assumed source of idiosyncratic income risk.[4]

---

[3] We abstract from disutility of work. Such a term would matter, for example, in a Nash bargaining set-up but has no consequences for our analysis.

[4] It is straightforward to allow also for idiosyncratic wage risk for employed workers.

There is also a continuum of capitalists of measure φ who own the firms in the economy. Capitalists maximize utility

$$U_{i,s}^c = \widehat{\mathbb{E}}_s \sum_{h=0}^{\infty} \beta_c^h c_{c,i,s+h}. \tag{19.4}$$

For simplicity, we assume that capitalists are risk neutral and discount utility at the rate β_c. The assumption of risk neutrality on the part of capitalists matters only to simplify part of the algebra. In subsequent sections of this chapter, we allow for risk averse capitalists. Capitalists' consumption baskets are defined by Eq. (19.2).

Firms. There is a continuum of monopolistically competitive firms indexed by j that are owned by the capitalists. Firms produce differentiated goods, $\mathbf{y}_j$, are price setters, and have access to a linear technology

$$\mathbf{y}_{j,s} = \exp(\mathbf{A}_s)\,\mathbf{n}_{j,s}, \tag{19.5}$$

where $\mathbf{A}$ is an aggregate productivity shock, and $\mathbf{n}_j$ is firm j's input of labor.

Firms hire labor in a matching market. At the end of each period, a fraction $\omega \in (0, 1)$ of existing worker–firm matches are exogenously dissolved. Firms make new hires by posting vacancies, $\mathbf{v}_j$, at the flow cost $\kappa > 0$ per vacancy, per period. Each vacancy is filled with probability $\mathbf{q}_s$ which firms take as given. Vacancies are posted at the beginning of the period and filled prior to production. The law of motion of employment in firm j is given as

$$\mathbf{n}_{j,s} = (1 - \omega)\,\mathbf{n}_{j,s-1} + \mathbf{q}_s \mathbf{v}_{j,s}. \tag{19.6}$$

Firms are monopolistically competitive and set the nominal price of their product, $\mathbf{P}_j$, subject to quadratic price adjustment costs following Rotemberg (1981). They maximize the objective function

$$\mathbf{\Phi}_{j,s} = \widehat{\mathbb{E}}_s \sum_{h=0}^{\infty} \beta_c^h \left[\frac{\mathbf{P}_{j,s+h}}{\mathbf{P}_{s+h}} \mathbf{y}_{j,s+h} - \mathbf{w}_{s+h}\mathbf{n}_{j,s+h} - \kappa \mathbf{v}_{j,s+h} - \frac{\phi}{2}\left(\frac{\mathbf{P}_{j,s+h}}{\mathbf{P}_{j,s+h-1}} - 1 \right)^2 \mathbf{y}_{s+h} \right], \tag{19.7}$$

where $\mathbf{P}$ is the aggregate price level; $\phi \geq 0$ quantifies price adjustment costs, and $\mathbf{y} = \int \mathbf{y}_j dj$ is aggregate output. Firms maximize the present value of profits given by Eq. (19.7) subject to (19.5), (19.6), and

$$\mathbf{y}_{j,s} = \left(\frac{\mathbf{P}_{j,s}}{\mathbf{P}_s} \right)^{-\gamma} \mathbf{y}_s, \tag{19.8}$$

$$\mathbf{v}_{j,s} \geq 0, \tag{19.9}$$

where Eq. (19.8) is the demand for variety j and Eq. (19.9) imposes that vacancies are nonnegative.

Matching. Households searching for jobs and firms with job vacancies meet in an anonymous matching market. The measure of new worker–firm matches, $\mathbf{m}$, is determined by a Cobb–Douglas matching function

$$\mathbf{m}_s = \bar{m}\mathbf{e}_s^{\alpha}\mathbf{v}_s^{1-\alpha}, \tag{19.10}$$

where $\mathbf{e}$ is the measure of searching workers, and $\mathbf{v} = \int \mathbf{v}_j dj$ is the measure of aggregate vacancies; $\bar{m} > 0$ is a constant and $0 < \alpha < 1$ denotes the elasticity of matches to the measure of searchers.

Letting $\theta = \mathbf{v}/\mathbf{e}$ be labor market tightness, the endogenously determined job finding and the vacancy filling rates are determined as:

$$\eta_s = \bar{m}\theta_s^{1-\alpha}, \tag{19.11}$$

$$q_s = \bar{m}\theta_s^{-\alpha}. \tag{19.12}$$

Wages. We assume that the real wage is determined as

$$\mathbf{w}_s = \bar{w}\left(\frac{\eta_s}{\bar{\eta}}\right)^\chi, \tag{19.13}$$

where $\bar{w}, \bar{\eta} > 0$ are constants. This specification assumes that real wages respond to the job finding rate with an elasticity of χ, so that real wages rise when workers are harder to hire. This assumption simplifies the incomplete markets model substantially, but it is straightforward to show that the Nash bargaining solution corresponds to a particular value of χ that is a complicated function of the deep parameters of the model.

Asset and budget constraints. Firms are owned by the capitalists who hold equity portfolios while households only have access to the bond markets. Capitalists have no access to bond markets and do not to participate in the labor market. These assumptions can be micro-founded assuming limited participation in equity markets and imposing the borrowing constraint in Eq. (19.17) below, see Ravn and Sterk (2021).

Let $\mathbf{b}_{i,s}$ be agents i's purchases of bonds at date s, $\mathbf{x}_{i,s}$ equity purchases, $\mathbf{R}_{s-1}$ the nominal interest rate, $\mathbf{R}_{x,s}$ the return on equity, and $\Pi_s = \mathbf{P}_s/\mathbf{P}_{s-1}$ the gross inflation rate between periods $s-1$ and s. The flow budget constraint for capitalists is

$$\mathbf{c}_{i,s} + \mathbf{x}_{i,s} \le \frac{\mathbf{R}_{x,s}}{\Pi_s}\mathbf{x}_{i,s-1} + \xi, \tag{19.14}$$

and we assume that they cannot go short on equity,

$$\mathbf{x}_{i,s} \ge 0. \tag{19.15}$$

Workers face a sequence of budget constraints

$$\mathbf{c}_{i,s} + \mathbf{b}_{i,s} \le \mathbf{w}_s\mathbf{n}_{i,s} + \xi\left(1 - \mathbf{n}_{i,s}\right) + \frac{\mathbf{R}_{s-1}}{\Pi_s}\mathbf{b}_{i,s-1} \tag{19.16}$$

and the borrowing constraint

$$\mathbf{b}_{i,s} \ge -\varkappa\mathbf{w}_s\mathbf{n}_{i,s}, \tag{19.17}$$

where $\varkappa > 0$. This borrowing constraint allows workers to issue debt if they are employed but not if they do not hold a job.

Monetary policy. The nominal interest rate is set by a central bank according to the interest rate rule

$$\mathbf{R}_s = \bar{R} \left(\frac{\boldsymbol{\Pi}_s}{\overline{\boldsymbol{\Pi}}} \right)^{\delta_\Pi} \left(\frac{\theta_s}{\bar{\theta}} \right)^{\delta_\theta} \exp\left(\varepsilon_s^R \right), \quad \bar{R} \geq 1, \tag{19.18}$$

where $\overline{\Pi}$ is an inflation target, $\bar{\theta}$ denotes steady-state labor market tightness, and ε_s^R is a monetary policy innovation. We allow the central bank to respond to labor market tightness because fluctuations in unemployment, due to the market incompleteness, can induce amplification of shocks.

Stochastic shocks. There are stochastic shocks to technology and to monetary policy. We assume:

$$\mathbf{A}_s = \rho_A \mathbf{A}_{s-1} + e_s^A, \tag{19.19}$$

$$\varepsilon_s^R = \rho_R \varepsilon_{s-1}^R + e_s^R, \tag{19.20}$$

where e^A is a productivity shock, and e^R is the monetary policy shock, and we impose $\rho_A, \rho_R \in (0, 1)$. We assume that e^A and e^R are mutually orthogonal, normally distributed variables with means 0 and variances σ_A^2 and σ_R^2, respectively.

Equilibrium. The economy displays limited heterogeneity in equilibrium. First, capitalists face no idiosyncratic risk therefore have identical consumption levels that we denote by $\mathbf{c}_{c,s}$. Second, unemployed workers would like to borrow, but are prevented from doing so because of the borrowing constraint. In equilibrium, they consume the endowment $c_{u,s} = \xi$ and will be in a corner solution. Third, employed workers have an incentive to save due to unemployment risk and are therefore on their Euler equations. However, bond market clearing implies that employed workers all consume their wage. We let $\mathbf{c}_{n,s}$ be the common consumption level for employed workers.[5]

We initially examine the properties of the economy in the vicinity of the steady-state where $\overline{\Pi} = 1$, so that the central bank targets price stability. Moreover, we focus on a symmetric equilibrium in which all firms set the same prices and make the same employment decisions.

The equilibrium conditions are then given by (19.5), (19.11), (19.12), (19.13), (19.18), and:

$$\mathbf{c}_{n,s}^{-\mu} = \beta_w \widehat{\mathbb{E}}_s \frac{R_s}{\Pi_{s+1}} \left[(1 - \omega (1 - \eta_{s+1})) \mathbf{c}_{n,s+1}^{-\mu} + \omega (1 - \eta_{s+1}) \xi^{-\mu} \right], \tag{19.21}$$

$$\gamma \mathbf{mc}_s = \phi (\Pi_s - 1) \Pi_s - \phi \beta_c \widehat{\mathbb{E}}_s (\Pi_{s+1} - 1) \Pi_{s+1} y_{s+1}/y_s + \gamma - 1, \tag{19.22}$$

$$\mathbf{mc}_s = \frac{1}{\exp(A_s)} \left(\mathbf{w}_s + \frac{\kappa}{\mathbf{q}_s} - \lambda_{v,s} - (1 - \omega) \beta_c \widehat{\mathbb{E}}_s \left\{ \frac{\kappa}{\mathbf{q}_{s+1}} - \lambda_{v,s+1} \right\} \right), \tag{19.23}$$

$$\mathbf{c}_{n,s} = \mathbf{w}_s, \tag{19.24}$$

$$\mathbf{n}_s = (1 - \omega) \mathbf{n}_{s-1} + \eta_s \mathbf{e}_s, \tag{19.25}$$

$$\mathbf{e}_s = 1 - n_{s-1} - \varphi + \omega n_{s-1}, \tag{19.26}$$

where $\mathbf{mc}_s$ denotes real marginal costs and $\lambda_{v,s} \geq 0$ is the Kuhn–Tucker multiplier on the vacancy nonnegativity constraint in Eq. (19.9). These equations represent the employed workers' intertemporal

---

[5] Challe and Ragot (2016) also study a setting with uninsurable unemployment risk and a degenerate wealth distribution in a setting with exogenous labor market transition rates.

Euler equation (19.21), firms' optimal price setting condition (19.22), the definition of real marginal costs (19.23), the determination of employed workers' consumption level (19.24), the law of motion of aggregate employment (19.25), and the law of motion of the measure of searchers (19.26).

The central new aspect of the model relative to complete markets' models is the modification of the Euler equation (19.21). Consider a log-linearization of the condition in the vicinity of the steady-state with price stability (and let $\bar{x}$ denote the steady-state value of x)

$$-\mu\left(\hat{\mathbf{c}}_{n,s} - \frac{1}{\Theta^{SS}}\widehat{\mathbb{E}}_t\hat{\mathbf{c}}_{n,s+1}\right) = -\widehat{\mathbb{E}}_s\left(\hat{\mathbf{R}}_s - \hat{\mathbf{\Pi}}_{s+1}\right) + \frac{\Theta^F}{\Theta^{SS}}\widehat{\mathbb{E}}_s\hat{\eta}_{s+1}, \tag{19.27}$$

where

$$\Theta^{SS} = 1 + \omega\left(1 - \bar{\eta}\right)\left(\left(\frac{\xi}{\bar{c}_n}\right)^{-\mu} - 1\right) \geq 1, \tag{19.28}$$

$$\Theta^F = \omega\bar{\eta}\left[\left(\left(\frac{\xi}{\bar{c}_n}\right)^{-\mu} - 1\right) - \chi\mu\left(1 - \bar{\eta}\right)/\bar{\eta}\right] \lesseqgtr 0. \tag{19.29}$$

Eq. (19.27) differs from its complete markets version because of (i) discounting, and because of (ii) a time-varying precautionary savings term. The former of these is present due to future consumption entering the left hand side with the coefficient $\mu/\Theta^{SS} \leq \mu$ while the second aspect is reflected by the last term on the right-hand side.

Discounting of future consumption in the log-linearized Euler equation, also referred to as "myopia" by Angeletos and Huo (2021), derives from the lack of insurance against unemployment risk which drives down the steady-state real interest rate. To see this, evaluate condition (19.21) in a stationary equilibrium without aggregate shocks:

$$\left(\frac{\bar{R}}{\bar{\Pi}}\right)^I = \frac{1}{\beta_w\Theta^{SS}} \leq \frac{1}{\beta_w}, \tag{19.30}$$

where the index "I" indicates the steady-state where inflation is on target. Thus, incomplete markets tilt the intertemporal allocation of consumption towards current consumption that is stronger the (i) larger is the consumption loss upon unemployment, $\xi/\bar{c}_n$, (ii) the more risk averse is the agent, and (iii) the larger is the unemployment risk of an employed worker, $\omega\left(1 - \bar{\eta}\right)$.

The time-varying precautionary savings term in Eq. (19.27) derive from variations in earnings risk captured by the last term on the right-hand side. While there are only aggregate shocks, at the individual worker level, due to incomplete markets, variations in the job finding rate impact on the idiosyncratic risk faced by households: uncertainty is *endogenous*.[6] The impact of the job finding rate on employed workers' consumption paths depends on the parameter Θ^F which may be positive or negative depending on the dominance of two different sources of earnings risk, namely job loss and real wage fluctuations. A currently employed worker faces unemployment next period with probability

---

[6] Juelsrud and Wold (2019) provide empirical evidence from Norwegian tax data indicating that job loss risk affects household savings.

$(1 - \omega(1 - \eta_{s+1}))$ in which case consumption declines to $\xi < c_n$. This risk will be higher in recessions due to worsening labor market conditions. On the other hand, wage procyclicality means that the drop in consumption in case of job loss will be larger in expansions. When job loss risk dominates, this wedge is positive, $\Theta^F > 0$, a case we refer to as *countercyclical endogenous earnings risk*. When $\Theta^F < 0$, wage procyclicality dominates and we refer to this case as *procyclical earnings risk*.

The countercyclical case is likely to be the more empirically relevant. For example, Broer et al. (2020b) study German administrative data and find that income risk for poorer households derive almost entirely from job loss risk while for richer households, job loss risk and wage risk (income risk for continued employment) appear about equally important. This would suggest that the countercyclical component deriving from job loss risk dominates in the aggregate. Hoeck (2020) estimates the elasticity of real wages of Danish workers to changes in labor market tightness studying firm level data and finds positive but very small elasticities. Moreover, countercyclical earnings risk implies, consistently with data, that real interest rates are procyclical as the precautionary motive drives down real returns in recessions, see Ravn and Sterk (2021).

When $\Theta^F > 0$, precautionary savings expand in recessions and decline in booms introducing an amplification mechanism. To see this, imagine a weakening labor market with a low job finding rate, η. This stimulates precautionary savings from the employed which translates into declining goods demand (at a given real interest rate). Due to sticky prices, firms respond to this through both a reduction in prices *and* in marginal costs. The latter has to come from real wage reductions and/or lower hiring costs. When the real wage elasticity is small, real marginal costs adjustments derive from hiring costs thus forcing firms to reduce vacancy postings. The latter induces a further increase in precautionary savings leading to amplification. Conversely, were earnings risk procyclical, $\Theta^F < 0$, the demand–supply interaction is stabilizing.[7]

In the subsequent sections we examine the role of these aspects of the incomplete markets model in applications to expectational shocks.

19.3 **News shocks**

A topic that has attracted much attention in macroeconomics is the extent to which general equilibrium models can generate news-driven business cycles, see, e.g., Beaudry and Portier (2006), Beaudry and Portier (2007), Jaimovich and Rebelo (2009), Kurmann and Sims (2021) Barsky and Sims (2011), or Schmitt-Grohe and Uribe (2011). We now examine the extent to which incomplete markets has implications for this topic through the mechanisms highlighted earlier.

We assume that agents have rational expectations and let $\mathbb{E}_s x_{s+h}$ denote the standard rational expectations operator. We focus on the impact of news shocks in the vicinity of a steady-state that implements price-stability, $\overline{\Pi} = 1$. Log-linearizing the equilibrium conditions around this steady-state delivers the

---

[7] Here we have assumed that unemployed workers receive endowments of the goods basket rather than tax financed transfers. Also, we have not included insurance through increasing marginal tax schedules for allowed for endogenous search effort choice. The importance of such issues have been examined by Kekre (2021) and McKay and Reis (2016b).

following set of equilibrium conditions:

$$\widehat{c}_{n,s} - \frac{1}{\Theta^{SS}} \mathbb{E}_s \widehat{c}_{n,s+1} = -\frac{1}{\mu} \left(\widehat{R}_s - \mathbb{E}_s \widehat{\Pi}_{s+1} - \frac{\Theta^F}{\Theta^{SS}} \mathbb{E}_s \widehat{\eta}_{s+1} \right), \tag{19.31}$$

$$\frac{\phi}{\gamma} \left(\widehat{\Pi}_s - \beta_c \mathbb{E}_s \widehat{\Pi}_{s+1} \right) = w \widehat{w}_s + \frac{1-\gamma}{\gamma} A_s + \frac{\kappa}{q} \frac{\alpha}{1-\alpha} \widehat{\eta}_s - (1-\omega) \beta_c \frac{\kappa}{q} \frac{\alpha}{1-\alpha} \mathbb{E}_s \widehat{\eta}_{s+1}, \tag{19.32}$$

$$\widehat{R}_s = \delta_\pi \widehat{\Pi}_s + \frac{\delta_\theta}{1-\alpha} \widehat{\eta}_s + \epsilon_s^R, \tag{19.33}$$

$$\widehat{w}_s = \chi \widehat{\eta}_s, \tag{19.34}$$

$$\widehat{c}_{n,s} = \widehat{w}_s, \tag{19.35}$$

$$\widehat{y}_s = A_s + \widehat{n}_s, \tag{19.36}$$

$$\widehat{n}_s = (1-\omega) \widehat{n}_{s-1} + \frac{\eta e}{n} \left(\widehat{\eta}_s + \widehat{e}_s \right), \tag{19.37}$$

$$e \widehat{e}_s = (\omega - 1) n \widehat{n}_{s-1}. \tag{19.38}$$

We assume that the stochastic processes for A_s and ϵ_s^R are given as:

$$A_s = \rho_A A_{s-1} + e_{s-m}^A, \tag{19.39}$$

$$\epsilon_s^R = \rho_R \epsilon_{s-1}^R + e_{s-m}^R, \tag{19.40}$$

where $0 \leq \rho_A, \rho_R < 1$ denote the persistence of productivity and monetary policy shocks, respectively. Thus, the date s innovations to productivity and monetary policy shocks, e_{s-m}^A and e_{s-m}^R, are news shocks which enter households' information sets $m \geq 0$ periods ahead of their realization (with $m = 0$ representing surprise shocks). It is straightforward to allow news shocks with anticipation horizons from 1 to m periods (the solution will characterize the impact of all of these) as well as for additional unanticipated shocks.

19.3.1 Analytical insights

We first consider the following special case:

Assumption 19.1. The monetary policy response to inflation is given as $\delta_\pi = 1/\beta_c > 1$.

When the central bank pursues price stability, $\bar{\Pi} = 1$, Assumption 19.1 ensures local determinacy of the equilibrium in the complete markets economy.[8] Combining (19.31)–(19.35) and inducing Assumption 19.1 yields the following first-order stochastic difference equation for $\widehat{\eta}$:

$$\mathbb{E}_s \widehat{\eta}_{s+1} = \Phi \widehat{\eta}_s + \Omega_A^\eta A_s + \Omega_R^\eta \epsilon_s^R, \tag{19.41}$$

where

$$\Phi = \frac{\Phi^N}{\Phi^D}, \tag{19.42}$$

---

[8] It is straightforward to allow for $\delta_\pi > 1/\beta_c$.

$$\Phi^N = \beta_c \mu \frac{\phi}{\gamma} \chi + w \chi + \beta_c \frac{\phi}{\gamma} \frac{\delta_\theta}{1-\alpha} + \frac{\kappa}{q} \frac{\alpha}{1-\alpha}, \tag{19.43}$$

$$\Phi^D = \beta_c \mu \frac{\phi}{\gamma} \frac{\chi}{\Theta^{SS}} + \beta_c \frac{\phi}{\gamma} \frac{\Theta^F}{\Theta^{SS}} + \beta_c (1-\omega) \frac{\kappa}{q} \frac{\alpha}{1-\alpha}, \tag{19.44}$$

$$\Omega^\eta_A = \frac{1-\gamma}{\gamma} \frac{1}{\Phi^D}, \tag{19.45}$$

$$\Omega^\eta_R = \beta_c \frac{\phi}{\gamma} \frac{1}{\Phi^D}. \tag{19.46}$$

Local determinacy of the equilibrium with price stability requires that $\Phi > 1$, i.e., that $\Phi^N > \Phi^D$. We make the following guess:

$$\widehat{\eta}_s = \Gamma^A_\eta A_s + \sum_{i=0}^{m-1} \tau_i^{\eta,A} e^A_{s-i} + \Gamma^R_\eta \epsilon^R_s + \sum_{i=0}^{m-1} \tau_i^{\eta,R} e^R_{s-i}. \tag{19.47}$$

Inserting the guess into (19.41) and using the method of undetermined coefficients gives us

$$\Gamma^A_\eta = \frac{(\gamma-1)/\gamma}{\Phi^N - \rho_A \Phi^D} > 0, \tag{19.48}$$

$$\tau_i^{\eta,A} = \Gamma^A_\eta \Phi^{-(m-i)} > 0, \tag{19.49}$$

$$\Gamma^R_\eta = -\frac{\beta_c \frac{\phi}{\gamma}}{\Phi^N - \rho_R \Phi^D} < 0, \tag{19.50}$$

$$\tau_i^{\eta,R} = \Gamma^R_\eta \Phi^{-(m-i)} < 0. \tag{19.51}$$

Given (19.48)–(19.51), the solution for the other variables are given as:

$$x_s = \Gamma^A_x A_s + \sum_{i=0}^{m-1} \tau_i^{x,A} e^A_{s-i} + \Gamma^R_x \epsilon^R_s + \sum_{i=0}^{m-1} \tau_i^{x,R} e^R_{s-i}, \tag{19.52}$$

$$\widehat{n}_s = \Gamma^A_n A_s + \sum_{i=0}^{m-1} \tau_i^{n,A} e^A_{s-i} + \Gamma^R_n \epsilon^R_s + \sum_{i=0}^{m-1} \tau_i^{n,R} e^R_{s-i} - \eta e (1-\omega) \widehat{n}_{s-1}, \tag{19.53}$$

where $x_s = \left(\widehat{\Pi}_s, \widehat{R}_s, \widehat{w}_s \right)$. The coefficients are given in the appendix.

19.3.1.1 *Productivity news*

Local determinacy implies that $\partial \eta_s / \partial A_s > 0$. Whether shocks are amplified or not by market incompleteness depends on its impact on the Φ^N and Φ^D. It follows from (19.42)–(19.44) that:

$$\frac{\partial \Gamma^A_\eta}{\partial \Theta^i} = \frac{\gamma-1}{\gamma} \frac{\rho_A}{\left(\Phi^N - \rho_A \Phi^D\right)^2} \frac{\partial \Phi^D}{\partial \Theta^i}, \quad i = F, SS, \tag{19.54}$$

$$\frac{\partial \Phi^D}{\partial \Theta^{SS}} = -\frac{1}{\left(\Theta^{SS}\right)^2} \frac{\beta_c \phi}{\gamma} \left(\chi \mu + \Theta^F \right) < 0, \tag{19.55}$$

$$\frac{\partial \Phi^D}{\partial \Theta^F} = \frac{\beta_c \phi}{\gamma} \frac{1}{\Theta^{SS}} > 0. \tag{19.56}$$

As long as $\rho_A > 0$, $\partial \Gamma_\eta^A / \partial \Theta^{SS} < 0$, a higher Θ^{SS} is equivalent to agents discounting more heavily future income prospects. However, incomplete markets also enters through Θ^F which determines the time-varying precautionary savings motive. When risk is countercyclical, this channel amplifies productivity while procyclical risk stabilizes productivity shocks. Similar insights can also be derived in a two-agent New Keynesian (TANK) setting, see Bilbiie (2020).

Both incomplete markets wedges depend on workers' consumption loss when they experience a transition to unemployment, $c^{rel} = \xi / c_n$.[9] We can therefore evaluate the consequences of introducing incomplete markets by examining the net effect on Γ_η^A of c^{rel}:

$$\frac{\partial \Gamma_\eta^A}{\partial c^{rel}} = \frac{\gamma - 1}{\gamma} \frac{\rho_A}{\left(\Phi^N - \rho_A \Phi^D\right)^2} \frac{\partial \Phi^D}{\partial c^{rel}}, \tag{19.57}$$

$$\frac{\partial \Phi^D}{\partial c^{rel}} = \frac{\beta_c \phi}{\gamma} \frac{\mu \omega \left(c^{rel}\right)^{-\mu-1}}{\left(\Theta^{SS}\right)^2} \left(\chi \mu (1 - \eta)(1 - \omega(1 - \eta)) - \eta\right). \tag{19.58}$$

The sign of $\partial \Gamma_\eta^A / \partial c^{rel}$ is determined by the sign of the bracket on the right-hand side of the expression for $\partial \Phi^D / \partial c^{rel}$. When the wage elasticity is low, a larger consumption drop upon unemployment (i.e., a lower c^{rel}) amplifies productivity shocks. Vice versa, when the wage elasticity is high, a higher consumption loss is stabilizing.

We now turn to the impact of news shocks about productivity. The expression in (19.49) shows that productivity news with a remaining anticipation horizon of $m - i > 0$ periods are discounted at the rate $\Phi^{-(m-i)}$. Since $\Phi > 1$ under local determinacy, more recent news (about productivity further out in the future) are therefore more heavily discounted. Such discounting have been referred to as "perverse" by Leeper et al. (2013) and the relationship between the rate of discounting and the unstable root of η, see Eq. (19.41), has been discussed by Mertens and Ravn (2010).

Thus, incomplete markets influence the economy's reaction to technology news both through Γ_η^A and Φ. Using the same logic as above, we find:

$$\frac{\partial \Phi}{\partial \Theta^{SS}} = \frac{\Phi^N}{\left(\Phi^D\right)^2} \frac{1}{\left(\Phi^{SS}\right)^2} \frac{\beta_c \phi}{\gamma} \left(\chi \mu + \Theta^F\right) > 0, \tag{19.59}$$

$$\frac{\partial \Phi}{\partial \Theta^F} = -\frac{\Phi^N}{\left(\Phi^D\right)^2} \frac{\beta_c \phi}{\gamma} \frac{1}{\Theta^{SS}} < 0, \tag{19.60}$$

$$\frac{\partial \Phi}{\partial c^{rel}} = -\frac{\Phi^N}{\left(\Phi^D\right)^2} \frac{\beta_c \phi}{\gamma} \frac{\mu \omega}{\left(\Theta^{SS}\right)^2} \left(\chi \mu (1 - \eta)(1 - \omega(1 - \eta)) - \eta\right) \left(c^{rel}\right)^{-\mu-1}. \tag{19.61}$$

The higher the Θ^{SS}, the stronger the agents discount news about future technology shocks. Recall that a higher Θ^{SS} also reduces the impact of *realized* productivity shocks. Thus, in tandem these two forces

---

[9] Kim (2020) discusses in detail further determinants of Θ^F and their impact on the forward guidance puzzle.

mute technology news. However, the introduction of incomplete markets also affects the economy's sensitivity to technology news through Θ^F. When earnings risk is countercyclical, a higher value of Θ^F increases the sensitivity of the job finding rate and other real variables to realized changes in productivity *and* implies less discounting. In this case, the net effect of incomplete markets on news shocks therefore depends on which of the wedges dominates quantitatively.

19.3.1.2 *Interest rate news*

These results extend to interest rates news shocks. News shock to the interest rate has attracted considerable attention in the low-interest rate environment that followed the Great Recession in the form of forward guidance. Del Negro et al. (2015) pointed out that the standard New Keynesian framework presents a *forward guidance puzzle* in the sense that it substantially overestimates the stimulating power of monetary policy announcement relative to empirical estimates. Moreover, and somewhat counterintuitively, the longer the news horizon, the larger the impact of monetary news shock in such models.

The key reason for why the standard NK economy presents such puzzles is the lack of discounting in the Euler equation which implies that preannounced future monetary stimuli have an immediate and potentially large impact the moment it is announced. Incomplete markets introduce such discounting and may therefore potentially address the puzzle. McKay et al. (2016) and McKay et al. (2017) argue that incomplete markets may indeed resolve the forward guidance puzzle. Inspecting the solutions in Eqs. (19.50)–(19.51), however, reveals the effect of expansionary monetary policy news shocks (negative shocks to the nominal interest rate) is parameter-dependent under incomplete markets. As for productivity news, discounting in the Euler equation mutes preannounced future interest rate reductions, while the time-varying precautionary motive amplifies them when endogenous earnings risk is countercyclical. Thus, as also stressed by Werning (2015), incomplete markets may actually worsen the forward guidance puzzle rather than resolve it.

19.3.2 **Quantitative analysis**

We now remove Assumption 19.1 and perform a numerical exercise by solving the model using a first-order perturbation around the steady-state with price stability. A period corresponds to a calendar month. The calibration targets are summarized in Table 19.1.

We assume an annual real interest rate of 4% and calibrate $\beta_c = 1.04^{-1/12}$. We set the coefficient of risk aversion, μ, equal to 2 and calibrate the consumption loss upon unemployment to 18%, an estimate in line with, e.g., Chodorow-Reich and Karabarbounis (2016).

We set the share of capitalists to be 0.1%. We target a monthly job finding rate of 34% implying an average unemployment duration of around three months, close to the US post-World War II experience. We set the monthly job separation rate equal to 3.58%. In combination with other parameters, this implies a steady-state unemployment rate of 6.5%. We normalize the constant term in the matching function, $\bar{m} = 1$ and set the elasticity of matches to the measure of searchers equal to 0.6. We set the wage elasticity, $\chi = 0.0283$, based on empirical estimates presented in the next section. Given these values, we obtain $\Theta^{SS} = 1.0115$ and $\Theta^F = 0.0046$ from Eqs. (19.28)–(19.29) implying that earnings risk is countercyclical. It follows that $\beta_w = 0.985$.

To calibrate ϕ which determines the degree of price stickiness, we exploit the relationship between the slope of the log-linearized optimal price setting equation delivered by our economy and the slope of the New Keynesian Phillips curve implied by a Calvo assumption on price adjustments. Let p_{dur} denote

Table 19.1 Calibration.

Parameter	Meaning	Value
$\bar{R}$	Steady-state gross real interest rate	$1.04^{1/12}$
μ	Coefficient of risk aversion	2
ξ	Home-production	$0.82\bar{w}$
γ	Elasticity of substitution	6
ω	Job separation rate	0.0358
$\bar{\eta}$	Job finding rate	0.34
ϑ	Steady-state hiring cost, fraction of wage bill	0.13
α	Matching function elasticity	0.6
p_{dur}	Average price contract length	6
χ	Real wage elasticity	0.0283
φ	Measure of capitalists	0.001
$\bar{\Pi}$	Inflation target	1
δ_π	Monetary policy response to inflation	1.5
δ_θ	Monetary policy response to labor market tightness	0
ρ_A	Persistence of productivity shocks	$0.95^{1/3}$
ρ_R	Persistence of interest rate shocks	0.5

Notes: One period corresponds to a calendar month.

the average price contract length, the slope of the NK Phillips curve is given as $\kappa_{NK} = p_{dur}(1 - \beta_c(1 - 1/p_{dur})/(1 - 1/p_{dur})$. We assume that $p_{dur} = 6$ months and accordingly set $\phi = \gamma/\kappa_{NK} = 177.8$.

Given these parameters, we can derive the steady-state real marginal costs and the steady-state real wage as:

$$\bar{mc} = \left(\phi(1 - \beta_c)\bar{\Pi}(\bar{\Pi} - 1) + \gamma - 1\right)/\gamma,$$

$$\bar{w} = \frac{\bar{mc}}{\bar{A} + (1 - \beta_c(1 - \omega))\vartheta\bar{n}/(\bar{v}\bar{q})},$$

where ϑ is the ratio of steady-state hiring costs to the wage bill which we calibrate to 13% and $\bar{v}$ is the steady-state measure of vacancies which is given as $\bar{v} = \omega\bar{n}/\bar{q}$. From these we find the vacancy posting cost parameter $\kappa = \vartheta\bar{w}\bar{n}/\bar{v}$ and the consumption level of the unemployed workers as $\xi = c_{rel}\bar{w}$.

We set $\delta_\pi = 1.5$ and $\delta_\theta = 0$. Finally, we assume that the persistence of TFP is 0.95 at the quarterly frequency, i.e., $\rho_A = 0.95^{1/3}$, and we set the persistence of monetary policy shocks equal to $\rho_R = 0.5$.

19.3.2.1 *Technology news*

Fig. 19.1 shows the impact of a news shock that raises productivity in the economy by 1% with a 6-month anticipation horizon. The productivity news stimulate the job finding rate as firms start building up employment gradually over time in anticipation of future higher productivity. Higher employment implies higher output and stimulates consumption through wages and lower precautionary savings and the economy expands ahead of the actual increase in productivity. Note that since firms invest in vacan-

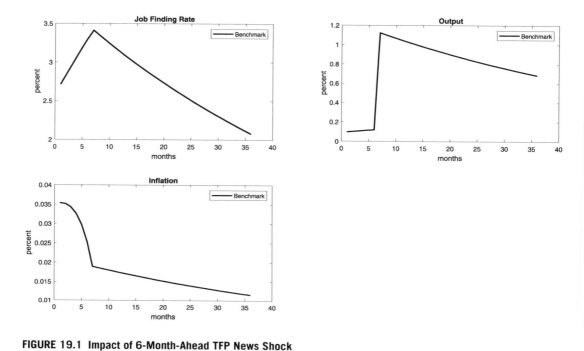

FIGURE 19.1 Impact of 6-Month-Ahead TFP News Shock

Notes: The figure shows percentage deviations of the variables from their steady-state values.

cies, also investment increases thus generating a Pigou cycle. An interesting result is that the demand effect is so strong that the TFP news shock increases inflation both during the anticipation period and after the actual increase in TFP.

Fig. 19.2 examines the determinants of the impact technology news on the job finding rate. We compare the benchmark model (continuous line) with four alternative economies. In the first we assume a tiny consumption loss upon unemployment which approximates complete markets (dotted line). The impact of TFP news is almost unchanged because "discounting" and amplification effects approximately cancel out: Incomplete markets lead to discounting, but also imply amplification of shocks through countercyclical endogenous earning risk. In the second alternative calibration, we increase the real wage elasticity to $\chi = 0.1$ but retain the incomplete markets assumption (dashed circled line). The higher real wage elasticity implies that the incomplete markets precautionary savings wedge is approximately acyclical, $\Theta^F \approx 0$, leading to substantial dampening relative to the complete markets results because the discounting effect dominates. Assuming instead a very low real wage elasticity, $\chi = 0.001$ (dashed line), implies substantial amplification of news shocks in the incomplete markets setting over the complete markets outcome because the amplification channel dominates the discounting channel. Last, we examine the importance of monetary policy allowing the central bank to respond to variations in labor market tightness and assume that $\delta_\theta = 0.05$. In this case, when firms start hiring ahead of the technology improvement, the central bank responds by increasing the nominal interest rate which

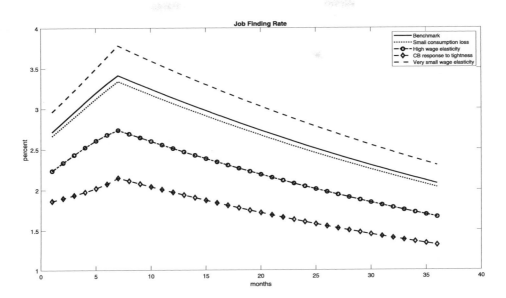

FIGURE 19.2 Determinants of Technology News Impact on Job Finding Rate

Notes: The figure shows percentage deviations of the variables from their steady-state values.

dampens the impact of the TFP news on the job finding rate and, hence, on output (dashed diamond line).

An interesting aspect of the closed form solutions for the impact of news on the job finding rate derived earlier in Eq. (19.47) is that whether incomplete markets makes the economy more or less sensitive to news depends, in general, on the news horizon.[10] In particular, the impact of news with anticipation horizon **m** on the job finding rate is given by $\Gamma_\eta^s \Phi^{-m}$ (where $s = A, r$). Since market incompleteness implies more discounting of future shocks through Φ, even when risk is countercyclical, it is potentially the case that while news with short anticipation horizons are amplified by incomplete markets, the opposite may be true for news about shocks far out in the future.

We examine this in Fig. 19.3 where we plot the response of the job finding rate in the first month to technology news for alternative news horizons going from one month up to four years. We show with the line without markers the incomplete markets economy and with the line with circle markers the complete markets case.[11] For short news horizons, the amplification mechanism dominates, but as the horizon grows, discounting becomes more important. Interestingly, in the incomplete markets case, when the news horizon goes above three years, agents practically ignore the news while they still have a sizeable effect under complete markets.

---

[10] We thank Marios Angeletos for suggesting this analysis.

[11] The calibration is the same as the benchmark model apart from price contracts assumed to correspond to one year.

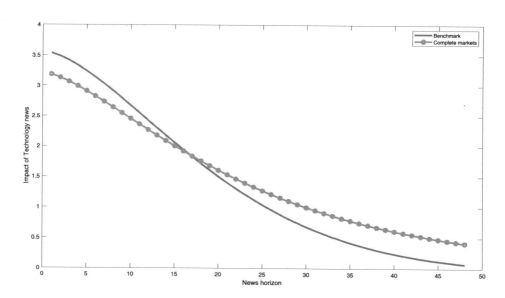

FIGURE 19.3 Amplification vs. Stabilization and the News Horizon

Notes: The figure shows percentage deviations of the job finding rate in response to technology news under incomplete markets (blue line) vs. complete markets (orange circled line).

19.3.2.2 *Monetary policy news*

In Fig. 19.4 we report the impact of 6-month-ahead forward guidance in the shape of a preannounced cut in the nominal interest rate. A preannounced interest rate cut stimulates the economy from the time of its announcement because firms start hiring once the news arrive which stimulates goods demand, and is inflationary both ahead of *and after* the monetary policy innovation. Given the response of interest rates to inflation, and the strength of the demand effect, nominal interest rates rise above their steady-state level even *after* the negative monetary policy innovation is implemented.

Fig. 19.5 examines the impact of forward guidance on the job finding rate in more detail. Symmetrically to technology news, the response of the economy to forward guidance are approximately the same in the baseline calibration (continuous line) and when assuming complete markets (assuming a minute consumption drop to job loss – the dotted line). A high real wage elasticity (dashed–circled line) instead implies stabilization of forward guidance shocks under incomplete markets, a finding that is consistent with McKay et al. (2016) and McKay et al. (2017). Increasing the degree of price rigidities to one year price contracts (dashed–diamond line) amplifies the impact of forward guidance. This result is explained by two properties of the incomplete markets economy. First, the stickier are prices, the more firms respond to shocks by adjusting hiring rather than prices which induces precautionary savings. Secondly, the smaller rise in inflation implies less response of nominal interest rates which amplifies further the impact of the news shock.

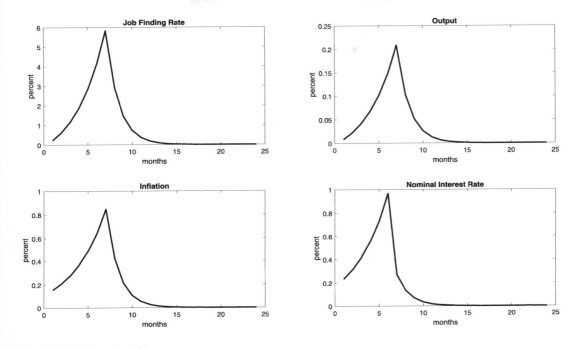

FIGURE 19.4 Forward Guidance

Notes: The figure shows percentage deviations of the variables from their steady-state values.

19.4 Channels underlying savings behavior

Since saving decisions of households play a central role in the amplification mechanism, we now delve deeper into the underlying behavior. We do so in the baseline economy calibrated as in Table 19.1. Recall that in equilibrium all households hold zero bonds. It is, however, important to note that is an *equilibrium* outcome. Unconstrained households (the employed) are in principle able to increase or reduce savings, but they choose not to do so in equilibrium. Underlying this decision, there are several opposing forces, which exactly offset each other. We uncover them by decomposing the savings response.

Let IRF^x be a T-length vector containing the Impulse Response Function (IRF) of an aggregated household decision variable x to an aggregate shock. Here, we study the response of aggregate bond holdings ($x = \mathbf{B}$) to a TFP shock. Following Auclert et al. (2021), we can express the model in sequence space and decompose the response (up to a linear approximation) as

$$IRF^{\mathbf{B}} = J^{\mathbf{B}}_{\mathbf{R}} \cdot IRF^{\mathbf{R}} + J^{\mathbf{B}}_{\mathbf{\Pi}} \cdot IRF^{\mathbf{\Pi}} + J^{\mathbf{B}}_{\eta} \cdot IRF^{\eta} + J^{\mathbf{B}}_{\mathbf{w}} \cdot IRF^{\mathbf{w}},$$

where J^x_y is a $T \times T$ matrix containing the *Jacobian* of variable x with respect to input variable y. The input variables are the equilibrium objects taken as given by the households, i.e., $y \in \{\mathbf{R}, \mathbf{\Pi}, \eta, \mathbf{w}\}$. As explained by Auclert et al. (2021), the kth column of J^x_y is the responses of x with respect to an

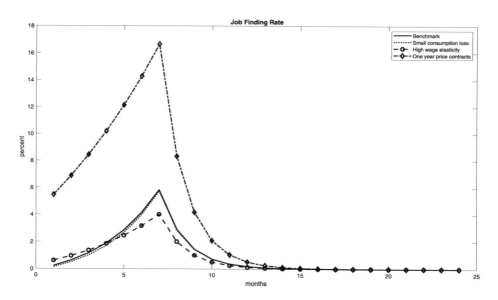

FIGURE 19.5 Determinants of Impact of Monetary Policy News

Notes: The figure shows percentage deviations of the variables from their steady-state values.

anticipated one time-change in variable y, k periods ahead, i.e., the partial-equilibrium responses to news shocks.[12]

We now apply the decomposition to the response of bond holdings to a TFP shock, based on the calibration described above. Fig. 19.6 plots the responses of TFP, as well as the variables $\mathbf{R}$, $\mathbf{\Pi}$, η, and $\mathbf{w}$, whereas Fig. 19.7 shows the decomposition of $\mathbf{B}$.[13] Following the shock, the job finding rate increases, as firms post more vacancies. This reduces the households' savings desire, as the precautionary motive weakens. On the other hand, wages increase somewhat, which strengthens the desire to save. As the economy expands and aggregate demand increases, inflation rises, that is, the model features "Keynesian Supply" effects, see Guerrieri et al. (2022). The persistent increase in inflation further weakens the households' desire to save, as it pushes down the real interest rate. The aggregate demand effects thus amplify the saving response. At the same time, in response to the increase in inflation, the central bank increases the nominal interest rate, which strengthens the household's desire to save. On net, these four forces cancel out, so that bond holdings are constant in equilibrium. However, the increase in inflation associated with the increase in aggregate demand must imply higher output, via the New Keynesian Phillips Curve. Quantitatively, the underlying forces are substantial, except for the wage response (as

---

[12] While Auclert et al. (2021) exploit the above decomposition to solve for equilibria in the sequence space. We instead solve the model in state space using a standard linearization method, but use the decomposition to improve our understanding of the savings channels. In Appendix 19.B we show how we implement the decomposition.

[13] This decomposition is entirely based on the saving decisions of the employed households, who are unconstrained. The unemployed households are constrained and do not react to prices, even in partial equilibrium.

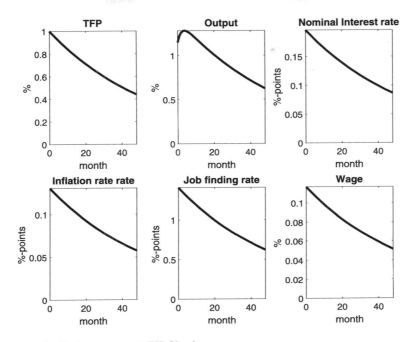

FIGURE 19.6 Impact of a Contemporaneous TFP Shock

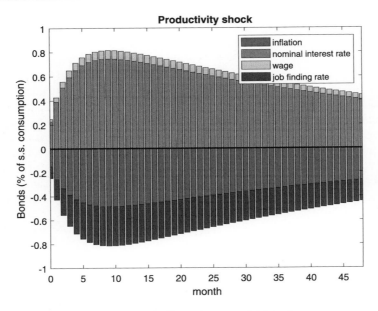

FIGURE 19.7 Decomposition of the Response of Bond Holdings to a TFP Shock

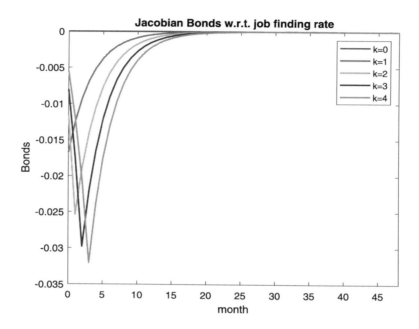

FIGURE 19.8 Jacobian of Bond Holdings with Respect to the Job Finding Rate

real wages are relatively sticky in the baseline calibration). The increase in the job finding rate corresponds to an increase in consumption of up to 2.5%, whereas the fall in inflation corresponds to a consumption increase of up to 4.1%. These effects are large, considering the fact that TFP increases only by 1%.

We can obtain further insights into the workings of the model by inspecting the Jacobians directly. Fig. 19.8 plots the first five columns of $J_\eta^\mathbf{B}$, the Jacobian of bonds with respect to the job finding rate. The first column ($k = 0$) is the response of bonds to a purely transitory and unanticipated increase in the job finding rate in the present period. This column is zero, since only the *expected* job finding rate enters into the Euler equation. Considering columns $k = 1, 2, 3, 4$, corresponding to anticipated increases in the job finding rate 1–4 periods ahead, we observe the Jacobians are negative, as households' desire to save reduces when job finding rates increase. Moreover, the Jacobians reach their minima in the period before the change in the job finding rate materializes. Nonetheless, the impact is substantially negative also in other periods, indicating anticipation and propagation.

Finally, let us consider the Marginal Propensity to Consume (MPC). One may be inclined to think that all households have an MPC of one, given that no households hold bonds. This, however, is not the case. The reason is that the employed households are not constrained, and would save part of any individual windfall in income, i.e., their MPC lies below one. Again, the fact that all households end up with zero savings is an equilibrium result. We can compute the intertemporal aggregate MPC matrix in the model as

$$MPC^C = (1 - \mathbf{u}) \cdot J_\mathbf{w}^{C_e}(1, 1) + \mathbf{u},$$

where $J_{\mathbf{w}}^{\mathbf{C_e}}(1, 1)$ is the upper left element of the Jacobian of consumption of the employed households with respect to the wage (or any other income flow), i.e., their contemporaneous MPC (the MPC of the unemployed equals one). We find an aggregate MPC in the first month of about 30%, which is roughly in line with estimates in the empirical literature.[14]

19.5 Noise shocks

Following Lorenzoni (2009), an extensive line of work has considered the extent to which "demand shocks" brought about by expectational shocks can generate macroeconomic fluctuations in models with imperfect information. In particular, in environments where agents receive noisy signals about changes in economic fundamentals, pure noise shocks may generate economic fluctuations which are transmitted over time through agents updating their beliefs and through standard business cycle transmission mechanisms, see, e.g., Barsky and Sims (2012), Blanchard et al. (2013), Boz et al. (2011), or Faccini and Melosi (2022). In what follows, we examine the role of incomplete markets in propagating such noise shocks. We extend the benchmark model in various dimensions and estimate formally key structural parameters, so that we can quantify the importance of incomplete markets.

19.5.1 Model

We retain the modeling of households outlined earlier, but now assume that capitalists are risk averse, symmetrically to working households:

$$\mathbf{U}_{i,s}^c = \widehat{\mathbb{E}}_s \sum_{h=0}^{\infty} \beta_c^h \frac{\mathbf{c}_{i,s+h}^{1-\mu} - 1}{1 - \mu}.$$

Apart from this, the three major changes concern the assumptions on the shocks to the economy, the information structure, and on technology.

Technology. We generalize the production technology to include capital and allow for variable capacity utilization,

$$\mathbf{y}_{j,s} = \exp\left(\mathbf{A}_s\right) \left(\mathbf{z}_{j,s} \mathbf{k}_{j,s}\right)^{\tau} \mathbf{n}_{j,s}^{1-\tau}, \tag{19.62}$$

where $\mathbf{z}_{j,s} \mathbf{k}_{j,s}$ is the input of effective capital, the product of the capital utilization rate, $\mathbf{z}_{j,s}$ and the capital stock, $\mathbf{k}_{j,s}$. The parameter $\tau \in (0, 1)$ is the elasticity of output to the input of effective capital.

Firms own the capital stock and the law of motion of capital is given as

$$\mathbf{k}_{j,s+1} = \left(1 - \delta\left(\mathbf{z}_{j,s}\right)\right) \mathbf{k}_{j,s} + \mathbf{i}_{j,s}, \tag{19.63}$$

where $\mathbf{i}_{j,s}$ denotes gross investment; $\delta\left(\mathbf{z}_{j,s}\right)$ is the depreciation rate which we assume is an increasing and convex function of the capital utilization rate, $\delta', \delta'' \geq 0$.

---

[14] In this calculation we let the mass of capitalists be zero, for simplicity. Otherwise the capitalists should be added to the unemployed as agents with an MPC of one, given that they are at the liquidity constraint.

Price setting. The firms' price setting in this setting has an additional term for the cost of the acquisition of capital. Firms maximize

$$\Phi_{j,s} = \widehat{\mathbb{E}}_s \sum_{h=0}^{\infty} \Lambda_{j,s,s+h} \left[\frac{P_{j,s+h}}{P_{s+h}} y_{j,s+h} - w_{s+h} n_{s+h} - \kappa v_{s+h} \right.$$

$$\left. - i_{s+h} - \frac{\phi}{2} \left(\frac{P_{j,s+h}}{P_{j,s+h-1}} - 1 \right)^2 y_{s+h} \right], \tag{19.64}$$

subject to (19.8), (19.6), and (19.62)–(19.63); $\Lambda_{j,s,s+h}$ denotes the capitalists' stochastic discount factor between periods s and $s + h$. In the symmetric equilibrium, this delivers the first order condition (19.22) but with the new definition of marginal costs given as

$$mc_s = \frac{1}{(1 - \tau) \exp(A_s) (z_s k_s / n_s)^\tau} \left(w_s + \frac{\kappa}{q_s} - (1 - \omega) \widehat{\mathbb{E}}_s \Lambda_{s,s+1} \frac{\kappa}{q_{s+1}} \right). \tag{19.65}$$

The first-order conditions for capital accumulation and for optimal capital utilization are:

$$1 = \widehat{\mathbb{E}}_s \Lambda_{c,s,s+1} \left((1 - \delta(z_s)) + \tau z_{s+1} \exp(A_{s+1}) (z_{s+1} k_{s+1})^{\tau-1} n_{s+1}^{1-\tau} \right), \tag{19.66}$$

$$\delta'(z_s) = \exp(A_s) (z_s k_s)^{\tau-1} n_s^{1-\tau}. \tag{19.67}$$

Shocks and information. The main new feature of the model relates to the information structure. We assume that the technology shock process is given as the sum of a persistent, A^P, and a transitory component:

$$A_s = A_s^P + \epsilon_s^T, \tag{19.68}$$

$$A_s^P = \rho_A A_{s-1}^P + \epsilon_s^P, \tag{19.69}$$

where ϵ_s^T, ϵ_s^P are two random shocks that are mutually orthogonal and normally distributed with means 0 and variances σ_T^2 and σ_P^2, respectively. Agents observe A_s but not the persistent and the transitory shock separately. In addition to observing A, agents also receive a noisy signal, Υ_s, about the persistent component of productivity,

$$\Upsilon_s = A_s + \epsilon_s^S, \tag{19.70}$$

where ϵ_s^S is normally distributed with mean zero and variance σ_S^2 and assumed orthogonal to the true productivity (and monetary policy shocks). Thus, innovations to ϵ_s^S may impact on agents' expectations but are pure noise.

Agents draw inference on the unobserved persistent component of productivity with the Kalman filter, see also Chapter 23 in this Handbook. Let $A_{s,t}^P$ denote the date t expectation of A_s^P. This expectation follows the law of motion

$$A_{s,s}^P = G A_{s-1,s-1}^P + K x_s^o, \tag{19.71}$$

where $\mathbf{x}_s^o = (\mathbf{A}_s, \Upsilon_s)'$ are the signals that the agents use for updating the beliefs about $\mathbf{A}_s^P$. Let $\epsilon_s = (\epsilon_s^P, \epsilon_s^T, \epsilon_s^S)'$, the vector $\mathbf{x}_s^0$ then follows the stochastic process

$$\mathbf{x}_s^o = \mathbf{CA}_s^P + \mathbf{D}\epsilon_s. \tag{19.72}$$

Monetary policy. We generalize the specification of the monetary policy rule in two dimensions. First, we introduce interest rate smoothing

$$\mathbf{R}_s = \mathbf{R}_{s-1}^{\delta_R} \left(\bar{R} \left(\frac{\Pi_s}{\bar{\Pi}} \right)^{\delta_\Pi} \right)^{1-\delta_R} e_s^R, \tag{19.73}$$

where e_s^R is the innovation to monetary policy. This innovation is given as

$$e_s^R = \epsilon_s^R + \psi \epsilon_s^S, \tag{19.74}$$

which accommodates the possibility that the central bank may react to noise shock directly. For simplicity, we have removed monetary policy responses to labor market tightness.[15]

19.5.2 Estimating the parameters

We are interested in evaluating the extent to which incomplete markets features affect the economy's response to expectational shocks. We estimate the deep structural parameters using an indirect inference approach.

19.5.2.1 Estimating the impact of noise shocks

We first estimate the impact of shocks unrelated to economic fundamentals in the U.S. We will think of the response of the economy to such shocks as estimates of how noise shocks impact on the economy. We derive these shocks by identifying autonomous changes in survey-based consumer sentiment data.[16]

For this purpose, we follow Lagerborg et al. (2021) and estimate the impact of autonomous changes in consumer confidence using an IV strategy adopting the Proxy SVAR estimator developed by Mertens and Ravn (2013). We estimate a VAR for the vector of observables, $\mathbf{Y}_t$, namely

$$\mathbf{Y}_s = \mathbf{A}(L)\mathbf{Y}_{s-1} + \mathbf{u}_s, \tag{19.75}$$

where the reduced form innovations, $\mathbf{u}_s$, are linear combinations of (unobserved) structural shocks, $\mathbf{e}_s$, namely

$$\mathbf{u}_s = \Omega_0 \mathbf{e}_s, \tag{19.76}$$

where Ω_0 is invertible and $\mathbf{Y}_s$ is assumed to be second-order stationary.

Let the first observable, $y_{1,s}$, be consumer confidence. Our aim is to identify an autonomous component of $e_{1,s}$, and then examine how such shocks impact on the economy. We do so with an external

---

[15]   When estimating the parameters, we typically have found little evidence of $\delta_\theta \neq 0$.
[16]   See also Chapter 18 in this Handbook for an alternative use of expectations data when estimating DSGE models.

instrument, z_s, which is required to fulfill the following identifying assumptions:

$$\mathbb{E}\left(e_{1,s}z_s\right) = \omega \neq 0, \tag{19.77}$$

$$\mathbb{E}\left(e_{i,s}z_s\right) = 0, \quad i \neq 1, \tag{19.78}$$

where Eqs. (19.77)–(19.78) are the relevance and exogeneity conditions.

We specify the vector of observables as $\mathbf{Y}_s = (ci_s, y_s, ur_s, r_s, cpi_s)'$ where ci_s is the University of Michigan's Index of Consumer Expectations, y_s is real industrial production, ur_s is the civilian unemployment rate, r_s is the federal funds rate, and cpi_s is the CPI. All variables except the federal funds rate are in logarithms and detrended with a fourth-order polynomial in time (including the federal funds rate). The sample period is 1965:1–2007:8 and the data are monthly. We use 18 lags in the VAR.

Following Lagerborg et al. (2021) the instrument adopted for $e_{1,s}$ is fatalities in public mass shootings in the U.S. which had seven or more victims excluding the perpetrator, see Lagerborg et al. (2021) for a discussion. We do not literally think of mass shootings as a measure for noise shocks to agents' information sets, but we use it as instrument to derive estimates of the dynamic causal effects of changes in consumer confidence unrelated to economic fundamentals. We find that the instrument is significant in the first stage and the weak instrument Robust F-statistic is 8.8. Given this, we adopt weak instrument robust inference using the procedure proposed in Montiel-Olea et al. (2021).

Fig. 19.9 illustrates the dynamic causal effects of a 1% deterioration in consumer confidence.[17] We show point estimates (continuous lines) along with 68% confidence bands (dotted lines). The results indicate that an autonomous deterioration in consumer confidence induces a recession which sees output dropping and unemployment rising. The drop in output is significant at the 90% level for forecast horizons going up to two years and the same is true for the rise in unemployment. At the same time, we find a drop in the nominal interest rate and an insignificant rise in the price level.[18]

19.5.2.2 *Estimation of structural parameters*

We estimate key structural parameters using a simulation estimator. We split the vector of structural parameters into Θ_1 and Θ_2; Θ_1 contains structural parameters that we calibrate rather than formally estimate discussed below; Θ_2 is the vector of parameters that we estimate.

Parameter Θ_2 is found by solving the following quadratic minimization problem:

$$\widehat{\Theta}_2 = \mathbf{argmin}_{\Theta_2}\left[\left(\widehat{\Lambda}_T^d - \Lambda_T^m\left(\Theta_2|\Theta_1\right)\right)' \mathbf{W}\left(\widehat{\Lambda}_T^d - \Lambda_T^m\left(\Theta_2|\Theta_1\right)\right)\right], \tag{19.79}$$

where $\widehat{\Lambda}_T^d$ is a vector of moments that are matched, $\Lambda_T^m\left(\Theta_2|\Theta_1\right)$ denotes the vector of equivalent moments from the theoretical model, and $\mathbf{W}$ is a weighting matrix.

We include in the vector of moments that we match (i) the F-statistic from the first-stage regression of the proxy SVAR model estimated earlier, (ii) the standard deviation of detrended TFP, and (iii) the impulse responses of consumer confidence, output, unemployment, the price level and the nominal

---

[17] Lagerborg et al. (2021) use a larger dimensional vector of observables and demonstrate the robustness of the results in a number of different dimensions.

[18] Ambrocio (2020) finds that increases in household income uncertainty estimated on European data appear to be inflationary. For the responses of other variables, see Lagerborg et al. (2021).

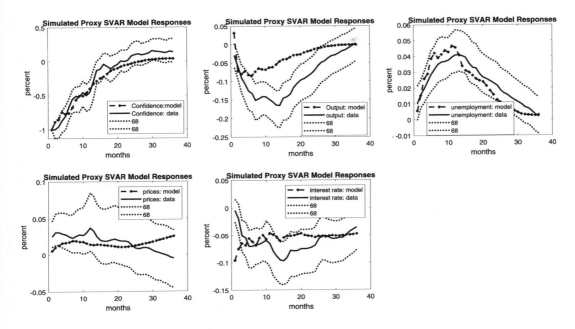

FIGURE 19.9 Model and Empirical Responses to Confidence Shock

Notes: The figure illustrates the proxy SVAR impact of consumer confidence shocks in the data and in the model.

interest rate in response to a sentiment shock for a forecast horizon of 36 months. The first-stage F-statistic is included because it helps identifying the importance of measurement error discussed further below. The standard deviation of TFP matters for the weights in the Kalman filter. We obtain estimates of capacity unadjusted TFP from Fernald (2012) detrended with a fourth-order time polynomial. This delivers an estimate of the standard deviation of TFP of 3.3% per month. We use the standard errors of the empirical estimates of the impulse responses to form the weighting matrix.

To match the estimated impulse responses we need to form a theoretical counterpart of the index of consumer expectations. We follow Barsky and Sims (2012) and assume that consumer confidence is given as:

$$\mathbf{CI}_s = (1 - \rho_{CI})\,\bar{\mathbf{CI}} + \rho_{CI}\mathbf{CI}_{s-1} + \mathbf{e}_{CI,s}, \tag{19.80}$$

$$\mathbf{e}_{CI,s} = \vartheta_1\left(\mathbf{A}_s - \rho_A\mathbf{A}^P_{s-1,s-1}\right) + \vartheta_2\left(\mathbf{A}^P_{s,s} - \rho_A\mathbf{A}^P_{s-1,s-1}\right) + \varepsilon_{CI,s}, \tag{19.81}$$

where $\rho_{CI} \in (-1, 1)$ is the persistence of consumer confidence measure, and $\varepsilon_{CI,s} \sim \mathcal{N}(0, \sigma_C^2)$ and orthogonal to other innovations.

The theoretical equivalents of the empirical impulse responses are computed as follows. Start with a guess on Θ_2^0:

Step 1. Given Θ_2^0, generate 200 sequences of artificial data from the model for sample periods of $T + R$ observations where T is the number of observations in the empirical sample. Eliminate the first R observations. Denote the $T \times 5$ vector of the model-based observables for the jth artificial sample by $\tilde{X}_j \left(\Theta_2^0 | \Theta_1 \right)$. Let $\tilde{\varepsilon}_j^S \left(\Theta_2^0 | \Theta_1 \right)$ be the $T \times 1$ vector of sentiment shocks.

Step 2. Add a small amount of measurement error to $\tilde{X}_j \left(\Theta_2^0 | \Theta_1 \right)$. Let $\widehat{X}^j \left(\Theta_2^0 | \Theta_1 \right)$ denote the resulting artificial samples of X and detrend it with a fourth-order time polynomial.

Step 3. Add measurement error to $\tilde{\varepsilon}_j^S \left(\Theta_2^0 | \Theta_1 \right)$ to obtain $\widehat{\varepsilon}_j^S \left(\Theta_2^0 | \Theta_1 \right) = \tilde{\varepsilon}_j^S \left(\Theta_2^0 | \Theta_1 \right) + m_j$ where $m_j \sim$ n.i.d.$(0, \sigma_m^2)$. Form the vector $\varepsilon_j^{*S} \left(\Theta_2 | \Theta_1 \right)$ where $\varepsilon_j^{*S} \left(\Theta_2^0 | \Theta_1 \right) = \widehat{\varepsilon}_j^S \left(\Theta_2^0 | \Theta_1 \right)$ for the K largest (absolute) values of $\left[\tilde{\varepsilon}_{ji}^S \left(\Theta_2^0 | \Theta_1 \right) \right]_{i=1}^{T}$ and zero otherwise where K is chosen to be the same as the number of shootings in the data.

Step 4. For each artificial dataset, estimate the model equivalents of the empirical proxy-SVAR moments using $\varepsilon_j^{*S} \left(\Theta_2^0 | \Theta_1 \right)$ as an instrument for $\mathbf{CI}_j \left(\Theta_2^0 | \Theta_1 \right)$. Let $\Lambda_T^m \left(\Theta_2^0 | \Theta_1 \right)^j$ denote the simulated equivalents of the vector of empirical moments for the jth artificial sample.

Step 5. Average the moments over the 200 replications, yielding $\Lambda_T^m \left(\Theta_2^0 | \Theta_1 \right)$.

Step 6. Evaluate the loss function (19.79). If this is smaller than ε^{crit} let $\widehat{\Theta}_2 = \Theta_2^0$. Otherwise update the guess for Θ_2^0 and return to Step 1.

The measurement error added in Step 2 is introduced to avoid stochastic singularity of the VAR estimated on the artificial data. We calibrate this source of measurement error. The measurement error added in Step 3, instead, is introduced in order to match the first-stage F-statistic. The selection of the K largest values of the noise shock as the instrument emulates the fact that we use fatalities in the K most dramatic shootings in the data as the instrument for consumer confidence in the data.

19.5.2.3 *Calibration and estimation results*

We calibrate parameters that are either hard to estimate or for which we believe there are good grounds for parametrizing using outside information rather than estimating. The vector of parameters that we calibrate at monthly frequency is $\Theta_1 = \left(\overline{R}, \beta_c, \xi, \mu, \gamma, \overline{u}, \overline{\eta}, \kappa, \tau, \delta\left(1\right), \delta''\left(1\right), \gamma, \overline{\Pi}, \phi, \delta_R, \sigma_R^2 \right)$, summarized in Table 19.2.

Most parameters are calibrated as in Table 19.1. We discuss the calibration of the extra parameters here. First, we allow for a 3% equity premium annually. Since capitalists do not face any idiosyncratic earnings risk, the latter determines their intertemporal discount factor at $\beta_c = 1.07^{-1/12}$.

Next, we assume that the steady-state unemployment rate equals 6.5%. Together with the calibrated monthly job finding rate, this implies that the monthly job separation rate, ω, equals 3.3%. Next, we assume that the vacancy cost parameter, κ, is consistent with an average hiring cost of 4.5% of the quarterly steady-state wage. Given these values, the steady-state incomplete markets wedge, $\Theta^{SS} = 1.0015$, and households' intertemporal discount factor is determined as $\beta_w = 1/\overline{R}\Theta^{SS} = 0.9854$.

We assume that the elasticity of output to employment, $1 - \tau$, is 65%. We normalize the steady-state capacity utilization rate, $\overline{z} = 1$ and calibrate the steady-state depreciation rate, $\delta\left(1\right)$, to match a capital-output ratio of 25 at the monthly frequency. This implies that $\delta\left(1\right) = 0.0024$; $\delta'\left(1\right)$ is calibrated to induce the steady-state capacity utilization of 1, and we set $\delta''\left(1\right)$ equal to 1 as well. The parameter ϕ

Table 19.2 Calibration.

Parameter	Meaning	Value
$\overline{R}$	Steady-state gross real interest rate	$1.04^{1/12}$
β_c	capitalists' discount factor	$1.07^{-1/12}$
μ	Coefficient of risk aversion	2
ξ	Home production	$0.82\,\overline{w}$
γ	Elasticity of substitution	6
$\overline{u}$	Steady-state unemployment rate	6.5%
$\overline{\eta}$	Job finding rate	0.34
ϑ	Steady-state hiring cost, fraction of wage bill	0.135
α	Matching function elasticity	0.6
τ	Output elasticity to capital	0.4
$\overline{K}/\overline{Y}$	Steady-state capital-output ratio	25
$\delta''(1)/\delta'(1)$	Elasticity of depreciation to capital utilization	1
p_{dur}	Average price contract length	6
φ	Measure of capitalists	0.001
$\overline{\Pi}$	Inflation target	1
δ_R	Interest rate smoothing	$0.7^{1/3}$
σ_R	Standard deviation of monetary policy shock	0.01

Notes: One period corresponds to a calendar month.

which determines the amount of nominal rigidities is calibrated by assuming an average price-contract length of six months which implies $\phi = 232.57$. We calibrate the amount of interest rate smoothing to $\delta_R = 0.7^{1/3}$, consistent with estimates of Rudebusch (2002). We set the variance of the monetary policy shocks to $\sigma_R^2 = 0.001^2$ which corresponds roughly to the variance of the Romer and Romer (2004) monetary policy shocks series.

We estimate the vector of parameters $\Theta_2 = (\chi, \delta_\pi, \psi, \rho_A, \sigma_T, \sigma_S, \sigma_P, \rho_{CI}, \vartheta_1, \vartheta_2, \sigma_C)$. We scale σ_T and σ_S by σ_P, and therefore estimate the ratio of the standard deviations of the transitory productivity shock and the noise shock to the standard deviation of the innovation to the persistent component of TFP. The parameter estimates are reported in Table 19.3.

Perhaps the most interesting parameter estimate is χ, the real wage elasticity, which we estimate to 2.83%. Given this parameter, it follows that $\Theta^F = 0.0046$ indicating that the endogenous earnings risk is countercyclical. We find a very moderate response of the nominal interest rate to inflation with δ_π estimated at 1.11. We also find that noise shocks impact on the monetary policy innovation. One interpretation of this result is that monetary policy responds to consumer confidence.

We estimate $\widehat{\rho}_A = 0.922$. The variance of transitory productivity shocks is estimated to be around one third higher than the variance of the innovations to the persistent component and we find substantial variance of noise shocks. Finally, we find $\widehat{\rho}_{CI} = 0.913$. The revisions to consumer confidence are dominated by the impact of changes in the subjective forecast of the persistent component of productivity relative to productivity innovations.

Table 19.3 Estimated Parameters.

Parameter	Meaning	Value
χ	Real wage elasticity	0.0283
δ_π	Monetary policy response to inflation	1.11
ψ	Monetary policy response to noise	0.0151
ρ_A	AR(1) coefficient of persistent technology shock	0.922
σ_P	Standard deviation of persistent technology shock	0.00146
σ_T/σ_P	Std. deviation of transitory technology shock relative to std. dev. of persistent technology shock	1.170
σ_S/σ_P	Standard deviation of noise shock relative to std. dev. of persistent technology shock	1.057
ρ_{CI}	Persistence of confidence	0.913
ϑ_1	Response of confidence to productivity innovation	4.528
ϑ_2	Response of confidence to change in forecast of persistent component of productivity	17.18
σ_c	Standard deviation of measurement error of confidence	0.0041
σ_m	Standard deviation of measurement error of proxy	0.000015

Notes: One period corresponds to a calendar month.

The dotted lines in Fig. 19.9 depict the simulated impulse response functions given $\widehat{\Theta}_2$. We match very well the impulse responses of consumer confidence and unemployment. The match to output is also good although output in the model is less affected by confidence shocks than in the U.S. data. As in the U.S. data, we find that the theoretical impulse responses indicate a small increase in inflation and a drop in the nominal interest rate in response to worsening consumer confidence.

19.5.3 Implications

Fig. 19.10 illustrates the expectations that agents form about the persistent component of technology conditional on either innovations to the persistent component of productivity or pure noise shocks. A positive innovation to the persistent productivity component leads agents to revise upward their estimates of the persistent component of productivity but initially by less than its actual increase. As higher productivity persists over time, agents' subjective expectations eventually catch up with the true component. A positive noise shock is initially confused with an increase in the persistent TFP component, but this confusion dissipates around three months after the noise shock.

Fig. 19.11 depicts the response of the economy to a negative noise shock. The shock triggers worsening consumer confidence and a recession which lasts five to six months. The recession witnesses a reduction in vacancy postings, rising unemployment, a drop in the job finding rate, lower output and consumption, and a drop in the utilization rate of the capital stock. On the nominal side, the central bank cuts the nominal interest rate both because of the contraction in demand, and because of the direct monetary response to consumer confidence. The monetary expansion induces a sustained increase in inflation from the second month onward. Therefore, while the noise shock generates a contraction in goods demand, it is inflationary.

In Fig. 19.12 we contrast the impact of noise shocks in the benchmark model with two alternative economies. In the first we increase the wage elasticity to $\chi = 0.1$ which makes earnings risk acycli-

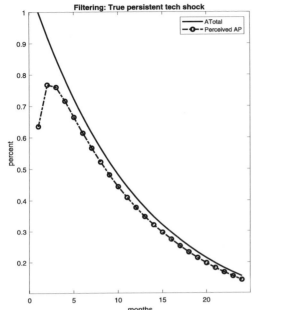
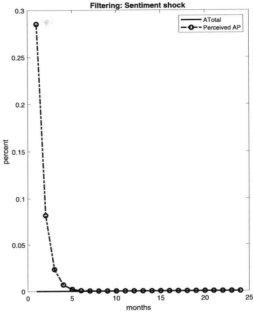

FIGURE 19.10 Beliefs and Shocks

Notes: The left panel illustrates the impact of a 1% increase in the persistent component of technology. The right panel illustrates the responses to a 1% positive noise shock.

cal (dashed–circled lines), in the second we reduce the consumption loss to 1% so that markets are approximately complete (dashed–squared lines). In order to focus entirely on these issues, we assume that $\psi = 0$ so that there is no direct monetary policy response to the noise shocks. In the benchmark economy, the drop in confidence generates an increase in unemployment that is almost an order of magnitude higher than under complete markets or when assuming acyclical earning risk. This much higher sensitivity to expectational shocks is echoed by the impact on the job finding rate, aggregate output, and aggregate consumption. The amplification mechanism derives the precautionary savings motive and the demand–supply interaction generated by price stickiness. When the consumption loss is small, the demand-side impact of expectational shocks is substantially reduced and noise shocks have only minor effects. Similarly, acyclical income risk neutralizes the impact of higher job loss risk on the precautionary savings motive. Thus, incomplete markets economies with countercyclical risk are much more prone to noise shocks than complete markets economies or acyclical risk economies.

19.6 Sunspots

In this section we demonstrate that incomplete markets in itself may be a source of purely expectations driven fluctuations. To this end, we employ the simple model from Section 19.2 of this chapter and

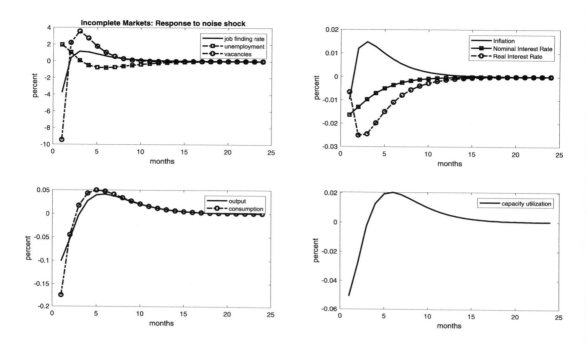

FIGURE 19.11 The Impact of Noise Shocks

Notes: The figure illustrates impact of a 1% negative noise shock.

abstract from stochastic changes in TFP and monetary policy shocks. We also retain the assumption of risk-averse capitalists.

Crucially, we now impose the nonnegativity constraint on firms' vacancy postings that we have ignored so far. We will show that under some circumstances, incomplete markets may generate self-fulfilling expectational equilibria in which firms stop posting vacancies and unemployment rises. In order to avoid a complete meltdown of the economy in this equilibrium, we assume that frictional hiring applies only to a subset of the hires made by firms. We implement this by modifying Eq. (19.9) with the assumption that a measure of vacancies $\mathbf{v_F} \geq 0$ can be posted for free, while each vacancy in excess of this measure, $\mathbf{v}_{j,s} - \mathbf{v_F}$, comes at the flow cost $\kappa > 0$ per period. We impose that

$$\mathbf{v}_{j,s} \geq \mathbf{v_F}, \quad \forall j, s. \tag{19.82}$$

One can think of free vacancies as capturing the fact that some jobs may be filled through informal channels without the need for firms to engage in costly hiring efforts.

The stationary equilibria of the economy are the solution to the following set of equations (letting "ss" denote a variable in a stationary equilibrium):

$$1 = \beta \frac{\overline{\mathbf{R}}}{\overline{\Pi}^{\delta_\Pi}} \Pi_{ss}^{\delta_\Pi - 1} \left[1 + \omega (1 - \eta_{ss}) \left(\left(\frac{\xi}{\mathbf{w}_{ss}} \right)^{-\mu} - 1 \right) \right], \tag{19.83}$$

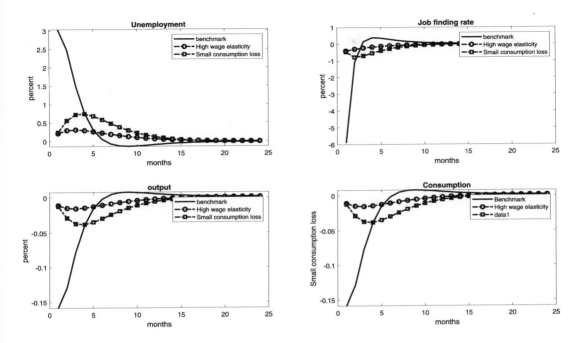

FIGURE 19.12 Noise Shocks and Incomplete Markets

Notes: The figure illustrates impact of a 1% negative noise shock.

$$\mathbf{mc}_{ss} = \frac{\gamma - 1}{\gamma} + \frac{\phi}{\gamma}(1 - \beta)(\mathbf{\Pi}_{ss} - 1)\,\mathbf{\Pi}_{ss}, \tag{19.84}$$

$$\mathbf{mc}_{ss} = \frac{1}{A}\left(\mathbf{w}_{ss} + (1 - (1 - \omega)\beta)\left(\frac{\kappa}{\mathbf{q}_{ss}} - \lambda_{v,ss}\right)\right), \tag{19.85}$$

$$\mathbf{w}_{ss} = \overline{w}\left(\frac{\eta_{ss}}{\overline{\eta}}\right)^{\chi}, \tag{19.86}$$

$$\mathbf{q}_{ss} = \overline{m}\left(\frac{\eta_{ss}}{\overline{m}}\right)^{-\alpha/(1-\alpha)}, \tag{19.87}$$

$$\mathbf{n}_{ss} = \frac{\eta_{ss}(1 - \psi)}{1 - (1 - \omega)(1 - \eta_{ss})}, \tag{19.88}$$

$$0 = \lambda_{v,ss}(\mathbf{v}_{ss} - \mathbf{v}_{\mathbf{F}}), \tag{19.89}$$

where $\lambda_v \geq 0$ is the Kuhn–Tucker multiplier on (19.82). Using (19.85)–(19.87), conditions (19.83) and (19.84) can be summarized by the following two equations in $(\mathbf{\Pi}_{ss}, \eta_{ss})$:

$$1 = \beta\overline{R}\left(\frac{\mathbf{\Pi_{ss}}}{\overline{\Pi}}\right)^{\delta_{\Pi}}\frac{1}{\mathbf{\Pi_{ss}}}\Theta^{ss}(\eta), \tag{19.90}$$

$$(\Pi_{\mathbf{ss}} - 1)\,\Pi_{\mathbf{ss}} = \frac{1 - \gamma + \frac{\gamma}{A}\left(\overline{w}\left(\frac{\eta_{\mathbf{ss}}}{\overline{\eta}}\right)^{\chi} + \left(\kappa\bar{m}\left(\frac{\eta_{\mathbf{ss}}}{\bar{m}}\right)^{-\alpha/(1-\alpha)} - \lambda_{v,ss}\right)(1 - (1-\omega)\beta)\right)}{1 - \phi\beta}, \qquad (19.91)$$

where $\Theta^{ss}(\eta)$ is given as

$$\Theta^{ss}(\eta) \equiv \left[1 + \omega(1 - \eta_{\mathbf{ss}})\left(\left(\frac{\xi}{\overline{w}\left(\frac{\eta_{\mathbf{ss}}}{\overline{\eta}}\right)^{\chi}}\right)^{-\mu} - 1\right)\right].$$

Let $\Pi^{PC}(\eta)$ be the inflation rate consistent with Eq. (19.91) as an implicit function of η. This schedule is vertical at the job finding rate corresponding to $\mathbf{v_{ss}} = \mathbf{v_F}$ and otherwise upward sloping as long as $\Pi > 1/2$, an assumption that we will impose. Similarly, let $\Pi^{EE}(\eta)$ denote the inflation rate as a function of the job finding rate consistent with (19.90). The slope of this schedule is given as:

$$\frac{d\Pi_{ss}}{d\eta_{ss}}\Big|_{EE} = -\frac{\Pi_{ss}}{\delta_{\pi} - 1}\frac{\partial\Theta^{ss}}{\partial\eta_{ss}}, \qquad (19.92)$$

$$\frac{\partial\Theta^{ss}(\eta)}{\partial\eta} = \mu\omega\frac{(1-\overline{\eta})}{\overline{\eta}}\left(\frac{\xi}{\overline{w}}\right)^{-\mu}\left[\chi - \left[\left(\frac{\xi}{\overline{w}}\right)^{-\mu} - 1\right]\right]. \qquad (19.93)$$

This slope is positive (negative) under the same conditions as $\Theta^{F} < 0$ (> 0). In a frictionless labor market or in the presence of actuarially fair unemployment insurance, Θ^{ss} is independent of η. In this case, since $\partial\Pi^{PC}/\partial\eta > 0$, the steady-state is unique. We refer to this stationary equilibrium as the "intended" steady-state (denoted by subscript $\mathbf{I}$) and impose that it displays local determinacy. In the intended steady-state, inflation is on target, $\Pi_{\mathbf{I}} = \overline{\Pi}$, vacancies are unconstrained, $\mathbf{v_I} > \mathbf{v_F}$, and the Kuhn–Tucker multiplier on the vacancy nonnegativity constraint is zero, $\lambda_{v,\mathbf{I}} = 0$. When endogenous earnings risk is procyclical, $\partial\Theta/\partial\eta > 0$, generating a negatively sloped $\Pi^{EE}(\eta)$. In this case, the steady-state uniqueness of the economy is preserved.

When endogenous earnings risk is countercyclical, instead, $\partial\Theta^{ss}/\partial\eta < 0$, and the $\Pi^{EE}(\eta)$ schedule becomes positively sloped. As long as the countercyclical risk is moderate, the stationary equilibrium remains unique. However, when this countercyclical earnings risk is sufficiently strong, $\Pi^{EE}(\eta)$ becomes steeper than $\Pi^{PC}(\eta)$ and another steady-state arises where $\Pi^{EE}(\eta)$ intersects the vertical segment of $\Pi^{PC}(\eta)$. Ravn and Sterk (2021) refer to this as the "unemployment trap" (indicated by $\mathbf{u}$) which features high unemployment and low inflation. In this stationary equilibrium, $\lambda_{v,\mathbf{u}} > 0$, and $\mathbf{v_u} = \mathbf{v_F}$. The equilibrium allocation and inflation rate in this steady-state solve:

$$\mathbf{n_u} = \frac{(1 - \xi)\,\eta_{\mathbf{u}}}{1 - (1 - \omega)(1 - \eta_{\mathbf{u}})} < \mathbf{n_I}, \qquad (19.94)$$

$$\eta_{\mathbf{u}} = \overline{m}\left(\frac{\mathbf{v_F}}{1 - \xi - (1-\omega)\,\mathbf{n_u}}\right)^{1-\alpha} < \eta_{\mathbf{I}}, \qquad (19.95)$$

$$\mathbf{w_u} = \overline{w}\left(\frac{\eta_{\mathbf{u}}}{\overline{\eta}}\right)^{\chi} < \overline{w}_I, \qquad (19.96)$$

$$\Pi_\mathbf{u} = \left[\beta \frac{\bar{R}}{\bar{\Pi}^{\delta_\Pi}}\left(1 + \omega\left(1 - \eta_u\right)\left(\left(\frac{\xi}{\mathbf{w}_u}\right)^{-\mu} - 1\right)\right)\right]^{1/(1-\delta_\Pi)} < \Pi_I. \qquad (19.97)$$

When the unemployment trap steady-state exists, there may also be temporary episodes where the equilibrium diverges from the intended steady-state. We will consider stochastic sunspot equilibria where the economy fluctuates between equilibria in the vicinity of the intended steady-state and of the unemployment trap. We model a negative sentiment shocks as a wave of pessimism where employed agents increase their desired savings due to doubts about future employment prospects. Pessimistic beliefs temporarily take the economy on a path towards a low-activity cumulative high-unemployment outcome until agents turn optimistic which returns to a path towards a high activity/low unemployment equilibrium.

Let ζ denote sentiments and assume that it follows a discrete two-state homogeneous Markov chain fluctuating between optimism, $\zeta_s = \zeta^o$, and pessimism, $\zeta_s = \zeta^p$, with transition probability matrix Υ^ζ. We define the transition probabilities by $p_{ij}^\zeta = \Pr\left(\zeta = \zeta^i | \zeta_{-1} = \zeta^j\right) \in [0, 1]$ for $j \in (o, p)$ where $\sum_i p_{ij}^\zeta = 1$. We solve for the decision rules by extending the state variables with the sunspot indicator:

$$\mathbf{n}_s = g_z\left(\mathbf{n}_{s-1}, \zeta_s\right), \quad \mathbf{n}_{s-1} \text{ given}, \qquad (19.98)$$

$$\mathbf{h}_s = g_h\left(\mathbf{n}_s, \zeta_s\right), \qquad (19.99)$$

where $\mathbf{h}_s = \left(\Pi_s, R_s, \eta_s, \mathbf{w}_s, \mathbf{mc}_s, \mathbf{c}_{c,s}, \mathbf{v}_s, \lambda_{v,s}\right)'$. When the equilibrium is unique, ζ is a redundant state variable, and the economy converges to the intended steady-state regardless of ζ. When the unemployment trap instead exists, the sunspot selects the equilibrium.

When agents are pessimistic, firms stop posting costly vacancies, $\lambda_{v,p}\left(\mathbf{n}\right) > 0$ and $\mathbf{v}_p\left(\mathbf{n}\right) = \mathbf{v}_F$, and the economy converges to a pessimistic sunspot limit where $\left(\mathbf{n}_p^l, \eta_p^l, \mathbf{w}_p^l, \Theta_p^l, \mathbf{v}_p^l\right) = (\mathbf{n}_\mathbf{u}, \eta_\mathbf{u}, \mathbf{w}_\mathbf{u}, \Theta_\mathbf{u}, \mathbf{v}_F)$ while $\left(\mathbf{mc}_p^l, \Pi_p^l, \mathbf{c}_{c,p}^l, \lambda_p^l\right)$ are the solutions to the following system of equations:

$$\left(\mathbf{w}_p^l\right)^{-\mu} = \beta\bar{R}\left(\Pi_p^l\right)^{\delta_\pi - 1}\left(\mathbf{w}_p^l\right)^{-\mu}\Theta_p^l$$

$$\times\left(p_{pp}^\zeta + \left(1 - p_{pp}^\zeta\right)\left(\frac{\Pi_o\left(\mathbf{n}_p^l\right)}{\Pi_p^l}\right)^{\delta_\pi - 1}\left(\frac{\mathbf{w}_o\left(\mathbf{n}_p^l\right)}{\mathbf{w}_p^l}\right)^{-\mu}\frac{\Theta_o\left(\mathbf{n}_p^l\right)}{\Theta_p^l}\right), \qquad (19.100)$$

$$\gamma\mathbf{mc}_p^l = (\gamma - 1) + \phi\left(1 - \beta p_{pp}^\zeta\right)\left(\Pi_p^l - 1\right)\Pi_p^l$$

$$- \phi\beta\left(1 - p_{pp}^\zeta\right)\left(\frac{\mathbf{c}_{c,o}\left(\mathbf{n}_p^l\right)}{\mathbf{c}_{c,p}^l}\right)^{-\mu}\left(\Pi_o\left(\mathbf{n}_p^l\right) - 1\right)\Pi_o\left(\mathbf{n}_p^l\right)\frac{n_o\left(\mathbf{n}_p^l\right)}{n_p^l}, \qquad (19.101)$$

$$\mathbf{mc}_p^l = \frac{1}{A}\left[\mathbf{w}_p^l + \left(1 - p_{pp}^\zeta(1 - \omega)\beta\right)\left(\frac{\kappa}{\mathbf{q}_p^l} - \lambda_p^l\right)\right]$$

$$- \left(1 - p_{pp}^\zeta\right)(1 - \omega)\beta \left(\frac{\mathbf{c}_{c,o}\left(\mathbf{n}_p'\right)}{c_{c,p}^l}\right)^{-\mu} \frac{\kappa}{q_o\left(\mathbf{n}_p'\right)}\Bigg], \tag{19.102}$$

$$c_{c,p}^l = \frac{A}{\xi}\left(1 - w_p' - \frac{\phi}{2}\left(\Pi_p' - 1\right)^2\right)\mathbf{n}_p' + \vartheta, \tag{19.103}$$

where $q_p' = \overline{m}^{1/(1-\alpha)}\left(\eta_p'\right)^{-\alpha/(1-\alpha)}$ and $\Theta_p' = 1 + \omega\left(1 - \eta_p'\right)\left(\left(\xi/w_p'\right)^{-\mu} - 1\right)$. In these expressions, $x_o\left(\mathbf{n}_p'\right)$ denotes the decision rule for variable x should agents become optimistic given the current employment level, $\mathbf{n}_p'$. Since firms stop posting costly vacancies while agents hold pessimistic beliefs, $\mathbf{v}_p' = \mathbf{v}_F$, the employment dynamics are given by:

$$\mathbf{n}_p = (1 - \omega)\left(1 - \eta_p\left(\mathbf{n}_{-1}\right)\right)\mathbf{n}_{-1} + \eta_p\left(\mathbf{n}_{-1}\right)(1 - \xi),$$

$$\eta_p\left(\mathbf{n}_{-1}\right) = \overline{m}\left(\frac{\mathbf{v}_F}{1 - \xi - (1 - \omega)\mathbf{n}_{-1}}\right)^{1-\alpha}.$$

The employment level in the pessimistic sunspot limit is the fixed point of this mapping. Since the job finding rate in the pessimistic sunspot limit is a function of the employment level only, and wages are determined by the job finding rate, job market outcomes in the pessimistic sunspot limit are identical to those in the unemployment trap steady-state. Thus, conditional upon existence of the pessimistic sunspot, monetary policy is unable to impact on the labor market outcomes as long as agents remain pessimistic. Inflation, marginal costs, entrepreneurial consumption, and the shadow cost of the lower bound on vacancies, instead, do respond to monetary policy because they are influenced by the policy functions that hold should the wave of pessimism turn to optimism.

When agents are optimistic, $\lambda_{v,o} = 0$ and $\mathbf{v}_{s,o} > \mathbf{v}_F$, and the decision rules solve the following system of equations:

$$(\mathbf{w}_o\left(\mathbf{n}_{-1}\right))^{-\mu} = \beta\overline{R}\left(\Pi_o\left(\mathbf{n}_o\right)\right)^{\delta_\pi - 1}(\mathbf{w}_o\left(\mathbf{n}_o\right))^{-\mu}\Theta_o\left(\mathbf{n}_o\right)$$

$$\times \left(p_{oo}^\zeta + (1 - p_{oo}^\zeta)\left(\frac{\Pi_p\left(\mathbf{n}_p\right)}{\Pi_o\left(\mathbf{n}_o\right)}\right)^{\delta_\pi - 1}\left(\frac{\mathbf{w}_p\left(\mathbf{n}_p\right)}{\mathbf{w}_o\left(\mathbf{n}_o\right)}\right)^{-\mu}\frac{\Theta_p\left(\mathbf{n}_p\right)}{\Theta_o\left(\mathbf{n}_o\right)}\right), \tag{19.104}$$

$$\gamma\,\mathbf{mc}_o\left(\mathbf{n}_{-1}\right) = (\gamma - 1) + \phi\left(\Pi_o\left(\mathbf{n}_{-1}\right) - 1\right)\Pi_o\left(\mathbf{n}_{-1}\right)$$

$$- \phi\beta p_{oo}^\zeta\left(\Pi_o\left(\mathbf{n}_o\right) - 1\right)\Pi_o\left(\mathbf{n}_o\right)\left(\frac{\mathbf{c}_{c,o}\left(\mathbf{n}_o\right)}{\mathbf{c}_{c,o}\left(\mathbf{n}_{-1}\right)}\right)^{-\mu}\frac{\mathbf{n}_o}{\mathbf{n}_{-1}}$$

$$- (1 - p_{oo}^\zeta)\phi\beta\left[\left(\frac{\mathbf{c}_{c,p}\left(\mathbf{n}_p\right)}{\mathbf{c}_{c,o}\left(\mathbf{n}_{-1}\right)}\right)^{-\mu}\left(\Pi_p\left(\mathbf{n}_p\right) - 1\right)\Pi_p\left(\mathbf{n}_p\right)\frac{\mathbf{n}_p}{\mathbf{n}_{-1}}\right], \tag{19.105}$$

$$\mathbf{mc}_o\left(\mathbf{n}_{-1}\right) = \frac{1}{A}\left(\mathbf{w}_o\left(\mathbf{n}_{-1}\right) + \frac{\kappa}{q_o\left(\mathbf{n}_{-1}\right)} - p_{oo}^\zeta(1 - \omega)\beta\left(\frac{\mathbf{c}_{c,o}\left(\mathbf{n}_o\right)}{\mathbf{c}_{c,o}\left(\mathbf{n}_{-1}\right)}\right)^{-\mu}\frac{\kappa}{q_o\left(\mathbf{n}_o\right)}\right)$$

$$- \frac{1}{A}\left(1 - p_{oo}^\zeta\right)(1 - \omega)\beta\left(\frac{\mathbf{c}_{c,p}\left(\mathbf{n}_p\right)}{\mathbf{c}_{c,o}\left(\mathbf{n}_{-1}\right)}\right)^{-\mu}\left(\frac{\kappa}{q_p\left(\mathbf{n}_p\right)} - \lambda_{v,p}\left(\mathbf{n}_p\right)\right), \tag{19.106}$$

$$\mathbf{c}_{c,o}(\mathbf{n}) = \frac{A}{\xi}\left(1 - \frac{\kappa}{\mathbf{n}}(\mathbf{v}_o - \mathbf{v_F}) - \mathbf{w}_o - \frac{\phi}{2}(\Pi_o - 1)^2\right)\mathbf{n}_o + \vartheta, \tag{19.107}$$

$$\mathbf{n_j} = (1 - \omega)\mathbf{n}_{-1} + \mathbf{q}_j\mathbf{v}_j, \quad j = o, p, \tag{19.108}$$

where $\Theta_o = 1 + \omega(1 - \eta_o)\left((\xi/w_o)^{-\mu} - 1\right)$ and $\mathbf{q}_j = \bar{m}\left(\frac{\eta_j}{\bar{m}}\right)^{-\alpha/(1-\alpha)}$.

We proceed by examining the dynamics of the economy in response to sunspot shocks in a numerical example. The (monthly) calibration will differ somewhat from the earlier exercises because, as explained above, sunspot dynamics arise when the incomplete markets wedge is *sufficiently* countercyclical.

We assume an annual real interest rate of 3.5% and set the inflation target equal to 4%. Consumption is now assumed to fall by 15% upon job loss. For this exercise, we assume significantly higher price stickiness and calibrate ϕ to target average price contract length of 18 months.

The elasticity of the matching function with respect to unemployment, α, is set to 50% and the monthly job separation rate, ω, is calibrated to 4% per month. We assume that vacancy costs are quite small and set κ to target hiring costs of around 2% of the wage bill in the intended steady-state. We impose that wages are rigid and set the wage elasticity parameter, $\chi = 0.0015$. We normalize average productivity to one. The inflation coefficient in the Taylor rule equals 1.5.

Next we assume that the steady-state unemployment rate equals 5% in the intended steady state. This implies that the monthly job finding rate, η_I, is equal to 43.2% so that the average unemployment duration upon job loss is around 2.3 months. We normalize $\overline{\mathbf{m}} = 1$. We calibrate the unemployment rate in the unemployment trap to be 8%. Should this level of unemployment be attained, the job finding rate declines to 31.5%.

We assume that the intended steady-state is absorbing, $\mathbf{p}_{oo}^{\zeta} = 1$, while the persistence of pessimism is calibrated to $\mathbf{p}_{pp}^{\zeta} = 0.85$. This implies that when agents turn pessimistic, this state will last on average for close to seven months. The rest of the parameters are set as in Table 19.1. We obtain the equilibrium paths from numerical approximations of the functions in (19.100)–(19.108). We use a global solver given that the economy may drift far away from the intended equilibrium when agents turn pessimistic. As in Mertens and Ravn (2014), we solve by time iteration using an endogenous grid method assuming piecewise linear policy functions on a discrete grid for employment, $\mathbf{n}$.

In Fig. 19.13 we illustrate the steady-state determination of the model with this calibration. There are two stationary equilibria, the intended steady-state and the unemployment trap due to strong countercyclicality of earning risk.

In Fig. 19.14 we illustrate the dynamics of the economy during a sentimental business cycle due to a wave of pessimism. The results correspond to the average outcomes of 2000 simulations of the model where in each of them we start out in the intended steady-state and then assume that agents at time 0 become pessimistic. We then simulate the Markov chain and we derive, through the large number of repetitions, smooth approximations of the average sunspot transition paths.

As pessimism sets in, output declines gradually reaching a maximum fall of approximately 1.2% relative to the intended steady-state after approximately three months. Also, unemployment rises more than a percentage point, inflation falls as does the nominal interest rate. The responses of output and inflation are hump-shaped because of two countervailing forces. First, as long as agents are pessimistic, firms stop posting costly vacancies, employment drops, and the economy approaches the negative sunspot limit. However, as time elapses, the probability that agents become positive again also increases. Averaging the results over many simulations, thus, introduces the hump-shaped dynamics.

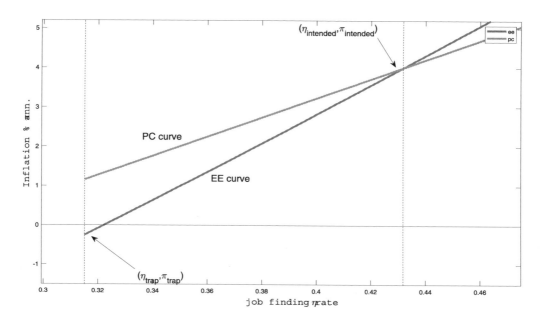

FIGURE 19.13 Steady-State Properties

Notes: The calibration is explained in the text.

The recession that is produced by the sunspot is very pronounced in the labor market because it derives from agents' pessimistic beliefs about adverse labor market outcomes which are confirmed by firms cutting back on hiring when the earnings wedge is countercyclical. Moreover, while inflation falls, its level remains positive (as it is assumed to be 4% in the intended steady-state) and the decline in inflation is moderate relative to the sunspot limit (which has a small amount of deflation). The reason for this is that agents are forward looking and there is always a positive probability that pessimism dissipates in which case inflation rises. One might relate these paths to the response of the economy to expectational shocks similar to those that were discussed in the previous section of this chapter that were estimated in response to innovations to survey evidence on consumer confidence. It is interesting to check the robustness of the results to key model parameters. We focus attention on the persistence of pessimism, $\mathbf{p}_{pp}^{\zeta}$, and the level of unemployment in the trap. We now look at two alternative calibrations, $\mathbf{p}_{pp}^{\zeta} = 0.9$, which implies an expected duration of the pessimistic state of 10 months, and $\mathbf{p}_{pp}^{\zeta} = 0.7$, where the average duration is 3.5 months, half of seven months assumed in the benchmark economy. Fig. 19.15 compares the responses of the benchmark (blue continuous line), with the high and low persistence economies (indicated with red lines with crosses and black lines with squares, respectively).

When the pessimistic state is very persistent, the economy experiences a significantly larger fall in output that occurs later (five months) after the onset of pessimism, a larger and more persistent rise in unemployment, and a sharper fall in prices. Results are symmetric when assuming low persistence of pessimism. Thus, the persistence of pessimistic beliefs determines the susceptibility of the economy to purely expectations driven fluctuations.

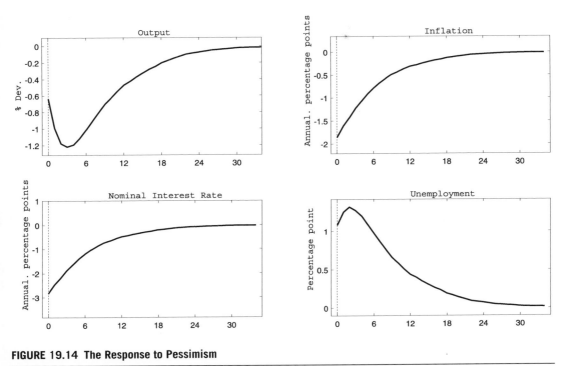

FIGURE 19.14 The Response to Pessimism

Notes: The figure illustrates the impact of agents becoming negative derived from simulating the model 2000 times and averaging the results.

In Fig. 19.16 we examine the sensitivity of results to the assumed level of unemployment in the low-activity steady state. We assume a dramatic case in which the unemployment rate in the trap is 11% (black line with squares), and a less dramatic case where we set $\mathbf{u}_u = 7\%$ (red line with crosses). Recall that in the benchmark economy $\mathbf{u}_u = 8\%$. The key insight of these experiments is that, the worse is the *potential* outcome, the larger are the real effects of a sentiment shocks. When $\mathbf{u}_u = 11\%$, output falls twice than in the baseline case and unemployment peaks at 7.2% relative to 6.2% in the baseline. In contrast, for $\mathbf{u}_u = 7\%$, the maximum decline in output and the increase in unemployment are both significantly muted. This suggests that economies that are more likely to experience high unemployment during crisis times are more susceptible to sentimental business cycles.

19.7 Conclusions

We have analyzed the impact of expectational shocks in an incomplete markets New Keynesian model with matching frictions in the labor market. In this framework, employed agents are subject to idiosyncratic income risk which introduces a precautionary savings incentive due to lack of unemployment insurance. Since firms face nominal rigidities, changes in aggregate demand impact on firms' hiring

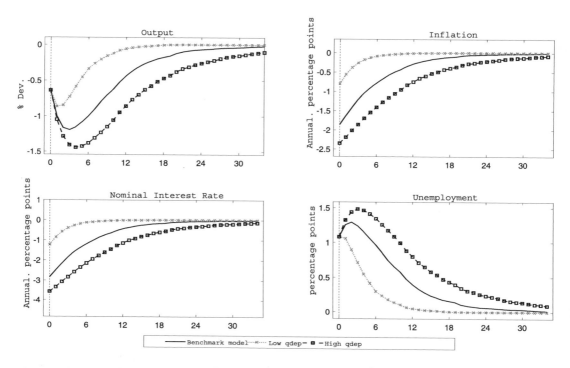

FIGURE 19.15 The Impact of the Persistence of Negative Beliefs

Notes: The figure illustrates the impact of agents becoming negative derived from simulating the model 2000 times and averaging the results.

decisions and because of matching frictions income risk becomes endogenous and depends on firms' hiring decisions.

Market incompleteness introduces two key features that determine the sensitivity of the economy to expectational shocks: (i) "discounting" in the Euler equation that determines (unconstrained) agents' intertemporal choices. Such discounting stabilizes expectational shocks as agents effectively become less forward looking; (ii) a time-varying precautionary savings motive that results in interactions between demand and supply which may either amplify or stabilize shocks. When employed agents' idiosyncratic income risk is countercyclical, incomplete markets induce amplification of shocks. Procyclical income risk instead stabilizes the economy. We have showed that countercyclicality of earnings risk induces sensitivity to expectational shocks including both news about future fundamentals, noise shocks, and stochastic sunspots. We argued that countercyclical earning risk is likely to be empirically relevant, but this topic deserves more attention, as there might be differences across different types of agents depending on their skill level and employment history. Thus, richer models will almost certainly be needed in order to reach firmer conclusions.

We have cast our analysis within a setup that allows for easy computation due to a degenerate equilibrium wealth distribution. This aspect has significant computational aspects but also comes with

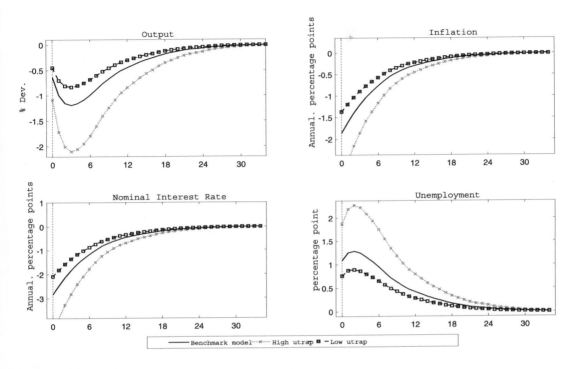

FIGURE 19.16 The Importance of the Size of the Unemployment Trap

Notes: The figure illustrates the impact of agents becoming negative derived from simulating the model 2000 times and averaging the results.

costs in terms of the ability to match relevant empirical moments such as the extent of wealth inequality or ex-ante heterogeneity in skills. It would be interesting to investigate richer settings in which these issues can be addressed. The incomplete markets setting also introduces differences in the incentive to acquire information across the wealth distribution and therefore in agents' expectations which would be very interesting to consider in more detail in future work, see, e.g., Broer et al. (2020a).

Appendix 19.A Solutions for news shocks

Using the solution for the job finding rate, it follows that the coefficients in Eqs. (19.52)–(19.53) are given as:

$$\Gamma_\Pi^A = \frac{\gamma/\phi}{1-\beta\rho_A}\left(\frac{1-\gamma}{\gamma} + \left(w\chi + \frac{\kappa}{q}\frac{\alpha}{1-\alpha}(1-\beta(1-\omega)\rho_A)\right)\Gamma_\eta^A\right), \tag{19.109}$$

$$\tau_{m-1}^{\Pi,A} = \beta\Gamma_\Pi^A + \frac{\gamma}{\phi}\left(\left(w\chi + \frac{\kappa}{q}\frac{\alpha}{1-\alpha}\right)\tau_{m-1}^{\eta,A} - (1-\omega)\beta\frac{\kappa}{q}\frac{\alpha}{1-\alpha}\Gamma_\eta^A\right), \tag{19.110}$$

$$\tau_{i<m-1}^{\Pi,A} = \beta\tau_{i+1}^{\Pi,A} + \frac{\gamma}{\phi}\left(\left(w\chi + \frac{\kappa}{q}\frac{\alpha}{1-\alpha}\right)\tau_i^{\eta,A} - (1-\omega)\beta\frac{\kappa}{q}\frac{\alpha}{1-\alpha}\tau_{i+1}^{\eta,A}\right), \tag{19.111}$$

$$\Gamma_\Pi^R = \frac{\gamma/\phi}{1-\beta\rho_R}\left(\left(w\chi + \frac{\kappa}{q}\frac{\alpha}{1-\alpha}(1-\beta(1-\omega)\rho_R)\right)\Gamma_\eta^A\right), \tag{19.112}$$

$$\tau_{m-1}^{\Pi,R} = \beta\Gamma_\Pi^R + \frac{\gamma}{\phi}\left(\left(w\chi + \frac{\kappa}{q}\frac{\alpha}{1-\alpha}\right)\tau_{m-1}^{\eta,R} - (1-\omega)\beta\frac{\kappa}{q}\frac{\alpha}{1-\alpha}\Gamma_\eta^R\right), \tag{19.113}$$

$$\tau_{i<m-1}^{\Pi,R} = \beta\tau_{i+1}^{\Pi,R} + \frac{\gamma}{\phi}\left(\left(w\chi + \frac{\kappa}{q}\frac{\alpha}{1-\alpha}\right)\tau_i^{\eta,R} - (1-\omega)\beta\frac{\kappa}{q}\frac{\alpha}{1-\alpha}\tau_{i+1}^{\eta,R}\right), \tag{19.114}$$

$$\Gamma_R^A = \delta_\Pi\Gamma_\Pi^A + \frac{\delta_\theta}{1-\alpha}\Gamma_\eta^A, \tag{19.115}$$

$$\tau_i^{R,A} = \delta_\Pi\tau_i^{\eta,A} + \frac{\delta_\theta}{1-\alpha}\tau_i^{\eta,A} \tag{19.116}$$

$$\Gamma_R^R = 1 + \delta_\Pi\Gamma_\Pi^R + \frac{\delta_\theta}{1-\alpha}\Gamma_\eta^R, \tag{19.117}$$

$$\tau_i^{R,R} = \delta_\Pi\tau_i^{\eta,R} + \frac{\delta_\theta}{1-\alpha}\tau_i^{\eta,R} \tag{19.118}$$

$$\Gamma_w^{S=A,R} = \chi\Gamma_\eta^{S=A,R}, \tag{19.119}$$

$$\tau_i^{w,A} = \chi\tau_i^{\eta,A}, \tag{19.120}$$

$$\tau_i^{w,R} = \chi\tau_i^{\eta,R}, \tag{19.121}$$

$$\Gamma_n^{S=A,R} = \frac{\eta e}{n}\Gamma_\eta^{S=A,R}. \tag{19.122}$$

$$\tau_i^{n,A} = \frac{\eta e}{n}\tau_i^{\eta,A}, \tag{19.123}$$

$$\tau_i^{n,R} = \frac{\eta e}{n}\tau_i^{\eta,R}, \tag{19.124}$$

and the solutions for employed workers consumption and for output equal the solution for real wages and employment, respectively.

Appendix 19.B Computing the Jacobians

To compute the Jacobians, we consider the decision problem of an employed household, which can be summarized by the following two equations:

$$\mathbf{c}_s^{-\mu} = \beta\mathbb{E}_s\frac{\mathbf{R}_s}{\Pi_{s+1}}\left[(1-\omega(1-\eta_{s+1}))\mathbf{c}_{s+1}^{-\mu} + \omega(1-\eta_{s+1})(\xi + \frac{\mathbf{R}_s}{\Pi_{s+1}}\mathbf{b}_s)^{-\mu}\right], \tag{19.125}$$

$$\mathbf{c}_s + \mathbf{b}_s = \mathbf{w}_s + \frac{\mathbf{R}_{s-1}}{\Pi_s}\mathbf{b}_{s-1}. \tag{19.126}$$

The equilibrium objects $\{\mathbf{R}_s, \Pi_s, \eta_s, \mathbf{w}_s\}$ are taken as exogenous, but stochastic from the households standpoint. To construct the Jacobians, we compute the response of $\mathbf{b}$ to a purely transitory news shock to each of the individual equilibrium objects k periods into the future, for any $k = 0, 1, \ldots, K$, with K being a truncation horizon. The Jacobians are constructed by collecting these responses on the columns of the matrix. The response to the news shocks can be computed using standard perturbation software, approximating the above equations around same steady state. After constructing the Jacobians, we apply the decomposition formula, plugging in the impulse responses from the full model.

References

Ambrocio, Gene, 2020. Inflationary Household Uncertainty Shocks. Working paper 5/20. Bank of Finland.

Angeletos, Marios, Huo, Zhen, 2021. Myopia and anchoring. The American Economic Review 111 (4), 1116–1200.

Angeletos, Marios, Lian, Chen, 2022. Confidence and the propagation of demand shocks. The Review of Economic Studies 88 (3), 1085–1119.

Auclert, Adrien, Bardóczy, Bence, Rognlie, Matthew, Straub, Ludwig, 2021. Using the sequence-space Jacobian to solve and estimate heterogeneous-agent models. Econometrica 89 (5), 2375–2408.

Auclert, Adrien, Rognlie, Matthew, Straub, Ludwig, 2019. The Intertemporal Keynesian Cross. Manuscript. Stanford University.

Barsky, Robert, Sims, Eric, 2011. News shocks and the business cycle. Journal of Monetary Economics 58 (3), 273–289.

Barsky, Robert, Sims, Eric, 2012. Information, animal spirits, and the meaning of fluctuations in consumer confidence. The American Economic Review 102 (4), 1343–1377.

Bayer, Christian, Luetticke, Ralph, Pham-Dao, Lien, Tjaden, Volker, 2019. Precautionary savings, illiquid assets, and the aggregate consequences of shock to household income risk. Econometrica 87 (1), 255–290.

Beaudry, Paul, Portier, Franck, 2006. Stock prices, news, and economic fluctuations. The American Economic Review 96 (4), 1293–1307.

Beaudry, Paul, Portier, Franck, 2007. When can changes in expectations cause business cycle fluctuations in neoclassical settings? Journal of Economic Theory 135 (1), 458–477.

Bilbiie, Florin, 2020. The new Keynesian cross. Journal of Monetary Economics 114, 90–108.

Blanchard, Olivier-Jean, L'Hullier, Jean-Paul, Lorenzoni, Guido, 2013. News, noise and fluctuations: an empirical investigation. The American Economic Review 103 (7), 1345–1370.

Boz, Emine, Daude, Christian, Durdu, C. Bora, 2011. Emerging market business cycles: learning about the trend. Journal of Monetary Economics 58 (6–8), 616–631.

Broer, Tobias, Kohlhas, Alexandre, Mitman, Kurt, Schlafmann, Kathrine, 2020a. Heterogeneous Information Choice in General Equilibrium. Manuscript. IIES, University of Stockholm.

Broer, Tobias, Kramer, John, Mitman, Kurt, 2020b. The Curious Incidence of Shocks along the Income Distribution. Manuscript. IIES, University of Stockholm.

Challe, Edouard, Ragot, Xavier, 2016. Precautionary saving over the business cycle. The Economic Journal 126 (590), 135–184.

Chodorow-Reich, Gabriel, Karabarbounis, Loukas, 2016. The cyclicality of the opportunity cost of employment. Journal of Political Economy 124 (6), 1563–1618.

Del Negro, Marco, Giannoni, Marc, Patterson, Christina, 2015. The Forward Guidance Puzzle. New York FED, Discussion Papers, 574.

Faccini, Renato, Melosi, Leonardo, 2022. Pigouvian cycles. American Economic Journal: Macroeconomics 14 (2), 281–318.

Farhi, Emmanuel, Werning, Ivan, 2019. Monetary policy, bounded rationality, and incomplete markets. The American Economic Review 109 (11), 3887–3928.

Fernald, John, 2012. A Quarterly Utilization Adjusted Series on Total Factor Productivity. Technical Report. Federal Reserve Bank of San Francisco.

Gornemann, Nils, Kuester, Keith, Nakajima, Makoto, 2016. Doves for the Rich, Hawks for the Poor: Distributional Consequences of Monetary Policy. CEPR Discussion Paper, no. 11233.

Guerrieri, Veronica, Lorenzoni, Guido, Straub, Ludwig, Werning, Ivan, 2022. Macroeconomic implications of COVID-19: can negative supply shocks bring about demand shortages? The American Economic Review 112 (5), 1437–1474.

Hoeck, Christian P., 2020. Wage Effects of Labor Market Tightness. Manuscript. University of Copenhagen and Danmarks Nationalbank.

Jaimovich, Nir, Rebelo, Sergio T., 2009. Can news about the future drive the business cycle? The American Economic Review 99 (4), 1097–1118.

Juelsrud, Ragnar E., Wold, Ella Getz, 2019. The Saving and Employment Effects of Higher Job Loss Risk. Working paper no. 17/2019. Norges Bank.

Kaplan, Greg, Moll, Benjamin, Violante, Giovanni L., 2018. Monetary policy according to HANK. The American Economic Review 108 (3), 607–743.

Kekre, Rohan, 2021. Unemployment Insurance in Macroeconomic Stabilization. Manuscript. Chicago Booth.

Kim, Chanwoo, 2020. Forward Guidance Puzzle under HANK & SAM. Manuscript. University College, London.

Kurmann, Andre, Sims, Eric, 2021. Revisions in utilization-adjusted TFP and robust identification of news shocks. Review of Economics and Statistics 103 (2), 216–235.

Lagerborg, Andresa, Pappa, Evi, Ravn, Morten O., 2021. Sentimental Business Cycles. Manuscript. Universidad Carlos III de Madrid and University College, London.

Leeper, Eric, Walker, Todd B., Yang, Shu-Chun S., 2013. Fiscal foresight and information flows. Econometrica 81 (3), 1115–1145.

Lorenzoni, Guido, 2009. A theory of demand shocks. The American Economic Review 99 (5), 2050–2084.

McKay, Alisdair, Nakamura, Emi, Steinsson, Jon, 2016. The power of forward guidance revisited. The American Economic Review 106 (10), 3133–3158.

McKay, Alisdair, Nakamura, Emi, Steinsson, Jon, 2017. The discounter Euler equation: a note. Economica 84 (336), 821–831.

McKay, Alisdair, Reis, Ricardo, 2016a. The role of automatic stabilizers in the U.S. business cycle. Econometrica 84 (1), 141–194.

McKay, Alisdair, Reis, Ricardo, 2016b. Optimal automatic stabilizers. The Review of Economic Studies 88 (5), 2375–2406.

Mertens, Karel, Ravn, Morten O., 2010. Measuring the impact of fiscal policy in the face of anticipation: a structural VAR approach. The Economic Journal 120 (544), 393–413.

Mertens, Karel, Ravn, Morten O., 2013. The dynamic effects of personal and corporate income tax changes in the United States. The American Economic Review 103 (4), 1212–1247.

Mertens, Karel, Ravn, Morten O., 2014. Fiscal policy in an expectations driven liquidity trap. The Review of Economic Studies 81, 1637–1667.

Montiel-Olea, Jose' L., Stock, James H., Watson, Mark W., 2021. Inference in structural vector autoregressions identified with an external instrument. Journal of Econometrics 225 (1), 74–87.

Ravn, Morten O., Sterk, Vincent, 2017. Job uncertainty and deep recessions. Journal of Monetary Economics 90, 125–141.

Ravn, Morten O., Sterk, Vincent, 2021. Macroeconomic fluctuations according to HANK&SAM: an analytical approach. Journal of the European Economic Association 19 (2), 1162–1202.

Reis, Ricardo, 2020. The People versus the Markets: a Parsimoneous Model of Inflation Expectations. Manuscript. London School of Economics.

Rendahl, Pontus, 2020. Fiscal policy in an unemployment crisis. The Review of Economic Studies 83 (3), 1189–1224.

Romer, Christina D., Romer, David H., 2004. A new measure of monetary shocks: derivation and implications. The American Economic Review 4 (94), 1055–1084.

Rotemberg, Julio J., 1981. Sticky prices in the United States. Journal of Political Economy 90 (6), 1187–1211.

Rudebusch, Glenn D., 2002. Term structure evidence on interest rate smoothing and monetary policy inertia. Journal of Monetary Economics 49 (6), 1161–1187.

Schmitt-Grohe, Stephanie, Uribe, Martin, 2011. What's news in business cycles? Econometrica 80 (6), 2733–2764.

Werning, Ivan, 2015. Incomplete Markets and Aggregate Demand. Manuscript. MIT.

Dampening general equilibrium: incomplete information and bounded rationality[☆]

George-Marios Angeletos[a,b] **and Chen Lian**[c,b]

aMIT, Cambridge, MA, United States
bNBER, Cambridge, MA, United States
cUniversity of California at Berkeley, Berkeley, CA, United States

20.1 Introduction

General equilibrium (GE) feedbacks—and the presumed ability of economic agents to understand them—are a central piece of modern macroeconomics. In some contexts (e.g., a Keynesian economy at the zero lower bound), they reinforce partial equilibrium (PE) effects, acting as "macroeconomic multipliers" that amplify exogenous shocks or raise policy effectiveness. In other contexts (e.g., competition over limited resources), they offset PE effects, helping stabilize aggregate outcomes or curtailing policy effectiveness. Either way, GE mechanisms limit the usefulness of PE intuitions and empirical works that focus on identifying PE effects.

In this paper, we review and synthesize recent research that studies how frictions in information and rationality arrest perceived and actual GE feedbacks. Our starting point is the standard modeling practice in macroeconomics, which combines a strong solution concept, Rational Expectations Equilibrium (REE), and a strong informational assumption, "full" or "complete" information. Following the literature, we refer to this combination as FIRE, a shortcut for Full Information Rational Expectations. But we also emphasize that, for our purposes, this combination has a very specific meaning: the "FI" half translates to common knowledge of aggregate shocks and the "RE" half translates to common knowledge of rationality. This hints at a deep connection between all the approaches considered in this paper, a connection that we make clear as we proceed.

Our main take-home lesson can be summarized as follows: relaxing either the "FI" or the "RE" half of FIRE, at least in the four ways considered in this chapter, amounts to anchoring the expectations of the responses of others to aggregate shocks or policy shifts and, thereby, dampening the GE effect of such shocks. Turning this lesson around, we conclude that the standard practice "overestimates" the potency of GE feedbacks—and crucially, this "bias" is largest when these feedbacks are stronger to

---

[☆] This chapter subsumes an older paper of ours, entitled "Dampening General Equilibrium: From Micro to Macro" (Angeletos and Lian, 2017). We have benefited from the comments of various colleagues, especially those of the editors, Rüdiger Bachmann, Wilbert van der Klaauw, and Giorgio Topa. Angeletos acknowledges the support of the National Science Foundation under Grant Number SES-1757198.

Handbook of Economic Expectations. https://doi.org/10.1016/B978-0-12-822927-9.00028-8

613

start with. This serves both as a warning for the state-of-the-art and as a direction for future research: to obtain reliable predictions for policy counterfactuals, it is important to make sure that the theory fits not only the usual type of microeconomic evidence (e.g., higher MPCs) but also survey evidence on the adjustment of beliefs.

But what are the four departures from FIRE that support this lesson? In what ways are they similar and in what ways are they different? What does the evidence tell us about them? And how should we choose among them, or between them and FIRE? The rest of this Introduction previews answers offered to these questions.

Four theories and their common ground

The first one, studied in Section 20.3, maintains rational expectations but accommodates incomplete information, along the lines of Morris and Shin (2002, 2006), Woodford (2003), Nimark (2017), and Angeletos and Lian (2018). The defining property of this approach is not the noise in the observation of the underlying shocks per se but rather the absence of common knowledge about them. Basically, the key is that agents worry that others may not share the same information with them. This anchors expectations of the behavior of others to the common prior, causing all agents to behave *as if* the GE feedback was lower to start with.[1]

The second approach, studied in Section 20.4, goes in the opposite direction, maintaining full information but replacing rational expectations with Level-k Thinking (Farhi and Werning, 2019; Iovino and Sergeyev, 2021) or two close variants of it, Reflective Equilibrium (García-Schmidt and Woodford, 2019) and Cognitive Hierarchy (Camerer et al., 2004). This amounts to assuming that the typical agent believes that other agents are less sophisticated than themselves and, as a result, less able to comprehend strategic interactions and GE feedbacks. And since the best response to such a belief is to act *as if* the actual GE feedback were smaller, this approach, too, translates to GE attenuation relative to FIRE.

Our description of the above two approaches suggests a deep connection between them. Indeed, both approaches can be viewed as complementary relaxations of strong common-knowledge assumptions: the first relaxes common knowledge of the shock, the second relaxes common knowledge of rationality. Furthermore, both approaches can be understood as anchoring higher-order beliefs to a certain default point: the common prior about the underlying shock in the first approach and the level-0 belief in the second approach. One subtle difference is that the common prior in the first approach is disciplined by the objective truth, while the level-0 belief in the second approach is a free parameter, which the analyst must choose judiciously. This difference and a minor "bug" aside,[2] the two approaches are close cousins to each other.

The third approach, Heterogeneous Priors, employed by Angeletos and La'O (2009) and Angeletos and Sastry (2021) and reviewed in Section 20.5, builds a bridge between the above two approaches. It

---

[1] Rational Inattention à la Sims (2003) and Sticky Information à la Mankiw and Reis (2002) can be viewed as subsets of the first approach, subject to the following qualification. These works have often emphasized the inertia in first-order beliefs, as opposed to that in higher-order beliefs. But GE attenuation is driven exclusively by the latter friction, which is what the literature cited in the main text focuses on. See also the review in Angeletos and Lian (2016).

[2] As explained in Section 20.4, this "bug" refers to the following issue: the plain-vanilla Level-k Thinking makes an ambiguous prediction when the GE feedback is negative, but this ambiguity goes away with an appropriate "smooth" variant of it, namely Reflective Equilibrium. We first pointed out this issue in Angeletos and Lian (2017), where we also drew an analogy to the relation between Cobweb and Tatonnement in Walrasian analysis.

decouples the first approach's relevant friction—the lack of common knowledge—from the pure noise in the observation of the underlying fundamentals. It allows for a sharp translation between the depth of knowledge and depth of rationality. And it allows a gain in tractability while preserving the common essence of the other two approaches.

The last quality is shared by Gabaix (2020)'s Cognitive Discounting, the fourth and final approach reviewed in this chapter. This concept introduces a form of underextrapolation, which ultimately produces a similar kind of GE attenuation as the other three approaches.

Applications

To simplify the exposition, most of the analysis in this chapter employs a static framework. But we show how the logic extends to dynamic settings, in which behavior is forward looking and the GE feedback runs across multiple periods. And we use this translation in Section 20.6 to review a number of topical applications, including why bounded rationality arrests the power of forward guidance at the zero lower bound (Angeletos and Lian, 2018; Farhi and Werning, 2019), or how it influences the relative merits of government spending and consumption taxes as means of regulating aggregate demand (Vimercati et al., 2021). We also discuss how to recast under this chapter's umbrella earlier applications that study business cycles and unemployment fluctuations (Angeletos and La'O, 2010; Venkateswaran, 2014), a literature that studies "competition neglect" (Camerer and Lovallo, 1999; Greenwood and Hanson, 2015), and even some recent decision-theoretic work on "narrow bracketing" (Lian, 2021).

Connecting the theory to evidence on expectations

Having emphasized the common ground and applicability of the various approaches under consideration, Section 20.7 clarifies the following three points, which relate to the available evidence on expectations.

First, all the approaches are tightly connected to under-reaction of average expectations to news. Such underreaction is evident in surveys of expectations. This offers not only support for the common ground of these theories but also a way to quantify the degree of GE attenuation.

Second, although GE attenuation equals underreaction of *expectations* relative to actual outcomes, it does not necessarily translate to underreaction of *actual* outcomes relative to FIRE. To put it differently, the same friction can either dampen or amplify aggregate fluctuations relative to FIRE. Which of the two cases obtains depends on whether the GE feedback is positive or negative to start with. When it is positive (i.e., it reinforces the PE effect), GE attenuation translates to dampened volatility and sluggish adjustment. And when it is negative (i.e., when it offsets the PE effect), GE attenuation translates to amplification and overshooting.

Finally, while all the approaches under consideration share similar testable predictions about the joint dynamics of aggregate outcomes and average expectations, they make distinct testable predictions about *individual* expectations. In particular, consider the following two empirical questions: first, what is the correlation between *average* forecast errors in one period and innovations of average forecasts in previous periods; and second, what is the corresponding correlation for *individual* forecasts. Our first approach (incomplete information) allows the answer to the first question to be positive but restricts the answer to the second question to be zero, because the forecast errors of rational agents cannot be predictable on the basis of their *own* past information. By contrast, all other approaches (Level-k Thinking, Cognitive Discounting, etc.) allow the answer to the second question be positive but also restrict that the answers to the two questions be exactly the same: if belief underreaction is due to a systematic bias, it ought to manifest equally in the predictability of individual and average forecast errors.

The available survey evidence suggests that, at least for professional forecasters, the reality is closer to the first scenario than the second. See Coibion and Gorodnichenko (2012, 2015) for average forecasts, Bordalo et al. (2020) and Broer and Kohlhas (2021) for individual forecasts, and Angeletos et al. (2021) for a synthesis. This, and a few additional considerations that we explain in due course, seem to favor incomplete information over the alternatives. That said, laboratory experiments offer ample support for Level-k Thinking and its variants,[3] including in settings that resemble macroeconomic interactions ("beauty contests").

Combining these observations with our main lesson (that all the approaches produce the same GE attenuation), we conclude that the first-order task is to move away from FIRE in the *common* direction of these approaches as opposed to running a horserace between them. Notwithstanding this point, we offer some additional guidance on the relative costs and benefits of each approach, on which ones are most tractable, and on which ones are most suitable for stationary environments (regular business cycles) versus nonstationary environments (unprecedented experiences).

20.2 **Framework**

In this section, we introduce an abstract setting, which stylizes PE and GE effects. We next show how it nests a simplified but micro-founded New Keynesian economy. We finally define and characterize the FIRE benchmark, which is the point of departure for the rest of the paper.

20.2.1 **PE and GE in a nutshell**

There is a continuum of agents $i \in [0, 1]$, each making a decision $c_i \in \mathbb{R}$. Anticipating our upcoming micro-foundation, we interpret c_i as individual spending. The optimal spending depends on an individual-specific fundamental θ_i (e.g., an agent-specific preference shock or an agent-specific interest rate) and her expectation of the aggregate spending,

$$c_i = \theta_i + \alpha E_i [c], \tag{20.1}$$

where α is a fixed scalar, $c = \int_{i \in [0,1]} c_i \, di$ is aggregate spending (an endogenous random variable), and $E_i [\cdot]$ is agent i's expectation (which, for now, does not have to be rational).

An agent's fundamental has both an aggregate and an idiosyncratic component, $\theta_i = \theta + \epsilon_i$, where θ is the aggregate component and ϵ_i is the idiosyncratic one. Implicit in (20.1) is the assumption that every agent knows perfectly her own fundamental (θ_i), regardless of what she knows about the aggregate shock (θ) and how she forms beliefs about the actions of others and aggregate activity (c). This lets us focus on how the latter kind of beliefs are formed and in particular on how they vary with the depth of the agents' knowledge and rationality.

---

[3] Nagel (1995); Stahl and Wilson (1994, 1995); Costa-Gomes et al. (2001); Costa-Gomes and Crawford (2006); Kneeland (2015); Mauersberger and Nagel (2018); Broer and Kohlhas (2021).

The aggregate counterpart of (20.1) is given by

$$c = \underbrace{\theta}_{\text{PE}} + \underbrace{\alpha \bar{E}[c]}_{\text{GE}}, \qquad (20.2)$$

where $\theta = \int \theta_i \, di$ and $\bar{E}[c] = \int E_i[c] \, di$ are the cross-sectional averages of θ_i and $E_i[c]$, respectively. This allows us to decompose the change in c triggered by any change in θ into a partial equilibrium (PE) and a general equilibrium (GE) effect. More specifically, the first term in (20.2) represents the average PE effect, for it captures the direct impact of θ on c, holding constant the average expectations of aggregate spending; and similarly the second term in (20.2) captures the average GE effect, or the indirect effect of θ on c via the feedback from aggregate spending to individual spending.

Note that the GE effect depends on the scalar α, which we treat as a fixed and commonly known parameter, and on the average expectation of the response of others, which is our focal point. In game-theoretic terms, α identifies the degree and form of strategic interaction; condition (20.2) is indeed mathematically the same as the best response in the kind of beauty-contest games studied in Morris and Shin (2002) and Angeletos and Pavan (2007). But for our purposes, α translates to the strength and direction of the GE feedback. When $\alpha > 0$, the GE effect works in the same direction as the PE effect, helping amplify it. When instead $\alpha < 0$, the GE effect works in the opposite direction of, and attenuates, the PE effect. In both cases, a higher $|\alpha|$ means a large absolute strength of the GE effect, but the direction of the GE effect, relative to the PE effect, switches sign with α.

Throughout, we restrict $\alpha \in (-1, 1)$ so that (20.2) is a contraction mapping. This in turn guarantees the following two key properties: first, that there will be a unique REE no matter the information structure; and second, that the Level-k Thinking solution converges to the unique REE as the depth of reasoning goes to infinity.[4]

20.2.2 Micro-foundation: a simplified New-Keynesian model

We now show how (20.1) may stylize a New Keynesian economy. To start with, suppose that there is a continuum of infinitely-lived consumers, as in Angeletos and Lian (2018), Garcia-Schmidt and Woodford (2019), and Farhi and Werning (2019). After the familiar log-linearization, the optimal consumption of any consumer i in any period t is given by the following relation:

$$c_{i,t} = (1 - \beta)a_{i,t} - \beta\sigma \left\{ \sum_{k=0}^{+\infty} \beta^k E_{i,t} \left[i_{t+k} - \pi_{t+k+1} \right] \right\} + (1 - \beta) \left\{ \sum_{k=0}^{+\infty} \beta^k E_{i,t} \left[y_{t+k} \right] \right\} + \sigma\beta\varrho_{i,t},$$

$$(20.3)$$

where $\beta \in (0, 1)$ is the subjective discount factor, $a_{i,t}$ is the consumer's asset position at the start of period t, y_t is aggregate income, i_t and π_{t+1} are the nominal interest rate and inflation between t and $t + 1$, and $\varrho_{i,t}$ is a discount rate shock. The corresponding aggregate shock is denoted by ϱ_t and serves the usual role: it is a proxy for an aggregate demand shock.[5]

---

[4] When instead $\alpha \notin (-1, 1)$, a "pandora box" opens: with rational expectations, there can be multiple equilibria; and with Level-k Thinking, the sensitivity of the level-k outcome to a free parameter (the arbitrarily chosen level-0 outcome) explodes to infinity as $k \to \infty$. The study of these possibilities is outside the scope of this chapter.

[5] Implicit in (20.3) is the simplifying assumption that all agents face the same interest rate and receive the same income.

Eq. (20.3) is basically the permanent income hypothesis, adjusted to accommodate shocks to preferences and interest rates. By aggregating it across i and imposing market clearing (more precisely, by assuming that agents themselves understand that $y_t = c_t$), we arrive at the following:

$$c_t = -\beta\sigma\left\{\sum_{k=0}^{+\infty}\beta^k\bar{E}_t\left[i_{t+k} - \pi_{t+k+1}\right]\right\} + (1-\beta)\left\{\sum_{k=0}^{+\infty}\beta^k\bar{E}_t\left[c_{t+k}\right]\right\} + \sigma\beta\varrho_t. \tag{20.4}$$

Under FIRE, we further have $E_{i,t}[\cdot] = \mathbb{E}_t[\cdot]$. The above can then be reduced to a representative consumer's Euler equation (plus the appropriate transversality condition). Away from FIRE, the above clarifies how aggregate spending in one period depends on expectations of monetary policy, inflation, and aggregate spending in all future periods.

Consider next the supply side of the economy. For simplicity, we assume that firms remain fully rational and fully informed, even though the consumers might not be so. In particular, we assume that firm behavior gets summarized in a standard hybrid NKPC,

$$\pi_t = \kappa c_t + \psi_{-1}\pi_{t-1} + \psi_{+1}\mathbb{E}_t[\pi_{t+1}], \tag{20.5}$$

where $\psi_{-1}, \psi_{+1} \geq 0$, $\psi_{-1} + \psi_{+1} \leq 1$, $\pi_{-1} = 0$. Note that this embeds the full-information rational expectation operator, and that this contains both a forward-looking and a backward-looking component, as in Clarida et al. (1999) and much of the applied New Keynesian literature.

Finally, consider monetary policy. To be able to reduce this infinite horizon economy to our simple static framework, we assume that monetary policy replicates flexible-price outcomes for all $t \geq 1$ (but not for $t = 0$). This translates to $c_t = i_t - \mathbb{E}_t[\pi_{t+1}] = 0$ for all $t \geq 1$. For $t = 0$, on the other hand, we impose the following Taylor rule:

$$i_0 = \phi_c c_0 + \phi_\pi \pi_0. \tag{20.6}$$

Note that this nests an interest-rate peg, or the ZLB, with $\phi_c = \phi_\pi = 0$. And more generally, it lets ϕ_c and ϕ_π parameterize how "passive" or "accommodative" monetary policy is (with higher values for ϕ_c and ϕ_π mapping to less accommodation).

Combining the above assumptions about monetary policy with Eqs. (20.4) and (20.5), and solving out for the inflation dynamics, we obtain the following equilibrium restriction at $t = 0$:

$$c_0 = \left(1 - \beta - \beta\sigma\left(\phi_c + \frac{\kappa}{1 - \psi_{+1}\chi}(\phi_\pi - \chi)\right)\right)\bar{E}_0[c_0] + \sigma\beta\varrho_0, \tag{20.7}$$

where $\chi \equiv \frac{1-\sqrt{1-4\psi_{+1}\psi_{-1}}}{2\psi_{+1}} \in (0, 1)$. This is readily nested in (20.2) with

$$\theta \equiv \sigma\beta\varrho_0 \quad \text{and} \quad \alpha \equiv 1 - \beta - \beta\sigma\left(\phi_c + \frac{\kappa}{1 - \psi_{+1}\chi}(\phi_\pi - \chi)\right).$$

That is, the aggregate fundamental equals the exogenous aggregate demand shock rescaled, and the degree of strategic interaction is pinned down by parameters that regulate aggregate demand (β, σ), aggregate supply ($\kappa, \psi_{-1}, \psi_{+1}$), and monetary policy ($\phi_c, \phi_\pi$).

Let us first consider the case of an interest rate peg, or fully passive monetary policy, in the sense of $\phi_c = \phi_\pi = 0$. In this case, the formula for α reduces to

$$\alpha = \underbrace{1-\beta}_{\text{Keynesian cross}} + \underbrace{\kappa \frac{\beta \sigma \chi}{1 - \psi_{+1} \chi}}_{\text{inflation-spending spiral}} > 0.$$

That is, the GE effect is positive (equivalently, the consumers' decisions are strategic complements) and comes from two parts. First, the "Keynesian cross": a consumer's optimal consumption increases with other consumers' consumption, which in turn determines her own income. And second, the "inflation-spending spiral": a higher aggregate spending today leads to an increase in inflation, which other things equal depresses the real interest rate and stimulates aggregate spending. These points explain why α increases both with $1 - \beta$, which herein measures the MPC or the slope of the Keynesian cross, and with κ, the slope of the Phillips curve.

As soon as monetary policy is active, in the sense that $\phi_c > 0$ and/or $\phi_\pi > 0$, a third GE effect comes into the picture. Higher aggregate spending now causes the monetary authority to raise the nominal interest rate, either directly (when $\phi_c > 0$), or indirectly via inflationary pressures (when $\phi_\pi > 0$). Other things equal, the increase in the nominal interest rate discourages private spending. It follows that this GE effect works in the opposite direction than the aforementioned two: it is the source of strategic substitutability among the consumers. Furthermore, when the Taylor rule is sufficiently steep (in the sense of a sufficiently high value for ϕ_c and/or ϕ_π), this negative GE effect may dominate, so that the overall GE feedback becomes negative ($\alpha < 0$). To put it differently, a sufficiently active, or hawkish, monetary policy turns consumer decisions from strategic complements to strategic substitutes.

20.2.3 Full Information Rational Expectations (FIRE)

Our benchmark is defined by imposing Rational Expectations Equilibrium (REE) along with full information, and indeed common knowledge of, the aggregate fundamental θ.

In any REE, equilibrium strategies, or the mappings from shocks to outcomes, are commonly known. Here, this translates to c being a commonly known function of θ. Along with the assumption that θ itself is commonly known, this guarantees that c is commonly known, too. That is,

$$E_i[c] = \mathbb{E}[c] = c, \tag{20.8}$$

where $\mathbb{E}[\cdot]$ is the full-information rational expectations operator. Using this in (20.2), we have[6]:

Proposition 20.1. *There is a unique equilibrium under FIRE and it is such that*

$$c = \underbrace{\theta}_{PE} + \underbrace{\frac{\alpha}{1-\alpha}\theta}_{GE} = \underbrace{\frac{1}{1-\alpha}}_{GE\ multiplier} \theta. \tag{20.9}$$

---

[6] All proofs follow from the argument in the main text and the details can be found in the appendix of the NBER working paper version of this paper.

In short, common knowledge of the underlying shock together with REE implies common knowledge of the responses of others to the shock. It is *as if* agents get together in the same room, perfectly coordinate their responses to the shock, and effectively act as a single and the same agent. It is in this sense that the GE adjustment is "perfect" under FIRE.

20.2.4 Beyond FIRE

The benchmark studied above combines rational expectations with full information. This is basically the same as imposing common knowledge of rationality and of information: everybody is both fully rational and fully informed, everybody knows this fact, everybody knows that everybody knows this fact, and so on. We say "basically" because of the following subtlety: in general, the outcomes that are consistent with common knowledge of rationality (also known as rationalizable outcomes) are a *superset* of the REE outcomes. But as long as there is a unique rationalizable outcome, which is the case in our setting for $\alpha \in (-1, +1)$, the two sets coincide. For our purposes, the "RE" half of FIRE is therefore synonymous to common knowledge of rationality—and similarly, the "FI" half is synonymous to common knowledge of θ and of the entire payoff structure.

These observations explain the two routes we take in the next two sections. In Section 20.3, we depart from FIRE by maintaining rational expectations, or common knowledge of rationality, but relaxing full information, or common knowledge of θ. In Section 20.4, we do the converse.

20.3 Incomplete information

As anticipated, in this section we relax the "FI" half of FIRE. More specifically, we maintain common knowledge of rationality but remove common knowledge of the underlying shock.

20.3.1 Removing common knowledge by adding idiosyncratic noise

In our FIRE benchmark, everybody knew θ perfectly and this fact was common knowledge. We now replace this assumption with the following alternative, which captures the essence of a large literature on incomplete information and higher-order uncertainty (e.g., Morris and Shin, 2002; Woodford, 2003; Angeletos and Lian, 2016, 2018):

Assumption 20.1. *(i) Nature draws θ from $\mathcal{N}\left(0, \sigma_\theta^2\right)$.*

(ii) Agents have imperfect and heterogeneous information about θ. In particular, an agent's information set is given by (θ_i, s_i), where s_i is a sufficient statistic of the agent's information about θ (and about others' information thereof) and is given by

$$s_i = \theta + \epsilon_i,$$

where $\epsilon_i \sim \mathcal{N}\left(0, \sigma^2\right)$ is orthogonal to θ and i.i.d. across i.

(iii) The above facts are common knowledge.

The first part specifies the agents' common prior about θ. The second part specifies each agent's private information. The last part makes sure that the subjective priors about all exogenous shocks coincide with the objective truth, a requirement embedded in the REE concept.

A few remarks are worth making about this assumption. First, the Gaussian specification is useful but not essential: it keeps the analysis tractable but does not drive the main insights. Second, the signal s_i is meant to summarize all the information that agent i has about the underlying aggregate shock, and thereby also about the information of others and the resulting aggregate activity. Third, the idiosyncratic noise in this signal could reflect not only the absence of relevant information but also cognitive limitations in processing such information, as in the literature on rational inattention (Sims, 2003; Mackowiak and Wiederholt, 2009). Finally, the fact that the noise is idiosyncratic as opposed to aggregate amounts to introducing higher-order uncertainty: every agent is uncertain not only about θ itself but also about what others know about θ, and hence also about what others know about others, and so on. As we will explain in due course, it is the second kind of uncertainty that translates to GE attenuation.

Our task now is to study how the informational friction changes equilibrium behavior relative to FIRE. To do this, let us first fix the language: by "equilibrium" in this section we mean a linear REE, or equivalently strategy of the form $c_i = a\theta_i + bs_i$ that solves (20.1) under rational expectations, for some coefficients a and b. Note that this imposes not only rational expectations but also linearity, which simplifies the subsequent analysis. But the linearity restriction is without any loss: a nonlinear REE does not exist in our setting because $\alpha \in (-1, 1)$ guarantees that there is a unique REE and Assumption 20.1 guarantees that this equilibrium is linear.

20.3.2 Main lesson: GE attenuation

From Assumption 20.1, we have that, for every i,

$$E_i[\theta] = \lambda s_i \qquad \text{with} \qquad \lambda \equiv \frac{\sigma_\theta^2}{\sigma_\theta^2 + \sigma^2} \in (0, 1]. \tag{20.10}$$

Note that λ is a monotone transformation of σ_θ^2/σ^2, the signal-to-noise ratio in an agent's information. And because varying the level of noise σ in $[0, +\infty)$ is equivalent to varying the coefficient λ in $[0, 1)$, we can think of λ as an exogenous parameter.

Aggregating the above, we get

$$\bar{E}[\theta] = \lambda\theta. \tag{20.11}$$

This allows one to interpret λ as a measure of how "attentive" or "aware" agents are on average, namely how much the average expectation of θ varies with innovations in θ. But whereas this interpretation emphasizes the degree of knowledge about the underlying aggregate shock, it is best to interpret λ as a measure of how well agents can predict one another's behavior. That is, as a measure of the extent of common knowledge or, equivalently, as a measure of how effectively they can coordinate with one another.

This point will become clearer in Section 20.3.3, where we expand on the role of higher-order beliefs, and in Section 20.5.1, where we decouple the relevant lack of common knowledge from noisy information about θ. But the following lemma, which follows from the above equation along with the fact that c must be proportional to θ in equilibrium, helps capture the essence.

Lemma 20.1. *In any equilibrium, the average rational expectation of c satisfies*

$$\bar{E}[c] = \lambda c. \tag{20.12}$$

This helps explain how a lower λ impedes coordination: under FIRE ($\lambda = 1$), behavior is perfectly coordinated in the sense that the typical agent expects others to respond as much as herself; and away from this benchmark, behavior is imperfectly coordinated in the sense that the typical agent worries that others will underreact.

How does this translate in dynamic settings? Let $\{\partial c_{t+\tau}/\partial \theta_t\}_{\tau=0}^{\infty}$ denote the impulse response function (IRF) of an aggregate outcome to an exogenous shock (e.g., that of aggregate output or inflation to a monetary shock) and let $\{\partial \bar{E}_{t+\tau} [c_{t+\tau}]/\partial \theta_t\}_{\tau=0}^{\infty}$ denote the corresponding IRF for the agents' average expectation of the same outcome. FIRE imposes $\partial \bar{E}_{t+\tau} [c_{t+\tau}]/\partial \theta_t = \partial c_{t+\tau}/\partial \theta_t$ for all τ: subjective and objective IRFs coincide. By introducing incomplete information, we have effectively imposed $|\partial \bar{E}_{t+\tau} [c_{t+\tau}]/\partial \theta_\tau| < |\partial c_{t+\tau}/\partial \theta_\tau|$ for all τ, or at least for τ small enough ("short run"). This dynamic translation is useful when connecting the theory to expectations evidence in Section 20.7.

Let us now return to our static setting and consider what Lemma 20.1 implies for actual behavior. By aggregating best responses, we obtain the following joint restriction on the actual outcome and the average expectation thereof:

$$c = \theta + \alpha \bar{E}[c].$$

Next, replacing $\bar{E}[c]$ from Lemma 20.1, we get

$$c = \theta + \lambda \alpha c. \tag{20.13}$$

This is the same fixed-point equation as that characterizing the FIRE outcome for an economy in which α is replaced by $\lambda \alpha$. In other words, it is *as if* the strategic interaction, or the GE feedback, has been attenuated towards 0 in proportion to the informational friction. We therefore reach the follow result, which contains the main lesson of this section:

Proposition 20.2. *There is a unique equilibrium such that*

$$c = \underbrace{\theta}_{PE} + \underbrace{\frac{\alpha \lambda}{1 - \alpha \lambda} \theta}_{GE} = \underbrace{\frac{1}{1 - \alpha \lambda}}_{GE\ multiplier} \theta. \tag{20.14}$$

By the same token, the following properties are true:

- *The aggregate outcome is the same as in a "twin" FIRE economy in which the GE parameter α in Eq. (20.2) has been replaced by $\lambda \alpha$.*
- *No matter whether $\alpha < 0$ or $\alpha > 0$, the absolute size of the GE effect is reduced, and the more so the smaller the degree of common knowledge, as measured by λ.*
- *When the GE feedback is positive ($\alpha > 0$), the friction translates to under-reaction of the actual outcomes to the underlying innovations, relative to FIRE; and when the GE feedback is negative ($\alpha < 0$), it translates to over-reaction relative to FIRE.*

By varying λ between 0 and 1, we can thus span all the values between the PE effect θ and the FIRE outcome $\frac{1}{1-\alpha}\theta$. For λ close to zero (meaning a sufficiently large departure from common knowledge), the total impact of the aggregate shock θ is arbitrarily close to its PE effect. But as λ increases (meaning a higher degree of common knowledge), the GE effect becomes more and more important. Importantly, all these properties hold true no matter whether the GE effect amplifies the PE effect ($\alpha > 0$) or dampens the PE effect ($\alpha < 0$). But how this translates in terms of the responsiveness of the aggregate outcome to the underlying innovations naturally depends on the direction of the GE feedback: the friction translates to *underreaction* (relative to FIRE) when the feedback is positive and to *over*-reaction when the feedback is negative.

The last point underscores how the friction under consideration is distinct from pure inattention, sparsity, or adjustment costs. These forces amount to attenuation of the PE effect and translate to underreaction regardless of α (indeed even if $\alpha = 0$). The friction under consideration, instead, amounts to attenuation of the GE effect and its translation to observables depends crucially on the sign and magnitude of α.

We will illustrate how this basic insight sheds new light on topical policy questions in Section 20.6. But let us offer here a first hint of what it may mean in applied terms. The HANK literature has emphasized that liquidity constraints and other frictions contribute to high MPCs and thereby to larger GE multipliers for monetary and fiscal policy. This was stylized in the example of Section 20.2, in which α was indeed related to the MPC. In this context, the above result suggests that the Keynesian multiplier may be muted in the short run, when it is likely that there is little common knowledge about the underlying innovations and one another's behavior (λ is small to start with), but may kick in over time as agents become more aware of the underlying innovations and one another's behavior (λ gets larger over time due to learning, as discussed in Section 20.5).

20.3.3 From rational expectations to higher-order beliefs (HOBs)

We now "dig deeper" to show how the insight developed above relates to a certain property of higher-order beliefs (the beliefs of the beliefs of others). For this purpose, we will borrow heavily from game theory, and we will echo Morris and Shin (1998, 2002, 2006) and Woodford (2003). But this does not mean that the above insight, or the accommodation of incomplete information more generally, requires that the economic agents themselves be "game theorists," i.e., engage in strategic or higher-order reasoning. Instead, the typical consumer or firm can be a "statistician" in the tradition of Muth (1961) and Lucas (1972): they only need to have a statistical model of how c and θ comove. The REE concept—with or without full information—imposes that the statistical model in people's minds is consistent with actual behavior, but is deliberately agnostic about how exactly agents learn this model in the first place.

We emphasize this point because it separates the approach taken here from that taken in the next section: by design, Level-k Thinking and its variants *require* that agents engage in deductive or higher-order reasoning. But for now, we put this point aside and proceed to translate our GE attenuation result from a property of the REE fixed point to the following property of higher-order beliefs: under incomplete information, higher-order beliefs (the beliefs of the beliefs of others) tend to react less to innovations than first-order beliefs (the beliefs of the fundamentals themselves).

To illustrate this property and its likely robustness, we proceed as follows. Go back to the best-response condition (20.1) but refrain, at least for the time being, from any assumption about what an agent knows about the underlying aggregate shock and the information, rationality or behavior of others. Aggregating this condition across i, we obtain

$$c = \theta + \alpha \bar{E}[c].$$

Note that this condition encapsulates individual rationality (optimality) for arbitrary expectations of c. Next, suppose that every agent believes that *other* agents are individually rational. Then, every agent can infer that the above condition holds, which implies that the average expectations of c must satisfy

$$\bar{E}[c] = \bar{E}[\theta] + \alpha \bar{E}[\bar{E}[c]] = \bar{E}[\theta] + \alpha \bar{E}^2[c],$$

where $\bar{E}^2[\cdot] \equiv \bar{E}[\bar{E}[\cdot]]$ denotes second-order beliefs. Iterating ad infinitum, we can express that the average expectations of c in terms of the higher-order beliefs of fundamentals,

$$\bar{E}[c] = \left(\sum_{h=1}^{\infty} \alpha^{h-1} \bar{E}^h[\bar{\theta}] \right), \qquad (20.15)$$

where $\bar{E}^h[\theta] \equiv \bar{E}[\bar{E}^{h-1}[\theta]]$ for all $h \geq 1$, and with the convention $\bar{E}^0[\theta] \equiv \theta$.

The following remarks help clarify what we have done:

1. In the above construction, "iterating ad infinitum" amounts to imposing common knowledge of rationality: the first iteration requires that agents know that others are rational, the second iteration requires that agents know that others are rational, and so on.

2. Had we stopped this process at some finite order K, instead of letting $K \to \infty$, we would have obtained

$$\bar{E}[c] = \left(\sum_{h=1}^{K} \alpha^{h-1} \bar{E}^h[\bar{\theta}] \right) + \alpha^K \bar{E}^{K+1}[c].$$

This restricts the subjective expectations of the aggregate outcome only up to a point, letting $\bar{E}^{K+1}[c]$ indeterminate (a "free variable"). As it will become clear in the next section, Level-K Thinking amounts to (i) stopping at some finite K and (ii) making a specific assumption about the value of $\bar{E}^{K+1}[c]$. Here instead we dispense of this "free variable" by letting $K \to \infty$, or by imposing "infinite rationality" in the precise sense of common knowledge of rationality.

3. In general, common knowledge of rationality is weaker than REE. But as mentioned earlier, the two notions are equal in our context, thanks to the restriction $\alpha \in (-1, 1)$. It follows that condition (20.15) can be read as follows: it describes the rational expectations of c for *arbitrary* information structures, including full information.

With the last point in mind, let us now explain how condition (20.15) specializes in the knife-edge of full information—and what changes away from this benchmark.

With full information, beliefs of all orders collapse to the underlying fundamental:

$$\bar{E}^h[\theta] = \bar{E}^{h-1}[\theta] = \cdots = \bar{E}^1[\theta] = \theta. \qquad (20.16)$$

This in turn implies that $\bar{E}[c] = c$, which can be read interchangeably as follows: (i) the expected response of c to any innovation in θ coincides with the actual response; (ii) agents face no uncertainty about one another's responses; and (iii) agents perfectly coordinate their responses.

When information is noisy, these properties remain true as long as all the noise is aggregate, that is, as long as all the information is "public" (in the precise sense of common knowledge). But they cease to hold as soon as once information is private, or the noise is idiosyncratic. And it is precisely the latter scenario that represents a "real" departure from FIRE.

Consider in particular the information structure assumed in the previous analysis. With this structure, we have that

$$\bar{E}[\theta] = (1 - \lambda)\mu_\theta + \lambda\theta,$$

where μ_θ corresponds to the prior mean (itself normalized to 0 for convenience), θ corresponds to the shock, and $\lambda \in (0, 1)$ parameterizes the precision of the available private information, or the degree of common knowledge. The above implies that

$$\bar{E}^2[\theta] = (1 - \lambda)\mu_\theta + \lambda\bar{E}[\theta] = (1 - \lambda^2)\mu_\theta + \lambda^2\theta$$

and, by induction,

$$\bar{E}^h[\theta] = (1 - \lambda^h)\mu_\theta + \lambda^h\theta$$

for all $h \geq 1$. We therefore see that, in response to any innovation in θ, beliefs of higher-order move less than beliefs of lower-order—to put it differently, higher-order beliefs are more anchored to the prior and less responsive to news.

This property is a robust implication of incomplete information and has been extensively discussed in the literature (Morris and Shin, 1998, 2002, 2003; Abreu and Brunnermeier, 2003; Woodford, 2003; Angeletos and Lian, 2016). The point here was to show how this property translates to GE attenuation, as well as to pave the way for some additional insights in the sequel. But keep in mind our earlier point: although this game-theoretic translation offers important insight, in the present approach agents themselves could still be "statisticians."

20.4 Bounded rationality

In this section, we recoup the "FI" half of FIRE but relax its "RE" half. In particular, we start by adapting the plain-vanilla version of Level-k Thinking from Farhi and Werning (2019) to our setting. For this version, GE attenuation obtains necessarily when $\alpha > 0$ but not when $\alpha < 0$. We then explain how this bug is resolved by two "smooth" variants, Reflective Equilibrium (García-Schmidt and Woodford, 2019) and Cognitive Hierarchy (Camerer et al., 2004).

20.4.1 Level-k Thinking

Level-k Thinking, also known as Limited-Depth Thinking, was developed in the experimental literature; see Nagel (1995), Stahl and Wilson (1994, 1995), Costa-Gomes et al. (2001), Costa-Gomes and Crawford (2006) for early contributions, and Crawford et al. (2013) for a survey. It was later imported into macroeconomics by García-Schmidt and Woodford (2019), albeit with a twist that we explain in the next subsection, and by Farhi and Werning (2019), which we follow here.

The concept is defined in a recursive manner. Let $k \in \{0, 1, \dots\}$. For $k = 0$, behavior is exogenously specified; and for any $k \geq 1$, behavior is given by the best response to the belief that all other agents are level-$(k - 1)$ thinkers. A higher k represents "deeper thinking" in the sense of incorporating more rounds of strategic interaction.

Putting this into math, let $\hat{c}^k$ and c^k, respectively, denote the conjectured (subjective) and the actual (objective) value of the aggregate outcome, c, when all agents are level-k thinkers. For each $k \geq 1$, the actual outcome c^k is the best response to the conjecture that the outcome will be $\hat{c}^k$; that is, $c^k = \theta + \alpha \hat{c}^k$. The conjecture in turn is given by the actual outcome for level-$(k-1)$ thinkers; that is, $\hat{c}^k = c^{k-1}$. Starting for an arbitrary $\hat{c}^1 = c^0$, we then have that the level-1 outcome is given by $c^1 \equiv \theta + \alpha c^0$ and, by induction, for any $k \geq 1$, the level-k outcome is given by

$$c^k = \theta + \alpha c^{k-1} = \sum_{j=0}^{k-1} \alpha^j \theta + \alpha^k c^0. \tag{20.17}$$

Because $\alpha \in (-1, 1)$, we immediately have that $c^k \to \frac{1}{1-\alpha}\theta = c^{\text{FIRE}}$ as $k \to \infty$, regardless of c^0. That is, as the depth of thinking grows without bound ("agents become infinitely rational"), the aggregate outcome converges to its FIRE counterpart regardless of the analyst's specification of c^0. But for any $k < \infty$, c^k remains anchored to c^0. This begs the question of what's the "right" parameterization of c^0.

This choice matters greatly for our purposes. So far, the value of c^0, and indeed the entire cross-sectional distribution of c_i^0, is a "free variable." In the experimental literature, it is common to let c_i^0 be i.i.d. across i, drawn from a uniform distribution with full support over the set of feasible actions. The alternative proposed by Farhi and Werning (2019) is to set $c_i^0 = 0$ for all i or, equivalently,

$$c^1 = \theta.$$

This translates as follows: "level-1 thinkers understand PE but not GE" (i.e., they behave as if there were no GE feedback). It follows that level-2 thinkers play $c^2 = \theta + \alpha\theta$, level-3 thinkers play $c^3 = \theta + (\alpha + \alpha^2)\theta$, and so on.

These iterations resemble adaptive expectations, except that the adjustment in beliefs happens instantaneously, not over real time, and on the basis of *hypothetical* outcomes (i.e., conjectures about the behavior of others), not on the basis of the observation of *actual* past outcomes. Furthermore, under the assumption that $c^1 = \theta$, these iterations can be interpreted as rounds of GE feedbacks: level-1 agents understand only PE; level-2 agents incorporate a single round of the GE feedback; level-3 agents incorporate two rounds; and so on.

Under this prism, FIRE translates to "infinite rounds of GE feedback", and bounded rationality translates to "finite rounds of GE feedback." This in turn suggests that Level-k Thinking should generate a similar form of GE attenuation as incomplete information, with lower sophistication (lower k) here translating to less information (lower λ) there. As it turns out, this logic is valid when the GE feedback is positive ($\alpha > 0$), but has to be qualified when the feedback is negative ($\alpha < 0$).

Proposition 20.3. *Suppose that the economy consists of a continuum of level-k agents, for some $k \geq 1$. Suppose further that level-0 agents are anchored to the prior, i.e., $c^0 = 0$. Then, the aggregate outcome is given by*

$$c = \underbrace{\theta}_{PE} + \underbrace{\frac{\alpha - \alpha^k}{1-\alpha}\theta}_{GE} = \underbrace{\frac{1-\alpha^k}{1-\alpha}}_{GE\ multiplier} \theta.$$

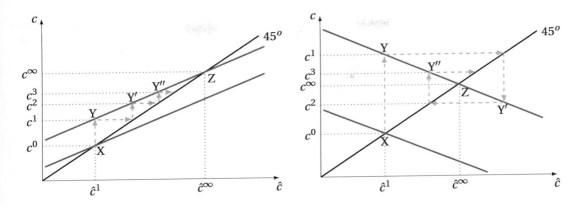

FIGURE 20.1 Level-k Thinking.

Furthermore, letting GE^k denote the GE effect in this economy and GE^{FIRE} its FIRE counterpart,[7] the following is true:

- When $\alpha > 0$, $|GE^k|$ is strictly increasing in k and bounded from above by $|GE^{FIRE}|$.
- When instead $\alpha < 0$, the above statement holds only for k odd. For k even, the opposite is true: $|GE^k|$ is strictly decreasing in k and bounded from below by $|GE^{FIRE}|$.

In other words, GE attenuation obtains in two cases: when the GE feedback is positive and the depth of thinking k is any finite number; or when the feedback is negative and k is odd. In both of these cases, level-k thinkers underestimate the response of others, not only relative to the FIRE counterpart but also relative to their *own* behavior; they therefore behave *as if* the GE feedback was smaller, i.e., as in a FIRE economy in which α is compressed towards zero. But the opposite is true when the GE feedback is negative and k is even. In this case, level-k thinkers *overestimate* the responses of others and, as a result, behave as if the GE feedback is larger.

We illustrate what's going on in Fig. 20.1. The left panel features strategic complementarity ($\alpha > 0$), and the right one features strategic substitutability ($\alpha < 0$). In either panel, the solid blue (dark gray in print version) lines represent the agent's decision rule (20.1) before and after the shock, namely for $\theta = 0$ and $\theta = 1$, respectively; $c^0 = 0$ identifies the level-0 outcome, which itself coincides with the preshock REE outcome; c^∞ identifies the postshock REE outcome. The level-1 response or, equivalently, the PE effect of the shock is captured by the vertical shift from point X to point Y. The frictionless GE effect ("infinite rounds") is captured by the shift from Y to Z. Note that the GE effect amplifies the PE effect when $\alpha > 0$ and offsets it when $\alpha < 0$. Finally, the dashed arrows represent the rounds of level-k thinking: level-1 is captured by the shift from X to Y (because level-1 coincides with PE); level-2 is captured by the shift from Y to Y'; and so on. It is then evident that Level-k Thinking captures incomplete GE adjustment when $\alpha > 0$, but opens the door to "GE overshooting" when $\alpha < 0$ and k is even.

---

[7] That is, $GE^k \equiv \frac{\alpha - \alpha^k}{1-\alpha}\theta$ and $GE^{FIRE} \equiv \frac{\alpha}{1-\alpha}\theta$.

Like others (García-Schmidt and Woodford, 2019; Angeletos and Sastry, 2021), we view this over-shooting as a bug, not a feature of Level-k Thinking. In Section 20.4.3 below, we thus explain how to fix this bug by a few appropriate amendments of this concept. With these fixes in place, and provided that one continues to assume that the level-1 outcome coincides with the PE effect, bounded rationality produces essentially the same kind of GE attenuation as that produced by incomplete information.[8] The deeper connection between the two approaches can indeed be understood by revisiting the discussion of higher-order beliefs from Section 20.3.3.

20.4.2 Parenthesis: back to higher-order beliefs

Recall that under rational expectations, and with or without full information, the aggregate outcome can be expressed as the following infinite sum:

$$c = \sum_{h=0}^{\infty} \alpha^h \bar{E}^h[\theta],$$

with $\bar{E}^0[\theta] \equiv \theta$, $\bar{E}^1[\theta] \equiv \bar{E}[\theta]$, $\bar{E}^2[\theta] \equiv \bar{E}[\bar{E}[\theta]]$, and so on. Under FIRE, we have $\bar{E}^h[\theta] = \theta$ for all h, and the above specializes to

$$c = c^{\text{FIRE}} = \sum_{h=0}^{\infty} \alpha^h \theta.$$

When we drop the "FI" half of FIRE along the lines of Section 20.3, we get $\bar{E}^h[\theta] = \lambda^h \theta$ for all $h \geq 0$, and therefore

$$c = c^{\text{inco}} = \sum_{h=0}^{\infty} \alpha^h \lambda^h \theta,$$

where $\lambda \in (0, 1)$ parameterizes the degree of common knowledge. Relative to FIRE, this amounts to discounting higher-order beliefs at an exponential rate. Finally, when we replace the "RE" half of FIRE with Level-k Thinking, we get

$$c = c^k = \sum_{h=0}^{k-1} \alpha^h \theta.$$

Relative to FIRE, this amounts to keeping the beliefs of order $h \leq k - 1$ intact and truncating the beliefs of order $h \geq k$.

Under this prism, both incomplete information and Level-k Thinking translate to "arresting the response of higher-order beliefs to the underlying shock." In the first case, this arresting takes the form of exponential discounting over h. In the second case, it takes the form of a truncation, or a step function over h. The second approach is less "smooth" than the first, but the essence is the same, especially if

---

[8] As a matter of fact, the above "bug" could have emerged even in our first approach, had we allowed for a more convoluted information structure.

the analyst feels comfortable to exchange the notion of less sophistication (lower k) for the notion of less information (lower λ).

20.4.3 Reflective equilibrium and cognitive hierarchy

The last paragraph hints that a "smooth" variant of Level-k Thinking may avoid the type of overshooting identified in the right panel of Fig. 20.1. Two such variants are readily available in the form of Reflective Equilibrium and Cognitive Hierarchy. The former was introduced by García-Schmidt and Woodford (2019) in the context of the New Keynesian model; the latter was developed by Camerer et al. (2004) and has been widely used in the behavioral and experimental literature (Crawford et al., 2013).

Let us start with Reflective Equilibrium. The basic idea is to preserve the essence of Level-k Thinking but recast the discrete iterations described in Section 20.4.1 with a continuous analogue. In particular, the depth of thinking k is now treated as a continuous variable in $(0, \infty)$ and the cognitive process is modeled as follows. Let $\hat{c}(k)$ and $c(k)$, respectively, denote the conjectured and actual values of the aggregate outcome, as functions of the depth of thinking.[9] The actual outcome is given by the average best response to the conjecture

$$c(k) = \theta + \alpha \hat{c}(k). \tag{20.18}$$

And the conjecture is given by as the solution to the following ODE:

$$\frac{d\hat{c}(h)}{dh} = c(h) - \hat{c}(h), \quad \forall h \in [0, k], \tag{20.19}$$

with the initial condition $\hat{c}(0) = 0$.

Eq. (20.19) requires that, as we move from step h to step $h + dh$, the conjecture is adjusted upwards if the conjecture at step h fell short of the corresponding outcome, and downwards otherwise. This captures the same essence as Level-k Thinking; but whereas that concept specifies these steps as discrete and requires that the conjecture in each step is given by the outcome in the previous step, Reflective Equilibrium allows the steps to be infinitesimally small and the adjustment to be continuous. As result, the bug is gone: the conjecture never overshoots the FIRE outcome.

One can visualize this with the help of Fig. 20.1 from Section 20.4.1. There (with plain-vanilla Level-k Thinking), as we varied k in $\{0, 1, 2, \dots\}$, the conjectures $\hat{c}^k$ and the outcomes c^k were jumping around in discrete steps. Here (with Reflective Equilibrium), as we vary k continuously in $(0, \infty)$, the pair $(\hat{c}^k, c^k)$ varies continuously along the segment between points Y and Z, guaranteeing that the outcome never overshoots relative to FIRE.[10] Translating this in terms of GE attenuation, we have the following result:

---

[9] These objects are also functions of θ and α, but these dependencies are suppressed to ease the notation.

[10] This brings to mind two older concepts developed to describe the off-equilibrium adjustment in Walrasian economies, namely Cobweb dynamics and Tatonnement. The first featured discrete adjustments, like Level-k Thinking. The second featured continuous adjustment, like Reflective Equilibrium. For a formalization of this parallel, see Angeletos and Lian (2017). Here, it suffices to say that Reflective Equilibrium avoids the overshooting property of Level-K Thinking for basically the same reason that Tatonnement avoided a similar overshooting property of Cobweb dynamics.

Proposition 20.4 (Reflective Equilibrium). *Suppose that agents are boundedly rational in the sense of Reflective Equilibrium, as specified above. There exists a function $\delta : [0, +\infty) \times (-1, 1) \to [0, 1)$ such that, when the depth of thinking is k, the aggregate outcome is given by*

$$c = \underbrace{\theta}_{PE} + \underbrace{\frac{\delta(k, \alpha)\alpha}{1 - \delta(k, \alpha)\alpha}\theta}_{GE} = \underbrace{\frac{1}{1 - \delta(k, \alpha)\alpha}}_{GE\ multiplier}\theta.$$

Furthermore, $\delta(k, \alpha)$ is strictly increasing in k, starting from 0 at $k = 0$ and converging to 1 as $k \to \infty$, regardless of the sign of α.

Reflective equilibrium therefore not only fixes the bug of the plain vanilla Level-k Thinking but also provides a tight connection to incomplete information: the two approaches generate the same kind of GE attenuation, with $\delta(k, \alpha)$ taking the place of λ. More succinctly, a lower depth of thinking under the present approach translates to a lower degree of common knowledge under our first approach (and vice versa).

Similar points apply to Cognitive Hierarchy. Motivated by the heterogeneity of observed choices and reported beliefs in experiments, this concept modifies the plain-vanilla Level-k Thinking in two ways. First, actual heterogeneity is introduced in the depth of thinking. And second, agents are allowed to understand the presence of such heterogeneity, albeit up to a point: an agent still thinks that she is at least as sophisticated as anybody else. With a judicious parameterization of the objective heterogeneity and of the subjective beliefs thereof, the distance between the average conjecture $\hat{c}$ and the corresponding best-response outcome c is a continuous function of a single parameter τ, which can be interpreted as the average sophistication in the population. The details are spelled out in Appendix A of the NBER working paper version of this paper. But the bottom line is this: relative to Reflective Equilibrium, this concept allows for heterogeneity but produces basically the same predictions for aggregate beliefs and aggregate outcomes.

20.5 Additional variants and dynamic extensions

In this section, we review the third approach, by Angeletos and La'O (2009) and Angeletos and Sastry (2021), which captures the common essence of the above two approaches while also being easier to use. We then discuss how the insights extend to dynamic settings, in particular the roles played by learning and forward looking behavior. We finally explain why the fourth approach, by Gabaix (2020), can be viewed as a close cousin of the other three approaches.

20.5.1 A bridge: heterogeneous priors, or shallow reasoning

We now discuss the approach taken by Angeletos and La'O (2009) and Angeletos and Sastry (2021). This approach mimics *both* incomplete information and Level-k Thinking (and its variants), while also being highly tractable and easily adaptable to richer settings.

The basic idea in Angeletos and La'O (2009) is to use heterogeneous priors to decouple the degree of common knowledge, or the extent of the coordination friction, from the precision of the available information. Think of this as revisiting the analysis in Section 20.3 and letting λ be a separate parameter from σ, the level of noise. Angeletos and Sastry (2021) further simplify that approach, highlight its tight connection to Level-k Thinking, and conclude that it captures interchangeably bounded depth of knowledge and bounded depth of rationality. Accordingly, they refer to this approach as "shallow reasoning." But one could also call it "anchored beliefs" or "lack of common knowledge of others' attentiveness."

Here, we follow the version of Angeletos and Sastry (2021), which amounts to the following joint assumption on the agents' actual information about θ and on their subjective beliefs about the information of others:

Assumption 20.2. *We shut down idiosyncratic shocks in fundamentals: $\theta_i = \theta$ for all i. All agents know θ and all agents are individually rational in the sense that they play according to the best response condition (20.1). However, this fact is not common knowledge. Instead, every agent believes (i) that the above fact is true for only a fraction λ of other agents, and that these agents share the same beliefs with herself; and (ii) that the remaining fraction $1 - \lambda$ of agents are uninformed about θ and that they therefore play $c_i = 0$.*

This approach resembles incomplete information in that it preserves common knowledge of rationality but drops common knowledge of the shock. But the latter property is no longer accomplished by adding nontrivial noise in the agents' own observation of θ. Instead, it is accomplished by introducing heterogeneous priors about one another's information. In a nutshell, all agents may *themselves* be perfectly informed about θ and nevertheless worry that other agents are *not*.

At the same time, this approach resembles Level-k Thinking and its two variants in the following regard: there, agents thought that they were smarter than the others; here, they think they are better informed than the others. Furthermore, it is straightforward to translate such beliefs about the informativeness of others to beliefs about the rationality of others: the proposed concept is indeed equivalent, in terms of both beliefs and behavior, to a variant of Cognitive Hierarchy in which the actual distribution of types has mass 1 at $k = \infty$, while the corresponding subjective beliefs have mass $1 - \lambda$ at $k = \infty$ and λ at $k = 0$.

In a nutshell, one can interpret λ interchangeably as the depth of knowledge and the depth of reasoning. Crucially, though, the present approach avoids the iterative nature of Level-k Thinking and instead preserves the fixed-point nature of REE: agents are statisticians, albeit with a misspecified model about the information of others. To put it differently, the present approach boils down to Bayesian Nash Equilibrium with heterogeneous priors.

Let us see what this means in practice. Let c be the actual outcome, or equivalently the action of the typical agent. Since this agent believes that only a fraction λ of the population are like herself (i.e., have the same information and play the same action), and that the remaining fraction is inactive, this agent's expectation of the aggregate outcome is given by

$$E_i [c] = (1 - \lambda) 0 + \lambda c = \lambda c.$$

The best response to this belief is

$$c_i = \theta + \alpha \lambda c. \tag{20.20}$$

Aggregating and solving for c, we get the following result:

Proposition 20.5. *Suppose that agents are shallow reasoners in the sense described in Assumption 20.2. The aggregate outcome is given by*

$$c = \underbrace{\theta}_{PE} + \underbrace{\frac{\alpha\lambda}{1-\alpha\lambda}\theta}_{GE} = \underbrace{\frac{1}{1-\alpha\lambda}}_{GE\ multiplier}\theta.$$

Note that this is the exact same characterization as that provided in Proposition 20.2 for our incomplete-information model. The difference, as anticipated in the beginning of this section, is that λ is now disconnected from how much agents know about the underlying shock and instead is more directly tied to the degree of common knowledge. At the same time, this approach preserves the bounded-rationality flavor of Level-k Thinking, for the reasons already explained. We conclude that the present approach bridges the other two approaches—and as evident from above analysis, it is more tractable than both of them.

20.5.2 Dynamics I: learning

So far the analysis has been confined to a static framework in order to deliver the key insights in a sharp and transparent manner. In applications, however, it is often central to allow for two different kinds of dynamics. The first (discussed in this subsection) has to do with learning over time, or the dynamics of beliefs. The second (discussed in the next subsection) has to do with intertemporal payoff interdependences, which make the decisions forward-looking actions.

To isolate the role of learning, we continue to assume that the GE feedback is static but let decisions be repeated over time, on the basis of time-varying fundamentals and beliefs. More specifically, we index time by $t \in \{0, 1, \dots\}$ and specify the optimal behavior at each t as follows:

$$c_{i,t} = \theta_{i,t} + \alpha E_{i,t}[c_t], \qquad (20.21)$$

where $c_{i,t}$ is the action (e.g., spending) of agent i in period t, $\theta_{i,t}$ is her payoff-relevant fundamental, c_t and θ_t are the corresponding aggregates, and $E_{i,t}$ is the agent's expectation in period t.

This is basically the same kind of dynamic setting as that considered in Woodford (2003) and Angeletos and La'O (2010). In the former, $c_{i,t}$ maps to the price set by a firm, $\theta_{i,t}$ to its nominal marginal cost, and $E_{i,t}[c_t]$ to its expectation of the aggregate price level; and in the latter, $c_{i,t}$ translates to the production of a firm, $\theta_{i,t}$ to its productivity, and $E_{i,t}[c_t]$ to its expectations of aggregate output (or aggregate demand). Putting aside the possible interpretations, the key observation here is that (20.21) rules out any feedback from the outcomes at $\tau \neq t$ to optimal behavior at t, which retains the static nature of the GE feedback and isolates the adjustment in beliefs as the only interesting dynamic element.

To illustrate, consider an aggregate shock to θ_0. With time passing, the agent receives more information about θ_0 (e.g., her own fundamental $\theta_{i,t}$) and gradually learns about θ_0. Because of such learning, the effective degree of information friction about θ_0 may decrease (equivalently, the effective degree of λ may increase) with the passage of time. For example, in the environment where the GE effect works in the same direction as the PE effect, such learning will let the GE multiplier increase with the age of the shock.

The basic idea that gradual learning can help generate sluggish responses is, of course, not new; a version of it can be found, e.g., in Sims (2003) and Mankiw and Reis (2002). But the subtler point first recognized by Woodford (2003), further pushed by Angeletos and Huo (2021), and echoed above is that the sluggishness in the aggregate outcomes implied by any given informational friction is larger the larger the macroeconomic complementarity or the GE feedback. This in turn helps explain why the form of sluggishness documented here is closely connected to the notion of GE attenuation, as well as why it may be more pronounced at the macro level than at the micro level (Angeletos and Huo, 2021), or more succinctly why macro hump shapes can be consistent micro jumps (Auclert et al., 2020).

Another important question is how exactly learning, or the adjustment in beliefs, takes place. Learning under full rationality, or Bayesian learning, is an important benchmark but not the only option. We refer the reader to Chapter 23 in this Handbook for a more detailed treatment of Bayesian learning with incomplete information, and to Chapter 25 in this Handbook for an alternative that emphasizes the spreading of beliefs from one agent to another.

20.5.3 Dynamics II: forward-looking behavior

In (20.2), the GE feedback is static; but modern macroeconomics emphasize forward looking behavior and intertemporal GE interactions. To illustrate, let us revisit the New Keynesian economy of Section 20.2.2. There, we assumed that the monetary policy replicated flexible-price outcomes for all $t \geq 1$. That assumption let us fix $E_{i,0}[c_t] = c_t = 0$ for all $t \geq 1$ and all i, muting the roles forward-looking behavior and dynamic GE interactions, and allowing us to reduce the entire economy to a static game at $t = 0$. But once we relax that assumption, the economy translates to a dynamic economy featuring not only a different decision at each t but also a GE feedback across t.

To see this more clearly, suppose that the discount rate shock follows an AR(1) process with persistence ρ and that prices are perfectly rigid, so that $\pi_t = 0$ for all t. The optimal consumption of an agent can then be expressed as follows:

$$c_{i,t} = -\beta\sigma \left\{ \sum_{k=0}^{+\infty} \beta^k E_{i,t}[i_{t+k}] \right\} + (1-\beta) \left\{ \sum_{k=0}^{+\infty} \beta^k E_{i,t}[c_{t+k}] \right\} + \frac{\beta\sigma}{1-\rho} \varrho_{i,t}. \qquad (20.22)$$

Next, assume the following Taylor rule for monetary policy:

$$i_t = \phi c_t, \qquad (20.23)$$

where $\phi > 0$ parameterizes how aggressively monetary policy responds to fluctuations in aggregate demand. Replacing the above into (20.22) and aggregating, we reach the following joint restriction between aggregate demand and expectations thereof:

$$c_t = \theta_t + \alpha \left\{ \sum_{k=0}^{+\infty} \beta^k \bar{E}_t[c_{t+k}] \right\}, \qquad (20.24)$$

where $\theta_t \equiv \frac{\beta\sigma}{1-\rho} \varrho_t$ and $\alpha \equiv 1 - \beta - \sigma\beta\phi$ can be interpreted as, respectively, the aggregate demand shock and the degree of dynamic macroeconomy complementarity. We then see clearly the following properties. First, the mathematical structure and interpretation of (20.24) is similar to the static analogue used in the rest of our chapter, except that now the outcome (aggregate spending) in any given period depends on the average expectations of the outcome not only in the same period but also in all future periods. And second, this dependence, or the overall dynamic GE feedback, is pinned down by the difference between the slope of the Keynesian cross $(1 - \beta)$ and the slope of the Taylor rule (ϕ).

The intuition for the last property is basically the same as that in Section 20.2.2: a larger MPC contributes towards a positive GE feedback, or strategic complementarity $(\alpha > 0)$; a less accommodative monetary policy contributes towards a negative GE feedback, or strategic substitutability $(\alpha < 0)$. What changes is that these feedbacks, or the strategic interactions, run across time.

Although this change is relatively minor at the conceptual level, it can raise nontrivial challenges at the computational level. This is particularly true for the incomplete-information approach; see Nimark (2008, 2017), Huo and Takayama (2021), and Angeletos and Huo (2021) for both a detailed discussion of the challenge and some ways to tame them. Level-k Thinking is significantly more manageable, as illustrated in Farhi and Werning (2019), because it shuts down any adjustment in beliefs. But if one is willing to abstract from learning, one can further maximize tractability by employing the approach in Angeletos and Sastry (2021). In the present context, for example, this approach translates to replacing the average subjective expectations $\bar{E}_t [c_{t+k}]$ in Eq. (20.24) with $\lambda \mathbb{E}_t [c_{t+k}]$, where $\mathbb{E}_t[\cdot]$ is the FIRE expectation operator and $\lambda \in (0, 1)$ measures the depth of knowledge or rationality. That is, Eq. (20.24) becomes

$$c_t = \theta_t + \lambda \alpha \left\{ \sum_{k=0}^{+\infty} \beta^k \mathbb{E}_t [c_{t+k}] \right\}. \tag{20.25}$$

Two properties are then evident: the insight about GE attenuation goes through; and the above approach is just as tractable as the FIRE benchmark.[11]

20.5.4 Cognitive discounting

We now turn to the approach taken by Gabaix (2020). This departs from FIRE by assuming that the *perceived* law of motion of the aggregate state of the economy is less persistent than the *actual* law of motion. Suppose in particular that a model's true law motion is given by

$$x_t = A x_{t-1} + B \epsilon_t,$$

where A and B are matrices, x_t is the state variable, and ϵ_t is the innovation. Gabaix (2020) assumes that the "behavioral agent" incorrectly perceives the law of motion to be $x_t = m \cdot (A x_{t-1} + B \epsilon_t)$, for some exogenous scalar $m \in (0, 1)$ that is interpreted as a "cognitive" discount factor.

To illustrate how this translates to GE attenuation, consider the New Keynesian example of the previous section. As long as the exogenous shock follows an AR(1) process, the FIRE outcome also follows an AR(1): it satisfies $c_t = \rho c_{t-1} + b^{\text{FIRE}} \epsilon_t$, where ϵ_t stands for the innovation in θ_t, ρ is the actual persistence of θ_t, and $b^{\text{FIRE}} > 0$ is a scalar pinned down by σ, β, ρ and ϕ. One can guess and

---

[11] One can further show that the exact same equation obtains with rational expectations and incomplete information as long as there is no learning, or at least as long as agents do not anticipate that there will be learning in the future. This point is proved in Angeletos and Lian (2018) and makes clear that the key simplification of Angeletos and Sastry (2021) is to abstract from learning, thus also bypassing the technical challenge of keeping track of the dynamics in the hierarchy of beliefs (Townsend, 1983).

verify that a similar property is true in the presence of cognitive discounting ($m < 1$),

$$c_t = \rho c_{t-1} + b\epsilon_t,$$

albeit for some $b \neq b^{\text{FIRE}}$. With this guess, the *perceived* law of motion becomes

$$c_t = \hat{\rho} c_{t-1} + \hat{b}\epsilon_t,$$

with $\hat{\rho} \equiv m\rho$ and $\hat{b} \equiv mb$. Together with the fact that future innovations are unpredictable, this implies that the subjective expectations satisfy $\bar{E}_t[c_{t+k}] = \hat{\rho}^k c_t = m^k \rho^k c_t$, while the objective, rational, expectations satisfy $\mathbb{E}_t[c_{t+k}] = \rho^k c_t$. It follows that

$$\bar{E}_t[c_{t+k}] = m^k \mathbb{E}_t[c_{t+k}], \tag{20.26}$$

which makes clear the following point: the present variant shares with all the other approaches in this chapter the property that the average expectations of the actions of others, or of the aggregate outcome, respond less to the underlying innovations than the actual outcome.

One subtle difference is that this kind of underreaction is predicted to increase with the horizon of forecasts, while this is not the case for other approaches in this chapter. With Angeletos and Sastry (2021), for example, we have $\bar{E}_t[c_{t+k}] = \lambda \mathbb{E}_t[c_{t+k}]$, where $\lambda \in (0, 1)$ is invariant to the forecast horizon k. Furthermore, when agents are incompletely informed but rational and there is learning over time, we effectively have that $\bar{E}_t[c_{t+k}] = \mu_k \mathbb{E}_t[c_{t+k}]$, where $\mu_k \in (0, 1)$ is an *increasing* function of k, opposite to (20.26). The intuition is that, when agents expect both themselves and others to learn, they also expect the friction in coordination to ease (formally, to reach higher levels of common knowledge). Notwithstanding this subtle difference, cognitive discounting is a close cousin of the other approaches in this chapter. And it shares with Angeletos and Sastry (2021) both a high degree of tractability and the treatment of the agents as "statisticians" rather than as "game theorists."

20.6 Applications

In this section, we illustrate how the abstract insights translate to specific applications.

20.6.1 Forward guidance at the zero lower bound

Consider a New Keynesian economy in a liquidity-trap recession, so that the central bank's hands are tied by the Zero Lower Bound (ZLB) on interest rates. The central bank may still attempt to stimulate aggregate demand by committing to keep interest rates low after the economy exits the trap and the ZLB ceases to bind. The basic New Keynesian model predicts that this kind of forward guidance can be extremely effective. But this does not appear to have been the case during the Great Recession, so this prediction became known as the "forward guidance puzzle" (Del Negro et al., 2015; McKay et al., 2016).

To understand this puzzle and our proposed resolution thereof, let us revisit the environment behind Eq. (20.24), pick an arbitrary $T \geq 2$ and make the following assumptions about monetary policy: $i_t = 0$ for $t \leq T - 1$ (this captures the role of the ZLB); i_T is chosen and announced at $t = 0$ (this captures the role of forward guidance); and finally for all $t \geq T + 1$, i_t is such that the flexible-price outcome, or $c_t = 0$, is henceforth obtained (this captures "return to norm"). The question of interest boils down to the following: how does c_0 varies with i_T, and in particular how does this response depend on T, the horizon of forward guidance?

To ease the exposition, let us address this question while abstracting from the role of inflation: prices are perfectly rigid, so that $\pi_t = 0$ for all t. Together with the above assumptions about monetary policy, this implies that Eq. (20.4) reduces to

$$
c_t = -\beta\sigma \left\{ \beta^{T-t} \bar{E}_t [i_T] \right\} + (1-\beta) \left\{ \sum_{k=0}^{T-t} \beta^k \bar{E}_t [c_{t+k}] \right\}, \tag{20.27}
$$

for all $t \leq T$ (and $c_t = 0$ thereafter). With FIRE, we further have $\bar{E}_t [i_T] = i_T$ and $\bar{E}_t [c_{t+k}] = c_{t+k}$, so that the response of c_t to the news about i_T can be calculated as follows:

$$
\frac{\partial c_t}{\partial i_T} = \underbrace{-\beta\sigma\beta^{T-t}}_{\text{PE}} + \underbrace{(1-\beta) \left\{ \sum_{k=0}^{T-t} \beta^k \frac{\partial c_{t+k}}{\partial i_T} \right\}}_{\text{GE}}. \tag{20.28}
$$

From this expression, we can see that, although the PE effect of i_T on c_t *decreases* with T, reflecting discounting at the individual level, the GE effect actually *increases* with T, because a large horizon translates to more periods over which the Keynesian feedback between income and spending can operate (or equivalently to a larger response in expected permanent income). Furthermore, these two conflicting effects happen to offset each other perfectly in the representative-agent version of the New Keynesian model, so that the following is true here:

Proposition 20.6. *Under FIRE, $\frac{\partial c_0}{\partial i_T} = -\sigma$ for all T.*

More succinctly, forward guidance about interest rates far in the future is predicted to be as effective as conventional monetary policy, which seems counterfactual. And if we relax the simplifying assumption of perfectly rigid prices, the puzzle gets even worse: under FIRE, the response of c_0 to any news about i_T increases with the horizon T. This is because allowing for nonrigid prices amounts to introducing an additional GE feedback between aggregate spending and inflation, which only adds to the income-spending multiplier.

The bottom line is that the puzzle is driven by GE feedbacks. But then it is an immediate corollary of this chapter's main theme that this puzzle is resolved, or at least eased, if we accommodate some bounds on the agents' depth of knowledge or rationality. For example, if we adopt the approach of Angeletos and Sastry (2021), we have that $\bar{E}_t [i_T] = i_T$ but $\bar{E}_t [c_{t+k}] = \lambda c_{t+k}$, so that (20.28) changes to the following:

$$
\frac{\partial c_t}{\partial i_T} = \underbrace{-\beta\sigma\beta^{T-t}}_{\text{PE}} + \lambda (1-\beta) \left\{ \sum_{k=0}^{T-t} \beta^k \frac{\partial c_{t+k}}{\partial i_T} \right\}. \tag{20.29}
$$

That is, the GE effect is effectively discounted by a factor equal to λ, helping the PE logic to "reign supreme." Indeed, solving the above fixed point problem, one can easily see that the power of forward guidance is attenuated and that the degree of attenuation increases not only with the friction in knowledge/rationality but also with the horizon T.

Proposition 20.7. *Suppose that there is a bound on agents' depth of knowledge or rationality, in the form of Angeletos and Sastry (2021). Then,*

$$\frac{\partial c_0}{\partial i_T} = \phi\left(\lambda, T\right) \left.\frac{\partial c_0}{\partial i_T}\right|_{FIRE}, \tag{20.30}$$

where $\phi(\lambda, T)$ is strictly bounded between 0 and 1, strictly increasing in λ for any $T \geq 1$, and strictly decreasing in T for any $\lambda \in [0, 1)$.

   Given what has been shown in this chapter, it should be no surprise that this result readily translates to rational expectations once information is incomplete (Angeletos and Lian, 2018), to Level-k Thinking (Farhi and Werning, 2019), and to Cognitive Discounting Gabaix (2020). As one moves across these approaches, the math changes a bit, but the essence is the same.

   The result as stated above directly extends to the full version of the New Keynesian model, which allows prices to adjust slowly. For a textbook calibration of that model and a modest value of the novel friction ($\lambda = 0.75$), Angeletos and Lian (2018) find that the attenuation effect can be quite sizable: at a horizon of 5 years ($T = 20$), the power of forward guidance could be as low as *one tenth* of its FIRE counterpart.[12] This number is of course sensitive not only to λ but also to all other parameters that regulate the potency of GE feedbacks, such as the slope of the Keynesian cross and the slope of the Phillips curve. By adopting a textbook calibration, Angeletos and Lian (2018) overestimates the latter but also underestimates the former. Accordingly, Farhi and Werning (2019) have emphasized that the documented attenuation effect is likely to be more pronounced in HANK economies that properly account for liquidity constraints and high MPCs than in an RANK economy. This circles back to our earlier point about the synergies between the type of frictions considered in this chapter and those traditionally considered in the literatures on incomplete markets and heterogeneity. For additional examples of this point, see Angeletos and Huo (2021) and Auclert et al. (2020).

20.6.2 Fiscal policy

We now turn to fiscal policy. In particular, we consider the question studied in Vimercati et al. (2021): which of the two fiscal tools, an increase in government spending or a reduction in consumption taxes, is more effective in stimulating aggregate demand when the economy is at the ZLB. Both types of fiscal stimuli are assumed to be financed by an increase in future lump sum taxes, so neither of them involves a labor distortion. The key issue, instead, is how expectations respond to the one versus the other.

   Because consumption taxes enter individual consumption in the exact same way as real interest rates, our preceding insights about forward guidance translate as follows: bounded rationality, or lack

---

[12] $\lambda = 0.75$ can be read as follows: every agent expects the typical other agent to be inattentive and not respond with probability 25%. Calibrating λ to the type evidence considered in Coibion and Gorodnichenko (2012, 2015) could have justified an even smaller value.

of common knowledge, reduces the stimulative power of future tax cuts but not so much that of current tax cuts, because the latter have a more pronounced, direct, PE effect. And since current taxes, unlike current monetary policy, are not constrained by the ZLB, this policy tool remains basically as effective as in FIRE—which is one key lesson in Vimercati et al. (2021).

But what about the other tool, government spending? Suppose, for simplicity, that the initial level of public debt is zero, so that the average asset position of the households is also zero. By aggregating the individual consumption functions, we now get that, unsurprisingly, aggregate demand depends on real interest rates and *disposable* permanent income:

$$c_t = -\beta\sigma \left\{ \sum_{k=0}^{+\infty} \beta^k \bar{E}_t \left[i_{t+k} - \pi_{t+k+1} \right] \right\} + (1-\beta) \left\{ \sum_{k=0}^{+\infty} \beta^k \bar{E}_t \left[y_{t+k} - T_{t+k} \right] \right\},$$

where T_t is the lump sum tax in period t. By the intertemporal budget constraint of the government, on the other hand, the present discounted value of taxes must equal the present discounted value of government spending. To the extent that consumers understand this basic fact, the above equation is replaced by

$$c_t = -\beta\sigma \left\{ \sum_{k=0}^{+\infty} \beta^k \bar{E}_t \left[i_{t+k} - \pi_{t+k+1} \right] \right\} + (1-\beta) \left\{ \sum_{k=0}^{+\infty} \beta^k \bar{E}_t \left[y_{t+k} - G_{t+k} \right] \right\},$$

where G_t is the government spending at t. Finally, by market clearing, $y_t - G_t = c_t$. And provided that consumers understand this property, too, the above reduces to

$$c_t = -\beta\sigma \left\{ \sum_{k=0}^{+\infty} \beta^k \bar{E}_t \left[i_{t+k} - \pi_{t+k+1} \right] \right\} + (1-\beta) \left\{ \sum_{k=0}^{+\infty} \beta^k \bar{E}_t \left[c_{t+k} \right] \right\}, \qquad (20.31)$$

which is *exactly* the same as Eq. (20.4) before.

This immediately implies that the following property extends from FIRE to all the alternatives studied in this chapter:

Proposition 20.8. *Holding constant the average expectations of real interest rates, aggregate private spending is invariant to the path of government spending, regardless of the depth of knowledge and rationality.*

By the same token, if prices are rigid and the monetary authority does not change interest rates in response to fiscal policy, the fiscal multiplier is one, again regardless of the depth of knowledge and rationality. This is indeed a corollary of Proposition 8 from Angeletos and Lian (2018).[13]

This lesson is different from that reported in Vimercati et al. (2021): that paper argues that, holding real rates constant, government spending crowds out private spending once agents are boundedly rational in the sense of Level-k Thinking. The apparent contradiction is due to a subtle difference in the specification of level-1 beliefs. Let us explain.

---

[13] That proposition, and similarly an extension in Vimercati et al. (2021), allows for prices to be nonrigid. This does not upset Proposition 20.8 above, but changes the prediction about fiscal multipliers, because government spending can now feed into inflation. For careful treatments of this case, see Section 6 of Angeletos and Lian (2018) and Section 3 of Vimercati et al. (2021).

In Section 20.4.1, and following Farhi and Werning (2019), we assumed that level-1 agents expect others not to respond to the underlying shock ($\hat{c}^1 = c^0 = 0$) and therefore act as if the shock had only a PE effect ($c^1 = \theta$). In the present context, this translates to the belief that the path of aggregate private spending is invariant to the path of government spending, or $\hat{c}_t^1 = 0$ for all t. By contrast, in Vimercati et al. (2021) the level-1 belief is that the path of aggregate *output* is invariant to the path of government spending, which translates to $\hat{c}_t^1 = -G_t$. That is, in response to an increase in government spending, level-1 consumers now expect other consumers to cut down their spending, which in turn motivates them to cut down their own spending despite the fact that government spending has no direct PE effect. As a result, the fiscal multiplier is lower than its FIRE counterpart for level-1 thinkers; and by induction, it remains so for any finite level of reasoning.

Which specification of level-1 beliefs is more plausible? The following remark offers some theoretical guidance: only the first specification is consistent with rational expectations and lack of common knowledge of the path of government spending. But the question is ultimately an empirical one: one can imagine conducting surveys that elicit the relevant subjective beliefs, whether in the messy real world or in a controlled experiment.

20.6.3 Other applications

We now discuss how the insights can find application outside the New Keynesian context—or even outside macroeconomics.

To start with, consider the incomplete-information RBC model of Angeletos and La'O (2010). This boils down to a game among the firms, with the best response of firm i given by

$$y_{i,t} = (1-\alpha)\chi a_{i,t} + \alpha E_{i,t}[y_t] \tag{20.32}$$

where $y_{i,t}$ is its output, $a_{i,t}$ is its TFP, $y_t = \int y_{i,t} di$ is aggregate output, and $\chi > 0$ and $\alpha < 1$ are fixed scalars. In this context, the empirically relevant case is $\alpha > 0$[14]; and this chapter's lesson about GE attenuation translates to under-reaction of aggregate output to aggregate TFP shocks. For some parameterizations, this attenuation can be sufficiently large that aggregate employment changes little, or even decreases, in response to a positive TFP shock, helping reconcile the RBC model with the evidence in Gali (1999).

Another flexible-price application is found in Venkateswaran (2014). Under our lens, that paper can be summarized as follows: incomplete information attenuates the GE feedback inside the Diamond–Mortessen–Pissarides model; and because that feedback is negative, this translates to larger unemployment fluctuations than under FIRE, helping ease the so-called Shimer puzzle.

Next, and moving from macroeconomics to IO, consider the works of Camerer and Lovallo (1999) and Greenwood and Hanson (2015) on "competition neglect." The latter concept refers to the idea that firms may fail to recognize that a favorable demand or supply shock will lead additional competitors to enter the industry, and as a result may cause the firms to overexpand in the short run. Under the prism of our analysis, the concept of competition neglect is the same as the concept of GE attenuation.

---

[14] In principle, α could be of either sign because it encapsulates two conflicting GE feedbacks: when other firms produce more, aggregate income goes up, which feeds to higher demand and higher returns for each firm; but they also push up the cost of labor or other inputs, which contributes in the opposite direction.

And in this particular context, GE attenuation translates to overreaction, or the kind of overinvestment documented in Greenwood and Hanson (2015), simply because the GE feedback works in the opposite direction to the PE effect.

Finally, let us turn to single-agent decision problems, the focus of Lian (2021). That paper shows how the theoretical tools and insights developed for *interpersonal* coordination frictions (as in Section 20.3) can be then used to study *intrapersonal* decisions and to provide a new way to think about narrow bracketing and mental accounting. This is formalized by assigning different decisions to different selves, who in turn share the same objective (the decision maker's utility) but make their respective decisions on the basis of different, nonnested, information.

20.7 Discussion: similarities, differences, and empirical backdrop

The key similarities of the various approaches considered in this chapter can be summarized as follows: they all can be understood as relaxations of one or another common-knowledge assumption; relative to FIRE, they all amount to discounting higher-order beliefs or, equivalently, to arresting the expected response of others to aggregate shocks; and they all ultimately translate to GE attenuation. We next expand on some of their key differences, of both conceptual and empirical nature. And we try to offer further guidance on when and how to use these approaches.

20.7.1 Key differences

Let us focus on our main two approaches, incomplete information and Level-K Thinking (or its variants). One key difference has already been emphasized: while Level-k Thinking requires that agents be "game theorists" (to reason recursively), incomplete information allows them to be "statisticians," in the tradition of Lucas (1972) and Muth (1961).

This cuts both ways. In the macroeconomic context, it does not seem a priori compelling—at least to us—to model the consumers or the firms as strategic players that actively engages in the kind of iterative reasoning articulated in Section 20.4. Instead, it seems more natural to model their thinking about the economy as a statistical model, which is what the incomplete information approach allows. On the other hand, the RE half of this approach, namely the assumption that the subjective statistical model in people's mind is the same as the objective truth, is hard to defend in the context of unusual circumstances, such as the Great Recession and the ZLB on monetary policy.

Another difference regards the scope for learning. Like other departures from rational expectations, Level-k Thinking begs the question of what agents do in the face of systematic discrepancies between their expectations and the realized outcomes. In the experimental literature, the estimated depth of thinking often increases with the rounds of play. Translating this into our context may suggest that the GE attenuation diminishes with the passage of time. But there is a problem: for this idea to be operational in a stationary environment, it would have to be that agents are at once "shallow thinkers" vis-a-vis recent shocks and "deep thinkers" vis-a-vis old shocks. Clearly, this makes no sense in the context of Level-k Thinking, at least insofar one takes this concept literally: an agent's reasoning capacity and her understanding of the economy may vary with her education and experience, but may not fluctuate with the age of recurring aggregate shocks.

Incomplete information (and its sibling, Rational Inattention) naturally avoids these problems. First, by maintaining rational expectations, this approach makes sure that agents are never presented with the conundrum of systematic discrepancies between their expectations and the realized outcome. And second, by allowing agents to accumulate more information about any given shock with the passage of time since the shock occurs, it naturally predicts that the degree of common knowledge is specific to each shock and increases with the age of the shock. More succinctly, incomplete information predicts that agents behave *as if* they are once shallow thinkers vis-a-vis recent shocks and deep thinkers vis-a-vis old shocks.

Last but not least, the two approaches share the same predictions about the time-series properties of *average* forecasts but have distinct predictions about the corresponding properties of *individual* forecasts. The same applies to cognitive discounting. We elaborate on this point in the next section and use it to highlight the combination of the survey evidence reported in Coibion and Gorodnichenko (2012, 2015), Bordalo et al. (2020), Angeletos et al. (2021) and elsewhere seems to favor incomplete information over all the alternatives.

All considered, we would offer the following guidelines: Incomplete Information, its siblings, Rational Inattention and Sticky Information, and the bounded-rationality alternatives of Angeletos and Sastry (2021) and Gabaix (2020) seem best suited for the study of "normal" business cycles and "systematic" policy rules. Furthermore, if one is willing to abstract from learning, the latter two approaches capture the essence while buying a lot of tractability. But we agree with Farhi and Werning (2019) that Level-k Thinking or some variants thereof may make sense in the context of unprecedented experiences, as well as that it offers another, plausible, and indeed complementary, way to model bounded rationality.

At the end of the day, it really depends on what the analyst wishes to achieve. If the main goal is to capture and quantify the degree of GE attenuation, the various approaches reviewed in this chapter are basically interchangeable. The key discipline from the data will then come in the form of measuring how much average expectations comove with realized outcomes, conditionally on a given policy shift or some other aggregate shocks. In our static, one-shock framework, this means measuring the ratio between the empirical counterparts of $\partial \bar{E}[c]/\partial \theta$ and $\partial c/\partial \theta$; and in a more realistic, dynamic, multishock context, it translates to the ratio between the empirical counterparts of $\{\partial \bar{E}_t[c_{t+\tau}]/\partial \epsilon_t\}_{\tau=0}^{\infty}$ and $\{\partial \mathbb{E}_t[c_{t+\tau}]/\partial \epsilon_t\}_{\tau=0}^{\infty}$.[15] Whether this ratio is matched in the theory by choosing a low degree of common knowledge, λ, a low depth of thinking, k, or a low cognitive discount factor, m, looks like a "detail" with regard to the aforementioned goal. But if the goal shifts to understanding and quantifying the adjustment of expectations over time, a theory that accommodates some form of learning seems necessary, and then incomplete information seems to be in a better position than the alternatives.

20.7.2 Empirical backdrop: underreaction in average vs individual forecasts

We now expand on the point made above regarding the available evidence on average and individual forecasts.

Under all the approaches considered in this chapter, GE attenuation is a direct consequence of the fact that agents underestimate one another's responses. A common testable prediction of all these

---

[15] In the latter case, one must read "ratio" as a measure of distance between the two IRFs. See, for example, Angeletos et al. (2021).

approaches is therefore the following: relative to actual outcomes such as inflation and GDP, the *average* expectations of these outcomes should underreact in response to identified shocks, or to past revisions of expectations.

This prediction and some close variants of it find empirical support in surveys of expectations (Coibion and Gorodnichenko, 2012, 2015; Angeletos et al., 2021). The available evidence on average forecasts therefore clearly favors these approaches over FIRE. But such evidence does not help distinguish between the various approaches. To accomplish this, we must look into *individual* forecasts.

If the first approach (incomplete information but rational expectations) is right, there can be underreaction in average forecasts but not in individual forecasts: an agents' forecast errors should be unpredictable by her own past forecast revisions, no matter what her information is. And if instead any of the other approaches is right, there should be the same level of underreaction at the aggregate and the individual level.

What does the evidence say about this? While there is, as already noted, evidence of underreaction in average forecasts, that is not the case for individual forecasts: if anything, individual forecasts appear to overreact a bit (Bordalo et al., 2020). This seems to favor incomplete information over the alternative: among the two general ways of relaxing FIRE and getting GE attenuation, that of dropping the "FI" half but maintaining the "RE" half is more consistent with the available evidence on expectations.

That said, the relevant available evidence on individual forecasts regards exclusively analysts and professional economists, leaving open the question of what goes on with regular consumers and firms. Furthermore, Level-k Thinking has found ample support in laboratory experiments, and so does the broader idea of "anchored" beliefs. All in all, we therefore view that the evidence is supportive of relaxing both the "FI" and the "RE" halves of the standard practice, and we iterate our recommendation from the previous section. Researchers may feel comfortable choosing their modeling strategy among the presented alternatives on the basis of the following two criteria: whether the main theme is GE attenuation or the dynamic adjustment in expectations; and which approach is most flexible and tractable.

20.8 Conclusion

GE effects, such as competitive pressures or Keynesian multipliers, are at the core of both theoretical and quantitative macroeconomics: they limit the usefulness of PE intuitions, and they often account for a significant fraction of the overall quantitative effects of aggregate shocks or policy interventions.

In this chapter, we have operationalized the notion that the standard modeling practice, which assumes FIRE, tends to overstate the potency of such GE effects. We did so by showing that plausible relaxations of either the "FI" or the "RE" half of this benchmark amount to anchoring the beliefs about the behavior of others and arresting GE feedback loops.

We illustrated this through specific examples. But the broader message can be summarized as follows. Perhaps there is more to "simplistic" PE intuitions than the macroeconomic theorist is trained to see. Perhaps the prevailing structural interpretations of the data are misleading because we have "overestimated" GE effects. And perhaps the policy maker should put more emphasis on policies that work through salient PE effects, as opposed to multi-layer GE effects, if she wishes to steer the economy in the short run.

Our framework was deliberately simple and abstract. This helped deliver the key insights in a transparent and flexible manner. It allowed us to shed light not only on the common ground of the various approaches but also on some key differences among them. And it let us offer the following guideline for how future researchers may choose among the different approaches: all approaches are equally good for the purpose of capturing the apparent underreaction in average expectations and the resulting GE attenuation; the approaches of Angeletos and Sastry (2021) and Gabaix (2020) accomplish this goal with maximal tractability; incomplete information gains ground in stationary settings with learning; and Level-k Thinking becomes more appealing in nonstationary or unfamiliar environments.

Finally, we would like to emphasize that the type of frictions studied here also helps accommodate "animal spirits" within a unique equilibrium framework. Angeletos and La'O (2013), Benhabib et al. (2015) and Huo and Takayama (2021) accomplished this by maintaining rational expectations but introducing incomplete information, making room for extrinsic fluctuations in higher-order beliefs. Furthermore, the resulting business fluctuations have the following quality: they resemble those of aggregate demand shocks, and capture salient features of the data, without a strict reliance on nominal rigidity and accommodative monetary policy.[16] But one can engineer basically the same fluctuations by replacing incomplete information with Level-k Thinking and by allowing the level-0 belief to be random, or by making an analogous modification of the other two approaches discussed in this chapter. Therefore, the key question is once again an empirical one: above, we asked how much expectations move with fundamentals; here, we must ask how much expectations move for extrinsic reasons.

All in all, the approaches reviewed in this chapter, and related work on rational inattention, hold promise to offer a better account of the joint stochastic behavior of observed expectations and observed outcomes, and a more reliable framework for macroeconomic policy evaluation. Recent quantitative explorations, such as those found in Angeletos and Huo (2021), Auclert et al. (2020), Chahrour and Ulbricht (2021), Mackowiak and Wiederholt (2015), Melosi (2017), and Qiu (2019), are encouraging; but the verdict is still open; see also Chapter 18 in this Handbook.

References

Abreu, Dilip, Brunnermeier, Markus K., 2003. Bubbles and crashes. Econometrica 71 (1), 173–204.

Angeletos, George-Marios, Collard, Fabrice, Dellas, Harris, 2018. Quantifying confidence. Econometrica 86 (5), 1689–1726.

Angeletos, George-Marios, Collard, Fabrice, Dellas, Harris, 2020. Business-cycle anatomy. The American Economic Review 110 (10), 3030–3070.

Angeletos, George-Marios, Huo, Zhen, 2021. Myopia and anchoring. The American Economic Review 111 (4), 1166–1200.

Angeletos, George-Marios, Huo, Zhen, Sastry, Karthik A., 2021. Imperfect macroeconomic expectations: evidence and theory. NBER Macroeconomics Annual 35 (1), 1–86.

Angeletos, George-Marios, La'O, Jennifer, 2009. Incomplete information, higher-order beliefs and price inertia. Journal of Monetary Economics 56, S19–S37.

Angeletos, George-Marios, La'O, Jennifer, 2010. Noisy business cycles. In: NBER Macroeconomics Annual 2009, vol. 24. University of Chicago Press, pp. 319–378.

---

[16] On this matter, see also Angeletos et al. (2018), Angeletos et al. (2020), Chahrour et al. (2021), Ilut and Saijo (2020), and Chahrour and Gaballo (2021).

Angeletos, George-Marios, La'O, Jennifer, 2013. Sentiments. Econometrica 81 (2), 739–779.

Angeletos, George-Marios, Lian, Chen, 2016. Incomplete information in macroeconomics: accommodating frictions in coordination. Handbook of Macroeconomics 2, 1065–1240.

Angeletos, George-Marios, Lian, Chen, 2017. Dampening General Equilibrium: from Micro to Macro. NBER Working Paper No. 23379.

Angeletos, George-Marios, Lian, Chen, 2018. Forward guidance without common knowledge. The American Economic Review 108 (9), 2477–2512.

Angeletos, George-Marios, Pavan, Alessandro, 2007. Efficient use of information and social value of information. Econometrica 75 (4), 1103–1142.

Angeletos, George-Marios, Sastry, Karthik, 2021. Managing expectations: instruments vs. targets. The Quarterly Journal of Economics.

Auclert, Adrien, Rognlie, Matthew, Straub, Ludwig, 2020. Micro jumps, macro humps: Monetary policy and business cycles in an estimated HANK model. NBER Working Paper 26647.

Benhabib, Jess, Wang, Pengfei, Wen, Yi, 2015. Sentiments and aggregate demand fluctuations. Econometrica 83 (2), 549–585.

Bordalo, Pedro, Gennaioli, Nicola, Ma, Yueran, Shleifer, Andrei, 2020. Overreaction in macroeconomic expectations. The American Economic Review 110 (9), 2748–2782.

Broer, Tobias, Kohlhas, Alexandre, 2021. Forecaster (mis-) behavior.

Camerer, Colin, Lovallo, Dan, 1999. Overconfidence and excess entry: an experimental approach. The American Economic Review 89 (1), 306–318.

Camerer, Colin F., Ho, Teck-Hua, Chong, Juin-Kuan, 2004. A cognitive hierarchy model of games. The Quarterly Journal of Economics 119 (3), 861–898.

Chahrour, Ryan, Gaballo, Gaetano, 2021. Learning from house prices: amplification and business fluctuations. The Review of Economic Studies.

Chahrour, Ryan, Nimark, Kristoffer, Pitschner, Stefan, 2021. Sectoral media focus and aggregate fluctuations. The American Economic Review 111 (12), 3872–3922.

Chahrour, Ryan, Ulbricht, Robert, 2021. Robust predictions for DSGE models with incomplete information. American Economic Journal: Macroeconomics.

Clarida, Richard, Gali, Jordi, Gertler, Mark, 1999. The science of monetary policy: a New Keynesian perspective. Journal of Economic Literature 37 (4), 1661–1707.

Coibion, Olivier, Gorodnichenko, Yuriy, 2012. What can survey forecasts tell us about information rigidities? Journal of Political Economy 120 (1), 116–159.

Coibion, Olivier, Gorodnichenko, Yuriy, 2015. Information rigidity and the expectations formation process: a simple framework and new facts. The American Economic Review 105 (8), 2644–2678.

Costa-Gomes, Miguel, Crawford, Vincent P., Broseta, Bruno, 2001. Cognition and behavior in normal-form games: An experimental study. Econometrica 69 (5), 1193–1235.

Costa-Gomes, Miguel A., Crawford, Vincent P., 2006. Cognition and behavior in two-person guessing games: An experimental study. The American Economic Review 96 (5), 1737–1768.

Crawford, Vincent P., Costa-Gomes, Miguel A., Iriberri, Nagore, 2013. Structural models of nonequilibrium strategic thinking: theory, evidence, and applications. Journal of Economic Literature 51 (1), 5–62.

Del Negro, Marco, Giannoni, Marc, Patterson, Christina, 2015. The Forward Guidance Puzzle. FRB of New York Mimeo.

Farhi, Emmanuel, Werning, Iván, 2019. Monetary policy, bounded rationality, and incomplete markets. The American Economic Review 109 (11), 3887–3928.

Gabaix, Xavier, 2020. A behavioral New Keynesian model. The American Economic Review 110 (8), 2271–2327.

Gali, Jordi, 1999. Technology, employment, and the business cycle: do technology shocks explain aggregate fluctuations? The American Economic Review 89 (1), 249–271.

Garcia-Schmidt, Mariana, Woodford, Michael, 2019. Are low interest rates deflationary? A paradox of perfect-foresight analysis. The American Economic Review 109 (1), 86–120.

Greenwood, Robin, Hanson, Samuel G., 2015. Waves in ship prices and investment. The Quarterly Journal of Economics 130 (1), 55–109.

Huo, Zhen, Takayama, Naoki, 2021. Rational Expectations Models with Higher Order Beliefs. Yale Mimeo.

Ilut, Cosmin, Saijo, Hikaru, 2020. Learning, confidence, and business cycles. Journal of Monetary Economics.

Iovino, Luigi, Sergeyev, Dmitriy, 2021. Quantitative Easing without Rational Expectations. Boconni Mimeo.

Kneeland, Terri, 2015. Identifying higher-order rationality. Econometrica 83 (5), 2065–2079.

Lian, Chen, 2021. A theory of narrow thinking. The Review of Economic Studies.

Lucas, Robert E., 1972. Expectations and the neutrality of money. Journal of Economic Theory 4 (2), 103–124.

Mackowiak, Bartosz, Wiederholt, Mirko, 2009. Optimal sticky prices under rational inattention. The American Economic Review 99 (3), 769–803.

Mackowiak, Bartosz, Wiederholt, Mirko, 2015. Business cycle dynamics under rational inattention. The Review of Economic Studies 82 (4), 1502–1532.

Mankiw, N. Gregory, Reis, Ricardo, 2002. Sticky information versus sticky prices: a proposal to replace the New Keynesian Phillips curve. The Quarterly Journal of Economics, 1295–1328.

Mauersberger, Felix, Nagel, Rosemarie, 2018. Levels of reasoning in Keynesian Beauty Contests: a generative framework. In: Handbook of Computational Economics, vol. 4, pp. 541–634.

McKay, Alisdair, Nakamura, Emi, Steinsson, Jón, 2016. The power of forward guidance revisited. The American Economic Review 106 (10), 3133–3158.

Melosi, Leonardo, 2017. Signalling effects of monetary policy. The Review of Economic Studies 84 (2), 853–884.

Morris, Stephen, Shin, Hyun Song, 1998. Unique equilibrium in a model of self-fulfilling currency attacks. The American Economic Review, 587–597.

Morris, Stephen, Shin, Hyun Song, 2002. Social value of public information. The American Economic Review 92 (5), 1521–1534.

Morris, Stephen, Shin, Hyun Song, 2003. Global games: theory and applications. In: Advances in Economics and Econometrics (Proceedings of the Eighth World Congress of the Econometric Society). Cambridge University Press.

Morris, Stephen, Shin, Hyun Song, 2006. Inertia of forward-looking expectations. The American Economic Review, 152–157.

Muth, John F., 1961. Rational expectations and the theory of price movements. Econometrica: Journal of the Econometric Society, 315–335.

Nagel, Rosemarie, 1995. Unraveling in guessing games: an experimental study. The American Economic Review 85 (5), 1313–1326.

Nimark, Kristoffer, 2008. Dynamic pricing and imperfect common knowledge. Journal of Monetary Economics 55 (2), 365–382.

Nimark, Kristoffer, 2017. Dynamic Higher Order Expectations. Cornell University Mimeo.

Qiu, Zhesheng, 2019. Level-k DSGE and monetary policy. City University of Hong Kong Mimeo.

Sims, Christopher A., 2003. Implications of rational inattention. Journal of Monetary Economics 50 (3), 665–690.

Stahl, Dale O., Wilson, Paul W., 1994. Experimental evidence on players' models of other players. Journal of Economic Behavior & Organization 25 (3).

Stahl, Dale O., Wilson, Paul W., 1995. On players' models of other players: theory and experimental evidence. Games and Economic Behavior 10 (1), 218–254.

Townsend, Robert M., 1983. Forecasting the forecasts of others. Journal of Political Economy, 546–588.

Venkateswaran, Venky, 2014. Heterogeneous Information and Labor Market Fluctuations. NYU Mimeo.

Vimercati, Riccardo Bianchi, Eichenbaum, Martin S., Guerreiro, Joao, 2021. Fiscal Policy at the Zero Lower Bound without Rational Expectations. NBER Working Paper 29134.

Woodford, Michael, 2003. Imperfect common knowledge and the effects of monetary policy. In: Knowledge, Information, and Expectations in Modern Macroeconomics: In Honor of Edmund S. Phelps.

Expectations data in structural microeconomic models[☆]

21

Gizem Koşar[a,b] and Cormac O'Dea[c,d,e]

[a]*Federal Reserve Bank of New York, New York, NY, United States*
[b]*CESifo, Munich, Germany*
[c]*Yale University, New Haven, CT, United States*
[d]*IFS, London, United Kingdom*
[e]*NBER, Cambridge, MA, United States*

21.1 Introduction

Across a wide range of applied research areas in economics, structural models are used both to understand the decision-making of economic agents and to evaluate the effects of counterfactual policies. In almost all cases, these models have been estimated using data on the choices agents make. A burgeoning literature, however, uses data on expectations instead of, or in addition to, data on observed choices. Expectations data can refer to data on how an economic agent believes some uncertain feature of reality will evolve or what choices the agents predict they will make in the future. This chapter discusses that literature.

There is no single accepted definition of a "structural" model.[1] The scope of this chapter is to discuss the literature in which: (i) the decision problem of the economic agent (usually an individual or household) is specified, (ii) that model is explicitly estimated, and (iii) that estimation involves the use of *micro* data on expectations. Our focus in this chapter is on structural models of individual and household decisions, with an emphasis on material not covered extensively elsewhere in this volume. For the literature on firms, see the recent review article by Aguirregabiria and Jeon (2020) and Chapters 2, 11, and 12 in this Handbook.[2] For the literature on financial market participants and investment and portfolio decisions, see especially Chapters 13 and 14 in this Handbook.

We start our discussion by outlining a simple model in Section 21.2. This model, a stylized version of that in van der Klaauw and Wolpin (2008), is of labor supply and savings decisions over the lifecycle. The purpose of the exposition of this model is threefold. First, it allows us to introduce the types of expectations data that have been used in the estimation of structural models. Second, it is used to

---

[☆] We are grateful to Rory McGee, Moritz Mendel, Dana Scott, Lindsey Uniat, Basit Zafar, and the editors for helpful comments. Boryana Ilieva provided excellent research assistance. The views expressed in this paper do not necessarily reflect those of the Federal Reserve Bank of New York or the Federal Reserve System as a whole.

[1] See Haile (2021) for a recent treatment which clarifies the use of various descriptions of empirical work.

[2] These chapters are, respectively, "Firm surveys" (Chapter 2), "The macroeconomic expectations of firms" (Chapter 11), and "Firm expectations about production and prices: facts, determinants, and effects" (Chapter 12).

illustrate *how* one can use expectations data in estimation and to highlight estimation issues particular to these data. Third, it allows us to motivate *why* expectations data can be valuable for identification and estimation of structural models.

The subsequent two sections then summarize the literature that uses expectations data in the estimation of structural models. We divide the literature according to a taxonomy provided by Manski (2004). In Section 21.3 we focus on papers in which data on expectations over future *states of nature* is used. These states of nature can be individual circumstances (e.g., future survival), economic conditions (e.g., earnings) or an aspect of policy (e.g., Social Security rules). In Section 21.4 we turn to the literature in which data on expectations over *choices* are used to estimate structural models. Choice expectations here encompass both statements of what choices agents expect to make in the future and choices that agents *would* make if faced with circumstances that are specified by the survey instrument. Section 21.5 concludes.

21.2 A model

To illustrate how and why one would use expectations data in the estimation of the parameters of a structural model, we first outline a simple life-cycle model. It is a simplified version of that in van der Klaauw and Wolpin (2008) and considers the consumption and labor supply choices of individuals who face uncertainty over the future in three dimensions: a demographic characteristic (their longevity), a feature of the economic environment (their earnings), and an aspect of economic policy (Social Security rules). We do not impose here that individuals have rational expectations – they may have expectations over the future distribution of those uncertain objects that will not coincide with the ex-post distribution in the population.

21.2.1 Specification

Demographics

Agents live for up to T periods. Time is discrete. Conditional on being alive in period t, each individual i has a probability $s_{i,t+1}$ of surviving to period $t + 1$.

Choices

Each agent i makes an extensive margin labor supply choice (p_{it}) each period until some retirement age $T^R < T$ and also decides how much of her resources to consume (c_{it}) each period. From age T^R, agents are retired and only make consumption decisions.

Economic environment

Wage offers (y_{it}) are assumed to be stochastic and are drawn from a distribution with mean μ and standard deviation σ. Wealth accrues interest at rate r. Agents enter each period t with a stock of assets, a_{it}.

Policy

Starting from the retirement age (T^R), all agents receive Social Security payments. Following van der Klaauw and Wolpin (2008), Social Security payments are the product of two terms:

$$ss_i = \kappa f(AIME_i). \tag{21.1}$$

The function $f(AIME)$ represents current Social Security rules, which depend on "average indexed monthly earnings" $(AIME)$, a function of the agent's earnings history; κ is a parameter which allows for the fact that Social Security rules may be different from those currently prevailing when the agents reach their claiming age. κ, a feature of future government policy, is not known; agents must form beliefs over it.

Preferences

Agents discount the future geometrically at rate β and have a utility function defined over consumption and leisure:

$$U(c_{it}, l_{it}) = \frac{(c_{it}^\nu l_{it}^{1-\nu})^{1-\gamma}}{1-\gamma}, \tag{21.2}$$

where l_{it} is leisure, which takes a value $l_{it} = 1 - h\mathbb{1}[p_{it} = 1]$, where the endowment of leisure is normalized to 1 and h is the fixed share of leisure that the agent forgoes in those periods in which she works; γ is the coefficient of relative risk aversion and ν governs the relative importance, to the agent, of consumption over leisure. Agents do not value wealth at death; so there is no bequest motive.

Expectations

We must make an assumption about agents' knowledge of the model's environment and their expectations about the future. The most common assumption in the literature is that agents have full information over the deterministic features of the problem and that they have rational expectations over all stochastic features. The latter means that the agents' subjective belief distribution of a given stochastic feature will be equivalent to the "objective" (according to the model) distribution of that feature.

The three stochastic model features here span three distinct types of "states of nature" that are relevant for decision-making under uncertainty. They are: (i) uncertain future personal or demographic states (here, survival), (ii) uncertain features of the economic environment (here, wage offers), and (iii) uncertain future policy features (here, Social Security). As we will discuss below, papers have used data on expectations in each of these domains to relax the assumption of rational expectations. To make clear that there can be a divergence between the objective distribution of some stochastic feature and agents' subjective beliefs, we will denote as $\bar{Z}_i$ the agent's subjective belief over any model object Z, and $\bar{\mathbb{E}}_i$ as the expectations operator with respect to the subjective belief distribution.

While we have outlined a model in which agents' expectations over model objects can differ from the objective distribution, we have not specified how those expectations are formed. This restriction is consequential: one of the advantages of explicitly modeling behavior is to be able to evaluate how those will evolve in counterfactual settings. Unless the expectation formation process is modeled, expectations will be assumed to stay unchanged in any counterfactual experiment. We will return to this issue in our discussion of the literature and in conclusion as a profitable direction for future research.

Recursive specification

The agent's decision problem in period t (we suppress i subscripts) can be expressed recursively through the value function:

$$V_t(\chi_t) = \max_{\{c_t, p_t\}} U(c_t, l_t) + \beta \bar{s}_{t+1} \bar{\mathbb{E}}_t V_{t+1}(\chi_{t+1}) \tag{21.3}$$

$$\text{such that} \begin{cases} a_{t+1} = (a_t + y_t \mathbb{1}[p_t = 1] - c_t)(1 + r) & \text{if } t < T^R, \\ a_{t+1} = (a_t + ss - c_t)(1 + r) & \text{if } t \geq T^R, \\ l_t = 1 - h\mathbb{1}[p_t = 1], \end{cases} \tag{21.4}$$

where $\chi_t = \{a_t, AIME_t\}$ collects the model's two state variables (assets and average indexed monthly earnings[3]), $\bar{s}_{t+1}$ represents the agents' perception of their survival probability, and $\bar{\mathbb{E}}$ indicates that the expectation is taken with respect to agents' subjective beliefs over other stochastic features.

Parameters

A set of model parameters is likely to be unknown to the researcher. This will include preference parameters (e.g., (β, γ, ν)) and potentially features related to expectations (e.g., the belief distribution over κ and the earnings distribution); θ collects these unknown model features.

Model solution

If θ were known, the model, once fully specified, could be solved using standard methods (see, for example, Adda and Cooper (2003)). The solution would imply decision rules (or policy functions) which relate the state variables to optimal consumption and labor supply decisions. Let us denote the consumption and labor supply decision rules at time t by

$$\tilde{c}_t(\chi_t, \theta), \quad \tilde{p}_t(\chi_t, \theta), \tag{21.5}$$

where we make it explicit that these depend on the unknown parameters (θ) and the state variables (χ_t). Let us further note that, just as the solution of the model implies trajectories of *choices* for agents, it also implies trajectories of *expectations of future choices* for those agents. A model parameterized by θ implies, for example, an expected value for any feature of behavior at all future ages $t + \tau$, or – to take a concept of expectations often measured in survey data – the probability of any single discrete outcome at age $t + \tau$. Examples of the latter that we highlight below include the probability of working at a particular age in the future or of having assets above a particular level at retirement, denoted respectively by

$$\mathbb{P}[\tilde{p}_{t+\tau} = 1 | t; \chi_t, \theta], \quad \mathbb{P}[\tilde{a}_{t+\tau+1} > \bar{a} | t; \chi_t, \theta]. \tag{21.6}$$

Before we turn to how expectations data are used in estimation, it is worth dwelling on the types of expectations data that are typically available.

---

[3] This is a function of lifetime earnings, on which Social Security payments in the U.S. are based. We do not include the law of motion here for it.

21.2.2 **Types of expectations data**

A useful taxonomy of expectations data comes from Manski's (2004) seminal article on the measurement of expectations. Two distinct types are data on expectations over states of nature and data on expectations over choices. We discuss both in turn, giving some examples from the Health and Retirement Study (HRS).

1. **Expectations over states of nature** relate to features of the economic and policy environment or of personal characteristics. These measured expectations often relate to beliefs over future realizations of stochastic events, though surveys also measure the extent of respondents' (potentially imperfect) understanding of some feature of the current environment. In the case of the model we have outlined, each possible combination of survival, earnings, and future Social Security rules comprise the states of nature.

   The HRS, for example, has asked respondents the following:

   • What is the percent chance that you will live to be 75 or more?
   • About how much do you expect the [future Social Security] payments to be in today's dollars?

2. **Expectations over choices** concern decisions individuals anticipate that they will make in the future, or that they would make under specified circumstances. In the case of the model we have outlined, these decisions are labor supply and consumption.

   The HRS asks individuals about their expectations of making certain decisions in the future:

   • Thinking about work in general and not just your present job, what do you think the chances are that you will be working full-time after you reach age 62?
   • Including property and other valuables that you might own, what are the chances that you (and your [husband/wife/partner]) will leave an inheritance totaling $10,000 or more?

This distinction between two types of expectations data can be used to characterize, in a straightforward manner, any feature in our simple model. In richer models, there may be features which straddle both groups – it could be that there are *choices* which are only possible if a particular *state of nature* arises. For example, in a frictional labor market where agents may not receive a job offer every period, the probability of working in a future period depends both on the realization of a state of nature (whether a job offer arrives) and on the choice the individual makes (whether the individual accepts the offer). Conversely, there could be *states of nature* which depend on *choices*. For example, in a model in which individuals invest in health, their survival risk could depend on their investment decisions. Expectations data on either states of nature or choices in each of these cases will contain information on the subjective expectations about the joint likelihood of the state of nature arising and the choice the individual will make. A further distinction worth drawing is that some data on expectations may encompass both groups by asking for expectations of a future *state of nature* conditional on a *choice* being made (for example, future earnings conditional on college choice). Therefore, the distinction between expectations about future states of nature and expectations about future choices will not always cleanly categorize data. Nevertheless, we rely on this useful distinction in organizing our discussion of the literature below.

21.2.3 **Identification and the role of expectations data**

Before turning to estimation, we discuss the role expectations data can play in the identification of parameters. A set of parameters is *identified* if different parameter values would, under the model, lead to different distributions of the observables.[4] Generally, the more limited the set of observables at hand is, the more restrictive the model will need to be to identify the features of interest. More specifically in the case of the model outlined above, without data on expectations over future Social Security payments, the conditions needed to identify β (patience) and κ (beliefs about future Social Security) will be more restrictive than those that would be needed for identification if such expectations data were available.

While the formal definition of identification of a structural parameter is a binary property that a model, paired with a joint distribution of observables, can have, researchers who estimate model parameters often more loosely characterize particular aspects of the data as "identifying" certain features of structure. Keane (2010) states that this (looser) notion of identification of model features relates to:
...

> "...what are the key features of the data, or the key sources of (assumed) exogenous variation in the data, or the key *a priori* theoretical or statistical assumptions imposed in the estimation, that drive the quantitative values of the parameter estimates, and strongly influence the substantive conclusions drawn from the estimation exercise?"[5]

In most estimated structural models, the observable variation that has been used to identify the parameters comes from data on *behavior*. However, if data on *expectations* over choices, the implications of those choices, or states of nature are measured, these can be used. Data on choices and data on choice expectations have related, but distinct, types of empirical content. Data on behavior in period t contain information about i's optimal behavior conditional on the information available in period t; data on expectations at time t of behavior in period $t + \tau$ contain information about optimal behavior in $t + \tau$ conditional on the information available in period t. In the next section, we will discuss how these two types of data can be used in estimation.

21.2.4 **Estimation**

In estimation, some parameters might be set with reference to the literature or might be credibly estimated without the solution of the model being used. In life-cycle models such as the one above, these could include the interest rate r, a parameter which is often directly estimated from time series data on interest rates. The survival curve $\{s_\tau\}_{\tau=1}^{T}$, might also be estimated using demographic data (if rational expectations are assumed) or by directly invoking expectations data on survival (which allows a relaxation of that assumption).

In general, however, most unknown parameters will be estimated by bringing implications of the model solution as close as possible, in some metric, to empirical analogues of those implications. In our

---

[4] More formally, features of data generating processes are "said to be identified if among the set of observationally equivalent structures [data generating processes], the value of that feature does not vary" (Matzkin (2013), following Hurwicz (1950)).

[5] Andrews et al. (2017) argue that much of the discussion of identification of the parameters of structural models using features of the data could be reframed in terms of "sensitivity" of the estimated parameters to features of the data.

discussion below, we specify what it means to bring chosen model implications "as close as possible" to the data for different estimation methods, highlighting how expectations data can be incorporated.

21.2.4.1 *Estimation methods*

Maximum likelihood estimation

In the specification of the model, we have made no distributional assumptions on preferences. Suppose we augment the model's preferences with a stochastic feature that has an assumed distribution. A simple example would be to augment the single period utility function by adding a shock to preferences, ϵ, with a distribution $F(\epsilon)$. The utility in period t would then be $U(c_t, l_t, \epsilon_t)$.[6] Suppose further that we have data on choices (assets holdings) and expectations (stated beliefs on the probability of working at a particular age in the future) for a sample of N individuals for T periods. For any given vector of preference parameters (θ), we can evaluate the likelihood of observing $\mathcal{D} = \{a_{it}, \mathbb{P}_{it}[p_{i\tau} = 1], i = 1, \ldots, N, t = 1, \ldots, T\}$ as the outcome of the model endowed with those parameters θ. That is, we can form the likelihood function

$$L(\mathcal{D}, \theta) = \prod_{i=1}^{N} L(\mathcal{D}_i, \theta). \tag{21.7}$$

The maximum likelihood estimate of θ is that parameter vector which maximizes the likelihood function. This is simply the usual likelihood estimator, applied in a context where some of the data are expectations. If the agent's problem lacks an analytical solution, and can only be solved numerically, or if there are missing state variables in the data for some or all observations, the evaluation of the likelihood function involves the solution of the model at θ and the simulation of behavior using implied decision rules. In that case, $\hat{\theta}$ is the simulated maximum likelihood estimate.

Method of simulated moments (MSM)

When evaluation of the likelihood function is infeasible or its computation is prohibitively time-consuming, nonlikelihood based simulation methods, such as MSM or indirect inference, might prove useful. In the case of MSM, a set of moments, which summarizes the behavior simulated from the model, is chosen. These moments, collected in $\hat{\mathbf{m}}(\theta)$, depend on unknown parameters θ. Parameter estimates are chosen such that the simulated moments are as close to the data moments $(\mathbf{m})$ as possible. That is, $\hat{\theta}$ is chosen to minimize the criterion function

$$\hat{\theta} = \arg\min_{\theta} \ (\mathbf{m} - \tilde{\mathbf{m}}(\theta))'\mathbf{W}(\mathbf{m} - \tilde{\mathbf{m}}(\theta)), \tag{21.8}$$

where $\mathbf{W}$ is a symmetric positive definite matrix.

Moments should be chosen such that their values are informative about the parameters to be estimated. As an example: given a desire to estimate the relative weight of consumption in the utility function (v), moments on labor supply would be candidates for inclusion in $\mathbf{m}$. All else equal, the higher is v, the higher labor supply will be. Data on labor supply, or expectations of future labor supply, can therefore help discriminate between settings where v is low (people place a relatively low value on

---

[6] The effect of ϵ_t on utility will often be choice specific – it could represent a shock to the marginal utility of consumption, or of leisure, for example.

consumption and a relatively high value on leisure) and settings where ν is high (the converse). Data on wealth over the life-cycle (or expectations of future wealth holdings) would similarly be informative for the discount factor (β).

Indirect inference

Indirect inference involves specifying an "auxiliary model," which relates the observables together in a computable manner. The auxiliary model need not be the true data generating process, but should be easily-computable. Indirect inference estimation involves choosing the parameters by minimizing the distance between the auxiliary parameters estimated using the observed data and those estimated using the model predictions (i.e., the data simulated using the model solution). Formally, let $\hat{\beta}_A$ be the estimated parameters of the auxiliary model using observed data y such that $\hat{\beta}_A = \arg\max_{\beta_A} L_A(y, \beta_A)$, and $\hat{\beta}_S$ be the estimated parameters of the auxiliary model using model predictions $y^S(\theta)$ such that $\hat{\beta}_S(\theta) = \arg\max_{\beta_S} L_A(y^S(\theta), \beta_S)$. Then the indirect inference estimate of preference parameters, $\hat{\theta}$, is defined as

$$\hat{\theta} = \arg\min_{\theta} \ (\hat{\beta}_S(\theta) - \hat{\beta}_A)' \mathbf{W}(\hat{\beta}_S(\theta) - \hat{\beta}_A), \tag{21.9}$$

where $\mathbf{W}$ is again a symmetric positive definite matrix. In this setup, both types of expectations data can be used in the estimation of the auxiliary model parameters. See Smith (1993) and Gourieroux et al. (1993) for the introduction of this method and van der Klaauw and Wolpin (2008) and Adda et al. (2022) for applications that use expectations data.

Non-full solution methods of estimation

The estimation methods we have outlined so far involve repeated solution of the model at many candidate parameter vectors as a particular function is either minimized (MSM criterion function) or maximized (a likelihood function). These methods are computationally expensive, especially in complex models where solving the model is time-consuming. Methods have been developed that allow for the estimation of parameters of dynamic models while avoiding the repeated solution of the model. These methods, developed by Hotz and Miller (1993), leverage "conditional choice probabilities" – the probability of a choice conditional on model states. We do not review this line of literature here (see the review article by Aguirregabiria and Mira (2010)), but we note that the key empirical input leveraged by these methods – measures of the probability that an individual will choose a particular discrete option in the future – are very much aligned with the concept of expectation measures often collected by surveys.[7]

21.2.5 Issues particular to structural estimation with expectations data
21.2.5.1 Constructing a model counterpart to expectations data

Bringing expectations data to bear on a structural model requires a precise determination of the model counterparts of what the expectations data measure. Often the data reflect objects for which the model has no single natural analogue. van der Klaauw (2012), studying occupational choice and using data

---

[7] See Pantano and Zheng (2013) for a method that uses subjective choice probabilities to allow for unobserved heterogeneity in estimation without full solution.

from the National Longitudinal Study of the High School Class of 1972, considers the response to the following question:

"What kind of work will you be doing when you are 30 years old? (circle one that comes closest to what you expect to be doing)."

There is no statistical analogue to which the answer to this question can be mapped, though the form of the question suggests that respondents might select the option with the highest choice probability (the mode), and this is how van der Klaauw (2012) interprets the answers. Delavande and Rohwedder (2011) similarly interpret the answer to the question "At what age do you expect to start collecting these [Social Security] benefits?" as the age at which claiming probability is highest.

A similar issue arises with questions that ask individuals what they expect for some continuous quantity. In their study of human capital and the return migration decisions of migrants, Adda et al. (2022) make use of a question that asks respondents "How long do you want to live in Germany?". One would not expect this to be an exact prediction of exactly how long the migrant will stay in Germany, but rather some summary measure which takes into account uncertainty. In constructing a model analogue, they assume that this reflects the median duration that a migrant will stay. van der Klaauw and Wolpin (2008) face a similar issue and interpret the number of dollars the respondents "expect" for [future Social Security] payments in today's dollars as expected values.

One type of data where a natural mapping to a model object does exist is when respondents are asked for choice probabilities. These are well defined objects in models of the type we are discussing. Surveys such as the HRS, its sister studies internationally, and the Federal Reserve Bank of New York's Survey of Consumer Expectations place a large emphasis on collecting expectations data in this form.[8] An additional advantage of probabilistic questions is in the richness of their empirical content. In the context of stated-choice experiments, Manski (1999) shows that the stated-choice approach may lead to different results than actual choices if the respondents are not provided with the full information that would be available to them when facing the actual choice problems. Elicited choice probabilities, on the other hand, can address the incompleteness of the scenarios by allowing respondents to express uncertainty over their choices. Moreover, they provide more information than choice experiments which elicit a single preferred option, as probabilities also contain some information related to respondents' rankings over choices.

21.2.5.2 *Use of data on choice expectations in maximum likelihood estimation*

The use of maximum likelihood techniques together with data that record respondents' stated choices or choice probabilities can lead to settings with discontinuous and nondifferentiable likelihood functions. During the repeated evaluation of the likelihood function in estimation, if, for a given trial parameter vector, the reported expected choice probability is not equal to the model-generated choice probability or the elicited "most-likely" choice is not equal to the one predicted by the model, numerical optimization can become difficult and standard inferential techniques may not be used. This issue, of course, is not limited to the use of expectations data. See van der Klaauw (2012) for a fuller discussion of a case

---

[8] In addition to being readily interpretable, choice probabilities are richer in empirical content than questions that solicit looser concepts of expectations and intentions. Juster (1966) notes that: "Intentions seem to have no informational content that a probability survey does not also have, and the probability survey is able to extract information that is not obtainable from intentions surveys."

where it occurs with expectations data and a proposed approach, which involves the assumption that individuals report their expectations (in this case, the most likely future choice) with an error, to deal with this issue.

21.2.5.3 *Focal point responses to probabilistic expectation questions*

A robust feature of data on probabilistic expectations is that there tends to be an excess mass of responses at certain focal points, e.g., 0%, 50%, and 100%. These masses in some cases display an implausible degree of certainty (0% or 100%), and in other cases may represent some bias in reporting (e.g., an excess mass at 50% could represent either rounding or a lack of understanding of the question or inability to formulate an answer; see Fischhoff and Bruine De Bruin (1999)).[9] Whatever the reason for such responses, it is unlikely that the underlying behavioral model to which the data will be applied will imply probabilities of future events that accord with these distributions. Using data contaminated by focal point biases to estimate a model which does not account for them means the model is not a correctly-specified data-generating process for the data in hand. Gan et al. (2005) develop a method for estimating individual-level survival curves in the presence of focal point biases, and subsequently use survival curves estimated through such an approach in a life-cycle model to study the interplay between subjective mortality risk and bequests. Blass et al. (2010) and Wiswall and Zafar (2018) show how to deal with these focal points in estimating preferences in a random utility model using choice expectations. This issue is also tackled by Hendren (2013), who uses subjective probability elicitations to study the role of private information in insurance rejections.

Our focus in this section has been on *how* expectations data might be used in the estimation of structural models. In Sections 21.3 and 21.4, we will turn to *why* one would use it, and we will discuss the applied literature that has done that.

21.3 Literature I: expectations over the states of nature

As we noted in Section 21.2.2, Manski's (2004) taxonomy for data on expectations draws a distinction between data on expectations over states of nature and data on expectations over choices. In this section, we discuss the literature that uses the former in the estimation of structural models. In Section 21.4, we discuss the literature on choice expectations. This taxonomy does not, of course, perfectly bisect the literature, and some papers will be referenced in both sections. We discuss most such papers in this section and defer some details on their use of choice expectations data to Section 21.4.

Dynamic structural models consider the behavior of agents making decisions today that yield payoffs both today and in the future. The future payoff will often depend on the realized state of nature: this could be the health of an individual, their earnings, the state of the economy, the state of economic policy, or some other unknown feature about the future state of the world. Agents make their decisions today based on the current payoff and their expectations about the future state of nature and, thus, about future payoffs. A classic identification problem (see Manski (1993) and Manski (2004)) involves separating the role of preferences from expectations over the future states of nature, since observed choices might be compatible with several combinations of preferences and expectations. The conventional res-

---

[9] See the discussions in Chapters 1, 7, 8, 9, and 10 in this Handbook on how to deal with focal points in different contexts.

olution to this identification problem in estimating choice models has been to use data on observed choices and realizations of that state of nature, together with an assumption of rational expectations. However, this approach does not allow for the possibility of subjective expectations being different than objective measures. An alternative approach to tackling this identification problem is to combine data on observed choices with subjective expectations to make inference on preferences. This alternative approach facilitates making weaker assumptions on the expectations formation rule. In fact, as Manski (2004) states, "...it is enough to assume that elicited expectations faithfully describe persons' perceptions of their environments." The literature we review in this section follows this second approach and combines data on observed choices with subjective expectations to estimate choice models.

We organize our discussion of this literature according to the way that the data are used. Section 21.3.1 discusses the literature that combines subjective expectations data with observed choices without a particular focus on modeling the belief formation process. Section 21.3.2 then discusses papers that emphasize the modeling of these beliefs.

21.3.1 Allowing for subjective expectations

An early example of using subjective expectations data in a choice model is by Nyarko and Schotter (2002), who elicit players' subjective expectations of opponents' behavior in a two-person game. The paper uses these elicited expectations in the estimation of this simple game, where the best response function of each player depends on that player's beliefs on the opponent's move. Comparing different assumptions on players' expectations, the authors find that the model that uses subjective expectations best predicts observed behavior. Other early examples include Lochner (2007), who studies the link between individuals' beliefs about own arrest probabilities and criminal behavior, and Delavande (2008), who studies contraception choice using data on elicited expectations of choice-specific outcomes (such as pregnancy, side effects, and protection from STDs), observed choice data, and a random utility model. The paper shows that there is substantial heterogeneity in choice-specific outcome expectations and that taking these into account rather than assuming everyone has full-information rational expectations (FIRE)[10] and homogeneous expectations matters for parameter estimates. In recent work, Miller et al. (2020) use similar data on beliefs about contraceptive attributes and a structural model to show the role of biased beliefs about pregnancy risk in driving the unmet need for contraception in Sub-Saharan Africa.

Education decisions often involve a trade-off between a cost that is to be incurred today and some future (uncertain) returns. Expectations over those returns, therefore, are central in models of education decisions and the literature using expectations data in structural models is larger than in other domains.[11] Early contributions by Arcidiacono et al. (2012) and Zafar (2013) implement surveys which directly measure expectations of how future earnings depend on major choice. Both studies also elicit measures of perceived ability or enjoyment of study under different choices of major. These data are used together with data on observed (and intended) major choices to estimate models of major choice taking into account subjective expectations of future returns. Wiswall and Zafar (2015) combine a survey eliciting students' expectations with an information treatment to estimate a structural model

---

[10] In what follows, we refer to full-information rational expectations when we use the term rational expectations.

[11] In this section we summarize only the papers which have used expectations data in the estimation of structural models. The broader literature using these data in education research is summarized in Chapter 7 in this Handbook.

of major choice.[12] Patnaik et al. (2020) also study major choice, but in their case, using a life-cycle model. Their aim is to separately identify the role of expectations over future earnings conditional on each major from the role of preferences (risk tolerance and patience), while allowing both beliefs and preferences to be heterogeneous.

Turning to different features of the college experience, Gong et al. (2021) quantify the consumption value of attending college. Using data on consumption in college and expectations of earnings post-college from the Berea Panel Survey (a survey which will be discussed further below), the authors, making use of the Euler equation, find a large consumption value of college. Delavande et al. (2020) model the time allocation of college students. They collect data on perceived academic and pecuniary returns to different time investments (e.g., studying, volunteering, internships) as well as measures of students' enjoyment of those activities. Estimating a model of time allocation during college, they find that differences in expectations play some role in explaining the heterogeneity in investments in college, but that the differences in the constraints students face (e.g., access to internships, work or family responsibilities) are more influential.

There are well-documented socio-economic gradients in undergraduate and postgraduate education and differences in perceived returns to college programs have been shown to be relevant in explaining these gradients. Attanasio and Kaufmann (2014), for example, investigate the role of own and parental expectations about future labor market risks in schooling decisions and how these links differ by the gender of the student. Kaufmann (2014) shows, with similar data, that children from poorer households require a greater perceived rate of return to attend college than do children from richer households. Hastings et al. (2015) show that lower-income students overestimate the returns to low-earning college degree programs and bring together a field experiment and a model of college demand to study the impact of providing accurate information to college students. Boneva et al. (2022) elicit the beliefs of undergraduates about returns to postgraduate education, expectations over college graduation, and the probability of getting a postgraduate degree. They estimate a choice model for postgraduate study using this data to study the role of differences in beliefs.

Giustinelli (2016) brings together expectations data and structural models to study *group* decision-making by parents and children over the choice of high school track. The challenge here is to separate the roles of each group member's preferences, their beliefs over uncertain choice-specific outcomes, and how the group comes to a decision. A unique data set, which brings together rich data on student and parental expectations over the long-run outcomes of each track choice as well as on the student's perceived enjoyment of each track, facilitates the estimation of a variety of models of decision-making: unilateral, bilateral, and nonstrategic.

Recent papers, by bringing together data on perceived admittance probabilities to schools or programs and models of applicant behavior highlight how allocation mechanisms can interact with subjective expectations. Kapor et al. (2020), for example, study the interplay between school assignment mechanisms and parental beliefs over students' acceptance probabilities. Allocation mechanisms that imply returns to strategic behavior can improve welfare relative to strategy-proof mechanisms by allowing participants to express the intensity of their preferences. However, if applicants (parents in their case) are misinformed about admittance probabilities, such allocations can be inefficient.[13] The authors

---

[12] See Section 21.4.2.2 for a detailed discussion of this paper.

[13] See also Arteaga et al. (2022) which highlights that, when information is costly to acquire, beliefs are central to the welfare of school applicants even when the allocation mechanism is strategy-proof.

survey households in a U.S. school district and estimate a model of school choice in which households are allowed to have erroneous subjective beliefs on the admittance probability. Using their estimated model they find that a switch from the baseline (nonstrategy proof) allocation mechanism to a strategy-proof allocation mechanism would *increase* welfare, whereas a planner who assumed parents have rational expectations would incorrectly believe it would *decrease* welfare. Tincani et al. (2021) also study admissions, but at the college level. They study a Chilean experiment, which guaranteed college admittance to the top 15% of students in treated high school classes. Survey data show that students overestimate their chances of guaranteed admission under this program. Treated students were found to respond to this experiment, which increased their admittance chances, by reducing their effort. To evaluate how decisions and outcomes (effort, application, admissions, and enrollments) would change if students had correct beliefs, the paper estimates a structural model of student decisions.

A large literature has investigated the extent to which stated survival probabilities differ systematically from objective survival probabilities.[14] Building on this literature, several recent papers bring estimated subjective survival curves into life-cycle models, relaxing the assumption that individuals' have rational expectations over their survival. Gan et al. (2015) estimate individual survival curves using reported survival probabilities from the HRS and use these in a model of wealth decumulation and bequests. They find that a model with subjective expectations better fits the observed decumulation and bequest behavior than a model with life table survival probabilities. Using methods developed by Gan et al. (2005), they account for the tendency of individuals to report probabilities at focal points (0 or 1).[15] Bissonnette et al. (2017) use the panel of survival expectations in the HRS and a life-cycle model to study the welfare losses associated with a divergence of subjective and objective survival probabilities, which they find are large. Heimer et al. (2019) find that young individuals are overly pessimistic about their survival, which, in a life-cycle model, causes them to undersave relative to what would be the case if they had accurate expectations. In contrast, the old are overly optimistic about their survival prospects, which causes them to decumulate wealth slower than they would if they had accurate expectations. de Bresser (2021) evaluates whether a life-cycle model can predict the retirement response to a pension reform in the Netherlands and finds that a model with subjective and heterogeneous survival probabilities can better explain the reform's impact than models with life table survival curves. Bairoliya and McKiernan (2021) also study retirement and Social Security claiming decisions, estimating a model using expectations data from the HRS. O'Dea and Sturrock (2021) study the implications of biases in subjective survival probabilities for the "annuity puzzle" – the fact that annuity demand is modest, despite the longevity insurance that it provides. They start from the fact (also shown by Teppa and Lafourcade (2013) and Wu et al. (2015)) that an annuity that is priced fairly can appear actuarially-unfair to an individual who is pessimistic about their survival chances. Then, using subjective survival curves estimated from the English Longitudinal Study of Ageing and a life-cycle model, they show that, in their setting, survival pessimism is one quantitatively important explanation for low annuity demand. Focusing on the implications of heterogeneity in survival expectations, Hosseini (2015) studies the role of adverse selection in annuity markets and estimates the heterogeneity in life expectancy using subjective expectations data from the HRS, while Foltyn and Olsson (2021) use subjective survival curves in an overlapping-generations model to show the role of expectations in driving wealth inequality.

---

[14] Early examples include Hamermesh (1985), Hurd and McGarry (1995), Hurd and McGarry (2002), and Hurd et al. (2005). See Chapters 8 and 10 in this Handbook for in-depth discussions.

[15] See also Comerford (2019) on modes of asking questions to mitigate biases in elicited survival expectations.

In measuring the nature and extent of risks over the life-cycle, it has been important to separately identify permanent and transitory shocks to income. Pistaferri (2001) shows how subjective expectations over future income, as well as data on income realizations, can be used to separately identify these different shocks. Attanasio et al. (2020b) apply this approach to study the extent to which households are able to smooth consumption in the face of income shocks. A crucial parameter in life-cycle models relates to the patience of the agents. Mahajan et al. (2020) provide results for the identification of the time-preference of potentially present-biased agents using an exclusion restriction on a variable that affects utility only through the perceived value of future states. Using data on the perceived malaria risk conditional on usage of insecticide-treated nets (ITNs), the paper examines the role of time inconsistency in the demand for ITNs.

A number of papers have used subjective expectations data in models of labor market decisions.[16] Arcidiacono et al. (2020) study occupational choice. They use a survey which elicited earnings beliefs conditional on major and occupational choice probabilities from undergraduates and then followed them after graduation as they made their actual choices. They document heterogeneity in earnings beliefs by occupation and find evidence of sorting on gains. Mueller et al. (2021) allow workers to have biased beliefs about the job finding rate and estimate a model of labor market transitions that incorporates a mapping between these beliefs and the actual rates, by targeting moments that include perceptions of the job finding rate at different points in an unemployment spell. Using these moments allows the authors to uncover the heterogeneity in the true job finding rates. Eisenhauer et al. (2021) document that women in Germany are overly optimistic about human capital accumulation in part-time work and use the estimated model to show that if agents had accurate beliefs, there would be a decline in part-time work and an increase in wages. Jäger et al. (2022) show that workers tend to anchor their beliefs about outside options to their current wage. This phenomenon, in an equilibrium model of labor supply, can provide one mechanism which sustains wage markdowns.[17]

A growing literature has shown the importance of investments in children (both of time and of resources), in developing their skills (see Cunha et al. (2010)). A series of recent papers has shown that parents often do not appreciate that the returns to these investments are large. Cunha et al. (2013) show that parents underestimate the productivity of investments and Boneva and Rauh (2018) document that parents believe the returns to late investments are greater than earlier investments, Attanasio et al. (2019) show that there is significant heterogeneity in beliefs across mothers and that they tend to underestimate the returns on investments, and Attanasio et al. (2020a) compare beliefs about returns to different types of investments. Embedding these beliefs into models of parents' decision-making is a profitable area for future research.

While a very large literature uses structural models to investigate the role of policy in shaping behavior, the literature which confronts uncertainty in the policy environment is much smaller. Contributing to this is the fact that the policy environment is a highly multidimensional object, which brings with it measurement challenges, as well as the fact that the nonstationarity in the policy environment precludes the use of realizations as estimates of what might happen in the future. As outlined in Section 21.2, van der Klaauw and Wolpin (2008) is an example of a paper that does introduce policy uncertainty, over

---

[16] See Chapter 22 in this Handbook for a detailed discussion of papers on the labor market that use expectations data.

[17] The papers discussed here use expectations data in the estimation of model features. Schneider (2020) uses data on choices and policy variation to identify expectations of beliefs over reemployment prospects.

Social Security benefits, into a model estimated using expectations data. Since then, evidence has accumulated documenting how agents consider the policy environment to be uncertain. Delavande and Rohwedder (2011) and Luttmer and Samwick (2018) both show this in the case of US Social Security. Ciani et al. (2022) complement this evidence by documenting that expectations are revised in advance of, as well as following, reform announcements and by showing that there is substantial heterogeneity in expectations, even after reform announcements.

21.3.2 Modeling subjective expectations

We now turn to the papers which emphasize the process by which expectations over states of nature are formed.[18] An early example is by Bellemare et al. (2008), who combine choice data in an ultimatum game with data on the proposer's expectations over the opponent's acceptance probability, by allowing reported beliefs to have measurement errors and to depend on preferences. Their results indicate that estimating the model using subjective expectations data leads to better in- and out-of-sample fits compared to those achieved assuming rational expectations.

A set of papers study the formation of expectations for college students using the Berea Panel Survey (BPS), an ongoing high-frequency panel in which expectations about future academic performance and future earnings are regularly measured.[19] Stinebrickner and Stinebrickner (2014a) study the choice students face between staying in college and dropping out. The paper specifies a discrete-choice model in which students decide, each semester, whether to stay in college or to drop out. In this setup, students learn about their ability, a process which the authors can estimate given their repeated measures of expected future academic performance. They find that learning about one's ability explains a large share of college drop-outs – poor academic performance makes the experience of being in college less enjoyable and also lowers the expected financial return to remaining in college. In a similar manner, Stinebrickner and Stinebrickner (2014b) estimate a model of major choice. They use data from the BPS on entering students' expectations about their major choice and data on their evolving expectations and performance through college, to study the reasons for the gap between the number of students who intend to major in science and those who ultimately do so. They find that overoptimism over own-aptitude for science is an important factor.

Delavande and Zafar (2019) study the choice between different types of universities in Pakistan. Their aim is to separate the roles played by the expectations of pecuniary returns to different choices from non-pecuniary features, such as the ideology of a school or parental approval. Their survey collects data on students' preference orderings over schools as well as their expectations about future outcomes conditional on school choice. The estimated model shows that nonpecuniary factors dominate expected earnings in driving college choice in this setting. In addition to collecting preference orderings given the actual cost of attending each college, survey respondents were asked for preference orderings assuming a counterfactual world where there were no financial constraints. Using this data, the authors validate

---

[18] As elsewhere in this chapter, our focus is on models of where the expectations formation process is brought into structural microeconomic models. See Chapter 23 in this Handbook for a dedicated treatment of learning models.

[19] The BPS has been an unparalleled resource for studying decisions made by college students (see Chapter 7 in this Handbook). Of particular relevance to the relaxation of rational expectations over earnings, a feature of many of the papers in this section, see Crossley et al. (2021) and Crossley et al. (2022). They find, as do d'Haultfoeuille et al. (2021) using other data, that departures from rational expectations are common.

their model by generating the predictions of the estimated model with the technology altered to relax financial constraints. They compare these predictions with the elicited preferences under the assumption of this counterfactual world and find a close correspondence between the two.

Learning models estimated using subjective expectations data are commonly used to explain labor market transitions. Conlon et al. (2018), for example, use data on expectations over future wage offers to estimate a job search model that allows for heterogeneous and potentially biased beliefs as well as learning about the wage offer distribution. They use elicited expectations on wage offers to identify the model's learning rule. They then show that incorporating expectations data in the estimation allows the estimated model to better fit the reported reservation wages, relative to a complete information model. Cortés et al. (2021) also focus on learning about job offers, but study gender differences in risk aversion, optimism, and updating of beliefs over the expected offer distribution in the labor market. They estimate a model of job search that incorporates these gender differences and allows beliefs to change over time. Their results show that the gender gap can be significantly reduced by providing accurate information to students. Hoffman and Burks (2020) study the quitting decision of truckers using a structural model which embeds a model of how they learn about their productivity. They make use of high-frequency survey data that include subjective expectations of truck drivers about their own future productivity (in terms of paid miles to be driven). The results indicate that drivers learn their true productivity over time, and that this learning is slower than what is predicted by Bayesian updating.

In Section 21.3.1 we discussed several papers that used survival expectations, where the focus was more on understanding the implications of survival than on modeling these expectations. Wang (2014) finds that smokers underestimate the implications of smoking for their longevity. Incorporating this channel in a model of smokers' choice of if and when to quit, the paper finds that smokers are estimated to be substantially less patient under rational expectations than they are found to be when subjective expectations are taken into account. Groneck et al. (2016) model the formation of survival beliefs using a model of Bayesian learning with cognitive limitations. They show that their model, calibrated with subjective expectations data from the HRS, can explain several regularities in the old-age savings behavior. See also Caliendo et al. (2020) who study the implications of ambiguity in survival expectations and Ludwig and Zimper (2013), de Bresser (2019), and Grevenbrock et al. (2021) on modeling the formation of survival expectations. Hentall-MacCuish (2021) estimates a life-cycle model that takes into account the belief formation process through agents' knowledge of their public pension entitlements. Using data on expectations of future entitlements to the UK's State Pension, the paper finds that accommodating endogenous, heterogeneous, and potentially erroneous beliefs helps the model explain bunching of labor market exits at the normal retirement age.

Hamilton et al. (2011) use data on the subjective expectations of a marketing manager to estimate a structural model of advertising decisions. By jointly estimating the manager's preferences with the actual and expected demand functions, they show that managers are overly-optimistic about advertising effectiveness. Studying financial decision-making, Bellemare et al. (2020) estimate a model of portfolio choice under uncertain return, incorporating ambiguity, loss-aversion preferences, and belief updating rules for how investors update their ambiguity, using elicited data on portfolio choices and stated beliefs over return distributions. Their results support dominant ambiguity aversion and belief updating and provide evidence against the hypothesis that loss aversion dominates ambiguity aversion for financial decisions.

In this section, we reviewed the literature that uses data on expectations of the states of nature in the estimation of structural models. In discussing these papers we emphasized whether the belief formation process was modeled. Modeling these beliefs explicitly is an important feature, as it allows researchers to evaluate the extent to which those beliefs would change in a counterfactual setting. We return to this in concluding the chapter when pointing to directions for future research.

21.4 Literature II: data on choice expectations

The second category of expectations data in Manski's (2004) taxonomy comprises data on choice expectations. These have many uses in the estimation of structural models. First, data on actual choices may not be available, and thus, data on choice expectations might be used as a substitute. Second, even when data on actual behaviors are available, researchers may still prefer eliciting choice expectations conditional on an explicitly specified economic environment, one which maps directly into the model's setting.[20] This allows the choice set and the characteristics of the individual choices to be specified in detail while eliciting choice expectations, making observable some characteristics which would be unobservable in revealed preference data.[21] Third, while eliciting choice expectations researchers can experimentally vary the choice attributes of interest, in doing so generating exogenous variation that can facilitate identification. Finally, in settings where data on choice expectations and revealed choices are both available, they can either be used together in estimation, improving efficiency as in van der Klaauw (2012), or if one is used in estimation, the other can be used for validating the model.

In the remainder of this section, we discuss how choice expectations data have been used in the literature to estimate structural microeconomic models. We will organize our discussion by distinguishing between data on unconditional choice expectations and data on conditional choice expectations. The difference between these two is whether the expectations are elicited conditional on an explicitly specified future environment. Section 21.4.1 discusses contributions that use data elicited through questions on what the respondent *will* do in the future without specifying any contingency about that future. Such questions are often found in large, general purpose household surveys. Section 21.4.2 discusses the set of papers that solicits choice expectations conditional on some future circumstances – what the respondent *would* do in those specified circumstances. These questions have often been developed in bespoke surveys developed for particular papers. Finally, Section 21.4.3 discusses the literature that uses "strategic survey questions," a type of design that elicits beliefs with the specific goal of identifying a particular feature of a given model.

21.4.1 Unconditional choice expectations

Unconditional choice expectations data take the form of a respondent's expected choices in the future, without the survey specifying any details of the environment the individuals will be facing when this actual decision will be made (other than perhaps their age or the time period in which the decision will be made). These choice expectations can be considered to be conditional only on the current information set of the individual.

---

[20] Such environments can be specified through future hypothetical scenarios. See Koşar et al. (2021) for an extensive discussion on the design of such choice experiments using hypotheticals.

[21] An example to this would be the unobserved components of jobs when the agent is choosing among different job options in a labor supply model, or the unobservable location attributes in a model of migration.

A very early contribution by Wolpin and Gonul (1985) tests whether data on expected retirement ages are consistent with those predicted by a labor supply model. They find that expectations data contain valuable information and highlight their use in estimating models of labor supply. Another early example is by van der Klaauw (2012), who studies the decision to become a teacher. He develops a dynamic model of career decisions under uncertainty, and shows how data on observed choices can be used together with choice expectations data to estimate parameters using simulated MLE. The data come from questions on the expected age 30 occupation of a sample with an average age of 25. The paper first estimates the model parameters using only choice data and then shows that the predictions from that estimated model are consistent with elicited choice expectations. The paper then estimates parameters using both realized choice data and choice expectations data and shows that these estimates are very close to those obtained using only realized choice data, but that the standard errors from the estimation that incorporates both types of data are smaller.[22]

The research design by van der Klaauw (2012) does not rely on expectations data for identification, but instead for efficiency and validation. However, choice expectations data are often particularly valuable for identifying certain parameters in a structural model. Adda et al. (2022) provide one such example, by studying the interplay between human capital choices and the return migration decisions of migrants. One decision migrants face is how much to invest in host-country-specific human capital (e.g., language), for which the returns vary with the intended duration of migration. To study this issue, the authors specify a model in which migrants, who differ in their preferences for living in their origin and host countries, are faced with human capital and return migration choices. Using repeated observations on the intended duration of stay from the German Socio-Economic Panel, the authors estimate the extent of heterogeneity in location preferences and the persistence of such preferences. In the absence of expectations data in this setting the most valuable observable that might identify heterogeneity and persistence in location preferences would be the level of language skills. However measured language skill has significant limitations for the purpose at hand as it is slow moving and, as language skills typically improve rather than deteriorate, it cannot be used to measure negative shocks to location preferences.

The papers we reviewed in this section so far use discrete choice expectations. An example of using probabilistic unconditional choice expectations is by van der Klaauw and Wolpin (2008). This was discussed in Section 21.3, with a focus there on their use of expectations data on policy uncertainty. In their paper, the authors also use data on choice expectations, specifically the probabilities of working at older ages and leaving a bequest. The value-added of expectations data in that context is to avail of measurements of model implications that cannot be available at the time of writing (since most of the sample were younger than 62 at the time of observation). McGee (2021) also leverages probabilistic data on bequest intentions – to identify the strength of bequest motives in a structural model developed to study how old-age wealth shocks are transmitted into savings, consumption, and bequests. The paper shows that, conditional on a rich set of observables, there is substantial heterogeneity in stated probabilities of leaving bequests among survey respondents in England. Expectations data are then used to separately identify precautionary saving motives from bequest motives.

---

[22] Somewhat similarly, but studying college major choice rather than occupational choice, both Arcidiacono et al. (2012) and Zafar (2013) combine data on observed choices with intended choices to estimate preferences. See Section 21.3 for a more detailed discussion of those papers.

21.4.2 Conditional choice expectations

Surveys often ask people what they expect to do in hypothetical future scenarios. The empirical content of these elicited responses is different from that of unconditional choice expectations. Consider a question which inquires about work expectations. Suppose, as in the HRS, individuals are asked about their probability of being in work at a future age, but without specifying anything about their circumstances at that age. The analogue of this, in the context of the simple model outlined in Section 21.2.1, would be $\mathbb{P}_i[\tilde{p}_{it+\tau} = 1]$, an individual's probability of being in work at age $t + \tau$, *integrating over all possible states of the world*. Suppose that, alternatively, individuals are asked to consider the probability that they will be in work conditional on some future state of the world (for example, based on their health status, as in Giustinelli and Shapiro (2019) who study the interplay between health and retirement). Denoting the state variable(s) which are considered in the question's conditioning as $\mathbf{x}$ and the realized future state as $\mathbf{x}^j$, the model analogue to this question would be $\mathbb{P}_i[\tilde{p}_{it+\tau} = 1 | \mathbf{x}_{t+\tau} = \mathbf{x}^j_{t+\tau}]$. This distinction naturally has implications for use of such data in estimation.

Choice expectations data elicited using hypothetical scenarios provide variation of a type not often available with data on observed choices. Whereas revealed preference data is observed in only one state of the world, creating selection problems that abound in economics, choice expectations can be assessed in many different states of the world. Similarly, whereas conditional choice expectations can be measured under conditions which have not (and may never) prevail, choice behavior can only be observed under conditions which actually have prevailed – as Ameriks et al. (2020a) note, there is "no obvious behavioral imprint of frustrated desires." Finally, soliciting choice expectations under multiple scenarios for the same individual leads to repeated observations that can be used to exploit within-person variation.

In the remainder of this section, we will classify studies based on whether they use stated discrete choice data (in Section 21.4.2.1) or choice probabilities (in Section 21.4.2.2) in the estimation of structural models. With stated choice expectations data, researchers elicit the most preferred choice or the preference ranking across different options. With probabilistic conditional choice expectations data, researchers instead elicit the probability of each option being chosen.[23]

21.4.2.1 Stated discrete choice data

A growing literature uses data on how employment decisions vary with job characteristics in the estimation of labor supply models. In this setting, observed data on choices are the outcomes of the interplay between individual preferences and market conditions – that is, the interplay between labor supply and labor demand. An advantage of using conditional choice expectations data here is that, by specifying carefully the terms of hypothetical job offers, labor demand can be held constant, allowing for identification of parameters which govern labor supply.[24]

Focusing on retirement decisions, van Soest and Vonkova (2014) study how individuals would trade off different combinations of retirement trajectories and income in retirement. Using conditional choice

---

[23] As noted in Section 21.2.5.1, probabilistic expectations data are richer in empirical content than stated choice data, in that a researcher needs some mapping to go from the former to the latter. Probabilistic choice expectations data are also more likely to be informative about rankings of options than are stated choice data.

[24] There is also a large literature in marketing, environmental, and natural resource economics that use discrete stated-choice experiments to recover preferences. We do not review that literature here – see Manski (1999, 2004) for two comprehensive reviews.

expectations data, which display respondents' most likely choices among different retirement scenarios that vary replacement rates and retirement ages, allows the authors to estimate preferences for pension plans that either may not exist or may be inaccessible to the respondents. The paper estimates the parameters of a labor supply model using simulated MLE. They find that the effect of financial incentives on retirement age are, in many cases, larger than those estimated with revealed preference data. The paper argues that this is due to the fact that more flexible choice options are presented to the respondents in the hypotheticals. Ameriks et al. (2020a) also study the transition into retirement and ask whether older individuals would work for longer if employment opportunities with more flexible schedules were available to them. The authors use a labor supply model and responses to the choices individuals would make if faced by hypothetical employment offers to resolve an identification problem – whether the abrupt fall in labor supply near retirement is due to supply-side factors (e.g., a high intertemporal elasticity of labor supply) or demand-side factors (e.g., nonconvexities in production technologies that make it unproductive for firms to hire part-time workers). They find that a latent desire to smooth leisure, identified using the data on conditional choice expectations, implies that demand-side factors play a substantial role.

Studying workers across the age distribution, Maestas et al. (2018) estimate the willingness-to-pay for job attributes using discrete stated-choice experiments that vary a broad set of job characteristics. Amenities are often correlated with other job characteristics in observational data. Hypothetical scenarios enable the authors to generate variation in these amenities (holding everything else constant), which can be used to recover preferences. Estimating a labor supply model with this data, they find substantial heterogeneity in preferences for different nonwage amenities across demographic groups and that accounting for this preference heterogeneity increases the measured wage inequality. Similarly, Koşar et al. (2022) tackle the problem of identifying heterogeneity in preferences, but for leisure. They design and implement a survey in which hypothetical wage-hours pairs are presented to respondents, who are asked to choose one of the job offers or unemployment. These data facilitate the estimation of preference heterogeneity in a canonical life-cycle model by providing exogenous variation in wages and weekly hours for the same individual – a richness seldom available with observational data. Using the estimated model, the authors show that the preference heterogeneity identified with the choice expectations data has important implications for the predicted responses to changes in tax policy and childcare subsidies.

Just as stated-choice data can be used to disentangle the role of labor demand and supply, they can similarly be used to isolate the workings of each side of the marriage market. Andrew and Adams-Prassl (2021) study the mechanisms driving school drop-out and early marriage for young girls in India. To separate the role of preferences of girls' families, the beliefs of those families about marriage market outcomes, and the preferences of grooms (the other side of the market), the authors design and implement a survey which elicits the stated choices of brides' families when presented with hypothetical vignettes that vary the outcomes over brides' completed education, brides' age of marriage, and grooms' characteristics. Using this induced exogenous variation in bride's and groom's characteristics, they estimate the parameters of a structural model of parental choice of daughter's education and marriage market behavior and show how the elicited choice data can be used to identify the parameters of parental utility function.

Finally, Lagakos et al. (2022) use discrete choice expectations data to validate the findings of a structural model of migration choices of rural migrants, estimated using data from a randomized field experiment where landless households in Bangladesh were offered one-time migration subsidies.

The estimated model generates a large nonmonetary utility cost of migration and the authors validate this result using responses from a discrete stated-choice experiment administered to the same sample. Bossavie et al. (2021) also study migration and use data on the expectations of migrants prior to migration in the estimation of their model.

21.4.2.2 *Probabilistic conditional choice expectations data*

The seminal empirical application of using elicited choice probabilities to estimate preferences is by Blass et al. (2010), who measure the willingness to pay for the reliability of electricity services using a hypothetical choice methodology. Following the theoretical discussion by Manski (1999), Blass et al. (2010) assume preferences follow a random utility model with random coefficients. The utility of individual i from alternative j is

$$U_{ij} = X_{ij}\beta_i + \varepsilon_{ij}, \tag{21.10}$$

where $\beta_i = b + \eta_i$ and X_{ij} denotes the observed characteristics of choice alternatives and personal attributes. The respondents observe X_{ij}, the characteristics of the choice alternatives stated in the scenarios. The probabilistic choice expectations they report reflect their uncertainty about their choice, which is captured by ε_{ij}. Manski (1999) calls this *resolvable uncertainty*, referring to the uncertainty respondents face about the unknown components of the environment that are not specified in the scenarios, but that would be known in an actual choice setting. Accounting for this type of uncertainty in a model, whether using data on probabilities of choices or data on a single most likely choice (such as in van der Klaauw (2012)) is pivotal, as the responses individuals give will conflate both information on their preferences and their assessments of how their environment will evolve.[25]

The identifying assumption to recover preferences here is that the scenario-specific unobserved terms, ε_{ij} for all $j \in \{1, \dots, J\}$, are *iid* and independent of the scenario attributes. This is generally achieved through the scenario design, where respondents are told that the choice alternatives vary only in the characteristics specified in the scenarios and are otherwise identical. It is common to further assume that ε_{ij} for each attribute j are *iid* with Type I extreme value distribution. With this assumption, the choice probabilities implied by (21.10) reduce to a multinomial logit form. Taking the log odds ratio leads to the linear mixed-logit model

$$\ln\left(\frac{q_{ij}}{q_{i1}}\right) = (X_{ij} - X_{i1})b + u_{ij}, \quad \forall j \in \{2, \dots, J\}, \tag{21.11}$$

where $u_{ij} = (X_{ij} - X_{i1})\eta_i$ and q_{ij} refers to the probability of respondent i choosing alternative j. Probabilistic expectations data (as discussed in Section 21.2.5.3) suffer from a rounding problem, where respondents tend to report expectations in increments of 5% or 10%. However, when choice probabilities are rounded to 0 or 1, the log odds ratio becomes undefined and thus, the least squares estimation cannot be implemented. To overcome this issue, Blass et al. (2010) assume η_i are normally distributed with mean 0, which implies that u_{ij} are also normally distributed around 0 conditional on X_{ij} and have a median of 0 conditional on X_{ij}. With this assumption, the median becomes

$$M\left[\ln\left(\frac{q_{ij}}{q_{i1}}\bigg|\mathbf{X}\right)\right] = (X_{ij} - X_{i1})b, \tag{21.12}$$

---

[25] With data on observed choices there is no resolvable uncertainty to account for.

and the parameters can be estimated using the Least Absolute Deviation (LAD) estimator. Since the median of a random variable is not affected by transformations that do not affect the ordering of values relative to the median, any zeros and ones can be suitably transformed and estimation can proceed.[26] Following Blass et al. (2010), researchers have used elicited choice probabilities to understand preferences for political candidates and voting behavior (Delavande and Manski, 2015), to estimate consumers' willingness to pay for electric power generated from different sources (Morita and Managi, 2015), and to estimate preferences for long-term care insurance products (Boyer et al., 2020), land-use scenarios (Shoyama et al., 2013), and postgraduate education (Boneva et al., 2022).

Wiswall and Zafar (2018) extend this methodology and apply it to study how preferences for workplace attributes affect the gender gap in labor market earnings. Instead of assuming $\beta_i = b + \eta_i$ as in Eq. (21.10), they allow β_i to freely vary in the population. This, together with the Type I extreme assumption on ε_{ij}, leads to the following linear mixed-logit model for the preferences in Eq. (21.10),

$$\ln\left(\frac{q_{ij}}{q_{i1}}\right) = (X_{ij} - X_{i1})\beta_i. \tag{21.13}$$

The authors use job choice probabilities elicited from undergraduates through hypothetical job scenarios that vary in attributes such as expected earnings, earnings growth, workplace flexibility, and dismissal probability, to estimate their model. Wiswall and Zafar (2018) assume these choice probabilities are reported with an error, which has a zero median conditional on the observed characteristics X_{ij} and takes a linear-in-log form. The final log odds ratio of the observed choice probabilities ($\widetilde{q}_{ij}$) becomes

$$\ln\left(\frac{\widetilde{q}_{ij}}{\widetilde{q}_{i1}}\right) = (X_{ij} - X_{i1})\beta_i + \omega_{ij}. \tag{21.14}$$

This can be estimated using the LAD estimator. Note that this formulation does not impose any distribution on the measurement errors (ω_{ij}), which, together with the rich variation created by the hypothetical scenarios, enables the estimation of this model separately for each individual to recover individual preferences. Koşar et al. (2021) follow the approach introduced by Wiswall and Zafar (2018) to recover the distribution of individual-level preferences for location characteristics and estimate the nonmonetary costs of moving. Gong et al. (2022) use a similar methodology and elicit location premiums to estimate the importance of nonpecuniary benefits in location decisions of college graduates from low-income backgrounds.

The papers discussed above use surveys that collect data on, but do not attempt to perturb, conditional choice expectations. Rather than using multiple hypothetical scenarios to vary the attributes and to identify their impact on choices, it is also possible to use information experiments. These involve shifting beliefs on certain choice-specific outcomes by providing information to the respondents. An early example of combining informational interventions, subjective conditional choice probabilities, and a model of decision-making is by Wiswall and Zafar (2015), who study college major choice. In their survey, the authors first elicit beliefs about respondents' own expected future earnings, labor market status, and marital status at age 30 conditional on receiving a degree in different majors, as well as their perceptions of the population distribution of these outcomes. Next, they give respondents

---

[26] Given the symmetry assumption, Blass et al. (2010) refer to the parameter estimates as mean preferences.

accurate information on the population characteristics of the graduates of each major. The revision in respondents' beliefs about their conditional, choice-specific outcomes as a result of the experimental design leads to panel data, which are then used to estimate a dynamic model of major choice, leveraging the within-individual variation in beliefs. The results show that heterogeneous tastes are the most important factor in driving major choice. The authors also show that estimation of the model using only cross-sectional expectations data, without taking into account the correlation of tastes with earnings expectations, overestimates the role of earnings in major choices. For more details and references on this estimation method, see Chapter 4 in this Handbook.

Following the approach by Wiswall and Zafar (2015), Ruder and Van Noy (2017) analyze how information on the population estimates of the earnings risk for college majors affect the preferences over these college majors and Baker et al. (2018) estimate the preferences of community college students for different college majors by experimentally manipulating their expected labor market outcomes through an information experiment.

21.4.3 Strategic survey questions

Conditional choice expectations data elicited using questions that are designed "strategically" to identify the features of a particular model have been termed "strategic survey questions" (SSQs). Utilizing this type of data to estimate model parameters goes back to Barsky et al. (1997), who obtained direct measurements of parameters governing risk tolerance, time preference, and intertemporal substitution using a survey using hypothetical scenarios. SSQs are designed alongside the parametric specification of preferences, since the hypothetical questions are designed with the identification of the parameters of the model in mind.

An early example of using SSQs to identify preference parameters in a structural model is by Ameriks et al. (2011), who study the reasons why annuities are rarely purchased, despite the fact that they can provide valuable longevity insurance. Two candidate explanations for this lack of demand have been a desire to avoid publicly-provided nursing home care, should it be necessary, and bequest motives, both of which have similar implications for wealth accumulation. To identify the parameters governing the strength of these motives, the authors develop two SSQs and use the mapping between the preference specification and the responses to these SSQs to estimate the preference parameters using simulated MLE. In a similar manner, Ameriks et al. (2020b) tackle the question of why many households retain wealth late into life, using a model that incorporates precautionary saving against health risks, the potential need for long-term care, and an uncertain lifespan. The authors combine observed wealth data and SSQs to jointly estimate risk aversion, aversion to publicly-provided long term care, and the strength of the bequest motive. They find that the risk of needing long-term care and bequest motives each have quantitatively similar roles in determining late-in-life saving. Using the same set of SSQs, Ameriks et al. (2016) estimate preferences in a life-cycle model with incomplete markets and stochastic health and mortality risks, to analyze why individuals hold little long-term care insurance even though they face significant late-in-life risks.

SSQs are commonly used to identify time preference and risk aversion parameters. Patnaik et al. (2020) recover parameters corresponding to constant relative risk aversion preferences and geometric discounting, using two separate games. The authors then use these parameters, along with probabilistic choice expectations and subjective beliefs on choice-specific outcomes, to estimate a model of college major choice. Ameriks et al. (2020c) use SSQs to jointly estimate *individual-level* risk tolerance as well as individuals' perceptions for the mean and variance of stock returns. Similarly, SSQs can also be used to analyze the state-dependence in marginal utility of consumption across health and disabled states, as in Brown et al. (2016).

21.5 Conclusion

This chapter discusses how expectations data can be, and have been, used in the estimation of structural microeconomic models. Data on individual or household expectations over future states of the world can be used to relax strong (and often-untested) assumptions on how expectations are formed, while data on expected future choices can be used to substitute for, and to complement, behavioral data, which have been the primary data source for estimating these models.

We conclude by noting two directions for future research. The first relates to the importance of measurement. The past two decades have seen a proliferation in the measurement of expectations, with the development of several dedicated high-quality surveys and with expectations questions now embedded in several general-use surveys.[27] Using this data, individuals' expectations have been shown to correlate with other features of their decision problems (preferences and constraints) in various areas. To the extent that measurement of those other features of decision problems do not have the same rich measurement base as do expectations, there is a risk of ascribing to expectations some role which should be shared with those (omitted) factors. Several recent papers that we review have made strides on measuring distributions of expectations alongside other dimensions of individual heterogeneity.

A second direction relates to the modeling of expectations formation. Many of the papers we review in this chapter do not model how individuals form their expectations. A common approach is to assume a specific form for expectations (e.g., rational expectations, if expectations data are not used) or to use elicited data to directly measure agents' expectations over future events, which are then assumed to be invariant to policy changes. However, the extent to which the process governing the formation of expectations varies with policy and which factors influence their formation are still very much open questions. In order to identify such processes, one would require expectations data with repeated observations and, ideally, a long time series. Several data sets that pioneered the elicitation of expectations, such as the Health and Retirement Study and the Federal Reserve Bank of New York's Survey of Consumer Expectations, have, by now, lengthy time series. These might facilitate the modeling of expectation formation processes in estimated structural models.

References

Adda, J., Cooper, R., 2003. Dynamic Economics: Quantitative Methods and Applications. MIT Press.

Adda, J., Dustmann, C., Görlach, J.-S., 2022. The dynamics of return migration, human capital accumulation, and wage assimilation. The Review of Economic Studies. Forthcoming.

Aguirregabiria, V., Jeon, J., 2020. Firms' beliefs and learning: models, identification, and empirical evidence. Review of Industrial Organization 56 (2), 203–235.

---

[27] See Chapter 1 in this Handbook.

Aguirregabiria, V., Mira, P., 2010. Dynamic discrete choice structural models: a survey. Journal of Econometrics 156 (1), 38–67.

Ameriks, J., Briggs, J., Caplin, A., Lee, M., Shapiro, M.D., Tonetti, C., 2020a. Older Americans would work longer if jobs were flexible. American Economic Journal: Macroeconomics 12 (1), 174–209.

Ameriks, J., Briggs, J., Caplin, A., Shapiro, M.D., Tonetti, C., 2016. The long-term-care insurance puzzle: Modeling and measurement. Working Paper 22726. National Bureau of Economic Research.

Ameriks, J., Briggs, J., Caplin, A., Shapiro, M.D., Tonetti, C., 2020b. Long-term-care utility and late-in-life saving. Journal of Political Economy 128 (6), 2375–2451.

Ameriks, J., Caplin, A., Laufer, S., Nieuwerburgh, S.V., 2011. The joy of giving or assisted living? Using strategic surveys to separate bequest and precautionary motives. The Journal of Finance 66 (13105), 519–561.

Ameriks, J., Kézdi, G., Lee, M., Shapiro, M.D., 2020c. Heterogeneity in expectations, risk tolerance, and household stock shares: the attenuation puzzle. Journal of Business & Economic Statistics 38 (3), 633–646.

Andrew, A., Adams-Prassl, A., 2021. Revealed beliefs and the marriage market return to education. Working paper.

Andrews, I., Gentzkow, M., Shapiro, J.M., 2017. Measuring the sensitivity of parameter estimates to estimation moments. The Quarterly Journal of Economics 132 (4), 1553–1592.

Arcidiacono, P., Hotz, V.J., Kang, S., 2012. Modeling college major choices using elicited measures of expectations and counterfactuals. Journal of Econometrics 166 (1), 3–16.

Arcidiacono, P., Hotz, V.J., Maurel, A., Romano, T., 2020. Ex ante returns and occupational choice. Journal of Political Economy 128 (12), 4475–4522.

Arteaga, F., Kapor, A.J., Neilson, C.A., Zimmerman, S.D., 2022. Smart matching platforms and heterogeneous beliefs in centralized school choice. The Quarterly Journal of Economics 137 (3), 1791–1848.

Attanasio, O., Boneva, T., Rauh, C., 2020a. Parental beliefs about returns to different types of investments in school children. The Journal of Human Resources. 0719-10299R1.

Attanasio, O., Cunha, F., Jervis, P., 2019. Subjective parental beliefs. Their measurement and role. Working Paper 26516. National Bureau of Economic Research.

Attanasio, O., Kaufmann, K., 2014. Education choices and returns to schooling: intrahousehold decision making, gender and subjective expectations. Journal of Development Economics 109, 203–216.

Attanasio, O., Kovacs, A., Molnar, K., 2020b. Euler equations, subjective expectations and income shocks. Economica 87 (346), 406–441.

Bairoliya, N., McKiernan, K., 2021. Revisiting retirement and social security claiming decisions. SSRN Working Paper 3896031.

Baker, R., Bettinger, E., Jacob, B., Marinescu, I., 2018. The effect of labor market information on community college students' major choice. Economics of Education Review 65, 18–30.

Barsky, R.B., Juster, F.T., Kimball, M.S., Shapiro, M.D., 1997. Preference parameters and behavioral heterogeneity: an experimental approach in the health and retirement study. The Quarterly Journal of Economics 112 (2), 537–579.

Bellemare, C., Kröger, S., Sossou, K.M., 2020. Optimal frequency of portfolio evaluation in a choice experiment with ambiguity and loss aversion. Journal of Econometrics. Forthcoming.

Bellemare, C., Kröger, S., van Soest, A., 2008. Measuring inequity aversion in a heterogeneous population using experimental decisions and subjective probabilities. Econometrica 76 (4), 815–839.

Bissonnette, L., Hurd, M.D., Michaud, P.-C., 2017. Individual survival curves comparing subjective and observed mortality risks. Health Economics 26 (12), e285–e303.

Blass, A.A., Lach, S., Manski, C.F., 2010. Using elicited choice probabilities to estimate random utility models: preferences for electricity reliability. International Economic Review 51 (2), 421–440.

Boneva, T., Golin, M., Rauh, C., 2022. Can perceived returns explain enrollment gaps in postgraduate education? Labour Economics 77.

Boneva, T., Rauh, C., 2018. Parental beliefs about returns to educational investments—the later the better? Journal of the European Economic Association 16 (6), 1669–1711.

Bossavie, L., Görlach, J.-S., Özden, Ç., Wang, H., 2021. Temporary migration for long-term investment. Policy Research Working paper 9740. World Bank Group.

Boyer, M., De Donder, P., Fluet, C., Leroux, M.-L., Michaud, P.-C., 2020. Long-term care insurance: information frictions and selection. American Economic Journal: Economic Policy 12 (3), 134–169.

Brown, J.R., Goda, G.S., McGarry, K., 2016. Heterogeneity in state-dependent utility: evidence from strategic surveys. Economic Inquiry 54 (2), 847–861.

Caliendo, F.N., Gorry, A., Slavov, S., 2020. Survival ambiguity and welfare. Journal of Economic Behavior & Organization 170, 20–42.

Ciani, E., Delavande, A., Etheridge, B., Francesconi, M., 2022. Policy uncertainty and information flows: Evidence from pension reform expectations. Economic Journal. Forthcoming.

Comerford, D.A., 2019. Asking for frequencies rather than percentages increases the validity of subjective probability measures: evidence from subjective life expectancy. Economics Letters 180, 33–35.

Conlon, J.J., Pilossoph, L., Wiswall, M., Zafar, B., 2018. Labor market search with imperfect information and learning. Working Paper 24988. National Bureau of Economic Research.

Cortés, P., Pan, J., Pilossoph, L., Zafar, B., 2021. Gender differences in job search and the earnings gap: Evidence from business majors. Working Paper 28820. National Bureau of Economic Research.

Crossley, T., Gong, Y., Stinebrickner, T.R., Stinebrickner, R., 2021. Examining income expectations in the college and early post-college periods: New distributional tests of rational expectations. Working Paper 28353. National Bureau of Economic Research.

Crossley, T.F., Gong, Y., Stinebrickner, R., Stinebrickner, T., 2022. The ex post accuracy of subjective beliefs: a new measure and decomposition. Economics Letters 210, 110160.

Cunha, F., Elo, I., Culhane, J., 2013. Eliciting maternal expectations about the technology of cognitive skill formation. Working Paper 19144. National Bureau of Economic Research.

Cunha, F., Heckman, J.J., Schennach, S.M., 2010. Estimating the technology of cognitive and noncognitive skill formation. Econometrica 78 (3), 883–931.

de Bresser, J., 2019. Measuring subjective survival expectations–do response scales matter? Journal of Economic Behavior & Organization 165, 136–156.

de Bresser, J., 2021. The role of heterogeneous expectations in life cycle models. CentER Discussion Paper 2021-034.

Delavande, A., 2008. Pill, patch, or shot? Subjective expectations and birth control choice. International Economic Review 49 (3), 999–1042.

Delavande, A., Del Bono, E., Holford, A., 2020. Academic and non-academic investments at university: the role of expectations, preferences and constraints. Journal of Econometrics. Forthcoming.

Delavande, A., Manski, C.F., 2015. Using elicited choice probabilities in hypothetical elections to study decisions to vote. Electoral Studies 38, 28–37.

Delavande, A., Rohwedder, S., 2011. Individuals' uncertainty about future social security benefits and portfolio choice. Journal of Applied Econometrics 26 (3), 498–519.

Delavande, A., Zafar, B., 2019. University choice: the role of expected earnings, nonpecuniary outcomes, and financial constraints. Journal of Political Economy 127 (5), 2343–2393.

d'Haultfoeuille, X., Gaillac, C., Maurel, A., 2021. Rationalizing rational expectations: characterizations and tests. Quantitative Economics 12 (3), 817–842.

Eisenhauer, P., Haan, P., Ilieva, B., Schrenker, A., Weizsäcker, G., 2021. Biased wage expectations and female labor supply. Working paper.

Fischhoff, B., Bruine De Bruin, W., 1999. Fifty–fifty=50%? Journal of Behavioral Decision Making 12 (2), 149–163.

Foltyn, R., Olsson, J., 2021. Subjective life expectancies, time preference heterogeneity, and wealth inequality. SSRN Working Paper 3895119.

Gan, L., Gong, G., Hurd, M., Mcfadden, D., 2015. Subjective mortality risk and bequests. Journal of Econometrics 188 (2), 514–525.

Gan, L., Hurd, M., McFadden, D., 2005. Individual survival curves. In: Wise, D. (Ed.), Analyses in Economics of Aging I. The University of Chicago Press, pp. 377–411.

Giustinelli, P., 2016. Group decision making with uncertain outcomes: unpacking child–parent choice of the high school track. International Economic Review 57 (2), 573–602.

Giustinelli, P., Shapiro, M.D., 2019. SeaTE: Subjective ex ante treatment effect of health on retirement. Working Paper 26087. National Bureau of Economic Research.

Gong, Y., Lochner, L., Stinebrickner, R., Stinebrickner, T.R., 2021. The consumption value of college. Working Paper 26335. National Bureau of Economic Research.

Gong, Y., Stinebrickner, T., Stinebrickner, R., Yao, Y., et al., 2022. The role of non-pecuniary considerations: Locations decisions of college graduates from low income backgrounds. Working Paper 20221. University of Western Ontario, Centre for Human Capital and Productivity.

Gourieroux, C., Monfort, A., Renault, E., 1993. Indirect inference. Journal of Applied Econometrics 8 (S1), S85–S118.

Grevenbrock, N., Groneck, M., Ludwig, A., Zimper, A., 2021. Cognition, optimism, and the formation of age-dependent survival beliefs. International Economic Review 62 (2), 887–918.

Groneck, M., Ludwig, A., Zimper, A., 2016. A life-cycle model with ambiguous survival beliefs. Journal of Economic Theory 162, 137–180.

Haile, P., 2021. Structural vs. reduced form: language, confusion, and models in empirical economics. http://www.econ.yale.edu/~pah29/intro.pdf.

Hamermesh, D.S., 1985. Expectations, life expectancy, and economic behavior. The Quarterly Journal of Economics 100 (2), 389–408.

Hamilton, B.H., Chan, T.Y., Makler, C., 2011. Using expectations data to infer managerial preferences. SSRN Working Paper 1830285.

Hastings, J., Neilson, C.A., Zimmerman, S.D., 2015. The effects of earnings disclosure on college enrollment decisions. Working Paper 21300. National Bureau of Economic Research.

Heimer, R.Z., Myrseth, K.O.R., Schoenle, R.S., 2019. YOLO: mortality beliefs and household finance puzzles. The Journal of Finance 74 (6), 2957–2996.

Hendren, N., 2013. Private information and insurance rejections. Econometrica 81 (5), 1713–1762.

Hentall-MacCuish, J., 2021. Costly attention and retirement. SSRN Working Paper 3363188.

Hoffman, M., Burks, S.V., 2020. Worker overconfidence: field evidence and implications for employee turnover and firm profits. Quantitative Economics 11 (1), 315–348.

Hosseini, R., 2015. Adverse selection in the annuity market and the role for social security. Journal of Political Economy 123 (4), 941–984.

Hotz, V.J., Miller, R.A., 1993. Conditional choice probabilities and the estimation of dynamic models. The Review of Economic Studies 60 (3), 497–529.

Hurd, M.D., McGarry, K., 1995. Evaluation of the subjective probabilities of survival in the health and retirement study. The Journal of Human Resources 30, S268.

Hurd, M.D., McGarry, K., 2002. The predictive validity of subjective probabilities of survival. The Economic Journal 112 (482), 966–985.

Hurd, M.D., Rohwedder, S., Winter, J., 2005. Subjective probabilities of survival: an international comparison. Working paper. RAND.

Hurwicz, L., 1950. Generalization of the concept of identification. In: Statistical Inference in Dynamic Economic Models. Cowles Commission.

Jäger, S., Roth, C., Roussille, N., Schoefer, B., 2022. Worker beliefs about outside options. Working Paper 29623. National Bureau of Economic Research.

Juster, F.T., 1966. Consumer buying intentions and purchase probability: an experiment in survey design. Journal of the American Statistical Association 61 (315), 658–696.

Kapor, A.J., Neilson, C.A., Zimmerman, S.D., 2020. Heterogeneous beliefs and school choice mechanisms. The American Economic Review 110 (5), 1274–1315.

Kaufmann, K.M., 2014. Understanding the income gradient in college attendance in Mexico: the role of heterogeneity in expected returns. Quantitative Economics 5 (3), 583–630.

Keane, M.P., 2010. Structural vs. atheoretic approaches to econometrics. Journal of Econometrics 156 (1), 3–20.

Koşar, G., Ransom, T., van der Klaauw, W., 2021. Understanding migration aversion using elicited counterfactual choice probabilities. Journal of Econometrics. Forthcoming.

Koşar, G., Şahin, A., Zafar, B., 2022. The work-leisure tradeoff: Identifying the heterogeneity. Working paper.

Lagakos, D., Mobarak, A.M., Waugh, M.E., 2022. The Welfare Effects of Encouraging Rural-Urban Migration. Staff Report 635. Federal Reserve Bank of Minneapolis.

Lochner, L., 2007. Individual perceptions of the criminal justice system. The American Economic Review 97 (1), 444–460.

Ludwig, A., Zimper, A., 2013. A parsimonious model of subjective life expectancy. Theory and Decision 75 (4), 519–541.

Luttmer, E.F., Samwick, A.A., 2018. The welfare cost of perceived policy uncertainty: evidence from social security. The American Economic Review 108 (2), 275–307.

Maestas, N., Mullen, K.J., Powell, D., von Wachter, T., Wenger, J.B., 2018. The Value of Working Conditions in the United States and Implications for the Structure of Wages. Working Paper 25204. National Bureau of Economic Research.

Mahajan, A., Michel, C., Tarozzi, A., 2020. Identification of time-inconsistent models: the case of insecticide treated nets. Working Paper 27198. National Bureau of Economic Research.

Manski, C.F., 1993. Adolescent econometricians: how do youth infer the returns to schooling?. In: Studies of Supply and Demand in Higher Education. University of Chicago Press, pp. 43–60.

Manski, C.F., 1999. Analysis of choice expectations in incomplete scenarios. Journal of Risk and Uncertainty 19, 49–66.

Manski, C.F., 2004. Measuring expectations. Econometrica 72 (5), 1329–1376.

Matzkin, R.L., 2013. Nonparametric identification in structural economic models. Annual Review of Economics 5 (1), 457–486.

McGee, R., 2021. Old age savings and house price shocks. Working paper 2021-4. University of Western Ontario Research Reports.

Miller, G., de Paula, Á., Valente, C., 2020. Subjective expectations and demand for contraception. Working Paper W20/7. Institute for Fiscal Studies.

Morita, T., Managi, S., 2015. Consumers' willingness to pay for electricity after the Great East Japan Earthquake. Economic Analysis and Policy 48, 82–105.

Mueller, A.I., Spinnewijn, J., Topa, G., 2021. Job seekers' perceptions and employment prospects: heterogeneity, duration dependence, and bias. The American Economic Review 111 (1), 324–363.

Nyarko, Y., Schotter, A., 2002. An experimental study of belief learning using elicited beliefs. Econometrica 70 (3), 971–1005.

O'Dea, C., Sturrock, D., 2021. Survival pessimism and demand for annuities. Review of Economics and Statistics. Forthcoming.

Patnaik, A., Venator, J., Wiswall, M., Zafar, B., 2020. The role of heterogeneous risk preferences, discount rates, and earnings expectations in college major choice. Journal of Econometrics. Forthcoming.

Pantano, J., Zheng, Y., 2013. Using Subjective Expectations Data to Allow for Unobserved Heterogeneity in Hotz-Miller Estimation Strategies. Working paper.

Pistaferri, L., 2001. Superior information, income shocks, and the permanent income hypothesis. Review of Economics and Statistics 83 (3), 465–476.

Ruder, A.I., Van Noy, M., 2017. Knowledge of earnings risk and major choice: evidence from an information experiment. Economics of Education Review 57, 80–90.

Schneider, U., 2020. Identifying and estimating beliefs from choice data–an application to female labor supply. Working paper.

Shoyama, K., Managi, S., Yamagata, Y., 2013. Public preferences for biodiversity conservation and climate-change mitigation: a choice experiment using ecosystem services indicators. Land Use Policy 34, 282–293.

Smith Jr, A.A., 1993. Estimating nonlinear time-series models using simulated vector autoregressions. Journal of Applied Econometrics 8 (S1), S63–S84.

Stinebrickner, R., Stinebrickner, T., 2014a. Academic performance and college dropout: using longitudinal expectations data to estimate a learning model. Journal of Labor Economics 32 (3), 601–644.

Stinebrickner, R., Stinebrickner, T.R., 2014b. A major in science? Initial beliefs and final outcomes for college major and dropout. The Review of Economic Studies 81 (1), 426–472.

Teppa, F., Lafourcade, P., 2013. Can longevity risk alleviate the annuitization puzzle? Empirical evidence from survey data. Working paper.

Tincani, M.M., Kosse, F., Miglino, E., 2021. Subjective beliefs and inclusion policies: Evidence from college admissions. UCL Working Paper.

van der Klaauw, W., 2012. On the use of expectations data in estimating structural dynamic choice models. Journal of Labor Economics 30 (3), 521–554.

van der Klaauw, W., Wolpin, K.I., 2008. Social security and the retirement and savings behavior of low-income households. Journal of Econometrics 145 (1–2), 21–42.

van Soest, A., Vonkova, H., 2014. How sensitive are retirement decisions to financial incentives? A stated preference analysis. Journal of Applied Econometrics 29 (2), 246–264.

Wang, Y., 2014. Dynamic implications of subjective expectations: evidence from adult smokers. American Economic Journal: Applied Economics 6 (1), 1–37.

Wiswall, M., Zafar, B., 2015. Determinants of college major choice: identification using an information experiment. The Review of Economic Studies 82 (2), 791–824.

Wiswall, M., Zafar, B., 2018. Preference for the workplace, investment in human capital, and gender. The Quarterly Journal of Economics 133 (1), 457–507.

Wolpin, K., Gonul, F., 1985. On the use of expectations data in micro surveys: the case of retirement. Report of the Employment and Training. Administration, U.S. Department of Labor, Washington, DC.

Wu, S., Stevens, R., Thorp, S., 2015. Cohort and target age effects on subjective survival probabilities: implications for models of the retirement phase. Journal of Economic Dynamics and Control 55, 39–56.

Zafar, B., 2013. College major choice and the gender gap. The Journal of Human Resources 48 (3), 545–595.

CHAPTER

Expectations data, labor market, and job search☆

22

Andreas I. Mueller[a,b,c,d] **and Johannes Spinnewijn**[e,c]

ªUniversity of Texas at Austin, Austin, TX, United States
ᵇNBER, Cambridge, MA, United States
ᶜCEPR, London, United Kingdom
ᵈIZA, Bonn, Germany
ᵉLondon School of Economics, London, United Kingdom

22.1 Introduction

Individuals' beliefs about their labor market prospects are an important determinant of their search behavior. In search-theoretic models of the labor market, job seekers balance the present costs of their search effort with the uncertain benefit of receiving a job offer. And when presented with an offer, job seekers trade off the value of the offer with the uncertain value of future offers they may receive if they reject the current offer and continue to search. Typically, search and acceptance decisions in the labor market context are viewed through the lens of models that impose rational expectations and assume that job seekers' know their labor market prospects or, at least, learn more about them through the process of job search.

In this chapter, we shed light on how expectations data can inform theories of the labor market and job search, but also on how expectations data can be used to test and relax the rational expectation assumptions in prior work. The chapter starts by reviewing existing surveys with data regarding job search expectations. An immediate observation is that these type of expectations are still relatively rare and only recently research started to use them more widely. While many surveys have adopted questions about job loss, only few data sources have adopted questions about the process of job search. This focus is often dictated by the sample frame of general population surveys and the associated small sample sizes of unemployed workers. One exception is the Survey of Consumer Expectations (SCE), which has collected by now a relatively large sample of unemployed job seekers along with their elicited beliefs (Federal Reserve Bank of New York, 2012–2019). Building on our own prior work, we will use the data from the SCE throughout the chapter to provide supporting evidence or illustrate specific methods. We start by illustrating a number of measurement issues that arise when eliciting beliefs about employment prospects. We stress the importance of panel data to measure beliefs and outcomes for the same individuals and ideally over the same horizon. This is critical to evaluate the predictive power of

---

☆ We thank Tristan Potter and Nate Vellekoop for their valuable comments and Ben Dahmen, Sebastian Ernst, and Anushka Mitra for their excellent research assistance.

Handbook of Economic Expectations. https://doi.org/10.1016/B978-0-12-822927-9.00030-6

677

beliefs, but also to measure potential biases in the elicited beliefs. We also illustrate the usefulness of collecting beliefs over different horizons or using alternative measures to deal with issues of bunching and other forms of measurement error.

An often cited advantage of expectations data is that it can help informing structural models and overcoming the challenge to separate the role of preferences and expectations in explaining individuals' behavior (Manski, 2004). This ambition has also been put forward in the context of models about the labor market (e.g., Manski and Straub, 2000; van der Klaauw, 2012). However, the multifaceted nature of the job search environment and the interdependence between beliefs and behavior make it difficult to put the theory into practice. We set up a stylized model of job search to highlight some key issues concerning beliefs about job finding and how they influence search behavior and outcomes. In practice, surveys often elicit individuals' *baseline* beliefs about their employment prospects or the unemployment risk they are facing. In theory, we would like to understand their impact on search behavior and for that we would need their *control* beliefs instead. Indeed, an important challenge in the context of job finding is that it is difficult to elicit beliefs about primitives such as the marginal return to search effort or the distribution of potential job offers. Instead, surveys have elicited beliefs about, for example, the probability of finding a job in a given time interval. While this is a relatively simple question to ask to a survey respondent, it mixes behavior and primitives, which makes it difficult in practice to identify the impact of beliefs on behavior. For example, job seekers may be optimistic about their job finding prospects because they search hard or they search hard because they are optimistic. We argue that instrumental variable approaches or field experiments that vary the information environment and that measure beliefs and behavior before and after treatment can address these issues of reverse causality. We see this as a promising avenue for future research and potentially a critical step towards embracing expectations data in our models of job search and the labor market.

We argue that a key benefit of expectations data in the labor market context so far has been in the identification of biases in beliefs and learning. The evidence strongly rejects the hypothesis of rational expectations – a standard assumption in models of labor market search. We focus our discussion on expectations data regarding outcomes of the job search process, such as expectations related to the chances of finding a job or expectations about job offers, and show how expectations data can be used to identify biases in job seekers' beliefs about their job finding prospects. We argue that one can identify biases for groups of individuals, but this requires panel data that elicits beliefs and outcomes for the same risk, over the same horizon and for the same set of individuals. We review recent evidence that consistently shows overoptimistic beliefs about job finding starting with Spinnewijn (2015) and also indicates a lack of updating in these beliefs. We specifically show evidence on how beliefs evolve over the unemployment spell, as studied by Mueller et al. (2021), and use the SCE to illustrate how beliefs respond to macroeconomic indicators when employed and unemployed. Importantly, if beliefs are biased and learning is limited, we expect this to affect the job seekers' search and acceptance behavior, with important implications for labor market policies such as unemployment insurance and job training programs. We discuss recent work that has extended the standard models of labor market search to study the importance of biases and learning for employment outcomes and policies.

While we argue that job seekers' beliefs are biased, this should not preclude researchers to use expectations data to learn about the labor market and search environment more generally. Pioneering research by Stephens (2004) has shown how individuals' expectations about their employment prospects are predictive of later outcomes. Following up on this, Hendren (2017) has shown how the relation between ex-ante expectations and ex-post realizations can be used to infer the extent of heterogeneity in ex-ante risk. Typically, this is a challenging task as ex-ante separation risk is not observed but only its random realization ex-post. With expectations data, to the extent that it is predictive of outcomes, one can leverage it to estimate the extent of heterogeneity in ex-ante risks. More recently, Mueller et al. (2021) apply this idea to the context of job finding and find substantial predictive power of beliefs about the probability of finding a job. They go one step further in showing how one can identify the extent of heterogeneity in the presence of biases either through nonparametric lower bounds or by jointly estimating it with a well-specified model of beliefs. These new methods have documented substantial heterogeneity across employed and unemployed workers and shed new light on long-standing questions regarding adverse selection in UI markets and the decline in job finding over the unemployment spell.

We hope that this chapter can serve as a guide for future research. To do so, we are: (i) presenting methods that use expectations data in labor and search theory, (ii) describing existing data sources and their comparative advantage to implement these methods, and (iii) trying to highlight some promising avenues and open questions for future research. Throughout we are heavily relying on our own work and experiences. This is an active research agenda with lots of excellent work of which providing a comprehensive and balanced overview is impossible. We refer interested readers to recent and related reviews by Cooper and Kuhn (2020) and Santos-Pinto and de la Rosa (2020).

The outline of this chapter is as follows: Section 22.2 describes existing data sources and discusses measurement issues. Section 22.3 sets up a framework that illustrates how beliefs influence search behavior and outcomes. Section 22.4 discusses how to empirically identify the impact of beliefs on behavior. Section 22.5 discusses how to identify biases in beliefs, their determinants and policy implications. Section 22.6 discusses how to leverage beliefs to identify heterogeneity in ex-ante risks in the context of the labor market. Section 22.7 concludes and outlines promising areas for future research.

22.2 Measurement

This section reviews a series of existing measures of expectations about labor market outcomes and highlight some measurement issues that arise.

22.2.1 Data sources

One of the first surveys that systematically collected information on expectations regarding job loss and job finding is the *Survey of Economic Expectations* (SEE). It was designed by Jeff Dominitz and Charles F. Manski and, running from 1994 to 2002, it randomly sampled nearly 10,000 respondents. It asked a question about job loss over the next 12 months to individuals with a job, as well as a question about job finding in the event of job loss. Table 22.1 provides the exact wording of the questions.[1] The SEE also asked questions about job finding to those looking for a job. Interestingly, it probed respondents first on how long they think it will take at most to find a job and then asked the probabilistic question about job finding over three different horizons, ranging from 2 weeks to 1.5 years.

Many surveys have adopted similar questions about job loss as the SEE. This includes the *Health and Retirement Survey* (HRS), which asked about the perceived probability of job loss over the next 12

---

[1] See also Table 1.1 in Chapter 1 in this Handbook for a list of surveys with probabilistic elicitations not restricted to the labor market.

Table 22.1 Selected Data Sources on Expectations about Job Loss and Job Finding.

Panel A. U.S. Data Sources

Survey	Years	Panel	Universe	Selected Survey Questions
SEE	1994–2002	None	Employed	"I would like you to think about your employment prospects over the next 12 months. What do you think is the PERCENT CHANCE that you will lose your job during the next 12 months?"
				"If you were to lose your job during the next 12 months... What do you think is the PERCENT CHANCE (or CHANCES OUT OF 100) that the job you eventually find and accept would be at least as good as your current job, in terms of wages and benefits?"
				"What do you think is the PERCENT CHANCE that you will leave your job voluntarily during the next 12 months?"
			Unemployed	"What is the PERCENT CHANCE (or what are the chances out of 100) that it will take you less than [X] to find a job that you will accept?"
				Asked for three different X, ranging from 2 weeks to 1.5 years.
HRS	1991–	Biennial	Individuals over 50 yrs old and their spouses	"What is the percent chance (0–100) that you will lose your job in the next 12 months?"
				"What do you think are the chances that you could find an equally good job in the same line of work within the next few months?"
KM	2009–2010	Weekly	UI recipients in New Jersey	"What do you think is the percent chance that you will be employed again within the next 4 weeks?"
				"How many weeks do you estimate it will actually take before you will be employed again?"
				"Do you think your chances of finding a job would increase if you spent more time searching for a job?"
				"How many weeks do you estimate it would take to become employed again if you spent an additional hour searching for a job every day?"
SCE	2012–	Monthly	Employed household heads	"What do you think is the percent chance that you will lose your current/main job during the next 12 months?"
				"What do you think is the percent chance that you will leave your current/main job voluntarily during the next 12 months?"
				"Suppose you were to lose your job this month. What do you think is the percent chance that within the following 3 months, you will find a job that you will accept, considering the pay and type of work"
			Unemployed household heads	"What do you think is the percent chance that within the coming 12 months, you will find a job that you will accept, considering the pay and type of work?"
				"And looking at the more immediate future, what do you think is the percent chance that within the coming 3 months, you will find a job that you will accept, considering the pay and type of work?"
SCE LMS	2014–	Quadri-mesterly	Household heads	"What do you think is the percent chance that four months from now you will be: (1) Employed (2) Employed and working for the same employer (3) Employed and working for a different employer (4) self-employed (5) Unemployed and looking for work (6) Unemployed and NOT looking for work"
				"What do you think is the percent chance that within the coming 4 months, you will receive at least one job offer?"
				"Over the next 4 months, how many job offers do you expect to receive?"
				"Think about the job offers that you may receive within the coming four months. Roughly speaking, what do you think the average annual salary for these offers will be for the first year?"
				"Think about the job offers that you may receive within the coming four months. Roughly speaking, what do you think the annual salary for the best offer will be for the first year?"
				"If you were to receive a job offer from another employer at a higher salary, what do you believe is the percent chance your current employer will match the salary offer?"

continued on next page

Table 22.1 (*continued*)

Panel B. Selected Data Sources in Other Countries

Survey (Country)	Years	Panel	Universe	Selected Survey Questions
HUS (Sweden)	1984–1998	Yearly	Employed	"How likely is it that you will keep your current job? Respond with a number between 0 and 100, where 100 means that it is completely certain that you will keep your job, 0 means that it is inconceivable and 50 means that both alternatives are equally likely."
GSOEP (Germany)	1999–	Yearly	Employed	"Do you expect to lose your job within the next two years?"
			Unemployed	"What is the probability of taking up a paid job within the next two years?"
BHPS (UK) Waves 6–7	1996–1997	Yearly	Employed	"In the next twelve months how likely do you think it is that you will: - Become unemployed? - Get a better job with your current employer? - Start a new job with a new employer? - Take up any work related training or education? - Start up your own business?"
LISS (Netherl.)	2008–	Quarterly/ Yearly	Employed	"Do you think that there is any chance that you might lose your job in the coming 12 months? You can indicate this in terms of a percentage. 0% means that you are sure that you will not lose your job, and 100% means that you are sure that you will lose your job." *Option for answering that "N/A since I am voluntarily leaving job."*
			Unemployed	Do you think that you have a chance of finding a job in the coming 12 months? You can indicate this as a percentage. 0% means that you are sure that you will not find a job, and 100% means that you are sure that you will find a job between now and 12 months.
DHS (Netherl.)	2005–	Yearly	Employed	"What do you think is the probability that you lose your jobin the next 12 months? You can fill in a number between 0 and 100."
CLP (Denmark)	2020–2021	Yearly	Employed	"Please think about your possible relationship with your current employer in 2021. Assign the probability in each possible case. The sum of the probabilities should be 100. 1. Staying with the current employer during 2021 2. Laid-off from current employer at some point during 2021 3. Quit from the current employer at some point during 2021 4. Separation for other reasons during 2021"

Notes: The table shows questions related to expectations about job loss and job finding in the Survey of Economic Expectations (SEE), Health and Retirement Survey (HRS), the Krueger–Mueller (KM) survey, the Survey of Consumer Expectations (SCE), the Labor Market Survey (LMS) module of the SCE, the Household Market and Nonmarket Activities panel survey (HUS), the German Socio-Economic Panel (GSOEP), the British Household Panel Survey (BHPS), the Longitudinal Internet Studies for the Social sciences survey (LISS), the DNB Household Survey (DHS), and the Copenhagen Life Panel (CLP). For the GSOEP, the panel structure is annual, but expectation questions are asked only every two years.

months, and the job finding probability in the event of job loss. The *Survey of Consumer Expectations* (SCE) adopted a similar structure, though it also probed respondents on what they think is their likelihood of leaving the current job. Examples in Europe are the *British Household Panel Survey* (BHPS) and, more recently, the survey of the *Copenhagen Life Panel* (CLP). Both ask directly about the mutually exclusive events of losing and quitting a job. Typically, the horizon for the job loss question is 12 months, except for the *German Socio-Economic Panel* (GSOEP), which asked about job loss over the next two years. It is likely that there are many other surveys that ask questions about job loss, though we focus here the attention on data sources that have been used for academic studies.

Surveys with questions about expectations related to job finding are more rare. While the SEE did ask questions about the probability of reemployment to unemployed job seekers, many other data sources do not include this type of question. A likely reason is that the sample of unemployed workers is typically just a small subsample of the surveyed population and thus sample size may be a limiting factor. The Survey of Unemployed Workers in New Jersey, also known as the *Krueger–Mueller* (KM) survey (Krueger and Mueller, 2011), directly targeted the universe of UI recipients in 2009–2010 in New Jersey and thus does not suffer from small sample issues. We received the opportunity to add questions to the KM survey that elicit beliefs about employment prospects in alternative ways. In particular, we asked unemployed job seekers both about their perceived probability of finding a job in the next 4 weeks, as well as the expected remaining time it would take them to find a job. We also added questions directly eliciting their beliefs about the returns to search, asking how much faster they would expect to find a job when searching more. The *Survey of Consumer Expectations* (SCE) asks all unemployed individuals about their perceived probability of finding a job in the next 3 and 12 months. It also does not suffer from small sample size as it has been continuously running since December 2012 and thus by now contains a relatively large subsample of unemployed workers. The GSOEP and the *Longitudinal Internet Studies for the Social Sciences Survey* (LISS) also ask belief questions about job finding, though the horizons for these questions seem long (12–24 months) given that most unemployed job-seekers typically find a job in less than a year. The *SCE Labor Market Survey* (LMS) is a special module of the SCE, which is administered in July, November, and March of every year since 2014, and asks questions about the perceived probability of a job offer as well as the expected number of job offers within the next four months. It asks these questions to all respondents, which makes sense to us, given the recent findings by Faberman et al. (2022) that many job seekers are actually employed, receiving a majority of job offers received. The SCE LMS also asks questions about expected offered wages. We found a few other surveys in other countries that ask questions about their expected wage in relation to their reservation wage, which are not included here.

While the seminal SEE sampled repeated cross-sections, most of the more recent studies have a panel dimension and/or are merged to administrative employment records. This is important because it allows (1) to compare elicited beliefs to actual outcomes and/or (2) to study the evolution of beliefs over time at the individual level.

22.2.2 Descriptive statistics

In this subsection, we provide some descriptive statistics with data from the SCE for the years 2013–2020. While the results here have been documented elsewhere, it is useful to illustrate these results in the SCE and we provide the references where applicable.

Table 22.2 reports the means of the elicited probabilities along with their realizations. Note that we restricted the sample of the SCE to responses with three consecutive follow-up interviews with information on labor force status. This is important since attrition would lead to undercounting of job finding.[2] The restriction to three consecutive follow-up interviews thus allows us to measure realized job finding as precisely as possible. We define the 3-month realized job-finding rate as the fraction of unemployed job seekers who reported being employed in at least one of the following three interviews. This limits any issues related to time aggregation, i.e., the possibility that someone finds a job but becomes unemployed again within the 3 month horizon.[3] Regarding job loss, we cannot compare the elicitation

---

[2] The SCE suffers from relatively little attrition and thus is well suited to compare elicitations with their realizations.

[3] In addition, we exclude survey answers where the answer to the elicited 12-month job finding question was smaller than (and thus inconsistent with) the 3-month job-finding probability, which amounts to about 12% of the sample.

Table 22.2 Means of Elicited and Realized Probabilities.

Variable	Sample	N	Mean	Std. error
3-Month Realized Job-Finding Rate	Unemployed	1720	0.403	0.011
3-Month Job-Finding Probability	Unemployed	1720	0.482	0.007
3-Month Job-Finding Probability in Event of Job Loss	Employed	44,466	0.553	0.001
3-Month Realized Job-Separation Rate	Employed	44,466	0.027	0.001
12-Month Realized Job-Separation Rate (Imputed)	Employed	44,466	0.103	0.003
12-Month Probability of Losing a Job	Employed	44,466	0.148	0.001
12-Month Probability of Leaving a Job	Employed	44,466	0.208	0.001

Notes: Survey weights are used for all estimates. Sample is restricted to unemployed or employed workers, ages 20–65, with three consecutive follow-up surveys in the SCE. The table shows the sample averages of some elicited and realized probabilities. The 3-Month Job Finding Probability for the employed refers to the elicited probability of finding a new job within 3 months in the event if job loss.

of the job loss probability to its realization over the same time horizon, since each individual has at most 11 follow up interviews. Instead, we decided to compute the average realization of the 3-month job loss probability, s_3, defined as the fraction of employed job seekers who were not employed in at least one of the following three interviews. We then impute the average realized 12-month probability as $s_{12} = 1 - (1 - s_3)^4$.

Table 22.2 shows that the unemployed tend to be over-optimistic in their job finding prospects, with the elicited 3-month job finding probability being 8 p.p. above the realized job-finding rates. Overoptimism among the unemployed has first been documented by Spinnewijn (2015) and been confirmed in other settings (see Section 22.5 for more details). The overoptimism seems even larger when comparing the unemployed's 3-month probability to the hypothetical job-finding probability elicited of the employed (in the event of job loss), but this could of course be explained by the negative selection into unemloyment.

The employed appear to be over-pessimistic when it comes to their probability of job loss, as the imputed 12-month realization of job loss – measured as the rate of transition from employment to unemployment – is 4.5 p.p. below the perceived one. The perceived probability of leaving the job is substantial, as 21% of employed expect to leave their job voluntarily over the next 12 months. There is no natural counterpart for the realization of job leaving in the SCE, as most quitters likely transition directly to a new job or to out of the labor force instead of becoming unemployed.

Panels (a) and (b) of Fig. 22.1 show the expected and realized job finding rate and job loss rate by year from 2013 to 2020. There is some positive comovement between realized and expected job finding, though perceptions appear somewhat more rigid than the realizations. This is even more apparent, when looking at the expectations of job loss, which appear to be completely stable in 2020. This latter finding seems puzzling, as job loss spiked up to unprecedented levels during the pandemic recession. Note, however, that the big waves in job loss in March and April 2020 were to a large degree unexpected and thus not captured by the elicitations of job loss in January and February of 2020. Moreover, these patterns may reflect selection as the pools of employed and unemployed changed rapidly over this period.

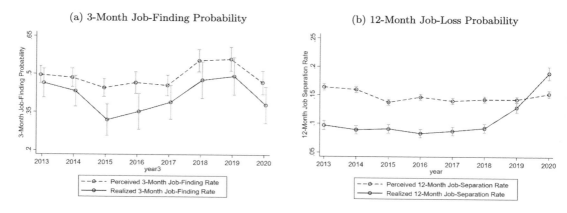

FIGURE 22.1 Expectations and Realizations of Job Finding and Job Loss, By Year in SCE

Notes: Survey weights are used for all estimates. Sample is restricted to unemployed or employed workers, ages 20–65, with three consecutive follow-up surveys in the SCE. Panel (a) shows the perceived and realized job-finding probability and panel (b) shows the perceived and realized job-loss probability. In panel (b), the 12-month separation rate is imputed based on realized 3-month transitions as explained further above in the text.

22.2.3 Predictive power of elicited beliefs

A central question regarding elicitations about labor market prospects is whether they predict actual job finding and job loss. Stephens (2004), Campbell et al. (2007), and more recently Hendren (2017) all look at the predictive value of beliefs about job loss in the HRS and find strong positive correlations with realizations. Mueller et al. (2021) look at the predictive power of beliefs about job finding and also find strong correlations between beliefs and realizations in the SCE. Relatedly, Conlon et al. (2018) show a strong positive correlation between the realized and expected number of job offers. With recent data from the SCE, we illustrate these sets of findings in Fig. 22.2. A common theme about both panel (a), which illustrates the predictive power of job loss expectations, and panel (b), which illustrates the predictive power of job finding expectations, is that the gradient between realized and elicited probabilities is less than one. This could be in principle the result of a systematic bias in the beliefs, where individuals overestimate how different their employment prospects are. The evidence that we discuss later in this chapter suggests that the opposite is true, with individuals' beliefs responding less than one-to-one to differences in their employment prospects. However, a slope of less than one can also arise due to random error in the beliefs.[4] Still, one should be cautious interpreting the muted slope as evidence against rational expectations as it can also be due to noise in the elicitation procedure, in particular when the concept covered by the elicitation question does not overlap perfectly with its realization. For example, job loss refers to the idea of losing the current job, whereas its realization – measured as the probability of transitioning from employment to unemployed – misses transitions of

---

[4] A slope of less than one has been found in other contexts such as survival and retirement, see Chapters 8 and 10 in this Handbook, respectively.

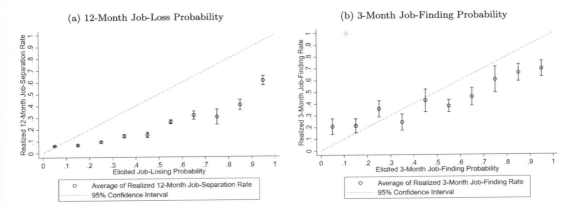

FIGURE 22.2 Realized Job Finding and Job Loss, By Bins of Elicited Beliefs

Notes: Survey weights are used for all estimates. Sample is restricted to unemployed or employed workers, ages 20–65, with three consecutive follow-up surveys in the SCE. Figures shows the 12-month E-to-U transition and the 3-month U-to-E rate by bins of the elicited beliefs about the probability of job loss (panel (a)) and job finding (panel (b)). Note that the 12-month job-separation rate is imputed based on realized 3-month transitions as explained further above in the text.

individuals who got an advance notice but found a new job before the previous one ended, but also includes some individuals who left their job voluntarily. In addition, our imputation of the 12-month transition rate based on the 3-month transition rate does not work if there is mean reversion of 3-month transition rates over the next 12 months. We turn to the issue of biases in more detail in Section 22.5.

22.2.4 Measurement issues

While qualitative questions about expectations may be useful in some contexts, we focus here on the quantitative questions, i.e., questions which ask the respondent to indicate a percent chance (or other quantitative measure) over a well-defined horizon. Of course, as mentioned in the previous paragraph about the predictive power of beliefs, issues related to the measurement of such elicitations are an important concern and we would like to elaborate on some of these issues here.

Nonclassical measurement error

Measurement errors in expectations may be of classical or nonclassical nature, with the latter especially likely at or near the bounds as individuals with a 0 cannot err on the negative and individuals with a true probability of 100 cannot err on the positive. Nonclassical measurement error introduces a number of problems, including potentially, on average, a positive or negative error. This is important when inferring biases in elicited expectations from the data, and it is thus advisable to probe the robustness of results by excluding surveys with expectations at or near 0 and/or 100.

Horizon

Individuals may find it difficult to think about a certain probability over horizons that are either too short or too long. Moreover, issues related to nonclassical measurement error are likely to be less common when choosing a horizon of the expectation question such that answers of 0 and 100 are uncommon. The SEE addressed this problem by probing respondents first about the maximum and minimum time till employment and then picking a horizon for the probability question based on the answer to these preliminary questions. Alternatively, a survey may just ask about different horizons for all respondents, which makes it easier to compare the elicitations to realizations. For example, the SCE asked about the probability of job finding over the next 12 and 3 months. This is a relatively simple approach and useful, because it also allows to detect inattentive survey answers. For example, if someone indicates that the probability of finding a job is 50% over the next 12 months but 60% over the next 3 months, it suggests that the person did not put much effort into filling out the survey questionnaire or has some fundamental difficulties with understanding the concept of probability.[5]

Bunching

A common source of measurement error is bunching in survey answers, which is most common at 50 for probability questions. While bunching per se is not necessarily a big issue when driven simply by rounding up or down, it may reflect a bigger problem of individuals indicating a percent chance of 50 if they have difficulty assessing the degree of risk. Multiple questions at different horizons, or questions about the expected remaining duration of the job or unemployment (as in KM survey) may be useful in this respect as they allow to see whether respondents who respond 50% on one question provide a different answer on the other question. Eliciting probabilities has the statistical advantage that it avoids ambiguity regarding the distributional moment one is hoping to elicit, but the disadvantage that individuals may not reason in probabilistic terms. We find in the SCE and in the KM survey that the alternative elicitations – either at different horizons or eliciting the expected remaining duration instead – are highly correlated, which is reassuring and suggests that many survey respondents submit responses that are consistent with each other (see Appendix D in Mueller et al., 2021 for details).

22.3 Illustrative framework

Individuals' beliefs about their employment prospects affect their search behavior, and vice versa. We can use the elicited beliefs discussed in the previous section to help understanding this relationship. In this section, we present a conceptual framework to highlight the key issues concerning beliefs and search behavior and how they affect employment outcomes. We refer to this framework in later sections.

We consider a stylized search model in which agents decide how much to consume, how hard to search for jobs and how to set their reservation wage. We define a vector of state variables, $h_{i,t}$, which captures both individual-specific characteristics *and* the agent's relevant employment and search history. For parsimony, we also include the stock of savings in the variable $h_{i,t}$. The arrival rate of job offers depends on the individual's search efforts $e_{i,t}$, but this mapping may be specific to the individual and dependent on her history, $\lambda\left(e_{i,t}|h_{i,t}\right)$. Job offers are drawn from a wage distribution $F\left(w|h_{i,t}\right)$, which again can be individual-specific and history-dependent. The unemployed agent's value at time t

---

[5] As mentioned earlier, we exclude these survey answers from figures and tables in this section.

is

$$U\left(h_{i,t}\right) = u\left(c_{i,t}, e_{i,t}|h_{i,t}\right)$$
$$+ \beta E\left[U\left(h_{i,t+1}\right) + \lambda\left(e_{i,t}|h_{i,t}\right)\int_{R_{i,t}}\left[V\left(w|h_{i,t+1}\right) - U\left(h_{i,t+1}\right)\right]dF\left(w|h_{i,t}\right)\right],$$

determined by her chosen search effort $e_{i,t}$, reservation wage $R_{i,t}$ and consumption $c_{i,t}$; $u(\cdot)$ denotes the per-period utility flow. The state vector $h_{i,t+1}$ builds on $h_{i,t}$, but depends on the agent's decisions (e.g., search, savings) at time t and shocks (e.g., productivity) at the start of $t+1$. The corresponding uncertainty is captured by the expectation operator E; $V\left(w|h_{i,t+1}\right)$ denotes the value of being employed at wage w in state $h_{i,t+1}$, including the agent's employment history. The continuation value when employed can be written in an analogue way with an additional term for separation into unemployment.

We now turn to the beliefs, referred to with a hat. The agent's job search behavior depends on her *beliefs* about the arrival rate and wage distribution. The perceived arrival rate $\hat{\lambda}\left(e|h_{i,t}\right)$ and wage distribution $\hat{F}\left(w|h_{i,t}\right)$, however, may differ from the true arrival rate and wage distribution, respectively. A job seeker thus sets her reservation wage $R_{i,t}$ to maximize her perceived continuation value at any time of the unemployment spell. At this reservation wage, the agent is indifferent between accepting a job and remaining unemployed, $\hat{U}\left(h_{i,t+1}\right) = \hat{V}\left(R_{i,t}|h_{i,t+1}\right)$. The job seeker also chooses to exert search effort $e_{i,t}$, trading off the cost of search and the perceived returns to search. Finally, the job seeker chooses her consumption $c_{i,t}$ depending on the perceived employment prospects, which in turn affect the continuation value when employed and unemployed.

The different dimensions of behavior and beliefs are intertwined. The resulting actual and perceived employment probability for unemployed agent i at time t given history $h_{i,t}$ equals respectively

$$T\left(h_{i,t}\right) = \lambda\left(e_{i,t}\left(h_{i,t}\right)|h_{i,t}\right)\left(1 - F\left(R_{i,t}\left(h_{i,t}\right)|h_{i,t}\right)\right), \tag{22.1}$$

$$\hat{T}\left(h_{i,t}\right) = \hat{\lambda}\left(e_{i,t}\left(h_{i,t}\right)|h_{i,t}\right)\left(1 - \hat{F}\left(R_{i,t}\left(h_{i,t}\right)|h_{i,t}\right)\right). \tag{22.2}$$

We can construct similar expressions to describe the job loss probability or the job to job transitions for employed workers. Note that, if individuals are uncertain about their beliefs and thus hold beliefs about the entire probability distribution, then Eq. (22.2) will have an additional covariance term. This is not relevant here, since we observe $\hat{T}$ rather than the objects on the right-hand side.

This stylized framework allows us to highlight some important factors determining the relationship between expectations and job search more generally:

Beliefs affect search

A job seeker's search strategy does not only depend on her preferences and the cost of search, but crucially depends on her beliefs, too. The decision to put in more effort depends in the first place on how much it will increase her chances to get an offer, $\hat{\lambda}'(e)$. The decision how to set her reservation wage depends in the first place on how it affects the share of acceptable job offers, $\hat{F}'(R)$. The different job search decisions also interact. In particular, when deciding how much effort e to put in, one needs to form beliefs about the type of wage offers one can expect, $\hat{F}\left(w|h_{i,t}\right)$. When deciding whether to accept a job or where to set one's reservation wage R, one needs to form beliefs about one's chances to get new job offers in the future, $\hat{\lambda}\left(e|h_{i,t+k}\right)$. In practice, job search is very diverse, requiring job seekers to make decisions in various dimensions. It is not just about how much time to spend, but also on the different modes of search to spend time on, e.g., through specific search platforms or through informal networks.[6] Similarly, it is not just about the wage one hopes for, but also about the types of jobs to search for. In principle, to understand the role of beliefs for job search, we would need to have a comprehensive understanding of individuals' beliefs on all of these dimensions.

Search affects beliefs

Not only do job seekers' choices depend on their beliefs, their beliefs will also depend on their choices. An agent will search more, the more she believes this increases her chances to get an offer. However, the overall effort she puts in will also affect her beliefs about her chances to get an offer. The endogenous relation between behavior and beliefs makes it challenging to separate the impact of beliefs on behavior, and vice versa. This challenge gets worse as we move away from primitives and consider beliefs at a higher level. Differences between the perceived and true employment probability $\hat{T}(h_{i,t}) - T(h_{i,t})$ could be driven by biases in the primitive beliefs, but then further magnified or mitigated by the choices made. To unpack the two channels in an empirical setting, we would need some exogenous variation that induces individuals to change their behavior and evaluate the impact on their beliefs, or that induces individuals to change their beliefs and evaluate the impact on their behavior. In both cases, we would also need to rely on an exclusion restriction that excludes any direct effect of the source of variation on the beliefs or the behavior, respectively.

Baseline vs. control beliefs

Given the multifaceted nature of job search and job seekers' beliefs, it is useful to distinguish between *baseline* and *control* beliefs as in Spinnewijn (2013, 2015). An individual's baseline beliefs refer to the risk an individual is facing, given her search behavior. For example, an individual is baseline-optimistic when she overestimates the probability to leave unemployment, conditional on her search effort and reservation wage, i.e., $\hat{T}(h_{i,t}) > T(h_{i,t})$. An individual's control beliefs refer to how much she can reduce her risk through her own behavior. For example, an individual is control-optimistic when she overestimates the impact of her own search effort on leaving unemployment, i.e., $\frac{\partial \hat{T}(h_{i,t})}{\partial e_{i,t}} > \frac{\partial T(h_{i,t})}{\partial e_{i,t}}$. The perception of the baseline unemployment risk is crucial to evaluate how much individuals would value any protection, mitigating the consequences of unemployment through unemployment benefits or precautionary savings. A baseline optimist would underappreciate the value of unemployment insurance and invest too little in precautionary savings as a consequence. The control beliefs are crucial for understanding individuals' search behavior and how much they would respond to changes in policy. While a control-pessimist exerts too little effort, financial incentives are ineffective when she believes to have little control over her employment prospects.

Heterogeneity

Beliefs and potential heterogeneity therein introduce another factor affecting individuals' behaviors differentially. However, beliefs also allow us to shed light on the importance of other dimensions of heterogeneity. A fundamental challenge is to understand how much of the heterogeneity in ex-post outcomes could be anticipated ex-ante. Some individuals receive job offers, while others do not. Some

---

[6] For example, see Holzer (1988) who argues that channel choices should relate to their costs and expected productivities.

of them are offered higher wages, while others are offered lower wages. But could they anticipate these differences ex ante? While we only observe the distribution of ex-post outcomes in the data, an individual's choice depends on the job offer probability, $\lambda\left(e|h_{i,t}\right)$, and wage distribution, $F\left(w|h_{i,t}\right)$, she is facing ex-ante. The predictive value of ex-ante elicited beliefs help us understand how much of the heterogeneity in ex-post outcomes was anticipated and allows to provide a lower bound on the overall importance of ex-ante heterogeneity in employment prospects.

Learning

Beliefs are not static, but evolve over time. Individuals learn. They respond to news or changes in the environment and update their beliefs accordingly. Like for heterogeneity, individuals' beliefs provide an opportunity to learn about the dynamics that are inherent to the search environment, but they also introduce their own dynamics that in practice may not be easily captured by standard models of learning. In a similar spirit, agents take search and consumption decisions jointly and their histories may influence future behavior. For example, if the job seeker is optimistic about the chances of finding a job, she will consume more than otherwise, but if she fails to find a job, the lack of savings may drive her to search more. Understanding how beliefs change and what they respond to is thus important, too.

22.4 Beliefs and behavior

Our conceptual work has illustrated how expectations wield a big influence on choices such as search effort and the reservation wage. But so do preferences. It is generally difficult to separate the role of preferences and expectations in explaining choice data (Manski, 1993, 2002, 2004). For example, a job seeker may search little because she is impatient and thus discounts heavily the expected gain from search or because she perceives the returns to search to be low. Similarly, a job seeker may set a low reservation wage because she is impatient and thus discounts the value of future offers or because she believes that the probability of sampling better offers is low (i.e., the option value of remaining unemployed is low). Expectations data about job finding are useful in this respect as they can help distinguish between preferences and expectations in explaining job search behavior. Alternatively, one can try to directly measure preferences, eliciting them through experiments or experimentally-validated survey questions.[7]

22.4.1 Structural models with expectations data

Despite the promise for expectations to help understanding job search behavior and separate the role of preferences, only a few papers have combined expectations data with data on search behavior and/or labor market transitions to inform structural models of job search. We already highlighted some challenges before, which can help explain why expectations data have not been embraced more in the structural labor literature. But there are definitely opportunities to be further exploited going forward.[8]

---

[7] For example, DellaVigna and Paserman (2005) show that measures of impatience are negatively correlated with search effort.

[8] See also Chapter 21 in this Handbook.

A first opportunity is to use expectations data in labor market models to improve the precision of estimated parameters. van der Klaauw (2012) shows this in the context of occupational choice. Assuming that the model underlying expectations data and choices are the same and that expectations data reflect optimal future behavior, he uses data on the expected future occupation to estimate a structural model of career choice and argues that a big gain in the efficiency stems from the fact that expectations allow to identify better unobserved types. We will return to this latter point in Section 22.6.

A second opportunity is that expectations data allow to drop the assumption of rational expectations. Conlon et al. (2018) and Mueller et al. (2021) estimate structural models of the labor market using data on both transitions *and* expectations. Their purpose is to show how deviations from rational expectations distort job seekers' behavior and affect employment outcomes. We will come back to this in Section 22.5.

A third opportunity lies in the combined use of expectations data and data on search behavior for the estimation of structural models of job search. Note that traditionally choice data such as search effort or the reservation wage are typically not directly observed and structural models infer behavior from transitions between labor market states and accepted wages. Recently, researchers have also started to use self-reported data on reservation wages and search effort (measured typically as time spent on job search activities) to estimate search models (e.g., Hall and Mueller, 2018; Potter, 2021), though they do not use elicitations of beliefs to inform the model. An interesting direction for future research would be to estimate search models with transition data, beliefs *and* behavior data on self-reported search effort and reservation wages. For example, DellaVigna et al. (2020) and Marinescu and Skandalis (2021) show that data on search effort informs the degree of reference-dependence in models of job search. Similarly, Ganong and Noel (2019) find that a model with present bias or myopia can account for the large consumption drops at UI exhaustion. Data on expectations about job finding or job offer arrival could further discipline the identification in this context, both increasing the precision of the estimates (as in van der Klaauw, 2012) and allowing for deviations from rational expectations (as in Conlon et al., 2018 and Mueller et al., 2021).

A final opportunity for expectations data in labor markets models is to shed light on general equilibrium forces, as they interact with beliefs and are important in shaping labor market outcomes more broadly. While this issue receives increasing attention in macroeconomics more generally, little work exists to date in the context of the labor market models, which typically rely on the rational expectations assumption. There are again a few exceptions. One is the recent paper of Menzio (2020) who shows that rigid beliefs about the probability of job finding lead to rigidity in bargained wages and amplify fluctuations in vacancy creation and unemployment. Also Mitra (2021) introduces biased beliefs about job finding in a search-and-matching model with endogenous search effort. In her framework, biased beliefs and shocks therein change job seekers' search effort, which in turn feeds into firms' incentives for vacancy creation. Finally, Balleer et al. (2021) introduce overoptimism about labor market prospects in a quantitative model of consumption and saving and explore the implications for aggregate wealth inequality. While we have not found other papers that use general equilibrium models, which deviate from rational expectations in the context of job search and job finding, we believe this is a promising avenue for future research.

22.4.2 Identification and empirical evidence

Separating the causal pathways between beliefs and behavior is challenging. An additional complication is that in practice it is difficult to elicit beliefs about primitives such as the returns and the shape of the wage offer distribution. Instead, researchers have resorted to elicit beliefs about job finding or the arrival rate of job offers, which reflect an amalgam of search inputs and beliefs about primitives. For example, the elicited job-finding probability reflects both search inputs and beliefs about the job-offer production function. To address these issues, one would like ideally to rely on exogenous variation in search behavior to study its impact on beliefs and exogenous variation in beliefs to study its impact on behavior. We address both causal pathways – the perceived returns to search and the impact of beliefs on search behavior – in what follows.

22.4.2.1 *The perceived return to job search*

We first consider different strategies to identify the perceived effect of search on employment prospects.

Exogenous variation

In an ideal experiment, we obtain exogenous variation in search behavior and study the impact on the perceived employment prospects. Following an instrumental variable (IV) approach, one can exploit variation in the costs of search related to instruments such as, e.g., differences in UI eligibility or the presence of severance pay, and then analyze the impact of resulting search behavior. This can in principle inform the primitives of the model (i.e., the beliefs about the marginal returns to search), but only if the exclusion restriction holds. In this spirit, Spinnewijn (2008) leverages the nonlinearity in unemployment benefits to estimate the impact of search efforts on both the perceived and actual remaining unemployment duration. An important complication in this respect is that the instrument may affect different behavioral dimensions, so that we cannot single out the impact of one specific behavior. The costs of search for example are likely to affect both search effort and the reservation wage and thus it is not possible to identify the marginal effect of either on job finding.[9]

A possible solution is to elicit beliefs about more narrow job search outcomes for which the exclusion restriction arguably holds. One example is to collect data on beliefs and realizations of job offer arrivals (such as in the SCE LMS) rather than job finding (as in the SCE and KM survey). Assuming that job offer arrival is only affected by search effort but not the reservation wage, one can then use the IV strategy to analyze the impact of search effort on beliefs about job offer arrival (the probability of receiving at least one offer or the number of offers). This assumption, however, holds only in a random search context, where job seekers' contact rate is independent of the reservation wage. If job seekers, however, apply to jobs that are acceptable, the reservation wage may affect the offer rate.

Another approach is to use multiple instruments, which allow to identify the marginal impacts of the different search behaviors when providing independent variation. This approach is illustrated in Table 22.3 with data from the KM survey, which contains information on both search efforts and the reservation wage. The table shows the results of linear regressions, which relate elicitations about job finding to self-reported measures of search effort and the reservation wage. Ordinary least square estimation in columns 1 and 3 shows that search effort is positively associated with the perceived probability of job finding whereas the reservation wage is negatively correlated with perceived job finding. As noted above, these coefficients may be biased due to endogeneity of search effort and the reservation wage to the perceived probability of finding a job. For this reason, we instrument search effort and the

---

[9] Another complication that violates the exclusion restrictions is when individuals learn about the uncertain search environment by engaging in search activities. For example, Banerjee and Sequeira (2021) find in a field experiment that unemployed youth in South Africa update their beliefs about job finding more if they are induced to search more.

Table 22.3 Linear Regressions of Elicitations on Time Spent on Job Search and the Reservation Wage.

	Elicited 1-Month Job-Finding Probability		Elicited Remaining Duration (Inverted)	
	OLS	IV	OLS	IV
Hours Spent on Job Search, Last Week/10	0.013**	0.118*	0.009	0.102*
	(0.006)	(0.065)	(0.006)	(0.059)
Log Hourly Reservation Wage	−0.061*	−0.160**	−0.085***	−0.280***
	(0.033)	(0.080)	(0.027)	(0.071)
Demographic Controls	X	X	X	X
Observations	4031	4031	3939	3939
R^2	0.128	0.103	0.099	0.102

Notes: *Survey weights are used in all regressions. All samples are restricted to unemployed workers, ages 20–65, in the KM survey. Expected remaining duration (inverted) is calculated as $1 - (1 - \frac{1}{x})^4$, where x is the elicited expected remaining duration of unemployment (in weeks). The columns 1 and 3 show results of OLS, whereas columns 2 and 4 use the following three variables as instruments: a dummy for whether the unemployed worker received severance pay, a measure of patience (i.e., based on choice of 20 now vs. 40 in 12 weeks) and a measure of self-reported risk aversion. Demographic controls include age, age squared, dummies for gender, race, ethinicity, and educational attainment. Robust standard errors (clustered at the individual level) are in parentheses. Asterisks indicate statistical significance at the *0.1, **0.05, and ***0.01 level.*

reservation wage with a dummy for the receipt of severance pay, a measure of impatience and a measure of self-reported risk aversion. These instruments should provide independent variation for search effort and the reservation wage. The exclusion restriction is now that all instruments affect elicited expectations only through these two behavioral dimensions. The results show big differences between the OLS and IV regressions in the relationship between the self-reported behavioral variables and the perceived job-finding probability. The contrast is particularly stark in the relationship for search effort, where 10 hours of additional job search have a 10–12 p.p. effect on the perceived job-finding probability in the IV specification compared to a 1 p.p. effect in the OLS specification. For the reservation wage, the IV specification also shows a substantially stronger effect, with a decrease of the perceived job-finding probability of between 1.6% and 2.8% for a 10% increase in the hourly reservation wage. The wedge is consistent with individuals who are more optimistic about their employment prospects searching less and setting their reservation wages higher, which attenuates the OLS estimates relative to the IV estimates. In future research, it would be valuable to refine these instruments, further gauge the plausibility of the exclusion restriction and compare the perceived returns to search to the actual returns to search.[10,11]

---

[10] As argued by DellaVigna and Paserman (2005), search effort is influenced more by present-bias whereas the reservation wage decision is a more forward-looking decision and influences the degree of impatience. Therefore, if one had some experimental measures of both present bias and impatience, this could provide a useful set of instruments for search effort and the reservation wage.

[11] The KM survey suffers from substantial attrition, in particular, for the subsample of observations with the belief questions and, thus, it is challenging to estimate the returns to search for the same sample.

Direct elicitations

Another way to address the endogeneity issue is to elicit beliefs directly about primitives. For example, how much do workers believe they improve their employment prospects by searching more or by lowering their reservation wage? This type of direct elicitations is clearly challenging, but we believe it is an avenue worth exploring more.

We briefly illustrate the potential of direct elicitations studying the following question we added to the KM survey[12]: "Do you think your chances of finding a job would increase if you spent more time searching for a job?", followed by a question "How many weeks do you estimate it would take to become employed again if you spent an additional hour searching for a job every day?" for those who answer with "yes" in the first question. One can compare the answer to the latter question to the baseline question about the expected remaining duration as shown in Table 22.1 to gauge the perceived return to one additional hour of job search per day, $\frac{\partial \hat{T}}{\partial e}$.[13] An important caveat is that only 12.6% of unemployed workers in the KM survey perceive there to be a positive return to job search at the margin. This is a striking observation by itself, but in hindsight we expect it would have been more informative to elicit the impact of searching less rather than searching more, or eliciting the marginal returns to search starting from a hypothetical number of hours.

Panel (a) of Fig. 22.3 shows the kernel density of $\frac{\partial \hat{T}}{\partial e}$ for those with a nonzero perceived marginal return along with descriptive statistics. For those with a positive perceived return, the return to 1 hour of job search is substantial with an average increase in the perceived job-finding probability of 16.5 p.p. Unconditionally, however, given the large fraction of zeros, the average return to job search is moderate with an increase in the perceived job-finding probability of 2.1 p.p. for 1 hour of job search per day. This is substantially lower than the IV estimates of the perceived marginal return to job search in Table 22.3, which is estimated at 7.1–8.3 p.p. for 1 hour per day.[14] Clearly, the IV estimates are identified of compliers that may differ from the average job seeker. Moreover, individuals may perceive the marginal returns to search as rapidly declining, potentially lowering the estimate using the direct elicitations. Interestingly, in panel (b) we find substantial heterogeneity in the perceived marginal return to search based on how much the job seekers searched in the last week, suggestive of strongly declining marginal returns to search.[15] This further illustrates the challenge to eliciting beliefs about primitives in the context of job finding, as it suggests that even the elicitation of the perceived marginal return to job search is endogenous to search effort.

---

[12] For eliciting the returns to search, we are only aware of our own attempt in the KM survey. Another paper directly eliciting perceived returns – not to search, but to training – is Alfonsi et al. (2020). They elicit job seekers' beliefs about their employment chances and expected earnings, both given their current skills and when following a training program. Interestingly, Bandiera et al. (2021) find that, on average, the beliefs elicited under the hypothetical training scenario and after having followed the training program coincide.

[13] To make this comparable to the perceived monthly job-finding probability in Table 22.3, we invert the expected remaining duration as $1 - (1 - \frac{1}{x})^4$, where $x = \hat{D}$ is the elicited expected remaining duration of unemployment in weeks (baseline) and $x = \hat{D}'$ the elicited expected remaining duration of unemployment in weeks (with 1 additional hour of job search per day). For those who say no to the first question, we assume that $\hat{D}' = \hat{D}$. The perceived return to 1 hour of job search per day in terms of the monthly job-finding probability, then is $\frac{\partial \hat{T}}{\partial e} = \hat{T}' - \hat{T}$.

[14] To get to these estimates, we multiply the estimates in Table 22.3 by 7/10.

[15] Note that if the marginal returns were constant, but heterogeneous (while marginal costs are homogeneous), we would expect the reverse relation with individuals perceiving higher returns searching more.

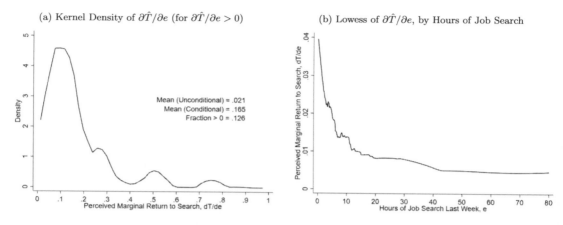

(a) Kernel Density of $\partial \hat{T}/\partial e$ (for $\partial \hat{T}/\partial e > 0$)   (b) Lowess of $\partial \hat{T}/\partial e$, by Hours of Job Search

Mean (Unconditional) = .021
Mean (Conditional) = .165
Fraction > 0 = .126

FIGURE 22.3 Elicitations of the Marginal Return to an Additional Hour of Search, $\partial \hat{T}/\partial e$

Notes: Survey weights are used for all estimates. Sample is restricted to unemployed workers, ages 20–65, in the KM survey. Panel (a) shows the kernel density estimate for the perceived marginal return to an additional hour of search per day. Panel (b) shows the fitted value of a locally weighted regression (Lowess) of elicited marginal return to an additional hour of search per day by time spent on job search last week. Note that marginal return to search is derived from a question about how the expected remaining duration is reduced by an additional hour of job search per day (if at all), which is then inverted and expressed as the perceived increase of monthly job-finding probability, $\partial \hat{T}/\partial e$.

A related identification issue arises when relating elicited beliefs about future wages to the elicited reservation wage. As recognized by the long literature on search-theoretic models of the labor market and put into sharp focus by Hornstein et al. (2011), the distribution of potential wage offers is critical for the reservation wage decision: unemployed job seekers who face a wide dispersion of potential offers will set a high reservation wage to increase the likelihood to sample a high-paying offer. Hornstein et al. (2011) argue, however, that search models calibrated with empirical measures of wage dispersion imply counterfactually long unemployment spells or low flow values of unemployment. A potential caveat, however, is that empirical measures of wage dispersion, inferred from wage realizations, may overstate the wage dispersion for the job offers individuals expect to receive. In particular, the measure of wage dispersion based on cross-sectional comparisons may reflect partly unobserved heterogeneity. Elicitations of the *distribution* of potential wage offers could address this issue.

The SCE LMS asks about the *average* expected offered wage, which under the assumption of random search is a primitive and thus can be related directly to reservation wages. Conlon et al. (2018) report that reservations wages are significantly related to their expectations about future offers, indicating that individuals who expect higher future wages, have a higher reported reservation wages. The SCE LMS also collects elicitations of the expected *best* offered wage and Fig. 22.4 plots the ratio of the best over the average expected wage offer. While it is not exactly clear what point in the distribution the "best" offer corresponds to, the figure suggests that a substantial fraction of job seekers do not perceive

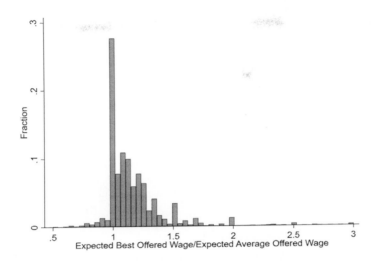

FIGURE 22.4 Histogram of the Ratio of Best over the Average Expected Offered Wage

Notes: Survey weights are used. Sample is restricted to ages 20–65, in the SCE LMS survey. The figure shows the histogram of the ratio of the elicitated expectation of the best wage offer received over the next 4 months over the elicited expectation of the average wage offer received over the next 4 months. Answers with values of less than 0.5 or more than 3 are trimmed from the sample.

any or very little dispersion in potential wage offers, with the ratio of the two being less than 1.1 for about 50% of job seekers.[16]

22.4.2.2 *Estimating the effect of beliefs on behavior*

We now turn to the opposite causal pathway and consider methods for estimating how beliefs affect search and other behavior. To empirically isolate the effect of beliefs on behavior, one ideally has information on the relevant beliefs and plausibly exogenous variation in those beliefs.

Direct elicitations

A first step is to elicit beliefs about primitives relevant for the behavior of interest. The second step is to relate those beliefs to behavior. This is a challenging task in the context of job finding, since elicitations are usually endogenous to search behavior as argued above. This is more feasible in the context of job loss, as layoffs are arguably exogenous, but still relevant for various dimensions of workers' behavior. Therefore, one can relate these elicitations directly to worker decisions. Stephens (2004) relates job loss expectations in the HRS to the consumption drop after job displacement and finds no effect. Hendren (2017) extends this by studying how job loss expectations and consumption evolve prior to displace-

---

[16] The SCE LMS asks follow-up questions on the percent chance that the best offer is more than 20% below or more than 20% above a critical value. While this is valuable, the reference value is the best offer, but – at least for the purposes here – it seems preferable to anchor these questions on the expected average wage offer.

ment, finding some anticipation effects. Campbell et al. (2007) find that qualitative measures of fear of job loss in the BHPS are associated with less subsequent wage growth. More recently, Lizama and Villena-Roldán (2021), find with data from the SCE that individuals who perceive a high likelihood of job loss are more likely to search for a new job, likely because they want to avert unemployment.[17] Pettinicchi and Vellekoop (2019) show that workers with higher job loss expectations reduce durable consumption such as cars, but also have more precautionary savings and less exposure to risky assets. Of course, it is possible that these cross-sectional comparisons are biased due to unobserved factors that are correlated both with the primitive and the worker search or consumption decision.

Exogenous variation

An alternative approach to gauge the role of beliefs for job search is to study how behavior responds to the arrival of new information. For example, one can look at search behavior before and after random events that shift expectations. In this spirit, Mitra (2021) uses data from the SCE and SCE LMS for an event study of the 2016 U.S. presidential election. She shows that after Trump's surprise election perceived labor market prospects improved in Republican relative to Democratic states, while time spent on job search activities declined in Republican states relative to Democratic ones, suggesting that search effort responds negatively to labor market prospects. Relatedly, Potter (2021) shows that search behavior increases after receiving (and rejecting) a job offer in the KM survey and he uses a structural model of job search to infer the impact on beliefs from the behavioral responses.[18] Conlon et al. (2018) document that expectations about the wage offer increase significantly if the respondent received a job offer with a wage that was above the previous expectation, though they do not look at the impact on search behavior associated with this change in expectation.

In the same vein, one can estimate the impact of beliefs on behavior through randomized information treatments, which affect behavior only through changes in beliefs. Card et al. (2012) study the effects of information provided about peer salaries on job satisfaction and the decision to engage in on-the-job search. Altmann et al. (2018) study the effects of information provided about job search strategies and the consequences of unemployment and find moderate treatment effects, which are concentrated among those at risk of long-term unemployment. Belot et al. (2019) find that information provided to job seekers on alternative occupations broadened their applications and increased the number of interviews attained. Finally, Roussille (2021) shows that, when a recruitment platform for engineers provided candidates with suggestions on what salary to ask for, the gender wage gap went to zero.

A common theme in this literature that uses event-study or information treatment designs to study the effect of beliefs on behavior is that typically it focuses either on elicitations of beliefs *or* behavior. More precisely, papers that employ structural techniques use empirical evidence on either and then use the structure of the model to infer the other, and papers that use information treatments typically estimate the reduced form of the information treatment on behavior. For future research, we believe it would be interesting to build on these papers and infer the impact of beliefs on job search in settings where both beliefs *and* behavior are elicited before and after the event or information treatment. This will allow to estimate the impact of beliefs on behavior directly from the data.

---

[17] Similarly, Stephens (2004) shows that a higher probability of job-loss is associated with a higher likelihood of a job-to-job transition.

[18] The KM survey also collects information on beliefs about job finding but only for a subsample of observations, see Mueller et al. (2021) for details.

22.5 Beliefs and biases

Traditional models of labor markets assume that workers have rational expectations about the risks they face. The direct measurement of workers' expectations through the elicitation of their beliefs allows to relax this assumption. The previous section discussed how beliefs affect behavior and how elicited beliefs can help separating its role from preferences. Importantly, if workers' beliefs are biased, these biases distort workers' behavior. Understanding these biases is therefore key for designing effective labor market policies. This section discusses the identification of biases in beliefs, the empirical evidence on biases in beliefs and its determinants, and the implications for policy.

22.5.1 Identification

The direct measurement of expectations allows to overcome important challenges when trying to identify how workers perceive the risk they face. First, it allows to relax the assumption of rational expectations. Second, it avoids the reverse mapping from ex post outcomes to ex ante expectations, which requires strong assumptions when risks are heterogeneous and dynamic as we discuss further in Section 22.6. However, the identification of biases poses some practical and conceptual challenges as well.

In the conceptual framework we introduced in Section 22.3, we consider an individual's beliefs to be optimistically biased if $\hat{T}(h_{i,t}) > T(h_{i,t})$, and vice versa.[19] The challenge in evaluating the accuracy of one's beliefs is that we cannot directly observe an individual's risk type, $T(h_{i,t})$. We can, however, observe realizations of the risk. Let us denote this by $R(h_{i,t})$, which equals 1 with probability $T(h_{i,t})$ and 0 otherwise. We can then construct a simple test for the bias in beliefs by comparing ex ante beliefs and ex post realizations, since

$$E_I(\hat{T}(h_{i,t})) = E_I(T(h_{i,t})) \Rightarrow E_I(\hat{T}(h_{i,t})) = E_I(R(h_{i,t})). \tag{22.3}$$

Here I refers to the specific group of individuals and time range over which we take the expectation. When rejecting the equality $E_I(\hat{T}(h_{i,t})) = E_I(R(h_{i,t}))$, we can conclude that expectations are on average biased in this group. Otherwise, expectations are on average correct, but can still be biased for any given individual in this group.

To implement this test, it is critical to compare the beliefs and realizations for the same risk. That is why it is very important to have elicitations of workers' beliefs and the corresponding labor market outcomes for the same workers. As discussed in Section 22.2, this requires not only quantitative elicitations of the beliefs about a well-defined risk for which the outcome is actually measurable. This also requires a panel survey or a survey that is linkable to other data to measure the relevant outcomes. Ideally, the outcome can be measured at the same horizon as the one used in the elicitation. Relatedly, it is important to use a time frame where differences between ex ante beliefs and ex post realizations cannot be rationalized by unexpected shocks at the macro level. For example, in the months right before the pandemic, individuals did not correctly anticipate the huge waves of job losses over the next months

---

[19] Moore and Healy (2008) refer to such types of overconfidence as *overestimation* and distinguish it from *overplacement* – the tendency to overestimate one's relative skills or performance – and *overprecision* – the tendency to overestimate the precision of one's beliefs.

(see Fig. 22.1). To sum up, at the individual level, we cannot expect workers to fully anticipate what will happen to them as individual outcomes as the random realization of a probability. However, at the group level, there is no reason for them to over- or underestimate their employment prospects, except when the studied group is subject to an aggregate shock.

For the interpretation of the test, we should also try to minimize the potential for elicitation noise to be systematic. As mentioned earlier, individuals may report a belief of 50% when their *true* belief is somewhere between $(50 - x)$% and $(50 + x)$%. Hence, if their risk type is in that interval, the measured bias may be simply due to the rounding that individuals do. Eliciting the beliefs in different ways or at different horizons will help in making a more compelling case that beliefs are indeed biased. Similarly, we want to avoid experimenter effects where individuals report beliefs to please the experimenter or the elicitation of beliefs is known to be linked to specific interventions. It is common in experimental belief elicitation to provide incentives to elicit participants' "true" beliefs, by mapping the ex-ante beliefs and ex-post realizations in a scoring rule (see Schlag and van der Weele, 2015 or Schlag et al., 2015 for a review). However, from a policy perspective, the goal is to measure the beliefs that are underlying individuals' behavior, potentially distorted for motivational reasons or to overcome other behavioral frictions. Hence, the "true" beliefs identified by providing incentives are not the most relevant ones.

We note that economists tend to trust more what individuals do than what they say in the spirit of the influential revealed preference paradigm. An alternative to using elicited beliefs is to look at the choices individuals make, like insurance or savings decisions. For example, Malmendier and Tate (2008) show how CEOs hold on for too long to their stock options as evidence for optimistic beliefs about their (firm) performance. In general, it is challenging to exclude that these choices cannot be rationalized by specific preferences rather than by specific beliefs. Recent work started studying how variation in the choice environment allows to separate preferences and perceptions (e.g., Ericson et al., 2021).

22.5.2 **Empirical evidence**

A large body of work in psychology and a rapidly growing literature in economics has documented substantial biases in beliefs (see, for example, Moore and Healy, 2008 or Santos-Pinto and de la Rosa, 2020 for reviews). People are shown to have overly optimistic beliefs in a variety of applications, both in experimental contexts and in the field. A number of recent papers have been documenting the importance of optimistic biases in labor markets as well.

To our knowledge, the first test for bias in labor market expectations was implemented by Spinnewijn (2015), who used a survey ran by a team of psychologists studying how couples handle depression during unemployment (Price et al., 1998).[20] A sample of 1487 unemployed job seekers in Michigan and Maryland were surveyed repeatedly between 1996 and 1998 and asked about their expectations in the question: "How many weeks do you estimate it will actually be before you will be working more than 20 hours per week?" In follow-up interviews, subjects were then asked when they actually started working. Spinnewijn (2015) simply links the reported expectations of unemployed job seekers to the actual outcomes of their job search to reveal a striking optimistic bias. On average, accounting for censored unemployment spells, the average remaining duration for the same sample of

---

[20] We also refer to the interested reader to the earlier version of Spinnewijn (2008), which contains a more comprehensive empirical analysis of the elicited beliefs, including an estimation of the perceived returns to search.

job seekers exceeded 23 weeks, which was more than three times longer than expected. This is a substantial wedge on average, with more than 80% of the job seekers underestimating the length of their unemployment spell. This wedge is unlikely to be rationalized by unexpected changes in the aggregate labor market conditions. However, the test is implemented for a specific sample in a specific context. The wording in the elicitation questions also leaves some ambiguity about whether the average number of weeks is what individuals are expected to report.

The optimistic bias in the beliefs held by unemployed job seekers is, however, corroborated using different types of elicitations and in different macroeconomic contexts. Mueller et al. (2021) report on the optimistic bias in beliefs from the KM survey and the SCE survey. As mentioned before, the KM survey elicited beliefs asking for the expected remaining duration and for the job finding probability. The optimistic bias is similar and very large again for both elicitation methods. In the SCE, probabilistic beliefs are elicited both at the three month and twelve month horizon. As shown in Table 22.2, at the three month horizon, we find an average optimistic bias (8 p.p.) indicating that job seekers perceive their chances to be 20% higher than they are. The overall bias is smaller than in the KM survey, but the optimistic bias is substantially larger for the long-term unemployed in both surveys. A number of recent papers (Abebe et al., 2020; Alfonsi et al., 2020; Bandiera et al., 2021; Banerjee and Sequeira, 2021) have fielded job search interventions in developing countries and also elicit job seekers' beliefs about their employment prospects. Despite the difference in contexts, all these papers consistently document optimistic biases in job seekers' expectations.

The elicited beliefs in Spinnewijn (2015) and Mueller et al. (2021) correspond to the baseline probabilities T in our conceptual framework. However, these optimistic beliefs could correspond to optimism about the specific dimensions of job search underlying these employment prospects. In particular, Conlon et al. (2018) have studied job seekers' expectations regarding the number of job offers they would receive and the wages that they would be offered, corresponding to the arrival rate λ and the wage offer distribution $F(w)$ in our conceptual framework. Conlon et al. (2018) find using the SCE that in general, workers tend to expect a much higher number of job offers than what they receive. The wage expectations are more accurate with only a small optimistic wedge between the average expected wage of $32.30 and average received wage offer of $30.40. Using similar elicitations in Switzerland, Arni (2017) reports overly optimistic beliefs on both the arrival rate and wage offers. Moreover, using an RCT intervention with coaching and counseling, he finds that job seekers' optimistic bias can be reduced. Relatedly, using the Linked IZA/IAB Evaluation Dataset from Germany, Drahs et al. (2018) look at the wages job seekers expect to be reemployed at and find that unemployed individuals overestimate their future net reemployment wage by 10% on average. Almost 40% expect to earn a wage which is very close to their last wage, but the average and the median job seeker obtain only 90% of their expected wage. Jäger et al. (2021) elicit workers' beliefs about their outside options in a special questionnaire in the GSOEP and find that most workers think their next-best job will pay exactly the same as their current one. Comparing the expected to actual wage changes associated with job transitions, they find that low-paid (high-paid) workers are overly pessimistic (optimistic) about their outside options. With correct beliefs, 13% of jobs would become nonviable (i.e., negative worker rent) at current wages. Finally, Cortés et al. (2021) find that among business majors men exhibit higher levels of optimism about their postgraduation earnings than women, and show that in a model of job search with biased beliefs this contributes to the realized gender earnings gap.

The above evidence mostly relates to the employment prospects of unemployed job seekers. However, also employed workers face the risk of unemployment. As reported in Table 22.2, in the SCE the perceived probability of losing a job is high relative to the separation rate to unemployment. However, it is substantially lower than the combined transition rate from employment to unemployment and non-employment and does not account for immediate job-to-job transitions after job loss. Therefore, it is not clear whether these differences reflect biases in the perceived probability of job loss or simply the imperfect overlap between the concept covered in the elicited probability and the realized transition. The HRS includes a question on involuntary job loss that relates more directly to the elicited beliefs. While focused on the predictive power of job loss expectations, Stephens (2004) finds a positive wedge between the perceived probability of job loss and the observed probability of job loss. This wedge is even more pronounced for later waves in the HRS, as reported in Hendren (2017). Both authors, however, caution the reader in interpreting this wedge as a pessimistic bias in beliefs.

Finally, employed workers do not only form beliefs about their unemployment risk, but also about their future productivity at a firm. These expectations affect the value of staying on a job and investing in firm-specific capital at this job or whether to consider alternative jobs. For example, Hoffman and Burks (2017) compare weekly productivity and productivity beliefs data for truckers in the US over two years and finds that workers' beliefs tend to systematically exceed realized productivity.

22.5.3 Determinants of biased beliefs

Since the seminal work by Kahneman and Tversky, psychologist and economists have formulated theories and collected evidence about how individuals form beliefs and update their beliefs based on personal observations and experience. Santos-Pinto and de la Rosa (2020) provide an excellent overview of explanations for overly optimistic beliefs. Individuals may prefer to have an optimistic belief about their own ability (Kunda, 1990), even though this could distort their decisions (e.g., Brunnermeier and Parker, 2005). Or individuals may distort their beliefs to mitigate the distorting impact of other behavioral biases like present bias or lack of self-control (e.g., Bénabou and Tirole, 2002; Heifetz et al., 2007a,b). These motivational effects may also affect how individuals' process information and update their beliefs. Understanding the sources of biases in beliefs is of course very challenging, but can be key to learn how to overcome these biases and reduce the potential behavioral distortions.

A first natural way to further our understanding of biases in beliefs in labor markets is to study observable factors they correlate with. Some prior work has studied how elicited beliefs themselves change with observables. Early examples are Manski and Straub (2000) and Stephens (2004). The notion that beliefs are responding to observables that are known to affect employment prospects is often seen as prima facie evidence that beliefs are predictive. However, there is relatively limited work that relates biases in beliefs to individuals' observable characteristics (e.g., Spinnewijn, 2015; Balleer et al., 2021). While more work would be valuable, for example, to inform the targeting of information treatments or debiasing policies, we need to be careful how to interpret differences in wedges for workers with different observables X. One interpretation is that *all* individuals in the population over- or underestimate the employment "returns" to individuals with these observables X and not just the individuals with these observables X. Therefore, policy makers may want to correct the population beliefs rather than the beliefs of individuals with those observables X. The alternative interpretation is that individuals with different observables are subject to different biases. This could be due to motivational reasons. Under this alternative interpretation targeting individuals with larger biases may not necessarily result in larger behavioral responses.

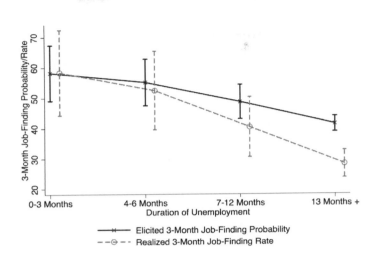

FIGURE 22.5 Perceived and Realized Job Finding in the SCE, by Duration of Unemployment

Notes: Survey weights are used for all estimates. Sample is restricted to unemployed workers, ages 20–65, with 3 consecutive follow-up surveys in the SCE.

Unemployment duration

In the context of unemployment, Spinnewijn (2008, 2015) and Mueller et al. (2021) link the biases in job seekers' beliefs to their reported search behavior and the duration of their unemployment spell. Spinnewijn (2008, 2015) finds that individuals who report higher search intensity experience significantly shorter unemployment spells, while the relation between search and the elicited expected duration of unemployment is smaller. This could indicate that job seekers underestimate the returns to search and thus are subject to biases in both their baseline and control beliefs. The relation with reported search efforts also points to another potential source of bias in beliefs, which is that individuals wrongly anticipate their behavior. For example, hyperbolic discounting or self-control issues imply that job seekers can overestimate their future search efforts when they are naive about their biases (DellaVigna and Paserman, 2005). The bias in beliefs about future behavior could explain why individuals who end up exerting less effort are more optimistic.

Mueller et al. (2021) show that the optimistic bias in baseline beliefs among job seekers is driven by the long-term unemployed. This observation is repeated in Fig. 22.5 with more recent data from the SCE, where we compare the beliefs and job finding of the short- and long-term unemployed, respectively. This links to two other potential sources of biases in beliefs. The first is a simple selection effect. Individuals with worse employment prospects may not perceive this as such, resulting in more optimistic individuals selecting into longer unemployment. This selection effect can interact with job seekers' behavior, for example, when optimistic job seekers are more selective or put in less effort and thus are more likely to remain unemployed. These type of selection effects underlying optimistic biases have been discussed in other contexts (e.g., van den Steen, 2004; Spinnewijn, 2017). Mueller et al. (2021) show that this type of dynamic selection is important for explaining the optimistic bias among long-term unemployed.

The second potential source is a lack of updating of beliefs. When job seekers have imprecise priors about their employability, we expect them to learn from prolonged spells of unemployment and revise their beliefs downward.[21] However, with data from the SCE and KM survey, Mueller et al. (2021) find that job seekers do not revise their beliefs downward as they remain unemployed. The lack of updating is surprising, but several explanations can be put forward. A first explanation is motivated beliefs where job seekers want to keep a positive self-image or value optimistic expectations even more as the lasting unemployment causes hardship. Biases in information processing and statistical reasoning can explain the persistence in beliefs, too. In particular, unemployed job seekers may be subject to the gambler's fallacy. By applying the law of small numbers, unsuccessful job seekers may infer from a series of bad draws (as their unemployment spell lasts) that the probability of a good draw increases (Rabin and Vayanos, 2010). Alternatively, the lack of updating may simply reflect stationary employment prospects over the spell of unemployment, see more on this in the next section. Stationary employment prospects also are consistent with Krueger and Mueller (2016), who show – using data from the KM survey – that reservation wages are nearly constant over the spell, and also with Marinescu and Skandalis (2021) and DellaVigna et al. (2020), who find that search activity is constant or even increasing, at least prior to the exhaustion of unemployment benefits.

The lack of learning and persistence in beliefs has been documented in other contexts. A large literature has studied the updating of beliefs in experimental settings more generally. Falk et al. (2006) study how beliefs evolve in a search experiment where the returns to search depend on subjects' relative performance on an initial task. Individuals update their beliefs depending on the success of their search efforts, but less than what would be predicted by Bayes' rule. A few papers have studied how beliefs evolve "in the field" in a labor market context.[22] Banerjee and Sequeira (2021) find in a field experiment that unemployed youth in South Africa update their beliefs about job finding more if they are induced to search more. This suggests that the lack of updating could be explained by inefficiently low search effort due to overoptimistic beliefs. Hoffman and Burks (2017) provide compelling evidence that truck drivers are not only overly optimistic about their productivity, but also that these optimistic beliefs are very persistent, up to two years after the first elicitations. Conlon et al. (2018) study workers' wage expectations and how they respond to a wage offer. They find that higher than expected salary offers cause workers' to update their beliefs about future wages upward, and vice versa. Estimating a structural model of learning, they show that this response is substantially stronger than what Bayesian updating would predict. They also elicit a direct measure of individuals' priors and they do not find that individuals with more precise priors update their beliefs less.

Business cycles

In addition to knowing how workers' beliefs respond to their personal circumstances, it is also important to understand how workers' beliefs and thus their behavior respond to aggregate circumstances. We already showed the time series of the perceived and realized job finding for the SCE in Fig. 22.1. Table 22.4 illustrates their relation further by showing how workers' perceptions respond to macroeconomic indicators.[23] The table shows that there is a clear and significant relationship between the

---

[21] See Bikhchandani and Sharma (1996) and Dubra (2004) for an analysis of learning with biased beliefs in standard search models.

[22] See Chapter 4 in this Handbook for a thorough analysis of this topic.

[23] Mueller et al. (2021) have reported a version of this table for the unemployed job seekers (see Appendix Table D.10).

Table 22.4 Linear Regressions of Elicitations on Aggregate Labor Market Variables.

Dependent Variable: Elicited 3-Month Job-Finding Probability	(1)	(2)	(3)	(4)	(5)
National Unemployment Rate	−1.582***	−0.588***			
	(0.161)	(0.175)			
× Unemployed	0.200	0.513			
	(0.638)	(1.194)			
National Job Openings Rate	3.351***	5.743***			
	(0.664)	(0.712)			
× Unemployed	−2.541	−1.726			
	(2.283)	(3.228)			
Pandemic		−0.067***			
		(0.013)			
× Unemployed		−0.018			
		(0.067)			
State Unemployment Rate			−1.891***	−1.884***	
			(0.141)	(0.145)	
× Unemployed			0.628	0.578	
			(0.527)	(0.505)	
Elicited Prob(Rise in Stock Prices)					0.220***
					(0.013)
× Unemployed					−0.127***
					(0.044)
Elicited Prob(Rise in US Unemployment)					−0.089***
					(0.012)
× Unemployed					0.004
					(0.045)
Demographics	×	×	×	×	×
State FE				×	
Observations	73,080	73,080	73,792	73,792	73,344
R^2	0.057	0.058	0.054	0.062	0.064

Notes: The sample period is 2012:12 to 2021:02. All samples are restricted to workers in the SCE, ages 20–65. Robust standard errors (clustered at the individual level) are in parentheses. Survey weights are used in all regressions.

monthly national unemployment and vacancy statistics and the elicited beliefs about job finding. Note that these regressions include both the employed and unemployed, and for the employed this refers to the probability of job finding in the event of job loss. We find a very similar relationship with the state unemployment rate, also when controlling for state fixed effects. Overall, the relationship between the beliefs and macroeconomic indicators seems less pronounced for the unemployed than the employed job seekers, though standard errors are very large. Compared to the employed job seekers, the relationship between the unemployed job seekers' beliefs and the national job openings rate is small and insignificant (column 1 in Table 22.4). Column 2 even indicates no relationship with the unemployment rate, once we control for the perceived impact of the Pandemic. This deserves further attention in the future, as the pattern is surprising; for the employed job seekers the elicited beliefs are only relevant conditional on becoming unemployed. The accuracy of beliefs thus matters more for the unemployed individuals, but they may have specific motivations to distort their beliefs. In spite of this difference, we do find a similar relationship for the employed and unemployed job seekers between the job seekers' beliefs and their elicited expectation that the unemployment rate will rise (column 5 in Table 22.4). This suggests that although the unemployed appear to be less informed about aggregate unemployment, they take into account their own perceptions about aggregate conditions.[24]

To unpack the correlation between macroeconomic expectations and personal expectations, Roth and Wohlfart (2020) vary exposure to expert forecasts and show how this exogenous variation changes macroeconomic and personal expectations. Moreover, the personal expectations respond more for individuals with higher exposure to macroeconomic risk. Emmler and Fitzenberger (2021) consider the German reunification and find even an overresponse in personal job loss expectations held by workers in East Germany. Kuchler and Zafar (2019) study the opposite direction and show that individuals who personally experience unemployment become more pessimistic about future nationwide unemployment.

While the overresponses in beliefs are seemingly opposite in nature to evidence for persistence in beliefs or lack of learning, prior work in psychology and experimental economics has also shown the tendency of individuals to rely too heavily on recent information, referred to as the "representative" heuristic (Kahneman et al., 1982). How the multitude of biases and heuristics can lead to persistence in beliefs in some settings vs. overresponses in others shows the importance of studying beliefs in a variety of contexts.

22.5.4 Policy implications

Understanding the biases in beliefs is important for designing effective labor market policies. The biases may affect the evaluation of standard labor market policies, but also open the door for information policies that help workers to correct these biases. While workers' perceived risks determine their decisions and their so-called "decision utility," the true risks will determine their so-called "true utility" and could be deemed more relevant to evaluate welfare. Hence, a policy maker who cares about workers' true utility needs to know the bias in beliefs to evaluate welfare. While most of the papers discussed above use workers' "true utility" to evaluate welfare, there is discussion in the literature regarding the appropriate welfare criterion (see Bernheim and Taubinsky, 2018).

Spinnewijn (2015) shows how biases in beliefs and the behavioral distortions they cause affect the evaluation of labor market policies. He starts from the Baily–Chetty formula (Baily, 1978; Chetty, 2006), which characterizes the optimal unemployment insurance (UI) generosity as a function of the consumption smoothing gains and the moral hazard costs. While both can be estimated empirically, this type of sufficient-statistics representation critically relies on the envelope theorem. This implies that any behavioral response to a change in the policy only has second-order impacts on the welfare of optimizing agents. However, when beliefs are biased and thus decisions are distorted, the behavioral response to a change in the policy and how this affects "true utility" can be of first-order. Spinnewijn (2015) shows how the moral hazard cost needs to be scaled by the bias in control beliefs, to account for the underlying distortion in search efforts, and how the consumption smoothing gain needs to be scaled

---

[24] See also Curtin (2003) who finds that expectations about changes in the unemployment rate are correlated with actual changes in the unemployment rate.

by the baseline bias, to account for the underlying distortion in intertemporal consumption smoothing. This type of internality corrections have been useful for standard policy formulae in other contexts too (e.g., Baicker et al., 2015; Allcott et al., 2019; Farhi and Gabaix, 2020). Moreover, biased beliefs may not only distort workers' choices, but also change the bargaining and interactions with potential employers. For example, Fang and Moscarini (2005) analyze the impact of biased beliefs on optimal wage-setting by firms. de la Rosa (2011) and Santos-Pinto (2008) show how biased beliefs affect both the wages and the power of incentives used by firms.

The presence of biases in beliefs that affect welfare also calls for policies that directly target these biases. Conlon et al. (2018) find sizeable welfare costs due to belief-induced search distortions, but show that the estimated learning process mitigates these distortions. Hoffman and Burks (2017) show that the optimistic bias in truckers' beliefs has only moderate impacts on their own welfare, but substantially increases firm profits. Moreover, as discussed in Section 22.4, a number of recent papers have studied the impact of specific policy interventions, either to provide information or additional job search assistance to improve job search outcomes. These interventions have had some mixed success and hopefully more general lessons can be learned in future work.

22.6 Beliefs and heterogeneity

This final section outlines how elicited beliefs can be used constructively to learn about the environment, above and beyond workers' expectations. We illustrate how beliefs can help uncover both heterogeneity and dynamics in employment risk – across and within job seekers, respectively – that is otherwise unobservable. Building on Hendren (2013, 2017), we start by writing down nonparametric lower bounds on heterogeneity in employment risk and then discuss issues related to biases and persistence in beliefs. We also discuss how beliefs can be leveraged to identify the scope for adverse selection in unemployment insurance markets and to separate dynamic selection from true duration dependence underlying the decline in job finding rates over the unemployment spell.

22.6.1 Identification

The prior section showed how subjective expectations can be used to relax the rational expectations assumptions commonly assumed in models of the labor market. What sometimes gets overlooked is that even when assuming rational expectations, one needs strong assumptions to infer ex-ante risk types from ex-post risk realizations. The challenge is most easily illustrated for binary risks. In Table 22.2 we reported that among the unemployed job seekers 40% enter employment again over the next three months. However, from the employment outcomes alone it is impossible to infer whether all of them faced a 40% probability to become employed, or whether 40% were certain to become employed and the remaining 60% were certain to remain unemployed. One solution is to have repeated employment observations for the same individual. For identifying income risk for employed workers, this would require a long time series of income observations for each individual (e.g., Chamberlain, 1984). Identifying the job finding probability for unemployed job seekers is even more challenging, because – as shown by Heckman and Singer (1984) – with single-spell data estimates are sensitive to assumptions about functional form of the distribution of types. Put more generally, the identification problem for an individual's risk translates to the identification of any heterogeneity or dynamics in individuals' risk.

Honoré (1993) provided a proof that identification can be obtained with multiple-spell data without relying heavily on functional form assumptions, and recently Alvarez et al. (2016) estimate a model with multiple-spell data from Austria. One potential limitation of this approach, however, is that it abstracts of any changes in types across spells (e.g., due to changes in savings, skills, health, etc.) and thus, only identifies the extent of heterogeneity that is fixed across spells.

Individuals' subjective expectations about these risks can help overcoming this identification challenge. For the estimation of income processes and for example tests of consumption smoothing hypotheses, it has been known for a while that subjective expectations can be useful, but there is some apparent reluctance in relying on subjective expectations in standard modeling, which could be explained by data availability, but also by the alternative assumptions that are required (see Jappelli and Pistaferri, 2010). For example, Pistaferri (2001) has shown how the extent to which innovations in income do not translate in updating of subjective income expectations can be used to identify transitory shocks and separate them from persistent shocks to income. However, to learn about the true income process, this requires again that expectations are rational. More recently, Hendren (2013, 2017) shows how we can use beliefs to learn about heterogeneity in employment risks – focusing on the risk of job loss for employed workers. Mueller et al. (2021) extend Hendren's approach for when expectations are not rational – focusing on the reemployment risk for unemployed job seekers.

The basic idea in Hendren (2013) relies on the variance decomposition. Presented in the context of our illustrative framework on job finding, we have

$$Var(T_{i,t}) \geq Var(E(T_{i,t}|X_{i,t})) \text{ for any } X_{i,t} \quad \Rightarrow \quad Var(T_{i,t}) \geq Var(E(R_{i,t}|\hat{T}_{i,t})). \qquad (22.4)$$

Any predictable variation in job-finding outcomes $R_{i,t}$ provides a nonparametric lower bound on the variance in job-finding probabilities $T_{i,t}$. While this holds for any set of observables $X_{i,t}$, job seekers' beliefs $\hat{T}_{i,t}$ may prove to be particularly predictive.

If individuals had perfect information about their employment prospects, the heterogeneity in job finding chances would be fully captured by the variance in elicited beliefs. That is, $Var(T_{i,t}) = Var(\hat{T}_{i,t})$. In general, beliefs can be subject to bias and elicited with error. Still, the predictive value of individuals' elicitations can help uncover the heterogeneity in true job-finding probabilities. For binary risks, the covariances of beliefs with ex-post job finding realizations and with ex-ante job-finding probabilities simply coincide, $cov\left(\hat{T}_{i,t}, T_{i,t}\right) = cov\left(\hat{T}_{i,t}, R_{i,t}\right)$. Hence, when elicited beliefs provide an unbiased – but potentially noisy – measure of individuals' job finding probabilities, the covariance between these beliefs and ex-post job finding outcomes exactly identifies the variance in ex-ante job-finding probabilities. That is, $var\left(T_{i,t}\right) = cov\left(\hat{T}_{i,t}, R_{i,t}\right)$, as shown by Hendren (2013). When beliefs are biased, we can still bound this variance using the Cauchy–Schwarz inequality (see Morrison and Taubinsky, 2019),

$$var\left(T_{i,t}\right) \geq \frac{cov\left(\hat{T}_{i,t}, R_{i,t}\right)^2}{var\left(\hat{T}_{i,t}\right)}. \qquad (22.5)$$

For a given variance in elicitations, a larger covariance between elicitations and realizations indicates less noise underlying the elicitations, and thus a larger variance in the job-finding probabilities themselves.[25]

The nonparametric bounds in (22.5) is robust to biases in beliefs. One can now go beyond partial identification by specifying a model of how beliefs relate to observable variation in job finding, as shown by Mueller et al. (2021). They consider the following linear model of job seekers' elicited beliefs:

$$\hat{T}_{i,t} = b_0 + b_1 T_{i,t} + \varepsilon_{i,t}. \tag{22.6}$$

In this model, $\varepsilon_{i,t}$ captures random error in the elicited beliefs (with $E(\varepsilon_{i,t}|T_{i,t}) = 0$), the intercept b_0 captures a bias in the elicitations that is common to all individuals, and the slope parameter b_1 captures the extent to which elicitations reflect the underlying job-finding rates. As a result, the covariance between the beliefs and actual job finding scales the variance in true job-finding rates with the slope parameter b_1,

$$cov(\hat{T}_{i,t}, R_{i,t}) = b_1 var(T_{i,t}). \tag{22.7}$$

Hence, if job seekers' elicitations underreact to variation in job finding ($b_1 < 1$), the covariance underestimates the variance in true job finding, and vice versa. Now one can leverage the variation in job-finding rates across individuals with different observable characteristics to learn about the slope parameter. Intuitively, this parameter is revealed by the compression of the differences in $\hat{T}$'s relative to the differences in T's across observable groups. For the linear model, this becomes

$$b_1 = \frac{E\left(\hat{T}_{i,t}|X_{i,t}\right) - E\left(\hat{T}_{i,t}|X'_{i,t}\right)}{E\left(R_{i,t}|X_{i,t}\right) - E\left(R_{i,t}|X'_{i,t}\right)}. \tag{22.8}$$

This relies on the assumption that the average bias is constant across workers with different observables (i.e., $E(\varepsilon_{i,t}|X_{i,t}) = E(\varepsilon_{i,t}|X'_{i,t}) = 0$), but this can be tested or relaxed if we can observe the same individual under different X's.[26]

22.6.2 Applications

We discuss two recent applications using the beliefs of job seekers to shed new light on two long-standing questions in economics.

Adverse selection in UI

A long-standing question in the unemployment literature is whether adverse selection can explain the absence of private markets for unemployment insurance (UI) and therefore rationalize the use of universal mandates in UI (see also Landais et al., 2021; Hendren et al., 2020). To shed light on this, Hendren

---

[25] Note that when the elicited beliefs are subject to noise, one can further tighten the bound by using multiple elicitations, $\hat{T}^k_{i,t}$ (see Morrison and Taubinsky, 2019 and Mueller et al., 2021).

[26] Mueller et al. (2021) use how individuals' job finding changes over the unemployment spell and show how the assumption that beliefs respond in the same way to variation in job finding across and within job seekers can be relaxed.

(2017) uses the elicited beliefs of employed workers in the HRS to estimate the heterogeneity in job loss probabilities and thus measure the scope for adverse selection. Building on Hendren (2013), this requires an estimate of the pooled-price ratio, i.e., $\frac{E(T_{i,t}|T_{i,t}\geq\bar{T})}{1-E(T_{i,t}|T_{i,t}\geq\bar{T})}$. Leveraging again the relationship between the elicited job-loss probabilities and the actual outcomes, Hendren (2017) provides nonparametric and parametric estimates of this statistic, which just like the variance crucially depends on the heterogeneity in job-loss probabilities. This relationship, also documented in Fig. 22.2, is very strong, even when controlling for a rich set of demographics and employment variables. The strong relationship translates into estimates for the pooled-price ratio that are as high as 300%. This indicates that for a private market to exist workers at the margin of buying UI would need to be willing to pay a mark-up of 300% relative to their cost in order to compensate private insurers for insuring individuals with even higher unemployment risk and who would be selecting the UI, too.[27]

Interestingly, Hendren (2017) also shows that individuals act on their elicited beliefs and self-insure against their perceived risk of job loss: spousal labor supply and consumption dynamics both significantly correlate with elicited unemployment risk. In particular, as individuals are surveyed closer to the moment they end up losing their job, they report higher perceived probabilities of job loss and they also report lower consumption levels. Hendren (2017) shows how these dynamics in self-insurance, scaled by the anticipated change in unemployment risk, can be used to infer how much workers value UI and finds that workers' willingness-to-pay is lower than a mark-up of 60% relative to their cost.

Duration dependence vs. dynamic selection

A long-standing question in macro- and labor economics is why employment prospects are worse for the long-term unemployed. Is it because long-term unemployment reduces a given worker's chances to find a job (e.g., due to skill depreciation)? Or is it because less employable workers select into long-term unemployment? Separating the role of duration-dependent forces from heterogeneity across job seekers has been a major empirical challenge (see Heckman and Singer, 1984; Machin and Manning, 1999). To shed light on this, Mueller et al. (2021) use the elicited beliefs of unemployed job seekers in the SCE to estimate the heterogeneity in job finding probabilities and measure the scope for dynamic selection.

Expressed in our stylized model, we have

$$E_t(T_{i,t}) - E_{t+1}\left(T_{i,t+1}\right) = E_t(T_{i,t} - T_{i,t+1}) + \frac{cov_t\left(T_{i,t}, T_{i,t+1}\right)}{1 - E_t\left(T_{i,t}\right)}, \qquad (22.9)$$

where the subindex t denotes the duration at which the job seekers are sampled to evaluate the corresponding moment. The challenge is thus to separate the true duration dependence in job finding, $E_t(T_{i,t} - T_{i,t+1})$, from dynamic selection of job seekers with worse reemployment prospects into prolonged unemployment, $cov_t\left(T_{i,t}, T_{i,t+1}\right)$. When cross-sectional differences in job finding are persistent over the unemployment spell, the dynamic selection term fully depends on the variance in job-finding probabilities, which can be estimated again using the covariance between elicited beliefs and actual job

---

[27] As mentioned, Hendren (2017) allows for beliefs to be elicited with noise, but not for them to be biased. Moreover, to translate the pooled-price ratio into a measure of adverse selection, one needs to assume that other dimensions of heterogeneity driving the selection of UI are orthogonal to the heterogeneity in risk.

finding. This variance, however, tends to overestimate the role of dynamic selection when some of the differences are transitory in nature. To separate the persistent differences in job finding, Mueller et al. (2021) show how one can use the relationship between realized job finding and the lagged rather than the contemporaneous beliefs. Furthermore, as discussed before, when job seekers under- or overestimate their differences, we need to scale the covariance by $1/b_1$ to obtain the variance in job finding. Comparing the difference in perceived and true job finding probabilities for the short- and long-term unemployed, they obtain an estimate of about 0.5 for b_1.

Putting these empirical moments together, Mueller et al. (2021) find that dynamic selection explains most of the observed negative duration dependence in job finding. A full parametric estimation of their model estimates this share to be 85%, leaving only 15% to be explained by true duration dependence. As mentioned before, Mueller et al. (2021) also find that job seekers are not significantly revising their beliefs downward as they remain unemployed. Simply using repeated elicitations of individuals' beliefs could have been a more direct solution to the challenge of identifying the dynamics of an individual's risk. This only works if individuals are not subject to biases more generally, but in this application also requires that individuals have perfect information. When job seekers have imperfect information instead, they should also learn about their employability from remaining unemployed and revise their beliefs downward. So it remains a puzzle why their perceived job finding does not decrease more rapidly as they remain unemployed. This persistence in their beliefs could also be part of the reason of why some job seekers remain unemployed for so long, as argued in Mueller et al. (2021).

22.7 Conclusion

We hope this chapter provides a stimulating guide for further work on belief elicitations in labor markets.

First, we have argued that an important advantage of belief elicitations is to shed light on biases in perceptions and the resulting distorted search behavior. Existing research shows a clear optimistic bias in elicited beliefs about job finding, which in turn raises questions about its sources as well as its implications. We believe it is important to better understand how biases distort search behavior. While existing research often relies on structural models to draw implications of distorted beliefs for behavior, we see promise in the instrumental variable approaches and field/natural experiments that rely on exogenous variation in beliefs or the information environment.

Second, and related to the discussion above, we believe that it is important to understand how beliefs about job prospects respond to changes in the macroeconomic environment as well as to study beliefs in equilibrium models of the labor market. For example, in a typical search-and-matching model with vacancy creation, if beliefs about job finding are sticky, then so will be bargained wages, which in turn may depress vacancy creation in response to a negative aggregate shock. While we present some evidence on the cyclicality of beliefs from the SCE in the present paper, a more systematic analysis with a longer time series and one that includes a comparison to actual outcomes would be of great value. The dynamics of beliefs over the business cycle may also inform macroeconomic models of aggregate consumption dynamics and the effects of stimulus policies. For all these reasons, it would be highly valuable if surveys aimed at collecting consistent time series of labor market expectations.

Third, a growing literature recognizes the importance of on-the-job search for labor market outcomes, yet with the exception of the SCE, elicitations about job prospects are typically limited to unemployed job seekers. Eliciting beliefs about job-to-job transitions and potential wages on other jobs, documenting potential biases and effects on search behavior thus seems a fruitful direction for future research.

Finally, despite the documented biases, we argued that one can leverage beliefs to learn about aspects of the job seekers' environment that are not observed otherwise. Elicited beliefs have a high predictive power for job finding, above and beyond the typical observable characteristics, suggesting that these elicitations reveal information that are typically private to the job seeker or, at least, not observable to the econometrician. This can be leveraged to learn about ex-ante heterogeneity in various settings, including but not limited to ex-ante heterogeneity in job loss, job finding, and wage offers.

References

Abebe, Girum, Fafchamps, Marcel, Falco, Paolo, Franklin, Simon, Quinn, Simon, Shilpi, Forhad, 2020. Matching Frictions and Distorted Beliefs: Evidence from a Job Fairs Experiment. Mimeo.

Alfonsi, Livia, Bandiera, Oriana, Bassi, Vittorio, Burgess, Robin, Rasul, Imran, Sulaiman, Munshi, Vitali, Anna, 2020. Tackling youth unemployment: evidence from a labour market experiment in Uganda. Econometrica 88 (6), 2369–2414.

Allcott, Hunt, Lockwood, Benjamin B., Taubinsky, Dmitry, 2019. Should we tax sugar-sweetened beverages? An overview of theory and evidence. The Journal of Economic Perspectives 33 (3), 202–227.

Altmann, Steffen, Falk, Armin, Jäger, Simon, Zimmermann, Florian, 2018. Learning about job search: a field experiment with job seekers in Germany. Journal of Public Economics 164, 33–49.

Alvarez, Fernando E., Borovickova, Katarina, Shimer, Robert, 2016. Decomposing Duration Dependence in a Stopping Time Model. NBER Working Paper No. 22188.

Arni, Patrick, 2017. What's in the Blackbox? The Effect of Labor Market Policy on Job Search Behavior, Beliefs and Non-cognitive Skills. A Field Experiment. IZA Discussion Paper 9617.

Baicker, Katherine, Mullainathan, Sendhil, Schwartzstein, Joshua, 2015. Behavioral hazard in health insurance. The Quarterly Journal of Economics 130 (4), 1623–1667.

Baily, Martin Neil, 1978. Some aspects of optimal unemployment insurance. Journal of Public Economics 10 (3), 379–402.

Balleer, Almut, Duernecker, Georg, Forstner, Susanne, Goensch, Johannes, 2021. Perceived and Actual Labor Market Risk. Mimeo.

Bandiera, Oriana, Bassi, Vittorio, Burgess, Robin, Rasul, Imran, Sulaiman, Munshi, Vitali, Anna, 2021. The Search for Good Jobs: Evidence from a Six-year Field Experiment in Uganda. Mimeo.

Banerjee, Abhijit V., Sequeira, Sandra, 2021. Spatial mismatches and imperfect information in the job search. CEPR Discussion Paper No. 14414.

Belot, Michele, Kircher, Philipp, Muller, Paul, 2019. Providing advice to jobseekers at low cost: an experimental study on online advice. The Review of Economic Studies 86 (4), 1411–1447.

Bénabou, Roland, Tirole, Jean, 2002. Self-confidence and personal motivation. The Quarterly Journal of Economics 117 (3), 871–915.

Bernheim, B. Douglas, Taubinsky, Dmitry, 2018. Behavioral public economics. In: Handbook of Behavioral Economics: Applications and Foundations, vol. 1, pp. 381–516.

Bikhchandani, Sushil, Sharma, Sunil, 1996. Optimal search with learning. Journal of Economic Dynamics and Control 20 (1), 333–359.

Brunnermeier, Markus K., Parker, Jonathan A., 2005. Optimal expectations. The American Economic Review 95 (4), 1092–1118.

Campbell, David, Carruth, Alan, Dickerson, Andrew, Green, Francis, 2007. Job insecurity and wages. The Economic Journal 117 (518), 544–566.

Card, David, Mas, Alexandre, Moretti, Enrico, Saez, Emmanuel, 2012. Inequality at work: the effect of peer salaries on job satisfaction. The American Economic Review 102 (6), 2981–3003.

Chamberlain, Gary, 1984. Panel data. Handbook of Econometrics 2, 1247–1318.

Chetty, Raj, 2006. A general formula for the optimal level of social insurance. Journal of Public Economics 90 (10–11), 1879–1901.

Conlon, John J., Pilossoph, Laura, Wiswall, Matthew, Zafar, Basit, 2018. Labor Market Search with Imperfect Information and Learning. NBER Working Paper No. 24988.

Cooper, Michael, Kuhn, Peter, 2020. Behavioral Job Search. Springer International Publishing, Cham.

Cortés, Patricia, Pan, Jessica, Pilossoph, Laura, Zafar, Basit, 2021. Gender Differences in Job Search and the Earnings Gap: Evidence from Business Majors. NBER Working Paper No. 28820.

Curtin, Richard T., 2003. Unemployment expectations: the impact of private information on income uncertainty. The Review of Income and Wealth 49 (4), 539–554.

de la Rosa, Leonidas Enrique, 2011. Overconfidence and moral hazard. Games and Economic Behavior 73 (2), 429–451.

DellaVigna, Stefano, Heining, Joerg, Schmieder, Johannes F., Trenkle, Simon, 2020. Evidence on Job Search Models from a Survey of Unemployed Workers in Germany. Mimeo.

DellaVigna, Stefano, Paserman, M. Daniele, 2005. Job search and impatience. Journal of Labor Economics 23 (3), 527–588.

Drahs, Sascha, Haywood, Luke, Schiprowski, Amelie, 2018. Job Search with Subjective Wage Expectations. Mimeo.

Dubra, Juan, 2004. Optimism and overconfidence in search. Review of Economic Dynamics 7 (1), 198–218.

Emmler, Julian, Fitzenberger, Bernd, 2021. Temporary overpessimism: Job loss expectations following a large negative employment shock. IZA Discussion Paper No. 14149.

Ericson, Keith Marzilli, Kircher, Philipp, Spinnewijn, Johannes, Starc, Amanda, 2021. Inferring risk perceptions and preferences using choice from insurance menus: theory and evidence. The Economic Journal 131 (634), 713–744.

Faberman, R. Jason, Mueller, Andreas I., Sahin, Aysegul, Topa, Giorgio, 2022. Job search behavior among the employed and non-employed. Econometrica 90 (4), 1743–1779.

Falk, Armin, Huffman, David B., Sunde, Uwe, 2006. Self-Confidence and Search. IZA Discussion Paper No. 2525.

Fang, Hanming, Moscarini, Giuseppe, 2005. Morale hazard. Journal of Monetary Economics 52 (4), 749–777.

Farhi, Emmanuel, Gabaix, Xavier, 2020. Optimal taxation with behavioral agents. The American Economic Review 110 (1), 298–336.

Federal Reserve Bank of New York, 2012–2019. Survey of consumer expectations. https://www.newyorkfed.org/microeconomics/sce/.

Ganong, Peter, Noel, Pascal, 2019. Consumer spending during unemployment: positive and normative implications. The American Economic Review 109 (7), 2383–2424.

Hall, Robert E., Mueller, Andreas I., 2018. Wage dispersion and search behavior: the importance of non-wage job values. Journal of Political Economy 126 (4), 1594–1637.

Heckman, James J., Singer, B., 1984. The identifiability of the proportional hazard model. The Review of Economic Studies 51 (2), 231.

Heifetz, Aviad, Segev, Ella, Talley, Eric, 2007b. Market design with endogenous preferences. Games and Economic Behavior 58 (1), 121–153.

Heifetz, Aviad, Shannon, Chris, Spiegel, Yossi, 2007a. The dynamic evolution of preferences. Economic Theory 32 (2), 251–286.

Hendren, Nathaniel, 2013. Private information and insurance rejections. Econometrica 81 (5), 1713–1762.

Hendren, Nathaniel, 2017. Knowledge of future job loss and implications for unemployment insurance. The American Economic Review 107 (7), 1778–1823.

Hendren, Nathaniel, Landais, Camille, Spinnewijn, Johannes, 2020. Choice in insurance markets: a pigouvian approach to social insurance design. Annual Review of Economics, 13.

Hoffman, Mitchell, Burks, Stephen V., 2017. Worker overconfidence: Field evidence and implications for employee turnover and returns from training. NBER Working Paper No. 23240.

Holzer, Harry J., 1988. Search method use by unemployed youth. Journal of Labor Economics 6 (1), 1–20.

Honoré, Bo E., 1993. Identification results for duration models with multiple spells. The Review of Economic Studies 60 (1), 241–246.

Hornstein, Andreas, Krusell, Per, Violante, Giovanni L., 2011. Frictional wage dispersion in search models: a quantitative assessment. The American Economic Review 101 (7), 2873–2898.

Jäger, Simon, Roth, Christopher, Roussille, Nina, Schoefer, Benjamin, 2021. Worker Beliefs About Outside Options. NBER Working Paper No. 29623.

Jappelli, Tullio, Pistaferri, Luigi, 2010. The consumption response to income changes. Annual Review of Economics 2 (1), 479–506.

Kahneman, Daniel, Slovic, Stewart Paul, Slovic, Paul, Tversky, Amos, 1982. Judgment Under Uncertainty: Heuristics and Biases. Cambridge University Press.

Krueger, Alan B., Mueller, Andreas I., 2011. Job search, emotional well-being, and job finding in a period of mass unemployment: evidence from high-frequency longitudinal data. Brookings Papers on Economic Activity, Spring 1 (1), 1–70.

Krueger, Alan B., Mueller, Andreas I., 2016. A contribution to the empirics of reservation wages. American Economic Journal: Economic Policy 8 (1), 142–179.

Kuchler, Theresa, Zafar, Basit, 2019. Personal experiences and expectations about aggregate outcomes. The Journal of Finance 74 (5), 2491–2542.

Kunda, Ziva, 1990. The case for motivated reasoning. Psychological Bulletin 108 (3), 480.

Landais, Camille, Nekoei, Arash, Nilsson, Peter, Seim, David, Spinnewijn, Johannes, 2021. Risk-based selection in unemployment insurance: evidence and implications. The American Economic Review 111 (4), 1315–1355.

Lizama, Carlos, Villena-Roldán, Benjamín, 2021. Avoiding Layoffs: on-the-job Search and Partial Insurance. Technical Report.

Machin, Stephen, Manning, Alan, 1999. The causes and consequences of longterm unemployment in Europe. In: Ashenfelter, Orley C., Card, David (Eds.), Handbook of Labor Economics, vol. 3, Part C. Elsevier, pp. 3085–3139.

Malmendier, Ulrike, Tate, Geoffrey, 2008. Who makes acquisitions? CEO overconfidence and the market's reaction. Journal of Financial Economics 89 (1), 20–43.

Manski, Charles, Straub, John, 2000. Worker perceptions of job insecurity in the mid-1990s: evidence from the survey of economic expectations. The Journal of Human Resources 06 (35), 447–479.

Manski, Charles F., 1993. Dynamic choice in social settings: learning from the experiences of others. Journal of Econometrics 58 (1–2), 121–136.

Manski, Charles F., 2002. Identification of decision rules in experiments on simple games of proposal and response. European Economic Review 46 (4–5), 880–891.

Manski, Charles F., 2004. Measuring expectations. Econometrica 72 (5), 1329–1376.

Marinescu, Ioana, Skandalis, Daphné, 2021. Unemployment insurance and job search behavior. The Quarterly Journal of Economics 136 (2), 887–931.

Menzio, Guido, 2020. Stubborn Beliefs in Search Equilibrium. Mimeo.

Mitra, Anushka, 2021. Macroeconomic Sentiments and the Job Search Behavior of Labor Market Participants. Mimeo.

Moore, Don A., Healy, Paul J., 2008. The trouble with overconfidence. Psychological Review 115 (2), 502.

Morrison, William, Taubinsky, Dmitry, 2019. Rules of thumb and attention elasticities: Evidence from under-and overreaction to taxes. NBER Working Paper No. 26180.

Mueller, Andreas I., Spinnewijn, Johannes, Topa, Giorgio, 2021. Job seekers' perceptions and employment prospects: heterogeneity, duration dependence, and bias. The American Economic Review 111 (1), 324–363.

Pettinicchi, Yuri, Vellekoop, Nathanael, 2019. Job loss expectations, durable consumption and household finances: Evidence from linked survey data. SAFE Working Paper.

Pistaferri, Luigi, 2001. Superior information, income shocks, and the permanent income hypothesis. Review of Economics and Statistics 83 (3), 465–476.

Potter, Tristan, 2021. Learning and job search dynamics during the Great Recession. Journal of Monetary Economics 117, 706–722.

Price, Richard H., Friedland, Daniel S., Vinokur, Anuram D., 1998. Job loss: hard times and eroded identity. In: Perspectives on Loss: A Sourcebook, pp. 303–316.

Rabin, Matthew, Vayanos, Dimitri, 2010. The gambler's and hot-hand fallacies: theory and applications. The Review of Economic Studies 77 (2), 730–778.

Roth, Christopher, Wohlfart, Johannes, 2020. How do expectations about the macroeconomy affect personal expectations and behavior? Review of Economics and Statistics 102 (4), 731–748.

Roussille, Nina, 2021. The central role of the ask gap in gender pay inequality. Mimeo.

Santos-Pinto, Luís, 2008. Positive self-image and incentives in organisations. The Economic Journal 118 (531), 1315–1332.

Santos-Pinto, Luis, de la Rosa, Leonidas Enrique, 2020. Overconfidence in labor markets. In: Handbook of Labor, Human Resources and Population Economics, pp. 1–42.

Schlag, Karl H., Tremewan, James, van der Weele, Joël J., 2015. A penny for your thoughts: a survey of methods for eliciting beliefs. Experimental Economics 18 (3), 457–490.

Schlag, Karl H., van der Weele, Joël J., 2015. A method to elicit beliefs as most likely intervals. Judgment and Decision Making 10 (5).

Spinnewijn, Johannes, 2008. Unemployed, but Optimistic: Optimal Insurance Design with Biased Beliefs. Mimeo.

Spinnewijn, Johannes, 2013. Training and search during unemployment. Journal of Public Economics 99, 49–65.

Spinnewijn, Johannes, 2015. Unemployed but optimistic: optimal insurance design with biased beliefs. Journal of the European Economic Association 13 (1), 130–167.

Spinnewijn, Johannes, 2017. Heterogeneity, demand for insurance, and adverse selection. American Economic Journal: Economic Policy 9 (1), 308–343.

Stephens, Melvin, 2004. Job loss expectations, realizations, and household consumption behavior. Review of Economics and Statistics 86 (1), 253–269.

van den Steen, Eric, 2004. Rational overoptimism (and other biases). The American Economic Review 94 (4), 1141–1151.

van der Klaauw, Wilbert, 2012. On the use of expectations data in estimating structural dynamic choice models. Journal of Labor Economics 30 (3), 521–554.

Theories of expectations 4

Bayesian learning[☆]

Isaac Baley[a,b,c,d] **and Laura Veldkamp**[e,f,d]
[a] University of Pompeu Fabra, Barcelona, Spain
[b] Center for Research in International Economics, Barcelona, Spain
[c] Barcelona School of Economics, Barcelona, Spain
[d] CEPR, London, United Kingdom
[e] Columbia University, New York, NY, United States
[f] NBER, Cambridge, MA, United States

23.1 Introduction

This chapter focuses on Bayesian learning. Learning is the process by which agents form beliefs. While many of the previous chapters consider how to measure beliefs, this chapter uses Bayesian tools to consider how agents form beliefs and the types of consequences these beliefs have for economic outcomes. In one class of models, agents know the true model of the economy and are only uncertain about which realization of the state will be drawn by nature. They use additional pieces of information (e.g., noisy signals) to form expectations about the state. In another class of models, agents are uncertain about the distribution of the state and also use Bayes' law to infer its moments or its shape, using a sample of observations.

Among models with Bayesian learning, there are models of passive learning and models of active learning. In passive learning models, agents are endowed with signals and/or learn as an unintended consequence of observing prices and quantities. One set of examples is models in which information is exogenous. Information may be an endowment or it may arrive stochastically. Endogenous information can also be learned passively. For example, information could be conveyed by market prices. This is still passive learning, because agents are not exercising any control over the information they observe.

Active learning is intentional. Information is chosen or is the direct result of a choice. This choice might involve purchasing information, choosing how to allocate limited attention, or choosing an action, while taking into account the information it will generate. Such models go beyond explaining the consequences of having information; they also predict what information agents will choose to have. Because an active-learning model can predict information sets on the basis of observable features of the

☆ For useful discussions and feedback, we thank Vladimir Asriyan, Andrés Blanco, Ana Figueiredo, Manolis Galenianos, Benjamin Hébert, Chad Jones, Boyan Jovanovic, Julian Kozlowski, Albert Marcet, Jordi Mondrià, Kristoffer Nimark, Luigi Paciello, Lubos Pastor, Luminita Stevens, Robert Ulbricht, Victoria Vanasco, Mirko Wiederholt, and Michael Woodford. Erfan Ghofrani, Ángelo Gutiérrez, Marta Morazzoni, Alejandro Rábano, and Judy Yue provided excellent research assistance. Baley acknowledges financial support from the Spanish Ministry of Economy and Competitiveness, through the Severo Ochoa Programme for Centres of Excellence in R&D (CEX2019-000915-S).

economic environment, pairing it with a passive-learning model in which information predicts observable outcomes results in a model in which observables predict observables. Such a model is typically empirically testable.

Economists often use the term learning to refer to a literature in which agents do not use Bayes' law to form their expectations. One example is adaptive least-squares learning, in which agents behave as econometricians, trying to discover the optimal linear forecasting rule for the next period's state. Evans and Honkapohja (2001) offer an exhaustive treatment of this literature. That is not our focus.

The chapter is organized as follows. Section 23.2 introduces a small set of mathematical tools needed to understand the material. Section 23.3 studies the implications of learning for economic activity given a set of beliefs. We discuss passive learning in signal extraction problems and coordination games with strategic motives in actions and in the use of information. Section 23.4 discusses several motives for active information acquisition and the most commonly used learning technologies. Finally, Section 23.5 surveys the growing literature on the data economy, in which economic activity generates data and the information in the data feeds back to affect economic activity. Within each section, we first describe the tools and then survey the many ways in which these tools have been used to answer important questions in economics and finance.

23.2 Mathematical preliminaries

A few basic concepts and mathematical tools are needed to understand this chapter. Bayes' law for univariate normal continuous variables appears repeatedly. In dynamic settings, this becomes the Kalman filter. For formal derivations and generalizations of Bayes' law and the Kalman filter, see Liptser and Shiryaev (2001) and Bernardo and Smith (2009).

23.2.1 Bayesian updating

Bayes' law

The probability of event A occurring, given that event B occurred, is

$$P(A|B) = \frac{P(B|A)P(A)}{P(B)}, \quad \text{with} \quad P(B) \neq 0. \tag{23.1}$$

This law comes from the definition of a conditional probability, $P(A|B) = P(A \cap B)/P(B)$.

For continuous random variables with smooth distributions, the probability of any discrete realization is zero. However, Bayes' law can also be applied to probability densities. Let f be a continuous random variable with a smooth distribution. Then the probability density of event A, given that event B occurred, is

$$f(A|B) = \frac{f(B|A)f(A)}{f(B)}, \quad \text{where} \quad f(B) = \int_{-\infty}^{\infty} f(B|A)f(A)\,dA. \tag{23.2}$$

Bayes' law for normal random variables

Suppose there is an unknown random variable θ and, according to agent's prior beliefs, $\theta \sim \mathcal{N}(\mu_\theta, \tau_\theta^{-1})$. In other words, before observing any additional information, θ was believed to be μ_θ

on average, with a precision of τ_θ. Note that the precision is the inverse of the variance (not the standard deviation). We will work with precisions because doing so generally renders the solutions simpler. Also, the agent sees a signal

$$s = \theta + \eta, \quad \eta \sim \mathcal{N}(0, \tau_s^{-1}). \tag{23.3}$$

The signal is an unbiased piece of data about θ with precision τ_s and is *conditionally independent* of $\mu_\theta - \theta$. That means that signals and priors are related only because they are both informative about θ, but their errors are independent. Independence implies that $\mathbb{E}[(\mu_\theta - \theta)(s - \theta)] = 0$. Given the prior information and the signal, the agent forms a posterior belief, also called a conditional belief, about the value of θ using Bayes' law

$$\hat{\theta} \equiv \mathbb{E}[\theta|s] = \frac{\tau_\theta \mu_\theta + \tau_s s}{\tau_\theta + \tau_s}. \tag{23.4}$$

With normal random variables, the posterior belief is simply a weighted average of the prior belief and the signal. Each is weighted by its relative precision. If a signal contains no information about θ, it would have zero precision. In this case, the posterior belief would be the same as the prior belief. The posterior (or conditional) variance also has a simple form

$$\hat{\Sigma} \equiv \mathbb{V}ar[\theta|s] = \frac{1}{\tau_\theta + \tau_s}. \tag{23.5}$$

The posterior precision (the inverse of the variance $\hat{\Sigma}^{-1}$) equals the prior precision τ_θ plus the signal precision τ_s. Every additional piece of independent information adds precision to the estimation.[1]

Survey evidence and "information-provision experiments" confirm that economic agents revise their beliefs in response to new information in ways broadly consistent with Bayes' law. See, for instance, Coibion et al. (2019) and Coibion et al. (2021) for the case of households and Coibion et al. (2018) and Chapter 11 in this Handbook for the case of firms.

23.2.2 The Kalman filter

When applied in dynamic models, the formula for Bayesian updating with normal variables becomes the Kalman filter. This learning applies when agents know the distribution but care about forecasting the actual realization of the variable. We specialize the state θ_t to follow a first-order Markov process and let s_t be an unbiased signal about θ_t. The system consists of two equations, one for the hidden state and one for its noisy observation:

$$\theta_{t+1} = \rho\theta_t + \varepsilon_{t+1}, \quad \varepsilon_{t+1} \sim \mathcal{N}(0, \tau_\theta^{-1}), \tag{23.6}$$

$$s_t = \theta_t + \eta_t, \quad \eta_{t+1} \sim \mathcal{N}(0, \tau_s^{-1}). \tag{23.7}$$

The two shocks ε and η are mutually independent and i.i.d. over time. The parameters $\rho \leq 1$ and (τ_θ, τ_s) are known, and prior beliefs are $\theta_0 \sim \mathcal{N}(\hat{\theta}_0, \Sigma_0)$. For all $t > 0$, let $\hat{\theta}_t$ denote the expectation of

---

[1] This observation is not always true. For instance, when agents learn about binomial random variables (e.g., learning a proportion), additional observations may actually reduce precision.

θ_t conditional on all the signals s observed up to, but excluding, time t, $\hat{\theta}_t \equiv \mathbb{E}[\theta_t | s_0, \ldots, s_{t-1}]$. Also let $\hat{\Sigma}_t \equiv \mathbb{V}ar[\theta_t | s_0, \ldots, s_{t-1}] = \mathbb{E}[(\theta_t - \hat{\theta}_t)^2]$ denote the conditional variance of θ_t. The following three recursive formulas describe how to update the mean and variance of beliefs:

$$\hat{\theta}_{t+1} = \rho\hat{\theta}_t + K_t(s_t - \hat{\theta}_t), \tag{23.8}$$

$$K_t = \rho \frac{\tau_s}{\hat{\Sigma}_t^{-1} + \tau_s}, \tag{23.9}$$

$$\hat{\Sigma}_{t+1} = \rho^2 \frac{1}{\hat{\Sigma}_t^{-1} + \tau_s} + \frac{1}{\tau_\theta}. \tag{23.10}$$

The term K_t is called the *Kalman gain*. It represents how much weight is put on the new information $(s_t - \hat{\theta}_t)$, relative to the old information in the prior belief $\hat{\theta}_t$ when forming the posterior belief $\hat{\theta}_{t+1}$. The higher the signal precision τ_s, the higher the weight placed on news. The Kalman gain is the analog of the term $\tau_s/(\tau_\theta + \tau_s)$ in (23.4). The conditional variance $\hat{\Sigma}_{t+1}$ can be similarly interpreted as the recursive analog of the Bayesian updating formula for posterior variance in (23.5). It is the inverse of the posterior precision, which equals the sum of the prior and signal precisions.

23.2.3 Learning the distribution of the state

In many setups, agents know the true distribution, but learn about the current state. For some applications, it is important that the distribution of random variables is not known. Pastor and Veronesi (2009) review finance models with parameter learning in more detail. Here, we provide the basics to aid in understanding the papers that follow. We start with a simple case, in which an agent knows the distribution is normal and learns the mean and/or variance by observing a sample of i.i.d. realizations of the state.

23.2.3.1 *Learning the mean*

Assume that the true distribution of the state is $\theta \sim \mathcal{N}(\mu_\theta, \tau_\theta^{-1})$. Suppose an agent knows the precision τ_θ but does not know the mean μ_θ. She holds prior beliefs about the mean that are normal, $\mu_\theta \sim \mathcal{N}\left(\mu_0, \tau_0^{-1}\right)$. After observing an i.i.d. sample of t realizations of θ, which are included in her date-t information set $\mathcal{I}_t = \{\theta_r | r \leq t\}$, the posterior belief is also normal,[2] $\mu_\theta | \mathcal{I}_t \sim \mathcal{N}\left(\mu_t, \tau_t^{-1}\right)$. The parameters evolve as[3]

$$\mu_t = \frac{\tau_0\mu_0 + t\tau_\theta\overline{\theta}}{\tau_t}, \qquad \tau_t = \tau_0 + t\tau_\theta, \qquad \overline{\theta} = \frac{1}{t}\sum_{r=1}^{t} \theta_r. \tag{23.11}$$

The posterior belief $\mu_t = \mathbb{E}[\mu_\theta | \mathcal{I}_t]$ is a weighted average of the prior mean μ_0 and the sample mean $\overline{\theta}$. The posterior precision $\tau_t = \mathbb{V}ar[\mu_\theta | \mathcal{I}_t]^{-1}$ is the sum of the prior precision τ_0 and the sample precision

---

[2] When prior and posterior distributions are in the same probability distribution family, as in this example, we say that they are conjugate distributions. Working with conjugate distributions is very tractable. Both normal and normal-gamma (used in the next section) are self-conjugate families.

[3] The Kalman filter formulas can be used to learn the mean by setting $\rho = 1$ and $\tau_\theta^{-1} = 0$.

$t\tau_\theta$, which grows linearly with the number of observations. As the number of observations increases ($t \to \infty$), the posterior belief converges to the sample mean $\mu_t \to \bar{\theta}$ and precision goes to infinity (uncertainty disappears), and since the sample mean converges to the true mean $\bar{\theta} \to \mu_\theta$, the truth is eventually revealed. In Section 23.3.1.2, we extensively discuss the literature that applies this type of learning structure to learn about a fixed characteristic (e.g., a worker's ability).

23.2.3.2 *Learning the precision*

Next, we consider a setting in which the precision is not known. With an i.i.d. data sample $\mathcal{I}_t = \{\theta_r | r \le t\}$, an agent now simultaneously learns about the mean and the precision of θ_t. The standard way to formalize this problem is to use a joint normal-gamma distribution. The precision is assumed to follow a gamma distribution $\tau_\theta \sim \Gamma(\alpha, \beta)$, with density $f(x|\alpha, \beta) \propto (\beta x)^{\alpha-1} e^{-\beta x}$, mean α/β and precision β^2/α. Conditional on the precision, the mean is normal. This formulation is convenient because when a normal mean and gamma precision are updated with data drawn from that same type of distribution, the posterior beliefs will also involve a normally distributed mean and a gamma-distributed precision. Given prior beliefs $\mu_\theta | \tau_\theta \sim \mathcal{N}\left(\mu_0, (\kappa_0\tau_\theta)^{-1}\right)$ and $\tau_\theta \sim \Gamma(\alpha_0, \beta_0)$, the posterior belief about the mean is $\mu_\theta | (\mathcal{I}_t, \tau_\theta) \sim \mathcal{N}\left(\mu_t, (\kappa_t\tau_\theta)^{-1}\right)$, with

$$\mu_t = \frac{\kappa_0\mu_0 + t\bar{\theta}}{\kappa_t}, \qquad \kappa_t = \kappa_0 + t, \qquad \bar{\theta} = \frac{1}{t}\sum_{r=1}^{t}\theta_r. \tag{23.12}$$

In turn, the parameters that govern the precision's posterior distribution $\tau_\theta | \mathcal{I}_t \sim \Gamma(\alpha_t, \beta_t)$ evolve as

$$\alpha_t = \alpha_0 + \frac{t}{2}, \qquad \beta_t = \beta_0 + \frac{1}{2}\left[\sum_{r=1}^{t}\left(\theta_r - \bar{\theta}\right)^2 + \frac{t\kappa_0(\bar{\theta} - \mu_0)^2}{\kappa_t}\right], \tag{23.13}$$

where $\mathbb{E}[\tau_\theta | \mathcal{I}_t] = \alpha_t/\beta_t$ and $\mathbb{V}ar[\tau_\theta | \mathcal{I}_t]^{-1} = \beta_t^2/\alpha_t$. As the sample size increases ($t \to \infty$), the posterior belief about the mean μ_t in (23.12) converges to the true value μ_θ and belief uncertainty goes to zero $\kappa_t^{-1} = 0$. Regarding the beliefs about the precision, both α_t and β_t in (23.13) go to infinity, but their ratio α_t/β_t converges to the true precision τ_θ and belief uncertainty goes to zero.

The normal-gamma approach is implemented by Cogley and Sargent (2005) to estimate the parameters of central bank policy rules and by Weitzman (2007), Bakshi and Skoulakis (2010), and Collin Dufresne et al. (2016) to study asset-pricing puzzles. Ghofrani (2021) shows that this framework generates persistent impacts of tail-event shocks.

23.2.3.3 *Nonparametric learning*

Finally, we consider a case where the functional form of the probability density is not known. Agents use an i.i.d. data sample $\mathcal{I}_t = \{\theta_r | r \le t\}$ to construct a frequentist (not Bayesian) estimate $\hat{f}_t$ of the true density f. A simple approach is to use a normal kernel density estimator

$$\hat{f}_t(\theta) = \frac{1}{tb_t}\sum_{s=0}^{t-1}\phi\left(\frac{\theta - \theta_{t-s}}{b_t}\right). \tag{23.14}$$

Here $\phi(\cdot)$ is the standard normal density function and b_t is the bandwidth parameter. As new data arrive, agents add the new observation to their data set and update their estimates, generating a sequence of beliefs $\{\hat{f}_t\}$. Belief changes tend to be very persistent, even if the θ_t shocks that caused the beliefs to change are transitory. This persistence arises from the martingale property of beliefs: On average, expected future beliefs are the same as current beliefs. As a result, any changes in beliefs induced by new information are approximately permanent. Kozlowski et al. (2020a,b) use this mechanism to generate belief scarring that explains the persistent effects of the Great Recession and the COVID pandemic.

23.3 Using signals to understand economic activity

This section examines the mechanisms though which agents' information affects economic activity. In this section, we take the agents' information sets as given. In other words, learning here is passive. First, we describe signal-extraction problems, in which agents try to disentangle permanent from transitory shocks or aggregate from idiosyncratic shocks. Then, we explore coordination games, in which strategic motives in actions render the use of information strategic as well.

23.3.1 Signal-extraction problems

In this environment, an agent's payoff depends on the distance from her action to an unknown stochastic target. This type of quadratic tracking problem is common because it is tractable. Also, one can map many models onto this framework by approximating objectives quadratically.

23.3.1.1 A tracking problem

The economy is populated by a continuum of agents indexed by $i \in [0, 1]$. Every agent chooses a continuous action $a_{it} \in \mathbb{R}$ to minimize the expected distance between her action and an unknown exogenous target a_{it}^* drawn by nature. Each agent solves the following problem:

$$\mathcal{L} = \min_{\{a_{it}\}_{t=0}^{\infty}} \mathbb{E}\left[\sum_{t=0}^{\infty} \beta^t (a_{it} - a_{it}^*)^2 \,\Big|\, \mathcal{I}_{i0}\right], \tag{23.15}$$

where $\beta < 1$ is the discount factor and $\mathcal{I}_{it}$ denotes agent i's information set at date t. Adding and subtracting the posterior belief $\hat{a}_{it}^* \equiv \mathbb{E}[a_{it}^*|\mathcal{I}_{it}]$ inside the payoff, distributing the expectation, and using the law of iterated expectations, we rewrite the problem in terms of posterior beliefs:

$$\mathcal{L} = \min_{\{a_{it}\}_{t=0}^{\infty}} \sum_{t=0}^{\infty} \beta^t \mathbb{E}\left[(a_{it} - \hat{a}_{it}^*)^2 |\mathcal{I}_{it}\right] + \sum_{t=0}^{\infty} \beta^t \hat{\Sigma}_{it}, \tag{23.16}$$

where we use the orthogonality of expectational errors $\mathbb{E}[(a_{it} - \hat{a}_{it}^*)(a_{it}^* - \hat{a}_{it}^*)|\mathcal{I}_{it}] = 0$ and define the posterior variance $\hat{\Sigma}_{it} \equiv \mathbb{E}[(\hat{a}_{it}^* - a_{it}^*)^2|\mathcal{I}_{it}]$. The problem is equivalent to minimizing the distance between actions and beliefs; the additional term involving the series of conditional variances $\{\hat{\Sigma}_{it}\}$ is a sunk cost that decreases utility but cannot be controlled by the agent because learning is passive. The first-order condition implies that the optimal action is the expected value of the target action,

$$a_{it} = \hat{a}_{it}^*. \tag{23.17}$$

The next two variants of this problem have different stochastic processes for the target action a_{it}^*.

23.3.1.2 Permanent vs. transitory shocks

In this class of models, the target action is idiosyncratic; it is specific to an individual. But a_{it}^* experiences permanent shocks and transitory shocks. Agents cannot distinguish between these permanent and transitory shocks, and their confusion is what generates interesting learning dynamics.

Suppose the target is an unknown, idiosyncratic, and fixed trait[4]

$$a_{it}^* = \theta_i. \tag{23.18}$$

The problem is analogous to learning a parameter (as in Section 23.2.3.1). Agents receive unbiased signals $s_{it} = \theta_i + \eta_{it}$ with noise $\eta \sim_{iid} \mathcal{N}(0, \tau_s^{-1})$. The transitory term prevents agents from backing out the permanent trait. Posterior beliefs are formed using the Kalman formulas in (23.8), (23.9), and (23.10) with $\rho = 1$ and $\tau_\theta^{-1} = 0$. Given initial values $(\hat{a}_{i0}, \hat{\Sigma}_{i0})$, the target forecast and its uncertainty evolve according to

$$\hat{\theta}_{it+1} = \hat{\theta}_{it} + \frac{\tau_s}{\hat{\Sigma}_{it}^{-1} + \tau_s}(s_{it} - \hat{\theta}_{it}); \qquad \hat{\Sigma}_{it+1}^{-1} = \hat{\Sigma}_{it}^{-1} + \tau_s. \tag{23.19}$$

Early applications of this setup were examined in labor markets. In Jovanovic (1979, 1984), worker–firm match quality—a fixed trait—is an experience good that is gradually revealed by noisy output performance. Learning generates a selection effect: Only the relationships with high match quality survive and job tenure becomes a sufficient statistic for match quality and uncertainty. Besides learning about a match-specific productivity term (Pries and Rogerson, 2005; Nagypál, 2007; Menzio and Shi, 2011), learning can be about innate worker skills in different occupations (Miller, 1984; Neal, 1999; Moscarini, 2001; Groes et al., 2014; Papageorgiou, 2014; Wee, 2016; Baley et al., 2021) or firm characteristics (Borovicková, 2016). In Gonzalez and Shi (2010) and Doppelt (2016), informational dynamics are driven by unemployment, as the posterior probability of being high skilled worsens with the length of unemployment spells.

Learning about idiosyncratic characteristics through noisy signals has also been used to examine technology choice (Jovanovic and Nyarko, 1996); entrepreneurship (Minniti and Bygrave, 2001); firm profitability (Pástor et al., 2009); exporters' demand (Timoshenko, 2015; Berman et al., 2019); durable consumption (Luo et al., 2015); firms' life-cycle (Arkolakis et al., 2018; Chen et al., 2020); and the impact of government policy (Pastor and Veronesi, 2012). Policymakers may also behave as Bayesian agents when learning about climate change parameters (Kelly and Kolstad, 1999) or the trade-off between inflation and unemployment (Cogley and Sargent, 2005; Sargent et al., 2006; Primiceri, 2006).

On the empirical front, Lee and Moretti (2009) use high-frequency data from political prediction markets to show that investors process information contained in polls in a Bayesian way. Others test learning by exploiting *tenure*—the duration of a relationship—as a proxy for uncertainty. Farber and Gibbons (1996) show that the wages of long-tenured workers correlate more with unobserved skills

---

[4] More generally, the target may follow a persistent process as in Section 23.2.2.

(measured via test scores); Kellogg (2011) shows that the productivity of an oil company and its drilling contractor increases with their joint experience; and Botsch and Vanasco (2019) show that loan terms become more correlated with unobserved firm characteristics as the duration of the lender–creditor relationship increases. Lastly, another set of papers exploits dynamic cross-sectional moments in the microdata, such as hazard rates, to discipline the speed of learning and recover the dynamics of information sets. Álvarez et al. (2011), Baley and Blanco (2019) and Argente and Yeh (2022) use price-adjustment hazards while Borovicková (2016) and Baley et al. (2021) use job separation hazards.

Keeping uncertainty alive

According to (23.10), belief uncertainty (forecast error variance) $\hat{\Sigma}_{it}$ continuously decreases until it reaches a minimum value in the long run. In particular, when agents learn about a fixed characteristic as in (23.19), uncertainty eventually disappears, $\hat{\Sigma}_\infty \equiv \lim_{t \to \infty} \hat{\Sigma}_{it} = 0$. In the cross-section, differences in uncertainty also disappear. In some setups, this is not a desirable feature—especially when models aim to explain the cross-sectional differences in uncertainty observed in the data.

The literature proposes various mechanisms to keep uncertainty dynamics active and to generate cross-sectional dispersion in uncertainty. Baley and Blanco (2019) develop a menu cost price-setting model in which firm productivity θ_i is subject to occasional shocks (fat-tail risk). Learning about fat-tailed shocks generates uncertainty cycles that translate into cross-sectional dispersion in the frequency of price adjustment and amplify the real effects of monetary policy. Senga (2018) explores the role of uncertainty cycles in a model with heterogeneous firms in explaining the level and cyclicality of the cross-sectional dispersion of sales growth. In Baley et al. (2021), uncertainty about workers' abilities jumps up when they endogenously switch their occupation and start learning about a new set of occupation-specific abilities. Uncertainty cycles about worker abilities explain features of labor market dynamics at the micro and macro levels.

23.3.1.3 *Aggregate vs. idiosyncratic shocks*

Agents can also be confused between aggregate and idiosyncratic factors. Suppose that the target action a_{it}^* is now a linear combination of an aggregate factor common across agents θ_t and an individual factor v_{it} specific to agent i,

$$a_{it}^* = (1 - r)\theta_t + r(v_{it} - \theta_t), \quad \text{with} \quad r \in [0, 1]. \tag{23.20}$$

For simplicity, the aggregate shock follows a random walk $\theta_t = \theta_{t-1} + \varepsilon_t$ with $\varepsilon_t \sim \mathcal{N}(0, \tau_\theta^{-1})$ and the idiosyncratic shock is i.i.d. across time and agents $v_{it} \sim \mathcal{N}(0, \tau_v^{-1})$. One noisy signal provides information about the sum of the two components $s_{it} = \theta_t + v_{it} + \eta_{it}$, with a common noise distribution $\eta_{it} \sim \mathcal{N}(0, \tau_s^{-1})$. With one signal and two shocks, agents cannot disentangle the components and mistakenly attribute part of an aggregate shock ϵ_t to an idiosyncratic shock v_{it}.

The confusion between aggregate and idiosyncratic shocks is at the core of the islands model of Phelps (1970) and Lucas (1972). In each island i, a representative agent chooses how much to work a_{it}, depending on the demand for her own good v_{it} relative to the aggregate demand θ_t. Setting $r = 1$, agents would like to work more only if they believe their relative price $v_{it} - \theta_t$ is high. Thus the nature of the shock matters. Agents see their own price s_{it}, but cannot tell whether their price is high because nominal demand θ_t is high or because island-specific real demand v_{it} is high. This mechanism gives rise to monetary nonneutrality. When money is abundant, aggregate demand increases, and most agents observe a high price for their good. Since they cannot disentangle the source of higher demand, they work harder and produce more. Money has real effects.

Hellwig and Venkateswaran (2009) also investigate the implications of signals that combine aggregate and idiosyncratic shocks, but in a nominal price-setting context in which firms choose their price a_{it} to be close to the target. Setting $r \in [0, 1/2]$ in (23.20), the optimal price depends positively on aggregate and idiosyncratic factors. In this case, the exact nature of the shock matters little for optimal pricing. When an aggregate shock occurs, firms mistakenly attribute it to a firm-specific shock, but adjust prices nevertheless. This increases the responsiveness to aggregate nominal shocks and reduces monetary nonneutrality. In the same spirit, Venkateswaran (2014) introduces confusion between idiosyncratic and aggregate productivity to a frictional labor market and argues that the increased responsiveness to aggregate shocks explains the large volatility in empirically observed labor market outcomes.

23.3.2 Using signals in strategic settings

We now consider coordination games. In Section 23.3.1, agents minimized the distance of actions from an unknown, exogenous state. In contrast, agents now also consider the distance between their action and the average action in the economy—which is an endogenous outcome. We introduce coordination motives through the target action a_{it}^*, which is a linear combination of an exogenous stochastic state θ_t and the average action in the economy a_t:

$$a_{it}^* = (1-r)\theta_t + ra_t, \quad \text{where} \quad a_t \equiv \int_0^1 a_{it}\, di, \quad \text{and} \quad r \in [-1, 1]. \tag{23.21}$$

The parameter r governs the type of strategic interaction. If $r = 0$, the optimal action is independent of the actions of others, as in the models in Section 23.3.1.2. When $r \neq 0$, actions become strategic. If $r > 0$, there is strategic complementarity, as the optimal action is increasing in the actions of others. If $r < 0$, there is strategic substitutability, as the optimal action is decreasing in the actions of others.

Next, we examine how coordination motives in actions generate coordination motives in the use of information. We make this point in a passive learning model in which information is exogenous. Section 23.4.6 revisits these models in the context of active learning models. Chapter 20 in this Handbook also uses this strategic setting to analyze how incomplete information and bounded rationality affect the response of aggregate outcomes to aggregate shocks. In their language, the direct effect of the fundamental θ—the first term in (23.21)—corresponds to partial equilibrium (PE) responses, while the indirect effect of θ through the average action a—the second term in (23.21)—corresponds to general equilibrium (GE) responses.

23.3.2.1 A beauty contest with exogenous signals

We simplify the tracking problem in (23.15) to a static model. Each agent chooses their action a_i to minimize the expected distance to the common target $a^* = (1-r)\theta + ra$, where $a \equiv \int_0^1 a_i\, di$ is the average action and θ is an unknown, exogenous state. Each agent solves the following problem:

$$\mathcal{L} = \min_{a_i} \mathbb{E}\left[(a_i - (1-r)\theta - ra)^2 \big| \mathcal{I}_i\right]. \tag{23.22}$$

The order of events is as follows. Nature draws the state θ from a normal distribution $\mathcal{N}(\mu_\theta, \tau_\theta^{-1})$ with mean μ_θ and precision τ_θ. These parameters are common knowledge and summarize all prior public information. Second, each agent receives a public signal z and private signal s that reveal additional information about the state: $z = \theta + \eta_z$ with $\eta_z \sim \mathcal{N}(0, \tau_z^{-1})$ and $s_i = \theta + \eta_{s,i}$ with $\eta_{s,i} \sim_{iid} \mathcal{N}(0, \tau_s^{-1})$, independent of s_j and z. The signals' precisions τ_z and τ_s are equal across agents. Finally, given their information set $\mathcal{I}_i = \{z, s_i\}$, each agent forms beliefs about θ and a, chooses an action a_i, and payoffs are realized. We look for a symmetric Nash equilibrium to solve the game.

Beliefs and equilibrium

According to the first-order condition, the optimal action is a convex combination of the belief about the state and the belief about the average action

$$a_i = (1-r)\mathbb{E}[\theta|\mathcal{I}_i] + r\mathbb{E}[a|\mathcal{I}_i]. \tag{23.23}$$

Averaging across agents, we get the average action as a function of the average beliefs

$$a = (1-r)\overline{\mathbb{E}}[\theta] + r\overline{\mathbb{E}}[a], \quad \text{where} \quad \overline{\mathbb{E}}[\cdot] = \int_i \mathbb{E}[\cdot|\mathcal{I}_i]\,di. \tag{23.24}$$

The aggregate action a can be described as an infinite sum of higher-order expectations. To see this, recursively substitute for a on the right side of (23.24) to get $a = \sum_{k=1}^{\infty}(1-r)r^{(k-1)}\overline{\mathbb{E}}^k[\theta]$, where the superscript k represents the kth-order average expectation. For example, $\overline{\mathbb{E}}^1[\theta] = \overline{\mathbb{E}}[\theta]$ is the average belief about θ, while $\overline{\mathbb{E}}^2[\theta] = \overline{\mathbb{E}}[\overline{\mathbb{E}}^1[\theta]]$ is the average belief about the average belief of θ, and so forth. Working with this infinite sum is complex. To avoid this, we follow Morris and Shin (2002) by conjecturing and then verifying a symmetric strategy.

Before we continue, we solve the full information problem in which the realization of θ is known. The optimal action is $a_i = (1-r)\theta + ra$. Integrating across agents yields $a = (1-r)\theta + ra$, or simply $a = \theta$, which implies that $a_i = \theta$ for all i. This is the unique Nash equilibrium.

Heterogeneous incomplete information

To compute the optimal action in (23.23) requires forming beliefs about the state θ and the average action a. To form beliefs about θ, we use Bayes' law:

$$\mathbb{E}[\theta|\mathcal{I}_i] = \frac{\tau_\theta \mu_\theta + \tau_z z + \tau_s s_i}{\tau_\theta + \tau_z + \tau_s}, \qquad \mathbb{V}ar[\theta|\mathcal{I}_i]^{-1} = \tau_\theta + \tau_z + \tau_s. \tag{23.25}$$

The best estimate is a convex combination of the prior mean μ_θ, the public signal z, and the individual signal s_i, with weights equal to their relative precisions. The posterior precision equals the sum of the precisions. Since precision is equal across agents, we denote it by $\Sigma^{-1} \equiv \mathbb{V}ar[\theta|\mathcal{I}_i]^{-1}$. Defining relative precisions as $\alpha_\theta = \Sigma\tau_\theta$, $\alpha_s = \Sigma\tau_s$, $\alpha_z = \Sigma\tau_z$, where $\alpha_\theta + \alpha_z + \alpha_s = 1$, we write the expected state as $\mathbb{E}[\theta|\mathcal{I}_i] = \alpha_\theta \mu_\theta + \alpha_z z + \alpha_s s_i$. To form beliefs about the average action $\mathbb{E}[a|\mathcal{I}_i]$, we guess and verify that the individual action is linear in the signals $a_i = \mu_\theta + \gamma_z(z - \mu_\theta) + \gamma_s(s_i - \mu_\theta)$, where the coefficients γ_z and γ_s are to be determined. Integrating the guess across agents, using the fact that the mean of the private signals s_i equals the true state θ, and taking expectations,

$$\mathbb{E}[a|\mathcal{I}_i] = \mu_\theta + \gamma_z(z - \mu_\theta) + \gamma_s(\mathbb{E}[\theta|\mathcal{I}_i] - \mu_\theta). \tag{23.26}$$

Substituting the beliefs about the state (23.25) and the average action (23.26) in the first-order condition (23.23), rearranging terms, and matching coefficients, we obtain the optimal weights on the public and the private signals

$$\gamma_z = \frac{\alpha_z}{1 - \alpha_s r}, \qquad \gamma_s = \frac{\alpha_s(1 - r)}{1 - \alpha_s r}. \tag{23.27}$$

We verify the conjecture that the action is linear in signals by checking that the weights on the prior μ_θ is $\gamma_\theta = 1 - \gamma_z - \gamma_s = \frac{\alpha_\theta}{1 - \alpha_s r}$. Finally, substituting the optimal action and the equilibrium average action into the loss function (23.22), we obtain

$$\mathcal{L} = (1 - r)^2 \left(\frac{\gamma_\theta^2}{\tau_\theta} + \frac{\gamma_z^2}{\tau_z} \right) + r^2 \frac{\gamma_s^2}{\tau_s}. \tag{23.28}$$

The expected loss decreases in the precision of both signals. Without additional externalities in payoffs, more information is always welfare improving.[5]

Optimal use of information

There are two key features of the solution. First, due to Bayesian updating, optimal actions a_i weight signals $\{z, s\}$ according to their precision. If signals are too noisy relative to the prior, the weight on the prior γ_θ dominates. If the public signal is very noisy relative to the private signal $\alpha_z < \alpha_s$, then the weight on the public signal is smaller $\gamma_z < \gamma_s$ and actions will not move much with z. As private heterogeneous signals become more important, dispersion in actions increases.[6] The opposite happens if the public signal is relatively more precise than the private signal. Second, the weight agents put on the public signal when forming their action γ_z is increasing in the value of coordination r. Agents who want to do what others do make their actions more sensitive to the information others know. Whenever there is strategic complementarity in actions ($r > 0$) we have $\gamma_z > \alpha_z$, which means that agents' actions react more to changes in public information than their beliefs do. Conversely, when there is substitutability in actions ($r < 0$), agents weight private signals more in their actions than in their beliefs.

Responsiveness to shocks

To describe the effects of information and coordination motives on aggregate outcomes, we define the *responsiveness to shocks* as the covariance of the average action with the state, normalized by fundamental volatility:

$$\frac{\mathbb{Cov}[a, \theta]}{\mathbb{Var}[\theta]} = \gamma_z + \gamma_s = \frac{\alpha_z + \alpha_s(1 - r)}{(1 - \alpha_s r)}. \tag{23.29}$$

It is equal to the sum of the weights on signals and thus depends on relative precisions. Also, this covariance is a measure of the informativeness of actions and could in principle be used to measure how much information the average agent has.

---

[5] With information externalities, more information can be welfare reducing (Morris and Shin, 2002; Angeletos and Pavan, 2007).

[6] Drenik and Perez (2020) exploit a historical episode—the manipulation of inflation statistics in Argentina—to show that a reduction in public signal precision τ_z increased the weight γ_s on private signals when forecasting inflation and generated larger cross-sectional price dispersion.

In the extreme case with perfect information, all agents set their action equal to the known state $a = \theta$ (there is no cross-sectional dispersion); responsiveness is highest at a value of 1 and expected welfare losses are zero $\mathcal{L} = 0$. At the other extreme with complete ignorance (both private and public signals have zero precision), actions equal the prior $a = \mu_\theta$ and do not correlate with the state (but are equal to each other). Responsiveness is lowest at a value of 0. Even if everyone takes the same action, utility losses arise because actions are far from the state.

Between these two informational extremes, the strength of strategic motives r matters for the optimal use of information and the implied responsiveness to shocks. In particular, the responsiveness measure in (23.29) decreases with r. We use this fact in the discussion that follows.

23.3.2.2 *Strategic complementarity and aggregate inertia*

With strategic complementarity ($r > 0$), agents want to do what others do, so they make their actions more sensitive to the information others know. To achieve this goal, agents' actions strongly comove with public information. For $r > 0$, the optimal weighting in (23.27) sets $\gamma_z > \alpha_z$ so that actions react more to public signals z than beliefs. Moreover, γ_z increases with the value of coordination r. With extreme complementarity ($r = 1$), all agents take the same action since welfare only depends on the closeness to others; agents completely ignore their private information ($\gamma_s = 0$) because it would only cause their choices to diverge. The dependence on public information generates *aggregate inertia* or delays in the adjustment of aggregate variables to shocks. Even if agents' private information tells them to adjust to changing economic conditions, they wait for others to do so. Thus responsiveness to shocks is low. In the language of Chapter 20 in this Handbook, the GE multiplier is attenuated.

Strategic complementarity arises naturally in Bertrand (price) competition, since firms have incentives to coordinate price-setting. They set a higher price if the competitor's price is higher, and vice versa. Woodford (2003) introduces price complementarity in the islands model of Lucas (1972) discussed in the previous section. Optimal prices not only depend on the state of nominal demand θ_t but also on the average level of prices charged by others a_t. Other settings that feature strategic complementarity include increasing returns to aggregate investment, technology spillovers, or speculative attacks.

23.3.2.3 *Strategic substitutability and aggregate volatility*

With strategic substitutability ($r < 0$), agents want to do the opposite of what others do. They weight private signals more in their actions than in their beliefs $\gamma_s > \alpha_s$ and their actions strongly move with private information. Information substitutability generates overreaction in the adjustment of aggregate variables to shocks, or *aggregate volatility*. That is, responsiveness is high. In the language of Chapter 20 in this Handbook, the GE multiplier is amplified.

In which environments is it natural to observe strategic substitutability? Market clearing is one mechanism that generates strategic substitutability through the equilibrium movement of prices. For instance, when firms compete by choosing quantities through Cournot competition, if a firm increases its production, its good becomes more abundant and its price goes down. Therefore, others want to produce less when one firm produces more. Similarly, consumers want to buy goods that others do not want to buy because the goods others demand will be more expensive. The same logic applies to financial investment, since investors want to buy assets with low demand, low price, and high return. Hiring decisions in frictional labor markets also feature strategic substitutability. The greater the aggregate number of vacancies posted in the economy, the lower the incentive of an individual firm to post vacancies. This mechanism is examined by Venkateswaran (2014) to explain labor market volatility. Lastly, models with returns to specialization are also situations in which agents want to behave differently from other agents.

The role of preferences

The simple games in this section consider either complementarity or substitutability motives. When both motives are present, the relationship between information and actions is more nuanced. Baley et al. (2020) make this point in a general equilibrium international trade model in which domestic firms choose how much to export based on their beliefs about foreign exports. Market clearing through the terms of trade introduces substitutability. Preference for a balanced consumption bundle introduces complementarity. The effect of information on export decisions depends on the relative strength of these two forces, which are encoded in agents' preferences.

23.4 Information choice and learning technologies

Active learning means that agents make choices to influence their future information sets. Whereas in the passive learning models in Section 23.3 signals were taken as given, now signals depend on choices. We present the two most commonly used learning technologies: sticky information, in which there is infrequent acquisition of perfect information, and rational inattention, in which there is frequent acquisition of noisy information. Finally, we discuss returns to scale in information acquisition and learning specialization.

23.4.1 Sticky information

Sticky information, also known as *inattentiveness*, is a learning technology in which most of the time agents get no information flow; occasionally, however, they observe the entire history of events. It is a lumpy informational flow, with periods of inaction followed by bursts of information processing. In settings in which an agent has to exert some effort to observe information but that information is not difficult to process, this technology makes sense. Examples include checking one's bank balance, looking up a sports score, or checking the current temperature. Dynamic models with information choice are notoriously hard to solve. Inattentiveness simplifies these problems by rendering the history of learning choices irrelevant each time an agent decides to learn.

23.4.1.1 *A beauty contest with infrequent information updating*

The following model introduces infrequent information updating to the tracking problem in (23.15). There is a continuum of agents $i \in [0, 1]$. Each agent chooses her action a_{it} to minimize its distance from an unknown stochastic target a_t^* that an agent with full information would set,

$$\mathcal{L} = \min_{\{a_{it},\, U_{it}\}} \mathbb{E}_0 \left[\sum_{t=0}^{\infty} \beta^t \left(\left(a_{it} - a_t^* \right)^2 + U_{it}\kappa_{it} \right) \Big| \mathcal{I}_{it} \right], \tag{23.30}$$

where $U_{it} \in \{0, 1\}$ is her decision to update the information set $\mathcal{I}_{it}$ at a cost $\kappa_{it} > 0$. The target is a convex combination of an exogenous unobserved state θ_t and the average action a_t:

$$a_t^* = (1 - r)\theta_t + ra_t, \quad \text{with} \quad a_t = \int_i a_{it} \, di. \tag{23.31}$$

The state follows a random walk $\theta_t = \theta_{t-1} + \varepsilon_t$ with i.i.d. innovations $\varepsilon_t \sim \mathcal{N}(0, \sigma^2)$. The following information cost, observed at the beginning of period t, nests two specifications in the literature:

$$\kappa_{it} = \begin{cases} \kappa & \text{with prob. } 1 - \lambda, \\ 0 & \text{with prob. } \lambda, \end{cases} \quad \text{with} \quad \lambda \in [0, 1]. \tag{23.32}$$

Setting $\kappa = \infty$ and $\lambda > 0$, this cost structure generates the (passive learning) sticky information model in Mankiw and Reis (2002), in which information arrives freely at an exogenous constant rate. Setting $\kappa > 0$ and $\lambda = 0$, this cost structure embodies active learning. It generates the costly information updating in Reis (2006a,b), in which agents face a fixed observation cost.

Information dynamics

An agent who last updated in period $\hat{\tau}$ enters period t with an information set that contains state realizations from every period up to and including $\hat{\tau}$, $\mathcal{I}_{i(t-1)} = \mathcal{I}_{\hat{\tau}} = \{\theta_\tau\}_{\tau=0}^{\hat{\tau}}$. If an agent chooses to update in the current period ($U_{it} = 1$), her new information set will contain all state realizations up to and including the current state, $\mathcal{I}_{it} = \mathcal{I}_t = \{\theta_\tau\}_{\tau=0}^{t}$. If the agent does not update in the current period ($U_{it} = 0$), she will not observe any new information, even endogenous information such as the average action ($\mathcal{I}_{it} = \mathcal{I}_{i(t-1)}$). Individual information sets $\mathcal{I}_{it}$ evolve according to

$$\mathcal{I}_{it} = \begin{cases} \mathcal{I}_{\hat{\tau}} = \{\theta_\tau\}_{\tau=0}^{\hat{\tau}} & \text{if } U_{it} = 0, \\ \mathcal{I}_t = \{\theta_\tau\}_{\tau=0}^{t} & \text{if } U_{it} = 1. \end{cases} \tag{23.33}$$

Equilibrium and optimal choices

An equilibrium is a sequence of information choices by every agent $\{U_{it}\}$ and actions $\{a_{it}\}$ that are $\mathcal{I}_{it}$-measurable and maximize (23.30), taking as given the choices of all other agents. The first-order condition dictates that agent i, who last updated at date $\hat{\tau}$, set her action equal to her expected target at time t,

$$a_{it} = \mathbb{E}\left[a_t^* | \mathcal{I}_{\hat{\tau}}\right] = (1 - r)\mathbb{E}[\theta_t | \mathcal{I}_{\hat{\tau}}] + r\mathbb{E}[a_t | \mathcal{I}_{\hat{\tau}}]. \tag{23.34}$$

Since the state is a random walk, $\mathbb{E}[\theta_t | \mathcal{I}_{\hat{\tau}}] = \theta_{\hat{\tau}}$. We guess and verify that the average action is also a random walk, $\mathbb{E}[a_t | \mathcal{I}_{\hat{\tau}}] = a_{\hat{\tau}}$. Let $\lambda_{t,\hat{\tau}}$ denote the measure of agents who last updated in period $\hat{\tau} \leq t$. Then the average action a_t is a weighted sum of the expected target of all agents: $a_t = \sum_{\tau=0}^{t} \lambda_{t,\tau} \mathbb{E}\left[a_t^* | \mathcal{I}_\tau\right] = \sum_{\tau=0}^{t} \lambda_{t,\tau} ((1 - r)\theta_\tau + ra_\tau)$. Recursively substituting for a_τ reveals that the average action is a weighted sum of all past innovations,

$$a_t = \sum_{\tau=0}^{t} \frac{\Lambda_{t,\tau}(1 - r)}{1 - r\Lambda_{t,\tau}} \varepsilon_\tau, \tag{23.35}$$

where $\Lambda_{t,\hat{\tau}} \equiv \sum_{\tau=\hat{\tau}}^{t} \lambda_{t,\tau}$ denotes the measure of agents who last updated between dates $\hat{\tau}$ and t. Substituting (23.35) in (23.31) tells us that the target action is $a_t^* = \sum_{\tau=0}^{t} \frac{1-r}{1-r\Lambda_{t,\tau}} \varepsilon_\tau$. Agents who last updated at date $\hat{\tau}$ set their action to $a_{it} = \mathbb{E}\left[a_t^* | \mathcal{I}_{\hat{\tau}}\right] = \sum_{\tau=0}^{\hat{\tau}} \frac{1-r}{1-r\Lambda_{t,\tau}} \varepsilon_\tau$. Their expected one-period loss (which agents compare to the information processing cost) depends on all the innovations since the last update,

$$\mathcal{L}_{t,\hat{\tau}} \equiv \mathbb{E}\left[\left(\mathbb{E}\left[a_t^* | \mathcal{I}_{\hat{\tau}}\right] - a_t^* | \mathcal{I}_{\hat{\tau}}\right)^2\right] = \sum_{\tau=\hat{\tau}+1}^{t} \left(\frac{1-r}{1-r\Lambda_{t,\tau}}\right)^2 \sigma^2. \tag{23.36}$$

The longer since an agent updated her information, the higher are the incentives to update in the current period. If information arrives exogenously, firms have no choice but to update at rate λ. In contrast, when information is actively chosen by paying the fixed cost κ, the updating policy consists of threshold dates such that agents who last updated at date $\hat{\tau} < \tau_t^*$ update at date t, whereas those who last updated at $\hat{\tau} > \tau_t^*$ find not updating to be strictly optimal. One equilibrium consists of staggered updating, which means that all firms update after a fixed number of periods T and each period a fraction $1/T$ of firms updates (Reis, 2006b).

Expression (23.36) highlights the updating complementarity. For any $\tau = \hat{\tau} + 1, \ldots, t$, the one-period loss increases with the strategic motive parameter—that is, $\partial \mathcal{L}_{t,\hat{\tau}} / \partial \Lambda_{t,t-\tau} > 0$—if and only if $r > 0$. When actions are complements ($r > 0$), there is complementarity in information acquisition: The more agents are aware of a shock that has occurred since the agent last updated, the higher the per-period loss of not being aware of this shock. The complementarity in updating information delays adjusting to changing economic conditions, or *inertia*. When actions are strategic substitutes ($r < 0$), the converse is true. This general principle, discussed in the static games of Section 23.3.2, reappears in dynamic settings.

23.4.1.2 *Applications of sticky information*

Sticky information has been extensively used to explain observed inflation inertia, because price-setting firms slowly update their information about money supply and demand. In Mankiw and Reis (2002) and Ball et al. (2005), firms passively update information on random dates. In Reis (2006b), the adjustment dates are actively chosen by paying an observation cost. Álvarez et al. (2016) generalize this setup to allow for heterogeneity in observation costs.

On the household side, sticky information has been put forward as an explanation for the equity premium puzzle (Gabaix and Laibson, 2001) and the excess sensitivity and excess smoothness puzzles of aggregate consumption (Reis, 2006a; Carroll et al., 2020). Auclert et al. (2020) show that embedding sticky expectations in a heterogeneous agent new Keynesian model reconciles the micro and macro responses to monetary policy shocks.

Inattentiveness is often mixed with adjustment costs in actions, by combining information updating with tools from the sS literature.[7] Bonomo and Carvalho (2004) and Álvarez et al. (2011, 2017) study price-setting problems in which firms pay an observation cost to discover their target price and a menu cost to change their price. Similarly, Álvarez et al. (2012) and Abel et al. (2013) study portfolio choice

---

[7] The sS literature considers models in which agents must pay a fixed adjustment cost to change their action. In these models, policy functions are typically characterized by an inaction region delimited by two thresholds $[s, S]$. Agents pay the adjustment cost and take action whenever their state falls outside this region; otherwise, agents remain inactive.

in which investors pay an observation cost to reveal the value of a risky asset and a transaction cost to adjust their portfolio. In these papers, small information and adjustment costs generate infrequent adjustment, yielding long periods of inertia.

On the empirical side, Klenow and Willis (2007) test inattentiveness models of price-setting by asking whether information revealed in past periods acts as a shock to prices in the current period. In a similar exercise with asset prices, Hong et al. (2007) and Cohen and Frazzini (2008) find that industry information affects the market index value with a lag. Andrade and Le Bihan (2013) document that professional forecasters fail to systematically update their forecasts and disagree when updating, all of which suggests inattention.

23.4.2 Rational inattention

The idea that economic agents have limited ability to process information, or to pay attention, is often referred to as *rational inattention*. Following Sims (2003), rational inattention has taken on a more specific meaning. Models that use rational inattention either bound the amount of information or charge agents a utility cost for information, in which the amount of information is measured according to how much it reduces entropy.

A large subset of the literature simplifies the problem by allowing agents to directly choose the precision with which they observe an exogenously specified set of normal signals. It turns out that with quadratic payoffs and normal priors, normal signals are optimal. We lay out such a quadratic-normal model in order to convey the main ideas from this literature.

23.4.2.1 *Measuring information: entropy and mutual information*

The standard measure of the quantity of information in information theory is Shannon *entropy* (Cover and Thomas, 1991). Entropy measures the amount of uncertainty in a random variable. For a random variable θ with density function f, entropy is defined as[8]

$$\mathcal{E}(\theta) \equiv -\mathbb{E}[\ln(f(\theta))].$$

(23.37)

Sims (2003) proposed modeling the informational content of a signal s about θ as the reduction in entropy achieved by conditioning on the additional information provided by the signal. This measure of uncertainty reduction is known as *mutual information*. It is defined as

$$I(\theta, s) \equiv \mathcal{E}(\theta) - \mathcal{E}(\theta|s),$$

(23.38)

where the second term is conditional entropy, $\mathcal{E}(\theta|s) = \mathcal{E}(\theta, s) - \mathcal{E}(s)$. The expectation in $\mathcal{E}(\theta, s)$ is taken over the realizations of (θ, s). With a normal state $\theta \sim \mathcal{N}(\mu_\theta, \tau_\theta^{-1})$ and a normal signal $s \sim \mathcal{N}(0, \tau_s^{-1})$, mutual information takes a simple form

$$I(\theta, s) = \frac{1}{2} \ln\left(1 + \frac{\tau_s}{\tau_\theta}\right).$$

(23.39)

Mutual information reflects the ratio of the posterior precision to the prior precision $(\tau_\theta + \tau_s)/\tau_\theta$. Mutual information increases with signal precision, since it generates a larger reduction in uncertainty.

---

[8] By using the natural logarithm, we express information units in *nats*, as opposed to *bits*, in which case the logarithm has base 2.

23.4.2.2 *A tracking problem with noisy information acquisition*

Consider a repeated tracking problem. The agent chooses the action a that minimizes the expected distance to an i.i.d. state $\theta \sim \mathcal{N}(0, \tau_\theta^{-1})$. She receives a noisy signal $s = \theta + \eta$, with precision τ_s. Two constraints govern how the agent can choose signal precision. The first is the capacity constrain, which takes the form of an upper bound $\kappa > 0$ on the mutual information of priors and prior plus signals. The second is a "no forgetting" constraint that requires mutual information to be nonnegative. The agent can increase capacity κ by paying a proportional utility cost $c\kappa$. The agent solves the following problem:

$$\mathcal{L} = \min_{\{a, \kappa\}} \frac{1}{2}\mathbb{E}\left[(a - \theta)^2 \,|s\right] + c\kappa \tag{23.40}$$

$$\text{such that } 0 \leq I(\theta, s) \leq \kappa,$$

where $I(\theta, s)$ is the mutual information for normal state and signals in (23.39). The solution to the problem takes place in two stages. In the first stage, the agent chooses how much attention to allocate to θ by choosing the total processing capacity κ. This choice determines the optimal signal precision τ_s. In the second stage, the agent receives a noisy signal s with the precision proportional to the attention allocated in the first stage and chooses the action.

To solve the model, we work backward. Suppose the agent receives signal s with precision τ_s. Conditional on this signal, the agent chooses the optimal action $a^* = \mathbb{E}[\theta|s] = \frac{\tau_s}{\tau_\theta + \tau_s}s$. The expected loss implied by the optimal action is $\mathbb{E}\left[(a^* - \theta)^2\right] = (\tau_\theta + \tau_s)^{-1}$. Since the expected loss decreases with signal precision, the capacity constraint will always bind and we set $\tau_\theta + \tau_s^* = \tau_\theta e^{2\kappa}$. Plugging the optimal action and binding capacity constraint into (23.40), and taking the first-order condition with respect to κ, we find the optimal attention capacity and the implied optimal signal precision. And conditional on these choices, we find the optimal action:

$$\kappa^* = \frac{1}{2}\ln\left(\frac{1}{\tau_\theta c}\right), \qquad (\tau_s^* + \tau_\theta)^{-1} = c, \qquad a^* = \max\{(1 - \tau_\theta c)s, 0\}. \tag{23.41}$$

This example illustrates key trade-offs of rational inattention models. The agent chooses signal precision by trading the costs of acquiring information with the benefits from better information. The agent increases attention κ^* if the state's volatility τ_θ^{-1} is high and if the marginal cost of acquiring information c is low. If the marginal cost is too large, the agent acquires no information and sets the action equal to the prior mean (zero in this example).

Tracking multiple states

Assume the agent tracks two i.i.d. states $(\theta_1, \theta_2) \sim \mathcal{N}(0, \Sigma)$, where Σ denotes the prior variance–covariance matrix. The agent chooses an action a to minimize the distance to both states subject to a bound on mutual information:

$$\mathcal{L} = \min_{\{a, \kappa\}} \frac{1}{2}\mathbb{E}\left[(a - \theta_1 - \theta_2)^2\right] + c\kappa, \tag{23.42}$$

$$\text{such that } 0 \leq \frac{1}{2}\ln\left(\frac{\det \Sigma}{\det \hat{\Sigma}}\right) \leq \kappa, \tag{23.43}$$

where $\hat{\Sigma}$ denotes the posterior covariance matrix. Mutual information with multivariate normal variables reflects the ratio of the determinants of the prior and the posterior variances.

The problem of tracking two states has a simple solution when the agent is allowed to choose the variance–covariance structure of the signals. To see this, define the target $\theta^* = \theta_1 + \theta_2$, and assume the agent receives a single noisy signal of this target. The problem can be restated as a single-state problem, with the optimal allocation of attention taking the same form as (23.41). This one signal allows the agent to achieve the same expected loss as two independent signals, while requiring lower mutual information.

Rationally inattentive agents generally prefer signals about a linear combination of the payoff-relevant states. However, restricting the set of signals to be independent and associated with a specific state is a plausible economic constraint in many settings. Following Maćkowiak and Wiederholt (2009), suppose the states are independent of each other and the agent receives two independent signals, $s_1 = \theta_1 + \eta_1$ and $s_2 = \theta_2 + \eta_2$, with respective precisions τ_{s1}, τ_{s2}. The prior Σ and posterior $\hat{\Sigma}$ variances are diagonal matrices, and the entropy constraint simplifies to

$$\frac{\hat{\Sigma}_{11}^{-1}\hat{\Sigma}_{22}^{-1}}{\tau_{\theta1}\tau_{\theta2}} \le e^{2\kappa}, \qquad \text{where} \quad \hat{\Sigma}_{ii}^{-1} = \tau_{\theta_i} + \tau_{si} \quad \text{for} \quad i = 1, 2. \tag{23.44}$$

The expected loss associated with the action is equal to $\mathbb{E}\left[(a^* - \theta)^2\right] = \hat{\Sigma}_{11} + \hat{\Sigma}_{22}$. In the case $c \ne 0$, total capacity κ can be chosen and the problem reduces to two independent single-state problems like (23.40). The optimal allocation of attention for each state is given by expression (23.41), replacing τ_θ with the corresponding precision of each state ($\tau_{\theta1}$ or $\tau_{\theta2}$). In the dual problem in which total capacity is fixed, the capacity constraint always binds. In this case, more attention to one state reduces the attention allocated to the other state. The ratios of posterior to prior precisions are increasing in the other state's precision:

$$\frac{\tau_{s1}^* + \tau_{\theta1}}{\tau_{\theta1}} = e^\kappa \sqrt{\frac{\tau_{\theta2}}{\tau_{\theta1}}}, \qquad \frac{\tau_{s2}^* + \tau_{\theta2}}{\tau_{\theta2}} = e^\kappa \sqrt{\frac{\tau_{\theta1}}{\tau_{\theta2}}}. \tag{23.45}$$

These expressions highlight a key lesson from multivariate rational inattention models: Agents optimally pay more attention to the more volatile state, as it generates larger welfare losses.

23.4.2.3 *Applications of rational inattention*

Following Sims (2003), the literature on rational inattention has rapidly expanded. One of the earliest applications is the price-setting model of Maćkowiak and Wiederholt (2009). Its core resembles the two-shock model in (23.42), where θ_1 represents monetary shocks and θ_2 idiosyncratic productivity shocks. Rationally inattentive firms optimally pay more attention to idiosyncratic shocks, since these are relatively more volatile than aggregate shocks, and thus underreact to monetary policy shocks. In this setting, Paciello and Wiederholt (2014) study optimal monetary policy and Maćkowiak and Wiederholt (2015) introduce rationally inattentive households. As with inattentiveness (Section 23.4.1), rational inattention gives rise to nominal rigidities and price inertia.

Unlike the simple static problems we presented, many applications feature dynamic settings in which states evolve persistently over time. This is technically challenging. Maćkowiak et al. (2018); Miao et al. (2019); and Afrouzi and Yang (2021a) study dynamic inattention problems and propose algorithms to solve them. Another strand of the literature provides axiomatic foundations (Caplin and Dean, 2015; de Oliveira et al., 2017; Ellis, 2018; Hébert and Woodford, 2019) and generalizations of entropy costs (Caplin et al., 2017; Hébert and Woodford, 2021).

Applications of rational inattention include portfolio allocation (Mondria, 2010); mutual fund management (Kacperczyk et al., 2016); discrimination against minorities (Bartoš et al., 2016); electoral competition (Matějka and Tabellini, 2021); international trade (Dasgupta and Mondria, 2018); insurance choice (Brown and Jeon, 2020); marriage markets (Cheremukhin et al., 2020); hiring decisions (Acharya and Wee, 2020); migration (Porcher, 2020; Bertoli et al., 2020); consumption (Luo, 2008; Kőszegi and Matějka, 2020); expectation formation (Fuster et al., 2020; Gutiérrez-Daza, 2022); and price-setting (Woodford, 2009; Stevens, 2020; Turén, 2020; Yang, 2020; Afrouzi and Yang, 2021b). Maćkowiak et al. (2020) provide a comprehensive review of this literature.

23.4.2.4 *Linear cost of signal precision*

Mutual information in (23.38) is one of several informational costs $I(\theta, s)$ employed in the active learning literature. A popular alternative is to specify costs that are linear in signal precision. In the case of two states and two signals, this constraint takes the form

$$\hat{\Sigma}_1^{-1} + \hat{\Sigma}_2^{-1} \leq \kappa. \tag{23.46}$$

Comparing (23.46) with (23.44), we see that entropy constrains the product of precisions, whereas the linear constraint bounds the sum of precisions.

While the entropy technology represents a process of increasingly refined search, linear technology models search as a sequence of independent explorations. Van Nieuwerburgh and Veldkamp (2010) and Myatt and Wallace (2012) use linear constraints to jointly study information acquisition and investment decisions in financial markets. Hébert and Woodford (2021) show that the linear constraint (23.46) can be obtained by assuming neighborhood-based information costs that capture notions of perceptual distance. Departures of mutual information in this direction have important welfare implications in general equilibrium, as examined by Angeletos and Sastry (2019) and Hébert and La'O (2020).

23.4.3 **Other learning technologies**

Agents' learning technology could involve a combination of both sticky information (inattentiveness) and noisy information acquisition (rational inattention). Agents may pay a fixed cost on discrete dates to observe perfect information about the current and past states of the economy. In between these updates, however, they may observe a flow of noisy information about the state. For example, Bonomo et al. (2022) develop a hybrid price-setting model with features from both learning technologies, and Coibion and Gorodnichenko (2012) consider both learning technologies and show that survey data favor models of noisy information.

A different learning technology developed by Woodford (2009); Stevens (2020); and Khaw et al. (2017) is a two-stage form of rational inattention: a decision whether to adjust and then how much to adjust. Although their two-stage adjustment is infrequent, like sticky information, the decision to adjust is nonetheless based on a continuous flow of information. The experimental data in Khaw et al. (2017) support this two-stage technology.

23.4.4 **Information choice as a source of inequality**

Information choice may exacerbate initial differences across agents when there are increasing returns in information. Increasing returns to information refers to the idea that an entity with more data values additional data more. Often, the reason is that when a firm or an economy gets more information it grows, invests more, or takes on more risky actions. But agents with larger investment or risky positions value information more. Thus more information raises the value of acquiring more information. In data economics, this same force is called the "data feedback loop."

Increasing returns in information appear naturally in production settings (Wilson, 1975). The more a firm learns how to improve its technology, the more it wants to produce and the more it produces, the more valuable information becomes. Firms that initially operate on a large scale are more likely to acquire information, produce with better technology, and grow faster than small firms. In the previous case, there were increasing returns to data acquisition. Increasing returns can also arise in data production. In Begenau et al. (2018), big data disproportionately benefits large firms. Because they have more economic activity, large firms produce more data. Abundant data improves investors' forecasts, which reduces investors' uncertainty and lowers the large firm's cost of capital. Lower investment costs enable large firms to grow even larger.

Information has increasing returns in portfolio problems because it can be used to evaluate one share of an asset or many shares of an asset. When a decision maker has lots of an asset, information about the asset's payoff is more valuable. Investors who are initially wealthier acquire more information because they have more asset value to apply that information to and they will also earn higher returns on their investments. Poor individuals may stay poor while the rich get richer. This mechanism has been shown to account for inequality in portfolio holdings of risky assets (Peress, 2004) and the increase in capital income inequality due to investor sophistication (Kacperczyk et al., 2019) and financial innovation (Mihet, 2021).

23.4.5 **Learning what others know**

Agents can acquire information by observing the behavior of others, and agents with information can share that information with others through their actions. Social learning may generate behavior that resembles irrationality, such as herds, bubbles, booms, and crashes, but that is completely rational. For a comprehensive discussion of social learning and its consequences, we refer to Chamley (2004) and Goyal (2011).

Next, we describe two recent evolutions of social learning.

Local learning

In certain settings, it is natural to observe the behavior of other agents who are geographically, culturally, socially, or economically "close." Moreover, agents may actively choose who forms part of the network of connections they obtain their information from (Herskovic and Ramos, 2020). The local learning that emerges generates similar beliefs and actions for members of the same group but different beliefs and actions across different groups. In the aggregate, local learning may slow the transmission of information.

The following papers examine local learning mechanisms. In Conley and Udry (2010), farmers learn a new agricultural technology from other farmers in their village; in Fogli and Veldkamp (2011), women learn the effects of maternal employment on children by observing nearby employed women;

in Buera et al. (2011), countries learn the impact of market-oriented policies from the experience of similar countries; in Galenianos (2013), firms learn an applicant's suitability for a job (match quality) when the applicant is referred to the firm; in Fernandes and Tang (2014), exporters learn the returns to exporting in foreign markets from neighboring firms' export performance; in Figueiredo (2018), high-school students learn the college premium from the wages of college-educated workers in their neighborhood; in Boerma and Karabarbounis (2021), households learn the returns to entrepreneurship from their dynasty's entrepreneurial experience. In another example of local learning, agents form housing market expectations based on local transactions; see Chapter 6 in this Handbook. The use of social networks for learning in the labor market is widespread and the subject of a large literature; see, for instance, Topa (2001, 2011). Other tools related to local transmission appear in Chapter 25 in this Handbook, which discusses epidemiological frameworks that can be used to study how social interactions may shape people's expectations.

News media

Agents also learn what others know through news media, which is a technology for aggregating and sharing information. One service the media provides is to select which events to report, and thus plays a large role as a source of *selected* information. In particular, the media may strategically choose to report unusual or extreme events to increase its number of users (Nimark and Pitschner, 2019). By focusing on certain observations, the media generates bias even among rational readers. In turn, this bias may increase volatility and can lead to aggregate fluctuations (Nimark, 2014; Chahrour et al., 2021).

Survey data can be useful in assessing the role the media plays in shaping expectations. In the context of households' expectations, Chapter 5 in this Handbook discusses survey evidence that points to a limited role for the media in explaining average inflation expectations. However, to the extent that Bayesian agents update their priors in response to a news report, the speed with which they update (in measured survey data) would depend on how intensely the topic is being covered (in traditional metrics for intensity of news coverage). Chapter 25 in this Handbook reviews the empirical evidence that aims to quantify this potential transmission channel.

23.4.6 Information choice in strategic settings

In settings with strategic behavior in actions, as in the coordination games of Section 23.3.2, an agent's choice to acquire information depends on others' information acquisition. Hellwig and Veldkamp (2009) and Hellwig et al. (2012) introduce information choice in the beauty contest game in (23.22). Agents choose their actions a_i to match an unknown target that depends on the exogenous state θ and the average action in the economy $a = \int_i a_i \, di$. But before playing the action game, agents choose how much to pay to acquire a common signal $z \sim \mathcal{N}\left(\theta, \tau_z^{-1}\right)$ and/or a private signal $s \sim \mathcal{N}\left(\theta, \tau_s^{-1}\right)$. The cost of information acquisition $\kappa\left(\tau_z, \tau_s\right)$ is increasing, convex, and twice differentiable in signal precisions. Each agent solves

$$\mathcal{L} = \min_{a_i, \tau_z, \tau_s} \mathbb{E}\left[(1-r)(a_i - \theta)^2 + r(a_i - a)^2 \Big| z, s_i\right] + \kappa(\tau_z, \tau_s), \tag{23.47}$$

The model is solved by backward induction. Taking agents' information as given, we solve the action game and compute expected utility as a function of information precision. That expected utility is the objective in the first-stage information choice game. With this objective, we can solve for optimal information choices.

The key result is that strategic motives in actions generate strategic motives in information choice. Information changes the economy's *responsiveness to shocks*, defined in (23.29) as the covariance of the average action with the state, normalized by fundamental volatility, $\mathbb{C}ov[a, \theta]/\mathbb{V}ar[\theta]$. That is what makes information more or less valuable.

When actions exhibit complementarity ($r > 0$) and other agents have precise information (high $\tau_z + \tau_s$), responsiveness is high. When the average action and the state covary, the agent faces more payoff uncertainty because if he chooses an action that turns out to be far from θ, it will also be far from a and he will be penalized twice. This added utility risk raises the value of accurate information. Information acquisition is complementary. Correlation in information choice induces further correlation in actions, such as financial investment (Veldkamp, 2006); production (Veldkamp and Wolfers, 2007); and price-setting (Gorodnichenko, 2008).

Conversely, when actions are substitutes ($r < 0$) and other agents have precise information (high $\tau_z + \tau_s$), responsiveness is again high, meaning that if the agent chooses an action that turns out to be far from θ, it will also be far from a. But in this case, that covariance reduces payoff uncertainty: Taking an action that is far from a confers a utility benefit, while being far from the state θ incurs a utility cost. The cost and benefit partially cancel each other. The risk of being far from the state θ hedges the risk of taking an action that is close to a. This hedging reduces the variability of overall utility. When others know more, the state and average action are more aligned and offset each other more effectively. The offset dampens utility fluctuations, and less utility risk lowers the value of information. Thus information is a strategic substitute because its value is less when others acquire more of it. Exploring strategic substitutability in information has a long tradition in the portfolio choice literature, starting with Grossman and Stiglitz (1980).

23.5 Theories of the data economy

Models of the data economy are learning models, like the ones we have examined so far. The key difference with this class of models is the two-way feedback between information and economic activity. Economic activity generates data and the information in the data feeds back to affect economic activity. In one class of models, data are modeled as ideas or knowledge. In another class, data are information that reduces uncertainty and guides decision-making. Both can speak to long-run growth and business cycle fluctuations.

23.5.1 Experimentation

Data economy models are examples of a broader class of models with active experimentation. Active experimentation means that an agent chooses an action that may generate information. The value of the information is explicitly incorporated into the agent's choice problem. Such problems often produce feedback between economic activity and information. Agents control the information flow (e.g., signal quality) through their actions. These actions, in turn, depend on the information agents learn.

In a class of models called bandit problems, all actions generate equally precise signals, but the decision is whether to act or not. In another class of models with experimentation, the signal precision depends on the agent's action. As a simple example, consider the quadratic tracking problem (23.16) in which the optimal action is set equal to a belief and thus depends on signal precision. In some cases, precision τ_s increases in the distance from the myopic target action a_{it}^*,

$$\tau_s = \phi(a_{it} - a_{it}^*)^2, \qquad \phi > 0. \tag{23.48}$$

Experimentation is costly because agents deviate from their target to obtain information. At the same time, experimentation brings benefits in the shape of more precise future information. A feedback loop between actions and information often arises. The optimal experimentation strategy solves a fixed-point problem that balances the current costs of deviating from the target against the benefits of better decision-making in the future.

Active learning through experimentation in optimal control problems in macroeconomics arises in Prescott (1972). Since Rothschild (1974), experimentation has been widely applied to price-setting models in which a monopolist learns about uncertain demand. Firms use their prices to learn about demand's slope or intercept (Balvers and Cosimano, 1990; Mirman et al., 1993; Keller and Rady, 1999; Willems, 2017). In these models, firms are willing to produce at negative revenue in order to obtain better information. Bachmann and Moscarini (2011) and Argente and Yeh (2022) build general equilibrium versions of this framework. Other applications of experimentation include investment and growth (Bertocchi and Spagat, 1998); optimal monetary policy (Wieland, 2000; Svensson and Williams, 2007); job mobility (Pastorino, 2009); and occupational choice (Antonovics and Golan, 2012).

23.5.2 Data and growth

We begin by exploring the connection between data and long-run growth. Consider an economy with a continuum of firms $i \in [0, 1]$. Each firm i produces output y_{it} using labor l_{it} and idiosyncratic productivity A_{it},

$$y_{it} = A_{it} l_{it}^\alpha, \quad \alpha \le 1. \tag{23.49}$$

Data D_{it} are generated as a by-product of economic activity. Data are generated through own output, with a "data-savviness" parameter z_i, or is produced by other firms B_{it},

$$D_{it} = z_i y_{it} + B_{it}. \tag{23.50}$$

A data-savvy firm harvests lots of data per unit of output; $B_{i,t}$ captures the fact that data are a nonrival good: The information produced by the activity of one firm can be used by others. Two main approaches have been explored to study the impact of data on productivity A_{it}: data as knowledge and data as information. These approaches differ starkly in their implications for long-run growth.

23.5.2.1 Data as knowledge

The first approach considers data as knowledge. We present a simplified version of the model by Jones and Tonetti (2020). Data D_{it} improves the quality of ideas and directly increases firm productivity A_{it}. Data relevance for productivity is mediated by the parameter η,

$$A_{it} = D_{it}^\eta. \tag{23.51}$$

Data from other firms B_{it}, produced with their output, may increase firm i's data at the *nonrivalry* rate $\tilde{z}_i$,

$$B_{it} = \int \tilde{z}_i y_{it} \, di. \tag{23.52}$$

If $\tilde{z}_i = 0$, then data are rival and data from other firms cannot be used by firm i. Higher values of $\tilde{z}_i$ indicate that firm i obtains more data generated by the production of the rest of the firms. Substituting B_{it} into (23.50), assuming symmetry ($z_i = \tilde{z}_i = z$ and $y_{it} = y_t$), and using the fact that firm i has measure zero yields $D_{it} = zy_t$. Then substituting A_{it} and D_{it} into (23.49) and rearranging, we obtain

$$y_t = z^{\frac{\eta}{1-\eta}} l_t^{\frac{\alpha}{1-\eta}}. \tag{23.53}$$

For $\eta > 1 - \alpha$, data production leads to increasing returns and long-run growth. This approach of equating data with knowledge is also used by Cong et al. (2021), in which data is used for R&D in an endogenous growth model, and by Abis and Veldkamp (2021), who study the impact of artificial intelligence (AI) in the investment management industry.

23.5.2.2 *Data as information*

The second approach considers data as information that reduces uncertainty and guides decision-making. Farboodi and Veldkamp (2021) consider data as information that is used in forecasting an optimal production technique. Firms face a signal-extraction problem, as in Section 23.3.1. They choose a production technique a_{it} to match the optimal technique $a_t^* = \theta_t + \varepsilon_t$ that consists of persistent θ_t and transitory ε_t components. Better forecasts of the optimal technique increase productivity A_{it},

$$A_{it} = \bar{A} - (a_{it} - \theta_t - \varepsilon_t)^2. \tag{23.54}$$

Firms receive a noisy signal s_{it} about θ_t. Its precision increases with data D_{it}, capturing data-driven improvements in forecasting,

$$s_{it} = \theta_t + \eta_{it}, \qquad \eta_{it} \sim \mathcal{N}(0, (\tau_s D_{it})^{-1}). \tag{23.55}$$

As in (23.50), data D_{it} come from own production and data shared by others. This structure generates a *data-feedback loop*. Large firms produce more data, which allows them to improve estimates of the optimal technique and increase output and future data. Nevertheless, since reducing a forecast error has a bounded value, data production cannot lead to long-run growth (the highest productivity, obtained with zero uncertainty, is $\bar{A}$).

Farboodi et al. (2019) apply a similar information structure to show that data production induces larger firms in steady state. Besides data arising from own production, data can be purchased in the market B_{it}. Differences in data savviness z_i can induce some firms to specialize in data production and grow faster than the rest.

23.5.3 Data and economic fluctuations

When analyzing business cycles, data inform regarding the current state of the economy, which is usually aggregate productivity. The feedback loop between data and economic activity amplifies or helps propagate the business cycle. Booms are times of high activity and information production.

To examine how data propagate business cycles, we make two assumptions. First, to produce, firms must pay a random idiosyncratic cost v_{it} that is i.i.d. across firms and time. Second, θ_t is an aggregate productivity shock identical across firms; it follows a two-state Markov process between a good state θ_g and a bad state θ_b, with $\theta_g > \theta_b$:

$$y_{it} = \theta_t l_{it}^\alpha - v_{it}, \qquad v_{it} \sim_{iid} \mathcal{N}(0, \sigma_v^2), \qquad \theta_t \in \{\theta_g, \theta_b\}. \tag{23.56}$$

Firms observe v_{it} but do not know θ_t. They receive a public signal s_t with a precision that increases with the number of active firms n_t in the economy:

$$s_t = \theta_t + \varepsilon_t, \qquad \varepsilon_t \sim \mathcal{N}(0, (n_t \tau_s)^{-1}). \tag{23.57}$$

A firm chooses to produce if its belief about productivity is high relative to the fixed production cost. When lots of firms believe that productivity is in the good state θ_g, there is high economic activity (large n_t) and information production (high signal precision). The opposite happens if firms believe productivity is low.

This structure generates an asymmetric flow of information over the cycle. When the economy is in the good state, signal precision is very high. According to Bayesian updating, firms put a high weight on unexpected news when updating their beliefs. Therefore, at the peak of the business cycle, an exogenous change from good times θ_g to bad times θ_b triggers a rapid adjustment in firms' beliefs and leads to an abrupt downward adjustment in production. In contrast, when times are bad, scarce information and high uncertainty slow belief updating. If the economy goes back to the good state, output will transition slowly.

This mechanism was proposed by Veldkamp (2005) to explain why many asset markets exhibit slow booms and sudden crashes and by Van Nieuwerburgh and Veldkamp (2006) to understand business cycle asymmetries, with slow expansions and sudden recessions. This mechanism is tested empirically by Ordonez (2013). Quantitative versions are developed by Saijo (2017) and Fajgelbaum et al. (2017), in which the level of aggregate investment determines the amount of information available to firms. In Straub and Ulbricht (2018), the ability of investors to learn about firm-level fundamentals declines during financial crises, which generates negative spillovers from financial distress onto the real economy. In all of these papers, there is a two-way interaction between the level of economic activity and aggregate uncertainty.

23.6 Conclusion

As the economy transforms itself from a physical production economy to a knowledge economy, understanding learning becomes more central to economics. Learning is the process whereby information is transformed into knowledge. Although we have described models in terms that suggest human beings are doing the learning, it may also be that in the future machines will do some of this learning for us. That does not render these problems less relevant. Machines will also work to solve signal-extraction problems, and algorithms will need to choose what data to process. The magnitude of the constraints may be quite different. But as data grow in abundance and value, understanding what signal extraction can reveal, the costs and benefits of this knowledge, and how it affects aggregate economic activity has never been more urgent.

References

Abel, A.B., Eberly, J.C., Panageas, S., 2013. Optimal inattention to the stock market with information costs and transactions costs. Econometrica 81 (4), 1455–1481.

Abis, S., Veldkamp, L., 2021. The changing economics of knowledge production. Available at SSRN 3570130.

Acharya, S., Wee, S.L., 2020. Rational inattention in hiring decisions. American Economic Journal: Macroeconomics 12 (1), 1–40.

Afrouzi, H., Yang, C., 2021a. Dynamic Rational Inattention and the Phillips Curve. Tech. Rep. CESifo.

Afrouzi, H., Yang, C., 2021b. Selection in Information Acquisition and Monetary Non-Neutrality. Tech. Rep. Columbia University.

Álvarez, F., Guiso, L., Lippi, F., 2012. Durable consumption and asset management with transaction and observation costs. The American Economic Review 102 (5), 2272–2300.

Álvarez, F., Lippi, F., Paciello, L., 2011. Optimal price setting with observation and menu costs. The Quarterly Journal of Economics 126 (4), 1909–1960.

Álvarez, F., Lippi, F., Paciello, L., 2016. Monetary shocks in models with inattentive producers. The Review of Economic Studies 83 (2), 421–459.

Álvarez, F., Lippi, F., Paciello, L., 2017. Monetary shocks in models with observation and menu costs. Journal of the European Economic Association 16 (2), 353–382.

Andrade, P., Le Bihan, H., 2013. Inattentive professional forecasters. Journal of Monetary Economics 60 (8), 967–982.

Angeletos, G.-M., Pavan, A., 2007. Efficient use of information and social value of information. Econometrica 75 (4), 1103–1142.

Angeletos, G.-M., Sastry, K., 2019. Inattentive Economies. Working Paper 26413. National Bureau of Economic Research.

Antonovics, K., Golan, L., 2012. Experimentation and job choice. Journal of Labor Economics 30 (2), 333–366.

Argente, D., Yeh, C., 2022. Product life cycle, learning, and nominal shocks. The Review of Economic Studies. Forthcoming.

Arkolakis, C., Papageorgiou, T., Timoshenko, O.A., 2018. Firm learning and growth. Review of Economic Dynamics 27, 146–168.

Auclert, A., Rognlie, M., Straub, L., 2020. Micro Jumps, Macro Humps: Monetary Policy and Business Cycles in an Estimated HANK Model. Working Paper 26647. National Bureau of Economic Research.

Bachmann, R., Moscarini, G., 2011. Business cycles and endogenous uncertainty. In: 2011 Meeting Papers, vol. 36. Society for Economic Dynamics, pp. 82–99.

Bakshi, G., Skoulakis, G., 2010. Do subjective expectations explain asset pricing puzzles? Journal of Financial Economics 98 (3), 462–477.

Baley, I., Blanco, A., 2019. Firm uncertainty cycles and the propagation of nominal shocks. American Economic Journal: Macroeconomics 11 (1), 276–337.

Baley, I., Figueiredo, A., Ulbricht, R., 2021. Mismatch cycles. Tech. Rep., Barcelona GSE Working Paper 1151.

Baley, I., Veldkamp, L., Waugh, M., 2020. Can global uncertainty promote international trade? Journal of International Economics 126, 103347.

Ball, L., Mankiw, N.G., Reis, R., 2005. Monetary policy for inattentive economies. Journal of Monetary Economics 52 (4), 703–725.

Balvers, R.J., Cosimano, T.F., 1990. Actively learning about demand and the dynamics of price adjustment. The Economic Journal 100 (402), 882–898.

Bartoš, V., Bauer, M., Chytilová, J., Matějka, F., 2016. Attention discrimination: theory and field experiments with monitoring information acquisition. The American Economic Review 106 (6), 1437–1475.

Begenau, J., Farboodi, M., Veldkamp, L., 2018. Big data in finance and the growth of large firms. Journal of Monetary Economics 97, 71–87.

Berman, N., Rebeyrol, V., Vicard, V., 2019. Demand learning and firm dynamics: evidence from exporters. Review of Economics and Statistics 101 (1), 91–106.

Bernardo, J.M., Smith, A.F., 2009. Bayesian Theory, vol. 405. John Wiley & Sons.

Bertocchi, G., Spagat, M., 1998. Growth under uncertainty with experimentation. Journal of Economic Dynamics and Control 23 (2), 209–231.

Bertoli, S., Moraga, J.F.-H., Guichard, L., 2020. Rational inattention and migration decisions. Journal of International Economics 126, 103364.

Boerma, J., Karabarbounis, L., 2021. Reparations and Persistent Racial Wealth Gaps. Tech. Rep. National Bureau of Economic Research.

Bonomo, M., Carvalho, C., 2004. Endogenous time-dependent rules and inflation inertia. Journal of Money, Credit, and Banking, 1015–1041.

Bonomo, M., Carvalho, C., Garcia, R., Malta, V., Rigato, R., 2022. Persistent monetary non-neutrality in an estimated menu-cost model with partially costly information. American Economic Journal: Macroeconomics. Forthcoming.

Borovicková, K., 2016. Job flows, worker flows and labor market policies. Tech. Rep. New York University.

Botsch, M., Vanasco, V., 2019. Learning by lending. Journal of Financial Intermediation 37, 1–14.

Brown, Z.Y., Jeon, J., 2020. Endogenous information acquisition and insurance choice. University of Michigan and Boston University Working Paper.

Buera, F.J., Monge-Naranjo, A., Primiceri, G.E., 2011. Learning the wealth of nations. Econometrica 79 (1), 1–45.

Caplin, A., Dean, M., 2015. Revealed preference, rational inattention, and costly information acquisition. The American Economic Review 105 (7), 2183–2203.

Caplin, A., Dean, M., Leahy, J., 2017. Rationally inattentive behavior: Characterizing and generalizing Shannon entropy. Tech. Rep. National Bureau of Economic Research.

Carroll, C.D., Crawley, E., Slacalek, J., Tokuoka, K., White, M.N., 2020. Sticky expectations and consumption dynamics. American Economic Journal: Macroeconomics 12 (3), 40–76.

Chahrour, R., Nimark, K., Pitschner, S., 2021. Sectoral media focus and aggregate fluctuations. The American Economic Review 111 (12), 3872–3922.

Chamley, C., 2004. Rational Herds: Economics Models of Social Learning, 1st edn. Cambridge University Press.

Chen, C., Senga, T., Sun, C., Zhang, H., 2020. Uncertainty, Imperfect Information, and Expectation Formation over the Firms's Life Cycle. Tech. Rep. CESifo.

Cheremukhin, A., Restrepo-Echavarria, P., Tutino, A., 2020. Targeted search in matching markets. Journal of Economic Theory 185, 104956.

Cogley, T., Sargent, T.J., 2005. The conquest of us inflation: learning and robustness to model uncertainty. Review of Economic Dynamics 8 (2), 528–563.

Cohen, L., Frazzini, A., 2008. Economic links and predictable returns. The Journal of Finance 63 (4), 1977–2011.

Coibion, O., Georgarakos, D., Gorodnichenko, Y., Kenny, G., Weber, M., 2021. The effect of macroeconomic uncertainty on household spending. Tech. Rep. National Bureau of Economic Research.

Coibion, O., Gorodnichenko, Y., 2012. What can survey forecasts tell us about information rigidities? Journal of Political Economy 120 (1), 116–159.

Coibion, O., Gorodnichenko, Y., Kumar, S., 2018. How do firms form their expectations? New survey evidence. The American Economic Review 108 (9), 2671–2713.

Coibion, O., Gorodnichenko, Y., Weber, M., 2019. Monetary policy communications and their effects on household inflation expectations. Tech. Rep. National Bureau of Economic Research.

Collin Dufresne, P., Johannes, M., Lochstoer, L.A., 2016. Parameter learning in general equilibrium: the asset pricing implications. The American Economic Review 106 (3), 664–698.

Cong, L.W., Xie, D., Zhang, L., 2021. Knowledge accumulation, privacy, and growth in a data economy. Management Science 67 (10), 6480–6492.

Conley, T.G., Udry, C.R., 2010. Learning about a new technology: pineapple in Ghana. The American Economic Review 100 (1), 35–69.

Cover, T.M., Thomas, J.A., 1991. Entropy, relative entropy and mutual information. Elements of Information Theory 2 (1), 12–13.

Dasgupta, K., Mondria, J., 2018. Inattentive importers. Journal of International Economics 112, 150–165.

de Oliveira, H., Denti, T., Mihm, M., Ozbek, K., 2017. Rationally inattentive preferences and hidden information costs. Theoretical Economics 12 (2), 621–654.

Doppelt, R., 2016. The hazards of unemployment. Working Paper.

Drenik, A., Perez, D.J., 2020. Price setting under uncertainty about inflation. Journal of Monetary Economics 116, 23–38.

Ellis, A., 2018. Foundations for optimal inattention. Journal of Economic Theory 173, 56–94.

Evans, G., Honkapohja, S., 2001. Learning and Expectations in Macroeconomics, 1st edn. Princeton University Press.

Fajgelbaum, P.D., Schaal, E., Taschereau-Dumouchel, M., 2017. Uncertainty traps. The Quarterly Journal of Economics 132 (4), 1641–1692.

Farber, H.S., Gibbons, R., 1996. Learning and wage dynamics. The Quarterly Journal of Economics 111 (4), 1007–1047.

Farboodi, M., Mihet, R., Philippon, T., Veldkamp, L., 2019. Big data and firm dynamics. AEA Papers and Proceedings 109, 38–42.

Farboodi, M., Veldkamp, L., 2021. A Growth Model of the Data Economy. Tech. Rep. Working Paper 28427. National Bureau of Economic Research.

Fernandes, A.P., Tang, H., 2014. Learning to export from neighbors. Journal of International Economics 94 (1), 67–84.

Figueiredo, A., 2018. Information frictions in education and inequality. In: 2018 Meeting Papers, vol. 804. Society for Economic Dynamics.

Fogli, A., Veldkamp, L., 2011. Nature or nurture? Learning and the geography of female labor force participation. Econometrica 79 (4), 1103–1138.

Fuster, A., Perez-Truglia, R., Wiederholt, M., Zafar, B., 2020. Expectations with endogenous information acquisition: an experimental investigation. Review of Economics and Statistics, 1–54.

Gabaix, X., Laibson, D., 2001. The 6d bias and the equity-premium puzzle. NBER Macroeconomics Annual 16, 257–312.

Galenianos, M., 2013. Learning about match quality and the use of referrals. Review of Economic Dynamics 16 (4), 668–690.

Ghofrani, E., 2021. Learning with uncertainty's uncertainty. Tech. Rep. UPF.

Gonzalez, F.M., Shi, S., 2010. An equilibrium theory of learning, search, and wages. Econometrica 78 (2), 509–537.

Gorodnichenko, Y., 2008. Endogenous information, menu costs and inflation persistence. Tech. Rep. National Bureau of Economic Research.

Goyal, S., 2011. Learning in networks. In: Handbook of Social Economics, vol. 1. Elsevier, pp. 679–727.

Groes, F., Kircher, P., Manovskii, I., 2014. The u-shapes of occupational mobility. The Review of Economic Studies 82 (2), 659–692.

Grossman, S.J., Stiglitz, J.E., 1980. On the impossibility of informationally efficient markets. The American Economic Review 70 (3), 393–408.

Gutiérrez-Daza, A., 2022. Inattentive Inflation Expectations. Tech. Rep. Universitat Pompeu Fabra.

Hébert, B., La'O, J., 2020. Information Acquisition, Efficiency, and Non-Fundamental Volatility. Tech. Rep. National Bureau of Economic Research.

Hébert, B., Woodford, M., 2019. Rational inattention when decisions take time. Tech. Rep. National Bureau of Economic Research.

Hébert, B., Woodford, M., 2021. Neighborhood-based information costs. The American Economic Review 111 (10), 3225–3255.

Hellwig, C., Kohls, S., Veldkamp, L., 2012. Information choice technologies. The American Economic Review 102 (3), 35–40.

Hellwig, C., Veldkamp, L., 2009. Knowing what others know: coordination motives in information acquisition. The Review of Economic Studies 76, 223–251.

Hellwig, C., Venkateswaran, V., 2009. Setting the right prices for the wrong reasons. Journal of Monetary Economics 56, S57–S77.

Herskovic, B., Ramos, J., 2020. Acquiring information through peers. The American Economic Review 110 (7), 2128–2152.

Hong, H., Torous, W., Valkanov, R., 2007. Do industries lead stock markets? Journal of Financial Economics 83 (2), 367–396.

Jones, C.I., Tonetti, C., 2020. Nonrivalry and the economics of data. The American Economic Review 110 (9), 2819–2858.

Jovanovic, B., 1979. Job matching and the theory of turnover. Journal of Political Economy 87 (5), 972–990.

Jovanovic, B., 1984. Matching, turnover, and unemployment. Journal of Political Economy 92 (1), 108–122.

Jovanovic, B., Nyarko, Y., 1996. Learning by doing and the choice of technology. Econometrica 64, 1299–1310.

Kacperczyk, M., Nosal, J., Stevens, L., 2019. Investor sophistication and capital income inequality. Journal of Monetary Economics 107, 18–31.

Kacperczyk, M., Van Nieuwerburgh, S., Veldkamp, L., 2016. A rational theory of mutual funds' attention allocation. Econometrica 84 (2), 571–626.

Keller, G., Rady, S., 1999. Optimal experimentation in a changing environment. The Review of Economic Studies 66 (3), 475–507.

Kellogg, R., 2011. Learning by drilling: interfirm learning and relationship persistence in the Texas oilpatch. The Quarterly Journal of Economics 126 (4), 1961–2004.

Kelly, D.L., Kolstad, C.D., 1999. Bayesian learning, growth, and pollution. Journal of Economic Dynamics and Control 23 (4), 491–518.

Khaw, M.W., Stevens, L., Woodford, M., 2017. Discrete adjustment to a changing environment: experimental evidence. Journal of Monetary Economics 91, 88–103.

Klenow, P.J., Willis, J.L., 2007. Sticky information and sticky prices. Journal of Monetary Economics 54, 79–99.

Kőszegi, B., Matějka, F., 2020. Choice simplification: a theory of mental budgeting and naive diversification. The Quarterly Journal of Economics 135 (2), 1153–1207.

Kozlowski, J., Veldkamp, L., Venkateswaran, V., 2020a. Scarring body and mind: the long-term belief-scarring effects of COVID-19. Tech. Rep. National Bureau of Economic Research.

Kozlowski, J., Veldkamp, L., Venkateswaran, V., 2020b. The tail that wags the economy: beliefs and persistent stagnation. Journal of Political Economy 128 (8), 2839–2879.

Lee, D.S., Moretti, E., 2009. Bayesian learning and the pricing of new information: evidence from prediction markets. The American Economic Review 99 (2), 330–336.

Liptser, R.S., Shiryaev, A.N., 2001. Statistics of Random Processes: I. General Theory, vol. 1. Springer Science & Business Media.

Lucas, R.E., 1972. Expectations and the neutrality of money. Journal of Economic Theory 4 (2), 103–124.

Luo, Y., 2008. Consumption dynamics under information processing constraints. Review of Economic Dynamics 11 (2), 366–385.

Luo, Y., Nie, J., Young, E.R., 2015. Slow information diffusion and the inertial behavior of durable consumption. Journal of the European Economic Association 13 (5), 805–840.

Maćkowiak, B., Matějka, F., Wiederholt, M., 2018. Dynamic rational inattention: analytical results. Journal of Economic Theory 176, 650–692.

Maćkowiak, B., Matějka, F., Wiederholt, M., 2020. Rational inattention: a review. CEPR Discussion Papers (15408).

Maćkowiak, B., Wiederholt, M., 2009. Optimal sticky prices under rational inattention. The American Economic Review 99 (3), 769–803.

Maćkowiak, B., Wiederholt, M., 2015. Business cycle dynamics under rational inattention. The Review of Economic Studies 82 (4), 1502–1532.

Mankiw, G., Reis, R., 2002. Sticky information versus sticky prices: a proposal to replace the new Keynesian Phillips curve. The Quarterly Journal of Economics 117, 1295–1328.

Matějka, F., Tabellini, G., 2021. Electoral competition with rationally inattentive voters. Journal of the European Economic Association 19 (3), 1899–1935.

Menzio, G., Shi, S., 2011. Efficient search on the job and the business cycle. Journal of Political Economy 119 (3), 468–510.

Miao, J., Wu, J., Young, E., 2019. Multivariate Rational Inattention. Boston University – Department of Economics – Working Papers Series WP2019-07. Boston University – Department of Economics.

Mihet, R., 2021. Financial Technology and the Inequality Gap. Swiss Finance Institute Research Paper Series 21-04 Swiss Finance Institute.

Miller, R.A., 1984. Job matching and occupational choice. Journal of Political Economy 92 (6), 1086–1120.

Minniti, M., Bygrave, W., 2001. A dynamic model of entrepreneurial learning. Entrepreneurship Theory and Practice 25 (3), 5–16.

Mirman, L.J., Samuelson, L., Urbano, A., 1993. Monopoly experimentation. International Economic Review, 549–563.

Mondria, J., 2010. Portfolio choice, attention allocation, and price comovement. Journal of Economic Theory 145 (5), 1837–1864.

Morris, S., Shin, H.S., 2002. Social value of public information. The American Economic Review 92 (5), 1521–1534.

Moscarini, G., 2001. Excess worker reallocation. The Review of Economic Studies 68 (3), 593–612.

Myatt, D.P., Wallace, C., 2012. Endogenous information acquisition in coordination games. The Review of Economic Studies 79 (1), 340–374.

Nagypál, É., 2007. Learning by doing vs. learning about match quality: can we tell them apart? The Review of Economic Studies 74 (2), 537–566.

Neal, D., 1999. The complexity of job mobility among young men. Journal of Labor Economics 17 (2), 237–261.

Nimark, K.P., 2014. Man-bites-dog business cycles. The American Economic Review 104 (8), 2320–2367.

Nimark, K.P., Pitschner, S., 2019. News media and delegated information choice. Journal of Economic Theory 181, 160–196.

Ordonez, G., 2013. The asymmetric effects of financial frictions. Journal of Political Economy 121 (5), 844–895.

Paciello, L., Wiederholt, M., 2014. Exogenous information, endogenous information, and optimal monetary policy. The Review of Economic Studies 81 (1), 356–388.

Papageorgiou, T., 2014. Learning your comparative advantages. The Review of Economic Studies 81 (3), 1263–1295.

Pástor, L., Taylor, L.A., Veronesi, P., 2009. Entrepreneurial learning, the IPO decision, and the post-IPO drop in firm profitability. The Review of Financial Studies 22 (8), 3005–3046.

Pastor, L., Veronesi, P., 2009. Learning in financial markets. Annual Review of Financial Economics 1 (1), 361–381.

Pastor, L., Veronesi, P., 2012. Uncertainty about government policy and stock prices. The Journal of Finance 67 (4), 1219–1264.

Pastorino, E., 2009. Learning in labor markets and job mobility. Unpublished manuscript. Department of Economics, University of Iowa.

Peress, J., 2004. Wealth, information acquisition, and portfolio choice. The Review of Financial Studies 17 (3), 879–914.

Phelps, E.S., 1970. Introduction: the new microeconomics in employment and inflation theory. In: Microeconomic Foundations of Employment and Inflation Theory, vol. 1, p. 23.

Porcher, C., 2020. Migration with Costly Information. Tech. Rep., Working Paper. Princeton.

Prescott, E.C., 1972. The multi-period control problem under uncertainty. Econometrica, 1043–1058.

Pries, M., Rogerson, R., 2005. Hiring policies, labor market institutions, and labor market flows. Journal of Political Economy 113 (4), 811–839.

Primiceri, G.E., 2006. Why inflation rose and fell: policy-makers' beliefs and us postwar stabilization policy. The Quarterly Journal of Economics 121 (3), 867–901.

Reis, R., 2006a. Inattentive consumers. Journal of Monetary Economics 53 (8), 1761–1800.

Reis, R., 2006b. Inattentive producers. The Review of Economic Studies 73 (3), 793–821.

Rothschild, M., 1974. A two-armed bandit theory of market pricing. Journal of Economic Theory 9 (2), 185–202.

Saijo, H., 2017. The uncertainty multiplier and business cycles. Journal of Economic Dynamics and Control 78, 1–25.

Sargent, T., Williams, N., Zha, T., 2006. Shocks and government beliefs: the rise and fall of American inflation. The American Economic Review 96 (4), 1193–1224.

Senga, T., 2018. A New Look at Uncertainty Shocks: Imperfect Information and Misallocation. Working Papers 763. Queen Mary University of London, School of Economics and Finance.

Sims, C., 2003. Implications of rational inattention. Journal of Monetary Economics 50 (3), 665–690.

Stevens, L., 2020. Coarse pricing policies. The Review of Economic Studies 87 (1), 420–453.

Straub, L., Ulbricht, R., 2018. Endogenous uncertainty and credit crunches. Available at SSRN 2668078.

Svensson, L.E., Williams, N.M., 2007. Bayesian and adaptive optimal policy under model uncertainty. Tech. Rep. National Bureau of Economic Research.

Timoshenko, O.A., 2015. Product switching in a model of learning. Journal of International Economics 95 (2), 233–249.

Topa, G., 2001. Social interactions, local spillovers and unemployment. The Review of Economic Studies 68 (2), 261–295.

Topa, G., 2011. Labor markets and referrals. In: Handbook of Social Economics, vol. 1. North-Holland, pp. 1193–1221. Chapter 22.

Turén, J., 2020. State-dependent attention and pricing decisions. Working paper. Pontificia Universidad Católica de Chile.

Van Nieuwerburgh, S., Veldkamp, L., 2006. Learning asymmetries in real business cycles. Journal of Monetary Economics 53 (4), 753–772.

Van Nieuwerburgh, S., Veldkamp, L., 2010. Information acquisition and portfolio under-diversification. The Review of Economic Studies 77 (2), 779–805.

Veldkamp, L., 2005. Slow boom, sudden crash. Journal of Economic Theory 124 (2), 230–257.

Veldkamp, L., 2006. Information markets and the comovement of asset prices. The Review of Economic Studies 73 (3), 823–845.

Veldkamp, L., Wolfers, J., 2007. Aggregate shocks or aggregate information? Costly information and business cycle comovement. Journal of Monetary Economics 54, 37–55.

Venkateswaran, V., 2014. Heterogeneous information and labor market fluctuations. working Paper.

Wee, S.L., 2016. Delayed learning and human capital accumulation: the cost of entering the job market during a recession. Unpublished manuscript, 18.

Weitzman, M.L., 2007. Subjective expectations and asset-return puzzles. The American Economic Review 97 (4), 1102–1130.

Wieland, V., 2000. Monetary policy, parameter uncertainty and optimal learning. Journal of Monetary Economics 46 (1), 199–228.

Willems, T., 2017. Actively learning by pricing: a model of an experimenting seller. The Economic Journal 127 (604), 2216–2239.

Wilson, R., 1975. Informational economies of scale. Bell Journal of Economics 6, 184–195.

Woodford, M., 2003. Imperfect common knowledge and the effects of monetary policy. In: Knowledge, Information, and Expectations in Modern Macroeconomics: In Honor of Edmund S. Phelps, p. 25.

Woodford, M., 2009. Information-constrained state-dependent pricing. Journal of Monetary Economics 56, S100–S124.

Yang, C., 2020. Rational inattention, menu costs, and multi-product firms: Micro evidence and aggregate implications. Tech. Rep. Federal Reserve Board.

Ambiguity☆

Cosmin Ilut[a,b] **and Martin Schneider**[c,b]
ᵃDuke University, Durham, NC, United States
ᵇNBER, Cambridge, MA, United States
ᶜStanford University, Stanford, CA, United States

24.1 Introduction

To introduce ambiguity, consider a simple thought experiment. Suppose we are uncertain about whether sea level rise will exceed one foot by the year 2050. Alternative models of climate change generate very different probabilities of this event. How should we value insurance in the face of such model uncertainty? A Bayesian with standard expected utility preferences assigns probabilities to all relevant events: he forms a prior over the different models and arrives at a prediction by averaging probability forecasts. Suppose for concreteness that this exercise delivers a conditional probability of one third.

Now suppose additional evidence leads all climate change models to *agree* on a probability of one-third for the event. In other words, scientific progress eliminates model uncertainty. For the Bayesian, this new information does not affect beliefs or behavior: model averaging still delivers a probability of one-third, and hence the same valuation of insurance. However, a complete lack of response is not obviously intuitive: new information should make us more confident in our assessment of the event, and this should be reflected in behavior as well. The expected utility model does not allow for a response since model uncertainty and uncertainty about events described by models are both treated as risk, that is, uncertainty with known odds. Reduction of compound lotteries then implies the same probability of one-third in both scenarios.

The term ambiguity refers to uncertainty when the odds are not known. Ambiguity averse agents are not confident enough to assign probabilities to events about which they have little information, such as what is the right model of climate change. The Ellsberg (1961) Paradox, reviewed below, illustrates that the distinction between ambiguity and risk is behaviorally meaningful; agents make choices that are inconsistent with the Bayesian model because they want to avoid ambiguity. Axiomatic models of rational choice consistent with the Ellsberg Paradox were developed in the 1980s. The key innovation was to represent preferences using sets of beliefs (Gilboa and Schmeidler (1989)). Uncertainty about probability assessments can then be described by the size of the belief set, similarly to how model uncertainty is handled in a related literature on robust statistics (for example, Huber (1981)).

☆ We thank Rudi Bachmann, Federico Bennett, Lautaro Chittaro, Florian Fiaux, Robert Garlick, Pamela Giustinelli, Monika Piazzesi, Giorgio Topa, Rosen Valchev, and Wilbert van der Klaauw for helpful comments.

When ambiguity averse agents evaluate a plan, they act *as if* they are relatively pessimistic about the plan, and more so the larger their belief set. Continuing our example, an ambiguity averse agent confronted with disagreement among climate change models has a large set of beliefs. An agent who is adversely exposed to sea level rise evaluates insurance as if sea level rise is relatively likely. In contrast, an agent who stands to gain from sea level rise behaves as if climate change has little effect. This endogenous adjustment of pessimism generates cautious behavior that is different in nature from what the Bayesian model can capture. In particular, news that all models agree collapses the set of beliefs to one, and behavior becomes less cautious.

Early applications of ambiguity aversion were mostly confined to finance, following the seminal papers on portfolio choice by Dow and Werlang (1992) and on asset pricing by Epstein and Wang (1994). The early 2000s then saw a surge of research on theoretical foundations for dynamic choice under ambiguity. Over the last decade, we have seen new applications in many fields of economics. Our goal in this chapter is to provide an overview of this work. We first compare models of ambiguity aversion and the standard Bayesian approach in four contexts: a consumption–savings problem, a portfolio choice problem, an asset pricing Euler equation, and a dynamic stochastic general equilibrium model of the business cycle. We then survey how the literature has used ambiguity aversion to understand aggregate fluctuations, asset pricing puzzles, decisions of heterogeneous agents in micro data, and optimal policy.

We emphasize three themes throughout the chapter. First, since ambiguity and risk are both concepts of uncertainty, models of risk aversion and ambiguity aversion naturally share many properties. Uncertainty of either flavor lowers welfare. Agents' desire to avoid uncertainty is a key force in asset markets: higher uncertainty can explain why some assets are cheaper than others, and why prices are lower in certain periods such as recessions. More generally, the desire to avoid uncertainty guides intertemporal decisions towards precautionary behavior: higher uncertainty leads to more savings, less hiring of workers, or less issuance of debt. Time variation in uncertainty can therefore generate economic fluctuations that coincide with drops in asset prices.

Second, a key difference between ambiguity and risk is that only the former can generate first order welfare effects of uncertainty. Intuitively, an ambiguity averse agent with a set of beliefs that differ in mean evaluates plans *as if* the worst case mean is low; uncertainty does not matter only for higher moments. There are two implications for applied work. One is technical: models with ambiguity-averse agents allow for precautionary savings, uncertainty premia and excess volatility of asset prices, but can still be characterized using standard *linear* approximation and estimation techniques that are common in macroeconomics. In particular, when ambiguity is assumed to move with the volatility of shocks, effects of stochastic volatility can also be studied with linear models.

First order welfare effects of ambiguity further generate inaction or inertia from uncertainty alone. Intuitively, an agent contemplating positive (negative) exposure to ambiguity evaluates plans based on low (high) mean payoffs and chooses zero exposure if both are sufficiently unfavorable. This feature leads to parsimonious explanations for a number of robust facts in micro data – for example, nonparticipation in asset markets that an investor is not familiar with, rigidity and memory in nominal prices, or lack of adoption of new technologies. We note that market frictions, technological rigidities, or curvature in utility is not required for the argument. This is contrast to results on inaction due to risk: for example, "wait-and-see" effects require irreversibility of investment, which induces curvature in the objective function.

Our third theme is that models of ambiguity aversion offer a way to *quantify* uncertainty that is conceptually more appealing and more tractable than standard practice, yet allows for similar discipline in specifying preferences. To elaborate, the standard approach to quantify models in macroeconomics and finance (i) estimates stochastic processes for exogenous fundamentals, such as productivity shocks or dividends, and (ii) assumes rational expectations: the estimated processes not only describe physical laws of motion, but also beliefs used to calculate agents' expected utility. As a result, agents in the model do not share researchers' doubts about model specification or the parameter uncertainty revealed by estimation. With agents that confident about the world, it is not surprising that the standard approach has run into many puzzles.

Quantitative models with ambiguity aversion capture doubts about model specification and parameter uncertainty through belief sets: they avoid puzzles by making agents less confident. Additional degrees of freedom are pinned down using survey data as well as model consistency criteria that relate actual and worst case laws of motion. At the same time, two attractive features of standard rational expectations modeling are retained. In particular, belief sets are typically parametrized by an interval of means centered around econometricians' point estimates: as in standard models, agents do not make systematic forecast errors. Moreover, agents have structural knowledge of the economy: they understand how endogenous variables depend on shocks as well as policy parameters and form belief sets accordingly. As in standard models, policy evaluation thus is not subject to the Lucas critique.

The rest of the chapter is structured as follows. Section 24.2 introduces preferences in a two period setting and studies savings and portfolio choice. Section 24.3 considers intertemporal preferences and studies consumption-based asset pricing and business cycle models. Section 24.4 reviews work that quantifies ambiguity using survey data. Section 24.5 covers aggregate models, Section 24.6 collects work that makes predictions for micro data, and Section 24.7 is about optimal policy. A conclusion flags open questions.

24.2 Static choice under uncertainty

We start with a two period setup and define preferences that reflect risk or ambiguity aversion. Our focus on applications leads us to discuss preferences only in terms of utility functions, as opposed to their axiomatic foundations. We refer the reader to Epstein and Schneider (2010) or Gilboa and Marinacci (2016) for a discussion of the main representation results.

24.2.1 Preferences

There are two dates 1 and 2 and one consumption good. At date 2, one of a finite number of states $\omega \in \Omega$ is realized. At date 1, an agent chooses not only date 1 consumption c, but also consumption $\tilde{c}(\omega)$ in each state ω at date 2. We refer to the pair $(c, \tilde{c})$ as a consumption *plan*. For all models we consider, preferences over consumption plans can be represented by

$$u(c) + \beta u(CE(\tilde{c})). \tag{24.1}$$

Here the function CE returns the certainty equivalent of uncertain date 2 consumption $\tilde{c}$, that is, the number $\bar{c}$ such that a plan with constant consumption $\bar{c}$ rather than $\tilde{c}(\omega)$ in all states ω at date 2 is indifferent to $(c, \tilde{c})$. The shape of CE reflects whether agents are averse to risk or ambiguity. The function u ranks certain consumption plans; throughout, it is smooth, strictly increasing and concave.

The agent's willingness to substitute intertemporally depends on the curvature of u. It can be measured, for example, by the intertemporal elasticity of substitution (IES) $\sigma(c) = -u'(c)/cu''(c)$.

Risk aversion. Let the probability P on the state space Ω denote the agent's subjective belief. In what follows, we use superscripts to distinguish between expectations formed under different beliefs, for example, $\mathbb{E}^P$ is the expectation under P. We define the certainty equivalent for the case of risk aversion by

$$v(CE(\tilde{c})) = \mathbb{E}^P\left[v(\tilde{c})\right], \tag{24.2}$$

where v is a strictly increasing and concave function.

Risk aversion is captured by curvature in v. Strict concavity of v implies $CE(\tilde{c}) < \mathbb{E}^P[\tilde{c}]$, that is, the certainty equivalent is valued less than mean consumption under the subjective belief. In this sense, the agent dislikes risky consumption plans. The degree of risk aversion can be measured, for example, by the coefficient of relative risk aversion $\gamma(c) = -cv''(c)/v'(c)$. In general, we allow $u \neq v$, so risk tolerance – the willingness to substitute across states – is distinct from the willingness to substitute over time, as in the large applied literature following Epstein and Zin (1989). In the special case $u = v$, we obtain the familiar time separable expected utility model $u(c) + \beta\mathbb{E}^P\left[u(\tilde{c})\right]$.

The Ellsberg Paradox. People prefer to know the odds of an event. In Ellsberg's thought experiment, such preference is revealed by the ranking of bets. To illustrate, consider bets that pay one dollar if an event occurs and zero otherwise. Compare two events: a risky event is known to occur with probability one-half ("known odds"), whereas no information is given about the other, ambiguous, event ("unknown odds"). It then makes sense to prefer a bet on the risky event to a bet on the ambiguous event. This is because we can be confident that the first bet is indeed fair, whereas the second bet might not be. By symmetry, it also makes sense to prefer a bet *against* the risky event – a bet that pays one dollar when it does not occur and zero otherwise – to a bet against the ambiguous event.

This intuitive "Ellsberg-type" behavior is incompatible with a single subjective belief on the state space. Indeed, a decision maker whose choice under uncertainty is represented by (24.1)–(24.2) has in mind a single probability not only for the risky event but also for the ambiguous event. Strict preference for a bet on the risky event therefore reveals that the subjective probability of the ambiguous event is smaller than one-half. At the same time, strict preference for a bet against the risky event implies a probability of the ambiguous event larger than one-half, a contradiction.

We note that the Ellsberg paradox not only reveals a problem with the standard expected utility model ($u = v$), but more broadly with any model that represents belief with a single probability, for example, the more general class (24.1)–(24.2) that distinguishes risk aversion from the willingness to smooth over time. This is why models of ambiguity aversion turn to sets of probabilities in order to capture Ellsberg-type behavior. We also emphasize that the paradox can be understood as a *rational* response to a lack of confidence in probability assessments – it is not limited to inexperienced subjects in the lab. Relatedly, it is not crucial that the odds of the risky event are exactly known, it is enough that we are confident to think about it in terms of probabilities.

Multiple priors. Let $\mathcal{P}$ denote a set of beliefs P on Ω. For the *multiple priors* model, introduced by Gilboa and Schmeidler (1989), the certainty equivalent is

$$v(CE(\tilde{c})) = \min_{P \in \mathcal{P}} \mathbb{E}^P\left[v(\tilde{c})\right]. \tag{24.3}$$

Agents with multiple priors preferences deal with ambiguity by acting *as if* they were using the most pessimistic belief from $\mathcal{P}$, a belief that we denote generically by P^*. In the special case where the set contains only a single probability, we are back to the risk aversion case (24.2). More generally, the size of the belief set describes agents' lack of confidence in probability assessments: a larger set reflects more ambiguity.

The multiple priors model is consistent with Ellsberg-type behavior because the "worst-case belief" P^* endogenously varies with the consumption plan. To see this, fix a state space and consider a set of beliefs that agree on the probability of an event S^r, say, but disagree on an event S^a such that $\min_{P \in \mathcal{P}} P(S^a) < P(S^r) < \max_{P \in \mathcal{P}} P(S^a)$. Here S^r represents a risky event to which the agent can attach a probability, whereas S^a is an ambiguous event that may or may not be more likely than S^r. An agent then prefers a bet on S^r to a bet on S^a because he evaluates the bet on S^a using $\min_{P \in \mathcal{P}} P(S^a) < P(S^r)$. At the same time, he prefers a bet against S^r to a bet against S^a since he evaluates the latter using the worst-case probability $1 - \max_{P \in \mathcal{P}} P(S^a) < 1 - P(S^r)$.

The Gilboa–Schmeidler axioms imply a representation (24.3) with *some* (subjective) set of beliefs $\mathcal{P}$. In applications, the set $\mathcal{P}$ is thus a primitive chosen by the modeler to describe behavior under ambiguity, much like the subjective belief P above is chosen to describe behavior under risk. One extreme choice is to let $\mathcal{P}$ contain only measures P_ω that put probability one on a single state ω, that is, agents consider a set of event realizations and evaluate plans by their performance under the worst-case *realization*. However, nothing in the theory restricts attention to that extreme: elements of $\mathcal{P}$ need not be degenerate. In applications, it often makes sense to make the set relatively small in order to fit agents' willingness to pay for insurance against ambiguity. As the example above shows, even a very small set generates choice that differs from expected utility.

Other models of ambiguity aversion. Several other models of preference have been developed to account for Ellsberg-type behavior; a detailed survey is Machina and Siniscalchi (2014). The most prominent models in applied work are multiplier preferences, proposed by Anderson et al. (2003) and axiomatized by Strzalecki (2011), as well as the smooth ambiguity model (Neilson (1993), Nau (2006), Klibanoff et al. (2005)).[1] Like multiple priors, these models work with sets of beliefs, and agents who evaluate a plan behave *as if* they are endogenously more pessimistic about that plan because unfavorable beliefs matter more for utility. Much of the intuition we discuss for multiple priors thus applies to all widely-used models.

The models differ from multiple priors in how belief sets enter the certainty equivalent function – in particular, they make the certainty equivalent a smooth function of consumption plans. As a result, welfare effects of uncertainty are not first order in the sense we describe below. Applications with multiplier or smooth ambiguity preference thus do not typically use linear methods, and do not emphasize qualitative differences from risk aversion related to inaction or inertia. The common denominator of all models that we emphasize in our review of applications is that they capture agents' concern with model uncertainty, which allows for better quantitative performance compared to models with risk aversion and rational expectations.

---

[1] Multiplier preferences are related to work on robust control in engineering. See Hansen and Sargent (2008) and Hansen and Sargent (2018) for an interesting recent extension that formalizes a concern for model misspecification. For a comprehensive survey of theoretical properties and applications of the smooth model, see Marinacci (2015).

24.2.2 Risk vs ambiguity: similarities and differences

The certainty equivalent functions for risk aversion (24.2) and ambiguity aversion (24.3) capture disutility from plans that vary across states. As a result, much of the standard intuition for behavior under uncertainty equally applies to both models. For example, a change in uncertainty that lowers the certainty equivalent of future consumption makes agents unhappy; they may respond by taking precautionary actions. The models differ, however, in what a change in uncertainty means. An increase in risk is typically captured by adding a mean-preserving spread in the distribution of date 2 consumption. An increase in ambiguity instead is an increase in the set of distributions used to evaluate date 2 consumption. This difference has important implications for modeling strategy and behavior.

Uncertainty without curvature. With risk aversion, utility costs of uncertainty are due to curvature in v. Indeed, if v is linear, a mean-preserving spread in the distribution of $\tilde{c}$ does not affect utility, since CE only depends on the mean $\mathbb{E}^P[\tilde{c}]$. This observation has led modelers who want to avoid curvature in utility for other reasons, say to eliminate wealth effects for tractability, to abstract from aversion to uncertainty altogether. For example, many papers on search markets or contracting within firms work with linear $u = v$.

The multiple priors model, in contrast, captures uncertainty aversion even when $u = v$ is linear. Suppose the beliefs $P \in \mathcal{P}$ differ in means, and consider utility

$$c + \beta \min_{P \in \mathcal{P}} \mathbb{E}^P[\tilde{c}]. \tag{24.4}$$

An increase in ambiguity – a larger set $\mathcal{P}$ – now lowers utility if it leads to a lower worst-case mean for the plan $\tilde{c}$. Incorporating ambiguity aversion thus allows tractable models without wealth effects that nevertheless feature compensation for uncertainty as part of contract design or prices in search markets.

Welfare costs of uncertainty. With risk aversion, the welfare costs of uncertainty are second order. The textbook result starts from a certain consumption plan $\tilde{c} = \bar{c}$ and adds a small mean preserving spread $\alpha \tilde{z}$, say, where $\mathbb{E}^P \tilde{z} = 0$. With concave v, welfare declines for any α, but the welfare loss scales with α^2, and so goes to zero faster than α. This property of risk preferences has far-reaching consequences for applications. It generates a strong appetite for risk taking: starting from certainty, a risky gamble is attractive even if it offers very small risk compensation, as long as that compensation declines linearly in α and hence more slowly than the welfare loss of uncertainty. More generally, it is a hallmark of quantitative models with risk aversion that agents are willing to tolerate high uncertainty in return for a small gain in the mean.

With multiple priors, in contrast, we can have first order welfare losses from uncertainty. Consider linear utility (24.4) with a set of beliefs that differ in means. Starting again at a certain consumption plan, add a random variable $\alpha \tilde{z}$ such that $\min_{P \in \mathcal{P}} \mathbb{E}^P \tilde{z} < 0 < \max_{P \in \mathcal{P}} \mathbb{E}^P \tilde{z}$, but all other moments are identical. The belief set that describes ambiguity is thus parametrized by an interval of means for $\tilde{z}$ that brackets zero: it contains beliefs with positive and negative means for $\tilde{z}$. Again utility declines for any α: the worst-case mean endogenously adjusts so its sign is opposite to that of α. The key difference is that the welfare loss from ambiguity is linear in α. In applications with multiple priors, mean and uncertainty can thus have the same order of magnitude.

Preference towards the timing of the resolution of uncertainty. It is common in applications with risk aversion to assume curvature in v to be much larger than in u so $\gamma(c)$ is much higher than the desire for consumption smoothing over time, measured by the inverse of the IES $\sigma(c)$. The assumption is particularly prominent in macroeconomics and finance in order to address asset pricing puzzles under rational expectations. However, it also implies that agents strictly prefer early resolution of uncertainty, that is, agents would pay to receive information even if they cannot adjust their consumption plans in response (see Epstein et al. (2014) for quantitative thought experiments). Standard expected utility agents with $u = v$ do not exhibit such behavior.

With multiple priors, modelers can avoid this tight connection between aversion to uncertainty and preference towards the timing of its resolution. In particular, multiple priors agents with $u = v$ are indifferent towards the timing of the resolution of uncertainty, just like standard expected utility maximizers.[2] For example, an agent with low IES but a large set of beliefs $\mathcal{P}$ also requires a lot of risk compensation, but would not pay up front for information unless he can use it in planning. Of course, if compensation for timing is desirable to match the data, then the multiple priors model can be augmented with $v \neq u$.

Uncertainty attitude versus beliefs. The two primitives that govern attitude towards risk – the belief P and the utility function v – permit a distinction between risk perception and risk attitude, respectively. At the same time, both work through the certainty equivalent, implying that changes in risk or risk aversion often have similar implications – for example, through intertemporal substitution behavior or required compensation.

Models of ambiguity aversion, in contrast, do not offer a distinction between attitude and beliefs. In particular, the set of beliefs $\mathcal{P}$ always reflects in part the agent's attitude towards ambiguity. Our Ellsberg paradox examples above illustrate this point: we used features of the set to describe events that are perceived as risky versus ambiguous. More generally, modelers often use the set of beliefs to encode different attitudes towards different sources of uncertainty. For example, perception of a source as ambiguous may be driven by a lack of information about it, which makes agents less confident in probability assessments.

Early quantitative work in economics relied heavily on the distinction between risk perception and risk attitude. The idea was to (i) obtain observable proxies for beliefs from survey data or statistical models and (ii) assume that a risk aversion coefficient is a "deep parameter" that can be transferred across settings; for example it can be measured in the laboratory and then used to calibrate models. As a result, low risk aversion coefficients measured in experiments were imposed on investors in financial markets.

More recently, the distinction between beliefs and attitude has arguably become less important. One reason is that the limits of assumption (ii) have become more clear. For example, Rabin (2000) provides a thought experiment to show that concavity as a source of risk aversion cannot deal well with plausible choices given small versus large risks. Moreover, the use of richer data sets and modern estimation techniques allows modelers to estimate preference parameters in many contexts. Of course, it is still useful to write parsimonious models such that behavior towards uncertainty depends on, say, a subjective conditional variance, a curvature parameters or the width of an interval of means for a belief set. But it is not crucial that any such parameter is transferable across settings.

---

[2] Strzalecki (2013) shows that multiple priors is the only model of ambiguity aversion that allows for indifference to timing. Intuitively, this is because other models capture ambiguity via nonlinear functions that affect timing preference, much like non-linearity of v does in the case of risk.

24.2.3 Savings and portfolio choice

In this section we illustrate how first order welfare losses from ambiguity shape behavior in two familiar applications. In a consumption savings problem, precautionary savings obtain even when utility is quadratic, and can therefore be characterized using linear approximations. In a portfolio choice problem, uncertainty leads to robust nonparticipation in markets even in the absence of transaction costs.

Precautionary savings. Consider a two-period consumption–saving problem. An agent is endowed with date 1 wealth w and uncertain date 2 labor income $\tilde{y}$. Savings s earn a certain gross interest rate R between dates 1 and 2. The agent chooses a consumption plan $(c, \tilde{c})$ and savings s to maximize utility (24.1) subject to the budget constraints

$$c = w - s; \quad s \geq 0,$$
$$\tilde{c} = Rs + \tilde{y}.$$

We abstract from timing effects by assuming $u = v$.

For both risk aversion and multiple priors, the condition for an interior optimum for savings takes the form of a consumption Euler equation

$$u'(w - s) = \beta R \mathbb{E}^{P^*}\left[u'(Rs + \tilde{y})\right] \tag{24.5}$$

The only difference between the models is the interpretation of P^*: with risk aversion, it is the unique subjective belief of the agent that is given as part of utility (24.2), whereas with multiple priors it is the worst-case prior that achieves the minimum when (24.3) is evaluated at the optimal consumption plan.

How does an increase in uncertainty affect savings? With risk aversion, we have the textbook result that income uncertainty increases savings if and only if utility exhibits prudence, that is, $u''' > 0$. In particular, the tractable case of quadratic utility rules out precautionary savings. Moreover, a linear approximation to (24.5), say around the point of certain labor income, cannot be used to study precautionary savings, since it would reflect at most second derivatives of u. As a result, the standard practice of solving general equilibrium models by linearization abstracts from precautionary savings effects.

With multiple priors, in contrast, precautionary savings requires only curvature in utility. To see this, assume income ambiguity $\tilde{y} = \bar{y} + \alpha \tilde{z}$, where $\bar{y}$ is a constant and $\tilde{z}$ is a random variable such that the interval of means brackets zero but all other moments are the same. The worst-case belief P^* is then the belief that implies the lowest – and hence a negative – mean for $\tilde{z}$. Regardless of the savings choice s and the parameter α, this belief minimizes expected utility. We then obtain the impact of uncertainty on savings by applying the implicit function theorem to (24.5):

$$\left.\frac{ds}{d\alpha}\right|_{\alpha=0} = \frac{1}{\Delta} Ru''(Rs + \bar{y}) \mathbb{E}^{P^*}[\tilde{z}] > 0,$$

where $\Delta > 0$ from the second order condition for optimality. Precautionary saving occurs as long as the agent is not willing to perfectly substitute consumption over time.

The example further illustrates two principles that are relevant also for understanding the quantitative applications we review below. First, for any given choice problem, there is an observational equivalence between ambiguity aversion and pessimism. Solving a decision problem with multiple priors involves first finding the worst-case belief, and then characterizing the solution given that belief, much like for the standard model. This feature is convenient for computation: we can often find the worst-case belief up front, as we did above, and then solve the problem with familiar tools. Importantly, the observational equivalence between ambiguity aversion and dogmatic pessimism (with a fixed prior) only holds for a given choice problem; it does not mean that we can simply replace the ambiguity aversion model by a model of dogmatic pessimism.

To see how observational equivalence does not extend beyond a given choice problem, compare responses to a change in the environment for an ambiguity-averse agent and an agent with a fixed prior. As a stark example, suppose the government introduces a transfer program that pays $-2\alpha\tilde{z}$ at date 2. In other words, the program subsidizes previously bad states and taxes good states, so much that it reverses their roles. Such a policy increases utility for the agent with the fixed prior: he now receives more income in the (previously bad) states he finds more likely. In contrast, for the ambiguity averse agent utility is unchanged: ambiguity about income is described by the same family of distributions as before, so the worst-case mean changes endogenously to put more weight on previously good, but now bad states. The agent's disutility stems from ambiguity, not mistaken belief, so a transfer program that leaves ambiguity unchanged is not beneficial.

A second principle is that curvature in the objective function matters for the effect of uncertainty. Indeed, the higher the curvature in u, or the more reluctant the agent is to substitute consumption over time, the more he responds to uncertainty by accumulating precautionary savings. Intuitively, the worry about a downward-sloping consumption path propels action. An agent with linear u still worries about uncertain income – utility is lower – but does not do anything about it. In many dynamic models, parameters that induce costs of uneven plans, such as adjustment costs, similarly strengthen precautionary behavior.

Portfolio inertia. To illustrate portfolio choice, we allow for two assets, but for simplicity abstract from the savings margin. Consider a mean–variance investor who maximizes end-of-period wealth. There is a bond with a constant risk-free rate of return as well as an asset with uncertain payoff that earns an excess return over the risk-free rate of $\tilde{R} = \bar{R} + \tilde{z}$. Assume that the belief set is such that the interval of means for $\tilde{z}$ brackets zero, and all other moments are the same. Let θ denote a zero-cost portfolio that is short in the bond and long in the uncertain asset. There are no borrowing or short sale constraints, so the agent solves

$$\max_{\theta} \min_{P \in \mathcal{P}} \left\{ \mathbb{E}^P \left[\tilde{R} \right] \theta - \frac{1}{2} \gamma \, var^P \left(\tilde{R} \right) \theta^2 \right\}. \tag{24.6}$$

Without ambiguity, the optimal portfolio is $\theta = \mathbb{E}^P \left[\tilde{R} \right] / \gamma \, var^P \left(\tilde{R} \right)$. The agent participates in the market whenever the (unique) subjective expected excess return is not exactly zero. As long as there is a small compensation for risk taking, the risk averse investor will take on risk, since the welfare loss is second order. Moreover, any change in the expected excess return alters the optimal portfolio.

With ambiguity, in contrast, nonparticipation ($\theta = 0$) is optimal whenever $\bar{R}$ is close enough to zero so $\min_{P \in \mathcal{P}} \mathbb{E}^P \tilde{R} < 0 < \max_{P \in \mathcal{P}} \mathbb{E}^P \tilde{R}$, a result due to Dow and Werlang (1992).[3] Indeed, if the agent contemplates going long (short) in the uncertain asset, the worst-case expected excess return is lower (higher) than zero, so the payoff (24.6) is negative and $\theta = 0$ is strictly better. The *endogenous*

---

[3] Bossaerts et al. (2010) and Asparouhova et al. (2015) confirm such behavior in experimental studies with laboratory asset markets.

switch to a pessimistic belief that depends on the action is crucial here. If instead $\bar{R}$ is sufficiently larger (smaller) than zero, then the solution is the same as under risk, but using the lowest (highest) mean of $\tilde{z}$. Put differently, the optimal portfolio policy as a function of $\bar{R}$ exhibits an inaction region, where the agent is out of the market and does not respond to changes in $\bar{R}$.

24.3 Dynamic choice and equilibrium

Dynamic applications require conditional preferences at every node of a decision tree. We thus describe briefly recursive versions of the models from Section 24.2.1. We continue to assume that time is discrete, but now use Ω to denote a period state space: one element $\omega \in \Omega$ is realized every period, and the history of states up to date t is $\omega^t = (\omega_1, \ldots, \omega_t)$. Consumption plans are now sequences of random variables $C = (C_t)_{t=0}^{\infty}$, where $C_t : \Omega^t \to \Re$ maps histories up to date t into consumption. We write $U_t(C; \omega^t)$ for utility from the consumption plan C conditional on the history ω^t.

For any plan C, conditional utilities solve the difference equation

$$u\left(U_t\left(C; \omega^t\right)\right) = u\left(C_t\right) + \beta u\left(CE\left(U_{t+1}\left(C; \omega^{t+1}\right)\right)\right), \tag{24.7}$$

where CE can be one of the certainty equivalent functions from Section 24.2.1. The probabilities involved in writing those functions are now understood to be one-step-ahead conditionals – at each node ω^t in the decision tree, they provide probabilities over the next state ω_{t+1}. When both u and v are power functions and belief sets are singletons, the utility process is common recursive utility under risk (Epstein and Zin, 1989). Recursive versions of multiple priors were axiomatized by Epstein and Schneider (2003) with $u = v$ and Hayashi (2005) for $u \neq v$.

We can summarize the primitives of recursive utility as functional forms for u and CE, a discount factor β, as well as an entire stochastic process of sets of conditional probabilities $\mathcal{P}_t(\omega^t)$ that describe beliefs about the next state ω_{t+1}. In the case of risk aversion only, all sets are singletons. In general, the dynamics of conditional beliefs can reflect changes in uncertainty, for example due to learning or uncertainty shocks. With risk aversion, such changes are captured only by higher moments under the singleton belief. With ambiguity aversion, fluctuations in the size of the belief set provide an additional dimension.[4]

Papers that provide axiomatic foundations for recursive utility consider families of conditional preference orderings, one for each history ω^t. Each conditional ordering satisfies the axioms justifying an atemporal model from Section 24.2, suitably modified for multiperiod plans. Moreover, conditional preferences at different histories are connected by dynamic consistency. The setup of the model further implies consequentialism, that is, utility from a consumption plan at history ω^t depends only on the consumption promised in future histories that can still occur after ω^t has been realized.

---

[4] Epstein and Schneider (2007, 2008) study learning under ambiguity. In particular, they propose functional forms such that the set of one-step-ahead conditionals can shrink as new data make agents more confident, but also expand when news is ambiguous.

24.3.1 Asset pricing

We now use the first order condition from the dynamic model (24.7) to study asset pricing. Consider an investor who has access, after every history ω^t, to a full set of contingent claims on states $\omega \in \Omega$ that can occur next period. In this section, we are no longer interested only in choice, but also in equilibrium asset price dynamics measured by an econometrician. We thus denote by P^0 the true probability over sequences of states and assume that its one-step-ahead conditionals $P_t^0 \left(\omega_{t+1} | \omega^t\right)$ have full support. For any one-step-ahead belief P_t, we can then define the random variable $d P_t / d P_t^0$ that makes a "change of measure" from the true Data Generating Process (DGP) to the belief: we have $d P_t / d P_t^0 \left(\omega^t, \omega_{t+1}\right) = P_t \left(\omega_{t+1} | \omega^t\right) / P_t^0 \left(\omega_{t+1} | \omega^t\right)$.

We write the price of a contingent claim that trades at date t after history ω^t and pays off one unit of the good if state ω_{t+1} occurs at date $t+1$ as $M_{t+1} \left(\omega_t, \omega_{t+1}\right) P_t^0 \left(\omega_{t+1} | \omega^t\right)$, so the pricing kernel M_{t+1} represents one-step-ahead state prices normalized by (true) probabilities. We denote by $\theta_{t+1} \left(\omega^t, \omega_{t+1}\right)$ the number of claims on state ω_{t+1} at $t+1$ purchased after history ω^t at date t. The agent's objective is to choose stochastic processes (C_t, θ_t) to maximize utility defined in (24.7) subject to the budget constraints

$$C_t + E_t^{P^0} [M_{t+1} \theta_{t+1}] = Y_t + \theta_t,$$

where Y_t is an exogenous income process and the conditional expectation represents expenditure on contingent claims.

In a complete market, absence of arbitrage implies that the unique pricing kernel M_{t+1} contains all information needed to price assets: the date t price Q_t of any asset with state-dependent payoff Π_{t+1} at date $t+1$ is given by

$$Q_t = \mathbb{E}_t^{P^0} [M_{t+1} \Pi_{t+1}] = Q_t^b \mathbb{E}_t^{P^0} [\Pi_{t+1}] + cov_t^{P^0} (M_{t+1}, \Pi_{t+1}), \tag{24.8}$$

where $Q_t^b = E^{P^0} [M_{t+1}]$ is the price of a risk-free bond and the covariance reflects the measured uncertainty premium – the difference between price and expected present value under the statistical model used by the econometrician.[5]

Since the econometrician recovers P^0 from the empirical distribution of prices, payoffs and consumption, we can view M_{t+1} and C_{t+1} as the data the model needs to explain. For a quantitatively successful asset pricing model, we want M_{t+1} to vary across states ω_{t+1}, so average premia can differ a lot across assets with different payoff profiles – for example, equity on average pays a larger premium than bonds. We also want M_{t+1} to vary with time t, so premia are volatile; for example, uncertainty generates low prices, and high expected excess returns for many uncertain assets in recessions.

Investor optimization places restrictions on the joint distribution of M_{t+1} and C_{t+1}. Let J_t denote the stochastic process of utility at the optimal consumption plan. We can use dynamic programming to show that optimal portfolio choice implies

$$M_{t+1} = \beta \frac{u' (C_{t+1})}{u' (C_t)} \frac{u' (CE (J_{t+1}))}{v' (CE (J_{t+1}))} \frac{v' (J_{t+1})}{u' (J_{t+1})} \frac{d P_t^*}{d P_t^0}, \tag{24.9}$$

---

[5] Dividing by the price Q_t, the covariance term is the conditional expected excess return $E_t[\Pi_{t+1}] / Q_t Q_t^b$, a measure of uncertainty premia that one would get for example by regressing excess returns on conditioning information.

where P_t^* is again the worst-case belief, which equals the unique subjective belief in the case of risk aversion.

In the benchmark case with time separable expected utility $u = v$ and rational expectations $P^* = P^0$, the pricing kernel is simply equal to the intertemporal marginal rate of substitution $\beta u'(C_{t+1})/u'(C_t)$. This model is soundly rejected by a large body of evidence. The other factors in (24.9) illustrate alternative approaches to generate larger premia due to preference for early resolution of uncertainty ($u \neq v$) or ambiguity aversion ($P^* \neq P^0$). We note that while J_{t+1} is not directly observable, it is related to consumption through (24.7), so observable counterparts can be constructed from consumption data, and possibly from wealth data using the budget constraint.

Intuitively, M_{t+1} indicates how bad a state is; the price of an asset is higher (and its premium lower) when it pays off relatively more in bad states, that is, it provides insurance. According to (24.9) a state can be bad for three reasons. First, future consumption is low – the standard effect from high marginal utility of consumption $u'(C_{t+1})$. Second, if the agent prefers early resolution of uncertainty – so there is more curvature in v than in u, then a state can be bad because future continuation utility is low, so the ratio $v'(J_{t+1})/u'(J_{t+1})$ is high. Importantly, utility can be low even if consumption at $t+1$ is high, say, because of bad news about consumption further in the future, a theme of the long-run risk literature. Finally, if the agent is ambiguity averse, then a state can be bad because it is very ambiguous, so its worst-case probability is much larger than its actual probability. Again here the future beyond next period matters – the worst-case can reflect beliefs about consumption in the long run, and it can do so even if $u = v$.

While compensation for ambiguity can be written as a covariance, much like compensation for risk, we emphasize that it generates premia even with risk neutrality. Indeed, with linear $u = v$, we have

$$cov_t^{P^0}(M_{t+1}, \Pi_{t+1}) = Q_t^b \left(\mathbb{E}_t^{P^*}[\Pi_{t+1}] - \mathbb{E}_t^{P^0}[\Pi_{t+1}] \right), \tag{24.10}$$

so the asset price in Eq. (24.8) becomes the worst-case present value $Q_t = Q_t^b \mathbb{E}_t^{P^*}[\Pi_{t+1}]$. The measured average excess return or premium then reflects only the difference between worst-case expected payoffs and expected payoffs measured by the econometrician.

We comment on two other properties of the pricing kernel that are important for quantitative performance. The first is that state prices – that is, cumulative products of one-step-ahead prices M_{t+1} – have a martingale component. As shown by Alvarez and Jermann (2005), a model without such a component has the property that very long horizon bonds have high premia relative to all other assets. As a result, standard business cycle models with trend stationary consumption and power utility are at odds with asset price data. Borovička et al. (2016) show that preference for early resolution introduces a martingale component. From (24.9), the cumulative product of changes of measure is also a martingale. This explains why multiple priors models can do a good job accounting for uncertainty premia even when consumption is trend stationary and there is no preference for early resolution.

A second property was highlighted by Ai and Bansal (2018), who build on the empirical work of Lucca and Moench (2015). It is a striking stylized fact that most of the equity premium in the US is earned through price jumps around macroeconomic announcement days, in particular monetary policy announcements. Ai and Bansal characterize the class of preferences that is consistent with price movements on pure news days, when nothing special happens to consumption. Both recursive utility with preference for early resolution and multiple priors belong to this class. The reason is apparent from (24.9): in both cases, the revelation of news about the far future, as opposed to only consumption, matter for the pricing kernel.

24.3.2 Business cycle models with uncertainty shocks

We consider a stylized model that can be solved in closed form, yet captures the main effects of uncertainty in quantitative models reviewed below. There are two goods: output of a numeraire consumption good Y_t is made from labor N_t according to the linear technology

$$Y_t = Z_t N_{t-1},$$

where Z_t is exogenous total factor productivity. The fruit of date $t-1$ labor effort thus only become available at date t. Since labor is an intertemporal decision, it depends on uncertainty. The resource constraint for the economy is $C_t = Y_t$.

To allow for flexible labor supply, we extend utility (24.7) to multiple goods. A consumption plan is a stochastic process for consumption and labor (C_t, N_t). Utility is defined recursively by

$$U_t = \frac{1}{1-\gamma} C_t^{1-\gamma} - \theta N_t + \beta \min_{P \in \mathcal{P}_t} \mathbb{E}^P [U_{t+1}],$$

where $\mathcal{P}_t$ is the process of one-step-ahead conditional belief sets, a singleton in the risk case.

Under the true data generating process, log TFP $z_t = \log Z_t$ is serially independent and normally distributed,

$$z_{t+1} = \mu_t - \frac{1}{2}\sigma_u^2 + u_{t+1}. \tag{24.11}$$

Here u is an iid sequence of shocks, normally distributed with mean zero and variance σ_u^2. The sequence μ is deterministic and unknown to agents.

Agents treat the unknown component μ_t as ambiguous. We parameterize their one-step-ahead set of beliefs at date t by a set of means $\mu_t^P \in [-a_t, a_t]$. The stochastic process a_t captures agents' perceived ambiguity about TFP; it evolves as

$$a_{t+1} = (1 - \rho_a)\bar{a} + \rho_a a_t + \varepsilon_{t+1}^a, \tag{24.12}$$

with long run mean $\bar{a} > 0$ and $0 < \rho_a < 1$. Periods of low $a_t < \bar{a}$ represent unusually low ambiguity about future productivity, whereas $a_t > \bar{a}$ describes periods of high uncertainty. We further assume that ε_t^a is independent of u_t.

Equilibrium and planner problem. We assume that labor and consumption goods are traded in competitive spot markets and there are complete financial markets. The welfare theorems then hold, and we can characterize competitive equilibrium allocations by solving the social planner problem: we maximize utility subject to the production function and the resource constraint. Using output as the only endogenous state variable, the Bellman equation is

$$V(Y, a) = \max_N \left\{ U(Y, N) + \beta \min_{\mu^P \in [-a,a]} \mathbb{E}^P \left[V\left(e^{\tilde{z}} N, \tilde{a}\right) \right] \right\},$$

where the conditional distribution of $\tilde{z}$ under belief P is given by (24.11) with $\mu_t = \mu^P$.

It is natural to conjecture that the value function is increasing in output. The worst-case belief P^* then has mean $\mu^{P^*} = -a$. Using normality of the shocks, we obtain a closed-form solution for log hours

$$n_t = \bar{n} - (1/\gamma - 1)\left(a_t + \frac{1}{2}\gamma\sigma_u^2\right), \qquad (24.13)$$

where $\bar{n}$ is constant. Substituting back into the Bellman equation verifies the conjecture that the value function is increasing in output.

Business cycle dynamics. According to (24.13), uncertainty reduces hours – and hence log output $y_t = z_t + n_{t-1}$ whether it is ambiguity, as measured by a, or risk, as measured by the product of the quantity of risk σ_u^2 and risk aversion γ. Intuitively, an increase in uncertainty has wealth and substitution effects. On the one hand, higher uncertainty lowers the certainty equivalent of future production. Other things equal, the resulting wealth effect leads the planner to reduce consumption of leisure and increase hiring. However, higher uncertainty also lowers the uncertainty-adjusted return on labor. Other things equal, the resulting substitution effect leads the planner to reduce hiring. The net effect depends on the curvature in felicity from consumption, determined by γ. With a strong enough substitution effect (low enough γ), an increase in uncertainty lowers hiring.

For $1/\gamma > 1$, an increase in ambiguity a generates a recession, even when productivity is not unusually low. Hours are below steady state only because the marginal product of labor is more uncertain, so the planner finds it optimal not to make people work. Conversely, an unusual increase in confidence – a drop of a_t below its long run mean – generates a boom in which employment and output are unusually high, but productivity is not. In other words, a phase of low realizations of a_t will look to an observer like a wave of optimism, where output and employment surge despite average productivity realizations. In the time series, allocations thus look like there is a countercyclical "labor wedge" between the marginal product of labor and the marginal rate of substitution of consumption for labor, a key feature of aggregate data.

Bounding ambiguity by observed volatility. How much variation in ambiguity is plausible? Ilut and Schneider (2014) propose a model-consistency criterion to bound the support of a. The idea is that even the most extreme forecasts implied by potential worst-case beliefs should be "good enough" in the long run. The concrete suggestion is to bound the support of ambiguity by $a \leq 2\sqrt{Var(z)}$, where $Var(z)$ is the observed long-run variance of z_{t+1} in (24.11). In other words, agents do not entertain forecasts outside a 95% confidence interval, centered around the long-run mean of z_{t+1}, given its observed variation. The criterion thus relaxes the rational expectations model-consistency criterion, which would collapse that interval of entertained beliefs to one number, but allows for more ambiguity when the data are more volatile.

A more general solution method In contrast to our stylized example, quantitative business cycle models include further state variables such as capital and thus require numerical tools. An advantage of modeling uncertainty as ambiguity is that popular first-order perturbation methods do not lose uncertainty effects such as precautionary savings or asset premia, in contrast to what happens with risk. Ilut and Schneider (2014) leverage this insight to propose a tractable four-step approach that generalizes what we did in this section with the stylized model to a broad class of models with stochastic ambiguity about means of shocks.

The first step conjectures the worst-case belief. When ambiguity is about shocks that increase surplus, such as TFP above, the natural conjecture is that the worst-case mean is as low as possible. The second step solves the model with worst-case beliefs using standard methods for expectational difference equations, for example linearization around the deterministic steady state (e.g., Sims (2002)). It delivers a steady state and law of motion used by the agent for planning. The third step verifies the conjecture: since the agent optimizes as if the worst-case dynamics were correct, we can check the (equilibrium) value function. For example, a conjecture of a low worst-case mean for some shock is verified if the value function is increasing in that shock.

Finally, with agents' perceived law of motion in hand, the last step describes model dynamics as measured by an econometrician. Here we take into account that exogenous variables follow the true DGP, not the worst-case dynamics perceived by agents. In particular, one-step-ahead conditional means of ambiguous shocks under the true DGP are more favorable – the difference is the gap between true and worst-case means. In our example above, agents plan *as if* TFP is always below trend, but realized TFP in fact has mean zero. Moreover, endogenous variables respond to the true exogenous shocks, but according to agents' pessimistic equilibrium response. In our example, hours move with ambiguity only because of agents' pessimistic perception of future TFP.

If step two characterizes the law of motion by linearization, then ambiguity about conditional means matters for the coefficients of the approximating linear law of motion. We have seen in Section 24.2.3 how precautionary savings under such ambiguity requires only curvature in utility, not a positive third derivative as with risk. It is therefore reflected in coefficients of a linearized consumption Euler equation. We have also seen in Section 24.3.1 how uncertainty premia in asset prices occur due to differences in worst-case versus true payoffs: while investors behave as if payoffs are low, so prices are below the present value of payoffs, actual payoffs are high, which generates high average excess returns from the perspective of the econometrician. With ambiguity about means, this effect is again present in the linear law of motion.

Volatility shocks and identification. The example law of motion (24.12) assumes that ambiguity is not connected to movements in actual TFP, the exogenous fundamental. Uncertainty about the future only responds to intangible information, such as signals about technological progress. Theory does not require this property. An alternative, proposed by Bianchi et al. (2018), makes ambiguity move with the volatility of fundamental shocks. In more turbulent times – that is, when larger shocks are expected – agents also find it harder to settle on a forecast of the future. Qualitatively, the model of Bianchi et al. (2018) thus works like a rational expectations model with stochastic volatility. The differences is that subjective uncertainty is captured by ambiguity. The estimation, in fact, allows ambiguity to move both with volatility and without it; the relative share of each type of movement is identified from the comovement of asset premia – which depend on subjective uncertainty – and conditional heteroskedasticity in fundamentals.

24.4 Quantifying ambiguity using survey data

In this section, we describe work that relates survey measures of ambiguity to experience and choice in the cross section of economic agents. We focus on large scale surveys, and do not cover the vast literature on experimental evidence reviewed for example by Trautmann and van de Kuilen (2015). We emphasize three takeaways. First, ambiguity aversion is a widespread phenomenon among both households and decision makers in firms. Second, variation in ambiguity is large, both in the cross-section of agents and in the time series for a given agent. It is at least partly accounted for by information, but not by sophistication. Third, measures of perceived ambiguity relate in sensible ways to observed choice. We conclude that survey evidence is consistent with rational behavior under ambiguity and hence a promising source for disciplining belief sets in structural models – in a final subsection we provide examples below for how this has been done.

Methodology. We distinguish two approaches to eliciting ambiguity. One follows the experimental literature and infers properties of preferences from choice, for example, by incorporating survey questions about (hypothetical) Ellsberg-type choice situations. It can in principle test axioms underlying specific models of ambiguity aversion. The second approach elicits stated "imprecise probabilities": it asks respondents about the likelihood of an event, but provides the option to answer with a range of probabilities. It has roots in psychology (for example, Wallsten et al. (1983)) and was first used in economics by Manski and Molinari (2010); it is also discussed in Chapters 7 and 26 in this Handbook. Asking for imprecise probabilities has recently become more prominent since it makes it easy to introduce questions about natural (not artificial) events into large scale surveys. An important agenda for future research is to compare the two approaches.[6]

Interpretation of imprecise probabilities needs to take into account that decision theory does not directly relate belief sets to survey responses. Belief sets only serve as devices to represent preferences – agents act *as if* they maximize with a belief set in mind. In particular, theory does not predict that ambiguity averse agents make pessimistic forecasts, just like the expected utility model does not predict that risk averse agents should do so.[7] Nevertheless, we can make two sharp statements. First, Bayesian respondents should answer questions about likelihoods with single probabilities. The frequency of imprecise probability answers thus measures the prevalence of non-Bayesian perception of uncertainty. Second, more ambiguity averse agents behave *as if* their belief sets are larger. If we are willing to make the additional assumption that such agents also state wider probability ranges in surveys, then we can rank ambiguity across agents, or for the same agent over time.

Evidence on households. Dimmock et al. (2016) elicit Ellsberg-style choice behavior among households in the American Life Panel. They show that, consistent with the theory described in Section 24.2.3, ambiguity aversion is negatively related to stock market participation and the portfolio weight on stocks, but positively related to own-company stock ownership and other measures of underdiversification. Bianchi and Tallon (2019) match survey responses to portfolio data from a large French financial institution. Ambiguity averse investors not only underdiversify and hence bear risk, but are also more active traders who earn higher average returns. Delavande et al. (2021b) add an incentivized choice module to the UK Household Longitudinal Study to assess various models of behavior under uncertainty. An interesting result is that women exhibit less ambiguity aversion, in contrast to earlier work on risk; it underscores the need for comprehensive measurement of uncertainty.

---

[6] For recent methodological advances in eliciting ambiguity perceptions about natural events from choice, see Baillon et al. (2018) or Abdellaoui et al. (2021).

[7] Recent work has tested this hypothesis in survey data. Under both risk or ambiguity, Eq. (24.8) says that uncertainty-adjusted expected returns should be equated across assets. However, subjective expected returns in surveys differ substantially across assets, see, for example, Adam et al. (2021) for securities and Kindermann et al. (2021) for housing returns.

Households prefer to communicate their uncertainty via imprecise probabilities for a diverse set of events, especially for those where information is scarce. Giustinelli et al. (2022) use the US Health and Retirement Study to show that about one-half of dementia-free older Americans perceive ambiguity about dementia and the need for long-term care and that ambiguity about the latter *conditional* on the hypothetical dementia state is substantially lower. Delavande et al. (2021b) elicit imprecise probabilities for a range of health and financial outcomes and documents widespread ambiguity. Delavande et al. (2021a) study ambiguity about COVID-19-related health outcomes and also ask about ambiguity conditional on hypothetical behavior to show that perceived returns from protective measures predict actual choice. We find such evidence on conditional beliefs particularly interesting to guide future modeling of learning and updating under ambiguity.

Evidence on firms. Bachmann et al. (2020) elicit imprecise probabilities about future sales growth from leading executives in German manufacturing firms, based on the ifo Business Survey. They present results from a quarterly panel over four years: even though sales growth is a short term, routine random variable for top executives, 25% of firms respond with imprecise probabilities in any given quarter, while 70% of firms do so at least once. Time variation in ambiguity is systematically related to credit spreads, familiar measures of uncertainty in financial markets. For example, the share of ambiguous responses spikes up in the 2015 Greek default crisis, especially for exporting firms. While there is considerable variation across firms, perception of ambiguity is unrelated to the use of statistical analysis inside the firm, and forecast mistakes are similar for precise and imprecise probability responses.

Quantifying models. Survey data have played a useful role in quantifying models of decision making under ambiguity. It is again helpful to distinguish two approaches. One is to jointly design the survey and the structural model to tightly connect survey answers to their model counterparts. An example is the pioneering study of Giustinelli and Pavoni (2017) who estimate a model of learning under ambiguity by Italian high school students who choose career tracks. The data follow students' beliefs and choices over several months. Ambiguity is again prevalent, as is lack of awareness of possible choices. Imprecise probabilities elicited from students provide moments that discipline the evolution of uncertainty. A main result is that the speed of learning depends importantly on parents' background.

An alternative approach is to use the *dispersion* in survey forecasts as a proxy for ambiguity. Ilut and Schneider (2014) draw on the Survey of Professional Forecasters to construct an observable counterpart for variations in ambiguity that drive the business cycle. The basic idea is that an ambiguity-averse representative household samples experts' opinions before making decisions, and stronger disagreement among experts leads to lower confidence in probability assessments. More formally, beliefs are parameterized by an interval for the one-quarter-ahead conditional mean of total factor productivity, where the interval is assumed to be monotonically related to the interdecile range of expert forecasts of output.[8] Forecast dispersion thus serves as an index of ambiguity – its volatility and comovement with other variables discipline the scope for uncertainty to matter.

---

[8] The mapping from survey forecast dispersion about output in the data to model beliefs about total factor productivity is a parametric function that respects the relationship between the variables in the model.

24.5 Aggregate applications

In this section, we review macro-finance models where ambiguity serves as a driver of the business cycle, asset prices, or both.

Ambiguity-driven business cycles. Ilut and Schneider (2014) propose and estimate a standard New Keynesian (NK) model with multiple priors utility. Ambiguity is about productivity, and its magnitude and fluctuations are disciplined by the dispersion in survey forecasts about GDP. The main result is that confidence shocks, that is, exogenous fluctuations in ambiguity, drive most of the business cycle. In particular, they generate comovement of hours, consumption and investment without strong reactions in inflation. The model thus meets the challenge put forward by Angeletos et al. (2020): models of demand-driven business cycle should be consistent with stable inflation. Intuitively, worry about productivity is not only a force for weak demand as households worry about future income, but also a force for high prices, as firms worry about future cost. The latter effect counteracts the deflationary force of weak demand.

Other papers in this area differ in how ambiguity is captured and what source of uncertainty it is about. Bidder and Smith (2012) consider a model with multiplier preferences and stochastic volatility; Bhandari et al. (2019) allow for shocks to agents' concerns for model misspecification. Related work analyzes the smooth ambiguity model with stochastic volatility (Backus et al. (2015)), learning about TFP (Altug et al. (2020)), or dispersed information (Pei (2018)). Masolo and Monti (2020), Michelacci and Paciello (2020) and Kroner (2021) propose quantitative models that use multiple priors preferences to focus specifically on ambiguity about monetary policy.

Ilut and Saijo (2021) go beyond exogenous ambiguity shocks to show how ambiguity is a *propagation mechanism* for standard fundamental shocks. Perceived uncertainty is endogenously higher in recessions, caused either by supply or demand shocks, because firms accumulate less information about themselves when they produce less. This depresses aggregate activity, since uncertainty-adjusted returns to working, consumption and investing are all lower. In other words, higher ambiguity in recessions *jointly* generates labor, consumption and investment "wedges" with respect to standard marginal conditions. The labor wedge works like in the simple model of Section 24.3.2. The consumption wedge occurs because precautionary savings pushes the risk-free rate below the growth rate of marginal utility. The investment wedge reflects equilibrium compensation for ambiguous returns on capital.

The model provides a unified explanation for comovement of major aggregates, as well as countercyclical correlated wedges, even though prices are fully flexible. The comovement result is surprising in light of Barro and King (1984) who showed that in a standard RBC model hours and consumption comove *only* in response to shocks to TFP or the disutility of work. New Keynesian models overturn this impossibility result through countercyclical markups. In Ilut and Saijo (2021), the endogenous countercyclical labor wedge allows labor and consumption to both fall *even conditional on demand* shocks, as in the data.

Asset pricing under ambiguity. A large literature studies asset pricing in representative agent endowment economies. Many early contributions are reviewed in detail in Epstein and Schneider (2010) and Guidolin and Rinaldi (2013). Ambiguity has been shown to generate the level and time-variation in the equity premium (e.g., Chen and Epstein (2002), Hansen (2007), Barillas et al. (2009) Hansen and Sargent (2010), Ju and Miao (2012), Chen et al. (2014), Bidder and Dew-Becker (2016), Collard et al. (2018), Gallant et al. (2019)), carry trade excess returns (Ilut (2012)), CDS spreads (Boyarchenko

(2012)), sovereign debt spreads (Pouzo and Presno (2016)), index options (Drechsler (2013)), or the variance premium (Miao et al. (2019)). Recent work studies asset pricing in production economies, where time-variation in premia arises from learning about an unobserved technology state, for example, Jahan-Parvar and Liu (2014), a process which further allows for time-varying volatility in Liu and Zhang (2021).

Bianchi et al. (2018) build on the points of Section 24.3 to study the joint dynamics of not only macro aggregates and asset prices in a production economy, but consider asset supply: they show that time varying ambiguity about technology generates observed fluctuations in shareholder payout and capital structure. Firms in the model face an increasing marginal cost of debt that is traded off against a tax advantage, as well as adjustment costs to equity. When ambiguity about future cost is high, shareholders worry more about the cost of debt, scale back leverage and lower payout. This mechanism accounts not only for the procyclicality of payout and debt, but also for medium term swings.

Importantly, ambiguity is not only about TFP, but also about operating costs that affect earnings but do not scale with production. The latter allows the model to account for high investment in times of high uncertainty, such as in the 1970s, whereas uncertainty about TFP generates low investment in recessions. Moreover, it helps reconcile volatile uncertainty premia with stable interest rates. Intuitively, operating cost is a small share of overall consumption, but a sizable share of shareholder payout, then uncertainty over these operating costs increases equity premia but affects uncertainty about future consumption only weakly, and thus has a small effect on precautionary savings and bond prices.

24.6 Heterogeneity and micro-to-macro applications

In this section we study review work that extends beyond the representative agent frameworks discussed so far. In particular, we discuss treatments of heterogeneous perceptions of uncertainty as well as micro-to-macro applications that use ambiguity to better account for behavior of heterogeneous firms, consumers and investors.

24.6.1 Heterogeneous perceptions of uncertainty

Heterogeneous ambiguity averse agents often act *as if* they disagree. One potential reason is heterogeneity in preferences. Ilut et al. (2016) study a model where more ambiguity averse households have larger belief sets about labor income and dividends. Equilibrium is then observationally equivalent to a model with persistent disagreement. The setup raises a computational challenge: in steady state, agents act *as if* they are on a transition path to *different* worst-case steady states. Ilut et al. (2016) thus propose a first order perturbation approach that solves jointly for steady state and transition dynamics. When quantified using US data on income and wealth, the model matches negative risk-free real rates, financial leverage and aggregate uncertainty premia. A key force is precautionary savings, which is reflected in the linear approximation and varies with aggregate uncertainty shocks.

Heterogeneity in the exposure to shocks can also make agents act *as if* they disagree. Michelacci and Paciello (2020) study a New Keynesian model with lenders and borrowers who receive ambiguous news of low future interest rates, a redistribution from lenders to borrowers. Each agent responds *as if* the news was unfavorable: under the worst-case belief, only lenders find the announcement credible. The main quantitative result is that this effect significantly weakens the power of ECB forward guidance. In

Saijo (2020), owners and non-owners of capital act as if they disagree about future capital taxes. While capital owners fear high taxes and substitute away from investment, nonowners fear low transfers from austerity and reduce consumption. Uncertainty generates a recession that is substantially stronger than in a representative agent benchmark.

In addition to the above papers on interaction in markets, a growing literature studies contracting with heterogeneous agents. Carroll (2019) reviews work on mechanism design that introduces ambiguity in standard principal/agent problems. Recent work in corporate finance studies capital structure choice under ambiguity in with bankruptcy costs (Izhakian et al. (2021)), asymmetric information (Malenko and Tsoy (2020)), dynamic moral hazard (Miao and Rivera (2016), Dicks and Fulghieri (2021b)) or allocation of control rights (Garlappi et al. (2017)). In political economy, multiple priors utility has been used to model parties that perceive ambiguity about voter preferences (e.g., Bade (2011)) as well as ambiguity-averse strategic voters, to explain selective abstention (Ghirardato and Katz (2006)) and show that abstention can be strong enough to prevent information aggregation (Ellis (2016)).

24.6.2 Inaction and inertia

Inaction due to first order effects of uncertainty helps understand a wide variety of phenomena. One important area is the behavior of nominal prices in micro data. Ilut et al. (2020) study price setting by ambiguity averse firms who learn about demand. The key idea is that uncertainty about the shape of a demand curve is local to every price point. A firm's uncertainty is therefore lowest near prices at which it has sold before. Formally, the model studies learning under ambiguity with sets of flexible Gaussian process distributions that allow many shapes of demand.

While local demand uncertainty could in principle be modeled as risk, in the presence of ambiguity aversion it implies price rigidity. For a firm that contemplates a price increase away from its current posted price, the worst-case is that the unknown demand function is very elastic at the higher price, so the firm loses a lot of sales from the price increase. For a price decrease, in contrast, the worst-case belief is a very inelastic demand, so the price cut does not stimulate sales much. This endogenous change in the worst-case belief forms a *kink* in the worst-case expected demand at previously posted prices, where the posterior uncertainty is the lowest.

Under ambiguity, firms thus behave *as if* they face time- and state-dependent costs of changing prices away from previously posted prices. Nominal prices stickiness emerges even without fixed ("menu") costs of changing prices. Moreover, in a quantitative evaluation based on micro-level pricing moments, the theory can account for facts that are difficult to explain with fixed costs: (i) price memory (the high likelihood of revisiting old price points), (ii) a decreasing price change hazard, and (iii) the coexistence of both small and large price changes. Related work in industrial organization includes Bergemann and Schlag (2011) who analyze a static optimal pricing problem with multiple priors over the distribution of buyers' valuations, Handel and Misra (2015) who consider a model with maxmin regret, and Handel et al. (2013) who develop theoretical and econometric arguments to identify consumer preferences from discrete choice data.

Inaction due to ambiguity also motivates a recent literature on technology adoption. In development economics, Warnick et al. (2011) and Ross et al. (2012) find that ambiguity aversion, and not risk aversion, constrains adoption of new farming technologies. Other recent work on slow adoption includes Kala (2019), Bryan (2019), Dougherty et al. (2020) and Norton et al. (2020). Moreover, technology adoption gives rise to interesting strategic interactions. Mukerji and Tallon (2004b) reviews work on games with ambiguity about the others' strategies (e.g., Dow and Werlang (1994), Eichberger and Kelsey (2002)) or payoffs (e.g., Azrieli and Teper (2011)). A key insight is that when individual payoff functions depends on others' actions, equilibrium worst-case scenarios may reflect a fear of "missing out," that is, not innovating or investing enough. In Beauchêne (2019), Bennett (2021), and Dicks and Fulghieri (2021a), various forms of payoff complementarity imply cautious individual decisions, but also equilibria that appear excessively *optimistic* from the perspective of an outside observer.

Nonparticipation in asset markets due to ambiguity has interesting equilibrium implications. Mukerji and Tallon (2001) and Mukerji and Tallon (2004a) model endogenously incomplete markets. In particular, ambiguity about relative prices can account for the observed lack of indexed debt. Condie and Ganguli (2011a,b, 2017) study models with informational inefficiency: private information is not fully revealed in equilibrium due to nonparticipation of informed investors. *Informational inertia* means that equilibrium stock prices do not reflect public information in some parts of the state space (see, for example, Illeditsch (2011), Illeditsch et al. (2021) and supporting evidence in Ben-Rephael and Izhakian (2020)). We finally note that ambiguity changes tradeoffs in evaluating real options. For example, in the job search model without recall of Nishimura and Ozaki (2004), an increase in ambiguity leads an agent to resolve uncertainty sooner and thus *stop* looking for a job, in contrast to the effect of an increase in risk (for other optimal stopping problems under ambiguity see Riedel (2009), Miao and Wang (2011), and Li (2019)).

24.6.3 Ambiguous information and asymmetric decision rules

Ambiguity can be due not only to prior lack of information, but also to ambiguous signals that are hard to interpret. Epstein and Schneider (2007, 2008) propose a model of learning from ambiguous signals: agents update beliefs with multiple likelihoods. Epstein and Halevy (2021) clarify the distinction between multiple priors and likelihoods and provide experimental evidence. A prominent special case is ambiguous signal quality: multiple likelihoods differ in precision. It implies that posterior beliefs respond asymmetrically to news: agents act *as if* bad (good) news are relatively more (less) precise. Early work applied this effect to asset pricing (for example, Epstein and Schneider (2008), Illeditsch (2011), and Ilut (2012)), we focus here on recent macroeconomic applications.

Ilut et al. (2018) show how asymmetric concave decision rules that respond more to bad than good news endogenously generate (1) negative skewness in both the cross-section and time series even if firm-level shocks are not skewed, and (2) countercyclical cross-sectional and time series volatility – this is because a bad aggregate shock lowers the average firm-level shock and leads the typical firm to respond more. The cross-sectional dispersion of actions thus increases in bad times even if the volatility of firm-level shocks is unchanged. Furthermore, Ilut et al. (2018) use Census data on U.S. manufacturing establishments to document that the relationship between employment growth and innovations to profitability is usually concave and argue for the empirical relevance of this asymmetry-driven mechanism as a unified and endogenous link between micro and macro moments.

Baqaee (2020) shows how ambiguity about inflation news endogenously generates downward wage rigidity, as in the data. Workers worry that inflation might lower real wages. When they observe news of ambiguous quality about future prices, they are more sensitive to inflationary than to deflationary news, and this is reflected in the equilibrium wage. Yoo (2019) estimates a model of consumption with an ambiguous quality of TFP signals that can deliver quantitatively relevant negative skewness in aggregate consumption responses. Kroner (2021) builds a New Keynesian model with two sectors that differ in the perceived ambiguity about the relevance of forward guidance signals. The asymmetric response mechanism implies that, as in the data, high-uncertainty sectors are endogenously more responsive to contractionary forward guidance and less responsive to expansionary forward guidance.

24.7 Policy implications

In general, an optimal policy problem with ambiguity features (i) ambiguity in the policy maker's objective and (ii) ambiguity in agents' utility, which is implicitly part of the policy maker's constraint set. While both features can be present and interact in the same study, they give rise to different effects, so we discuss their effects in two subsections.

24.7.1 Ambiguous policy objectives

There is a long tradition of studying policy uncertainty as risk – a prominent theme is the Brainard principle: monetary policy should be less aggressive if key features of the economy are unknown. Manski (2011, 2013) argues that partial identification of policy effects point to ambiguity as a way to capture policy markers' uncertainty.

Whether cautious behavior under ambiguity leads to attenuated or more aggressive policy actions depends on the source and structure of ambiguity. Barlevy (2011) reviews literature on attenuation, which occurs when the policy maker is not confident in the *sign* of the net welfare gain from a policy, a version of the "Brainard principle." At the extreme, inaction due to ambiguity may lead the policy maker to not intervene at all, as in the social insurance model of Kocherlakota and Phelan (2009).

However, cautious optimal stabilization policy may also respond more aggressively to shocks. In Sargent (1999) and Coenen (2007), persistent shocks create bigger losses. With ambiguity about persistence, caution calls for more aggressive action. In Giannoni (2002) and Leitemo and Söderström (2008), aggressive policy stems from uncertainty about feedback effects between multiple policy objectives. Woodford (2010) and Adam and Woodford (2012) show how history dependence in optimal policy becomes stronger when the policy-maker is uncertain about agents' model misspecification.

A related literature studies the performance of a given set of (usually simple) policies across a small but importantly *nonnested* set of standard models that have substantially different propagation mechanisms (see, for example, Levin et al. (2003), Levin and Williams (2003), Kuester and Wieland (2010), and the survey in Taylor and Williams (2010)). The overall policy performance is computed as a weighted average of the policy's utility outcomes conditional on each model. Robust policies are then those that do "well enough" even when the model where that policy does the worst has most of the weight.

Finally, we briefly mention the growing interdisciplinary literature on ambiguity and environmental policy. Climate scientists report high uncertainty about key parameters such as the climate sensitivity to greenhouse emissions. Similarly, the economic costs and benefits of adopting environmental policies are highly uncertain, but are crucial for quantitative models (for example, Palmer and Stevens (2019)). For frameworks to capture such uncertainty as ambiguity, see Lange and Treich (2008), Asano (2010), Millner et al. (2010), Millner et al. (2013). Examples of dynamic, quantitative economic models of climate change with ambiguity are Lemoine and Traeger (2016), Lemoine and Rudik (2017), Barnett et al. (2020), Barnett et al. (2021), and Hansen (2021).

24.7.2 Optimal policy with ambiguity-averse agents

When policy changes, ambiguity averse agents' endogenously pessimistic beliefs adjust, as discussed in Section 24.2. The optimal policy problem thus changes, even if the policy maker itself is not ambiguity averse, as emphasized in Hansen and Sargent (2008) and Hansen and Sargent (2015).

Consider first fiscal policy. Karantounias (2013) studies optimal taxation when agents have multiplier preferences. Procyclical tax policy dampens the private agents' effective pessimism, which allows the government to issue debt at a higher equilibrium bond prices and reduce the welfare losses arising from distortionary taxes. Similar setups are studied in Karantounias (2020) and Ferriere and Karantounias (2019). Young (2012) and Bennett et al. (2022) study optimal macroprudential policy in a related setting. A key point there is that policies depend on whether the planner is ambiguity averse or not. In Ilut and Saijo (2021), the government spending multiplier is larger than under rational expectations because the generated increase in economic activity also endogenously raises agents' confidence.

For monetary policy, Ilut and Saijo (2021) show that an interest rate rule that reacts to the credit spread would significantly lower output variability because it stabilizes the variation in endogenous uncertainty and thus in the equilibrium worst-case beliefs. Benigno and Paciello (2014) show in a quantitative NK model that optimal policy under paternalism involves less inflation stabilization and alleviates inefficiencies through a lower average markup. In Baqaee (2020), although fluctuations are costly and asymmetric, the standard policy prescription of an inflationary bias is undone in equilibrium by the endogenously-formed household expectations.

A number of papers have explored policy with heterogeneous ambiguity averse agents. Lensman and Troshkin (2022) analyze optimal mechanisms for public good provision when agents are uncertain about the distribution of private valuations. They find that uncertainty can lead to simple implementations of efficient policies. Caballero and Krishnamurthy (2008) derive a role for a lender of last resort when bank portfolios are ambiguous. Easley and O'Hara (2009) and Brock and Manski (2011) study regulation of credit markets.

We finally comment on welfare costs. Quantitative business cycle models with risk typically exhibit low welfare costs, which has led some macroeconomists to emphasize policy aimed at economic growth (a first order effect) relative to stabilization. As we have seen above, however, ambiguity has *first order* welfare effects. As a result, Ilut and Schneider (2012) and Baqaee (2020) find *welfare cost* of business cycles that are orders of magnitude larger than the standard Lucas (1987) number based only on risk (see also Barillas et al. (2009) for a discussion).

The same property can generate large welfare costs of *policy uncertainty*. In the linearized New Keynesian model of Saijo (2020), fiscal policy uncertainty leads to heterogeneous worst-case beliefs and altered aggregate dynamics. In Masolo and Monti (2020), ambiguity about monetary policy generates a low frequency drift in agents' worst-case beliefs about inflation. In Michelacci and Paciello (2020), ambiguity in monetary policy communication ignites concerns over redistribution.

24.8 Concluding remarks

We mention two areas where we see the greatest need for future research. The first is to incorporate ambiguity into a wider variety of models with heterogeneous agents and aggregate uncertainty. Currently, most quantitative models fall into one of two categories. On the one hand, a very active literature on economic policy and inequality allows for rich heterogeneity consistent with micro data on income and wealth, but nevertheless assumes that there are no premia for aggregate uncertainty. On the other hand, models that feature such premia allow only for stylized heterogeneity. One reason is presumably that fast computational methods rely on linear approximations that cannot handle risk premia. As we have shown, ambiguity premia are captured easily using linear methods and are therefore straightforward to introduce into models with rich heterogeneity.

Another area where we look forward to both theoretical and quantitative advances is the endogenous evolution of belief sets. Our review of the applied literature has described a number of mechanisms by which changes in uncertainty move prices and quantities. In other words, the literature has made a lot of progress understanding how beliefs shape data. We feel that for the other direction, how data shape beliefs, existing quantitative work has only scratched the surface, in particular with respect to learning about a world that is constantly evolving due to structural change. We expect that the new literature that directly collects survey data on ambiguity can help distinguish between alternative feedback mechanisms from data to beliefs. A combination of theory and evidence should thus lead us to models of the joint dynamics of uncertainty and observables, with causal effects running in both directions.

References

Abdellaoui, M., Bleichrodt, H., Kemel, E., l'Haridon, O., 2021. Measuring beliefs under ambiguity. Operations Research 69, 599–612.

Adam, K., Matveev, D., Nagel, S., 2021. Do survey expectations of stock returns reflect risk adjustments? Journal of Monetary Economics 117, 723–740.

Adam, K., Woodford, M., 2012. Robustly optimal monetary policy in a microfounded New Keynesian model. Journal of Monetary Economics 59, 468–487.

Ai, H., Bansal, R., 2018. Risk preferences and the macroeconomic announcement premium. Econometrica 86, 1383–1430.

Altug, S., Collard, F., Cakmaklı, C., Mukerji, S., Özsöylev, H., 2020. Ambiguous business cycles: a quantitative assessment. Review of Economic Dynamics 38, 220–237.

Alvarez, F., Jermann, U.J., 2005. Using asset prices to measure the persistence of the marginal utility of wealth. Econometrica 73, 1977–2016.

Anderson, E.W., Hansen, L.P., Sargent, T.J., 2003. A quartet of semigroups for model specification, robustness, prices of risk, and model detection. Journal of the European Economic Association 1, 68–123.

Angeletos, G.-M., Collard, F., Dellas, H., 2020. Business-cycle anatomy. The American Economic Review 110, 3030–3070.

Asano, T., 2010. Precautionary principle and the optimal timing of environmental policy under ambiguity. Environmental & Resource Economics 47, 173–196.

Asparouhova, E., Bossaerts, P., Eguia, J., Zame, W., 2015. Asset pricing and asymmetric reasoning. Journal of Political Economy 123, 66–122.

Azrieli, Y., Teper, R., 2011. Uncertainty aversion and equilibrium existence in games with incomplete information. Games and Economic Behavior 73, 310–317.

Bachmann, R., Carstensen, K., Lautenbacher, S., Schneider, M., 2020. Uncertainty is more than risk–survey evidence on Knightian and Bayesian firms. Working Paper.

Backus, D., Ferriere, A., Zin, S., 2015. Risk and ambiguity in models of business cycles. Journal of Monetary Economics 69, 42–63.

Bade, S., 2011. Electoral competition with uncertainty averse parties. Games and Economic Behavior 72, 12–29.

Baillon, A., Huang, Z., Selim, A., Wakker, P.P., 2018. Measuring ambiguity attitudes for all (natural) events. Econometrica 86, 1839–1858.

Baqaee, D.R., 2020. Asymmetric inflation expectations, downward rigidity of wages, and asymmetric business cycles. Journal of Monetary Economics 114, 174–193.

Barillas, F., Hansen, L.P., Sargent, T.J., 2009. Doubts or variability? Journal of Economic Theory 144, 2388–2418.

Barlevy, G., 2011. Robustness and macroeconomic policy. Annual Review of Economics 3, 1–24.

Barnett, M., Brock, W., Hansen, L.P., 2020. Pricing uncertainty induced by climate change. The Review of Financial Studies 33, 1024–1066.

Barnett, M., Brock, W., Hansen, L.P., et al., 2021. Climate Change Uncertainty Spillover in the Macroeconomy. NBER WP No 29064.

Barro, R.J., King, R.G., 1984. Time-separable preferences and intertemporal-substitution models of business cycles. The Quarterly Journal of Economics 99, 817–839.

Beauchêne, D., 2019. Is ambiguity aversion bad for innovation? Journal of Economic Theory 183, 1154–1176.

Ben-Rephael, A., Izhakian, Y.Y., 2020. Should I stay or should I go? Trading behavior under ambiguity. Rutgers University. Mimeo.

Benigno, P., Paciello, L., 2014. Monetary policy, doubts and asset prices. Journal of Monetary Economics 64, 85–98.

Bennett, F., 2021. Strategic Complementarity and Ambiguity Aversion: a portfolio choice application. Duke. Mimeo.

Bennett, F., Montamat, G., Roch, F., 2022. Robust Optimal Macroprudential Policy. Mimeo.

Bergemann, D., Schlag, K., 2011. Robust monopoly pricing. Journal of Economic Theory 146, 2527–2543.

Bhandari, A., Borovička, J., Ho, P., 2019. Survey data and subjective beliefs in business cycle models. NYU. Mimeo.

Bianchi, F., Ilut, C., Schneider, M., 2018. Uncertainty shocks, asset supply and pricing over the business cycle. The Review of Economic Studies 85, 810–854.

Bianchi, M., Tallon, J.-M., 2019. Ambiguity preferences and portfolio choices: evidence from the field. Management Science 65, 1486–1501.

Bidder, R., Dew-Becker, I., 2016. Long-run risk is the worst-case scenario. The American Economic Review 106, 2494–2527.

Bidder, R., Smith, M.E., 2012. Robust animal spirits. Journal of Monetary Economics 59, 738–750.

Borovička, J., Hansen, L.P., Scheinkman, J.A., 2016. Misspecified recovery. The Journal of Finance 71, 2493–2544.

Bossaerts, P., Ghirardato, P., Guarnaschelli, S., Zame, W.R., 2010. Ambiguity in asset markets: theory and experiment. The Review of Financial Studies 23, 1325–1359.

Boyarchenko, N., 2012. Ambiguity shifts and the 2007–2008 financial crisis. Journal of Monetary Economics 59, 493–507.

Brock, W.A., Manski, C.F., 2011. Competitive lending with partial knowledge of loan repayment: some positive and normative analysis. Journal of Money, Credit, and Banking 43, 441–459.

Bryan, G., 2019. Ambiguity aversion decreases the impact of partial insurance: evidence from African farmers. Journal of the European Economic Association 17, 1428–1469.

Caballero, R.J., Krishnamurthy, A., 2008. Collective risk management in a flight to quality episode. The Journal of Finance 63, 2195–2230.

Carroll, G., 2019. Robustness in mechanism design and contracting. Annual Review of Economics 11, 139–166.

Chen, H., Ju, N., Miao, J., 2014. Dynamic asset allocation with ambiguous return predictability. Review of Economic Dynamics 17, 799–823.

Chen, Z., Epstein, L., 2002. Ambiguity, risk, and asset returns in continuous time. Econometrica 70, 1403–1443.

Coenen, G., 2007. Inflation persistence and robust monetary policy design. Journal of Economic Dynamics and Control 31, 111–140.

Collard, F., Mukerji, S., Sheppard, K., Tallon, J.-M., 2018. Ambiguity and the historical equity premium. Quantitative Economics 9, 945–993.

Condie, S., Ganguli, J., 2017. The pricing effects of ambiguous private information. Journal of Economic Theory 172, 512–557.

Condie, S., Ganguli, J.V., 2011a. Ambiguity and rational expectations equilibria. The Review of Economic Studies 78, 821–845.

Condie, S., Ganguli, J.V., 2011b. Informational efficiency with ambiguous information. Economic Theory 48, 229–242.

Delavande, A., Del Bono, E., Holford, A., 2021a. Perceived Ambiguity about COVID-related Health Outcomes and Protective Health Behaviors among Young Adults. Working Paper.

Delavande, A., Ganguli, J., Mengel, F., 2021b. Uncertainty Attitudes, Subjective Expectations and Decisions under Uncertainty. Working Paper.

Dicks, D., Fulghieri, P., 2021a. Uncertainty, investor sentiment, and innovation. The Review of Financial Studies 34, 1236–1279.

Dicks, D.L., Fulghieri, P., 2021b. Uncertainty, Contracting, and Beliefs in Organizations. UNC Kenan-Flagler. Mimeo.

Dimmock, S.G., Kouwenberg, R., Mitchell, O.S., Peijnenburg, K., 2016. Ambiguity aversion and household portfolio choice puzzles: empirical evidence. Journal of Financial Economics 119, 559–577.

Dougherty, J.P., Flatnes, J.E., Gallenstein, R.A., Miranda, M.J., Sam, A.G., 2020. Climate change and index insurance demand: evidence from a framed field experiment in Tanzania. Journal of Economic Behavior & Organization 175, 155–184.

Dow, J., Werlang, S.R.d.C., 1992. Uncertainty aversion, risk aversion, and the optimal choice of portfolio. Econometrica, 197–204.

Dow, J., Werlang, S.R.d.C., 1994. Nash equilibrium under Knightian uncertainty: breaking down backward induction. Journal of Economic Theory 64, 305–324.

Drechsler, I., 2013. Uncertainty, time-varying fear, and asset prices. The Journal of Finance 68, 1843–1889.

Easley, D., O'Hara, M., 2009. Ambiguity and nonparticipation: the role of regulation. The Review of Financial Studies 22, 1817–1843.

Eichberger, J., Kelsey, D., 2002. Strategic complements, substitutes, and ambiguity: the implications for public goods. Journal of Economic Theory 106, 436–466.

Ellis, A., 2016. Condorcet meets Ellsberg. Theoretical Economics 11, 865–895.

Ellsberg, D., 1961. Risk, ambiguity, and the Savage axioms. The Quarterly Journal of Economics, 643–669.

Epstein, L.G., Farhi, E., Strzalecki, T., 2014. How much would you pay to resolve long-run risk? The American Economic Review 104, 2680–2697.

Epstein, L.G., Halevy, Y., 2021. Hard-to-Interpret Signals. University of Toronto. Mimeo.

Epstein, L.G., Schneider, M., 2003. Recursive multiple-priors. Journal of Economic Theory 113, 1–31.

Epstein, L.G., Schneider, M., 2007. Learning under ambiguity. The Review of Economic Studies 74, 1275–1303.

Epstein, L.G., Schneider, M., 2008. Ambiguity, information quality, and asset pricing. The Journal of Finance 63, 197–228.

Epstein, L.G., Schneider, M., 2010. Ambiguity and asset markets. Annual Review of Financial Economics 2, 315–346.

Epstein, L.G., Wang, T., 1994. Intertemporal asset pricing under knightian uncertainty. Econometrica 62, 283–322.

Epstein, L.G., Zin, S.E., 1989. Substitution, risk aversion, and the temporal behavior of consumption and asset returns: a theoretical framework. Econometrica, 937–969.

Ferriere, A., Karantounias, A.G., 2019. Fiscal austerity in ambiguous times. American Economic Journal: Macroeconomics 11, 89–131.

Gallant, A.R., Jahan-Parvar, M.R., Liu, H., 2019. Does smooth ambiguity matter for asset pricing? The Review of Financial Studies 32, 3617–3666.

Garlappi, L., Giammarino, R., Lazrak, A., 2017. Ambiguity and the corporation: group disagreement and underinvestment. Journal of Financial Economics 125, 417–433.

Ghirardato, P., Katz, J.N., 2006. Indecision theory: weight of evidence and voting behavior. Journal of Public Economic Theory 8, 379–399.

Giannoni, M.P., 2002. Does model uncertainty justify caution? Robust optimal monetary policy in a forward-looking model. Macroeconomic Dynamics 6, 111–144.

Gilboa, I., Marinacci, M., 2016. Ambiguity and the Bayesian paradigm. In: Readings in Formal Epistemology. Springer, pp. 385–439.

Gilboa, I., Schmeidler, D., 1989. Maxmin expected utility with non-unique prior. Journal of Mathematical Economics 18, 141–153.

Giustinelli, P., Manski, C.F., Molinari, F., 2022. Precise or imprecise probabilities? Evidence from survey response related to late-onset dementia. Journal of the European Economic Association 20, 187–221.

Giustinelli, P., Pavoni, N., 2017. The evolution of awareness and belief ambiguity in the process of high school track choice. Review of Economic Dynamics 25, 93–120.

Guidolin, M., Rinaldi, F., 2013. Ambiguity in asset pricing and portfolio choice: a review of the literature. Theory and Decision 74, 183–217.

Handel, B.R., Misra, K., 2015. Robust new product pricing. Marketing Science 34, 864–881.

Handel, B.R., Misra, K., Roberts, J.W., 2013. Robust firm pricing with panel data. Journal of Econometrics 174, 165–185.

Hansen, L.P., 2007. Beliefs, doubts and learning: valuing macroeconomic risk. The American Economic Review 97, 1–30.

Hansen, L.P., 2021. Central Banking Challenges Posed by Uncertain Climate Change and Natural Disasters. Becker Friedman Institute for Economics Working Paper No. 2021-64.

Hansen, L.P., Sargent, T.J., 2008. Robustness. Princeton University Press.

Hansen, L.P., Sargent, T.J., 2010. Fragile beliefs and the price of model uncertainty. Quantitative Economics 1, 129–162.

Hansen, L.P., Sargent, T.J., 2015. Four types of ignorance. Journal of Monetary Economics 69, 97–113.

Hansen, L.P., Sargent, T.J., 2018. Structured ambiguity and model misspecification. Becker Friedman Institute for Economics Working Paper No. 2018-77.

Hayashi, T., 2005. Intertemporal substitution, risk aversion and ambiguity aversion. Economic Theory 25, 933–956.

Huber, P.J., 1981. Robust Statistics. Wiley.

Illeditsch, P.K., 2011. Ambiguous information, portfolio inertia, and excess volatility. The Journal of Finance 66, 2213–2247.

Illeditsch, P.K., Ganguli, J.V., Condie, S., 2021. Information inertia. The Journal of Finance 76, 443–479.

Ilut, C., 2012. Ambiguity aversion: implications for the uncovered interest rate parity puzzle. American Economic Journal: Macroeconomics 4, 33–65.

Ilut, C., Kehrig, M., Schneider, M., 2018. Slow to hire, quick to fire: employment dynamics with asymmetric responses to news. Journal of Political Economy 126, 2011–2071.

Ilut, C., Krivenko, P., Schneider, M., 2016. Uncertainty aversion and heterogeneous beliefs in linear models. Duke Univ. Mimeo.

Ilut, C., Saijo, H., 2021. Learning, confidence, and business cycles. Journal of Monetary Economics 117, 354–376.

Ilut, C., Schneider, M., 2012. Ambiguous business cycles. NBER Working Paper No. 17900.

Ilut, C., Schneider, M., 2014. Ambiguous business cycles. The American Economic Review 104, 2368–2399.

Ilut, C., Valchev, R., Vincent, N., 2020. Paralyzed by fear: rigid and discrete pricing under demand uncertainty. Econometrica 88, 1899–1938.

Izhakian, Y., Yermack, D., Zender, J.F., 2021. Ambiguity and the tradeoff theory of capital structure. Management Science.

Jahan-Parvar, M.R., Liu, H., 2014. Ambiguity aversion and asset prices in production economies. The Review of Financial Studies 27, 3060–3097.

Ju, N., Miao, J., 2012. Ambiguity, learning, and asset returns. Econometrica 80, 559–591.

Kala, N., 2019. Learning, adaptation, and climate uncertainty: Evidence from Indian agriculture. MIT Sloan School of Management. Mimeo.

Karantounias, A.G., 2013. Managing pessimistic expectations and fiscal policy. Theoretical Economics 8, 193–231.

Karantounias, A.G., 2020. Doubts about the model and optimal policy. Federal Reserve Bank of Atlanta WP 2020-12.

Kindermann, F., Le Blanc, J., Piazzesi, M., Schneider, M., 2021. Learning about housing cost: Survey evidence from the German house price boom. NBER Working Paper 28895.

Klibanoff, P., Marinacci, M., Mukerji, S., 2005. A smooth model of decision making under ambiguity. Econometrica 73, 1849–1892.

Kocherlakota, N., Phelan, C., 2009. On the robustness of laissez-faire. Journal of Economic Theory 144, 2372–2387.

Kroner, N., 2021. Firm-Level Uncertainty and the Transmission of Forward Guidance to Investment. UT Austin. Mimeo.

Kuester, K., Wieland, V., 2010. Insurance policies for monetary policy in the euro area. Journal of the European Economic Association 8, 872–912.

Lange, A., Treich, N., 2008. Uncertainty, learning and ambiguity in economic models on climate policy: some classical results and new directions. Climatic Change 89, 7–21.

Leitemo, K., Söderström, U., 2008. Robust monetary policy in the New Keynesian framework. Macroeconomic Dynamics 12, 126–135.

Lemoine, D., Rudik, I., 2017. Managing climate change under uncertainty: recursive integrated assessment at an inflection point. Annual Review of Resource Economics 9, 117–142.

Lemoine, D., Traeger, C.P., 2016. Ambiguous tipping points. Journal of Economic Behavior & Organization 132, 5–18.

Lensman, T., Troshkin, M., 2022. Implications of uncertainty for optimal policies. Journal of Economic Theory 199.

Levin, A., Wieland, V., Williams, J.C., 2003. The performance of forecast-based monetary policy rules under model uncertainty. The American Economic Review 93, 622–645.

Levin, A.T., Williams, J.C., 2003. Robust monetary policy with competing reference models. Journal of Monetary Economics 50, 945–975.

Li, J., 2019. The k-armed bandit problem with multiple priors. Journal of Mathematical Economics 80, 22–38.

Liu, H., Zhang, Y., 2021. Financial uncertainty with ambiguity and learning. Management Science.

Lucas, R.E., 1987. Models of Business Cycles, vol. 26. Basil Blackwell, Oxford.

Lucca, D.O., Moench, E., 2015. The pre-FOMC announcement drift. The Journal of Finance 70, 329–371.

Machina, M.J., Siniscalchi, M., 2014. Ambiguity and ambiguity aversion. In: Handbook of the Economics of Risk and Uncertainty, vol. 1. Elsevier, pp. 729–807.

Malenko, A., Tsoy, A., 2020. Asymmetric information and security design under Knightian uncertainty. Univ. of Toronto. Mimeo.

Manski, C.F., 2011. Choosing treatment policies under ambiguity. Annual Review of Economics 3, 25–49.

Manski, C.F., 2013. Public Policy in an Uncertain World. Harvard University Press.

Manski, C.F., Molinari, F., 2010. Rounding probabilistic expectations in surveys. Journal of Business & Economic Statistics 28, 219–231.

Marinacci, M., 2015. Model uncertainty. Journal of the European Economic Association 13, 1022–1100.

Masolo, R., Monti, F., 2020. Ambiguity, monetary policy and trend inflation. Journal of the European Economic Association 19, 839–871.

Miao, J., Rivera, A., 2016. Robust contracts in continuous time. Econometrica 84, 1405–1440.

Miao, J., Wang, N., 2011. Risk, uncertainty, and option exercise. Journal of Economic Dynamics and Control 35, 442–461.

Miao, J., Wei, B., Zhou, H., 2019. Ambiguity aversion and the variance premium. Quarterly Journal of Finance 9, 1950003.

Michelacci, C., Paciello, L., 2020. Ambiguous policy announcements. The Review of Economic Studies 87, 2356–2398.

Millner, A., Dietz, S., Heal, G., 2010. Ambiguity and climate policy. NBER Working Paper No. 16050.

Millner, A., Dietz, S., Heal, G., 2013. Scientific ambiguity and climate policy. Environmental & Resource Economics 55, 21–46.

Mukerji, S., Tallon, J.-M., 2001. Ambiguity aversion and incompleteness of financial markets. The Review of Economic Studies 68, 883–904.

Mukerji, S., Tallon, J.-M., 2004a. Ambiguity aversion and the absence of indexed debt. Economic Theory 24, 665–685.

Mukerji, S., Tallon, J.-M., 2004b. An overview of economic applications of David Schmeidler's models of decision making under uncertainty. In: Uncertainty in Economic Theory, pp. 299–318.

Nau, R., 2006. Uncertainty aversion with second-order probabilities and utilities. Management Science 52, 136–145.

Neilson, W.S., 1993. Ambiguity aversion: an axiomatic approach using second order probabilities. Mimeo.

Nishimura, K.G., Ozaki, H., 2004. Search and Knightian uncertainty. Journal of Economic Theory 119, 299–333.

Norton, B.P., Hoel, J.B., Michelson, H., 2020. The demand for (fake?) fertilizer: using an experimental auction to examine the role of beliefs on agricultural input demand in Tanzania. In: Agricultural and Applied Economics Association Annual Meeting.

Palmer, T., Stevens, B., 2019. The scientific challenge of understanding and estimating climate change. Proceedings of the National Academy of Sciences 116, 24390–24395.

Pei, G., 2018. Ambiguity, Pessimism and Economic Fluctuations. University of Zurich. Mimeo.

Pouzo, D., Presno, I., 2016. Sovereign default risk and uncertainty premia. American Economic Journal: Macroeconomics 8, 230–266.

Rabin, M., 2000. Risk aversion and expected-utility theory: a calibration theorem. Econometrica 68, 1281–1292.

Riedel, F., 2009. Optimal stopping with multiple priors. Econometrica 77, 857–908.

Ross, N., Santos, P., Capon, T., 2012. Risk, ambiguity and the adoption of new technologies: experimental evidence from a developing economy. In: Conference, Brazil, International Association of Agricultural Economists.

Saijo, H., 2020. Redistribution and fiscal uncertainty shocks. International Economic Review 61, 1073–1095.

Sargent, T., 1999. Comment on 'Policy rules for open economies' by Laurence Ball. In: Monetary Policy Rules, vol. 31. University of Chicago Press, pp. 144–154.

Sims, C.A., 2002. Solving linear rational expectations models. Computational Economics 20, 1–20.

Strzalecki, T., 2011. Axiomatic foundations of multiplier preferences. Econometrica 79, 47–73.

Strzalecki, T., 2013. Temporal resolution of uncertainty and recursive models of ambiguity aversion. Econometrica 81, 1039–1074.

Taylor, J.B., Williams, J.C., 2010. Simple and robust rules for monetary policy. In: Handbook of Monetary Economics, vol. 3. Elsevier, pp. 829–859.

Trautmann, S.T., van de Kuilen, G., 2015. Ambiguity attitudes. In: The Wiley Blackwell Handbook of Judgment and Decision Making, vol. 1, pp. 89–116.

Wallsten, T.S., Forsyth, B.H., Budescu, D.V., 1983. Stability and coherence of health experts' upper and lower subjective probabilities about dose—response functions. Organizational Behavior and Human Performance 31, 277–302.

Warnick, J.C.E., Escobal, J., Laszlo, S.C., 2011. Ambiguity aversion and portfolio choice in small-scale Peruvian farming. The B.E. Journal in Economic Analysis & Policy 11.

Woodford, M., 2010. Robustly optimal monetary policy with near-rational expectations. The American Economic Review 100, 274–303.

Yoo, D., 2019. Ambiguous information, permanent income, and consumption fluctuations. European Economic Review 119, 79–96.

Young, E.R., 2012. Robust policymaking in the face of sudden stops. Journal of Monetary Economics 59, 512–527.

Epidemiological expectations☆

25

Christopher Carroll and Tao Wang

Johns Hopkins University, Baltimore, MD, United States

While mass media play a major role in alerting individuals to the possibility of an innovation, it seems to be personal contact that is most relevant in leading to its adoption. Thus, the diffusion of an innovation becomes a process formally akin to the spread of an infectious disease.
— Arrow (1969)

A very natural next step for economics is to maintain expectations in the strategic position they have come to occupy, but to build an empirically validated theory of how attention is in fact directed within a social system, and how expectations are, in fact, formed.
— Simon (1984)

If we want to know why an unusually large economic event happened, we need to list the seemingly unrelated narratives that all happened to be going viral at around the same time and affecting the economy in the same direction.
— Shiller (2017)

An idea is like a virus. Resilient. Highly contagious. And even the smallest seed of an idea can grow. —Cobb
— The movie *Inception* (2010)

25.1 Introduction

It is a commonplace, in academia and popular culture, that ideas spread like diseases: they can be "infectious" or "go viral." The proposition is hardly new; as Shiller (2017) points out, it can be found at least as far back as Hume (1748), whose ideas thoroughly infected the work of his friend Smith (1776).[1] Indeed, in fields other than economics, debates about how to model belief dynamics are largely about

☆ Thanks to the participants in the *Handbook of Economic Expectations* Conference for insightful comments, and the editors for comments that substantially improved the paper. Thanks also to Sebastian Benthall, Francesco Bianchi, Jennifer Manning, and Adrian Monninger for feedback on earlier drafts, Charles Manski, Matthew Jackson, Robert Shiller, David Hirshleifer, Cars Hommes, Leif Anders Thorsrud, Byoung-Hyoun Hwang, and Cris Moore for further comments; and special thanks to Mridul Seth for help in using the `NDLib` and `NetworkX` python libraries to produce our SIR Model Notebook.

[1] See Rasmussen (2017).

Handbook of Economic Expectations. https://doi.org/10.1016/B978-0-12-822927-9.00034-3

which particular models of social communication are most suitable for understanding the spread of which kinds of ideas.[2]

"Expectations" are just a category of ideas. So upon being told that expectations play a critical role in structural economic modeling, a scholar who was not an economist might suppose that epidemiological approaches would be a standard part of the economist's toolkit for modeling expectations – unless there were good reason to believe that economic ideas are immune to social influence. But evidence for social transmission of economic ideas is plentiful – see Section 25.4.4.

Still, it would not be accurate to say that an "epidemiological expectations" (EE) approach is a standard way of constructing formal models of economic phenomena – a conventional off-the-shelf alternative, say, to a "rational expectations" (RE) approach, the "Rational Inattention" (RI) approach advocated by Sims (2003), the "diagnostic expectations" model of Bordalo et al. (2018), or a number of bounded rationality approaches (e.g., Gabaix (2020) or Ilut and Valchev (2020)).

This is perhaps because nowhere has a focused attempt been made to define what would constitute an EE treatment of an economic question. For the purposes of this survey, we will think of a full-fledged EE treatment as incorporating the following elements:

1. **A mechanism –** An explicit and rigorous mathematical description of a process by which ideas are communicated between agents ...
2. **Implying expectational dynamics –** ... that generates observable expectation dynamics at the level of individuals or populations ...
3. **With economic consequences –** ... and those expectations have knock-on implications for an observable outcome (often, prices, quantities, or market values) that is the primary subject of the economic analysis.

We have identified three fields in economics – technological diffusion (Section 25.4.1), asset pricing (Section 25.4.2), and macroeconomics (Section 25.4.3) – with sets of papers that satisfy all these criteria, even if in some cases the work has not mainly been thought of as "epidemiological" until now. In addition, we survey the proliferating evidence that social interactions drive expectations and corresponding behaviors (Section 25.4.4); draw connections between the EE approach and a separate literature on financial contagion (Section 25.4.5); and present selected examples of research outside of economics that might be particularly interesting for economists (Section 25.4.6).

25.2 Background and motivation
25.2.1 Expectational heterogeneity

In their introduction to the *Handbook of Microeconomics*, Browning et al. (1999) wrote that the most universal lesson of microeconomics is that "people are different in ways that importantly affect their economic behavior."

---

[2] A recent article in *Nature Scientific Reports* begins "Opinion formation cannot be modeled solely as an ideological deduction from a set of principles; rather, repeated social interactions ... are consequential in the construct of belief systems." (Nedić et al., 2019).

Since then, a great deal of the progress in macroeconomics has come from incorporating microeconomic heterogeneity "in ways that importantly affect" macroeconomic behavior. (See "Macroeconomics and Heterogeneity" in the latest *Handbook of Macroeconomics*, Krueger et al. (2016)).

But few models in the HA-Macro literature have allowed for differences in agents' expectations about variables like stock returns (where everyone's realized outcome will be identical) – though disagreements on such subjects are rife and people make choices that correspond to their expressed beliefs (Giglio et al., 2021).[3]

Partly, the failure to incorporate expectational heterogeneity reflects the fact that until recently there was not widespread awareness among macroeconomists that measurable expectation differences have power to explain observable microeconomic behavior. Evidence of the recent change in attitudes can be seen in the published discussions in the 2017 *NBER Macroeconomics Annual* of Manski (2018)'s paper surveying the literature on the measurement of expectations (in which Manski himself has been the leading figure). The commissioning of this *Handbook*, and the proliferation of new research summarized herein, are among the many other indications of a sea-change in the profession's attitudes.

25.2.2 Epidemiological models

We will use the word "classical" to refer to epidemiological models that descend from Kermack and McKendrick (1927), who formulated the problem as one of tracking the size of "compartments" of the population in different disease states ("Susceptible" to infection, "Infected," or "Recovered"; S, I, and R for short) under a "random mixing" assumption in which all members of the population were equally likely to encounter each other in a time interval. These assumptions allowed formulation of the problem as a set of nonlinear differential equations.

A newer literature uses the tools of "network theory" to study models in which the "nodes" in a graph are people and the "edges" are social links between nodes. Erdős et al. (1960) originated this literature with a model in which connections among agents were a "random graph" (the network analog of the "random mixing" assumption), so the only parameter was "degree": the number of connections each agent had. Subsequent work relaxed the random graph assumption, allowing meaningful definition of an agent's "neighbors," and showed that a "clustering coefficient" is a useful measurement of the extent to which a person's neighbors know each other.[4]

While the classical and the network-theory approaches seem quite different, it turns out that a "random graph" network can be configured to produce an arbitrarily close approximation to the classical problem, by assuming that at any date t each node is in one of the three states $\{S, I, R\}$, and that "edges" are the links by which an infection can pass from an infected to a susceptible person (our SIR model in Section 25.3.2 is constructed in exactly this way; see Newman (2002) and Jackson (2010) for canonical analyses of epidemics on networks, and Easley and Kleinberg (2010) for a textbook focused on markets).

Networks can also be used to study a great many other essentially epidemiological questions that could not even be formulated in the classical setup.

---

[3] One example is Velásquez-Giraldo (2022), who shows that household portfolio choice models yield much more reasonable results when the model is calibrated with survey respondents' self-reported stock market expectations than when calibrated with beliefs like the empirical history of stock returns.

[4] A standard reference for economists is the textbook by Jackson (2010).

One particularly interesting result is the "Small World" effect explained by Watts and Strogatz (1998), who show that even when a network's "clustering coefficient" is high, a small sprinkling of random links to "distant" nodes has remarkable power to make a network "completely connected" (or nearly so). Barabási et al. (2016)'s summary is that when network models are calibrated to match facts about human connections, the "interconnectedness" phenomenon is extremely robust.

This provides a satisfying explanation for a phenomenon first documented by Milgram (1967), who famously found that, on average, any two randomly selected people in the U.S. were able to identify intermediate links of personal friends and friends-of-friends (and so on) by which they were connected, with the typical length of the chain involving only six people – they have "six degrees of separation."[5]

Moore and Newman (2000) demonstrate that the patterns of the spread of diseases on "small worlds" networks can be quite similar to those of the classical SIR model – under certain assumptions about the nature of the interactions that occur over the links. But a subsequent literature has shown that, even in a network whose link structure satisfies the "small worlds" requirements, the ultimate outcome depends sensitively not only on the structure of the network but also on the exact nature of the interactions. Even in a fully connected world, it is easy to construct models in which disagreement persists indefinitely and and subpopulations converge to different beliefs, if some agents are 'stubborn' (Acemoğlu et al., 2013) or prone to confirmation bias (Sikder et al., 2020).

25.2.3 Expectational tribes

If there were no evidence that differences of opinion could matter for important economic decisions, the case for epidemiological modeling would be weaker. We therefore conclude this our "background and motivation" with some evidence of a recent clear failure of "identical beliefs" with consequences for measured choices in an area core to both micro and macro modeling, namely financial risk-taking.

Meeuwis et al. (2021), using data on millions of retirement investors, show that after Donald Trump's surprise victory in the U.S. 2016 Presidential election, investors likely to be affiliated with Republican Party (inferred from campaign donations at the zip code level) increased the equity share in their portfolio, while (likely) Democrats rebalanced into safe assets (see Fig. 25.1). These choices occurred at exactly the same time that consumer sentiment surveys showed that self-identified Republicans had suddenly become more optimistic, and Democrats more pessimistic, about the economy's prospects over the next few years.[6]

25.3 What insights can the epidemiological framework offer?
25.3.1 What is an epidemiological framework?

We will say that ideas, beliefs, "narratives," or other mental states that affect behavior (henceforth, "expectations") result from an "epidemiological" process whenever they are modeled as resulting from some social interaction.

---

[5] This provides another example of crossover appeal in popular culture, having spawned John Guare (1990)'s play "Six Degrees of Separation," a movie adaptation, a popular parlor game, and other byproducts like calculators for the degrees of separation between academics.

[6] The New York Fed blog post *"Political Polarization in Consumer Expectations"* also finds partisan differences in consumer expectations.

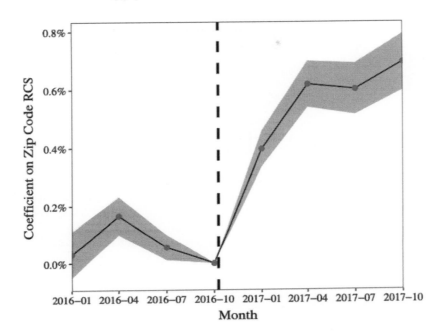

FIGURE 25.1 Portfolio Responses to the 2016 U.S. Election

Note: Reproduced from Meeuwis et al. (2021), this figure reports regression coefficients of equity share on zip-code-level campaign contribution share to Republican candidates over an interval spanning the election.

Table 25.1 Common Source SI Model.		
Date t	**Susceptible$_t$**	**Infected$_t$**
0	1	0
1	$(1-p)$	$1-(1-p)$
2	$(1-p)^2$	$1-(1-p)^2$
$\vdots$	$\vdots$	$\vdots$
n	$(1-p)^n$	$1-(1-p)^n$

Transmission need not be person-to-person; it can reflect exposure to a "common source." (Cosmic radiation to which everyone is exposed can cause diseases like cancer). In the context of beliefs, a natural interpretation of such a "common source" is news media (a point to which we return below).

In the simplest epidemiological model, a continuous population is partitioned among infected people I and those who are susceptible S but not yet infected, and the infectiousness of the "common source" is time-independent at probability p. For a population at discrete date zero with a susceptible population of size 1, the dynamics of such a common-source SI model are given by Table 25.1, with the obvious implication that as n approaches infinity the entire population eventually becomes infected.

Table 25.2 Transmissible SI Model.

Date t	Susceptible$_t$	Infected$_t$
0	S_0	I_0
1	$S_0 - \beta S_0 I_0$	$I_0 + \beta S_0 I_0$
2	$S_1 - \beta S_1 I_1$	$I_1 + \beta S_1 I_1$
$\vdots$	$\vdots$	$\vdots$
n	$S_{n-1} - \beta S_{n-1} I_{n-1}$	$I_{n-1} + \beta S_{n-1} I_{n-1}$

This framework can be extended in many directions. The usual next step is for the disease to be transmitted as a result of "random mixing" where each susceptible person who encounters an infected person becomes infected with a fixed probability. Given a nonzero initial infected fraction I_0, the fraction infected and susceptible evolve per Table 25.2.

The best-known epidemiological framework adds an R state that can designate either recovery or "removal" (via, say, death), yielding the "classical" SIR models. The SIR framework has rich and interesting implications, such as the potential for "herd immunity" which comes about when a high enough proportion of the population has either Recovered or otherwise been Removed (say, by vaccination) from the Susceptible compartment.

Options proliferate from there.[7] A framework in which there are two possible outcomes of the infection, recovery or death, receives the acronym SIRD. If the disease is one in which it is necessary to track the proportion who have been Exposed but are not yet (and may never become) infected, the result is an SEIR model – and so on.

In some dimensions, close analogies can be drawn between the two applications. Like an infected disease, an idea/opinion/certain view of the economy can spread via interpersonal contacts from those who have held it already, i.e. the infected (I) to those who are exposed to it (E) or who are potentially receptive to them (S), and it may also be forgotten, i.e. recovery (R). Furthermore, the agents could be either ex-ante homogeneous or heterogeneous and the transmission of the expectations could be specific to agent types and their locations in the network.

25.3.1.1 *Adapting the disease metaphor to expectations*

Basic epidemiological models usually study the dynamics of a single disease in a population, with a natural terminal stage like recovery or death. Economists will often be interested in keeping track of how expectations change about an aggregate variable like stock prices, which does not have a terminal point and in which many competing opinions may infect different people at the same time.

An advantage of network-theory tools is that they can easily accommodate ways in which an economic application may call for such modifications. It is trivial to represent as many competing "diseases" (e.g., theories of stock prices) as desired, and there is no need to specify a "recovery" state.

To take a more complex example, in classical epidemiological models it would be painful to capture dynamics of a disease in which people become "more infected" after repeated contact with other

---

[7] For a general introduction to these model basics, we refer the reader to the Wikipedia page https://en.wikipedia.org/wiki/Compartmental_models_in_epidemiology# Transition_rates. Prominent examples include Bailey et al. (1975), Anderson et al. (1992), Hethcote (2000), Brauer (2017).

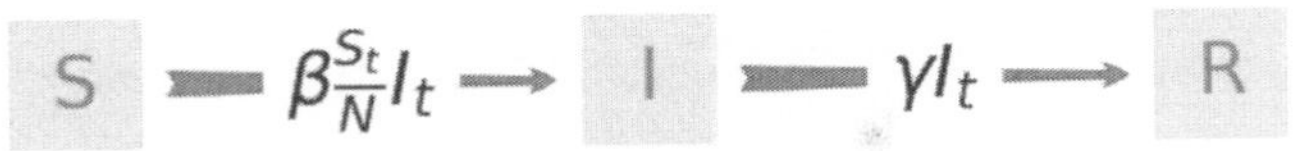

$$S \longrightarrow \beta\frac{S_t}{N}I_t \longrightarrow I \longrightarrow \gamma I_t \longrightarrow R$$

FIGURE 25.2 A SIR model of stock investors

Note: This graph plots the transitions between different compartments in the SIR model of stock investors described in Shiller and Pound (1989).

infected people. But in a network model, it is easy to capture the proposition that a person may need to be exposed to an idea more than a certain number of times, or from more than a given number of sources, before they will adopt it – as proposed in Granovetter (1978), and as implemented in Jackson and Yariv (2007).[8]

25.3.2 One example

Here, we provide a specific example of an economic question formulated in a thoroughgoing epidemiological way. Our present purpose is not to extract economic insights – we do that in Section 25.4.2 below – but simply to illustrate how the epidemiological toolkit works.

Shiller and Pound (1989) use an SIR model to capture how interest in particular stocks spreads[9]; we examine a model almost identical to theirs. At date t, a large population of investors measured by the real number N is divided into three "compartments" (see Fig. 25.2); I_t investors are currently "infected" with interest in a certain stock; S_t investors are not infected but are "susceptible" to becoming interested; and R_t measures investors who have been "infected" but have "recovered" from the infection.[10]

Under "random mixing," each person is expected to have contact with χ others, randomly selected from the entire population. The only kind of contact with any consequence is between an infected and a susceptible person: Such an encounter has a probability τ of causing the susceptible person to become infected.

Epidemiological models typically define a parameter β that combines consequences of the rate of social contact χ and the rate of transmission upon contact, τ, namely

$$\beta = \tau \chi. \tag{25.1}$$

The expected number of new infections generated in period t (corresponding to the decline in the number of susceptible persons) can now be calculated: Fraction S_t/N of an infected person's contacts will be susceptible, so the number of newly generated infections per infected person will be $\tau \times \chi \times (S_t/N)$. The "infected" population also changes because every infected person recovers with a probability of γ per period.

Putting these elements together, the changes in the population in different compartments are given by

---

[8] See the interesting discussion of such "threshold models" in Glasserman and Young (2016).

[9] This paper builds on the earlier work comparing the efficient market hypothesis of stock prices and an alternative model incorporating social dynamics Shiller (1984).

[10] For our purposes here, we do not need to define the exact consequences of "recovery." See below (or see the original paper) for further discussion.

$$\Delta S_{t+1} = -\beta I_t (S_t/N),$$

$$\Delta I_{t+1} = \beta \frac{S_t}{N} I_t - \gamma I_t, \qquad (25.2)$$

$$\Delta R_{t+1} = \gamma I_t.$$

The simplest special case of the SIR model is one with a recovery rate of $\gamma = 0$, in which case the model reduces to the transmissible SI model discussed in Section 25.3.1. Another straightforward case is $\beta < \gamma$, in which from any starting point the population of infected persons I gradually dies down to zero.

The interesting cases emerge when the "basic reproduction ratio" $\mathcal{R}(0) = (\beta/\gamma)$ exceeds one (this $\mathcal{R}(0)$ is unrelated to the R used elsewhere to measure the recovered population), because $\mathcal{R}(0) > 1$ guarantees that an initial arbitrarily small infection will grow, at least for a while (assuming that at the beginning everyone is susceptible, $S_0/N = 1$).

To illustrate the model's implications, we configure it with four combinations of parameter values taken from Shiller and Pound (1989), characterizing two different kinds of investors and two categories of stocks.

We calculate the quantitative implications using one of the best of the many computational toolkits for analyzing such models that have proliferated in recent years: NDlib lets users specify an arbitrary network structure on which a disease might spread. We exploit the above-mentioned fact that a random-mixing SIR model can be approximated with an *ex-ante* generated random graph when the transmission probability τ and the average number of connections χ in the graph are configured such that their product is equal to the calibrated infection rate β (see Eq. (25.1)).[11]

In Fig. 25.3 the vertical axis measures the populations of S, I, and R investors; time since the initial date of infection is on the horizontal axis. Also plotted is the limiting size of the recovered compartment.

Two common patterns emerge. First, since in all four cases the basic reproduction ratio $\mathcal{R}(0)$ is greater than 1, in all four cases there is an outbreak. The size of the infected population first expands to its maximum value and then gradually levels off to zero, exhibiting a hump-shaped "viral curve" characteristic of SIR models. Second, in all scenarios, the system ultimately converges to a steady-state where most people have cycled through infection and recovery. Even in the case with the smallest reproduction ratio, the proportion who cycle through the process of Infection and Recovery is almost 85%, implying a high degree of infectiousness. Under other configurations, the limiting size of the infected-then-recovered "compartment" R is close to 100%.

The main difference in the parameterizations is the speed with which these eventualities play themselves out, which varies considerably. (For a discussion of the model's economic (as distinct from epidemiological) content see Section 25.4.2).

25.4 **Literature**

Fig. 25.4 provides a citation map of papers in the literatures we discuss here; the thin lines represent a citation from the later paper to the linked earlier one.

---

[11] See the companion Jupyter Notebook of this paper for our implementation.

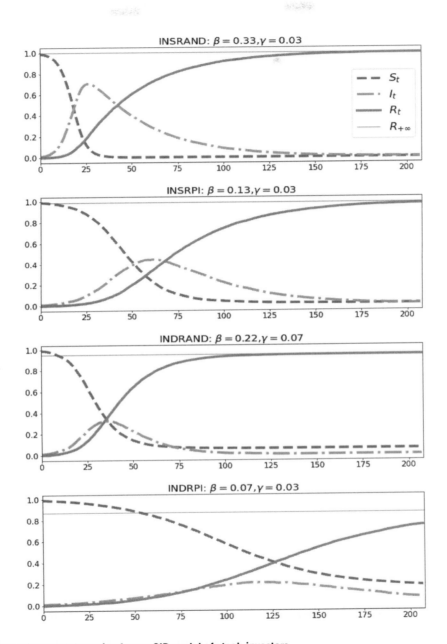

FIGURE 25.3 Simulated dynamics from a SIR model of stock investors

The four figures respectively simulate an SIR model under calibrations corresponding to Shiller and Pound (1989)'s parameter estimates for (1) institutional investors for a randomly selected stock (INSRAND); (2) institutional investors for a rapidly rising stock (INSRPI); (3) individual investors for a random stock (INDRAND); and (4) individual investors for a rapidly rising stock (INDRPI). The susceptible population S is dashed; dashed–dotted line shows the size of the I compartment, and the recovered population R is solid. The horizontal thin solid line corresponds to the limiting size of compartment of R in the long run. To reproduce these figures, see the companion Jupyter Notebook.

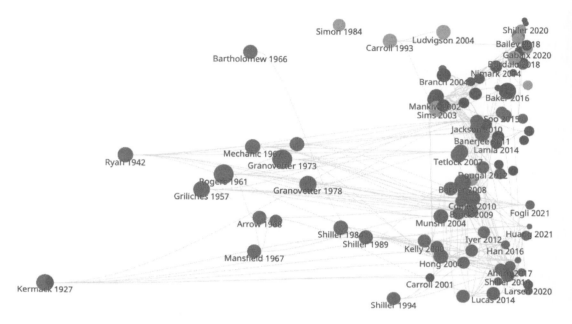

FIGURE 25.4 Literature map of cited papers

Note: Papers we have identified as having a strong epidemiological flavor in three literatures in economics: technological diffusion (red (gray in print version)), asset markets (purple (mid gray in print version)), and macroeconomic expectations (blue (dark gray in print version)). Papers in yellow (light gray in print version) have no epidemiological content but are cited in the text as having content that may be interesting to EE modelers. See https://app.litmaps.co/shared/89EF6E28-98E7-4406-AA0F-BE8045A0571C for an interactive version.

25.4.1 Diffusion of technology

Arrow (1969) argues that the process of knowledge diffusion may account for international differences in both levels and dynamics of income per capita. He conjectures that knowledge diffusion is influenced by factors that he explicitly compares to those that influence the spread of disease including (1) the perceived reliability of the sender (which affects infectiousness); (2) socioeconomic traits (which affect exposure and susceptibility); (3) the understandability of information by the receiver (degree of immunity); and so on.

Arrow's interpretation puts technological diffusion squarely in the realm of EE modeling, under the mild further assumption that what spreads is the "expectation" that adoption of the technology will yield higher productivity (see Banerjee et al. (2013), discussed below, for survey evidence confirming that people adopt a technology when they expect it to be beneficial).

In closely related work, Rogers et al. (1962) popularized a theory of the "diffusion of innovations" based on a meta-analysis of studies of the spread of ideas in academic disciplines.[12] The factors that this literature identifies as determinants of the dynamics of diffusion are directly interpretable as corresponding to the "infectiousness" of the idea, the degree to which populations are "exposed" to the idea, and many of the other elements of epidemiological models.

Young (2009) presents a broad survey of how alternative epidemiological models generate different shapes of "adoption curves" with consequent effects on the path of economic growth. He shows how the shape of diffusion curves differs in models of "inertia" (a SI common-source model), "social influence" (a threshold model), "contagion" (a transmissible SI model), and "social learning," where learning is based on observed actions of others.[13]

The aforementioned Banerjee et al. (2013) estimates an epidemiological model based on the real-world network and pattern of diffusion of microfinance in Indian villages, providing direct evidence for word-of-mouth diffusion of beliefs through a social network.

Lucas and Moll (2014) construct an economy containing agents with a distribution of levels of productivity, and consider the dynamics of aggregate productivity under several alternative assumptions about how agents with lower productivity "learn" from agents with higher productivity. Agents solve an optimization problem to determine the intensity of their search effort, which affects the likelihood of encountering an agent with a learnable "better technology."

Not only are mechanisms of the spread of technology and disease comparable, they may interact. Fogli and Veldkamp (2021) develop a model in which the structure of the networks connecting people ("nodes") allows the authors to explore the roles of the three dimensions central to the network theory literature that has developed since Erdős et al. (1960): "degree," "clustering," and "sprinkling" (see Section 25.2.2). Both productivity and disease spread through these connections, so the dynamics of productivity and disease are connected. The model highlights a trade-off between the speed of technological diffusion and disease spreading, which affect economic growth outcomes in opposite directions.

25.4.2 Financial markets

Academic models of financial markets traditionally assume investors choose stocks based on self-generated rational beliefs about future returns. But popular treatments have emphasized social communication, and ideas with a distinctly epidemiological flavor, since the first published description of the first publicly traded securities (De La Vega (1688)'s account of the trading of shares of the East India company on the Amsterdam stock exchange). MacKay (1850)'s vivid prose has made his (thoroughly epidemiological) descriptions of the Dutch Tulip mania and other financial episodes of "The Madness of Crowds" a classic of English literature. This popular emphasis on the importance of social interactions has continued to the present: Michael Lewis (2011)'s bestseller about the financial crisis of 2008–2009 goes so far as to suggest that one of the reasons a particular analyst was able to perceive the housing bubble early was his temperamental indifference to other people's opinions.

---

[12] Though Rogers was a sociologist, we include his work in the discussion here because it has had such a strong impact on the subsequent economics literature.

[13] We do not survey a large parallel literature on technology/innovation diffusion in economics that features the role of social learning, as this work is not explicitly built upon epidemiological frameworks. Examples include Munshi (2004), Comin and Hobijn (2010), and so on.

The academic tide seems now to be turning in this popular direction. Hirshleifer (2020)'s Presidential Address to the American Finance Association urged the profession take up the study of the social transmission of ideas as "[a] key but underexploited intellectual building block of social economics and finance," and argues that such models may be able to make sense of patterns that are difficult to understand with traditional models. Akçay and Hirshleifer (2021) make a broad argument that there are important biases in the transmission of ideas from one person to another which "shape market outcomes." Kuchler and Stroebel (2021) propose "social finance" as the name for a field that would study the role of social interactions, and argue that new data and new methods could advance the field quickly.

These are by no means the first academics to propose a role for social transmission of financial ideas. But the proportion of efforts that could be described as constituting a full-fledged EE analysis, as opposed to piecemeal evidence or provocative theoretical exercises, is small.

An early example of such a comprehensive approach is Shiller and Pound (1989), used in Section 25.3.2 to delineate the elements of the generic SIR model. Now we interpret its content as an economic model. Shiller and Pound (1989) surveyed individual active investors to understand the sources of information that generated their initial interest in the stock they had most recently purchased (which they designate as "randomly selected" – RAND), and in a set of stocks that have been "rapidly rising." (RPI). Their separate survey of institutional investors used a different methodology to designate RAND and RPI stocks.

Their survey-based estimates of the epidemiological parameters for both individual (IND) and institutional (INS) investors indicate considerable heterogeneity in infection rates both within and between the groups. The estimates also suggest that infectiousness differs between RAND and a RPI stocks. Interestingly, the RAND category is more (interpersonally) "infectious" than the rapidly rising category; the authors speculate that public news sources will already have widely covered rapidly rising stocks, so that interpersonal communications are unnecessary to attract attention.

Fig. 25.3 shows compartmental dynamics under their median estimates (of infection and removal rates) for individual and for institutional investors, and for randomly selected versus rising stocks, respectively.

The epidemiological parameters are estimated from a sample of highly interested and motivated investors – which is why it is not surprising that all parameterizations were ones in which R (the proportion of investors who would eventually become interested in a stock) converges to a high value.

The results can now also be interpreted in temporal terms. The authors note that a fully rational model with no private information would imply that spikes in trading volume should immediately follow news events, while the epidemiological model is consistent with long and variable lags. It takes around half a year for the interest of institutional investors in the randomly selected stocks to reach its peak and a little more than a year for a rapidly rising stock. For individual investors, the population interested in RAND reaches its peak after 40 weeks, while interest in RPI takes 2.5 years to peak.

The paper also argues that in a special case where the infection rate is close to the removal rate, and the size of the pool of interested investors is driven by serially uncorrelated shocks, stock prices could follow a random walk, because the change in the level of "interest" would be nearly unforecastable.[14]

---

[14] Shiller (1984) elaborates on this logic by allowing the presence of both rational investors ("smart money") and social-dynamics driven investors. The presence of unforecastable social dynamics undermines the conclusion that a random walk implies full rationality.

Remarkably little of the large literature citing Shiller and Pound (1989) has involved meaningful epidemiological modeling; most has either been nonstructurally empirical, or has used a modeling framework that cannot really be characterized as "epidemiological." A likely reason for this lack of followup is the nonexistence of direct data on either of the two key components of the model: beliefs (about, say, stock prices); and social connections. We have found only two subsequent papers that estimate parameters of a structural epidemiological model of stock investors using microdata.

Shive (2010) uses an SI ("susceptible–infected") model to figure out how to construct a reduced-form empirical regressor that aims to capture social influences among investors ($I_t S_t/N$ in our equation (25.2)). The author assumes that the key social infection channels are at the municipal level, and estimates the time-series dynamics of ownership within municipalities. Controlling for standard variables (demographics, news sources, price dynamics, and others), the author estimates the β coefficient in Eq. (25.2). The estimated β is highly statistically significant, indicating at a minimum that there is some local dynamic pattern to stock purchases which is captured by "proportion locally infected last period" (S_t/N in our equation (25.2)).

The second example is Huang et al. (2021), which estimates an epidemiological model of diffusion of financial news among geographical neighbors. The paper reports a time-average estimate of the reproduction ratio $\mathcal{R}$ between 0.3 to 0.4 (equivalent to $(\beta S_t/N)/\gamma$ in the SIR model above). Since the estimated reproduction ratio is below 1, their results imply that news of this kind does not lead to an epidemic of stock trading. The authors also find stronger transmission between investors of the same characteristics (age, income category, and gender), confirming the usual presumption of homophily (people trust others with similar backgrounds); and between senders and receivers with high past performance, the natural interpretation of which the kind of "transmission bias" discussed by Han et al. (2022), in which people are more likely to boast about their investments in winners than to mention their losing bets.

A final example of an EE model in asset markets is an impressive model of housing price fluctuations by Burnside et al. (2016), which shows how incorporating social interactions can generate booms and busts. A foundational assumption is that agents differ in their beliefs (optimistic or skeptical) about the fundamental value of housing (and the model collapses to a Rational Expectations equilibrium under some simple alternative assumptions). Although it is a random-mixing model, the paper has a mechanism with implications similar to those of the simplest epidemiological model of "superspreaders" (in which some agents have many more social connections than others): Their agents differ in the degree of confidence they have in their opinions (whether optimistic or pessimistic) and those with greater confidence are more likely to convert those who have less confidence. Because it is calibrated using survey data on house price expectations, the model satisfies all our criteria for a full-fledged EE model.

Another literature that deserves brief mention is the work on "Agent Based Computational Finance" (see the survey of that title by LeBaron (2006)). It would be straightforward to reinterpret much of this work as exploring epidemiological models of expectations of asset prices, and epidemiological terminology is sometimes explicitly invoked in the literature. Economists interested in constructing formal EE models would do well to delve into that literature for ideas that could be reinterpreted (or relabeled) to purpose. We have chosen not to survey this literature partly because there are a number of excellent surveys already available, and partly because the literature has not mainly interpreted itself as modeling the dynamics of expectations (and has mostly not tested its models with data on expectations).

25.4.3 Macroeconomic expectations

We have identified only a few papers in macroeconomics (excluding finance; see above) that either constitute full-fledged EE modeling exercises or are closely related to such models.[15]

25.4.3.1 *Sticky expectations*

Carroll (2003) presents an epidemiological model in which the dynamics of aggregate consumer inflation expectations follow a "sticky expectations" equation,

$$M_t[\pi_{t+1}] = (1 - \lambda)M_{t-1}[\pi_t] + \lambda\mathbb{E}_t[\pi_{t+1}], \qquad (25.3)$$

where $M_t[\pi_{t+1}]$ reflects mean consumer expectations at date t for inflation at date $t + 1$, and $\mathbb{E}_t[\pi_{t+1}]$ is a "rational" expectation with which an individual consumer might be infected.

This analytical solution for aggregate dynamics of expectations is possible because the paper employs the simplest tool in the epidemiological toolkit: the common-source susceptible–infected (SI) model whose dynamics we presented in Table 25.1.[16] The idea is that consumers' expectations of inflation stem from exposure to (common) news media sources. The consequence is a population distribution of beliefs in which a proportion of the population $(1 - \lambda)^n$ holds the belief previously held by professional forecasters n periods in the past. The model collapses to the rational expectations model as the parameter λ approaches 1, making it easy to examine the consequences of the epidemiological deviation from RE.

Another implication – inflation expectations are a result of the degree of exposure to news stories – leads to a straightforward prediction: The speed at which inflation expectations move toward professionals' expectations will depend on the intensity of news coverage of inflation. Carroll (2003) found some support for this; Lamla and Lein (2014) and Larsen et al. (2021) find further evidence that a greater intensity of news coverage of inflation leads to more accurate expectations in the population.

The SI model provides a plausible (and testable) microfoundation for the work of Mankiw and Reis (2002), who simply assume that the dynamics of inflation expectations are given by a process like (25.3); they call this a "sticky information" assumption,[17] and argue that the macroeconomic implications of a New Keynesian model in which expectations work this way match a variety of facts (most notably, the sluggishness of inflation dynamics) that standard NK models cannot capture. Mankiw and Reis (2007) extend the analysis of their earlier paper to a general equilibrium context with goods, labor, and financial markets, and point out explicitly that the stickiness that drives the core results in their new model can be motivated by an epidemiological model.

An example closely related to the overtly epidemiological work on inflation expectations is Branch (2004), who considers a model in which agents who have different inflation forecasting rules meet each other and the rules that work better are adopted.

A number of recent papers including Shibata et al. (2019), Carroll et al. (2020), and Auclert et al. (2020) have applied the same SI epidemiological model used in Carroll (2003) to model the behavior of consumers whose attention to macroeconomic news may be spotty even if they are very well informed about their own idiosyncratic circumstances. The consequence is that aggregate consumption exhibits

---

[15] See Chapters 5 and 23 in this Handbook for nonsocial models of macroeconomic expectations formation.

[16] See Easaw and Mossay (2015) for a version that adds social learning between households.

[17] See Chapter 23 in this Handbook for an alternative potential microfoundation.

"excess smoothness" in a way that matches macro data well, while at the same time predictions about microeconomic behavior are consistent with the micro facts that have been used to discipline the new generation of HA-Macro models.

25.4.3.2 *Sentiment and the business cycle*

Section 25.4.4 summarizes evidence of macroeconomic effects of consumer sentiment or "animal spirits." Most of the theoretical work in this area[18] resembles the theoretical work in on financial contagion: It examines questions like existence of an equilibrium (or multiple equilibria), but does not focus on understanding social interaction mechanisms by which the equilibrium could come about, and does not use expectations data to test the model.

Angeletos and La'O (2013) is an exception. It rationalizes sentiment-driven business cycle fluctuations with a theoretical model with an explicit epidemiological mechanism. The paper defines the "sentiment shocks" as extrinsic belief shocks that neither affect fundamentals (such as technology and preferences) nor the beliefs about these fundamentals and shows that these shocks still drive equilibrium outcomes under the critical assumption that imperfect communication prevents agents from achieving common knowledge. The paper explores aggregate belief and output dynamics after an exogenous sentiment shock hits a fraction of agents and gradually spreads via random mixing. The paper computes population flows between what an epidemiologist would describe as three "compartments" (uninformed, informed, and fully informed about productivity). Such dynamics induce "fad-like" or boom–bust dynamics of both aggregate beliefs and realized outputs.

25.4.3.3 *Learning of macroeconomic equilibria*

Brock and Hommes (1997) model the dynamics of beliefs using a model in which there is a population of forecasting rules that agents can adopt, and in which the agents periodically construct a predictor by choosing combinations of forecasting rules whose performance has been better. The dynamics in the model are described as reflecting the 'survival of the fittest.' Arifovic et al. (2018) examine an economy with agents who have different macroeconomic forecasting rules. Aggregate dynamics evolve as agents discard their own rules when they encounter others whose rules have proven more effective. Another way of describing this would be to say that more effective rules are more infectious. The paper also discusses the potential role of professional forecasters and the extent to which their views can spread to the population at large – in our terminology, because their views are more "viral."

The paper is an example of an "agent-based modeling" approach, which Tesfatsion (2006) has argued has application to many subfields of economics. Haldane and Turrell (2019) make a strong case for a broad reinterpretation of these kinds of models as epidemiological, particularly in the macroeconomic context. Though most such models do not use expectations data to test their implications (an exception is the work of Hommes (2006); see also Branch (2004)), it is a short leap from the assumption that successful decision rules spread to an interpretation that what spreads is a set of expectations that would induce the decision rule that is spreading.

As with the work on agent based modeling in finance, we chose not to attempt a summary of this literature because excellent comprehensive surveys already exist (see, e.g., Dawid and Gatti (2018)). But readers interested in these subjects would do well to absorb this literature (and especially the work of Hommes).

---

[18] For example, Angeletos and La'O (2010), Benhabib et al. (2015), Angeletos et al. (2018).

25.4.4 **Nonstructural empirical evidence**

Above we cite efforts to construct and calibrate structural models of epidemiological models. Here, we touch upon literatures that collect evidence in ways not targeted to constructing structural models, but that may nevertheless be useful in guiding the construction of structural EE models.

25.4.4.1 *Directly measured social networks*

Direct data on social interactions have only very recently become available to researchers. One of the first papers to use such data is Allen et al. (2018), who use data from peer-to-peer (P2P) FinTech platforms to examine effects of social connections on consumer and small business loans. They find that P2P loan demand in a given locale increases faster it has previously been growing in its socially connected locales, even when they are geographically distant. Cookson and Niessner (2020) use data from a social media investing platform to examine sources of disagreement across investors who are in direct communication with each other.

Several papers have used data from Facebook. Bailey et al. (2018a, 2019), using data on individual users' social networks, show that people who happen randomly to have social-network friends in distant cities where home prices have increased are more optimistic about their local housing market, and more likely to buy, than people whose remote friends happen to live in places where house prices declined.[19]

Bailey et al. (2018b) constructed an aggregated social-connectedness-index (SCI) using the universe of Facebook users, which calculates the Facebook connections between any two zip codes in the U.S., as well as the connections of each zip with foreign countries. There is already a burgeoning literature using these data (much of it outside of economics). Among selected early results in economics, Makridis (2019) shows that a rise in a locality's sentiment caused by events in socially connected areas has a substantial effect on nondurables spending. Makridis and Wang (2020) find that during the COVID-19 crisis, the severity of the decline in consumption in a county was partly explained by the severity of the epidemic in the places to which that county had especially dense social ties – even when those places were geographically distant. Ratnadiwakara (2021) shows that individuals who are socially connected to someone affected by Hurricane Harvey are more likely to purchase flood insurance policies after the event.

25.4.4.2 *Papers using proxies for social connections*

In the absence (until very recently) of direct evidence about the nature and frequency of social contacts between people, economists have naturally used proxies. Hong et al. (2005) found that fund managers tend to buy similar stocks to other fund managers in the same city. Hvide and Östberg (2015) found that a person's stock market investment decisions are positively correlated with those of coworkers. Cohen et al. (2008) show that fund managers place larger bets (that perform better) on firms to whose employees they are socially connected. Social interaction also affects stock market participation and stock choices (Hong et al., 2004; Brown et al., 2008; Ivković and Weisbenner, 2007). In the context of housing market investment, one paper that explicitly emphasizes the transmission of information or beliefs by social contacts, and specifically suggests epidemiological mechanisms as a way to model the channels of transmission, is Bayer et al. (2021), which shows that novice investors were more likely to enter the market (in speculative ways) after seeing that their immediate neighbors had invested.

---

[19] See Chapter 6 in this Handbook for a discussion of various drivers of housing price expectations.

Finally, there is a large literature finding "peer effects" on people's financial choices; a natural interpretation is that in many cases such effects likely reflect epidemiological transmission of beliefs. But much of this literature has been content to document the existence of such correlations while remaining mute on the mechanism. (See Kuchler and Stroebel (2021) for a comprehensive survey.)

25.4.4.3 *Public media*

News media are not the only "broadcast" (one-to-many) way in which ideas are transmitted. We use the term "Public Media" to encompass all such sources (e.g., websites, podcasts, books, etc.) whose natural interpretation is as a "common source" of infection.

Finance. Rather than attempting to summarize the diffuse literature on the relationship between public media and financial markets, we refer the reader to "The Role of Media in Finance" by Tetlock (2015). Here we highlight just a few contributions that are particularly noteworthy for our purposes.

Dougal et al. (2012) attempt to measure the impact of the opinions of individual *Wall Street Journal* columnists on market outcomes; this is a particularly clear example of a result with a straightforward interpretation using a "common source" epidemiological model. Soo (2015) used news sources to construct an index of "animal spirits" in the housing market and argued that this index had predictive power for housing prices. Choi (2022) proposes that systematic deviations of household financial choices from the normative advice offered by optimizing models may reflect decisionmakers' infection with ideas common in personal finance books.

Macroeconomics. A substantial literature (mostly outside of economics, cf. Soroka et al. (2015); Damstra and Boukes (2021)) characterizes the nature of news coverage of macroeconomic developments (see Bybee et al. (2020) for recent work by economists), but the slow-moving nature of macroeconomic outcomes makes it difficult to distinctly identify consequences of the nature of the coverage from the consequences of the economic events themselves. Nimark (2014) is nevertheless able to show that particularly surprising events seem to have identifiable macroeconomic consequences out of proportion to what might be judged to be their appropriate impact.[20]

An indirect approach is to attempt to measure the effect of news coverage on consumer sentiment, and then to rely upon a separate literature that has found that consumer sentiment has predictive power for economic outcomes (Ludvigson, 2004; Carroll et al., 1994). One example is a clever paper by Doms and Morin (2004) who show that consumer sentiment is driven by news coverage by finding episodes where other news events have crowded out economic news.[21]

Perhaps the most notable recent work relating media to macroeconomics has been that of Baker et al. (2016), who use news sources to construct an index of "economic policy uncertainty" and find that it has predictive power for macroeconomic outcomes beyond what can be extracted from the usual indicators. The uncertainty the authors measure might be affected by the structure of interactions in the media ecosystem; the extensive literature on "fake news" (see Allcott and Gentzkow (2017) discussed elsewhere) and the incentives faced by suppliers of commentary would surely admit the possibility that uncertainty might be introduced or amplified by epidemiological mechanisms. One way to test for

---

[20] See also Chahrour et al. (2021) provide evidence that coverage about newsworthy events that affect particular sectors but are unrepresentative of broader developments can affect broader hiring decisions.

[21] For further evidence that news coverage is a key source of people's views, see Lamla and Maag (2012), though see Pfajfar and Santoro (2013) for a skeptical view.

the epidemiological alternative might be consider alternative scenarios for the policies that might be manifested as competing "narratives" about how policymakers will behave; the uncertainty would then be about which narrative would turn out to be correct.[22]

That leads us to our next topic.

25.4.4.4 *Epidemiology and "narrative economics"*

Robert Shiller has repeatedly speculated that the driving force in aggregate fluctuations, both for asset markets and for macroeconomies, is the varying prevalence of alternative "narratives" that people believe capture the key "story" of how the economy is working (his earliest statement of this view seems to be Shiller (1995)).

After presenting a popular case for the idea in Akerlof and Shiller (2010), he has recently returned to the theme; our opening quote from him makes it clear that he thinks narratives spread by "going viral." See Shiller (2017, 2019) for extended treatments.

There are formidable obstacles to turning Shiller's plausible idea into a quantitative modeling tool. One is the difficulty of identifying the alternative narratives competing at any time, and reliably measuring their prevalence. Shiller (2020) made an initial effort at this. By combining historical news archives and internet search records, he identified six economic narratives that have circulated since 2009, which he labeled as "Great Depression," "secular stagnation," "sustainability," "housing bubble," "strong economy," and "save more." (See also Ash et al. (2021) and the references therein.)

Larsen and Thorsrud (2019) take up the challenge of quantifying media narratives, deriving virality indexes, and conducting Granger causality tests to determine the extent to which viral narratives can predict or explain economic outcomes. The authors find episodes in which their methodology identifies "narratives" that have "gone viral," with measured economic consequences.

25.4.4.5 *Social communication in animals*

A large literature (Whiten, 2021) documents many examples of the social transmission of behaviors and "ideas" in populations of animals, and argues that the epidemiological mechanisms by which novel ideas spread are similar to those in human populations (Whiten et al., 2016). Results from this literature could be useful because animal populations are easier to experiment on. For example, in one such experiment, Kendal et al. (2015) find that ideas are more likely to spread from dominant chimpanzees to subordinate ones than vice-versa.

Recent work in cognitive science (Kendal et al., 2018) argues that biological mechanisms of "social learning" are common across species and between humans and animals (Carcea and Froemke, 2019). Again, laboratory experiments to uncover the role of potential neurological mechanisms of transmission (e.g., "mirror neurons") may be more feasible in animals than in humans.

Results from these literatures have the potential to shape economists' perceptions of the most plausible mechanisms of social transmission of ideas among humans.

25.4.5 Contagion

In the epidemiology literature and in ordinary usage the word "contagion" means essentially "epidemic of a transmissible disease." Large literatures in economics and finance describe themselves as investi-

---

[22] See Eliaz and Spiegler (2020) for a model of such mechanisms.

gating economic or financial "contagion." But for reasons we articulate here, most of this work is quite different from what we define as an EE modeling approach.

Diamond and Dybvig (1983)'s canonical model of "bank runs" has two RE (self-fulfilling) equilibria. In one, all depositors attempt to withdraw their savings from the bank, causing it to fail; in the other, nobody wants to withdraw their savings and the bank remains sound. But the paper's model fails our first criterion for an EE model: There is no dynamic process by which ideas "spread" so it has no testable implications for measured expectational dynamics at either the micro or the macro level. Most of the theoretical work about "contagion" is of this kind – that is, about multiple equilibria without any testable description of transmission or dynamics (much less measurement) of expectations.

Nothing intrinsic to the questions this literature addresses prohibits construction of genuinely epidemiological models – indeed, work by Iyer and Puri (2012) makes an excellent start by collecting data on detailed dynamics of bank withdrawals among members of a social network during a bank run episode. The authors write: "we want to understand ... contagion in bank runs. In order to model this, we draw on a long, time honored literature on contagion of infectious diseases in the epidemiology literature." (Note the explicit invocation the epidemiology literature, presumably to head off possible confusion with whatever might be meant by "financial contagion.")

They proceed to note that "the parallel [to infection] in bank runs is the probability of running as a result of contact with a person who has already run." The paper reports an estimated transmission probability (corresponding to τ in Eq. (25.1)) of 3.6% via social network connections and of 6% through neighborhood connections. Despite the straightforward structural implications of these estimates, the authors stop without using them to parameterize and simulate an SI model of the bank run they study. (These would be interesting steps to take for someone interested in advancing the EE agenda.)

Another branch of the "financial contagion" literature that has aimed to understand the panic occasioned by the 2008 collapse of Lehmann Brothers explores the idea that markets can be vulnerable to the failure of entities that are "too interconnected to fail." This literature has examined datasets on the interconnections between financial institutions, using many of the same tools (network theory, random graphs, etc) described above. But what has been modeled as being transmitted along the network connections is usually financial flows (rather than ideas or expectations), because financial flows are what the datasets measure. The models therefore involve assumed mechanical consequences of disruptions to such flows. Despite the overarching "contagion" metaphor, the low-level elements of the transmission process generally do not mainly aim to model the transmission of expectations at either the micro or the aggregated level. (See Glasserman and Young (2016) for a summary of this literature and Cabrales et al. (2015) for a deep dive).

25.4.6 Noneconomic applications

This section highlights elements of epidemiological modeling in other fields that might be of most value to economists. We focus on three areas:

1. The spread of news, fake news, and rumors
2. The diffusion of scientific ideas
3. The dissemination pattern of internet content such as memes

Daley and Kendall (1964)'s proposal that rumors spread like diseases spurred a literature exploring variants of the classical epidemiological model. A highly-cited example (Jin et al., 2013) estimates a model using the diffusion patterns of news about eight real events among Twitter users, including the Boston marathon bombings and the resignation of Pope Benedict, and rumors such as the Mayan doomsday. In each case, the model matches the dynamics reasonably well.

Vosoughi et al. (2018) found that falsehood spreads on the internet faster than the truth, possibly because the interesting falsehoods have a greater capacity to produce emotional arousal. Similarly, Berger and Milkman (2012) claim that "content that evokes high-arousal positive (awe) or negative (anger or anxiety) emotions is more viral. Content that evokes low-arousal, or deactivating, emotions (e.g., sadness) is less viral." Zannettou et al. (2018) found that the content of a meme affects its virality: racist and political memes are particularly viral.

Kohlhas and Walther (2021) attempt to explain evidence that people seem to underreact to events that are not very surprising, but overreact to surprising events. The authors attempt to model this using a combination of ideas from Sims's rational inattention framework and the Bordalo–Shleifer diagnostic expectations model, but to the extent that surprising events elicit emotional arousal, this paper may also be connected to the noneconomic literature.

Allcott and Gentzkow (2017) used a post-2016-election U.S. survey to analyze the importance of social media for fake news consumption, exposure to fake news, and partisan composition. The paper models profit-maximizing firms who supply fake news in order to appeal to consumers subject to confirmation bias. This seems a natural extension of standard epidemiological models to incorporate the production side of the content – "infectiousness" of certain ideas in subpopulations is an incentive for the production of content that will become "viral" because of a high reproductive number in the targeted subpopulation.

Another potential determinant of the degree to which ideas spread is explored in Acemoğlu et al. (2010), who show that the presence of "forceful" agents (who are immune to others' opinions) may lead to the persistence of misinformation. The key insight is that heterogeneity in infectiousness can reflect characteristics of the sender ("forcefulness") as well as the receiver.

Epidemiological models have also been effectively used to study the spread of scientific ideas. For example, Bettencourt et al. (2006) find that epidemiological models perform well in explaining the spread of Feynman diagrams through theoretical physics communities.

Internet memes are a favorite topic of noneconomist modelers (Dawkins, 1978). Bauckhage (2011) shows that epidemiological models do a good job capturing the growth and decay of some famous memes. Wang and Wood (2011) finds that a modified SIR model allowing for the reinfection of the "recovered" fits the propagation dynamics of various viral memes well. A large literature has followed their work.

25.4.7 Future directions

25.4.7.1 New tests of competing models

One attractive aspect of the EE modeling approach is that it opens the possibility of testing competing models of an aggregate outcome using patterns in the cross-section and panel dynamics of microeconomic expectations. Since there are often many competing models that are able to fit aggregate patterns roughly equally well (stock price dynamics, say) it should be possible to winnow down the field of plausible contenders using their different predictions about microeconomic expectations data.[23]

25.4.7.2 *New kinds of survey data*

Common tools from epidemiological practice could usefully be imported into expectational surveys – particularly tools that epidemiologists use to track the source of an infection (e.g., "contact tracing"). After a person's expectations have been elicited, at least a small amount of extra time should sometimes be allocated to asking "why do you believe [x]." In many cases the respondent might have a useful response: "A friend told me" or "I read it in the newspaper," or "I did some research on the internet."[24]

Several times we have mentioned evidence that information from certain sources, or of some kinds, was more infectious; other evidence indicated that certain recipients are more susceptible to infection. Direct survey questions asking respondents which sources of information they find most persuasive, and why, might prove very helpful in thinking about the most appropriate assumptions for our models.

25.4.7.3 *New and big data*

There is also a rapidly expanding body of work that tries to answer economic questions by analyzing "big data" on textual/conversational information using natural language processing (NLP). (See Gentzkow et al. (2019) for an overview.) As those tools get more sophisticated, they might become usable for creating reliable methods for tracking the content of narratives in the manner required to turn Shiller's "narrative economics" ideas into practical tools of current analysis.

Separately, it is not beyond imagining that at some point, and to the extent that corporate interests and privacy considerations permit, it will be possible to train AI algorithms to comb through social network communications to identify economic narratives, and to measure the ways in which they spread. Because such a source would have direct measures of social connections between agents, it might be possible to construct a thoroughly satisfactory epidemiological model of Shiller's narrative theory of economic fluctuations – and to see how effective it is. But that date is still some distance in the future.

25.4.8 **Literature summation**

Ideas that we would term "epidemiological" have emerged independently in scholarly fields that (ironically) seem largely unaware of each others' existence. Different terminology and methodological tools have developed for ideas that are close cousins; this likely has hindered the ability of participants in distant fields to recognize deep commonalities in their work.

For example, the work on "social learning" in macroeconomics studies the propagation of competing forecasting rules via agent interactions in simulated populations. If it were couched as being about the spread of beliefs in the efficacy of the rules, this work would have satisfied our criteria that

---

[23] A few such exercises have already been performed: Carroll (2001) shows that the time-series dynamics of micro-level *disagreement* in inflation expectations matches reasonably well the predictions of his baseline SI/sticky expectations model. Coibion and Gorodnichenko (2012) compare the implications of sticky expectations to those of a Kalman filter, and conclude that the dynamics of the cross-section indicate substantial rigidity in beliefs whichever framework is used.

[24] Arrondel et al. (2020) provide an example of this approach. They not only elicited survey respondents' stock market expectations, but also the size and financial expertise of the social circles within which they discuss financial matters. The paper finds that social interactions affect stock market beliefs mostly through information channels, instead of social preferences.

it addressed a substantive economic question using a mechanism by which beliefs were transmitted by social interaction. But authors in this literature often do not describe their models in explicitly epidemiological terms, nor do they typically propose testing their models by querying simulated agents about their expectations, and comparing simulated expectations data to actual expectations data.

Nor does this work take much notice of Shiller's longstanding view that economic dynamics reflect the competition of "narratives" that "go viral." "Social learning" models' forecasting rules are arguably exactly how one might want to make a computational representation of what Shiller calls a narrative, and the economic dynamics that result from the increasing prevalence of the rules that succeed in "tournaments" are a good candidate for a computational representation of the consequences of what might be meant by the claim that "narratives" can "go viral."

One of our ambitions is for this survey to infect scholars with the idea that it is useful to describe their models in a common language drawn as much as possible from the familiar domains of epidemiological modeling and network theory: Infectiousness, susceptibility, transmissibility, exposure, immunity, mixing, homophily, reproduction rates, degree distributions, clustering, and so on (in place of miscellaneous other words that in practice are synonymous with the epidemiological term).

25.5 Conclusion

Many of the obstacles, real and perceived, to the construction of what we call full-fledged Epidemiological Expectations models have lessened over the last two decades.

A large body of evidence now finds that opinions on economic questions are sharply heterogeneous, and that people's choices are related to their (surveyed) opinions.

Data from social networks now provide the possibility of directly observing the key mechanisms of the social transmission of ideas – as has already been done in a few cases of economic models (and many more cases outside of economics).

Other work based on measures of "clustering" like geographical proximity or shared workplaces has found robust evidence of social transmission of ideas, while another strand of research has explored the ways in which each news outlet can be modeled as a source of heterogeneity in beliefs if news stories have degrees of either exposure or infectiousness less than 100%.

The recent successes achieved by the HA-Macro literature from incorporating measurable heterogeneity in nonexpectational variables seem likely to tempt scholars to see what more can be accomplished with structural models of expectational heterogeneity calibrated to match empirically measured expectations. While there are other mechanisms for generating heterogeneity, given the copious evidence of epidemiological transmission of beliefs and the rich toolkits for epidemiological modeling, EE modeling seems a natural choice.

An EE approach is by no means applicable only to macroeconomic questions; expectations are at the heart of all sorts of economic questions. Available tools allow economists to expand their imagination far beyond the limits of "classical" epidemiological models. A particularly attractive direction that any literature written by economists is likely to take is to apply the discipline's sophisticated tools for analyzing purposive behavior, as is done, for example, in the paper by Lucas and Moll (2014) whose agents optimally expose themselves to the possibility of infection with new ideas in the hopes of improving their productivity – something scholars have done since time immemorial.

References

Acemoğlu, D., Como, G., Fagnani, F., Ozdaglar, A., 2013. Opinion fluctuations and disagreement in social networks. Mathematics of Operations Research 38 (1), 1–27.

Acemoğlu, D., Ozdaglar, A., ParandehGheibi, A., 2010. Spread of (mis)information in social networks. Games and Economic Behavior 70 (2), 194–227.

Akçay, E., Hirshleifer, D., 2021. Social finance as cultural evolution, transmission bias, and market dynamics. Proceedings of the National Academy of Sciences 118 (26).

Akerlof, G.A., Shiller, R.J., 2010. Animal Spirits: How Human Psychology Drives the Economy, and Why It Matters for Global Capitalism. Princeton University Press.

Allcott, H., Gentzkow, M., 2017. Social media and fake news in the 2016 election. The Journal of Economic Perspectives 31 (2), 211–236.

Allen, L., Peng, L., Shan, Y., 2018. Social interactions and peer-to-peer lending decisions. Technical report, Working Paper. Zicklin School of Business, Baruch College, New York.

Anderson, R.M., Anderson, B., May, R.M., 1992. Infectious Diseases of Humans: Dynamics and Control. OUP, Oxford.

Angeletos, G.-M., Collard, F., Dellas, H., 2018. Quantifying confidence. Econometrica 86 (5), 1689–1726.

Angeletos, G.-M., La'O, J., 2010. Noisy business cycles. NBER Macroeconomics Annual 24 (1), 319–378.

Angeletos, G.-M., La'O, J., 2013. Sentiments. Econometrica 81 (2), 739–779.

Arifovic, J., Schmitt-Grohé, S., Uribe, M., 2018. Learning to live in a liquidity trap. Journal of Economic Dynamics and Control 89, 120–136.

Arrondel, L., Calvo Pardo, H.F., Giannitsarou, C., Haliassos, M., 2020. Informative social interactions. Available at SSRN 3171564.

Arrow, K.J., 1969. Classificatory notes on the production and transmission of technological knowledge. The American Economic Review 59 (2), 29–35.

Ash, E., Gauthier, G., Widmer, P., 2021. Text semantics capture political and economic narratives. arXiv preprint. arXiv:2108.01720.

Auclert, A., Rognlie, M., Straub, L., 2020. Micro jumps, macro humps: Monetary policy and business cycles in an estimated hank model. Technical report. National Bureau of Economic Research.

Bailey, M., Cao, R., Kuchler, T., Stroebel, J., 2018a. The economic effects of social networks: evidence from the housing market. Journal of Political Economy 126 (6), 2224–2276.

Bailey, M., Cao, R., Kuchler, T., Stroebel, J., Wong, A., 2018b. Social connectedness: measurement, determinants, and effects. The Journal of Economic Perspectives 32 (3), 259–280.

Bailey, M., Dávila, E., Kuchler, T., Stroebel, J., 2019. House price beliefs and mortgage leverage choice. The Review of Economic Studies 86 (6), 2403–2452.

Bailey, N.T., et al., 1975. The Mathematical Theory of Infectious Diseases and Its Applications. Charles Griffin & Company Ltd, 5a Crendon Street, High Wycombe, Bucks HP13 6LE.

Baker, S.R., Bloom, N., Davis, S.J., 2016. Measuring economic policy uncertainty. The Quarterly Journal of Economics 131 (4), 1593–1636.

Banerjee, A., Chandrasekhar, A.G., Duflo, E., Jackson, M.O., 2013. The diffusion of microfinance. Science 341 (6144).

Barabási, A.-L., et al., 2016. Network Science. Cambridge University Press.

Bauckhage, C., 2011. Insights into internet memes. In: Proceedings of the International AAAI Conference on Web and Social Media, vol. 5.

Bayer, P., Mangum, K., Roberts, J.W., 2021. Speculative fever: investor contagion in the housing bubble. The American Economic Review 111 (2), 609–651.

Benhabib, J., Wang, P., Wen, Y., 2015. Sentiments and aggregate demand fluctuations. Econometrica 83 (2), 549–585.

Berger, J., Milkman, K.L., 2012. What makes online content viral? Journal of Marketing Research 49 (2), 192–205.

Bettencourt, L.M., Cintrón-Arias, A., Kaiser, D.I., Castillo-Chávez, C., 2006. The power of a good idea: quantitative modeling of the spread of ideas from epidemiological models. Physica A: Statistical Mechanics and its Applications 364, 513–536.

Bordalo, P., Gennaioli, N., Shleifer, A., 2018. Diagnostic expectations and credit cycles. The Journal of Finance 73 (1), 199–227.

Branch, W.A., 2004. The theory of rationally heterogeneous expectations: evidence from survey data on inflation expectations. The Economic Journal 114 (497), 592–621.

Brauer, F., 2017. Mathematical epidemiology: past, present, and future. Infectious Disease Modelling 2 (2), 113–127.

Brock, W.A, Hommes, C.H, 1997. A rational route to randomness. Econometrica 65 (5), 1059–1095.

Brown, J.R., Ivković, Z., Smith, P.A., Weisbenner, S., 2008. Neighbors matter: causal community effects and stock market participation. The Journal of Finance 63 (3), 1509–1531.

Browning, M., Hansen, L.P., Heckman, J.J., 1999. Micro data and general equilibrium models. In: Handbook of Macroeconomics, vol. 1. Elsevier, pp. 543–633. Chapter 8.

Burnside, C., Eichenbaum, M., Rebelo, S., 2016. Understanding booms and busts in housing markets. Journal of Political Economy 124 (4), 1088–1147.

Bybee, L., Kelly, B.T., Manela, A., Xiu, D., 2020. The structure of economic news. Technical report. National Bureau of Economic Research.

Cabrales, A., Gale, D., Gottardi, P., 2015. Financial contagion in networks. In: The Oxford Handbook of the Economics of Networks. Oxford University Press.

Carcea, I., Froemke, R.C., 2019. Biological mechanisms for observational learning. Current Opinion in Neurobiology 54, 178–185.

Carroll, C.D., 2001. The epidemiology of macroeconomic expectations. Technical report. National Bureau of Economic Research.

Carroll, C.D., 2003. Macroeconomic expectations of households and professional forecasters. The Quarterly Journal of Economics 118 (1), 269–298.

Carroll, C.D., Crawley, E., Slacalek, J., Tokuoka, K., White, M.N., 2020. Sticky expectations and consumption dynamics. American Economic Journal: Macroeconomics 12 (3), 40–76.

Carroll, C.D., Fuhrer, J.C., Wilcox, D.W., 1994. Does consumer sentiment forecast household spending? If so, why? The American Economic Review 84 (5), 1397–1408. https://www.econ2.jhu.edu/people/ccarroll/SentAERCarrollFuhrerWilcox.pdf.

Chahrour, R., Nimark, K., Pitschner, S., 2021. Sectoral media focus and aggregate fluctuations. The American Economic Review 111 (12), 3872–3922.

Choi, J.J., 2022. Popular personal financial advice vs. the professors. Unpublished manuscript.

Cohen, L., Frazzini, A., Malloy, C., 2008. The small world of investing: board connections and mutual fund returns. Journal of Political Economy 116 (5), 951–979.

Coibion, O., Gorodnichenko, Y., 2012. What can survey forecasts tell us about information rigidities? Journal of Political Economy 120 (1), 116–159.

Comin, D., Hobijn, B., 2010. An exploration of technology diffusion. The American Economic Review 100 (5), 2031–2059.

Cookson, J.A., Niessner, M., 2020. Why don't we agree? Evidence from a social network of investors. The Journal of Finance 75 (1), 173–228.

Daley, D.J., Kendall, D.G., 1964. Epidemics and rumours. Nature 204 (4963), 1118.

Damstra, A., Boukes, M., 2021. The economy, the news, and the public: a longitudinal study of the impact of economic news on economic evaluations and expectations. Communication Research 48 (1), 26–50.

Dawid, H., Gatti, D.D., 2018. Agent-based macroeconomics. In: Handbook of Computational Economics, vol. 4, pp. 63–156.

Dawkins, R., 1978. The Selfish Gene.

De La Vega, J., 1688. Confusion de Confusiones. Amsterdam.

Diamond, D.W., Dybvig, P.H., 1983. Bank runs, deposit insurance, and liquidity. Journal of Political Economy 91 (3), 401–419.

Doms, M.E., Morin, N.J., 2004. Consumer sentiment, the economy, and the news media. Technical Report 2004-09. Federal Reserve Bank of San Francisco.

Dougal, C., Engelberg, J., Garcia, D., Parsons, C.A., 2012. Journalists and the stock market. The Review of Financial Studies 25 (3), 639–679.

Easaw, J., Mossay, P., 2015. Households forming macroeconomic expectations: inattentive behavior with social learning. The B.E. Journal of Macroeconomics 15 (1), 339–363.

Easley, D., Kleinberg, J., 2010. Networks, Crowds, and Markets: Reasoning About a Highly Connected World. Cambridge University Press.

Eliaz, K., Spiegler, R., 2020. A model of competing narratives. The American Economic Review 110 (12), 3786–3816.

Erdős, P., Rényi, A., et al., 1960. On the evolution of random graphs. Publications of the Mathematical Institute of the Hungarian Academy of Sciences 5 (1), 17–60.

Fogli, A., Veldkamp, L., 2021. Germs, social networks, and growth. The Review of Economic Studies 88 (3), 1074–1100.

Gabaix, X., 2020. A behavioral New Keynesian model. The American Economic Review 110 (8), 2271–2327.

Gentzkow, M., Kelly, B., Taddy, M., 2019. Text as data. Journal of Economic Literature 57 (3), 535–574.

Giglio, S., Maggiori, M., Stroebel, J., Utkus, S., 2021. Five facts about beliefs and portfolios. The American Economic Review 111 (5), 1481–1522.

Glasserman, P., Young, H.P., 2016. Contagion in financial networks. Journal of Economic Literature 54 (3), 779–831.

Granovetter, M., 1978. Threshold models of collective behavior. American Journal of Sociology 83 (6), 1420–1443.

Guare, J., 1990. Six degrees of separation: a play. Vintage.

Haldane, A.G., Turrell, A.E., 2019. Drawing on different disciplines: macroeconomic agent-based models. Journal of Evolutionary Economics 29 (1), 39–66.

Han, B., Hirshleifer, D., Walden, J., 2022. Social transmission bias and investor behavior. Journal of Financial and Quantitative Analysis 57 (1), 390–412.

Hethcote, H.W., 2000. The mathematics of infectious diseases. SIAM Review 42 (4), 599–653.

Hirshleifer, D., 2020. Presidential address: social transmission bias in economics and finance. The Journal of Finance 75 (4), 1779–1831.

Hommes, C.H., 2006. Heterogeneous agent models in economics and finance. In: Handbook of Computational Economics, vol. 2, pp. 1109–1186.

Hong, H., Kubik, J.D., Stein, J.C., 2004. Social interaction and stock-market participation. The Journal of Finance 59 (1), 137–163.

Hong, H., Kubik, J.D., Stein, J.C., 2005. Thy neighbor's portfolio: word-of-mouth effects in the holdings and trades of money managers. The Journal of Finance 60 (6), 2801–2824.

Huang, S., Hwang, B.-H., Lou, D., 2021. The rate of communication. Journal of Financial Economics.

Hume, D., 1748. An Enquiry Concerning Human Understanding. Andrew Millar.

Hvide, H.K., Östberg, P., 2015. Social interaction at work. Journal of Financial Economics 117 (3), 628–652.

Ilut, C.L., Valchev, R., 2020. Economic agents as imperfect problem solvers. Technical report. National Bureau of Economic Research.

Ivković, Z., Weisbenner, S., 2007. Information diffusion effects in individual investors' common stock purchases: covet thy neighbors' investment choices. The Review of Financial Studies 20 (4), 1327–1357.

Iyer, R., Puri, M., 2012. Understanding bank runs: the importance of depositor-bank relationships and networks. The American Economic Review 102 (4), 1414–1445.

Jackson, M.O., 2010. Social and Economic Networks. Princeton University Press. Google-Books-ID: rFzHin-VAq7gC.

Jackson, M.O., Yariv, L., 2007. Diffusion of behavior and equilibrium properties in network games. The American Economic Review 97 (2), 92–98.

Jin, F., Dougherty, E., Saraf, P., Cao, Y., Ramakrishnan, N., 2013. Epidemiological modeling of news and rumors on Twitter. In: Proceedings of the 7th Workshop on Social Network Mining and Analysis, pp. 1–9.

Kendal, R., Hopper, L.M., Whiten, A., Brosnan, S.F., Lambeth, S.P., Schapiro, S.J., Hoppitt, W., 2015. Chimpanzees copy dominant and knowledgeable individuals: implications for cultural diversity. Evolution and Human Behavior 36 (1), 65–72.

Kendal, R.L., Boogert, N.J., Rendell, L., Laland, K.N., Webster, M., Jones, P.L., 2018. Social learning strategies: bridge-building between fields. Trends in Cognitive Sciences 22 (7), 651–665.

Kermack, W.O., McKendrick, A.G., 1927. A contribution to the mathematical theory of epidemics. Proceedings of the Royal Society of London. Series A, Containing Papers of a Mathematical and Physical Character 115 (772), 700–721.

Kohlhas, A.N., Walther, A., 2021. Asymmetric attention. The American Economic Review 111 (9).

Krueger, D., Mitman, K., Perri, F., 2016. Macroeconomics and household heterogeneity. Handbook of Macroeconomics 2, 843–921.

Kuchler, T., Stroebel, J., 2021. Social finance. Annual Review of Financial Economics 13.

Lamla, M.J., Lein, S.M., 2014. The role of media for consumers' inflation expectation formation. Journal of Economic Behavior & Organization 106, 62–77.

Lamla, M.J., Maag, T., 2012. The role of media for inflation forecast disagreement of households and professional forecasters. Journal of Money, Credit, and Banking 44 (7), 1325–1350.

Larsen, V.H., Thorsrud, L.A., 2019. Business cycle narratives. Technical report, CESifo Working Paper.

Larsen, V.H., Thorsrud, L.A., Zhulanova, J., 2021. News-driven inflation expectations and information rigidities. Journal of Monetary Economics 117, 507–520.

LeBaron, B., 2006. Agent-based computational finance. In: Handbook of Computational Economics, vol. 2, pp. 1187–1233.

Lewis, M., 2011. The Big Short: Inside the Doomsday Machine. Penguin UK.

Lucas, R.E., Moll, B., 2014. Knowledge growth and the allocation of time. Journal of Political Economy 122 (1), 1–51.

Ludvigson, S.C., 2004. Consumer confidence and consumer spending. The Journal of Economic Perspectives 18 (2), 29–50.

MacKay, C., 1850. Memoirs of Extraordinary Popular Delusions and the Madness of Crowds. Lindsay and Blakiston.

Makridis, C., 2019. The effect of economic sentiment on consumption: Evidence from social networks. Available at SSRN 3092489.

Makridis, C., Wang, T., 2020. Learning from friends in a pandemic: Social networks and the macroeconomic response of consumption. Available at SSRN 3601500.

Mankiw, N.G., Reis, R., 2002. Sticky information versus sticky prices: a proposal to replace the new Keynesian Phillips curve. The Quarterly Journal of Economics 117 (4), 1295–1328.

Mankiw, N.G., Reis, R., 2007. Sticky information in general equilibrium. Journal of the European Economic Association 5 (2–3), 603–613.

Manski, C., 2018. Survey measurement of probabilistic macroeconomic expectations: progress and promise. NBER Macroeconomics Annual 32 (1), 411–471.

Meeuwis, M., Parker, J.A., Schoar, A., Simester, D.I., 2021. Belief disagreement and portfolio choice. The Journal of Finance.

Milgram, S., 1967. The small world problem. Psychology Today 2 (1), 60–67.

Moore, C., Newman, M.E., 2000. Epidemics and percolation in small-world networks. Physical Review E 61 (5), 5678.

Munshi, K., 2004. Social learning in a heterogeneous population: technology diffusion in the Indian green revolution. Journal of Development Economics 73 (1), 185–213.

Nedić, A., Olshevsky, A., Uribe, C.A., 2019. Graph-theoretic analysis of belief system dynamics under logic constraints. Scientific Reports 9 (1), 1–16.

Newman, M.E., 2002. Spread of epidemic disease on networks. Physical Review E 66 (1), 016128.

Nimark, K.P., 2014. Man-bites-dog business cycles. The American Economic Review 104 (8), 2320–2367.

Nolan, C., 2010. Inception [motion picture]: the shooting script. Technical report, Producers: Christopher Nolan, Emma Thomas; Director: Christopher Nolan; Screenwriter: Christopher Nolan; Studios: Legendary Pictures, Syncopy.

Pfajfar, D., Santoro, E., 2013. News on inflation and the epidemiology of inflation expectations. Journal of Money, Credit, and Banking 45 (6), 1045–1067.

Rasmussen, D.C., 2017. The Infidel and the Professor. Princeton University Press.

Ratnadiwakara, D., 2021. Flooded social connections. Quarterly Journal of Finance 11 (04), 1–15.

Rogers, E.M., et al., 1962. Diffusion of innovations. In: Diffusion of Innovations.

Shibata, A., Shintani, M., Tsuruga, T., 2019. Current account dynamics under information rigidity and imperfect capital mobility. Journal of International Money and Finance 92, 153–176.

Shiller, R.J., 1984. Stock prices and social dynamics. Brookings Papers on Economic Activity 1984 (2), 457–510.

Shiller, R.J., 1995. Conversation, information, and herd behavior. The American Economic Review 85 (2), 181–185.

Shiller, R.J., 2017. Narrative economics. The American Economic Review 107 (4), 967–1004.

Shiller, R.J., 2019. Narrative Economics: How Stories Go Viral and Drive Major Economic Events. Princeton University Press. Google-Books-ID: HciXDwAAQBAJ.

Shiller, R.J., 2020. Popular economic narratives advancing the longest us economic expansion 2009-2019. Technical report. National Bureau of Economic Research.

Shiller, R.J., Pound, J., 1989. Survey evidence on diffusion of interest and information among investors. Journal of Economic Behavior & Organization 12 (1), 47–66.

Shive, S., 2010. An epidemic model of investor behavior. Journal of Financial and Quantitative Analysis, 169–198.

Sikder, O., Smith, R.E., Vivo, P., Livan, G., 2020. A minimalistic model of bias, polarization and misinformation in social networks. Scientific Reports 10 (1), 1–11.

Simon, H.A., 1984. On the behavioral and rational foundations of economic dynamics. Journal of Economic Behavior & Organization 5 (1), 35–55.

Sims, C.A., 2003. Implications of rational inattention. Journal of Monetary Economics 50 (3), 665–690.

Smith, A., 1776. The Wealth of Nations (1776). W. Strahan and T. Cadell, London.

Soo, C., 2015. Quantifying Animal Spirits: News Media and Sentiment in the Housing Market. SSRN Scholarly Paper ID 2330392. Social Science Research Network, Rochester, NY.

Soroka, S.N., Stecula, D.A., Wlezien, C., 2015. It's (change in) the (future) economy, stupid: economic indicators, the media, and public opinion. American Journal of Political Science 59 (2), 457–474.

Tesfatsion, L., 2006. Agent-based computational economics: a constructive approach to economic theory. In: Handbook of Computational Economics, vol. 2, pp. 831–880.

Tetlock, P.C., 2015. The role of media in finance. In: Anderson, S.P., Waldfogel, J., Stromberg, D. (Eds.), Handbook of Media Economics. In: Handbook of Media Economics, vol. 1. North-Holland, pp. 701–721. Chapter 18.

Velásquez-Giraldo, M., 2022. Beliefs, stockholding and wealth accumulation throughout the life cycle. Unpublished manuscript.

Vosoughi, S., Roy, D., Aral, S., 2018. The spread of true and false news online. Science 359 (6380), 1146–1151.

Wang, L., Wood, B.C., 2011. An epidemiological approach to model the viral propagation of memes. Applied Mathematical Modelling 35 (11), 5442–5447.

Watts, D.J., Strogatz, S.H., 1998. Collective dynamics of 'small-world' networks. Nature 393 (6684), 440–442.

Whiten, A., 2021. The burgeoning reach of animal culture. Science 372 (6537), eabe6514.

Whiten, A., Caldwell, C.A., Mesoudi, A., 2016. Cultural diffusion in humans and other animals. Current Opinion in Psychology 8, 15–21.

Young, H.P., 2009. Innovation diffusion in heterogeneous populations: contagion, social influence, and social learning. The American Economic Review 99 (5), 1899–1924.

Zannettou, S., Caulfield, T., Blackburn, J., De Cristofaro, E., Sirivianos, M., Stringhini, G., Suarez-Tangil, G., 2018. On the origins of memes by means of fringe web communities. In: Proceedings of the Internet Measurement Conference 2018, pp. 188–202.

Open issues

Looking ahead to research enhancing measurement of expectations

26

Charles F. Manski

Northwestern University, Evanston, IL, United States

26.1 Introduction

There is by now extensive empirical evidence that survey respondents are willing and able to report expectations in probabilistic form. Economists have sought to learn what expectations persons hold and they have used expectations data to help understand and predict choice behavior. Analysis of probabilistic expectations has become part of normal economic science.

An early review article by Manski (2004) described the emergence of this field of empirical study and summarized a range of initial applications. More recent review articles by Hurd (2009), Armantier et al. (2013), Delavande (2014), Schotter and Trevino (2014), and Manski (2018a) have respectively described research measuring expectations of older persons, inflation, populations in developing countries, subjects making decisions under uncertainty in lab experiments, and macroeconomic expectations. This Handbook reviews many additional studies. The scope for informative future applied research using expectations data seems unlimited.

Economists have usually presumed that measured probabilistic expectations accurately express the beliefs that persons hold regarding uncertain events. Yet the willingness and ability of persons to report probabilistic expectations does not necessarily imply that they think probabilistically and use subjective probability distributions to make decisions. It has long been known that persons also respond to questions seeking point predictions of uncertain events or verbal assessments of likelihood. Nevertheless, persons need not use point predictions or verbal assessments of likelihood to make decisions. What the empirical evidence shows is that, however they think and act, persons are willing and able to report their beliefs in multiple forms – as point predictions, verbal assessments of likelihood, or probabilistic expectations.

The literature measuring probabilistic expectations has by now matured to the point where we should do more than take such measurements at face value. We should strive to understand more deeply how persons respond to the questions that have been posed on surveys and how they would respond if expectations were measured in different ways. We should also strive to improve our very limited understanding of how persons revise expectations as they obtain new information. Basic research seeking to enhance measurement of expectations can improve our general understanding of behavior and increase the contributions made by studies in specific applied settings.

Handbook of Economic Expectations. https://doi.org/10.1016/B978-0-12-822927-9.00036-7

In this chapter I describe research, most of it recent, that seeks to enhance measurement of expectations and I look ahead to encourage future study of major open questions. Section 26.2 summarizes efforts to measure and interpret rounding in reported probabilities. Section 26.3 conjectures that persons may sometimes hold imprecise probabilities, summarizes a study that measures imprecision, and calls for further research on imprecision. Section 26.4 considers the large problem of understanding expectations formation with receipt of new information. Section 26.5 discusses hypotheses that persons may sometimes confound their expectations and preferences.

The research discussed in this chapter has been selected to exemplify broad issues in the measurement of expectations. The chapter does not aim to review all related work. Readers will find material connected to the concerns of the chapter throughout this Handbook.

26.2 Rounding reported probabilities

Rounding is the practice of reporting one value when a real number lies in an interval. Rounding of responses to questions eliciting probabilistic expectations has been found to be common. See Dominitz and Manski (1997), Manski and Molinari (2010), Kleinjans and van Soest (2014), and Giustinelli et al. (2021).

Rounding poses challenges for econometric analysis of expectations data. Ignoring rounding generates measurement error. The measurement error induced by rounding is not the classical type where observed data equal true values plus white noise. Hence, econometric analysis based on the familiar errors-in-variables framework is not appropriate. Indeed, no general theoretical predictions can be made on the direction of the bias of estimates obtained using rounded expectations data as if they were accurate measures of underlying beliefs.

The extent of rounding in responses is not directly observable and may vary across persons and questions. There are no firm conventions for rounding elicited probabilities. Questionnaires do not request that respondents round to a specified degree. Hence, researchers cannot be sure how much rounding there may be in survey data. Respondents may vary in their rounding practices, which are unknown to data users.

26.2.1 Inferring rounding from response patterns

I discuss two related studies that have attempted to infer rounding practices by studying response patterns across questions. Manski and Molinari (2010) studied respondent-specific response patterns across all expectations questions asked in the 2006 wave of the Health and Retirement Study (HRS). We found strong evidence of rounding, with the extent differing across respondents. We proposed use of a person's response pattern across questions to infer the person's rounding practice, the result being interpretation of reported numerical values as interval data.

Giustinelli et al. (2021) substantially expanded study of respondent-specific rounding by analyzing responses across all expectations questions in the core HRS between 2002 and 2014. We initially studied each wave of the HRS separately and found that the respondent-specific rounding patterns reported by Manski and Molinari (2010) using 2006 HRS data are stable across waves. We then pooled data across waves. We found that about half of the respondents provide more refined responses in the tails of the 0–100 scale than the center. About 5% of respondents gave more refined responses in the center than the tails. Respondents tended to report 25 and 75 more frequently than other values ending in 5. Rounding practices varied somewhat across question domains.

Extending Manski and Molinari (2010), we developed a framework that interprets each numerical response given by a respondent as an interval. We proposed a two-stage algorithm. The first stage classifies each respondent into one of a set of mutually exclusive and exhaustive rounding types and places an upper bound on the amount of rounding each respondent is inferred to apply when reporting their expectations. The second stage assigns an interval to each of the respondent's original point responses, which represents the range of values in which the respondent's underlying true belief is plausibly deemed to lie based on the respondent's inferred rounding type. Within a question domain, a respondent's rounding type is a bivariate vector of the form (tail, center) rounding, partitioning the 0–100 scale into two symmetric tails (0–24 and 76–100) and a center (25–75).

We used this framework to study how rounding tendencies vary with observable characteristics of the respondents. We found that higher levels of educational attainment and of cognition are associated with a tendency to give more refined responses (less rounding) across all scale segments and question domains. The association of rounding with age appears to be nonlinear, with youngest (50–59) and oldest (80+) respondents displaying a higher tendency to round than respondents in the intermediate age groups (60–69 and 70–79).

26.2.2 Possible reasons for rounding

The reasons why respondents round are not well understood. Some authors have devoted special attention to responses of 0%, 50%, and 100%, sometime called "focal responses." Fischhoff and Bruine de Bruin (1999) and Bruine de Bruin et al. (2002) hypothesized that some respondents use 50% to signal epistemic uncertainty, by which they mean that knowledge is too weak to place any probability on uncertain events. Hudomiet and Willis (2013) conjectured that respondents form full subjective distributions for the probability of an event and then report whichever of the values (0, 50, 100) is closest to the mode of their distribution. Kleinjans and van Soest (2014) developed and estimated a panel-data structural econometric model to analyze response patterns to each of six expectations questions in the HRS. Their analysis aimed to investigate the extent to which probability reports are determined by genuine underlying probabilistic beliefs, rounding, a tendency to give focal responses, and selective item nonresponse.

Researchers have also investigated how respondents' propensity to give focal responses varies with the survey technology (e.g., with survey mode, features of the percent-chance scale, etc.). In an online survey with a nationally representative sample of the Dutch population, Bruine de Bruin and Carman (2018) found that elicitation of percent-chance expectations using a visual linear scale with a clickable slider significantly reduced the use of focal responses relative to a more traditional open-ended mode, without affecting the predictive validity of responses and survey satisfaction of respondents.

The HRS expectations studied by Giustinelli et al. (2021) were elicited by a combination of computer-assisted, in-person or phone, interviews by means of traditional open-ended percent-chance questions. We analyzed each individual's reports of (0, 50, 100) percent jointly with that individual's responses to the entire set of expectations questions asked. We found that only a small fraction of respondents in any wave, between 2% and 4%, gave responses that were exclusively in the (0, 50, 100) group.

Rather than focus on interpretation of focal responses, Manski and Molinari (2010) viewed rounding broadly and hypothesized that respondents may round to simplify communication and/or to convey partial knowledge. Consider a person who responds "30%" to a probabilistic expectations question. The person may actually hold a subjective probability of $1/3 \approx 0.333$ for the event under consideration but, thinking that an interviewer does not want to receive such a specific value on the percent chance scale, rounds to 30 to simplify communication. Or the person may perceive the future as partially ambiguous and, hence, not feel able to place a precise probability on the event. Thus, a response of "30%" could mean that a respondent believes that the percent chance of the event is in the range [20, 40] but feels incapable of providing finer resolution.

The conjecture that rounding may be used by respondents to express imprecision of beliefs leads naturally to design of questions that directly elicit imprecise probabilities. This work is discussed next.

26.3 Imprecise probabilities
26.3.1 Background

When considering expectations for uncertain events, applied economists have generally assumed that persons hold precise subjective probabilities. Yet some have long been concerned that this may not be the case (e.g., Keynes, 1921; Knight, 1921; Ellsberg, 1961), especially when available information is limited. This broad idea is variously called ambiguity, Knightian uncertainty, or deep uncertainty.

A simple way to formalize the idea is to suppose that a person holds a set of subjective distributions for an unknown event, not a single distribution, thus yielding lower and upper probabilities for events. Such a person may then be said to have imprecise probabilities or multiple priors. In the statistics literature, Dempster (1968) and Shafer (1976) developed a generalization of the Bayesian theory of subjective probability, featuring upper and lower probabilities, and a rule of conditioning that generalizes Bayesian updating. Further efforts followed, sometimes called *robust Bayesian analysis* (e.g., Berger, 1994). These include the Walley (1991) *imprecise probabilities* framework and the work of Kuznetsov (1991) and Weichselberger (2000) on *interval statistical models* and *interval probabilities*. Related ideas appear in research on philosophy of science, including Levi (1974, 1980) and Kyburg (1961, 1983).

Manski (2000) connected imprecise probabilities with partial identification in econometrics. Empirical research combines assumptions with data to draw conclusions about objective probability distributions. Partial identification occurs when credible assumptions combined with unlimited data drawn by a specified sampling process partially reveals a distribution.

Research to date on imprecise probabilities has largely been theoretical. Psychologists have occasionally elicited imprecise probabilities in experimental settings (e.g., Wallsten et al., 1983; Budescu and Wallsten, 1987). Behavioral economists have sought to infer imprecise probabilities from observations of choice behavior in experiments (e.g., Camerer and Weber, 1992). Very little has been known about the precision of the probabilistic expectations people hold in real life when making decisions with uncertain consequences. The prevalence and nature of imprecision may vary across people and contexts. Hence, there has been a need to perform empirical research studying broad populations in contexts of substantive importance.

With this in mind, Manski and Molinari (2010) performed a pilot study in which respondents were asked to answer a sequence of questions about an uncertain event of interest. The elicitation procedure starts from the conventional precise percent-chance format, which requires respondents to report precise percent chances as numbers between 0 and 100, and then used two probing questions to learn more about the nature of respondents' expectations. The first probe asked whether the reported probability was intended to be an exact number or was rounded/approximated. When the response is rounded/approximated, a second probe permitted the respondent to give an exact precise probability or an imprecise probability, stated as a range.

26.3.2 Imprecise probabilities of dementia

Giustinelli et al. (2022) have performed a full-scale study applying the question format proposed by Manski and Molinari (2010) to study expectations of dementia and related choices connected to long term care (LTC), matters of important personal consequence. Specifically, we elicited expectations of developing late-onset dementia and LTC decisions—purchasing LTC insurance or entering a nursing home—among over 1600 dementia-free respondents in the Health and Retirement Study.

We conjectured that expectations regarding these events may be imprecise because available research on the prevalence of dementia does not provide evidence on personalized risk that persons will develop dementia. Medical researchers have developed online tools that predict the chance that persons with specified attributes will develop cardiovascular disease and breast cancer. However, there currently exists no similar tool predicting personalized risk of dementia. The prediction task may be difficult for lay people. Hence, we conjectured that many persons may hold imprecise expectations of their dementia risk – and also LTC outcomes, which may depend on dementia expectations.

We found that nearly half of respondents held imprecise probabilities of developing late-onset dementia. Similar fractions expressed imprecision regarding purchase of LTC insurance and entering a nursing home. Across LTC and dementia outcomes, over 60% of respondents expressed imprecision at least once. Respondents with imprecise probabilities varied in the extent of their imprecision, with the distribution of interval widths featuring a median of 20 points and a dispersion of 70 points as measured by the difference between the 9th decile (80%) and 1st decile (10%). Importantly, imprecision appeared to vary with respondents' conditioning information, with the prevalence of imprecise LTC probabilities decreasing substantially when LTC expectations are conditioned on hypothetical knowledge of the dementia state.

For each outcome, the elicitation procedure generates two measures of subjective expectations as percent chance among respondents who round or approximate their initial report: an initial rounded point-probability and a post-probe response which may be an unrounded point-probability or an interval probability. Taking advantage of this data structure, we compared the initial reports elicited through the standard HRS format with the reports obtained after our probing questions. When doing so, we viewed the initial response as a potentially error-ridden measure of the true subjective probability and the post-probe response as a more accurate measure of the truth. We investigated how the error-ridden measure varies as a function of the underlying true probability.

We found that individuals holding precise probabilities have a tendency, when asked using the standard format, to overreport very small probabilities compared to their post-probing reports. They also tended to under-report large probabilities. A similar pattern was exhibited by respondents holding imprecise probabilities, compared with the lower bound of the interval that they report post probing, conditional on the width of the interval. About 30% of respondents with imprecise probabilities reported an interval that does not include the initial point report.

This pattern, combined with rounding of initial reports by precise-probability respondents, implies that use of initial point-reports for prediction of economic decisions that depend on dementia probabilities can lead to incorrect predictions. We illustrated using a simple model for study of LTC insurance purchase with uncertain dementia state. Our analysis adapted a model of medical decision making under ambiguity in Manski (2018b). The findings suggest that dementia expectations affect decisions regarding purchase of LTC insurance. They indicate that many older Americans make LTC decisions under ambiguity, rather than by maximizing subjective expected utility as economists usually assume.

26.3.3 Looking ahead

Looking beyond the context of dementia, Giustinelli et al. (2022) considered our work as a natural next step advancing the research program on measuring expectations. We were intrigued by the fact that respondents were willing and able to answer expectations questions in multiple ways. Even if they held imprecise probabilities, respondents readily reported a single value when asked to do so.

We view our work as contributing to a new phase of measuring expectations, with important questions still to be addressed. Considerations of survey space emerge immediately: the probing questions in our module add length to the HRS instrument. While the empirical evidence suggests that our sequence of probes successfully elicits imprecise probabilities, more effective question formats might be possible. For example, a survey could directly offer to respondents the possibility to report their beliefs as intervals. Direct elicitation of intervals requires less survey space than asking a sequence of probing questions. It does not prompt respondents to think more deeply about the questions they are asked to answer. An open question is whether surveys should seek quick responses to expectations questions or should encourage the deeper thought that a probing sequence may stimulate. Our finding that pre-probe precise probabilities are sometimes not contained within post-probe probability intervals suggests that probing has cognitive implications.

It is also an open question whether imprecise probabilities should be elicited in all contexts, or only in those where imprecision seems a prominent concern. We found that unconditional LTC expectations exhibit much more imprecision than LTC expectations conditional on hypothesized dementia status. This may be a context-specific finding, or it may be that provision of conditioning information generically affects the precision of beliefs. Study of this question seems intellectually interesting and may help to learn the contexts in which imprecision is a salient feature of expectations.

26.4 Studying expectations formation

Econometric models of decision processes often are used to predict behavior following policy interventions or other events that may alter expectations. When this is so, prediction of behavior requires an understanding of expectations formation. Macroeconomists have long been sensitive to this requirement, it being a central feature of the Lucas (1976) critique of macroeconomic policy evaluation.

Lucas powerfully called attention to the importance of understanding expectations formation when one attempts to predict the outcomes of new macroeconomic policies. He pointed out that optimizing individuals and firms may update their expectations following receipt of new information and revise decisions accordingly. He observed that the econometric models used in the 1970s to predict macro policy outcomes lacked microfoundations. He criticized the failure of these models to distinguish anticipated policy changes, whose enactment should not affect expectations, from unanticipated changes, whose enactment may affect expectations. Given his critique of the then-prevalent econometric practice, Lucas might have recommended that economists initiate empirical research on expectations formation in order to improve macroeconomic policy analysis. However, he made no such recommendation. Instead, he advocated that macroeconomists should assume that economic agents have rational expectations.

Experimental psychologists and economists have long studied how persons update objective probabilities following receipt of sample data in highly structured settings like those presented in textbook statistics exercises. A concern has been to test adherence to and characterize departures from application of Bayes Theorem; see, for example, Tversky and Kahneman (1974) and El-Gamal and Grether (1995). However, it is difficult to draw lessons from this work for expectations formation in real life, where the information that persons receive rarely maps cleanly into a textbook exercise in probability updating. Bayesian updating, which expresses new information through the likelihood function, presumes that data are generated by a well-defined sampling process. Expectation formation in real life requires persons to assimilate government announcements, media reports, personal observations, and other forms of information that may be generated in obscure ways.

26.4.1 Microeconomic analysis of expectation formation

One can learn something about updating in real life by eliciting expectations repeatedly from persons, observing how they change over time, and seeking to interpret the observed changes as responses to accumulation of new information. Microeconomists have performed an eclectic set of empirical studies of this type, generally eliciting precise probabilities.

One subject of interest has been formation of earnings expectations. Dominitz (1998) elicited earning expectations at six-month intervals from a spring 1993 cohort of respondents to the Survey of Economic Expectations (SEE) who were reinterviewed in fall 1993. He examined the association between revisions to expectations and the earnings that respondents realized between interviews. Zafar (2011) elicited expectations of the returns to alternative college majors from a cohort of college sophomores who were re-interviewed a year later. He examined how expectations were updated following student course experiences during the sophomore year.

Another topic has been updating of expectations of equity returns. Dominitz and Manski (2011) elicited expectations of equity returns at six-month intervals from respondents to the Michigan Survey of Consumers. Our analysis of the data suggests that the population may be composed of a mixture of *expectation types*, each updating expectations in a stable but different way. We presented an exploratory analysis to learn about the prevalence of different types, focusing on three types suggested by thinking in orthodox and behavioral finance. These are a *random-walk (RW) type*, who believes that returns are independent and identically distributed over time, a *persistence (P) type*, who believes that recent stock market performance will persist into the near future, and a *mean-reversion (MR) type*, who believes that recent market performance will be reversed in the near future.

One can also learn about updating from information experiments embedded in surveys, which elicit expectations before and after provision of specified information. Delavande (2008) explored how women revise their expectations about contraceptive effectiveness following receipt of new information. As part of her survey studying contraceptive expectations and choices, Delavande introduced a hypothetical new contraceptive to her respondents, elicited prior expectations for its effectiveness, and then elicited posterior expectations after providing various forms of further information. To analyze the prior and posterior expectations data, she developed the creative idea of an "equivalent random sample," this being the random sample evidence that would lead a Bayesian statistician to make the same revision to expectations as a given respondent was observed to make.

Wiswall and Zafar (2015) designed and executed a survey of college undergraduates that first elicited expectations about their major choices and the returns to alternative majors. They next provided information to respondents on the empirical distribution of earnings of students who had graduated with different majors. They then again elicited expectations following provision of this information. They used the data on prior and posterior expectations to analyze expectations updating by the respondents.

Armantier et al. (2016) first elicited respondent expectations of inflation in the year ahead. They then conducted an information experiment in which they randomly provided some respondents with information about past-year average food price inflation, some with professional economists' median forecast of year-ahead inflation, and others with no information. They subsequently asked all respondents for their expectations of inflation in the year ahead. Their experiment generated an informative panel data set that enabled them to examine how provision of new information induces respondents to update their inflation expectations.

Similarly, Armona et al. (2016) used a survey information experiment to examine how consumers revise expectations for home prices. They first elicited respondents' beliefs about past and future local home price changes. They then presented a random subset of the respondents with factual information about past changes and reelicited expectations.

26.4.2 Studying expectations formation to inform macro policy analysis

While the modern literature measuring probabilistic expectations has until recently developed mainly with a concern for applications to microeconomics, there is enormous potential for use of probabilistic expectations data in macroeconomics as well. I concluded my early review article (Manski, 2004) with a call for study of expectations formation, writing (p. 1371):

> "Looking beyond measurement, I see a critical need for basic research on expectations formation. Understanding how persons revise their expectations with receipt of new information often is a prerequisite for credible use of econometric decision models to predict behavior."

Multiple microeconomic studies have been performed subsequently, summarized above, but there remains a critical need for sustained research on expectations formation. Indeed, understanding expectations formation is even more essential to macroeconomics than it is to microeconomics. I have argued previously (Manski, 2004, 2018a) that macroeconomists have little basis to assume that persons hold rational expectations.

Consider, for example, research on the operation of equity markets. A microeconomist may want to learn the distribution of risk and time preferences in a population of potential investors. To achieve this objective, he may obtain a random sample of the population, measure their expectations of returns to equities and other assets, observe their portfolio choices, and use the data to estimate a structural econometric model that assumes each member of the population makes a choice that maximizes expected utility. A macroeconomist may want to use the estimated structural model to predict the dynamics of equity prices that would occur after announcement of an unanticipated change in fiscal or monetary policy. To achieve this objective, one needs to do more than measure the current expectations of equity returns in the population of investors. One needs also to forecast how investors update their expectations after announcement of the policy change and as they observe the subsequent market dynamics.

Similarly, consider research on labor markets. A microeconomist may want to learn the distribution of labor-leisure preferences in a population of potential workers. To achieve this objective, he may obtain a random sample of the population, measure their expectations of life-cycle after-tax earnings under alternative labor-supply choices, observe their actual choices, and use the data to estimate a structural model that assumes each person chooses labor supply to maximize expected utility. A macroeconomist may want to use the estimated structural model to predict the dynamics of market wages and aggregate employment after announcement of an unanticipated policy change, such as a change in the income tax schedule. To achieve this objective, one needs to do more than measure current expectations of life-cycle earnings in the population. One needs to forecast how persons would update their expectations after they learn of the new policy and as they observe the subsequent dynamics of the labor market.

Macroeconomists are increasingly becoming sensitive to these issues. Multiple chapters in this Handbook describe recent empirical studies.

26.4.3 **The potential contribution of expectations measurement**

Measurement of expectations can enable more fruitful study of expectations formation. To make progress, I urge measurement and analysis of the revisions to expectations that agents make following occurrence of unanticipated shocks. In Section 26.4.1, I described some studies that have performed two types of such research. Both types first measure expectations at a specified point in time and then measure revised expectations after provision of new information. They differ in how the new information is provided and when revised expectations are measured.

Some studies reinterview persons at later points in time and examine the revisions to expectations that they make following the occurrence of actual new events. Other studies provide information within the survey and then elicit posterior expectations immediately. Studies of the former type are appealing because they examine real-time revisions to expectations in response to actual informational shocks, but they have the disadvantage that the researcher may not know what new information respondents obtained. Studies of the latter type have opposing advantages and disadvantages: the researcher controls provision of new information, but the setting is artificial.

To give a sense of what may be learned with data of the first type in a macroeconomic setting, Engelberg et al. (2011) considered the expectations of professional macroeconomic forecasters. Their first analysis displayed in a figure the subjective medians and IQRs for 2001 GDP growth elicited from thirteen forecasters who participated in the Survey of Professional Forecasters (SPF) in both 3Q2001 and 4Q2001. Thus, they showed GDP growth expectations before and after the terrorist attacks of September 11, 2001. Each forecaster was depicted by an arrow whose tail is his 3Q2001 prediction and whose tip is his 4Q2001 prediction.

Examination of the 3Q2001 predictions shows moderate heterogeneity in GDP growth expectations prior to the attacks. Across the SPF panel, the subjective median forecast varied from 0.011 to 0.018 and the subjective IQR varied from 0.005 to 0.013. The terrorist attacks and the policy response that followed provide a classic case of an unanticipated shock. It was found that nearly all forecasters revised their median forecast downward between 3Q2001 and 4Q2001, but the magnitude of the revision varied greatly across forecasters. The median forecast of four forecasters remained essentially unchanged. Eight forecasters reduced their median growth forecast moderately (by about 0.025 to 0.01). One reduced his median forecast substantially, lowering it from 0.015 to −0.005. Forecasters also varied in the direction of revisions to their subjective IQRs, with some becoming more certain about output growth and others becoming less certain.

The evident heterogeneity across forecasters in GDP growth predictions is hard to reconcile with the assumption of rational expectations. It is similarly hard to reconcile with the RE assumption the strong heterogeneity of forecasts in the second analysis of the paper, which showed 3Q2005 inflation predictions and the revisions that forecasters made to these predictions in 4Q2005, after Ben Bernanke's nomination to be Chair of the Fed Board. An RE assumption is plainly inconsistent with the observed heterogeneity in the expectations of the SPF panel if forecasters have common knowledge of the state of the economy. To rescue the RE assumption would require that SPF members possess differential private information that makes their prior predictions and revisions to expectations vary across forecasters.

I expect that study of revisions to expectations such as performed by Engelberg et al. (2011) will enable macroeconomists to make progress learning about expectations formation. However, I do not think that measurement of revisions to expectations per se will suffice to guide macroeconomic policy analysis. To develop credible models of expectations formation, it will be important to study how persons obtain and interpret new information over time.

Economists have generally modeled revision to expectations as a process of Bayesian updating, which expresses new information through the likelihood function. This presumes that data are generated by a well-defined sampling process. However, revision of macroeconomic expectations in real life requires persons to assimilate many forms of information that may be generated in obscure ways.

Introspecting about how I revise my own macroeconomic expectations after receipt of new information, I often find it difficult to conjecture an explicit sampling process. Hence, I am unable to consciously update in the Bayesian manner. Yet I somehow do revise my expectations and find that I can express a posterior subjective probability distribution. If my experience is typical, it will be a challenge to develop realistic models of expectations formation by individuals and firms.

26.5 Confounding beliefs and preferences

Economic research on decision making has long assumed that persons separate their beliefs and preferences. The distinction between beliefs and preferences is expressed in decision theory by supposing that a person choosing an action from a choice set C, specifies a state space S that lists all possible states of nature, and a state-dependent utility function $U(c, s)$ that values each action $c \in C$ in each state $s \in S$. The utility function expresses preferences. The state space expresses a basic form of belief, differentiating between those states that can possibly occur and those that cannot. Placing a precise or imprecise probability distribution on the state space may strengthen the specification of beliefs.

Although separation of beliefs and preferences remains a standard assumption of applied economic analysis, some economists have theorized about choice behavior with modes of decision making that confound beliefs and preferences. See, for example, Akerlof and Dickens (1982), Caplin and Leahy (2001), Brunnermeier and Parker (2005), Gollier and Muermann (2010), Cochrane (2011), and Bénabou and Tirole (2016).

26.5.1 Evidence in research measuring probabilistic expectations

Measuring expectations in a survey is a well-defined task if persons separate their beliefs and preferences. It is less clear how to interpret expectations data if persons confound beliefs and preferences.

There has long been concern that the verbal questions used in attitudinal research may be susceptible to confounding. For example, if one asks a person to state whether it is "likely" or "unlikely" that an event will occur, the concern has been that the person's interpretation of these words may depend on the nature of the event. One of the most basic arguments for elicitation of probabilistic rather than verbal expectations has been that probability provides a well-defined absolute numerical scale for responses. Hence, there is reason to think that responses may be comparable across persons and events.

Accepting the traditional decision theoretic separation of beliefs and preferences, modern research eliciting probabilistic expectations has assumed that responses measure beliefs alone, not beliefs confounded with preferences. The empirical evidence has broadly seemed consistent with this assumption. Survey responses usually have high face validity. They often are reasonably accurate when compared with objective frequencies, even if not so much as to warrant being called rational expectations. Moreover, there has been considerable success, in the sense of obtaining sensible findings, using elicited probabilistic expectations to replace expectations assumptions when estimating econometric models of expected utility maximization.

These generalizations notwithstanding, there have been occasional settings in which elicited probabilistic expectations may confound beliefs and preferences. Teenagers interviewed in the 1997 cohort of the National Longitudinal Survey of Youth often gave highly inaccurate responses when asked to predict their chance of dying in the next year or the next several years. Their responses tended to wildly overstate the chance of dying, relative to the empirical evidence in life tables; see Fischhoff et al. (2000). One might speculate that their responses conflated the risk of dying with the severity of the event. On the other hand, analysis of HRS data on the expectations of older adults to survive to age 75 has shown these expectations to be reasonably accurate when compared to life tables; see Hurd and McGarry (1995). It may be that older adults can think separately about the risk of death and its finality, but teenagers are not able to do so.

Measurement of risk of crime victimization may be another setting in which persons confound beliefs with preferences. The attitudinal research literature has long been concerned with confounding of responses to verbal questions in this domain. Numerous surveys ask respondents about their fear of crime (see Warr, 1994). Ferraro and LaGrange (1987) argue that such questions confound two concepts—the perceived risk of crime and the emotional response to crime—that need not be strongly associated. In fact, they argue that the empirical evidence suggests these two phenomena are not strongly positively related and, for some criminal activities, may be negatively related.

Dominitz and Manski (1997) analyzed probabilistic expectations of burglary elicited in the SEE in 1994. We found a pervasive tendency of respondents to overpredict the risk of burglary in the year ahead. Among men, the mean subjective probability of burglary was 0.16, whereas the realized rate at which SEE respondents had been victims of burglary in the previous year was 0.05. Among women, the mean subjective probability was 0.17 and the realized fraction burglarized was 0.03. Our findings on beliefs about risk victimization corroborated the conventional wisdom that Americans perceive crime to be far more prevalent than it actually is (see Bursik and Grasmick, 1993; Chapter 4 in this Handbook). We could not, however, offer a compelling rationale for the phenomenon. In personal communications, some researchers suggested to us that persons tend to be pessimistic about the likelihood of traumatic events. Yet we found no tendency towards pessimism regarding other adverse events—job loss and absence of health insurance—that arguably are as traumatic as burglary.

It is not clear whether confounding of beliefs and preferences explains teenager overstatement of the risk of mortality and adult overstatement of the risk of crime victimization. If confounding does explain these empirical phenomena, one must ask why researchers have not found analogous overstatements when eliciting probabilistic expectations of other personal risks.

26.6 **Conclusion**

Economists were long hostile to measurement of expectations. In my early review of the modern literature (Manski, 2004), I wrote that caution is prudent, but hostility is not warranted. By the early 2000s, we had already learned enough that I felt able to recommend that economists should abandon their antipathy to measurement of expectations. I felt comfortable asserting that persons usually respond informatively to questions eliciting probabilistic expectations for personally significant events. I observed that the unattractive alternative to measurement of expectations is to make unsubstantiated assumptions.

Writing now, I can easily reinforce what I wrote then. We have amassed a substantial body of data on the probabilistic expectations of a wide spectrum of persons regarding many uncertain events. These new data and the analyses they have enabled strongly corroborate my belief that researchers should measure expectations and use the data to study economic behavior under uncertainty. At the same time, we still have much work ahead to enhance measurement of expectations, the objective being to improve our understanding of important behaviors. The impressive scope of this Handbook demonstrates how much has been accomplished and will undoubtedly guide future research in fruitful directions.

References

Akerlof, G., Dickens, W., 1982. The economic consequences of cognitive dissonance. The American Economic Review 72, 307–319.

Armantier, O., Bruine de Bruin, W., Potter, S., Topa, G., Van der Klaauw, W., Zafar, B., 2013. Measuring inflation expectations. Annual Review of Economics 5, 273–301.

Armantier, O., Nelson, S., Topa, G., van der Klaauw, W., Zafar, B., 2016. The price is right: updating of inflation expectations in a randomized price information experiment. Review of Economics and Statistics 98, 503–523.

Armona, L., Fuster, A., Zafar, B., 2016. Home Price Expectations and Behavior: Evidence from a Randomized Information Experiment. Staff Report No. 798. Federal Reserve Bank of New York.

Bénabou, R., Tirole, J., 2016. Mindful economics: the production, consumption, and value of beliefs. The Journal of Economic Perspectives 30, 141–164.

Berger, J., 1994. An overview of robust Bayesian analysis. Test 3, 5–124.

Bruine de Bruin, W., Carman, K., 2018. Measuring subjective probabilities: the effect of response mode on the use of focal responses, validity, and respondents' evaluations. Risk Analysis 38, 2128–2143.

Bruine de Bruin, W., Fischbeck, P.S., Stiber, N.A., Fischhoff, B., 2002. What number is "fifty–fifty?": redistributing excessive 50% responses in elicited probabilities. Risk Analysis 22 (4), 713–723.

Brunnermeier, M., Parker, J., 2005. Optimal expectations. The American Economic Review 95, 1092–1118.

Budescu, D., Wallsten, T., 1987. Subjective estimation of precise and vague uncertainties. In: Wright, G., Ayton, P. (Eds.), Judgmental Forecasting. Wiley, pp. 63–81.

Bursik, R., Grasmick, H., 1993. Neighborhoods and Crime. MacMillan, New York.

Camerer, C., Weber, M., 1992. Recent developments in modeling preferences: uncertainty and ambiguity. Journal of Risk and Uncertainty 5, 325–370.

Caplin, A., Leahy, J., 2001. Psychological expected utility theory and anticipatory feelings. The Quarterly Journal of Economics 116, 55–80.

Cochrane, J., 2011. Presidential address: discount rates. The Journal of Finance 66, 1047–1108.

Delavande, A., 2008. Measuring revisions to subjective expectations. Journal of Risk and Uncertainty 36, 43–82.

Delavande, A., 2014. Probabilistic expectations in developing countries. Annual Review of Economics 6, 1–20.

Dempster, A., 1968. A generalization of Bayesian inference. Journal of the Royal Statistical Society, Series B 30, 205–247.

Dominitz, J., 1998. Earnings expectations, revisions, and realizations. Review of Economics and Statistics 80, 374–388.

Dominitz, J., Manski, C., 1997. Perceptions of economic insecurity: evidence from the survey of economic expectations. Public Opinion Quarterly 61, 261–287.

Dominitz, J., Manski, C., 2011. Measuring and interpreting expectations of equity returns. Journal of Applied Econometrics 26, 352–370.

El-Gamal, M., Grether, D., 1995. Are people Bayesian? Uncovering behavioral strategies. Journal of the American Statistical Association 90, 1137–1145.

Ellsberg, D., 1961. Risk, ambiguity, and the Savage axioms. The Quarterly Journal of Economics 75, 643–669.

Engelberg, J., Manski, C., Williams, J., 2011. Assessing the temporal variation of macroeconomic forecasts by a panel of changing composition. Journal of Applied Econometrics 26, 1059–1078.

Ferraro, K., LaGrange, R., 1987. The measurement of fear of crime. Sociological Inquiry 57, 70–101.

Fischhoff, B., Bruine de Bruin, W., 1999. Fifty–fifty = 50%? Journal of Behavioral Decision Making 12, 149–163.

Fischhoff, B., Parker, A., Bruine de Bruin, W., Downs, J., Palmgren, C., Dawes, R., Manski, C., 2000. Teen expectations for significant life events. Public Opinion Quarterly 64, 189–205.

Giustinelli, P., Manski, C.F., Molinari, F., 2021. Tail and center rounding of probabilistic expectations in the health and retirement study. Journal of Econometrics. https://doi.org/10.1016/j.jeconom.2020.03.020.

Giustinelli, P., Manski, C.F., Molinari, F., 2022. Precise or imprecise probabilities? Evidence from survey response on late-onset dementia. Journal of the European Economic Association. https://doi.org/10.1093/jeea/jvab023.

Gollier, C., Muermann, A., 2010. Optimal choice and beliefs with ex ante savoring and ex post disappointment. Management Science 56, 1272–1284.

Hudomiet, P., Willis, R.J., 2013. Estimating second order probability beliefs from subjective survival data. Decision Analysis 10 (2), 152–170.

Hurd, M., 2009. Subjective probabilities in household surveys. Annual Review of Economics 1, 543–564.

Hurd, M., McGarry, K., 1995. Evaluation of the subjective probabilities of survival in the health and retirement study. The Journal of Human Resources 30, S268–S292.

Keynes, J., 1921. A Treatise on Probability. MacMillan, London.

Kleinjans, K., van Soest, A., 2014. Rounding, focal point answers and nonresponse to subjective probability questions. Journal of Applied Econometrics 29, 567–585.

Knight, F., 1921. Risk, Uncertainty, and Profit. Houghton-Mifflin, Boston.

Kuznetsov, V., 1991. Interval Statistical Models. Radio i Svyaz Publications.

Kyburg, H., 1961. Probability and the Logic of Rational Belief. Wesleyan University Press.

Kyburg, H., 1983. Epistemology and Inference. University of Minnesota Press.

Levi, I., 1974. On indeterminate probabilities. The Journal of Philosophy 71, 391–418.

Levi, I., 1980. The Enterprise of Knowledge. MIT Press, Cambridge, MA.

Lucas, R., 1976. Econometric policy evaluation: a critique. In: Carnegie-Rochester Conference Series on Public Policy, vol. 1, pp. 19–46.

Manski, C., 2000. Identification problems and decisions under ambiguity: empirical analysis of treatment response and normative analysis of treatment choice. Journal of Econometrics 95, 415–442.

Manski, C., 2004. Measuring expectations. Econometrica 72, 1329–1376.

Manski, C., 2018a. Survey measurement of probabilistic macroeconomic expectations: progress and promise. NBER Macroeconomics Annual 32, 411–471.

Manski, C., 2018b. Credible ecological inference for medical decisions with personalized risk assessment. Quantitative Economics 9, 541–569.

Manski, C., Molinari, F., 2010. Rounding probabilistic expectations in surveys. Journal of Business and Economic Statistics 28, 219–231.

Schotter, A., Trevino, I., 2014. Belief elicitation in the laboratory. Annual Review of Economics 6, 103–128.

Shafer, G., 1976. A Mathematical Theory of Evidence. Princeton University Press, Princeton, NJ.

Tversky, A., Kahneman, D., 1974. Judgement under uncertainty: heuristics and biases. Science 185, 1124–1131.

Walley, P., 1991. Statistical Reasoning with Imprecise Probabilities. Chapman & Hall, London.

Wallsten, T., Forsythe, B., Budescu, D., 1983. Stability and coherence of health experts' upper and lower subjective probabilities about dose—response functions. Organizational Behavior and Human Performance 31, 227–302.

Warr, M., 1994. Public perceptions and reactions to violent offending and victimization. In: Reiss, A., Roth, J. (Eds.), Understanding and Preventing Violence, vol. 4. National Academy Press, Washington, DC.

Weichselberger, K., 2000. The theory of interval probability as a unifying concept for uncertainty. International Journal of Approximate Reasoning 24, 149–170.

Wiswall, M., Zafar, B., 2015. Determinants of college major choice: identification using an information experiment. The Review of Economic Studies 82, 791–824.

Zafar, B., 2011. How do college students form expectations. Journal of Labor Economics 29, 301–348.

Index